W9-AVB-431

LAW IN ITS APPLICATION TO BUSINESS

REVISED EDITION

LAW

IN ITS APPLICATION TO BUSINESS

William H. Schrampfer

PROFESSOR
CHAIRMAN, DEPARTMENT OF
INDUSTRIAL ADMINISTRATION
IOWA STATE COLLEGE

HOLT, RINEHART AND WINSTON · NEW YORK

JANUARY, 1961

Library of Congress Catalog Card Number: 52-5599
27784-0112

To

FRANCES
JO ANN
and
BETTY

PREFACE TO REVISED EDITION

The objective of this book is to present a basic treatment of that area of American law which finds its application to business and economic life. The present volume retains the philosophy of the first edition, the attempt to portray the practical operational significance of law in the field of man's varied business and economic pursuits. It is to this purpose that the revised product differs in the following significant respects:

1. The reorientation as a whole has been to place greater stress upon principles of greatest practical importance, retaining, however, a complete pattern of basic relationships of subject matter so as to avoid in so far as is possible fragmentation and consideration of isolated principles of law.

2. The text material has been written and the cases selected to place greater emphasis upon the preventive aspects of law which will acquaint the student with desirable business procedures and practices. It is of paramount importance to learn how to keep out of trouble.

3. Practically all the text material has been rewritten and much of it reoriented.

4. Much of the text material has been expanded and the number of illustrations greatly increased. Two new chapters covering Insurance and Landlord and Tenant have been added.

5. Many new cases have been introduced and the total number of cases has been materially increased. Most of the new cases are modern, and many of them indicate significant trends.

6. The problem material has been greatly expanded, introducing fairly long fact situations from cited cases. This will give students further opportunity for independent analysis and application of legal principles—an opportunity to acquire the ability to use intelligently the legal principles at his command as guides in the conduct of business affairs.

I owe a debt of gratitude to many who have been instrumental either directly or indirectly in making this revision possible. I am grateful to my former students, who patiently and sometimes unwittingly submitted themselves to the testing of the material used. I am especially indebted to Professor C. A. Phillips, of the College of Commerce, State University of Iowa, for his many helpful suggestions and confidence-inspiring encouragement; to Professor W. H. Thompson of the Industrial Economics staff, Iowa State College, for the reading of the manuscript and his constructive suggestions; to Professor Allen W. Goodspeed, University of West Virginia, for the technical assistance he has rendered, to attorneys William Hammond Short, of Chapman and Cutler, Chicago, Illinois, and Thomas B. Roberts of Brammer, Brody, Charlton, Parker and Roberts, Des Moines, Iowa, for the many ways in which they have been helpful; to Frances N. Schrampfer, Marie

Smith and Carla Hansel for the preparation of the manuscript. To the many users who have made constructive suggestions I publicly extend my heartfelt thanks and invite them and others to give me their criticisms, unfavorable or favorable. It is in all humility my sincere hope that their suggestions and my ten years of additional experience and studied effort have made this volume a better teaching instrument.

WILLIAM H. SCHRAMPFER

Ames, Iowa
January, 1952

CONTENTS

► INTRODUCTION

1. THE NATURE AND SOURCE OF LAW 3

I. *Social Control by Laws* 3
II. *Basis and Development of Law* 6
III. *The Body of Our Law* 8

2. LEGAL RIGHTS, DUTIES, AND REMEDIES 14

I. *Concept of Legal Rights and Duties* 14
II. *Remedies at Law and at Equity* 16
III. *Legal Procedure* 19
IV. *Courts* 24

► I. CONTRACTS

3. INTRODUCTION TO LAW OF CONTRACTS 31

I. *Role of Contracts in Business* 31
II. *Basic Concept of a Contract* 31
III. *Elements of a Contract* 32
IV. *Meaning of Enforceability of Contracts* 33
V. *Contracts Classified* 33

4. OFFER AND ACCEPTANCE—AGREEMENT THE BASIC ELEMENT 36

I. *Nature of Offer and Acceptance—The Agreement* 36
II. *Requisites of a Legally Acceptable Offer* 37
III. *Duration of Offer* 40
IV. *The Acceptance* 42
V. *Need for Certainty of Terms* 46
VI. *Options* 47

5. CONSIDERATION 88

I. *Elements of Consideration* 88
II. *The Rule of Consideration Applied and Illustrated* 92
III. *Promises Enforceable without Consideration* 97

6. VOIDANCE OF CONTRACTS 130

I. *Incompetent Parties* 130
II. *Fraud* 135

III. *Innocent Misrepresentation* 139
IV. *Mistake of Fact* 139
V. *Duress* 144
VI. *Undue Influence* 144

7. **FORM OF THE CONTRACT—THE STATUTE OF FRAUDS** 185

I. *Parol Evidence Rule* 185
II. *Types of Contracts Required to Be in Writing by Statute of Frauds* 185
III. *Acknowledgment Before Notary* 192

8. **ILLEGAL AGREEMENTS** 219

I. *Agreements in Violation of Common Law or Statutory Enactment* 219
II. *Agreements Contrary to Public Policy* 220
III. *Particular Types of Contracts Considered* 221

9. **ASSIGNMENT OF RIGHTS AND DELEGATION OF DUTIES** 251

I. *Assignment of Contractual Rights* 251
II. *Delegation of Duties Distinguished* 255
III. *Third Party Beneficiary Contracts* 256

10. **PERFORMANCE, CONTRACTUAL CONDITIONS, AND BREACH** 274

I. *Remedies for Nonperformance* 274
II. *Excuses for Nonperformance* 276
III. *Conditions in Contracts* 278
IV. *The Doctrine of Anticipatory Breach* 283

11. **DISCHARGE OF CONTRACTUAL OBLIGATIONS** 316

I. *By Operation of Law* 316
II. *By Mutual Agreement* 317
III. *By Arbitration and Award* 318
IV. *Material Alteration* 318
V. *Payment by Negotiable Instrument* 319
VI. *Tender of Performance* 319

► II. AGENCY

12. **NATURE AND CREATION OF AGENCY RELATIONSHIP** 329

I. *Servant and Agent Distinguished* 329
II. *Servant Distinguished from Independent Contractor* 329
III. *Principal and Agent—The Law of Business Representation* 330
IV. *Creation of Agency* 331

13. RIGHTS AND LIABILITIES OF PRINCIPAL TO THIRD PARTY FOR ACTS OF AGENT 351

I. *Agent's Authority the Basis of Liability* 351
II. *Express Authority* 351
III. *Implied or Apparent Authority* 353
IV. *Secret Limitations* 355
V. *Liability for Torts of Agent* 356
VI. *Agent Acting for Undisclosed Principal* 357
VII. *Rights of Third Party* 359

14. RIGHTS AND LIABILITIES AS BETWEEN AGENT AND THIRD PARTY 381

I. *Liability of Agent on Authorized Contracts* 381
II. *Liability of Agent Resulting from Unauthorized Contracts* 382
III. *Implied Warranty as to Principal* 383
IV. *Right of Third Party to Recover Money Paid to Agent* 383
V. *Agent's Tort Liability* 384
VI. *Liability Based on Fraud* 385

15. RIGHTS AND DUTIES AS BETWEEN PRINCIPAL AND AGENT 394

I. *Duties of Agent to Principal* 394
II. *Duties of Principal to Agent* 399
III. *Agent's Right of Lien* 400

16. TERMINATION OF AGENCY RELATIONSHIP 427

I. *By Agreement* 427
II. *Implied from Nature of Undertaking* 428
III. *Termination Resulting from Acts of Parties* 428
IV. *Termination Resulting from Operation of Law* 429
V. *Requirement of Notice of Termination* 429
VI. *Irrevocable Agencies* 430
VII. *Agencies Irrevocable to a Degree* 431

► III. NEGOTIABLE INSTRUMENTS

17. INTRODUCTION TO LAW OF NEGOTIABLE INSTRUMENTS 443

I. *Negotiable Instruments Classified* 443
II. *Creation and Transfer of Credit by Use of Negotiable Instruments Illustrated* 447
III. *Consequences of Transfer by Negotiation—Assignment Distinguished* 447

18. REQUIREMENTS FOR NEGOTIABLE INSTRUMENTS 450

I. *Writing and Signature* 450
II. *Unconditional Promise or Order* 451

III. *Payable in a Sum Certain in Money* 454
IV. *Certainty of Time of Payment* 458
V. *Payable to Order or Bearer* 462

19. **TRANSFER OF NEGOTIABLE INSTRUMENTS—NEGOTIATION** 487

I. *Transfer of Order Paper without Indorsement* 487
II. *Negotiation of Order Paper* 488
III. *Negotiation of Bearer Paper* 491
IV. *Surrender to Drawee Distinguished from Negotiation* 491

20. **RIGHTS OF HOLDERS—HOLDERS IN DUE COURSE** 501

I. *Holders Distinguished* 501
II. *Rights of Holder through Holder in Due Course* 501
III. *What Constitutes a Holder in Due Course* 502
IV. *Payee as Holder in Due Course* 507
V. *Defenses* 508

21. **LIABILITY OF PARTIES** 537

I. *Primary and Secondary Parties Distinguished* 537
II. *Contractual Undertakings of Primary Parties* 537
III. *Contractual Undertaking of Secondary Parties* 540
IV. *Accommodation Parties* 542

22. **PRESENTMENT, DISHONOR, PROTEST, AND NOTICE** 553

I. *Conditions Precedent to Liability of Secondary Parties* 553
II. *Presentment for Payment* 553
III. *Presentment for Acceptance* 558
IV. *Notice of Dishonor* 559
V. *Protest* 564

23. **CHECKS** 583

I. *Nature of Checks* 583
II. *Relationship between Drawer and Drawee Bank* 583
III. *Drawee's Obligations* 583
IV. *Certification of Checks* 584
V. *Drawer's Liability* 585

24. **DISCHARGE OF NEGOTIABLE INSTRUMENTS** 591

I. *Discharge of Instruments* 591
II. *Discharge of Secondary Parties* 594

► IV. PERSONAL PROPERTY AND RELATED TOPICS

25. PERSONAL PROPERTY 601

I. *Property in General* 601
II. *Personal Property Distinguished from Real Property* 602
III. *Personal Property Classified* 605
IV. *Processes of Acquiring Title to Personal Property* 605
V. *Joint Ownership of Property* 613

26. THE LAW OF SALES 642

I. *Subject Matter* 642
II. *Time of Passing of Title* 643
III. *Warranties* 650
IV. *Rights and Remedies of Seller* 654
V. *Rights and Remedies of Buyer* 657
VI. *Bills of Lading and Warehouse Receipts as Negotiable Documents of Title* 659

27. BAILMENTS 691

I. *Nature of Bailments* 691
II. *Distinguishing Characteristics* 691
III. *Classification of Bailments* 694
IV. *Duties of Bailee* 694
V. *Limitation of Liability by Contract* 697

28. SECURITY INTERESTS IN PERSONAL PROPERTY 714

I. *Liens* 714
II. *Pledges* 717
III. *Chattel Mortgages* 720
IV. *Conditional Sales* 725
V. *Trust Receipts* 729

► V. REAL PROPERTY AND RELATED TOPICS

29. REAL PROPERTY 751

I. *Ownership Interests Classified* 751
II. *Joint Estates* 755
III. *Methods of Acquiring Title* 756
IV. *Steps in a Real Estate Transaction* 758

30. REAL ESTATE MORTGAGES 782

I. *Nature of Real Estate Mortgages* 782
II. *Nature of Mortgagee's Interest* 782

III. *Form, Execution, and Recording* 783
IV. *Transfer of Mortgaged Property* 785
V. *Transfer of Mortgagee's Interest* 786
VI. *Payment and Release of Mortgage* 787
VII. *Foreclosure Proceedings* 788

31. LANDLORD AND TENANT 797
I. *Nature of Relationship* 797
II. *The Lease* 798
III. *Tenancies Classified* 798
IV. *Termination of Tenancies* 799
V. *Rights and Liabilities of Parties* 802
VI. *Rent* 806

32. LIENS UPON REAL PROPERTY 823
I. *Judgment Liens* 823
II. *Mechanics' Liens* 824
III. *Tax Liens* 828

VI. BUSINESS ORGANIZATIONS

33. DISTINGUISHING FEATURES AND FORMATION OF PARTNERSHIP 837
I. *Essential Elements* 837
II. *Contract of Partnership* 840
III. *Partnership Name* 841
IV. *Partnership as Legal Entity* 841
V. *Partnership Property* 842
VI. *Instances of Partnership Liability without Existence of Partnership in Fact* 844
VII. *Limited Partnership Distinguished* 845

34. RELATIONS OF PARTNERS TO THIRD PERSONS: THEIR POWERS AND LIABILITIES 859
I. *Agency Character of Partnership* 859
II. *Extent and Nature of Partners' Liability* 863
III. *Liability of Incoming Partner* 865

35. RELATIONS OF PARTNERS TO ONE ANOTHER: THEIR RIGHTS AND DUTIES 874
I. *Rights and Duties Established by Partnership Agreement* 874
II. *Fiduciary Character of Relationship* 874
III. *Right of Participation in Management* 875
IV. *Right to Information* 876

V. *Right to an Accounting* 877
VI. *Right of Reimbursement and Contribution* 878
VII. *Right to Receive Compensation for Services* 878
VIII. *Rights in Respect to Partnership Property* 879
IX. *Profits, Surplus, and Losses* 880

36. **DISSOLUTION AND TERMINATION OF PARTNERSHIP** 892

I. *Dissolution Distinguished* 892
II. *Causes of Dissolution* 892
III. *Status of Partnership and Partners after Dissolution* 898

37. **CHARACTER AND FORMATION OF BUSINESS CORPORATIONS** 915

I. *Classification of Corporations* 916
II. *Legal Concepts of Corporations* 917
III. *Formation* 923
IV. *Steps Preliminary to Corporate Existence—Promotion* 927

38. **POWERS, DURATION, AND TERMINATION OF CORPORATIONS** 948

I. *Source of Authority to Act* 948
II. *Express Powers* 953
III. *Powers Implied from Those Expressly Conferred* 954
IV. *Ultra Vires Acts* 958
V. *Duration and Termination* 961

39. **STOCKHOLDERS' POSITION** 986

I. *Methods of Becoming Stockholders* 986
II. *Transfer of Stock* 988
III. *Rights of Stockholders* 992
IV. *Limited Liability* 999

40. **CORPORATION MANAGEMENT AND CONTROL** 1014

I. *Stockholders' Right of Management* 1014
II. *By-Laws* 1015
III. *Directors* 1017
IV. *Administrative Officers* 1020

► VII. SURETYSHIP AND INSURANCE

41. **SURETYSHIP** 1039

I. *Nature of Relationship* 1039
II. *Creation* 1039
III. *Nature and Extent of Surety's Liability* 1040
IV. *Rights of Surety or Guarantor* 1042

V. *Defense Available to Surety* 1043
VI. *Discharge of Surety by Acts of Creditor* 1044

42. CONTRACTS OF INSURANCE 1054

I. *Insurance Distinguished* 1054
II. *Insurable Interest* 1055
III. *Insurance Contracts* 1055
IV. *Reasons Permitting Avoidance of Contract* 1056
V. *Extent of Recovery* 1060
VI. *Coinsurance Clauses* 1061
VII. *Concurrent Insurance* 1061
VIII. *Subrogation* 1062

TABLE OF CASES 1075

INDEX 1083

Introduction

Chapter

1. THE NATURE AND SOURCE OF LAW

2. LEGAL RIGHTS, DUTIES, AND REMEDIES

1 INTRODUCTION:

THE NATURE AND SOURCE OF LAW

► I. SOCIAL CONTROL BY LAWS

Group life is productive of frictions and conflicts. This is attested to by the hundreds of thousands of cases that annually come before our courts. These many conflicts stem primarily from the instinctively acquisitive and self-protective nature of man—a self-interest that brings him into conflict with others. With the evolution of our present-day highly complex, interrelated, and interdependent economic order, points of contact between individuals have become manifold and the possibilities of friction have become increasingly great.

Since the dawn of history, man has been striving to evolve better standards of behavior for the purpose of obtaining harmonious relations. Although man is far from having achieved the ideal, his evolutionary processes have both consciously and unconsciously done much to facilitate an orderly and harmonious social existence. He has developed precepts of morality and religion that have given him a strong consciousness of right and wrong; he has come to accept the force of public opinion; he has adopted codes of professional ethics; and he has developed various kinds of social institutions, such as the family, the church, and business and fraternal organizations. These are powerful social control mechanisms. Without them, man's behavior toward his fellow men would be much less virtuous than it is. Within their framework are the standards of conduct through which the ideal society could be realized.

Were all its members to achieve that state of perfection which the constant application of the principles of religion and morality make possible, society would have no need for positive agencies of control. That day seems far distant, and organized society will long find it necessary to induce desired standards of conduct by positive means—by positive agencies of control. Of these agencies, our legal system is most important; through it society has promulgated rules and standards of conduct which its members and its governing bodies are expected to observe—rules that prescribe that which must be done, that which must not be done and that which it is permissible to do. Those who fail to comply with these rules subject themselves to the consequences such as society has provided, which are at times harsh and drastic. These rules and standards to which organized society gives sanction through its courts are laws. For practical purposes the law is as Justice Holmes stated, "The prophecies of what the courts will do in fact, and nothing more pretentious, . . ." *

* *The Path of the Law,* 10 Harvard Law Review 457.

A. LAWS AS RULES REQUIRING OR PROHIBITING CONDUCT

Much of our law consists of rules of conduct designed to obtain certain behavior from individuals and government. Stated in another way, one of the primary functions of our legal system is to set up and define standards of conduct that society expects will be followed for the sake of order. Unless these standards of conduct are observed, society can, through its judicial machinery:

(1) Force compliance;
(2) subject the delinquent individual to punishment by the state;
(3) subject the delinquent individual to monetary liability to another; or
(4) use a combination of the above.

To illustrate:

(1) The Federal Constitution provides that:

"Congress shall make no law respecting an establishment of religion, or prohibiting the free exercise thereof; or abridging the freedom of speech, or the press; or the right of the people peaceably to assemble, and to petition the Government for a redress of grievances."

This is only one of the many provisions in our legal system requiring a certain behavior of the various branches of our federal government.

(2) The Federal Constitution provides that (Section 10, Clause 1) "No state shall . . . pass any . . . law impairing the obligation of contracts." This is an illustration of one of the numerous standards of conduct imposed upon the states.

(3) Society prohibits the individual from driving his automobile without a permit or while intoxicated. His failure to comply with this standard of conduct subjects him to punishment by organized society.

(4) The individual is expected to conduct himself in a certain way in respect to the person and property of others. Thus, it is expected that one merchant will not disparage—belittle—the goods of another, that he will not appropriate to his own use a trade-mark of another, and that he will not induce the employees of another to break their contracts of employment. The failure to comply with these standards of conduct will make the offender liable to money damages for such injury as he has caused and, if necessary, society will force compliance in the future through the use of an injunction.

(5) Society expects that one individual will not convert the property of others to his own use. Thus, if A takes it upon himself to use B's car without the latter's consent, he may be punished by society and be required to pay money damages to B or return the car if B should so choose.

(6) The individual is prohibited from engaging in certain activities without a demonstration of his qualifications. A prerequisite to the practice of medicine is, for example, the obtaining of a certificate of qualification.

B. LAWS AS RULES OF PERMISSIVE CONDUCT

All laws do not require the doing of certain things or prohibit the doing of others. The student of business law should appreciate that many laws grant individuals the privilege of certain conduct.

To illustrate:

(1) Minors are by law extended the privilege of disaffirming their contracts.

(2) The individual is, upon the basis of his insolvency, given the privilege to petition for a discharge of his obligations by bankruptcy proceedings.

(3) Society accords the individual the privilege of protecting his original creations by copyright or patent.

(4) Creditors have the privilege of obtaining liens against debtors. For example, one who improves real property has the election of obtaining a claim against the property for payment—a mechanics' lien.

(5) The individual has the privilege of making a distribution of his property by will. Should the individual fail to avail himself of this privilege, his property will, upon his death, be distributed in the manner provided by legislative law. The individual thus has the privilege of making his own will or letting the legislature make it for him.

(6) Individuals have the privilege of associating themselves as partners in the conduct of a business enterprise.

(7) The individual has the privilege of conducting his affairs through the use of an agent—a business representative.

C. LAWS AS STANDARDS FOR SOLUTION OF CONFLICTS

It seems appropriate to the author that the student of business law should also accept the point of view that much of our law is a declaration of rules and standards that are employed for the solution of conflicts as they arise. These rules and standards serve the courts as guides in determining what the outcome of controversies should be as they come before them.

To illustrate:

(1) Let us suppose that A has failed to supply B with certain merchandise as he had agreed to do. B brings action against A in a court to recover money damages. This conflict between A and B may be decided in favor of one or the other by such considerations as (a) the form of the agreement (whether it was oral or written), or (b) the amount involved, or (c) whether the agreement was based upon what the law calls "a consideration."

(2) Creditors making claim against the assets of a bankrupt will be given an order of priority in accordance with established rules and standards. Thus, wages will, to a certain extent, be paid before general creditors can obtain payment.

(3) The right of the holder of a promissory note to collect from the maker may be determined by the form of the instrument—whether the note is in negotiable form. The holder of a negotiable note may recover from the maker under circumstances that would deny him the right to recover on a non-negotiable note.

(4) Creditors of a debtor may come into conflict when one has a claim upon the real property of the debtor and the other has a claim upon the personal property. The conflict will arise from their inability to agree upon what property is real and what property is personal. The rights of the respective claimants will be determined by an application of the legal standards set up for the purpose of distinguishing real and personal property.

To the businessman, the many rules and standards by which conflicts are resolved are of real importance. They serve him as guides in determining the business practices and procedures necessary for the protection of his own interests. The reader of the following chapters will come to realize the need of conducting daily business affairs within the pattern of these legal standards. A few of the many things he will come to appreciate are

(1) the danger of leaving a promissory note in the hands of the holder after it has been paid;

(2) the need of giving notice under various circumstances for the protection of a right of legal action or to avoid liability;

(3) the danger of contracting with a minor;

(4) the possible desirability of owning property jointly as joint tenants; and

(5) the need of placing chattel mortgages and other types of instruments upon the public records.

► II. BASIS AND DEVELOPMENT OF LAW

"Breach for breach, eye for eye, tooth for tooth: as he hath caused a blemish in a man, so shall it be done to him again." * No longer is this ancient law one of mankind's principles of justice. With the passage of time man's changing precepts of right and wrong have been consistently reflected in his laws. History is replete with evidence that laws of mankind reflect his customs, habits, traditions, and morals. It should be apparent that our criminal laws are the outgrowth of man's moral development. Individuals do not abstain from murder because the law prohibits it. Their self-restraint is founded upon the generally accepted moral principle that it is wrong to kill another, regardless of provocation. The general practice of abstaining from homicide did not come from the law; the law instead came from the accepted moral standard that it is wrong to kill one's fellow man.

An illustration of man's customs and usages forming the basis of the law is found in the Civil Practice Act of California of 1851, which provided:

> "in actions respecting mining claims, proof shall be admitted of the customs, usages, or regulations established and in force at the bar, or diggings, embracing such claims; and such customs, usages, or regulations, when not in conflict with the constitution and laws of this State, shall govern the decisions of the action."

In *Farnsworth* v. *Albert*, 79 F. Supp. 27 (1948), the court said:

* Leviticus 24:10.

> ". . . in accordance with the custom prevailing in the building trade in New Orleans, an offer by the sub-contractor to a general contractor to do work is irrevocable after the contractor has used the estimate of the sub-contractor as a basis for his offer to the owner, and the owner has accepted the general contractor's bid . . ."

Throughout this book will be found many instances of law being based upon custom and usage.

Since our laws find their basis in the experiences of group life and since they stand as evidence of what have come to be the accepted standards of conduct, the accepted practices, and the preferred way of life, it follows that with man's changing social, economic, and political conditions his laws also change. Legislative bodies in making laws and courts in deciding controversies are constantly giving reflection of changed conditions and crystallizing changed public policy.

> "Law is a growth, an evolution; not a thing, like Jonah's gourd, grown overnight. It is born with the needs of the people as those needs develop themselves . . . and adapted to these varying wants and needs of an advancing civilization." *Moss Point Lumber Co.* v. *Harrison Co.,* 89 Miss. 448.
>
> "Law is the rule of reason applied to existing conditions. Obviously, when conditions change there must be a corresponding change in the law, else it would cease to be a rule of reason and would become a mere arbitrary static rule. Law indicating, as it does, the just relations that obtain under given conditions, can be static only so long as the conditions to which it applies remain static. It does not prevent new conditions from arising, for if it did, and could, progress would be arrested. On the contrary, it aims to adjust relations to conditions as they exist when rights or obligations are claimed under them, and in proportion as it does that equitably it performs its true function. Whenever it arrests or clogs true progress it ceases to function truly. To do justice, then, under existing conditions, is its paramount office—all else, even the most venerable precedents, must yield to that office." *Milwaukee* v. *Milwaukee Electric R. Etc. Co.,* 173 Wis. 400.

The reader recognizes the need of legislative bodies to be responsive to public opinion. Laws which are not in keeping with the prevailing social policy of the public will be disregarded and difficult to enforce. The adoption and the necessary subsequent repeal of the Eighteenth Amendment to the Federal Constitution is a good illustration in point.

As an illustration of law evolving from changed conditions: the advent and general usage of the airplane has greatly modified the principle that "to whomever the soil belongs, he owns also to the sky and to the depths." The court in *Swetland* v. *Curtis Airports Corporation,* 55 F. (2d) 201, in keeping with "the traditional policy of the courts to adapt the law to the economic and social needs of the time," refused to enjoin the defendant from flying aircraft above the plaintiff's land.

► III. THE BODY OF OUR LAW

To the layman, a law usually suggests a ruling by a governmental body—a ruling by formal declaration or enactment. While it is true that many of our laws come into being in such manner, it is not the exclusive method by which laws originate under our legal system. The body of our law consists of two component parts:

(1) The law as found in the reported cases, which is called the *unwritten law* and is also referred to as the *common law;* and

(2) that law which comes into being by formal declarations or enactments by various governmental bodies and agencies.

A. CASE LAW—COMMON LAW RULES

The rules and standards as found declared in the reported cases constitute a major part of our legal system. The reader will find in the following chapters the repeated use of the term *common law rule.* This term has reference to the law as enunciated by the judges in the controversies that have come before them for solution.

There are three primary forces responsible for the shaping of our case law. They are (1) custom, (2) precedent, and (3) the judges.

1. *Case Law as Law of Custom*

"The common law is a system of general customs applicable to the rights of man in all the various pursuits and relations of life." *Spears* v. *Ward,* 48 Ind. 541.

Historically, case law was a direct reflection of the customary conduct and practices of the people themselves. In the early development of the common law system in England, the judges of the courts undoubtedly did formulate laws (their decisions) upon the basis of the general customary "law" of the land—the customary practices to which the community had given its common consent. This development was brought about very largely by the failure of any governmental authority properly to develop and administer rules of conduct, such being left to the people themselves. Subsequently the courts, during the course of their development, accepted the customary rules as formulated by the people themselves as being the law. To illustrate: In early England the merchant classes, due to the inadequacies of the then existing system of law and courts, developed their own rules and regulations governing their commercial transactions. The basis of these rules was very largely universal customs and usages adhered to by merchants. This body of rules came to be known as the *lex mercatoria,* the law merchant. In time the common-law courts recognized its existence and embraced it as part of the law of the land.

As said in *Cook* v. *Renick,* 19 Ill. 598:

". . . it began to insinuate itself into the common law, by the courts taking judicial notice of it, till its fibres became so intimately interwoven with the body of the common law itself, that no one could draw the line of demarcation between the two; and the common law, ever improving and adapting itself to the requirements of commerce, and the wants of the subject, finally, by progressive judicial decisions, the law merchant, or at least, that portion of it which was of universal application throughout the realm, was recognized by the courts without proof of its existence, and from that time forth, it became absorbed by and really constituted a part of the common law."

Custom today does not play the important part that it once did in the development of case law. There are those who believe that it plays a very small part indeed.* Custom is, however, followed by virtue of the many court decisions in which it is embodied, these decisions standing as precedents for future conduct.

2. *Case Law as Law of Precedent* (*Stare Decisis*)

The laws as declared by judges in the reported cases stand as judicial precedents to be applied to like or similar cases in the future. The courts are by honor bound to the traditional *doctrine of precedent,* to the doctrine that past decisions are controlling unless for controlling reasons they should not be followed. The doctrine of precedent introduces a strong element of stability into our legal system. Kent, in his *Commentaries* (Vol. 1, p. 476), succinctly and clearly characterized the doctrine as follows:

"A solemn decision upon a point of law arising in any given case, becomes an authority in a like case, because it is the highest evidence which we can have of the law applicable to the subject, and the judges are bound to follow that decision so long as it stands unreversed, unless it can be shown that the law was misunderstood or misapplied in that particular case. If a decision has been made upon solemn argument and mature deliberation, the presumption is in favor of its correctness; and the community have a right to regard it as a just declaration or exposition of the law, and to regulate their actions and contracts by it. It would, therefore, be extremely inconvenient to the public, if precedents were not duly regarded and implicitly followed. It is on the notoriety and stability of such rules that professional men can give safe advice to those who consult them; and people in general can venture with confidence to buy and trust, and to deal with each other. If judicial decisions were to be lightly disregarded, we should disturb and unsettle the great landmarks of property. When a rule has been once deliberately adopted and declared, it ought not to be disturbed unless by a court of appeal or review, and never by the same court, except for very cogent reasons, and upon a clear manifestation of error; and if the practice were otherwise, it would be leaving us in a state of perplexing uncertainty as to the law."

---

* See Gray, *Nature and Sources of the Law,* Sec. 634.

3. *Case Law as Judge-Made Law*

Case law is frequently called *judge-made law.* Undoubtedly, to an extent, this view of case law is valid. Although the doctrine of precedent introduces a strong element of stability into our legal system, we must realize that the common law by its very nature possesses a flexibility of application not inherent in statute law. The courts have no restraints in applying the recognized fundamental principles of the common law to new and changed conditions as they arise. As the court said in *Ketelson* v. *Stilz,* 184 Ind. 702:

> "Since courts have had an existence in America, they have never hesitated to take upon themselves the responsibility of saying what are the proper rules of common law."

The court in *Mitchell* v. *State,* 179 Miss. 814, spoke thus:

> ". . . The common law, . . . both in its substantive and in its adjective features, is not now, never has been, and never will be, static or stagnant. It has been one of the proudest boasts of the common law that it has within itself the potency of steady improvement, and this by judicial action, so long as that action is in accord with existing fundamental legal principles. It is the duty of courts, as attested by numerous decisions in this court, and in all courts throughout the nation, not only to keep the common law and its processes of enforcement abreast, or nearly so, with the substantial innovations of time, with the higher moral and material attainments in the general progress of enlightened civilization, proceeding always, however, upon established fundamental legal principles . . . but also it is equally the duty of courts to see that the state of the law shall continually profit by the experiences and observations of the past and that, when such experiences have definitely disclosed a mischievous imperfection in previous precedents, the mischief shall be removed by recourse to another, and a fitter, legal principle."

In the sense, then, that judges apply the basic underlying principles of our legal system to new or changed conditions, they do make law. In *Williams* v. *Miles,* 68 Neb. 463, the court observed:

> "The theory of our system is that the law consists, not in actual rules enforced by decisions of the courts at any one time, but the principles from which those rules flow; that old principles are applied to new cases, and the rules resulting from such application are modified from time to time as changed conditions and new states of facts require."

Thus, with the development of such things as the telegraph, the railroads, the advanced methods of industrial production, and the radio, new situations arose that were not covered by any actual rules of law. The judges were prepared to develop legal rules in these areas as the need arose—rules that were in harmony with the basic principles of the common law system.

But since judges are human beings, they are at times motivated by their own social, economic, or political philosophies in arriving at their decisions. Case law is to a very large extent "the product of the judges and not of the people." There can be no absolute certainty as to what the ruling of a court may be.

B. LAW BY ENACTMENT OR DECLARATION

The so-called *written law* consists of formal declarations or enactments by the various governmental bodies and agencies. It includes our Federal Constitution, the constitutions of the states, statutory enactments by legislative bodies, those rules and regulations of administrative bodies and commissions which have the binding force and effect of law, and city ordinances.

1. *Status and Functions of Statute Law*

As constitutional law is paramount to and controlling over statute law, so is statute law paramount to and controlling over common law. Consequently, common law rules and standards are applied only in those instances where there are no applicable written laws.

In our legal system, legislative enactments perform three primary functions:
(1) The codification of existing common law rules;
(2) the abolition or modification of judge-made case law; and
(3) the declaration of new rules of law.

a. Codification. Although the major portion of the rules of conduct that govern our everyday life is of the common law variety, there has been an increasing disposition to codify our case law. An examination of any state code will attest to this fact. Many of the legislative enactments found in the various state codes are compilations of common law rules. It is not the aim of such legislation to change the existing law but rather to reduce it to an orderly form and to clarify its application. Much of this codification of common law rules has resulted from the movement for uniformity of the laws of the various states. The Commission on Uniform State Laws has recommended various uniform acts, some of which have been enacted by a substantial majority of the states. One, the Uniform Negotiable Instruments Law, has been passed by every state in the Union. In some of our states, moreover, an effort has been made to codify the entire substantive law.

b. Abolition and Modification of Common Law. It is frequently charged that the common law processes are inadequate as a means of evolving rules of law to meet the rapidly changing conditions that characterize our modern existence. Thus, it is alleged that the conservatism and stability resulting from the doctrine of precedent have given the judges a backward rather than a forward point of view. Dicey, in his *Law and Public Opinion* (p. 369), said:

> "If a statute . . . is apt to reproduce the public opinion not so much of today as of yesterday, judge-made law occasionally represents the opinion of the day before yesterday."

It must be admitted that precipitous changes can be effected by legislation, whereas a change by the common law processes is a slow and gradual evolution. It is likewise true that the courts are not disposed to make fundamental changes in the traditional law. The author has been impressed by the number of recent cases in which the courts, although they recognized the desirability of a change, have refused to depart from the traditional law on the grounds that changes of a fundamental nature are legislative functions. President Wilson, in speaking before the American Bar Association on October 20, 1914, said:

> "Have we got to a time when the only way to change law is by statute? The changing of law by statute seems to me like mending a garment with a patch . . . I should hate to think that the law did not derive its impulse from looking forward rather than from looking backward."

Certainly the courts of today fail to display the vigor of the early common law courts in the development and application of the common law. The making of fundamental changes in our judicially declared common law rules has, therefore, very largely fallen to the lot of the legislative bodies. The fact that the judge-made law is retroactive in its application is a strong deterrent to fundamental changes by court decision. And it is actually the belief of many that, under our system of government, the initiation of law is a legislative function and should in no wise be exercised by the judiciary.

c. Declaration of New Rules of Law. The rapid development of our highly complex capitalistic exchange economy created social problems with which the common law was not prepared to cope. The conduct of much of man's economic activity by the use of large aggregates of the factors of production created a tremendous power of control over the individual contributors of capital and labor as well as over the consumer. A situation developed in which the individuals found themselves quite helpless to protect their self-interests, a situation in which those in control could exploit the individual to the detriment of the common welfare. This called for a redefinition and further crystallization of individual and collective rights with a view to the preservation and furtherance of social gains. The earlier common-law philosophy of individualism—the philosophy that the consequences of a given situation were the concern only of the individuals involved—has been greatly modified by social legislation.

A very large proportion of our modern legislation has concerned itself with the many social and economic problems that have resulted from the rapid development of our modern economic order. This remedial social legislation has dealt with matters such as unemployment compensation, minimum wages, maximum hours of work, compensation for occupational injuries, working conditions, economic security for the aged and those in a necessitous condition, the conservation of natural resources, and fair trade practices. Besides these, there are the laws providing for the regulation of business institutions said to be burdened with a public interest. State and federal legislative enactments whereby transportation agencies, public utilities, financial institutions, and insurance companies are subjected to detailed regulation constitute one of the more important phases of legislative action.

This type of law can be viewed as social engineering—the setting up of desirable goals and the means by which it is hoped they will be achieved.

2. *Relation of Courts to Statute and Constitutional Law*

Under our system of government, it is recognized that one of the functions of the judiciary is the interpretation of statute law and constitutional provisions. Statutes are not always drafted with such clarity of expression as to obviate the need for judicial interpretation. And, even though the language of a statute is clear and unambiguous, it is quite impossible for a legislative body to foresee all possible contingencies that might arise. Therefore, the courts are frequently called upon to determine the meaning of legislative enactments and the factual situations to which they were intended to apply. Unquestionably, the findings of the courts are at times contrary to the legislative intent. It thus becomes obvious that statute law is, upon final analysis, what the courts declare it to be. The process of judicial interpretation of statutory enactments and constitutional provisions constitutes an important source of law.

Review Questions

1. The statement has been made that "law is a luxury." Do you agree?
2. Enumerate the various social techniques that in your estimation have a tendency to contribute toward social control.
3. Would you include education in the above enumeration?
4. By what means does society seek to obtain observance of the rules of conduct established by its legal system?
5. Illustrate a rule of law as being a standard for the solution of a conflict between individuals.
6. What is the unwritten law as distinguished from the written law?
7. The common law, as we know, is found in the reported cases. To what, then, does the term *unwritten* have reference when it is used to designate the common law?
8. What governmental authority, if any, was instrumental in bringing the *law merchant* into being?
9. Where would you expect to find the greater degree of stability (not inflexibility), in case law or statute law?
10. Suppose that a problem were to come up before an Illinois court for which there was no judicial precedent in Illinois. Judicial precedent can be found in a number of eastern states as well as in a number of western states; however, the rule in the eastern states is different from the rule in the western states. How would the Illinois court proceed to solve the problem?
11. Can case law be effectively used for purposes of "social engineering"?
12. To what extent do the judges exercise influence over statute law?
13. In deciding a controversy, a court finds that the applicable case-law rule is different from the applicable statute-law rule. Which rule will prevail?

2 INTRODUCTION:

LEGAL RIGHTS, DUTIES, AND REMEDIES

▶ I. CONCEPT OF LEGAL RIGHTS AND DUTIES

The fundamental purpose of our legal structure is to make possible the existence of an orderly and harmonious society—a society in which both the individual and the group as a whole are afforded protection in their varying pursuits and activities. Specifically, such protection is accomplished by our system of legal rights and correlative legal duties. A legal right can be regarded as an interest which society will protect by imposing upon another or others a duty to respect it. These are foundation stones of orderly group life.

Legal rights and their corresponding duties, which the individual possesses or which he may acquire, can be classified as being either *contractual* or *noncontractual.*

A. CONTRACTUAL RIGHTS

Contractual rights and duties are those which arise out of a voluntarily created factual relationship, called a *contract.* Contractual rights are self-made rights. In essence, a contract is an agreement whereby individuals make commitments to each other about their future conduct. Our highly specialized exchange economy operates largely upon the basis of promises as to future conduct, and its orderly operation is achieved by the fact that individuals are held responsible for the contractual assurances they make. If an individual fails to fulfill a contractual obligation, the other party to the contract—who holds the corresponding right—may sue and receive such redress as society provides under the circumstances. Redress for breach of contract is usually money damages to the extent of the loss occasioned by the failure of performance. Under some circumstances, however, the individual will be required to carry out in fact his contractual undertaking.

The subject of contracts is of fundamental importance to the business student, for all business transactions and relationships are predicated upon the legal rights and corresponding legal duties that arise out of contractual undertakings. It is no exaggeration to say that our present-day cooperative exchange economy could not function without the sanctity of the contract. The contract affords an effective control mechanism, which makes possible the conduct of commercial affairs in relative peace and harmony. Businessmen feel secure in the conduct of their business affairs because they know that society protects their contractual rights. The redress that society gives to individuals whose contractual rights are not realized prevents those who have the corresponding legal duties from repudiating them with impunity.

B. NONCONTRACTUAL RIGHTS

Noncontractual legal rights and duties are those which exist by reason other than a contract. It is quite beyond the scope of this work even to indicate the many and varied noncontractual legal rights that society has seen fit to recognize in its quest for social control. In general, noncontractual rights and duties can be placed in three categories:

(1) Those which are common to all members of organized society;

(2) those which arise out of certain relationships and exist as between the individuals in the relationship; and

(3) those which exist between organized society and the individual.

1. *Legal Rights Common to All Members of Society*

Many legal rights accrue to the individual because of the fact that he is a member of our organized society—rights that are common to all members of society. The individual himself does nothing to acquire such basic rights as to be secure in (1) his person, (2) his reputation, (3) the use and enjoyment of his property, (4) his family relations, and (5) his business relations. These rights represent broad standards of conduct that the members of organized society have evolved to promote and protect their individual and collective welfare. They thus form an inherent part of our social organization. It is the duty of every member of the group to respect these rights. Any intentional, negligent, or reckless interference with them constitutes a legal wrong for which society gives the injured individual some form of redress. Such a wrong against the individual is designated as a *tort*. Bishop, in his *Non-contractual Liability*, Section 73, defines a tort as being "a breach of a duty which the law in distinction from a mere contract has imposed."

2. *Legal Rights Arising Out of Relationships*

Individuals may acquire legal rights and have imposed upon them legal duties by virtue of certain factual situations. If Mr. Lorch, for instance, takes a wife, the law attaches to this factual relationship—the marital status—legal duties with corresponding legal rights. It is, for example, the duty of the husband to provide the wife with the necessities of life. Should he fail in this respect, he becomes legally responsible to reimburse those who discharge his legal duty for him. By the same token, A, who enters the employ of B in the capacity of an agent, binds himself thereby to assume a course of behavior toward his employer B in keeping with the established standards governing agency relationships. A, the agent, has, for example, the legal duty to obey the instructions of his employer B. In the course of his study, the student will encounter other relationships, many of which are created by contract, to which the law attaches the legal duty to pursue a certain course of conduct.

3. *Collective Rights*

For its collective welfare, society prohibits certain acts and activities. These prohibitions establish standards of conduct that all members of the organized group are expected to observe. It is the right of society in its aggregate capacity to demand that the individuals of the group adhere to these standards of social behavior. Conduct in violation of one's duty to organized society is called a *crime,* for which society through its representatives may take punitive action.

Many acts which are regarded as crimes—wrongs against organized society—are also torts—wrongs against individuals. Thus the taking of an individual's property by force is a wrong against him for which he as an individual can obtain redress and it is also a wrong against organized society for which it may punish the wrongdoer. Other torts will readily suggest themselves as criminal acts. It should also be recognized that certain acts are purely crimes and not torts. The acts of treason, disorderly conduct, disobedience of traffic regulations, vagrancy, and contempt of court are inimical to the public interest and yet may not be harmful to any particular individual.

► II. REMEDIES AT LAW AND AT EQUITY

The failure to respect a legal right constitutes a legal wrong. It is axiomatic that society provides redress to every individual who has suffered a legal wrong. The nature of the remedies available to injured parties—those who have been legally wronged—depends upon the circumstances in the individual case. Our system of jurisprudence operates under a dual system of remedies, making available *remedies at law* and *remedies at equity.* Remedies at law are administered by law courts and remedies at equity are administered by equity courts. In some states, there is an actual physical distinction between law courts and equity courts; in other states, one court has jurisdiction over both law and equity cases. An understanding of the distinction between remedies at law and equitable remedies is fundamental to a study of law.

This division of our legal system upon the basis of legal and equitable remedies is historical in its origin. The early common law courts found themselves in the position where they could give relief only under well-defined factual circumstances.

> "The common law courts paid such deference to forms and precedents that they became slaves to them. Their jurisdiction was thus circumscribed. They adhered to certain precise writs and rigid forms of action which were not sufficiently comprehensive to enable them to give . . . any redress in many others. In such cases the aggrieved person was remediless, except he could get a hearing of the king himself." *Dalton* v. *Vanderveer,* 8 Misc. 484, 29 N.Y.S. 342.

History indicates that as appeals to the king became more numerous he referred them to the chancellor, who was directed to do justice. The next logical step was the creation of the chancellor's court to decide cases that did not fall into the scheme of remedies developed by the common-law courts. This was the origin of the modern court of equity and of equitable principles. It marked the beginning of the recognition of many rights that could not be given recognition by the common-law courts as long as they persisted in adhering to the established rigid forms of procedure and limited remedies.

> "The office of chancellor had been established before the Norman conquest, he being the personal adviser and representative of the crown; and there had long existed the special council, composed of the chancellor, the treasurer, the chief judiciary and others appointed by the king, a body which usually took cognizance of causes which other judges were incapable of determining. From the existence of these officials, and out of the large number of judicial complaints there arose the jurisdiction of the chancellor acting in the name and place of the sovereign. As the representative of the king, he exercised grace, tempered the strict rules of law by considerations of equity, absolved suitors from engagement into which they had been induced to enter by fraud, accident or mistake, and gave remedies for which the courts of the common law were owing to the fixed nature of their proceedings inadequate." *Shenehon* v. *Illinois L. Ins. Co.,* 100 Ill. App. 281.

A. BASIS OF EQUITY JURISDICTION

The basis of equity jurisdiction today is still, as it was at its origin, the inadequacy of a remedy at law. A court of equity will grant relief whenever there is no available remedy at law or the available remedy is imperfect or impracticable in its administration of prompt justice.

> "If the remedy at law is doubtful, difficult, not adequate to the object, not so complete as in equity, nor so efficient and practicable to the ends of justice and its prompt administration, then equity will take jurisdiction." *Rumbarger* v. *Yokum,* 174 Fed. 55.

B. NATURE OF EQUITABLE REMEDIES

The need for an enlargement of remedial law can be more fully appreciated if we consider the nature of the remedies that were and are today available in the law courts. In general, courts of law give only two forms of redress, namely: (1) money damages, and (2) the restoration of real or personal property to one from whom it is being unjustly withheld. The common-law courts did not develop protective or preventive remedies. Neither did the remedies available in all instances give complete and adequate redress for the legal injury suffered. The development and growth of equitable principles and the resultant remedies are a consequence of the inability of the law courts to administer complete and adequate justice. Some of the more important equitable remedies that were developed to supplement the restricted remedies at law follow.

1. *Specific Performance*

A court of law cannot enforce a contract in the literal sense of the word. It can award the party who has not realized his rights a sum of money to compensate for the injury suffered. In the event that the contract relates to subject matter which is unique, a monetary award to the injured party may be most inadequate. To illustrate:

Let us suppose that A has contracted for the purchase of 100 bushels of potatoes of a certain grade and variety from B at $1.00 a bushel. Should he fail to deliver the potatoes as he promised, A's remedy of money damages would be adequate. By recovering the difference between the contract price and the market price of potatoes, he could place himself in as good a position as he would have occupied had the contract been performed. Generally speaking, a breach of contract for the sale of personal property can adequately be taken care of by the awarding of money damages to cover the actual injury suffered.

Now let us suppose that the object contracted for was an invention, a thing unique. Money damages would hardly be adequate as a remedy. Therefore, equity would make available the remedy of specific performance. Equity would decree that B *specifically perform* his contractual promise. By the same token, courts of equity will require the performance of real-estate contracts. A refusal to observe a decree of an equity court constitutes a contempt of court. Consequently, B's failure to comply with the court order would be held a contempt of court, which would subject him to a fine or to imprisonment.

2. *Injunction*

Law courts cannot prevent the commission of an injury and can award redress only after the injury has been suffered. Equity, however, can prevent the commission of a wrong by the remedy of an *injunction*. To illustrate:

A has sold his business establishment to B. Although A has agreed not to compete with B, nonetheless A makes preparations to establish a competing business enterprise. B would have no remedy in a court of law until A would have actually violated the contract. By that time, however, an action for damages would be of little value to B, because of the impossibility of estimating the amount of money damages the violation would cause B. Under such circumstances, equity would issue an injunction ordering A to refrain from violating his contract. It thus administers preventive justice, a function which the law courts do not perform.

3. *Rescission*

The equitable remedy of *rescission* can be characterized as being a phase of protective justice. The remedy of rescission consists of relieving parties of their contractual undertakings if the circumstances require such a course of procedure. When granting relief from contractual commitments, a court of equity, if it sees fit, may restore the parties to their original positions. Well-recognized grounds upon which equity will rescind or cancel a contract are cases in which:

(1) Contractual assent was induced by fraud, duress, or undue influence;

(2) the contractual commitment was the result of a mistake; or

(3) a contracting party as a matter of law was not possessed of contractual capacity as, for example, one of unsound mind.

4. *Equitable Titles or Interests*

Equity recognizes that, under certain circumstances, individuals have equitable interests in property even though the legal title is held by others. A trustee holds legal title to property for the benefit of another (the beneficiary), and a corporation holds legal title for the benefit of the stockholders. In these cases, equity will protect the rights of the beneficiaries. In equity, the legal title holders have the obligation to use and to apply the property faithfully in the manner of the trust reposed in them.

During the course of his study, the student will encounter other equitable forms of relief. He will come to realize that equity in conjunction with strictly legal remedies makes possible a well-rounded system of justice.

► III. LEGAL PROCEDURE

A litigant has the absolute right to bring suit in a court of law, whereas in a court of equity he will be heard only by petition—by grace of the court. Equitable relief has been said to rest within the sound discretion of the court. "A court of equity acts only when and as conscience demands." *Deweese* v. *Reinhard,* 165 U.S. 386.

In a court of law it is the litigant's right to have issues of fact determined by a jury. The function of a jury whenever used is to serve as a fact-finding body. In a court of equity, however, the right to trial by jury does not exist. The chancellor may submit an issue of fact to a jury, but the jury's finding is not binding upon him. This course of procedure is adopted only "to inform the conscience of the chancellor."

A. TRIAL PROCEDURE

A study of law through the use of case material necessitates an understanding of the fundamentals of legal procedure—of the basic steps followed in the prosecution of a civil action to its conclusion. It is especially important that the student have knowledge of the procedural steps preliminary to the actual court trial—those steps by which the limits of the controversy between the plaintiff and the defendant are established. Only through an understanding of the conflicting contentions of the parties and a knowledge of the manner in which they arose can the student fully appreciate the application of the principles of law to the factual situation presented by the case.

The individual states have full control over the procedure followed in their courts for both civil and criminal cases. However, their judicial sovereignty is subject to the qualification that such procedure must not deny the individual the fundamental rights protected by the Federal Constitution. The Fourteenth Amendment of the Federal Constitution makes it obligatory for the states not to "deprive any person of life, liberty, or property without due process of law." * In the case of *Penroyer* v. *Neff,* 95 U.S. 714, it was said that *due process of law* means a course of legal procedure according to the rules and principles that have been established in our system of jurisprudence for the protection and enforcement of private rights. The United States Supreme Court has said many times that a procedure which gives reasonable notice and affords a fair opportunity to be heard before the issues are decided meets the requirements of due process of law.

The court said in *Simon* v. *Craft,* 182 U.S. 437, that the due process clause

> ". . . does not necessitate that the proceedings in a State court should be by a particular mode, but only that there shall be a regular course of proceedings, in which notice is given of the claim asserted and an opportunity afforded to defend against it."

While the details of procedure differ in the various states, the basic pattern is the same. In general, provision is made for

(1) notice to the defendant of the suit;

(2) the filing of the parties' pleadings with the clerk of the court for the purpose of resolving the controversy to specific issues;

(3) the trial;

(4) appeal of the case from the original trial court to an appellate court for review and final determination.

1. *The Notice*

The first step in a legal action consists of giving notice to the defendant of the impending suit. Unless the requirements of notice have been met, the court has no jurisdiction over the defendant. It is the notice *to* the defendant that gives the court the right and power to act *against* the defendant. A proceeding against an individual who has not been given the required notice and who has not waived notice is a nullity.

Notice of the impending action against the defendant is accomplished by serving him with a document usually called a *summons.* The summons informs the defendant that proceedings have been instituted against him and that, unless he takes steps to defend, his default will be noted and a judgment entered against him. The summons briefly relates the plaintiff's cause of action against the defendant and informs the latter that the plaintiff's complaint, which fully sets out his grievance, will be on file with the clerk of the court. In some jurisdictions, a copy of the plaintiff's complaint is served with the summons.

It is usually required that the notice be served upon the defendant personally,

* The Fifth Amendment applies only to the Federal Government.

but under certain circumstances provision is made for leaving the notice with a member of the defendant's household. In some instances it is possible to get jurisdiction over the defendant by publishing the notice in a newspaper of general circulation in the county in which the action is to be brought.

2. *Pleading—Establishing Issues*

The pleadings that are filed with the clerk of the court by the parties to the action perform the function of resolving the controversy to a specific issue or issues. *Pleading* is the process whereby the plaintiff and the defendant formally declare their contentions regarding the controversy with a view to determining definitely the nature of the dispute. As the court said in *Parliman* v. *Young,* 2 Dak. 174:

> "Pleadings . . . are composed of the written allegations of the parties, terminating in a single proposition, distinctly affirmed on one side, and denied on the other, called the issue."

There can be no trial before a court until the issue or issues between the parties have been determined. The court in *Treadgold* v. *Willard,* 81 Ore. 658, characterized the pleadings as being

> ". . . the formal written allegations by the parties of their respective demands and defenses, and . . . employed to state the ultimate facts which, when uncontroverted or when established by evidence at the trial . . . afford the foundation upon which a judgment or decree must necessarily rest."

a. Plaintiff's Complaint. The first pleading in an action is the plaintiff's *complaint,* in which he states the facts that constitute his cause of action against the defendant. In this way the defendant is apprised of the facts that the plaintiff expects to prove during the course of the trial.

> "Where a petition states facts which show that the plaintiff has been wronged, show of what such wrongs consist, and the amount of damage plaintiff has sustained thereby, and further show that defendant perpetrated such wrongs and is liable to plaintiff therefor, and prays judgment for the amount of damages sustained by reason of such wrongs, it states a cause of action." *Smith* v. *Gardner,* 37 Okla. 183.

b. Defendant's Defense. Unless the defendant enters his appearance and pleads a defense against the plaintiff's allegations, a judgment will be entered against him by default. There are various ways in which the defendant may interpose a defense to the facts alleged by the plaintiff. The defendant may, for example, file a *demurrer* to the complaint. A demurrer raises the question of whether the complaint is sufficient as a matter of law to support the plaintiff's action. It thus brings up a question of law to be decided by the court. If the court concludes that the plaintiff has not pleaded facts that constitute the commission of a wrong by the defendant, the demurrer will be sustained. Then, unless the plaintiff pleads further, the defendant need do nothing more.

A complaint that sufficiently states a cause of action must be answered by the defendant. The defendant's answer may take various forms. It may be a categorical denial of the plaintiff's allegations. Obviously, this would raise an issue of fact to be tried by the court. If one party alleges certain facts to be true and the other party denies their truth, an issue has been established. Not infrequently the defendant in his answer will admit to the truth of the plaintiff's allegations and then will proceed to plead other facts, which are designed to defeat the plaintiff's cause of action. This is known as *answering by confession and avoidance.* To illustrate:

Step 1. The plaintiff in his *petition* has alleged that the defendant's negligent conduct was the proximate cause of a personal injury.

Step 2. The defendant *answers* by admitting his negligent conduct and alleging that the plaintiff's own conduct contributed to his injury. (As a matter of law, contributory negligence on the part of the plaintiff will bar recovery.) As yet no issue has been raised. It is now incumbent upon the plaintiff to take the initiative.

Step 3. The plaintiff may file a *demurrer* questioning the sufficiency of the defense as a matter of law, or he may file a reply to the facts alleged by the defendant. If he files a denial, the controversy has been resolved to an issue. In some jurisdictions, the new matter pleaded is deemed controverted without need of reply.

Another type of pleading with which the student should be acquainted is the *counterclaim,* which may be employed by the defendant. Strictly speaking, it is not a defense to the matters alleged in the plaintiff's complaint, but is a statement of fact allegedly constituting a cause of action against the plaintiff. In some jurisdictions the pleading of a counterclaim is conditioned upon an admission of the allegations contained in the complaint, but, as a general rule, the counterclaiming defendant may either deny or admit the plaintiff's allegations. To illustrate:

Upon the basis of past business dealings, Jones has acquired an obligation of $2,000 to Smith. Jones refuses to pay the obligation since, he contends, Smith has not performed a contract that the parties had entered into. Smith denies the existence of a contract such as Jones alleges and brings an action to recover his $2,000. In his answer, Jones admits the obligation of $2,000 and *counterclaims* for damages for the alleged breach of contract by Smith. If Jones is not successful in establishing a contract, there will be no damages and Smith will get a judgment entitling him to his $2,000. However, if Jones is successful in establishing a breach of contract and damages of $1,500, such damages will stand as a set-off against the $2,000 which Jones has admitted he owed Smith.

3. *Trial of Issues*

After an issue has been established by the pleadings of the litigants, the case is ready for trial before the court. If the issue is one of law, the decision rests entirely with the judge. It is his function to pass upon all matters of law, including the rules of procedure for the conduct of the trial, and to see that these rules —designed to ensure fair play—are adhered to. If a question of fact has been raised by the pleadings, it is submitted to the jury for determination. The jury in a trial serves as the fact-finding body. The conflicting evidence and testimony of the parties is heard by the jury, and from it the jury is required to determine what the true facts are. In the event that no conflicting evidence is submitted, the judge can take cognizance of such and direct a verdict for the party who successfully established his allegations without submitting the case to the jury. In such an event, it is necessary only to apply the law to the obvious facts. Where, however, the case is submitted to the jury upon an issue of fact, it is the jury which renders the verdict. Before the jury retires to deliberate upon the evidence, the judge issues instructions to them for their guidance in arriving at the proper verdict. These instructions inform the jury about the various laws that might be applicable, depending on what facts it is going to consider as true. The jury applies the law, in accordance with the judge's instructions, to the facts as they are found.

After the verdict has been rendered, it is customary for the losing party to submit to the court a motion for a new trial. This motion is based upon alleged irregularities in the course of the trial. If the motion is denied, a judgment is recorded in keeping with the verdict. The only further recourse available to the losing party (or the winning party if, for example, he is dissatisfied with the amount awarded him) is an appeal of the case to a higher court for a review of the proceedings in the trial court.

B. REVIEW PROCEDURE

The reader should also appreciate that cases can be appealed only from those trial courts which are "courts of record." A court of record is one in which the proceedings are recorded "for a perpetual memorial and testimony." As will be pointed out, it is this record that forms the basis for the appeal court's review of the case.

Cases tried in "courts not of record" can be appealed *for trial upon their merits* in some other trial court. For example, in Iowa Justice of the Peace courts (as is usual with Justice of the Peace and other small-claims courts) are courts not of record, and the Code provides for appeal for trial upon the merits in either a district or a superior court within the county.

Courts are of two types, namely, (1) *trial courts* or, as they are called, *courts of original jurisdiction,* and (2) *courts of appeal.* The function of an appeal court is to review cases after their trial in a court of original jurisdiction. In no sense of the word does an appeal court try a case.

In essence, an appeal consists of:

(1) Transferring a certified record (or an abstract of the record) of the proceedings in the trial court to the appeal court. This record forms the basis for the court's review of the case.

(2) Filing of briefs by the litigants. The party who initiates the appeal (the appellant) will first file his brief, in which he will set forth his contentions as to what conclusion the appeal court should arrive at. The other party (the appellee) will then file a brief in which he answers the contentions of the appellant. The

brief will also cite decided cases as legal authority in support of the arguments that are presented.

(3) In some states, the litigants are entitled to present oral arguments before the court, whereas in other states the arguments are confined to the briefs. The right of oral argument is dependent upon statute or the rules of the particular court.

(4) Disposition of the case by the court. The court, after reviewing the case as it was tried in the lower court and after giving consideration to the arguments of the parties, will render its decision in the form of a written opinion. The opinion will state the principles of law upon which the court has based its conclusion. The court's opinion will be to affirm, modify, or reverse the decision of the lower court. The court will then either (a) render a final judgment or (b) send the case back to the lower court for retrial or for further proceedings consistent with the court's opinion.

► IV. COURTS

A. FEDERAL COURTS

Under our dual system of government, a dual system of courts exists—state and federal. The federal judiciary is entirely separate from, and independent of, the judiciary of the various states. Article III, Section 1 of the Constitution of the United States provides:

> "The Judicial Power of the United States, shall be vested in one supreme Court, and in such inferior Courts as the Congress may from time to time ordain and establish."

Congress has seen fit to supplement the Supreme Court with the federal district courts and the circuit courts of appeals. Since the Supreme Court was primarily an appeal court, it was necessary for Congress to establish trial courts, courts in which cases can originate. The *federal district courts* are courts in which federal cases are initiated. The *circuit courts of appeals,* on the other hand, are exclusively appeal courts, established for the purpose of reviewing cases appealed from the district courts. They are not trial courts and have no original jurisdiction. Their sole function is to review the record of the proceedings of such cases as are appealed from the district courts or, in some instances, from decisions of commissions. The Supreme Court's original and appellate jurisdiction is provided for by Article III, Section 2:

> "In all cases affecting ambassadors, other public Ministers and Consuls and those in which a State shall be Party, the supreme Court shall have original Jurisdiction. In all the other Cases before mentioned, the supreme Court shall have appellate Jurisdiction, both as to Law and Fact, with such Exceptions, and under such Regulations as the Congress shall make."

1. *Extent of Judicial Power*

The term *jurisdiction* is generally employed to designate the extent of a court's judicial powers. If a person or a thing is said to come within the jurisdiction of the court, it means that the court has the right to apply the law in respect to that person or thing. A court's jurisdiction is determined by either its constitutional or its legislative grant of powers, which are to be exercised within designated territorial limits.

The limits of action of the federal judiciary are established by Article III, Section 2, of the Constitution of the United States, which reads:

> "The judicial Power shall extend to all Cases, in Law and Equity, arising under this Constitution, the Laws of the United States, and Treaties made, or which shall be made, under their Authority;—to all Cases affecting Ambassadors, other public Ministers and Consuls;—to all Cases of admiralty and maritime Jurisdiction;—to Controversies to which the United States shall be a Party; to Controversies between two or more States;—between a State and Citizens of another State;—between Citizens of different States;—between Citizens of the same State claiming Lands under Grants of different States, and between a State, or the Citizens thereof, and foreign States, Citizens or Subjects."

This, however, is subject to the Eleventh Amendment to the Constitution, which says:

> "The Judicial power of the United States shall not be construed to extend to any suit in law or equity, commenced or prosecuted against one of the United States by Citizens of another State, or by Citizens or Subjects of any Foreign State."

The Constitution does not specifically confer any jurisdiction upon inferior federal courts. It merely prescribes the limits of judicial power that Congress may confer upon them. The district courts and circuit courts of appeals have, therefore, only such jurisdiction as is conferred upon them by act of Congress. The Constitution specifies merely the original jurisdiction of the Supreme Court, to which Congress cannot add or from which it cannot detract. The Supreme Court does not have any appellate jurisdiction other than that provided for by congressional enactment.

2. *Concurrent and Exclusive Jurisdiction*

Although the state and federal judiciaries are independent of each other, they enjoy concurrent jurisdiction over many matters. As a matter of fact, state courts have equal jurisdiction with the federal courts in all matters in which jurisdiction has not been reserved exclusively to the federal courts.

> "Legal or equitable rights, acquired under either system of laws (state or federal), may be enforced in any court of either sovereignty competent to hear and determine such kind of rights and not restrained by its constitution in the exercise of such jurisdiction. Thus, a legal or equitable right acquired

under State laws, may be prosecuted in the State courts, and also, if the parties reside in different States, in the Federal courts. So rights whether legal or equitable, acquired under the laws of the United States, may be prosecuted in the United States courts, or in the State courts, competent to decide rights of the like character and class; subject, however, to this qualification, that where a right arises under a law of the United States, Congress may, if it see fit, give to the Federal courts exclusive jurisdiction. . . . This jurisdiction is sometimes exclusive by express enactment and sometimes by implication." *Claflin* v. *Houseman,* 93 U.S. 130, 23 L. Ed. 833.

The federal judicial code enumerates the classes of cases in which the jurisdiction of the federal courts is exclusive. For example, it includes cases arising under the bankruptcy laws, the patent laws, and the copyright laws; cases arising under antitrust legislation; admiralty and maritime cases; and actions against ambassadors or consuls. The federal judicial code also specifies what cases can be appealed to the Supreme Court from state courts. For example, controversies involving the Federal Constitution may be appealed to the United States Supreme Court after they have been decided by a court of last resort in a state.

B. STATE COURTS

There is a considerable variation in the composition of the court systems of the forty-eight states. However, each system consists of various courts of original jurisdiction and one or more courts of appellate jurisdiction. The student should inquire into the structure of the judiciary and the jurisdiction of the various courts in his own state.

Review Questions

1. What is the basic distinction between contractual and noncontractual rights?
2. What is the basic distinction between a tort and a crime?
3. May the same act of an individual be both a tort and a crime?
4. What is the nature of the remedies available in a court of law?
5. What was the historical basis for the development of equitable remedies?
6. What determines whether a court of equity will make a remedy available to an injured party?
7. X contracts to sell his secret formula for the manufacture of tooth paste to Y. In the event that X fails to perform the contract, would Y have an equitable remedy?
8. Why will a court of equity require a party who has contracted to sell real property to perform the contract specifically?
9. Explain what is meant by *preventive* justice.
10. For the purpose of protecting his interests, would a stockholder, in an action against the corporation, bring the suit in a court of law or a court of equity?
11. Does a litigant have the right to a trial by jury under all circumstances?
12. Explain how an action by the plaintiff against the defendant may result in a judgment for money damages in favor of the defendant.
13. Define *due process of law* as the term is used in the Federal Constitution.

14. A conflict arises between A and B as to the ownership of certain household goods. They are agreed upon the facts and come into court upon a stipulation of facts. Is a jury necessary?
15. What is the purpose of the pleadings in a legal action.
16. Enumerate the courts of original jurisdiction in your states indicating those which are courts of record.
17. What is the nature of appeal from a court not of record?
18. When a case is appealed from the trial court, is it retried by the appeal court?
19. Residing in Ohio, X brings an action for breach of contract against a Delaware corporation doing business in Ohio. Could the action be brought in either a state court or in a federal district court?
20. The state legislature passed a law imposing a special tax upon those businesses engaged in the sale of butter substitutes. Engaged in this business, A instituted legal action contending the law was in violation of the Fourteenth Amendment of the Federal Constitution, which provides that "No state shall deny any person within its jurisdiction the equal protection of the laws." The trial court held against him and the state appeal court—the court of last resort—sustained the trial court. Does A have any further recourse?

I

Contracts

Chapter

3. INTRODUCTION TO LAW OF CONTRACTS

4. OFFER AND ACCEPTANCE—AGREEMENT THE BASIC ELEMENT

5. CONSIDERATION

6. VOIDANCE OF CONTRACTS—INCOMPETENT PARTIES, FRAUD, MISTAKE, DURESS, AND UNDUE INFLUENCE

7. FORM OF THE CONTRACT—THE STATUTE OF FRAUDS

8. ILLEGAL AGREEMENTS

9. ASSIGNMENT OF RIGHTS AND DELEGATION OF DUTIES

10. PERFORMANCE, CONTRACTUAL CONDITIONS, AND BREACH

11. DISCHARGE OF CONTRACTUAL OBLIGATIONS

3 CONTRACTS:

INTRODUCTION TO LAW OF CONTRACTS

► I. ROLE OF CONTRACTS IN BUSINESS

The law of contracts occupies a position of prime importance in its application to the field of business. Contracts are the medium through which our exchange economy functions. Stated in broad terms, such phases of business as employment, selling, buying, use of credit, transportation, shifting of risk, storing, manufacturing, and renting are accomplished through the use of contracts. Most of our forms of business organization—partnerships, corporations, business trusts, and the various forms of cooperatives—owe their very existence to these instrumentalities called contracts. Some appreciation of the place of the law of contracts in business will readily follow from a study of the following chapters, whose aim it is to establish, develop, and apply the more important principles that pertain to this type of human engagement.

The reader should constantly bear in mind that contracts are also control mechanisms facilitating the orderly conduct of our economic affairs. The student of business certainly must know how the interests of society are served by the use of these control mechanisms. The law of contracts should not be regarded as a set of abstract rules of conduct applying to the individual case, but rather as expressions of public policy with a view to obtaining better social control. In some instances, opinions will differ as to how well this public policy is conceived.

► II. BASIC CONCEPT OF A CONTRACT

The law of contracts can very properly be characterized as the law of promises. Section 1 of the *Restatement of the Law of Contracts* defines a contract as follows:

> "A contract is a promise or a set of promises for the breach of which the law gives a remedy, or the performance of which the law in some way recognizes as a duty."

A contract is basically a relationship resulting from a voluntary agreement between persons. To this relationship the law attaches the legal rights and corresponding legal duties such as the parties have agreed upon. A contractual relationship consists of an exchange of promises or an exchange of a promise for an act. If such a relationship exists, the person to whom such a promise is made acquires the legal right to expect a realization of the contents of the promise. The one who makes the promise (the promisor), on the other hand, assumes the corresponding legal duty to fulfill such expectation. Therefore, it is said that a contract is an agreement that is legally enforceable, an agreement "for the breach of which the law gives a remedy, or the performance of which the law in some way recognizes as a duty."

It should be realized that, although a contract is founded upon an agreement, not all agreements are contracts. A and B agree that they will accompany each other to an ice-cream social; B fails to carry out his promise and escorts C instead. This was not an agreement that created a legal obligation. Legally, there is no recourse against B for his failure to fulfill his promise to A. Should A and B, however, agree to accompany each other to the altar for the purpose of joining in the bonds of matrimony, the agreement creates legal rights and legal duties. If either party fails to do as promised, the other would have legal redress available. Society sanctions the enforceability of only such agreements as are of some economic significance and importance in the maintenance and the operation of the accepted social order. As a group, we are little concerned with the question of whether individuals live up to their purely social engagements, but social as well as individual welfare demands that engagements which entail contemplated economic consequences, and which are compatible with social objectives, be enforced. It is not, for example, in keeping with the accepted social standards to sanction an agreement whereby A promises to pay B $100 if a horse named Sonny Joe runs faster than the other horses competing with him in a race, and B, in turn, promises to pay A $50 if Sonny Joe is outdistanced by any of his competitors.

► III. ELEMENTS OF A CONTRACT

A contract is a factual relationship, consisting of certain recognizable facts. These facts, which are necessary to the existence of a contract, are commonly called the *essential elements of a contract.* They are: (1) an offer and an acceptance—the agreement, (2) a valid consideration, (3) competent parties, and (4) a legal object.

These elements are enumerated in the *Restatement of the Law of Contracts,* Section 19, as follows:

"(a) A promisor and a promisee each of whom has legal capacity to act as such in the proposed contract;

"(b) a manifestation of assent by the parties who form the contract to the terms thereof, and by every promisor to the consideration for his promise, except as otherwise stated;

"(c) a sufficient consideration except as otherwise stated;

"(d) the transaction, though satisfying the foregoing requirements, must b one that is not void by statute or by special rules of the common law."

It is the objective of Book One to establish with some degree of certainty

(1) the factual requirements necessary to the existence of the above contract essentials;

(2) the factual circumstances which may prevent the existence of a contractual relationship; and

(3) the factual circumstances which may effect the termination of a contractual relationship.

► IV. MEANING OF ENFORCEABILITY OF CONTRACTS

The term *enforceable* as used in this discussion must not be taken too literally. It does not necessarily mean that the delinquent party can be made to do as agreed. As here employed, enforceability means that society makes available some form of redress to a party who fails to realize his reasonable expectations under a contractual promise.

If there has been a failure of performance, society will enforce a contract in the sense that through its established machinery—the courts—it may give the following forms of redress, depending upon the circumstances.

(1) The payment of a sum of money in lieu of performance, which we will call from this point on the *remedy of money damages.*

(2) The actual performance of the promise:

(a) By the use of the *equitable remedy of specific performance* which is used when the performance of the contract requires positive action. For example, the contractual undertaking to convey title to real property as distinguished from a contractual undertaking to refrain from doing a certain thing.

(b) By the use of the *equitable remedy of injunction* which is used when the performance of the contract consists of refraining from doing a certain thing.

(3) Relieving the contracting parties of their contractual commitments and placing them back in their original positions insofar as is possible. This is the *equitable remedy of rescission.*

► V. CONTRACTS CLASSIFIED

In the following chapters, contracts will at different times be designated and characterized as being either express, implied, bilateral, unilateral, executed, executory, void, voidable, unenforceable, formal, informal, or quasi. It seems desirable that the reader should, as a prelude to the study of the subject matter of contracts, have some comprehension of the meaning of these terms.

A. EXPRESS AND IMPLIED CONTRACTS

An *express* contract is the result of the written or spoken words of the parties; these words establish the contractual relationship. The agreement and its terms are declared by the parties and are not left to inference.

An *implied* contract, on the other hand, originates from the acts or conduct of the parties, such acts and conduct as lead to the reasonable inference that a contractual relationship was intended. If A, for example, goes into a hardware store where he is well known and walks out with a hedge clipper, saying to the clerk, "I'll be seeing you, Shorty," a contract has been entered into, for these circumstances give rise to the reasonable implication that A intends to pay the regular price for the clipper, and the clerk gives his assent.

It is a common occurrence for parties to an agreement to fail to express themselves in regard to major terms, leaving such to implication. Services are frequently bargained for without any agreement as to the price. Under such circumstances, it is logical to infer an intention to pay a reasonable price for the benefit obtained.

B. BILATERAL AND UNILATERAL CONTRACTS

A *bilateral* contract is created by an exchange of promises. A promises to marry B, and B promises to marry A; this is a bilateral agreement.

A *unilateral* contract is an exchange of a promise for an act. At B's request, A extends $500 worth of credit to C, and B agrees to pay this sum in the event of C's default. This is a unilateral contract, consisting of A's act in exchange for B's promise of repayment.

C. EXECUTED AND EXECUTORY CONTRACTS

An *executed* contract is one that has been fully performed by all parties. It is obvious, of course, that a contract may at a given time be at one of the various stages of execution. An *executory* contract is one upon which no performance has taken place.

D. VOID AND VOIDABLE CONTRACTS

A *void* contract is no contract. It is an agreement under which neither the parties nor third persons can acquire any legal rights. If A and B enter into an agreement to carry out acts prohibited by a statute, the agreement would be void.

A *voidable* contract is, as the term suggests, subject to being avoided by one or both of the parties. It is an agreement which is in every sense of the word a contract until such time as an election is made to avoid it. Contracts of minors belong in this category. The law gives them the right to choose whether or not they wish to be bound by their agreements.

E. UNENFORCEABLE CONTRACTS

An *unenforceable* contract is one which cannot be established in a court of law. As a matter of public policy, claimants are, under certain circumstances, required to have written proof of contracts as a condition of their enforcement. Under circumstances requiring written evidence, an oral contract would be unenforceable. Claimants are likewise required to assert their rights within a specified statutory period of time. Unless they take steps legally to enforce their contracts within this time period, the agreements become unenforceable.

F. FORMAL AND INFORMAL CONTRACTS

Most contracts are not required to conform to a set form or pattern. Such contracts are referred to as being *informal* or simple.

Formal contracts are those which are required to meet established standards of form, such as negotiable instruments, or those executed under seal. Sealed contracts, although still prevalent in some jurisdictions, are no longer in general use.

G. QUASI CONTRACTS

Quasi contracts are frequently called *implied contracts* or *contracts implied in law*. However, they are not contracts in the true sense of the word. *Quasi contract* is merely a legal theory designed for the purpose of giving individuals the right to recover money or property where such will serve the ends of justice. Let us suppose, for example, that A makes payment of an obligation to B, when in fact it should have been made to C, who is the lawful claimant. To allow B to keep the payment would be to enrich him unjustly. In order to prevent this, therefore, the law makes available a basis of recovery. In effect, the law imposes upon B the duty to return the payment made to him. Another case of a quasi-contractual obligation would be the duty imposed on a husband to reimburse a third person for the necessities of life which the third person has furnished to his wife.

As the court said in *Conkling's Estate* v. *Champlin*, 193 Okla. 79, 141 P. (2d) 569:

> "A 'quasi' or constructive contract is an implication of law. An 'implied' contract is an implication of fact. In the former the contract is a mere fiction, imposed in order to adapt the case to a given remedy. In the latter, the contract is a fact legitimately inferred. In one, the intention is disregarded; in the other, it is ascertained and enforced. In one, the duty defines the contract; in the other, the contract defines the duty."

Review Questions

1. Explain how contracts are control mechanisms.
2. It has been said that "contractual rights are self-made rights which exist or fail as a result of the parties themselves." What does this mean?
3. What determines whether an agreement is a contract?
4. What are the possible remedies available to the injured party for a breach of contract?
5. X accepts professional services from Y, a physician. It has never been agreed between X and Y that these services are to be paid for. Is there a contract?
6. Illustrate a bilateral contract as distinguished from a unilateral contract.
7. What is a quasi contract?

4 CONTRACTS:

OFFER AND ACCEPTANCE—AGREEMENT THE BASIC ELEMENT

► I. NATURE OF OFFER AND ACCEPTANCE—THE AGREEMENT

A. AS AN EXCHANGE OF ASSURANCES

Let the statement be recalled that a contract to which the law attaches legal rights and corresponding legal duties consists of a voluntary exchange of promises or an exchange of a promise for an act. The law of contracts can very appropriately be characterized as the law of assurances. A contract in essence consists of an exchange of assurances (by promise or act) between individuals—assurances which they are then expected to live up to. These assurances are generally called the offer and the acceptance.

Obviously, the initial step in arriving at an agreement is the making of an offer by one person to another, the offer being in the nature of a proposal by the offeror to the offeree. Usually this offer is in the form of a promise—an assurance—conditioned upon the offeree's giving a price, in the form either of an act or of a promise, generally a promise.

Similarly, the acceptance may be viewed (1) as an assurance from the offeree that the price asked for in the offer will be forthcoming, and (2) as an implied request that its price be the promise made by the offeror.

B. AS A MEETING OF MINDS

To have a valid offer and acceptance, the one must be the exact counterpart of the other. There must be present a manifest intention that the parties are agreeing upon the same thing. This does not require that the parties be of a mind as to every particular but that they have come to agreement as to the thing in respect to which they are contracting. Thus, if A proposes to sell his car to B for the price of $500 and B accepts, he cannot object that he was of the mind that A's car was a 1940 Ford when in fact it was a 1940 Chrysler. The minds of the parties had apparently met upon one and the same thing, namely A's car, be it what it may.[1]

To require an actual meeting of the minds rather than an apparent meeting of the minds would make it nigh impossible to establish a contract.

In *Kyle* v. *Kavanagh,* 103 Mass. 356, the defendant had agreed to purchase of the plaintiff four lots on Prospect Street in the city of Waltham. There were,

[1] Allen v. Bissinger, p. 48.

however, two different Prospect Streets in Waltham, the plaintiff having in mind the street on which he owned the lots and the defendant having in mind the other. The court held that there was no agreement, since the parties had different things in mind. The substance of the contract had not been identified in the minds of the parties.

► II. REQUISITES OF A LEGALLY ACCEPTABLE OFFER

The problem at this point is to determine what constitutes in the eyes of the law an acceptable offer, an offer of such a nature that upon its acceptance the law, in effect, says to the parties, "You are now expected to live up to your commitments or suffer the consequences such as society provides."

There are two essentials to the existence of a legally acceptable offer, namely, (1) communication from the offeror to the offeree and (2) an indication of an apparent intent to contract.

A. NEED OF COMMUNICATION

One of the prerequisites to the existence of an offer which by acceptance can be translated into a contract must, of necessity, be a communication of the offer to the offeree from the offeror or his authorized agent.[2] By the very nature of things there can be no agreement unless the offeror in the first instance gives expression of his intention or willingness to enter into a contract with the offeree. This is accomplished by communication, by making known to the offeree such intention or willingness. The communication may be through the medium of the spoken word, letter, telegram, messenger, newspaper, placard, or handbill, or even through an act.

Application of this principle is important in those situations where one renders services or goods to another without knowledge that an offer has been made or where no offer in fact exists. Compliance with an offer of reward is in itself not sufficient to make the offeror liable. Merely meeting the terms of an offer is not an adequate acceptance; the one who acts upon an offer made must also have knowledge of the existence of the offer as a prerequisite to recovery.[3]

Communication of the offer as a requisite to the existence of a legally acceptable offer does not mean communication of the actual terms of the offer. Communication of the fact that contractual consequences are intended is sufficient. Accordingly, if one signs a contract in ignorance of its contents, to say that he was not aware of the terms of the offer is immaterial.[4] It is sufficient that he was aware of the fact that a contractual proposal was being made. The moral is: before signing a contract, read the fine print.

---

[2] Green v. Smith, p. 50.
[3] Smith v. Vernon County, p. 52.
[4] Sunderman v. Roberts, p. 53.

B. NEED OF INTENT TO CONTRACT

A true contract is an intentional relationship, existing only if the parties apparently intend to acquire legal rights and to assume corresponding legal obligations. Before there can be an acceptable offer, some indication of this intention or willingness to contract must be given.

1. *Actual Intent Not Requisite*

As the term *intent* is used here, it does not mean the actual state of mind of the offeror, but rather the intent as it is made apparent to the offeree through expressions or the circumstances surrounding the transaction.

No absolute test can be applied in determining the presence of intent to contract; the general test is whether the offeree in a particular instance is reasonably justified in believing that the offeror has indicated his willingness to be bound to a contractual commitment. It is a question of fact whether an intent to be bound by a contractual undertaking can reasonably be attributed to the offeror under the given circumstances, regardless of what his secret intent might have been. Therefore it is possible, as is brought out in the following subdivision, that an offeror may be held to his proposal despite the fact that he said something which he did not intend to say, and, on the other hand, it is possible that he may avoid being held to a proposal despite the fact that it reflected his actual intent.

2. *Intent Deduced from Expressions*

Whether a statement is to be interpreted as an offer is dependent upon whether it can reasonably be interpreted to demonstrate an intent on the part of the asserter to contract. Obviously, a reasonable person is not justified in relying upon proposals made as jokes or motivated by great emotional strain. To illustrate:

In *Higgins* v. *Lessig,* 49 Ill. App. 459, the defendant upon discovering the theft of his $15 harness exclaimed that he would "give $100 to know who stole his harness." The court said that such a statement "should be regarded rather as an extravagant exclamation of an excited man than as manifesting an intention to contract."

The following illustrates a situation under which apparent intent to contract is present regardless of the actual intent of the offeror. In the case of *Harmon* v. *Foley,* 62 Wis. 584, the plaintiff claimed to have purchased from the defendant some cattle for $161.50 in accordance with the defendant's offer. The defendant, however, had intended to state the price as $261.50. The court concluded that there was no justification for finding that the plaintiff was or should have been aware of the fact that if the defendant's offer was $161.50, such was a mistake and never his real intent. The bid of $161.50 was to the plaintiff the apparent intent of the offeror regardless of his actual intent.* If the defendant's offer had read $26.15, such could obviously not have been relied upon.

---

* Mistake is treated more specifically in Chap. 6, p. 139.

3. *Advertisements and Price Quotations and Other Invitations to Contract*

Advertisements, price quotations, and preliminary negotiations must be distinguished from offers to contract. Usually they contain no expression of intent to make a contractual commitment.[5] Advertisements, *unless positively indicating a willingness to be bound,* are viewed as mere invitations to the public to deal —invitations to make offers upon the terms indicated in the advertisements. To illustrate:

In *Lovett* v. *Frederick Loeser and Co.,* 207 N.Y.S. 753, the facts were that the defendant had advertised in a newspaper that it would sell and deliver and install certain "well known standard makes of radio receivers at 25% to 50% reduction" from the advertised list price. The plaintiff had selected two from among those radios named and the defendant refused to perform. The court said:

> "Defendants' advertisement is nothing but an invitation—and is not an offer which may be turned into a contract by a person who signifies his intention to purchase some of the articles mentioned in the advertisements."

In *Anderson* v. *Wisconsin Central Railway Co.,* 107 Minn. 296, the court said:

> "A merchant advertises that on a certain day he will sell his goods at bargain prices; but no one imagines that the prospective purchaser, who visits the store and is denied the right to purchase, has an action for damages against the merchant. He merely offers to purchase, and, if his offer is refused, he has no remedy, although he may have lost a bargain, and have incurred expense and lost time in visiting the store."

Likewise, in the letting of contracts and the sale of goods upon the basis of bids, the call for bids is not construed as an offer. The acceptance of the bid by the advertiser consummates the contract.[6] Section 21 of the *Uniform Sales Act* reads:

> "A sale by auction is complete when the auctioneer announces its completion by the fall of the hammer, or in other customary manner. Until such announcement is made, any bidder may retract his bid; and the auctioneer may withdraw the goods from sale unless the auction has been announced to be without reserve.
>
> "Where notice has not been given that a sale by auction is subject to a right to bid on behalf of the seller, it shall not be lawful for the seller to bid himself or to employ or induce any person to bid at such a sale on his behalf, or for the auctioneer to employ or induce any person to bid at such sale on behalf of the seller or knowingly to take any bid from the seller or any person employed by him. Any sale contravening this rule may be treated as fraudulent by the buyer."

---

[5] Nebraska Seed Co. v. Harsh, p. 54.

[6] Anderson v. Wisconsin Cent. Ry. Co., p. 56.

4. *Intent Deduced from Circumstances—Implied Intent*

An individual's conduct may reasonably lead another to believe that contractual consequences were intended. Thus, if A requests, or accepts without request, goods or services of B, it is implied in the absence of unusual circumstances—circumstances suggestive that the goods or services were intended to be free—that A intends to be bound for the value of the thing rendered.[7, 8] Should A request the services for another rather than for himself, it would require special circumstances to give rise to the implication that A, instead of the one to whom the services were rendered, intended to be bound for the price.[9]

► III. DURATION OF OFFER

An offer to contract may cease to exist for various reasons. The offeree must recognize the possibilities of termination of an offer prior to an attempted acceptance, which termination may become effective in some instances without notice to the offeree.

A. TERMINATION BY PROVISION IN OFFER

The offer may provide for the time of its duration. For example, it may specify that acceptance must be made within the week, by return mail, or by the happening of a certain event.[10]

B. TERMINATION BY REVOCATION

An offer may be withdrawn by the offeror at any time before acceptance. This is true not only when the offeror has declared to the offeree that the offer will remain open for a certain period of time, but also when the offer itself stipulates its period of existence.

To be effective, the revocation must be brought to the knowledge of the offeree. Whenever the offeror employs some agency of communication (such as the mails), the revocation does not become operative until the communication actually reaches the offeree. However, notice of revocation need not come directly from the offeror; notice from any source is sufficient. Whenever the offeree is made aware of facts that should reasonably be regarded by him as an indication that the offeror no longer intends to contract, the offer is effectively terminated. Should the offeree have knowledge of acts by the offeror that are inconsistent with the offer, such as the selling of the object of the offer to another, it is interpreted as a revocation.

---

7 Austin v. Burge, p. 57.
8 In re Fox's Estate, p. 59.
9 Broadway v. Jeffers, p. 60.
10 Caldwell v. Cline, p. 61.

1. *Revocation of Offers Publicly Made*

An offer may be directed to a specified individual, to a specified group of individuals, or to the public generally. Revocation of a public offer may be made effective without actual notice to the various offerees. Under such circumstances, the offeror cannot possibly have knowledge of all persons to whose attention the offer has come. Therefore, before an acceptance has taken place the offeror can effect a revocation by using the same medium through which the offer was made. The withdrawal merely requires the same amount of publicity as was given the offer. To hold otherwise would make public offers irrevocable.

C. TERMINATION BY DEATH OR INSANITY

Death or insanity has no effect upon a contractual relationship unless the contract so provides, or unless it can be implied from the nature of the contract that the parties conditioned the contract upon the continued existence of the person. If, however, either party dies or is adjudged insane before acceptance of the offer, the offer terminates as a matter of law. Even though the offeree has no notice of the death or insanity of the offeror, the termination is effective. In this manner the law charges the offeree with notice of the termination of the offer. This rule makes possible the infliction of a real hardship upon an offeree who has acted upon the assumption that a contract exists. Nevertheless, this is the well-established rule of law. A change by legislative action has been suggested.

D. TERMINATION BY EXPIRATION OF REASONABLE TIME

In view of the fact that the circumstances which motivate the making of an offer frequently change—such as a change in the price of a commodity—the offeree cannot regard an offer as remaining open for acceptance for an indefinite time. Fair play demands some rule that will prevent the offeree from accepting an offer at a point of time when it would be greatly to his advantage and correspondingly to the disadvantage of the offeror. The courts have adopted what has been called a *rule of convenience* to forestall such possibilities. According to this rule, an offer terminates upon the expiration of a *reasonable length of time*.

Obviously, the application of this inflexible rule depends upon what is to be regarded as a reasonable length of time in a given instance.[11] Reasonableness of time, like a rubber yardstick, has no definite length; it depends upon the circumstances of the particular situation. Consequently, no definite test for its determination is available. Factors that would have a material bearing in determining a reasonable length of time would be: (1) the nature of the subject matter (for example, an offer to buy or sell a perishable object would remain in existence for a much shorter time than an offer concerning something of a more permanent nature); (2) relative stability of the market price; (3) method used to communicate the offer (a telegram implies haste).

[11] Minnesota Linseed Oil Co. v. Collier White Lead Co., p. 63.

E. TERMINATION BY REJECTION

Whenever the offeree declines to accept the offer or commits any act which the law interprets as a rejection, the offer is terminated once and for all. The basis of termination by rejection is that the offeree indicates by such action that he has no intention of contracting. A counteroffer or a conditional acceptance, which is in effect a counteroffer, constitutes an expression of intent not to contract upon the basis of the offeror's proposal.[12] Such will automatically terminate the offer. Care must be exercised in distinguishing a mere inquiry regarding the possibility of different terms or a comment upon the terms of the offer from a counteroffer.[13]

► IV. THE ACCEPTANCE

The acceptance is the indicated or apparent intent of the offeree to accept the rights and assume the obligations proposed in the offer. Section 63 of the *Restatement of the Law of Contracts* states:

> "Acceptance of an offer is an expression of assent to the terms thereof, made by the offeree in a manner requested or authorized by the offeror. If anything except a promise is requested . . . (unilateral offer) no contract exists until part of what is requested is performed or tendered. If a promise is requested no contract exists until that promise is expressly or impliedly given."

Our basic problem at this point is to determine under what circumstances a promise by the offeree constitutes an acceptance and under what circumstances an act by the offeree constitutes acceptance. For this purpose it is necessary to distinguish between a unilateral offer (one in which the offeror asks for an act as acceptance) from a bilateral offer (one in which the offeror asks, not for an act, but for a promise as acceptance).

A. ACCEPTANCE OF UNILATERAL OFFER

A unilateral offer is accepted by a completion of the act called for in the offer. A promise to do the act will not serve as an acceptance. Thus, if A offers to pay B $50 for the return of his lost wrist watch, he wants the act performed and not a promise that it will be performed.

The one to whom a unilateral offer is made must recognize that until the act called for is, in the eyes of the law, accomplished, the offer stands as unaccepted and may be revoked by the offeror. B, in the above illustration, would have no cause for complaint if A, in spite of B's earnest assurance that he would give the matter his best efforts, should withdraw the offer.

It is held, however, by a majority of the courts that after the offeree has started to perform (as distinguished from preparation to perform) the act called for,

---

[12] Lerback v. Re Mine, p. 64.

[13] Byford v. Gates Bros. Lumber Co., p. 66.

the offer may not be revoked. This rule is stated in Section 45 of the *Restatement of the Law of Contracts* thus:

> "When an offer for a unilateral contract has been made and the offeree in response thereto has given, tendered, or performed, a part of the consideration requested, the offeror is bound to give the offeree the time stated in his offer to complete performance; or if no time was stated, a reasonable time." *

1. *Notice of Performance*

As stated above, the performance of the act called for by the offer constitutes the acceptance. This would indicate that the offeree need give no notice to the offeror that performance has taken place, and such is the rule. Unless the offeror either expressly or impliedly requests communication of the fact that performance has been completed, the performance in itself will be a sufficient acceptance. If the offeror desires notice, he must make that part of the price he requests in his offer, which then would require of the offeree the additional act of giving notice within a reasonable period of time after performance. Section 56 of the *Restatement of the Law of Contracts* states the circumstances under which notice is required as being where "the offeror has no adequate means of ascertaining with reasonable promptness and certainty that the act or forbearance has been given." To illustrate the above points:

a. The Act as Acceptance. The court in *Midland Nat. Bank of Minneapolis* v. *Security Elevator Co.*, 161 Minn. 30, observed that: "A simple illustration is the supposed case of A's saying to B, 'If you want my horse for $200, go to the stable and get him.' If, without a word to A, B takes the horse, the contract is complete. In such case, communication of the acceptance to the offeror has never been suggested as prerequisite to the completion of the contract of sale."

Under such circumstances, knowledge of the performance of the act will, in the usual course of events, come quickly and readily to the offeror.

b. Implied Request for Notice of Acceptance. If A writes B, "I will pay you $20 if you will check the enclosed list of names for errors in spelling," it can reasonably be implied that A desires that B communicate to him the results of his findings. This act is not of such a nature that knowledge of its completion will come quickly and readily to the offeror, and it is in the results of the act that A is primarily interested.

c. Offers of Guaranty. Offers of guaranty are unilateral in nature. For example, if A promises B that he will guarantee the credit of C to the extent of $1,000 for any goods sold to C or any advances of money made to C by B, the fact of having sold goods or having advanced money would constitute an acceptance of the offer. However, in many of our states, it is the rule that even though the extension of credit is an acceptance of the offer, the guarantor will be relieved of his responsi-

---

* See Case No. 14, p. 418.

bility unless he is given notice of the acceptance (advancing of credit) within a reasonable time.[14] Consequently, it follows that one relying upon a promise of guaranty should give notice immediately upon selling goods or advancing money upon the credit of the third party.

2. *Part Performance As Acceptance*

An act to be acceptance must be in compliance with the terms and conditions of the offer. It should be recognized, however, that performance need not be exact and literal. If the offeree has in good faith given what the courts regard as substantial performance, the acceptance is complete.[15] A full treatment of substantial performance will be found in Chapter 10.

B. ACCEPTANCE OF BILATERAL OFFER

Usually an offer is bilateral in form, requesting for its acceptance a promise from the offeree. However, it is not at all times clear whether the offeror intends his offer to be accepted by a return promise or by the performance of an act. A may, for example, say to B, "I will pay you $500 if you will build the garage according to the plans and specifications I have submitted." It is very probable that, according to A's intention, a promise rather than the performance of the act should constitute an acceptance. Consequently, the law provides a presumption in favor of an offer being bilateral rather than unilateral.

Section 31 of the *Restatement of the Law of Contracts* reads:

> "In case of doubt it is presumed that an offer invites the formation of a bilateral contract by an acceptance amounting in effect to a promise by the offeree to perform what the offer requests, rather than the formation of one or more unilateral contracts by actual performance on the part of the offeree."

As previously stated, the acceptance is the assurance on the part of the offeree that the price asked in the offer will be forthcoming. The acceptance must be in compliance with the offer—its counterpart.[16] The promise need take no special form; any words or acts indicative of an intent to become bound by the terms of the offer are sufficient. In fact, as will be seen presently, a contract may result without the offeree's intention being brought to the attention of the offeror.

1. *Time of Acceptance Becoming Effective: Mode of Communication*

It is said that the offeree must communicate his acceptance to bind himself and the offeror to a bilateral contract. This does not necessarily mean that he must actually notify the offeror of his intention to be bound. The existence of a contract is dependent only upon the existence of a common intent, an apparent meeting of the minds of the contracting parties. The following rules apply in determining the time at which an acceptance becomes effective, the time at which a meeting of minds occurs:

---

[14] Rothchild Bros. v. Lomas, p. 67.
[15] Scott v. People's Monthly Co., p. 68.
[16] Anderson v. Stewart, p. 69.

(1) Any provisions in the offer as to mode or time of acceptance must be complied with absolutely.[17] Should the offeror make the offer subject to receipt of the acceptance, there can be no contract until the acceptance is actually communicated to the offeror.

(2) If the offeror specifies a mode of communication in his offer, the acceptance becomes effective upon its being placed with the specified agency. Thus, if the offeror directs that an answer be sent by return mail, he is designating the mail as his authorized agency of communication. Under such circumstances, the posting of the letter of acceptance would consummate the contract.

(3) If the offeror specifies no mode of communication in his offer, he impliedly requests the offeree to employ the medium used in making the offer. Depositing the indicated assent with the agency impliedly held out constitutes an effective acceptance. For example, if a letter of acceptance is posted in response to an offer received by mail, it is an effective expression of assent to contract even though the letter is delayed or lost in transit.

(4) If the offeree uses a mode of communication other than that impliedly held out by the offeror, the acceptance is not effective until actually received by the offeror.

(5) If the offeror uses no agency of communication, circumstances may impliedly authorize the offeree to choose such agency as would customarily be employed in such a situation. Thus, if it is customary to use the mails, such is the impliedly authorized mode of communication.

(6) In the absence of a duty to speak, silence on the part of the offeree can never constitute an acceptance.[18, 19]

2. *Acceptance of Bilateral Offer by Act*

It is possible that the offeree's promise—his assent to contract—may be implied from his acts. Thus, if A orders goods from B—a bilateral offer—and B sends the goods to A, of which act A acquires notice, the act will be equivalent to a promise, providing the notice was imparted to A before the offer has terminated.

> "When goods are sent in compliance with an order, and are accepted by the vendee, of course no question as to his liability for the price can arise. If they are sent immediately upon the receipt of the order, *or within what would be reasonable time for giving assent thereafter,* and a bill of lading or equivalent document is sent to the vendee, as is usually the case; or if he is informed of the arrival of the goods at their destination, that also is sufficient notice of the vendor's assent." (Italics supplied) *Crook* v. *Cowan,* 64 N.C. 743.

Regardless, good practice would be to immediately, or within a reasonable time, send a formal acceptance of the offer.

---

17 Spratt v. Paramount Pictures, Inc., p. 71.
18 Sell v. General Electric Supply Corporation, p. 72.
19 Cole-McIntyre-Norfleet Co. v. Holloway, p. 73.

3. *Sufficiency of Statement As Acceptance*

In the absence of a further showing of the intention of the parties, the better view seems to be that a letter acknowledging the receipt of an order, coupled with the words, "The same shall have prompt attention," or "prompt and careful attention" is not in itself an acceptance which will prevent a withdrawal of the order by the buyer, or bind the seller to fill the order.

► V. NEED FOR CERTAINTY OF TERMS

The very term agreement implies a certainty of understanding. To make a contract, the terms must be sufficiently clear, definite, and certain, so as to enable a court to determine with *reasonable certainty* what the undertakings of the parties are. Unless such certainty exists, there is no contract.[20] Parties in contracting should make the terms of the agreement as meaningful as possible and leave nothing to chance. To do otherwise might lead to misunderstanding and litigation.

Certainty of obligation may exist without having the exact measure of the obligation fixed. If the court can by the application of reasonable standards determine what the approximate undertakings of the parties were, the agreement will be upheld.[21, 22] Many cases have come before the courts involving offers to purchase or to sell an uncertain quantity of goods. For example, A may, at an agreed price, promise to purchase of B all the coal he will need in the operation of his manufacturing plant for the coming year, or A may promise to buy all the coal he desires.

In *Cold Blast Transportation Co.* v. *Kansas City Bolt & Nut Co.,* 114 Fed. 77, the court said:

> "The rules applicable to contracts of this class may be thus briefly stated: A contract for the future delivery of personal property is void, for want of consideration and mutuality, if the quantity to be delivered is conditioned by the will, wish, or want of one of the parties; but it may be sustained if the quantity is ascertainable otherwise with reasonable certainty. An accepted offer to furnish or deliver such articles of personal property as shall be needed, required or consumed by the established business of the acceptor during a limited time is binding, and may be enforced, because it contains the implied agreement of the acceptor to purchase all the articles that shall be required in conducting this business during this time from the party who makes the offer.
>
> "But an accepted offer to sell or deliver articles at specified prices during a limited time in such amounts or quantities as the acceptor may want or desire in his business, or without any statement of the amount or quantity,

---

[20] Corthell v. Summit Thread Co., p. 75.
[21] Packard Forth Worth v. Van Zandt., p. 76.
[22] Costelli v. Tolibia, p. 77.

is without consideration and void, because the acceptor is not bound to want, desire or take any of the articles mentioned."

In *Crane* v. *Crane,* 105 Fed. 869, the court said:

> ". . . It is within legal competency for one to bind himself to furnish another with such supplies as may be needed during some certain period for some certain business or manufacture or with such commodities as the purchaser has already bound himself to furnish another. Reasonable provision in business requires that such contracts, though more or less indefinite, should be upheld. Thus a foundry may purchase all the coal needed for the season, or a furnace company its requirements in the way of iron, or a hotel its necessary supply of ice. . . . So, too, a dealer in coal in a given locality may contract for such coal as he may need to fulfill his existing contracts, regardless of whether delivery by him to his customers is to be immediate or in the future. In all these cases . . . it will be observed that although the quantity under contract is not measured by any certain standard, it is capable of an approximately accurate forecast. The capacity of the furnace, the needs of the railroad or the requirements of the hotel are, within certain limits, ascertainable by the vendor."

An agreement that fails to state the time for performance will not ordinarily fail because of uncertainty. It is implied that the agreement is to be performed within a reasonable time after it was entered into.[23] Where, however, the agreement contemplates the continuing performance of an act, the time period over which performance is to continue must be supplied by the parties.[24]

► VI. OPTIONS

An option is a contract giving one party the right to accept an offer. For example, A contracts to give B the right to purchase his home within a specified period of time for a specified price. An option is thus an offer which cannot be withdrawn because of the fact that a consideration has been given for it. This will become more meaningful after the reader has been introduced into the next chapter.

---

[23] Vanlandingham v. Jenkins, p. 78.
[24] Undercliff Corp. v. Consolidated Ed. Co., p. 79.

CASES

CASE NO. 1

Franklin W. Allen v. Bissinger & Company. 62 Utah 226, 219 Pac. 539, 31 A.L.R. 376 (1923)

CHERRY, J. . . . This is an action at law by the plaintiff to recover fees for furnishing defendant a copy of the official report of certain proceedings before the Interstate Commerce Commission. A trial before the court resulted in findings and judgment for the plaintiff, from which the defendant has appealed. . . .

On July 20, 1918, plaintiff sent letters to various large shippers of freight, including defendant, as follows:

"Dear Sir:

At the request of the Director General of Railroads the Interstate Commerce Commission will conduct an investigation concerning the reasonableness and propriety of the descriptions, rules, regulations, ratings, and minimum weights provided in proposed consolidated freight classification No. 1, prepared by the special committee appointed by the United States Railroad Administration to consolidate the official, western, and southern classifications. . . .

"A summary of the changes recommended in the proposed consolidated classification is inclosed. As these are of unusual interest and importance, those who want copies of the official reports of these hearings, which will be furnished at the usual rate fixed by the Commission, should advise us at once, so that we may make enough to supply them without delay."

On July 31, 1918, the defendant wrote plaintiff:

"We will be interested in your official report of the different changes in the handling of freight and would ask you to put our name down for a copy of same."

On August 5, 1918, the plaintiff wrote defendant:

"Please accept our thanks for your order of July 31, for one copy of the official report of the proceedings in the Consolidated Classification Case No. 10204, which will have our prompt attention."

. . . . .

On October 10, 1918, the defendant wrote the plaintiff:

"We are just in receipt of another allotment of your Interstate Commerce Commission report, and want to say to you that this is something that we cannot use at all, and there is no use of you sending us anything further. . . .

"In ordering these from you in the first place we expected to find all the information we wanted in one volume and did not think we were going to get a full library.

"Trusting you will look at this matter as a business proposition, with kindest regards."

To this the plaintiff replied on October 15, 1918:

"Replying to your letter of October 10, if agreeable to you, we will accept your cancellation effective at the end of the hearing of September 27. A copy of the report having already been made for you up to that point, we cannot accept cancellation of your order for that part of the report, because we cannot return to our employees and get credit for the labor which they have expended in making the copy for you."

. . . . . .

Plaintiff sent defendant a statement of the amount due, amounting to $1,047.50, and received in response the following letter, dated December 20, 1918:

"Your first and only statement of prices and account under date of December 14 just received. We are certainly surprised at the price you attempted to charge for same, and amount of these goods (8,380 pages) attempted to put upon us.

"Referring once again to this matter, as stated before, these reports are absolutely useless to us, and we absolutely refuse to pay this account, and hold these goods subject to your orders."

. . . The manager of defendant corporation testified that during the summer of 1918 he had had difficulties with respect to shipping regulations; that his attention was attracted to a circular inclosed in the plaintiff's first letter, purporting to be a summary of the important changes recommended in the proposed consolidated freight classification; that he had this circular in mind when he wrote the letter dated July 31. He denied receiving the plaintiff's letter dated August 5. He stated that the material sent him was not what he had ordered; that none of the shipments contained any report of the different changes relating to freights; that the material sent by the plaintiff was of no value to him; that he did not use it in any way; and that it was of no value whatsoever to the defendant in the business in which it was engaged.

. . . It is insisted by appellant that the correspondence did not create a contract, because the offer contained in plaintiff's letter was not accepted, and hence the minds of the parties never met. . . .

Of course, if the defendant's letter was not an acceptance of the particular thing plaintiff offered, there was no contract. The parties must contract ad idem. . . .

In 13 C.J. 265 the rule is stated as follows:

"The apparent mutual assent of the parties, essential to the formation of a contract, must be gathered from the language employed by them, and the law imputes to a person an intention corresponding to the reasonable meaning of its words and acts. It judges of his intention by his outward expressions, and excludes all questions in regard to his unexpressed intention. If his words or acts, judged by a reasonable standard, manifest an intention to agree to the matter in question, that agreement is established, and it is immaterial what may be the real, but unexpressed, state of his mind upon the subject."

The offer of the plaintiff was to furnish one specific thing, viz., a copy of the official report of the hearings. There was no uncertainty or ambiguity in the offer. The thing offered was described with fairness and verity. The defendant's response to the offer was:

"We will be interested in your official report of the different changes in the handling of freight, and would ask that you put our name down for a copy of same."

. . . Under the circumstances, we think the communications of the parties above referred to, judged by a reasonable standard, manifest an intention to agree upon the same thing, and that the evidence was sufficient, as a matter of law, to support the finding of the trial court that the plaintiff's offer was accepted by the defendant. . . .

Judgment affirmed.

CASE NO. 2

Green v. Smith. 146 Va. 442, 131 S.E. 846, 44 A.L.R. 1175 (1926)

CHINN, J. . . . Defendant's automobile was first placed at plaintiff's garage some time in the early part of the year 1918. . . . Mrs. Green at the time was an old lady, and her daughter, Mrs. B. R. Dunn, who resided with her . . . looked after her affairs. There was no formal contract between the parties, but plaintiff advised Mrs. Dunn of the terms and regulations then in effect at his garage for the regular monthly storage of automobiles, which were accepted by the defendant by leaving the car in his custody. According to the terms thus agreed to, in addition to certain other specified services, plaintiff contracted to deliver the car at the owner's residence and take it back to the garage once each day when requested by the owner. . . In January, 1920, plaintiff had printed what he called a "folder," which bore on the title page this inscription:

"Service Rates

. . . . .

Effective on and after January 1, 1920"

The center or inside pages of the folder contained a schedule of charges for divers specified services performed by the garage and other printed matter, which, so far as pertinent, read as follows:

"Delivery Service

"Delivery and calling for car once each way daily (see note). An extra charge of 25 cents each way will be made for extra trips (see note) . . .

"Note: The owner agrees to accept our employees as his or her agent and to absolve this garage from any liability whatsoever arising while his or her car is in the hands of said employees at the request of and as agent of the owner. . . ."

The folder was mailed to all the patrons of the garage, . . . and copies were also placed by the employees of the garage, on several occasions, in defendant's car, as well as all other cars kept at the garage on regular storage. . . .

On October 1, 1920, after Mr. Moore had been injured by one of the regular employees while taking Mrs. Green's car from her residence to the garage to be stored for the night, and after suit had been instituted by Moore against the plaintiff in the instant case to recover damages for said injuries, at the suggestion of his counsel, plaintiff mailed another copy of the folder to Mrs. Green, accompanied by the following letter:

"Richmond, Va., Oct. 1, 1920.

"Mrs. A. D. Green, City—Dear Mrs. Green: Please sign both of the inclosed service rate cards, returning one to us some time to-day, and retaining one for your own files.

"No cars will be delivered after today unless this has been done.

"Very truly yours,
Richmond Electric Garage
E. D. Smith."

The above letter was received by Mrs. Green and promptly answered as follows:

"109 S. 3rd St., Richmond, Va.
Oct. 1st, 1920

"Richmond Electric Garage, Howard M. Smith, Proprietor—Dear Sir: In compliance with your request in your letter of even date, I am inclosing agreement of acceptance of your service rates; said agreement being effective on and after this date and until revoked. You will notice that I have marked out "effective on and after January 1, 1920", as this is the first intimation of such rules and agreement, especially as to the delivery of cars.

"Cordially yours,
A. D. Green By B. R. Dunn."

The defendant, Mrs. Green, on account of her advanced age and infirmities, did not appear at the trial of the instant case, but it was testified by Mrs. Dunn that she acted as agent for her mother, and that she had no knowledge or intimation of the terms contained in the folder until her attention was called to it by plaintiff's letter to Mrs. Green of October 1, 1920, inclosing a copy of same with a blank form of acceptance stamped on the title page as . . . stated. This witness also testified that she had received several folders previous to that date with plaintiff's monthly bills, but had not paid any attention to them. It does not appear that Mrs. Green herself ever received or saw a copy of the folder. . . .

It is manifest, however, that, before one can be held to have accepted the offer of another, whether such offer is made by word or act, there must have been some form of communication of the offer; otherwise there could be no assent, and in consequence no contract . . . In the instant case the plaintiff relies upon the "note" printed in the folder as constituting the terms of the proposed contract, on the fact that said folder was mailed to Mrs. Green on several occasions with her monthly bills and placed in her car, as a communication of said terms, and on her conduct in continuing to keep her car in his garage as an implied acceptance of the terms specified in said note. The question, therefore, of whether Mrs. Green agreed to, and is bound by, the terms of the "note" in the main depends upon whether the means employed by the plaintiff to communicate such terms were sufficient, under the circumstances, to constitute her act in the premises an implied acceptance of the said terms. The rule as to when the delivery of a paper containing the terms of a proposed contract amounts to an acceptance is thus stated in 13 C.J. at page 277:

> "A contract may be formed by accepting a paper containing terms. If an offer is made by delivering to another a paper containing the terms of a proposed contract, and the paper is accepted, the acceptor is bound by its terms; and this is true whether he reads the paper or not. When an offer contains various terms, some of which do not appear on the face of the offer, the question whether the acceptor is bound by the terms depends on the circumstances. He is not bound as a rule by any terms which *are not communicated* to him. But he is bound by all the legal terms which are communicated. This question arises when a person accepts a railroad or steamboat ticket, bill of lading, warehouse receipt, or other document containing conditions. He is bound by all the conditions whether he reads them or not, *if he knows that the document contains conditions.* But he is not bound by terms *of which he is ignorant, even though he may know that the ticket or document contains writing, unless he knows that the writing contains terms, or unless he ought to know that it contains terms, by reason of previous dealings or experience or by reason of the form, size, or character of the document.*"

. . . In Newman v. National Shoe & Leather Exch., 26 Misc. 388, 56 N.Y. Supp. 193, the plaintiff placed a claim for collection in the hands of a New York collection agency that he had employed on several occasions, and which delivered to him a paper which on its face was an ordinary receipt; but, appearing on the reverse side, under the caption "Collection Department," were printed the agency's rates of commission, and a clause stating that they did not guarantee clients against loss from the dishonesty of an attorney or the suspension of a bank. The agency sent the claim to an attorney, who collected it and failed to account for the proceeds. The plaintiff thereupon sued the agency for the amount. He admitted possession of the receipt by mail or by being handed to him, but testified that the conditions on the back of the paper were never brought to his attention, and that he did not know of any limitation of defendant's liability. In the course of its opinion, the court said:

> "Where a party receives a paper which, from the circumstances of the transaction, he has a right to regard simply as a receipt or voucher, and no notice is given to him that it embodies the terms of a special contract, or is intended to subserve any other purpose than a receipt, his omission to read the paper is not per se negligence, and he is not, as a matter of law, bound by its terms. . . . The defendant, in order to relieve itself from liability, is bound to establish the contract. . . . In the absence of any circumstances or limitation indicating it to be anything other than an ordinary voucher, he was justified in so regarding it. The minds of the parties did not meet on the subject of a contract embracing the restriction invoked; hence it cannot avail the defendant."

. . . There was nothing on the face of the folder nor in its form or character, to indicate that it contained the terms of the contract which plaintiff has attempted to establish in this case, or any other contract imposing obligations of such a nature upon the defendant. The paper only purported to contain a schedule of rates for services at plaintiff's garage, and defendant had no reason, on account of her previous dealings with the plaintiff or otherwise, to know that plaintiff proposed, by mailing the folder to her along with his monthly bill, and placing a copy of it in her car, to commit her to a new contract of such unusual terms. . . . If plaintiff proposed to form a special contract of this kind, he should have, at the least, called Mrs. Green's attention to the terms contained in the folder, as he undertook to do, upon the advice of counsel, after the accident to Mr. Moore.

Under these circumstances we are of the opinion that the plaintiff has failed to establish the contract alleged in his declaration in the manner that the law requires, and is not, as a matter of law, entitled to recover over from Mrs. Green the damages he was compelled to pay Mr. Moore for the negligence of his servant. . . .

For the foregoing reasons, the judgment complained of will be reversed and judgment entered for the defendant.

CASE NO. 3

Smith v. Vernon County. 188 Mo. 501, 87 S.W. 949 (1905)

LAMM, J. . . . The cases are in hopeless conflict on this question.

On the one side is a line holding to the theory that knowledge of the offer of a reward is not necessary. The reasoning of this line of cases is felicitously expressed in Auditor v. Ballard, 72 Ky. 572, thus:

> "But it is said that the appellee is not entitled to the reward because he did not know, at the time he arrested the fugitive and delivered him to the jailor, that one had been offered, and therefore the services could not have been performed in consideration of

the reward. If the offer was made in good faith, why should the state inquire whether appellee knew that it had been made? Would the benefit to the state be diminished by a discovery of the fact that the appellee, instead of acting from mercenary motives, had been actuated solely by a desire to prevent the escape of a fugitive and to bring a felon to trial? And is it not well that all may know that whoever in the community has it in his power to prevent the final escape of a fugitive from justice, and does prevent it, not only performs a virtuous service, but will entitle himself to such reward as may be offered therefor?"

On the one side is a line holding to the theory that knowledge of the offer and a resulting reliance upon it in performing services are essential elements in the recovery of a reward. This line of cases is based on the theory, everywhere recognized, that an offer of a reward is the same as any other contractual offer, and must be known and accepted by being acted upon. If the promise of a reward is to be brought, as seems sensible, within the classification of a contract, it is impossible to see how any other conclusion can be logically arrived at; for in every contract there must be an aggregatio mentium, and how can a meeting of the minds exist without the acceptance of an offer, express or implied, or arising, at least, from some fiction of law? That the absence of knowledge of the offer and the absence of performance of services on the faith of the offer are barriers to recovery is reasoned out on principle by a philosophical writer, Dr. Wharton (1 Whar. on Contracts, p. 50 et seq.); by Story (1 Story on Con. (5 ed.) sec. 493), and other authors, and is the doctrine of many courts of last resort, and is within the rationale of other cases, where the point was not directly involved.

CASE NO. 4

Sunderman v. Roberts. 213 S.W. (2d) 705 (Tex.) (1948)

NORVELL, J. Upon the completion of the taking of the evidence, the trial judge, being of the opinion that the law issues only were involved, discharged the jury and rendered judgment for the plaintiff, Lela Roberts, and against the defendant, Paul E. Sunderman, for the sum of $3,178.17. This recovery was based upon a clause in the deed whereby the defendant had agreed to pay off an indebtedness of $3,500, secured by a lien against certain real property which he had conveyed to plaintiff.

The plaintiff, Lela Roberts, and the defendant had formerly been husband and wife. They were divorced on the 12th day of July, 1944. In contemplation of this divorce the parties entered into an agreement, bearing date of July 6, 1944, settling their respective community property rights. This agreement provided that:

> "1. Paul E. Sunderman . . . First Party agrees to transfer, perfect and vest title of the following property in Second Party . . . (property described) . . . and First Party will pay off and discharge same as his personal obligation, in accordance with the written instruments evidencing said indebtedness and lien, so long as Second Party remains single and retains ownership of said property."

On July 11, 1944, Paul Sunderman executed a deed conveying the real property described in the contract to Lela Sunderman, which omitted the restriction contained in the contract with reference to Mrs. Sunderman's remaining single and retaining ownership of the property.

Lela Sunderman married Roy E.

Roberts on July 17, 1945. Prior to this time Paul E. Sunderman was delinquent upon installments of the assumed indebtedness but contends that his liability should be limited to installments which became due on or before the date of his former wife's remarriage. In other words, Sunderman contends that his liability should be measured by terms of the original agreement of July 6, 1944.

Appellant's first contention is fully answered by the recent case of Baker v. Baker, 207 S.W. (2d) 244, 249, by this court, in which Mr. Justice Murray reviewed applicable authorities and quoted with approval the following from Devlin on Deeds:

"No rule of law is better settled than that where a deed has been executed and accepted as performance of an executory contract to convey real estate, the contract is functus officio, and the rights of the parties rest thereafter solely in the deed." Devlin, Law of Deeds, Vol. 2, § 850a. See also 14 Tex. Jur. 875, § 101.

In our opinion the trial judge correctly ruled as a matter of law, that appellant was not entitled to a reformation of the deed. As to certain matters there was a dispute in the testimony, but this does not lessen the effect of controlling circumstances which compel the sustaining of the deed as written.

The following facts are however undisputed. Prior to signing the deed, Sunderman was afforded an opportunity to read it. No one prevented him from doing so. . . . The alleged "mistake" —omission of a certain language from the deed—is readily apparent from a reading of the deed. There is nothing latent about it. . . . Any one able to read the English language and laboring under no mental disability would be able to discover upon a mere reading of the deed that Sunderman's liability was not limited to the payment of installments accruing prior to his wife's remarriage. In situations similar to this, the law does not leave property rights dependent upon parol evidence and the imperfect memories of witnesses.

"It will not do for a man to enter into a contract, and, when called upon to respond to its obligations, to say that he did not read it when he signed it, or did not know what it contained. If this were permitted, contracts would not be worth the paper on which they are written. But such is not the law. A contractor must stand by the words of his contract; and, if he will not read what he signs, he alone is responsible for his omission." Indemnity Insurance Co. of North America v. W. L. Macatee & Sons, 129 Tex. 166, 101 S.W. (2d) 533, 556, quoting from Upton v. Tribilcock, 91 U.S. 45, 50, 23 L.Ed. 203, 205. . . .

The judgment appealed from is affirmed.

CASE NO. 5

Nebraska Seed Co. v. Harsh. 98 Neb. 89, 152 N.W. 310 (1915)

MORRISSEY, C. J. Plaintiff, a corporation, engaged in buying and selling seed in the city of Omaha, Neb., brought this action against the defendant, a farmer residing at Lowell, Kearney county, Neb. The petition alleges:

That on the 26th day of April, 1912, the plaintiff purchased of and from the defendant 1,800 bushels of millet seed at the agreed price of $2.25 per hundredweight, F.O.B. Lowell, Neb., which said purchase and contract was evidenced by writing and correspondence passing between the respective parties of which the following is a copy:

"Lowell, Nebraska, 4—24—1912.

"Neb. Seed Co., Omaha, Neb.—

Gentlemen: I have about 1800 bu. or thereabouts of millet seed of which I am mailing you a sample. This millet is recleaned and was grown on sod and is good seed. I want $2.25 per cwt. for this seed f.o.b. Lowell.

"Yours truly,

H. F. Harsh."

Said letter was received by the plaintiff at its place of business in Omaha, Neb., on the 26th day of April, 1912, and immediately thereafter the plaintiff telegraphed to the defendant at Lowell, Neb., a copy of which is as follows:

"4—26—12.

"H. F. Harsh, Lowell, Nebr.—Sample and letter received. Accept your offer. Millet like sample two twenty-five per hundred. Wire how soon can load.

"The Nebraska Seed Co."

On the same day, to wit, April 26, 1912, the plaintiff, in answer to the letter of the said defendant, wrote to him a letter and deposited the same in the United States mail, directed to the said defendant at Lowell, Neb., which said letter was duly stamped, and which the plaintiff charges that the defendant in due course of mail received. That a copy of said letter is as follows:

"4—26—12.

"Mr. H. F. Harsh, Lowell, Neb.—Dear Sir: We received your letter and sample of millet seed this morning and at once wired you as follows: "Sample and letter received. Accept your offer. Millet like sample two twenty-five per hundred, wire how soon can load." We confirm this message have booked purchase of you 1800 bushels of millet seed to be fully equal to sample you sent us at $2.25 per cwt. your track. Please be so kind as to load this seed at once and ship to us at Omaha. We thank you in advance for prompt attention. When anything further in the line of millet to offer, let us have samples.

"Yours truly,

The Nebraska Seed Co."

It alleges that defendant refused to deliver the seed, after due demand and tender of the purchase price, and prays judgment in the sum of $900. Defendant filed a demurrer, which was overruled. He saved an exception to the ruling and answered, denying that the petition stated a cause of action; that the correspondence set out constituted a contract, etc. There was a trial to a jury with verdict and judgment for plaintiff, and defendant appeals.

In our opinion the letter of defendant cannot be fairly construed into an offer to sell to the plaintiff. After describing the seed, the writer says, "I want $2.25 per cwt, for this seed f.o.b. Lowell." He does not say, "I offer to sell to you." The language used is general, and such as may be used in an advertisement, or circular addressed generally to those engaged in the seed business, and is not an offer by which he may be bound, if accepted, by any or all of the persons addressed.

"If a proposal is nothing more than an invitation to the person to whom it is made to make an offer to the proposer, it is not such an offer as can be turned into an agreement by acceptance. Proposals of this kind, although made to definite persons and not to the public generally, are merely invitations to trade; they go no further than what occurs when one asks another what he will give or take for certain goods. Such inquiries may lead to bargains, but do not make them. They ask for offers which the proposer has a right to accept or reject as he pleases." 9 Cyc. 278e.

The letter as a whole shows that it

was not intended as a final proposition, but as a request for bids. It did not fix a time for delivery, and this seems to have been regarded as one of the essentials by plaintiff, for in his telegram he requests defendant to "wire how soon can load."

"The mere statement of the price at which property is held cannot be understood as an offer to sell." Knight v. Cooley, 34 Iowa 218.

We do not think the correspondence made a complete contract. To so hold where a party sends out letters to a number of dealers would subject him to a suit by each one receiving a letter, or invitations to bid, even though his supply of seed were exhausted. In Lyman v. Robinson, 14 Allen (Mass.) 242, 254, the Supreme Court of Massachusetts has sounded the warning:

"Care should always be taken not to construe as an agreement letters which the parties intended only as a preliminary negotiation."

Holding, as we do, that there was no binding contract between the parties, . . . the judgment of the district court is reversed.

CASE NO. 6

Anderson et al. v. Wisconsin Cent. Ry. Co. 107 Minn. 296, 120 N.W. 39, 20 L.R.A. (N.S.) 1133

ELLIOT, J. The Wisconsin Central Railway Company, having acquired certain real property, . . . advertised that . . . the buildings thereon would be sold at public auction. Bids for a certain house had been made until the amount offered amounted to $675. Anderson then increased his bid $5, . . . The auctioneer refused to consider this bid, because, as he stated, the amount of the raise was too insignificant. After waiting for a time to give Anderson an opportunity to increase it, the auctioneer announced that the house was sold to the last previous bidder for $675. Anderson demanded to know why the auctioneer had not accepted his bid, and on the same day he tendered the $680, and it was refused. Before this tender was made, a bill of sale of the building had been executed and delivered to the party to whom the building had been knocked down. Anderson then brought this action for damages, and recovered a verdict for $1,500. The defendant appealed.

The jury, under proper instructions, found that the property was offered without express reservations as to the amount of the bids, that the bid of $5 was made in good faith, and that under the circumstances the amount was not so small as to justify the auctioneer in declining to consider it on that ground. For the purpose of the argument, we assume the correctness of the respondent's claim that an advertisement or announcement of an auction sale which does not state limitations and conditions is equivalent to the announcement that the sale will be without reserve. The issue of law is thus clearly defined.

The custom of selling goods at auction is as old as the law of sale. In Rome military spoils were disposed of at the foot of the spear—*sub hastio*—by auction, or increase. In later times we find a mode of auction called a "sale by the candle," or by the "inch of candle," which consisted of offering the property for sale for such a length of time as would suffice for the burning of an inch of candle. In Holland they inverted the usual process, and put the property up at a price usually greater than its value, and then gradually lowered the price until some one closed the sale by accepting the offer, thus becoming the purchaser.

In view of the general prevalence of the custom of selling by auction, it is remarkable that no very early cases are found in the English reports. The parent case of Payne v. Cave, 3 Term R. 148, was decided by Lord Kenyon, C.J., sitting at Guildhall in 1788. The plaintiff offered a distilling apparatus for sale, including a pewter worm, at public auction, on the usual conditions that the highest bidder should be the purchaser. There were several bidders for the worm, of whom Cave, who bid 40 pounds, was the last. The auctioneer dwelt on this bid for some time, until Cave said: "Why do you dwell? You will not get more." The auctioneer stated that he was informed that the worm weighed at least 1,300 hundredweight, and was worth more than £40. The bidder then asked him if he would warrant it to weigh so much, and, receiving an answer in the negative, he declared that he would not take it. The worm was then resold on a subsequent day for £30, and an action was brought against Cave for the difference. Lord Kenyon ruled that the bidder was at liberty to withdraw his bid at any time before the hammer fell, and nonsuited the plaintiff. On motion to set aside the nonsuit, it was contended that a bidder is bound by the conditions of the sale to abide by his bid, and could not retract; that the hammer is suspended, not for the benefit of the bidder, or to give him an opportunity for repenting, but for the benefit of the seller; and that in the meantime the person who bid last is a purchaser, conditional upon no one bidding higher. But the court thought otherwise, and held that the auctioneer was the agent of the vendor, and that the assent of both parties was necessary to make the contract binding, and "that is signified on the part of the seller by knocking down the hammer, which was not done here until the plaintiff had retracted."

. . . . .

On principle and authority the correct rule is that an announcement that a person will sell his property at public auction to the highest bidder is a mere declaration of intention to hold an auction at which bids will be received; that a bid is an offer which is accepted when the hammer falls, and until the acceptance of the bid is signified in some manner neither party assumes any legal obligation to the other. At any time before the highest bid is accepted, the bidder may withdraw his offer to purchase or the auctioneer his offer to sell. The owner's offer to sell is made at the time through the auctioneer, and not when he advertises the auction sale. . . . As the advertisement in this case was a mere statement of intention to offer the property for sale at public auction to the highest bidder, the respondent's bid did not complete either a contract of sale or a contract to make a sale.

The order is therefore reversed, with directions to enter judgment for the defendant.

CASE NO. 7

Austin v. Burge. 156 Mo. App. 286, 137 S.W. 618 (1911)

ELLISON, J. This action was brought on an account for the subscription price of a newspaper. The judgment in the trial court was for the defendant. It appears that plaintiff was publisher of a newspaper in Butler, Mo., and that defendant's father-in-law subscribed for the paper, to be sent to defendant for two years, and that the father-in-law paid for it for that time. It was then continued to be sent to defendant, through the mail, for several years more. On two occasions defendant paid a bill presented for the subscription price, but each time directed it to be stopped. Plaintiff denies the order to stop, but for the purpose of the case we shall assume that defendant is correct. He testified that, notwithstanding the order to stop it, it was continued to be sent to him, and he continued to receive and read it, until finally he removed to another state.

We have not been cited to a case in this state involving the liability of a person who, though not having subscribed for a newspaper, continues to accept it by receiving it through the mail. There are, however, certain well-understood principles in the law of contracts that ought to solve the question. It is certain that one cannot be forced into contractual relations with another and that therefore he cannot, against his will, be made the debtor of a newspaper publisher. But it is equally certain that he may cause contractual relations to arise by necessary implication from his conduct. The law in respect to contractual indebtedness for a newspaper is not different from that relating to other things which have not been made the subject of an express agreement. Thus one may not have ordered supplies for his table, or other household necessities, yet if he continues to receive and use them, under circumstances where he had no right to suppose they were a gratuity, he will be held to have agreed, by implication, to pay their value. In this case defendant admits that, notwithstanding he ordered the paper discontinued at the time when he paid a bill for it, yet plaintiff continued to send it, and he continued to take it from the post office to his home. This was an acceptance and use of the property, and, there being no pretense that a gratuity was intended, an obligation arose to pay for it.

A case quite applicable to the facts here involved arose in Fogg v. Atheneum, 44 N.H. 115, 82 Am. Dec. 191. There the Independent Democrat newspaper was forwarded weekly by mail to the defendant from May 1, 1847, to May 1, 1849, when a bill was presented, which defendant objected to paying on the ground of not having subscribed. Payment was, however, finally made, and directions given to discontinue. The paper changed ownership, and the order to stop was not known to the new proprietors for a year; but, after being notified of the order, they nevertheless continued to send it to defendant until 1860, a period of 11 years, and defendant continued to receive it through the post office. Payment was several times demanded during this time, but refused on the ground that there was no subscription. The court said that:

> "During this period of time the defendants were occasionally requested, by the plaintiff's agent, to pay their bill. The answer was, by the defendants, 'We are not subscribers to your newspaper.' But the evidence is the defendants used or kept the . . . newspapers, and never offered to return a number, as they reasonably might have done, if they would have avoided the liability to pay for them. Nor did they ever decline to take the newspapers from the post office."

The defendant was held to have accepted the papers, and to have become liable for the subscription price by implication of law.

The preparation and publication of a newspaper involves much mental and physical labor, as well as an outlay of money. One who accepts the paper, by continuously taking it from the post office, receives a benefit and pleasure arising from such labor and expenditure as fully as if he had appropriated any other product of another's labor, and by such act he must be held liable for the subscription price. On the defendant's own evidence, plaintiff should have recovered.

The judgment will therefore be reversed, and the cause remanded.

CASE NO. 8

In re Fox's Estate. 131 W.Va. 429, 48 S.E. (2d) 1, 7 A.L.R. (2d) 1 (1948)

LOVINS, J. . . . Nellie M. Fox, the claimant, is the wife of Merley Fox, a son of decedent, and resides in Sharon, Pennsylvania. Elizabeth E. Fox seems to have resided in Morgantown, Monongalia County, West Virginia, but on a date, not clearly shown in the record, she went to live with her son and daughter-in-law at their home in the State of Pennsylvania. On December 18, 1942, while at the home of her son, she fell and sustained a broken hip. By reason of that injury she was confined to her bed for about seven months and to her room until her death on February 20, 1946, a period of thirty-eight months.

During the time of decedent's illness, claimant performed various nursing services, prepared and served meals to decedent in her room. Her claim against the estate is based on those services, but no charge is made against decedent's estate for room and board.

During her illness, decedent made various statements to the daughters and son-in-law of claimant, to the effect that she would pay claimant for the care bestowed upon her; that Merley Fox and claimant would not regret their services to her; and that she felt obligated to claimant for such services.

Elizabeth E. Fox left a will by which she directed that all her property be sold by the executor of her will, and, from the proceeds of the sale thereof, she bequeathed two hundred dollars to a son, O. L. Fox; five hundred dollars to the son, Merley Fox, the husband of claimant; and disposed of the residue of the proceeds of sale of her property by bequeathing such proceeds to her four children and their descendants "equally share and share alike." The will was probated by the County Court of Monongalia County on February 25, 1946, the order of probate reciting that decedent was a resident of said county and had died therein on February 20, 1946; but it seems that she died in the Town of Sharon, Pennsylvania.

The estate having been referred to a commissioner of accounts, the said commissioner received and filed the claim of Nellie M. Fox for thirty-eight months' services, commencing on December 18, 1942, and ending on the date of decedent's death on February 20, 1946, at thirty dollars a month, amounting to eleven hundred and forty dollars. E. D. Faux, a son of decedent, filed a counter-affidavit, denying the legality of the claim and objecting to the allowance thereof. Claimant, together with her two daughters and her son-in-law, testified in support of the claim. No proof was offered by E. D. Faux or any other person in opposition to the claim. It appears from the commissioner's report that the gross amount of the estate of Elizabeth E. Fox was $4,762.55, and that the executor of her will had made disbursements of $1,785.46.

The commissioner, in his report, denied the claim of Nellie M. Fox, and she excepted to said report. . . . the Circuit Court of Monongalia County over-ruled the exceptions and confirmed the report. Nellie M. Fox now brings the case here by writ of error.

In the opinion of the comparatively

recent case of In re Roberts' Estate, 350 Pa. 467, 39 A. (2d) 592, 593, the Supreme Court of Pennsylvania makes a similar review and collation of prior expressions of that Court, and therein states the basic principle as follows:

"The applicable principles of law are comprehensively stated in Re Mooney's Estate, 328 Pa. 273, page 274, 194 A. 893, 894, where Mr. Justice Drew said: '(Claimant's) burden . . . is extremely heavy. We have said many times that claims of this nature must be subjected to the closest scrutiny, being objects of just suspicion . . . and must be established by evidence clear, precise and indubitable. . . .' "

Furthermore, under the law of Pennsylvania, a person presenting a claim such as here considered, must overcome a presumption that any services rendered were paid for from time to time, while they continued. . . . No such presumption exists under the laws of this State, although, of course, the ordinary burden of proving nonpayment does rest upon claimant. . . .

Applying these principles to the admissible proof offered by claimant in support of her claim, it is obvious that no express contract has been proved. Nor do we hesitate to say that the proof offered to establish the existence of an implied contract is not sufficient. There is no evidence that decedent and claimant agreed upon a price for the services rendered. The only proof offered is testimony relative to declarations made by decedent, as hereinbefore stated. Such declarations were indefinite and of such a nature that more than one inference could be drawn therefrom. There is no basis for a clear inference that decedent intended to compensate claimant on a contractual basis, or that claimant expected remuneration for the services rendered. The declarations of decedent do not constitute "clear proof of circumstances from which (a contract) is necessarily implied," as required by Ireland v. Hibbs, supra. That being true, it is even more apparent that such declarations do not constitute evidence of an implied contract which is "clear, precise and indubitable," as required by In re Roberts' Estate, supra. . . .

CASE NO. 9

Burnette Broadway v. W. A. Jeffers. 194 S.E. 642, 114 A.L.R. 1244 (1938)

BAKER, J. . . . These actions were instituted and prosecuted to judgment by respondents for the recovery of compensation for professional services rendered and hospitalization furnished to appellant's son, William Jeffers, an adult not residing with appellant. . . .

As a general rule, a request by a parent to a surgeon or physician to attend an adult child does not create an implied contract to pay for the services rendered by the physician or surgeon. However, this is not a rule of invariable application, for the conditions and circumstances surrounding the parties at the time the request is made, as well as the utterances on the subject, must be taken into consideration, and if, under the facts and circumstances, the physician or surgeon is justified in believing and relying on the parents' intention to pay for the services rendered, although there is no express promise to pay therefor, an implied contract is created, making the parent liable for the reasonable value of the services rendered. Of course, if there is nothing in the facts and circumstances suggesting to the physician or surgeon that the parent intends to assume the legal obligation to pay, at the time the request for services is made, the parent is no more legally liable for services rendered to his adult child, living away from his home, than he would be for the services requested to be rendered to a total stranger. . . .

In Williston on Contracts, Vol. 1, at page 43, in section 36, it is stated:

"An offer need not be stated in words. Any conduct from which a reasonable person in the offeree's position would be justified in inferring a promise in return for a requested act or a requested promise by the offeree, amounts to an offer. The common illustration of this principle is where performance of work or services is requested. If the request is for performance as a favor, no offer to contract is made, and performance of the work or services will not create a contract; but if the request is made under such circumstances that a reasonable person would infer an intent to pay for them (and this is always a question of fact under all the circumstances of the case) the request amounts to an offer, and a contract is created by the performance of the work. . ."

. . . There is no express contract disclosed by the testimony in the case at bar, and if appellant is to be held legally responsible for services rendered to his son, William Jeffers, by respondents, such liability must of necessity be created by an implied contract; . . .

When appellant arrived at the Summerville Infirmary, he was advised that he could employ any surgeon he preferred to perform the necessary surgical operation, or an ambulance would be called to carry his son to another hospital. Thereupon, appellant advised Dr. Tupper that he wished to have him perform the operation; that he would like to have them do everything possible for his wounded son and to spare no expense.

We must not be unmindful of the relationship of appellant and the wounded man. If the statements made by appellant had related to a stranger or a mere acquaintance, we do not think that any liability would have been established by the evidence; but such is not true of the case at bar. Here we have a father, upon being advised of his wounded son's condition, coming a long distance after night and upon finding his own flesh and blood upon the verge of expiration, asks about other doctors and surgeons, and then, after conferring with other persons present, advises Dr. Tupper to proceed with the operation and to spare no expense. . . .

The circuit judge instructed the jury that there was such a thing as an implied contract, and gave the jury the following illustration:

"For instance, suppose you go to a lawyer's office, and, without saying anything about the price, get him to take a case for you, or prepare some legal document, that is what is known as an implied contract and the law says that you will have to pay him a reasonable fee for his services."

We find no error in the charge in this respect, and the exception thereabout is overruled. . . .

Judgment for respondents affirmed.

CASE NO. 10

Caldwell v. Cline. 109 W.Va. 533 (1930)

LIVELY, P. In this chancery suit for the specific performance for a contract for the sale and exchange of real estate, the chancellor sustained a demurrer to plaintiff's bill of complaint and dismissed the bill. Plaintiff appeals.

According to the allegations contained in the bill, W. D. Cline, . . . addressed a letter, dated January 29, 1929, to W. H. Caldwell, . . . in which Cline proposed to pay to Caldwell the sum of $6,000 cash and to deed to Caldwell his land on Indian Creek in exchange for Caldwell's land known as the McKinsey farm. The letter further provided that Cline "will give you (Caldwell) eight days in which" to accept or reject the offer. Caldwell received the letter at Peterstown on February 2, 1929. On February 8, 1929, the offeree wired Cline as follows: "Land deal is made. Prepare deed to me. See letter." The telegram reached Cline on February 9, 1929. Upon Cline's refusal to carry out the terms of the alleged agreement, plaintiff instituted this suit for specific performance; . . .

The first ground relied upon by defendant to sustain his demurrer to the bill is that the offer and acceptance are too vague and uncertain. These qualities can certainly not be attributed to defendant's offer. The uncertainty in the offer, if any, relates to the question as to when an offer becomes completed, and not to the duration of the offer. The letter provides for acceptance within eight days, which is indeed a mathematical certainty. If there is any vagueness in the acceptance telegram, it is as to the intendment of the offeree in the use of the words "See letter," for it is not clear whether the words refer to defendant's offering letter, or to one confirming offeree's telegraphic acceptance. A letter purporting to accept an offer, which, in reality, varied the terms thereof, would constitute a defense; but, in the instant case, the record contains only the bill and the demurrer, and the bill relates to but one letter, which is the offering letter of defendant. Without more, the telegram of acceptance appears sufficient to constitute an unconditional acceptance.

Defendant's main contention is that the offer was not accepted within the time limit specified in the offer, and counsel for defendant, in his brief, states the law to be as

> "the time for acceptance runs from the date of the offer and not from the date of its delivery."

The subject of contract by mail began with the English case of Kennedy v. Lee, 3 Meriv. and was followed a few years later by Adams v. Lindsell, 1B & Ald. 681 (1818), and courts have had no hesitation in recognizing the validity of simple contracts thus made. Adams v. Lindsell, *supra*, was an action for nondelivery of a lot of wool. On September 2, 1817, the defendant wrote from St. Ives to the plaintiffs, living in Bromsgrove, making an offer of a lot of wool on stated terms, one of which was contained in this phrase, "receiving your answer in due course of post." The letter was misdirected, and, in consequence, was not delivered to plaintiffs until September 5th, when an acceptance was sent by return of post and reached defendants on the 9th. Meanwhile, on the 8th, the wool had been sold to other parties. The court, adjudging that a contract had been made upon the posting of the acceptance, stated "that defendants must be considered in law as making, during every instant of the time their letter was traveling, the same identical offer to the plaintiffs." Taken literally, it would follow that an offer was made at the instant the letter is mailed. That the quoted statement from Adams v. Lindsell lends difficulty is recognized and criticized by an eminent writer, who finds "the truth of the matter" stated thus in Bennett v. Cosgriff, 38 L.T. Rep. (N.S.) 177:

> "A letter is a continuing offer or order, or statement by the sender which takes effect in the place where the person to whom it is sent receives

it." Williston, Contracts, Vol. I, p. 50. And other courts and text-writers have followed the rule that, where a person uses the post to make an offer, the offer is not made when it is posted, but when it is received. See Restatement of Law of Contracts, Amer. Law Inst., § 23. The reason for such a rule is clear. When contracting parties are present, words spoken by one party must strike the ear of the other before there can be mutual assent. So *inter absentes,* letters, which perform the office of words, must come to the knowledge of the party to whom they are addressed before they are accorded legal existence. . . .

As in other contracts, to consummate a contract for the sale of land, there must be mutual assent, and, where the proposal to sell stipulates a limited time for acceptance, it is essential, to constitute a valid contract, that the acceptance be communicated to the proposer within the time limited. Dyer v. Duffy, 39 W.Va. 148.

The letter, proposing that Cline "will give you eight days" to accept or reject the offer, is, without more, conclusive of the offeror's intention; and, the unconditional acceptance having been received by Cline within the specified time limit, the result was a concurrence of the minds of the contracting parties upon the subject-matter of their negotiations, in other words, a consummated contract and one which equity may enforce.

The contention of defendant, relied upon as a third ground in his demurrer, that acceptance could be made only by letter, is without merit, since the offer did not provide the means of communication. Lucas v. Telegraph Co., 131 Iowa, 669.

. . . we reverse the decree of the lower court and reinstate plaintiff's bill of complaint.

CASE NO. 11

Minnesota Linseed Oil Co. v. Collier White Lead Co. Fed. Cas. No. 9, 635, 4 Dill. 431 (1876)

Plaintiff sues to recover $2,150 claimed for oil sold to defendants whose counterclaim is based upon the following circumstances. On July 31, plaintiff by telegram offered to sell a certain amount of linseed oil to defendant at a certain price, which telegram was transmitted late in the evening of July 31 and delivered to defendant the morning of August 2. On August 3, 8:53 A.M., defendant made what he contends was an acceptance of plaintiff's offer by depositing a telegram with the telegraph office.

NELSON, D.J. . . . In the case at bar the delivery of the message at the telegraph office signified the acceptance of the offer. If any contract was entered into, the meeting of minds was at 8:53 of the clock, on Tuesday morning, August 3rd, and the subsequent dispatches are out of the case. Pars. Cont. 482, 483.

The rule is not strenuously dissented from on the argument, and it is substantially admitted that the acceptance of an offer by letter or by telegraph completes the contract, when such acceptance is put in the proper and usual way of being communicated by the agency employed to carry it; and that when an offer is made by telegraph, an acceptance by telegraph takes effect when the dispatch containing the acceptance is deposited for transmission in the telegraph office, and not when it is received by the other party. Conceding this, there remains only one question to decide, which will determine the issues: Was the acceptance of defendant deposited in the telegraph office Tuesday, August 3rd, within a reasonable time, so as to consummate a contract binding upon the plaintiff?

It is undoubtedly the rule that when a proposition is made under the circumstances in this case, an acceptance concludes the contract if the offer is still open, and the mutual consent necessary to convert the offer of one party into a binding contract by the acceptance of the other is established, if such acceptance is within a reasonable time after the offer was received.

The better opinion is, that what is, or is not, a reasonable time, must depend upon the circumstances attending the negotiation, and the character of the subject matter of the contract, and in no better way can the intention of the parties be determined. If the negotiation is in respect to an article staple in price, there is not so much reason for an immediate acceptance of the offer, and the same rule would not apply as in a case where the negotiation related to an article subject to sudden and great fluctuations in the market.

The rule in regard to the length of time an offer shall continue, and when an acceptance completes the contract, is laid down in Parsons on Contracts (Vol. 1, p. 482). He says:

> "It may be said that whether the offer be made for a time certain or not, the intention or understanding of the parties is to govern. . . . If no definite time is stated, then the inquiry as to a reasonable time resolves itself into an inquiry as to what time it is rational to suppose the parties contemplated; and the law will decide this to be that time which as rational men they ought to have understood each other to have had in mind."

Applying this rule, it seems clear that the intention of the plaintiff, in making the offer by telegram, to sell an article which fluctuates so much in price, must have been upon the understanding that the acceptance, if at all, should be immediate, and as soon after the receipt of the offer as would give a fair opportunity for consideration. The delay, here, was too long and manifestly unjust to the plaintiff, for it afforded the defendant an opportunity to take advantage of the change in the market and to accept or refuse the offer as would best subserve its interests.

Judgment will be entered in favor of the plaintiff for the amount claimed. . . .

CASE NO. 12

Lerback v. Re Mine. 188 Ore. 429, 216 P. (2d) 266 (1950)

LATOURETTE, J. On the 28th day of April, 1945, the plaintiffs and defendant entered into a certain written contract, by the terms of which plaintiffs agreed to sell to defendant all of the merchantable timber on a certain parcel of land in Marion County, Oregon. Defendant agreed to pay plaintiffs for said timber as it was cut at certain rates per thousand feet. The defendant went onto the property and started cutting timber. On the 15th day of October, 1946, plaintiffs sent to defendant the following offer:

> "I hereby offer for sale all of the timber located in Section 18, Twp. 9S, R. 4 E. WWM., Marion County, State of Oregon, together with all of the land in the S ½ of same section of which we are in position to give you title insurance.
>
> "The price is $27,000.00. Terms: $15,000.00 cash less the amount Mr. Re Mine has paid on his contract to December 15, 1946. Balance of $12,000.00 due on or before July 15, 1947.
>
> "Upon receipt of $12,000.00 title insurance and deed on S ½ of Sec. 18, Twp. 9S, R. 4 E. will be issued.

"The above to be considered as a 60 day option."

The 60-day option was later extended by plaintiffs to February 1, 1947.

On the 1st day of February, 1947, defendant issued a check in the amount of $8,500 to the Clatsop County Bank at Seaside, Oregon, and coincident therewith, filed with the Bank the following escrow instructions:

"I have handed you the sum of $8500.00 which I direct that you hold until you have received from Jens Lerback, and I have accepted, a contract of sale from him to myself, for the sale of all the timber located in Section 18, Twp. 9S R. 4 E. WWM., Marion County, State of Oregon.

"Upon receipt by you and acceptance by me, of the above described documents, you will pay to Jens Lerback the funds herein deposited.

"If you have not received the above document, or I have not accepted it, on or before April 1, 1947, you will terminate the escrow and return the funds to me.

"This agreement is binding upon the heirs, executors, successors and/or assigns of all the parties hereto.

"It is expressly understood and agreed that the printed provisions on the reverse hereof are a part of these instructions to the same extent and effect as though typed hereon."

On the reverse side is the following:

"You shall have the right to retain and are hereby given a lien upon, all documents and other things of value at any time held by you hereunder until all your compensation, fees, costs, and expense shall have been paid. . . ."

Thereupon the Bank notified plaintiffs of such escrow instructions, but plaintiffs refused to accept the $8,500 and withdrew their offer.

Plaintiffs then brought action to recover payments due on the timber contract. Defendant by answer sought specific performance of the alleged offer and acceptance contract. The trial court denied specific performance and awarded the plaintiffs judgment in the sum of $1,853.16, being the amount which the defendant owed for timber already cut.

This appeal turns on the point of whether or not the deposit of $8,500 and escrow instructions amounted to an acceptance of the offer of plaintiffs to sell the timber and land involved. It is agreed that the amount defendant paid on the contract dated April 28, 1945, was the difference between the $15,000 and the $8,500 tendered. Plaintiffs contend that defendant's attempted acceptance of such offer did not meet the terms of the offer and was not an unqualified and unconditional acceptance thereof, whereas, defendant contends that such deposit and escrow instructions were unequivocal and unconditional and constituted a binding contract between the parties.

It is the law that where an offer to sell is made the acceptance of such an offer must conform literally with the terms of the offer and must be unequivocal, absolute and unconditional. . . .

Plaintiffs' offer first described the property to be sold; second, it set out the purchase price and terms of sale; and, third, it granted a 60-day option.

The defendant's alleged acceptance in no wise indicated an agreement on the part of the defendant to pay the balance of $12,000 and that alone would negative the theory of a completed contract; furthermore, defendant's escrow arrangements called for (1) a contract from plaintiffs as a condition precedent to the payment of the $8,500 over to plaintiffs; (2) an acceptance of the same by the defendant; and, (3) the Bank to have the right to retain and to hold a lien upon the contract and the deposit until all of the Bank's compensation, fees, costs and expenses were paid.

In our opinion the acceptance as evidenced by such escrow instructions did not conform to the terms of the offer and was equivocal, not absolute and not unconditional, and was therefore not such an acceptance as is contemplated by law in order to make a binding contract.

For the foregoing reasons, the judgment of the lower court is affirmed.

CASE NO. 13

Byford v. Gates Bros. Lumber Co. 216 Ark. 400, 225 S.W. (2d) 929 (1950)

GEORGE ROSE SMITH, J. In this case the trial judge directed a verdict for the plaintiffs. . . .

The pivotal question is whether Mrs. Byford bound herself to settle certain debts owed by her daughter, Dorothy Cole, to the appellees. . . . The appellees had furnished labor and materials for an uncompleted skating rink on the restaurant property, and in the decree they were given judgments for their claims. . . .

At this point Mrs. Cole appealed to her mother, the appellant, for assistance in saving the home. On November 16 Mrs. Byford, through her former attorney, submitted separate offers of settlement to the attorneys for the appellees. Each offer referred to the other and made it a condition that both be accepted. We discuss only the offer to Gates Brothers, as it presents the more difficult of two similar problems. The Gates Brothers' judgment against the Coles was for $4,036.92. In her letter Mrs. Byford offered to pay Gates Brothers $3,000 and to . . . release to Gates Brothers the lumber in the unfinished rink. In return Gates Brothers was to satisfy its judgment. . . . The letter concluded: "Please advise whether or not this is acceptable to your client."

On November 19 the attorneys for Gates Brothers replied:

> "We are authorized by Gates Bros. to accept the settlement offered in your letter to us dated the 16th inst., provided, the cash settlement is paid promptly and a reasonable time is allowed for removal of the lumber from the skating rink, which I suggest should be 90 days in view of the season of the year we are in. . . ."

The appellant's most forceful argument is that the Gates Brothers letter did not amount to an acceptance of the proposed settlement for the reason that additional terms were suggested. We recognize the familiar rule that if the offeree proposes new conditions he is really making a counter-offer that must in turn be accepted by the other party. But it is well settled that the offeree's acceptance is not conditional merely because it recites terms that would in any event have been implied from the original offer. Restatement, Contracts, § 60. That is the situation here. Gates Brothers asked that the money be paid promptly and that a reasonable time be allowed for removal of the lumber. Since the sale that Mrs. Byford sought to avert was only eleven days away, it is evident that the offer itself contemplated prompt payment by Mrs. Byford. And the law would allow a reasonable time for removal of the lumber; so this requirement in the acceptance added nothing to the contract. Even though Gates Brothers "suggested" that ninety days would be a reasonable time, there still came into existence a binding contract by which Gates Brothers could remove the lumber within a period fixed by law as reasonable, whether greater or less than ninety days. See Restatement, Contracts, § 62.

Upon this point our earlier cases are controlling. In Bushmeyer v. McGarry, 112 Ark. 373, 166 S.W. 168, 169, an offer to sell land provided that the abstract of title would be left with an Oklahoma bank, but the letter of acceptance directed that the abstract be forwarded to the vendee in Arkansas. The seller did forward the abstract but later attempted to avoid the contract on the theory that the vendee's counterproposal had not been accepted. We upheld the contract, saying:

"It is true the letter of acceptance introduces a change in details, in that . . . it is asked in this letter that the abstract be forwarded for inspection. Now, that was not a substantial change in the terms, but merely a detail which the defendant promptly acceded to by forwarding the abstract as requested. It was not such a change as amounted to a qualification of the original offer."

To the same effect is Skinner v. Stone, 144 Ark. 353, 222 S.W. 360, 11 A.L.R. 808. . . .

Affirmed.

CASE NO. 14

Rothchild Bros. v. Lomas. 75 Ore. 395, 146 Pac. 479

The defendant addressed to the plaintiff the following letter:

"Portland, Oregon, February 24, 1912.

"Messrs. Rothchild Bros., City—Gentlemen: I hereby agree to stand as surety for I. D. Watson to you on any credit which you may extend to him not exceeding the sum of $500, and hereby guarantee the payment of such account to that amount.

"(Signed) Leroy Lomas."

Between February 25, 1912, and May 6 of the same year, the plaintiff sold and delivered to Watson, at the latter's request, upon credit, certain liquors to the amount of $976.63. I. D. Watson became insolvent and was unable to pay. The plaintiff had repeatedly demanded of defendant the payment of $500 which the latter refused. A general demurrer was filed, but judgment was rendered for plaintiff and defendant appealed.

BURNETT, J. . . . Nothing appears anywhere obliging the plaintiff to do anything by reason of the defendant's writing quoted above. Under these circumstances, the letter is at best but a mere offer by the defendant to assume a contractual relation with the plaintiff,

As said in Saint v. Wheeler, 95 Ala. 362, 10 So. 539, 36 Am. St. Rep. 210:

"The undertaking of guaranty in a case like this is primarily an offer, and does not become a binding obligation until it is accepted, and notice of acceptance has been given to the guarantor. Till this has been done, it cannot be said that there has been that meeting of the minds of the parties which is essential to all contracts."

The rule is thus concisely laid down in Davis Sewing Machine Co. v. Richards, 115 U.S. 524, 527:

"A contract of guaranty, like every other contract, can only be made by the mutual assent of the parties. If the guaranty is signed by the guarantor at the request of the other party, or if the latter's agreement to accept is contemporaneous with the guaranty, or if the receipt from him of a valuable consideration, however small, is acknowledged in the guaranty, the mutual assent is proved, and the delivery of the guaranty to him or for his use completes the contract. But if the guaranty is signed by the guarantor without any previous request of the other party, and in his absence, for no consideration moving between them, except future advances to be made to the principal debtor, the guaranty is in legal effect an offer or proposal on the part of the guarantor, needing an acceptance by the other party to complete the contract."

After construing the contract there in question the learned jurist closes his opinion with this language:

"The guarantors had no notice that their sufficiency had been approved, or that their guaranty had been accepted, or even that the original contract had been executed or assented to by the plaintiff, until long afterward, when payment was demanded of them for goods supplied by the plaintiff to the principal debtor."

Under the principles thus laid down, the complaint in the instant case fails to state a cause of action against the defendant. It goes no further than to declare an offer by the defendant without disclosing whether it was ever accepted or not, or, if accepted, whether notice of the same was imparted to the defendant. Hence there is wanting the mutuality necessary to support any valid contract.

Judgment reversed and cause remanded.

CASE NO. 15

Scott v. People's Monthly Co. 209 Iowa 503, 228 N.W. 263, 67 A.L.R. 413 (1929)

WAGNER, J. The plaintiff seeks to recover the sum of $1,000 for the claimed performance, by her, of an alleged contract growing out of an offer of prizes in a "Word-building Contest." It is her claim that she is entitled to the first prize ($1,000) for submitting to the defendant the "largest correct list of words" made from the letters in the word "determination." The defendant denied liability, upon the ground that the list submitted by plaintiff was not responsive to, and did not comply with, the terms and conditions of the offer of prizes made by it, and that the same did not constitute a substantial compliance or performance under and in accordance with the rules of the contest.

When the appellant mailed her list of words, she attached thereto a letter, in which she states:

"There are words in this list which I know are not good under the rules, but judges do not always follow the rules strictly, and to protect myself against such a possibility I included everything I could find. There are good words in this list which do not appear in their vocabulary places, but they are good words just the same."

Appellant testifies, as a witness, that she had studied and examined the rules, was familiar with them, including rule 5, and that she did not follow that rule.

Appellant's action is founded upon contract. Did the action of the appellant, in submitting her list, containing a vast volume of words known by her to be incorrect under the rules, amount to an acceptance of appellee's offer? Was it substantial performance under and in accordance with the rules? . . .

In 34 Cyc. 1731, we find the following apt language:

"An offer of or promise to pay a reward is a proposal merely or a conditional promise, on the part of the offerer, and not a consummated contract. It may be said to be in effect the offer of a promise for an act, and the offer becomes a binding contract when the act is done or the service rendered in accordance with the terms of the offer."

It is the doing of the act in accordance with the terms and conditions of the offer which completes the contract. In other words, to make a binding and enforceable contract, the act must be done in accordance with the terms and conditions of the offer. Was there a performance by the appellant, in accordance with the terms and conditions of the offer? In 34 Cyc. 1743, it is aptly stated:

> "Substantial compliance with the terms of the offer is in general sufficient. However, substantial compliance at least with the conditions of the offer must be shown in order to authorize recovery."

Substantial performance permits only such omissions or deviations as are inadvertent or unintentional.

It was appellee who made the offer and fixed the rules. To constitute an acceptance by the appellant, it was necessary for her to substantially comply with the terms and conditions fixed in appellee's offer. Unless she did so, then there was no meeting of the minds, and no contract. Intentional violation of the rules, the terms of the offer, is not substantial performance. Other contestants, who substantially complied with the rules, should not lose to one who intentionally and deliberately violated them. Appellant was under no obligation to send appellee a list of words. She could do so or not, at her own election, but, to be entitled to a prize, it was incumbent upon her to substantially comply with the terms and conditions of appellee's offer. She could not, by making her list, make a rule to suit herself.

CASE NO. 16

Anderson v. Stewart. 149 Neb. 660, 32 N.W. (2d) 140 (1948)

WENKE, J. Appellants Alma Anderson and Clyde Anderson, who are wife and husband and who were plaintiffs below, brought this action for the purpose of having the court require the appellee, Hallie Stewart, to specifically perform the terms of the contract which they allege she entered into with them. From a decree dismissing their petition, motion for new trial having been overruled, appellants appeal. . . .

It is either admitted or the record establishes that the appellee, who is a widow and who was the defendant below, was and is the owner of the north half of Lot 15 and all of Lots 16, 17, and 18, Block 23 of Railroad Addition to the town of Imperial, Chase County, Nebraska; that on February 23, 1946, appellee entered into a lease with appellants renting to them this property for the period from March 25, 1946, to March 25, 1947; that this lease contained the following provision:

> "Lease subject to sale with the option to parties of the second part to purchase same;"

and that this provision was understood and construed by the parties to the lease to give appellants the first opportunity to buy this property if the appellee should decide to sell during the term of the lease.

Having decided to sell, appellee, in accordance with this understanding did, on July 6, 1946, send a letter from her home at Eagle, Nebraska, to Mrs. Anderson, at Imperial, Nebraska, where the Andersons live. In this letter, . . . she advised Mrs. Anderson as follows:

> "I have had an offer of $6500 for the property where you are now living and have decided to sell. In the contract we have, is a statement that I am to give you folkes the first opportunity to buy, so what do you wish to do?"

Although there was additional correspondence between the parties in relation to this offer, however, it was not in any manner modified thereby and remained in effect until the appellee, on July 30, 1946, wrote to Mrs. Anderson advising as follows: "I hereby withdraw my offer and the place is not for sale at any price." This letter Mrs. Anderson received on July 31, 1946.

However, the evidence shows that on July 30, 1946, Mrs. Anderson wrote to appellee as follows:

> "Jess Nothnagle was over Sunday and we did not make satisfactory arrangements so we have decided to exercise our option and are enclosing deed which, when you have signed it before a Notary will you please send it to the Farmers & Merchants bank where the $6500.00 is on deposit. . . ."

This letter was mailed by Mrs. Anderson on July 31, 1946, at Imperial, Nebraska, before she received the letter of appellee dated July 30, 1946.

> " 'An acceptance may be transmitted by any means which the offerer has authorized the offeree to use and, if so transmitted, is operative and completes the contract as soon as put out of the offeree's possession, without regard to whether it ever reached the offerer, unless the offer otherwise provides.' Restatement, Contracts, § 64." Corcoran v. Leon's, Inc. 126 Neb. 149, 252 N.W. 819, 820.

> " 'The request or authorization to communicate the acceptance by mail is implied . . . where a person makes an offer to another by mail and says nothing as to how the answer shall be sent.' 13 C.J. 300; (17 C.J.S., Contracts, § 52.)" . . .

> "Revocation of an offer may be made by a communication from the offeror received by the offeree which states or implies that the offeror no longer intends to enter into the proposed contract, if the communication is received by the offeree before he has exercised his power of creating a contract by acceptance of the offer." Restatement, Contracts, § 41, p. 49.

We find the acceptance was mailed before the letter withdrawing the offer was received and, under these principles, a contract was entered into if the acceptance was unconditional, for, as set forth in 55 Am. Jur., Vendor and Purchaser, § 16, p. 483:

> "The acceptance of an offer to buy or sell real estate must be an unconditional acceptance of the offer as made; otherwise no contract is formed. There must be no substantial variation between the offer and the acceptance. If the acceptance differs from the offer or is coupled with any condition that varies or adds to the offer, it is not an acceptance, but is a counterproposition. Thus, it is held that an acceptance specifying a different place for the delivery of the conveyance or payment of the price from that stated in the offer or implied as a matter of law is not a sufficient unconditional acceptance."

As stated in 66 C.J., Vendor and Purchaser, p. 523:

> ". . . an acceptance of an offer to sell or purchase real estate must be identical with the offer and unconditional, and so if the offeree accepts conditionally or introduces a new term or condition into the acceptance, or in any other manner makes a counteroffer, the acceptance is not effectual." . . . (Cases cited)

It will be observed that while the offer made no reference thereto, the acceptance directed the appellee to send the deed to the Farmers & Merchants Bank at Imperial, Nebraska, and that payment of the purchase price would be made there. While it might be argued that the language used in the letter of July 30, 1946, merely requested that the deed be sent to the bank at Imperial and did not require that it be done as a condition of their acceptance, however, the letter of Mrs. Anderson to appellee dated July 31, 1946, mailed immediately following receipt of appellee's letter withdrawing the offer, and her subsequent letter of August 6, 1946, clearly show that appellants did intend appellee should be required to send the deed to the bank as a requirement of their acceptance and did intend that the money should be paid there where they said it was on deposit.

We said in Lopeman v. Colburn, 82 Neb. 641, 118 N.W. 116:

> "In order to convert an offer into a contract to sell real estate, the vendee must accept the offer as made. Acceptance of an offer to sell land, but fixing a place other than the residence of the vendor or the place named in the offer, for the payment of the consideration and delivery of the deed, is not an unconditional acceptance so as to bind the vendor."

The vendor not living in Central City the court went on to say:

> "It is also clear that it was not the province of the vendee to compel the vendor to deliver the deed and receive the consideration in Central City.
>
> "If no place for payment is specified in the offer, where the negotiations are carried on by correspondence, it is implied that payment is to be made to the vendor in the city where he resides." 66 C.J., Vendor and Purchaser, p. 525, note 23b.
>
> "If no place for delivery is specified (1) the vendor is entitled to have the transaction closed where he lives." 66 C.J., Vendor and Purchaser, p. 525, note 24a.

Here the appellants had no right to purchase under their agreement unless, during the term of their lease, the owner should decide to sell. Having decided to do so appellee was under legal obligation to offer the property to the appellants and give them a reasonable time to either accept or reject her offer before selling to another on the same terms. Appellee gave the appellants the benefit of this provision by offering the property to them. This offer she was under no obligation to keep open for any definite length of time but could withdraw at any time she desired provided it had not been unconditionally accepted. This she did. Under these circumstances she would be required to give the appellants the same opportunity to buy should she again decide to sell the property during the term of the lease. Nevertheless, she was not obligated to keep the offer made open for the term thereof. The appellants not having unconditionally accepted the offer before it was withdrawn cannot . . . have it enforced and, in the absence of any evidence to show that the appellee has sold or conveyed the property to another during the term of the lease, are not in position to complain. . . .

While cases are cited which hold contrary to the principles herein announced they are few in number and do not in our judgment represent a sound rule for the reason that owners of property have the absolute right to make the terms and conditions upon which they are willing to sell their property and any offer to do so must be unconditionally accepted if the owner is to be bound thereby. Courts should not qualify this right. See Whellchel v. Waters, 152 Ga. 614, 11 S.E. 25; Curtis Land & Loan Co. v. Interior Land Co., 137 Wis. 341, 118 N.W. 853. . . .

We have come to the conclusion that the decree of the trial court is correct and it is therefore affirmed.

CASE NO. 17

Spratt v. Paramount Pictures, Inc. 35 N.Y.S. (2d) 815 (1942)

BEVENGA, J. The plaintiff brought this action to compel defendant to issue to plaintiff ninety shares of its common stock, to which plaintiff claims he is entitled by reason of the privilege of conversion granted to holders of defendant's preferred stock under the terms of defendant's certificate of incorporation.

The certificate of incorporation provides that, in the case of shares called for redemption, the preferred stock shall be convertible

> "only up to and including the day which shall be two weeks prior to the redemption,"

and that before the holder of such preferred stock shall be entitled to convert the same into common stock,

> "he shall surrender the certificate or certificates for the stock to be converted to the corporation at the office of any transfer agent for the common stock."

Concededly, plaintiff's stock was called for redemption. The redemption date was February 3, 1942. The last day, therefore, on which the preferred stock was convertible was January 20, 1942. The question presented is whether the mailing by plaintiff of his certificates for shares of preferred stock on January 20, 1942, at York, S.C., so that it was not received at the office of the transfer agent in New York until January 22, 1942, is sufficient compliance with the provisions of the certificate of incorporation.

Plainly, the certificate of incorporation not only fixes the time within which the privilege of conversion must be done, but also prescribes the manner in which it must be exercised. The preferred stock is convertible

> "only up to and including January 20, 1942, by surrendering the certificates of stock to be converted to the corporation."

In other words, the certificate of incorporation calls not only for the acceptance of the offer within the time fixed, but the surrender of the certificate within that time. Compliance with both of these conditions is a prerequisite to the plaintiff's right to convert his preferred stock into common stock. Since the plaintiff failed to comply with these conditions, he has waived or lost that right.

It is true, as plaintiff argues, that an offer is deemed to be accepted as soon as a letter of acceptance, duly addressed and stamped, is deposited in a post office or letter box. But this rule applies only in cases where the offer is transmitted by mail. The theory is that the offeror, by using the mail as his agent to transmit the offer, has given the offeree implied authority to use the same agency to receive the reply. The rule does not apply where the offer prescribes the time, place, mode of acceptance, or other matters which the offeror may insert in and make a part of the offer.

CASE NO. 18

Sell, et al. v. General Electric Supply Corporation. 227 Wis. 242, 278 N.W. 442 (1938)

MARTIN, J. . . . On March 17, 1937, R. W. Cooke, a salesman representative of the defendant, called upon the plaintiffs, who at that time were without a line of electric refrigerators in their store. After some negotiations, plaintiffs gave Cooke an order for five refrigerators at specified prices. This order was signed by Cooke. He testified the order was taken subject to approval by his superiors at their Milwaukee office. Plaintiffs claim an outright agreement of sale was made. At the time the order was taken, plaintiffs executed, in blank, a note, attached to a form of trust receipt used by the General Electric Contracts Corporation, and at the same time delivered to Cooke a check for 10 per cent of the purchase price of said refrigerators, payable to the General Electric Contracts Corporations. General Electric Contracts Corporation is an independent sales financing corporation, affiliated with the General Electric Supply Corporation and the General Electric Company. . . .

On April 2, 1937, the General Electric Contracts Corporation notified the plaintiffs that they would extend credit to them and would purchase their customers' contracts. No definite date of delivery was stated in the order or agreed upon. On April 5, 1937, the defendant wired plaintiffs as follows:

"Extremely sorry we are unable to ship refrigerators as requested Stop Therefore check for ten percent of initial order is being returned."

And on April 6, 1937, defendant wrote plaintiffs as follows:

"Supplementing our telegram of April 5th in reference to your order for Hotpoint refrigerators, we are extremely sorry that we are unable to ship this merchandise to you as originally intended.

"The delay in securing refrigerators from our factory has seriously handicapped us in securing enough refrigerators for our established dealers and rather than disappoint you after shipping a few refrigerators, we believe it will be for the best if we do not attempt to establish another dealer outlet. . . ."

The plaintiffs . . . contend that . . . the order . . . was accepted by the defendant by retaining the order and not disaffirming the transaction until April 5th. . . .

This letter definitely rejected any negotiations theretofore had, looking to the possible appointment of the plaintiffs as the local dealer in Wausau.

Generally speaking an offeree has a right to make no reply to offers, and his silence and inaction cannot be construed as an assent to the offer.

In Morris F. Fox & Co. v. Lisman, supra, speaking of the above rule, the court said:

"This rule is of course subject to exceptions. If the relations between the parties have been such as to give to silence the significance of an assent to the offer, the offeree's silence may amount to an implied acceptance. Hobbs v. Massasoit Whip Co., 158 Mass. 194, 33 N.E. 495. Or, if the conduct of the offeree is such as to lead the offeror to believe that the offer has been accepted, there may be an acceptance by estoppel. 1 Page, Contracts, § 161."

In the instant case, there were no former relations between the parties. The only manifestations to the offeror by the defendant are the telegram and confirming letter, above quoted, each rejecting the offer. The fact that the letter indicates that the offeree had originally intended to accept is of no consequence because an unmanifested intent to accept is of no legal consequence. There is no evidence from which the court or jury might find a contractual acceptance. The defendant's motion for a directed verdict should have been granted.

Judgment reversed.

CASE NO. 19

Cole-McIntyre-Norfleet Company v. A. S. Holloway. 141 Tenn. 679, 214 S.W. 817, 7 A.L.R. 1683 (1919)

LANSDEN, CH.J., delivered the opinion of the court:

This case presents a question of law, which, so far as we are advised, has not been decided by this court in its exact phases. March 26, 1917, a traveling salesman of plaintiff in error solicited and received from defendant in error, at his country store in Shelby county, Tennessee, an order for certain goods, which he was authorized to sell. . . .

After the order was given, the defendant heard nothing from it until the 26th of May, 1917, when he was in the place of business of plaintiff in error, and told it to begin shipment of the meal on his contract. He was informed by plaintiff in error that it did not accept the order of March 26th, and for that reason the defendant had no contract for meal.

The defendant in error never received confirmation or rejection from plaintiff in error, or other refusal to fill the order. The same traveling salesman of plaintiff in error called on defendant as often as once each week, and this order was not mentioned to defendant, either by him or by his principals, in any way. Between the day of the order and the 26th of May, the day of its alleged rejection, prices on all of the articles in the contract greatly advanced. . . .

The contract provided that it was not binding until accepted by the seller at its office in Memphis, and that the salesman had no authority to sign the contract for either the seller or buyer. It was further stipulated that the order should not be subject to countermand. . . .

From this evidence the circuit court found as an inference of fact that plaintiff in error had not acted within a reasonable time, and therefore its silence would be construed as an acceptance of the contract. The question of whether the delay of plaintiff in error was reasonable or unreasonable was one of fact, and the circuit court was justified from the evidence in finding that the delay was unreasonable. Hence the case, as it comes to us, is whether delay upon the part of plaintiff in error for an unreasonable time in notifying the defendant in error of its action upon the contract is an acceptance of its terms.

We think such delay was unreasonable, and effected an acceptance of the contract. . . .

It is undoubtedly true that an offer to buy or sell is not binding until its acceptance is communicated to the other party. The acceptance, however, of such an offer, may be communicated by the other party either by a formal acceptance, or acts amounting to an acceptance. Delay in communicating action as to the acceptance may amount to an acceptance itself. When the subject of a contract, either in its nature or by virtue of conditions of the market, will become unmarketable by delay, delay in notifying the other party of his decision will amount to an acceptance by the offerer. Otherwise, the offerer could place his goods upon the market, and solicit orders, and yet hold the other party to the contract, while he reserves time to himself to see if the contract will be profitable. . . .

An earnest petition to rehear has been filed, and we have re-examined the question with great care. The petition quotes the text of 13 C.J. p. 276, as follows:

"An offer made to another, either orally or in writing, cannot be turned into an agreement because the person to whom it is made or sent makes no reply, even though the offer states that silence will be taken as consent, for the offerer cannot prescribe conditions of rejection, so as to turn silence on the part of the offeree into acceptance."

And further:

"In like manner mere delay in accepting or rejecting an offer cannot make an agreement." . . .

The quotation from C.J. contemplates the case of an original offer, unaccompanied by other circumstances, and does not apply to this case, where the parties had been dealing with each other before the contract, and were dealing in due course at the time.

It is a general principle of the law of contracts that, while an assent to an offer is requisite to the formation of an agreement, yet such assent is a condition of the mind, and may be either express or evidenced by circumstances from which the assent may be inferred, . . . Acceptance of an offer may be inferred from silence. This is only where the circumstances surrounding the parties afford a basis from which an inference may be drawn from silence. There must be the right and the duty to speak, before the failure to do so can prevent a person from afterwards setting up the truth. We think it is the duty of a wholesale merchant, who sends out his drummers to solicit orders for perishable articles, and articles consumable in the use, to notify his customers within a reasonable time that the orders are not accepted; and if he fails to do so, and the proof shows that he had ample opportunity, silence for an unreasonable length of time will amount to an acceptance, if the offerer is relying upon him for the goods.

The petition to rehear is denied.

CASE NO. 20

Corthell v. Summit Thread Co. 192 Me. 94, 167 Atl. 79 (1933)

Plaintiff Corthell entered into an agreement with his employer, the defendant, which contained the following:

"R. N. Corthell agrees that he will turn over to the Summit Thread Company all future inventions for developments, in which case, reasonable recognition will be made to him by the Summit Thread Company, the basis and amount of recognition to rest entirely with the Summit Thread Company at all times.

"All of the above is to be interpreted in good faith on the basis of what is reasonable and intended and not technically."

STURGIS, J. . . . Corthell turned several patents over to the company during the term of the contract. The plaintiff has never received any compensation. . . .

No contention is made that the term "reasonable recognition," as used . . . , means other than reasonable compensation or payment for such inventions as the plaintiff turned over.

There is no more settled rule of law applicable to actions based on contracts than that an agreement, in order to be binding, must be sufficiently definite to enable the court to determine its exact meaning and fix exactly the legal liability of the parties. Indefiniteness may relate to the time of performance, the price to be paid, work to be done, property to be transferred, or other miscellaneous stipulations of the agreement. If the contract makes no statement as to the price to be paid, the law invokes the standard of reasonableness, and the fair value of the services or property is recoverable. If the terms of the agreement are uncertain as to price, but exclude the supposition that a reasonable price was intended, no contract can arise. And a reservation to either party of an unlimited right to determine the nature and extent of his performance renders his obligation too indefinite for legal enforcement, making it, as it is termed, merely illusory.

In the instant case, the contract of the parties indicates that they both promised with "contractual intent," the one intending to pay and the other to accept a fair price for the inventions turned over. "Reasonable recognition" seems to have meant what was fair and just between the parties, that is, reasonable compensation. . . .

CASE NO. 21

Packard Fort Worth v. Van Zandt. 224 S.W. (2d) 896 (Tex.) (1949)

MCDONALD, CH.J. Appellant at the times material herein was a retail dealer in Packard automobiles in Forth Worth. Appellee alleged that on December 17, 1946, he and appellant entered into an agreement for the sale by appellant to appellee of a certain model Packard automobile for $2200, to be delivered on or about January 25, 1947. In a non-jury trial appellee was awarded damages for breach of said contract. . . .

It is undisputed that on December 17, 1946, an instrument in writing, styled "New Car Order," was signed by appellee and was accepted by appellant. The automobile to be purchased was described in the order. . . .

Nothing was said in the order with respect to accessories such as spare tire, radio, heater, etc. Nothing was said in the order with respect to the price to be paid for the automobile. The order did contain two paragraphs reading as follows:

"It is further agreed that no representation or agreement made to, by, or between the parties hereto, prior to, or at the time of the acceptance hereof, shall be binding upon either of the parties hereto, unless the same is printed or written in this order. No salesman's agreement is binding on The Dealer. All terms and conditions of this sale are expressed in this agreement, and any promises or understanding not herein specified in writing are hereby expressly waived.

"It is further understood and agreed that the above set out statements cover the entire contract and agreement between the parties hereto."

An executory contract of sale should set a certain or definite price, or else refer to some guide or standard from which the price is capable of ascertainment. . . . The rule as stated in 55 C.J. 68, quoted with approval in Lewis v. Pittman, Tex. Civ. App., 191 S.W. (2d) 691, 695, is that:

"It is also essential to a valid sale or contract of sale that the parties thereto, either expressly or impliedly, agree upon and fix with reasonable certainty the price or consideration to be paid for the property sold, or provide some method or criterion by which it can be definitely ascertained."

There can be circumstances under which a promise to pay a reasonable price may be implied. But appellee does not seek to recover on the theory that the contract impliedly called for payment of a reasonable price, or a price fixed by O.P.A. regulations, or a price listed by the manufacturer of the automobile. He argues that the written order did not contain the entire contract of the parties—that a part of their agreement was made orally. He argues that the salesman agreed with him when the order was signed that the car would be sold to him for $2200.

"It is settled that a contract of sale may be partly oral and partly in writing. In other words the contract may consist of an oral agreement and a written agreement, the one supplementing the other and each containing one or more of the terms and conditions agreed on." 37 Tex. Jur. 137.

But is it also settled that

". . . when an apparently complete written agreement declares, in effect, that it embodies all the terms of the contract, parol evidence of an agreement by one party, not specified in the writing, is inadmissible although

the adverse party alleges that the writing does not set forth the entire contract." 37 Tex. Jur. 184.
Many cases could be cited in support of the rule last stated. . . .

. . . The parties may have agreed to all that was set out in the written contract, but they failed to agree in the writing on a vital matter, to-wit, the price. . . .

. . . Insofar as the judgment awards appellee a recovery for damages for breach of the alleged contract, it is reversed and judgment is here rendered that he take nothing. . . .

CASE NO. 22

Castelli v. Tolibia et al. 83 N.Y.S. (2d) 554 (1948)

BEVENGA, J. . . . Castelli then binds himself to waive his interest in the corporation if Mrs. Tolibia will pay him the value of his stock "on the basis of net worth, plus the value of the good will of the business" as of the end of 1941. . . .

Shortly after the execution of the agreement, Castelli left for Italy, with the understanding that he would return in the fall when the "exact figures" could be computed. When Castelli returned in November, 1947, he and his accountant were permitted full and complete access to the books and papers of the corporation, in order to determine the "exact figures."

While the examination of the books was in progress, Castelli served notice, revoking the agreement. . . .

The question still remains whether the compromise agreement is sufficiently definite and certain to render it legally enforceable. The argument that it is vague and indefinite is based, in large part, upon the use of the terms "net worth" and "good will" in the provision that Castelli would waive his interest in the corporation, if Mrs. Tolibia would pay him the value of his stock "on the basis of net worth, plus the value of the good will of the business" as of the end of 1941.

It is well settled that, to render a contract enforceable, absolute certainty is not required; it is enough if the promise or agreement is sufficiently definite and explicit so that the intention of the parties may be ascertained "to a reasonable degree of certainty." Varney v. Ditmars, 217 N.Y. 223, 228, 111 N.E. 822, Ann. Cas. 1916B, 758. A contract cannot be ignored as meaningless, except as a last resort. "Indefiniteness must reach the point where construction becomes futile." Cohen & Sons v. M. Lurie Woolens Co., 232 N.Y. 112, 114, 133 N.E. 370, 371. Nor can a contract be rejected as uncertain, if it can be rendered certain by reference to something certain; the maxim being, *Id certum est quod certum reddi potest*—that is certain which may be rendered certain. Wells v. Alexandre, 130 N.Y. 642, 645, 29 N.E. 142, 143, 15 L.R.A. 218; Williston on Contracts, Rev. Ed., § 47. Thus, agreements to sell or to buy what will be "needed" or "required" have been enforced with little difficulty, where the surrounding circumstances indicated the approximate scope of the promise. Stern v. Premier Shirt Corporation, 260 N.Y. 201, 203, 204, 183 N.E. 363, 364. Furthermore, where the terms of the contract are not absolutely certain, the parties in effect agree to refer the matter to a court or jury in the event they cannot agree. Worthington v. Beeman, 7 Cir., 91 Fed. 232, 236; 17 C.J.S., Contracts, § 616, p. 1284.

Applying these principles, it would seem that the intention of the parties is reasonably certain. The terms "net worth" and "good will" have well-defined meanings. The "net worth" of a business is the remainder after deduction of liabilities from assets (W. H. Miner, Inc. v. Peerless Equipment Co., 7 Cir., 115 F. (2d) 650, 655; 45 C.J. 1389); the "good will" is the element of value which inheres in the fixed and favorable consideration of customers arising from an established and well-known and well-conducted business. Randall v. Bailey, Sup., 23 N.Y.S. (2d) 173, 177, 178, affirmed 262 App. Div. 844, 29 N.Y.S. (2d) 512, affirmed 288 N.Y. 280, 43 N.E. (2d) 43; 38 C.J.S., Good Will, § 1, p. 948.

It may be that, while the net worth of a business can be determined with almost mathematical certainty (see Olson v. Harvey, 68 Colo. 180, 185, 186, 188 Pac. 751), its good will cannot be so determined. But, however difficult the problem may be, it nevertheless presents an issue of fact to be determined by a court or jury. Von Au v. Magenheimer, 115 App. Div. 84, 87, 100 N.Y.S. 659, 661, affirmed 196 N.Y. 510, 89 N.E. 1114; Pett v. Spiegel, Sup., 202 N.Y.S. 650, 658; 38 C.J.S., Good Will, § 6, pp. 953, 954. The provision lays down a method or measure of valuation. Adopting it, the parties can, with the assistance of an accountant, compute valuation with reasonable certainty. If they disagree, it can be determined by a court or jury. This is everyday practice in cases involving damages for loss of good will. Cramerton Milk v. Nathan & Cohen Co., 231 App. Div. 28, 35, 36, 246 N.Y.S. 259, 267, 268, and cases cited. No reason suggests itself why the practice should not be followed here. . . .

CASE NO. 23

Vanlandingham v. Jenkins. 207 Miss. 882, 43 So. (2d) 578 (1949)

MONTGOMERY, J. The appellee, W. A. Jenkins, was the owner of a house and lot in the City of Clarksdale, which he turned over to Holcomb and Longino, Inc., Real Estate Agents, for sale. He did so under what is known as an agency contract, a part of which was as follows:

> "The title is good and abstract of title and taxes will be furnished at my expense."

Thereafter Charles Longino, Jr., of the real estate firm, contacted H. C. Vanlandingham and Ernest Vanlandingham, who are brothers, and as a result thereof an agreement was reached between them. . . .

At the time this agreement, which was oral, was reached, the Vanlandinghams put up $400 as earnest money with the real estate firm. On being notified of the sale Jenkins requested Honorable E. M. Yerger, an attorney of Clarksdale, to prepare the necessary papers for closing the deal. . . . Mr. Yerger informed the real estate firm that he would not have time to get up a complete abstract of title, but that he would make a thorough examination of the record and that very probably the Vanlandinghams would accept his opinion on the title, and, if not, then they would have a few days additional time to furnish an abstract. With this understanding, Mr. Yerger prepared the paper and notified Holcomb and Longino that they were ready for execution. . . .

. . . the Vanlandinghams demanded an abstract of title. Mr. Yerger explained that he had examined the records and was prepared to give them his opinion of title, and would furnish his abstract within a few days, as soon as it could be gotten up from the records. The Vanlandinghams refused to close the trade without the abstract of title, and Mr. Yerger told them he would have to set another day for the closing of the transaction, after the abstract had been prepared. This conference was in the late afternoon, and after adjournment the Vanlandinghams notified Mr. Yerger that the trade was off, and they would not go through with their contract. . . .

. . . we do not feel that the Vanlandinghams were entitled to rescind the oral contract because of the failure to immediately furnish an abstract of title. The true rule is stated in 52 A.L.R. at page 1481, as follows:

> "Where the contract contains a stipulation obligating the vendor to furnish an abstract of his title to the vendee, but no particular time is fixed in which it is to be furnished, an implication arises that the abstract is to be furnished within a reasonable time in view of all the circumstances, and compliance by the vendor with this implication is obligatory."

The proof here does not show that any particular time was fixed in which the abstract of title was to be furnished, and the implication arises that it was to be furnished within a reasonable time in view of all of the circumstances and where, as here, the vendor had reason to believe that it would not be required at all, he would be entitled to a reasonable time for furnishing it when thereafter demanded, and the vendee has no right to rescind the contract without giving a reasonable time for the furnishing of the abstract. . . .

CASE NO. 24

1501 Undercliff Ave. Corp. v. Consolidated Edison Co. 83 N.Y.S. (2d) 264 (1948)

EDER, J. . . . The basis of each of plaintiffs' causes of action is the following guaranty provision in the written order of March 22, 1929, Exhibit A, annexed to the complaint, which reads as follows:

> "The refrigerators are guaranteed for a period of one year after delivery *and thereafter free labor service is continued.*"

This clause, in my opinion, does not constitute an enforceable contract; it is indefinite and incomplete; the nature and extent of the "free labor service" is nowhere defined and no period is specified during which "free labor service" is to be "continued." The rule is clearly set forth in Varney v. Ditmars, 217 N.Y. 223, 228, 111 N.E. 822, 824, Ann. Cas. 1916B, 758:

> "It is elementary in the law that, for the validity of a contract, the promise, or the agreement, of the parties to it must be certain and explicit, and that their full intention may be ascertained to a reasonable degree of certainty. Their agreement must be neither vague nor indefinite, and, if thus defective, parol proof cannot be resorted to."

Fundamental gaps are left unfilled; whether this be intentional or from inadvertence, the result is the same; the so-called contract in respect of those features is left in the realm of conjecture, indefiniteness and uncertainty. There is no escape, in my opinion, from the fact that these are essential features to constitute a valid contract. They are absent here, and it is my view that they may not be supplied by parol proof. The contract is therefore void for uncertainty. . . .

Review Questions

1. A contractual agreement is said to consist of a *meeting of the minds* of the parties. What does this mean?
2. What two essentials are necessary to the existence of an offer that will, upon acceptance, become a contract?

3. Does the legal requirement of communication of the offer mean that the offeree must have actual knowledge of the terms of the offer?
4. Are all the terms of a proposed contract found in the offer?
5. What is apparent intent? What justification is there for basing a contract upon apparent intent rather than real intent?
6. What element is lacking in advertisements that prevents their being offers to contract?
7. Illustrate an offer containing a provision whereby certainty of obligation is introduced into the contract in the future.
8. By what various methods may an offer to contract cease to exist?
9. How can an offer that has been publicly made be withdrawn by the offeror?
10. In applying the rule that an offer terminates upon the expiration of a reasonable length of time, what test is used in determining *a reasonable length of time?*
11. Illustrate the revocation of an offer by an act of the offeror.
12. What justification is there for holding that an offer terminates upon the death of the offeror without notice of such fact to the offeree?
13. Illustrate rejection of an offer by conditional acceptance.
14. What constitutes acceptance of a unilateral offer?
15. May a unilateral offer be withdrawn before the act called for by the offer is completed?
16. Why is an offer of guaranty a unilateral offer?
17. Under what circumstances is an acceptance complete when posted? What is the theory underlying this principle?

Problems for Discussion

1. X offered a substantial reward for the return of a bearer corporate bond which he had lost. Y found the bond and upon discovering X's name penciled thereon, returned it to X, who said nothing concerning the reward. Later in the day, Y read the offer of reward in a newspaper and made claim against X. Is Y entitled to the reward?
2. The defendant, the St. Louis Union Trust Co., advertised that it "allows interest on deposits." Stone deposited money with the defendant corporation in reliance upon this advertisement but in ignorance of the rate of interest (4 per cent) and the time and manner of its computation. It is Stone's contention that the 4 per cent should be paid him on his current account. Should Stone be allowed the 4 per cent interest? (*Stone* v. *St. Louis Union Trust Co.,* 150 Mo. App. 331)
3. X sent Y an offer in the form of a written agreement for the latter's signature. Being in a hurry to get to a football game, Y signed it without having ascertained its contents. Later he discovers that the written agreement contains provisions he would like to avoid. He contends that since he never had knowledge of the contents of the proposal made to him by the offeror, there was no communication of the offer and consequently no contract. Answer this contention.
4. X offered to buy certain merchandise from Y. The day following the receipt of this offer, Y sold his business establishment to Z, who then notified X that the

terms of his offer were accepted and the goods were being sent. X refused to accept the merchandise and Z sued to recover the purchase price. Result?

5. Without being requested to do so, X offered to operate the retail business of his brother Y during the latter's illness. Y told X that he didn't expect to be absent long, but if X insisted he would be very happy about the matter. X worked for one month and when Y refused to pay him he sued to recover for his services. Result?

6. On December 15, 1945, plaintiff wrote defendant concerning a lot: "If you have not sold, I of course, am the logical purchaser. . . ." On December 16, defendant wrote: "If you should be interested in this (lot), would be glad to hear from you. Size of lot, 20 by 100, price $1,000."

    Two days later, plaintiff telegraphed: "Will accept your proposition of $1,000 . . . and will get contract and check to you within a day or so."

    The next day plaintiff wrote: "Inclosed you will find contracts in the usual form and also my check for $100 as evidence of good faith, and will you please sign and return one copy to me, so that title company can institute search?"

    On December 23, defendant advised plaintiff that the lot had been sold. Plaintiff brought an action for specific performance. Did he succeed? (*Patrick* v. *Kleine,* 215 N.Y.S. 305)

7. This action was brought against the administrator of the estate of Ruth W. Anderson, deceased, seeking to recover money for which it is claimed the estate is liable. The cause was tried to the court without a jury, and resulted in findings of fact, conclusions of law, and judgment sustaining the plaintiff's right to recover in the sum of $413.95. From this judgment the defendant appeals.

    On September 3, 1920, Ruth W. Anderson, a lady more than seventy years of age, was very ill. At that time she was a resident of the city of Seattle. The respondent was her stepson, and resided at Indiana, Pennsylvania. On this date Mrs. Martha C. Deutsch, a friend of Mrs. Anderson for a number of years, sent a telegram to the respondent, and on the following day he left his home and came to Seattle, arriving there on September 8th. He remained in Seattle for approximately a week, when he returned to his home, and some days later Mrs. Anderson died. . . . The respondent claimed that he had made the trip at the special instance and request of his stepmother, and that the expenses thereof, together with some incidental expenses that he had been put to for her benefit while he was in Seattle, should be paid out of the funds of the estate. Decide. (*Cramer* v. *Clark,* 121 Wash. 507, 209 Pac. 688)

8. Nelson wrote Failing in respect to certain real estate, "I will not sell for less than $56,000." Failing contends this to be an unqualified offer that was accepted by him when he wired Nelson, "Will accept your offer $56,000 net." What do you think? (*Blakeslee* v. *Nelson,* 207 N.Y.S. 676)

9. Defendant offered a reward of $100 for the recovery of a set of old double harness, worth perhaps $15, which had been taken from him. Plaintiff's version of the language used was that defendant said: "I will give $100 to any man who will find out who the thief is and will give a lawyer $100 for prosecuting him," using rough language and epithets concerning the thief. Is plaintiff, who recovered the harness, entitled to the reward? (*Higgins* v. *Lessig,* 49 Ill. App. 459)

10. Plaintiff seeks to recover for services from February 1, 1945, to January 1, 1946, upon the following proposition made him by defendant: "If you boys will go on and continue the way you have . . . and get me out of this trouble and get these jobs started that were in the office three years, on the first of next January, I will close my books and give you a fair share of my profits." Result?
11. A agrees to furnish the B creamery all the butter tubs to be used in B's business for the period of one year. The price per tub was agreed upon, but A seeks to avoid the agreement because of the uncertainty of the number of tubs to be supplied. Will he succeed?
12. Lorberry agreed to sell Brooks 25,000 tons of freshly mined anthracite coal of a specified grade, deliveries to be completed within three months. Brooks agreed to pay for all coal shipped and accepted during any month at "the price which Brooks will receive for all coal sold during the month less a 10 per cent commission." Lorberry refused to deliver coal to Brooks, who sued for breach of contract. Result? (*Amsbry Brooks* v. *Federal Surety Co.,* 113 W.Va. 404, 168 S.E. 384)
13. Suppose in question No. 12 the parties had agreed that Brooks would pay the market price of coal at the time of his sales, less a 10 per cent commission. Would your conclusion be the same?
14. In May, 1837, the following offer was published for about one week in the daily papers of Boston: "The frequent and successful repetition of incendiary attempts renders it necessary that the most vigorous efforts should be made to prevent their recurrence. $1,000 will be paid by the city for the conviction of any person engaged in these nefarious practices. Samuel A. Eliot, Mayor." In January, 1841, an extensive fire occurred, and plaintiffs, suspecting one Marriot, were successful in bringing about his prosecution. Are plaintiffs entitled to the reward? (*Loring* v. *City of Boston,* 7 Metc. [Mass.] 409)
15. An offer contained the following statement: "We agree that this offer may be accepted any time prior to April 10, and that we will not withdraw it before such time." Can the offeror, providing the offer has not been accepted, withdraw the offer before April 10?
16. Henry B. Ste. Marie apprehended one Surratt and claimed a $25,000 reward which had been publicly offered by the War Department. Sometime prior to the apprehension, the offer had been publicly withdrawn by use of the same means as that through which the offer had been made. Ste. Marie contends that since the revocation was never communicated so as to come to his knowledge, it was ineffective and a contract was formed by his compliance with the request. Answer this contention. (*Shuey* v. *U.S.,* 92 U.S. 73)
17. X sent Y an offer and in his letter stated, "Unless I hear from you within the week, I will conclude that you have accepted my offer." X failed to hear from Y within the week. Is there a contract?
18. This was an action by a railroad corporation established at Minneapolis in the State of Minnesota against a manufacturing corporation established at Columbus in the State of Ohio. The petition alleged that on December 19, 1879, the parties made a contract by which the plaintiff agreed to buy of the defendant, and the defendant sold to the plaintiff, two thousand tons of iron rails of the weight of 50 lbs. per yard, at the price of $54 per ton gross, to be delivered free

on board cars at the defendant's rolling mill in the month of March, 1880, and to be paid for by the plaintiff in cash when so delivered. The answer denied the making of the contract. It was admitted at the trial that the following letters and telegrams were sent, and were received in due course by the parties, through their agents:

December 5, 1879. Letter from plaintiff to defendant:

"Please quote me prices for 500 to 3,000 tons 50-lb. steel rails, and for 2,000 to 5,000 tons 50-lb. iron rails, March, 1880, delivery."

December 8, 1879. Letter from defendant to plaintiff:

"Your favor of the 5th inst. at hand. We do not make steel rails. For iron rails, we will sell 2,000 to 5,000 tons of 50-lb. rails for fifty-four ($54.00) dollars per gross ton for spot cash, F.O.B. cars at our mill, March delivery. . . . If our offer is accepted, shall expect to be notified of same prior to Dec. 20, 1879."

December 16, 1879. Telegram from plaintiff to defendant:

"Please enter our order for twelve hundred tons rails, March delivery, as per your favor of the eighth. Please reply."

December 16, 1879. Letter from plaintiff to defendant:

"Yours of the 8th came duly to hand. I telegraphed you today to enter our order for twelve hundred (1,200) tons 50-lb. iron rails for next March delivery. at fifty-four dollars ($54.00) F.O.B. cars at your mill. Please send contract. . . ."

December 18, 1879. Telegram from defendant to plaintiff, received same day:

"We cannot book your order at present at that price."

December 19, 1879. Telegram from plaintiff to defendant:

"Please enter an order for two thousand tons rails, as per your letter of the eighth. Please forward written contract. Reply. . . ."

After repeated similar inquiries by the plaintiff, the defendant, on January 19, 1880, denied the existence of any contract between the parties.

The jury returned a verdict for the defendant. Decide. (*Minneapolis & St. Louis Ry. Co.* v. *Columbus Rolling Mill Co.,* 119 U.S. 149, 30 L.Ed. 376)

19. Plaintiff alleges a contract for all the cattle-carrying space on the Warren Line for the May sailings from Boston to Liverpool at the rate of 52 shillings and 6 pence per head. At half past eleven the defendants telegraphed plaintiff: "Subject prompt reply, will let you May space, fifty-two six." This was received at sixteen minutes past twelve, and twelve minutes later an acceptance was wired which was not received by defendants until twenty minutes past one. At one, the defendants wired a revocation which was received at forty-three minutes past one. Was there a contract? (*Bauer* v. *Shaw,* 168 Mass. 198)
20. The following letter evidenced the basis of plaintiff's suit for breach of contract:

"Tyler Brokerage Company, Ltd.
Tyler, Texas
December 2, 1947

"S. Skeen Staley, Jr.
312 Lacy Building,
Dallas 1, Texas.

"Dear Sir:

"This will confirm our sale to you of 600 tons of soil pipe and fittings to be delivered at the rate of 100 tons per month starting in January 1948 and to be completed during June 1948.

"As quoted, the price on victory weight pipe, sizes 2" through 6" will be list price plus 23½% f.o.b. cars Tyler, Texas. On fittings 2" through 6" the price will be list price plus 29½% f.o.b. cars Tyler, Texas.

"The terms on this sale will be sight draft B/L attached payable at the Tyler State Bank & Trust Company, Tyler, Texas. . . .

"Yours very truly
Tyler Brokerage Company, Ltd.
By W. H. Heller."

The trial court concluded that the letter relied upon entirely as the basis of a binding contract was unenforceable. (*Staley* v. *Harvey*, 226 S.W. (2d) 897)

21. Defendant concluded his offer to supply plaintiff with crude oil with the following: "We extend to you a refusal of making the contract on the above basis for the term of sixty days from this date."

Before the expiration of the sixty-day period defendant wrote plaintiff: "We wish to advise you that we withdraw our offer of July 31 . . . You will therefore consider the same canceled."

Two days later, however, the plaintiff replied as follows: "Dear Sirs: We hereby notify you that we accept and will fully carry out the option and contract given to us. . . . We hereby repudiate your attempted withdrawal of said option and contract as expressed in your letter to us, dated Pittsburgh, Pa., September 25, 1893." Is there a contract?

22. The material facts in the case are: When the plaintiff was about twelve years of age, in the absence of other home, she went to live with the defendant, her brother-in-law. This was in the year 1885. For the first three or four years she was sent to school, and during the whole period she lived in the family as the defendant's own daughter might have done. She was furnished with a comfortable room, with suitable clothing and other necessaries, was supplied with money for shopping and other purposes, accompanied the defendant's wife on various pleasure trips, went to the World's Fair with money furnished by the defendant, received numerous presents at Christmas and other times, and was treated by the defendant with great kindness and consideration in every way. On her part, the plaintiff rendered services such as might have been required and expected from a daughter; attending to the marketing, and assisting in the care of the young children. In addition to these services the plaintiff assisted the defendant in his store, attending to customers, looking after entertainments the defendant had in charge, and doing whatever else the exigencies

of the business, and her own capacities, from time to time suggested. According to the plaintiff's testimony, a conversation took place four years before August, 1894, late one evening, in the store of the defendant. This conversation was repeated several times in the plaintiff's testimony and was given by her as follows: "Mr. Durst asked me if I was tired. I said, 'Yes, sir'; and he said, 'How long have you been with me now?' and I told him 'Five years'; and he said, 'Well, when you are with me ten years, I will give you one thousand dollars.' " On another occasion defendant remarked that when she (the plaintiff) should get married he would give her $1,000, and a $500 diamond ring. Defendant does not positively deny either of these conversations, except as to the time of the first, but intimates that he was not in earnest, but jesting.

The trial court allowed the plaintiff to recover. Decide. (*Plate* v. *Durst*, 24 S.E. 580, 42 W.Va. 63)

23. The defendant, by Brucks & Peyser, its agents, wrote the plaintiff as follows:

"Outlet Embroidery Co., June 15, 1929
412 6th Avenue,
New York City

"Gentlemen:

"Enclosed please find copy of your order placed with us today, terms on same 3/10 days, delivery as soon as possible.

"We have cabled this order today to England as these goods will be made up special for you.

"Please send us your confirmation of same by return mail.

"Also note that the price of $3.10 per box on your Fil D'Angora brand which we are to ship to you is subject to change pending tariff revision.

"Yours very truly,
Brucks & Peyser
Morell Peyser

"All Prices Subject to Change Pending Tariff Revision."

Accompanying this letter was an order specifying quantities and colors, and repeating the statement that the price was to be $3.10 per box. The plaintiff, on receipt of the letter and its inclosure, made answer as follows:

"Brucks & Peyser, June 17, 1929
100 Fifth Avenue
New York, N.Y.

"Gentlemen:

"Received your letter dated June 15, 1929, enclosing copy of my order.

"We confirm the same as requested.

"We hope you will deliver the merchandise as soon as possible and avoid last season's delays.

"Very truly yours,
Outlet Emby. Supply Co., Inc."

Three days later (June 20, 1929) the defendant canceled its acceptance, and notified the plaintiff that it would refuse to make delivery.

The plaintiff sues for the damages resulting from the refusal. (*Outlet Embroidery Co.* v. *Derwent Mills,* 254 N.Y. 179)

24. The defendants, on or about August 1, 1914, signed a paper which reads as follows:

"Brooklyn, N.Y., August 1, 1914.

"Undersigned hereby authorizes the publishers of the Butchers' Advocate to insert our ad. to occupy ¼ page in Butchers' Advocate for one year and thereafter until publishers have order to discontinue the ad., for which we agree to pay $8.00 per insertion.

"Safety Auto Trolley,
J. W. Berkof."

The plaintiff proceeded under this authorization to publish advertisements for the defendant. Some time in September the defendants notified the plaintiff to discontinue the advertisement, but the plaintiff nevertheless continued to insert same in each issue, and has recovered a judgment for the sum of $416, the price named for the insertion of the advertisement for one year. Decide. (*Butchers' Advocate Co.* v. *Berkof,* 158 N.Y.S. 160)

25. Defendants, proprietors of a medical preparation called "The Carbolic Smoke Ball," inserted in the *Pall Mall Gazette* of November 13, 1891, and in other newspapers, the following advertisement:

"£100 reward will be paid by the Carbolic Smoke Ball Company to any person who contracts the increasing epidemic influenza, colds, or any disease caused by taking cold, after having used the ball three times daily for two weeks according to the printed directions supplied with each ball. £1,000. is deposited with the Alliance Bank, Regent Street, showing our sincerity in the matter. Price, 10s., post free."

Plaintiff, a lady, on the faith of this advertisement, bought one of the balls at a chemist's and used it as directed, three times a day, from November 29, 1891, to January 17, 1892, when she was attacked by influenza. Hawkins, J., held that she was entitled to recover the £100. Decide. (*Carlill* v. *Carbolic Smoke Ball Co.,* 1 Q.B. 256)

26. On April 20, 1895, appellee wrote appellant the following letter:

"St. Louis, Mo., April 20, 1895.

"Gentlemen:

"Please advise us the lowest price you can make us on our order for ten carloads of Mason green jars, complete, with caps, packed one dozen in a case, either delivered here, or f.o.b. cars your place, as you prefer. State terms and cash discount.

"Very truly,
Grunden-Martin W. W. Co."

To this letter appellant answered as follows:

"Grunden-Martin Wooden Ware Co., Fairmount, Ind., April 23, 1895
St. Louis, Mo.

"Gentlemen:

"Replying to your favor of April 20, we quote you Mason fruit jars, complete, in one-dozen boxes, delivered in East St. Louis, Ill.: Pints, $4.50, quarts, $5.00, half gallons, $6.50 per gross, for immediate acceptance, and shipment not later than May 15, 1895; sixty days' acceptance, or 2 off, cash in ten days. Yours truly,

"Fairmont Glass Works

"Please note that we make all quotations and contracts subject to the contingencies of agencies of transportation, delays or accidents beyond our control."

For reply thereto, appellee sent the following telegram on April 24, 1895;

"Fairmount Glass Works, Fairmount, Ind.

"Your letter twenty-third received. Enter order ten carloads as per your quotation. Specifications mailed. Grunden-Martin W. W. Co."

In response to this telegram, appellant sent the following:

"Fairmount, Ind., April 24, 1895.

"Grunden-Martin W. W. Co., St. Louis, Mo.:

"Impossible to book your order. Output all sold. See letter. Fairmount Glass Works."

Appellee insists that, by its telegram sent in answer to the letter of April 23d, the contract was closed for the purchase of 10 carloads of Mason fruit jars. Appellant insists that the contract was not closed by this telegram, and that it had the right to decline to fill the order at the time it sent its telegram of April 24. The court below gave judgment in favor of appellee. Decide. (*Fairmount Glass Works* v. *Grunden-Martin Wooden Ware Co.*, 51 S.W. 196, 106 Ky. 659)

27. Jones, by telegram, offers to buy Smith's 100 shares of stock in the X Corporation for $55 a share. Two weeks later Smith sends Jones a telegram in which he states that he is accepting the offer. Jones refuses to deal since the stock has declined in market value to $37 a share. Can Smith recover for breach of contract?
28. X had received an offer from Y by mail. X immediately posted a letter of acceptance but shortly thereafter induced the postmaster to return the letter to him. Had a contract been consummated?
29. X offered to sell Y his house. Y answered, "I will accept your offer if you can furnish me with a good title to the property." Is this a conditional acceptance?
30. X presented the following letter to Y: "This will introduce my friend X; let him have $2,500 worth of merchandise on account and I will guarantee payment. Signed S." Y did as requested but before he had an opportunity to communicate such fact to S, he received a letter from S revoking the guaranty. In the event of default of payment by X, can Y hold S?

5 CONTRACTS:

CONSIDERATION

Let us recall that we characterized the law of contracts as the law of promises. And let us keep in mind that the law of contracts is basically and primarily concerned with determining what promises society recognizes as being enforceable.

Promises (contractual promises), to be enforceable, must in general have the element of consideration present. It is the purpose of this chapter (1) to establish what consideration consists of, (2) to demonstrate its application to typical commercial situations, and (3) to establish the situations under which promises are enforceable without need of consideration.

► I. ELEMENTS OF CONSIDERATION

A. CONSIDERATION IS A PRICE

In establishing the characteristics of consideration, it will be helpful to recognize that consideration is found in both the offer and the acceptance. Offer and acceptance must embody the element of legal consideration if they are to obtain the status of a contract. As was stated in the previous chapter, the offer is usually made in the form of a promise (it may, however, take the form of an act) conditioned upon the offeree's giving a price either in the form of an act or a promise. Similarly, the acceptance may be viewed both as (1) an assurance from the offeree that the price asked in the offer will be forthcoming, and (2) impliedly requesting as its price the promise made or the act performed by the offeror.

In the preceding paragraph lies the basic concept of consideration: it is the price *which the promisor requests for his promise.* This is the bargain theory of consideration, the purchase of a promise for a price. (If you will do something for me, I will do something for you.) It is not sufficient that the promise and the price merely coincide; they must be the motive for each other—they must have been bargained for. A promise that has been purchased for a price is a contractual promise and consequently enforceable, whereas a gratuitous promise stands unenforceable.

The above may be diagrammatically illustrated thus:

(1) Having two promisors—a bilateral contract—the promisors request as the price for their promises the promises of each other. See figure 1.

(2) Having only one promisor—a unilateral contract—the promisor requests the act of the other contracting party as the price for his promise. See figure 2.

B. PRICE AS DETRIMENT TO PROMISEE OR BENEFIT TO PROMISOR

The fact that a price has been requested and given for a promise does not necessarily constitute consideration. The price, in order to be consideration, must meet the requirement of being a *legal detriment* to the *promisee* or *legal benefit* to the *promisor*. Legal detriment means a *promise to give up* (forego) or *the actual giving up* (foregoing) of a legal right, privilege, or immunity. By the same token, legal benefit means the advantage to the promisor in receiving something either tangible or intangible to which he was not previously entitled.[1, 2, 3]

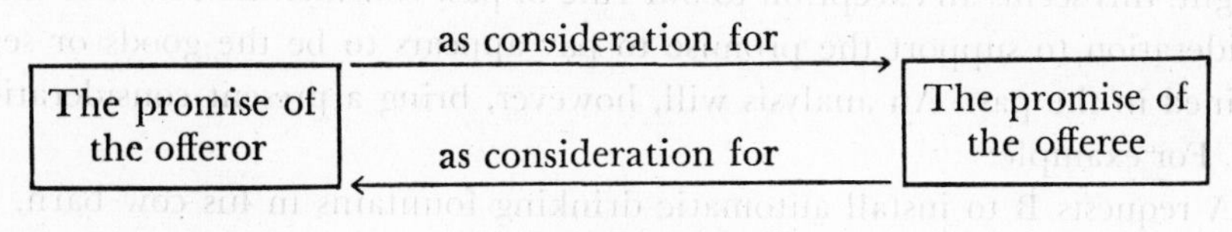

Figure 1

Figure 2

Combining the two elements of consideration, we can then conclude that consideration is the price that the promisor requests for his promise, providing such price is a legal detriment to the promisee or a legal benefit to the promisor. Thus, if A proposes marriage to B, and B accepts, there is a bilateral contract in which the two promisors are requesting each other to give up the right to remain footloose and fancy free. The promise to give up this right constitutes a legal detriment to the two promisees. By the same token, receiving the promises is a benefit to the respective promisors.

C. PAST CONSIDERATION

To be binding, a promise must be supported by a present or future consideration—something bargained for, and given or foregone by the promisee *at the time*

1 Miller v. Bank of Holly Springs, p. 99.
2 Coast Natl. Bank v. Bloom, p. 100.
3 Speroff v. First Central Trust Co., p. 101.

of the making of the promise. Therefore, it is generally said that past consideration will not support a present promise.[4] To illustrate:

Dill sold a mechanical contrivance to Thompson, which developed various alleged ailments. When Thompson complained to Dill and professed great dissatisfaction, Dill promised to service the machine for one year. This promise is not supported by a present consideration. The price paid (or the promise to pay) in the past will not support the present promise.

Special mention must be made of those situations where services and goods are obtained upon request without any agreement at the time as to compensation or price. Unless the circumstances show that such were intended as a gift, a subsequent promise to pay a specified amount will be legally enforceable. On first thought, this seems an exception to our rule of past consideration in that the only consideration to support the promise to pay appears to be the goods or services obtained in the past. An analysis will, however, bring a present consideration to light. For example:

A requests B to install automatic drinking fountains in his cow barn, nothing being said about the price. This relationship implies a promise on the part of A to pay a reasonable amount upon performance of the request. Upon performance, B has the corresponding right to receive a reasonable amount. The subsequent promise by A to pay a specified amount, $500, to which B gives his assent, is supported by a present consideration. B has, by his promise to accept $500, given up his legal right to a reasonable compensation for the installation.

D. ADEQUACY OF CONSIDERATION

Generally any consideration that the parties agree upon, regardless of its value, is adequate to support a promise. A thing of no value, however, cannot serve as consideration.[5] The value of the consideration in relation to the promise is a matter that is left entirely to the determination of the offeror and offeree. They and not the courts make the bargain.[6] The court in *Nelson* v. *Brassington,* 64 Wash. 180, said "The trial court found that the fair market value of the several articles of personal property sold by the respondent to the appellant approximated the sum paid as the consideration for the sale, and hence concluded that there was no consideration for the remaining part of the agreement not to enter into business within the prohibited territory. But this is not the correct test. Courts in transactions of this kind do not inquire into the adequacy of the consideration. This, in the absence of fraud or over-reaching, is solely the business of the parties. The court inquires only into the legality of the consideration, not whether the party to be bound made an improvident bargain."

Although the courts will not pass upon the adequacy of the consideration itself, it is recognized that a consideration of small value in relation to the value of the promise may suggest and be evidence that the transaction is founded upon

---

[4] Plowman v. Indian Refining Co., p. 102.
[5] Grant v. Aerodraulics Co., p. 104.
[6] Hood v. Cline, p. 106.

fraud, duress, or undue influence. Where a debtor transfers his assets for a nominal consideration, it will be viewed as evidence of an attempt to defraud creditors. It is self-evident that gross inadequacy may also be indicative of a lack of intent to contract.

1. *Exception to Rule of Adequacy*

As an exception to the above rule, it is well established that, in the case of an exchange of things of like kind, as money for money, the consideration must be equal. This rule is based upon the fact that the value of money is fixed and certain. How can it be said that the parties are bargaining if one promises to pay $1,000 for a return promise to pay $1? The technical artificiality of consideration is suggested by the fact that a promise to give an article, regardless of its value, would support the $1,000 promise.

E. REQUIREMENT OF MUTUALITY OF CONSIDERATION—ILLUSORY PROMISE

Where a contract imposes no definite obligation on one party to perform, it lacks mutuality of obligation or consideration, which is the same thing. A promise that imposes no definite obligation is called illusory—a *nudum pactum*—and is in reality no promise.

In a bilateral agreement both parties must be bound or neither is bound.[7, 8] The courts speak of this requirement as *mutuality of obligation.* This is in fact the principle of certainty of obligation (which was considered in the preceding chapter) viewed from the point of view of consideration. To illustrate:

Mr. H agreed to give Mr. L the exclusive agency to sell grapes from the H Grape Farm. Mr. L accepted the commission with the stipulation that he could have the agency "as long as he wished." The promise of Mr. L was obviously no promise since he might not wish to have the agency. He has bound himself to nothing. *He has not promised to suffer a legal detriment.* Consequently, his illusory promise cannot serve as a consideration to make the promise of Mr. H binding. Obviously, an exclusive agency contract would have been created if in our illustration above the seller had agreed to sell for a five-year period at a 25 per cent commission and had agreed not to sell any other line of grapes.

The above case contains a promise by Mr. H which can be accepted to the extent of the performance by Mr. L. Let us assume that Mr. L is to receive a 25 per cent commission on all sales. H would then become bound to his promise for all sales consummated by L; the act of selling would furnish the consideration to support the promise.

---

[7] International Shoe Co. v. Herndon, p. 107.
[8] Crawford v. Baker, p. 108.

▶ II. THE RULE OF CONSIDERATION APPLIED AND ILLUSTRATED

A. EXISTING LEGAL OBLIGATIONS AS CONSIDERATION

By a strict application of the doctrine of consideration, existing legal obligations, whether contractual or noncontractual, cannot serve as consideration. A promisor is suffering no legal detriment by promising to do or by doing that which he is already bound to do.

1. *Noncontractual Obligations*

The execution of, or a promise to execute, a noncontractual duty as imposed by law—statutory or otherwise—is, therefore, not sufficient as consideration for a promise given in return. This applies to such duties as that of peace officers to make arrests, witnesses to appear to testify, trustees to perform their trust duties, finders to return the property to the true owners, parents to care for their minor children, and individuals to refrain from illegal acts.

2. *Contractual Obligations to Promisor or Others*

Upon the same reasoning as applied above to noncontractual duties, a promise to fulfill, or the fulfillment of, a duty arising out of a contractual relationship will not meet the requirements of legal consideration. Therefore, it is generally held that a promise of additional compensation as an inducement to complete performance of a contract is not enforceable. Under such circumstances, to be secure in the promise for additional compensation the obligor must make certain that a new consideration is introduced into the agreement.[9, 10]

At times, contracting parties find it desirable to modify or to introduce new terms into an existing contract. The introduction of new terms into a contract will not give rise to the presumption that the parties have rescinded the old contract and substituted a new agreement therefor. The new terms must be supported by a new consideration.* For example:

A landlord and tenant enter into a five-year lease, whereby the tenant agrees to pay $10 an acre per year. After three years, they agree that for the remaining two years the tenant will pay only $6 an acre. This does not constitute a rescission of the five-year contract, but rather an attempt at modification of the contractual obligation of the tenant. The landlord can still recover $10 per acre for the remaining two years unless the tenant has *given consideration* (doing anything or agreeing to do anything he is not legally bound to do) to support the promise to collect only $6 an acre. The promise to pay $6 an acre is not a legal detriment to the tenant since he is already bound to pay $10 an acre for a period of five years.

---

* Some states provide by statute that an agreement to change or modify a contract is enforceable without consideration if in writing. See N.Y. Personal Property Law, McK. Consol. Laws, C. 41, § 33(2).

9 Leggett v. Vinson, p. 110.

10 Scott v. Duthie, p. 111.

It is generally held that such an agreement will be enforced to the extent of its performance.

An exception to the general rule, which can at least be countenanced in good conscience, has been established in a relatively few states to apply *where unforeseen substantial difficulties or obstacles* present themselves in the performance of the contract. This exception is founded entirely upon equitable precepts—here the conscience of equity creeps into the law.[11]

B. ACCORD AND SATISFACTION

Numerous problems of consideration arise out of agreements dealing with the discharge of claims or obligations—arising from either contract or tort—upon terms other than the performance originally expected by the claimant or creditor. *Any arrangement by which a substitute settlement is accomplished is called an accord and satisfaction.* The *accord* is the agreement of the parties to abide by the proposed terms in settlement of the original claim or obligation. In effect the claimant or creditor agrees to give up his recourse to legal action for a price. The *giving and accepting of this price constitutes the satisfaction and must stand as consideration to bind the claimant or creditor to this promise to wipe out his original demands.* This price may take either the form of a *promise* or an *act.*

1. *Compromise Agreements*

For varying reasons, in the conduct of business and personal affairs, disagreements and disputes as to respective legal rights and legal duties arise between individuals and may result in litigation. Realizing the desirability of avoiding law suits, the parties in many instances settle their differences by a compromise agreement—a special type of accord and satisfaction.

> This agreement made this ______ day of ______ 19___, between ______, of ______, and ______, of ______.
>
> Whereas a dispute exists between the parties hereto as to their respective rights and liabilities in regard to ______ (statement as to the nature of the dispute),
>
> And whereas the parties hereto desire to effect a just and amicable settlement of such dispute and to compromise and adjust such dispute without resorting to litigation,
>
> Now, therefore, in consideration of the mutual promises of each other hereinafter set forth, the undersigned agree as follows: (Statement of facts agreed to).

Such an agreement need not be formally executed; any understanding in provable form is sufficient. By the use of divers theories of consideration the courts universally uphold agreements to settle conflicting claims where such claims are *honestly* asserted. Amicable settlement of controversies is a desirable

[11] King v. Duluth, p. 112; see also Dahl v. Moss and Son, p. 307.

practice to which the courts have given every encouragement. Consequently they have never found it difficult to establish consideration in agreements to settle differences. Some of the varying theories of consideration which can be found in the written opinions of courts are that the consideration consists of (1) the settlement of the dispute; (2) the mutual release of the respective rights of the parties; (3) the avoidance of the expense and bother of litigation; and (4) the agreement to abide by the result of the settlement.

a. Compromise of Dispute Over Amount Due. A compromise agreement is used for the purpose of extinguishing an obligation the amount of which is in dispute.

In the business world, it is a matter of common occurrence that obligors will dispute in good faith the amount claimed due and owing by the creditor. Whenever the parties agree upon an amount in settlement of the dispute, the payment and acceptance of such amount will discharge the original claim of the creditor.[12, 13] Thus, if a debtor reasonably believes that the amount claimed by the creditor is not the true measure of the obligation and sends a check for a lesser amount than the claim, marking the check "Payment in full of all obligations to date," the acceptance of such will discharge the creditor's claim. The parties have in this way compromised their differences. A dishonest pretense of a claim, used by the debtor merely for its nuisance value, will not support a compromise agreement; a dispute must in fact exist.[14, 15]

Generally the above rule applies even in those cases in which the amount due the creditor is not in itself disputed and in which the debtor claims a setoff against the amount due. The minority view demands that the conflicting claims must be based upon the same transaction.

b. Forbearance to Sue As Consideration. A promise to give up the right to bring legal action is consideration to support a promise under circumstances where (1) recovery would be certain, or (2) where there is at least a reasonable possibility that the action would not fail.[16] To illustrate:

(1) In the case of *Conn* v. *Conn,* 192 Iowa 58, the plaintiff, holder of X's promissory note, which was past due, promised to refrain from bringing suit against the maker in consideration of the defendant's promise to become a surety on the note. The court, in allowing the plaintiff recovery on the defendant's promise as a surety, said, "A promise to forbear bringing suit either for a fixed or a reasonable period of time stands as consideration for a promise made."

(2) Believing he has a right of action against B for injuries sustained in an automobile collision, A agrees to forbear bringing suit in consideration of B's promise to pay him a specified sum of money.

---

[12] Schnell v. Perlmon, p. 114.
[13] Eckert-Fair Const. v. Capitol Steel, p. 115.
[14] Hogue v. Natl. Automotive, p. 116.
[15] Am. L. Ins. Co. v. Williams, p. 117.
[16] Murphy v. Henry, p. 118.

2. *Release Agreements*

Under the heading "Compromise Agreements," attention was given to problems of consideration arising in the compromise of controversial claims. We shall now take up the possibilities of extinguishing by contract existing obligations or liabilities based upon recognized causes of action. Contracts whereby such can be accomplished are called *releases.*

a. Payment of Lesser Sum to Discharge Greater Obligation. A release agreement is used for the purpose of extinguishing an obligation the amount of which is not in dispute. As a matter of business practice, creditors at times find it expedient or necessary to accept payment of a sum less than that admittedly due, acknowledging it to be in discharge of the obligation in full. Legally, such payment is generally not a discharge of the obligation even if the creditor gives the debtor a receipt for payment in full. The creditor, in accepting the lesser amount or agreeing to accept the lesser amount, is promising the debtor that he will not collect the unpaid balance. Unless the debtor gives some consideration, he cannot hold the creditor to this promise. The courts generally hold that the debtor, by paying a lesser amount than is recognized as being due, is only doing part of that which he is already legally bound to do. This is no legal detriment to the debtor and, consequently, will not stand as consideration. Thus the promise of the creditor not to collect the balance is not binding. The debtor cannot be assured that the obligation is fully discharged unless some consideration is introduced into the release agreement. For example:

A is B's debtor to the extent of $1,000. A pleads his inability to pay and B accepts or agrees to accept $500 in discharge of the obligation in full. Nevertheless, B can still recover the unpaid balance of $500. However, if B's promise is conditioned upon payment of the $500 plus the doing of some act by the debtor A which he is not legally bound to do—as turning over to B his Model T Ford—the promise of discharge would be enforceable. The assuming of some *new* obligation by the debtor is consideration.

There need be no argument on the undesirability of a rule which permits the luring of a debtor into a false security. The author has been impressed with the almost unanimous refusal of students to accept this principle as being sound. The rule that payment and an acceptance of a lesser amount will not discharge a greater obligation is followed in the majority of states. There is, however, a present trend away from this undesirable rule as evidenced by the following: [17]

(1) In Arkansas and Connecticut, it is held that a receipt of payment in full discharges the obligation.

(2) In some states the courts have seen fit to break away from the rule. And others have upon a *slight* consideration held that the payment of the lessor sum is a full discharge.[18]

The court in *Jones* v. *Perkins,* 29 Miss. 139, said·

"A rule of law which declares that under no circumstances, however

[17] Rye v. Phillips, p. 119.

[18] Engbretson v. Seiberling, p. 120.

favorable and beneficial to the creditor, or however hard and full of sacrifice to the debtor, can the payment of a less sum of money at the time and place stipulated in the original obligation, or afterwards, for a greater sum, though accepted by the creditor in full satisfaction of the whole debt, ever amount in law to satisfaction of original debt, is absurd, irrational, unsupported by reason and not founded in authority, as has been declared by courts of the highest respectability, and of last resort, even when yielding reluctant assent to it. We decline to adopt or to follow it."

(3) In a number of states the common law principle has been either abrogated or modified.*

(4) The states of Pennsylvania and Utah have enacted the Uniform Written Obligations Act under which a written promise may be made enforceable without a consideration or a seal. The Pennsylvania act reads as follows:

"A written release or promise, hereafter made and signed by the person releasing or promising, shall not be invalid or unenforceable for lack of consideration, if the writing also contains an additional express statement, in any form of language, that the signer intends to be legally bound."

b. Release of Obligation Evidenced by Negotiable Instrument. If the obligation upon which the lesser amount has been paid is evidenced by a negotiable instrument, as a promissory note, an intentional cancellation of the instrument will discharge the obligation in full.

Cancellation of an instrument is accomplished by some act of the holder in connection with the instrument, showing that the instrument has been discharged. It may consist of impressing the instrument with unmistakable evidence that the obligation has been satisfied, by mutilating or completely destroying it, or by surrendering it to the obligor. An intentional cancellation by the holder discharges the instrument regardless of whether or not it has been paid in full.

c. Composition with Creditors. It is possible for a debtor who is insolvent or in embarrassed financial circumstances to discharge his obligations by a *composition agreement* with his creditors. That is, he may propose to his creditors that he pay them a certain percentage of the amounts owing. If they assent, such agreement becomes binding *upon the assenting creditors* only. Those who have not assented to the arrangement are still entitled to press their claims for the full amount due them. A composition agreement reads as follows:

> We, the undersigned, unsecured creditors of X, agree to accept 50 cents on the dollar in full settlement of our claims against X, as represented by the amount set forth opposite our names as subscribed below, provided all other unsecured creditors accept the same proposition of their claims in full settlement.

* Alabama, California, Georgia, Indiana, Maine, North Carolina, South Dakota, Tennessee, Virginia. See particularly New York Statutes, Chap. 12, § 243.

The usual theory upon which the courts have declared composition agreements enforceable has been that the promise of each creditor to be satisfied with a lesser amount is the consideration to support the promises of the other creditors. According to such reasoning, the agreement is made in reality between the creditors for the benefit of the debtor, regardless of whether such was intended by the creditors. Where a debtor is actually insolvent, his giving up of the privilege of availing himself of a discharge of his obligations by bankruptcy may serve as consideration to make the promises of the creditors binding. Nevertheless, the composition agreement is recognized as an entirely valid method of discharging a debtor's obligations. From the social and business points of view, it must be regarded as a desirable means of untangling financial snarls.

► III. PROMISES ENFORCEABLE WITHOUT CONSIDERATION

The early common law courts, in their desire to enlarge the field of enforceable promises, did not at all times adhere strictly to the requirement of consideration. In certain classes of cases, promises became enforceable and continue to be enforceable to the present day, even though unsupported by consideration in the orthodox sense of the word. The important exceptions follow.

A. PROMISE TO PAY OBLIGATIONS DISCHARGED BY OPERATION OF LAW

1. *Promise to Pay Debt Outlawed by Statute of Limitations*

Through statutory provisions, the states specify the periods of time within which various types of legal actions must be brought. A failure to comply has the effect, generally, of depriving the injured party of his legal remedy. In those instances where there has been a failure to take action on a contractual obligation within the time provided, the obligation is said to have become outlawed—discharged by operation of law. By the use of various theories—legal fictions—the courts have consistently applied the rule that a promise to pay a debt outlawed by statute is enforceable without any new consideration.[19] It is frequently said that such a promise is founded upon a moral consideration arising out of a preexisting obligation. However, some states require by statute that the new promise be in writing.*

2. *Promise to Pay Debt Discharged by Bankruptcy Proceedings*

Similarly, if an insolvent debtor who has been relieved of his obligations through bankruptcy proceedings (which is a discharge by operation of law) subsequently promises to pay, this new promise may be enforced against him, although no consideration is presently given to support the promise.[20]

* Local statutes should be consulted as to the possibility of the obligation being revived by part payment or unqualified acknowledgment.

[19] Hunt v. Lyndonville Sav. Bank and Trust Co., p. 122.

[20] Garrison v. Marshall, p. 123.

B. SUBSCRIPTION PROMISES

Offers of subscriptions for charitable, educational, religious, or similar purposes are generally enforceable without consideration. The offer of subscription becomes binding upon acceptance. The acceptance need not be expressly made, nor need the subscriber ordinarily be notified of the acceptance. Where liability or expense is incurred in reliance upon the subscription, an acceptance is implied.

The subscription offer cases are another indication of the willingness of the courts to depart from the established doctrine of consideration to make promises enforceable. Upon the conviction that it is socially desirable to have such promises binding on subscribers, the courts have indulged in varying theories of consideration.[21]

The court in *Barnes* v. *Perine,* 12 N.Y. 18, in speaking of this situation, said:

> "An attempt to reconcile all the cases which have been adjudged, touching the validity of voluntary engagements to pay money for charitable, educational, religious or other public purposes, would be fruitless; . . . it will be found that there is, to some extent, a want of harmony in the principles and rules applied as tests of validity to that class of undertakings . . . and judges . . . have been willing nay apparently anxious to discover a consideration which would uphold the undertaking as a valid contract."

C. CONTRACTS UNDER SEAL

In states where the common law seal is still recognized, contracts executed with the attendant formalities of *affixing a seal and delivering the instrument* stand enforceable without consideration.[22] The acts of sealing and delivering the contract are taken as being conclusively expressive of the intent of the parties to be bound. These acts are regarded as being symbolic of the studied and deliberated undertakings of the contracting parties and thus lend credence to the facts evidenced by the instrument. As said by the court in *Storm* v. *United States,* 94 U.S. 76:

> ". . . the seal imports a consideration or renders proof of consideration unnecessary . . . the instrument binds the parties by force of the natural presumption that an instrument executed with so much deliberation and solemnity is founded upon some sufficient cause."

A seal is defined in *The Restatement of the Law of Contracts,* § 96, as follows:

> "A seal is a piece of wax, a wafer or other substance, affixed to the paper or other material on which a promise, release or conveyance is written, or a scroll or sign, however made, on such paper or other material, or an impression made thereon; provided that by a recital or by the appearance of the document an intention of the promisor, releasor or grantor is manifested that the substance, scroll, sign or impression shall be a seal."

And Section 97 reads:

---

21 Allegheny College v. National Chautauqua County Bank, p. 123.

22 Thomason v. Bescher, p. 125.

"A written promise is sealed if the promisor affixes or impresses a seal on the document or adopts a seal already thereon."

Since in most states the common law status of sealed contracts has been altered by statutes, local provisions should be consulted. Many states have entirely abolished private seals and make the enforceability of contracts contingent upon the presence of a valid consideration. It should be recognized, however, that approximately half of the states still recognize the binding force and effect of a contract under seal. In these states, a contract is valid if it has either a seal or a consideration.

D. WRITTEN CONTRACTS WITHOUT CONSIDERATION

In some jurisdiction, written contracts are declared by statute to *import* a consideration; a consideration will be implied from the writing. *This places the burden upon the party defending against the written instrument to show that it was without consideration.* If the defendant can establish that the agreement is without consideration, it will be unenforceable. Such a statutory provision is Section 9440 of the 1939 Iowa Code, which reads:

"All contracts in writing signed by the party to be bound by his authorized agent or attorney, shall import a consideration."

CASES

CASE NO. 1

Miller v. Bank of Holly Springs. 131 *Miss.* 55, 95 *So.* 129, 31 *A.L.R.* 698 (1923)

ANDERSON, J. . . . In June, 1918, appellant purchased through appellee United States war saving stamps of the maturity value of $1,000, which he left on special deposit with appellee for safekeeping. These stamps were placed by an officer of the appellee in its said vault. In the summer or early fall of 1919 the vaults of a good many banks over the country were being burglarized, and United States Liberty bonds and war saving stamps stolen therefrom. Appellant, learning of this fact through the public press, approached Mr. Fort, who was the active president of appellee bank as well as a director therein, and stated to him that, in view of these burglaries, he was uneasy about his war saving stamps remaining in appellee's said vault, and therefore desired to remove them to another bank for safekeeping. Mr. Fort in response stated that if appellant would permit his stamps to remain in appellee bank, he would, in order to assure their safety, put them in the Corliss safe, where the money of the bank was kept; . . . Thereupon appellant agreed that the stamps should remain on deposit with appellee upon condition that they were put in that safe. In November, 1919, appellee's vault was burglarized, and the appellant's stamps stolen therefrom, appellee having failed to place them in its Corliss safe as agreed, which was not burglarized, and therefore appellant's loss was caused by appellee's breach of its agreement. . . .

Appellee contends that said contract of deposit was without consideration moving to it; therefore it held said deposit merely as a gratuitous bailee, and is not liable to appellant for its loss unless such loss was caused by appellee's negligence, and, there being no evidence of such negligence, the action of the trial court in directing a verdict for appellee was authorized.

There is a sufficient consideration for a promise if there be any benefit to the promisor or any loss, detriment, or inconvenience to the promisee. The consideration to be sufficient in law need not be adequate. The consideration is sufficient if the person to whom the promise is made refrains from doing anything which he has the right to do, whether there be any actual loss to him, or actual benefit to the party making the promise or not. . . . Lawson, Contr. 2d . . . page 117, illustrates the principle thus:

> "If A promise B to pay him $5 if he will not eat a dinner, or $10 if he will not wear his best coat for a day, B's abstaining from eating his dinner and refraining from wearing his coat are sufficient to support A's promise, for B has a legal right to do both of these things. In a New York case, an uncle promised a nephew that if he would refrain from drinking liquor, using tobacco, swearing, and playing certain games for money until he came of age, he would pay him $5,000. The nephew kept his side of the bargain, but, when sued for the money, the uncle claimed that the agreement was not founded on a valid consideration. But the court said: It is sufficient that he restricted his lawful freedom of action within certain limits upon the faith of his uncle's agreement. . . ."

Applying these principles to the case here: Appellant had the right to remove his war saving stamps to another bank than appellee's for safe-keeping. Appellee induced appellant to refrain from doing so by promising to remove said stamps into its Corliss safe and there keep them. It seems clear that under the authorities referred to there was sufficient consideration for said contract, and it bound appellee to do what it therein agreed to do.

CASE NO. 2

Coast National Bank v. Bloom. 113 N.J. 597, 174 A. 576, 95 A.L.R. 528 (1934)

The question in this case is whether a bank director's note given as his contribution to a reserve fund made up of notes and cash contributed by directors to make good a depletion of capital by depreciation of assets and prevent a threatened closing of the bank is supported by a valuable consideration.

HEHER, J. . . . There was a judgment for plaintiff . . . in an action upon a promissory note, dated June 26, 1931, in the sum of $1,500, made by defendant to it. . . .

There was . . . evidence to support the finding that some benefit accrued to appellant from the making of the promise in question, and this constituted a consideration within the accepted definition of the term. The directors who gave their notes secured a tangible benefit which accrued directly from the contract. The requirement ordinarily stated for the sufficiency of consideration to support a promise is, in substance, a detriment incurred by the promisee, or a benefit received by the promisor, at the request of the promisor. . . .

Williston on Contracts, § 102:

> "Consideration is, in effect, the price bargained for and paid for a promise. It may be given to the promisor or to some other person, or by the promisee or by some other person. It matters not from whom the consideration moves or to whom it goes. If it is bargained for as the exchange for the

promise, the promise is not gratuitous. . . ."

Appellant here indisputably gained an advantage—one that he sought as the price for his promise. . . .

He conceived that the continued operation of the bank on a solvent basis would redound to his advantage. He therefore derived a benefit sufficient as a consideration to support the promise. The extent to which appellant was benefited is immaterial. A very slight advantage to one party or a trifling inconvenience to the other is a sufficient consideration to support a contract. . . .

Whatever consideration a promisor assents to as the price of his promise is legally sufficient consideration. Legal sufficiency does not depend upon the comparative economic value of the consideration and of what is promised in return.

CASE NO. 3

Speroff v. First-Central Trust Co. 149 Ohio St. 415, 79 N.E. (2d) 119, 1 A.L.R. (2d) 1150 (1948)

In the Municipal Court of Akron the plaintiff, Vassil Speroff, sued to recover from the defendant, The First-Central Trust Company, the amount of a check which he had drawn on the defendant but which he later notified the defendant not to pay, but which the defendant nevertheless did pay.

As a defense, the defendant pleaded further that the plaintiff signed the following:

Stop Payment Request to
The First-Central Trust Co.
Akron, O.
April 26, 1945

Please stop payment on:
Check No. ________ Dated 5-1-25
Payable to the order of J. C. Hardman
Endorsed) For the
Signed) By ________ Sum of $60

The undersigned hereby agrees to indemnify the First-Central Trust Company against any loss resulting from nonpayment of said check, and it is expressly understood that you will in no way be held responsible if you should pay this check through inadvertency or oversight.

Signed—Vassil Speroff . . .

The trial court . . . rendered a judgment for the defendant.

On an appeal to the Court of Appeals on questions of law the judgment of the trial court was reversed and a final judgment was rendered for the plaintiff on the grounds that the statement or release signed by the plaintiff is void for want of consideration . . .

WEYGANDT, CH.J. The single question of law before this court is whether the statement or release signed by the plaintiff constitutes a valid defense to his action.

In his opinion in the case of Cincinnati H. & D.R. Co. v. Metropolitan Nat. Bank, 54 Ohio St. 60, on page 71, 42 N.E. 700, on page 702, 56 Am. St. Rep. 700, 31 L.R.A. 653, Judge Spear summarized the law relating to banks and depositors as follows:

"As applicable to such case we believe that reason and the great preponderance of authority establish the following conclusions: The relation of bank and general depositor is simply the ordinary one of debtor and creditor, not of agent and principal, or trustee and cestui quie trust. The bank agrees with its depositor to receive his deposits, to account with him for the amount, to repay to him on demand, and to honor his checks to the amount of his credit when the checks are presented; and for any breach of that agreement the bank is liable to an action by him. . . ."

In the case of Kahn, Jr., v. Waltoin, 46 Ohio St. 195, 20 N.E. 203, 204, this court held:

> "A bank check, being an order on the bank by the drawer to pay his money as therein directed, is revocable by him before its presentation for payment, unless the bank on which it is drawn has accepted or certified it, or otherwise become committed to its payment. . . ."

Hence, the plaintiff clearly had the right to countermand or revoke the check. According to the facts as alleged in the defendant's amended answer and admitted by the plaintiff's demurrer, the check was issued April 26, 1945, and was countermanded or revoked later the same day. However, nearly a month thereafter on May 22, 1945, the defendant nevertheless paid the check. In its amended answer the defendant alleges that this "was occasioned solely by inadvertence and/or oversight." . . .

The members of this court, after a careful study of the authorities, are of the opinion that the decision of the Court of Appeals in the instant case is sustained by the better reasoning. This plaintiff was not required to sign anything. The defendant bank was aware that a check

> "is simply an order which may be countermanded and payment forbidden by the drawer any time before it is actually cashed or accepted"

and that an order to stop payment may be either oral or in writing so long as it conveys to the bank a definite instruction to that effect. Under the reciprocal rights and obligations inherent in the relationship existing between a bank and its depositors, it was the duty of the defendant not to pay the check after receiving such an order from the plaintiff depositor. Hence, when the plaintiff was asked to sign a statement or release to the effect that the bank would not be held responsible if it should pay the check through inadvertency or oversight, this was something new—an element that concededly had not previously existed in their relationship. What benefit or consideration was received by the plaintiff as the promisor and what detriment was suffered by the defendant bank as the promisee as a result of the new statement or release? Clearly there was no compliance with either of these fundamental requirements as to a consideration. On the contrary, the plaintiff promisor thereby received no benefit but suffered a detriment, and the promisee suffered no detriment but received a benefit.

Consequently the Court of Appeals was not in error in holding the purported release void for want of consideration. . . .

CASE NO. 4

Plowman v. Indian Refining Co. 20 F. Supp. 1 (1937)

LINDLEY, J. The theory of plaintiffs is that on July 28, 1930, the vice president and general manager . . . called the employees, who had rendered long years of service, separately into his office and made with each a contract, to pay him for the rest of his natural life a sum equal to one-half of the wages he was then being paid. The consideration for the contracts, it is said, arose out of the relationship then existing, the desire to provide for the future welfare of these comparatively aged employees and the provision in the alleged contracts that the employees would call at the office, for their several checks, each payday. . . .

The employees were retained on the pay roll, but, according to their testimony, they were not to render any further services, their only obligation being to call at the office for their remittances. . . .

The payments were made regularly until June 1, 1931, when they were cut off and each of the employees previously receiving the same was advised by defendant's personnel officer that the arrangement was terminated. . . .

Presented also is the further question of whether, admitting the facts as alleged by plaintiffs, there was any consideration for a contract to pay a pension for life. However strongly a man may be bound in conscience to fulfill his engagements, the law does not recognize their sanctity or supply any means to compel their performance, except when founded upon a sufficient consideration.

The long and faithful services of the employees are relied upon as consideration; but past or executed consideration is a self-contradictory term. Consideration is something given in exchange for a promise or in reliance upon the promise. Something which has been delivered before the promise is executed, and, therefore, made without reference to it, cannot properly be legal consideration. . . .

It is further contended that there was a moral consideration for the alleged contracts. The doctrine of validity of moral consideration has received approval in some courts, but quite generally it is condemned because it is contrary in character to actual consideration. . . .

Upon the same ground, appreciation of past services or pleasure afforded the employer thereby is not a sufficient consideration. So Williston says (Contracts, Vol. 1, p. 230):

> ". . . no motive, such as love and respect, or affection for another or a desire to do justice, or fear of trouble, or a desire to equalize the shares in an estate, or to provide for a child, or regret for having advised an unfortunate investment, will support a promise."

Plaintiffs have proved that they were ready, willing, and able to travel to and report semimonthly to the main office. But this does not furnish a legal consideration. The act was simply a condition imposed upon them in obtaining gratuitous pensions and not a consideration. The employees went to the office to obtain their checks. Such acts were benefits to them and not detriments. They were detriments to defendant and not benefits. This was not consideration. . . .

We have merely a gratuitous arrangement without consideration, and therefore, void as a contract. . . .

Viewing the testimony most favorably for the plaintiffs, despite the desirability of the practice of liberality between employer and employee, the court must decide a purely legal question—whether under plaintiff's theory there were valid contracts. The obvious answer is in the negative. Consequently, there will be a decree in favor of defendant dismissing plaintiffs' bill for want of equity. . . .

CASE NO. 5

Grant v. The Aerodraulics Company.
88 Calif. 718, 199 P. (2d) 745 (1948)

SHINN, J. This is an appeal by the Aerodraulics Company, a copartnership, and its members both as partners and individually, from a judgment on the pleadings awarding David Grant the sum of $7,000 and cancelling a contract between the parties. It appears to be conceded by both parties that cancellation was properly decreed, and the only substantial question before us concerns the correctness of money award . . .

. . . plaintiff Grant's complaint sets forth . . . the terms of a written contract, dated November 8, 1943, where by plaintiff granted to defendant partnership (herein referred to as the Company) an exclusive world-wide license to produce and sell for commercial use only a hydraulic unloading valve invented by plaintiff. By the terms of this contract the company was obligated "to apply for and procure a patent upon the device at its own expense, to diligently exploit, manufacture, use and sell said valve for commercial purposes," and to take reasonable measures to promote its use and sale. The Company further was required to pay plaintiff as

> "a minimum guaranteed royalty for said exclusive license for commercial use only, the sum of Ten Thousand Dollars ($10,000.00), whether sales of said valve be made or not."

This so-called "primary royalty" was to be payable in stated installments pending the outcome of the patent application, with the balance thereof to become immediately due and payable when letters patent were issued by the United States Patent Office. An additional "reserve royalty" based on net sales was also provided for.

In respect to termination on the license, the contract contained the following provisions: . . .

> "Company may not terminate or revoke this Agreement unless the basic design of said invention is unworkable and cannot be used advantageously . . . In the event of cancellation by Company, Inventor shall retain all payments previously made to him and Company shall have no right to reimbursement thereof."

. . . the complaint alleges that letters patent were issued in respect to the said valve on May 8, 1945; that the balance of the sum of $10,000 as provided in the contract then became due and payable; that the defendants have paid $3,000 thereon, leaving a balance of $7,000 due, owing, and unpaid; and that demand in writing for said sum has been made, but defendants have failed and refused to pay said sum in whole or in part. . . .

Defendants deny, however, that they are indebted to plaintiff, and as an affirmative defense, allege the following:

> "That during the summer of 1945 plaintiff and defendants orally agreed that in consideration of the payment by the Aerodraulics Company to plaintiff of the sum of One Thousand Dollars ($1000.00), payable Five hundred Dollars ($500.00) in the month of October, 1945, that said agreement described in plaintiff's complaint, should thereupon be cancelled, terminated and of no further force and effect whatsoever; that The Aerodraulics Company paid to plaintiff at said time the sum of $500.00, and on or about the 17th day of October, 1945 tendered to plaintiff the additional sum of $500.00, as in said agreement provided which sum plaintiff refused to accept."

As a second affirmative defense, the

answer quotes paragraph 13 of the contract as set forth above, alleges that

"the basic design of plaintiff's invention is unworkable and cannot be used advantageously,"

and alleges that on that ground a written notice of election to cancel the contract was given plaintiff on November 13, 1945.

. . . According to the settled rule of construction,

"the exercise of an option to terminate prevents liability for further transactions but does not affect obligations which have already accrued." 17 C.J.S., Contracts, § 404, p. 893, and cases cited; . . .

An oral cancellation, however, is subject to the rules concerning contracts in general and hence must be supported by a sufficient consideration to be enforceable. Haberman v Sawall, 72 Cal. App. 576, 582, 237 Pac. 776; Hooke v. Great Western Lumber Co., 54 Cal. App. 681, 683, 202 Pac. 492. Construing the affirmative defense most favorably to defendants, it appears that the consideration for plaintiff's agreement to terminate the contract and cancel the undisputed debt of $7,000 then due consisted of the payment of one thousand dollars in two equal installments, and a release by the Company of all its rights under the contract. Since the amount of the indebtedness was undisputed, however, payment by the Company of the lesser sum of $1,000 could not constitute a valid consideration for its cancellation, or for the termination of plaintiff's contractual rights against the Company. . . . Restatement, Contracts, § 76(a); 1 Williston on Contracts, Rev. Ed., § 120.

"It is an uniform rule of law that a consideration for an agreement is not adequate when it is a mere promise to perform that which the promisor is already legally bound to do." General Motors Acceptance Corp. v. Brown, 2 Cal. App. (2d) 646, 650, 38 Pac. (2d) 482, 484.

Appellants contend that ample consideration may be found in the termination of their exclusive world-wide license to manufacture and sell plaintiff's invention. It may be conceded that, as a general rule, a mutual cancellation of executory contractual rights is supported by a valid interchange of consideration. Sistrom v. Anderson, 51 Cal. App. (2d) 213, 219, 124 P. (2d) 372; Haberman v. Sawall, 72 Cal. App. 576 582, 237 Pac. 776; Hooke v. Great Western Lumber Co., 54 Cal. App. 681, 683, 202 Pac. 492; Restatement, Contracts, § 406 and comment a; 1 Williston on Contracts, Rev. Ed., § 102A, pp. 327–8. However, in the foregoing cases and others cited by appellants, the rights which were yielded up were unquestionably of value to the respective parties, and since each was legally privileged to continue to assert those rights prior to the cancellation agreement, each suffered a legal detriment in giving them up.

The facts pleaded by appellants in the present case present an entirely different situation, in which the authorities cited by them are not controlling, for two reasons. First, the elementary rule that a court of law will not inquire into the adequacy of consideration for a contract . . . does not preclude the necessity of a showing that the consideration has some value at least. See Restatement, Contracts, § 80, comment a; . . . It is well settled that something which is completely worthless cannot constitute a valid consideration . . . In accordance with this rule, it has been held that want of consideration is a good defense to an action on a note given in return for the assignment of valueless rights in an invention (Craddick v. Emery, 93 Wash. 648, 161 Pac. 484), or to an action on a contract for the sale of a void and worthless patent. Herzog v. Heyman, 151 N.Y. 587, 45 N.E. 1127, 56 Am. St. Rep. 646. Turning to defendants' verified answer, . . . we find a clear implication that the exclusive license granted to the Company was in fact valueless. It would seem to follow from the cases cited above that the termination of the Company's apparently worthless rights, which it has neither intended nor attempted to exercise, does not constitute the giving up of anything of any value, and hence does not meet the requirements of valid consideration. . . .

The judgment is affirmed.

CASE NO. 6

Hood v. Cline. 35 Wash. (2d) 192, 212 Pac. (2d) 110 (1949)

ROBINSON, J. Plaintiffs, John F. Hood and his sister, Ida Hood Brown, brought this action seeking a decree rescinding the sale of their remaindermen's interest in a 310-acre wheat and pea farm located in Walla Walla county, Washington, and Umatilla county, Oregon. The gist of their action was fraudulent concealment and misrepresentation on the part of the purchasers Wilbur A. Toner and Robert L. Cline. . . .

The farm in question formerly belonged to John A. Hood, the father of appellants, who died in 1938. In his will, he left a life interest in his property to Augusta Hood, his widow, and appellants' stepmother, and an undivided one-half of the remainder interest to each of the appellants. . . .

Appellants' final charge of fraud is based on their contention that Mr. Toner misrepresented the value of the farm, and that the consideration they received for their interests therein was inadequate. It can hardly be doubted that Mr. Toner's estimate of the value of the land, including both remainder interest and life estate, at $30,000, was low. Considering that there were 310 acres in the farm, this estimate suggested a value of slightly less than $100 an acre. Appellants' expert witnesses, who were appointed through the State of Washington realty board and who seemed completely impartial, estimated that the property was worth $175 or $180 an acre in 1945. . . .

It is the general rule, however, that, if a representation is as to value, which is a matter of opinion, it will not, in general, avoid the contract, at least in the absence of a fiduciary relation. See 1 Perry on Trusts 282 § 173. . . . Therefore, we are unable to say that this representation amounted to fraud, and we are brought to a consideration of the question of the adequacy of the slightly less than $17,000 actually received by appellants in exchange for their remainder interest.

. . . it has very generally been held in this country that the sale of reversionary or remainder estates will not be set aside for inadequacy of consideration when there is no fraud or imposition shown. . . .

One's natural sympathies in this case are with the appellants who may well have sold their interests in the farm for less than it was worth. Certainly, hindsight indicates that they made a poor bargain . . . as is stated in the headnote to Opie v. Pacific Investment Co., 26 Wash. 505, 67 Pac. 231, 56 L.R.A. 778:

> "Mere inadequacy of consideration will not afford cause for rescission of a contract on the ground of fraud, where the parties have dealt at arm's length, with avenues of information open to the one claiming fraud, and

where the agreement is entered into after the exercise of the independent judgment of each of the parties." . . .

CASE NO. 7

International Shoe Co. v. Herndon. 135 S.C. 138, 133 S.E. 202, 45 A.L.R. 1193 (1926)

COTHRAN, J. . . . Action upon an account for goods sold and delivered, amounting to $467.59, between April 4, 1923, and June 23, 1923.

The defendant . . . set up a counterclaim in substance as follows: That in March, 1915, he bought a bill of shoes from the plaintiff, in consideration of which the plaintiff

> "entered into a parol agreement with the defendant, C. H. Herndon . . . wherein it contracted and agreed that the defendant should have the exclusive sale of plaintiff's shoes at Walterboro, and should be the only person, firm or corporation to handle said line of shoes, at said place, said parol agreement further providing that the defendant should have the exclusive agency as long as he would handle said shoes and as long as he wished to handle same";

. . . that in May, 1923, the plaintiff violated said agreement by selling its shoes to two or more merchants in Walterboro, all to his damage in loss of profits and injury to his reputation as a merchant, in the sum of $2500. . . .

The contract set up in the counterclaim is not declared upon as a unilateral contract, but as a bilateral one a contract by which the defendant agreed to buy a certain bill of goods, and in consideration thereof the plaintiff agreed to give him the exclusive sale of the shoes at Walterboro.

It is very true that mutuality of obligation is not an essential element in unilateral contracts. . . . But in bilateral contracts, where the consideration is sought to be sustained upon mutual promises, the contract consists of the several engagements of the parties; the engagement of one being the consideration for the engagement of the other, and the combined engagements constituting the contract. In order to accomplish this result, it is manifest that the promise or engagement of one of the parties, which is sought to be held as the consideration for the promise or engagement of the other, must be an absolute engagement of such party; for if it is not, the contract is lacking in mutuality, notwithstanding the absolute character of the engagement of the other party. . . .

It will be observed that this alleged engagement is not only indefinite as to time, quantity, price and terms, but it is accompanied by no corresponding engagement on the part of the defendant; he binds himself to nothing; he could, under it, order one or a thousand pairs of shoes, or none at all; at a price unknown, not agreed upon, and upon indefinite terms.

Under such circumstances, it cannot be considered as partaking of any of the elements of an absolute, binding, enforceable engagement, such as will constitute the consideration for the defendant's engagement, the essential element of a valid contract. . . .

In Fowler v. Gray, 168 Ind. 1, 79 N.E. 897, 7 L.R.A. (N.S.) 726, 120 Am. St. Rep. 344, it is said:

> "This rule is founded upon a want of mutuality. The term contract implies mutual obligation, and in general contracts, other than options, are not enforceable unless both parties thereto are bound, so that an action could be maintained by each against the other."

In that case a contract with a heating plant to furnish heat at a certain rate per annum was held lacking in mutuality, where the heat from the plant rested in the discretion of the consumer.

. . . We think therefore that the alleged contract, for the breach of which the defendant asks damages, was lacking in consideration and mutuality, and that the plaintiff's demurrer should have been sustained.

The court is not unmindful of the principle that where the contract has been fully executed, the party who has received the benefit of such performance will not be heard to urge the lack of mutuality of obligation on the part of the party performing in the contract as originally appearing . . . But this is not such a case, the defendant is not seeking recovery for any act of performance upon his part; but for profits which he would have made under a contract which must be held to have been lacking in consideration and mutuality.

The judgment of this court is that the order of the circuit court overruling the plaintiff's demurrer to the defendant's counterclaim be reversed, and that the case be remanded to that court, with direction to enter an order sustaining the same, and of judgment in favor of plaintiff upon the amount sued upon admitted by the answer.

CASE NO. 8

Crawford v. Baker. 207 Ga. 56, 60 S.E. (2d) 146 (1950)

Mrs. J. M. Crawford filed her equitable complaint in the Superior Court of Fulton County, against J. E. Baker, H. C. Posey, and Fred J. Baker, doing business as Stratford Coal Company, and American Oil Company, in which she alleged that on June 23, 1945, she and J. E. Baker entered into and signed a written contract as follows:

"Georgia, Fulton County: This contract made and entered into this 23rd day of June, 1945, between Mrs. J. M. Crawford, hereinafter referred to as party of the first part, and Mr. J. E. Baker, hereinafter referred to as party of the second part; witnesseth: That the party of the first part hereby agrees to furnish and install certain equipment for the operation of a gasoline filling station, located at 2879 Gordon Road, and operated by party of the second part, or any dealer to whom he may lease premises during the term of this contract, said equipment being a rotary lift, and furthermore, said station having been paved with concrete at the expense of party of the first part. Other equipment already in use at said location includes one electric computing pump, one 10 gal. visible pump, also two 550, underground tanks, which is owned by party of the first part.

"Title to the above named property is retained by party of the first part, and upon expiration of this contract party of the first part shall have the right to remove said equipment from the premises.

"Party of the second part agrees that for and in consideration of the furnishing of the above-named equipment by the party of the first part that for a period of 7½ years, expiring December 31, 1952, he will sell only and purchase only for resale in the operation of said business, petroleum products handled by the party of the first part.

"That the parties hereto agree that this contract shall be binding and in effect upon the signing hereof, and that any successor or purchaser or assigns of the party of the second part in the operation of said service station shall be bound hereby.

"Signed in duplicate, this day and year first above written."

It was further alleged: that, at the time of the execution of the contract, the plaintiff was and had been, and since said date has continued to be, a tank truck dealer for Texas Company, engaged in the wholesale distribution of Texaco petroleum products . . . that in pursuance of her contract she furnished and continues to furnish to the individual defendants certain of the equipment referred to in the contract . . . for the benefit of the defendants, J. E. Baker and his lessees, in the operation of the gasoline filling station mentioned in the contract; that in pursuance of the contract she spent $350 for concrete paving in and around the gasoline filling station for the purpose of improving the station operated by the defendant J. E. Baker, this paving and furnishing of equipment being done in conformity with provisions of the contract and in consideration of the defendant J. E. Baker's agreement that he would sell and purchase for resale in the operation of the filling station only the products handled by the plaintiff . . . that in the latter part of December, 1949 . . . the defendant, American Oil Company, advised the other defendants that their contract with the plaintiff was void and unenforceable; that this company made such statements for the purpose of maliciously inducing the other defendants to breach their contract with the plaintiff . . .

To this petition the defendants demurred generally upon the ground that the same is insufficient as a matter of law to constitute a cause of action.

To the judgment of the trial court sustaining this demurrer and dismissing the petition, the plaintiff excepts. . . .

HAWKINS, J. It is contended by the defendants in error that the trial court properly sustained the demurrer and dismissed the petition, upon the ground that "the contract was unenforceable because it is unilateral and without mutuality; . . . that it purports to bind the defendant in error, J. E. Baker, and his assigns for a period of seven and one-half years to sell only and purchase only for resale in the operation of said business petroleum products handled by the party of the first part. There is no corresponding obligation on the part of the plaintiff in error to sell petroleum products to the defendant in error, J. E. Baker. There is no mutuality of obligation to sell and purchase. . . ."

While it is true that the contract in this case imposes upon the plaintiff no obligation to sell petroleum products to the defendant, we cannot agree with the contention of the defendants that this renders the contract so wanting in mutuality as to invalidate it. The rule here invoked by the defendants that the obligations of a contract must be mutually binding before they can be enforced applies where mutual promises are relied on as furnishing or constituting the consideration for the contract. . . . It is not true, as insisted by the defendants, that "a contract, to be enforceable, must impose an obligation upon both parties." The rule that agreements which are optional and not binding on one party are also optional and not binding on the other applies only to agreements which are wholly executory and consist of mutual promises, each the consideration for the other. . . .

"Mutuality of obligation is not required where there is other consideration than a promise." 12 Am. Jur. 509, § 114.

In the instant case, the petition alleges that the plaintiff furnished the equipment and made the improvements upon the filling station property, which were accepted by the defendant operators of the filling station. The contract was, therefore, based upon a valid and valuable consideration moving from the plaintiff to and received by the defendants, and was not invalid as being unilateral and without mutuality. In Hendler Creamery Co. v. Lillich, 152 Md. 190, 136 Atl. 631, 60 A.L.R. 207, it is held that a contract by the terms of which a creamery company agrees to install free of cost a mechanical refrigerating plant in a drugstore, to remain for three years, in consideration of which the druggist agrees to buy and use the said company's ice cream and other frozen products during said term, exclusive of any other company's frozen products, and to refrain from and refuse permission for advertising any such commodities other than the said company's, is not void for lack of mutuality, although the creamery company does not agree to sell and furnish such products. . . .

Judgment reversed. . . .

CASE NO. 9

Leggett et al. v. Vinson. 155 Miss. 411, 124 So. 472 (1929)

COOK, J. The appellee testified that he entered into the written contract . . . under the terms of which he agreed to furnish all the labor and material of every kind and character for the construction of such building, . . . that he began work under this written contract and continued for about seven weeks, when he discovered that he could not complete the work at the price fixed in this contract without suffering great loss, and so informed Dr. Leggett; . . . that Dr. Leggett asked appellee to get his bills together so that they could go over them. The appellee did get his bills together and the bills showed that it would cost about $1000 more than the contract price to complete the job. Dr. Leggett said, "Go ahead and complete the job like we started and I will pay you time and pay the bills."

Appellants assign as error the action of the court below . . . in refusing the peremptory instruction which was requested by them at the conclusion of all the evidence; the contention of appellants in this regard being that under the alleged oral contract the appellee assumed no burdens or obligations other than those already imposed by the written contract, and therefore the oral agreement of appellants, if made, was without consideration.

While there is some authority to the contrary, notably from the courts of Massachusetts, Indiana, and Illinois, the great weight of authority seems to establish as the general rule the proposition that a promise to do that which a party is already legally bound to do is not a sufficient consideration to support a promise by the other party to the contract to give the former an additional compensation or benefit, and such a promise cannot be legally enforced although the other party has completed his contract in reliance upon it; and with this general rule, prior decisions of this court are in accord. . . .

In the case of McGovern v. City of New York, 234 N.Y. 377, 138 N.E. 26, 30, 25 A.L.R. 1442, McGovern and others entered into a contract with the city of New York to build a subway, and afterwards, on account of an unforeseen advance in the price of labor and material, a later contract was entered into for increased compensation for the same work, and the court held . . . that:

> "The plaintiffs, therefore, did nothing more than it was their duty to do without additional reward. . . . We hold, then, that the defendant's promise is unenforceable for lack of a consideration to support it." . . .

In the case of Ayres v. Railroad Co., 52 Iowa, 478, 3 N.W. 522, a contractor threatened to stop construction work because it was unprofitable, and the railroad company agreed to pay the debts incurred by the contractor if he would continue, and after the performance of the contract in reliance on this promise, it was sought to enforce the promise, but the court held:

> "An agreement to do what one is already under a legal obligation to do does not constitute a consideration for a contract." . . .

It is undoubtedly true that the parties to a contract may modify it, or waive their right under it, and ingraft new terms upon it, and in such case the promise of one party will be sufficient consideration for the promise of the other. But where the promise of one is merely a repetition of a subsisting legal promise, and the duties, obligations, and burdens imposed upon such party by the contract are in no way varied, altered, or changed, there is no consideration for the promise of the other. Such is the case made by the appellee's proof, and therefore the alleged promise of appellant was without consideration. . . .

CASE NO. 10

Scott v. Duthie & Co. 125 Wash. 470, 216 Pac. 853, 28 A.L.R. 328 (1923)

MACKINTOSH, J. . . . This appeal arises from the sustaining of a demurrer to a complaint which alleges that, on December 23, 1918, the appellant was a department foreman in the shipyard owned and operated by the respondent; that the employment was for an indefinite term; that on that date the respondent made a promise as follows:

> ". . . J. F. Duthie & Co. promises the general department foremen now in its employment that upon the completion of its contract with the shipping board the company will divide as a bonus one-half million dollars among those of its general department foremen who continue in its employment until the completion of that contract. . . ."

As stated by the appellant, the question here is:

> "Where an employer promises a bonus or a share of the profits to an employee employed for an indefinite term, to be paid if he works continuously for a given period, is the employer bound by his promise when the employee accepts the offer by performance?" . . .

The argument that the appellant cannot recover the bonus for the reason that he was paid his regular salary while in the respondent's employ overlooks the very idea conveyed by the word "bonus," which is "an allowance in addition to what is . . . stipulated." Standard Dict. The complaint shows that the appellant was free to quit his work at any time, and therefore was under no obligation to do the thing which the respondent was seeking to accomplish by its offer. The compliance with the terms . . . created a contract supplementary to the contract of employment. By this supplementary contract the respondent agreed to reward the appellant for remaining in its employ and refraining

> "from accepting employment elsewhere until this company shall complete the ships." . . .

See also . . . 212 Fed. 716, where the court said:

> "The objection mainly relied upon at the trial and here was that this promise of a bonus, if made, was nudum pactum because the plaintiff, being bound to do his best for his salary, gave nothing in the way of consideration to support the promise of a bonus. This would be true if the plaintiff were legally bound to con-

tinue in the employment of the defendant to the end of the season. But he was not and could have quit work at any time. . . ."

The distinction between a promise of a gift to one for doing what he is obliged to do and the promise of a bonus to one for doing what he is not obliged to do seems to us real.

The judgment is reversed, with instructions to overrule the demurrer.

CASE NO. 11

King v. Duluth, M. & N. Ry. Co. 61 Minn. 482, 63 N.W. 1105 (1895)

START, C.J. . . . This is an action brought by the plaintiff, as surviving partner of the firm of Wolf & King, to recover a balance claimed to be due for the construction of a portion of the defendant's line of railway . . .

The complaint for a first cause of action alleges, among other things, substantially, that in January, 1893, the firm of Wolf & King entered into three written contracts with the president and representative of the defendant for the grading, clearing, grubbing, and construction of the roadbed of its railway for a certain stipulated price for each of the general items of work and labor to be performed; that the firm entered upon the performance of such contracts, but in the latter part of February, 1893, in the course of such performance, unforeseen difficulties of construction involving unexpected expenses, and such as were not anticipated by the parties to the contracts, were encountered. That the firm of Wolf & King found that by reason of such difficulties it would be impossible to complete the contracts within the time agreed upon without employing an additional and an unusual force of men and means, and at a loss of not less than $40,000 to them, and consequently they notified the representative of the defendant that they would be unable to go forward with the contracts, and unable to complete or prosecute the work. Thereupon such representative entered into an agreement with them modifying the written contracts, whereby he agreed that if they would go forward and prosecute the said work of construction, and complete said contract,

> "he would pay or cause to be paid to them an additional consideration therefor, up to the full extent of the cost of the work, so that they should not be compelled to do the work at a loss to themselves";

that in consideration of such promise they agreed to forward the work rapidly, and force the same to completion, in the manner provided in the specifications for such work and referred to in such contracts. . . .

It is entirely competent for the parties to a contract to modify or to waive their rights under it and ingraft new terms upon it, and in such a case the promise of one party is the consideration for that of the other; but where the promise to the one is simply a repetition of a subsisting legal promise, there can be no consideration for the promise of the other party; . . . But where the party refusing to complete his contract does so by reason of some unforeseen and substantial difficulties in the performance of the contract, which were not known or anticipated by the parties when the contract was entered into, and which place upon him an additional burden not contemplated by the parties, and the opposite party promises him extra pay or benefits if he will complete his contract and he so promises, the promise to pay is supported by a valid consideration. In such a case the natural inference arising from the transaction, if unmodified by any equitable considerations, is rebutted;

and the presumption arises that by the voluntary and mutual promises of the parties their respective rights and obligations under the original contract are waived, and those of the new or modified contract substituted for them. Cases of this character form an exception to the general rule that a promise to do that which a party is already legally bound to do, is not a sufficient consideration to support a promise by the other party to the contract to give the former an additional compensation or benefit. . . .

On the other hand, where no unforeseen additional burdens have been cast upon a party refusing to perform his contract, which make his refusal to perform, unless promised further pay, equitable, and such refusal and promise of extra pay are all one transaction, the promise of further compensation is without consideration; and the case falls within the general rule; and the promise can not be legally enforced, although the other party has completed his contract in reliance upon it. This proposition, in our opinion, is correct on principle and supported by the weight of authority. What unforeseen difficulties and burdens will make a party's refusal to go forward with his contract equitable, so as to take the case out of the general rule and bring it within the exception, must depend upon the facts of each particular case. They must be substantial, unforeseen, and not within the contemplation of the parties, when the contract was made. *They need not be such as would legally justify the party in his refusal to perform his contract,* unless promised extra pay, or *to justify a court of equity in relieving him from the contract;* for they are sufficient if they are of such a character as to render the party's demand for extra pay manifestly fair, so as to rebut all inference that he is seeking to be relieved from an unsatisfactory contract, or to take advantage of the necessities of the opposite party to coerce from him a promise for further compensation. Inadequacy of the contract price which is the result of an error of judgment, and not of some excusable mistake of fact, is not sufficient.

The cases of Meech v. City of Buffalo, 29 N.Y. 198, where the unforeseen difficulty in the execution of the contract was quicksand, in place of expected ordinary earth excavation, and Michaud v. McGregor (decided at the present term), 63 N.W. 479, where the unforeseen obstacles were rocks below the surface of the lots to be excavated, which did not naturally belong there, but were placed there by a third party, and of the existence of which both parties to the contract were ignorant when the contract was made, are illustrations of what unforeseen difficulties will take a case out of the general rule.

Do the allegations of fact contained in plaintiff's first alleged cause of action bring his case within the exception? Clearly not, for eliminating all conclusions and considering only the facts alleged, there is nothing to make the case exceptional, other than the general statement that the season was so extraordinary that in order to do the stipulated work it would require great and unusual expense, involving a large use of powder and extra time and labor for the purpose of blasting out the frozen earth and other material which was encountered. What the character of this material was, we are not told, or what the other extraordinary conditions of the ground were. The court will take judicial knowledge of the fact that frozen ground on the Missabe Range, where the work was to be performed, in the month of February, is not unusual or extraordinary. It was a matter which must have been anticipated by the parties, and taken into consideration by them when this contract was made. The most that can be claimed from the allegations of the complaint is that the contractors had made a losing bargain and refused to complete their contract, and the defendant, by its representative, promised them that if they would go forward and complete their contract, it would pay them an additional compensation; so that the total compensation should be equal to the actual cost of the work.

CASE NO. 12

Schnell v. Perlmon. 238 N.Y. 362, 144 N.E. 641 (1924)

Action by Harry Schnell and others, copartners under the firm name of H. Schnell & Co., against Sol Perlmon, trading under firm name of Detroit Celery & Produce Co. From a judgment of Second Judicial Department of Appellate Division of the Supreme Court, unanimously affirming a judgment in favor of plaintiffs, entered upon a verdict directed by the court, defendant appeals . . .

CRANE, J. . . . The facts, briefly stated, therefore are: The plaintiffs sold to the defendant onions for an agreed price. The shipment in part was rotten and decayed. The defendant notified the plaintiffs of the fact, sending to them the government reports made by the food products inspector. The defendant paid for the goods which were in good condition, deducting $801.29 for those which he claimed to have been decayed. The payment was made by checks and notes and accompanying letters, notifying the plaintiffs that if accepted by them they would be in full payment of the amount due, and the balance, $801.29, the amount of the deduction, would thus be paid by agreement or by accord and satisfaction (to use the legal terms). The claim put forth by the defendant for deduction was apparently made in good faith and in view of the government reports seems to be reasonable and fair. . . .

The general rule is that a liquidated claim—that is, a claim which is not disputed, but admitted to be due—can not be discharged by any payment of a less amount. . . .

In this case before us, the full amount claimed by the plaintiffs was not admittedly due. The fact that the contract called for a stated amount or an amount which could be easily figured according to deliveries did not make the claim liquidated within this meaning of the law as applied to accord and satisfaction. . . . The amount claimed by the plaintiffs and specified in the contract was repudiated by the defendant. He denied that he owed the money. He disputed the plaintiffs' demand. The contract had not been fulfilled and completed. Deliveries had not been made as called for. . . .

. . . It was a disputed claim. The plaintiffs knew it was disputed. They knew also that the checks and notes which they received and cashed were received in full payment of their disputed claim. They could not under these circumstances keep the money and reject the conditions attached to payment. Having accepted payment and the conditions attached, the balance of $801.29 has been satisfied. . . .

Not only do we find in this case before us an honest dispute regarding the amount due, but we also find a consideration for the release of the balance due in the surrender by the defendant of his claim for damages under the breach of warranty and the satisfaction of his debt or claim against the plaintiffs. . . .

Therefore the judgments below must be reversed, and judgment directed for the defendant dismissing the complaint, with costs in all courts.

CASE NO. 13

Eckert-Fair Const. Co. v. Capitol Steel & Iron Co. 178 F. (2d) 338 (1949)

MCCORD, C.J. Capitol Steel & Iron Company, a corporation domiciled at Oklahoma City, Oklahoma, brought this suit against Eckert-Fair Construction Company, a corporation located and doing business at Dallas, Texas, for a balance claimed to be due and owing for work and labor performed and materials furnished defendant during the erection of the Fat Stock Show Buildings at Fort Worth, Texas. The erection of the buildings was completed in January, 1948, and a controversy thereafter arose between the parties hereto as to the amount owing for extra materials furnished and work and labor done under their contract. The dispute continued for about six months, during which time the parties through their representatives met and attempted to reach an agreement as to the balance due. After two or three meetings and conferences they finally failed to agree.

The record reveals that on July 21, 1948, defendant wrote the plaintiff a letter in which it itemized all charges and countercharges claimed between them under their contract up to that date, arriving at a balance of $20,268.71 in favor of plaintiff. A check for that amount was enclosed which recited "Final Payment Stock Show Contract." This letter with check enclosure was received and the check was cashed on July 23, 1948. On August 7, 1948, plaintiff answered defendant's letter of July 21st, and stated that it was not willing to settle the account on the basis of defendant's calculations. . . .

On November 24, 1948, plaintiff brought suit to recover an alleged balance. . . .

The case was tried to the court without a jury, and judgment was rendered for plaintiff in the aggregate sum of $5,728.70. . . .

We are of opinion that decision here must turn upon whether the depositing of the check by the auditing department of the plaintiff was such an acceptance as to constitute an accord and satisfaction binding upon it as a subcontractor. The burden of proof was on the defendant to show (1) that it tendered the amount paid in full satisfaction of the debt; (2) that there was an acceptance of the sum tendered; and (3) that such acceptance was by the plaintiff or one authorized by it to act, or else there was a subsequent ratification by plaintiff of the acts of its agents in the alleged accord and satisfaction, all to the end that it be shown the minds of the parties have met in accordance with recognized contractual principles in effectuating an accord and satisfaction. Thus, the entering into an agreement for an accord and satisfaction is the making of a new and independent contract in which the minds of the parties must meet, the parties who act must be so authorized, or there must be an acceptance by way of ratification. . . .

A careful consideration of the entire record evidence in this case leads us unerringly to the conclusion that defendant has failed to discharge its burden of proving an acceptance or ratification by plaintiff sufficient to constitute the alleged accord and satisfaction. After the check was deposited by the auditing department of the plaintiff it is without dispute that upon the return of Mr. Shubert, plaintiff's representative, a letter was written within a reasonable time rejecting the settlement offer, and advising that the amount paid had been credited to defendant's account. Consequently, there is no sufficient proof that the minds of these parties have ever met in effectuating the alleged accord and satisfaction, or that the check was accepted by an agent having authority to enter into such contract on behalf of plaintiff. . . .

CASE NO. 14

Hogue v. National Automotive Parts Ass'n. 87 F. Supp. 816 (1949)

. . . .

KOSCINSKI, D.J. Plaintiff had verdict for unpaid wages and overtime under the provisions of the Fair Labor Standards Act, 29 U.S.C.A. § 201 et seq.

. . . Plaintiff claimed approximately $3,900.00; the jury awarded her $2,075.00.

. . . The final and most important issue raised by defendant is that of compromise and settlement.

Following separation from her employment with defendant, the Wage and Hour Division was consulted by plaintiff relative to her claim for unpaid and overtime compensation. As a result of an investigation made by the Wage and Hour representatives the defendant on August 1, 1946, in a letter to the plaintiff, enclosed a check for $258.71 payable to her. The letter read as follows:

"Loretta M. Hogue
1320 Philip Avenue
Detroit 15, Michigan

"Dear Miss Hogue,

We are informed by the Wage and Hour Division of the U.S. Department of Labor that it has been determined that $315.49 gross salary is due you. We therefore are enclosing our check for $258.71 which covers this amount after making proper deductions for social security and withholding tax. The attached Payroll Deductions slip and Withholding Statement, Form W-2, give the detailed amounts of these deductions.

"It is understood that the payment of this amount releases us from all claims which you may have against us under the Fair Labor Standards Act or otherwise.

"Please date, sign and return to us both copies of the enclosed receipt for unpaid wages.

"Yours very truly,
National Automotive Parts Assn.
(Signed) Myron L. Buck"

The check was held by plaintiff for about six months before being cashed by her. In the meantime plaintiff again consulted the representatives of the Wage and Hour division who informed her in effect that she could cash the check and retain the proceeds, and that she could then commence suit against defendant for any further sum of money claimed to be due her.

. . . A "dispute" to invoke the doctrine of accord and satisfaction must be an honest, genuine, or bona fide dispute advanced in good faith and resting on a substantial basis, or founded on some reasonably tenable or plausible ground, and need not be in fact established or based upon solid foundation, but there must be some justification therefor and not a mere arbitrary refusal to pay.

The evidence in this case fails to disclose that plaintiff at any time conferred with or discussed the amount of her claim or number of hours for which she claimed regular or overtime compensation; nor is there any evidence that she at any time waived her claim to liquidated damages. The most that can be said here is that she went to the Wage and Hour Division for information concerning collection of the money she claimed was due her from the defendant. The Wage and Hour Division representatives were public officials and not plaintiff's representatives. They were acting in the performance of their duties as public officials and enforcing the provisions of the Fair Labor Standards Act.

The amount represented by the check was paid to plaintiff not on the basis of a "bona fide dispute" between the plaintiff and defendants, but because of enforcement activities of government officials.

There is a total lack of proof of any negotiations between plaintiff and defendant which could remotely be called a "bona fide dispute," in the proper definition and application of that phrase to the evidence in this case. The defendant simply refused to recognize the validity of plaintiff's claim.

A person cannot create a "dispute" sufficient as consideration for compromise by a mere refusal to pay an unliquidated claim. Burns v. Northern Pacific Ry. Co., 8 Cir., 134 F. (2d) 766, 770.

Since the defendant complied with the Wage and Hour Division's finding that plaintiff had an absolute right to the amount represented by the check, there was no valid consideration for the "release" claimed by defendant, as she received only what was due her beyond any doubt, since the defendant did not appeal this determination by the Wage and Hour Division of the Department of Labor.

CASE NO. 15

American L. Ins. Co. v. Williams. 234 Ala. 469, 175 So. 554 (1937)

FOSTER, J. . . . This is a suit on a policy of industrial life insurance issued by appellant on the life of Nathaniel Williams without a physical examination. . . .

The policy was issued August 26, 1935; insured died January 6, 1936. The policy contained a clause that if the death of the insured occurred within nine months from the date of delivery of the policy on account of any of the following diseases, pulmonary disease, chronic bronchitis, cancer, or disease of the heart, liver, or kidneys, liability under it was limited to a return of the premiums paid.

. . . Defendant claimed that insured died of a pulmonary disease, to wit, tuberculosis, and also claimed an accord and satisfaction, in that on January 7, 1936, defendant paid plaintiff, who was the beneficiary, the sum of $1.20, alleged to be the amount of premiums which had been paid in so far as this insured was concerned, when she executed a receipt to defendant for said sum in which the recital is made that it is

> "in full for all claims against said company upon (the) policy issued on the life of Nathaniel Williams." . . .

But regardless of the question of whether there was fraud or its equivalent in procuring the receipt as a contract of accord and satisfaction, another inquiry is, whether an accord and satisfaction under those circumstances was supported by a sufficient consideration. In 1 C.J.S., Accord and Satisfaction, p. 504, it is said,

> ". . . a transaction of this character is clearly distinguishable from one in which the whole of a claim or demand is in dispute and there is paid and received in settlement the amount which the debtor believes or concedes to be due or is willing to pay."

The authorities reason that the payment of an amount admitted to be due in respect to one feature of a transaction cannot be the basis of an agreement to forego another feature of it, though the latter is disputed or unliquidated. . . .

So that plaintiff was not precluded from her claim now made that insured did not die from a pulmonary disease, because of the alleged accord and satisfaction, whether it was procured by fraud or not. It was not based on sufficient consideration . . .

CASE NO. 16

Murphy v. Henry. 311 Ky. 799, 225 S.W. (2d) 662 (1950)

. . . . .

CLAY, C. This is an appeal from a Circuit Court judgment confirming an order of the Morgan County Court probating the will of Thomas Greene Henry. Appellant prayed that the probate be set aside because the will was void. The answer pleaded a compromise agreement between appellant and appellee, and asserted appellant had no interest in the estate involved.

Appellant and appellee are the only heirs at law of the deceased. On October 4, 1945, he executed a will bequeathing $500 to the former, and most of the remaining estate to the latter. He remarried two days after he executed the will; his former wife, mother of the two parties involved, having theretofore departed this world. He died in 1947, leaving an estate with an estimated value of approximately $15,000.

Shortly after her father's death, appellant consulted an attorney regarding the possibility of breaking the will. She was advised that it would be necessary to establish her father was of unsound mind, and she was not inclined to contest the will on this ground. A week or so later, after several conferences regarding the probate of the will between appellant, appellee, and their attorneys, appellant relinquished any claims she might have under the will and any interest she might have in her father's estate under the laws of descent and distribution. In consideration for this compromise, she was paid the sum of $2,500 cash by appellee. Thereafter the will was probated.

Appellant's position is that the compromise agreement is not binding, because appellee furnished no consideration for her agreement to accept less than the amount she would inherit in the event her father died intestate. This contention is based on the argument that the subsequent marriage of her father revoked the will he had executed two days earlier; that this fact or legal result was known to appellee; and in settling with her, he relinquished nothing but a groundless claim.

The parties apparently are not in disagreement concerning the applicable principle of law. It is well settled in this state, as in others, that forbearance to prosecute a doubtful claim asserted in good faith will constitute adequate consideration for a compromise agreement. . . . On the other hand, good faith alone is not sufficient if the claim is utterly groundless. Hardin's Administrators et al. v. Hardin, 201 Ky. 310, 256 S.W. 417, 38 A.L.R. 756. The cases cited by appellant recognize the above principles in holding that forbearance to sue on a groundless claim, *known to be so,* will not constitute consideration for a compromise.

It is well to bear in mind in this type of case that the question does not concern the actual legal validity of the claim, nor is it necessary that the person asserting it would be successful in a subsequent judicial proceeding. The problem is whether or not there was a *bona fide* settlement of *doubtful* rights, which the courts encourage. See 11 Am. Jur., Compromise and Settlement, § 7 . . .

Turning now to the facts shown in this case, we find the following situation. Under the will appellant was bequeathed the sum of $500. If the will was valid and unrevoked, this is all she would have received from her father's estate, and appellee would be entitled to substantially all the rest. Under KRS

394.090 a will is revoked by a subsequent marriage except under certain circumstances. Appellee consulted a reputable attorney about this will. His attorney advised him of the legal effect of the statute, but also expressed his opinion that there had been a prenuptial agreement between the deceased and his present widow, in view of which circumstance the will might be upheld in spite of the statute. This opinion was based upon an examination of legal authorities, one of them being the case of Stewart, etc., v. Mulholland, etc., 88 Ky. 38, 10 S.W. 125, 21 Am. St. Rep. 320.

We thus find that appellee, acting on competent legal advice in good faith, believed that the will might be upheld. Whether this claim could be successfully litigated is not the vital question before us, and we do not pass upon it. However, it was at least a doubtful one, and certainly was not groundless.

The evidence shows, as was pointed out by the Circuit Court in an able opinion, that after the question was raised, negotiations between the parties and their attorneys were conducted in good faith by all parties in an honest effort to settle a family controversy. Appellee was paid a substantial sum, as was likewise the deceased's widow who entered into a settlement at the same time. Since appellee relinquished his full claim under the will, which at least rose to the dignity of a doubtful one asserted in good faith, he furnished appellant adequate consideration for the compromise. . . .

The judgment is affirmed.

CASE NO. 17

Rye v. Phillips. 203 Minn. 567, 282 N.W. 459, 119 A.L.R. 1120 (1938)

STONE, J. . . . Action by indorsee, not a holder in due course, upon a promissory note . . .

The answer sets up a defense in the nature of a release or an accord and satisfaction . . . in the words:

"That in the early part of the year 1930, one Kooima, referred to in the complaint herein, held and owned the note described in the said complaint; at that time the plaintiff was the owner of a Chevrolet car, . . . and the defendant then was hopelessly insolvent and unable to pay his debts or obligations, all of which the plaintiff and Kooima then well knew. The plaintiff at that time approached the defendant and Kooima and offered to purchase said note from Kooima by turning over said car, valued at $250 and no more. As a part of said transaction and as consideration for same defendant agreed to turn over to plaintiff *livestock* or *produce* of the value of $250, or some livestock and the balance in cash, and to pay the car license on said plaintiff's car that he was then and there trading to Kooima. In pursuance of said agreements, carried out, defendant turned over to plaintiff livestock and cash aggregating the amount admitted as paid in the complaint, and additionally paid the said car license fee to the plaintiff; all of which was a compromise and settlement of all liability on the part of the defendant on said note referred to in the complaint herein."

On the ground that the answer failed to plead a defense, plaintiff objected to the introduction of any evidence. The objection was sustained, and plaintiff's motion for directed verdict granted upon the ground that

"a mere promise of a creditor to receive, and of the debtor to pay, a sum less than the debt in full satisfaction of it, is without consideration, and binds neither party." . . .

The doctrine thus invoked is one

of the relics of antique law which should have been discarded long ago. It is evidence of the former capacity of lawyers and judges to make the requirement of consideration an overworked shibboleth rather than a logical and just standard of actionability.

In Oien v. St. Paul City Ry. Co., 198 Minn. 363, 373, 270 N.W. 1, we made such observations concerning it that the bar should have been advised thereby that we were ready to label the proposition as a museum piece of the law and shelve it accordingly. . . .

Its true status is accurately stated in Selected Readings on the Law of Contracts (MacMillan 1931) 325, as follows:

"And the rule is commonly thought to be a corollary of the doctrine of consideration. But this is a total misconception. The rule is older than the doctrine of consideration and is simply the survival of a bit of formal logic of the mediaeval lawyers."

The law has been changed by statute in at least ten of our states. Id. 328. But, being a judge-made rule, no vested rights depending on it, judges are just as competent to get rid of it as the legislature.

There is more than one ground of logic and good law upon which this old and indefensible rule may be discarded. There is no reason why a person should be prevented from making an executed gift of incorporeal as well as corporeal property. Why should a receipt in full for the entire debt not be taken in a proper case as sufficient evidence of an *executed gift* of the unpaid portion of the debt? Again, where there is proof, or on adequate evidence a finding, that a completed legal act such as a waiver has set a matter at rest, why is it necessary to search for any consideration?

The modern view is that a new promise to pay a debt barred by the statute of limitations or discharged in bankruptcy is binding without consideration. I Restatement, Contracts, §§ 86, 87. In that field at least, judges have recognized the futility of their former efforts to create a synthetic consideration where there was no actual consideration.

What has just been said may appear mere dictum, but judicial frankness justifies it to the end that both bar and public may be advised of our attitude.

. . . the paragraph of the answer above quoted pleads a defense. It avers a new contract, not alone between plaintiff and defendant, but between both of them and Kooima, the payee of the note. Furthermore, it shows that the agreement was executed. The new tripartite contract pleaded had *plenty of consideration.* Kooima got an automobile instead of cash for his note. Plaintiff got the note. Insofar as defendant agreed to turn over livestock and pay the license tax he assumed new obligations which were not his as maker of the note. Hence, it is immaterial whether the obligation substituted by the new contract for the old one under the note would or would not be the latter's equivalent in money value.

For these reasons it was reversible error to exclude defendant's offered evidence in support of his defense and to direct a verdict for plaintiff.

CASE NO. 18

Engbretson v. Seiberling et al. 122 Iowa 522, 98 N.W. 319 (1904)

Action to enjoin the enforcement of an execution held by W. H. Carter, assignee of J. F. Seiberling & Co., on the ground that the judgment on which the execution issued had been fully satisfied. . . .

MCCLAIN, J. . . . It appears from the allegations of plaintiff's petition, which are in accordance with the evidence introduced on the trial, that J. F. Seiberling & Co., being the owners of a judgment recovered by them against this plaintiff for $256, accepted from such judgment debtor the sum of $65 in cash and his promissory note for $25 in full satisfaction of said judgment. J. F. Seiberling & Co. subsequently assigned the judgment to W. H. Carter, who caused execution to issue thereon. It is further averred and proved that at the time the agreement was made to accept the partial payment in full satisfaction Engbretson was insolvent. The sole question for our consideration is whether the acceptance from an insolvent debtor of part payment in full satisfaction of a claim is founded upon such consideration that the entire debt is thereby discharged. The general rule that an agreement to accept part payment in full satisfaction is invalid for want of consideration, and the usual exceptions to that rule, have been often considered by this court, and a general citation of authorities on the subject is unnecessary. . . . But in none of these cases, nor in any others decided in this state, do we find an express exception, such as that insisted upon by the plaintiff in this case. We do, however, find suggestions in each of those cases indicating the existence of the thought that perhaps such an exception should be made in a proper case. In Marshall v. Bullard, 114 Iowa 462, it is said:

> "If, however, such an agreement is supported by any new consideration, though insignificant or technical merely, if valuable, it will be upheld. Thus, if a part is to be and is paid before due, or at a place other than that at which the obligor was legally required to pay, or a payment is made in property, no matter what its value, or by the debtor in composition with his creditors generally, in which they agree to accept less than their demands, the consideration is held to be sufficient."

And it was decided in that case that if the debtor, having no other way of obtaining the money which he was to pay in satisfaction of the debt, induced another to pay it for him, the acceptance of a less sum than the full amount of the debt thus procured to be paid by another would support an agreement to discharge the entire debt. . . . And in Stroutenberg v. Huisman it is said, as a reason for sustaining the full release of a judgment on part payment, that

> "the settlement avoided litigation, settled the dispute, canceled the judgment, and secured the payment of $75 from the insolvent debtor . . ."

In Curtiss v. Martin, 20 Ill. 557, the court, after stating the general rule, says (at p. 577):

> "But if a smaller sum be taken by way of compromise of a controverted claim, or from a debtor in failing circumstances, in full discharge of the debt, no reason is perceived why it should not be binding on the parties."

In Dawson v. Beall, 68 Ga. 328, it is held that an agreement by a debtor not to go into bankruptcy, and thereby be discharged from the payment of the debt, furnishes a sufficient consideration to support a contract by the debtor to take less than the full amount thereof, . . . In view of the fact that, as indicated by the prior decision on the question in this state, the rule that an agreement to accept part payment in full satisfaction is without consideration is purely technical, and subject to many exceptions which the courts have ingrafted upon it from time to time in order to avoid to some extent the injustice which is recognized as frequently resulting from its strict application, we are led to adopt as valid and reasonable the exception which has been hinted at or suggested, rather than authoritatively announced, in the cases already cited. Our conclusion is therefore that plaintiff in this case had a good defense to the enforcement of the judgment against him, and that his action to enjoin the further enforcement of the judgment should not have been dismissed as being without equity.

Reversed.

CASE NO. 19

Hunt v. Lyndonville Sav. Bank & Trust Co. 103 F. (2d) 852 (1939)

GARDNER, C.J. . . . It appears from the evidence and was found by the court that on the 14th of May, 1924, defendant Harry Hunt procured a loan of $10,000 from the New England Securities Company and executed a deed of trust as security conveying 320 acres of land, and on the 9th of December, 1924, he secured another loan from the same company in the sum of $20,000 and executed a deed of trust conveying 640 acres of land as security. Both of these loans prior to their maturity were assigned and transferred to the plaintiff Lyndonville Savings Bank and Trust Company. The $10,000 loan by its terms became due December 1, 1929, and the $20,000 loan became due April 1, 1930. . . . No payments were made on the principal of either loan. Suits for foreclosure were filed January 7, 1937.

On the 10th of July, 1933, Hunt conveyed all of the land covered by both mortgages to his daughter, Genevieve Hunt, also named as defendant, and on the same date his daughter reconveyed the property to him. Each of these deeds described the indebtedness involved in the foreclosures and the land was conveyed expressly subject to the deeds of trust. The conveyance from Hunt to his daughter was recorded February 7, 1935, and plaintiffs' representative learned of its provisions shortly thereafter. The deed from Genevieve Hunt to her father, Harry Hunt, although actually delivered, was never recorded. . . .

The lower court found that there had been a written acknowledgment of the debts within five years before the institution of the suits, and that defendants were estopped to plead the statute of limitations. . . .

In considering whether there has been a sufficient acknowledgment in writing to toll the statute of limitations, the question to be determined is the intention of the debtor. It is generally held to be sufficient if, by fair construction, the writing constitutes an admission that the claim is a subsisting debt unaccompanied by any circumstances repelling the presumption of the party's willingness or intention to pay. . . .

. . . When Hunt accepted from his daughter the conveyance with its recital of the existing mortgages and that the conveyance was subject to the obligations secured thereby, he adopted that instrument and its recitals as his own, and he thereby acknowledged that he owed these obligations to plaintiff. Even if he had been a stranger to plaintiff's mortgages, he was by this transaction brought into contractual relations with the plaintiffs by which he in effect agreed with plaintiffs to accept the property subject to plaintiffs' mortgages. . . . This estopped Hunt from denying the validity of the mortgages and arrested the running of the statute of limitations, and the suits to foreclose were instituted within five years from that date. . . .

CASE NO. 20

Garrison v. Marshall. 117 Kan. 722, 233 Pac. 119 (1925)

Defendant being hopelessly involved in debt entered into a composition agreement with his creditors. The property was sold and the proceeds were distributed pro rata among the creditors by the trustee. Sometime later the defendant gave the trustee his promissory note for the amount of the unpaid balance due his creditors. This is an action on said note. The debtor claims a discharge of liability to his creditors by virtue of the composition and that there was no consideration given for the note. The trustee alleges that the note since given in payment of an obligation which had been discharged by operation of law needs no consideration to support it.

MARSHALL, J. . . . The plaintiff contends that the moral obligation of the defendant to pay his creditors in full was a sufficient consideration for the note and cites Brown v. Akeson, 74 Kan. 301, 86 Pac. 299, and Robinson v. Jacobia, 115 Kan. 36, 221 Pac. 1113. In Brown v. Akeson, a judgment had become barred by the statute of limitations, and was therefore dormant. The judgment debtor made a new promise to pay the judgment, and executed a chattel mortgage to secure its payment. The court held that there was sufficient consideration for the new promise. In Robinson v. Jacobia, the debtor had been discharged by proceedings in bankruptcy. Afterward, a new promise was made. There the court said:

> "The extinguishment of a debt by an order of discharge made in a bankruptcy proceeding does not extinguish the moral obligation of the debtor to pay it, and such moral obligation constitutes a sufficient consideration for a new promise by the debtor to pay the debt."

Other authorities are cited to the same effect. Those promises were made where the obligation to pay the debt had become unenforceable by operation of law. In the present case the obligation to pay the creditors had become unenforceable by agreement of the parties. The authorities make a distinction between the two classes of obligations.

In 17 A.L.R. 1335, is found a note which reads:

> "While, as has been seen, the cases are nearly unanimous in upholding the validity of a new promise without a new consideration, after a discharge by operation of law in bankruptcy or insolvency proceedings, they, with a few exceptions unite in holding that a new promise, after a voluntary discharge by act of the parties, is invalid without a new consideration, even when the debt, or a portion of it, is unpaid."

Judgment for defendant affirmed.

CASE NO. 21

Allegheny College v. National Chautauqua County Bank of Jamestown. 246 N.Y. 369, 159 N.E. 173, 57 A.L.R. 980 (1927)

CARDOZO, CH.J. . . . The plaintiff, Allegheny College, is an institution of liberal learning at Meadville, Pennsylvania. In June, 1921, a "drive" was in progress to secure for it an additional endowment of $1,250,000. An appeal to contribute to this fund was made to Mary Yates Johnston, of Jamestown, New York. In response thereto, she signed and delivered on June 15, 1921, the following writing:

"Estate Pledge, Allegheny College
Second Century Endowment
Jamestown, N.Y., June 15, 1921

"In consideration of my interest in

Christian education, and in consideration of others subscribing, I hereby subscribe and will pay to the order of the treasurer of Allegheny College, Meadville, Pennsylvania, the sum of five thousand dollars; $5,000.

"This obligation shall become due thirty days after my death, and I hereby instruct my executor, or administrator, to pay the same out of my estate. This pledge shall bear interest at the rate of — per cent per annum, payable annually, from —— till paid. The proceeds of this obligation shall be added to the endowment of said institution, or expended in accordance with instructions on reverse side of this pledge.

Mary Yates Johnston."

On the reverse side of the writing is the following indorsement:

"In loving memory this gift shall be known as the Mary Yates Johnston Memorial Fund, the proceeds from which shall be used to educate students preparing for the ministry, either in the United States or in the Foreign Field.

"This pledge shall be valid only on the condition that the provisions of my will, now extant, shall be first met.

Mary Yates Johnston."

The subscription was not payable by its terms until thirty days after the death of the promisor. The sum of $1,000 was paid, however, upon account in December, 1923, while the promisor was alive. The college set the money aside to be held as a scholarship fund for the benefit of students preparing for the ministry. Later, in July, 1924, the promisor gave notice to the college that she repudiated the promise. Upon the expiration of thirty days following her death, this action was brought against the executor of her will to recover the unpaid balance.

The law of charitable subscriptions has been a prolific source of controversy in this state and elsewhere. We have held that a promise of that order is unenforceable, like any other, if made without consideration. . . . On the other hand, though professing to apply to such subscriptions the general law of contract, we have found consideration present where the general law of contract, at least as then declared, would have said that it was absent. . . .

A classic form of statement identifies consideration with detriment to the promisee sustained by virtue of the promise. . . . So compendious a formula is little more than a half truth. There is need of many a supplementary gloss before the outline can be so filled in as to depict the classic doctrine.

"The promise and the consideration must purport to be the motive each for the other, in whole or at least in part. It is not enough that the promise induces the detriment or that the detriment induces the promise if the other half is wanting." Wisconsin & M. R. Co. v. Powers, 191 U.S. 379, . . .

If A promises B to make him a gift, consideration may be lacking, though B has renounced other opportunities for betterment in the faith that the promise will be kept.

The half truths of one generation tend at times to perpetuate themselves in the law as the whole truths of another, when constant repetition brings it about that qualifications, taken once for granted, are disregarded or forgotten. The doctrine of consideration has not escaped the common lot. As far back as 1881, Judge Holmes, in his lectures on the Common Law (p. 292), separated the detriment which is merely a consequence of the promise from the detriment, which is in truth the motive or inducement, and yet added that the courts "have gone far in obliterating this distinction." The tendency toward effacement has not lessened with the years. On the contrary, there has grown up of recent days a doctrine that a substitute for consideration or an exception to its ordinary requirements can be found in what is styled "a promissory estoppel." . . . Certain at least it is that we have adopted the doctrine of promissory estoppel as the equivalent of consideration in connection with our law of charitable subscriptions. So long as those decisions stand, the question is not merely whether the enforcement of a charitable subscription can be squared with the doctrine of consideration in all its ancient rigor. . . .

We have said that the cases in this state have recognized this exception, if exception it is thought to be. Thus, in Barnes v. Perine, 12 N.Y. 18, the subscription was made without request, express or implied, that the church do anything on the faith of it. Later, the church did incur expense to the knowledge of the promisor, and in the reasonable belief that the promise would be kept. We held the promise binding, though consideration there was none except upon the theory of a promissory estoppel. . . . Very likely, conceptions of public policy have shaped, more or less subconsciously, the rulings thus made. Judges have been affected by the thought that "defenses of that character" are

> "breaches of faith towards the public, and especially towards those engaged in the same enterprise, and an unwarrantable disappointment of the reasonable expectations of those interested." W. F. Allen, J., in Barnes v. Perine, supra, p. 24, . . .

It is in this background of precedent that we are to view the problem now before us. The background helps to an understanding of the implications inherent in subscription and acceptance. This is so though we may find in the end that without recourse to the innovation of promissory estoppel the transaction can be fitted within the mould of consideration as established by tradition.

The promisor wished to have a memorial to perpetuate her name. She imposed a condition that the "gift" should be known as the "Mary Yates Johnston Memorial Fund." The moment that the college accepted $1,000 as a payment on account, there was an assumption of a duty to do whatever acts were customary, or reasonably necessary, to maintain the memorial fairly and justly in the spirit of its creation. The college could not accept the money and hold itself free thereafter from personal responsibility to give effect to the condition. . . . More is involved in the receipt of such a fund than a mere acceptance of money to be held to a corporate use. . . .

We think the duty assumed by the plaintiff to perpetuate the name of the founder of the memorial is sufficient in itself to give validity to the subscription within the rules that define consideration for a promise of that order. When the promisee subjected itself to such a duty at the implied request of the promisor, the result was the creation of a bilateral agreement. . . .

The subscriber does not say: I hand you $1,000, and you may make up your mind later, after my death, whether you will undertake to commemorate my name. What she says in effect is this: I hand you $1,000, and if you are unwilling to commemorate me, the time to speak is now.

CASE NO. 22

Thomason v. Bescher. 176 N.C. 622, 97 S.E. 654, 2 A.L.R. 626 (1918)

There were facts in evidence tending to show that on June 18, 1918, J. C. and

W. M. Bescher, two tenants in common in a tract of land, entered into a written contract under seal, giving plaintiff Thomason the option to purchase the timber thereon, . . .

HOKE, J., delivered the opinion of the court:

It is the accepted principle of the common law that instruments under seal require no consideration to support them. Whether this should rest on the position that a seal conclusively imports a consideration, or that the solemnity of the act imports such reflection and care that a consideration is regarded as unnecessary, such instruments are held to be binding agreements, enforceable in all actions before the common-law courts. Speaking to the question in Harrell v. Watson, 63 N.C. 454, Pearson, Ch.J., said:

> "A bond needs no consideration. The solemn act of sealing and delivering is a deed; a thing done, which, by the rule of the common law, has full force and effect, without any consideration. Nudum pactum applies only to simple contracts."

A similar position is stated with approval in Professor Mordecai's Lectures, at page 931, and Dr. Minor, in his Institutes (pt. 1, vol. 3, p. 139), says:

> "In all contracts under seal a valuable consideration is always presumed, from the solemnity of the instrument, as a matter of public policy and for the sake of peace, and presumed conclusively; no proof to the contrary being admitted, either in law or equity, so far as the parties themselves are concerned."

While there is much diversity of opinion on the subject, we think it the better position, and sustained by the weight of authority, that the principle should prevail in reference to these unilateral contracts or options when, as in this case, they take the form of solemn written covenants under seal; and its proper application is to render them binding agreements, irrevocable within the time designated, and that the stipulations may be enforced and made effective by appropriate remedies, when such time is reasonable, and there is nothing offensive and unconscionable in the terms of the principal contract.

As heretofore stated, there are opposing decisions on the question, holding that a written option without valuable consideration, though under seal, may be recalled at any time before notice of acceptance given. Some of these . . . are dependent on statutes which change or modify the effect given to seals under the principles of the common law. In others, there being nothing in the record to present it, the mind of the judges was not specially called to the distinctions existent, and usually observable, between a mere offer to sell without consideration and without seal, and one that is effective as a binding agreement by reason of the seal. . . .

Review Questions

1. What distinguishes a gratuitous promise from a contractual promise?
2. What is the bargain theory of consideration?
3. Every price that a promisor requests for his promise is not a legal consideration. Explain.
4. What is the detriment theory of consideration?
5. What serves as the consideration in a unilateral contract? What is the consideration in an executory bilateral contract?

6. Will a past consideration support a present promise? Illustrate past consideration.
7. What constitutes adequacy of consideration?
8. Why is it that an existing legal obligation cannot serve as consideration to support a promise?
9. Can a peace officer recover an offer of reward for performing his official duties?
10. Why would it be unwise as a matter of public policy to allow peace officers to share in rewards for accomplishing things in the line of their duties?
11. A and B have contracted for the sale and purchase of a house. Subsequently they mutually agree to call the transaction off. What is the consideration that makes this new agreement binding?
12. What is a compromise agreement? What is an agreement of release? What is a composition agreement with creditors?
13. What is the effect of accepting a check upon which the statement appears, "Payment in full of all obligations to date," which check is for less than the amount that is admittedly due and owing?
14. What is the significance of the Uniform Written Obligations Act?
15. Would a check, like the one in Question 13, after it gets back to the drawer, properly indorsed by the creditor, satisfy the requirements of the Uniform Written Obligations act?
16. An insolvent debtor agrees to give his creditors 50 cents on the dollar. This proposal is accepted by the creditors. What is the consideration to support the promise of the creditors to be satisfied with the amount agreed upon?
17. What is the consideration to support a promise to pay an obligation that has been outlawed by the statute of limitations or by discharge in bankruptcy?
18. What is a contract under seal? Does your state recognize the common law seal?

Problems for Discussion

1. X and Y exchange promises of marriage. What is the consideration?
2. The entire agreement is expressed in the following writing: "I agree to transfer unto X all my right, title, and interest in and to my share of the A, B Partnership. Signed A." Can X hold A to this agreement?
3. The trial court found that defendant promised plaintiff the sum of $5,000 "if he would refrain from drinking liquor, using tobacco, swearing, and playing cards or billiards for money until he should become twenty-one," and that he "in all things fully performed his part of said agreement." Defendant contends that the agreement was without consideration. What is your reaction? (*Hamer v. Sidway*, 124 N.Y. 538)
4. X gave Y his promissory note for $10,000, which was payable sixty days after X's death. The note contained a statement that X was motivated by his affection for Y and his desire that Y should be assured of economic security. Can Y be assured that he can recover on the note?
5. Joe and John were both negotiating for the position of manager of the X hotel. Joe offered John $100 if he would withdraw his application. John complied with this request, but since a third party was the successful candidate for

the position, Joe refuses to pay. He contends that, since he received nothing of value for his promise to pay the $100, he is not obligated. What do you think?

6. A widow promised to pay her deceased husband's note upon realizing the income from certain lands. Is her promise enforceable after her income is realized?
7. Motivated by fear that B would divulge A's past history, A promised (by promissory note) to pay B $1,000. B in no way induced or influenced A to make the promise. Can B enforce the promise?
8. Plaintiff contracted for the purchase of defendant's business. Some time after this agreement, plaintiff and defendant entered into another agreement, whereby defendant, in consideration of the sale of the business, promised not to engage in the same business in that locality. Is this agreement binding?
9. Plaintiff contracted to do certain construction work for defendant. Before the work was completed, plaintiff told defendant that he was losing money on the job and that he didn't have enough money to carry the contract to its conclusion. Defendant asked, "How much more will it take?" To which plaintiff answered, "$1,000." Defendant then said, "Go ahead and complete the job and I will pay you up to $1,000." Plaintiff completed the contract. Can he recover the $1,000?
10. X accepted $150 from Y in discharge of the latter's $200 promissory note, of which X was the holder. What would be the effect of this transaction under the following circumstances?
    (1) The note was at the time past due and was retained by X after payment.
    (2) The note was at the time not yet due and payable.
    (3) The note was at the time of payment surrendered to Y.
11. A purchased an automobile from B, and being dissatisfied he refused to pay the balance of $200 on the purchase price. Subsequently he tendered B $100 in discharge of the obligation in full, which B accepted. Is B prevented from recovering the $100 balance?
12. Plaintiff alleges and the proof shows that in March, 1946, he and the defendant entered into a verbal agreement whereby plaintiff was employed to sell defendant's home for a sum which was to net the defendant $6,200, plaintiff to have any sum over and above this price in payment of his services. Plaintiff advertised the property in a local paper for sale at the price of $6,500, and secured a purchaser for that price who was ready and willing to make the purchase. The defendant was notified, but refused to go through with the sale, stating that he had changed his mind and had sold the property to someone else. On the appeal, the defendant urged that there was no consideration for the alleged contract. (*Isaac* v. *Dronet,* 31 So. (2d) 299)
13. Having become insolvent, A made an assignment for the benefit of his creditors. His creditors agreed to release him from all liability in consideration of payment of 25 per cent of their claims. B, a creditor who signed the agreement, now brings an action to recover the balance of his claim, contending that A gave no consideration to support B's promise to be satisfied with 25 per cent. Will he succeed?
14. X was in B's employ as a bookkeeper. X, being dismayed by the dirty windows in his employer's establishment, took it upon himself to wash them after office hours. B was pleased by X's enterprise and initiative and to reward him prom-

ised that there would be a $25 bonus in his next pay check. Not finding the expected fruits of his labor in his next check, X comes to you for advice.

15. Plaintiff being unable to procure the type of tile specified in his contract with defendant, it was agreed that plaintiff could use a different type of tile and that defendant would pay the extra cost. (*Sasso* v. *K.G. & G. Realty Const. Co.,* 98 Conn. 571, 120 Atl. 158) Did plaintiff recover on defendant's promise?
16. Plaintiff Connell had received two monthly payments for disability under an accident policy with the defendant. After examination of plaintiff by defendant's doctor who reported no disability at the time of examination, defendant sent plaintiff the following communication: "In view of this, the only thing that we can do is make payment up to and including June 9, the date that the examination was completed. This involves benefits for 22 additional days for which we are glad to enclose draft for $73.33." On the face of the draft was a recital that it was "in full settlement of any and all claims." Also on the draft was the following: "For and in consideration of the amount shown, I hereby release . . . Provident Life from any and all liability arising from the claim thereon referred to." Plaintiff in taking action for additional benefits contends the release is not binding. (*Connell* v. *Provident Life and Accident Ins. Co.,* 224 S.W. (2d) 194)
17. The defendant set up a counterclaim for damages on account of the breach of a contract whereby the plaintiff, a manufacturer of cigars, agreed to sell in the future to the defendant, a dealer, as many of a certain brand as the defendant might desire, and to continue to do so during the life of the brand as long as the defendant desired to sell them. Decide. (*Santaella* v. *Lange,* 155 Fed. 719)
18. The plaintiff contracted to build a basement under the defendant's house. He encountered conditions which were described as follows: "The house stood on a hard crust about three feet thick, and the foundation of that house didn't extend through that hard crust. It was built on that crust and the more we got through that the more we got into a swamp like the bottom of an old creek, black muddy stuff and soft."

    The plaintiff upon refusing to continue with the project was induced to carry it to its completion upon the defendant's promise to stand the extra costs involved. After completion the defendant refused to pay more than the original contract price and plaintiff took action to recover the additional expenses caused by the unusual conditions he had encountered. Decide. (*Linz* v. *Schuck,* 106 Md. 220, 67 Atl. 286)

6 CONTRACTS:

VOIDANCE OF CONTRACTS

The circumstances under which a contract is entered into may be such as to make it legally possible for one or both of the parties to be relieved of their contractual commitments. If present at the time of the making of the contract, those facts that form the basis upon which the courts may grant such relief can be classified as follows: (1) incompetent parties; (2) fraud—intentional misrepresentation; (3) innocent misrepresentation; (4) mistake; (5) duress; (6) undue influence.

► I. INCOMPETENT PARTIES

Recall that one of the essential requisites to a binding contractual relationship is *competent parties.* The term *competent parties* refers to persons who, upon giving assent to a contract, will be held responsible for their commitments. The term *incompetent parties* denotes persons who are, as a matter of law, deemed incapable of giving binding assent to a contract. Consequently, incompetent parties are allowed to avoid their contracts at their discretion. Incompetent parties are· (1) infants—minors; (2) insane persons; (3) intoxicated persons; (4) corporations; (5) married women.

A. INFANTS

1. *Contractual Liability of Infants*

Infants are ordinarily persons below the age of twenty-one years,* but local statutes should be consulted. Iowa, for example, makes two exceptions:

(1) Minors attain their majority upon marriage.

(2) Females may enter into binding contracts for marriage at the age of eighteen years.

Infants, like adults, have the privilege of entering into contracts. Infancy is not a prohibition to contracting. However, to protect those of tender years against their youthful indiscretions, the law gives infants the right to avoid their contracts and get a return of any consideration they have given. Unless an infant chooses to avoid a contract, there is, as far as he is concerned, a valid contract upon which he can demand performance by the other party. The moral is that one dealing with a minor does so at his own peril.

---

* An infant reaches his majority on the first moment of the day preceding his twenty-first birthday.

2. *Disaffirmance*

No particular mode of disaffirmance is required. Any indication of intention by word or by act not to be bound by the contract is sufficient.[1] A positive declaration of such intention to the other contracting party is, of course, most certain. The right to avoid may usually be exercised during the period of minority and always within a reasonable time after majority is attained. Some states adhere to the view that an infant may not disaffirm during his minority. A rule such as this, forcing the infant to look to the uncertain future for redress, may work to his serious disadvantage. Such future redress will avail him little if for practical reasons recourse against the other party would be futile at the time of his majority. If the objective of the law is to be accomplished, infants must, of necessity, be given the right to avoid their contractual obligations during minority.

a. Disaffirmance under Executory Contract. Disaffirmance presents no serious problems if the contract remains wholly unperformed. In such an event the infant has no liability unless, upon attaining majority, he ratifies the agreement by indicating his intent to be bound. Accepting performance would be a ratification. Unless ratification takes place, remaining passive constitutes an effective disaffirmance.[2]

b. Disaffirmance When Infant Alone Has Performed. If the infant alone has given his consideration, he may refuse to accept performance from the other contracting party and take action to recover that which he has given under the contract.

c. Disaffirmance under Executed Contract. The fact that the infant has received performance under the contract in no way affects his right to disaffirmance. The disaffirming infant is, however, required to return that which he has received by virtue of the contract and which is remaining within his control. The right of disaffirmance is subject to the infant's duty to restore the other contracting party to his former position to the fullest extent possible. Consequently, as a general rule an infant may recover his consideration even though he has dissipated or disposed of the consideration he has received under the contract.[3] Where it affirmatively appears that the minor during his minority has squandered or lost the property, he will not be required to give anything in return for his consideration. The courts hold minors to varying degrees of accountability as a condition to exercising the right of disaffirmance. Regardless of such, the fact is that one dealing with a minor is courting the possibility of litigation.

In giving protection to those of immature judgment, the law should not, however, lend itself as an instrument whereby infants can take advantage of others to their own profit. As stated in Kent's *Commentaries,* "The privilege of infancy is to be used as a shield and not as a sword." Although the right of an infant to

---

[1] Tatum v. Montgomery Banking Co., p. 145.
[2] Cassella v. Tiberio, p. 146.
[3] Block v. Means, p. 148.

avoid his contractual obligations is paramount to the interests of the other contracting party, there is an increasing disposition on the part of the courts not to disregard the latter.[4]

There is no harmony of opinion among the courts as to whether an infant upon changing the form of the consideration he received can elect to disaffirm the contract without making restitution to the other contracting party. An infant buys a horse and then trades it for a cow; can it be said that the cow is what he received by virtue of the original contract? *The general rule is that the infant must return only the consideration remaining in his hands in specie.* When the consideration received by the infant has been translated into a different form, he is no longer under obligation to make restoration. Such a rule certainly suggests the possibility of an infant's using the protection afforded him by law "as a sword" rather than "as a shield." In a few jurisdictions the consideration may be traced from one form to another.

d. Disaffirmance When Other Party Alone Has Performed. An infant who has received performance must comply with the rules of restoration as established above in order to avoid his executory promise. Retention, use, or disposition of the property after the effective period of infancy has terminated will be interpreted as a ratification of the agreement.

e. Recovery of Property Transferred to Third Person. The general common law rule is that an infant who has transferred property to another may recover it, although it has subsequently been transferred to another. Thus if M, a minor, sells and transfers a car to A, who in turn transfers it to B, the minor M can recover the car from B.

In those states that have adopted the Uniform Sales Act this rule, as it applies to personal property, has been changed. Section 24 reads, "Where the seller of goods has voidable title thereto, but his title has not been avoided at the time of the sale, the buyer acquires a good title to the goods, provided he buys them in good faith, for value and without notice of the seller's defect of title."

3. *Infants in Business*

It seems to the writer that the privilege of infancy is needlessly arbitrary. With present-day facilities for training and learning, many minors are possessed of an intellect and business sagacity far in advance of that of the average adult. There seems little reason why an infant should be possessed of such complete immunity where he engages in business ventures the same as an adult. In granting relief, the common law, however, makes no distinction as to the nature or purpose of an infant's contract. Some states have, by statute, shown a disposition to place a greater responsibility upon infants if they engage in business the same as adults and the other contracting party has no notice of the infancy.

There is no limitation on infants' becoming business partners. Infants may and do enter into partnership agreements. A partnership agreement is no more

[4] Goerke v. Nicholson, p. 149.

binding upon an infant than are his other contracts and is voidable at the infant's election.

An infant may also avoid personal liability for any partnership obligations. It has been held that an infant may disaffirm the contracts of the partnership without disaffirming the partnership agreement. Note that the right of an infant partner to avoid partnership obligations relates only to his personal unlimited liability which the law imposes upon a partner. An infant's share of the partnership assets is subject to liabilities incurred by the partnership to the same extent as the interest of an adult partner.

4. *Infants' Liability for Necessities*

Infants may avoid their contracts for necessities as well as their other contracts. The courts have, however, seen fit to impose liability upon them for the *reasonable value* of any necessities obtained. This liability is not dependent upon a promissory expression but is based rather upon the theory of quasi contract.[5] Where the contract price for necessities furnished is reasonable, the contract is in effect being enforced.

No hard and fast rule can be established for determining what things are necessities to infants. In general it can be said that necessities are those things that are necessary to supply the personal needs and requirements of the individual as those needs and requirements are determined by his station and circumstances in life. Things which may constitute necessities to one may not be necessities to another. As stated in *Davis* v. *Caldwell,* 12 Cush. (Mass.) 512:

> "The term 'necessaries,' in this rule of law, is not used in its strictest sense, nor limited to that which is required to sustain life. That which is proper and suitable to each individual, according to his circumstances and condition in life, are necessaries."

The services of a private tutor, for example, may constitute a necessity to a minor who has an estate sufficient to meet his every need and want, but it could hardly be regarded as such in the case of a minor who has no means of support. If a parent or guardian takes care of an infant's personal needs, things furnished the child by others can obviously not be claimed to constitute necessities.

The broad limits of necessities which are generally observed by the courts were established by Lord Coke when he wrote:

> "An infant may bind himself to pay for his necessary meat, drink, apparel, necessary physic, and such other necessaries, and likewise for his good teaching or instruction whereby he may profit himself afterward." Coke, Litt., 172a.

It is generally held that things which do not relate to the personal requirements of the infant cannot qualify as necessities. Consequently, contracts pertaining to an infant's property or to his business pursuits cannot be contracts for necessities.

An infant's liability for the reasonable value of necessities extends also to necessities for those who are dependent upon him. An infant could thus be held

[5] Gregory v. Lee, p. 150.

responsible for necessities furnished to his wife and child under a contractual commitment.

B. INSANE PERSONS

Mental incompetents cannot be held to their contractual undertakings. Mental incompetency is not easy to define, since no precise formula can be applied in determining whether an individual is endowed with a mental capacity sufficient to bind him to his contractual commitments. The general test of mental incompetency is whether the individual's mental faculties are so impaired as to render him incapable of understanding the nature and the consequences of his acts in the transaction in question. The court in *Sprinkle* v. *Wellborn,* 140 N.C. 163, said:

> ". . . the measure of capacity is the ability to understand the nature of the act in which he is engaged and its scope and effect, or its nature and consequences; not that he should be able to act wisely or discreetly, nor to drive a good bargain, but that he should be in such possession of his faculties as to enable him to know at least what he is doing and to contract understandingly."

It is quite generally held that contracts of insane persons, prior to an adjudication of insanity, are voidable. Like infants, they are generally required to return the consideration that they have received by virtue of the contract as a condition to avoiding the contract.[6]

Contracts entered into by an individual after he has been adjudged insane and a conservator appointed to take charge of his affairs are regarded as being void. Third persons are charged with notice of the incompetent's status and are required to deal with his appointed representative.

C. INTOXICATED PERSONS

Intoxication to a degree "so as to suspend the reason and create impotence of mind at the time of entering into the contract" constitutes contractual incompetency. Consequently, one who has contracted while in such a condition may within a reasonable time after his return to sobriety avoid his contractual undertaking. A failure to disaffirm within a reasonable time will be interpreted as an affirmance of the contract.

D. CORPORATIONS

Theoretically, a corporation can exercise only such powers as are granted to it by the incorporating state, which powers are contained in the corporation's charter. A contract with a corporation, which is not authorized by the corporation's charter, may not be binding upon the corporation. Consequently, anyone contracting with a corporation should, for his own protection, have first determined that the corporation is competent to do the things provided for in the contract.*

---

* See p. 926.

[6] Sparrowhawk v. Erwin, p. 151.

E. MARRIED WOMEN

"At common law, the moment a woman married, she ceased to exist as an entity, but simply became merged in her husband." *Kerner* v. *McDonald,* 60 Neb. 663. Consequently, under common law a married woman has no contractual capacity. Very generally this disability has been removed by statute in the various states, but let it be recognized that in some states there is a survival of this disability to an extent. Local statutes should be consulted.

► II. FRAUD

When, by fraud or deceit, one has been induced to give contractual assent, he may, upon the basis of such, rescind the contract.

A. CONCEPT OF FRAUD

> "Fraud is manifold in its devices, and its ingredients cannot be so defined as to include all cases, save by such general statements as must after all, refer the question to the judgment of the jury upon the facts." *Hanger* v. *Evans,* 38 Ark. 334, 336.

It has been declared as a matter of public policy that the establishing of the limits of fraud is not to be desired. "Messieurs, fraud-feasors would like nothing half so well as for courts to say they would go thus far and no further in its pursuits." *Stonemets* v. *Head,* 248 Mo. 243, 263, 154 S.W. 108.

In very general terms, fraud is said to be any cunning, artifice, or deceitful practice used to cheat or deceive another. Fraud is a tort, a failure to comply with a duty imposed upon the individual by law.

B. ELEMENTS OF FRAUD

The essential elements necessary to the existence of fraud upon the basis of which a contract may be rescinded are:

(1) A false representation—misrepresentation—by expression or conduct of facts material to the transaction;

(2) knowledge that the facts represented are untrue or asserted as being true without knowledge of their truth;

(3) intent to induce action—the giving of contractual assent;

(4) action undertaken in justifiable reliance upon the representation; and

(5) injury as result of such action.

1. *Meaning of False Representation*

Within the bounds of the law, the term *false representation* has great latitude in its application. Broadly speaking, *anything* producing a false impression upon the mind of the other party qualifies as a false representation. The law is not concerned with the form in which the deceit is accomplished but rather with the fact that a deception has been achieved.

a. Deliberate Lying. Deliberate and intentional lying is the most obvious type of false representation, a practice with which everyone is familiar.

b. Evasive, Deceptive, or Partial Answers. The failure to disclose a true state of affairs by giving deceptive, evasive, or partial answers to inquiries can be as misleading as any positive statement. A half-truth can be as misleading as a falsehood.

c. Acts or Conduct. The cases are numerous in which a falsehood was accomplished by act or conduct. False impressions can be produced as effectively by conduct as by words.[7] The act of drawing a check leads one reasonably to believe that the drawer is declaring that he has funds in the bank to which the check is directed. A witness to a forged instrument is making a representation by his conduct as effectively as though he were to say, "The signature on this instrument is the signature it purports to be." Mixing gold in samples of ore would, in all probability, be more effective than a declaration in words.

Conduct that *actively conceals or suppresses* material facts is misrepresentation. For example, introducing a foreign substance into the transmission of a car for the purpose of concealing the true state of affairs would be a misrepresentation.

d. Nondisclosure of Facts. Ordinarily it is not misrepresentation if there is a failure to give information or disclose facts (silence) which, if known to the other party, would dissuade him from dealing. In the absence of exceptional circumstances "it is the right of every man to keep his business to himself." Only when the law creates a duty to speak does silence constitute one of the necessary elements of fraud. Parties dealing at arm's length may have a moral obligation to disclose any knowledge that the other party might be pleased to have, but the law makes no such requirement.[8] As the court said in *Harris* v. *Tyson,* 34 Pa. 374:

> "A person who knows that there is a mine on the land of another may nevertheless buy it. The ignorance of the vendor is not of itself fraud on the part of the purchaser. A purchaser is not bound by our laws to make the man he buys from as wise as himself."

Relationship of Trust and Confidence. Whenever there is a relationship of trust and confidence between the contracting parties, there is a legal duty imposed upon them to make a full disclosure of all facts material to the contract. A failure to do so is misrepresentation—an intent to mislead and deceive. Some of the more evident relationships of trust and confidence are: agent to his principal; one partner to another; attorney to client; corporate officers to stockholders; and trustee to the beneficiary. For example:

A is employed by B as the general manager of his properties. A discovers that a certain piece of property has a unique value and contracts to purchase it from B for less than its true value, not having disclosed its unique qualities to B. B can rescind the agreement upon the basis of fraud.

If one of the contracting parties places reliance in the other party to make

[7] Fischetto v. Quigley Co., p. 153.

[8] Oates v. Taylor, p. 155.

known certain information material to the contract, a confidential relationship is created requiring a full disclosure of such information. To illustrate:

(1) In the case of *Williamson* v. *Harris,* 167 Mo. App. 347, the purchaser of property told the seller that he would have to rely upon the seller's honor to tell him the truth about the fertility of the soil. The court held that the seller's nondisclosure of the fact that he had found it necessary to use fertilizer was misrepresentation of fact.

(2) In *Evans* v. *Palmer,* 137 Iowa 425, the court said, "If it is known by the vendor that the purchaser relies upon the vendor's knowledge of value, it is his duty to disclose truthfully his knowledge of the entire matter."

Superior Position of Knowledge. The law imposes a duty to speak when one is in a superior position of knowledge, if the circumstances are such that the knowledge is not readily available to the other party. Thus, a purchaser of property has the right to expect his vendor to disclose any hidden defects of which he has knowledge. A failure to do so is misrepresentation.

2. *Facts Material to Transaction*

Any misrepresentation of fact that serves as an inducement to give contractual assent is material to the transaction. In other words, any fact is material that, had its falsity been known, would have prevented the obtaining of contractual assent.

a. Opinions Distinguished. Expressions of opinion are not expressions of fact, since they are expressions of *honest belief* and not of knowledge. Expressions of future expectations, such as "the stock will have a material increase in value," are statements of opinion and not fact.[9]

Clearly, if the parties stand on an *equal footing* as to the availability of knowledge—when an equal opportunity to form and exercise independent judgment exists—that which is asserted as an opinion should not be relied upon. When, however, the asserter—as an expert—is in a superior position of knowledge, the other party has the right to rely upon such assertion of opinion.[10] To illustrate:

In *Turk* v. *Botsford,* 70 Ore. 198, the defendant, who alone was familiar with the circumstances, induced the plaintiff to contract to cut timber at a distant place by expressions of opinion as to the amount the plaintiff could earn and the length and conditions of employment. The facts did not develop in accordance with the expectations as expressed in the opinion and the court, in holding that such constituted fraud, said:

> "A matter of opinion may amount to an affirmation of fact, when, for example, the parties are not dealing upon equal terms, and one of them has, or is presumed to have, means of information not equally open to the other."

b. State of Mind as a Fact. The courts have said that "the state of a man's mind is as much a question of fact as is the state of his digestion." Consequently, a misrepresentation of one's state of mind is a misrepresentation of fact. Fraud by mis-

---

[9] Tetreault v. Campbell, p. 157.

[10] Traylor Eng. Co. v. Nat'l Cont. Corp., p. 158.

representation of mind may come about either through the making of a contractual promise with the intent not to perform or the making of an assertion as an opinion when in fact the assertion is not an honest belief. To illustrate:

In *Donaldson* v. *Farwell*, 93 U.S. 631, the evidence established the fact that the purchaser of property was at the time of the purchase insolvent and had no intent to pay. The court said:

> ". . . a party not intending to pay, who as in this instance, induces the owner to sell him goods on credit by . . . his intent not to pay for them, is guilty of a fraud which entitles the vendor . . . to disaffirm the contract and recover the goods."

3. *Need For Reliance*

One cannot have been deceived when he has placed no reliance upon the false representation made to him. If a party relies upon his own judgment or upon some other inducement, he can have no cause to complain.[11] Thus, even though a seller makes false representations relative to the qualities of the goods, and the buyer nevertheless makes his own tests and investigations, he has not relied upon the statements of the seller.[12]

Reliance in itself is not sufficient; the law requires that the reliance be justified. In general, it can be said that such statements as reasonable men would take into consideration in deciding to contract may be relied upon.[13] This excludes dealers' talk, puffing, exaggerated statements, and optimistic assurances as things that can be relied upon.[14] Granted that sellers are fully conscious of the fact that they are stretching the truth when making such vague statements as "the best buy in town," "the best car on the market," "will wear like iron," the law does not hold them responsible for their obviously false optimism. Statements of this nature are such as to be mistrusted and would be fully discounted by reasonable men.

C. EFFECT OF FRAUD

Fraud is also a *tort,* a wrong against the individual. As a result, in addition to rescission of the contract, the injured party may maintain an action for money damages. When the contract is executed, he may

(1) affirm the contract and sue in tort for the deceit to recover damages suffered, or

(2) avoid the contract and get a return of his consideration. When the rescission does not fully repair the injury, a tort action may be maintained to recover damages.

When the contract is executory, the injured party may

(1) affirm the contract and sue in tort, or

(2) elect not to perform the contract and use fraud as a defense in the event of suit for breach of contract.

The individual circumstances will dictate which course of action is most ad-

---

11 McIntyre v. Lyon, p. 160.
12 Owen v. Schwartz, p. 161.
13 Babb v. Bolyard, p. 164.
14 Henning v. Kyle, p. 165.

vantageous to the injured party. Unless the injured party takes measures within a reasonable time to enforce his rights to rescind (and until he does so), the contract is effective.[15]

► III. INNOCENT MISREPRESENTATION

Innocent misrepresentation or innocent concealment of material facts can be as harmful as though such were intentionally done. A purchaser's position, for example, is not improved by the fact that he was induced to buy upon the basis of an innocent misstatement rather than a fraudulent assertion.[16]

Consequently, one may avoid a contract if his contractual assent has been induced by innocent misrepresentation. As in the case of fraud, it becomes a question of whether the representation has been justifiably relied upon. So-called dealer's talk, puffing, and mere opinions cannot be taken seriously. If facts asserted are peculiarly within the knowledge of the asserter, there is no question concerning the right of the other party to rely upon the facts as represented. Thus, if A innocently misstates material facts in a life-insurance application, the company can avoid the insurance contract upon discovery that the facts are not as they were represented. Of necessity, in passing upon the application, the insurer must rely upon many facts as stated by the applicant.

Unlike fraud, innocent misrepresentation will not serve as a basis for a tort action for damages, nor does an innocent asserter in any way violate a criminal law. An essential to criminal prosecution is criminal intent—an intent to do wrong. Thus, one obtaining property by false pretenses (intentional misrepresentation) intends to commit a wrong and subjects himself to criminal prosecution. However, obtaining property by innocent misrepresentation would not be a criminal wrong, since the intent to do wrong is lacking.

A. SUBSEQUENT DISCOVERY THAT REPRESENTATION IS FALSE

If one subsequently discovers the falsity of a representation made in belief of its truth and passively allows the other party to act, he is misrepresenting a fact by his failure to speak. Similarly, by the weight of authority, where a true representation subsequently becomes false to the knowledge of the one who made the assertion, he has the imperative duty to communicate such to the other party in order to prevent the taking of any action in reliance on the original representation. A failure to so communicate is fraud.

► IV. MISTAKE OF FACT

Mistake means the *misapprehension of fact,* an assumption of fact that is not true, a state of mind that is not in accord with the facts. Whether one can be relieved of a contract entered into upon the basis of a mistake is basically dependent upon the nature of the mistake.

[15] Franco v. Voursney, p. 166.
[16] Williams v. Green, p. 167.

A. MISTAKE OF ONE PARTY—UNILATERAL

As a general rule, a mistake by one of the contracting parties, which serves as the inducement to contract, will not serve as a basis for relief from the contract. This is as it should be. The party who made the mistake should be made to take the consequences of his own failure to properly ascertain the facts. There would be no justice in affording him relief at the expense of the other contracting party, who was innocent in the matter.

1. *Erroneous Expression of Intent*

In making a contract, the essential thing is not what a party believes he is saying or what he intends to say, but rather that which he does say. The law ascribes to a person such intention as is reasonably apparent to the other contracting party.[17] It is of rather common occurrence that a party will contract for a price that has been arrived at by a mistake, for example, by miscalculation of figures. Thus, if A agrees to sell his tractor to B for $676, he cannot subsequently get out of the agreement by pleading a mistake, in that he had intended to say $767. Under the circumstances, B is justified in believing that A meant what he said. To illustrate:

In the case of *H. L. Tatum* v. *Coast Lumber Co.*, 16 Idaho 471, the plaintiff agreed to furnish certain tools and machinery for $5,134.80. It was later discovered that a mistake of $1,060 had been made in computing the price. The defendant paid the $5,134.80 and the plaintiff brought action to recover the $1,060, contending he should be relieved of his mistake—that because of the mistake, the minds of the parties had never met.

The court, in denying the plaintiff recovery, said:

> "In *Brown* v. *Levy*, 29 Tex. Civ. App. 389, the court held quite recently that, where a person makes an offer to erect a building for a certain amount, and the other party accepts it, there is a consummated and binding agreement, although the bidder in adding up the items of his estimate made a mistake in the total, and consequently made the bid $10,000 less than it should have been.
>
> ". . . No court, so far as we are advised, has ever held a contract void or invalid on account of a unilateral mistake of which the other party was not aware. . . . In 15 *Am. & Eng. Ency. Law*, p. 628, it says: 'In order that a mistake may come within the cognizance of a court of equity, it must be shown to be: First, material, or the moving cause of the complaining party's action; second, mutual, or shared in by both parties to the transaction. . . .'
>
> "Contracts are the deliberate and voluntary obligations of parties capable of contracting, and they must be accorded binding force and effect. Those who enter into them must understand that they have a meaning and that they cannot be lightly tampered with. If a vendor can be heard to come into court and repudiate his contract on the ground that it had never been really

---

17 Steinmeyer v. Schroeppel, p. 168.

consummated for the reason that he made a mistake in computing the prices of the various articles involved in the transaction, he might, with equal reason, insist that he had made a mistake in computing the profit he expected to realize out of the transaction. No such proposition can be tolerated. The owner of property is supposed to know what it is worth, and at least know what he is willing to take for his property. The purchaser may likewise exercise his free will and choice as to whether he will purchase property at a given price. After he has received the property, understanding that he is to pay a fixed price for it, he cannot be compelled to pay a different and greater price simply because the vendor was careless or negligent in the transaction of his own business."

a. Known or Obvious Mistake. When the party to whom an erroneous expression of intent has been made has knowledge of the error, or if the facts are such that he ought to know of the error, no binding contract can result.[18] The law will not and should not allow one to knowingly take advantage of another's mistake. To illustrate:

In the case of *Tyra* v. *Cheney,* 129 Minn. 428, the court held that where a mistake in the price was made in a written bid following an oral estimate and bid, the person to whom the bid was offered could not take advantage of the obvious mistake and bind the bidder.

b. Transmission of Offer by Telegram. In the case of *Holtz* v. *Western Union Telegraph Co.,* 294 Mass. 543 (1936), the plaintiff had employed the defendant to transmit a message to the Penn Shoe Company quoting shoes at a price of $1.75 a pair. The message was transmitted as reading $1.25 instead of $1.75. The Penn Shoe Company placed an order and when billed for $1.75 a pair they refused to pay more than the $1.25 a pair. The court concluded that "the plaintiff was not bound by the price of $1.25 per pair. . . . The message as delivered . . . was not the plaintiff's order. . . . The parties were never in agreement as to terms."

In support of its conclusion, the court said:

"There is conflict in the authorities as to the liability of the sender in case of mistake in the transmission of an offer or acceptance by telegram. It is held in some jurisdictions that a party making an offer by telegram is responsible for the correct transmission of his message and is bound by it in the terms in which it is actually delivered to the person addressed. This is on the theory that the carrier of the message is the agent of the sender. . . . It is held in other jurisdictions that the telegraph company is in no proper sense a private agent of the sender of the message. . . . We are of opinion that a telegraph company is not in any strict and proper sense the agent of the sender in transmitting a message, but is a public service corporation subject to duties and liabilities incident to those of a common carrier of intelligence for hire. This question was fully discussed with ample review of the conflicting authorities in *Western Union Telegraph Co.* v. *Cowin & Co.,*

[18] Cunningham Mfg. Co. v. Rotograph Co., p. 169.

20 F. (2d) 103. It there was held in conclusion that the sender of a message in nowise controls the service rendered by the telegraph company. The latter selects its own instrumentalities, its own particular employees, and its own methods for transmitting a message. The sender employs the telegraph company to deliver to the addressee of the message, not the original message filed, but a true copy thereof. Such being the character of a telegraph company and the nature of the service it renders, it logically follows that the relation between the sender and the telegraph company is not that of principal and agent in the usual sense of those terms but rather that of employer and independent contractor, that the telegraph company is authorized only to transmit the message filed by the sender, and that if it goes beyond that authority and delivers a message containing an offer in terms different than the original message filed by the sender for transmission, the latter is not bound by the offer as expressed in the erroneous message delivered. . . ."

2. *Mistake Relating to Motive or Expectation*

Under no circumstances will a mistake as to facts that serve as the motive for contracting or relate to the expected results of the contract afford the mistaken party relief. An expression of contractual assent influenced by a mistaken idea as to the value or quality of a thing is binding. Even if the other party knows that such a mistake has been made, the contract is enforceable.

"Courts cannot deprive one party of the advantage which superior judgment or better information may give, nor inquire as to how the parties would have contracted if each had known the same facts as to the condition of the market or other extrinsic matters, where the sources of information were equally open to both." * *Oliver* v. *Oliver,* 118 Ga. 362.

B. MISTAKE OF BOTH PARTIES—BILATERAL

The courts have many times declared that a mutual mistake as to material facts—one which goes to the substance of the contract—will make the contract voidable. The court in *Young Co.* v. *Springer,* 113 Minn. 382, said that such a mistake consists of "a clear showing of a misunderstanding, reciprocal and common to both parties, in respect to the terms and subject matter of the contract, or some substantial part thereof." A mutual mistake of a fact which is not of the essence of the agreement—which does not go to the substance—has no effect upon the contract. There is no absolute test which can be used for the purpose of determining whether a mistake goes to the substance of a contract. Such requires an application of that rare talent called judgment. The following illustrations will give the reader an appreciation of the problem.

(1) When the mistake pertains to the existence of the subject matter, the contract is voidable.[19] In such a case there never would be anything upon which the minds of the parties could meet.

* See Nondisclosure of Facts, p. 136.
[19] Graham v. Atchison etc., p. 171.

In the case of *Riegel* v. *American Life Ins. Co.*, 153 Pa. 134, the court allowed the plaintiff rescission of a contract under which she had surrendered a $6,000 insurance policy for a paid-up policy of $2,500. This was done upon the assumption that the party insured was still in existence when as a matter of fact he had been deceased for nine years. The court said:

". . . The general rule is that an act done or contract made under a mistake of a material fact is voidable and relievable in equity. The fact must of course be material to the actual contract; for, though there may be an accidental mistake or ignorance of the facts, yet, if the act or contract is not materially affected by it, relief will not be granted. Thus, A buys from B an estate to which the latter is supposed to have an unquestionable title. It turns out, upon due investigation of the facts unknown at the time to both parties, that B has no title; as, if there be a nearer heir than B, who was supposed to be dead, but is in fact living. In such a case, equity would relieve the purchaser and rescind the contract. But suppose A buys from B an estate the location of which was well known to each of them, and they mutually believed it contained 20 acres when in fact it contained only 19¾ acres, and the difference would not have varied the purchase in the view of either party; in such a case the mistake would not be ground for rescission of the contract.

"It makes no difference in application of the principle that the subject matter of the contract be known to both parties to be liable to a contingency which may destroy it immediately; for, if the contingency has, unknown to the parties, already happened, the contract will be avoided, as founded on a mutual mistake of a matter constituting the basis of the contract.

"The principle is illustrated by familiar examples, employed by text writers, thus: A agrees to buy a certain horse from B. It turns out that the horse is dead at the time of the bargain, though neither party was then aware of the fact. The agreement is void. A agrees to buy a house belonging to B. The house was previously destroyed by fire, but the parties dealt in ignorance of that fact. The contract, not being for sale of the land on which the house stood, was not enforceable. So, too, A, being entitled to an estate for the life of B, agreed to sell it to C. B was dead, but both parties were ignorant of the fact. The agreement was avoided.

"For similar reasons, a life insurance contract cannot be revived by payment of the premium within the time allowed for that purpose by the original contract, but after the life had dropped, unknown to both insurer and assured, although it was in existence when the premium became due. . . .

"It is therefore adjudged . . . that the contract under which said exchange of insurance polices was made be rescinded; that the paid-up policy for $2,500 be surrendered and canceled; that the original policy of insurance be reinstated as of date of its surrender; and it is further adjudged and decreed that the defendant company pay to the plaintiff the sum of $6,000 with interest."

(2) By the same token, there is no contract if the mistake pertains to the iden-

tity of the subject matter.[20] The classical illustration is the case of *Kyle* v. *Kavanagh,* 103 Mass. 356, in which the defendant agreed to purchase of the plaintiff four lots in Waltham on Prospect Street. The defendant submitted evidence that he had in mind a parcel of land on another Prospect Street in Waltham. The court concluded that, upon the basis of mistake as to identity of the subject matter, there was no contract.

(3) A mistake as to the value of the subject matter of the contract does not go to the substance of the contract.[21] Thus is has been held that the sale of a valuable stone, when both parties act upon the assumption that it is of little value, is not voidable.

(4) By the same token, it has been held that a mutual mistake as to the quality of the subject matter is not material.

(5) A mutual mistake as to the acreage contained in a tract of land may or may not make the contract voidable, depending upon the circumstances.[22]

► V. DURESS

Duress is the use of means that will prevent one of the contracting parties from exercising his free will. The use of either force or threats to induce contractual assent against the free will of the person so coerced is duress and because of such the contract can be rescinded.

The Restatement of the Law of Contracts, § 493, reads:

"Duress may be exercised by

"(a) Personal violence or a threat thereof, or

"(b) Imprisonment, or threat of imprisonment, except where the imprisonment brought about or threatened is for the enforcement of a civil claim, and is made in good faith in accordance with law, or

"(c) Threats of physical injury, or of wrongful imprisonment or prosecution of a husband, wife, child,[23] or other near relative, or

"(d) Threats of wrongfully destroying, injuring, seizing or withholding land or other things, or

"(e) Any other wrongful acts that compel a person to manifest apparent assent to a transaction without his volition or cause such fear as to preclude him from exercising free will and judgment in entering into a transaction."

► VI. UNDUE INFLUENCE

The Restatement of the Law of Contracts, § 497, reads:

"Where one party is under the domination of another, or by virtue of the relation between them is justified in assuming that the other party will not act in a manner inconsistent with his welfare, a transaction induced by

20 Am. Nat'l Bank v. West, p. 172.
21 Costello v. Sykes, p. 174.
22 Enequist v. Bemis, p. 175.
23 Meylink v. Minnehaha Co-op. Oil Co., p. 177.

unfair persuasion of the latter, is induced by undue influence and is voidable." [24]

Undue influence may arise out of the following situations:

(1) "The principle applies to every case when influence is acquired and abused, where confidence is reposed and betrayed." *Smith* v. *Kay,* 7 H.L. Cas. 750. Family and other relations, such as those between business associates, attorney and client, trustee and beneficiary, fall within the above.

(2) Advantage is taken of another's mental weakness.

(3) Advantage is taken of another's position of necessity and distress.

A contract induced by undue influence, as well as a contract made under duress, may be avoided by the injured party because of lack of real assent.

In those cases where the law recognizes a relationship of trust and confidence —a so-called fiduciary relationship—between contracting parties, it is generally presumed that undue influence exists. In *Curtis* v. *Fisher,* 406 Ill. 102, the court stated the presumption thus:

> ". . . transactions of parties standing in a fiduciary relation are *prima facie* voidable on grounds of public policy; that they will be closely scrutinized by a court of equity and relief granted unless the parties claiming the benefit of the contracts show by clear and convincing proof that they have acted in good faith and have not betrayed the confidence reposed in them.
>
> "Important factors in determining whether a particular transaction is fair include a showing by the fiduciary (1) that he has made a free and frank disclosure of all the relevant information which he had; (2) that the consideration was adequate; and (3) that the principal had competent and independent advice before completing the transaction."

CASES

CASE NO. 1

Tatum v. Montgomery Banking Co. 33 Ala. App. 186, 31 So. (2d) 311 (1947)

CARR, J. On June 6, 1946, James Ward, a minor, borrowed a sum of money from the Montgomery Banking Company. To secure the loan, Ward gave a mortgage on an automobile. On July 2d following Ward sold the mortgaged car to D. L. Tatum, one of the defendants in the court below. On July 15, 1946, the minor made a monthly payment on the indebtedness to the mortgagee. It was not until some time in August, 1946, that the banking company learned that the car had been sold as indicated. No other payments were made on the mortgage debt.

This suit is by the Montgomery Banking Company against D. L. Tatum and others for the conversion of the automobile and also for damages for the destruction of the mortgage lien. The cause was tried by the court below without the aid of a jury and resulted in a judgment in favor of the plaintiff. The

[24] Stieber v. Vanderlip, p. 178.

defendant, Tatum, alone, brings this appeal.

. . . The only question urged in brief is that the trial court should have held that the sale of the automobile by the minor was in legal effect a rescission of the contract with the plaintiff, and thereafter the mortgage agreement was void. The insistence follows that, because of this fact, no rights could be asserted against the purchaser of the car in the manner attempted in this case. . . .

It is a legal truism that an infant may avoid his contract either before or after he arrives at majority. Ex parte McFerren, 184 Ala. 223, 63 So. 159, 47 L.R.A., N.S., 543, Ann. Cas. 1915B, 672. This may be done in various ways, the question of ultimate concern being did the act show an unequivocal renunciation of or a clear intent not to abide by the terms of the contract. 43 C.J.S., Infants, p. 173.

It is equally well established by the authorities that disaffirmance of a contract by a minor is largely a question of intention, and this must be determined by all the facts and circumstances indicating a purpose to be no longer bound by the contractual undertaking. . . .

We entertain the view that in the case at bar the fact that the infant sold the mortgaged property did not of itself close the mind of the court against a further inquiry into the evidence to ascertain whether or not the minor intended to avoid the contract. It is without dispute in the record that the mortgagor made one monthly payment on the mortgage indebtedness after he sold the automobile. There was other testimony relating to the sale transaction that the court was privileged to consider and weigh.

. . . We are convinced that the judgment of the court below should not be disturbed. It is ordered, therefore, that it be affirmed.

CASE NO. 2

Cassella v. Tiberio. 150 Ohio St. 27, 80 N.E. (2d) 426, 5 A.L.R. (2d) 1 (1948)

ZIMMERMAN, J. . . . On April 20, 1933, Lee Tiberio, Rosa Tiberio, his wife, and Louis Tiberio, his son, the latter then being 19 years of age, affixed their signatures to a cognovit note in the sum of $4,024.22, payable to the order of Guiseppe (Joseph) Cassella. The consideration for such note was loans of money previously made to Lee Tiberio by Guiseppe Cassella. Thereafter, the note was sold, transferred and set over to Lena Cassella, niece of Guiseppe, who took judgment thereon by confession on August 21, 1939, . . .

The judgment became dormant and Lena Cassella moved for a conditional order of revivor. The Tiberios were directed to show cause why the judgment should not be revived. . . . Objection was made by Louis Tiberio for the reasons (1) that he had signed the note as a witness only and (2) that he was a minor when he affixed his signature thereto. The court overruled the objections as being untenable on a motion for revivor and ordered the judgment revived.

Thereafter, Lee and Louis Tiberio filed separate petitions, . . . to vacate the judgment, . . the cause came on to be heard on its merits before the court and a jury, resulting in verdicts against both Lee and Louis Tiberio. . . .

Louis Tiberio's motion for judgment notwithstanding the verdict was sustained, and judgment was entered in his favor.

From this latter judgment an appeal was taken by Lena Cassella to the

Court of Appeals, which affirmed the judgment. . . .

The trial court, in rendering judgment for Louis Tiberio notwithstanding the verdict, and the Court of Appeals, in approving such determination, adopted the rule that where an infant enters into a contract out of which he derives no benefit, it is not binding on him unless he ratifies the same after becoming of age.

On the other hand, counsel for Lena Cassella stoutly maintain that the contract made by Louis Tiberio when he signed the note was voidable, that his failure to disaffirm within a reasonable time after reaching majority constituted ratification, and that the fact that the transaction was of no benefit to him is immaterial.

In 12 Am. Jur. 507, § 9, we find the following statements:

> "An executory contract is one in which a party binds himself to do, or not to do, a particular thing, whereas an executed contract is one in which the object of the agreement is performed and everything that was to be done is done. . . . Another distinction between an executory and an executed contract is that the former requires affirmative action for its establishment, but the latter remains in force until disaffirmed."

In 27 Am. Jur. 808, § 82, under the general heading "Infants," it is categorically stated that

> "the great weight of authority is to the effect that omission to disaffirm within a reasonable time does not ratify an executory contract, provided the former infant does not retain possession of the consideration. . . . It seems, however, that an executed contract, voidable on the ground of infancy is deemed to be ratified by the failure of the former infant to disaffirm it within a reasonable time after reaching majority."

Certainly, a written and signed promise to pay money comes within the classification of an executory contract so far as the promisor is concerned.

For a practical application of the rule, attention is directed to the case of Nichols & Shepard Co. v. Snyder, 78 Minn. 502, 81 N.W. 516, where it is held in the syllabus written by the court:

> "The contract of an infant is simply voidable, and in law there is a marked distinction between his executed contract and his contract merely executory. As to the latter he may always interpose his infancy as a defense in an action for its enforcement, and he is not bound by such a contract unless he has affirmed or ratified it, after he has arrived at maturity, by some sufficient act or deed."

Such rule is particularly appropriate in a situation like the one presented by the instant case.

Looking at the matter realistically, we see no good reason why, when an infant receives something of value under a contract which is executory as to him, he should not be held to the bargain if he retains the thing and does nothing by way of disaffirmance for an appreciable length of time after reaching legal age. See 27 Am. Jur. 756, § 12.

In our opinion the executed contract of an infant is and should be binding upon him by his failure to disaffirm it within a reasonable time after attaining majority, but where the contract is wholly executory and it is apparent the infant has received no benefits, a different conclusion is in order. 43 C.J.S., Infants, p. 169. Compare Mestetzko v. Elf Motor Co., 119 Ohio St. 575. . . .

As we are of the opinion that the judgments below were correct, the judgment of the Court of Appeals is affirmed.

Judgment affirmed.

CASE NO. 3

Block v. Means. D.C., 64 A. (2d) 163 (1949)

HOOD, A.J. Plaintiff purchased from defendant a motor scooter, paying therefor $336.35. Approximately three weeks after its purchase the scooter was stolen from in front of plaintiff's home and has never been recovered. Thereafter plaintiff, through his mother as next friend, brought this action to recover the purchase price on the ground that at the time of the purchase and at the time suit was filed he was an infant. He obtained judgment for the full purchase price, and defendant has appealed.

Plaintiff was a little over nineteen years of age when he purchased the scooter. The trial court, which had heard the case without a jury, in a memorandum denying the motion for new trial indicated that it had found as a fact (1) that at the time of the transaction no reference was made by plaintiff to his age and no inquiry concerning it was made by defendant, (2) that the scooter was not a necessary for plaintiff, and (3) that plaintiff had not been emancipated. There was ample evidence to support these findings.

Appellant's first contention is that an infant cannot disaffirm his contract without first restoring the other party to the status quo. The settled authority in this jurisdiction is to the contrary.

> "The inability of the infant to place the other party in status quo does not affect the right of disaffirmance." Gannon v. Manning, 42 App. D.C. 206, 209, citing MacGreal v. Taylor, 167 U.S. 688, 17 Sup. Ct. 961, 42 L. Ed. 326.

Appellant argues, however, that the Supreme Court in Myers v. Hurley Motor Co., Inc., 273 U.S. 18, 26, 47 Sup. Ct. 277, 279, 71 L. Ed. 515, 50 A.L.R. 1181, ruled that actions of this sort are equitable in nature and are to be determined on equitable principles, and appellant says that equity requires that one who disaffirms a contract must restore the consideration he had received. We do not understand the Myers case to go that far. Its ruling appears to be confined to the following:

> "When an infant of mature appearance, by false and fraudulent representations as to his age, has induced another person to sell and deliver property to him, it is against natural justice to permit the infant to recover money paid for the property without first compelling him to account for the injury which his deceit has inflicted upon the other person."

In the instant case the infant did not misrepresent his age, so there is no basis here for saying that appellant has been injured by any deceit on the infant's part. And the highest court of this jurisdiction has ruled that the Myers case does not make restoration a prerequisite to disaffirmance. In Mutual Life Ins. Co. of New York v. Schiavone, 63 App. D.C. 257, 258, 71 F. (2d) 980, 981, 94 A.L.R. 962, in which the Myers case was cited, it was held that an infant's

> "inability to return the consideration and restore the status quo does not deprive him of his right to repudiate."

Appellant also contends that the trial court was in error in not holding that the scooter was a necessary, and in not holding that the infant had emancipated himself and was therefore liable on the contract. As already stated, the trial court found adversely to appellant on these questions and was amply supported by the evidence in so finding. Furthermore, emancipation does not give an infant enlarged capacity to contract. Williston, Contracts, § 225 (rev. ed.); Wickham v. Torley, 136 Ga. 594, 71 S.E. 881, 36 L.R.A., N.S., 57; Schoenung v. Gallet, 206 Wis. 52, 238 N.W. 852, 78 A.L.R. 387.

Affirmed.

CASE NO. 4

R. J. Goerke Co. v. Nicolson. 5 N.J. Sup. 412, 69 A. (2d) 326 (1949)

DONGES, J.A.D. This is an appeal from an order of the Union County District Court denying appellant's application to set aside a judgment against defendant and in favor of plaintiff.

On November 5, 1946, appellant made personal application to respondent's credit manager, Mary Zack, to open a charge account. The appellant furnished credit data to the said credit manager, which data was incorporated in a printed application. The application contained the further provision that the applicant expressly represents that she is of full legal age, etc. The application was signed by Florence R. Nicolson, the appellant, and was witnessed by Mary Zack.

Between November 15, 1946, and November 27, 1946, there were charges to this account in the sum of $493.15. A credit of $100 was made on January 8, 1947, leaving a balance of $393.15.

. . . On April 1, 1947, a judgment was entered in favor of respondent and against appellant. Subsequently, the appellant's salary was garnisheed with her employer.

On or about February 1, 1949, the court below reopened the judgment for the purpose of taking testimony as to whether the judgment should be set aside. The court permitted the entire case to be tried on the merits, and appointed one Stewart Cooley as guardian for the appellant.

Appellant asserted that she was an infant at the time the purchases were made, and that she did not recall being asked if she was of full age or of having read the provision concerning age in the application.

Mary Zack, the credit manager, testified that she asked appellant if she was of full age and received an affirmative reply. She also stated that she read the provision relating to age to the appellant and that appellant looked like she was of legal age.

At the conclusion of the hearing, the judge concluded that the appellant was estopped from setting up the plea of infancy. . . .

That contracts of infants are voidable by them generally must be conceded. However, in a proper case, an infant may be estopped from asserting infancy as a defense.

In La Rosa v. Nichols, 92 N.J.L. 375, 105 Atl. 201, 203, 6 A.L.R. 412 (E. & A. 1918), the court said:

"It seems anomalous indeed that youth of sufficient age and capacity, although less than 21 years old, may be convicted of crime, and be held liable for their torts, and yet not be liable on their contracts when apparently of sufficient capacity to make them, and when they procure their making by fraud."

In the instant case, it does not appear that the infant returned any of the articles purchased. There is ample, competent evidence in the record to indicate that the appellant misrepresented herself to be of full age and that she appeared to the credit manager to be an adult.

Under circumstances such as these, an infant will not be permitted to use as a sword her plea of infancy which in fact was given to her as a shield.

The appeal is dismissed with costs.

CASE NO. 5

Gregory v. Lee. 64 Conn. 407, 30 Atl. 53 (1894)

TORRANCE, J. The complaint in this case alleges that on the 1st of June, 1892, the defendant, being a student in Yale College, entered into a contract with the plaintiff, by which he leased a room for the ensuing college year of 40 weeks, at an agreed rate of $10 per week, payable weekly, and immediately entered into possession of said room, and has neglected and refused to pay the rent of said room for the 10 weeks ending February 7, 1893. The answer, in substance, is as follows: On or about September 15, 1892, the defendant agreed to lease a room in the house of the plaintiff for the ensuing college year of 40 weeks, at the agreed rate of $10 per week, payable weekly; that he then entered into possession of said room, and occupied it till December 20, 1892; that on said day he gave up possession of said room, and ceased to occupy the same, and then paid to the plaintiff all he owed her for such occupation and possession up to that time; that immediately thereafter he engaged at a reasonable price another suitable room elsewhere, and continued to possess and occupy the same until the end of said college year; that during all of said period he was a minor, and a student in said college; and that on December 20, 1892, he refused to fulfill said agreement with the plaintiff to occupy or pay for said room for the remainder of said 40 weeks, and has always refused to pay for the time during which he did not possess or occupy said room. . . .

Under the facts stated, it must be conceded that this room, at the time the defendant hired it, and during the time he occupied it, came within the class called "necessaries," and also that to him during said period it was an actual necessary, for lodging comes clearly within the class of necessaries; and the room in question was a suitable and proper one, and during the period he occupied it was his only lodging room.

> "Things necessary are those without which an individual cannot reasonably exist. In the first place, food, raiment, lodging, and the like. About these there is no doubt."

. . . So long, then, as the defendant actually occupied the room as his sole lodging room it was clearly a necessary to him, for the use of which the law would compel him to pay; but as he paid the agreed price for the time he actually occupied it, no question arises upon that part of the transaction between these parties. The question now is whether he is bound to pay for the room after December 20, 1892. The obligation of an infant to pay for necessaries actually furnished to him does not seem to arise out of a contract in the legal sense of that term, but out of a transaction of a quasi-contractual nature; for it may be imposed on an infant too young to understand the nature of contract at all. And where an infant agrees to pay a stipulated price for such necessaries, the party furnishing them recovers not necessarily that price, but only the fair and reasonable value of the necessaries. . . . This being so, no binding obligation to pay for necessaries can arise until they have been supplied to the infant; and he cannot make a binding executory agreement to purchase necessaries. For the purpose of this case, perhaps, we may regard the transaction which took place between these parties in September, 1892, either as an agreement on the part of the plaintiff to supply the defendant with necessary lodging for the college year, and on the part of the defendant as an executory agreement to pay an agreed price for the same from week to week; or we may regard it as what, on the whole, it appears the parties intended it to be, a parol lease, under which possession was taken, and an executory agreement on the part of the defendant to pay rent. If we regard it in the former light, then the defense of infancy is a good defense; for in that case the suit is upon an executory contract to pay for necessaries which the defendant refused to take, and never has had, and which, therefore, he may avoid. If we regard the transaction as a lease under which possession was taken, executed on the part of the plaintiff, with a promise or agreement on the part of the defendant to pay rent weekly, we think infancy is equally a defense. As a general rule, with but few exceptions, an infant may avoid his contracts of every kind, whether beneficial to him or not, and whether executed or executory. . . .

In this case the defendant gave up the room and repudiated the agreement, so far as it was in his power to do so, in the most positive and unequivocal manner. The plea of infancy, . . . must prevail, . . .

CASE NO. 6

Sparrowhawk v. Erwin. 30 Ariz. 238, 246 P. 541 (1926)

LOCKWOOD, J. From the record the facts . . . appear to be as follows: Cyrus W. and Emma E. Erwin were husband and wife . . . the former made application in the name of his wife to . . . defendant, for a loan of $2,000, and offered as security therefore certain real estate situated in Phoenix which he claimed was the community property of himself and wife. Defendant inspected the premises and found them to be good security for the amount of the loan, and a title report showed good title in Emma E. Erwin. . . . Mrs. Erwin read over the note and mortgage, apparently understanding them, and seemed satisfied therewith, signing and delivering them to the defendant; they also being signed by her husband. Erwin requested that the check be made payable to him and Mrs. Erwin was asked if that would be all right, to which she replied, "Yes." A check was then made out in his name, and delivered to him. His wife asked him to let her see it, and she looked at it and then handed it back to her husband, and the Erwins left the office.

The money, with the exception of some $125.20, was used entirely by Erwin for his separate purposes, and in no manner inured to the benefit of his wife. Several days after, the circumstances of this transaction came to the knowledge of plaintiff herein, who is the daughter of Emma E. and stepdaughter of Cyrus W. Erwin, and she applied for letters of guardianship of her mother on the ground of the incompetency of the latter. These letters were granted on the 23d day of April, and a week later she brought this suit, setting up that at the time of the execution of the note and mortgage aforesaid, her mother, by reason of old age and weakness of body and mind, was unable to take care of herself and her property, and that at the time of signing said instruments was not competent and did not have the requisite mental faculties to transact the affair. She also alleged that defendant company knew, or could have known, of Mrs. Erwin's incompetency by the exercise of reasonable prudence on its part, and prayed that the note and mortgage be canceled, and set aside.

. . . The court, . . . made findings of fact expressly negativing the finding of competency made by the jury, and holding that Mrs. Erwin did not have mental capacity sufficient to understand what she was doing when she signed the note and mortgage. It further found that she had received only $125.20 of the $2,000 loaned by defendant, and that the latter had no knowledge of any circumstances which would cause a reasonably prudent person to doubt her capacity, and had acted in good faith in all respects during the transaction. Judgment was rendered on the findings against plaintiff. . . .

There is only one question of law raised which it is necessary for this court to determine to decide this case. There is no dissent from the general proposition that the contract of an incompetent person is invalid. There is a conflict of authorities, however, upon the question of whether such a contract is void or merely voidable. A few of the states hold that such an agreement is absolutely void, but plaintiff admits that the great weight of authority supports the rule that, where a contract with an insane person has been entered into in good faith, without fraud or imposition, for a fair consideration, and without notice of the infirmity, and before an adjudication of insanity, and has been executed in whole or in part, it will not be set aside, unless the parties can be restored to their original position. She, however, claims there is this exception to the general rule, that although the other party to a contract has parted with an adequate and valuable consideration, yet, where the incompetent has not received the benefit thereof, the contract will be set aside without the necessity of his returning it. It is the contention of defendant, on the other hand, that it is immaterial as to whom the consideration passed; the test being whether or not the other party to the contract had in good faith and at the request of the incompetent parted with the consideration. These respective rules contended for are both supported by very respectable authority, and are in hopeless conflict.

The contention of defendant is best typified by the case of Edwards v. Miller, 102 Okla. 189, 228 Pac. 1105, in which the court used the following language:

"This rule deals with cases where the party contracting with the lunatic acted in good faith, and such theory the evidence in the record established here. It makes no difference that the lunatic received no actual benefit from the money expended by the other party in good faith in discharging the duties imposed upon him by the contract. If the lunatic and his relatives and friends, and those upon whom rests the moral or legal duty to protect him in his unfortunate mental condition fail to have his mental incapacity judicially determined, so that others may learn of his condition, and the mental condition and appearance of the lunatic are such that he causes even the cautious and prudent individual with whom he deals to believe in good faith that he is a fully competent person, then simple justice demands that innocent third persons be not made to suffer and lose moneys actually paid out by them in good faith in carrying into effect the contracts made by them with such lunatic whose mental condition and actions make him appear to them to be a fully competent individual. The reason of the rule requires with equal force the restitution of moneys thus expended, though the lunatic did not profit thereby, as well as where he did so. . . ."

. . . We are of the opinion that upon the whole the rule of Edwards v. Miller, supra, will, in the majority of cases, prove the most satisfactory. In much the greater number of cases arising under a state of facts similar to this, while the action is nominally for the benefit of the estate of the incompetent, yet as a matter of fact any recovery would inure eventually—in the greater part at least—to some relative or heir, and not to the incompetent. There might be merit in the contention that, if the sole benefit of the recovery were actually to go to the incompetent, his equity is at least equal, though we cannot see where it is superior to that of the innocent other party to the contract. But certainly there is no comparison as between an heir and one who has in good faith advanced money to one whom the relatives and heirs have allowed to remain in a position where he might injure another.

The equitable maxim that, where the equities are equal, the parties will be relegated to their remedy at law, is one which, in our opinion, can well be applied in cases of this nature, and we therefore adopt the rule set forth in the Edwards Case, supra, as the law of Arizona.

The judgment . . . is affirmed.

CASE NO. 7

Fischetto Paper Mill Supply v. Quigley Co. 3 N.J. 149, 69 A. (2d) 318 (1949)

WACHENFELD, J. The appellant sued for the purchase price of certain merchandise delivered to wit, waste paper. Delivery was admitted but the respondent disputed the quantity received and the amount due. . . .

The appeal concerns the issues arising out of a counterclaim filed by the respondent in which it alleges it purchased and paid for shipments of waste paper for a long time, from December 1940 to July 1945, and during this period was cheated and defrauded by the appellant because the weights of the shipments so made were overstated, resulting in payments over and above the reasonable value of the merchandise received to the extent of approximately $15,000. The jury returned a verdict of $9,499.62 for which judgment was accordingly entered and is presently under consideration.

The case involves a somewhat complicated state of facts in reference to the proof submitted by the respondent on its counterclaim endeavoring to show it had been defrauded by paying for merchandise never actually received.

The counterclaim alleges there was a scarcity of the commodity at the time and the appellant refused to sell and deliver any waste paper unless the weighing thereof was waived and the appellant's representation as to the true weight accepted and payment made at the prevailing market price. It further alleges that between December 1940 and July 1945 various quantities of waste paper were delivered to the Old Bridge plant which were represented by the appellant to weigh 4,774,724 pounds and the respondent, relying upon said representation, paid therefor, including the cost of truckage, the sum of $38,555.07. It then charges that in truth only 2,589,791 pounds of waste paper were actually delivered and the appellant had thus cheated and defrauded the respondent to the extent of $15,365.25.

Fischetto Paper Mill Supply, Inc., is a closely held family corporation and has been supplying waste paper to the respondent for many years. Quigley Company has factories in South River and Old Bridge, New Jersey. It manufactures, amongst other products, high temperature insulated fire brick, of which burnt waste paper is a component part. The paper is chopped up and added to other ingredients in precise proportions ascertained by weighing, after which the whole mixture is put in kilns where the paper and other inflammable materials are burned out, leaving a porous and insulated brick. . . .

Some time in 1943 the respondent discovered at the Old Bridge plant a shortage in the book inventory of materials in relation to all of the products used in production. They were operating at full capacity but their auditors were unsuccessful in ascertaining the cause of the shortage. As a result of an anonymous telephone call in May 1945, the respondent's plant manager became suspicious of the correctness of the certificates showing the quantity of paper delivered. The next load was therefore weighed and was found to total only 28,195 pounds instead of 41,955 pounds, the amount stated in the receipt. On the following delivery the total load was found to weigh only 19,516 pounds instead of the 29,635 pounds represented. . . .

It is contended there was error by the trial court in not directing a verdict against the respondent and in holding it had made out a case of fraud. . . .

The rule as to fraud is clear and has been consistently followed in our courts.

> "In Byard v. Holmes, 34 N.J.L. 296, the rule was laid down that, to maintain an action on the case of deceit, the plaintiff must allege with reasonable certainty, and be prepared to prove, (1) that the defendant made some representation to the plaintiff, meaning that he should act upon it; (2) that such representation was false, and that the defendant, when he made it, knew it to be false; and (5) that the plaintiff, believing such representation to be true, acted upon it, and was thereby injured." Koschucki v. McGarry, 104 N.J.L. 65, 139 Atl. 31 (E. & A. 1927).

The appellant now argues, as nearly as we can ascertain from its brief, that one of the important elements in a charge of fraud is the intent with which the representation was made, and it is urged "throughout the transcript nowhere is there any proof of intent on the part of the plaintiff." Likewise, it is asserted "there was no reliance on any representation and without it, no fraud" and "there just is no representation by the plaintiff to the defendant that can be found anywhere in this record."

These contentions are hardly tenable in view of the record. Although it was partly conflicting, there nevertheless was ample testimony to indicate there had been a system of weighing and checking each load of paper which was discontinued upon the insistment of the appellant, the respondent being induced to agree to the suggestion because of the scarcity of the supply occasioned by war demands, plus the fact that it was to receive a weight certificate specifying the amount of merchandise delivered. Certainly, by inference at least, it was intended the purchaser should rely upon the certificates. Otherwise they would have no purpose or utility. In fact, the company's treasurer testified he had "been taking the word of the Fischetto Company for the amount of paper that they had delivered."

Although the respondent was aware of a marked shortage in material, it was unsuccessful in solving the problem until the receipt of the anonymous phone call, which caused the actual checking and weighing of the next two deliveries. This shed considerable light on what formerly had been a mystery.

The testimony to the effect that some of the weighmaster's certificates were not authentic but were prepared by the appellant and the figures put on after the seal had been affixed was most significant. It is difficult to conceive this as an honest transaction with such spurious documents as its foundation. They surely were not calculated to give a financial advantage to the respondent. The intent to defraud, we think, was amply proved and there was direct testimony as to the reliance upon the representations made.

In so far as "representation" is concerned, the appellant apparently takes the position that there must be an actual oral or written statement embodying the inducement in order to form the basis of a charge of fraud. Here the representations relied upon by the respondent were the statements contained in the weighmaster's certificates and the receipts prepared and issued by the appellant. The presentation of these to the respondent at the time of the delivery of the paper constituted the representations, which, if false, are a sufficient basis for an action in fraud and deceit. Whether or not they were false under these circumstances was a question of fact to be determined by a jury. . . .

The judgment is affirmed.

CASE NO. 8

Oates v. Taylor. 31 Wash. (2d) 898, 199 P. (2d) 924 (1948)

SCHWELLENBACH, J. This is an appeal from a judgment rendered against Appellant W. F. Taylor and the marital community composed of Taylor and wife, in the sum of $2,462.81.

W. F. Taylor has been for some time a builder and contractor in Seattle. About February 1, 1946, he started to work as building superintendent, for J. R. Huson, Inc., a corporation which was building a number of houses. About a month later it developed that Huson Inc., was bankrupt, having liabilities of $139,000.00 and assets of $82,000.00. Home Finders, Inc. was then organized, . . . The new corporation took over the Huson business, . . .

About August 29, 1946, the financial affairs of the corporation became so involved that Taylor threatened to quit . . . It was then decided that portions of the funds received would be turned over to him. He deposited these funds to the account of Home Finders, Inc., and then disbursed the funds to laborers and materialmen to whom the corporation was indebted.

On January 10, 1947, the corporation entered into a contract to build a home for Mr. Oates. We quote that portion of the agreement which is material to the questions in issue.

"The cost of said residence to be the sum of Nine Thousand Six Hundred Fifty and agreed that the above figure covers the house complete, including the lot, and that the determining factor as to what is included therein shall be the plans and specifications attached hereto.

"The said purchaser agrees to pay the sum $500.00 as earnest money and $2500.00 when the basement is started. The balance of the purchase price ($6650.00) shall be paid as follows:

"$665.00 upon the basement being poured and completed.

665.00 when the house is framed and roofed.

1330.00 when the house is plastered.

1995.00 when the millwork is completed as per the plans and specifications. . . ."

The earnest money payment of $500.00 was retained by the corporation. When Oates was first asked to pay the $2,500.00 he refused to do so until the basement was actually started. He testified that the representatives of the corporation came to him on a Saturday and told him that they wanted the $2,500.00. He went down to the lot and the basement had not been started. They said that they would be there the next day. Monday they called him and said that they had started the basement. He went down again and no work was started, and he refused to make the payment. They called that afternoon and said the work had been commenced. The next day he found that the bulldozer was there ready to start, and he gave them the check for $2,500.00.

On February 24, 1947, when the basement was completed, $665.00 was paid and turned over to Taylor. On March 21, 1947, the house was framed and roofed, and another $665.00, together with an additional $125.00 for a dormer, was paid and turned over to Taylor.

In the meantime, the financial affairs of the corporation had gotten into a precarious condition. . . .

. . . Lawrence Justice (the salesman who negotiated the original contract with Oates) and Taylor went to see Mr. Oates. Justice did most of the talking. The testimony is in dispute as to what transpired at this meeting. Something was said about needing the money to pay other bills, and also to buy a carload of hardwood flooring, to be used, partly in the Oates house and partly in other houses being built by the corporation. Oates was told that if he advanced the money, he would not have to make the next payments when they became due under the contract. He told them that by June 1st he would have to be out of the house that he was then living in, and they promised to cooperate by having his house ready by that time. He then agreed to give them the check the next day. . . .

The next day he went to the office with the check for $2,565.08. . . .

This check . . . was turned over to Taylor, who then went out with his Home Finders, Inc. checkbook and paid the laborers and materialmen. He did not receive any of this money himself.

After paying the bills, Taylor left the company. Before he left he asked Mr. Omtvedt, who succeeded him as superintendent, to rush the completion of the Oates house. . . .

A new contractor was brought in to complete the house. Oates was compelled to pay the bills as they came in, thus resulting in the total cost to him of $12,112.81, which included the check for $2,565.08. This became necessary because of threats to file liens against the house for work done.

This action alleging fraud was commenced against Taylor and wife, . . .

To constitute "actionable fraud" the representations must have been made as to a material matter, with a knowledge of their falsity. They must have been made with the intention that they should be acted upon by the other party; and he must have acted in reliance upon them to his injury. . . .

". . . It is settled that the suppression of a material fact which a party is bound in good faith to disclose is equivalent to a false representation. Where the law imposes a duty on one party to disclose all material facts known to him and not known to the other, silence or concealment in violation of this duty with intent to deceive will amount to fraud as being a deliberate suppression of the truth and equivalent to the assertion of a falsehood. The concealment of a fact which one is bound to disclose is an indirect representation that such fact does not exist, and constitutes fraud." 37 C.J.S., Fraud, § 16a, p. 244.

. . . in Perkins v. Marsh, 179 Wash. 362, 37 P. (2d) 689, 690, where the premises had been leased as a retail automobile business, the basement to be used as a storage and salesroom for used automobiles, we held that failure to reveal that the premises were never fit for the purposes for which they were leased by reason of the fact that the basement was continually wet during the rainy season, presented a case of fraudulent concealment. We there said:

> "It is true that, in the absence of a duty to speak, silence as to material fact does not of itself constitute fraud. Farmers' State Bank of Newport v. Lamon, 132 Wash. 369, 231 Pac. 952, 42 A.L.R. 1072. However, the concealment by one party to a transaction of a material fact within his own knowledge, which it is his duty to disclose, is actual fraud. If appellants intentionally concealed some fact known to them which it was material for respondents to know, that constituted a fraudulent concealment; that is, the concealment of a fact which one is bound to disclose is the equivalent of an indirect representation that such fact does not exist, and differs from a direct false statement only in the mode by which it is made."

It will thus be seen that the duty to speak does sometimes arise when the parties are dealing at arm's length. That duty arises where the facts are peculiarly within the knowledge of one person and could not be readily obtained by the other; or where, by the lack of business experience of one of the parties the other takes advantage of the situation by remaining silent. However, a party cannot be permitted to say that he was taken advantage of, if he had means of acquiring the information, or if, because of his business experience or his prior dealings with the other, he should have acquired further information before he acted.

Here, there was no fiduciary relationship. The parties were dealing at arm's length. It can be assumed that, had respondent been aware of the precarious financial condition of the corporation, he would not have advanced the money. Did appellant owe respondent the duty to speak? Respondent was an experienced businessman. He knew that, under the terms of the contract, he was not obligated to make any payments at that time. He had been put on notice of the business dealings of the corporation because it had tried to obtain the $2,500.00 payment before it started the basement. He knew that part, at least, of the advancement, was to be used for the purpose of paying general corporation bills. Under the circumstances, it was his duty to investigate further before making an advancement not required under the terms of the contract. But he was interested in getting into the house by June 1st, so he took a chance. Under all of the facts in this particular situation, there was no duty on the part of appellant to speak, and his silence did not constitute actionable fraud. . . .

The judgment is reversed.

CASE NO. 9

Tetreault v. Campbell. 115 Vt. 349, 61 Atl. (2d) 591 (1948)

JEFFORDS, J. This is an action of fraud and deceit based on alleged false and fraudulent representations leading up to the sale of the defendants' farm and personal property thereon to the plaintiffs. The case was tried by jury with a resulting verdict and judgment for the plaintiffs and it is here on exceptions of the defendants. . . .

The court charged the jury as follows:

> "There is also another claim in this case, with regard to representations by the defendants that the farm and personal property was worth $40,000. With regard to this claim, such a representation is ordinarily a matter of opinion and not deemed fraudulent, but it may be otherwise. If it is made as an assertion of fact, and with the purpose that it shall be so received, and it is so received, it may

amount to a fraud. A statement of value may be of such a character and may be so made and intended and so received as to constitute a fundamental misrepresentation. Whether this is so in this case, it is for you to say. No certain rule can be laid down for your guidance. Each case must necessarily depend upon its own facts in a large measure. The character and the reputation of the parties, their respective intelligence, the subject matter of the bargain, and all the circumstances must be considered in determining that issue, because, as we have told you before, that if an assertion of value is made as an assertion of fact, that amounts to fraud." . . .

Statements appear in many of our cases to the effect that representations as to value are ordinarily regarded as matters of opinion and so not fraudulent in a legal sense. But if they are made as assertions of facts, and with the purpose that they shall be so received, and are so received, they may amount to fraud. That whether such statements are to be taken as mere opinions or as statements of facts depends upon the circumstances of the particular case; so whether fraud was intended is usually, though not always, a question for the jury. . . .

In Belka v. Allen, 82 Vt. 456, 74 Atl. 93, the statement in question was that the "farm carried wood and timber enough to pay for it." This court held that this statement depending as it must upon estimate and judgment alone, and that predicated upon data uncertain if not conjectural, was so plainly a mere expression of opinion and recommendation that the court below committed no error in ruling that it would not support the action.

An examination of the remainder of the cases just above cited shows that in each there was some fact or circumstance from which the maker of the statement in question knew or should have known that it was not true. It was for this reason that it was held in each of these cases that it could be found that the statements were made not as mere opinions but as assertions of facts.

In the present case there are no facts or circumstances tending to show that the maker of the representation that the farm and personal property was worth $40,000 knew or should have known that this was not so. As far as it appears it was merely an expression of opinion as to the value and thus the statement comes within the general rule as to such statements as recognized and applied in Belka v. Allen, supra.

Judgment reversed and cause remanded.

CASE NO. 10

Traylor Eng. & Mfg. Co. v. National Container Corp. 70 A. (2d) 9 (Del.) (1949)

Action to recover the balance of the purchase price of a rotary kiln and auxiliary equipment sold by plaintiff to defendant. The answer sets up . . . counterclaim for damages . . . fraud in connection with procuring the contract. . . .

. . . These representations are as follows:

"(1) that plaintiff would give individual and personal engineering service and advice and would make a survey to ascertain defendant's individual requirements with reference to defendant's lime kiln problems, particularly with a view toward increasing the quantity and improving the quality of lime; (2) that the long kiln had been satisfactorily developed for use in the paper industry and that it had manufactured similar kilns for others in the paper industry which were operating satisfactorily; (3) that the long kiln was a preferable substitute for defendant's short kiln; (4) that the fuel consumption in operation of the said kiln and auxiliary equipment manufactured by plaintiff would be less than sixty-five gallons of oil per ton of lime produced; (5) that the kiln would easily produce seventy tons of high quality lime per day; (6) that the kiln would operate economically and without trouble with plaintiff's up to date temperature control; (7) that lime rings could not and would not form in the kiln; (8) that the quantity of dust from the kiln would not be noticeable; (9) that the lining in the kiln would last from three to five years; (10) that the kiln was entirely automatic and when the correct temperatures were set on the controls, the soda content of the mud and amount of mud would not affect its operation since automatic controls would take care of its operation; and (11) that defendant's savings and benefits would justify the expense of purchasing and installing the long kiln." . . .

LAYTON, J. . . . Plaintiff maintains that . . . the oral representations complained of by defendant as actionably fraudulent in character consist merely of dealer's talk, puffing or statements concerning future events for which an action for deceit will not lie. . . .

Do the oral representations alleged to have been made by plaintiff to defendant constitute actionable fraud? Vol. 37 C.J.S., Fraud, § 3, lays down a comprehensive definition of fraud:

"Comprehensively stated, the elements of actionable fraud consist of: (1) A representation. (2) Its falsity. (3) Its materiality. (4) The speaker's knowledge of its falsity or ignorance of its truth. (5) His intent that it should be acted on by the person and in the manner reasonably contemplated. (6) The hearer's ignorance of its falsity. (7) His reliance on its truth. (8) His right to rely thereon. (9) And his consequent and proximate injury. Many other statements of the elements have been made, some of which are couched in different language and most of which are less comprehensive in that they fail to mention one or more of the elements stated above."

Pennsylvania adheres generally to the principles above stated. Emery v. Third National Bank, 314 Pa. 544, 171 Atl. 881. Plaintiff contends that the representations which Defendant points to as fraud are mere puffing or expressions of opinion. A very thin line divides those statements which are, from those which are not, actionably fraudulent. I have given careful consideration to some of the cases holding that statements which are characterized as dealer's talk or puffing, statements as to future events and those promissory in nature only are not actionable. Deming v. Darling, 148 Mass. 504, 20 N.E. 107, 2 L.R.A. 743; Grove v. Economical Life Ins. Co., 80 Atl. 809; Dawe v. Morris, 149 Mass. 188, 21 N.E. 313, 4 L.R.A. 158, 14 Am. St. Rep. 404; and Nye Odorless Incinerator Corp. v. Felton, 5 W.W. Harr. 236, 162 Atl. 504. But I feel that the representations alleged to have been made here go farther than dealer's talk. Defendant had a right to rely upon Plaintiff's purported special knowledge of the construction, operation and performance of its own lime kilns. At least one representation seems to have been of an existing fact, and several others as to future performance of the kiln were known to have been false when made. In a strikingly similar case, Bareham v. McFarland & Kane, 228 App. Div. 396, 240 N.Y.S. 123, 126, the appellate division of the Supreme Court of New York upheld defendant's theory of this phase of its case in the following language:

"The first defense alleges that, in order to induce the defendant to purchase the heating plant, the plaintiff falsely and fraudulently represented to the defendant 'that said heating plant would adequately and satisfactorily heat the premises owned by defendant, . . . and would give much better heat than coal; that it would heat said building to 70° F. in zero weather; that the fuel oil required to produce adequate heat in said building would not cost more than eight to ten percent in excess of the coal required in the heater then in use upon said premises, and would, in no event, exceed $350 for the season; that the gas for the pilot light would not cost to exceed $1 a month, and that the electricity would not run over $5 to $6 a month, and that the heater would run smoothly and give entire satisfaction.' There is an allegation that the plaintiff knew that said representations were false, and that defendant relied thereon in making the purchase.

. . . . .

"While the alleged misrepresentations in the case at bar relate to what the heating plant will do when it is installed in defendant's home, it must be remembered that the heater was either in existence at the time the statements were made, or, if it had not actually been assembled and set up, was one of a specified, definite, and certain type, which had previously been manufactured and sold, and was not an article which was to be constructed in the future, the characteristics of which were largely conjectural. What was said could easily be understood to relate to the inherent capacity, character, and quality of the heater, and what it was actually capable of doing. Giving to it such interpretation, the representations were more than mere 'dealer's talk,' or a prophecy of what would occur in the future; they were positive statements of existing facts, concerning which the plaintiff had superior and peculiar knowledge. That being so, they could be made the basis of an action in fraud.

"The decisions of the courts indicate a disinclination to extend the rule which permits a dealer, in order to sell his wares, to indulge with impunity in statements of opinion, which turn out to be untrue."

It is clear from the language of the case just quoted, and from many others considered, that the statement of an opinion not in fact entertained but made to deceive, is as actionable as the misrepresentation of a past or present fact.

CASE NO. 11

McIntyre v. Lyon. 325 Mich. 167, 37 N.W. (2d) 903 (1949)

CARR, J. On or about May 17, 1941, plaintiff purchased from the defendant Lyon Screw Products, Inc., 1,000 shares of its capital stock for which he paid $1 per share. From time to time he inquired of defendants concerning the value of the stock and the progress of the company. It is his claim that in response to each such inquiry he was advised that his stock was worth $1.50 per share. On or about September 30, 1943, he sold it to the company for $1,500, endorsing the certificate and acknowledging receipt of the consideration. In December, 1944, he filed suit in equity alleging that defendants had fraudulently misrepresented the value of the stock, that at the time of the sale by him it was worth approximately $30 per share, that the representation was known to defendants to be false, that it was made for the purpose of inducing plaintiff to sell his stock, that he relied thereon and that he suffered injury in consequence.

. . . the circuit judge concluded from the evidence that the value of the stock was in fact misrepresented by defendants, and that it was worth at the time of the transaction in question approximately $6.50 per share. . . .

It is the claim of the appellants that plaintiff failed to make out a cause of action in that his proofs did not show that he relied on the alleged misrepresentation of the defendants as to value of the stock. . . .

Plaintiff's testimony indicates that he did not have confidence in the management of the defendant corporation. . . . His explanation as to what occurred at the time of the sale of the stock by him is set forth in his testimony on direct examination, in response to questions by his counsel, as follows:

"Q. Did you inquire at that time as to the business conditions of the corporation?

"A. I asked him how things were going, and he said, 'Well you can sell your stock now and get out while you can make a $500 profit on your thousand dollar investment.'

"Q. Who told you that? A. Mr. McCrory.

"Q. Did you have any further conversation with them that day? A. No. I just sold my stock, and that was all."

Interrogated further on cross-examination with reference to the matter, he testified as follows:

"Q. At the time of this sale, you say you made an inquiry of Mr. McCrory again, what the stock was worth? A. Yes, sir.

"Q. And then what did you tell him? A. I asked him if there was any way of me finding out exactly what the stock was worth, because all I could do was take their word for it. And he said it was a closed corporation and you had no right to look at any books or anything.

"Q. And how did that make you feel? A. That made me more suspicious that something was wrong.

"Q. In other words, that your stock was worth more than that? A. Yes.

"Q. And yet you sold it. A. I figured if I didn't get out at that time I would lose the stock I had.

"Q. And maybe you thought the stock was worth less than that. A. I thought it was worth more.

"Q. Yet, feeling that it was worth more, you sold it. Why? A. The way things were going I thought I would probably take a loss from it."

. . . The conclusion cannot be avoided that plaintiff did not at the time have confidence in the defendants, that he did not believe their statement as to the value of the stock, and that he made the sale for the reasons indicated by him rather than in reliance on the alleged misrepresentation. . . .

CASE NO. 12

Owen v. Schwartz. 85 App. D.C. 302, 177 F. (2d) 641, 14 A.L.R. (2d) 1337 (1949)

LEDERLE, D.J. This is an appeal from a judgment of no cause for action based upon a verdict directed in favor of defendant-appellees by the trial court at the close of the evidence presented by plaintiff-appellant. . . .

On April 22, 1947, plaintiff, Miss Thelma F. Owen, filed her complaint against defendant Max C. Schwartz, a real-estate broker, and defendants Theodore S. and Grace L. Grape, owners of real estate, who had engaged defendant Schwartz as their sales agent. Plaintiff sought return of a $5,000 forfeit-money deposit she had paid to defendant Schwartz, as the admitted agent for defendants Grape, whereby plaintiff was to purchase from defendants Grape a house known as 3351 Mt. Pleasant Street, N.W., Washington, D.C., with some adjoining land. The complaint alleged fraud in the inducement in that defendant Schwartz had made two material oral misrepresentations upon which plaintiff had relied, namely, "that the land to be conveyed was 1¼ acres . . ." alleging further that plaintiff had notified defendants of her election to rescind promptly upon learning of such fraud, but that defendants had refused to honor such election and return her $5,000. The complaint also alleged that the contract did not contain a description of the land. . . . The answer admitted that the tract contained substantially less than one acre, but denied the fraud. . . .

The record discloses that, as plaintiff learned shortly after signing the contract, the area of the land was half of the alleged 1¼ acres, being actually only ⅝ of an acre, . . .

As to the alleged representation that the tract contained 1¼ acres when in fact it contained only one half that acreage, defendants rely upon general statements appearing in a number of cases to the effect that where the means of knowledge are at hand and equally available to both parties, and the subject of purchase is alike open to their inspection, if the purchaser does not avail himself of these means and opportunities, he will not be heard to say that he has been deceived by the vendor's misrepresentations; that, if, having eyes, he will not see matters directly before them, where no concealment is made or attempted, he will not be entitled to favorable consideration when he complains that he has suffered from his own voluntary blindness and has been misled by overconfidence in the statements of another; and the same reasoning applies when the complaining party does not rely upon the misrepresentations, but seeks from other quarters means of verification of the statements made, and acts upon the information thus obtained. Such statements must be interpreted in the light of the peculiar facts and circumstances involved in the case where the pronouncements were made. Viewed in such a way, the statements do not militate against plaintiff's position on this phase of the case. Considering these cases in the order cited in defendants' brief, we find the following:

Shappirio v. Goldberg, 1904, 192 U.S. 232, 24 Sup. Ct. 259, 48 L. Ed. 419, involved a claimed misrepresentation as to the boundaries of an irregularly shaped city lot. The deed correctly described each boundary of the lot by feet and inches, and the irregular shape of which the purchaser complained was apparent on the face of the deed. Before contracting, the purchaser had given this correct description to his real-estate agent for investigation and checking. Actually, there was no showing of any reliance upon the alleged misrepresentations, as the purchaser had relied upon his own agent's investigation of the boundaries based upon a correct and complete written description. . . .

Farrar v. Churchill, 1890, 135 U.S. 609, 10 Sup. Ct. 771, 34 L. Ed. 246, involved sale of a plantation and incorrect statements in a written memorandum as to acreage cleared and acreage above the Mississippi overflow, which memorandum was given to the prospective purchaser by the vendor's sales agent upon the agent's express statement to the prospective purchaser that he had never seen the plantation, knew nothing of it or of the statements in the memorandum and that the prospective purchaser should make his own investigation. The prospective purchaser spent a whole day at the plantation, inspecting it on horseback throughout its length and breadth before signing the contract to purchase, and also, was given possession two months before receiving the deed from which he asked relief. Here, again, was a case of no reliance upon the misstatements.

Slaughter's Adm'r v. Gerson, 1872, 13 Wall 379, 20 L. Ed. 627, was a suit to collect the purchase price of a steamboat which defendant steamboat operator had purchased from plaintiff upon plaintiff's express statement that he knew nothing about steamboats and that the prospective purchaser should examine it himself and talk to its captain before signing the contract. The purchaser defended on the ground that plaintiff had misrepresented that the boat loaded drew only 3 feet of water, and that actually it drew 6 feet and had gone aground in 5 feet near one dock on the purchaser's route, which had only 3 feet of water. The judgment for the plaintiff was affirmed, and the Supreme Court pointed out that there was evidence showing that, prior to the purchase, defendant-purchaser and his son, who became captain of the boat after purchase, with two of the defendant's carpenters, made a run in the boat from Baltimore to New York, examined the boat thoroughly and measured the draft, and defendant was informed by plaintiff's captain and defendant's own men that the draft was greater than his maximum limit of 3 feet and, therefore, not fit for his purposes. Again, we have a case of no reliance upon anything said by the seller and a detailed technical examination made by the purchaser.

On page 936 of 35 L. Ed., in Farmsworth v. Duffner, 1891, 142 U.S. 43, 12 Sup. Ct. 164, 168, the Supreme Court succinctly sums up this whole case thus:

"This is the whole case presented by the record. The vendors pretended to sell only a tax-title. They specially guarded themselves against any rights of actual settlers. The validity of their title and the extent of it were matters apparent on the records, and open to the inspection of the purchaser. [The purchaser] did not act on their representations that the title was good, but brought his own counsel from home to examine those records, and acted upon his judgment of the title (and also spent two days with the county surveyor). The conduct of the defendants (vendors) supports their testimony, that they believed there was validity to their title."

Rescission at the suit of the purchaser was refused . . . there had been no reliance upon statements made by the seller.

Graziani v. Arundell, 1924, 55 App. D.C. 21, 299 Fed. 886, involves the claim of the purchaser, who had examined the premises, that the seller had represented that there were 5 rooms on the second floor of a 3-floor building.whereas there were only 3 rooms on this floor. Certainly, examining a floor where there are only 3 rooms instead of 5 is a far cry from two ladies looking at a house and adjoining land which defendant real-estate expert says contains 1¼ acres when it contains only ⅝ of acre. The true distinction was expressed thus in Starkweather v. Benjamin, 1875, 32 Mich. 305–306:

"The defense rested mainly on the ground that the purchaser saw the land, and was as able to judge its size as Starkweather. We do not think the doctrine that where both parties have equal means of judging there is no fraud, applies to such a case. The maxim is equally valid, that one who dissuades another from inquiry and deceives him to his prejudice is responsible. It cannot be generally true that persons can judge of the contents of a parcel of land by the eye. When any approach to accuracy is needed, there must be measurement. When a positive assurance of the area of a parcel of land is made by the vendor to the vendee, with the design of making the vendee believe it, that assurance is very material, and equivalent to an assurance of measurement."

Defendants then cite a number of state court cases which have adopted the so-called "Massachusetts Rule," to the effect that if the true boundaries are pointed out, misrepresentations as to area are not actionable . . . the Massachusetts courts recognize a split of authority on this subject. This court has not adopted the rigid "Massachusetts Rule." . .

. . . from the record presented here, it does not appear that the boundaries of the trace in question were pointed out to plaintiff or her sister or that they knew or could have located such boundaries. Plaintiff and her sister were rooming-house operators. They were assured by defendant Schwartz, an experienced real-estate expert, that the tract contained 1¼ acres. . . .

The judgment appealed from is reversed and the case remanded to the trial court for a new trial.

CASE NO. 13

Babb v. Bolyard. 72 A. (2d) 13 (Md.) (1950)

MARKELL, J. This is an appeal by defendant from a judgment for $900, entered on the verdict of a jury . . . in an action for deceit by the buyer against the seller of a used 1946 Buick automobile.

The purchase was negotiated and contracted for in Cumberland on January 27, 1947, and consummated the same day. The price was $3,000. . . . Plaintiff went to defendant's "used car lot" and was looking at the Buick. He says Frantz came out and asked him if he was interested in the car, he said he would like to have one, and asked Frantz the price of the car . . . then Frantz said,

> "Well, this car sells for $3,000; that is what the Buick dealer sells it for, and it is a great car";

the next day a dealer at Keyser told him that the price of a new Buick was $1,986; you could not get any new car . . . at that time; (the Cumberland Buick dealer had a waiting list a year long) . . . if he had known that the price of a new Buick of the same model was $1,986, he would not have bought this car and paid $3,000 . . .

Repeated decisions of this court have established rules and precedents which must govern the decision in the instant case.

> "It is well settled by all the authorities that the fraud must work an actual injury to the party complaining, and it must appear that he not only did in fact rely upon the fraudulent statement, but had a right to rely upon it in the full belief of its truth, for otherwise it was his own folly or fault, and he cannot ask of the law to relieve him from the consequences." Reynolds v. Evans, 123 Md. 365, 367, 91 Atl. 563, 564.

It is generally held that a representation as to value is only an expression of opinion, not a statement of fact. . . .

In any event, he had not "the right, as a person of ordinary business prudence," to rely upon the alleged misrepresentation of the dealer's price of new Buicks. If new cars had been obtainable, used cars would not have brought a premium, and the market price of new cars might have been a material fact in the purchase of a used car. Whether even then a purchaser would have had a right to rely on a representation as to the dealer's price of new cars, instead of finding out by going or telephoning to a dealer, we need not decide. In the circumstances we think the price of new Buick "futures" was not material to an immediate purchase of a used Buick. In a free market a misrepresentation of the market price of a new Rolls-Royce or a horse and buggy would hardly be material in a purchase of a used Buick. If a person bought Pennsylvania Railroad shares on a misrepresentation of the latest price on the New York Stock Exchange, the fact represented would be material, but we are not prepared to say the purchaser would have the right to rely on the representation instead of picking up a daily newspaper and ascertaining the truth. A housewife who brought a bag of flour from a grocer could not maintain an action for deceit in a misrepresentation of the Chicago price of grain "futures."

Defendant's request for a directed verdict and his motion for judgment *n.o.v.* should have been granted.

Judgment reversed with costs.

CASE NO. 14

Henning v. Kyle. 190 Va. 247, 56 S.E. (2d) 67 (1949)

MILLER, J. Betty K. Kyle and Z. T. Kyle, plaintiffs below and here so designated, instituted this action against Ruth S. Henning, who will be hereinafter referred to as defendant. They claimed damages for alleged breach of contract because of defendant's refusal to pay for certain real estate that she had agreed to purchase from them. . . .

The defense asserted to the action was that plaintiffs and their agent had induced defendant to sign the contract of purchase by fraudulent representation of material facts. . . .

Where parties deal at arm's length, the statement of matters of opinion by the owner or his agent, though found by the jury to be untrue, not being representations of factual matter which are material, seldom justifies avoidance of the contract for the purchase of real estate. Especially is this true when the purchaser is then availing or has availed himself of an independent investigation and inspection of the property.

In justification of her refusal to pay the purchase price and in substantiation of her claim that plaintiffs and their agent induced her to sign the contract by false representation of material facts which she believed to be true, defendant, on this the second trial, said:

> "They said it was a substantial, well-built house and had been built by the contractor for his own use and it was easy to heat and that I wouldn't have to worry about a thing, all I would have to do was move in, that it was in good repair in every way. . . .
>
> "They told me it was in excellent condition and it was a substantial, well-built house and all I had to do was move in, wouldn't have to worry about anything, that it was easy to heat and the plumbing was in good condition."

These are all the representations of alleged material facts offered in evidence by defendant. To establish their untruth, she testified that she had to "make repairs on the oil burner and plumbing," that "the oil burner had worn out and needed a new generator" though it had been stated to be in fine running condition, and that "the plumbing was worn around the joints and the sinks were stopped up." The extent or character of these ordinary defects often existing in a house several years old, as this was shown to be, is not given, nor is the cost to remedy them stated. . . .

On motion of plaintiffs the defendant testimony was stricken out and this evidence rejected. The court evidently concluded that the statements testified to by defendant as having been made to her by plaintiffs and their agent and which she claimed induced her to buy were not representations of material fact but mere "puffing" or permissible "dealers' talk." . . .

Upon the authorities heretofore cited in this opinion, and the reasons given, we conclude that under the circumstances of this case the statements testified to by defendant on the second trial which were made to her by the agent and by the owners of the premises were expressions of opinion rather than false representations of material facts which would avoid the sale, and hence the judgment of the lower court is affirmed.

Affirmed.

CASE NO. 15

Franco v. De Voursney. 2 N.J. Sup. 359, 63 A. (2d) 900 (1949)

FREUND, J. This action is brought by plaintiffs to rescind the sale of a lakeside bungalow, because of the misrepresentation by defendant vendors that ownership of the property carried with it lake privileges, domestic water supply and the right to membership in a community club which owns the lake and water facilities.

No formal contract of sale was entered into, but early in June, 1946, the plaintiffs made a down payment. Several days later, the balance of the purchase price was paid and a deed delivered to the plaintiffs, who took possession of the property on June 29, 1946. On July 7, 1946, the plaintiffs were told by the club officers that they would have to apply for membership in the club. That same day they filed their application and the following day the club notified them by letter that their application had been rejected and accordingly lake and club privileges would be denied to them.

Plaintiffs testified that they promptly advised defendants of these developments and demanded the return of the purchase price and that defendants promised to take back the property. After remonstrating unsuccessfully with the club officers in an attempt to have plaintiffs accepted as members, defendants, on July 21st and again on July 28th, refused plaintiffs' demand to take back the property. Early in August, the domestic water supply was shut off, so that plaintiffs had no water and neither lake or club privileges. However, the complaint in this proceeding was not filed until March 5, 1948, over a year and a half after the discovery of the alleged fraud.

. . . the plaintiffs, having discovered the fraud and having been refused the return of the purchase price, delayed instituting a suit for over a year and a half—a period of time which all the cases hold to be a bar to rescission. Where fraud has been committed and the fraud discovered, the failure to take advantage of available remedies with diligence and promptitude is generally regarded as an acquiescence and a bar to any equitable relief. Dennis v. Jones, Err. & App. 1888, 44 N.J. Eq. 513, 14 Atl. 913, 6 Am. St. Rep. 899. Furthermore, the plaintiffs continued to occupy the property at least for occasional weekends during 1946, 1947 and 1948. Under such circumstances, the failure to institute suit and the occupancy of the premises after the discovery of the fraud

"afforded plenary proof of an election . . . not to rescind, to which conclusive effect should have been given."

Faulkner v. Wassmer, Err. & App. 1910, 77 N.J. Eq. 537, 77 Atl. 341, 343, 30 L.R.A., N.S., 872, where a delay of four months was held a bar. . . .

In Kazepis v. North Jersey Holding Co., Err. & App. 1932, 111 N.J. Eq. 342, 162 Atl. 595, 596, the facts were somewhat similar to those in the instant case, in that the plaintiffs placed the matter in the hands of an attorney who demanded rescission, but suit was not brought until a year after the discovery of the fraud. The court held

"This is fatal to the right or remedy of rescission. The defrauded party to a contract has but one election to rescind, which he must exercise with reasonable promptitude after the discovery of the fraud, and, when he once elects, he must abide by his decision. . . ."

CASE NO. 16

Williams v. Green. 23 Fed. (2d) 796 (1928)

HAYES, D.J. On December 30, 1922, the Commercial National Bank of Wilmington, N.C., was closed by reason of its insolvency and C. L. Williams was appointed receiver, agreeably to the statutes relating to national banks. In this capacity he brought an action against T. A. Green to recover on a promissory note of $4,000 held by the bank. The defendant admitted the execution of the note, but alleged that on May 26, 1922, through the false and fraudulent representations of T. E. Cooper, a director, and C. E. Bethea, a director and active vice president, of the bank, he had been induced to purchase $5,000 par value of the capital stock of the bank from W. B. Cooper, president and a large stockholder of the bank, and a brother of T. E. Cooper; . . . that the bank took the note from Cooper with knowledge of the fraud; . . .

There is evidence to show that T. E. Cooper was a director and a stockholder, and that C. E. Bethea was an active vice president in charge of the bank and a director and stockholder; that W. B. Cooper owned about $40,000 of the stock, and was president of the bank; that T. E. Cooper, Bethea, and other stockholders and officers of the bank thought W. B. Cooper was injuring the bank, and that they solicited the defendant and asked him to buy $5,000 worth of W. B. Cooper's stock, and represented to him that the stock was worth $112 to $116 a share, and supplied him a financial statement of the bank, representing that the value of the stock was $112 or $116, and that its assets and bills receivable compared favorably with any bank in North Carolina; that these representations were made on May 26, 1922, and the bank was closed by the Comptroller of the Currency as insolvent, on December 30, 1922; that an examination of its assets revealed a large amount of worthless notes, and on which the interest had not been paid, which notes had been due for many years; that an assessment of 100 cents on the dollar was levied against the stockholders; that at the time of the trial on February 28, 1927, the receiver had been able to pay only 15 per cent. dividend to its creditors, and that the stock was worth nothing on May 26, 1922; that T. E. Cooper and C. E. Bethea knew the bank was insolvent, or made the representations that it was solvent for a fact without knowing it to be true; that Green relied upon the representations, and was induced to execute the note and to pay his $1,000 by reason thereof. . . .

While it is true that Mr. Bethea claimed that he did not know of the bank's insolvency, still he had access to its books, and particularly its bills receivable, from which he should have discovered its insolvent condition. He prepared a statement and submitted the same to Mr. Green, which represented the stock to be worth from $112 to $116 per share, when, as a fact, it was worth nothing. We think the evidence was sufficient to take the case to the jury on the theory either that Bethea, having access to the records of the bank, knew the representation as to the value of the stock to be false, or that, knowing and intending that they would be relied upon by Green, he made them with reckless disregard of truth.

It is not necessary that actual knowledge of the falsity of the representations should be known to the party making them.

"Whether the party, thus misrepresenting a fact, knew it to be false, or made the assertion without knowing whether it were true or false, is wholly immaterial; for the affirmation of what one does not know, or believe to be true, is equally, in morals and law, as unjustifiable as the affirmation of what is known to be positively false. And even if the party innocently misrepresents a fact, by mistake, it is equally conclusive; for it operates as a surprise and imposition on the other party. Or, as Lord Thurlow expresses it, in Neville v. Wilkinson, 'it misleads the parties contracting, on the subject of the contract.'" Smith v. Richards, 13 Pet. 26, 10 L. Ed. 42.

"A person who makes representations of material facts, assuming or intending to convey the impression that he has actual knowledge of the existence of such facts, when he is conscious that he has no such knowledge, is as much responsible for the injurious consequences of such representations, to one who believes and acts upon them, as if he had actual knowledge of their falsity." Lehigh Zinc, etc., Co. v. Bamford, 150 U.S. 665, 673, 14 Sup. Ct. 219, 221 (37 L. Ed. 1215). . . .

After a careful examination of the record, we find no reversible error in the trial below.

Affirmed.

CASE NO. 17

Steinmeyer et al. v. Schroeppel. 226 Ill. 9, 80 N.E. 564, 10 L.R.A. (N.S.) 114 (1907)

CARTWRIGHT, J., delivered the opinion of the court:

. . . On June 10, 1905, appellee was about to erect a building for himself, and left at the office of appellants an itemized list of lumber, containing thirty-four items, on which he desired them to give him a price. Appellants' bookkeeper set down upon that list, opposite each item, the selling price, but did not add up the column. If correctly added the column would have footed up $1867. One of the appellants made the addition and by mistake made the total $1446.

. . . Appellants did not furnish the lumber, and appellee purchased it at the next lowest bid from another firm and sued appellants for the difference between what he paid for the lumber and what they had agreed to furnish it for. . . .

The jurisdiction of equity to grant the remedy of cancellation because of a mistake of fact by one party to a contract is well recognized. Mutual consent is requisite to the creation of a contract, and if there is a mistake of fact by one of the parties going to the essence of the contract, no agreement is, in fact, made. If there is apparently a valid contract in writing, but by reason of a mistake of fact by one of the parties, not due to his negligence, the contract is different with respect to the subject matter or terms from what was intended, equity will give to such party a remedy by cancellation where the parties can be placed *in statu quo*. The ground for relief is, that by reason of the mistake there was no mutual assent to the terms of the contract. The fact concerning which the mistake was made must be material to the transaction and affect its substance, and the mistake must not result from want of the care and diligence exercised by persons of reasonable prudence under the same circumstances. In this case the mistake was in the addition of the figures set down by the bookkeeper. The price of each item was written correctly, but appellants claimed that one item of about $400 was placed somewhat to the right, and in adding the column the 4 was counted in the ten-column instead of the hundred-column. If that was done it does not account for the difference of $421. But if it did, it would only show a want of ordinary care and attention. If the figures were not exactly in line, the fact could hardly escape notice by a competent businessman giving reasonable attention to what he was doing. There was no evidence tending to prove any special circumstances excusing the blunder. . . .

A mistake which will justify relief in equity must affect the substance of the contract, and not a mere incident or the inducement for entering into it. The mistake of the appellants did not relate to the subject matter of the contract, its location, identity or amount, and there was neither belief in the existence of a fact which did not exist or ignorance of any fact material to the contract which did exist. The contract was exactly what each party understood it to be and it expressed what was intended by each. If it can be set aside on account of the error in adding up the amounts representing the selling price, it could be set aside for a mistake in computing the percentage of profits which appellants intended to make, or on account of a mistake in the cost of the lumber to them, or any other miscalculation on their part. If equity would relieve on account of such a mistake there would be no stability in contracts, and we think the appellate Court was right in concluding that the mistake was not of such character as to entitle appellants to the relief prayed.

The judgment of the Appellate Court is affirmed.

CASE NO. 18

Cunningham Mfg. Co. v. Rotograph Co. 30 App. D.C. 524, 15 L.R.A. (N.S.) 368 (1908)

VAN ORSDEL, J. . . . It appears that, on March 7, 1906, the appellee . . . sent a letter to the appellant . . . inclosing a sample of a new card it was publishing of various Washington views. The letter stated that the regular price of the cards was $15 per thousand, but it was making a price to jobbers of $1 per thousand. The evidence produced by appellee shows that this letter was copied on a typewriter by a stenographer from a circular letter, and through some mistake, the price was inserted at $1 per thousand, when $10 per thousand was the price quoted in the circular letter and the price intended to be quoted to appellant. To this letter appellant replied as follows:

> "In answer to your letter of the 7th inst., will say, your sample card sent us is very good and owing to the price you quote us the stock must be faulty in some way or your stenographer made a mistake in the price. If the stock is good and price is correct as quoted us, will take several thousand."

The general sales manager of the appellee company . . . testified that on receipt of this letter he looked up the copy of the circular letter from which the letter sent to appellant had been copied (no copy of the letter sent having been retained), and replied by letter to the effect that the cards were first class in every respect, but they were being sold at cost, and they would guarantee them in every respect. On receipt of this letter, appellant wrote a letter ordering 25,000 cards as per samples at price quoted in appellee's original letter, giving the date. The price of $1 per thousand, however, was not mentioned in this letter. Appellee, not having the full number in the subjects ordered, shipped to appellant by freight 22,585 cards. . . . That he sent bill to defendant by mail same afternoon that goods were shipped. The bill is as follows:

"New York, March 20, 1906
"Cunningham Mfg. Co.,
Washington, D.C.,
to The Rotograph Co., Dr.
22585 Style S. at $10 . . . . . . $225.85"

. . . Appellant immediately wrote plaintiff the following letter, calling its attention to the discrepancy between the bill and the price quoted:

"We have just received your bill for postal cards and return it for correction. The price of these cards is $1 instead of $10 as you bill them. We refer you to your letter of the 7th inst., when you sent us sample and price."

The receipt of plaintiff's letter of March 22, 1906, contained the first intimation he had as to the alleged mistake. The letter reads as follows:

"Gentlemen:—In reply to your valued favor, we beg to inform you that there is evidently an error some place. The price of the cards as quoted you was ten dollars ($10) per thousand. and not $1. The duty alone on these cards costs us $2.25 per thousand, and you can readily understand that it would be impossible for us to sell same at any such price as $1 per thousand. If the price we give you is not satisfactory at $10 per thousand, we would request that you send us the cards immediately as we have orders that will take up all the stock. Kindly return us the letter in which you state that you are quoted $1 per thousand."

In reply to a question by the court, witness said that the reason he did not return the goods after receipt of plaintiff's letter was because he had in good faith made a contract with plaintiff to deliver the cards at $1 per thousand, and had received the goods, and he did not desire to cancel it.

. . . It is evident that there was not such a meeting of the minds of the parties in fixing the consideration as would constitute a contract. Before there can be a contract, the minds of the parties must meet honestly and fairly, without mistake or mutual misunderstanding, upon all the essential points involved in the transaction composing the contract. If one of the parties, through mistake, names a consideration that is out of all proportion to the value of the subject of negotiation, and the other party, realizing that a mistake must have been committed, takes advantage of it and refuses to let the mistake be corrected when it is discovered, he cannot, under these conditions, claim an enforceable contract. The law is that, where there is a mistake that amounts to a mutual misunderstanding, or that on its face is so palpable as to place a person of reasonable intelligence upon his guard, there is not a meeting of the minds of the parties, and, consequently, there can be no contract. . . .

Appellant company, by its refusal to return the goods when the mistake was discovered and its election to retain them, will be deemed to have accepted the goods at the price for which they were billed, thereby creating a new and enforceable contract, for which it must be held liable.

CASE NO. 19

Graham v. Atchison, T. & S.F. Ry. Co.
176 Fed. (2d) 819 (1949)

YANKWICH, D.J. The appellant, George H. Graham, the plaintiff below, a brakeman in the employ of the appellee, the defendant below, began, on August 30, 1946, an action for damages for personal injuries under the Federal Employers' Liability Act. . . .

The plaintiff was injured on July 6, 1945, at Needles, California. . . . While in the hospital, he talked, on August 18, to Dr. Morrison, Chief Surgeon of the hospital, who told him to go back to work. The plaintiff gave this version of his conversation with Dr. Morrison:

"Q. And what did he tell you? A. Well, he told me to go back to work if I possibly could, that the company was very short of men and that they needed to keep the trains operating—the war was still on, and to go back and take it easy, that I would be all right in thirty or sixty days. . . ."

The facts relating to the release, signed by the plaintiff, as they were told by him from the stand were these:

Mr. Sims, Assistant Claims Adjuster in Los Angeles, called on him while he was at the hospital. . . . Nothing definite came of the meeting. About September 25, he saw a Mr. Evan Lewis, Claim Adjuster, who, at first, offered him $1,200 or $1,300 in settlement of the claim, stating, however, that "the Los Angeles office" would not accept it. He finally went to the Los Angeles claims office and signed a release on October 1, 1945, receiving at the same time, a check for $1,050. The release reads:

"For the sole and only consideration of $1,050, the receipt of which is hereby acknowledged, I hereby release and forever discharge the Atchison, Topeka & Santa Fe Railroad Company, Coast Lines, its agents and employees from any and all claims and demands which I have now or may hereafter have on account of any or all injuries, including any injuries which may hereafter develop as well as those now apparent, sustained by me at or near Needles, California, on or about July 6, 1945, while employed as brakeman. . . ."

. . . On February 13, 1946, an X-ray of the spine was taken by Dr. Fenlon, who then advised the plaintiff that he had an injury to his spine. Medical testimony at the trial was to the effect that these X-rays showed the identical crushed disc disclosed by X-rays taken at the hospital in August, 1945.

. . . The defendant moved for a directed verdict, . . . upon the general ground that there was no evidence before the court to impugn the validity of the release. . . .

. . . the court directed the jury to return a verdict in favor of the defendant. . . .

What may be the result if the patient acts upon the physician's statement was summed up by the court in Matthews v. Atchison, T. & S.F. Ry. Co., supra, 54 Cal. App. (2d), at p. 558, 129 P. (2d) at p. 441:

"It was believed by plaintiff, and if it was also believed by the physician, the case is one of mutual mistake. If the statement was not believed by the physician, we have a case of fraud. In either case the plaintiff was entitled to rescind, and it is not disputed here that the steps he took were sufficient to accomplish that result." . . .

It is clear from the testimony that the X-rays taken at the hospital in August, 1945, showed the crushed disc. The plaintiff was not informed of that fact; he did not learn of it until February 13, 1946. . . .

In the present state of the record, we cannot say whether Dr. Morrison's failure to disclose the true condition was willful or whether he did not read the X-rays correctly. In the last analysis, however, the matter is unimportant. For, if the doctor was mistaken, as was the plaintiff, as to the existence of a permanent injury, we have a case of mutual mistake. If the mistake was only on the part of plaintiff, but was induced by the carelessness of Dr. Morrison, there was the type of mistake for which the cases . . . grant relief. See especially Great Northern R. Co. v. Fowler, 136 Fed. 118; Great Northern R. Co. v. Reid, 245 Fed. 86. If there was willfulness in the failure to disclose, we have a case of fraud. In any of the three situations, the broad terms of the release (*"including any injuries which may hereafter develop"*) did not stand in the way of rescission. . . .

The trial court having erred in granting the motion for a directed verdict, the judgment on the verdict in favor of the defendant is reversed and a new trial is ordered.

CASE NO. 20

American Natl. Bank v. West. 307 Ky. 831, 212 S.W. (2d) 314 (1948)

FELTS, J. The American National Bank, administrator of Mrs. Vera L. Cryer, deceased, sold her personal effects at auction. At this sale Mrs. Karen M. West bought among other things a box of deceased's old clothes for $9.50. She later found in a pocket of a bathrobe in this box two of deceased's rings—a cameo of small value and a diamond of the value of $2,500. . . .

On learning of their discovery the administrator demanded them as property of the estate. Mrs. West refused to surrender them. The administrator filed a bill of replevin to recover them. In her answer Mrs. West claimed they had passed to her under the sale as part of the contents of the box of clothes. . . .

The Chancellor submitted to the jury only one issue:

> "Was it or not the intention of the parties and one of the terms of sale of the box to Mrs. West, which box contained the rings in question, that the purchaser got title to all its contents, including said rings?"

The jury were unable to agree and complainant moved the Chancellor to withdraw the issue and to enter a decree for complainant because the evidence raised no question of fact or issue for the jury. The Chancellor granted this motion, held there was no evidence of any intention of the parties the one to sell and the other to buy these rings, and entered a decree awarding recovery of them to complainant. . . .

In conducting the sale the auctioneer offered each article or box separately, and when it was sold his clerk made a record of the number, the price, a brief description of the thing sold, and the name of the purchaser. The auction lasted three days, and Mrs. West attended and made a number of different purchases. She saw this box of clothing the day before it was offered for sale. It was a pasteboard box containing items of deceased's personal clothing and nothing else except the rings which, unknown to everyone, had been secreted by deceased in the bathrobe pocket. The top of this box was open and a dress or coat was exposed to view. While Mrs. West said she did not look into this box, she did state that prospective bidders looked into the boxes that were open "if they wanted to."

If these rings could have been found before the sale, the auctioneer would have sold them separately as he did other items of jewelry of deceased. . . .

A sale must rest on mutual consent of the parties as to all its terms, *including the identity of the thing sold.* Where there is no consensus ad idem there can be no sale. So it is generally held that valuables secreted by a decedent in articles of personal property do not pass by the personal representative's sale of such articles, but upon discovery are held by the purchaser as the property of the decedent's estate. Huthmacher v. Harris, 38 Pa. 491, 80 Am. Dec. 502; Evans v. Barnett, 6 Pennewill [Del.] 44, 63 Atl. 770; Bowen v. Sullivan, 62 Ind. 281, 30 Am. Rep. 172; Durfee v. Jones, 11 R.I. 588, 23 Am. Rep. 528; Livermore v. White, 74 Me. 452, 43 Am. Rep. 600; 46 Am. Jur., Sales, § 147, p. 325; Benjamin on Sales, 6th ed. 78; 1 Mechem on Sales, § 273, p. 256. . . .

To take the case out of this general rule, appellant relies on what she testified the auctioneer announced as the terms on which the sales would be made. . . .

She testified that he announced that

"everything was to be sold and what you bought, there was no comeback on that, you were guaranteed nothing, of the contents or anything, except the title, after you buy it, it is yours";

that

"it was an understood fact, that you would buy whatever was there and the title was yours, anything was yours, whatever you bought belonged to you";

that

"whatever you bought in the box (referring to no box in particular but generally to all of them) it was yours." . . .

Giving this testimony its utmost effect, we think it did not constitute any evidence that the parties understood, contemplated, or intended that these rings of the value of $2,500 should pass by the sale of this box of comparatively valueless old clothes, which sold for $9.50. These terms of sale did not apply at all until a sale had actually been made. They did not impose on the parties a contract they never intended to make; they were merely to strengthen the contract which the parties did intend to make; not to entrap them into one which they had no idea of making.

Appellant relies on Crespin v. Puncheon, 7 V.L.R. 203 (Australia, 1881). . . . That was an auction sale of salvage from a shipwreck. Plaintiff purchased four bales which the catalogue described as "newspaper." But with this description the catalogue also stated:

"If any error is made in describing the quality of any of the lots it shall not vitiate the sale but the purchaser shall be bound to take the article sold with all its faults as it lies here, packages full or empty, contents not known or guaranteed."

It turned out that these four bales contained not newspaper but calico, which was much more valuable. The seller refused to deliver the bales and the buyer sued for damages for nondelivery. The court held that the effect of the above quoted condition was that the parties contracted to sell and buy a "chance" and to run the risk of whatever might be the contents of the packages.

Clearly that case is no precedent for a decision of this case, since the facts are wholly different. There the parties were uncertain of the contents and specially contracted to cover such uncertainty or risk. Here there was no uncertainty in the minds of the parties as to the contents of this box of clothes. The auctioneer had put the clothes in the box, left it open for inspection, and stated it contained clothes. Appellant understood this. But that these valuable rings were hidden in the bathrobe pocket was a thing of which neither party had any idea and a thing about which both were mistaken. This mistake prevented any meeting of the minds and any contract or sale of the rings. . . .

The decree of the Chancellor is in all things affirmed. The costs of the appeal are adjudged against appellant and the surety on her appeal bond. . . .

CASE NO. 21

John P. Costello v. Alice G. Sykes. 143 Minn. 109 (1919)

LEES, C. Appeal from order sustaining a demurrer to the complaint on the ground that it failed to state a cause of action. In substance the material allegations are as follows:

The Calhoun State Bank was a Minnesota banking corporation, having, according to its books, a paid-in capital of $35,000, a surplus of $5,250, and undivided profits of $6,000. Respondents were stockholders. The par value of a share of stock was $100. If the bank's capital was unimpaired, and it had the surplus and undivided profits shown by its books, a share of stock was worth at least $136. Respondents sold ten shares of stock to appellant for $1,360. At the time of the sale the parties to the transaction believed that the bank's capital had not been impaired, that its assets and liabilities were as set forth in its books, that it had the surplus and profits referred to, that its books were kept correctly, and that the book value of its stock was not less than $136 per share. In fact, it had neither surplus nor undivided profits. Its employees had kept its books so as to conceal defalcations of which they were guilty, and its stock was worth but $60 per share. Such employees are insolvent, and there is no way of making good their defalcations. The parties to the sale were mutually mistaken as to the assets of the bank, the actual value and the book value of its stock, and the amount of its surplus and undivided profits. Upon discovering the truth, appellant tendered the stock to respondents and demanded repayment of the purchase price, and, his demand being refused, sues for a rescission of the contract of sale.

The sole question presented is whether the mistake alleged is of such a character as to give rise to a right to rescind.

The subject-matter of the contract of sale was ten shares of the capital stock of the bank. *There was no mistake as to its identity or existence.* A mistake relating merely to the attributes, quality, or value of the subject of a sale does not warrant a rescission. Neither does a mistake respecting something which was a matter of inducement to the making of the contract, where the means of information were open alike to both parties, and each was equally innocent, and there was no concealment of facts and no imposition. A leading case is Kennedy v. Panama, N. Z. & A. Royal Mail Co., L.R. 2 Q.B. 580. Like the one at bar, it involved a contract for the sale of corporate stock. The corporation owned and operated a line of steamships. Both parties bona fide believed that it had obtained a valuable contract to carry government mails, but it turned out that the contract was made without authority. The government refused to ratify it, and so the value of the stock was much less than the parties supposed.

It was contended, as it is here, that there was a difference in substance between shares in a company with and shares in a company without such a contract, that this was a difference which went to the very root of the matter involved, and that, therefore, the purchaser was entitled to rescind. The contention did not meet with the court's approval, and it was held that the case was one of innocent misapprehension, that a rescission could not be had, and that there was not such a complete difference in substance between what was supposed to be and what was taken as would constitute a failure of consideration. The purchaser got the very shares he intended to buy and they were far from being of no value. Such are the facts in the case at bar, for appellant got the shares he intended to buy and they were far from being of no value. His complaint is that they are worth but $60, instead of $136, each. The Kennedy Case has been widely and approvingly cited by courts of last resort in this country. . . .

In Chapman v. Cole, 12 Gray (Mass.) 141, plaintiff gave defendant a gold piece, believing it was 50 cents, and was allowed to recover it back on the ground, as stated by the court, that there was a mistake as to the identity of the subject matter of the transaction.

If the question were one of first impression, we should not be inclined to open up a new field for litigation by adopting the rule that a contract for the sale of corporate stock may be rescinded merely because both parties were mistaken about the nature or extent of the assets or liabilities of the corporation, if the means of information are open alike to both and there is no concealment of facts or imposition. Upon the sale of a note both parties may be mistaken as to the solvency of the maker, or of an indorser or guarantor of payment, and may deal on the assumption that the paper is good when in fact the unknown insolvency of the parties liable for its payment makes it worthless.

In the absence of fraud or inequitable conduct on the part of the seller of property of that kind, we had supposed the buyer could not have a rescission. He can always protect himself against possible loss by requiring the seller to guarantee or secure the payment of the paper. See Day v. Kinney, 131 Mass. 37; Burgess v. Chapin, 5 R.I. 225.

We think this should be the rule when stock in a corporation is the subject of a contract of sale, and conclude that the learned trial judge correctly disposed of the case, and the order sustaining the demurrer is affirmed.

CASE NO. 22

Enequist v. Bemis. 115 Vt. 209, 55 A. (2d) 617, 56 A. (2d) 5, 1 A.L.R. (2d) 1 (1947)

MOULTON, CH.J. On February 26, 1938, the parties to this action entered into a written contract whereby the defendants agreed to sell and convey to the plaintiff, and the plaintiff agreed to purchase, certain real estate,

> "described approximately as follows: Two hundred and seventy-five (275) acres located in the town of Westminster, Vermont, known as the farm of Ernest E. Bemis and more fully described in the deed of said premises."

. . . The contract price was $4,200 of which $420 was paid by the plaintiff to the defendants at the time of signing the contract, as that instrument provided that it should be, and the balance was due at the time set therein for the delivery of the deed, and the possession of the premises, April 30, 1938, at 11 A.M.

The contract further provided as follows:

> "It is understood and agreed that the property herein described has been inspected by the Buyer or the Buyer's duly authorized agent; that the same is and has been purchased by the said Buyer solely as a result of said inspection."

The transaction was not consummated and the plaintiff has brought this action to recover the sum of $420 which has not been repaid to her by the defendants, together with interest thereon. . . . The plaintiff filed . . . an additional count to the declaration, which contains allegations that the contract for sale was entered into between the parties; that before April 30, 1938, it became apparent that the defendants were unable to convey 275 acres of land; that she rescinded the contract and demanded the return of the $420 down payment, which was refused. That thereafter the defendants conveyed the property to third persons, thus making it impossible for them to carry out the contract.

The cause was tried by jury and resulted in a directed verdict for the defendants. . . .

The plaintiff here and below has taken the position that the parties labored under a mutual mistake in estimating the acreage of the farm, and that therefore there was no meeting of their minds upon the subject matter, and no contract existed, which gave the plaintiff the right to the return of the money that she had paid. . . .

The defendants maintain that the contract was for the sale of the specified tract of land, that is, for a sale in gross and not by the acre; that the statement of the approximate acreage was mere matter of description; that the plaintiff, or her authorized agent, had inspected the property before execution of the contract; and that she contracted in reliance upon the information thus obtained regarding its contents.

Where a contract has been entered into under a mutual mistake of the parties regarding a material fact affecting the subject matter thereof, it may be avoided in a court of law at the instance of the injured party, and an action lies to recover money paid under it. . . . The mistake must be one vitally affecting a fact or facts on the basis of which the parties have contracted; and where they have mutually assumed a certain state of facts to exist and contracted on the faith of that assumption, relief from the bargain should be given if the assumption is erroneous. 5 Williston, Contract (Rev. Ed.) par. 1544, p. 4334. Restatement, Restitution, par. 9 (3), par. 16, comment c. But in the absence of a mistake of this nature, . . .

> "one of the parties can no more rescind the contract without the other's express or implied assent, than he alone could have made it." Fay v. Oliver, 20 Vt. 118, 122, 49 Am. Dec. 764.

It is clear that this contract was for a sale in gross. The phrases "described approximately as," in the agreement, and "more or less" in the deed from the defendants to the McDougals, referring to the acreage in each instance, are the same in meaning. They are words of safety and precaution, intended to cover some slight and unimportant inaccuracy and, where the property is described by metes and bounds, and the identity of the tract is in issue, are regarded as a mere matter of description, since the boundaries control the quantity actually conveyed. . . .

But it has been held in numerous decisions that where the disparity between the estimated and the actual quantity of land is palpable and unreasonable, and the contract for sale, or the deed, was the result of a mutual mistake as to this fact, the injured party is entitled to relief.

In Darling v. Osborn, 51 Vt. 148, on foreclosure proceedings the defendant sought a reduction of the amount due on his note secured by a purchase-money mortgage, on the ground of a mutual mistake as to the acreage of the real estate. The property consisted of two lots, described by number in the deed, "supposed to contain 100 acres each, more or less." It appeared that one of the lots contained slightly over 60 acres, and the other 53 acres, and that the statement as to quantity was due to the mutual mistake of both parties to the deed and was relied upon by the defendant. In granting the desired relief the court said (quoting with approval from Couse v. Boyles, 4 N.J. Eq. 212, 3 H. W. Green 212, 216, 38 Am. Dec. 514):

> "When land is sold as containing so many acres, more or less, if the quantity, on an actual survey or estimation, either overrunning or falling short of the contents named be small, no compensation should be recovered by either party. But if the variance is considerable, the party sustaining the loss should be allowed for it; and this rule should prevail when it arises from mistake only, without fraud or deception."

. . . It has many times been held that under such circumstances a court of equity will grant rescission of the instrument upon application of the injured party to the contract. . . .

If it is shown that the hazard or gain or loss, whatever it may be, was accepted by the parties and entered into the contract, relief will be refused. . . . But where the contract is for the payment of a gross sum for a tract of land upon the estimate of a given quantity with the phrase "more or less" or its equivalent, the presumption is that the contract is not one of hazard. . . . The vendee does not ipso facto take all risk of quantity so as to preclude the claim of a mistake, where the difference between the estimate and the actual acreage is unreasonable. . . .

The equitable principle of the decisions above mentioned applies in the present case. The plaintiff agreed to purchase a designated parcel of land, containing, with allowance for slight and unimportant inaccuracies, 275 acres. By their deed to the McDougals, the defendants conveyed all and the same land as containing 200 acres, with the same allowance. The latter description was an admission by them that the farm consisted of only about that quantity. . . . There was, therefore, evidence upon which the jury could find that there was an unreasonable difference in acreage between the quantity stated in the contract for sale and the amount actually embraced within the limits of the property, and that this discrepancy was material and such as to go the essence of the contract. . . . In the absence of any showing of special facts and circumstances the natural inference is that in a sale of agricultural land the element of quantity enters into the transaction and affects the consideration agreed to be paid. . . .

We are of opinion, therefore, that the issues of mutual mistake and reliance thereon should have been submitted to the jury, and that there was error in the direction of the verdict. . . .

Judgment reversed and cause remanded. . . .

CASE NO. 23

Meylink v. Minnehaha Co-op. Oil Co.
283 N.W. 161 (South Dakota) (1938)

SMITH, J. . . . Plaintiff alleged that defendant had coerced him into paying defendant the sum of one thousand dollars by threatening to prosecute plaintiff's son for embezzlement. The issues made up by these allegations and defendant's denials were submitted to a jury. The verdict was for plaintiff. Thereafter the court entered judgment for defendant notwithstanding the verdict, upon grounds which had been urged by defendant in a motion for a directed verdict made at the conclusion of the testimony. . . .

Plaintiff testified that he would not have caused the payment to have been made had it not been for the threats.

Although plaintiff made repeated efforts to induce defendant to make repayment for the reason that the son was not actually short in his accounts, this action was not started until December, 1936. . . .

That settlements or contracts made under the coercive influence of threats of arrest and imprisonment will be set aside, is the established law of this and other jurisdictions. . . It logically follows that a payment procured from a parent by threatening arrest and imprisonment of his child may be recovered if the fear induced by such threats did in fact operate as the coercive cause of the payment by overcoming the will and free agency of the parent. . . .

The burden of respondent's argument here deals with the third ground of its motion. We are told that the circumstances, including the lapse of time and the opportunity for reflection and consultation, as disclosed by plaintiff's evidence, established as a matter of law that the payment was voluntary. That this contention is supported by respected authority we must admit. . . . That the circumstances of a particular case, including an extreme lapse of time between threat and action, might be such as to render it entirely reasonable for a court to determine as a matter of law that the questioned act was the result of a judgment formed by a free and uncontrolled mind, must also be conceded. However, a rule which denies all possibility of coercion whenever there has been time for consultation and reflection, no matter how short the time, and notwithstanding the fact that no disinterested advice had in reality been had, in many instances will lead to results unsupported by actual facts, and is founded upon assumptions that human experience does not sustain. Modern doctrine measures the reaction of the particular individual involved to the threat made. 17 Am. Jur. 884. Such a threat made to a certain type of parent would be more apt to gain than lose in potential with the passage of a few cruel days of contemplation. It therefore seems more logical and more in accordance with realities to hold that these are but circumstances of the particular case to be considered by the triers of the fact in arriving at a determination as to whether the claimant was in fact bereft of free agency. Restatement, Contracts, § 492, comment (c).

It follows that we are of the opinion that the learned trial court erred in entering a judgment notwithstanding the verdict. The judgment is reversed, and the trial court is instructed to re-instate the verdict of the jury.

CASE NO. 24

Stieber v. Vanderlip. 136 Neb. 862, 287 N.W. 773 (1939)

JOHNSEN, J. This is a suit to cancel a contract for support and the conveyances executed in connection therewith and to require an accounting.

The term defendants is used in this opinion to refer to Etta May Vanderlip, plaintiff's daughter, and to Bryan Littrell and Louis J. Patz, who were the attorneys for both parties in the transaction. . . .

The petition alleges in substance that defendants had conspired to defraud plaintiff of all her property; that they secured her signature to conveyances of the real estate involved, in favor of defendant, Mrs. Vanderlip, while plaintiff, by reason of age and illness, was unable to understand or transact business; and that they were able to obtain possession of the property from her because of her condition and the confidence which she reposed in them by virtue of the trust, professional and confidential relationships which they had previously borne to her.

The contract for support and the conveyances involved were executed on June 2, 1936. Plaintiff claimed that she had no knowledge that she had executed the contract or made unconditional conveyances of title to her daughter. She was at the time approximately eighty years old. The trial court made the following finding with respect to her condition:

"During the trial of this cause, and while the plaintiff was upon the witness-stand, the court gave careful consideration and scrutiny to her testimony, her appearance and her demeanor. A portion of the time while she was on the stand she appeared to have her full mental faculties, while at other times she was confused and bewildered. From a full consideration of all the evidence in the case, the court is of the opinion that because of her age and the general debility with which she suffered at the time of the happening of the transactions involved herein, she did not have her full mental faculties, and was a person who was easily persuaded, and was lacking in stability."

As to the previous relationships of the parties, defendant Mrs. Vanderlip had been making her home with plaintiff since . . . 1930, and, according to the recitation in the contract for support, she had, for two years, "nursed, administered to the needs, and cared for" plaintiff. Littrell and Patz had been Mrs. Vanderlip's attorneys in some preceding litigation and had then been engaged by plaintiff to look after her interests in the Fred Stieber estate. Patz made social visits at plaintiff's home, took her to "movie" shows, and on occasion brought out refreshments. Littrell used to chauffeur plaintiff downtown in his automobile, and, at times when he was busy, had his father do so. . . .

On June 2, 1936, according to plaintiff, Mrs. Vanderlip told her that Patz wanted her to come to his office to execute some papers. She had had some previous conversation with Patz about a suit against her by the Citizens State Bank of Bennett, Nebraska. It appeared that one of Mrs. Vanderlip's sons at one time had induced plaintiff to sign a blank note, which he had fraudulently used to obtain a loan at the Bennett bank. Patz had suggested to her, so she said, that she ought to execute deeds to her property, so that, if judgment was recovered against her, it could not be collected on execution. It seems to have been her impression that it was on this matter she was being called to Patz's office. What she actually executed, however, was a contract between herself and Mrs. Vanderlip, which Patz had previously prepared, and in which she agreed to convey all her property to Mrs. Vanderlip, in consideration of an obligation on the part of the daughter to provide her with a home and support. . . . After a careful consideration of all the evidence contained in the one thousand page bill of exceptions, however, the conviction is clear that plaintiff did not know or understand that she had executed a contract for support and had given her daughter her property as a consideration therefor. She thought she had merely executed some deeds which were to be held by Patz, as a protection to her, until the claim of the Bennett bank had been disposed of. This is apparent, not merely from her words, but also from her actions, and when we consider that there is involved an eighty-year old woman, past the age of guile and calculation, her simple actions are demonstratively significant. When she subsequently learned that Mrs. Vanderlip had made a settlement of her son's obligation to the Bennett bank and that there was accordingly no outstanding liability against her, plaintiff went to Patz's office and requested back her deeds, insisting that there was now no necessity for him to hold them longer for her. In this incident there is no self-serving calculation, but a manifestation of simple, honest understanding. Incidentally, Patz up to that time had kept the deeds in his file unrecorded, except as to one piece of property in Kansas. After plaintiff's request for their return, he promptly had all of them recorded. . . . It is unnecessary for us here to comment upon defendants' motives. They may have been intended to be in plaintiff's best interest, although some of the things which were done throughout their relationship with plaintiff can hardly merit professional acclaim. . . . The trial court rightly held that Littrell and Patz occupied a confidential relationship to plaintiff, whose responsibility was not lessened because they were also representing Mrs. Vanderlip in the transaction. Mrs. Vanderlip, too, bore a confidential relationship to her mother, in view of the latter's age, physical infirmity, mental instability, and the situation arising out of the fact that she was making her home with plaintiff and exercising daily care and supervision over her. Defendants knew that plaintiff reposed trust and confidence in them. They knew she was old and unstable. Patz, as previously indicated, had tried to protect himself against her instability by insisting that she give him a purportedly irrevocable power of attorney.

By virtue of their past relationships to plaintiff, and her age, physical infirmity and mental stability, it was the duty of all the defendants to see that no possible advantage was taken of her. Neither Mrs. Vanderlip nor Littrell and Patz in her behalf could deal at arm's length with plaintiff. Nor could they enter into a transaction with her of personal benefit to any of them, where as here, she was without independent advice, unless it was convincingly clear that she knew just what she was doing and, with a full understanding of the transaction, was willing to enter into it. . . . The rule as to confidential or fiduciary relations applies to any transaction or situation of advantage, in which confidence is rightfully reposed on one side and a resulting superiority and opportunity for influence is thereby created on the other. In any such case where confidence is known, or may reasonably be expected, to exist as a fact, whether it is of a legal, moral, social, domestic or personal character, equity will scrutinize the transaction critically —and especially so where age, infirmity and instability are involved—to see that no inequitable action has been taken and no injustice has occurred. Its purpose is not merely to satisfy itself of absence of pressure or influence, but to be certain that the fullest and fairest explanation possible has been made, and that complete knowledge, understanding, intention, consent and freedom of action duly existed.

The preponderance of the evidence clearly brings the facts of this case within the foregoing rules. . . .

Review Questions

1. Are incompetent parties prohibited from entering into contracts?
2. What is the reasoning underlying the principle that infants' contracts are voidable?
3. What is your reaction to the application of the principle that an infant may use his infancy "as a shield but not as a sword" to cases in which he has received the benefits of the contract?
4. Are infants liable for the contract price of necessities?
5. The rule that infants are subject to liability for the value of necessities contracted for is subject to what limitation?
6. What argument is there for the view that an infant should be allowed the right of disaffirmance during the period of minority?
7. What reason supports the rule that an infant may not disaffirm a contract for realty until after majority?
8. The argument has been presented that to allow an infant to disaffirm a contract during the period of minority would logically necessitate allowing him to disaffirm the disaffirmance. Discuss.
9. What are the possible legal consequences if an infant induces contractual consent by representing himself as an adult? Will such a misrepresentation prevent him from disaffirming the contract?
10. Can an infant be held to his contract for the purchase of a taxicab to be used for the purpose of making a livelihood?
11. In general terms, what is fraud?
12. Enumerate the various means whereby fraud may be accomplished.
13. Illustrate fraud by active concealment.
14. When is a failure to disclose facts fraudulent?
15. What determines whether a fact that has been misrepresented is material to the transaction?
16. When will a false opinion be regarded as a misrepresentation of fact?
17. What is the effect of fraud upon a contract?
18. How do the legal consequences of innocent misrepresentation differ from those arising from intentional misrepresentation?
19. A, in an application for life insurance, states that he is thirty-four years of age when in fact he is only thirty-two. Does such misrepresentation make the contract voidable?
20. What is meant by the statement that fraud is a tort?
21. What limitations are there to the equitable remedy of rescission for a bilateral mistake? Construct a fact situation covering one of these limitations.
22. Formulate a statement as to when a remedy of rescission will be available for a unilateral mistake.
23. In what respect does duress differ from undue influence?
24. Why are corporations classed as incompetent persons?

Problems for Discussion

1. A, an infant, contracted for instruction in aviation. Upon completion of the course of instruction A seeks to recover the tuition he has paid. Will he suc-

ceed? Would a delay for nearly a year after attaining his majority before disaffirming the contract constitute a ratification?

2. A, a minor, buys a radio from B for $45 cash. A subsequently sells the radio to C for $50 and dissipates the money. Can he recover the $45 he has paid B?
3. Suppose in the facts above that the radio was sold to C the day after A attained his majority. What would be your conclusion?
4. A, a minor, becoming dissatisfied with conditions at home, leaves his father's bed and board. B furnishes A board and lodging for one month. Can B recover from A?
5. Plaintiff an 18-year-old orphan purchased a used car of the defendant for the sum of $203.85. The car was purchased for the purpose of going to and from the plaintiff's place of work which was six miles distance from the place where he lived. Plaintiff being dissatisfied with his purchase tendered a return of the car and brought an action to recover the purchase price. Decide. (*Chambers* v. *Dunmeyer Chev. Co.,* 74 Ohio App. 235)
6. On December 11, 1931, plaintiff, then 19 years old, applied to the defendant for $25,000 insurance on his life for the benefit of his mother and sister, and for which a policy was issued December 14th. One month before the application his father, president of a Washington bank where plaintiff was employed, had died, leaving a will by which plaintiff, his mother, and sister were equal beneficiaries of a trust fund of $100,000.

   His only other resources were a salary of $80 per month from the bank and an agency for an insurance company producing sundry hopes at that time and little else thereafter.

   The father's estate was soon found to be insolvent; the trust fund did not materialize; the bank closed; and the infant lost his employment, when the policy was seven months gone.

   On December 28, 1932, the plaintiff repudiated his contract and demanded return of the premium paid, which was refused, and the suit followed. Decide. (*Mutual Life Ins. Co.* v. *Schiavone,* 71 Fed. (2d) 980)
7. X is induced to sell Y certain real property upon the basis of the following representation by Y: "If you will sell to me at the price of $5,000, I will within one year erect no less than ten houses upon the property which I will guarantee will increase the value of your adjoining property." Y never did as he represented he would. Can X avoid the agreement because of fraud?
8. X sells Y his car without revealing the knowledge that it has traveled many more miles than are indicated by the speedometer. Is this fraud?
9. Defendant gave plaintiff an option to purchase a portion of his hotel for $15,000. Defendant contends the option is voidable because of plaintiff's failure to disclose the fact that a large factory was to be located in the city where the hotel was located. Is this contention sound?
10. Plaintiff had agreed to purchase a half interest in defendant's business for $3,000—one half to be paid in cash and the balance in installments of $100 once a month. The agreement was induced by defendant's representations that the 1945 profits accruing to plaintiff from the business would be sufficient to pay the installments as they came due, and would reimburse plaintiff for his down payment; that defendant could, with the capital contributed by plaintiff, get the wholesale business and that there was no competition to fear. In view

of the fact that plaintiff's expectations did not materialize, is this actionable fraud?

11. Plaintiff recovered the purchase price of cattle sold to defendant under the following circumstances:

Plaintiff made no disclosure to defendant of the fact that the cattle were sick nor that they were reported to have the fever. Defendant bargained for the cattle on Sunday afternoon, and on Monday morning completed the contract at $3.75 per cwt., and at once shipped them to Chicago. Thirty died on the way; twenty were condemned by the health officer. It is shown beyond all question that they all had the Texas fever.

The court, by the first instruction given at the request of the plaintiff, told the jury that "if plaintiff made no representations to defendant as to the health or condition of said cattle to influence defendant to believe said cattle were sound or in healthy condition, but on the contrary, defendant bought said cattle on actual view of the same, and relying on his own judgment as to their health and condition, then the jury will find for the plaintiff; . . . and, if the cattle were bought by the defendant in the manner above stated, it makes no difference whether said cattle, or any of them, were, at the time of said sale, affected with Texas fever or other disease, or whether plaintiff did or did not know of their being so diseased, as, under such circumstances, he would buy at his own risk and peril." Decide. (*Grissby* v. *Stapleton,* 94 Mo. 423, 7 S.W. 421)

12. In an action to recover the purchase price of a cash register, the defendant sets up as a defense the contention that the contract was induced by fraudulent representations of the plaintiff's agent to the effect that the use of the cash register would save the expense of a bookkeeper, as the books could be kept by the machine, and would also save half of one clerk's time. Should defendant be allowed to rescind the agreement because of fraud? (*Cash Register Co.* v. *Townsend,* 135 N.C. 652)

13. Fully aware of his own insolvency, A buys goods from B without disclosing his insolvency. Is this a fraudulent misrepresentation?

14. For the sum of $400, A purchased a $7,000 judgment from B, which the latter held against C. A failed to reveal to B the knowledge—which he acquired from the public records—that C had died leaving a considerable estate. Is this fraud?

15. X, an expert in gold-mining stocks, sold Y 1,000 shares in the Bear Cat Mining Company. Y was induced to buy upon the basis of X's opinion to the effect that "This gold-mining company has the best prospects of any company that has come into existence in the last five years, and at the risk of my reputation I will say it will pay 25 per cent in dividends." After five years, the company had never paid any dividends and the facts were that the general investment community had at all times regarded the prospects of the company as extremely doubtful. May Y avoid the agreement with X?

16. Meyers during negotiations for the sale of his restaurant to Monroe stated that the new building being erected across the street was to be a dormitory housing university students. The new building subsequently turned out to be a university restaurant which materially affected Monroe's business. Upon trial Meyers sought to excuse himself by testifying that in fact he did not know the purpose of the building as he paid no attention to it. Decide. (*Meyers* v. *Monroe,* 226 S.W. (2d) 782)

17. When he sold Smith a steam shovel, Jones grossly misrepresented its characteristics. B, in making the purchase, said, "I doubt the machine can do what you say, but I'll take a chance." Finding that his doubts were justified, he seeks to avoid the contract because of fraud. Result?
18. X employed fraud to induce Y to sell him certain property. However, X did pay Y better than a fair value for the property. What recourse would Y have against X?
19. Plaintiff sold defendant a tract of land. Unknown to both parties, oil had been discovered in the immediate vicinity and plaintiff could have realized many times the purchase price. Can plaintiff rescind upon the basis of mutual mistake?
20. X contracted to sell Y his interest in a partnership. The value was fixed at $5,000 upon the basis of the books of the partnership. Unknown to X and Y at the time of the agreement was the fact that the books of the partnership did not reveal the true state of affairs, as they had been falsified by the partnership's bookkeeper. Upon discovering that the partnership interest is worth much less than $5,000, may Y avoid the contract because of mistake?
21. X dictated an offer to Y in which he agreed to sell corn at 90 cents a bushel. In transcribing the letter, the stenographer wrote "80 cents a bushel." The offer was sent without the error having been discovered. Y immediately accepted. Upon discovering the mistake, can X avoid the agreement?
22. Mrs. Lemke, a collector of antiques, agreed to pay Quincy $105 for a piece of glassware, under the mistaken belief that it was of rare value. Upon discovering her error—upon discovering that the same glassware could be purchased in any dime store—can she avoid the agreement because of mistake?

7 CONTRACTS:

FORM OF THE CONTRACT—THE STATUTE OF FRAUDS

► I. PAROL EVIDENCE RULE

There is no general requirement that, to be enforceable or to be used as a defense in an action, contracts must be in any special form or be evidenced in writing. However, the desirability of reducing a contract to writing cannot be denied. Oral agreements lend themselves to contradiction, whereas written contracts are protected from such by the rule that parol evidence may not be used to contradict a written contract.

If the written contract appears *to be complete* and is *understandable,* it cannot be changed by the use of oral evidence. For this reason it is also necessary for the parties to a contract to reduce to writing any changes made in the contract after it is written.[1] To illustrate:

In the case of *Thompson* v. *Fitzgerald,* (Tex.) 105 S.W. 334, it was held that the plans and specifications contained in a written contract could not be changed by a subsequent oral agreement of the parties.

► II. TYPES OF CONTRACTS REQUIRED TO BE IN WRITING BY STATUTE OF FRAUDS

No contract can be legally enforced or used as a defense unless it can be established by proof. This proof of a contract may fail either from (1) the unavailability of sufficient evidence as a matter of fact, or (2) the inability to use available evidence because of some rule of law. The Statute of Frauds is such a rule of law: it prevents the use of oral evidence as proof of certain kinds of contracts. It is generally a statute of evidence, requiring written proof to maintain an action in connection with the types of contracts specified therein.

> ". . . The object of the statute is to prevent the assertion of verbal understandings . . . and to obviate the opportunity for fraud and perjury. It is not a mere rule of evidence, but a declaration of public policy. In the absence of equities sufficient of themselves to take the case out of the statute, it operates as a limitation upon judicial authority to afford a remedy unless renounced or waived by the party entitled to claim its protection. . . . Both parties are presumed to have known that either might take advantage of the terms of the statute. . ." *Haskell* v. *Heathcote,* 69 A. (2d) 71 (1949)

The purpose of the Statute of Frauds is well indicated by the title of the

[1] Seitz v. Brewer's Refrigerating Co., p. 193.

original statute, "An Act for the Prevention of Fraud and Perjuries," which was enacted in England in 1676 and upon which the American statutes have been modeled. The statutes of the various states contain substantially similar provisions. Although there are slight variations, the following provisions, taken from the 1946 Iowa Code, are typical:

> "Section 11285, *Statute of frauds.* Except when otherwise specially provided, no evidence of the following enumerated contracts is competent, unless it be in writing and signed by the party charged with performance or by his authorized agent.
>
> "Subsection 1. Those made in consideration of marriage.
>
> "Subsection 2. Those wherein one person promises to answer for the debt, default, or miscarriage of another, including promises by executors to pay the debt of the decedent from their own estates.
>
> "Subsection 3. Those for the creation or transfer of any interest in lands except leases for a term not exceeding one year.
>
> "Subsection 4. Those that are not to be performed within one year from the making thereof.
>
> "Section 9933. A contract to sell or a sale of any goods or choses in action shall not be enforceable by action unless . . . some note or memorandum in writing of the contract or sale be signed by the party to be charged or his agent in that behalf."

A. CONTRACTS IN CONSIDERATION OF MARRIAGE (SUBSECTION 1)

Note that the statute quoted above reads contracts in *consideration of marriage* and *not marriage contracts.* There need be a writing only in those instances in which marriage is a consideration to support a promise other than one of marriage. Mutual promises to marry do not fall within the Statute of Frauds, and therefore they are enforceable in oral form. Should William say to Mary, "If you will marry me, Mary, I will give you half of the farm," and should Mary accept this proposal, a contract in consideration of marriage would result that would require written evidence for its enforceability.

B. CONTRACTS TO ANSWER FOR DEBT OF ANOTHER (SUBSECTION 2)

The terms *debt, default, or miscarriage* as used in the statute are generally taken to mean any existing binding legal obligation.

The term *of another* means exactly what it says, namely, that the promisor accepts the responsibility of another's obligation, which responsibility is collateral and secondary to such original and primary obligation. The promisor's undertaking is in the nature of a guaranty, being intended to guarantee the obligation of another, not to replace it.[2, 3] To illustrate:

[2] Workman Inc. v. Lincoln, p. 193.

[3] Collier v. Brown, p. 194; see also Somers & Sons v. Le Clerc, p. 194.

(1) A owes the X garage $200 for repairs on his car, which the garage is holding by right of their lien. B tells the X garage to let A have the car and promises to pay the repair bill. It would appear that B intends to accept the $200 obligation as his primary undertaking rather than as a guaranty of A's obligation. Should B agree to pay upon the condition of A's release from the obligation, it would, of course, clearly be a primary undertaking. Now let us suppose that B tells the X garage to let A have the car and promises to meet the obligation if A should fail to pay. In that case, the undertaking of B is a guaranty of A's obligation; it is secondary rather than primary and would be unenforceable in oral form.

(2) In *Ledlow* v. *Becton,* 36 Ala. 596, the defendant, without having received authority from X, acted as X's buying agent in contracting with the plaintiff for goods and services to be furnished to an employee of X. The defendant orally "guaranteed" to the plaintiff that X would pay. The plaintiff, upon not receiving payment from X, brought an action on the defendant's oral promise to pay if X did not. The court held that the promise by the defendant was primary and not secondary, and enforceable in oral form. Since the defendant was not authorized to act for X, the latter could have no primary obligation to which the defendant's promise could be secondary.

(3) In *Southern R. Co.* v. *Hazelwood,* 45 Ind. App. 478, the defendant orally promised the plaintiff that it would pay for medical services rendered one of its injured employees if the latter did not pay. The defendant had entered into a contract of settlement with the employee whereby it had agreed to pay all medical expenses. In an action by the plaintiff upon the oral promise, the defendant contended it was unenforceable, being as they said, "a promise to pay the debt of another." The court held the oral promise enforceable, saying that the contract of the defendant with the injured employee made this its primary obligation.

1. *Promises Primarily for Benefit of Promisor*

If the object of the promisor in promising to answer for the debt, default, or miscarriage of another is to accomplish some purpose other than to guarantee the obligation, the promise is primary even though incidentally it would stand as a guaranty of the obligation: this would be true, for example, when the promise of the promisor is intended for his own benefit. To illustrate:

(1) In the case of *Wills* v. *Cutler,* 61 N.H. 405, the defendant purchaser of a manufacturing enterprise, orally promised the employees that he would pay all back wages due to them from the former owner. The court held that the undertaking to pay this obligation was merely incidental to the primary or main purpose of the promise, which was to induce the employees to continue work for the benefit of the defendant, and consequently was enforceable in oral form.

(2) In *McCormick* v. *Johnson,* 31 Mont. 266, the facts were: X owed the plaintiff a sum of money; the defendant orally promised the plaintiff that he would pay X's debt, in consideration of the defendant giving the plaintiff an agency for the sale of defendant's coal. This was held to be not an undertaking to pay the debt of X, but an original promise for the benefit of the defendant—the promisor.

C. CONTRACTS PERTAINING TO REAL PROPERTY (SUBSECTION 3)

1. *Nature of Interest in Real Property*

This provision of the Statute of Frauds does not encompass all contracts that affect real property. It applies only to those contracts which contemplate the transfer or the creation of any title, ownership, or possessory interest in and to realty.[4] Suppose that A agrees to raze a building situated on B's land and to accept 50 per cent of the salvage as his compensation. While this agreement relates to real property, it does not create or transfer an interest in land as contemplated by the above section and consequently need not be in writing to be enforceable.

In many instances, the applicability of the statute is dependent upon a determination of whether the contract involves real or personal property. In very general terms, real property is land or anything that is permanently attached as part of the land.

2. *Sale of Things to Be Removed*

It is the rule in some states that a sale of buildings, timber, and other things permanently attached to the realty is a transfer of an interest in real property, even though it is contemplated that they are to be removed. However, in some states it is held that where removal is immediately contemplated, the contract is one for the sale of personal property and not realty.[5] Therefore the only safe rule is to have such a transaction evidenced by a writing. Obviously, if the agreement between the buyer and seller is unequivocally clear that the title is not to pass to the buyer until after severance, it is a contract for the sale of personal property.

3. *Change of Position in Reliance upon Oral Contract*

In the event that one of the parties, in reliance upon an oral contract for the creation or transfer of an interest in real property, substantially changes his position, a court of equity may give him protection by enforcing the oral contract.[6, 7] His change of position must be to such an extent that it is impossible to place him back in his former status. To illustrate:

In *Veeder, Rec.* v. *Horstmann et al.,* 85 N.Y. App. Div. 154, the court in passing upon the enforceability of an oral agreement under which possession had been taken said: "The company not only entered into the possession of the real property under said agreement and remained in the exclusive possession thereof, but expended large sums of money in permanent and substantial improvements. Where improvements are substantial and permanent in character and are such as would not have been made except in reliance on the contract, specific performance will be decreed. Where the circumstances are peculiar and exceptional and where in

---

[4] Walker v. Walker, p. 195.
[5] Rankin v. Ridge, p. 195.
[6] Halligan v. Frey, p. 198.
[7] Cottrell v. Nurnberger, p. 199.

case the contract is not carried out it will result in a fraud upon some of the parties to the contract, equity should and will lend its aid to defeat the fraud."

4. *Leases Not Exceeding One Year*

Leases not exceeding one year need not be in writing to be enforceable. The period of one year is usually determined not from the time the lease is entered into but from the time of the commencement of the term of possession. Thus, if A on January 1 orally agrees to lease certain premises of B for a period of one year, with possession to be given on March 1, the term (for the purpose of satisfying the statute) is computed from March 1 and not January 1, and the agreement would be enforceable in its oral form.

D. CONTRACTS OF LONG DURATION (SUBSECTION 4)

In determining whether, as the statute says, a contract is to be performed within one year from the making thereof, the provisions of the contract and the nature of the performance required must be taken into consideration.

Thus, a contract is not of long duration:

(1) If the contract expressly provides that performance is to be accomplished within the year, providing such is possible.[8]

(2) If in the absence of any specified agreement by the parties as to the time for performance, the contract is capable of being performed within the year, as the courts say, in the normal course of events. Thus a contract may not as a matter of fact be performed within the year and still be enforceable in oral form. To illustrate:

A agrees to build B a home, the contract specifying no time for performance. This contract is capable of being performed within the year and is enforceable in oral form even though it takes A two years to complete the house.

(3) If performance is dependent upon the happening of some event which might happen within the year, even though it does not happen within the year. To illustrate:

A and B, joint owners of promissory notes, orally agree that upon death of either the survivor would be the sole owner. Even though this contract goes beyond the year, it is enforceable since it could have been performed within the year.

(4) If parties specify the maximum time for performance or liability as exceeding one year, providing they contemplate the possibility of performance within the year. To illustrate:

In the case of *Groce* v. *West Lumber Co.,* (Tex.) 165 S.W. 519, an oral contract allowed the buyer four years within which to remove certain property. The court held the agreement enforceable.

In *Philip Carey Mfg. Co.* v. *Southern Construction Co.,* 2 Ala. App. 292, an oral contract guaranteeing a roof for five years was held to be enforceable in oral

[8] Nickerson v. Harvard College, p. 201.

form. The court said, "The contingency upon which the liability is to accrue may happen within one year."

A contract is of long duration:

(1) If by express terms it provides for performance that will extend beyond a year from its making.[9]

(2) If the contract stipulates no definite period of time but its performance within one year is impossible or highly improbable. To illustrate:

In the case of *Swift* v. *Swift,* 46 Cal. 266, an oral contract whereby a borrower agreed to repay the money out of the profits from nut-bearing trees that at the time of the agreement were not yet planted was held unenforceable.

E. CONTRACTS PERTAINING TO PERSONAL PROPERTY (SECTION 9933)

The salient features of this provision of the Statute of Frauds which requires that a contract to sell or a sale of any personal property to be enforceable must be in writing are:

(1) It applies to all forms of personal property including choses in action. The general rule is that stocks, bonds, mortgages, and other evidences of indebtedness are included within its provisions.

(2) It applies only to contracts for the sale of property at or above a stated value. In the original draft of the Uniform Sales Act, this section was made to apply where the value of the property was $500 or upwards. This amount ranges from $30 to as much as $2,500 in the statutes of the various states. Some statutes (as in Iowa) contain no stated amount; this brings all contracts for the sale of personal property within the operation of the statute.

(3) Part delivery of the goods or choses in action and an acceptance of same by the buyer will take the contract out of the operation of the statute and so allow it to be enforced in its oral form. Whether there has been a delivery and acceptance is, of course, a question of fact, which is largely a matter of determining whether control of the goods has been relinquished to the buyer.[10]

(4) Part payment for the goods by the buyer will also serve to make an oral contract enforceable. Payment within the meaning of the statute is any value that has been received by the seller as a consideration for the sale of the goods. It must be given in discharge of part of the purchase price.[11]

(5) If the goods under the contract are to be manufactured by the seller especially for the buyer and are not suitable for sale to others in the ordinary course of the seller's business, the statute does not apply.[12] Contracts for articles of this kind are enforceable in oral form. This rule has been embodied in the Uniform Sales Act and is very generally followed.

---

[9] McGirr v. Campbell, p. 202.
[10] Mayer v. Randolph, p. 204.
[11] Maryatt v. Hubbard, p. 205.
[12] Murphy v. Munson, p. 207.

F. NATURE OF WRITING REQUIRED AND SIGNATURE

The writing required under the Statute of Frauds need not take the form of a formally executed contract. The statute requires only such writing as is sufficient to establish the transaction with reasonable certainty; any writing, regardless of its nature, must contain all the essential terms of the contract if it is to be adequate. The Statute of Frauds merely requires written evidence equal to its proposed end—the establishing of the agreement with reasonable certainty. A letter, a telegram, a receipt, a memorandum of sale, or even a check *may* be adequate proof.[14, 15]

The proof required need not be contained in a single writing. A combination of writings that clearly indicate that they mutually relate to the same transaction may be used to establish all the essential terms of a contract.

In the case of *Alba* v. *Strong,* 94 Ala. 163, 10 So. 242, it was observed that:

> "The following propositions must be regarded as settled by the former decisions of this court beyond controversy: First. That to authorize the specific enforcement of an agreement to sell land, all the terms of the agreement must have been agreed on, leaving nothing for negotiation. Second. That all the terms of the agreement, viz., the names of the parties, the subject-matter of the contract, the consideration and the promise, must be in writing, signed by the party sought to be charged, or by his agent thereunto authorized in writing. Third. That it is not essential that the paper evidence of the agreement be in any particular form, provided it contain the substance, as stated above. Fourth. That the written evidence of the terms of the agreement need not all be expressed in one paper. If expressed in two or more papers it will be sufficient, if collectively they contain enough, and refer to each other, and show the connection with sufficient clearness, without the aid of oral testimony. If, however, oral testimony is required to connect the papers, or to supply any essential term of the contract, then there is a failure to make a case for specific performance. . . ."

It is not necessary that the writing date from the time of entrance into the contract. The written evidence may be supplied at any time prior to the commencement of an action on the contract.[13]

Both parties to the contract need not sign the writing. Generally, only the signature of the party to be charged with performance is required—the one who would be in default of performance. Unless the defendant's signature appears upon the writing, he cannot be held.[16] In some states, the rule is that a contract for the sale of land is enforceable when signed by the seller, and the buyer's signature is not required.

---

[13] Pitek v. McGuire, p. 208.
[14] Martin v. Seigel, p. 212.
[15] Weber v. DeCecco, p. 213.
[16] Andre v. Ellison, p. 214.

G. PART PERFORMANCE UNDER ORAL CONTRACT

Part performance will not in itself make an oral agreement enforceable, with the exception of those for the sale of personal property. Neither taking possession of, nor making payment of rent on real property will, for example, take an oral lease out of the operation of the statute so as to make it enforceable. When, however, one of the parties to an unenforceable oral contract refuses to perform, after the other party has given part performance, the latter can get a return of the consideration given or recover a reasonable value for the benefit which the other party has received.

> "It is the general law that although a contract may be . . . unenforceable because within the Statute of Frauds, yet, if one party thereto has performed, he may recover in an action of quantum merit the reasonable value of his services." *Gutowsky* v. *Jones,* 178 Fed. (2d) 60

► III. ACKNOWLEDGMENT BEFORE NOTARY

A. TO MAKE ELIGIBLE FOR RECORDING

There is no general requirement that a written contract to be valid must be acknowledged at the time of its execution. The purpose of the acknowledgment is usually to make the contract or instrument eligible for placing of public record —recording.*

An acknowledgment consists of:

(1) An admission by the party or parties executing the contract that the execution is their voluntary act and deed. This gives considerable assurance that the contract is free of fraud or coercion.

(2) A verification by the officer (the notary) taking the acknowledgment that (a) the party or parties executing the contract personally appeared before him, (b) were personally known or properly identified to him, and (c) signed in his presence. (This is a real protection against a forgery if the notary properly performs his function.)

The acknowledgment must conform with the requirements of the statute in the state where it is taken. The exact language of the statute should be used.

B. TO MAKE CONTRACT VALID

To a limited extent, provisions can be found in the various state codes requiring certain types of contracts and instruments to be acknowledged as a prerequisite to their validity. Thus, in Iowa, it is provided that a contract of assignment of wages by the head of a family, to be valid, must be signed by both husband and wife and acknowledged before an officer authorized to take acknowledgments. Local statutes should be consulted.

---

* See p. 721 for purpose of recording.

CASES

CASE NO. 1

Seitz v. Brewers' Refrigerating Co. 141 U.S. 510, 35 L. Ed. 837 (1891)

FULLER, CH.J. . . . The position of the plaintiff in error is, in the first place, that the evidence on his behalf tended to show an agreement between himself and defendant in error, entered into prior to or contemporaneously with the written contract, independent of the latter and collateral to it, that the machine purchased should have a certain capacity and should be capable of doing certain work, that the machine failed to come up to the requirements of such independent parol contract; that this evidence was competent; and that the case should therefore have been left to the jury.

Undoubtedly the existence of a separate oral agreement as to any matter on which a written contract is silent, and which is not inconsistent with its terms, may be proven by parol, if under the circumstances of the particular case it may properly be inferred that the parties did not intend the written paper to be a complete and final statement of the whole of the transaction between them. But such an agreement must not only be collateral, but must relate to a subject distinct from that to which the written contract applies; that is, it must not be so closely connected with the principal transaction as to form part and parcel of it. And when the writing itself upon its face is couched in such terms as import a complete legal obligation without any uncertainty as to the object or extent of the engagement, it is conclusively presumed that the whole engagement of the parties, and the extent and manner of their undertaking, were reduced to writing. . . .

There is no pretense here of any fraud, accident or mistake. The written contract was in all respects unambiguous and definite. The machine which the company sold, and which Seitz bought, was a No. 2 size refrigerating machine, as constructed by the company, and such was the machine that was delivered, put up and operated by the brewery. A warranty or guaranty that the machine should reduce the temperature of the brewery to 40 degrees Fahrenheit, while in itself collateral to the sale, which would be complete without it, would be part of the description and essential to the identity of the thing sold; and to admit proof of such an engagement by parol would be to add another term to the written contract, contrary to the settled and salutary rule of this subject. . . .

CASE NO. 2

Workman, Inc. v. Lincoln et al. 250 N.Y. 518, 166 N.E. 307 (1929)

PROSKAUER, J. . . . Defendants, as agents for a foreign principal, contracted to sell furs to the plaintiff. In consideration of the making of the contract they orally warranted that the goods delivered by their principal would conform with the contract. The complaint has been dismissed on the ground that the promise was within the statute of frauds. . . .

. . . The agreement of an agent to answer for his principal is, of course, made effectual as a contract when supported by the consideration of making of the contract. But the statute of frauds is intended to safeguard against the false claim of the making of such secondary agreement. It is based upon the sound consideration of public policy that an agent should be protected against the plausible claim which might often be falsely asserted that he engaged to insure his principal's performance. . . .

Here the defendants were to become liable only in the event of their principal's default.

We conclude therefore that the order appealed from should be affirmed.

CASE NO. 3

Collier v. Brown. 19 La. App. 567, 141 So. 405 (1932)

TALIAFERRO, J. Plaintiff instituted this suit against defendants to recover a balance due him on an open account. . . .

The lower court gave judgment against both defendants. Brown has appealed.

. . . Plaintiff is engaged in retail mercantile business in the village of Campti, La. The defendant Willard was in possession of a portable sawmill and moved it on the lands of defendant Brown for the purpose of manufacturing Brown's timber . . . into ties. Brown sold his timber to Willard and purchased the output of the mill. Beyond this, Brown appears to have had no interest in the activities. . . . About the time the mill began operations, Brown accompanied Willard to plaintiff's place of business and made them acquainted and informed Collier that Willard purposed to start the sawmill to running and then and there arrangements were made for Willard to open an account with plaintiff. The following testimony of plaintiff reflects his understanding of what was said and done at the time, namely:

"Mr. Brown brought Mr. Willard around and made him acquainted with me, and told me he was going to operate a little mill around there and let him have what he needed and he would see that it was paid." . . .

The merchandise purchased by Willard was first entered on small charge slips showing his name, with itemized list of articles purchased and price of each item. Thereafter, the record of the purchases was transferred to the ledger and carried into an account against Brown. He kept in touch with the account from time to time, and, as Willard desired him to do so, made payments thereon, giving check or cash to Willard for that purpose. Payments thus made were charged to Willard by Brown. This mode of business continued until Brown notified plaintiff to discontinue Willard's account, and thereafter nothing was sold him on credit. . . .

It is certain plaintiff would not have extended credit to Willard, a total stranger to him, but for Brown's voluntary agreement to see that the account would be paid. By introducing Willard, under the circumstances, and recommending him to plaintiff for credit, Brown impliedly vouched for his honesty, and evinced an interest in Willard because of the fact that he was preparing to manufacture Brown's timber into ties and Brown expected to profit by purchasing the output of the mill.

Viewed in the light of all the circumstances, Brown's meaning and intent with regard to Willard's account cannot be misunderstood. It is equally clear as to whom the credit was really given. If there had been any doubt on these two propositions, Brown has removed same by his own construction of his relationship to plaintiff. He kept in touch with Willard's dealing with plaintiff, and made payments on the account for him, and, when Willard's business was in such condition as to cause apprehension as to his ability to pay his debts,

Brown notified plaintiff to discontinue the account. . . .

Brown did not become the surety for Willard, nor the guarantor of his account, but became bound as principal with him for the payment of the account. Two persons may be bound as principals for the same debt, when, as between them, only one in reality should pay it.

The lower court held that defendants were bound as principals for the payment of plaintiff's account, and we think this holding correct. . . .

CASE NO. 4

Walker v. Walker. 231 N.C. 54, 55 S.E. (2d) 801 (1949)

Civil action to impress a trust upon defendant's title to certain real property.

On October 3, 1932, F. J. Walker and wife, for a valuable consideration, conveyed a ten-acre tract of land by warranty deed to defendant, their son. In the summer of 1933 defendant asked his father to repurchase the property. F. J. Walker then borrowed $300 which he paid to defendant for the repurchase. Defendant said his deed had been lost or misplaced and as soon as he could find it he would destroy it and thus revest title in F. J. Walker. No paper writing or memorandum was signed. Instead, the contract was wholly oral. After the agreement of repurchase was entered into, F. J. Walker took possession of the land and remained in possession thereof until the time of his death. On October 19, 1947, F. J. Walker died. On October 28, 1947, defendant filed his deed for registration. These are the facts disclosed by the allegations in the complaint and the testimony offered when considered in the light most favorable to plaintiffs.

Plaintiffs, heirs at law and devisees of F. J. Walker, instituted this action for judgment that defendant hold title to said land as trustee for the use and benefit of plaintiffs. The defendant denied the oral agreement to sell and reconvey and pleaded the statute of frauds. . . .

BARNHILL, J. . . . The plaintiffs ground their action on an oral agreement by defendant to reconvey the premises to F. J. Walker, by the destruction of his unrecorded deed, and his alleged fraudulent misrepresentations in respect to the loss of the deed and his consequent inability to destroy it. He agreed to revest title in his father by destroying his unrecorded deed to the locus. This he failed to do. Now he should be compelled to comply with his agreement or else be declared trustee for the use and benefit of plaintiffs. So they contend. Their position finds no support in law or equity.

The contract to reconvey, if made, was voidable at the election of defendant. . . . Upon his denial of the contract and plea of the statute of frauds, it became wholly unenforceable. . . .

In disavowing the contract and refusing to abide by its terms, defendant was exercising a legal right and his exercise of a legal right in a lawful manner cannot be made the basis of a charge of fraud such as would impress a trust upon his title to the property. . . .

The judgment below is affirmed.

CASE NO. 5

Rankin v. Ridge. 53 N.M. 33, 201 P. (2d) 359, 7 A.L.R. (2d) 510 (1948)

BRICE, C.J. The plaintiffs (appellees) brought this suit to recover for timber cut from their land under an oral contract made between their predecessor in title and the defendants (appellants). The defendants by cross action sued plaintiffs for $24,500 damages claimed to have been sustained by them because of the refusal of the plaintiffs to permit the defendants to continue to cut timber under the terms of the contract after the plaintiffs purchased the property. . . .

The case is here on the question of whether the trial court erred in dismissing the cross complaint on plaintiffs' motion.

The allegations of the cross complaint, which are taken to be true for the purpose of our decision, are substantially as follows:

. . . By the terms of this contract the cross-complainants were to move a small sawmill upon the premises, and commence to saw and remove the merchantable timber therefrom in a "reasonably continuous manner," until all thereof had been removed and sawed. . . . Before Gibbs sold the ranch to cross-defendants he notified them of this contract, and they bought the ranch subject to the rights of cross-complainants, and upon the agreement that they would carry out the obligations of Gibbs in said contract. The cross-defendants have admitted their liability by making their complaint in writing herein against these cross-complainants, and by accepting the benefits of said contract, and bringing suit to compel performance on the part of these cross-complainants. The cross-complainants cut and removed approximately 96,574 board feet of timber. On April 8, 1947, the cross-defendants without excuse notified and demanded in writing that the cross-complainants remove their machinery from said property and refrain from cutting and removing any more timber. The cross-defendants have failed, refused and neglected to carry out the terms of the contract and cross-complainants have been refused entry upon the premises.

There were approximately one million board feet of merchantable timber upon the premises and cross-complainants have been damaged to the sum of $24,000. In addition thereto the cross-defendants had felled and cut some timber upon the premises previous to the notice, which timber they were not allowed to remove or saw; to their damage $500.00. . . .

The question is whether the trial court erred in dismissing the cross-complaint, upon the theory that the contract was within the statute of frauds.

It is a general rule that the sale of growing timber is within the fourth section of the Statute of Frauds, in that the trees are a part of the reality. . . .

However, according to the decisions of a number of courts (the writer believes the majority of those that have decided the question, including the courts of England), a contract for the sale of trees to be immediately severed from the freehold by the vendee is not a sale of an interest in land. (Cases cited)

It is held that the phrase "immediate severance" as before used, contemplates a severance as soon as it reasonably can be done under the existing circumstances. Cheatham v. Head, 203 Ky. 489, 262 S.W. 622.

The language of the contract here involved, regarding time of severance, clearly brings it within the definition of "immediate severance."

On this subject we quote from various texts, as follows:

"Definition of 'Goods.'

"Goods, within the meaning of the Statute, are:

"(a) Chattels personal, except current money bargained for as a medium of exchange;

"(b) Crops unsevered from the land, whether matured or not at the time when by the terms of the bargain they are to be sold, if they are of a kind subject to yearly cultivation;

"(c) Things attached to or forming

part of the realty which are agreed to be severed therefrom before sale or promptly after the formation of the contract."

Comment:

. . . Though strictly whatever is attached to the land is part thereof, crops which are the subject of yearly planting or cultivation, that is fructus industriales, have been classified under the Statutes as goods rather than part of the land. On the other hand fructus naturales while growing are part of the land; but under the circumstances stated in Clause (c) even fructus naturales have been held withdrawn from the operation of the provision of the Statute relating to land. Clause (c) covers also things attached to land other than fructus naturales, such as minerals or ice, or even buildings." Restatement, Contracts, § 200 and comment a

"In England the law has gone to great length in supporting the validity of an oral contract to sell standing trees. In Marshall v. Green, there was a parol sale of thirty-two trees 'to be got away as soon as possible.' After six of the trees had been cut down the seller countermanded the sale, but the buyer continued to cut, and the action was brought by the seller because of this. The court held that 'where the thing sold is to derive no benefit from the land, and it is to be taken away immediately, the contract is not for an interest in land.' Since part of the trees had been taken away the section of the Statute relating to goods was satisfied and the bargain was held to be enforceable. The same doctrine has prevailed in several of the United States, prior to the passage of the Sales Act and, though 'the courts of most of the American States that have considered the question (have held) expressly that a sale of growing or standing timber is a contract concerning an interest in land,' the Sales Act, copying as it has, the definition of 'goods' so far as concerns this question, from the English Statute, has adopted the English rule that any growing object attached to the soil is to be treated as goods, if by the terms of the contract it is to be immediately severed. A contract to cut and market timber belonging to another in return for a share of the proceeds is a contract of hire and is enforceable." Williston on Contracts (Rev. Ed.), § 516. . . .

The tendency of the later decisions is toward the holding that if the sale is made upon the condition that the trees are to be "immediately severed" from the soil, as the phrase has been defined herein, the contract is not within the fourth section of the Statute of Frauds. This view was adopted by the authors of the uniform sales act, Williston on Contracts, § 521, which, however, has not been adopted here.

The great weight of authority holds that the sale of crops (fructus industriales), matured or not, is not within the statute; also there is much authority that the sale of grass uncut, and buildings attached to the soil to be immediately removed, are not within the Statute of Frauds. . . .

We will not further pursue this quest. We conclude that the sale was that of personal property, not within the Statute of Frauds.

The plaintiffs were not only aware of the defendants' (cross-plaintiffs) contract with plaintiffs' grantor, but agreed to carry out its terms as a part of the consideration for the purchase of the property. . . .

The judgment is reversed and cause remanded to the district court with instructions to set aside its judgment, reinstate the case upon the docket of the court and proceed to a hearing thereof not inconsistent herewith. . . .

CASE NO. 6

James F. Halligan v. Charles A. Frey. 161 Iowa 185, 141 N.W. 944 (1913)

Action to enjoin defendant from commencing an action or in any way interfering with plaintiff in the possession of certain premises in the city of Davenport, which, it is claimed, plaintiff leased of defendant in the year 1908 for the term of ten years, from and after the 1st day of July in said year. Defendant denied the execution of the lease; pleaded the statute of frauds, . . . decree for plaintiff, and defendant appeals.

DEEMER, J. . . . defendant proposed to plaintiff that if he (plaintiff) would give up his lease on the Harrison street property and lease 212 West Fourth street, with the basement, he (defendant) would let the same to him for the term of ten years. . . . Plaintiff moved into the premises on the strength of the agreement and expended something more than $700 in buying additional furniture and fixtures to better adapt it to his use. . . . Plaintiff signed the lease and . . . moved into the property and paid the agreed rental down to and including May, 1910. Defendant refused to accept the rental for any further time and immediately served notice upon plaintiff to quit. . . .

Plaintiff insists that the case is not within the statute: (1) Because of part performance on his part; (2) because defendant is estopped from denying the oral lease; and (3) for the reason that defendant cannot avail himself of the statute; because, to permit him to do so, would allow him to perpetrate a fraud. . . .

Neither taking possession of the property, under an oral lease, nor the payment of rent thereunder, will take the case from under the statute. . . .

Again, the written memorandum of agreement, or lease, must be signed by the party to be charged. It is not enough that it be signed by the plaintiff alone. . . .

But the statute was intended to prevent perjury and fraud, and cannot be used as an instrument whereby to perpetrate a fraud. And this rule is peculiarly applicable to equitable actions, such as this. . . .

The rule is thus summarized by Pomeroy, in his work on Equity Jurisprudence (§§ 921, 1293, and 1294):

> "The statute of frauds was enacted for the purpose of preventing fraud and cannot be made an instrument of shielding, protecting, or aiding the parties who rely upon it in the perpetration of the fraud or the consummation of a fraudulent scheme. . . ."

Where any agreement is made verbally which the statute requires should be in writing or the execution of a written agreement is prevented through the fraud of one party and the other party is induced to accept and rely upon the verbal agreement as binding and valid, a court of equity will not permit a *fraudulent party to set up the statute of frauds as a defense,* but will enforce the contract against him although it is merely verbal. . . .

Courts of equity have established the principles which they apply in various circumstances that it shall not be used as an instrument for the accomplishment of fraudulent purposes. Designed to prevent fraud, it shall not be permitted to work fraud. This principle lies at the basis of the doctrine concerning part performance, but is also enforced wherever it is necessary to secure equitable results.

. . . where a promise is made, such as is shown in this case, and on the strength thereof plaintiff surrenders another lease, goes to the expense of moving and places valuable improvements upon the property which are designed for that property alone, and is finally presented with a written lease, drawn by the defendant covering the agreement as originally made, which lease he signs on his part and pays rent thereunder for ten months, and then is threatened with removal unless he consents to an advance in the rental to $60 per month, it is perfectly plain that defendant is attempting to use the statute of frauds as an instrument whereby to perpetrate a fraud upon the lessee and equity will give such lessee protection. If it did not, it would be a humiliating confession that a court of chancery is helpless and incapable of affording relief where the law is deficient, and is unable to prevent fraud and deception. . . .

The general doctrine upon which the rule is based is founded upon estoppel. All the elements thereof are present here, and we think the trial court was clearly correct in overruling the demurrer and in rendering the decree as prayed.—Affirmed.

CASE NO. 7

Cottrell v. Nurnberger. 131 W.Va. 391, 47 S.E. (2d) 454, 5 A.L.R. (2d) 1298 (1948)

HAYMOND, J. This suit was instituted in the Circuit Court of Kanawha County by G. J. Cottrell, Jr., and eight other persons who own lots in Falls View Addition, in Jefferson District, Kanawha County, as plaintiffs, to enjoin the defendants, J. S. Nurnberger, Ray Wheeler and R. H. Harrison, their successors, grantees and assigns, from using a lot designated as Lot No. 45 of that addition except as a playground and a recreational area and for other community purposes, for the enjoyment and the benefit of the plaintiffs and other lot owners, and to obtain a decree imposing upon the foregoing lot, for their benefit, a covenant to restrict its use to those purposes. . . .

Nurnberger subsequently sold the lots in the addition now owned by the respective plaintiffs to them or their predecessors in title and, in making the sales, represented to the various purchasers that, in addition to the beach and playground areas shown on the map, a level lot comprising about an acre of land, located in the center of the addition and designated as Lot No. 45, was reserved solely and exclusively for playground, recreational and other community purposes for the use and benefit of the purchasers, and that he would construct a well and a well house on that lot for their common use and benefit. . . .

The defendant, Nurnberger, is the owner of the lot upon which the plaintiffs seek to impose the restrictive covenant and, according to the allegations of the bill of complaint, notwithstanding the "promises, representations and restrictions" made by him in connection with the sales of the lots, he has entered into negotiations with the defendants, Wheeler and Harrison, for the sale of that lot to them to be used as a hotel site. The defendants have undertaken the construction of a hotel upon the lot which will deprive the plaintiffs of their use of it as a playground and recreational area and for other community purposes and will cause irreparable damage to their lots and summer homes. . . .

It should be observed that the statements mentioned and contained in the bill of complaint, laid to the defendant Nurnberger, . . . and which were relied upon by the plaintiffs to restrict his use of the lot in question to a playground, recreational area, and other community purposes for the benefit of the plaintiffs, are not alleged to have been incorporated in any deed or other writing. . . .

It is obvious that the right claimed and sought to be enforced by the plaintiffs, if it in fact exists, is created by and arises from an easement and not by virtue of a license, and as the decisive questions in this case involve the method of creating a valid easement and the availability to the defendants of the defense of the Statute of Frauds in connection with a verbal agreement or arrangement. . . .

Though the distinction between an easement and a license may, in a particular instance, be difficult to determine and has given rise to many conflicting decisions involving that question, the essential characteristics of the two are materially different. An easement creates an interest in land; a license does not, but is a mere permission or personal and revocable privilege which does not give the licensee any estate in the land. . . . In the Missouri Case of Fuhr v. Dean, 26 Mo. 116, 69 Am. Dec. 484, the Court, discussing the difference between a license and an easement, citing the Massachusetts case of Cook v. Stearns, 11 Mass. 533, 536, said that

> "a license is technically an authority to do something on the land of another without passing an estate in the land, and a license to do a particular act does not invade the policy of the law that requires conveyances of title or interest in land to be in writing, for it may amount to nothing more than an excuse for an act which would otherwise be a trespass; but an easement cannot be acquired without a deed, or prescription which implies one." . . .

From these authorities, and many others that could be cited, it is clear that the restriction which the plaintiffs seek to impose upon the lot owned by the defendant Nurnberger, if valid and effective, is an easement; that it is within the provisions of Section 3, Article 1, Chapter 36, Code 1931, which require a contract for the sale of land, or a note or memorandum of such contract, to be in writing and signed by the party to be charged. . . .

The plaintiffs cite and rely upon the cases of Tufts v. Copen, 27 W. Va. 623, 16 S.E. 793, and Sanford v. First City Company, 118 W.Va. 713, 192 S.E. 337, in support of their asserted right to impose the claimed restrictions upon Lot No. 45. In the Tufts case, . . . it appears that the plaintiff entered into an oral contract with the defendant, a married woman, by which she agreed that he might construct and operate a tramroad over her lands. He paid and she accepted the agreed consideration for the right of way. She permitted him to construct the tramway at great expense and to operate it for several months. She then obstructed the tramroad by building a fence across it and by that means deprived him of its use. This Court held that by her conduct she was estopped to obstruct the road or to repudiate her oral agreement and that a court of equity would not permit her, after allowing the work to be completed and to be in operation, to destroy its entire usefulness by means of the obstruction. In that case to permit the defendant to deny the easement would cause the plaintiff to be deprived of the use of valuable property which, in reliance upon his right to the easement, he had placed upon it. Here the plaintiffs are subjected to no such loss and no equitable estoppel has occurred. In the Sanford case this Court held that equity would enforce by specific performance a parol contract for an easement when it appears that the party seeking to establish the easement under the contract has performed it in whole or in part to the extent that to refuse to enforce performance of it would be tantamount to a fraud upon the party claiming the easement. In that case the denial of an easement, in favor of the owners of a building, upon a strip of land on which the lessee of an adjoining lot had erected a wall of the building with the acquiescence of the lessor, the predecessor in title of the owners of the building, would have deprived them of the use of one of its main walls and destroyed its value. As already indicated, there is no allegation in the bill of complaint of any acts and conduct upon the part of the defendant Nurnberger which establish any fraud upon the plaintiffs or which create an equitable estoppel against the defendants. Because of the different factual situation which existed in the Tufts case and in the Sanford case, as compared to that disclosed by the allegations of the bill of complaint in the case at bar, the holdings in those cases have no application here.

The allegations of the bill of complaint that the plaintiffs paid the purchase price for the lots conveyed in an amount in excess of that which they otherwise would have paid except for the representations with respect to Lot No. 45, and that they entered into possession of that lot, which since 1941, has been used and occupied as a playground, recreational area, and for other community purposes, do not show such part performance of the oral agreement by the plaintiffs as is necessary to render the Statute of Frauds inapplicable. The payment of the purchase price, even though excessive, is not of itself part performance which will remove the agreement from the operation of the statute. . . .

Nor does the alleged possession of the lot by the plaintiffs amount to the exclusive possession which is necessary to constitute part performance. To entitle a person to specific performance of a parol agreement the possession must be actual, notorious and exclusive. Kee v. Simmons, . . . There is no allegation to that effect or that the plaintiffs made any improvements upon Lot No. 45. They simply improved the lots which they purchased and to which they hold title under their respective deeds, and those lots are their own properties. . . .

For the reasons stated the ruling of the Circuit Court of Kanawha County in refusing to sustain the demurrer of the defendants is reversed.

CASE NO. 8

Nickerson v. President and Fellows of Harvard College. 289 Mass. 484, 11 N.E. (2d) 444, 114 A.L.R. 414 (1937)

LUMMUS, J. . . . G. L. (Ter. Ed.) c. 259, § 1, so far as material to this case, reads: "No action shall be brought: . . . Fifth, Upon an agreement that is not to be performed within one year from the making thereof; Unless the promise, contract or agreement upon which such action is brought, or some memorandum, or note thereof, is in writing and signed by the party to be charged therewith or by some person thereunto by him lawfully authorized."

The method of computing time under words like those of the statute, is firmly established in this Commonwealth. The "making" of an agreement means, for the purpose of computing time, the day on which the agreement is made. The law reckons in days, not commonly in fractions of days; and an agreement made at six o'clock in the morning stands on the same footing with one made at eleven o'clock in the evening. The words "from the making" of the agreement exclude the day on which it is made. The year begins with the following day, and ends at the close of the first anniversary of the day on which the agreement is made. . . .

The foregoing method of computing time has been applied to cases under the section of the statute of frauds in question. The result of such application is, that an agreement made on March 9 for employment for a term of one year is not within the statute if the term is to begin either on that day or the next day, March 10. . . .

In the present case there is no doubt that the agreement, whatever it was, was made on March 9, 1931; that the plaintiff actually went to work on March 16, 1931; and that he was discharged on October 9, 1931. He testified that the term of his employment was to be one year beginning with the time when he should go to work. . . .

The plaintiff's description of the time when his employment was to begin was in various forms. Perhaps the most favorable to him was that he was to go to work whenever the defendant should send for him, which was to be "in a very short time, possibly a day or two." Clearly he was not to begin work on the very day on which the contract was made. But we think the defendant could have required him to begin work on the next day, March 10. Under the contract there were a number of different periods of one year, beginning on different days, that would have satisfied the contract; the election among those periods was given to the defendant; and as one of those periods was such that, if it had been chosen by the defendant, the agreement could have been performed within one year from the making thereof, the agreement is not within the statute of frauds, and no memorandum was required. . . .

We think that the direction of a verdict for the defendant was in error. . . .

CASE NO. 9

McGirr v. Campbell. 75 N.Y.S. 571 (1902)

INGRAHAM, J. . . . The parties to this action were engaged as copartners in the business of gathering, shipping, and selling manure in the then city of New York, and while so engaged, on the 20th of April, 1897, entered into a *verbal* agreement, whereby the defendant sold to the plaintiff certain personal property, and the business theretofore conducted with the good will thereof, . . . The complaint alleges that it was a part of that agreement that the defendant "would not again enter into or carry on the business of gathering, shipping, or selling manure, or either of them, in the then city of New York, until the last of said notes became due and payable, namely, twenty-seven months after the 20th day of April, 1897"; then in or about the month of April, 1898, the defendant did, in breach of his said agreement, enter into and carry on the business of gathering, shipping and selling manure in the city of New York . . . the defendant . . . alleging that the agreement which is sought to be enforced is void as being within the statute of frauds, it being an agreement not to be performed within one year. . . . This agreement is analogous to a contract for an employment which was to continue for a longer period than one year, and such agreements have always been held to be within the statute. Drummond v. Burrell, 13 Wend. 307, was a case where the defendant agreed to work two years from the date of the agreement for the plaintiff, and the plaintiff agreed to pay him $100; and the court, in holding that this agreement was within the statute of frauds, says:

"When was the agreement to be performed? The defendant was to occupy two years in performing his part of the agreement. Of course, he could not perform within one year. When was the plaintiff to pay the $100? On this point the contract is silent in terms, but, as the payment is to be made in consideration of the services, those services are a condition precedent to the payment, and must be performed in full, before payment can be enforced. The money was then to be paid at the end of two years, and, of course, not within one year. The contract, then, by its terms, was not to be performed within one year."

. . . It is claimed, however, that this contract is not within the statute, because, it being a personal covenant on the part of the defendant, it cannot last beyond his life, and therefore the real agreement was that he would perform it for 27 months, or so long as he lived within that time; and, as he might have died within the year, the contract was not one which, by its terms, could not be performed within a year. This construction of the statute is supported by the case of Knowles v. Hull, 97 Mass. 207, and several other cases in that state. . . . A contract for a copartnership to continue for 27 months would be within the statute, although upon the death of either partner there would be an instantaneous dissolution of the copartnership. In 8 Am. & Eng. Enc. Law (1st Ed.) p. 688, it is stated that a contract

"to continue to do an act for a period greater than one year, or to refrain from doing during such a period,"

is within the statute. The note to this section says:

"Where the contract will be fully performed by the death of the party during the term, the courts of Massachusetts hold the statute does not apply (Doyle v. Dixon, 97 Mass., 208, 93 Am. Dec. 80), but the law elsewhere is stated in the text."

In the note on page 691 it is said:

"Where, however, the death of any person will simply put an end to the contract, leaving it unperformed, the fact that the death may happen within the year will not take the agreement out of the statute."

And the cases to which attention is there called seem to establish that the general rule adopted in this country and in England is that stated in the text. . . .

Taking this contract in question in its entirety, it was clearly contemplated that it was not to be performed by either party within a year. The plaintiff agreed to pay for the business partly by notes, the payment of which was extended for 27 months, and the defendant was to refrain from entering business similar to that carried on by the copartnership for a like period. . . . The defendant agreed, assuming that the testimony of the plaintiff was correct, that he would not carry on this business for 27 months. It seems to me it was clearly within the intention of the parties that the contract was not to be performed within a year, and thus was within the statute. Such an agreement is, I think, clearly within the spirit of the statute, for, as said by Dayley, J., in Boydell v. Drummond, 11 East. 159:

"The mischief meant to be prevented by the statute was the leaving to memory the terms of a contract for longer time than a year. The persons might die who were to prove it, or they might lose their faithful recollection of the terms of it."

A contract restricting the right of an individual to carry on a particular trade or business would seem to be one which was within the class of contracts that the statute intended should be evidenced by a writing. It is a contract to restrain the liberty of the individual, and, if it is good for 27 months, it is good for 20 years, or the life of the promisor; and thus a restraint upon the power of an individual to earn his livelihood would be valid for many years, depending upon the uncertain recollection of conversations, and without the certainty of proof as to the contract that the statute intended should be presented.

I think the contract was within the statute. . . .

CASE NO. 10

Maher v. Randolph. 257 N.Y. 80, 9 N.E. (2d) 786, 111 A.L.R. 1309 (1937)

LOUGHRAM, J. . . . As owners of 240 shares of the stock of a corporation formed under a co-operative ownership plan, plaintiffs held a lease of an apartment in a building erected by the corporation. This apartment, with its furnishings, they let to the defendant for a term to expire on May 15, 1935. The furnishings included three pairs of draperies worth about $150.

On May 5, 1935, the parties entered into an oral agreement for sale by the plaintiffs and purchase by the defendant of the 240 shares of stock for $4,000. In the course of this transaction the defendant inquired whether the plaintiffs "would consent to include the draperies in the sale," and the plaintiffs answered: "Very well, the draperies are yours." Before the time fixed for delivery of the stock and for payment of the first installment of the purchase price, the defendant withdrew from the transaction.

This is an action for breach of the contract of purchase and sale. The defense is the statute of frauds relating to personal property.

"A contract to sell or a sale of any goods or choses in action of the value of fifty dollars or upwards shall not be enforceable by action unless the buyer shall accept part of the goods or choses in action so contracted to be sold or sold, and actually receive the same, or give something in earnest to bind the contract, or in part payment, or unless some note or memorandum in writing of the contract or sale be signed by the party to be charged or his agent in that behalf." Personal Property Law (Consol. Laws, c. 41), § 85, subd. 1.

The question is whether there was such an acceptance and actual receipt of the curtains by the defendant as to make the contract enforceable. . . .

Prior to the enactment in 1911 (Laws 1911, c. 571) of section 85 of the Personal Property Law as part of the Uniform Sales Act, it was settled for us that the mere words of the bargain are not sufficient evidence to satisfy the statute in a case where the buyer already has possession of the goods under some prior and independent transaction of the parties. . . .

Plaintiffs contend that the law was changed by subdivision 3 of section 85. It is thereby provided:

> "There is an acceptance of goods within the meaning of this section when the buyer, either before or after delivery of the goods, expresses by words or conduct his assent to becoming the owner of those specific goods."

The argument of the plaintiffs, as we understand it, is that acceptance by a buyer in independent possession includes an actual receipt; that an acceptance may now be evidenced by words without an act; and that, therefore, such a transaction, though resting in words alone, is no longer condemned by the statute.

. . . The validity of this view of the

statute, as we are aware, has been doubted and denied. But with the policy of the law as there declared in 1848 the Legislature did not see fit to interfere prior to the enactment of the foregoing subdivision 3 of section 85 of the Personal Property Law in 1911. Under the circumstances, we cannot find in section 85 a sufficient expression of intention to overturn so long and so settled a course of decision.

FINCH, J. . . . dissenting: We are no longer bound by Young v. Ingalsbe, 208 N.Y. 503, 102 N.E. 590. The rule enunciated therein has been the subject of much criticism and is contrary to the great weight of authority. 2 Williston on Contracts (Rev. Ed.) § 554; American Law Institute, Restatement of the Law of Contracts, § 202; Burdick, A Statute for Promoting Fraud, 16 Col. Law Rev. p. 273. In 1911 New York adopted the Uniform Sales Act which in paragraph 3 of section 4, provides that

> "There is an acceptance of goods within the meaning of this section when the buyer, either before or after delivery of goods, expresses by words or conduct his assent to becoming the owner of those specific goods." (Personal Property Law, Consol. Laws, c. 41, § 85, subd. 3)

Most of the other states which have adopted the Uniform Sales Act construe this to mean that where goods are already in possession of the buyer, acceptance may be evidenced by words. Williston, op. cit. supra, § 557. The statute having been amended, we are no longer bound by the earlier cases and, especially in view of our adoption of the Uniform Statute, no valid reason appears for continuing to follow a rule which seems to be counter to the new statute and is out of harmony with the rule generally adopted. . . .

CASE NO. 11

Maryatt v. Hubbard. 33 Wash. (2d) 325, 205 P. (2d) 623, 8 A.L.R. (2d) 245 (1949)

Defendant, on whose land was a greenhouse, orally agreed to sell it to a neighbor for a certain price. The neighbor sent the seller a check for the amount, which the seller endorsed for deposit, but before depositing it had an opportunity to sell her residence to one who insisted that the greenhouse be included. She then returned the check, and the would-be purchaser of the greenhouse had one built and sued for the difference between the cost and the purchase price. The statute of frauds was set up as a defense. . . .

BEALS, J. . . . The action was tried to the court, sitting without a jury, and resulted in the entry of findings of fact and conclusions of law in plaintiffs' favor, followed by a judgment against defendant, in the sum of $301.81, together with plaintiffs' costs.

From this judgment, defendant has appealed.

Appellant's assignments of error present one question of law, namely, whether or not the evidence shows that the parties made a valid and binding contract for the purchase and sale of the greenhouse.

Appellant relies upon Rem. Rev. Stat. § 5836-4, the statute of frauds, which provides, in part, as follows:

> "(1) A contract to sell or a sale of any goods or choses in action exceeding the value of $50 shall not be enforceable by action unless the buyer shall accept part of the goods or choses in action so contracted to be sold or sold, and actually receive the same, or give something in earnest to bind the contract, or in part payment, or unless some note or memorandum

in writing of the contract or sale be signed by the party to be charged or his agent in that behalf."

Appellant contends that the delivery of Mr. Maryatt's bank check to appellant, and its acceptance and retention by her for a considerable period of time, did not constitute a payment or, in any other way, a compliance with the section of the statute above quoted.

In the case at bar, the evidence shows, beyond question, that appellant had agreed to sell, and respondents had agreed to purchase, the greenhouse for the sum of $175. There was, of course, no delivery or partial delivery, and there was no note or memorandum of the contract, in writing, signed by the appellant.

If a binding contract between the parties was made, it was because of the delivery of the check, and its retention and endorsement by appellant. Apparently, no such question has ever been directly passed upon by this court. . . .

Whether or not a check, or other form of negotiable paper, is accepted as a payment, under the circumstances here shown or under other similar circumstances, depends upon the intention of the parties, and, in deciding such a question, the court or jury should consider the actions of the parties in connection with the transaction.

In the case of Coffman v. Fleming, 301 Mo. 313, 256 S.W. 731, the supreme court of Missouri adopted the opinion of the court of appeals affirming a judgment of the circuit court in favor of the plaintiff. It was held that a sale, for future delivery, of personal property for more than $50 was binding upon the defendant, who had accepted the plaintiff's check for $50 and held the check for two or three weeks before tendering it back to the plaintiff, who has refused to accept it. The court held that the question of whether the plaintiff accepted the check as part payment was one of fact, to be determined by the jury. It appeared that the plaintiff's check was good, and would have been cashed upon presentation, and that the record contained nothing to indicate that the defendant had any doubt as to the plaintiff's solvency when the contract was entered into.

The supreme court of Iowa, in the case of Rohrback v. Hammill, 162 Iowa 131, 143 N.W. 872, which was tried as an action for damages for breach of a parol contract for the transfer of an interest in real estate, affirmed a judgment in favor of the plaintiff. The action was tried to a jury, which returned a verdict, the defendant appealed. It appeared that, at the time the oral contract was entered into, the plaintiff delivered to the defendant his check for $500, and that the defendant later returned the check to the plaintiff and refused to carry out the contract. The defendant contended that the contract was void, under the statute of frauds. The court quoted at length from the opinion in the case of Conde ve. Dreisam Gold Mining Co. 3 Cal. App. 583, 86 Pac. 825, the quotation concluding with the following:

> " 'We do not, however, understand the rule to require that there should be express words or writing of the parties agreeing that the check should be absolute payment. The circumstances and the conduct of the parties taken together may show an express understanding that the check is taken in satisfaction of the debt, or estop the creditor from claiming the contrary. As here, for example, the check was sent for the express purpose of payment, and was retained under circumstances implying that it was so accepted. It has been held that unreasonable delay in returning a check may make it equal to payment.' " . . .

In the case of Charles R. Ablett Co.

v. Sencer, 130 Misc. 416, 224 N.Y.S. 251, it was held that the delivery to the plaintiff of the purchaser's check was sufficient to take an oral contract for the purchase of goods exceeding $50 in value without the statute of frauds. It appeared that, when the check was delivered, the seller (plaintiff in the action) gave the defendant a receipted bill for the merchandise, and that, subsequently, the defendant purchaser stopped payment on the check and the plaintiff brought suit thereon. The court denied the defendant's motion to set aside the verdict of the jury and for a new trial.

In the case at bar, there is little, if any, substantial conflict in the evidence. Appellant desired to sell the greenhouse, and the parties agreed upon a price which was satisfactory to all concerned. After the delivery of the check to appellant, she was still satisfied with the contract and endorsed the check. When, upon cross-examination . . . appellant was asked whether she received the check in fulfillment of the contract, she answered: "Well, at that time, yes, that's so."

At a later date, when she found a purchaser for the entire property, which evidently she had not anticipated selling when she made the contract with respondents for the sale of the greenhouse, and the purchaser insisted that the greenhouse be included in the sale, appellant repudiated her contract with respondents and returned their check, with the letter referred to above.

The trial court found that appellant accepted the check in full payment for the greenhouse, and this finding is amply supported by the evidence.

Apparently, appellant did not decide to sell her home until after January 1, 1947. Certainly she reached that decision some days after respondents' check was delivered to her. When her endorsement was placed thereon is uncertain. On cross-examination, appellant testified that she received the check, recognizing that it represented payment by respondents of the agreed price for the sale of the greenhouse. She never questioned Mr. Maryatt's credit or that the check would be paid upon presentation. . . .

. . . judgment appealed from is affirmed. . . .

CASE NO. 12

Murphy v. Munson. 95 Cal. A. 306, 212 Pac. (2d) 603 (1949)

THOMPSON, J. This is a suit to recover the purchase price of a portable sawmill and equipment sold to defendant for the agreed price of $4,207.14 and the delivery of which the purchaser refused to accept. The answer denied the material allegations of the complaint and pleaded, as a further defense, the statute of frauds. Civil Code, § 1624a. The agreement to purchase the sawmill was in writing, which was signed in defendant's name by his amanuensis, at his request. It was in the form of a letter, the terms of which were dictated to defendant's clerk, Mr. Miller, who took memoranda of the terms and order for the machine, and subsequently wrote them out on one of defendant's printed letterheads and signed defendant's name to it as he had been requested to do.

. . . At the written request of the defendant, the standard machine which was ordered was altered, to the detriment of plaintiffs, and new parts were purchased and installed at a cost of $525. The court adopted findings favorable to the defendant, and judgment was rendered that plaintiffs take nothing by this action. . . .

In defendant's letter to plaintiffs dated August 20th, he requested plaintiffs to make specified alterations and changes in the standard Farquhar Saw

Mill as advertised by the addition of
"a third headblock and a top-saw rig to carry a 40 inch saw to be used in connection with a 60 inch bottom saw."

Plaintiffs agreed to do so and wrote defendant August 29th saying that they had ordered the requested parts at a cost of $525, but suggested the use of a 36 inch saw instead of the requested 40 inch saw. September 6, 1947, defendant accepted that proposed change of saws and thereby ratified the former agreement of purchase, including his authorization to sign his name thereto. That letter reads:

"Sept. 6, 1947

"Gentlemen:

"We have your letter of August 29 in regard to the top-saw attachment and additional head-block.

"We will use the 36 inch saw instead of the 40 inch saw as we first intended and approximately 60 day shipment will be all right as we intend to install the mill this winter.

"Yours very truly
(Signed) W. H. Munson."

The machine and equipment were crated and ready for shipment, but defendant subsequently refused to accept delivery. This suit was then commenced to recover the agreed purchase price.

The correspondence between the parties in this case clearly constitutes a valid binding agreement for the purchase and sale of the sawmill and equipment in question. The letters from the defendant were written on his own printed letterheads, and his name was signed to each letter. The plaintiffs were led to believe they were dealing directly with the defendant himself. The letters were signed with the defendant's name, by his direct authorization. While that authorization was general and not specific as to each letter, the evidence was adequate to show his authorization. More-over, he subsequently ratified and approved that agreement to purchase the machinery. . . . The signatures of the defendant to those letters, under the circumstances of this case, fully meet the requirements of § 1624a of the Civil Code and comply with the statute of frauds, for they were signed by "his agent in that behalf." Moreover, that section of the code provides that

"if the goods are to be manufactured by the seller especially for the buyer and are not suitable for sale to others in the ordinary course of the seller's business, the provisions of this section shall not apply."

There is evidence in this case that the alterations and changes made in the standard machine at defendant's request rendered it unsalable to others in the ordinary course of plaintiffs' business. They testified that they tried to sell the machine as altered, and were unable to do so. . . .

The judgment is reversed and the court is directed to ascertain the sum due and owing to plaintiffs and to render judgment in their favor for that amount. . . .

CASE NO. 13

Pitek v. McGuire. 51 N.M. 364, 184 Pac. (2d) 647, 1 A.L.R. (2d) 830 (1947)

Summary of Decision: The defendant, a woman 76 years old, residing in Chicago, owned six contiguous lots in Albuquerque, New Mexico. The plaintiff began negotiations by letter for the purchase of these lots and after the defendant's refusal of an offer of $3,500 asked her to put a price upon them; in reply the defendant stated she thought the lots ought to be worth about $12,000. Subsequently the plaintiff carried on oral negotiations with the defendant at her home, in the course of which a purchase price of $11,000 was agreed upon, the plaintiff giving the defendant a down-payment check for $500 with an indorsement:

> "To be applied on purchase of property on E. Central Ave., Albuquerque, N.M., Bernalillo Co."

Later the defendant executed a warranty deed to plaintiff, correctly describing the property, which she mailed to her attorney, who wrote the plaintiff that he was holding the deed for him; but before the deed was delivered the defendant, having discovered that the property, which she has not seen for several years during which time land values had greatly increased, was worth a great deal more than the purchase price, declined to go through with the purchase. . . .

BRICE, CH.J. . . . This action was brought to enforce the specific performance of a contract for the sale and purchase of real estate; and the questions are (1) was the contract within the statute of frauds? . . .

The trial court concluded that the defendant was the owner of the property in question; that the contract was void and unenforcible because within the statute of frauds of the states of New Mexico and Illinois. . . .

The findings of the trial court satisfy us that the plaintiff has established all facts necessary to a recovery, if a memorandum of the contract was signed by the defendant that satisfies the requirements of the statute of frauds. . . .

To satisfy the statute of frauds the contract itself must be in writing; or if verbal, then there must have been some writing subsequently made however informal, stating each of its essential elements, signed by the person to be charged, or by his authorized agent acting for him.

The essentials of such contracts have been stated as follows:

"A memorandum, in order to make enforceable a contract within the statute, may be any document or writing, formal or informal, signed by the party to be charged or by his agent actually or apparently authorized thereunto, which states with reasonable certainty, (a) Each party to the contract either by his own name, or by such a description as will serve to identify him, or by the name or description of his agent, and (b) the land, goods, or other subject-matter to which the contract relates, and (c) the terms and conditions of all the promises constituting the contract and by whom and to whom the promises are made." Restatement, Contracts, § 207.

"Generally speaking, a memorandum in writing meets the requirements of the statute of frauds that certain contracts shall be evidenced by writing if it contains the names of the parties, the terms and conditions of the contract, and a description of the property sufficient to render it capable of identification." 49 A.J., Statute of Frauds, § 321.

The only writings signed by defendant having reference to the oral contract were the deed sent to her attorney, and that on the check which was endorsed by her. . . .

The only land defendant owned in the City of Albuquerque situated on East Central Avenue at the time the check was endorsed by defendant, was lots 3 to 8 inclusive, of Block 4, Mankato Place Addition to the city of Albuquerque, which consisted of six contiguous lots fronting 150 feet on that avenue. She did own property beyond the city limits of Albuquerque, fronting on an extension of East Central Avenue, but the description excludes that property. It is evident that the memorandum had reference to the Mankato Place property, or some part of it. One or more of the lots would come within the description. If the description had been "all of payee's property fronting on East Central, etc.," or "property fronting 150 feet on East Central, etc.," the description would have been sufficient. But, while the property is in one tract, it is divided into lots, any one or more of which is "property on East Central Avenue, etc."

The plaintiff asserts that the memorandum written on the check, supplemented by previous correspondence and a description of the property contained in an undelivered deed executed by the defendant after she received the check, satisfied the statute of frauds.

A question is whether the correspondence between the parties antedating the making of the oral agreement may be used as evidence to supplement the description of the property written on the check.

The fourth section of the statute of frauds does not prohibit the making of an oral contract for the sale of tenements, etc. Such a contract may be in writing or oral, but unless it is in writing (that is, if oral), then "some memorandum or note thereof shall be in writing," etc. to legally prove it.

There is a difference between a contract in writing and a memorandum of a parol contract as contemplated by the statute of frauds. The former may be made up of letters and telegrams or any other character of writing or writings, which together will constitute a contract, or it may be a formal contract. But if the contract made is oral, it is written evidence to prove that the particular contract was made that must be produced. The writings need not in themselves amount to a contract or be addressed to the other party. It is sufficient as evidence if the person to be bound signs any statement or document in which he admits that the parties made the oral contract, sufficiently stating therein its essential terms, 2 Williston on Contracts (Rev. Ed.), §§ 567, 579 (a); no matter what may be his purpose in making the writing, or to whom it is addressed. 2 Williston on Contracts (Rev. Ed.), § 568, 579; 1 Restatement, Contracts, § 209.

If the description on the check can be supplemented by the letters written prior to the time the parties entered into the oral contract of sale and purchase, then the description of the property is adequate. The contents of these letters consist of negotiations for the sale and purchase of the property in suit. . . .

It is commonly said that a memorandum may be made at any time subsequent to the making of the oral contract and prior to suit. Williston on Contracts (Rev. Ed.), § 590. But appellant insists that the memorandum required by the statute of frauds may be made prior to the making of a contract. There are statements in text books to that effect. 49 A.J., Statute of Frauds, §§ 317 and 335; 2 Williston on Contracts, § 590. But each of these texts has reference to contracts resulting from a written offer orally accepted. The offer bound the offerer when so accepted by the offeree, but the contract thus made was not oral. We have reference to contracts in which the offer and acceptance are oral.

Appellant cites Restatement of Law of Contracts, § 214, as follows:

> "A signed memorandum that correctly states the terms of a contract satisfies the statute, whether the memorandum is made before or at the time of the formation of the contract, or at any subsequent time during its existence."

This text is supported by the following illustration:

"A and B, in January, 1925, enter into an enforceable written contract within the statute, for one year's employment. In January, 1926, they agree orally to enter into another contract 'on the terms expressed in our contract of last year.' There is a sufficient memorandum of the new contract." Illus. 1, § 214.

We do not agree that this illustration correctly states the law and we have found no supporting cases. The assumed agreement stated as an illustration, had expired by its terms; and being within the statute of frauds, it could not be revived and extended by parol. No contract within the statute of frauds that has expired by its terms can be revived and extended by parol. Reason and authority are against it. Thompson v. Robinson, 65 W.Va. 506, 64 S.E. 718, 17 Ann. Cas. 1109; Smith v. Taylor, 82 Cal. 533, 23 Pac. 217, 220; 49 A.J., Statute of Frauds, § 7; 37 C.J.S., Frauds, Statute of, § 113. See Ann. 17 A. & E. Ann. Cas. 1111.

We are of the opinion that a contract wholly oral, and within the statute of frauds, may not be proved by a writing made prior to the meeting of the minds of the parties. Handy v. Barclay, 98 Conn. 290, 119 A 227; Massie-Wilson Grocery Co. v. Carroll, Brough, Robinson & Humphrey, 105 Okla. 56, 231 Pac. 1084; Jacobson v. Perman, 238 Mass. 445, 131 N.E. 174; Mead v. Leo Sheep Co., 32 Wyo. 313, 232 Pac. 511; Rabe v. Danaher, 2 Cir., 56 P. (2d) 758; 37 C.J.S., Frauds, Statute of, § 171.

But this does not necessarily mean that a sufficient memorandum may not consist partially of writings made prior to the making of the oral agreement. If such prior writings are referred to in, and thereby made a part of, a memorandum or writing subsequently made so it can be said that the prior writings are incorporated therein, it is not objectionable on that account.

We are of the opinion that the letters in evidence cannot be resorted to to aid the faulty description of the property in the memorandum written on the check. . . .

Ordinarily an undelivered deed in the possession of the grantor or his attorney, that does not contain, or refer to, the terms of an oral agreement to sell and purchase real estate; or which does not refer to a writing made in pursuance thereof, or in which writing it is not referred to, cannot be used as evidence to prove the identity of the particular property that was the subject of an oral contract or complete an insufficient description thereof contained in the memorandum. Carr v. Maxon Estate Inc., 26 N.M. 308, 191 Pac. 137; Swain v. Burnette, 89 Cal. 564, 26 Pac. 1093; Day v. Lacasse, 85 Me. 242, 27 Atl. 124; Hartenbower v. Uden, 242 Ill. 434, 90 N.E. 298, 29 L.R.A., N.S. 738; Burns v. Huseman, 266 Ill. 212, 107 N.E. 462. See authorities pro and con in Ann. 100 A.L.R., p. 196 et seq.

This deed was sent by defendant from Chicago to her attorney in Albuquerque who wrote plaintiff regarding it: "I am holding . . . a deed from Katherine McGuire to you and your wife as joint tenants," and this is all that is stated regarding it. If defendant or her attorney had sent plaintiff the deed for examination, or to close the transaction, with a statement that it has been executed for such purpose or purposes, it could have been considered as supplementing the memorandum written on the check. . . .

The decree of the district court should be affirmed, and it is so ordered. . . .

CASE NO. 14

Martin v. Seigel. 35 *Wash.* (2*d*) 223, 212 *Pac.* (2*d*) 107 (1949)

SCHWELLENBACH, J. This is an appeal from a decree dismissing an action for specific performance of a contract to sell real property. . . .

On June 24, 1948, the following Earnest Money Agreement was entered into. . . .

"Seattle, Washington June 24, 1948 —Received from *Lois M. Martin* (*Widow*) the sum of *$1,000.00* Dollars as part payment on this his (her) agreement to purchase from Frank L. McGuire, Inc., Agent for owner, the following real property *at 309 E. Mercer and furniture as per inventory* in the City of Seattle, County of *King*, State of Washington, at the agreed price of *$18,500* Dollars, the balance of the down payment to be paid as follows: . . ."

On August 5, 1948 a policy of title insurance was furnished, which described the property:

"In The County of King, State of Washington

"Lot one (1) and north 10 feet of lot two (2), block thirty-two (32), Supplementary Plat of Pontius Second Addition to Seattle, according to plat thereof recorded in volume 5 of plats, page 76, records of said county."

This is the correct legal description. . . .

The general rule with regard to the sufficiency of legal descriptions to satisfy the statute of frauds in contracts for the sale of real property is stated in 49 Am. Jur. 658, Statute of Frauds, § 349:

". . . In general, a description of the property in a contract for the sale of real estate may be sufficient to satisfy the statute of frauds even though it is not in such particulars as to render unnecessary a resort to extrinsic evidence to apply the description to the subject matter; the description is considered sufficient if with the assistance of external evidence it can be applied to the property intended to the exclusion of all other property. It follows that evidence of extrinsic circumstances is admissible within limitations in aid of a description the words of which standing alone would not identify the subject matter of the contract positively. A writing relied upon to constitute the memorandum must in and of itself furnish the evidence that the minds of the parties met as to the particular property which the one proposed to sell and the other agreed to buy; when such evidence is not found in the writing, it cannot be supplied by parol, but if it is found there, parol evidence of extrinsic circumstances may be resorted to for the purpose of specifically designating the property to which both parties are shown to have referred by the terms of the writing."

In 37 C.J.S., Frauds, Statute of, § 188, p. 674, we find the following:

"In transactions affecting urban property a description of the property by street and number is a sufficient description where the city or town in which it is located is stated either in the caption or the body of the instrument or may be ascertained from the writing. Ordinarily, however, an omission of the city or town in which the property is located renders the description insufficient where it contains nothing from which the omitted statement may be inferred."

In Broadway Hospital & Sanitarium v. Decker, 49 Wash. 586, 92 Pac. 445, 446, we affirmed a judgment dismissing an action for specific performance, where the memorandum described the property to be sold as: "House No. 322 Broadway," because the writing did not show the state, county, or city where the property might be found. See also, West v. Cave, 98 Wash. 237, 167 Pac. 747, where the property was described as the "J. T. Arrasmith place." Rogers v. Lippy, 99 Wash. 312, 169 Pac. 858, L.R.A. 1918C, 583, where the writing stated: "my stock ranch located in sections 9, 17 and 21 township 3 south, range 13 east, Sweetgrass county, Mont." Nelson v. Davis 102 Wash. 313, 172 Pac. 1178, 1179, "One lot and store building in Wenda(e)ll, Idaho, in the county of Gooding, state of Idaho." . . .

It will thus be seen that this court is at variance with the more liberal rule which permits parol testimony to explain what particular property the parties had in mind when they contracted to transfer real property described merely by a street number. We do not care to recede from the rule adopted by us, which has been stated in a long line of decisions over a number of years, and known and followed by the members of the bar and title men. We do not apologize for the rule. We feel that it is fair and just to require people dealing with real estate to properly and adequately describe it, so that courts may not be compelled to resort to extrinsic evidence in order to find out what was in the minds of the contracting parties. . . .

In the interests of continuity and clarity of the law of this state with respect to legal descriptions, we hereby hold that every contract or agreement involving a sale, conveyance or interest in platted real property must contain, in addition to the other requirements of the statute of frauds, the description of such property by the correct lot number(s), block number, addition, city, county and state. . . .

Applying the above rule to the facts in the present case, it is apparent that the legal description of the property in question is insufficient and, therefore, the agreement set forth in the earnest money receipt is . . . unenforceable. . . .

CASE NO. 15

Weber v. De Cecco. 1 N.J. Sup. 353, 61 Atl. (2d) 651 (1948)

HANEMAN, J. This is a suit seeking to restrain the defendant-landlord from interfering with the quiet and peaceful possession of the plaintiff-tenants. The facts as alleged in the pleadings . . . demonstrate that on or about September 1, 1939 the parties hereto entered into a written lease signed by the plaintiffs and the defendant. . . .

Alfred E. Weber testified that sometime prior to September 1, 1944, that being the date of the expiration of the term provided for in said lease, he requested the defendant to renew the lease for an additional term of five years. . . . Sometime subsequent to September 1, 1944 the defendant requested the plaintiffs to produce and deliver to him the original lease. Thereafter, and still within the month of September 1944, the defendant returned the original lease, in the body of which had been inserted the following provision: "renewed for sixty months (60) from the first day of September, 1944." . . .

On the cardinal questions there is no dispute. The lease dated 1939 was delivered to the defendant after the expiration of the term therein provided, for the purpose of obtaining a renewal. Defendant typed the words above quoted in the body of the lease, above the signatures written in 1939, with the intent of renewing the lease for a period of sixty months and then delivered the same to plaintiffs.

The very narrow and restricted

question here involved is whether the lease, as offered in evidence, complies with Revised Statutes 25: 1–1, N.J.S.A.

It is conceded that the alleged tenancy commencing September 1, 1944, being for a period longer than three years, must be in writing "and signed by the parties." Defendant contends that the alleged lease, as offered, does not comply with such statute, in that it was not physically signed in 1944. We are, therefore, confronted with the question as to whether, under the facts, the signatures appended to the lease on September 1, 1939 can be considered the signatures to a lease, the term of which was to commence September 1, 1944.

It is to be remembered that the section above referred to is a portion of our Statute of Frauds which we obtained from the English statute entitled "An Act for the Prevention of Frauds and Perjuries." This statute was originally enacted to prevent fraud and perjury in the enforcement of obligations depending for their evidence on the memory of witnesses by requiring certain enumerated contracts and transactions to be evidenced by a writing signed by the parties. There is no requirement in the statute that the signature be in definite or particular form. It has been held that typewritten or printed names, signatures in ink or pencil, or any name or symbol used by a party with the intention of constituting it his signature, is sufficient to comply with the statutory requirements. 37 C.J.S., Frauds, Statute of, § 202; 40 Am. Jur. par. 377.

Restatement Contracts, par. 210, reads as follows:

> "The signature to a memorandum under the Statute may be written or printed and need not be subscribed at the foot of the memorandum, but must be made or adopted with the declared or apparent intent of authenticating the memorandum as that of the signer."

It is therefore apparent that in the first instance the lease would have been effective if it contained a name, initial or symbol affixed thereto by the parties with the intention that it should be recognized as their signatures.

It is as well a compliance with the statutes if the parties adopt a prior signature made by them with the intent to authenticate the instrument. 37 C.J.S., Frauds, Statute of, § 202.

It therefore follows that the question of whether the insertion of the phraseology extending the term of a written lease originally signed by the parties but not thereafter re-signed is a compliance with the Statute of Frauds, turns upon the intention of the parties. It revolves about whether they intended to adopt the original signatures. Under the facts, it seems clear that the lease was delivered to the defendant with the intention of obtaining a renewal thereof; that the defendant inserted the phraseology for this purpose, and by his redelivery to plaintiffs signified his willingness to adopt the original signature and so to be bound. . . .

CASE NO. 16

Andre v. Ellison. 324 Mass. 665, 88 N.E. (2d) 340 (1949)

. . . .

WILKINS, J. This is an action of contract by the buyer against the seller for breach of a contract for the sale of land in Ludlow. . . . One of the defences is the statute of frauds. . . . The District Court judge found for the plaintiff. The Appellate Division vacated the finding, and ordered judgment for the defendant. The plaintiff appealed.

The alleged written contract is as follows:

"Ludlow, Mass. Mar. 8, 1947, Received of John B. Andre Five Hundred Dollars first payment on land west side of Miller Street. Balance to be paid forty-five dollars per acre on delivery of deed on or before May 1, 1947. (Signed) Mr. F. H. Ellison."

The land is the southerly portion of a large tract owned by the defendant and not separated by any distinguishing marks from the defendant's remaining land. During the negotiations the parties stood on the premises and indicated where the line was to run to divide the southerly portion to be purchased by the plaintiff from the northerly portion to be retained by the defendant.

The alleged written contract standing alone fails to meet the requirements of the statute of frauds, as it does not contain a description which applies to one parcel of land only. Michelson v. Sherman, 310 Mass. 774, 778, 39 N.E. (2d) 633, 139 A.L.R. 960. This the plaintiff concedes. His contention is rather that a memorandum of an oral agreement sufficient to satisfy the statute may be found if the writing of March 8, 1947, is considered with other writings in the light of the evidence. See Frost v. Kendall, 320 Mass. 623, 626, 70 N.E. (2d) 521; Tampa Shipbuilding & Engineering Co. v. General Const. Co., 5 Cir., 43 F. (2d) 309, 85 A.L.R. 1184. These other writings are a survey and a deed made subsequent to the memorandum at the defendant's request but not bearing his handwritten signature. The survey shows that boundaries to which the parties orally agreed, and the deed describes those boundaries accurately by metes and bounds. The survey bears the stamped imprint of the name of the surveyor and the legend "Land Survey for Frank Ellison. Land West of Miller St. Ludlow Mass. 3/17/47." To the deed a wafer seal is affixed opposite the blank for the signature of the defendant, who is described therein as the grantor.

The survey and the deed cannot be considered as signed by the defendant. There is nothing to indicate that his printed or typed name or the seal was adopted by the defendant as his signature with the intent of authenticating either writing as his own. Cabot v. Haskins, 3 Pick. 83, 95; Boardman v. Spooner, 13 Allen 353, 357–358, 90 Am. Dec. 196; Irving v. Goodimate Co., 320 Mass. 454, 459, 70 N.E. (2d) 414, 171 A.L.R. 326; Restatement, Contracts, § 210. Williston, Contracts (Rev. Ed.), § 585. . . .

It likewise could not be found that these independent unauthenticated writings were brought to the attention of the parties and were so united in their minds with the signed writing of March 8, 1947, that taken together these writings have been adopted to express their purpose. . . . No survey is referred to in the writing of March 8, 1947. The actual survey made thereafter means no more than would any other survey of land of the defendant on the west side of Miller Street. In Baker v. Hall, 158 Mass. 361, 33 N.E. 612, relied upon by the plaintiff, it appears from the original papers that the sketch was physically incorporated as well as expressly referred to, in the memorandum. The writing of March 8, 1947, refers vaguely to "delivery of deed." Any deed of real estate of the defendant on the west side of Miller Street would satisfy that description. . . .

Order of Appellate Division affirmed.

Review Questions

1. What is the parole evidence rule?
2. What is the purpose of the Statute of Frauds?
3. How does a contract in consideration of marriage differ from a simple marriage contract?
4. What is a secondary obligation as distinguished from a primary obligation?
5. Does the Statute of Frauds require written evidence for the enforceability of primary obligations?
6. Construct a fact situation illustrating an undertaking to answer for the debt, default, or miscarriage of another.
7. Does the Statute of Frauds require written evidence for the enforceability of every contract that in any way pertains to real property?
8. Under what circumstances will an oral agreement for the transfer of an interest in real property be enforceable?
9. What is the justification for computing the period of leases for a year from the day that the term commences rather than from the day that the lease is executed?
10. What determines whether a contract is one of long duration?
11. Illustrate a contract that is not of long duration although the time of performance has exceeded one year.
12. What are *choses in action* as distinguished from *goods?*
13. Is an oral contract for the sale of corporate securities enforceable?
14. What events will take an oral contract for sale of goods or choses in action out of the operation of the statute?
15. Does the Statute of Frauds require written evidence in the form of a formally executed contract?
16. The Statute of Frauds requires only the signature of "the party to be charged." What does this mean?
17. What does an acknowledgment of a legal instrument consist of?

Problems for Discussion

1. Plaintiff purchased a heating plant from defendant upon the latter's oral warranty to the effect that the heating plant was of sufficient capacity to properly heat plaintiff's building. The heating plant proved to be inadequate and plaintiff sued for breach of the warranty. Defendant produced a written contract under which the sale was made and the contract contained no such warranty. Defendant contends that plaintiff should not be allowed to establish the warranty by oral proof. Result?
2. Defendant made the following oral promise to plaintiff: "You give all the goods they want to Harris and Rogers and charge directly to them, and the first of every month you bring in the bill and I will pay it." Plaintiff sued defendant to recover for goods delivered to Harris and Rogers. Did he recover?
3. In *Wray* v. *Cox,* 86 Miss. 638, the defendant told the plaintiff to supply a third party with certain goods and orally stated, "I will see you paid." Would you hold this oral promise to be enforceable?

4. The principal stockholder in the X corporation orally promised a creditor of the corporation that he would, upon failure of the corporation to pay, discharge the obligation. Is this promise enforceable?
5. X leased property to Y, who then sublet the property to Z. At the time of the sublease, Y owed X three months' rent, which Z orally agreed to pay to X. Can X hold Z to this promise?
6. Suppose in the facts above that Z made the oral promise to X at the termination of the lease and in consideration of X's letting Z have the premises for another year. Would your conclusion be different?
7. Defendant, a large stockholder, director, and vice-president of the X corporation, orally promised plaintiff at the time of the latter's purchase of 6,000 shares of stock in the X corporation that in the event the stock became worthless the defendant would pay to plaintiff the sum of $1,500. The stock became worthless and in an action on the oral promise, defendant contended he was a guarantor and the promise was not enforceable. Result? (*Kilbride* v. *Moss,* 113 Colo. 432)
8. X orally contracts to sell Y standing timber and at the time of the agreement Y pays X $2,000 on account. What is the importance of determining whether this is a contract for realty or personal property?
9. X orally contracted to sell Y certain real property. Y made a down payment and took possession of the premises. X refuses to execute a deed to the property. Can Y force performance?
10. Plaintiff took possession of real property under a long-term oral lease with defendant and expended $47,000 in preparing the property for his use. Is the oral lease enforceable?
11. X, by letter, offered to sell Y a certain piece of real property. Y accepted the offer by telephone. When X learned Y's intent to place a modernistic house upon the premises, he refused to convey title to Y. Can Y force performance?
12. The XY Partnership orally agreed to admit Z, one of their employees, as a partner for a period of five years. Is this promise enforceable?
13. X called Y—a fire-insurance agent—on the telephone and requested insurance on a designated piece of property for a period of three years. Y assured X that the matter would be taken care of. X suffered a loss the next day and upon seeking to recover was met with the defense that the oral undertaking was not enforceable. What is your decision?
14. An oral agreement had been made that the Ritz Carlton Valet Service could remain as a tenant "so long as the 150 Central Park South, Inc. owned the premises." The tenant took occupancy of the premises in August, 1946, and this action to test the enforceability of this agreement was commenced two years later at which time the premises were still owned by 150 Central Park South, Inc. The tenant urged that since the lease was capable of performance within a year it was enforceable. Decide. (*Central Park South* v. *Ritz Carlton Valet Serv.,* 93 N.Y.S. (2d) 478)
15. Plaintiff brought action for specific performance based upon a writing to sell "Lot no. 60 on the South side of Jefferson Street in that part of the City of Montgomery, formerly known as New Philadelphia." Decide. (*Jones* v. *Pettus,* 39 So. (2d) 12)
16. The agreement alleged to this cause of action was orally entered into during

the month of December, 1946. The agreement provided for payment, in addition to the plaintiff's salary, based upon the amount by which the defendant's net sales for 1947 should exceed a certain fixed quota. Decide. (*McCants* v. *Emeerol Mfg. Co.*, 81 N.Y.S. (2d) 770)

17. X orally contracted to sell Y forty tons of coal at $11 a ton. Is this agreement binding in your state?
18. X orally contracted to construct a set of false teeth for Y. Is this oral agreement binding?

8 CONTRACTS:

ILLEGAL AGREEMENTS

An illegal agreement is not enforceable; therefore, it cannot qualify as a contract. Such agreements are said to be *void*. This means that the law will not give aid to either party but will leave them exactly as they are found, unless extraordinary circumstances demand intervention.

Illegality of an agreement may result from the following causes:

(1) Violation of some rule of common law;

(2) violation of some statutory enactment;

(3) violation of that which is conceived as being in the best interest of society. Such agreements are usually designated as being contrary to that "unruly horse," public policy.

► I. AGREEMENTS IN VIOLATION OF COMMON LAW OR STATUTORY ENACTMENT

Any agreement is illegal that is not in keeping with, or that is prohibited by, a positive rule of law, whether statutory or common. The law cannot lend its aid to the furthering of that which it seeks to prevent. One who agrees to the performing of an act that is contrary to the established legal standards of conduct can be given no redress for a failure to realize his expectations under such an agreement. It would not lead to obtaining the contemplated social control if legal remedies for the violation of agreements of this nature were made available. Illegal agreements would be:

(1) Those agreements that contemplate the commission of a crime or a civil wrong. To illustrate:

> X agrees to steal Y's car for Z in consideration of the latter's promise to pay X $200. X cannot enforce the agreement.
>
> In *Nichols* v. *Ruggles*, 3 Day (Conn.) 145, the contract provided for the printing of literary works by the plaintiff in violation of the copyright. This was a wrong against the copyright holder and the contract could not be enforced against the defendant, who had promised to pay for the printing.

(2) Those agreements that provide for the commission of acts that are either prohibited, declared illegal, or declared void by statute or ordinance. The imposition of a penalty for the commission of an act may in itself be a sufficient indication of the legislative intent to prohibit such act.

(3) Those agreements entered into by persons in respect to activities denied them because of their failure to obtain the necessary certificate or license as required by statute or ordinance, providing the purpose in requiring the certificate

or license is to give protection to the public rather than to raise revenue.[1, 2] To illustrate:

It has been held by the courts that unlicensed attorneys, physicians, and schoolteachers could not enforce the contracts under which they rendered services. Obviously the purpose of requiring professional people to obtain licenses is to protect the public against those who are not qualified.

In *Albertson & Co.* v. *Shenton,* (N.H.) 98 Atl. 516, the plaintiff had sold the defendant a ring, without having acquired a peddler's license as required by statute. The court held the agreement void and denied him the right to recover upon the grounds that the statute was not merely for the purpose of obtaining revenue. They said:

> "Its purpose in part is to protect the public by preventing unsuitable persons, those not of good moral character, from engaging in the business regulated."

In *Walker* v. *Baldwin,* 103 Md. 352, the plaintiff sold realty for the defendant without having obtained a license to carry on the business of a real estate broker. The court allowed him to recover for his services upon the basis that the statute was a revenue measure and not for the protection of the public.

In *Wood* v. *Krepps,* 168 Cal. 382, it was held that an ordinance requiring a license by pawnbrokers was primarily for the purposes of administrative convenience and securing revenue.

▶ II. AGREEMENTS CONTRARY TO PUBLIC POLICY

In present-day society, the rights of the individual members are subservient to those of the group as a whole. To accomplish its economic and social objectives, organized society places numerous limitations upon the activities of its members by restriction or requirement. Our public policy consists of the established rules of conduct and accepted principles and standards whereby these objectives are to be accomplished. Broadly speaking, *public policy* can be said to be that intangible something which is regarded as being socially desirable and in the best interest of society as a whole.

There are many agreements which are injurious to, or have a tendency to be injurious to, the public welfare even though they are not contrary to public policy as established by positive law. Any activities that tend to defeat social objectives (whether or not these objectives are declared by a positive rule of law) are contrary to public policy. The phrase *agreements contrary to public policy* is used to designate those agreements which contravene public policy not declared by positive law.

The principle that agreements contrary to public policy are illegal is as extensive in scope of application as are human relations. And while this has led to some difference of judicial opinion in declaring agreements illegal, there is substantial

---

[1] Rosasco Creameries v. Cohen, p. 227.

[2] Gardner v. Reed, p. 228.

harmony of opinion on certain classes of cases. We must bear in mind, however, that public policy may greatly vary with time and place.

In *Trist* v. *Child*, 21 Wall (U.S.) 441, the court observed:

"Lord Mansfield said: 'Many contracts which are not against morality, are still void as being against the maxims of sound policy.'

"It is a rule of the common law of universal application, that where a contract express or implied is tainted with either of the vices last named, as to the consideration or the thing to be done, no alleged right founded upon it can be enforced in a court of justice.

"Within the condemned category are:

"An agreement—to pay for supporting for election a candidate for sheriff; to pay for resigning a public position to make room for another; to pay for not bidding at a sheriff's sale of real property; to pay for not bidding for articles to be sold by the government at auction; to pay for not bidding for a contract to carry the mail on a specified route; to pay a person for his aid and influence in procuring an office and for not being a candidate himself; to pay for procuring a contract from the government; to pay for procuring signatures to a petition to the Governor for a pardon; to sell land to a particular person when the surrogate's order to sell should have been obtained; to pay for suppressing evidence and compounding a felony; to convey and assign a part of what should come from an ancestor by descent, devise or distribution; to pay for promoting a marriage; to influence the disposition of property by will in a particular way."

► III. PARTICULAR TYPES OF CONTRACTS CONSIDERED

A. CONTRACTS IN RESTRAINT OF TRADE

"Among the most ancient rules of the common law is the one that bonds in restraint of trade are void. As early as the second year of Henry V (A.D. 1415), we find by the Year Books that this was considered old and settled law." *Alger* v. *Thacher*, 19 Pick. (Mass.) 51.

Restatement of the Law of Contracts, § 513, states:

"A bargain is in restraint of trade when its performance would limit competition in any business or restrict a promisor in the exercise of a gainful occupation."

Various reasons have been alleged to support this rule. From the point of view of public policy the basic considerations seem to be that

(1) contracts in restraint of trade subject *the public* to the harmful effects of monopoly; [3] and

(2) they tend to deprive the public of the services of men in their most useful capacities.

---

[3] Buckalew v. Niehuss, p. 229.

1. *Statutory Provisions*

The reader should take cognizance of the state and federal statutes prohibiting contracts and combinations in restraint of trade. These have been specifically designed to prevent monopolistic combinations of business units and monopolistic mutual-benefit trade practices between competing business units. Although such combinations and practices were illegal as a matter of common law, the public has had little, if any, protection from their harmful effect. For the only consequence of common law illegality is the unenforceability of the contract between the parties. Under our prohibitory statutes, the contracting parties subject themselves to fine and imprisonment, and any such combination can be dissolved and unlawful practices prevented.

The Sherman Antitrust Law, passed by Congress in 1890, has served as a model for the various state statutes dealing with this subject. The basic provisions read:

> "Every contract, combination in the form of trust or otherwise, or conspiracy, in restraint of trade or commerce among the several states, or with foreign nations, is hereby declared to be illegal. Every person who shall make such contract, or engage in any such combination or conspiracy, shall be deemed guilty of a misdemeanor. . . ."

In their application of this statute, the courts have been guided by the common law rule of reason, which rule is discussed in the following section.

B. CONTRACTS REASONABLY IN RESTRAINT OF TRADE

Not all contracts in restraint of trade are, however, regarded as contrary to public policy. Society gives its sanction to such contracts as are said to be "reasonably in restraint of trade." The designation *reasonably in restraint of trade* is in itself of no significance. This has been the courts' way of saying that if the objectives of agreements, even though these agreements are in restraint of trade, are paramount to the public interest, they are reasonable and consequently enforceable.

1. *Agreements Not to Compete Accompanying Sale of Business*

An asset of considerable value can be the intangible element of good will that an established business or professional enterprise enjoys. Purchasers generally recognize that unless they can benefit from the good will at least to the extent of being protected against competition with the seller, the physical assets may be of little value. Sellers must be able to give such protection in order fully to capitalize upon their established good will and to sell to their best advantage. The courts recognize that agreements are not contrary to public policy if sellers agree not to re-engage in competition with the business sold.[4] However, the restriction may not extend beyond what is necessary in the individual case in order to accomplish this purpose.[5] The courts will not uphold agreements whose objectives are primarily the elimination or restriction of competition.[6]

---

[4] Heuer v. Rubin, p. 230.

[5] Irving Investment Corp. v. Gordon, p. 232.

[6] Losquadro v. Rubel Corp., p. 233.

Considerations similar to those relating to the protection of good will apply to those cases in which a buyer of property agrees not to use it in competition with that retained by the seller.

2. *Transfer of Good Will Without Specific Restrictions*

A transfer of a business property including the good will, without any specific restrictions not to compete, places very few limitations upon the seller. The courts have held that the seller may, under such circumstances, freely engage in a competing business but that he may not solicit business from the customers of the firm he has sold. To allow him to solicit former customers would have the effect of depreciating the value of the property he has transferred.

3. *Agreements by Employees or Retiring Partners Not to Compete*

For the protection of their business undertakings, employers can restrain their employees by contract from entering into competition with them upon leaving their employ.[7, 8] At times it is necessary to entrust employees with valuable trade secrets. There is little reason why an employer should not be allowed to protect himself from competition based upon his own property rights. In many instances, employees are brought into close touch with the public by the very nature of their employment and are consequently personally instrumental in establishing and maintaining good will to the benefit of the employer. Unless restrained, an employee might easily convert the good will of his employer's business to his own good.

Obviously, the above considerations also apply to a partner retiring from a business. As long as the restraint is no broader as to time or area than is necessary to give the required protection to the business, the agreements are not regarded as being contrary to public policy.

C. INTERFERENCE WITH GOVERNMENTAL FUNCTIONS

The functions of letting and making contracts by public officials present especially inviting fields for the use of improper means in their procurement. As would be expected, any agreement made in connection with the award of a contract is illegal if its objective *tends* to influence the judgment of a public official, regardless of whether it actually does or not. The interests of society cannot be served best if the public cannot avail itself of free competition in the letting of contracts. Consequently, any agreements whose objectives tend to prevent competitive bidding are against public policy.

It is illegal to award a public contract to an official who has a voice or influence, by virtue of his public office, in letting the contract. This is equally true if a contract is awarded to a business firm of which such a public official is a member or in which he has a personal financial interest. Thus, when a board of supervisors voted to retain one of its members as legal counsel, the resulting agreement was

[7] Miller Laboratories, Inc. v. Griffin, p. 234.
[8] May v. Young, p. 235.

held to be contrary to public policy and, consequently, illegal. Human nature has not yet reached so high a plane that the interest of the public will not be sacrificed by public officials who have an adverse personal interest.

D. WAGERING CONTRACTS

The essence of a wagering contract is that one of the parties will win at the expense of the other and that the winner is determined very largely by chance. Under the common law such agreements were recognized as being enforceable. This is substantially the present-day English rule. From an early time, the American people have regarded agreements of this nature as being contrary to public policy, and the courts have refused to extend their aid to participants.[9] Most of our states have statutes prohibiting or at least placing definite limitations upon wagering agreements.

1. *Insurance Contracts*

Insurance contracts are basically wagering agreements. In a life insurance contract, for example, the parties wager upon the continued existence of a life. Since they offer, however, a method of distributing and shifting the individual's risk of loss to all those insured and, thus, are socially beneficial, they stand as an exception and are legally enforceable, providing the *insurer* has what is called an *insurable interest.* Unless an insurable interest exists, the contractual undertaking is a wager and unenforceable.[10]

a. Insurable Interest in a Life. Insurable interest in a life consists of a reasonable expectation of benefit or advantage, pecuniary or otherwise, from the continued existence of that life. It is the person who obtains the policy that must have such an interest. Thus, an insurable interest exists between husband and wife and between persons engaged to be married. An employer has an insurable interest in the life of his employee, and a creditor has an insurable interest in the life of his debtor, though only to the amount of the obligation. A policy in excess of the obligation is an illegal wagering agreement. It is common practice for a creditor to insure the life of his debtor; certainly he has a reasonable expectation of financial benefit from the continued existence of that life. Business partners have an insurable interest in each other. In the case of *Phillips' Estate,* 238 Pa. 423, the court said:

> "The affection naturally to be regarded as prevailing between brothers and sisters, and the well-grounded expectation that in case of need they will render each other pecuniary aid, is considered sufficient to support an insurable interest."

The insurable interest in a life need exist only at the time that the contract is entered into. If it subsequently ceases to exist, the contract of insurance is nevertheless valid.

[9] Jasper v. Rossman, p. 237.

[10] Ellison v. Independent Life & Accident Ins. Co., p. 238.

The reason for requiring an insurable interest was stated in *Workman* v. *Brown,* 112 Ga. 545, thus:

> "The public policy which prevents one person from insuring the life of another in whose life he has no insurable interest is based upon the presumption that a temptation would be held out to the one taking out the policy to hasten . . . the time when he should receive the amount of the insurance named in the policy."

b. Insurable Interest in Property. One has an insurable interest in property if he will be benefited by its continued existence or if he will suffer a pecuniary loss by its impairment or destruction. Obviously, an ownership interest is not essential to the existence of an insurable interest. Thus, a mortgagee has an insurable interest in the mortgaged property, a tenant in the property he has leased, a stockholder in the property of the corporation, a contractor in the building he is constructing, and a bailee in the property in his possession.

The insurable interest in property must exist at the time of the making of the contract and also at the time of the loss of or injury to the property. Thus, a mortgagee's interest in the debtor's (mortgagor's) property would cease to exist when the mortgage debt is paid, and any contract of insurance held upon the property by the mortgagee for his own benefit would become invalid at that time.

2. *Futures Contracts*

Contracts dealing in "futures" constitute another exception to the general rule. If goods are sold for future delivery at a certain price with the intent that delivery of the goods is to be made (and the contract so solemnly declares), the transaction is not regarded as a wagering agreement. If, however, such an agreement is made with the intent that the parties will settle by a payment of the difference between the contract price and the price at the delivery date, then the agreement is merely a wagering contract and void.[11] The legality of the agreement is dependent upon the intent of the parties, which, obviously, is difficult to ascertain. It is a matter of common knowledge that many of the "futures" transactions entered into through the various commodity exchanges in fact contemplate a settlement upon a cash basis, regardless of the text of the contracts.

E. AGREEMENTS TO PERPETRATE FRAUD

A fraud is a tort, a legal wrong against an individual. Consequently, an agreement between two persons that would result in the perpetration of a fraud upon another, or upon the public generally, is illegal and unenforceable. To illustrate:

In *McCullough* v. *Dogget* (Okla.) 54 P. (2d) 184, it was held that a buyer, returning an automobile to the seller as being unsatisfactory, could not recover on the dealer's agreement to return the buyer's money if the seller would find it possible to resell the automobile as being new. The court said that the agreement had for its object the perpetration of fraud on a third person.

---

[11] Young v. Stephenson, p. 239.

F. USURY

Usurious contracts are those contracts which intentionally provide for a rate of interest greater than that allowed by law as a compensation for the future use of money. All the states have enacted statutes fixing the maximum amount of interest that may be charged and prohibiting the charging of a greater rate. Early statutes usually held usurious contracts to be absolutely void and unenforceable. Modern statutes have greatly modified the penalty. The Iowa statute, for example, provides that the creditor may recover only his principal, but also requires that the debtor pay seven per cent per annum upon the loan into the school fund of the county in which the action was brought.

Whether a charge is regarded as interest for the use of money is a question of fact. Unless the charge is for a consideration other than for the use of money, it is interest. For example, the lender cannot charge the maximum rate of interest and in addition extract a bonus or commission for the making of the loan. However, charges for legitimate services are proper. They must be essential to the making of a loan, such as legal and recording fees, a charge for procuring insurance on property given as a pledge to secure a loan, or the expense incurred for a guaranty of payment of the borrower's note. A charge for property that is greater when it is sold upon credit than if sold for cash would not be usurious if the parties acted in good faith. The risk incident to financing a deferred payment contract is an adequate consideration for the greater charge. It is generally recognized that the sale of negotiable paper by a holder at a discount greater than the maximum rate of interest is not usurious. After negotiable paper has been issued, it is regarded as being personal property and may be sold for whatever it can bring.

The student should take note of local interest statutes as they apply to loan associations, pawnshops, small loan companies, and corporations. As a general rule, corporations are free to contract for any rate of interest.

G. SUNDAY CONTRACTS

Under the common law, Sunday contracts are not illegal. However, there is considerable variation today among the states as to the status of contracts entered into on a Sunday. No generalizations can be made here; the statutes of the state in which the contract is entered into should be consulted.[12, 13]

► IV. EFFECT OF ILLEGALITY

The parties to an illegal agreement cannot invoke the aid of the courts in the event of a breach of the agreement. Whether the agreement stands wholly executory or wholly or partially executed, the parties are left in whatever position they are found.[14, 15]

---

12 Goldberg v. Mitchell, p. 241.
13 Greene v. Birkmeyer, p. 242.
14 Fitzsimons v. Eagle Brewing Co., p. 243.
15 Stone v. Freeman, p. 244.

Like every good rule of law, this one also has its exceptions. Those of most general application are:

(1) Public policy may require intervention even though the parties stand in equal guilt, and, as a result of intervention, one may benefit.[16]

(2) If the parties do not stand in equal guilt, the one least guilty may be granted relief.[17] One may be induced by fraud, for example, to enter into what he subsequently discovers to be an illegal agreement.

(3) Relief will not be denied to those for whose protection a statute has been designed. If it is the purpose of a prohibitory statute to protect certain individuals from others, to refuse aid to those for whom the protection is designed would instead be placing a penalty upon them. Thus, under a statute declaring interest over a given rate to be illegal, a borrower may recover the excess interest paid if the purpose of the statute is to give protection to needy borrowers.

(4) If the illegal purpose is not carried out, the agreement may generally be repudiated.

CASES

CASE NO. 1

John E. Rosasco Creameries v. Cohen. 276 N.Y. 274, 11 N.E. (2d) 908, 118 A.L.R. 641 (1937)

FINCH, J. . . . The plaintiff, a milk dealer, brought this action to recover approximately $11,000 as the agreed and reasonable value of milk sold and delivered to the defendants, who are also milk dealers. The answer admits the sale and delivery of milk. . . . As an affirmative defense, it alleges that the plaintiff was not licensed as a milk dealer in accordance with the Agriculture and Markets Law (Consol. Laws, c. 69) during the period when it sold the milk to the defendants. . . .

Illegal contracts are generally unenforceable. Where contracts which violate statutory provisions are merely malum prohibitum, the general rules does not always apply. If the statute does not provide expressly that its violation will deprive the parties of their right to sue on the contract, and the denial of relief is wholly out of proportion to the requirements of public policy or appropriate individual punishment, the right to recover will not be denied. . . .

The statute involved does not expressly provide that contracts made by unlicensed milk dealers shall be unenforceable, although it does make a violation of the so-called milk control law a misdemeanor punishable by a fine of not less than $25 nor more than $200 or by imprisonment for not less than one month nor more than six months, or both. In the case at bar, if the contract is declared unenforceable, the effect will be to punish the plaintiff to the extent of a loss of approximately $11,000 and permit the defendants to evade the payment of a legitimate debt. Nor was the statute enacted for the purpose of protecting dealers such as the defendants. The primary purpose of the statute is to protect producers. Little danger to the public health is involved by the sale of

[16] Delgado v. Delgado, p. 245.

[17] Stevens v. Berger. p. 247.

milk by unlicensed dealers, the statute itself providing that dealers who have less than 3,000 pounds of milk a month and those selling milk in any quantity in markets of 1,000 population or less, may be exempted from its requirements. This distinguishes the case at bar from those involving health and morals.

. . . Nothing in this statute reveals an implied intent to deprive unlicensed dealers of the right to recover the reasonable value of the milk sold by them, and where the wrong committed by the violation of the statute is merely malum prohibitum, and does not endanger health or morals, such additional punishment should not be imposed unless the legislative intent is expressed or appears by clear implication. . . .

CASE NO. 2

Gardner v. Reed. 207 Miss. 306, 42 So. (2d) 206 (1949)

MC GEHEE, CH.J. This is a suit for damages on account of the breach of a contract on the part of the defendants, Maurice T. Reed and others, doing business as the M. T. Reed Construction Company, for the purchase from the plaintiff, A. H. Gardner, of 200 tons of sulphate of ammonia, a commercial fertilizer. . . .

The defendants deny liability on two grounds, . . . that the plaintiff failed to comply with the requirements of Chapter IV of the Mississippi Code of 1942 as a seller of commercial fertilizer, and particularly the requirements for registration as a dealer therein, the purchase of stamps, the payment of inspection fees, and the giving of notice to the Commissioner of Agriculture of the shipments. . . .

. . . the provisions of the code chapter hereinbefore mentioned make it a misdemeanor for a seller of fertilizer to sell, or offer to sell, the same without compliance with the various statutory provisions. It does not provide for a forfeiture of the purchase price by the seller in the event of non-compliance. If we should read such a provision into the statute, it would render the same highly penal. For instance, if the failure to comply by the seller would prevent his recovery of the purchase price, then in the instant case the defendants could have received the fertilizer, used it, and declined to pay for same. If the Legislature had intended to impose a penalty so drastic, it should have been declared so by statutory enactment. . . .

The contract covered the purchase of a lawful commodity, and was not malum in se but merely malum prohibitum. Cf. Levinson v. Cox, 127 Miss. 250, 90 So. 1; Hartford Fire Insurance Company v. Knight, 146 Miss. 862, 111 So. 748; and Huddleston v. McMillan Brothers, 112 Miss. 168, 72 So. 892.

It is true that in the cases above mentioned the statutes involved were for the protection of the public revenue, whereas the statutes here involved are both for the raising of revenue to defray the expenses of the Department of Agriculture in connection with such shipments as well as for the protection of the farmers in their purchase of mixed fertilizers; but since the contract here involved was to cover the sale of a commodity, the sale of which is not prohibited by law, and there is no statutory provision declaring such a contract to be void and unenforceable for failure to comply with the provisions thereof, but makes such failure a criminal offense instead, we are aligning ourselves with the decisions of other jurisdictions which hold that in the absence of a statutory provision declaring a forfeiture, none will be imposed. We follow the case of Niemeyer v. Wright, 75 Va. 239, 40 Am. Rep. 720, and other similar holdings, although there are cases in some jurisdictions holding to the contrary.

Since the amount of the damages is clearly shown by the undisputed evidence, . . . a judgment will be rendered here accordingly in favor of the appellant in the sum of $1,750 and all costs.

Reversed and judgment here for the appellant.

CASE NO. 3

Buckalew v. Niehuss. 249 Ala. 585, 32 So. (2d) 299 (1947)

SIMPSON, J. This suit is to enforce a covenant in a deed restricting the use of the conveyed property to residential purposes only.

Appellant Niehuss in 1937 purchased from E. E. Jackson Lumber Company its entire community site of Riderwood, which it had owned and used in connection with its sawmill operations, comprising some 700 acres of land. The lumber company owned the residences where the employees lived and operated the only mercantile establishment in the village, and after ceasing operations the property was sold to Niehuss. . . .

Appellant Jewel Buckalew succeeded to the title of one of these lots and thereafter her husband, appellant Otis Buckalew, started erecting a store building on it for the purpose of carrying on a mercantile business. This suit was instituted by Niehuss to enjoin such use of the property on the basis of this covenant in the deed, of which the appellants had notice before the purchase and contemplated improvement of the lot.

. . . The sole question is whether the reservation should be enforced. . . .

The real contention in the case is that the restriction incorporated in the deed is contrary to public policy as in restraint of trade and tending to create a monopoly. Able counsel have supported the contention with cogent and ingenious argument, but we are persuaded the current of opinion sustains a contrary view and that to hold otherwise would upset a rule of property long prevailing in this jurisdiction. . . .

A restriction was upheld and enforced in Robbins v. Webb, 68 Ala. 393, where the owners and proprietors of a public warehouse on a navigable river conveyed the adjoining land and as a part of the sale received a covenant from the grantees not to allow a warehouse or place of shipping or receiving goods on the conveyed premises. In upholding the validity of the restriction, the court said: "The contract in question was not void as against the public policy. Contracts restraining the exercise of any trade, profession or business, are legal when there is a fair and reasonable ground for the restriction, and they are confined to a limited locality, not unreasonably large or extensive.

The case of Morris & Morris v. Tuskaloosa Mfg. Co., 83 Ala. 565, 3 So. 689, 690, is similar to the case at bar and is regarded by us as decisive of the question here litigated. There the owners and operators of cotton mills sold a part of their lands with the reservation that it should be used

> "as a residence only, and not for the purpose of a trading-house, or house or place for the sale of groceries, liquors, or merchandise of any kind or description whatever."

The owner of the servient estate was enjoined from carrying on a mercantile business on the property conveyed. The same complaint of monopoly and contention of invalidity as in restraint of trade was urged but the court, speaking through Mr. Chief Justice Stone, affirmed the validity of such a reservation and answered that

"to recognize such doctrine (that the

restriction was void as tending to create a monopoly), would be to place a very dangerous restraint on the power of alienation, which is supposed to be inherent in the ownership of property." 83 Ala. at page 573, 3 So. at page 692.

But it is argued that the instant case is to be distinguished because Niehuss owned the entire property and by selling the thirteen pieces with the stated restriction, in effect inhibited the carrying on of any mercantile business by anyone else in the community and had the effect of controlling the economy of the village and allowed him to sell his merchandise at his own price. Under the circumstances disclosed by the evidence, in the light of the holdings in our former cases, this was his right and he could no more be required to relinquish that right than to sell any of his property which he did not wish to sell. Nor could appellants, taking possession under a conveyance containing such a restriction, afterward throw off the restraint and maintain the right to an unqualified use of the estate. We deem it not amiss to observe also that the residents of the village were not required to patronize his store. There were other trading centers conveniently accessible where they might and did trade and the Buckalews were free to carry out their contemplated business on any other property in the neighborhood they might acquire free of such restriction. There is nothing in the reservation violative of sound public policy or just legal principles. . . .

CASE NO. 4

Heuer et al. v. Rubin. 142 N.J. Eq. 792, 61 Atl. (2d) 567 (1948)

. . . . .

BIGELOW, V.C. This is a suit to enforce a covenant in restraint of trade contained in a schedule which was part of a bill of sale. The bill of sale sets forth

"that we, Irving Miller and Max Rubin, trading as Rahway Public Market"

in consideration of $2,100, do sell to the complainants

"all the goods and chattels particularly described and mentioned in the schedule hereto annexed and made part hereof."

The schedule first lists store fixtures and equipment and an auto truck, and then continues:

"It is hereby understood and agreed by and between the parties hereto that the said parties of the first part, Max Rubin and Irving Miller, will not engage in the fruit and vegetable business within the city limits of the City of Rahway, County of Union and State of New Jersey.

"It is further understood and agreed that this bill of sale shall include the good will of the Rahway Public Market, and also the lease"

of the premises where the market was conducted.

The sale was consummated in 1942 and complainants took over and have since operated the business known as the Rahway Public Market. Six years after the sale, Max Rubin, who was one of the vendors and is the defendant, purchased for himself, his son, his son-in-law, and another person, all the capital stock of Quality Fruit and Vegetable Market, Inc., which conducts a fruit and vegetable business in Rahway in the immediate neighborhood of complainants store. Complainants thereupon filed their bill and now move for an injunction . . . restraining Rubin from participating in the business of the Quality Fruit and Vegetable Market. Rubin, in his answering affidavit, says that he is not an officer of the Quality Fruit and Vegetable Market, Inc., and that its business will be conducted by his son and by his son-in-law, while he, the defendant, will only operate a concession in the store for the sale of dairy products and fancy groceries.

At the time of the sale in 1942, the business which Rubin and Miller conducted had been closed down for three weeks and all the fruit and vegetables which were the stock in trade had been disposed of. The principal subjects of the sale were store fixtures and a truck. . . .

A contract in restraint of sale is considered contrary to public policy and unenforceable, unless it is ancillary to a transfer of good will or other subject of property, or to an existing employment or contract of employment. Bond Electric Co. v. Keller, 113 N.J. Eq. 195, 166 Atl. 341; Glantz v. Willow Supply Co., 139 N.J. Eq. 523, 53 A. (2d) 346. Defendant urges that since the business of the Rahway Public Market had been shut down three weeks before the sale, there could have been no good will to preserve, or to sell, but this does not follow. Good will, the value of a trade name, may persist for several years after the use of the name has been discontinued. A transfer of good will is sufficient to support a contract in restraint of trade, although the good will is of very slight value.

A contract in restraint of trade must be reasonable. The present covenant is limited to the City of Rahway, and is not limited in time. The territorial limit is obviously reasonable in these days of automobiles and of shopping by telephone. When such a covenant is reasonably limited in point of space, it is not objectionable that it be unlimited in point of time. Scherman v. Stern, 93 N.J. Eq. 626, 117 Atl. 631; Schwartz v. Van Der Plate & Co., 132 N.J. Eq. 132, 27 A. (2d) 209.

The obligation not to engage in the fruit and vegetable business in Rahway was undertaken by Rubin and Miller jointly. Defendant argues that it left him at liberty to enter business by himself, or with anyone except Miller; that the covenant is broken only if he and Miller jointly engage in business. . . . Every contract must be interpreted in the light of the purpose which the parties presumably sought to accomplish. The agreement of the sellers of a business not to compete is intended to protect the good will by making sure that old customers will not resume trading with the sellers. If either one of the partners who conducted the business before the sale should start anew in the neighborhood of the old store, some of the former customers would doubtless resort to him rather than to the purchaser of the business, although probably not so many as if both partners should again go into business together. In order to give reasonable effect to the covenant, it should be construed, in the absence of strong indications to the contrary, to prohibit the sellers, either jointly or separately, from setting up a competing business.

The words of the covenant "not to engage in the fruit and vegetable business," do not include words generally found, such as "directly or indirectly" or as "principal or employee," etc. I question whether defendant is prohibited by his contract from having a stock interest in a competing corporation, or from participating at all in its management, or from acting as its buyer. . . . But I am satisfied that he is debarred from using his personal acquaintance with his old customers to draw them away from complainants.

I will advise an order restraining defendant from frequenting the store of Quality Fruit and Vegetable Market while it is open to the public, and from participating in its business in such a way as to bring to the attention of any of its customers, or prospective customers, his interest in the Market, or as to lead them to believe that he is an officer or employee of the Market.

CASE NO. 5

Irving Investment Corporation v. Gordon. 3 N.J. 217, 69 A. (2d) 725 (1949)

CASE, J. The primary question is whether a corporate lessor may lawfully burden a lessee with a covenant in restraint of trade when the covenant is effective against property not involved in the lease and is made for the benefit of another corporation with which the lessor has no privity and in which it has no interest.

Irving Investment Corporation, one of the plaintiffs, owned a property located at . . . 147 Mulberry Street, in the City of Newark. Defendants, David Gordon and Irving Gordon, were, . . . at . . . 145 Mulberry Street, and for sixteen years and more had, as partners, there engaged in business as electrical contractors and in selling electrical motors, tools and equipment. Plaintiff, Newark Hardware & Plumbing Supply Company, a corporation, rented a property . . . numbered 148, from David Meyers and wife and had there conducted, for many years, a business which included the sale of radios, heaters and stoves. The stock in both plaintiff corporations was closely held by David Meyers and the members of his family. The two corporations had no interest in each other. The sole point of contact, if it may be so called, was that holders of shares in one were also holders of shares in the other.

On September 1, 1946, the defendants, uncertain of their tenure at 145 Mulberry Street, and with the purpose of transferring their business to the new location, entered into a five year lease with Irving Investment Corporation for the premises at number 147. The lease contained these covenants:

> ". . . Lessees covenant and agree not to engage in same or similar line of business as the said Newark Hardware and Plumbing Supply Co., except as hereinto set forth, within a radius of one-eighth of a mile from demised premises nor place signs advertising such a business within said area, so long as Newark Hardware & Plumbing Supply Co. shall continue in said business at 148–50 Mulberry St., Newark, N.J., either directly or indirectly, as principals, agents, servants or otherwise."

However, the necessity for the contemplated change of location never arose. Defendants bought their old store premises and continued the business there. They sublet the newly demised premises for the same uses as theretofore, namely the first floor as a saloon and the upper floors as lodgings.

Plaintiffs, the one as covenantee and the other as the person for whose benefit the restrictive covenants were imposed, filed their joint complaint in the Superior Court, Chancery Division, setting up the covenants, alleging that defendants, at their 145, were selling and advertising articles of merchandise in violation thereof, and seeking injunction and damages. . . . The court . . . found that the restrictive covenants were invalid and unenforceable with respect to any area or place outside the confines of the demised premises and granted summary judgment to the defendants. . . .

As a general rule, an agreement in unreasonable restraint of trade is illegal and void, but an agreement in reasonable restraint of trade is valid. That statement hardly needs citation of authorities. The difficulty arises in the application of the broad principle to the facts of a given case. A slight narrowing of the rule was stated by Vice Chancellor Backes in Stevens & Thompson Paper Co. v. Brady, 106 N.J. Eq. 410, 151 Atl. 92, 93 (Ch. 1930) as follows:

> "Contracts in general restraint of trade are condemned in law as against public policy. Partial restraints that serve to promote and protect trade are countenanced, but guardedly enforced."

We are not so much concerned with limitations as to time or space as we are with the interest that is to be served by the restraint; and a more pertinent expression in that respect is the quotation approved in Voices, Inc. v. Metal Tone Mfg. Co., Inc., 119 N. Eq. 324 . . .

> "A restraint to be reasonable must be such only as to afford a fair protection to the interests of the party in favor of whom it is given and not so large as to interfere with the interests of the public." . . .

Irving Investment Corporation is merely the owner of land which is not benefited by the restraint. It is neither a merchant nor a manufacturer; it has no interest in the goods or in the places where the goods are sold, or in the profits or losses entailed in the merchandising of them. The property which it owns is not the locus of any business affected by the covenants and has no present prospect of being so. The restraints have no reasonable relation to the rents or the reversion. . . .

Not only has the Irving Investment Corporation no interest in the Newark Hardware & Plumbing Company, or any of its doings; the Newark Hardware & Plumbing Company has no interest in the Irving Investment Corporation.

It is fairly clear that the main objective of the covenants was to prevent close competition with No. 148 by No. 147; indeed Meyers, president of Irving Investment Corporation, president of Newark Hardware & Plumbing property, said under examination that he would not have granted the option to purchase No. 147 if it hadn't been for the covenants, adding:—"I don't want any competitor right on top of me." . . . and the covenants were inserted in anticipation not only of the use of No. 147 by the defendants under its lease for business that would be competitive with No. 148, but of the possible exercise by the defendants of their option to purchase. The unwillingness to sell, or even to lease, a property subject to such possibilities of harmful competition is understandable; and it may be supposed with reasonable assurance that the several restraints were imposed and accepted with respect only to the property which was the subject matter of the lease, and that the continued use of No. 145 by the defendants was not then in the mind of anyone. . . .

Conceding that there are instances where a person, for whose benefit a contract is made, may, although not a party to the contract and not a contributor to the consideration, sue thereon, we further find that since the contract is not, as to the covenants in application to No. 145, valid between the immediate parties, it may not form a basis for relief in those respects at the suit of the designated beneficiary.

CASE NO. 6

Losquadro Coal Corporation v. Rubel Corporation. 86 F. Supp. 774 (1949)

FAKE, CH.J. . . . The action seeks a declaratory judgment based upon the extent and meaning of a certain contract in writing between the parties to this suit dated August 1, 1947. It appears that the defendant herein, Rubel Corporation, was and for some time had been engaged in the manufacture, sale, and distribution of ice in the States of

New York and New Jersey, and the party of the second part was the owner and operator of a coal, oil and ice business located on Park Avenue, Weehawken, and also on New York Avenue, Jersey City. The Losquadro Coal Corporation, desiring to sell its business to the Rubel Corporation, entered into the contract above mentioned, making the sale for the sum of $2250 and coupling the sale with a covenant in restraint of trade. . . .

The covenant prohibits the vendor, Losquadro Coal Corporation, and its officers from entering into the ice business in any way, directly or indirectly, for a period of five years anywhere within the State of New Jersey, . . .

It is contended by the defendant that plaintiffs are guilty of a breach of the terms of the contract in that they did engage in the ice business within the County and State covered. . .

In the case of Schultz v. Johnson, 110 N.J. Eq. 566, 160 Atl. 379, Vice Chancellor Leaming said:

> "The obligations arising from covenants of this nature have been considered by our courts so frequently that almost every aspect of the subject has been determined. A review of the cases seems unnecessary."

So here I will not burden the record further than to say: It is well established in New Jersey that a covenant, such as that in the instant case, is void because its restriction goes

> "beyond the territory in which the business which was sold was transacted at the time of the sale," and "beyond any extension of that territory, by expansion of the business sold, as might have been reasonably contemplated by the parties, at the time of the sale."

Many cases are cited in the plaintiff's brief, and may be found in the digests and reported opinions. They all tend to the conclusion that the covenant here is void. . . .

CASE NO. 7

E. S. Miller Laboratories, Inc., v. Griffin. 200 Okla. 398, 194 P. (2d) 877, 3 A.L.R. (2d) 519 (1948)

GIBSON, J. On December 25, 1945, plaintiff in error, a manufacturer and seller of pharmaceutical, chemical and biological products, engaged the services of defendant in error as salesman for a particular territory. By the terms of the contract it was provided that in event the latter left the employment he would not work in said territory for any other pharmaceutical company or distributor for a period of two years thereafter. . . .

. . . In plaintiff's petition it is alleged that on April 1, 1947 defendant, in violation of said agreement, left the service of plaintiff and immediately entered the employ of another pharmaceutical company, a competitor of plaintiff, and is working for such competitor in said territory, in violation of said provision of the contract. And, alleging plaintiff is without adequate remedy at law, a permanent injunction is prayed for. Defendant demurred generally to the petition. The demurrer was sustained and judgment rendered for defendant. Plaintiff appeals from the judgment.

The only question involved on appeal is whether the provision of the contract is in restraint of trade, and therefore against public policy and void.

Plaintiff's contention is reflected in the following statement in the brief:

> "The authorities at common law to sustain a contract as in the instant case are overwhelming, and there can be no question but that at common law this contract is valid.
>
> "What is the effect of the Oklahoma Statute on this situation? It is the contention of the plaintiff that the

Oklahoma Statute is only declarative of the common law rule, and as such must be interpreted as being subject to the same qualifications as the common law rule." . . .

The applicable Oklahoma statutes Tit. 15 O.S. 1941 §§ 217, 218 and 219, are as follows:

"Sec. 217. Every contract by which any one is restrained from exercising a lawful profession, trade or business of any kind, otherwise than as provided by the next two sections, is to that extent void.

"Sec. 218. One who sells the good will of a business may agree with the buyer to refrain from carrying on a similar business within a specified county, city or part thereof, so long as the buyer, or any person deriving title to the good-will from him carries on a like business therein.

"Sec. 219. Partners may, upon or in anticipation of a dissolution of the partnership, agree that none of them will carry on a similar business within the same city or town where the partnership business has been transacted, or within a specified part thereof." . . .

We are in accord with the holdings of the California and North Dakota courts as to the effect of the statutes upon the common law rules. From this it must follow that since the restraint herein comes within neither of the exceptions recognized in sections 218 and 219 it is void and unenforceable . . . that the restraint is within the purview of section 217 is clear and not questioned. . . .

CASE NO. 8

May v. Young. 125 Conn. 1, 2 A. (2d) 385, 119 A.L.R. 1445 (1938)

HINMAN, J. . . . The plaintiff is an industrial engineering firm engaged in the business of installing systems covering sales and administrative expenses, budgets, accounting and cost methods, overhead rates, factory, clerical, direct and indirect labor, production planning and scheduling, inventories and other cost elements. It was organized in 1925 and has since served seventeen hundred business firms in forty-four States and in Canada. Its systems are installed by a specially qualified and trained personnel, and a particular job may last one month or many depending on the extent of the work undertaken. It has developed solutions of particular industrial problems which are preserved in its confidential records, as are schedules of its rates and charges, a list of the clients served and a list of prospective clients being contacted. The defendant entered into the employ of the plaintiff on August 1st, 1929, and continued therein until July 1st, 1936, and served the plaintiff in cities west of the Mississippi River. . . .

On July 1st, 1935, the plaintiff and the defendant entered into a written contract setting forth that the plaintiff used in its business certain data and information and certain trade secrets which would be communicated to the defendant by virtue of his employment and which the plaintiff desired to protect and preserve for its own use, and by which the defendant agreed to serve the plaintiff and it agreed to employ him indefinitely so long as his services were satisfactory but reserved the right to terminate the agreement at any time upon seven days' notice in writing. The contract included an agreement by the defendant that he would not,

"while this contract remains in effect or at any time within two years thereafter . . . enter into the employ of any client of the (plaintiff),"

and that in case of violation of this or other related provisions the plaintiff shall be entitled to an injunction and "as liquidated damages" the sum of $10,-000. The defendant thereafter worked under that contract until about July 1st, 1936, when his employment was terminated by the plaintiff in accordance with the provisions of the contract.

In 1932 the defendant, as an employee of the plaintiff, had performed services, including production schedules, for the Waterbury Buckle Company and in April, 1936, had solicited that company for further work to be done later in 1938 by the plaintiff. Inefficiencies existed in the production of the Waterbury Buckle Company and it was desirous of securing assistance in correcting them, and on December 22d, 1936, the defendant entered into employ as a production manager, his duties involving the speeding up and increasing of production, services similar to which were included in those performed by the plaintiff in its business.

. . . the trial court concluded, correctly, that the only provision of the contract which the defendant violated was that forbidding him to enter into the employ of any client of the plaintiff within two years after the termination of his employment by the plaintiff. The principal question on this appeal concerns the validity of the further conclusion that this provision

> "is contrary to public policy, void, and if enforced against the defendant would impose undue hardship upon him."

A covenant restricting the activities of an employee during or after the termination of his present employment, in order to be valid and enforceable, must be partial, or restricted in its operation either as to time or place, on some good consideration, and

> "must be reasonable, that is, it should afford only a fair protection to the interests of the party in whose favor it is made, and must not be so large in its operation as to interfere with the interests of the public." Cook v. Johnson, 47 Conn. 175, 176, 36 Am. Rep. 64.

Of the principal consideration affecting the validity of restrictive contracts on grounds of public policy, one is injury to the public by being deprived of the restricted party's industry or services, the other the injury to the party himself by being precluded from pursuing his occupation and thus being prevented from supporting himself and family.

> "But if neither of these evils ensue and if the contract is founded on a valid consideration and a reasonable ground of benefit to the other party, it is free from objection, and may be enforced." Oregon Steam Navigation Co. v. Winsor, 20 Wall. 64, 87 U.S. 64, 68, 22 L. ed. 315.

The restriction here involved being only from engaging with clients of the plaintiff, leaving open to the defendant all other opportunities for employment, cannot be held so to involve either of these consequences as to invalidate it on grounds of public policy. . . .

It is apparent from the finding that the business of the plaintiff is of a somewhat unusual nature involving the development and use of systems and methods and the accumulation of records and data which may well be regarded as partaking of the nature of trade secrets, and constituting an enterprise which could not be confined within narrow territorial limits as in the most commonly occurring cases involving dealings with commercial customers in one community or section. . . . Employments which involve acquisition of confidential knowledge involved in the business and acquaintance with the employer's clientele are regarded as particularly appropriate to restrictions against the use of such knowledge in competition with the employer. . . .

The designation of this sum as liquidated damages does not necessarily make it such rather than a penalty. If the provision was inserted for the purpose of deterring the defendant from breaching his contract and of penalizing him for doing so, instead of specifying a sum which the parties in good faith agreed upon as representing the damages which would ensue from a breach, it is to be regarded as imposing a penalty. . . .

In such a case recovery will be limited to the actual damage and if no damage is proven no recovery may be had. . . .

The finding that the plaintiff proved, and the conclusion that it suffered, no damage as a result of the employment of the defendant by the Waterbury Buckle Company are warranted, and there was no error in refusing to award damages.

CASE NO. 9

Jasper v. Rossman. 41 N.W. (2d) 310 (S.D.) (1950)

ROBERTS, J. Plaintiff brought this action to recover the balance alleged to be due for certain merchandise sold and delivered to the defendant. The answer set up the defense that the articles purchased were gambling devices and that the purchase being void as against public policy there was no valid consideration for the promise to pay. . . . The court . . . made findings and conclusions of law in favor of defendant. . . .

The court found that plaintiff, doing business under the name of Specialty Sales Company in Minneapolis, Minnesota, sold to the defendants certain merchandise consisting of punch boards, Dormeyer mixers, and novelties . . . that the value of the mixers was the sum of $388.50; that the agreed price of the punch boards was $370.62. . . .

. . . The question to be determined is whether there is basis in the record for denial of recovery because use of these punch boards would be contrary to law and against public policy.

In the case of Ferguson v. Yunt, 13 S.D. 20, 82 N.W. 509, this court said: "Courts do not lend their aid to parties engaged in transactions in violation of law, and betting gambling contracts are uniformly held to be contrary to the policy of the law, and illegal.

"The test to determine whether the plaintiff is entitled to recover, is his ability to establish his case without any aid from the illegal transaction. If his claim or right to recover depends upon a transaction which is malum in se, or prohibited by legislative enactment, and that transaction must necessarily be proved to make out his case, there can be no recovery."

The general rule that the law will not aid either party has been applied to illegal transactions other than gambling. . . . The defense of illegality prevails, not as a protection to the defendant, but as a disability in plaintiff. The reasons for refusing the aid of the court become even stronger when the property is liable to proceedings by the state to enforce a forfeiture.

There have been many decisions to the effect that, where the sale is of an article that may or may not be used for an illegal purpose, it is no defense to an action to recover the price that the seller knew of the purpose of the buyer to devote it to the commission of a minor offense, without some further evidence implicating the seller. . . .

Thus, in Rose v. Mitchell, 6 Colo. 102, 45 Am. Rep. 520, the court observed:

"To say that a bare knowledge that the article sold was capable of unlawful use, and that it probably would be put to such use by some remote vendee, is sufficient to vitiate a sale, would be a conclusion too far fetched for legal consideration, applicable to the law of contracts. Such a rule would operate to vitiate sales of ordinary playing cards, billiard tables, race horses, and many other articles and kinds of property of legitimate trade, which are capable of being made the means of gambling, contrary to statute. Such a rule would impose an unreasonable restraint upon commerce and trade."

Accordingly, it was held in J. M. Brunswick & Balke Co. v. Valleau, 50 Iowa 120, 32 Am. Rep. 119, that the plaintiff who sold to the defendant a billiard table could recover the price notwithstanding his knowledge at the time of the sale that the table was to be used in a saloon where, as it appeared from the evidence, gambling was almost universally carried on in connection with billiard tables.

The case before us rests upon different facts than those in the cases referred to. . . . The seller of punch boards brought the action to recover their price. The court held that the only practical use to which these articles could be put was to conduct a game of chance and that the seller could not recover. . . . True, the sale of punch boards in this state is not expressly prohibited, but their use for selling of chances to win money or prizes is unlawful. The ordinary use, if not the only use, of the punch boards sold by plaintiff was for gaming or lottery purposes and for these reasons plaintiff cannot maintain this action.

CASE NO. 10

Ellison v. Independent Life & Accident Ins. Co. 216 S.C. 475, 58 S.E. (2d) 890 (1950)

STUKES, J. Plaintiff operates a retail store in Belton. Roy Gregory, now deceased, was mayor and occupied the city hall which was next-door to plaintiff's store. For many years Gregory had been an insurance agent and was the general agent in Belton for Life Insurance Company of Virginia. Although only forty-eight years old he suffered a heart attack several years before the transaction under review and was retired from his former employment. He continued to serve as mayor.

He was in plaintiff's store on Oct. 4, 1948, in social conversation with plaintiff and with defendant's agent, Hammond. There were also present plaintiff's clerk, one Watkins, and Lawrence Ellison, of the same surname but no relation, who was agent at Belton for another life insurance company. The subject of insurance was broached and the testimony thereabout of defendant's agent Hammond will be first summarized. He entered the store he said to purchase a soft drink and found plaintiff talking to Ellison who Hammond understood was trying to sell plaintiff a policy. Gregory asked Hammond if he could write a policy for him whereupon Hammond inquired his age, quoted the weekly premium and filled an application. Upon inquiry as to beneficiary, Gregory first mentioned his wife and plaintiff interjected that he should be the beneficiary, to which Gregory agreed and the application was so written. Under instruction from plaintiff his clerk, Watkins, took cash from the money-drawer of the store and paid Hammond the amount of the first premium. . . .

He procured the issuance of the policy from defendant's Anderson office and delivered it to plaintiff or his clerk, Watkins, for him. After the death of the insured the witness, accompanied by another agent of defendant, tendered refund of the amount of the premium to plaintiff who declined it. . . .

. . . authorities conform to the rule that one cannot obtain valid insurance upon the life of another in whom he has no insurable interest; but it is generally held that one may procure insurance on his own life and make it payable to whomever he will if in good faith and not to cover a wagering policy. The latter follows from the precept that everyone has an insurable interest in his own life. 29 Am. Jur. 312, Insurance, § 355; 44 C.J.S., Insurance, § 202, p. 899. 2 Appleman on Insurance Law and Practice, Ch. 45, Insurable Interest, § 761 et seq., p. 77 et seq. This was the consideration which moved the lower court to find for respondent and it renders irrelevant the cases of contrary facts cited in the brief. There was no evidence or finding of fraud, or deception of appellant in this connection. The circumstances and surroundings of the negotiations negate that. They took place in a "fishbowl" without indication of *mala fides* or attempt to "cover" an unlawful transaction. Applicable is the following oft-quoted excerpt from the well-reasoned opinion in Crosswell v. Connecticut Ind. Ass'n, 51 S.C. at pages 116, 117, 28 S.E. at page 205:

> "A sound public policy requires the enforcement of contracts deliberately made which do not clearly contravene some positive law or rule of public morals. It is surely not a sound policy to permit insurers to contract to insure the lives of persons, receive premiums therefor as long as the insured, the beneficiary, or the assignee will continue to pay, and then, when the time comes for the insurers to pay what they agreed to pay, allow them to escape their contract on the ground of want of insurable interest in the life insured, unless it clearly appears that such contracts are pernicious and dangerous to society. Courts should not annul contracts on doubtful grounds of public policy. In such matters it is better that the legislature should first speak." . . .

Judgment affirmed.

CASE NO. 11

Young v. Stephenson. 82 Okla. 239, 200 Pac. 225, 24 A.L.R. 978 (1921)

MCNEILL, J., delivered the opinion of the court:

This action was commenced in the district court of Tulsa county by James A. Stephenson, William Hargis Walker, and S. de Zell Hawley against F. A. Young. The allegations of the petition were that said plaintiffs had sold to F. A. Young 6,000 shares of stock of Okmulgee Producing & Refining Company for $15 per share, and received in payment certain cash and three notes in the sum of $14,400 each, and an agreement upon behalf of Young to pay $19,550 in thirty days; that all of said amounts were due and unpaid, and judgment was prayed for said amounts and interest.

The defendant, Young, answered, pleading . . . the transaction was a gambling contract dealing in futures and was void. . . .

The court rendered judgment for the plaintiffs for the full amount sued for, and the defendant, Young, has appealed from said judgment. . . .

The facts relating to this transaction, as testified to by Mr. Walker, are as follows:

"Dr. Hawley and myself went to

Okmulgee on March 20, 1918. We were discussing Okmulgee Producing & Refining Company conditions. Mr. Young was at that time general manager of the company and a director. Mr. Young said if we would buy 2,000 shares apiece at the market price he would guarantee us in thirty days $15 a share for the stock if we would pay him $1 a share bonus. . . . Mr. Hawley, Mr. Stephenson, and myself, after discussing it, decided we would do that, and we purchased 6,000 shares at $9.70 per share, paying $58,200 therefor. We then sent him this telegram: 'Hawley, Stephenson and myself have purchased 6,000 shares Okmulgee to-day for our joint account.' We received the following telegram from Young in reply: 'Your wire received. I confirm my guaranty as per premium plan.' . . ."

On the 17th day of May, 1918, the stock was not worth the sum of $15 per share, but was only worth about $7 per share, and the parties made a settlement whereby Mr. Young purchased the stock, agreeing to pay $15 per share, or $90,000, therefor. Mr. Walker's testimony upon this point was as follows:

"At that time Mr. Young paid $15,000 in cash. He had previously paid $4,000, and we credited him with a dividend of $2,250. He gave us three notes of $14,400 each, which left a balance of $19,550 due on the contract. We also allowed him the $6,000 for making the guaranty. . . ."

In support of the contention that the so-called contract was a mere wagering contract and void, the plaintiff in error relies upon the principle of law announced in cases where parties purchased goods or property for future delivery at a certain price, and the goods were not intended to be delivered, but instead thereof one party was to pay the other the difference between the contract price and the market price of the goods at the date designated in the contract. If this is such a contract, the same is merely a wagering contract and void. . . . It is, however, contended by the defendant in error that this is not a wagering contract, nor, strictly a contract of guaranty or suretyship, but is an original undertaking in consideration of a certain premium to insure the value of property.

In considering this question, our first inquiry will be to consider what is an insurance contract. It is defined in Elliott on Contracts, vol. 5, § 4020, as follows:

"In a general sense, insurance is a contract, for a consideration, to pay a sum of money upon the happening of a particular event or contingency."

In the case of State v. Hogan, 8 N.D. 301, 45 L.R.A. 166, 73 Am. St. Rep. 759, 78 N.W. 1051, the supreme court of North Dakota there stated:

" 'A corporation which undertakes to guarantee a fixed revenue per acre from farming lands, and which, in order to do so, contracts, for a specified consideration, to pay such fixed amount per acre for the crop grown upon said land, irrespective of its value,' has been held to be an insurance company within the meaning of a statute regulating insurance companies and agents, and defining insurance as 'a contract whereby one undertakes to indemnify another against loss, damage, or liability arising from an unknown or contingent event.' . . ."

It is essential in the contract of insurance that the insured have the interest in the property insured.

The rule as to the different characters of insurance as stated in Elliott on Contracts, vol. 5, § 4028, is as follows:

"Almost any contingent or unknown event, however, whether past or future, which may damnify a person having an insurable interest, or create a liability against him, may be insured against. Whatever has an appreciable pecuniary value and is subject to loss or deterioration, or of which one may be deprived, or that he may fail to realize, whereby his pecuniary interest is or may be prejudiced, may properly constitute the subject-matter of insurance."

That all insurance contracts have an element of wager in the same is stated in vol. 5, Elliott on Contracts, § 4031, as follows:

"In an ordinary contract the thing given or done by one party is considered as an equivalent of what is given or done by the other, but an element of wager enters into every insurance contract. If no loss occurs, the insurer gains the amount of the premium; if loss occurs, the insured receives the amount of his loss, which is generally much greater than the premium. By reason of this element of chance the contract is said to be aleatory."

A case which, we think, is very analogous, is the case of Elliot v. Hayes, 8 Gray, 164, stated:

"A guaranty that the owner of stock in a corporation shall receive dividends thereon, of a specified amount for a certain number of years, he paying to the contractor all he receives above that amount, is valid."

In the body of the opinion the court stated:

"If the contract in the present case had been put into the form of a policy of insurance, it is certain that it would not have been a wager policy."

This case is referred to in 2 L.R.A. 184, in the note, as follows:

"A guaranty that the owner of stock in a corporation shall receive dividends thereon of a specified amount, for a certain number of years, by paying to the guarantor all he receives above that amount, is valid. It is not a wager, but 'not only in words, but also in its plain design, a guaranty to the plaintiffs of a certain yearly profit on railroad stock owned by them' . . ."

We will now direct our attention to wagering contracts. A wagering contract has been defined to be a contract by which two or more parties agree that a certain sum of money or other thing shall be paid or delivered to one of them on the happening or not happening of a certain event. Bouvier's Law Dict. (Rawle's Rev.).

One of the conditions in a gambling or wagering contract is, there is no opportunity for both sides to make gains. One must gain and the other must lose. . . .

It is true the contract provides not only against loss, but it provides that the value of the stock should be of a certain value upon a certain date. On the 17th day of May, the date the settlement was made between the parties, the stock was only worth the sum of $7 per share, or about $42,000, and by reason of this fact the plaintiffs had sustained an actual loss of over $16,000. This contract was not dealing in futures, because the stock was actually purchased. It was not a wager, but was a contract to guarantee against this kind and character of a loss. . . .

For the reasons stated, the judgment of the trial court is affirmed.

CASE NO. 12

Goldberg v. Mitchell. 322 Mich. 662, 34 N.W. (2d) 515 (1948)

REID, J. This is a bill for specific performance of a land contract for the sale of real estate . . . The defendants raised the defense, among other things, that the contract in question was signed on Sunday. . . .

Plaintiff Louis Goldberg swore as a witness that the transaction occurred on Monday, November 26, 1945, the date of the contract. He was to some extent corroborated by the testimony of his wife, Sarah Goldberg. Defendants claim the contract was signed on Sunday, November 25, 1945. The trial court properly held that the burden of proof was on the defendants to show that the signing of the contract occurred not on Monday, the date of the contract, but on Sunday.

The controversy in this case is principally factual. The trial court had an abundant opportunity to observe at first hand the whole matter of the giving of the testimony in person by plaintiff's witnesses and the five witnesses for defendants. His conclusion was that the transaction actually took place and the signing of the contract sued on actually occurred on Sunday, November 25, 1945. In that conclusion we concur. It follows that the contract sued on is void under our statute, . . . which is as follows:

"No person shall keep open his shop, warehouse, or workhouse, or shall do any manner of labor, business, or work, or be present at any dancing, or at any public diversion, show, or entertainment, or take part in any sport, game, or play on the first (1st) day of the week. The foregoing provisions shall not apply to works of necessity and charity, nor to the making of mutual promises of marriage, nor to the solemnization of marriages. And every person so offending shall be punished by fine not exceeding ten (10) dollars for each offense."

"The contract, being a Sunday contract, was not voidable merely, but was absolutely void; it was not and could not be ratified." Dabits v. Hauser, 210 Mich. 414, 177 N.W. 951.

CASE NO. 13

Greene v. Birkmeyer. 8 N.J. 217, 73 A. (2d) 728 (1950)

BIGELOW, J.A.D. The case turns upon R.S. 2:207–1, N.J.S.A., the pertinent part of which reads:

"No traveling, worldly employment or business, ordinary or servile labor or work either upon land or water, except works of necessity or charity . . . shall be done, performed, used or practiced by any person within this State on the Christian Sabbath, or first day of the week, commonly called and hereinafter designated as Sunday."

On Sunday, December 5, 1948, the plaintiff agreed to buy land provided he were able to borrow on it a certain sum. At the same time, he deposited $500 with the vendor on account of the purchase. The plaintiff sues for the return of the $500, alleging that he was unable to obtain the mortgage, and also that he refuses to fulfill the contract because it was made upon the Sabbath. The District Court was of the opinion that since the contract was made on Sunday, the plaintiff had a right to disaffirm and recover back his deposit. Judgment followed accordingly, and the defendant appeals.

It is, of course, apparent that the bargain for the real estate and the deposit of $500 thereon, were business dealings forbidden by the statutes. That a contract made on Sunday will not be enforced or a transaction on that day will not be given effect, is abundantly established. An action cannot be maintained for the amount due on a promissory note made on Sunday. Reeves v. Butcher, 31 N.J.L. 224 (Sup. Ct. 1865). Or for an accounting of commissions upon a contract made on Sunday. Gennert v. Wuestner, 53 N.J.Eq. 302, 31 Atl. 609 (Pitney, V.C., 1895). Or for the specific performance of an agreement for the sale of real estate, executed and delivered on Sunday. . . . A notice to a tenant, given on Sunday, that after the expiration of his term, the rent will be increased to a certain amount, is without effect and the tenant, remaining in possession, is liable only at the old rate. . . . One who, on Sunday, repairs a boiler pursuant to a contract, even though made on a weekday, cannot recover. . . .

Business dealings in violation of the Sunday law are on a par with contracts forbidden by other statutes. . . . It is the rule in many states that where money has been paid on a contract which is illegal, the party making the payment may repudiate the contract, provided it still remains executory, and may recover the money, even though the parties are in *pari delicto*. Greenberg v. Evening Post Ass'n, 91 Conn. 371, 99 Atl. 1037 (Conn. 1917); Harrington v. Bochenski, 140 Md. 24, 116 A. 836 (Md. 1922); Duane v. Merchants Legal Stamp Co., 227 Mass. 466, 116 N.E. 873 (Mass. 1917). See 17 C.J.S., Contracts, § 275. . . . The foregoing view of the law, applied to gambling contracts, was stated by Chief Justice Green in our Supreme Court in Huncke v. Francis, 27 N.J.L. 55. . . .

With respect to illegal contracts in general, we take it that the law in New Jersey will not aid one guilty party to recapture a payment that he has made to the other. Dicta in the cases on the Sunday statute present the same rule. . . .

The plaintiff in the action before us was himself guilty of violating the express command of the statute. The law will not help him out of the situation in which his own illegal conduct has placed him, and so the judgment must be reversed.

CASE NO. 14

Fitzsimons v. Eagle Brewing Co. 107 F. (2d) 712, 126 A.L.R. 681 (1939)

CLARK, C.J., delivered the opinion of the court:

The facts of the case at bar are reminiscent. The plaintiff-appellant, a Baltimorean, operating as the Camden Products Company (New Jersey), manufactured malt syrup, a primary ingredient in the brewing of beer. The defendant-appellee, a brewery, for reasons undisclosed by the record but easily conjecturable by United States Judges, lost its permit for the manufacture of near beer, the then legal kind, 27 USCA §§ 4, 58; R. 45. Nothing daunted, it continued the purchase of plaintiff's malt and in those purchases enjoyed the enthusiastic co-operation of the plaintiff seller. In other words and in plainer English, the plaintiff sold malt syrup in large quantities to a wildcat brewery and is now squealing because the learned trial judge had more regard for the public interest than it had. We say the judge because the defense of illegality was not interposed by a welsher but, as was not only proper but necessary, by the court sua sponte. . . .

> ". . . the rule of public policy that forbids an action for damages for breach of such an agreement is not based on the impropriety of compelling the defendant to pay the damages. That in itself would generally be a desirable thing. When relief is denied it is because the plaintiff is a wrongdoer, and to such a person the law denies relief. Courts do not wish to aid a man who founds his cause of action upon his own immoral or illegal act. If from the plaintiff's own statement or otherwise it appears that

the bargain forming the basis of the action is opposed to public policy or transgresses statutory prohibitions, the courts ordinarily give him no assistance. The court's refusal is not for the sake of the defendant, but because it will not aid such a plaintiff." 2 Restatement, Contracts § 598, p. 1110. . . .

The principal case gives us the easiest example of an illegal contract. We are not troubled with a violation of the sometimes vague rules of the common law, . . . or even vaguer and more varying tenets of morals, . . . or public policy. . . . Our contract cannot be performed without the violation of an express statute, 27 USCA § 13. That statute contains an express prohibition and does not merely impose a penalty. We are not concerned then with some confusion evinced by the courts re that type of statutes. . . .

All this is just about conceded. What is not conceded is a question of timing. As there is a conflict of laws as to place, so there may be a conflict of laws as to time. As Professor Williston puts it:

"It may sometimes happen that a bargain is illegal when it is made either because of the illegal purpose of the parties to it or for other reasons, and that when the bargain is performed the transaction has become lawful either because the purpose of the parties has changed or because changes in the law or other external circumstances have made that lawful which was previously unlawful." 6 Williston on Contracts, § 1758, p. 4992.

The appellant urges that the validity of the agreement does not depend upon the law at the time it was made. In so doing, he runs counter to the overwhelming weight of authority. 6 Williston on Contracts, § 1758, above cited, 12 Am. Jur. § 165; 15 Am. & Eng. Ency. of Law (2nd Ed.) p. 942; 2 Restatement, Contracts, § 609, p. 1128. The cases cited in support of these texts hold that the subsequent repeal of a prohibitive statute does not authorize recovery under the contract originally forbidden.

We cannot understand any other view. By definition your purpose is to discourage action deemed harmful. You are not interested in the consequences of acts but in the mental processes of the actor. Those processes precede both the acts and a fortiori their consequences and the relevant state of law is that existing at the time of the processes and not at the time of the consequences. The law breaking mens rea has reference to the time of contemplated breach. The medicine tastes nasty when it is swallowed. . . .

CASE NO. 15

Stone v. Freeman. 298 N.Y. 268, 82 N.E. (2d) 571, 8 A.L.R. (2d) 304 (1948)

. . . DESMOND, J. The suit is by a broker or agent for his commissions earned in arranging a sale by defendant, who is a jobber of clothing, to the French Purchasing Mission, in New York City, in 1946. However, the sole question here is as to the sufficiency of two counterclaims. For present purposes, those counterclaims may be treated as one, since each alleges these same things: that defendant (vendor) agreed to pay, and did pay to plaintiff (broker) certain sums on plaintiff's agreement that he would divide those sums with an employee or representative of the French Supply Council (vendee), but that plaintiff paid to that French representative part only of the latter's agreed share, wherefore defendant, in these counterclaims, sues for return of the part so assigned to the French representative but not paid to him. The question of law is aptly stated in appellants' brief thus (p. 2):

> "May a seller of goods, who has agreed with his broker that the broker shall divide his commissions with the buyer's purchasing agent and has paid the broker moneys intended to be so divided, recover back from the broker a portion of such moneys intended to be paid to the buyer's purchasing agent but not yet so paid?"

Both courts below answered that question in the affirmative. We answer it in the negative.

These counterclaims plainly allege a conspiracy (see Penal Law, Consol. Laws, c. 40, § 580) to violate section 439 of the Penal Law, which makes it a misdemeanor to give or offer such a commission or bonus to a purchasing agent. The contract or arrangement between plaintiff and defendant was thus illegal, criminal and unenforcible. . . . It is the settled law of this State (and probably of every other State) that a party to an illegal contract cannot ask a court of law to help him carry out his illegal object, nor can such a person plead or prove in any court a case in which he, as a basis for his claim, must show forth his illegal purpose. . . .

For no court should be required to serve as paymaster of the wages of crime, or referee between thieves. Therefore, the law

> "will not extend its aid to either of the parties" or "listen to their complaints against each other, but will leave them where their own acts have placed them." Shermerhorn v. Talman, 14 N.Y. 93, 141.

Conforming to that settled rule, this court and its predecessor have several times held that when an agent receives money to be spent for illegal purposes, his principal may not recover back so much of that money as the agent has failed so to spend, particularly when the illegal purpose has been partly or wholly attained and a part of the money expended therefor. . . .

. . . a broker or agent who knowingly participates in a criminal scheme is a principal, and in pari delicto with the one who employs him, so that neither may sue the other. Such is the New York law and it disposes of this case. Insofar as the Restatement of the Law of Agency (§ 412) is to the contrary, we do not concur in it.

We point out that we are passing on the precise question here involved, and no other. This is not a case where a mere agent or depository, receiving money for his principal, refuses to pay it over, on the ground that it was the fruit of an illegal contract between his principal and another. . . . Nor are we deciding what the result would be had this defendant repented of his wrong, and demanded back his money, before any attempt had been made by plaintiff to bribe the purchasing agent. . . .

CASE NO. 16

Delgado v. Delgado. 42 N.M. 582, 82 P. (2d) 909, 118 A.L.R. 1175 (1938)

BICKLEY, J. . . . Action by plaintiffs to set aside a warranty deed made and executed by the mother of defendant and the plaintiffs on the ground that the deed was made for the purpose of placing the title to the property described in the deed in the defendant so that the tax exemption laws of this state would apply to said property and for that purpose only. . . . The defendant particularly denied that the deed was made to defendant for the purpose of obtaining exemption from taxes as an ex-service man. . . .

The statute said to be violated is Sec. 141–1408, Code of 1929. It imposes a penalty of a fine and/or imprisonment for claiming an exemption on property not owned. . . .

Ordinarily where parties to illegal contracts are in pari delicto, a court will leave them where it finds them whether the contract is executory or executed, refusing relief to both. This action of the court gives no validity to the transaction, but deprives the parties of their right to either enforce the contract or to be relieved from it. . . . But the plaintiffs contend there is a well recognized exception to this rule; that is where such contracts are against the public policy of the state or against public interests. There are authorities supporting this view.

> "Although the parties are in pari delicto, yet the court may interfere and grant relief at the suit of one of them, where public policy requires its intervention, even though the result may be that a benefit will be derived by a plaintiff who is in equal guilt with defendant." . . . 13 C.J., Title "Contracts," § 441.

It is not invariable that an act done in violation of a statutory prohibition is absolutely void. A survey of the statute said to be violated must be made in order to discover the legislative intent. The statute in question does not declare that a conveyance of property to a person entitled to exemption with intent to secure said exemption to such person not entitled thereto shall be absolutely void as between the parties to the transaction. The statute says that persons violating the provisions of the act shall be punished by a fine or imprisonment in the penitentiary or by both such fine and imprisonment, at the discretion of the court, and any or all the property conveyed with intent to violate any of the provisions of this act shall escheat to the state upon proper proceedings therefor. The question arises whether the legislature having delineated certain penalties has not excluded others than such as are declared in the statute itself. . . .

It is to be noted that the statute is penal in character and must therefore be strictly construed, and also that the statute contains no provisions that the forbidden conveyance shall be void between the parties. We see no reason why the title may not repose in one of the parties as well as the other until the state shall successfully prosecute proper proceedings to escheat the property to the state. In other words, adverting to the 13 C.J. text, "Contracts," § 441, quoted supra, if the transaction was as the trial court found it to be, no "greater public good can be subserved by action than by inaction" in the case at bar.

BRICE, J., dissenting:

The object of the transfer of this property was to defraud the state of its revenues. The parties to the transaction were in pari delicto, and the heirs of Mrs. Delgado have no rights superior to those she had at the time of her death.

The State of New Mexico in an appreciation of its soldiers, enacted,

> "real and personal property of every soldier shall be exempt from taxation in the sum of two thousand dollars." . . .

I conclude that the deed in question was void, as I find nothing in the statute to indicate that the legislature intends that contracts made in its violation should be valid.

It is true as the majority opinion holds, that ordinarily where parties to illegal contract are in pari delicto, the court will leave them where it finds them, whether the contract is executory or executed, refusing relief to both, and that this action of the court gives no validity to the transaction, but deprives the parties of all right to either enforce the contract or be relieved from it. There is a well recognized exception to this rule; and that is, where such contracts are against the public policy of the state, or against public interests. (See 13 C.J. "Contracts," § 441.) . . .

The rights of the State are grossly violated by such unconscionable acts on the part of ex-soldiers and their relatives. To leave the parties where the court finds them would deprive the State of taxes due it for several past years, as well as future revenue. Consideration for the public welfare should be paramount; and in my opinion requires relief, notwithstanding, it may benefit the heirs of Mrs. Delgado, who otherwise would be entitled to no relief.

It is the public policy of this state, expressed in its constitution and statutes, that property subject to taxation shall bear its proportion of the burden of taxes which must be collected for the expense of government. As between the parties to this suit the court is neutral. It is not interested in the transaction except to prevent a fraud against the state; otherwise it would leave the parties where they have placed themselves.

The opinion of the majority is an invitation to those who, in like situations, are willing to abuse a privilege granted to them by a generous state government, to defraud it of its revenue. . . .

CASE NO. 17

Stevens v. Berger. 255 Wis. 55, 37 N.W. (2d) 841 (1949)

WICKHEM, J. On February 15, 1947 defendants leased to plaintiff as living quarters the second floor of their home and also a garage, occupancy to be given on or before April 1, 1947. The rent for one month was paid and accepted. Defendants agreed to allow plaintiff to store his household goods on part of the premises without charge. Upon getting lease plaintiff had rugs altered to the premises leased, employed movers and sustained other expenses . . . the remodeling work was done under a permit from the federal housing expediter and certain materials for remodeling could not be had by defendants without such a permit. On May 30, 1947 defendants informed plaintiff that the remodeling was being done under such a permit which required them to give renting preference for thirty days to a veteran of World War II. Defendant, Harry Berger, admitted to plaintiff that in the fall of 1946 he had in accordance with regulations posted on his premises a placard giving notice that the work was being done under a permit and also stating the renting regulations but that he had removed the placard before plaintiff had come to view the premises. The trial court took the position that the lease was illegal at its outset; that it was unenforceable and could not be the basis for a claim for damages.

We are of the view that the ruling of trial court was erroneous. Assuming that under the circumstances of this case a lease by defendants to plaintiff would be an illegal contract, plaintiff might nevertheless be in a position to recover if he was not in pari delicto with defendants. In this situation if plaintiff did not know that the premises were built under the housing act and especially if this ignorance was fostered by removal of the required placard from the premises and by defendants' silence plaintiff would not be a wrongful participant in an illegal contract and its illegality would not preclude him from recovering damages from a guilty defendant. See Restatement, Contracts, § 598, comments (a) and (b).

Judgment reversed and cause remanded with directions to vacate summary judgment and for further proceedings according to law.

Review Questions

1. Illegality of an agreement may result from what causes?
2. (a) What is your concept of *public policy?* (b) Would you regard an agreement on the part of an employee to refrain from getting married during an extended period of employment as being contrary to public policy?
3. In what respect does the common law illegality of a contract in restraint of trade differ from its illegality under modern antitrust statutes?
4. Why are agreements that interfere with the operation of governmental functions regarded as being contrary to public policy?
5. Are agreements to lobby illegal?
6. What is the test of a contract reasonably in restraint of trade?
7. Why does the purchaser of a business enterprise find it necessary to prevent the seller from engaging in a like business within the same locality?
8. What is the test of a wagering contract?
9. What element is essential to make an insurance contract legal?
10. How does an insurable interest in a life differ fundamentally from an insurable interest in property?
11. What is a futures contract? What test is employed in determining the enforceability of such an agreement?
12. What is usury?
13. Construct a fact situation illustrating usury although the stipulated rate of interest does not exceed the maximum fixed by law.
14. What qualifications must be made of the general rule that the parties to an illegal agreement are left in whatever position they are found?

Problems for Discussion

1. X, Y, and Z, who are dealers in livestock, agree not to compete with each other in designated areas. Is this agreement valid?
2. The members of an association of contractors had mutually agreed that none of the members would bid on any contract for which a nonmember was a bidder. X, a member of the association, violated this agreement. Action is taken by the association to recover the fine provided for in the contract in the event of its violation. Result?
3. A sells his bowling alley to B. In order to protect B, he agrees not to engage in a similar business in the county for a period of five years. In violation of the agreement, A opens a bowling alley in the county at a point forty miles removed from his original business. Is B entitled to enjoin A from violating the agreement?
4. Plaintiff bought defendant's chiropractic business establishment upon the agreement that defendant would not engage in that profession in that community for a period of three years. When plaintiff failed to qualify for chiropractic practice, defendant resumed his practice. Plaintiff seeks an injunction to prevent defendant from violating his agreement. Result?
5. Sloss organized a corporation and, without meeting the requirements of the Blue Sky Law, proceeded to sell stock. Among other things, the law prohibited

the sale of stock without first having obtained a permit. Keane subscribed for 100 shares and paid $2,000, which was one half of the total subscription price. What are the rights of the parties under this agreement?

6. X sold his business establishment in the city of Keokuk to Y without having agreed to refrain from entering into a similar business. He immediately organized a competing business and actively engaged himself in notifying his former customers of his new venture. Is it his legal right to do this?

7. Three persons, decedent Edward C. Garratt, defendant A. H. Baker, and defendant John Callahan, all married men, were engaged in business as partners. They entered into an agreement by the terms of which each agreed that in the event of the death of any one of them, the two survivors would pay to the widow of the deceased partner the sum of $500 per month as long as they and she should live. Edward C. Garratt died November 19, 1932. Plaintiff is his surviving widow. The other partners paid the monthly sum above specified for some time, and then refused to make further payments. Plaintiff brought this action for $4,750, the amount alleged to be in arrears.

   The position of the defendants, in which the lower court concurred, was that the agreement as set forth in the complaint was an illegal wagering contract. Decide. (*Garratt* v. *Baker,* 5 Cal. (2d) 745)

8. The plaintiff brought action to recover for printing "tickets or slips of paper" to be used by the defendant in games of chance. The lower court held in favor of the plaintiff. Decide. (*Hart Publications* v. *Kaplan,* 37 N.W. (2d) 814)

9. This case involves the enforcement of an arbitration award in payment for certain painting work performed by interior decorators as part of their agreed services. The propriety of such recovery is challenged upon the ground that the decorators were not shown to be licensed contractors at the time of performance of the work in question.

   "It is unlawful for any person to engage in the business or act in the capacity of a contractor within this State without having a license therefor. . . ." Bus. & Prof. Code, § 7028. As defined by statute, a "contractor" is "any person . . . who . . . undertakes to . . . himself or *by or through others,* construct, *alter, repair, add to,* subtract from, *improve* . . . any building. . . ." Decide. (*Franklin* v. *Nat C. Goldstone Agency,—Calif.—,* 204 P. (2d) 37, 1949)

10. Defendant agreed to pay plaintiff $500 if the latter would obtain a pardon for defendant. The pardon was obtained primarily through the efforts of plaintiff. Can he recover?

11. Although aware of the fact that the property would be used for an illegal purpose, plaintiff sold defendant property under a conditional sales contract. Should plaintiff be allowed to recover the purchase price or repossess the property as provided for in the contract?

12. A sued his wife for a divorce. She took steps to contest the action. Then A gave his wife his promissory note for $5,000 in consideration of her withdrawal of all opposition to the divorce proceedings. Can the wife collect upon the note?

13. X agrees to pay Y $100 if the latter will fail to appear as a witness in a criminal trial. Y complies and sues to recover the $100 from X. Result?

14. X, a trucker, hauled "merchandise" into the state for Y without knowledge of the fact that the merchandise consisted of spiritous liquors. Under the state

statute, such an act was prohibited. When Y brought an action to recover for his services, X set up the defense of illegality. Result?

15. Plaintiff, who is a sister of the city clerk, paid money over to X with directions for him to pay the money to the city to cover shortages in the clerk's account if the city should agree not to prosecute the clerk. Then plaintiff withdrew from this plan and ordered X to return the money to her. In violation of her directions, he paid the money to the city. The city resists repayment upon the grounds that the transaction was illegal. Results?
16. A agreed to loan B money at the maximum rate of interest, on the condition that B would purchase his winter's supply of coal from A at an excessive price. Would such a transaction be usurious?
17. Jones made a wager of $1,500 with Smith that a Democrat would be the next incumbent in the White House. Brown was appointed stakeholder. One week before the election, Jones—for reasons best known to himself—called the bet off and demanded a return of the $1,500 from Brown, who refused. The outcome of the election was as Smith wagered it would be, and Brown paid Smith the money. Jones brought an action to recover the $1,500. Did he succeed?

9 CONTRACTS:

ASSIGNMENT OF RIGHTS AND DELEGATION OF DUTIES

► I. ASSIGNMENT OF CONTRACTUAL RIGHTS

A. NATURE AND FORM

Contractual rights are property—assets—and as such can be transferred by the owner to another.

Endorsed on the back of a written contract is the following:

> I, (*the assignor*), the party of the second part in the within written contract, for and in consideration of one dollar and other valuable consideration to me in hand paid, the receipt whereof is hereby acknowledged, do hereby sell, assign, and convey unto (*the assignee*) all my right, title, and interest, in, to, and under the said within contract, including all rights of action to me accrued or hereafter to accrue thereunder, together with all other rights of whatever nature or kind under said contract in connection therewith.
>
> (Signed) The Assignor

The above instrument is called an *assignment,* such as may be used by a contracting party to transfer his *contractual right to performance* to a third party. Technically, an assignment is the transfer of the right to performance, and this transfer is evidenced by the instrument. The party who transfers his contractual right to performance is the *assignor,* and the party to whom it is transferred is the *assignee.* Generally, no particular form is required for an assignment. Usually it may be oral or written without need of any formality attending its execution.

If the assignment is written on a paper other than the contract whose rights are being assigned, care must be exercised to identify properly the rights being transferred.

B. LIMITATIONS TO ASSIGNMENT OF RIGHTS

There are few limitations to the assignment of contractual rights. Ordinarily, it is of little or no consequence to whom an obligor discharges his duties under the contract. On the other hand, there is every reason why contractual rights, being property, should be readily transferable. The right of disposition is one of the characteristics of our institution of private property. To hold otherwise would be placing, without reason, a restriction upon the freedom of commercial transactions.[1] This right of assignment is generally given protection by the courts and

[1] State St. Furniture Co. v. Armour & Co., p. 259.

Iowa has by statute declared that, even when the contract between the parties specifies that no rights thereunder may be assigned, an assignment thereof is nevertheless valid.

1. *Rights not Assignable—Personal Rights*

Rights involving a personal relationship between the contracting parties cannot be assigned.[2] To illustrate:

Rights to personal services are not transferable by assignment without the consent of the person who has the obligation to perform such services. As a matter of public policy, it would be undesirable to force one to work for a party not of his own choosing. It should be recognized that a contract to accomplish a certain result in accordance with certain standards is not a contract for personal services. Thus, if A agrees to build B a house according to plan and specifications, it is not a contract for personal services unless the parties have agreed that A alone should perform. In the absence of such an understanding, B could transfer his rights to have the house built to C without the consent of A.

2. *Assignment of Wages*

Wage earners frequently resort to the use of assignment to obtain the present value of their future income or to discharge existing obligations. As a general rule, future wages as well as wages earned may be assigned. Future wages are such as may accrue under an existing contract of employment, even though the period of employment or the amount of wages to be earned is uncertain.

There are many statutory declarations in respect to assignment of wages. Some states prohibit and declare void the assignment of future wages; others specify the form that an assignment must take to be valid. Iowa, for example, requires the assignment of wages by the head of a family to be in writing and, if the assignor is married, the assignment must be signed by both husband and wife and the execution acknowledged before an officer authorized to take acknowledgments. The purpose of these statutory provisions is to give protection to wage earners and their families. Local statutes should be consulted.

C. POSITION OF ASSIGNEE UNDER ASSIGNMENT

1. *Rights Against Party Obligated to Perform Right Assigned (The Obligor)*

An assignee can stand in no better position than his assignor. Rights under a simple contract cannot be transferred to the prejudice of the party upon whom rests the obligation to perform. Therefore, while a transfer by assignment vests in the assignee the same rights possessed by the assignor, it also subjects him to (1) any claims or defenses the obligor might have against the assignor up to the time of notice to the obligor of the assignment, or (2) which might subsequently arise out of the same contract or transaction which gave rise to the rights assigned.[3]

---

2 Crane Ice Cream v. Terminal, p. 260.

3 William Iselin & Co. v. Saunders, p. 263.

(1) In the case of *Sinclair Rfg. Co.* v. *Rosier,* 104 Kan. 719, the defendant had purchased oil to the amount of $1,500 from the Chanute Co. on open account. The defendant had a claim against the Chanute Co. for $1,400 representing inspection fees paid under an unconstitutional inspection law, leaving the defendant a net obligation of $100 to the Chanute Co. The Chanute Co. assigned this open account to the plaintiff, and the defendant, when sued, set up a counterdemand to the amount of the inspection fees paid. The court held that since the defendant had a valid claim for the fees paid against the Chanute Co. (the assignor), he would also have the same claim as a setoff against the rights of the plaintiff as assignee. Consequently, the defendant's obligation to the assignee was no greater than his obligation to the assignor.

The court said:

> "It has been determined that, when demands exist between parties, one of them cannot defeat the demands of the other by an assignment, but that the assignee takes the assigned claim subject to any defense or demand that the other party holds against the assignor prior to the assignment. . . ."

(2) In the case of *Chambers* v. *Lancaster,* 160 N.Y. 342, it was held that a subcontractor (the assignee) to whom a part of a contract had been assigned could not recover from the owner, even though that part of the contract was fully performed, unless the contractor (assignor) had completed the rest of the contract, which would entitle him to recover. The rights of the subcontractor (the assignee) were subject to all claims that the owner would have against the contractor for default of performance of the contract as a whole.

2. *Rights Against Assignor*

An assignment need not be supported by a consideration. A gratuitous assignment, like any other gratuitous promise, may be revoked by the assignor at any time before the assignee has realized performance from the obligor. The revocation is not effective until the obligor has been notified.

Usually assignments are based upon a consideration. Consideration gives an assignment the status of a contract, under which the assignee becomes the owner of the rights assigned. Consequently, the assignor has no right to defeat the realization of the rights by the assignee. In every assignment supported by consideration, the assignor impliedly warrants: first, that he has a title which has no defects (such as defenses available to the obligor or a prior assignment by the assignor); second, that he will do nothing to defeat the realization of the rights assigned (such as making a subsequent assignment or accepting performance of the rights assigned). Should there be a breach of warranty, the assignee has legal recourse against the assignor for damages.

As a general rule, there is no implied warranty that the rights assigned will be realized. The assignor impliedly assumes no responsibility to the assignee for a default of performance. In some states, an exception to the above rule has been made if the right assigned is a claim for the payment of money. Even in these jurisdictions, the responsibility of the assignor is not based upon the default itself but depends rather upon the fact that the assignee has exhausted his available remedies against the debtor without success.

3. *Need of Giving Notice*

For his own protection, the assignee, immediately upon receiving an assignment, should give notice to the obligor, as follows:

> I hereby give you notice that by an agreement dated the ______ day of ________, 19___, and made between ________ of ________, of the one part, and myself, of the other part, the debt of ________ dollars owing by you to the said ________ has been absolutely assigned to me, my executors, administrators, and assigns; and further take notice that you are hereby required to pay to me, or such person as I may appoint to receive the same, the said debt of ________ dollars on or before the ______ day of ______ next, and in default thereof I shall pursue such remedies as are allowed by law for the recovery of the said debt. Dated this ______ day of ________, 19___.
>
> To *The Obligor.* (Signed) *The Assignee*

The assignee by giving such notice protects himself from the following:

(1) Performance by the obligor to the assignor. Unless notified, the obligor is within his right to discharge his obligation to the party with whom he contracted. In such an event, the assignee's recourse would be against the assignor for breach of implied warranty.

(2) Available defenses of setoff or counterclaim arising out of some other transaction. Any defenses that the obligor acquires subsequent to the giving of notice are not available against the assignee.

(3) Subsequent assignees. In some jurisdictions, as between successive assignees, the one first to give notice has priority rather than the one who first obtained the assignment. In the event the assignee fails to realize upon the assigned rights because of a prior assignment, he may look to the assignor for breach of implied warranty.

Good business practice dictates that a party who is contemplating accepting rights by assignment should communicate with the obligor (the party from whom he will expect performance) for the purpose of determining whether there has been another assignment or whether any claims have been made against the rights. For example:

Banks frequently accept life insurance policies with a cash value as security for loans. Before they advance the funds to the borrower, they usually communicate with the insurance company to determine whether they have notice of any other claims upon the rights under the policy.

► II. DELEGATION OF DUTIES DISTINGUISHED

It again becomes necessary to emphasize the fact that for every contractual right there is a reciprocal duty. These inseparable twins, rights and corresponding duties, are the very essence of a contract.

For the sake of clarity and in view of the fact that a contract is composed of both rights and duties, the use of the term *assignment* will be limited here to a transfer of contractual rights, although it is commonly said that a contract can be assigned. It is possible, however, for a contracting party to entrust the performance of his obligation to a third party. In other words, contractual duties may be *delegated* rather than assigned.

The reader should recognize then that the three following situations are possible:

(1) A transfer of contractual rights without a transfer of the duties which serve as the consideration for the rights. Thus, A may assign his right to wages which he has already earned.

(2) A transfer of contractual duties without a transfer of the contractual rights which serve as consideration for the rights. Thus, a contractor may delegate his contractual obligation to perform a certain phase of the work to a subcontractor. In such a case the contractor pays the subcontractor directly for the performance of the work and the contractor collects from the party for whom the work was performed.

(3) A transfer of both. Thus, a tenant may sublet the premises to another with the understanding that the subtenant will pay the rent. The tenant has in this way assigned his right to the use of the premises and has delegated his duty to pay rent.

The entrusting of performance to a third party does not relieve the original obligor of his duty to perform. Should there be a failure of performance, the injured party could still look for satisfaction to the party with whom he contracted.*

Under a bilateral contract, it frequently happens that an assignment of the rights is accompanied by a delegation of the performance of duties to the assignee. It is important to recognize that under no circumstances can a contracting party discharge his duty to perform by delegating the performance to another person. He can divest himself of his rights under the contract, but not of his obligations by means other than a proper legal discharge or the consent of the party holding the corresponding rights. To illustrate:

If A sells real estate to B upon which there is a $10,000 mortgage in favor of C, and it is agreed between A and B that B alone is to pay the amount of the mortgage obligation to C, there has been a delegation of A's obligation to B. This in itself does not relieve A of his obligation to C should B fail to pay. C can still look to A for payment.

---

* The right of the injured party to legal recourse against the party to whom the duty was delegated is treated under Third Party Beneficiary Contracts, p. 256.

A. DISCHARGE OF CONTRACTUAL OBLIGATIONS BY NOVATION

A contracting party will be relieved of his contractual duties by their transfer to a third party, providing the consent of the other contracting party is obtained. An arrangement like this is called a *novation.* In essence, by mutual consent of the parties, a new obligor is substituted for the old obligor, who is thereby *discharged of his obligations.* The party entitled to performance of the transferred obligations agrees to look to the substituted party for satisfaction and can no longer look to the original obligor.

B. LIMITATIONS TO DELEGATION OF DUTIES

A party to a contract has no cause for complaint if his justifiable expectations under the contract are realized. The test of performance does not depend upon the person from whom the performance is obtained but rather on whether that which was bargained for is realized. Consequently, when a realization of contractual rights is not dependent personally upon the original obligor, he may delegate his duties to a third party, from whom the other contracting party is obligated to accept performance. X contracts to construct for Y a factory in accordance with certain plans and specifications. Performance is not dependent upon X personally. Others can build according to plans and specifications equally as well as X. Hence, the duty to build may be delegated, and Y can have no objection. Likewise, the payment of money is not dependent upon the debtor personally and therefore may be delegated. A partner, upon retiring from a firm, may delegate to the continuing partners his duty to pay existing partnership creditors. He does not, however, thereby relieve himself of his obligations to the creditors. As a matter of law, his liability to the firm's creditors remains primary, although in effect he stands as a surety for the payment of such obligations.

Duties cannot be delegated, then, in those instances where performance as bargained for is dependent upon the original obligor personally.[4] This personal obligation may result (1) when the personal services of the obligor are bargained for or (2) when the relationship between the parties is one of trust and confidence. For example, at times it is necessary that the party entitled to performance entrust the obligor with money or property by means of which the performance is made possible. In such a case, the party entitled to performance cannot be made to rely upon the integrity of anyone other than the party with whom he bargained.

► III. THIRD PARTY BENEFICIARY CONTRACTS

In our law, the anomalous situation exists wherein one may acquire contractual rights without contracting. This may become possible under a type of agreement known as a *third party beneficiary contract,* a contract that inures to the *direct benefit of a third party.*[5] The test of direct benefit is well stated in *Penn. Steel Co.* v. *New York City R. Co.,* 194 Fed. 543, where the court said:

[4] Smith v. Zuckman, p. 265.

[5] Spires v. Hanover Fire Ins. Co., p. 266; see also U.S. v. Huff, p. 293.

"There is no real and substantial reason why, if the parties to a contract recognize the interest of a third person in it and desire and intend to give him a right of action upon it, they should not be able to do so. And the prevailing doctrine in this country is contrary to the English rule. It is generally held, subject to qualifications, that a third person may sue upon a promise made to another for his benefit. . . ."

A. DONEE TYPE DISTINGUISHED FROM CREDITOR TYPE

Third party beneficiary contracts can be classified as being either of the *donee* or *creditor* type. In the donee type, the benefit to the third party is a gratuity, the third party beneficiary having no relationship other than that of a donee to the contracting parties. Suppose, for example, that A sells B a quantity of hay and B promises A to pay the purchase price of $100 to X. Having no obligation to X, A intends the $100 to be a gift. X stands as a donee beneficiary under this contract between B and A.

Usually, but not necessarily, the beneficiary named by the insured in a life insurance contract is a donee.

The distinguishing characteristic of the creditor type is that the beneficiary stands in the position of a creditor to one of the contracting parties. Let us suppose that in the illustration above A *owed* X $100. In that event, X would stand as a creditor beneficiary under the contract between B and A. Obviously, by requesting B to pay the purchase price to X, A intends to have his creditor paid. Let us note that B, by assuming to pay X, has accepted the *delegation* of this duty, which in itself, however, does not discharge A from his obligation.

If under an insurance contract the beneficiary is a creditor of the insured, it is a third party beneficiary contract of the creditor type.

A very practical illustration of the creditor type of third party beneficiary contracts relates to the purchase of real property that is encumbered by a mortgage. Generally, the purchaser, in taking over the mortgage indebtedness as part of the purchase price, agrees with his grantor (the mortgagor) to pay the mortgagee; the purchaser *assumes* the mortgage obligation. The mortgagee,[6] who is the creditor of the grantor (the mortgagor), stands as a creditor beneficiary under the contract between the grantor and the purchaser. The fact that the mortgagor has *delegated* to the purchaser his duty to pay the mortgage indebtedness does not relieve the mortgagor from his responsibility to the mortgagee. In effect, the purchaser becomes the principal debtor of the mortgage obligation, and the grantor (the original mortgagor) stands as his surety.

B. RIGHT OF BENEFICIARY TO SUE

It cannot be categorically stated that a third party beneficiary may bring legal action to enforce the promise that inures to his benefit. The right to sue is dependent upon the nature of the contract or the jurisdiction within which the

[6] Guardian Depositors Corp. v. Brown, p. 268.

action is to be brought. The uncertainty of the situation becomes apparent from the following:

(1) All states allow beneficiaries under insurance policies to sue the insurer.

(2) A majority of the states allow creditor beneficiaries to sue.

(3) Some states allow recovery to donee beneficiaries and not to creditor beneficiaries.

(4) In some states, the opposite of (3) is true.

(5) Some states allow recovery to both donee and creditor beneficiaries. Certain intricate variations could be added to the above.

C. RIGHT OF CONTRACTING PARTIES TO RESCIND

The rights of a beneficiary under a third party beneficiary contract are as absolute as any other contractual rights, being subject only to the terms of the contract. After the beneficiary has accepted or claimed the benefits, the contracting parties cannot rescind the contract without the consent of the beneficiary unless the contract itself gives them this right, unless the rights of the beneficiary were acquired subject to such a condition in the contract.[7, 8] To illustrate:

(1) X has insured his life with the Y Insurance Company and has named Z as the beneficiary. X cannot change the beneficiary without the consent of Z unless he has reserved the right to change the beneficiary in the insurance contract.

(2) In *Bassett et al.* v. *Hughes,* 43 Wis. 319, Hughes transferred all his property to his son, the defendant, who agreed to pay all his father's debts. The plaintiff, who held a note against the father, was notified of this fact. When the plaintiff brought an action against the defendant for the payment of the debt, it was the defendant's contention that he was no longer obligated, since he and his father had rescinded the contract. The court, in holding the defendant liable, said:

> "It is settled in this state that when one person, for a valuable consideration, engages with another to do some act for the benefit of a third person, the latter may maintain an action against the former for a breach of such engagement. . . .
>
> "It is quite immaterial, if the defendant's covenant to pay his father's debts was afterwards rescinded by mutual agreement between the parties to it. Before that was done, the plaintiffs had been informed of the covenant, and made no objection thereto; indeed the fair inference from the testimony is, that the plaintiffs fully assented thereto. . . . After such notice and assent, the covenant could not be rescinded to the prejudice of the plaintiffs, without their consent."

---

[7] O'Connell v. Brady, p. 269.

[8] Waller v. Waller, p. 271.

CASES

CASE NO. 1

State Street Furniture Co. v. Armour & Co. 345 Ill. 160, 177 N.E. 702 (1931)

ORR, J. . . . As a defense to the action brought by the plaintiff . . . under its wage assignment, the defendant filed an affidavit of merits, which, among other things recited that the employee whose wages were involved had prior to the date of the assignment entered into a written contract with defendant as follows:

> "For and in consideration of my employment by Armour & Co. . . . I do hereby covenant and agree, as a part of my contract of employment, that I will not sell, transfer, set over or assign in any manner . . . any right to or claim for wages or salary, in whole or in part, due me or to become due me from Armour & Co., . . . without the consent in writing of Armour & Co.; . . ."

Prior to the date of the assignment the defendant had given written notice to numerous firms, including the plaintiff, that it had entered into such a contract with all of its employees and would no longer honor wage assignments. It was therefore the contention of the defendant that because of such contract and notice the subsequent assignment of wages without its consent was null and void. On motion of the plaintiff the trial court struck the defendant's affidavit of merits because it failed to set forth any legal defense to the statement of claim. The defendant elected to stand on its affidavit of merits, and upon its refusal to plead further a default was entered against it, followed by an assessment of damages and judgment. . . .

The principal question presented is whether the affidavit of merits filed by the defendant stated a legal defense to the plaintiff's claim. In other words, by reason of the employment contract was the assignment of wages void, since the written consent of the defendant was not obtained thereto? The determination of this section is of great importance to all mercantile firms which sell goods on the installment plan.

The right of an employee to make an assignment of his wages has long been recognized in this State, and the privilege of using and contracting for the disposal of wages is both a liberty and a property right. . . . Property includes every interest in any and everything subject to the ownership of man, and the right to dispose of that interest is a property right. . . . The relationship between employer and employee with respect to unpaid wages is that of debtor and creditor, and the right of the employee to those wages is a chose in action and as such may be assigned. . . . This court has not only held that assignments of wages may be enforced as to past services, but has also sanctioned such assignments as to wages to be earned in the future under an existing employment if such assignment is made for a valuable consideration and untainted with fraud. . . .

. . . . .

The defendant further asserts that a partial assignment of a debt due or to become due cannot be made without the consent of the debtor. But the assignment here is of the entire claim and no question of partial assignment of a debt due or to become due is involved. Where the assignment is of the entire claim the consent of the debtor is not required, as it is of no concern to the defendant in whose name the suit for wages due the employee is instituted. . . . . Where the employer owes the employee for wages earned, the contract of employment has, to the wages earned, ceased to be a bilateral contract with mutual rights and duties. It has then become a unilateral contract or debt, with an absolute obligation on the part of the employer to pay and an absolute right on the part of the employee to receive his pay. . . . When one has incurred a debt, which is property in the hands of the creditor, the debtor cannot restrain its alienation as between the creditor and a third person any more than he can forbid the sale or pledge of other chattels. A debt is property, which may be sold or assigned, subject to the ordinary rules of the common law in determining the rights of the assignee, and, when untainted with fraud, its sale offers no ground for complaint by the debtor. . . .

Judgment affirmed.

CASE NO. 2

Crane Ice Cream Company v. Terminal Freezing & Heating Company. 147 Md. 588 (1925)

PARKE, J. The appellee and one W. C. Frederick entered into a contract for the delivery of ice by the appellee to Frederick, and, before the expiration of the contract, Frederick executed an assignment of the contract to the appellant; and on the refusal of the appellee to deliver ice to the assignee it brought an action on the contract against the appellee to recover damages for the alleged breach. . . .

. . . At the execution of the contract the Terminal Freezing & Heating Company, appellee, was a corporation engaged in the manufacture and sale of ice at wholesale within the state of Maryland, and William C. Frederick made and sold ice cream in Baltimore, where his plant was located. . . .

The contract imposed upon the appellee the liability to sell and deliver to Frederick such quantities of ice as he might use in his business as an ice cream manufacturer, to the extent of 250 tons per week, at and for the price of $3.25 a ton of 2,000 pounds on the loading platform of Frederick. The contractual rights of the appellee were (a) to be paid on every Tuesday during the continuation of the contract, for all ice purchased by Frederick during the week ending at midnight upon the next preceding Saturday; (b) to require Frederick not to buy or accept any ice from any other source than the appellee, except in excess of the weekly maximum of 250 tons; (c) to annul the contract upon any violation of the agreement by Frederick; and (d) to sustain no liability for any breach of contract growing out of causes beyond its control. The converse of these rights and liabilities of the appellee were the correlative liabilities and rights of Frederick under the contract. . . .

As soon as the appellee learned of this purported assignment and the absorption of the business of Frederick by the appellant, it notified Frederick that the contract was at an end, and declined to deliver any ice to the appellant. . . .

It may be stated as a general rule that a contract cannot be enforced by or against a person who is not a party to it, but there are circumstances under which either of the contracting parties may substitute another for himself in the rights and duties of the contract without obtaining the consent of the other party to the contract. The inquiry here is if the facts bring the case within the scope of the general rule, and the answer must be found from a consideration in detail of the relation of the parties concerned, the subject-matter of the contract, its terms, and the circumstances of its formation. . . .

Whether the attempted assignment of these rights, or the attempted delegation of these duties, must fail because the rights or duties are of too personal a character, is a question of construction to be resolved from the nature of the contract and the express or presumed intention of the parties.

The contract was made by a corporation with an individual, William C. Frederick, an ice cream manufacturer, with whom the corporation had dealt for three years, before it executed a renewal contract for a second like period. The character, credit, and resources of Frederick had been tried and tested by the appellee before it renewed the contract. Not only had his ability to pay as agreed been established, but his fidelity to his obligation not to buy or accept any ice from any other source up to 250 tons a week had been ascertained. In addition, the appellee had not asked in the beginning, nor on entering into the second period of the contract, for Frederick to undertake to buy a specific quantity of ice, or even to take any. Frederick simply engaged himself during a definite term to accept and pay for such quantities of ice as he might use in his business, to the extent of 250 tons a week. If he used no ice in his business, he was under no obligation to pay for a pound. In any week, the quantity could vary from zero to 250 tons, and its weekly fluctuation, throughout the life of the contract, could irregularly range between these limits. The weekly payment might be nothing, or as much as $812.50; and for every week a credit was extended to the eighth day from the beginning of every week's delivery. From the time of the beginning of every weekly delivery of the ice to the date of the payment therefor, the title to the ice was in the purchaser, and the seller had no security for its payment except in the integrity and solvency of Frederick. The performances, therefore, were not concurrent, but the performance of the nonassigning party to the contract was to precede the payments by the assignor.

When it is also considered that the ice was to be supplied and paid for, according to its weight on the loading platform of Frederick at an unvarying price, without any reference either to the quantity used, or to the fluctuations in the cost of production, or to market changes in the selling price, throughout three years, the conclusion is inevitable that the inducement for the appellee to enter into the original contract and into the renewal lay outside the bare terms of the contract, but was implicit in them, and was the appellee's reliance upon its knowledge of an average quantity of ice consumed, and probably to be needed, in the usual course of Frederick's business, at all times throughout the year, and its confidence in the stability of his enterprise, in his competency in commercial affairs, in his probity, personal judgment, and in his continuing financial responsibility. The contract itself emphasized the personal equation by specifying that the ice was to be bought for "use in his business as an ice cream manufacturer," and was to be paid for according to its weight "on the loading platform of the said W. C. Frederick." . . .

. . . The assigner had his simple plant in Baltimore. The assignee, in its purchase, simply added another unit to its ice cream business which it had been, and is now, carrying on

> "upon a large and extensive scale in the city of Philadelphia and state of Pennsylvania, as well as in the city of Baltimore and state of Maryland."

The appellee knew that Frederick could not carry on his business without ice wherewith to manufacture ice cream at his plant for his trade. It also was familiar with the quantities of ice he would require, from time to time, in his business at his plant in Baltimore, and it consequently could make its other commitments for ice with this knowledge as a basis.

The appellant, on the other hand, might wholly supply its increased trade acquired in the purchase of Frederick's business with its ice cream produced upon a large and extensive scale by its manufactory in Philadelphia, which would result in no ice being bought by the assignee of the appellee, and so the appellee would be deprived of the benefit of its contract by the introduction of a different personal relation or element which was never contemplated by the original contracting parties. Again, should the price of ice be relatively high in Philadelphia, in comparison with the stipulated price, the assignee could run its business in Baltimore and furnish its patrons, or a portion of them, in Philadelphia, with its product from the weekly maximum consumption of 250 tons of ice throughout the year. There can be no denial that the uniform delivery of the maximum quantity of 250 tons a week would be a consequence not within the normal scope of the contract, and would impose a greater liability on the appellee than was anticipated.

Moreover, the contract here to supply ice was undefined except as indicated from time to time by the personal requirements of Frederick in his specified business. The quantities of ice to be supplied to Frederick to answer his weekly requirements must be very different from, and would not be the measure of, the quantities needed by his assignee, and, manifestly, to impose on the seller the obligation to obey the demands of the substituted assignee is to set up a new measure of ice to be supplied, and so a new term in the agreement that the appellee never bound itself to perform. . . .

Under all the circumstances of the case, it is clear that the rights and duties of the contract under consideration were of so personal a character that the rights of Frederick cannot be assigned nor his duties be delegated without defeating the intention of the parties to the original contract. When Frederick went out of the business of making ice cream, he made it impossible for him to complete his performance of the contract, and his personal action and qualifications upon which the appellee relied were eliminated from a contract which presupposed their continuance. Frederick not only attempted an assignment, but his course is a repudiation of the obligations of the contract. He is not even alleged to be ready to pay for any ice which might be delivered after the date of the purporting assignment, but the allegations of the declaration simply aver that the assignee alone had undertaken to perform the further contractual obligations of the assignor. Frederick, however, cannot be heard to say that he has not repudiated a contract, whose contemplated performance his own act has made it impossible for him to fulfill.

While a party to a contract may, as a general rule, assign all his beneficial rights, except where a personal relation is involved, his liability under the contract is not assignable *inter vivos*, because anyone who is bound to any performance whatever or who owes money cannot by any act of his own, or by any act in agreement with any other person than his creditor or the one to whom his performance is due, cast off his own liability and substitute another's liability. If this were not true, obligors could free themselves of their obligations by the simple expedient of assigning them. A further ground for the rule is that not only is a party entitled to know to whom he must look for the satisfaction of his rights under the contract, but, in the familiar words of Lord Denman, in Humble v. Hunter, 12 Q.B. 317:

> "You have a right to the benefit you contemplate from the character, credit, and substance of the person with whom you contract."

For these reasons, it has been uniformly held that a man cannot assign his liabilities under a contract, but one who is bound so as to bear an unescapable liability may delegate the performance of his obligation to another, if the liability be of such a nature that its performance by another will be substantially the same thing as performance by the promisor himself. In such circumstances, the performance of the third party is the act of the promisor, who remains liable under the contract and answerable in damages if the performance be not in strict fulfillment of the contract. . . .

As it is the opinion of the court that the judgment below was in accordance with the principles of law applicable to the facts admitted by the demurrer, the judgment will be affirmed. . . .

CASE NO. 3

William Iselin & Co. v. Saunders. 231 N.C. 642, 58 S.E. (2d) 614 (1950)

Civil action by assignee to collect a non-negotiable chose in action from debtor.

There was sharp conflict between the pleadings and evidence of the parties.

The testimony of the plaintiff, a corporation of Columbus, Ohio, made out this case against the defendants, retailers of dry goods at Kings Mountain, North Carolina:

On October 18, 1946, the defendants, acting through their agent, Consolidated Clothiers, of New York City, New York, gave the Falcon Sportswear Company, a clothing manufacturer of St. Louis, Missouri, an unconditional written order for 100 pairs of "all wool redyed serge" pants at an agreed price of $9.50 per pair. The Falcon Sportswear Company expressed 100 pairs of pants conforming to the order from St. Louis to the defendants at Kings Mountain in two equal consignments on the 23rd and 28th days of January, 1947, and forthwith assigned its account against the defendants for $950.00, the total price of the goods, to the plaintiff, which took the account in good faith and for a valuable consideration while the merchandise was en route from St. Louis to Kings Mountain. Upon the subsequent arrival of the goods at Kings Mountain, the defendants unjustifiably refused to accept or pay for them, and the express company returned the consignments to St. Louis, where the Falcon Sportswear Company declined to receive them. The plaintiff brought the action to recover the sum of $950.00 on the assignment after the defendants had refused its demand for payment.

The evidence of the defendants presented the following version of the events antedating the litigation:

The defendants had no direct contractual relations of any kind with either the Falcon Sportswear Company, or the plaintiff. On October 18, 1946, David L. Saunders, one of the defendants, visited the office of the Consolidated Clothiers in New York City, and gave the Consolidated Clothiers, which was either an independent wholesale dealer in dry goods or a selling agent of the Falcon Sportswear Company, a provisional order for 50 pairs of pants, which the Consolidated Clothiers then and there exhibited to him. The Consolidated Clothiers took this order from David L. Saunders on the specific condition that it would not be valid unless it should be approved by his partners, the defendants D. D. Saunders and W. L. Davis, who were then in Kings Mountain. They refused to confirm the provisory order, and immediate notice of that fact was given the Consolidated Clothiers. The defendants had no further connection with or notice of any of the matters resulting in this litigation until the consignments and the invoices covering them reached Kings Mountain. The invoices recited that the Falcon Sportswear Company was shipping the goods to the defendants on its own account, and had assigned the sale price to the plaintiff. The defendants inspected the consignment of January 23, 1947, immediately after its arrival at Kings Mountain; discovered that it contained 50 pairs of very inferior pants, which did not correspond in kind and quality with the sample exhibited to David L. Saunders by the Consolidated Clothiers three months previously; and rejected the goods. When the consignment of January 28, 1947, reached Kings Mountain, the defendants declined to inspect or accept it because they had not ordered it. The defendants gave the Falcon Sportswear Company prompt notice of their rejection of each of the shipments, and caused the express Company forthwith to return them to St. Louis, where the Falcon Sportswear Company refused to receive them.

The Court submitted this single issue to the jury: "Are the defendants indebted to the plaintiff, and if so, in what amount?" The jury answered the issue "$950.00," and the court rendered judgment for the plaintiff accordingly. . . .

ERVIN, J. The transactions giving rise to this litigation are susceptible of several constructions which would have afforded the defendants either complete or partial exoneration from liability to the Falcon Sportswear Company if it had sued the defendants directly upon the claim now in suit. . . .

Upon a fourth view, the testimony in the record justifies the inferences that the defendants had had no dealings with the Falcon Sportswear Company, and had never held the Consolidated Clothiers out as authorized to act for them; that on or about October 18, 1946, the defendants employed the Consolidated Clothiers as a special agent with the limited power to buy not exceeding 50 pairs of pants for them; that the Consolidated Clothiers exceeded its limited authority, and undertook to enter into a contract with the Falcon Sportswear Company in the name of the defendants, purporting to bind the defendants to purchase 100 pairs of pants from the Falcon Sportswear Company at a price of $9.50 per pair; that the Falcon Sportswear Company endeavored to perform this alleged contract on its part by shipping 100 pairs of pants in two equal consignments from St. Louis to the defendants at Kings Mountain; and the defendants forthwith refused to accept the consignments, and caused them to be returned to St. Louis, where the Falcon Sportswear Company declined to receive them. If this was the state of things, the defendants were liable to the Falcon Sportswear Company for the price of only 50 pairs of the pants. This is true because a special agent can only contract for his principal within the limits of his authority, and a third person dealing with such an agent must acquaint himself with the strict extent of the agent's authority and deal with the agent accordingly. . . .

Notwithstanding the testimony tending to negative or minimize liability of the defendants to the plaintiff's alleged assignor, i.e., the Falcon Sportswear Company, the court instructed the jury in a portion of the charge, which is the subject of the ninth assignment of error, to award the plaintiff the full amount sued for, i.e., $950.00, in response to the only issue submitted to it in case it

> "should find from the evidence, and its greater weight, that the account in question was sold and assigned to the plaintiff for a valuable consideration and without any notice of fault before maturity, and that the same has not been paid by the defendants."

In so charging the jury, the court committed substantial error, entitling the defendants to a new trial. The instruction contravenes the well-settled principle that the assignee of a nonnegotiable chose in action, though he buys it for value, in good faith, and before maturity, takes it subject to all defenses which the debtor may have had against the assignor based on facts existing at the time of the assignment or on facts arising thereafter but prior to the debtor's knowledge of the assignment. . . . This rule is the inescapable corollary of the bedrock proposition that the assignor of a nonnegotiable chose in action cannot confer upon the assignee a greater right than he possesses.

The verdict and judgment are vacated, and the defendants are granted a new trial.

CASE NO. 4

Smith v. Zuckman. 203 Minn. 535, 282 N.W. 269 (1938)

Plaintiff's intestate and defendant had entered into a written contract whereby former agreed to use his "best efforts to solicit contracts" for advertising film service, such to be displayed by defendant in latter's theater; also that he would make contracts with individuals and business concerns requiring payment by such parties to defendant at a certain rate per week. Defendant agreed to show

> "at every performance the film ads (so) contracted for, . . . and to display same while the audience is seated."

He also agreed that he would not show

> "advertising slides or films other than those furnished by first party (plaintiff's intestate)."

This suit was brought by plaintiff administrator to recover damages for breach of contract and for injunctive relief. There is no claim that defendant failed to perform any contract duty prior to the demise of plaintiff's intestate. Defendant's general demurrer was sustained. . . .

OLSON, J. . . . Plaintiff's claim is founded upon the theory that the contract, not having been cancelled by notice as provided for therein, continues to exist in full force and effect and that he as administrator succeeded to all the rights of his decedent. It is not claimed that defendant had defaulted in respect of any service rendered or other monetary obligation incurred prior to the time he refused to accept the administrator's services in lieu of those theretofore rendered by the other contracting party. There is no claim of any new or substitute contract having been made effective between plaintiff as administrator and defendant. So we come directly to the point made by the court, that plaintiff's intestate entered into "personal obligations" with defendant and that, this being so, the administrator is incapable of rendering the service that decedent had promised to perform.

Generally speaking, where one undertakes a duty, especially, one of personal service, he cannot assign such duty to another. It would be strange indeed if one who owes money or is bound to any performance to another could by any act of his own or by agreement with a third person, not a party to the agreement, divest himself of the duty so assumed and substitute another in his place. Of course,

> "One who is subject to a duty though he cannot escape his obligation may delegate performance of it provided the duty does not require personal performance. In the absence of express agreement to the contrary there will be no such requirement if the duty is of such character that performance by an agent will be substantially the same thing as performance by the obligor himself. *The performance in such a case is indeed in legal contemplation rendered by the original obligor, who is still the party liable if the performance is in any respect incorrect* . . ."

On the other hand,

> "If the duty does require personal performance it cannot be discharged by any performance by another even though it would serve the purpose as well or better than the performance of the one who contracted to render it." 2 Williston, Contracts (Rev. Ed.) § 411. . . .

The same author (§ 411A) furnishes numerous citations of cases of attempted delegations of duties which the courts refused to enforce because such duties were personal. Cases within that class are, amongst many, those involving contracts to give a home and support to a relative . . . contracts whereby one undertakes to carry on a farm for another on a crop share basis; to plant and care for an orchard; to one who in return for a promised commission undertaken to assist in the sale of land; similarly, where contractual duty involved the exclusive agency to sell certain goods; to a contract to place advertising and supervise the advertising matter "as to style and contents." . . .

Nor do we think plaintiff's argument that the contract here involved bears upon its face an intent to bind the "successors and assigns" of the parties is of any moment. That question was disposed of adversely to plaintiff's contentions in Marvel v. Phillips, 162 Mass. 399, 401, 38 N.E. 1117, 1118, 26 L.R.A. 416, 44 Am. St. Rep. 370, where the court said:

> "A contract to render such services and perform such duties is subject to the implied condition that the party shall be alive and well enough in health to perform it. Death or a disability which rendered performance impossible discharges the contract. Neither Phillips nor his estate is bound to furnish a substitute, nor is the plaintiff bound to accept one. . . ."

We think the court was right in sustaining the demurrer, and its order in the premises is affirmed.

CASE NO. 5

Spires v. Hanover Fire Ins. Co. 364 Pa. 52, 70 A. (2d) 828 (1950)

STERN, J. The issue here involved . . . is whether an insurance company must account for the performance of its obligations under a policy of fire insurance to anyone other than the named insured.

Plaintiffs in September, 1944 leased a tract of land owned by them to one Mary E. Kaehler. . . . The land contained an aeroplane hangar and was laid out as an airport. . . . The lessee agreed

> "to keep the buildings now erected or to be erected upon said premises insured against loss by fire, at her own cost and expense," and also to "keep all runways and hangars in good condition and proper repair at her own proper cost and expense."

. . . the lessee took one Louis A. Raub as a partner in the operation of the airport. In November, 1946 they—

the partners—obtained from the Hanover Fire Insurance Company a policy which provided that the company, for the term of three years,

> "to an amount not exceeding Fifteen Thousand Dollars, does insure Louis A. Raub and Mary Eileen Kaehler . . . to the extent of the actual cash value of the property at the time of loss, . . ."

The property insured was described as including the one story building known as Hangar No. 1 (which was the hangar on the premises when the lease was executed). . . .

A fire occurred in March, 1947 which resulted in a total loss of Hangar No. 1 and other property on the leased premises. Kaehler and Raub settled with the Insurance Company for the loss occasioned by the fire but in an amount which did not include the value of Hangar No. 1. They refused to file a proof of loss in regard to that hangar and they refused also to institute any action against the Insurance Company for the loss sustained by its destruction. Thereupon plaintiffs themselves filed a proof of loss and brought the present action against the Insurance Company to recover for that loss, averring in their complaint all the facts above stated.

. . . the only ground upon which they assert a right of action is their contention that the insurance was taken out for their benefit in pursuance of the provision to that effect in the lease.

There are two reasons why this claim is untenable. The first is that their contention that the insurance was carried primarily for their benefit is unwarranted. The lease provided that the lessee was to keep the hangars in good condition and repair at her own cost and expense; she thereby obligated herself to restore plaintiffs' hangar at the time of the termination of the lease even though it were meanwhile destroyed by fire or other accident: Hoy v. Holt, 91 Pa. 88, 36 Am. Rep. 659; Girard Trust Co., Agent, v. Tremblay Motor Co., 291 Pa. 507, 518, 140 Atl. 506, 510. In view of that obligation the lessee had a primary and paramount insurable interest of her own in the policy, that interest being the value of the property which she was bound to replace: Imperial Fire Insurance Co. v. Murray, 73 Pa. 13. A policy of fire insurance is a personal contract of indemnity against such loss as the *insured* may sustain; the insurance is not of the property as such, but of the *interest of the insured* in the property. . . .

The other reason why plaintiffs cannot recover on the policy is because, whatever incidental interest they may have had therein, and even if, *as between them and the lessee,* they were meant to be a beneficiary thereof, they are not referred to in the *policy itself* as an intended beneficiary; indeed it does not appear that the Insurance Company ever knew of the lease from plaintiffs to Kaehler, or even that any such persons as plaintiffs existed. To be a third party beneficiary entitled to recover on a contract is not enough that it be intended by *one* of the parties to the contract and the *third person* that the latter should be a beneficiary, but *both parties to the contract* must so intend and must indicate that intention in the contract; in other words, a promisor cannot be held liable to an alleged beneficiary of a contract unless the latter was within his contemplation at the time the contract was entered into and such liability was intentionally assumed by him in his undertaking; the obligation to the third party must be created, and must affirmatively appear, in the contract itself: Klingler v. Wick, 266 Pa. 1, 6, 7, 109 Atl. 542, 543; 17 C.J.S., Contracts, § 519(c), pp. 1127–1130; 12 Am. Jur. 831, 832, § 280; 833, 834, § 281. The fact, therefore, that plaintiffs would be incidentally benefited would not give them a right to recover on the policy by virtue of any arrangement between them and Kaehler where the Insurance Company assumed no obligation to them in the policy but believed itself to be insuring only the interest of the persons named therein.

It is true that a third party beneficiary may be in contemplation without being specifically or individually designated: for example, there is a type of policy frequently taken out by a bailee covering goods in his possession "on account of whom it may concern," or by "trust and commission," or with similar clauses; in such cases the bailor may recover on the policy. The present policy contained an "in trust or on commission" clause but only with respect to the personal property, not the land and hangars. . . .

CASE NO. 6

Guardian Depositors Corporation of Detroit v. Brown. 287 N.W. 798 (Mich.) (1939)

BUTZEL, CH.J. In 1929, Simeon G. Trevethan and wife executed a first mortgage of which plaintiff subsequently became the owner by a series of mesne assignments. In the same year the mortgagors conveyed the mortgaged property to defendants Roy E. Brown and Lillian K. Brown. The warranty deed provided that it was

> "subject to a mortgage in the sum of $2,640 being principal and interest due to date on said mortgage, which second parties (defendants) assume and agree to pay."

Pursuant to this contract of assumption, defendants made some payments on the property to the mortgagee. However, it appears from the meager record before us that the mortgage was foreclosed by advertisement in 1934 and a sum insufficient to pay the amount of the debt was realized.

In 1938, plaintiff brought suit at law to collect the deficiency from defendants, relying on the express assumption of the mortgage as a contract for plaintiff's benefit within the operation of Act No. 296, Pub. Acts 1937 (Stat. Ann. § 26.1321). The first section of this act, which had an effective date of October 29, 1937, is as follows:

> "Any person for whose benefit a promise is made by way of contract, as hereinafter defined, shall have the same right to enforce said promise that he would have had if the said promise had been made directly to him as the promisee." . . .

At the threshold of a discussion of the rights of third party beneficiaries, we are confronted with such a mass of law that we can make no attempt to survey it within the confines of a single opinion. The English rule prohibiting beneficiaries from suing on a contract has, to greater or lesser degree, been abandoned or radically modified by exceptions and qualifications in almost every State of the Union. See Williston, Contracts, Rev. Ed., Chap. XIV, 1029; annotation in 81 A.L.R. 1271. Today in most States both a donee and a creditor beneficiary can sue at law and in equity to enforce rights under the contract. See Restatement, Contracts, Chap. IV, 151. Michigan, however, has been one of the few remaining jurisdictions which have adhered to the old rule. Many of our statements to the effect that a third party cannot sue even though the contract was made for his benefit are collected in the concurring opinion of Mr. Justice Potter in People's Savings Bank v. Geistert, 253 Mich. 694, 235 N.W. 888. But there have been incursions into this rule as demonstrated by the cases cited in Smith v. Thompson,

250 Mich. 302, 230 N.W. 156, 73 A.L.R. 1389. This latter decision, our last definitive utterance on the question, went far toward bringing our law in accord with the almost unanimous view elsewhere. . . . All question has been removed by Act No. 296, which broadly empowers third party beneficiaries to sue as promisees. This statute must be regarded as highly remedial and subject to a liberal construction to effect the corrective purposes of the legislature in passing it. . . .

. . . we hold that plaintiff may properly avail itself of the provisions of Act No. 296. . . .

CASE NO. 7

O'Connell v. Brady. 136 Conn. 475, 72 A. (2d) 493 (1950)

DICKENSON, J. The plaintiff in this action of interpleader sought to recover the proceeds of a life insurance policy in which his decedent was the insured. The insurer, the Metropolitan Life Insurance Company, and the beneficiary in the policy, Phoebe Brady, were named defendants. . . . The defendant claimed that she was the beneficiary under the policy and had made certain premium payments on it, and that the plaintiff's decedent had never exercised his privilege of changing the beneficiary. The plaintiff claimed that his decedent had done all in his power to effect a change of beneficiary but had failed to because of the conduct of the defendant, and that he had an equitable right to the proceeds. He has appealed from a judgment for the defendant.

Undisputed facts are that in 1918, when Eugene Brady, the plaintiff's decedent, and the defendant were husband and wife, Brady took out a twenty-payment policy of life insurance with the Metropolitan Life Insurance Company in the amount of $1,000 in which the defendant was named as beneficiary. The policy contained a provision that the insured might designate a new beneficiary by filing a written notice thereof with the company accompanied by the policy for indorsement. Part of the premiums of the policy were paid out of the defendant's earnings. The policy became paid up in 1938. The two lived together until 1939 when Brady left his wife after he had refused to surrender the policy in return for its cash value. . . . On May 6, 1942, Brady submitted an application for a duplicate policy to the company on its form, in which he indicated that he believed the original policy was lost because of

> "separation between husband and wife about three years ago. Policy was in wife's possession but she will not admit it is either lost or in her possession now. She is beneficiary."

The application was not accepted by the company because it had not been duly executed by the beneficiary. On June 12, 1945, Brady obtained a decree of divorce from the defendant on the grounds of desertion. On several occasions, both before and after the divorce, Brady asked his attorney Mr. Healey to obtain the policy from the defendant, as he wished to change the beneficiary. He was told that defendant could not change the beneficiary until he found the original policy. On July 30, 1945, Mr. Healey wrote the defendant requesting the policy. On August 3, 1945, he received a letter from her stating that the policy was mislaid or lost at the time Brady left home. . . . Under the rules of the company, the only way Brady could have effected a change in the beneficiary without the signature of the defendant or possession of the policy was by the submission of proof that the contract was in the defendant's possession and she had refused to surrender it. With such proof the company would have notified the defendant that unless enjoined by legal process it would grant the insured's request. So far as appears, Brady took no steps after June, 1945, to attempt to have the insurer change the beneficiary. He died April 27, 1948, with the policy still in force but mislaid or lost.

The trial court further found that no request was ever made of the defendant to sign any forms in support of an application for a duplicate policy or for a change of beneficiary; that the defendant never refused to surrender the policy; that Brady never gave written notice to the insurer that he wished to change the beneficiary; that by proper application Brady could have obtained a duplicate policy, change of beneficiary, or cash value; and that he failed to take the required measures. . . . We find no evidence that the defendant was asked to sign such a statement or that she refused to sign one. We must accept the finding that she did not refuse to as the true statement of the fact.

In Bachrach v. Herrup, 128 Conn. 74, 20 A. (2d) 395, there was a provision in a life insurance policy for a change of beneficiary similar to that before us. The right to change was reserved to the insured and the policy provided that such change should become effective only upon written notice to the company and indorsement by it of the policy. The wife was the insured and the husband was the named beneficiary. They separated and the husband refused to give the wife the policy. She wrote the company to learn whether the beneficiary could be changed in any other manner. She executed a company form for a change of beneficiary to the plaintiff and forwarded it to the company together with a statement of the reasons why she could not produce the policy. Upon her death the person claiming under the change of beneficiary brought an action against the original beneficiary and the insurance company and the parties interpleaded. We said, 128 Conn. at page 76, 20 A. (2d) at page 396:

> "The general rule is that a change of beneficiary can only be effected by following the mode prescribed by the policy, however clear the intention to make the change may be. Insurance companies usually require, as in this case, that the original policy be surrendered for indorsement. To this rule there is a well recognized exception and a change is recognized where the insured has done all in his power to comply therewith but has failed because the policy is beyond his control. Vance, Insurance (2d Ed.) § 148 . . ."

Summarized, our decisions indicate that the beneficiary takes a vested right when there is no provision in the policy for a change of beneficiary and that when there is such a provision the insured desiring a change of beneficiary must comply with the requirements of the policy or at least make every reasonable effort to comply with them in order to obtain relief through equitable principles.

The case before us is distinguished factually from Bachrach v. Herrup, supra, and the trial court was not in error in holding that it did not come within the exception to the rule. While there was a written application for a duplicate policy, there was none for a change of beneficiary. Later, in 1945, Brady requested a change of beneficiary of the company but there is no claim that he made a written application for a change, and a plaintiff's exhibit states that the company's records do not indicate the reason why the insured abandoned his attempts to obtain a duplicate policy. So far as appears, he took no steps to change the beneficiary from 1945 to the time of his death in 1948.

. . . If Brady believed that the policy was in the possession of his wife, he could have taken legal measures to compel her to surrender it. He took no such action. . . .

CASE NO. 8

Waller v. Waller. 341 Ill. App. 204, 93 N.E. (2d) 113 (1950)

TUOHY, J. . . . Emerging from lengthy pleadings is the fundamental question whether the assignee of a policy-holder may surrender life insurance policies for their cash value without the consent of all irrevocable beneficiaries. . . .

The complaint herein was filed by William Waller, Jr., and Virginia Waller Hill, as trustees, seeking a decree that they are the owners of three insurance policies, one issued by the Massachusetts Mutual Life Insurance Company and two by the National Life Insurance Company, by virtue of an assignment from the insured; and that the trustees are vested with the full and complete ownership of all incidents of ownership of the policies excepting the power to change the beneficiaries, *but including full right to surrender said policies.*

. . . Supporting our conclusion is the general rule stated in Richards, The Law of Insurance (4th Ed. by Rowland H. Long, 1932), sec. 328. . . .

"The effect of failure of the insured to reserve the right to change the beneficiary is to give the beneficiary a property right in the policy of which he may not be divested except by due process of law. Upon the maturity of the policy the proceeds are payable to the beneficiary. The insured cannot assign, or pledge the policy or receive a loan value or surrender and receive the cash value of the policy without the consent of the beneficiary. Nor can the insured and insurer acting together deprive the beneficiary of his right." . . .

Review Questions

1. Distinguish an assignment of contractual rights from a delegation of contractual duties.
2. Construct a fact situation illustrating a limitation to the assignment of contractual rights.
3. Are there any limitations to the assignment of wages in your state?
4. Explain the statement that "an assignee can stand in no better position than his assignor."
5. What is the position of an assignee under an assignment made without consideration?
6. What implied warranties does the assignor make under a contract of assignment?
7. Does the assignor warrant that the assignee will be able to realize upon the assigned rights?
8. Why should an assignee give immediate notice of the assignment to the party who is obligated to perform the assigned rights?
9. What is a contract of novation?
10. What is the test of a third party beneficiary contract?
11. What distinguishes the donee type of third party beneficiary contract from the creditor type?

12. X owes Y $100 and Y owes Z $100. X and Y agree that X will pay Z $100, in this way discharging X's obligation to Y and Y's obligation to Z. What kind of contract was entered into between X and Y?

Problems for Discussion

1. A contracted to remodel B's house for the sum of $1,500. Subsequently, but before the remodeling took place, B sold the house to C. They agreed that C would pay A the $1,500 as part of the purchase price and that B was no longer to be liable to A. Neither B nor C paid A. Which of these parties is liable to A, and upon what basis can the liability be established?
2. X contracted for the personal services of Y for the performance of a certain task. Y assigned his right to the payments that would become due him to Z. X contends this cannot be done, since the contract is one for personal services. Answer the contention.
3. X, upon the hopes that he would obtain employment from Y, made an assignment of his anticipated wages to Z. Is this a valid assignment?
4. X is employed by Y under a contract that gives Y the right to discharge X at will. X assigns his future wages to Z. Is this a valid assignment?
5. A was awarded a scholarship in the X business college and then sold it to B. Is B, as the assignee, entitled to the benefits and privileges enumerated in the scholarship?
6. The plaintiff sues as assignee of a contract dated December 11, 1900, between W. E. Kelly & Co. and the Dunton Lumber Company, and complains that the defendant has failed and refused to deliver to him lumber covered by the contract. Under the contract the lumber company sold to Kelly & Co. the entire cut of white pine lumber for 1901, except so much as it should need for its retail trade in the city of Rumford Falls, agreeing to retain not the best of the lumber but only an average grade for that trade. Delivery was to be f.o.b. cars at Rumford Falls, Kelly & Co. to pay within 10 days from date of invoice. The logs were to be cut in lengths of 12, 14, and 16 feet, but Kelly & Co. agreed to accept some lumber shorter than 12 feet, not less than 8 feet, and some longer than 16 feet. The trial judge held that this contract was not assignable, and that, therefore, the plaintiff had no right of action. Decide. (*Demarest* v. *Dunton Lbr. Co.,* 161 Fed. 264)
7. Plaintiff was doing business as a wine and liquor merchant under a trade-name, and entered into a contract with the defendant, a California corporation, for the shipment to him in New York of 750 barrels of wine by monthly deliveries, extending over a year beginning December, 1912, as directed by plaintiff, and to be paid for 30 days after each shipment arrived. The contract was negotiated through the New York manager of the defendant, subject to the approval of the home office in San Francisco. Notification dated October 2, 1912, was sent by mail to the plaintiff from the New York office, advising him of defendant's final acceptance of the contract. Is this contract assignable? (*Gargiulo* v. *Calif. Wineries,* 171 N.Y.S. 855)
8. X engaged Y, an attorney, to represent him in a certain matter. Y, being too busy to give the matter his attention, turned it over to a friend, Z. Z, without

the knowledge of X, properly carried out Y's undertaking to X. Is X liable for the service performed?

9. To secure a bond for faithful performance of a contract with the city, Poanessa made an assignment of all rights to accrue under the contract to the surety company that had furnished the bond. Subsequently, Poanessa made an assignment of the same rights to one Lloyd to secure certain advances made by the latter. Lloyd immediately gave notice of the assignment to the city. Both Lloyd and the surety company, who had never given notice of the assignment, now make claim against the city for the funds due under the contract. Who will prevail? (*Adamson* v. *Poanessa,* 180 Cal. 157)
10. X was indebted to Y for a certain sum of money. Y assigned the right to receive the money to Z. X, without having received any notice of the assignment, made settlement of the obligation with Y. What are the rights of Z (a) against X? (b) against Y?
11. A borrowed $5,000 from B. In order to secure the obligation, A executed a mortgage in favor of B. A then sold the property encumbered by the mortgage to C, who assumed and agreed to pay the $5,000 obligation to B as part of the purchase price for the property. The debt was never paid, and B foreclosed the mortgage. The property was sold under foreclosure proceedings for $3,000. Who is responsible to B for the deficiency of $2,000?
12. X sold his business establishment to Y, who agreed to pay all of X's business creditors. What are the rights of the creditors against Y?
13. X insured his life with the A Insurance Company, naming his wife Y as beneficiary. The contract of insurance did not provide that X reserved the right to change the beneficiary named. May X change the beneficiary without obtaining the consent of Y?

10 CONTRACTS:

PERFORMANCE, CONTRACTUAL CONDITIONS, AND BREACH

► I. REMEDIES FOR NONPERFORMANCE

A failure of performance is a breach of contract making available to the injured party some form of legal redress unless performance is legally excused. The nature of the remedy available to the injured party is dependent upon the circumstances of the individual case. Remedies for breach of contract may be (1) money damages, (2) specific performance, or (3) injunction.*

A. MONEY DAMAGES

1. *Measure of Money Damages*

The remedy of money damages is available to the injured party for any unexcused breach of contract.[1] The injured party has the burden of proving what damages he has in fact suffered as a direct result of the failure of performance by the other party. The measure of recoverable damages is that amount which will place the injured party in substantially the same position he would have been in had performance taken place. Thus, if A agrees to furnish B one ton of paper at $80 and then fails to perform, the measure of damages would be the difference between the contract price and the price B would have to pay to get the paper elsewhere. Generally a party who is in breach of contract cannot recover payments he has made under the contract.[2]

2. *Liquidated Damages*

At times contracts will contain provisions specifying the amount of damages that are to be paid in the event of breach. Thus, a construction contract might provide that, if the contractor has not completed performance by the time provided for in the contract, he will pay a certain amount per diem until performance is completed. Such liquidated damages are enforceable and binding upon the parties providing they have in good faith pre-estimated the damages that would result from a breach.[3, 4] As the court said in *U.P.R. Co.* v. *Mitchell Tie Co.*, 190 Fed. 318,

> "Where the amount of damages for breach is uncertain and difficult of ascertainment, and the agreement discloses the intention of the parties to fix a sum certain as damages, the contract will be enforced."

---

* See p. 18 for a treatment of Specific Performance and Injunction as remedies for breach of contract.

[1] Lamm v. Shingleton, p. 284.

[2] Bisner v. Mantell, p. 286.

[3] Simms v. Bovee, p. 286.

[4] Advance Amusement Co. v. Franke, p. 287.

If, however, the provision is introduced for the mere purpose of serving as a penalty in the event of nonperformance, it is not binding. To illustrate:

(1) In the case of *Knox Rock Blasting Co.* v. *Grafton Stone Co.,* 16 Ohio Cir. Ct. 21, the contract provided that the licensee of machinery would upon the expiration of the contract pay twice the contract license fee, should he continue to use the machinery without renewal of the contract. The court held this provision was intended to be a penalty and not an attempt to determine damages.

(2) In the case of *Wilhelm* v. *Eaves,* 21 Ore. 194, the court said:

> "The contract, when analyzed, contains some sixteen different stipulations of varying degrees of importance, the damages for a breach of some of which would be easily ascertainable; and yet it is provided that $200 shall be paid as stipulated damages for a breach of any of them, even the most unimportant. It is not to be supposed the parties intended their agreement to have any such effect, and following the above well established rule in such cases, the stipulated sum must be construed as a penalty . . ."

(3) In the case of *Beury* v. *Fay,* 73 W. Va. 460, a contract for an exchange of several thousand acres of mineral and timber land provided that a $10,000 deposit could, upon default of the depositor, be retained by the other party. The court held this to be an agreed compensation for breach of contract and not a penalty designed to force performance.

(4) In *Dopp* v. *Richards,* 43 Utah 333, the court held that a provision in a contract for the sale of land giving the seller the right to retain payments made in the event of a breach will be regarded as an agreement for damages rather than a penalty, where such payments bear a reasonable relationship to the rental value of the land.

3. *Duty to Prevent or Reduce Damages*

In the event of a breach of contract, the law imposes upon the injured party the duty to keep the damages as low as is reasonably possible.[5] The court in *Hall* v. *Paine,* 224 Mass. 62, said:

> "It is a rule of fair dealing that when one is deprived of the fruits of a contract, he must use the efforts of a reasonably prudent man to put himself in as good a position as he would have been if the contract had not been abrogated. He cannot lie idly by and expect to recover all losses which such inaction may entail as damages for breach of the contract. He must be reasonably active and diligent to recoup his loss."

To illustrate:

(1) In the case of *Hodges* v. *Fries,* 34 Fla. 63, the plaintiff contracted to lease a store building from the defendant, which contract the latter then broke by refusing to give the plaintiff possession. The court held that the plaintiff had failed in his duty to mitigate damages by refusing to accept another store building in the same vicinity, which building was equally well suited to his purpose.

(2) In the case of *A. B. Frank Co.* v. *A. H. Motley Co.,* 37 S.W. 868, the plain-

[5] Bomberger v. McKelvey, p. 289.

tiff contracted to sell certain goods for the defendant, which contract the plaintiff then failed to carry out. The court held that the defendant was not entitled to damages in that he held the goods after the breach until they were no longer salable. It was his duty to make a reasonable effort to sell.

(3) In the case of *Ware Bros.* v. *Cortland Cart. Co.,* 210 N.Y. 122, the defendant contracted for an advertisement in plaintiff's trade publication, which advertisement was to be carried in a particular location for one year. Before the expiration of the year, the defendant repudiated the contract but the plaintiff refused to consent and continued the advertisement to the conclusion of the year. The court held that it was the plaintiff's duty, after notification that the defendant was terminating the contract, to exercise reasonable diligence to find an advertiser for the same period of time and the same space. He could not, however, be required to split up the time or space covered by the contract.

(4) An employee, in the event of a breach of contract by the employer, is under duty to make a reasonable effort to obtain employment of like or similar nature.

An injured party who has failed to minimize damages is precluded from recovering those damages which he could have prevented, although he is allowed to recover those damages which were unpreventable.

► II. EXCUSES FOR NONPERFORMANCE

A contracting party cannot always be held to a performance of his undertakings. Certain exceptional situations may arise, which will legally excuse him from fulfilling his contractual obligations. Excuses for nonperformance are, however, the exception rather than the rule. Ordinarily a contractual liability is not discharged by a subsequent impossibility or inability to perform.[6, 7] In *Berg* v. *Erickson,* 234 Fed. 817, the court said:

> "The general rule is that one who makes a positive agreement to do a lawful act is not absolved from liability for a failure to fulfill his covenant by a subsequent impossibility caused by an act of God, or an unavoidable accident, because he voluntarily contracts to perform it without any reservation or exception, which, if he desired, he could make in his agreement, and thereby induces the other contracting party, in consideration of his positive covenant, to enter into and become bound by the contract."

For their protection the contracting parties must provide in the contract against any contingencies that might arise to render performance impossible or unduly burdensome.[8] The broad application of this need will be more fully comprehended after the exceptions are established.

A. IMPOSSIBILITY CREATED BY LAW

If performance of a contract is subsequently prohibited by domestic law or its performance becomes contrary to law, performance is excused. Thus, a change in

6 Raiser v. Jackson, p. 292.
7 U.S. v. Huff, p. 293.
8 Glens Falls Indemnity Co., v. Perscall, p. 294.

zoning laws which prevents the erection of a building as contracted for will excuse the contractor from performing and will relieve him from liability under the contract. Likewise, a lease for premises to be used for an undertaking that is subsequently prohibited by statute is thereby terminated without further liability on the part of the lessee.

B. DESTRUCTION OF SUBJECT MATTER

A agrees to paint the house of B. Before performance, the house burns. Both parties are excused from their contractual obligations by a destruction of the subject matter essential to performance of the contract. In contracts whose performance is dependent upon the continued existence of certain subject matter, the courts *imply* that the parties assume their contractual obligations upon the *condition* that the subject matter will remain in existence.[9]

The above rule has been held not to apply to a destruction of subject matter that is to be the source of performance. The destruction of a producer's manufacturing plant will not excuse the producer from his contractual commitments. Should A agree to furnish B with a specified quantity of hay, he could not excuse his performance by the fact that his hay crop was consumed by grasshoppers. He would still be bound to perform as he had agreed. However, performance will be excused if the source of performance is specified in the contract and performance becomes impossible from such source.[10] Should A, in the last illustration, agree to furnish the hay from his own acreage, he would be relieved of his liability for failure of performance.

C. DEATH OR PERSONAL INCAPACITY

Death or personal incapacity will be a legal excuse for nonperformance only if the contract provides, either expressly or by reasonable construction, for personal performance by one of the contracting parties.* Unless personal services are bargained for, the physical inability of the one obligated to perform will not excuse performance, and, in the event of his death or physical incapacity, his personal representatives are bound to perform.

D. PREVENTION OF PERFORMANCE

The law does not allow one to benefit by his own dereliction. Accordingly, a party to a contract cannot enforce the other party's promise when he himself caused its nonperformance. Or conversely stated, performance of a contract is excused if it is prevented or made impossible by the adverse party. The party prevented from carrying out his part of the contract may treat it as broken and may immediately bring an action for damages.

---

* See Smith v. Zuckman, p. 265.

9 U. S. Fidelity v. Parsons, p. 295.

10 Snipes Mt. Co. v. Benz Bros. & Co., p. 297.

E. WAIVER OF PERFORMANCE

The injured party to a contract may relinquish any rights accruing to him by virtue of a breach of promise or by a failure of compliance with a condition. Any unequivocal indication of intention to forego the remedies available for a breach constitutes a waiver of performance. Waiver of performance is said to be the equivalent of performance.

F. ACT OF GOD

The writer has all too frequently encountered the belief among laymen that an act of God will excuse performance of a contract and will relieve the obligor of liability. While there are some expressions to this effect, an analysis of the cases will not bear out this conclusion. An obligation voluntarily assumed by contract will not be annulled by an act of God. Only where the law imposes a liability without the consent of the obligor will an act of God serve to relieve liability. Upon these grounds, a common carrier is relieved of his extraordinary law-imposed liability for the safe carriage of freight.*

► III. CONDITIONS IN CONTRACTS

A. CONDITIONS PRECEDENT

Contracts, in addition to the terms of performance, also contain conditions. A condition precedent in a contract is an understanding by the parties, either express or implied, that the acquiring of any contractual rights or the duty to perform is contingent upon fulfillment of a certain event. To illustrate:

(1) Where the condition is collateral to the terms of performance:

(a) A agrees to purchase certain property of B should the legislature pass a pending bill by July 1. A has no obligation to perform unless the specified event happens.

(b) In the case of *Mascioni* v. *Miller, Inc.*, 261 N.Y. 1, a contract between the plaintiff, a subcontractor, and the defendant, the principal contractor, provided that payments were to be made from the principal contractor to the subcontractor as they were received by the principal contractor from the party for whom the work was being done. The court interpreted this provision as being a *condition* and held that, since the principal contractor had never received payment from the owner, he had no obligation to pay the subcontractor. It may be that the parties had included this provision in their contract for the sole purpose of fixing the convenience of time of payment, but they had failed to clearly indicate the purpose.

(2) Where a term of performance is also a condition:

A agrees to work for B upon the condition that B will furnish him with adequate housing. A has no obligation to perform, nor does B acquire any contractual rights against A until the condition—furnishing housing—is fulfilled.

* See p. 695.

B. EXPRESS AND IMPLIED CONDITIONS

By express agreement, the parties may make the obligation to perform contingent upon the happening of any extraneous or collateral event. They may also, by agreement, make performance of *any term of the contract*—regardless of how inconsequential it may be to the whole—a condition precedent to (1) the acquiring of any rights by the party who is obligated to fulfill the condition, and (2) any obligation of the other party to perform.

Performance of a contractual term may assume the status of a condition without express provision to that effect by the contracting parties, as, for example, the time for performance may be implied as a condition. And likewise it may be implied that the obligation to perform a contract is conditioned upon the continued existence of a certain state of facts or upon the happening of a certain event.[11]

C. EFFECT OF FAILURE OF CONDITION

The effect of nonfulfillment of a condition is to give the injured party the right to rescind the agreement. When the condition in a contract is performance, the nonfulfillment of the condition, of necessity, also results in a breach of contractual promise. In such a case, the party who failed to realize the performance provided for as a condition may (1) elect to rescind upon the failure of the condition or (2) waive the condition and sue for money damages for the breach.

D. SUBSTANTIAL PERFORMANCE AS CONDITION

> "Under the common law rule, the express stipulations of the contract were required to be strictly performed and a substantial compliance with its terms was not sufficient. This rule has been much relaxed of late, and under the recent decisions of most of the courts of this country, the performance of the contract is not in all cases required to be literal and exact. The more equitable rule has been generally adopted which permits a recovery by one who in good faith attempts to perform his contract and does so substantially, although there may be a slight deviation or some technical and unimportant omission or defect." *Denton* v. *Atchison*, 34 Kan. 438.

The *doctrine of substantial performance* is readily recognized as applying to those situations which lend themselves by their very nature to a failure of a strict technical performance. For example, in carrying out construction and building contracts that call for performance in accordance with plans and specifications, it is admittedly difficult to achieve perfection in every detail. It has also been held that making an article substantially like the model is sufficient performance.

This means, then, that substantial performance given in good faith is a condition precedent to the right of recovery. Unless the party who is obligated to perform has substantially performed, he has no right to recover for this partial performance, unless he has rendered some benefit to the other party, which the latter has accepted and retained. In that event, the reasonable value of the benefit can be

[11] Duris v. Iozzi, p. 298.

recovered. When he has substantially performed, he can recover only to the extent of the performance, the injured party being entitled to receive damages for the partial breach.

> "Where one party to a contract has received and retained the benefits of a substantial partial performance of the agreement by the other party who has failed to completely fulfill all his convenants, the first party cannot retain the benefits and repudiate the burdens of the contract, but he is bound to perform his part of the agreement, and his remedy . . . is limited to compensation in damages." *Kauffman* v. *Raeder,* 108 Fed. 171, 54 L.R.A. 247.

Substantial performance is not easily defined, there being no absolute test. In essence, it means performance to a degree where the breach will be inconsequential and can be readily compensated for by damages. The failure to perform any material part of the contract will be a failure of the condition of substantial performance and will entitle the injured party to rescind the agreement.[12] To illustrate:

(1) In the case of *Harris* v. *Sharples,* 202 Pa. 243, the defendant has ordered catalog covers from the plaintiff in accordance with proofs submitted by the plaintiff to the defendant. In printing the covers, the plaintiff put the defendant's firm name at the bottom of the last page, which was a deviation from the proofs. The defendant refused to accept the goods and plaintiff brought an action to recover contending substantial performance. The court held that the plaintiff had not sufficiently complied with performance and was not allowed to recover.

(2) In *North American Wall Paper Co.* v. *Jackson Construction Co.,* 153 N.Y.S. 204, it was held that under a contract for work for $3,200, a performance to the extent of $2,750 did not constitute substantial performance.

1. *Recovery Under Willful Breach*

The general rule seems to be that when performance of a contract is willfully abandoned, no recovery can be had for a partial performance.[13] This, without doubt, appears to be the rule as applied to construction and labor contracts. Willful abandonment of contracts may be costly.

E. TIME AS A CONDITION

As a general rule, in the absence of express provision, the time for performance in a contract is not a condition precedent.[14] The parties may, of course, agree that the time for performance is to be a condition.[15] In that event, the time provision must be met exactly or the injured party may rescind for the failure of the condition. The terminology usually used to make time a condition is "time is of the essence."

When the time provision is not a condition, the party who is obligated to perform will have a reasonable period of time after the expiration of the stipulated

[12] Cohen v. Eggers, p. 299.
[13] Sward v. Nash, p. 300.
[14] Klapka v. Shrauger, p. 302.
[15] Dodge v. Galusha, p. 303.

time within which to complete performance.* Thus, if A agrees to deposit a deed in escrow on March 1, he would, in the absence of the time provision being a condition, have a reasonable time after March 1 within which to perform. If, however, the parties had agreed that "time is of the essence," the time provision would be a condition giving the other party the right to rescind if not complied with absolutely.

In certain types of contracts, the time for performance is of such obvious importance to the contract as a whole that the courts recognize time as of the essence; they will by implication regard the time provision as a condition. Under some circumstances, it is entirely logical to presume that the intention of the parties must have been that performance was to be accomplished in strict accordance with the time provision in the contract. This applies particularly to option contracts, contracts whose subject matter is unstable in value or perishable, and mercantile contracts. In the latter, as in most other commercial transactions, prompt compliance with the time provisions is the accepted standard of the business community.[16]

F. PERSONAL SATISFACTION AS A CONDITION

It is not uncommon for a contract to provide that payment by one of the contracting parties is conditioned upon performance that will be entirely satisfactory to the party promising to pay. A may, for example, commission B to construct for him a set of artificial teeth and agree to pay upon the condition that the result will be entirely satisfactory to him. Or he may contract for the installation of a furnace and condition payment upon the fact that the furnace be satisfactory to him. Such contracts, in which one party agrees to perform to the satisfaction of the other, are generally treated by the judiciary under two categories. The courts distinguish between (1) cases where the performance relates to the taste, fancy, or sensibility of the promisor and (2) those where the performance relates to something that is desired for its commercial value or mechanical fitness.

1. *Taste or Fancy of Promisor*

> "If the subject matter of the contract is a coat or a painting, for which the promisor agrees to pay upon the condition that the coat or the painting is to his satisfaction, he is not obligated to accept or pay for it, if he is not satisfied, though the coat may be of the best material and workmanship and style, or the painting executed in the most artistic and skillful manner and an exact likeness of the original. But this does not give the promisor a cause of action against the tailor or painter for damages for breach of contract because the coat or painting did not satisfy the fanciful taste or capricious mental state of the promisor. It is quite enough that he, in such case, is not required to accept and pay for the coat or the painting, if he is not satisfied, without assigning any

* Section 276 of *Restatement of the Law of Contracts:* "Unless the nature of a contract is such as to make performance on the exact day agreed upon of vital importance, or the contract in terms provides that it shall be so, failure by a promisor to perform his promise on the day stated in the promise does not discharge the duty of the other party." . . .

[16] Sunshine Cloak v. Roquette, p. 305.

reason therefor, except that he is not satisfied. He may not, at the same time, insist that the tailor keep on making coats for him or the painter painting pictures, until the indefinable and fanciful taste of his mind is satisfied, and upon his refusal so to do, subject him to a claim for damages for breach of contract." *Midgley* v. *Campbell,* 38 Utah 293, 112 PAC. 820.

2. *Commercial Value or Mechanical Fitness*

Where the object of the performance is not to gratify the personal taste or preference of the promisor but is rather to obtain a thing that is wanted for its commercial value or mechanical fitness, the courts have generally applied a different rule. Under such circumstances, performance to the satisfaction of the promisor is taken to mean performance that would be satisfactory to the mind of a reasonable man.[17] Consequently, if A contracts for the installation of a furnace and agrees to pay upon the condition that the furnace's operation is satisfactory to him, he could not arbitrarily elect to be dissatisfied.

G. APPROVAL OF THIRD PERSON AS A CONDITION

A promise can be conditioned upon the approval of some third party. A contract to buy land may, for example, provide that the buyer is not obligated unless his attorney approves the title to the land. In building and construction contracts, the promise to pay is at times conditioned upon obtaining an architect's certificate that gives approval to the performance. It is generally held by the courts that if the approval is arbitrarily or unreasonably withheld by the third party, the approval may be dispensed with.[18]

H. CONCURRENT CONDITIONS

Concurrent conditions in a contract may be viewed as mutual conditions precedent, for both parties have the obligation to perform before either can be held in default. A common illustration of this is an agreement in which a transfer of title to property by one party is conditioned upon payment by the other party, and payment, in turn, is conditioned upon the transfer of title. These conditions are concurrent; performance of each party is dependent upon the performance of the other.

It would be pointless to require actual performance when in all likelihood there will be no reciprocal performance. In the illustration above, there should be no need for the purchaser to make actual payment before he can declare the other party in default and elect either to sue for damages or to rescind the agreement. Therefore, the law requires, as a fulfillment of the condition precedent to legal redress, a *tender* of performance in lieu of actual performance. And unless the tender is made within the required time of performance of the contract, both parties will stand in default and the contract continues in force. If no time for

[17] Winkelman Co. v. Barr, p. 306.
[18] Dahl v. Moss & Son, p. 307.

performance is stipulated in the contract, performance within a reasonable time is implied.

The term *tender* as here used means an indicated readiness and willingness, accompanied by the ability, of one of the contracting parties to perform his part of the contract.

> "If a contract calls for successive acts, first by one party and then by the other, there is no breach by one if the precedent act has not been performed by the other; but if the contract contemplates concurrent acts, it is sufficient to put one party in default that the other party is ready, willing and offers to perform his part of the contract." *Osgood* v. *Skinner,* 211 Ill. 229.

I. CONDITIONS SUBSEQUENT

A condition subsequent in a contract is one which, if met or fulfilled, serves to annul the contract—to relieve the contracting parties from further obligation. To illustrate:

(1) A promissory note contained the following provision:

> "The makers shall be personally liable for the full amount of such advances, subject to the condition that, if the United States Department of Agriculture War Board of the county identified by the state and county code appearing in the identification number on this note (or such other agency or person as the Regional Agricultural Credit Corporation of Washington, D.C., may designate to make the certification herein required) certifies that: (1) The makers have used the amount advanced for producing the crops for the production of which the advances were made; (2) The makers have provided for insurance on such crops to the extent and in the manner required by the Regional Agricultural Credit Corporation of Washington, D.C., to protect its interest in such crops; (3) The makers in good faith have diligently applied principles of good husbandry to the production of such crops."

This is a condition subsequent in that proper certification serves to relieve the makers of the note from any further obligation.

(2) A fire insurance policy provides, "no liability shall exist under this policy for loss or damage in or on vacant or unoccupied buildings, unless consent for such vacancy or inoccupancy be indorsed hereon." This is a condition subsequent.

► IV. THE DOCTRINE OF ANTICIPATORY BREACH

It is possible that a breach of contract may result from the *conduct* of one of the parties rather than from a failure to perform in accordance with the contract provisions. Should one party, by his conduct, justifiably lead the other to believe that performance will not be forthcoming at the time when due under the contract, the latter may elect to treat the contract as ended and may immediately bring an action for damages upon the anticipatory breach.[19] Anticipation that there will be

[19] Williams v. Mutual Benefit Assoc., p. 309.

a breach is clearly justified by conduct such as an outright renunciation or a person's placing himself in a position where he can no longer perform.[20]

This principle of anticipatory breach applies only where the contract is wholly executory. If the one party has already performed his part and the other party then refuses to perform, this cannot be treated as an anticipatory breach. In such a case, the injured party has no right of action until there has been an actual breach, that is, until the time allowed for performance in the contract has expired. To illustrate:

If A sells goods to B upon ninety days' credit and after delivery of the goods B denies the obligation to pay, A cannot bring an action to recover until the ninety-day period has expired.

Likewise, if A makes payment to B for goods to be delivered in ninety days and B then renounces the contract, A cannot bring action until the ninety-day period has expired.

CASES

CASE NO. 1

Lamm v. Shingleton. 231 N.C. 10, 55 S.E. (2d) 810 (1949)

Plaintiff's first husband, Larry Waddell, died 3 August 1946. She employed the defendant undertakers to conduct the funeral and purchased from them a casket and vault. The vault was composed of two sections: a base on which the casket rested and a metal cover or lid which fitted over the casket and locked to the base with ratchet locks at each end. The defendants represented and warranted that it was watertight and would protect the body from water for years.

On Wednesday before Thanksgiving Day, plaintiff discovered that the vault, during a very rainy spell of weather, had risen above the level of the ground, the top of one end being about six inches above the ground level. She reported the condition to defendants and to the cemetery authorities. Defendants (or the cemetery authorities) undertook to reinter the body.

On the following Saturday, employees of defendant and of the cemetery authorities met at the grave for the purpose of placing the vault in an adjoining grave prepared for that purpose. Plaintiff was present. When the vault, including the base, was raised, it was discovered that water and mud had entered it, and the casket was wet.

The plaintiff offered evidence tending to show that the vault was not locked and had not been locked at the time of the original interment. The defendants contended and offered evidence tending to show that the vault was securely locked, that to remove the vault from the original grave it was necessary to use a lever . . . that the lever slipped, struck the top or lid, and dislodged the locks at one end, permitting the water and mud to enter at that time.

Plaintiff testified that "seeing the vault out of the ground that first time" caused her considerable shock and made her extremely nervous as a result of which she became a nervous wreck. She also testified that while the men were about the grave after a discussion about getting the mud out of the vault, defendant Shingleton said he was not go-

[20] Miller & Sons Bakery Co. v. Selikowitz, p. 309.

ing to get it out and "To hell with the whole damned business, it's no concern of mine," and that this language made her so nervous she could hardly stand up. . . .

When the plaintiff rested, the court dismissed the cause of action for damages for breach of warranty. . . .

BARNHILL, J. . . . This is essentially an action for damages for breach of contract. Plaintiff alleges a contract to furnish a casket and watertight vault and conduct the funeral and inter the body, the breach thereof by failure to lock the vault, and damages resulting from the breach. The further allegation that the defendants' failure to lock the vault at the time of the burial, as a result of which water and mud entered the vault and forced its top to the surface, was due to their negligence and carelessness does not convert it into an action in tort.

The defendants held themselves out as specially qualified to perform the duties of an undertaker. When they undertook to conduct the funeral of plaintiff's deceased husband they impliedly covenanted to perform the services contemplated by the contract in a good and workmanlike manner. Any breach of the duty thus assumed was a breach of the duty imposed by the contract and not by law.

So then, the primary question posed for decision is this: Is mental anguish an element of damages to be considered by the jury in an action for the breach of the contract alleged and, if so, must plaintiff show that the breach amounted to a willful tort?

"A party to a contract who is injured by another's breach of the contract is entitled to recover from the latter damages for all injuries and only such injuries as are the direct, natural, and proximate result of the breach or which, in the ordinary course of events, would likely result from a breach and can reasonably be said to have been foreseen, contemplated, or expected by the parties at the time when they made the contract as a probable or natural result of a breach." 15 A.J. 449, § 51; 25 C.J.S. Damages, § 24, p. 481. . . .

. . . contracts are usually commercial in nature and relate to property or to services to be rendered in connection with business or professional operations. Pecuniary interest is dominant. Therefore, as a general rule, damages for mental anguish suffered by reason of the breach thereof are not recoverable. Some type of mental anguish, anxiety, or distress is apt to result from the breach of any contract which causes pecuniary loss. Yet damages therefor are deemed to be too remote to have been in the contemplation of the parties at the time the contract was entered into to be considered as an element of compensatory damages. McCormick on Damages 592, § 145; 15 A.J. 599, § 182; Annotations 23 A.L.R. 372, 44 A.L.R. 428, 56 A.L.R. 659.

The rule is not absolute. Indeed, the trend of modern decisions tends to leave it in a state of flux. Some courts qualify the rule by holding that such damages are recoverable when the breach amounts in substance to a willful or independent tort or is accompanied by physical injury. 15 A.J. 599, 603; Hall v. Jackson, 24 Colo. App. 225, 134 Pac. 151. Still others treat the breach as an act of negligence and decide the question as though the action were cast in tort, and thus confuse the issue. Thus, to some extent the courts have modified the common law rule.

In this process of modification a definite exception to the doctrine has developed. Where the contract is personal in nature and the contractual duty or obligation is so coupled with matters of mental concern or solicitude, or with the sensibilities of the party to whom the duty is owed, that a breach of that duty will necessarily or reasonably result in mental anguish or suffering, and it should be known to the parties from the nature of the contract that such suffering will result from its breach, compensatory damages therefor may be recovered.

Thus we have held that such damages may be recovered in an action for breach of contract of marriage, Allen v. Baker, 86 N.C. 91, 40 Am. Rep. 444; Annotation 41 L.R.A., N.S., 842, and for breach of contract to transmit a death message, Russ v. Western Union Telegraph Co., 222 N.C. 504, 23 S.E. (2d) 681; Johnson v. Western Union Telegraph Co., 175 N.C. 588, 96 S.E. 36; Betts v. Western Union Telegraph Co., 167 N.C. 75, 83 S.E. 164, when the meaning or import of the message and the interest of the addressee or beneficiary of the contract is made known to the telegraph company at the time the message is accepted for transmittal. Thomason v. Hackney & Moale Co., 159 N.C. 299, 74 S.E. 1022, 47 L.R.A., N.S. 1120.

The tenderest feelings of the human heart center around the remains of the dead. When the defendants contracted with plaintiff to inter the body of her deceased husband in a workmanlike manner they did so with the knowledge that she was the widow and would naturally and probably suffer mental anguish if they failed to fulfill their contractual obligation in the manner here charged. The contract was predominantly personal in nature and no substantial pecuniary loss would follow its breach. Her mental concern, her sensibilities, and her solicitude were the prime considerations for the contract, and the contract itself was such as to put the defendants on notice that a failure on their part to inter the body properly would probably produce mental suffering on her part. It cannot be said, therefore, that such damages were not within the contemplation of the parties at the time the contract was made.

. . . cause remanded for trial upon the issues raised by the pleadings. . . .

CASE NO. 2

Bisner v. Mantell. 95 N.Y.S. (2d) 793 (1950)

See *p. 678.*

CASE NO. 3

Simms v. Bovee. D.C., 68 A. (2d) 800 (1949)

CAYTON, CH.J. Appellee Bovee brought suit in the Small Claims and Conciliation Branch of Municipal Court for return of a deposit on a contract for the purchase of an automobile from Simms Motor Company. Bovee was awarded $50. . . .

The contract was in the form of an "Order for Used Car" and a cash receipt. By these Bovee engaged to purchase a Chevrolet sedan for $130, less the deposit of $25. The cash receipt reads:

> "Received of Elmer W. Bovee
> Twenty-five & no/100 dollars
> Deposit on 1934 Chev Eng. # 00-426311 Car #
> Balance to be paid 3 pymts. of 2 wks apart @ 35.00 per week starting May 11, 1949 & ending June 8, 49
> No deposit to be refunded if contract is cancelled.
> Sold As Is"

. . . On May 25 he paid $35 more on his contract, and thereafter made no further payments to the vendor. . . .

On June 13, 1949, Bovee filed suit in the small claims court "For return of deposit left with the defendants during

May, 1949." His claim was for $60, on which he entered a voluntary credit or reduction of $10, in order to bring it within the $50 jurisdiction of the small claims branch. At the trial the facts above recited were brought out, and as we have said, the trial judge awarded judgment to plaintiff. . . .

We think it clear that the motor company had every right, legal and equitable, to retain the money paid toward the purchase of the second (Chevrolet) automobile, as expressly provided in writing, and that it was error to rule otherwise. No showing of fraud, duress, or mistake was presented at the trial, and as we have recently held, courts have no right to relieve parties to contracts merely because certain provisions may operate disadvantageously to them.

We do not overlook the general rule that the law does not favor forfeitures. But we note that in this jurisdiction it has been held that parties to a contract may agree in advance to damages for breach of contract without reference to the actual damages found at the time of the breach, and that only when such agreement provides for a penalty is it void or unenforceable. And in the case before us there was nothing to show that the provision was for a penalty; nor did the trial judge so hold. As we view the matter, this contract provided for liquidated damages, even though not expressly stated as such. Nor does it come within the general tests set out by the courts as converting such a stipulation into a penalty. There was no evidence of any circumstances which would make this provision "grossly excessive," "unjust and oppressive," "unreasonable," "extravagant" or "disproportionate" as a matter of law. Rather it seems to meet the common qualifications since "it may fairly be allowed as compensation for the breach."

There is no doubt that it was the purchaser alone who breached the contract, and that such breach was without legal cause or justification, the vendor being at all times ready to perform. That being so, the law is clear, as enunciated by many decisions that the purchaser had no right to demand the return of the payments he had made.

Reversed, with instruction to enter judgment for defendants.

CASE NO. 4

Advance Amusement Co. v. Franke. 268 Ill. 579, 109 N.E. 471 (1915)

CARTER, J., delivered the opinion of the court:

Plaintiff, the Advance Amusement Co., brought suit . . . to recover $2,500 deposited by it with [defendant] pursuant to certain provisions of a lease between said parties . . . as to a theater building . . . at a rental of $350 per month. By reason of default and failure to pay rent for December and a portion of that for November, 1912, the lessor, after giving the statutory five days' notice, brought suit for the possession of the premises and obtained judgment therefor. . . . On a trial in the municipal court without a jury, a judgment was entered in that court against said landlord (Franke) and in favor of said amusement company, for the sum of $2,500 so deposited, less the amount of rent that had accrued and remained unpaid at the date of the termination of the lease. That judgment, on appeal to the Appellate Court, was affirmed.

The first question urged here is whether the $2,500 deposited with plaintiff in error (defendant) should be considered liquidated damages, or, as held by the Appellate Court, a penalty. Section II of the lease between the parties provided that said sum was

"to be held by the party of the first

> part as security for the faithful performance by the party of the second part of the covenants and agreements in this rider and in the indenture of lease to which this rider is attached . . . which said sum of twenty-five hundred dollars ($2,500) shall be applied by said party of the first part as rental reserved for the said premises for each of the last seven and one-seventh months of the term herein demised, provided that prior to the application of each of said month's rental said second party shall not be in default in any of the terms, covenants and conditions in this rider or in the indenture of lease." . . .

By section 12 it was further covenanted and agreed that

> "in the event that the indenture of lease to which this rider is attached shall be terminated by reason of a breach by party of the second part of any of the terms and conditions in said indenture of lease contained, by said party of the second part to be kept and performed, then and in such event the party of the first part may, at his option, retain as and for full liquidated damages the said sum of $2,500 or such portion thereof as may at such time be in the hands of the party of the first part under the terms hereof, and thereafter the party of the second part shall have no further right, claim or interest in and to the said sum of $2,500 or any part thereof."

As was said by this court in Gobble v. Linder, 76 Ill. 157, no branch of the law is involved in more obscurity by contradictory decisions than whether a sum named in an agreement to secure performance will be treated as liquidated damages or a penalty, and as each case must depend upon its own peculiar and attendant circumstances, general rules of law on this question are often of little practical utility. While the intention of the parties on this question must be taken into consideration, the language of the contract is not conclusive. The courts of this state, as well as in other jurisdictions, lean toward a construction which excludes the idea of liquidated damages and permits the parties to recover only damages actually sustained. . . . This court has said that the rules deducible from the cases may be stated as follows:

> "First, where by the terms of a contract a greater sum of money is to be paid upon default in the payment of a lesser sum at a given time, the provision for the payment of the greater sum will be held a penalty; second, where by the terms of a contract the damages are not difficult of ascertainment according to the terms of the contract and the stipulated damages are unconscionable, the stipulated damages will be regarded as a penalty; third, within these rules parties may agree upon any sum as compensation for a breach of contract." . . .

This and all other courts seem to agree upon the principle that a stipulated sum will not be allowed as liquidated damages unless it may be fairly allowed as compensation for the breach. (1 Sedgwick on Damages, 9th ed., § 407, and cases cited.) We have frequently said that courts will look to see the nature and purpose of fixing the amount of damages to be paid, and if it appears to have been inserted to secure the prompt performance of the agreement it will be treated as a penalty and no more than actual damages proved can be recovered. . . . In general a sum of money in gross, to be paid for the non-performance of an agreement, is considered as a penalty. Tayloe v. Sandiford, 7 Wheat. 13; 1 Sedgwick on Damages (9th ed.), § 402.

. . . . .

The lease specifically states that this sum of $2,500 was deposited to be held by the party of the first part "as security." There is nothing in any other part of the contract that conflicts with this statement. On the contrary, the entire contract, read together, is in full harmony with the conclusion that said sum was held as security. There is nothing in the nature of this contract that would make it especially difficult to ascertain the amount of damages for its breach, as there is in that class of cases where one has agreed to give his personal services to another for a certain length of time and repudiates the contract, or where one has sold out the good will of a business with the agreement not to enter into the same kind of business in a specified number of years or within a limited territory. The proof in this record shows that there was no special difficulty in proving the actual damages. Furthermore, it seems quite clear from reading all the terms of this contract together, that the parties did not intend to agree that this sum was liquidated damages, for one of the provisions was that the first party might, "at his option, retain" said sum. This provision is not consistent with the view that the parties adjusted in advance the damages that might arise by any breach of contract. The argument of counsel for plaintiff in error would require the holding that the $2,500 should be retained as liquidated damages whether the lease was violated less than a year before it expired the same as if it were violated within a few months after it was entered into. Such a construction of the contract violates the great fundamental principle which underlies our whole system,

> "that of compensation; the great object of this system is to place the plaintiff in as good a position as he would have had if his contract had not been broken." (Sedgwick on Damages, 9th ed., § 406, p. 779.)

To put this construction upon it, under circumstances that might readily arise, would work great oppression and hardship. In the light of the circumstances in this case the Appellate Court rightly held this sum a penalty and not liquidated damages.

CASE NO. 5

Bomberger v. McKelvey. 35 Cal. (2d) 607, 220 P. (2d) 729 (1950)

GIBSON, CH.J. Plaintiffs brought this action against D. P. McKelvey to recover a sum of money promised for the demolition and removal of a building which stood on real property purchased by McKelvey from plaintiffs. . . .

Early in 1946 defendants purchased twelve lots in the City of Modesto for the purpose of constructing a building and adjoining parking facilities for rental to a chain grocery store. Four of these lots, including lots 15 and 16, were acquired from plaintiffs for $60,000. At this time lots 15 and 16 were improved by a business structure occupied by the Hills. . . .

During negotiations for the sale of the lots the Hills agreed to surrender their lease upon payment of $4,000 by defendants, less $300 per month rent after March 1, 1946, and to vacate the premises "immediately upon the completion" of a new building to be built for the Hills by plaintiffs elsewhere in Modesto. . . .

It was orally agreed that defendants would pay plaintiffs $3,500 upon the demolition and removal of the old building on lots 15 and 16. During the various conversations relating to the transaction defendants stated that they did not want the old building or any part of it, and it appears that lots 15 and 16 were to be used as a parking lot by the chain store. Plaintiffs informed defendants that they intended to use whatever material they could from the old building in constructing the new one for the Hills.

The oral agreement was confirmed by a letter from defendants to plaintiffs on March 11, 1946, wherein defendants recited that plaintiffs were to "remove the existing improvements therefrom" and that in consideration for this defendants would pay them $3,500. The letter further stated that if plaintiffs were prevented by strikes, government regulations, or the like, from completing the new building, the Hills could continue to occupy the old building and the time of its "removal" should be "extended to coincide with the completion of said new building." In reliance upon this letter and the agreement to tear down the old building, plaintiffs changed the plans for the new building "to fit the possible use of salvage" from the old building, namely, plate glass and skylights, and for this reason did not order those items, which were then scarce and could be obtained only after a delay of at least 90 to 120 days. In addition sheet metal for skylights was under priority by reason of governmental restrictions. There is testimony that the new building could not be completed without the glass and skylights from the old one.

Plaintiffs commenced construction of the new store for occupancy by the Hills, but due to governmental restrictions defendants were unable to get materials for the contemplated chain store and parking lot. Because of this delay defendants on August 2, 1946, notified plaintiffs that construction of the chain store building was not contemplated in the immediate future, that until further written notice plaintiffs were not to proceed with the demolition. . . .

Toward the end of October plaintiffs removed the plate glass and skylights from the old building and completed the new building for the Hills. About October 30 the Hills abandoned the old building, and plaintiffs thereupon entered defendants' premises and demolished and removed the building. On November 1 the Hills moved to the new store constructed for them by plaintiffs. . . .

Defendants refused to pay either the agreed price of $3,500 due upon demolition of the old building or the unpaid balance of $2,500 due to the Hills for surrender of the lease. The Hills assigned their claim to plaintiffs, who brought the present action to recover both amounts.

. . . The principal question for our determination is whether plaintiffs could ignore the express notification from defendants not to enter the land and not to demolish the building.

It is the general rule in California and in practically all other jurisdictions that either party to an executory contract has the power to stop performance of the contract by giving notice or direction to that effect, subjecting himself to liability for damages, and upon receipt of such notice the other party cannot continue to perform and recover damages based on full performance . . . This is an application of the principle that a plaintiff must mitigate damages so far as he can without loss to himself. . . .

The reason for this rule is twofold: Ordinarily a plaintiff is interested only in the profit he will make from his contract, and if he receives this he obtains the full benefit of his bargain; on the other hand, performance by the plaintiff might be useless to the defendant, although he would have to pay the entire contract price if the plaintiff were permitted to perform, and this would inflict damage on the defendant without benefit to the plaintiff. . . . If these reasons are not present, the rule is not applied. For example, where the plaintiff is not interested solely in profit from the agreement but must proceed with the work in order to fulfill contract obligations to others, or where refraining from performance might involve closing a factory, damages may be inadequate and the plaintiff may have a right to continue performance. Southern Cotton-Oil Co. v. Heflin, 5 Cir., 99 Fed. 339; 5 Williston on Contracts, Rev. Ed. 1937, § 1299, p. 3696. It has likewise been held that where a contractor has started work and has reached a point where it would be impracticable to attempt to make a reasonable estimate of damages, or where to complete the work will diminish damages or at least not enhance them, the contractor may go forward and complete performance.

The general rule is also subject to the jurisdiction of equity to order specific performance of the contract, and, apparently in recognition of this principle, it has been held that in cases where damages will not afford adequate compensation and where specific performance will lie, the plaintiff may continue to perform, in spite of a notice to stop, and thereafter recover on the basis of his continued performance. . . .

In the present case the trial court granted relief similar to that which has been allowed under this exception to the general rule. The court determined that plaintiffs acted properly in performing the contract on their part and that, having performed, they were entitled to the full amount of $6,000 due under the agreement. In the light of the foregoing, we must consider whether the facts bring this case within the reasons underlying the general rule or the reasons for the exception, and we must determine whether there is sufficient evidence to show that plaintiffs would have been entitled to specific performance and that damages would have been inadequate.

. . . the agreement involved here did not provide simply for the payment of money in return for the performance of services. As we have seen, it was contemplated that plaintiffs were to keep all salvaged material. During the negotiations for the agreement they informed defendants that they planned to use as much of this material as they could in constructing the new building for the Hills, and, in reliance on the contract, they altered the plans for the new building to permit use of the glass and skylights from the old one. These materials were then scarce, and sheet metal for the skylights was under priority. . . . Except for the glass and skylights the new building was completed sometime in October, and the lack of these materials left it exposed to the weather and apparently unsuitable for occupation by the Hills. Thus it is obvious that an essential element of the rule giving one party the power to stop performance by giving notice not to perform is lacking here since plaintiffs were not interested solely in the profit to be derived from tearing down the old building and selling the salvage, but they had an additional interest in obtaining actual performance of the agreement so that they could secure scarce materials and complete the new building.

The fact that the agreement involved property which was scarce and under priority is of particular importance in the present case. There are analogous decisions in other jurisdictions holding that a purchaser does not have an adequate remedy at law and may obtain specific performance of a contract to sell materials if he needs them in his business and cannot obtain them or their equivalent within the local marketing area.

. . . the adoption of the Uniform Sales Act exemplifies a tendency to liberalize the requirements for specific performance of contracts to sell or transfer personal property. See 2 Williston on Sales, Rev. Ed. 1948, § 601; cf. Sanford v. Boston Edison Co., 316 Mass. 631, 56 N.E. (2d) 1, 3, 156 A.L.R. 644, stating that there is a "growing tendency" to allow specific performance where damages are not the equivalent of the performance. . . .

The judgment is affirmed.

CASE NO. 6

Raisor v. Jackson. 311 Ky. 803, 225 S.W. (2d) 657 (1950)

. . . . .

CLAY, C. This suit was brought by appellant, the buyer, to recover damages for the seller's breach of a contract to convey real estate. Following the trial Court's instructions, a verdict was returned in appellant's favor for nominal damages of $1. These instructions authorized the jury to award substantial damages (the difference between the contract price and the reasonable market value of the property) only in the event it found appellee acted in bad faith and was guilty of positive or actual fraud. . . .

On February 14, 1947, the property was sold to appellant at a public auction for $22,252. He complied with the terms of sale by making a down payment of $4,500. A few days later when appellant called on appellee to convey the property, the latter advised he could not do so because his wife, who owned an undivided one-half interest therein, refused to join in the deed. The down payment was returned to appellant, and shortly thereafter appellee and his wife sold the property to another party. On the trial there was evidence the land had a reasonable market value in excess of the sale price.

. . . Appellant insists the breach of contract entitled him to recover for the loss of his bargain.

. . . As set forth in Restatement, Contracts, § 455, impossibilities arising from the inability of the promisor to perform an act do not discharge the duty created by the contract. In the comment to this section, the vital distinction is noted between "the thing cannot be done" and "I cannot do it." It is said in 12 Am. Jur., Contracts, § 370:

> "If a promise is conditioned upon the act or consent of a third person, the condition must be performed. But the inability to control the actions of a third person, whose co-operation is needed for the performance of an undertaking, is ordinarily not to be regarded as an impossibility avoiding the obligation. One who engages for the act of a stranger must procure the act to be done, and the refusal of the stranger without the interference of the other party to the contract is no excuse. The performance of an absolute promise is not excused by the fact that a third person refuses or fails to take action essential to performance."

From what has been said above, it is obvious that the matter of good faith is not material in the type of case we are considering. The seller has simply undertaken to do something which he finds he cannot do. His intentions or motives are without significance. As stated in the case of Doherty v. Dolan, 65 Me. 87, 91, 20 Am. Rep., 677:

> "The pecuniary damages are the same to the vendee, whether the mo-

tive of the vendor in refusing to convey is good or bad. It is a difficult thing to ascertain whether or not a vendor is actuated by good faith in his refusal to convey. There can easily be frauds and deceits about it. The vendor is strongly tempted to avoid his agreement, where there has been a rise in the value of the property. The vendee, by making this contract, may lose other opportunities of making profitable investments. The vendor knows, when he contracts, his ability to convey a title, and the vendee ordinarily does not. The vendor can provide in his contract against such a contingency as an unexpected inability to convey."

. . . For the reasons stated, the judgment is reversed, with directions to grant appellant a new trial and for proceedings consistent herewith.

CASE NO. 7

United States v. Huff. 165 F. (2d) 720, 1 A.L.R. (2d) 854 (1948)

LEE, C.J. The owners of adjacent tracts of land near Camp Barkeley, in Taylor County, Texas, executed leases covering the lands to three named trustees in order to permit the trustees to make a blanket lease of all the tracts to the federal Government for use as the site of an Army training and maneuver camp and an artillery firing and target range. The trustees executed a blanket lease dated January 2, 1941, to expire July 1, 1943. The appellees, plaintiffs below . . . were the tenants . . . of the tracts of land included in the blanket lease. At the time of the execution of the blanket lease these tenants were using and occupying the different tracts for the purpose of raising sheep and goats and were permitted to continue such use and occupancy during the term of the lease. The complaint in each case alleges that the acts of the Government or its agents and employees, particularly set forth in the petition, constituted negligence which caused loss of and damage to sheep and goats. . . .

Appellant contends that the appellees not being parties to the lease cannot sue upon the contract. We think the lease was drawn with the double purpose of benefiting both the owners of the lands in question and their tenants, appellees. Paragraphs 12 and 13 of the lease read as follows:

"12. The Government will not be liable during the life of this lease, or any renewal thereof, for the loss of, or damage of any nature to livestock that may be on said premises, save and except the loss of, or damage to, said livestock due to negligence on the part of the Government or its agents or employees.

"13. The Government shall have the right, during the existence of this lease, to let down any wire on the now existing wire fences, with the understanding that following the crossing of said fences by the troops, the Government will restaple the said wire to the posts, and leave the fence in as good condition and repair as it was at the time of entry upon the leased premises by the Government."

The record shows that the only livestock on the leased premises was livestock belonging to the tenants, appellees. Clearly, therefore, paragraph 12 must be held to have been drawn with rights of the tenants in the minds of the contracting parties. Patently paragraph 13 protects both the owners' property in the fences and the tenants' interest in keeping their livestock enclosed to prevent straying. If the owners' property interest in the fences were the only, or even the primary, interest to be protected, it could have been protected merely by an agreement on the part of the Government to replace or pay for removed fences at the termination of the lease. But the paragraph in question provides for replacement of the fences *following the passage of the troops,* and we think the inescapable conclusion must be that the agreement was intended by the parties also to benefit the tenants in their business of raising livestock. This conclusion is fortified by the fact that the Government expressly agreed that during the term of the lease, the tenants in possession might remain upon the lands and continue in business. . . . It is evident that at least in these quoted paragraphs and clauses the Government lease is charged with obligation toward the tenants, that they are third-party beneficiaries of the contract, and that, therefore, they may sue upon it. Williston on Contracts, § 356A; Restatement, Contracts, § 133.

. . . it is probably true as the lower court pointed out, that the lease created an impossible situation. Clearly, it must have been supposed by all the parties that the use of the lands by the Government as a maneuver area would be entirely compatible with continued use of the same lands by the appellees as livestock ranges. That supposition was proved erroneous. The evidence shows that fulfillment of the contract would have been unreasonably difficult, if not impossible. But

> "the common law regards a promise as binding according to its terms, even though it proves impossible of performance, unless the promisor can show that it falls within an excepted clause." Williston on Contracts, §§ 1967, 1979; Restatement, Contracts, § 467.

Upon this theory, the Government is clearly liable, under the Tucker Act, upon its contract. . . .

CASE NO. 8

Glens Falls Indemnity Co. v. Perscallo.
96 Cal. (2d) 799, 216 P. (2d) 567 (1950)

DRAPEAU, J. Plaintiff bonded the defendant Nick Perscallo for the faithful performance of a contract with the State of California to build a portion of the state highway. The defendant failed to complete his contract and the plaintiff was required under the terms of the bond to pay for its completion. Plaintiff advanced the money to the defendant for payments to workmen and for material. . . .

Fifty-seven thousand thirty-one dollars and thirty-one cents ($57,031.31) was found and adjudged due from defendant to plaintiff. . . .

From the judgment defendant appealed.

Defendant contends: . . . that the Court made no finding on defendant's presented issue of impossibility of performance of his contract with the State. . . .

Defendant's contention as to impossibility of performance of the contract may be stated by quoting from his brief:

> "The second defense was that the alleged contract with the State of California had been terminated and the performance excused by unanticipated circumstances designated as commercial frustration, without fault of the defendant; that the State of California cancelled the contract thereby releasing the defendant from all obligations thereon.
>
> "The third defense was that because of large war orders, the prohibition against sale of materials necessary to defendant, the issuance of inadequate priorities, the performance of the contract by the defendant was made impossible; that the con-

tract had been executed when the parties contemplated that the materials would be available *but the contemplated means of performance ceased* thereafter to exist and by reason thereof the defendant was discharged from further performing and the condition of the bond was not broken.

"The fourth defense alleged that it was impossible for the defendant to carry out the contract with the State except by violation of law and rule and regulations of war; that the performance of the contract was made impossible by the act of law."

The excuse of commercial frustration, like that of impossibility, is a conclusion of law drawn by the court from the facts of a given case. . . .

If the possibility of governmental regulation is reasonably foreseeable there can be no commercial frustration of a contract. Mere difficulty, or unusual or unexpected expense does not establish frustration or impossibility of performance of a contract. . . .

The contract was dated December 13, 1941. The Japs attacked the United States at Pearl Harbor December 7, 1941. For months before Pearl Harbor any American citizen should have been able to foresee the imminence of war with the axis powers. So the defense of commercial frustration does not help the defendant under the facts of this case. . . .

The judgment is affirmed.

CASE NO. 9

United States Fidelity & G. Co. v. Parsons. 147 Miss. 335, 112 So. 469, 53 A.L.R. 88 (1927)

This is an action on a building contractor's bond to recover for a failure of the contractor to rebuild a house destroyed by fire before its completion.

MC GOWEN, J. . . . The fourth and tenth grounds of the demurrer challenge the right of the owner to demand a completed building, because of the provisions of exhibit A as follows:

"The owner is to carry fire insurance on the building and the contractor is to pay his pro rata of the cost."

And the demurrer asserts that this agreement in the contract for protection by fire insurance stands in lieu of the contract to erect a new building, and that this agreement for fire insurance relieves the contractor of the duty to rebuild, and shows that the contract was not breached by failure or refusal to rebuild, there being no express provision in the contract that in case of fire the contractor will rebuild. In other words, in the absence of an express provision, appellant contends that the provision for carrying fire insurance constitutes one of the exceptions to the general rule to the effect that the contract implies that the house shall be rebuilt in case it is destroyed by fire, and especially where the insurance has been carried and collected and retained by the owner, as shown in this bill.

On this question, the general rule is that where a house is destroyed by fire, and the contractor having agreed to furnish labor and material and construct a completed house for the owner, that he takes the risk of the incompleted house being destroyed by fire, unless he protects himself by expressly contracting that he shall not be held liable for an act of God, or other untoward circumstance, against which he is not willing to be bound.

The common-law rule is that where the duty is imposed on a party for performance, his non-performance shall be excused if it be rendered by an act of God, but where by his contract the party engages to do an act, it is deemed to be his own folly and fault that he does not expressly provide against such contingencies and exempt himself in certain events. In the instance of an absolute and general contract, the performance is not excused by an inevitable incident or other contingency. . . . Destruction by fire would excuse the non-performance of a duty created by law, but would not excuse a breach of that duty created by contract. The party must contract against such contingencies, or abide and suffer the loss entailed by failure to so contract as to relieve himself from liability.

Counsel for appellants argue very forcibly and plausibly that the agreement on the part of the owner to carry insurance amounted to an exception to the general rule which we have stated. In the case of Piaggio v. Somerville, 119 Miss. 6, 80 So. 342, Chief Justice Smith very clearly stated these exceptions where he said:

> "There are, however, certain classes of events the occurring of which are said to excuse from performance because 'they are not within the contract,' for the reason that it cannot reasonably be supposed that either party would have so intended had they contemplated their occurrence when the contract was entered into, so that the promisor cannot be said to have accepted specifically nor promised unconditionally in respect to them. . . . These three classes are: First, a subsequent change in the law, whereby performance becomes unlawful . . . Second, the destruction, from no default of either party, of the specific thing, the continued existence of which is essential to the performance of the contract . . . And, third, the death or incapacitating illness of the promisor in a contract which has for its object the rendering by him of personal services. . . ."

Applying these exceptions to the case at bar, it cannot be said that the agreement to carry fire insurance is in any way related to any change of the law, or that the agreement to carry fire insurance renders impossible the obligation of the contractor to rebuild the house after destruction, nor can it be said that the fire insurance provision invokes the exception

> "that the destruction from no default of either party of the specific thing, the continued existence of which is essential to the performance of the contract."

It might be said on a casual reading that this building was destroyed by fire, and therefore the continued existence of that which is essential to the performance of the contract was essential and did apply. But there was no building in existence when the parties contracted originally, and the contract undertook to create that which did not exist before, and therefore that which he undertook and partially created was not originally essential to the performance of the contract, nor can it be said that the carrying of fire insurance has any relation to this exception. The application of this exception to the rule is illustrated in the books, as where a contractor undertakes to repair a building already in existence, and that which was in existence at the time the contract was entered into is destroyed, by fire, or otherwise, then this exception to the general rule is applicable because that upon which the contractor depends to add to or repair is non-existent.

Another illustration is where a hotel building existed, and the contractor agreed to build an annex thereto, and before such annex was completed the hotel and annex were destroyed by fire. Then the exception applies, and the contractor is under no duty to rebuild the annex, because that to which it was to be attached has been destroyed and the contractor is thus relieved; so far as he is concerned an impossibility has arisen.

Counsel argues that because the building partially created was destroyed by fire, being insured at the time, this would relieve the contractor and place him within the second exception quoted, supra. To our minds, the fact that the parties agreed to insure the house is an additional reason for saying that said parties contemplated a completed building, and a rebuilding of said house in case of its destruction by fire.

. . . the owner contends that she is entitled to a new building as well as the excess of insurance arising from the old building. That would be inequitable and unjust. . . . The said excess insurance must be applied to the erection of the new house. She cannot "eat the cake and have it too."

CASE NO. 10

Snipes Mountain Co. v. Benz Bros. & Co. 162 Wash. 334, 298 Pac. 714 (1931)

PARKER, J. . . . The plaintiff, Snipes Mountain Company, seeks reformation of a written contract for the sale of one hundred tons of potatoes by it to the defendant, Benz Bros. & Co., and recovery of an unpaid balance claimed to be due upon the agreed purchase price of sixty-four tons of the potatoes delivered under the contract. The reformation sought is to have the written contract show that the potatoes contracted to be sold were only potatoes growing upon certain specified land, to the end that the plaintiff will be entitled to recovery for the potatoes grown upon that land, all of them having been delivered under the sale contract, though amounting only to sixty-four tons. . . .

During the negotiations leading up to the signing of the written contract, two members of the defendant's firm visited the growing crop of potatoes on the plaintiff's land, knowing that was all the potatoes being grown by the plaintiff during the season of 1929. The potatoes were then found to be in promising condition, having matured to the extent that they were then from about the size of a walnut to about the size of a hen's egg. Those participating in the negotiations were then well convinced that the crop would yield considerably more than one hundred tons, and then so expressed themselves. The evidence shows practically conclusively that all who conducted the negotiations and participated in the execution of the contract contemplated that it was a contract for the sale and purchase of one hundred tons of those particular potatoes, and no others; and that, in so far as the written contract failed to expressly so provide, there occurred a mutual mistake of the parties in its preparation. The contract was by the decree reformed by inserting therein between the words "potatoes" and "graded" the words "grown during the year 1929 on the following described premises: (Here follows a description of the land, being the land on which the members of the defendant's firm saw and examined the growing potatoes.)" We are of the opinion that the evidence well supports the reformation portion of the decree.

. . . The evidence renders it plain that the failure of the crop to yield one hundred tons or more was not in the least the fault of the plaintiff. The small yield, less than half the normal yield, was wholly the result of a partial crop failure from natural causes. The plaintiff harvested and delivered to the defendant the whole of the crop, constituting sixty-four tons of potatoes. To that extent the contract was strictly performed by the plaintiff. The applicable law, we think, is well stated in general terms in a note in 12 A.L.R. 1288 by the editors, as follows:

"Whether or not a contract for the sale of produce to be delivered at a certain future date contemplates that it shall be grown on a particular tract of land, so that a failure of the crop on that land will excuse nondelivery, is often a close question of construction of the particular contract. The rule appears to be that if the parties contemplate a sale of the crop, or of a certain part of the crop, of a particular tract of land, and by reason of a drought or other fortuitous event, without the fault of the promisor, the crop of that land fails or is destroyed, non-performance is to that extent excused; the contract, in the absence of an express provision controlling the matter, being considered as subject to an implied condition in this regard. . . ."

We are of the opinion that the failure of the crop to produce more than sixty-four tons of potatoes absolved the plaintiff from liability for its failure to deliver to the defendant any additional potatoes, and that therefore the plaintiff is entitled to recover from the defendant the unpaid portion of the purchase price of the sixty-four tons of potatoes delivered; and that the defendant is not entitled to damages as claimed by it.

The judgment is affirmed. . . .

CASE NO. 11

Duris v. Iozzi. 6 N.J. Super. 530, 70 A. (2d) 793 (1949)

STEIN, J.S.C. Local 441 is a local trade union whose primary purpose is the representation of employees of Phelps Dodge Copper Products Corporation in collective bargaining. United Electrical, Radio and Machine Workers of America, International Union (hereinafter called UE) became an affiliate of the Congress of Industrial Organizations (hereinafter called CIO) on November 16, 1938, pursuant to the issuance of a certificate of affiliation by the CIO. Local 441 was chartered on December 10, 1940, by the UE-CIO while UE was an affiliate of CIO.

In its organizing campaign preceding the formation of Local 441, UE-CIO sought support by virtue of its affiliation with CIO, advertising that affiliation and its ability to protect and advance the interests of the Phelps Dodge employees by drawing on the moneys, personnel, experience and prestige of CIO.

On or about November 2, 1949, CIO expelled UE-CIO on grounds of defiance by UE of CIO policy in organizational, economic and political matters. At the same time CIO chartered a new international union known as International Union of Electrical, Radio and Machine Workers, CIO (hereinafter called IUE-CIO). IUE-CIO is now the national organization affiliated with CIO, with CIO jurisdiction to represent employees in the electrical, radio and machine industries.

. . . Meetings of Local 441 were held . . . the membership, by a vote of approximately 800 to 30, voted in favor of disaffiliating itself from UE and in favor of affiliating with IUE-CIO. Local 441 thereupon applied to IUE-CIO for a charter which it received and now holds as Local 441 IUE-CIO. All of the former officers of Local 441 UE-CIO signed the application for a charter to IUE-CIO, including the plaintiff Duris. . . .

Plaintiffs who in essence represent the interests of the United Electrical, Radio and Machine Workers of America, seek injunction preventing Local 441 from spending any of its funds, from receiving from Phelps Dodge any union dues checked off by Phelps Dodge from the wages of its employees under the aforesaid agreements, and restraining defendants from taking any steps "in pursuance of their plan to have UE Local secede from the UE" and from using the name Local 441 either alone or in a combination with any other name, and from using its office at 105 Bayway Avenue, Elizabeth, New Jersey, or preventing or attempting to prevent the use of office by UE. . . .

The defendants contend that the contract between Local 441 and UE is to be found in the body of the writings consisting of the CIO constitution, the certificate of affiliation granted by CIO to UE-CIO, the International constitution, the charter issued by UE-CIO to Local 441, and the constitution of the Local . . . defendants contend that the principal and fundamental question is whether in view of the situation which has arisen by reason of expulsion of UE from the CIO resulting in the loss of its affiliation with the latter, the contract between UE and Local 441 terminated and rendered void Article 18 Section O of the UE constitution which provides that

> "disbandment, dissolution, secession or disaffiliation of any local shall be invalid and null and void if seven or more members indicate their desire to retain the local charter."

Defendants in support of such contention cite Clark v. Fitzgerald, N.Y. Super. Ct. Spec. Term, Part III, 93 N.Y.S. (2d) 768, 774. That was likewise a suit for injunction in which the UE issued charters to locals including Local 450 UE and in which the facts and circumstances were identical with the instant case. Justice Eder in that held:

> ". . . Under the circumstances, in such a situation as is here extant, it is my view that it must be held that with the expulsion of United Electrical from CIO the contract between United Electrical and Local 450 terminated, and that article 18, Section O, of the constitution of United Electrical was rendered nugatory and eliminated. To hold, in the circumstances, that article 18, Section O, none the less continues operative, and that the Local is bound to continue membership in the UE, even though the basic objective and inducing cause for joining with UE, viz., UE's affiliation with CIO, has been rendered impossible of continuance by UE's expulsion, is to give to this provision an unreasonable, unwarranted and unjustified construction. . . ."

With this holding by Justice Eder I agree. . . .

. . . Where the continued existence of a state of facts (here an affiliation) is an implied condition going to the essence of the contract, the destruction of that state of facts puts an end to the contract itself. The obligation is no stronger or more enduring than the foundation upon which it rests and will not survive the latter's collapse. . . .

Preliminary injunction is denied.

CASE NO. 12

Cohen v. Eggers. 220 N.Y.S. 109 (1927)

FINCH, J. This appeal involves the question of whether the plaintiffs can be said to have performed substantially the contracts which they made to build two houses. . . . The action is to foreclose a mechanic's lien. The trial court has found that the plaintiffs did not perform in mixing and laying the cement for the cellars and the runways to the garages, in accordance with the specifications, resulting in the disintegration of the finished work, and he has made an allowance of $1,200 for this failure to perform, being $600 for each of the houses. In addition, this record shows that the plaintiffs have failed to perform the contracts also in the following respects:

The specifications required the roofs "to be thoroughly flashed and guaranteed waterproof." The roofs of both houses leaked badly during the first rainstorm, which occurred about a week after the defendants took possession. Investigation showed that the flashings had been improperly installed. Each house had to have a portion of the roof removed, flashings properly installed, and the roofs, and incidentally some stucco, relaid. In addition, the specifications in connection with both houses required sheet rock ceilings to be installed in the garages. This was not done. Further, specifications called for concrete pillars under the porches and sun parlors of each house. Wooden posts were substituted. The specifications also called for brick coping on stoops and bluestone treads on cellar stairs. Instead of this, cement was substituted.

The principles of law pertaining to the question of substantial performance are clear in their application to the facts in this case. In the latest case upon the subject, namely, Jacob & Youngs v. Kent, 230 N.Y. 239, 129 N.E. 889, the specifications of a building contract required the plaintiff to provide wrought iron pipe for the plumbing, of the grade known as "standard pipe" of "Reading manufacture." The plaintiff instead installed similar pipe known as "Cohoes" pipe. It appears from the opinion that the difference between the two pipes was as follows:

> "Reading pipe is distinguished from the Cohoes pipe and other brands only by the name of the manufacturer stamped upon it at intervals of between six and seven feet. Even the defendant's architect, although he inspected the pipe upon arrival, failed to notice the discrepancy."

Even such a slight deviation from the specifications presented a close question as to whether the plaintiff had had the performance under his contract to which he was entitled. The Court of Appeals held that there was substantial performance, but three members of the court dissented. In the case at bar the failure to perform the contract on the part of the plaintiffs is far greater than in Jacob & Youngs v. Kent, supra. This is so, considering alone the failure to comply with the specifications in connection with the cementing of the cellars and runways to the garages. . . .

. . . In addition, as already noted, the plaintiffs failed to comply with the specifications in respect of the roofing, the ceilings of the garages, concrete pillars under the porches and the sun parlors, brick copings on step, and bluestone treads on cellar stairs. In the case at bar, therefore, there cannot be said to have been substantial performance. The plaintiffs cannot therefore recover upon their contract.

The plaintiffs urge that by moving into the premises the defendants waived the defects. The authorities, however, are to the contrary. In Crawley v. Weiner, 236 N.Y. 357, 140 N.E. 724, Judge Crane, for the Court of Appeals, said:

> "The house was built upon the defendants' property. They could move into it, live in it, and in this sense accept it, without waiving any defects in construction." . . .

CASE NO. 13

Sward v. Nash et al. 230 Minn. 100, 40 N.W. (2d) 828 (1950)

. . . . .

GALLAGHER, J. Plaintiff is a building contractor. He sought a mechanic's lien in the amount of $1,793.95 for services and material furnished defendant Alice

C. Nash in the erection of a commercial garage. Defendant . . . disputed the terms of the oral contract under which plaintiff claimed a lien and asserted that plaintiff was entitled to no lien because he claimed more than was due him; that the work was defective and not in accord with the terms and conditions of the contract; and that plaintiff left the work voluntarily before completion of the building in violation of the contract. Defendant counterclaimed for loss of additional rent from the new building because of plaintiff's alleged failure to complete it on time and for sums expended to correct defects in the building caused by plaintiff's faulty workmanship. The trial resulted in findings and in a verdict for plaintiff for $1,500. Defendant's motion for a new trial was denied, and she appeals from the judgment. . . .

The rule in this state, in the case of building contracts, is that if the facts show that a contractor has substantially performed his contract, although there were minor defects in his work, he is entitled to recover the contract price, less the sum necessary to cure the defects. . . . However, the doctrine of substantial performance does not apply when the omissions or departures from the contract are intentional or so substantial as not to be capable of remedy, so that even though the owner received an allowance out of the contract price he still would not receive what he contracted for. Elliott v. Caldwell, 43 Minn. 357, 45 N.W. 845, 9 L.R.A. 52. If the contract is entire and performance is wilfully abandoned before completion, there can be no recovery on the contract or in *quantum meruit.* Johnson v. Fehsefeldt, 106 Minn. 202, 118 N.W. 797, 20 L.R.A., N.S., 1069; Groves v. John Wunder Co., 205 Minn. 163, 286 N.W. 235, 123 A.L.R. . . .

The exact terms of the contract are in dispute. Plaintiff and his wife testified that the agreement was made orally at plaintiff's home on December 18, 1945, that he was to work only until April 1, 1946; that he was to receive a $750 flat fee for supervision of the work and, in addition, was to receive $75 per week as a working foreman; that his work was to involve only the structure proper and did not include plumbing, heating, and electrical construction; and that defendant was to furnish the materials for the job. Defendant's agent, D. P. Blomquist, who acted for defendant in all matters involved in this case, denied that there was any agreement for weekly compensation. However, this issue was left to the jury, who allowed plaintiff weekly compensation in addition to the $750. In connection with the amount of work contemplated by the contract, Blomquist testified that the understanding was that the building could be *substantially* completed and that at the time the contract was made he told plaintiff that he could "see most of the materials to substantially complete that building." When asked what state of completion the building had reached when plaintiff left the job, Blomquist testified that the doors, windows, interior and electrical work, floor, and plumbing were incomplete. However, on cross-examination, he indicated that the plumbing and electrical work was to be done by others. . . . Accepting Blomquist's evidence in its entirety, it appears that when plaintiff left the work on March 29, 1946, he had completed all the exterior work with which he was chargeable, except for installation of sash, doors, and windows.

There is no direct testimony as to how much of the interior finishing the contract bound plaintiff to do, but an examination of the record indicates to us that only the structural part was involved, and that was substantially completed. The undisputed evidence shows that the carpenters, who with the masons and laborers constituted the force which plaintiff was employed to supervise, were laid off by defendant on April 4, 1946, very shortly after plaintiff ceased work. It appears that at that time the structure, as such, was substantially completed. Laying aside the evidence of failure by Blomquist to procure needed materials, with resulting unavoidable delay of plaintiff's operations, it appears that the structure proper, with the exception of some doors and windows, was complete at the time plaintiff left the job. Inasmuch as Blomquist characterized the agreement as one to "substantially" complete the building, we feel justified in concluding as a matter of law, setting aside minor defects which we shall consider later, that plaintiff had substantially completed any contract which the evidence warranted the jury in finding and that there was no intentional and unexcused abandonment of the work. While defendant alleged that the workmanship was in several respects defective, she does not contend that the defects and omissions were intentional. A reading of the record convinces us that the trial court was warranted in instructing the jury that the defects were not such as to prevent substantial performance. It properly instructed the jury that they were to deduct the cost of correcting the defects from any verdict that they might find for plaintiff.

CASE NO. 14

Klapka v. Shrauger. 135 Neb. 354, 281 N.W. 612 (1938)

PAINE, J. . . . This is an action for the rescission of a land sale contract and to recover the payment of $1,000 made by the plaintiff to the defendant at the time the contract was executed. . . .

The contract was dated August 20, 1936, and provides for the sale of the 120-acre farm for $7,000, of which $1,000 cash was paid by check that night. Defendant was to pay one-half of the 1936 taxes, and possession of the premises was to be given March 1. Then follows this paragraph:

> "Party of the first part to execute a warranty deed showing the above land to be clear of all encumbrance, and deposit the same in escrow with the Citizens State Bank, Pawnee City, Nebraska, and to be delivered to the party of the second part upon his paying $3,000 and executing a first mortgage on the above land for $3,000 at five percent to run for two years from March 1st, 1937, to the party of the first part."

A careful examination of this contract discloses that it contains no statement to the effect that time is of the essence of this contract. . . .

The defendant received a written notice, dated February 27, 1937 from Attorney Witte, . . . in which she is notified that said attorney has examined the agreement signed up August 20, 1936, and the abstract of title, and that she has breached the agreement by not depositing in escrow a deed that would convey title to said real estate, and that she must of necessity breach the agreement further on March 1, 1937, because it will be impossible for her to convey title that day; that his client elects to and does rescind the agreement; . . .

The petition of the plaintiff admits the execution of the contract, and charges that upon the date the contract was executed the defendant owned only a one-third interest in the land she contracted to convey, one-third interest belonging to her daughter, Ena June Shrauger, who was then a minor and incapable of conveying said real estate, . . . that the defendant's breaches of said contract are material, and for that reason the plaintiff has elected to and has rescinded the contract, and asks judgment for return of the $1,000 cash payment. . . .

Plaintiff also alleged in his petition that on March 1, 1937, the defendant tendered to the plaintiff a deed executed by the defendant and by her son, John Sterling Shrauger, and also executed by Ena June Shrauger, who was a minor, who would arrive at her majority June 13, 1937. . . .

"The decided weight of authority now is that any deed of an infant is voidable only, so that the title passes by it and remains in the grantee until some clear act of disaffirmance is done by the grantor after coming of age." 8 R.C.L. 949, § 23. See Curtice Co. v. Kent 89 Neb. 496, 131 N.W. 944, 52 L.R.A., N.S., 723.

"It is not every breach of a contract or failure exactly to perform—certainly not every partial failure to perform—that entitles the other party to rescind. A breach which goes to only a part of the consideration, is incidental and subordinate to the main purpose of the contract, and may be compensated in damages and does not warrant a rescission of the contract; the injured party is still bound to perform his part of the agreement, and his only remedy for the breach consists of the damages he has suffered therefrom. A rescission is not warranted by a mere breach of contract not so substantial and fundamental as to defeat the object of the parties in making the agreement." 12 Am. Jur. 1020, § 440. See Schlake v. Healey, 108 Neb. 35, 187 N.W. 427.

Many cases hold that, where time is not of the essence of the contract, the vendor is entitled to a reasonable time and opportunity to secure or perfect the title. In such cases a sudden determination to end the transaction will not be permitted without giving the vendor a reasonable length of time in which to perform. The question as to what is a reasonable time is one for the court to determine. If the time of such performance is uncertain and indefinite, the other party is not required to keep himself in readiness to perform; but, on the other hand, if the date of possible and probable performance is fixed and definite, and not far in the future, courts will be liberal in allowing the vendor a reasonable time to perform where there is no provision in the contract that time is of the essence of the contract.

The plaintiff was put in peaceable possession of the farm on September 1, and remained so until several days after March 1, when he voluntarily moved out. This court cannot see what hardship he would have suffered in remaining in possession a short time longer until the daughter could affirm her deed already given by giving an additional deed after she became of age.

This court has reached the conclusion that the trial court erred in entering its decree for the plaintiff, and the same is hereby Reversed.

CASE NO. 15

Dodge v. Galusha. 151 Neb. 753, 39 N.W. (2d) 539 (1949)

CHAPPELL, J. This was an action in equity to obtain specific performance of an oral contract to convey real estate. . . .

With regard to plaintiff's action, the decree found that plaintiff and defendant . . . had entered into a contract substantially as claimed by plaintiff, but that time was of the essence of the contract, and plaintiff, having failed to perform within such time, was not entitled to specific performance. . . .

Plaintiff, an elderly man not in

the best of health, owned a residence property in Marion. He was and had been in possession thereof during all times here involved. Defendant bid in the aforesaid property for $1,700 at a tax foreclosure sale on April 5, 1948, and thereafter obtained a sheriff's deed on May 21, 1948. . . .

In October, 1948, defendant employed counsel to obtain possession of the property from plaintiff. . . .

While the foregoing matters were respectively pending or not yet enforced, plaintiff, his son, defendant, and their respective counsel, entered into negotiations for settlement. The result thereof was that plaintiff was temporarily left in possession, and contract was made, whereby defendant agreed to sell the property to plaintiff upon receipt of $2,000 cash, which money was to be left at the First National Bank of McCook, to be there available and payable to defendant on or before December 22, 1948, and when the money was there for defendant, he was to then tender a deed to the property. . . .

Plaintiff negotiated and arranged to obtain two loans. One was for $700 upon the son's insurance policies. The other was for $1,300 upon the property itself. The proceeds of the first were obtained by plaintiff and left with the bank on December 22, 1948. The proceeds of the other loan, and a mortgage on the property, executed by plaintiff to secure payment thereof, were also left with the bank on December 22, 1948. Without dispute, however, the mortgage was not to be delivered to the mortgagee and such proceeds were not to be paid to plaintiff or to be available and payable to either plaintiff or defendant until, as instructed by the loaner, the bank had received from plaintiff an abstract of title with legal opinion thereon showing title approved by the bank. Defendant gave the bank no instructions whatever, and took no part in that transaction.

Such abstract was not even ordered by plaintiff until after December 22, 1948. It was not certified until January 19, 1949. A legal opinion thereon, addressed to plaintiff and approving title, was not completed until January 22, 1949, and neither the abstract nor opinion was delivered to the bank until January 23, 1949. That was the first date upon which the $2,000 became available and payable to either plaintiff or defendant. It will be observed that such date was more than a month after the date upon which plaintiff was required to perform under the specific terms and conditions of the agreement. Thereafter, defendant refused to perform, and on February 9, 1949, plaintiff filed this action. . . .

. . . as said in Restatement, Contracts, § 276(e), p. 407:

"In a suit for specific performance of a contract for the sale or purchase of land, considerable delay in tendering performance does not preclude enforcement of the contract where the delay can be compensated for by interest on the purchase money or otherwise, unless

"(i) the contract expressly states that performance at or within a given time is essential, . . ."

. . . in Jewett v. Black, 60 Neb. 173, 82 N.W. 375, 377, this court said:

"It is now firmly established everywhere that time may be made the essence of a contract, and it will be so regarded even in equity, if it affirmatively and clearly appear that the parties intended that time should be essential. In 3 Pomeroy, Equity Jurisprudence (2d ed.), § 1408, it is said: 'Time may be essential. It is so whenever the intention of the parties is clear that the performance of its terms shall be accomplished exactly at the stipulated day.' No particular form of words is necessary to express the intention of the parties. If they have clearly indicated their purpose that the contract shall be void if not performed within the prescribed time, that is sufficient. It is the business of the courts to enforce agreements actually made, and not to make new ones, or relieve parties from obligations which they have deliberately assumed. Between the plaintiff and Sanford it was expressly stipulated that time should be of the essence of the contract; not, of course, by the use of these very words, but by the employment of terms almost as explicit. . . ."

As stated in 55 Am. Jur., Vendor and Purchaser, § 114, p. 590:

"If the agreement is that the vendor will convey provided that the purchaser shall on a certain day pay a specified sum, time is deemed of the essence of the agreement and the payment of the sum on such day is a condition precedent to the creation of any right in the purchaser to the performance of the agreement. It has also been held that where the purchaser deposits the purchase price in a bank under an agreement made at the time with the vendor that he shall receive it upon delivery by him to the bank of the instruments of title named in the conditions of deposit within a specified time, the vendor is entitled to receive it only on compliance with such conditions within such time, as time is of the essence of the contract. It is generally held that a provision authorizing the vendor to declare a forfeiture of the rights of the purchaser on his default in making the payments stipulated for renders time of the essence of the contract, and a court of equity cannot relieve the purchaser of the effect of a forfeiture for such cause if promptly asserted by the vendor." . . .

In the light of the foregoing authorities and the circumstances appearing in the record before us, we conclude that time was of the essence of the contract, and that plaintiff, having failed to perform within the time, was not entitled to specific performance. . . .

CASE NO. 16

Sunshine Cloak & Suit Co. v. Roquette et al. 30 N.D. 143, 152 N.W. 359 (1915)

Action by plaintiff to recover $173.25 as an amount due on ladies' cloaks and suits sold defendant. The evidence indicated that defendant ordered the goods with the understanding that they were to be shipped by August 15, they being fall goods. They were shipped on September 28 and arrived October 12 and were immediately returned to the plaintiff. Defendant appeals from a judgment for the plaintiff.

CHRISTIANSON, J. . . . It is doubtless true, as appellant contends, that time is never considered as the essence of a contract, unless by its terms it is expressly so provided. . . . But, although it is true that time is never considered as the essence of the contract, unless it is so provided by the terms thereof, still it is not necessary to declare in so many words "that time is of the essence of the contract," but it is sufficient if it appears that it was the intention of the parties thereto that time should be of the essence thereof.

The supreme court of Iowa, in considering this question in Bamberger Bros. v. Burrows, 145 Iowa 441, 450, said:

"In the law of sales it is a settled rule that time may be of the essence of the contract; and, when a time for delivery is fixed it is generally so regarded. Therefore, if the seller fails to make delivery on the date so fixed, the buyer may rescind or recover damages for the seller's breach of contract. . . ."

In Cleveland Rolling Mill Co. v. Rhodes, 121 U.S. 255, that court said:

". . . In the contracts of merchants time is of the essence. The time of shipment is the usual and convenient means of fixing the probable time of arrival, with a view of providing funds to pay for the goods, or of fulfilling contracts with third parties. . . ."

We are satisfied that the agreement to ship on August 15 was a condition precedent.

Judgment reversed.

CASE NO. 17

D. W. Winkelman Co. v. Barr. 178 F. (2d) 341 (1949)

ALLEN, C.J. This appeal arises out of an action based upon a contract for the laying of sewers, mains and service lines in Oak Ridge, Tennessee, which was part of the wartime construction for atomic bomb development. Appellee was subcontractor under appellant's principal contract, and an arrangement was entered into on February 3, 1944, under which appellee secured labor and equipment, brought it a considerable distance to Oak Ridge and constructed main line sewers and house connections. The superintendent of inspectors in charge certified that the appellee completed his work in a very workmanlike manner. On March 31, 1944, appellant terminated the contract upon the ground that the Government had cancelled a substantial part of the work assigned to appellee. Appellant itself later completed the work. This litigation ensued and resulted in a judgment allowing appellee recovery of $323.18 for work done, and $5,347.62 as prospective profits. . . .

It is contended . . . that the provision that *the agreement may be terminated by either party on five days' notice if it proves unsatisfactory* renders the agreement a contract at will and destroys its mutuality. . . .

Appellant cites certain decisions from federal courts and various states as authority for the proposition that when a contract contains such a phrase a party thereto has the absolute right to determine for himself whether the work as done effected a satisfactory result. . . . This contract was made in Tennessee, to be performed within that state, and is governed by the law of Tennessee. The cases cited from that jurisdiction, so far from requiring reversal, support the decision of the District Court. In Tennessee the courts follow the *general rule* that where a contract involves feelings, taste, or sensibilities and provides that a price bid in a sale must be satisfactory the buyer has an absolute right to determine for himself whether the article furnished or work done is satisfactory. But where the contract involves operative fitness or mechanical utility, performance is held to be sufficient if it reasonably ought to satisfy a reasonable man. . . .

In Peck-Williamson Heating & Ventilating Co. v. McKnight & Merz, 140 Tenn. 563, 205 S.W. 419, 423, strongly relied on by appellant, the court stated:

"There is a conflict in the authorities as to the meaning of the term 'satisfactory,' so used in a contract. It is held, perhaps by the weight of authority, that where such term appears in the contract, the party in whose favor it was reserved has the absolute right to determine the question, and to act accordingly—that is, either accepting or rejecting the work, provided his act is not merely capricious. Other authorities hold that such term is fully met where the work, as done, should be satisfactory to a reasonable man. Without now deciding between these two views, it is sufficient to say that this particular term was not lightly used in the contract. It was made the subject of correspondence between the parties. Complainant was very loath to use it, saying it had had so much trouble with agreements in which this word appeared that it had ceased to admit such term into its contracts. Williamson insisted, and would sign no other; thereupon the complainant yielded. So we think the parties must have understood that Williamson was to have the absolute right to determine for himself whether the work as done effected a result satisfactory to himself."

It could hardly be contended on the facts of this record that the cited case controls here, nor that the drastic construction urged by appellant was within the contemplation of the parties when the contract was made. This record does not reveal that there was any discussion at that time or later as to the meaning of the somewhat vague cancellation clause. The circumstances surrounding the arrangement, which involved wartime contracts with the Government, indicate that the phrase was inserted mainly in order to protect the principal contractor in case the Government should cancel its contracts. But if appellant, whose vice president inserted this phrase in the letter, intended the cancellation clause to ensure satisfactory performance, the proper test would seem to be as declared in Ragsdale v. Byer, 150 Tenn. 496, 513, 266 S.W. 91, whether the performance would be acceptable or satisfactory to a reasonable man.

While appellant's answer herein set up that appellee did not perform the work in a satisfactory manner, at the trial appellant's agent refused to testify that the contract was terminated for that reason, and the positive evidence of the inspectors in charge was distinctly to the contrary. . . .

We conclude that the District Court correctly held that the contract was enforceable, and breached by appellant. The findings as to damages are carefully worked out and based upon positive testimony.

The judgment is affirmed.

CASE NO. 18

Dahl v. Edwin Moss and Son. 136 Conn. 147, 69 A. (2d) 562 (1949)

MALTBIE, CH.J. This is an action arising out of contract wherein the plaintiff, an electrical contractor, seeks damages from the defendant, for material and labor which he furnished and which he claims were not called for by the contract . . . the material portion of which was as follows:

> "Furnish all necessary labor and materials for a complete job of Electrical Work all in strict accordance with plans, specifications, and addenda prepared by Albert Kahn Associates and subject to the approval of Albert Kahn Associates, for the sum of $103,000.00."

Albert Kahn Associates was the firm of architects in charge of the construction of the building and we shall hereafter refer to it as the architect. . . .

Included in the plaintiff's work was the laying of 10,000 feet of underfloor duct, a device for carrying electric and other wires beneath the floor surface. In submitting his bid, the plaintiff contemplated using a round fiber duct, which would cost $1,500. The plaintiff incorporated the round fiber duct in the list of materials he proposed to use, which was submitted to the architect. The architect disapproved the use of this duct, stating that in its opinion the duct did not meet the specifications, . . . A General Electric Company duct met the approval of the architect but would cost the plaintiff substantially more than the duct he proposed to install. He told Moss that he could not proceed with job if the General Electric duct was required. Moss then directed the plaintiff to install the General Electric duct and said that the defendant would take care of the additional cost. . . .

. . . clearly it was not intended that the plaintiff could install any fiber duct it chose which would meet the requirements as to area and wires to be carried, but that the particular type of duct to be used was subject to the approval of the architect. It had the right under the contract to disapprove the round duct proposed by the plaintiff if in so doing it did not act improperly.

The trial court found that the duct proposed by the plaintiff met the requirements of the specifications and also, after reciting that the architect stated the contrary to be true and that the duct would not install an underfloor duct system, found that opinion of the architect was erroneous; and one of the conclusions of the court was that the rejection of the duct was unreasonable and unwarranted. Even if we assume that the trial court was correct in these respects, the plaintiff can gain no advantage thereby. Under the contract, the decision of the architect was binding upon the plaintiff if it was made in good faith; that the duct did not meet the specifications was true when the requirement of the architect's approval is taken into consideration; and, if the architect's statement that the round duct would not install an underfloor duct system was mistaken, that would not invalidate its decision unless it acted in bad faith or under circumstances amounting to it. Chatfield Co. v. O'Neill, 89 Conn. 172. . . . The trial court's conclusion that the decision of the architect was unreasonable and unwarranted is insufficient to invalidate the disapproval of round duct by it.

Finally, the plaintiff seeks to recover on the basis of the promise made to him by Moss that the defendant would take care of the additional cost due to the purchase and installation of General Electric duct. As approval by the architect of the type of duct was required by the specifications, the plaintiff in installing a duct which was so approved was doing no more than he was required to do by the contract; and Moss's promise therefore lacked consideration and would ordinarily be unenforceable. Blakeslee v. Water Commissioners, 106 Conn. 642, 652, 139 Atl. 106, 55 A.L.R. 1319; Williston, Contracts (Rev. Ed.) § 130. The plaintiff relies upon an exception to that rule which we stated in the Blakeslee case as follows; 106 Conn. at page 655, 139 Atl. at page 111:

> "Where the contractor can justify his refusal to proceed with the contract by showing that he is confronted with circumstances not contemplated when the contract was made which render its performance impossible or unduly onerous and promisor, being informed of the situation, induces him by a promise of additional compensation to proceed with it, the contractor's right to that compensation ought justly to be recognized."

. . . cases in other jurisdictions . . . clearly condition the exception upon a situation which was not within the contemplation of the parties when the contract was made. In this instance, disapproval by the architect of a duct which the plaintiff might propose to use cannot be held to have been outside the contemplation of the parties when the contract was made. The exception, then, has no application.

CASE NO. 19

Williams v. Mutual Benefit Health & Accident Ass'n. 100 F. (2d) 264 (1938)

MC CORD, C.J. . . . William R. Williams, appellant, sued at law to recover damages of Mutual Benefit Health & Accident Association, appellee. It is without dispute that the insurance company insured appellant as against accident. The appellant complains that he was permanently and totally disabled by reason of accident; that the policy was in force and effect at the time; that due and proper notice was given to the insurance company; and that the policy of insurance provided that in the event of permanent and total disability by reason of accident that the insurance company would pay to the insured, the appellant, the sum of two hundred dollars per month.

The appellant further complains that the insurance company wholly and completely repudiated its contract of insurance and informed the insured that it would not pay him in any event. . . . Thereupon appellant sued for anticipatory breach of the contract. The trial court sustained special exception which challenged the sufficiency of the petition to state a cause of action. The appellant refused to amend his petition and his case was dismissed, and from that ruling he appeals to this court. . . .

The petition alleges a breach of the insurance contract by charging that the appellee insurance company told Williams

> "that it would not pay him in any event according to the terms of its policy, to-wit, a monthly indemnity, . . . advised plaintiff that even though a doctor of their choice advised them that he was totally disabled, they would not pay the monthly indemnity provided in the policy issued to him."

This is an allegation of repudiation and abandonment of the insurance contract by the insurance company. When one who is obligated by contract to make money payments to another, absolutely repudiates and abandons the obligation without just excuse, the obligee is

> "entitled to maintain his action in damages at once for the entire breach, . . ." . . .

The appellee insurance company contends that the quoted declaration of its agent that it would not pay the monthly indemnity in accordance with the terms of its contract, was not an absolute and unequivocal repudiation of the contract. The Texas cases hold that the doctrine of anticipatory breach is not applicable to cases where the insured "merely denies liability or claims defenses under the terms of the policy." . . . The case at bar does not fall within the protection of that rule. Here the refusal to pay was "in any event," and the petition in all things speaks a good complaint for anticipatory breach. . . .

The trial court's ruling is reversed and the cause is remanded for a trial on its merits.

CASE NO. 20

Miller & Sons Bakery Co. v. Selikowitz. 8 N.J. Super. 118, 73 A. (2d) 607 (1950)

BIGELOW, J.A.D. The respondent, Miller and Sons Bakery Co., agreed to buy the business conducted by the appellant Selikowitz, and paid $2,000 on account of the purchase price when the contract was signed November 17, 1948. One of the stipulations of the contract read:

> "The seller agrees to procure an employment agreement with James

Koye, with the restrictive covenant (2 yrs.) not to engage in a similar business or to take the customers of the seller, at a salary of $63.00 per week, for a period of one year. If the seller cannot obtain such an agreement, the purchaser may, at his option, declare this contract void, and be entitled to a return of his deposit in full, without damages to either party."

The buyer later assumed to exercise his option to avoid the contract, and the question in the suit is whether the circumstances gave him the right to make that election. On November 26, the seller's lawyer, Harold J. Sklarew, wrote to Lewis S. Jacobson, attorney for the buyer, as follows:

"I am enclosing, herewith, copy of contract which I negotiated between Selikowitz and his driver, James Koye. It was necessary for me, upon Koye's request, to make the contract for two years in order to get a two year restrictive covenant. . . . Please let me know whether the same meets with your approval, so we can at least dispose of this question at the closing."

Benjamin Miller testified that on November 28 or 29, he had a talk with Selikowitz:

"I told him I can't take the business with such an agreement (meaning the agreement with Koye). He says, 'That is the best agreement I can get. Otherwise the deal is off.' "

On cross examination, Benjamin restated what he had said to Selikowitz: "The deal is off. You can't get a contract and the deal is off." Samuel Miller corroborated his brother Benjamin, but Selikowitz denied that the conversation took place. Benjamin Miller testified that on November 27 or 28 he had a similar conversation with Sklarew. This also is denied.

On December 1, Jacobson wrote Selikowitz "to effectively cancel" the agreement to buy the business. . . . The letter avers that the contract with Koye which had been signed

"varies materially and substantially from the one contemplated in the agreement and undertaken by you with my client. I must therefore insist upon the return of the deposit forthwith so that the declaration of the contract as being void under the option given to my client is given full force and effect and the option on the part of my client (the purchaser) is that he declares this contract void by virtue of the failure on your part to perform the conditions precedent."

Sklarew, to whom Jacobson had sent a copy of the foregoing letter, immediately replied under date of December 2:

"I certainly feel that the contract prepared with James Koye is one which would be materially beneficial to Koye and Miller, in the long run. However, since your client desires to be technical, I suggest that you prepare the contract in accordance with Mr. Miller's requirements, and I will have the parties sign the same, or if you will instruct me what changes you wish to be made, I will redraft the same. I will await your further instructions."

Jacobson rejoined, by letter dated December 3, that his client

"takes the position that he wishes to avail himself of the option, which he has done, to give no effect to the contract by virtue of the variance in the employment agreement which had already been executed."

Now, the agreement of sale signed November 17, did not call for passage of title until January 3, 1949, at which time the bill of sale "and all other agreements and instruments are to be delivered." On December 6, Sklarew again wrote Jacobson:

"There is no duty upon my client to supply you with an employment agreement until the date of closing. At that time I will provide such an agreement duly executed exactly in accordance with the terms of the contract. Under the circumstances, your client doesn't have the right to exercise his option to cancel the agreement, and we will hold him strictly accountable to the same."

Each side stood firm and on December 17, two weeks before the time set for fulfillment of the executory clauses of the contract, the respondent brought suit for return of the sum of $2,000 which had been paid on account. . . . The action then came on for trial which resulted in a verdict for plaintiff in the sum of $2,000. . . .

The subject of anticipatory breach of contract has been discussed at length by counsel, as an aid in determining the operation of the option clause in the contract and also because the rules relating to anticipatory breach may have some direct relevancy to the issue here. Upon a vital breach of contract by one party, the opposite party may sue for damages resulting from the breach, or he may treat the contract as terminated, and maintain *assumpsit* for a return of the consideration paid on account. Ordinarily no action for damages or for restitution can be maintained until the time for performance has come and there has been an actual failure to perform. But when one party announces clearly and unequivocably that he will not or cannot fulfill the contract, the opposite party may bring suit without awaiting the day set for performance. . . . Or if a party puts it out of his power to fulfill his contract, the result is the same, that is, the other party may sue forthwith. . . .

The plaintiff argues that when the seller, Selikowitz, signed a contract with Koye, for two years' employment, he disabled himself from fulfilling the terms of his bargain with plaintiff which called for a one-year contract with Koye. But any contract with Koye depended, of course, on Koye's consent. It was as possible after he had signed the two years' contract as before that he might agree to one year. Selikowitz did not put it out of his power to fulfill his agreement with Miller.

There is another rule relating to anticipatory breaches that has not been brought into the case by the pleadings, or request to charge, or otherwise, and which has not been argued before us but which we will mention in order not to seem to discard it by silence. An anticipatory breach is nullified as the basis of an action for damages, if the repudiation of the contract is withdrawn before the injured party brings his action or otherwise materially changes his position.

. . . the action turns on whether the buyer, Miller and Sons Bakery Co., was in such a position that the option provision of the contract gave the buyer the right on December 1 to "declare this contract void." The principles that apply to breach of contract and rescission which we have been discussing, aid us in reaching our decision that Selikowitz' statement that the two-year agreement with Koye "is the best agreement I can get. Otherwise the deal is off," created a situation where the buyer had a right to elect that the contract should be void. There was sufficient evidence to sustain the verdict. . . .

The judgment is affirmed.

Review Questions

1. What remedies may be available for a breach of contract and what, if any, are the limitations to their availability?
2. What is the measure of money damages available for breach of contract?
3. What are liquidated damages?
4. What is the test applied in determining whether a liquidated damage provision is enforceable?
5. What duty is imposed upon a party who has failed to realize his rights under a contract, as a condition to his right to recover damages?
6. To what extent is a contracting party's inability to perform a legal excuse for nonperformance?
7. When will inability occasioned by an act of God serve as an excuse for nonperformance of a contract?
8. Can it be said that a condition in a contract is an "if and when clause"? Explain.
9. Illustrate (a) a condition that is collateral to performance of the contract, and (b) a condition that is also a term of performance in the contract.
10. What remedy is available to the injured party for the failure of a condition in the contract?
11. What is the doctrine of substantial performance?
12. What are the rights of the party who has failed to substantially perform a contract to recover for his part performance?
13. Can a party who has substantially performed a contract recover the contract price?
14. Construct a fact situation in which the time for performance of the contract would be implied as being a condition.
15. What is the significance of the phrase "time is of the essence" when introduced into a contract?
16. What are concurrent conditions?
17. Construct a fact situation illustrating an anticipatory breach of contract.
18. What is the limitation to the right to bring action upon an anticipatory breach of contract?

Problems for Discussion

1. X contracted to furnish Y articles manufactured under a patent held by X. When X refused to perform, Y brought an action for specific performance. Did he succeed?
2. A contract for the sale of road-grading machinery provided that should the buyer fail to perform he would pay 25 per cent of the purchase price and an additional 10 per cent as attorney's fees. Is this provision enforceable?
3. Plaintiff contracted to manufacture machines for defendant. In an action for breach of contract against defendant, may he show that plaintiff occupied his whole time in fulfilling a contract with a third party and that the profits under this contract offset the loss suffered by defendant's breach of contract?
4. This is an action at law brought by the Stanford Motor Company, a partnership, against Edmund J. Westman. The purpose of the action is to recover

$500 as stipulated liquidated damages based on the defendant's breach of an automobile repurchase agreement. At the conclusion of defendant's evidence, plaintiff moved for a directed verdict. This motion was sustained and judgment entered accordingly.

The contract provided as follows:

"Stanford Motor Company

Broken Bow, Nebr., October 4th, 1947

For One Dollar and other valuable considerations, I hereby agree with Stanford Motor Co. I will not sell, barter, trade or assign Buick 4 Door Sedan Model 71 Serial No. 447 27 392 Motor No. 4908 330 7, to any person within six months from the above date, without first offering to resell it to the Stanford Motor Company, Broken Bow, Nebraska, at a price not exceeding the purchase price less a reasonable amount for usage. This constitutes a repurchase option, for the violation of which purchaser agrees to pay Stanford Motor Company the sum of five hundred dollars ($500) as liquidated damages."

The record discloses that appellee thought that if the purchasers of its new cars immediately put the cars on the "gray market" where new used cars were at that time selling far above list price, it would cause the buying public in the trade area of Broken Bow to feel, and possibly believe, that appellee was actually selling the new cars it received on the "gray market," thus damaging its business reputation in that community. Its purpose in adopting the above policy was to prevent this from happening and thus protect its good will. Decide. (*Stanford Motor Company* v. *Westman,* 39 N.W. (2d) 841)

5. Charles Pembroke and Mary Pembroke, his wife, instituted an action against the appellees for the recovery of liquidated damages under a written agreement for the purchase and sale of real property entered into by and between the parties to this appeal.

The written agreement upon which the plaintiffs predicated their action contained the following pertinent provisions:

"Received of Jay Caudill and his wife Emma Caudill, hereinafter called the purchaser, $6,200.00. . . . Cash, check, as earnest money and in part payment on account of the purchase price . . . the total purchase price being $67,500.00. . . . Payment to be made as follows: Cash, earnest money as acknowledged above, $6,200.00, cash upon closing deal, $34,400.00, balance of $26,900.00 covered by two mortgages in amounts of $19,400.00 and $7,500.00, respectively, to be assumed by purchaser at present rate of interest and amortization payments.

"5. That in case of the failure of the purchaser to make either of the payments, or any part thereof, or to perform any of the covenants on his part made or entered into, this contract shall, at the option of the Seller, be terminated and voided and the purchaser shall forfeit said earnest money; and the same shall be retained by the Seller as liquidated damages, and the escrow agent is hereby authorized by the purchaser to pay over to the seller the said earnest money.

"6. That time is an essential part of this agreement. . . ."

The trial court sustained the demurrer on the ground that the clause in the contract was one providing for a penalty and not liquidated damages and that hence there could be no recovery without pleading and proof of the sustainment of actual damages. Decide. (*Pembroke* v. *Caudill,* 37 So. (2d) 538)

6. Defendant, during wartime, at the insistence of the government, accepted government orders to such an extent that he was forced to cancel his contracts to make civilian goods. Would you exonerate him for his nonperformance? (*Mawhinney* v. *Nullbrook Woolen Mills,* 231 N.Y. 290, 132 N.E. 93)
7. X was employed as a lobbyist by the Y Mutual Benefit Association. Under the contract of employment, he was to serve until the adjournment of Congress at a monthly stipend of $1,000. One month after his employment, X was wrongfully discharged. He availed himself of the opportunity to take a much needed vacation. After Congress adjourned he hurried back from the vacation to bring suit against the Y Mutual Benefit Association. What are his rights of recovery?
8. X contracted to ship Y 1,000 head of cattle. While the cattle were en route, they were held up by the imposition of quarantine regulations, thus preventing X from fulfilling the contract in the manner he had contemplated. Is X liable to Y for damages?
9. Defendant had contracted to supply plaintiff with certain wood paving blocks. In an action for damages for nonperformance, defendant contended that his inability to perform was caused by a shortage of railroad cars and that consequently he was legally excused from performance. Answer this contention.
10. Defendant contracted with plaintiff—who, in turn, had contracted for the construction of a school building for the city X—to furnish all labor and material necessary to complete all millwork requirements. Defendant failed to perform, and in an action for damages his defense was that the destruction of his millwork factory by fire made it impossible for him to perform as he had agreed. Is this a good defense?
11. A had agreed to erect a number of oil derricks for B. While the derricks were in the process of construction, A was fatally injured. B brought an action against the personal representative of A for failure to complete the performance. The representative of A contends that the death of A excused further performance. Result?
12. X had practically completed his contract to construct a business building for Y when the building was completely destroyed by fire. Neither X nor Y had insured the building. Is X obligated to complete the structure in accordance with the contract?
13. An opera singer agreed to appear six days before the beginning of his engagement for the purpose of rehearsals. He appeared only two days before the opening, and the manager refused to honor the contract. Can the opera singer recover for breach of contract?
14. Suppose that in Problem 13 the opera singer had arrived two days after the scheduled opening of his concert. Would your answer be the same?
15. The plaintiff built a country residence for the defendant at a cost of upwards of $77,000, and now sues to recover a balance of $3,483.46 remaining unpaid. The work of construction ceased in June, 1914, and the defendant then began to occupy the dwelling. There was no complaint of defective performance until March, 1915. One of the specifications for the plumbing work provides that "all wrought-iron pipe must be well-galvanized, lap-welded pipe of the grade known as 'standard pipe,' of Reading manufacture." The defendant learned in March, 1915, that some of the pipe, instead of being made in Reading, was

the product of other factories. The plaintiff was accordingly directed by the architect to do the work anew. The plumbing was then incased within the walls, except in a few places where it had to be exposed. Obedience to the order meant more than the substitution of other pipe. It meant the demolition at great expense of substantial parts of the completed structure. The plaintiff left the work untouched, and asked for a certificate that the final payment was due. Refusal of the certificate was followed by this suit.

The evidence sustains a finding that the omission of the prescribed brand of pipe was neither fraudulent nor willful. It was the result of the oversight and inattention of the plaintiff's subcontractor. Reading pipe is distinguished from Cohoes pipe and other brands only by the name of the manufacturer stamped upon it at intervals of between 6 and 7 feet. Even the defendant's architect, though he inspected the pipe upon arrival, failed to notice the discrepancy. The plaintiff tried to show that the brands installed, though made by other manufacturers, were the same in quality, in appearance, in market value, and in cost, as the brand stated in the contract—that they were, indeed, the same thing, though manufactured in another place. The evidence was excluded, and a verdict directed for the defendant. Decide. (*Jacob* v. *Kent,* 230 N.Y. 239)

16. X, manager of an advertising agency, agreed to pay Y $500 a month upon the condition that he obtain at least two clients for the agency monthly. It was also agreed that if Y should fail to refrain from the use of intoxicating liquors, he would receive only $200 a month. During the first month, Y obtained the required number of clients but he failed in his resolve of abstinence. Can X enforce the provision to pay Y only $200?
17. X sold a stock of merchandise to Y, agreeing to make delivery on June 1. Y, however, was to make payment on May 15. Y failed to do as he had undertaken, and X sued him for breach of contract. Y set up the defense that X had made no tender of the merchandise as required by law. Is Y correct in his contention?
18. A and B entered into a contract whereby A agreed to convey his farm to B by warranty deed on June 1 and B agreed to pay the purchase price in cash on the same day. B paid $100 down as "earnest money." Neither A nor B did anything to consummate the deal on June 1. On June 15, A requested B to drop into his office "sometime soon, and I will execute the deed." B now elects to drop the deal and recover his deposit. What are the rights of A and B against each other?
19. Plaintiff agreed to install a heating system for defendant. It was also agreed that payment was to be made when the system was accepted as being satisfactory to defendant. Does defendant's dissatisfaction necessarily mean that plaintiff cannot recover?

11 CONTRACTS:

DISCHARGE OF CONTRACTUAL OBLIGATIONS

Of necessity, some of the methods by which contractual obligations are or may be terminated have already been considered in previous chapters. For example, there was the right of unilateral rescission based on a lack of real intent due to such things as mistake, fraud, and duress, and the right of rescission because of incompetency. In the chapter on performance it was shown that under certain circumstances a contracting party is legally excused from fulfilling his contractual obligations and that the right of rescission exists for a breach of a condition or a failure of substantial performance. This chapter will deal with the termination of contractual obligations by methods that have not been specifically considered heretofore.

► I. BY OPERATION OF LAW

A. STATUTE OF LIMITATIONS

By statutory provisions the states specify the periods of time within which various types of actions must be brought. A failure to comply generally has the effect of depriving the injured party of his legal remedy. Whenever there has been a failure to take action on a contractual obligation within the time provided, the obligation is said to have become outlawed. For all intents and purposes, the contractual liability has been discharged, since it can no longer be enforced. Some statutes specifically declare that the promise is discharged by lapse of time.

The periods of time allowed for the bringing of action upon the various types of contracts should be ascertained from local statutes. Usually, different periods of time are specified for written and for oral contracts.

The court in *Bettman* v. *Cowley,* 19 Wash. 207, characterized statutes of limitations as being "statutes of repose, intended to put at rest controverted questions of fact, to insure to a degree certainty in testimony by compelling its production before it is affected by the infirmities of memory."

B. BY BANKRUPTCY

Under the federal bankruptcy statute, known as the Bankruptcy Act, an insolvent debtor may be relieved of his various obligations by the proper procedure.

C. BY JUDGMENT

It is self-evident that when a judgment has been obtained for a breach of contract, the contractual obligation is wiped out. The judgment debt takes the place of the contractual promise and represents an entirely different type of obligation.

► II. BY MUTUAL AGREEMENT

A. MUTUAL RESCISSION

Agreements that are *wholly executory* may be terminated by an agreement of the parties not to hold each other bound. The consideration to support their mutual promises consists of the promises of each to the other to give up the legal right to hold the other to his obligation under the contract.

A partially executed contract—one which has been performed by only one of the parties—cannot be discharged by a mere agreement to that effect. The party who has not performed his part of the contract has given no consideration to support the promise of discharge.*

B. BY NOVATION

A *novation* is defined as a bilateral agreement for the substitution of one obligation for another. It is a situation in which an old obligation is discharged and a new obligation substituted in its place. The obligee agrees to look to the new obligation for satisfaction. A failure to realize upon the new obligation, however, will not revive the old one. When, therefore, the parties change the terms of an existing contract, a novation has been effected. Let us suppose that A owes B $100 on an open-book account, which is secured by a chattel mortgage on A's car. If B accepts a promissory note payable in one year in discharge of the original obligation, he can no longer resort to the old obligation and the security for satisfaction, both being discharged by acceptance of the note—by a novation.

A novation can also be effected by the substitution of a new party for one of the original contracting parties.† All parties must agree, in this case, that the obligee will look only to the new obligor for satisfaction.[1] A contracts, for example, to drill a well for B but finds it impossible to proceed with the work because of financial difficulties. He induces X to take over the contract and secures B's consent that he, A, will be released from his contractual obligation.

C. ACCORD AND SATISFACTION

An accord and satisfaction is an arrangement whereby a contractual obligation is discharged by a substitute performance. To have an accord and satisfaction, it is necessary that the substitute performance be completed before the original obligation is discharged. In this respect it differs from a novation, under which not a per-

* See page 92.

† See page 256.

[1] Somers & Sons v. Le Clerc, p. 320.

formance but a mere obligation is substituted for the original obligation. Under a novation, moreover, the new agreement completely discharges the old one, whereas, under an agreement of accord and satisfaction, the new agreement must be fully performed before the old one is discharged. The *accord* is the making of the new agreement and the *satisfaction* is its performance in discharge of the original obligation.

► III. BY ARBITRATION AND AWARD

The right of settling controversies by arbitration and award has long been recognized under the common law as another method by which contractual obligations may be discharged. If there is a controversy respecting their rights and obligations, contracting parties may submit the disagreement to friendly third parties and agree to abide by their findings. In this way, the matter can be cheaply and expeditiously disposed of with the possibility of avoiding future litigation.

The arbitration proceedings are not binding upon the parties until and unless they allow the arbiters to complete their findings and make an award. The award liquidates the obligation that under the contract was in dispute. Unless the obligor honors the award, the obligee can bring a legal action and reduce it to a judgment.

Many states provide statutory procedure for the submission of controversies to arbitration and award. Usually neither party has the right to revoke the submission without the consent of the other, and the award is given the force and effect of a jury verdict, upon which a judgment may be entered.

► IV. MATERIAL ALTERATION

Any person who takes it upon himself to materially alter a contract or who makes himself a party to a material alteration without consent of the other party thereby deprives himself of all rights under the original contract. Neither has he, of course, any rights under the contract in its altered form. A material alteration consists of any change that will have the effect of altering the contractual obligation or the legal relationships of the parties, as those rights and relationships were evidenced by the original writing. To illustrate:

In *Griffen Grocery Co.* v. *Carson Grocery Co.*, 174 Okla. 96, the defendant had entered into a written contract with the plaintiff whereby the latter agreed to ship flour on open account. The plaintiff subsequently changed the contract to read "payment upon delivery by the carrier." Defendant refused to carry out the contract in its altered form; the plaintiff sued. The court denied the plaintiff the right to recover, holding this change to be a material alteration. They said:

> "An alteration of a written contract becomes material when it may have the effect to enlarge, extend, or diminish the duties, liabilities, or obligations of the obligor or promisor, in any manner not in contemplation of the parties at the time of execution, if done without the knowledge or consent of the party to be bound."

An instrument so altered ceases to be the contract executed, and the law does not make new contracts or enforce new and different liabilities, not in contemplation of the parties when they contracted. The right to disaffirm an altered contract must, however, be exercised within a reasonable period of time.[2]

▶ V. PAYMENT BY NEGOTIABLE INSTRUMENT

As a matter of business convenience, performance of a contractual obligation to pay a specific sum of money is frequently accomplished by the use of a negotiable instrument, such as a check. The acceptance of the check by the creditor will not in itself discharge the obligation unless such has been specifically agreed to. In the absence of such an agreement, acceptance of the check as a discharge of the obligation is conditioned upon the check being collectible.[3] Thus, if A indorses a check upon which X is the drawer to B as payment of an obligation, this will not constitute performance on the part of A unless B can realize upon the check.

▶ VI. TENDER OF PERFORMANCE

A. TENDER OF MONEY

A creditor need not accept performance until the obligation is due. It is his right to continue in his position as a creditor until the maturity date. He has no right, however, to refuse payment at maturity. If the debtor makes a proper tender of payment, its refusal by the creditor will have the following effect:

(1) It will not discharge the obligation to pay.

(2) It will, however, relieve the debtor of any further interest obligation upon the debt.

(3) It will prevent the creditor from recovering court costs from the debtor if he subsequently brings suit.

(4) It will serve to release the creditor's security interest in any property which was given to secure the debt. Thus, if the debtor has given his creditor a chattel mortgage upon his car, a tender of payment of the obligation will release the encumbrance upon the car.

The tender of payment must be for the exact amount due.[4] It has been held, for example, that where a tender is too small by nine cents it is, in effect, no tender. And, as a general rule, a tender in the form of a check, even if certified, is not sufficient.*

B. TENDER OF SPECIFIC ARTICLE

Where the contractual obligation is to deliver a specific thing, a tender of such thing will fully discharge the obligation. If the thing tendered is refused, the

* See Cornelius v. Cook, p. 322.

[2] Martin v. Hartley, p. 321.

[3] Cornelius v. Cook, p. 322.

[4] Aviation Industries v. East & West Ins. Co., p. 324.

tenderer holds the property as a bailee for the other party. After the refusal of the tender, the property is held by the one who made the tender at the risk and expense of the party to whom it was tendered.

Local statutes should be consulted as to the requirements and effect of tender.

CASES

CASE NO. 1

Somers & Sons v. Le Clerc. 8 A. (2d) 663, 124 A.L.R. 1494 (Vt.) (1939)

SHERBURNE, J., delivered the opinion of the court:

This is an action of contract in which it is alleged that in consideration of the discharge of an indebtedness due from the defendant's mother the defendant promised to pay it out of the rents and profits of her mother's real estate and out of the proceeds from its sale. The case comes here upon exceptions to the direction of a verdict in favor of the defendant.

It was conceded that the plaintiff had a valid account against the defendant's mother, and, viewing the evidence most favorably to the plaintiff, it appeared that on February 12, 1934, the defendant came to the plaintiff's store and had a talk with Fred I. Somers, plaintiff's general manager, in which she said that her mother could not pay the account, and he said that he wished someone to assume responsibility, whereupon she said that she would assume the account in her name and make small monthly payments, and stated that she was going to look after her mother's property and affairs, that they hoped they could sell the property for enough to clean up their accounts, and that they would pay in full if they sold for enough to pay what they owed. At this time she paid ten dollars on account, and he directed the bookkeeper to transfer the account into defendant's name and to send future statements to her. . . .

. . . For the purposes of this case it is unnecessary to go as far as § 421 of the Restatement of Contracts does where it provides:

> "A payment or other performance by a third person, accepted by a creditor as full or partial satisfaction of his claim discharges the debtor's duty in accordance with the terms on which the third party offered it. But the debtor on learning of the payment or other performance has power by disclaimer within a reasonable time to make the payment or other performance inoperative as a discharge."

But we do hold, particularly in view of the relationship of the parties, their living together, the mother's inability to pay and the long time that has elapsed, that, in the absence of any showing to the contrary, the jury could have rightfully inferred that the defendant's assumption of her mother's debt was either authorized or subsequently ratified by her mother. Hence the jury could have found that the plaintiff discharged the account against the mother upon the defendant's promise to assume it. The validity of the account having been conceded, such findings would have made out a novation by substitution of a new debtor, which requires a mutual agreement between the three parties, the creditor, his immediate debtor, and the intended new debtor, by which the liability of the last named is accepted in discharge of the original debt. Peters v.

Estate of Poro, 96 Vt. 95, 107, 117 Atl. 244, 25 A.L.R. 615; Manley Bros. Co. v. Somers, 100 Vt. 292, 297, 137 Atl. 336. The former case and the cases cited therein show that the discharge of the original debt is a sufficient consideration for the new promise, and that the new promise is not within the statute of frauds, P.L. 1675, requiring a special promise to answer for the debt of another to be in writing, but is an independent contract and provable as such. Both cases hold that a novation is never presumed, but that there must be a clear and definite intention on the part of all concerned that such is the purpose of the agreement, and that the existence of such an intention may be found, although there is nothing positive in the agreement, it being a question to be decided from all the circumstances. Such an intention could have been found by the jury.

Judgment reversed, and cause remanded.

CASE NO. 2

Martin v. Hartley. 208 Miss. 112, 43 So. (2d) 875 (1950)

LEE, J. Appellees, J. K. Hartley and wife Ellen Hartley, instituted this suit against appellant, J. C. Martin, Sr., to cancel a lease contract on certain land. . . . The lower court declined to cancel the lease. . . .

The issue was clear cut, and the substantial facts were as follows: During the month of October 1944, the appellees were property owners in the town of State Line. Appellant was in the sawmill business, and desired to lease from the appellees a site on which to locate a mill, yard, etc. Hartley and Martin went upon the land, viewed the same and agreed upon the terms. Subsequently, Martin prepared the lease contract himself, using, as he claimed, the description, which was given him by Hartley, and mailed the instrument to Hartley for signature and acknowledgment by himself and wife. Thereafter the instrument, acknowledged December 11, 1944, was received by Martin. The sawmill was installed and full operations were commenced. There was no friction of any kind between the parties. A large portion of the property was used by the appellant in connection with the business for about a year and a half without objection or protest from the appellees—their residence was situated nearby, and they could see and observe what was going on. Finally appellant was about to move one of his employees into a house on this land, when Hartley went to him and protested that the employee was undesirable. Up to this point, there is no substantial dispute. Nothing had marred the apparent satisfactory relations between the parties.

During the conversation about the undesirable employee, Hartley charged that Martin had encroached on the "still lot," which was reserved; that he had expressly written this into the lease before signing, and asked to see the lease. Martin said he was unable to locate it —it was Saturday, a payday—but that he would find it and let him see it the next week. Thereupon Hartley procured counsel and instituted this proceeding. . . .

The evidence for the appellees tended to show that when the lease was received, there was no reservation of the "still lot"—a lot on which a turpentine still was located; that before acknowledging, Hartley wrote on the margin where the description began with pencil, "still lot reserved"; that the pencil writing was erased; that "100 feet x 100 feet still lot reserved" was written with typewriter in lieu thereof, without the knowledge or consent of appellees; that the "still lot" was actually 200 by 272 feet; that this type was heavier than that in the body of the description. In other words, the instrument had been deliberately altered after its execution. . . .

On this issue of fact, the learned chancellor was warranted in finding that the appellant had altered the instrument. He heard the witnesses, observed their demeanor on the stand, and saw the original instrument itself. It is elemental that this Court will not reverse a chancellor on a finding of fact, where such finding is sustained by substantial evidence. . . .

The complaint of appellees . . . is that, since the court found that the appellant . . . had made a material alteration in the contract, the same should have been cancelled. To this end, they cite a number of cases. . . .

In those cases, the aggrieved parties knew nothing of the alteration, as here, but, in addition, did nothing to evidence acquiescence in the result of the alteration. On the contrary, they acted timely. In the case here, appellees stood by for a year and a half without objection or protest and permitted Martin to occupy, use, enjoy the benefits of this parcel of land, and make a large investment thereon, as though he had the legal right thereto. But for the friction over moving the alleged disagreeable employee, we are justified in believing that this contract would not have been questioned. They must, therefore, be held to have acquiesced, and thereby consented to such use of this land. To direct the cancellation of the contract, under such circumstances, would be in conflict with the well known principles of equitable estoppel. See 19 Am. Jur. 678, as follows:

> ". . . The rule is well recognized that where a party with full knowledge, or with sufficient notice or means of knowledge, of his rights and of all the material facts remains inactive for a considerable time or abstains from impeaching a contract or transaction, or freely does what amounts to a recognition thereof as existing, or acts in a manner inconsistent with its repudiation and so as to affect or interfere with the relation and situation of the parties, so that the other party is induced to suppose that it is recognized, this amounts to an acquiescence and the transaction, although originally impeachable, becomes unimpeachable." . . .

CASE NO. 3

Cornelius v. Cook. 213 S.W. (2d) 767 (Tex.) (1948)

LONG, J. On the 9th day of November, 1938, appellants F. M. and G. W. Cornelius borrowed $100.00 from Mary Dell Cook and as security therefor, executed a deed of trust covering each of their 1/16th interest in a one-half section of land. . . . Nothing was paid upon the indebtedness and the appellee Mary Dell Cook foreclosed the same under the power given in the deed of trust and sold the property through a trustee and on September 7, 1943, received from the trustee a deed to all of the interest of the appellants in such one-half section of land.

Appellants instituted this suit to cancel the trustee's deed upon the ground that appellee had been tendered the entire amount due upon such debt prior to foreclosure. . . .

The controlling question presented is, did appellants, prior to the foreclosure proceedings, make legal tender to appellee of the total amount of principal and interest due on the note. If they did make legal tender, then the trial court should have granted appellants' motion for judgment and should have entered a judgment in their favor. On the other hand, if legal tender was not made, then the trial court was correct in granting appellee's motion for judgment. . . .

The parties to this suit all reside in Texarkana, Arkansas. Gail Cornelius, the son of appellant F. M. Cornelius, in July, 1943, was a soldier in the United States Army. He came home on a furlough and he and his father had a conversation with appellee, Mary Dell Cook, with reference to the note due her by his father and his uncle. We quote from the testimony of F. M. Cornelius as follows:

"Q. Mr. Cornelius, talk so the Jury can hear, and tell only what you did. A. Me and my son went over there, and he said, 'Now, Mary Dell, here is your money, a check for your money. All you have got to do is get the note and sign it.' And she said, 'I haven't got it, but as Uncle Bill is going to sell it, let him alone until he sells the place and we will settle up then.' And then he said, 'Here is your money; all you have got to do is get the note, and it will be square,' and she refused. All I could do was offer."

The burden of proving a tender rests upon the party alleging a tender. 62 C.J., p. 698, § 101. It is not contended that appellants tendered Mary Dell Cook any money. All the evidence shows that the only tender made was a check. The evidence fails to show the amount of such check. The check was not offered in evidence and no explanation is given as to why it was not offered. There is no evidence showing upon what bank the check was drawn nor is there any evidence that Gail Cornelius had an account with any bank. The evidence fails to show that if appellee had accepted the check that the same would have been paid when in due course of business it might have been presented to the bank. The law is settled that for a check to have the effect of payment, the drawer thereof must have sufficient funds to his credit in the bank to pay the same or proof must be made that such check, when presented in the usual course of business, would be paid by the bank on which it is drawn. . . .

It is further the law that in order to make a valid tender, the thing to be tendered must be actually produced and offered to the party entitled thereto and the tenderer must place the money or property in such a position that his control over it is relinquished for a sufficient time to enable the tenderee, if he so desires, to reduce it to possession by merely reaching out and laying hold of the money or thing. . . . There is no showing in this record that the check was ever placed in such a position that Mary Dell Cook could reach out and lay hold of it or that Gail Cornelius ever surrendered his control over the check at any time. He told her, in effect, if and when she got the note and signed it, he would give her the check. The check was not then offered her but the offer was predicated upon appellee getting possession of the note and signing it.

Ordinarily, a tender of a debt payable in money must be made by money and a tender of a check is not sufficient. We recognize the rule that under certain circumstances, the offer of a check in payment of a debt will constitute a tender. In other words, where the tender is refused on account of a specific objection, then if the tenderee does not object because the tender is not made in money, he waives his right to thereafter insist the tender was not made of money. As we view the evidence in this case, appellee did not unqualifiedly refuse to accept the tender. If it should be held that she did refuse such tender, there is nothing in the record showing upon what ground or grounds such refusal was predicated. However, in view of the holdings made above, it is not necessary that we pass upon the question of waiver in this case.

. . . Under the facts there was no legal tender as a matter of law.

CASE NO. 4

Aviation Industries v. East and West Ins. Co. 211 P. (2d) 156 (Idaho) (1949)

PORTER, J. This is an action to recover on a policy of insurance for damages to an aircraft. An aircraft belonging to the respondent was flown on July 23, 1946, from Coeur d'Alene to Boise. . . .

The aircraft was delivered to respondent March 12, 1947, together with a bill for $2,717.94 for repairs and replacements, which bill was paid by respondent. The appellant having refused to reimburse the respondent, this action was instituted for the recovery of such sum, less $300 cash deductible as provided by the policy. . . . By its answer, appellant admitted that the damage to said airplane amounted to the sum of $1,665.72 and tendered said sum, less the cash deductible, in full settlement of respondent's claim. A trial was had to the court sitting without a jury which resulted in a judgment in favor of respondent in the sum of $2,130.99 with interest thereon from March 13, 1947, together with costs in the sum of $16.10. From such judgment appellant prosecutes this appeal.

. . . By specifications of error Nos. VI and VII, appellant complains of the allowance of interest and costs to the respondent on the ground that no interest after the tender by appellant, and no costs should have been allowed. This would be true if the court had found that the amount due was the amount of the tender. However, where the amount found due by the court was in excess of the tender, then, costs were properly allowable. Section 12–110, I.C. Also, the amount tendered being less than the amount found due by the court, such tender did not estop the accumulation of interest upon any part of the debt. Smith v. Faris-Kesl Const. Co., 27 Idaho 407, 150 Pac. 25.

. . . judgment of the trial court . . . affirmed.

Review Questions

1. What do you believe to be the public policy underlying the requirement that aggrieved parties must take legal action within a specified period of time?
2. Construct a fact situation illustrating a mutual rescission.
3. Construct a fact situation illustrating a novation by the substitution of a new obligation and one illustrating the substitution of a new party.
4. What are the elements of an accord and satisfaction?
5. In what respect is an accord and satisfaction different from a novation?
6. What statutory provision is made in your state for settling controversies by arbitration and award?
7. What test is applied in determining whether a contractual alteration is material?
8. When will a delivery and acceptance of a check as payment of a debt constitute a legal discharge of the debt?
9. Can a creditor be required to accept payment of a debt before it is due?

10. What is the effect of a tender of payment?
11. What constitutes a sufficient tender?

Problems for Discussion

1. A is B's tenant under a five-year lease. After the lease had run for two years, A and B mutually agreed to reduce the rent by one half for the duration of the five-year term. Has there been a mutual rescission of the original five-year lease?
2. Defendant leased a hotel building from plaintiff and immediately assigned the lease to X without the knowledge or consent of plaintiff. In an action to recover rent, defendant contends that a novation had been effected and that he is no longer a party to the lease. Result?
3. A contracted to furnish B with certain nursery stock. Unable to furnish the varieties contracted for, A proposed to B that he furnish other specified varieties for the same price. This proposal was accepted by B, and the substitute varieties were delivered. In view of the fact that the substituted nursery stock was of substantially less value than that originally contracted for, can B recover from A for breach of the original contract?
4. A leased premises from B; the lease provided that the landlord B agreed "to put heater, range, and plumbing in good order." Subsequent to the time of execution of the lease, B obliterated this clause in the lease. A contends he is released from any further obligation under the lease. Result?
5. The plaintiffs made a contract with Moulton and Bromley, as partners, to build a machine. After a small part of the work had been done, the partnership was dissolved and Moulton gave notice of this to plaintiffs and informed them he would no longer be responsible for the contract. Plaintiffs agreed to release Moulton from the contract and agreed to look solely to Bromley. Plaintiffs completed the machine and now look to Moulton for the contract price. Decide. (*Collyer* v. *Moulton,* 9 R.I. 90)
6. Plaintiff sold his retail grocery and meat stock and business, together with the tools and store fixtures, to defendants on a title retaining contract. For the balance of the purchase price, plaintiff accepted defendants' note for $2,500. Defendants ran the business for a time and then sold it, with plaintiff's consent, to one Schadel. Schadel gave plaintiff his note for $2,500, and later gave a chattel mortgage on the stock to secure it; but plaintiff did not surrender defendants' note. Schadel was not successful; he was soon in bankruptcy. Failing to receive his pay from Schadel, plaintiff brought this action on the old note given by defendants. Decide. (*Ceabuske* v. *Smolary,* 229 Mich. 100)
7. X met his creditor Y at a public meeting and tendered payment of the debt. Y refused to accept payment, since he was uncertain as to the amount due and was in no position to ascertain the facts. Was this a sufficient tender?
8. Would the statement by a debtor to his creditor, "I am going to pay you," without displaying the money constitute a valid tender?

Agency

Chapter

12. NATURE AND CREATION OF AGENCY RELATIONSHIP

13. RIGHTS AND LIABILITIES OF PRINCIPAL TO THIRD PARTY FOR ACTS OF AGENT

14. RIGHTS AND LIABILITIES AS BETWEEN AGENT AND THIRD PARTY

15. RIGHTS AND DUTIES AS BETWEEN PRINCIPAL AND AGENT

16. TERMINATION OF AGENCY RELATIONSHIP

12 AGENCY:

NATURE AND CREATION OF AGENCY RELATIONSHIP

Employment relationships result from the desire of individuals to use others to accomplish given tasks. Depending very largely upon the nature of the tasks to be performed, employment relationships are classified as being either those of (1) master and servant, (2) independent contractor, or (3) principai and agent.

► I. SERVANT AND AGENT DISTINGUISHED

A servant is an employee whose function is personally to perform a task or tasks for the master, he being, in their performance, subject to the control and direction of his employer. One employed, for example, as a bookkeeper or an elevator operator would be a servant. An *agent,* on the other hand, is one who is employed to act for and in place of the employer. The agent is the representative of the principal (the employer) in the transaction of business with others. If A is employed to make purchases for his employer B, he occupies the status of an agent rather than that of a servant, since his assignment relates to the transaction of business with third persons. He is not merely performing a task, but is acting in the place of his employer. Obviously, an agent may also act in the capacity of a servant.

The principles of law applying to the relation of principal and agent also govern the more limited relation of master and servant.

► II. SERVANT DISTINGUISHED FROM INDEPENDENT CONTRACTOR

Although the term *servant* in its everyday usage denotes a person engaged in domestic service, its legal meaning is much broader. A servant is conceived as being an employee, other than an agent, who, while accomplishing an assigned task, is under the direction of and within the control of the master—the employer. In legal contemplation, an employee while in the performance of the employer's work is the embodiment of the employer. In effect, an employer extends his legal personality by making use of an employee and is held responsible for the acts done by his employee in the course of the employment.

The reader should recognize that it is possible to engage a person to accomplish a given task in a capacity other than as an employee. Thus, if A engages B to build a garage, and if B while performing the work is under the control and direction of A, a master and servant relation exists. However, if A engages B to accomplish the task of building the garage and B's only obligation to A is to accomplish the result, B stands as an independent contractor and not as an employee. An independent contractor is one who is engaged to accomplish a given result—one who is under contract to carry a task to its conclusion and who is free to choose his own course of procedure and conduct toward such an end.[1, 2, 3] As said by the court in *Moreland* v. *Mason*, 260 Pac. 1030:

> "An independent contractor is defined as one who renders services in the course of an occupation, representing the will of the employer only as to the results of the work, and not as to the means by which it is accomplished."

There are very practical reasons for the need to make the above distinction. In the first place, as a general rule, an independent contractor is alone responsible for his acts and conduct in the course of accomplishing the task, whereas an employer stands responsible for the similar acts and conduct of an employee.[4] In the second place, under modern social legislation it becomes necessary to distinguish between these capacities of employment. Thus, under workmen's compensation statutes, employees and not independent contractors are entitled to benefit payments for injuries suffered in the course of their employment, and under social security legislation, both state and federal, the compensation paid to employees only is subject to taxation.

► III. PRINCIPAL AND AGENT—THE LAW OF BUSINESS REPRESENTATION

From the point of view of modern business practice, that phase of employment relationships designated as *agency*—principal and agent—is of fundamental importance. The law of agency can very properly be viewed as the law of business representation. The function of an agent is to represent the employer in business and commercial affairs. This means that an agent is one who is empowered by the employer to contract with others for the benefit of and on behalf of the employer and to accomplish such things as the employer himself could do.

The need for business representatives is a necessary concomitant of an exchange economy that covers a market area national and international in scope. Business ventures exceeding the one-man size call for the employment of representatives in varying capacities. Well known to the business student is the present-day practice of conducting commercial and industrial affairs through various forms of business organizations such as the corporation and the partnership, which are capable of acting only through representatives.

A. THE PRINCIPAL

The law of agency is based upon the fundamental concept that he who does an act through another does it himself. The law recognizes that, generally, where a

---

[1] Glenn, Collector of Int. Rev. v. Beard, p. 335.
[2] Capitol City Lumber Co. v. Cash, p. 336.
[3] Party Cab Co. v. U.S., p. 338.
[4] Ozan Lumber Co. v. McNeeley, p. 340.

principal has the legal capacity to do a thing himself, the same may be done through a representative. To illustrate:

In the case of *McNulty* v. *Dean,* 154 Wash. 110, the question arose whether a statute giving the judgment debtor the right to retain possession of the property during the period of redemption required personal possession by the debtor. The court said:

> ". . . It is the right to possession which the statute grants, and it places no restriction on the manner in which the right may be exercised. In the absence of special restrictions, the general rule is that a person may do through the agency of another whatever he is empowered to do in his own proper person, and we find nothing in the statute, or in the situation presented, which prevents the operation of the rule in this instance."

It is inconceivable, however, that one should be allowed to serve a jail sentence by proxy or take an oath—the object of which is to search the conscience—through another. Voting, the performance of contracts for personal services, and the execution of wills are other acts that must be attended to personally. In some instances, statutes specify personal performance of certain acts.

B. THE AGENT

The question of whether an individual is qualified to act as an agent is very largely a matter of fact and not of law. The law prescribes no general requirements that one must possess to be a business representative of another. The selection of one who can act in the capacity of an agent is essentially a matter of choice by the principal. Thus, a minor may be appointed as an agent. His principal will be held responsible for his acts, although the minor agent may avoid all liability. Partnerships and corporations may also serve in the capacity of agents. Many such organizations serve as agents for others, for example, banking institutions.

1. *Legal Limitations*

An attorney at law usually serves his client as an agent. Here is an instance where the law has prescribed that an individual serving in such an agency capacity be possessed of certain qualifications. Other agents who must usually meet specific requirements as prescribed by law are brokers, realtors, auctioneers, and warehousemen.

It is also recognized that a person who has an interest that is adverse to the principal's cannot act as the latter's agent. Thus, an individual could not act as agent for both the buyer and the seller in the same transaction.*

► IV. CREATION OF AGENCY

A. BY AGREEMENT OF PARTIES

An agency relationship results from a contract of employment between the principal and the agent. The requirement for an agency to exist as a matter of

* See page 395 for a full treatment.

fact is an offer of appointment by the principal and an acceptance of the appointment by the agent. Its existence is dependent upon the intent of the parties. This intention must find expression either in words or in conduct between the principal and agent. To establish an agency, it is necessary to show either an actual expression of intent to that effect or some connection between the principal and the agent from which it may reasonably be inferred or implied that an agency relationship was intended.

An agency relationship may be created by, and exist under, an agreement unsupported by consideration.[5] The acts of an agent under a gratuitous appointment are as binding upon the principal as where consideration is present. The practical effect of a gratuitous agency is that while the agreement to act is executory, it is not binding on either of the parties. Should, however, a gratuitous agent enter upon performance of his commission, he is legally bound to perform properly and completely in accordance with his promise and to subject himself to all the duties of an agent to his principal.

1. *Form of Appointment and Authorization*

With few exceptions, the appointment of an agent may take any form. For most purposes, a parol authorization to act is as valid as is one in writing. When the agent is required to execute a formal document under seal, his authority must, however, be derived from an instrument under seal. The importance of this rule greatly diminished with the abolition of private seals in most of our states. Many states specify by statute the mode and form of appointment requisite for the exercise of agency powers for certain purposes. The most common of these requirements is that an agency dealing with, or conveying title to, real property must be in writing and executed in a certain manner. By way of illustration, Section 10049 of the 1939 Iowa Code provides: "Declarations or creations of . . . powers in relation to real estate must be executed in the same manner as deeds of conveyance."

In some states, an agent must be authorized in writing to enter into all contracts controlled by the Statute of Frauds.

B. AGENCY BY RATIFICATION

Aware of the fact that B is a pigeon fancier, A took it upon himself as a favor to B to contract for what he regarded as a unique specimen. A professed to act for and on behalf of B although no agreement of employment had ever been consummated. Obviously, B is not bound by the act of his alleged agent A. B may choose, however, to sanction the assumed agency relationship and thereby give validity to the transaction; the effect would be the same as though the agency had existed in the first instance. Such a sanction is legally known as a *ratification*. Ratification, then, means giving approval to or confirming an unauthorized act.

An effective ratification is dependent upon the existence of the following facts:

---

[5] Georgeson v. Nielsen, p. 342.

(1) The self-appointed agent must have acted for and on behalf of the alleged principal. He must have disclosed the identity of the principal for whom he professed and intended to act in such a manner as to make him ascertainable.[6]

(2) The ratification of an act relates back to the time of the commission of the act, and the rights of the parties are determined as of that time. For that reason, the ratifying principal must have not only the legal capacity to authorize the act at the time of ratification, but must also have been in existence and legally capable of performance himself at the time of the act by the professed agent. This has an important bearing upon the liability of the alleged agent. To illustrate:

(a) In the "pigeon fancier" illustration above, A, without B's ratification of the contract, is personally liable upon the contract. Should B ratify, A is relieved of this liability. The ratification relates back to the time the contract for the pigeon was entered into, which makes B a party to the contract as of that time. A was, thus, in effect acting for a disclosed principal and consequently has no liability under the contract.

(b) It is a customary, proper, and necessary practice for promoters to enter into contracts on behalf of corporations prior to their formation. A promoter may, for example, profess to act as an agent in entering into an option contract for the purchase of property to be used by the contemplated corporation. Upon coming into being, the corporation cannot ratify such contract since the corporation was not in existence and capable of acting at the time of its consummation. If a corporation takes over a promoter's contract, it becomes a party to the contract as of the time of the adoption and not as of the time it was entered into. Since the corporation cannot ratify the contract, the promoter remains personally liable upon the contract.

Let us suppose that X, a promoter, acting as the agent of a proposed corporation, contracts for the purchase of property that is to be used by the corporation after its formation. The corporation upon coming into existence adopts the contract of purchase. The corporation becomes a party to the contract as of the time of adoption and not as of the time the contract was entered into. Thus, X was not acting for a principal at the time he contracted and he remains personally liable. If the corporation becomes insolvent before the purchase price is paid, X can be looked to for payment.

(3) A valid and binding ratification is further dependent upon the condition that the ratifier be possessed of full knowledge of the facts pertaining to the transaction.[7, 8] To illustrate:

(a) Let us suppose that A had entered into the employ of B without any agreement as to the rate of pay. Since A and B could come to no understanding upon this matter, X, an attorney, took it upon himself in behalf of A to negotiate a settlement with B. The figure of 60 cents an hour was agreed upon,

---

[6] Valaske v. Wirtz, p. 343.
[7] Bond Rubber Corp. v. Oates Bros., p. 344.
[8] Kirkpatrick v. Williams, p. 345.

10 per cent of which was to be taken in merchandise. The rate of 60 cents an hour being quite satisfactory to A, he ratified the settlement. He had not, however, been apprised of the fact that 10 per cent was to be taken in merchandise. Consequently, the ratification was not binding.

Under certain circumstances, the ratifier has the duty of ascertaining the true state of affairs surrounding the transaction to be ratified. Should he be in possession of the means of ascertaining the material facts, the ratification is binding without an actual knowledge of such facts. The same holds true where a knowledge of the facts is deliberately waived.

1. *Form of Ratification*

Like the appointment or authorization of an agent, the act of ratification is usually not required to take any particular form. Ordinarily, any indicated assent to be bound is sufficient.[9] An acceptance of the benefits resulting from the assumed agent's act is interpreted as an intention by the alleged principal to be bound. An acceptance of the benefits also carries with it an assumption of the obligations. A ratification must cover the act as a whole and not in part only. In those instances where the appointment or authorization of an agent is required to be in a certain form, the ratification must take like form.

C. AGENCY AS A MATTER OF LAW—ESTOPPEL

In the interests of justice and equity, the law may recognize the existence of an agency relationship even though none exists as a matter of fact. Such an agency is based upon an estoppel brought about by the conduct of the alleged principal. An *estoppel* is a rule of law that prevents one from asserting the true state of affairs. The essentials for its existence are: (1) a change of position by a person in (2) justifiable reliance upon (3) the conduct of another. Consequently, where one, by his action or failure to act, allows another to change his position in the reasonable belief that an agency exists, the law will invoke an agency by estoppel even though none in fact exists. To illustrate:

In *Hannon* v. *Siegel-Cooper Co.,* 167 N.Y. 244, the facts were that A was engaged in the practice of dentistry, having his office in the defendant's department store. The defendant advertised the dental practice as being one of its departments when in fact A was carrying on the practice on his own account. The plaintiff sued the defendant for damages suffered as a result of unskillful treatment of her teeth by A. The defendant had, by his actions, given others the right to believe that A was his employee—that an agency relation existed. Consequently, the defendant was held liable upon the basis of an agency by estoppel.

[9] Sullivan v. Bennett, p. 346.

CASES

CASE NO. 1

Glenn, Collector of Internal Revenue v. Beard. 141 F. (2d) 376 (1944)

MC ALLISTER, J. The Collector of Internal Revenue levied and collected Social Security taxes from appellee, who, thereafter, filed a petition in the district court for refund and was awarded a judgment therefor. The court held that appellee was not an employer; that the workers, upon whose asserted employment the taxes were levied, were independent contractors; . . .

The question presented by this appeal is whether the workers in question are independent contractors, exempt from the provisions of the statute, or whether they are employees, subject to the Act.

Appellee maintains studios in Kentucky, where, for many years, she has engaged women to make comforters, quilts, and similar articles. The women do the work in their homes on farms, within a 25-mile radius of a studio. Appellee supplies materials stamped with designs, and specifications for the work are agreed upon. The material and thread, together with the specifications or instructions, are delivered to the worker at the time of the signing of a contract by the worker and appellee. The contract provides that the homeworker will work the material according to the specifications; that the work may be done at such times—within a designated period—and at such places, as are agreeable to the worker; and that, further, the worker may do the work personally or by agents of her selection. It is also provided that, upon completion of the specified work and its delivery to the appellee, a certain price will be paid to the worker, who is responsible for any damage or injury to the materials while they are in her possession.

There was no supervision of the work and appellee never even called at the homes of the workers to inspect the work. . . . Appellee had no right to withdraw the work from a homemaker while it was being worked upon and within the time limit provided by the contract. Other individuals and companies were engaged in the same kind of business as appellee, and often homeworkers would be engaged in working on various materials for several such concerns at the same time, interspersing such work with their household duties. They only worked when they wanted to, and at such times in the year as their farm duties permitted them.

According to the pertinent regulations of the Commissioner of Internal Revenue, promulgated under Title IX of the Social Security Act, it is provided:

> "In general, if an individual is subject to the control or direction of another merely as to the result to be accomplished by the work and not as to the means and method of accomplishing the result, he is an independent contractor, not an employee."

Treasury Regulation No. 90, Art. 205. The Regulation is in harmony with the assumption that the Act took over the term "employee" as the common law knew it,

> "for it enumerates the generally accredited determinants in such cases, of which the most important is the putative employer's control over the employee's business."

. . . As was said in Ruth Bros. v. Stambaugh's Adm'r, 275 Ky. 677, 122 S.W. (2d) 501:

> "The main question in all cases of this type is whether or not the one who is claimed to be an independent contractor has contracted to do the work according to his own methods and without being subject to the control of his employer except as to the result of his work."

We agree with the conclusion of the district court that the homeworkers were independent contractors and not employees.

In a case concerned with similar homeworkers, this court recently held that they were covered by the provisions of the Fair Labor Standards Act (Walling v. American Needlecrafts, Inc., 139 F. (2d) 60), and appellant relies upon that decision as determinative of the question before us. In the Needlecrafts case, however, the controlling factor was the broad statutory definition of employ. " 'Employ' includes to suffer or permit to work." It was held in the case above referred to that, from the legislative history of the statute in question, and of the subsequently proposed and rejected amendments thereto, there was evinced the intention of Congress, for the purposes of fair labor standards, to treat homemakers as any other type of employee. The fact that such workers may be independent contractors does not, of itself, exclude them from the application of the Fair Labor Standards Act; they are embraced in the classification of employees, within the intendment of that statute, if they are *suffered* or *permitted* to work. But there is no such definition or provision relating to employment or employees in the Social Security Act. . . . Employment under this statute is to be understood in its ordinary sense, as meaning the legal relationship of employer and employee; . . .

The Social Security Act must be liberally construed to effect its purposes

> "to save men and women from the rigors of the poor house as well as from the haunting fear that such a lot awaits them when journey's end is near,"

as said by Mr. Justice Cardozo in Helvering v. Davis, 301 U.S. 619, 57 Sup. Ct. 904. However, almost half of all the persons gainfully occupied in the United States are excluded by Congress from the benefits of the statute. We are unable to construe the Act to include appellee within its ambit, or, within its provisions, such individuals as the independent contractors in this case.

The judgment of the district court is affirmed.

CASE NO. 2

Capitol City Lumber Co. v. Cash. 214 Ark. 35, 214 S.W. (2d) 363 (1948)

MC FADDIN, J. Appellees recovered judgment against appellant for $645, as damages for the wrongful cutting and removing of timber. . . .

. . . it is admitted by both Smith and Cash . . . that the Lumber Company could cut and remove from the land all of the pine timber eight inches and above at the stump.

On October 5, 1947, Cash and Smith instituted this action against the Lumber Company, claiming that the Lumber Company had cut and removed from the land 430 trees, each of which was less than eight inches in diameter at the stump. The plaintiffs claimed actual damages in the sum of $645. . . .

Independent Contractor Issue. In the trial the Lumber Company undertook to show that J. C. Hester—the man who was in charge of collecting the felled trees and sawing them into lumber on the lands—was an independent contractor. The Lumber Company thus sought to escape liability by shifting the fault of cutting small trees to Hester, as independent contractor. The trial judge refused to submit to the jury any phase of the independent contractor theory, and this refusal is assigned as error. In fact, this is the assignment argued at the greatest length.

We have a multitude of cases stating the test to determine when the relationship of independent contractor exists. . . . In Wheeler & Co. v. Fitzpatrick, 135 Ark. 117, 205 S.W. 302, 304, Mr. Justice Wood used this language:

"Says Judge Elliott: 'An independent contractor may be defined as one who in the course of an independent occupation prosecutes and directs the work himself using his own methods to accomplish it and represents the will of the company only as to the result of his work.' 3 Elliott on Railroads, p. 1586, § 1063."

The contract between the Lumber Company and Hester was oral; and the Lumber Company sought to establish the terms of the contract by Hester. Here is his testimony on this phase of the case:

"Q. What was your agreement with the Capitol City? A. Well, I had a contract to cut that stuff and they paid me so much delivered at the mill at Little Rock.

"Q. You ran the mill on that property. A. Yes, sir.

"Q. They had their cutters? A. I was supposed to cut the logs.

"Q. Did they furnish cutters on this tract? A. Yes.

"Q. Their cutters cut the logs there and your mill sawed it up and you delivered it, after it had been sawed, to Little Rock? A. That's right.

"Q. You had a contract with them by the thousand to do this work? A. Yes.

"Q. Did they pay their own cutters? A. They paid it and held it out of my wages.

Again he testified:

"Q. They hired the cutters? A. They had their own. I didn't have any and they sent theirs out there.

"Q. Capital City sent men out to cut the timber? A. That's right.

"Q. You didn't have anything to do with them? A. Nothing more than if I were out there and noticed them cutting under eight inches I would have stopped them.

Q. You didn't do that? A. No, I didn't."

From this evidence, it is clear that the Lumber Company paid a certain amount per thousand for all timber cut, sawed and delivered; but it is also clear that the Lumber Company sent its own men on the land, who cut the trees without any supervision of, or instructions from, Hester, the alleged independent contractor. This last-mentioned fact—established by the Lumber Company's own witness—is the antithesis of the independent contractor relationship, and fully justified the trial court's refusal to submit to the jury any issue concerning independent contractor. Hester was not an independent contractor insofar as concerned the cutting of the trees, because the Lumber Company sent its own employees (cutters) into the woods, and they cut the trees without any supervision of, or instructions from, Hester. So appellant's assignment on this point is without merit. . . .

Affirmed.

CASE NO. 3

Party Cab Co. v. United States. 172 Fed. (2d) 87, 10 A.L.R. (2d) 358, cert. den. 338 U.S. 818, 70 Sup. Ct. 62 (1949)

MAJOR, CH.J. This is an appeal from a judgment adverse to the plaintiff (the taxpayer), . . . in a suit to recover from the defendant taxes alleged to have been illegally assessed and collected under the provisions of Title VIII and IX of the Social Security Act, . . .

Plaintiff is an Illinois corporation organized

"to operate taxicabs and automobiles for hire as a public and private carrier of freight and passengers; to buy and sell and deal in automobiles."

The question for decision is whether the persons designated as the drivers of plaintiff's taxicabs are, under the terms of the Act, its employees whose earnings are wages so as to make the plaintiff liable for the tax sought to be recovered. . . .

That we are presented with a perplexing problem is evident from the opposing results which have been reached and the contrariety of views expressed in a number of cases.

A study of the cases where the question has been considered discloses that varying facts account in no small measure for the contrary results which have been reached. Another factor which has played a large part is the policy pursued by the Social Security Board (hereinafter referred to as the Board) and the courts in the broadening of the concept of the term "employee" and the consequent inclusion within the coverage of the Act of a number of persons who are not in ordinary usage looked upon as employees. . . .

This brings us to a consideration of the facts. . . .

The drivers paid the plaintiff $8.00 for the use of a cab during the day shift and $9.00 for its use during the night shift. The drivers paid for the gas and oil which they used in operating the cabs, but all other expense such as maintenance, upkeep, license fees were paid by the plaintiff. Occasionally the plaintiff called meetings of the drivers to give instructions on such subjects as safe driving, forbidding drinking while on duty, how to avoid and what to do in case of accidents. The drivers had no business telephones and although not required to do so, accepted calls received in plaintiff's office. Their principal business was derived by cruising the streets of the city. The drivers had no license to operate taxicabs for hire and the operation was conducted under licenses owned by the plaintiff. The drivers received all their pay or compensation from the public. They were required to make no report to the plaintiff as to the amount so earned and received, and the plaintiff had no interest therein.

This court in Williams v. United States, 7 Cir., 126 F. (2d) 129, decided that the leader of a dance orchestra was not an employee of the establishment for which the orchestra performed. In doing so, we applied the common law test, and the Board here relies heavily upon the factors there enumerated, such as the right to hire and discharge persons doing the work, the method and determination of the manner of the payment of the workmen, whether or not the person doing the work is engaged in an independent business or enterprise, particularly, whether he stands to make a profit on those workers under him, which party furnishes the tools or materials with which the work is done, and who has control of the premises where the work is done. The factors thus enumerated are not inconsistent with Treasury Regulation 90, promulgated under the Social Security Act, which emphasizes "generally the relationship exists when the person for whom services are performed has the right to control and direct the individual who performs the services, not only as to the result to be accomplished by the work but also as to the details and means by which that result is accomplished. That is, an employee is subject to the will and control of the employer not only as to what shall be done but how it shall be done. . . . In general, if an individual is subject to the control or direction of another merely as to the result to be accomplished by the work and not as to the means and methods for accomplishing the result, he is an independent contractor, not an employee."

Thus it appears that the most important factor in determining the employer-employee relationship is that of control which the former either exercises or has the authority to exercise over the latter. In this connection, the court below found that the plaintiff did exercise

"a reasonable amount of control over the methods and means by which the drivers performed their services."

As to the control which plaintiff exercised over the drivers, the Board in its brief states:

"The taxpayer controls whether a particular individual works, when his working shift begins, how long it may last, when it ends, which taxicabs he is allowed to use, and the fact that only a particular driver may operate a taxicab during the shift in question," and it states further, "and a much more realistic and effectual control is found in the undisputed fact that violation of the taxpayer's rules or regulations might result in the taxpayer's refusing to allow the offender to take out a taxicab again."

The weakness of this argument on control lies in the fact that the elements relied upon by the Board are matters which concern the plaintiff's business rather than the services performed by the drivers. The matter of control which is material is that which the plaintiff exercised over the drivers during the period they were in possession of the cabs rather than what the plaintiff might do either prior or subsequent to such period. Considered in this light, any control exercised by the plaintiff was quite meager.

During this so-called period of employment the plaintiff had no control over the area of operation or the number of miles which the cab was to be operated. It could not require the drivers to accept a call for a taxi received by it, to telephone the office or report his whereabouts, and could not require a driver to purchase gasoline or oil from it, or to account for fares collected or for tips or gratuities received. In fact, it appears that a driver had the same freedom as to the manner and means to be employed in the operation of a taxicab as would be possessed by any other car owner or driver. The remuneration which he received was dependent solely upon his own energy, initiative and business acumen, and the plaintiff was not interested in how much money a driver made. Thus it appears that the plaintiff had little, if any, control over the details, means, and method by which the drivers performed their services, and while the plaintiff no doubt was interested in the operation to the extent that it was in the interest of its business that the public be satisfactorily served, we are unable to discern how it had any considerable authority over the accomplishment of such a result. . . .

The Board argues that the drivers are not independent contractors and, therefore, they must be employees. It is pointed out that the drivers have no capital investment, no business telephone, no regular place of business and do not advertise. . . . It is hardly accurate however, to say that the drivers have no capital investment, when they furnish the oil and gas and the labor by which they earn a livelihood. In fact, the relation between the plaintiff and the drivers appears more like some kind of a joint venture, where in the plaintiff provides the facilities for a fixed charge and the drivers contribute the fuel, their skill, energy and labor. It is pointed out that the drivers have no opportunity for profit and loss of investment, but this ignores the fact that the amount of their earnings is dependent wholly upon their own efforts. Assuming, however, that the drivers cannot be properly classified as independent contractors in the common acceptance of that term, it does not necessarily follow that they are "employees" within the meaning of the Act. . . .

Another factor which we think strongly militates against the employer-employee relationship is that the "wages" which afford the basis for the tax were received from the public and not the plaintiff. And the services performed by the drivers and for which such "wages" were received were rendered directly to the public. Thus the public received the benefit of their services and compensated them therefor. . . .

While there is room for argument on both sides of the question presented for decision, we are of the view that under the amended definition of the term "employee," taking into consideration as we must the congressional purpose and direction, the drivers under the circumstances of the instant case are not included within the term. It follows that the tax was illegally assessed and collected and that the plaintiff was entitled to recover. . . .

CASE NO. 4

Ozan Lumber Co. v. McNeely. 214 Ark. 657, 217 S.W. (2d) 341, 8 A.L.R. (2d) 261 (1949)

MILLWEE, J. Appellant, Ozan Lumber Co., has appealed from judgments rendered against it and C. M. Kirby in favor of appellees, Ruth McNeely, Pearl McClelland, J. V. McClelland, Jr., a minor, and Wallace Moorehead, for damages on account of injuries resulting from a collision of an automobile in which appellees were riding and a truck owned and operated by C. M. Kirby at the time of the collision. . . .

The original complaints alleged that C.M. Kirby was the driver of the log truck and working for Ozan Lumber Co. and for himself at the time of the collision. Amendments to the complaints were later filed alleging that

> "the defendant, Ozan Lumber Company, was further negligent in employing C. M. Kirby to haul logs for it, knowing that he was a reckless, careless and negligent driver, or at least had this knowledge prior to the time of the accident complained of herein and was negligent in retaining him."

The answers of appellant denied generally the allegations of the complaint and specifically that Kirby was acting for it in any capacity at the time of the accident, . . . The cases were consolidated for trial resulting in judgments aggregating $36,000. Kirby has not appealed. . . .

Although Kirby was called as a witness by appellees to show that he was operating the truck which he left on the highway about 3:00 P.M., he was not questioned as to the manner of his operations under the written contract. The only other evidence showing the method of Kirby's operations was that appellant paid one claim voluntarily and another after suit for damages resulting from collisions in which Kirby was involved. These collisions occurred two or three years prior to the one involved here and the jury's consideration thereof was limited to the question as to whether appellant engaged Kirby knowing that he was a careless, reckless and incompetent contractor. . . .

After appellees introduced testimony showing that Kirby was engaged in hauling logs for appellant at the time of the injuries complained of, the burden rested upon the company to show that Kirby was an independent contractor. . . . To discharge this burden appellant introduced its written contract with Kirby, executed on September 22, 1947, and under which Kirby was operating the truck at the time of the collision five days later. . . . We do not set out the terms of the written contract but it is sufficient to say that under our decisions it established the relationship of employer and independent contractor between appellant and Kirby, unless there was other substantial evidence that the written contract was modified by the practice under it indicating a right of control reserved by appellant over Kirby's manner of doing the work. Although a written contract creates the relation of employer and independent contractor, such relation may be destroyed by conduct of the employer through direction of means and methods of producing physical results and it becomes a question of fact for the jury if there is any substantial evidence to show that such conduct became operative. . . .

The jury gave an affirmative answer to the following special interrogatory submitted by the court:

> "Do you find from a preponderance of the evidence in this case that defendant, Kirby, was an employee of defendant, Ozan Lumber Company, at the time complained of herein?"

When the testimony in the instant case is considered in the light most favorable to appellees, we find no substantial evidence showing a modification of the written contract by the practice under it sufficient to support the verdict on this question. It follows that reversible error was committed by the trial court in submitting this issue to the jury.

Much of the testimony offered by appellees was directed to the proposition that appellant was negligent in employing or contracting with Kirby knowing that he was a reckless, careless, and negligent truck driver or operator. Appellant contends that, since the evidence discloses that C. M. Kirby was an independent contractor, it is not responsible for his acts. . . . One of the well recognized qualifications to this rule is that the employer must have used ordinary care to select a contractor of proper skill and prudence. Shearman & Redfield on Negligence, Rev. Ed., Vol. 1, § 174. . . . The authors of Restatement of the Law, Torts, Vol. 2, § 411, state:

> "One who employs an independent contractor to (a) do work which involves risk of bodily harm unless it is skillfully and carefully done, or (b) perform a duty which the employer owes to third persons, is subject to liability for bodily harm caused by the failure to exercise reasonable care to employ a competent contractor."

The following illustration is given in application of the rule at page 1112:

> "A, a builder, employs B, a teamster, to haul material from a nearby railway station to the place where A is building a house. A knows that B's trucks are old and in bad condition and that B habitually employs inexperienced and inattentive drivers. C is run over by a truck carrying A's material and driven by one of B's em-

ployees. A is liable to C if the accident is due either to the bad condition of the truck or the inexperience or inattention of the driver." . . .

In the instant case, if the relationship of employer and independent contractor existed between appellant and Kirby, the company is not liable to appellees unless it was negligent in selecting the contractor, Kirby, and his reputation as an incompetent, reckless and negligent truck driver or operator thus becomes a pertinent issue in the case. . . .

. . . For the error indicated the judgment against appellant is reversed; and since the cause does not appear to have been fully developed, it will be remanded for a new trial. . . .

CASE NO. 5

Georgeson v. Nielsen et al. 214 Wis. 191, 252 N.W. 576 (1934)

Georgeson had borrowed a trailer to haul cattle he had purchased. Dennis, a friend of Georgeson, offered the use of his car which was equipped with a trailer hitch. A collision took place while Dennis and Georgeson, with the use of Dennis's car, were transporting the cattle. Georgeson's contention is that the collision resulted from the negligence of Dennis which negligence cannot be imputed to him since he was merely a guest of Dennis.

NELSON, J. Georgeson contends that the court erred in denying his motion for judgment on the verdict it rendered. In support of this contention it is argued that the undisputed facts show that the relationship existing between Dennis and Georgeson was that of host and guest and it was therefore improper to impute the negligence of Dennis to Georgeson. While there is some basis for the argument if only the conversation between Georgeson and Dennis . . . , as testified to by them, is considered, the undisputed fact is that Dennis was engaged in performing Georgeson's job, namely, transporting cattle for him. It was clearly Georgeson's enterprise which Dennis and Georgeson were furthering. What was done was done for the benefit of Georgeson. Although, according to the testimony, Dennis was not to receive any compensation, it is our opinion that, while he was engaged in transporting the cattle for Georgeson, he was a gratuitous agent of Georgeson and the relationship of agency, not that of host and guest, existed between them.

"Agency is the relationship which results from the manifestation of consent by one person to another that the other shall act on his behalf and subject to his control, and consent by the other so to act. . . .

"(a) The relationship of agency is created as the result of conduct by the parties manifesting that one of them is willing for the other to act for him subject to his control, and that the other consents so to act. The principal must in some manner indicate that the agent is to act for him, and the agent must act or agree to act on his behalf and subject to his control.

"(b) It is not necessary that the parties intend to create the legal relationship or to subject themselves to the liabilities which the law imposes upon them as a result of it. On the other hand, there is not necessarily an agency relationship because the parties to a transaction say that there is, or contract that the relationship shall exist, or believe it does exist. Agency results only if there is an agreement for the creation of a fiduciary relationship with control by the fiduciary." Restatement, Agency § 1, p. 8.

Since the agency was gratuitous, neither party was under any obligation to continue the relationship. Sec. 16,

Restatement, Agency. But so long as Dennis continued in Georgeson's enterprise, the agency continued. As before stated, it was Georgeson's work or enterprise that was being performed. He directed Dennis where to go to get the cattle and directed him where to transport them. While Dennis could have terminated the relationship at any time and was not under the control of Georgeson as to just how he should operate his automobile, he was, in our opinion, the agent of Georgeson while engaged in transporting the cattle.

Judgment reversed and new trial granted.

CASE NO. 6

Valaske v. Wirtz. 106 F. (2d) 450 (1939)

ARANT, C.J., delivered the opinion of the court:

For several years John St. Clair and Chris Demetral were partners in the operation of a restaurant in Hamilton, Ohio, known as The Gold Dollar Café. . . . On October 27, 1937, they filed a voluntary petition in bankruptcy, and the partnership was duly adjudged bankrupt. Appellant claimed to be a secured creditor by virtue of a mortgage executed to him by St. Clair. The referee denied appellant's claim, the District Court affirmed his order and this is an appeal from that judgment.

The mortgage upon which appellant bases his claim was executed by St. Clair on March 16, 1932, upon

> "all the grantor's two-thirds interest in the goods and chattels in The Gold Dollar Café."

It was given to secure the repayment of $500, borrowed by St. Clair in December, 1931, and $750, borrowed when the mortgage was executed, these loans being evidenced by the individual promissory note of St. Clair. Appellant claims that the money was used for partnership purposes, that the note is a firm obligation and that the mortgage is a lien upon two-thirds of the partnership property. The referee and the District Court held that the mortgage covered only St. Clair's two-thirds interest in the partnership property.

Appellant's first contention is that Demetral's advance knowledge or subsequent ratification of the transaction between himself and St. Clair not only made the note a partnership obligation but secured it as well by a mortgage upon two-thirds of the partnership. . . . Since previously allowed secured claims and other priorities exceed the proceeds from the sale of the partnership property, appellant's right to participate in the distribution is dependent upon his mortgage establishing a priority over general creditors of the firm. . . .

Conceding this partnership to have been of the type in which each partner has authority to borrow money for the firm, there is nothing to indicate that St. Clair intended to exercise such power on the occasion in question. On the contrary, the form of his note indicates that he intended to obligate himself individually rather than the partnership, in which event his subsequent use of the money received for partnership purposes doubtless made him a creditor of the firm. But if there can be any doubt as to whether St. Clair intended the note to bind him alone or the firm, it is clear, from the language of the mortgage, that he did not intend that it should bind the partnership property. In words as clear and unequivocal as could have been selected, he conveyed his individual two-thirds interest, which was two-thirds of the residue remaining after payment of firm creditors. . . . In consequence, a contention that the mortgage was binding upon firm property when it was executed cannot be sustained.

Nor could a subsequent ratification have this effect. It is well established in the law of agency that an unauthorized act can be ratified only when the act done was accompanied by a profession that it was done as the representative of another. . . . If the other, thereafter, with knowledge of the facts, expressly or impliedly, approves the act professed to have been done on his behalf, he is bound as fully as if he had authorized it in advance. . . . But profession to act for the other is a condition precedent to the existence of the other's power to ratify. The ratification of an unauthorized act of a partner is governed by this requirement. . . .

As already stated, St. Clair probably did not intend to act as agent for the firm when he borrowed the money and clearly did not do so when he executed the mortgage. Nor did he profess in either instance to act for the partnership. Consequently, his acts could not be ratified. . . .

The judgment of the District Court is affirmed.

CASE NO. 7

Bond Rubber Corporation v. Oates Bros. 136 Conn. 248, 70 A. (2d) 115 (1949)

ELLS, J. The plaintiff brought this action against the defendant, a trucking company, to recover damages for the alleged violation by the latter of its duty properly to collect the price of three C.O.D. shipments. Judgment was for the defendant and the plaintiff has appealed. . . .

The plaintiff, a Connecticut corporation, operates a manufacturing plant at Derby. The defendant, a common carrier by motor truck, has its office and place of business about three miles distant, in the town of Shelton. On September 12 and 16, 1947, the plaintiff turned over to the defendant two C.O.D. shipments of merchandise for delivery to a customer in New York. On September 17, the defendant delivered both shipments and accepted an uncertified check drawn on the consignee's bank in New York City and made out to the order of the plaintiff. The check was dated September 19. A similar delivery was made on September 22 and the driver accepted an uncertified check dated September 26 and payable to the order of the plaintiff. The defendant mailed each check to the plaintiff on the day following its receipt. Attached to each check was a C.O.D. remittance slip showing the date of delivery. With the knowledge of the plaintiff, its bookkeeper marked the account as "paid" and deposited the checks in the bank in the ordinary course of business, the first on September 23 and the second on September 26. The first C.O.D. remittance slip was receipted by the plaintiff as of September 23 and mailed to the defendant, who received it on September 24; the second one was receipted by the plaintiff without date and mailed to the defendant, who received it on September 27. Both checks were returned to the plaintiff as unpaid because of insufficient funds and duly protested. On a number of occasions prior to the shipments in question, and in one instance thereafter, the plaintiff accepted from this same consignee uncertified checks which the defendant had taken in payment of C.O.D. shipments. . . .

The defendant concedes that under the C.O.D. bills of lading it was required by regulations of the Interstate Commerce Commission to collect cash or obtain certified checks, but it contends that the trial court was not in error in concluding that the plaintiff, by its unqualified acceptance of the uncertified checks, waived the requirement and ratified the acts of the defendant in accepting them.

A carrier receiving merchandise on a C.O.D. shipment acts as bailee to transport the goods and as agent to collect the price; if it fails to carry and deliver the goods to the person and on the conditions stated by the shipper, it is liable as a bailee; for breach of its duty to act as agent for the shipper in the collection of the price, it is liable for whatever loss has resulted from its failure to perform its duty to collect. Mogul, Inc. v. C. Lewis Lavine, Inc., 247 N.Y. 20, 22, 159 N.E. 708, 57 A.L.R. 934. The present case involves an agency, and the trial court concluded that the plaintiff ratified the acts of the defendant in accepting uncertified checks.

"The acceptance of the results of the act with an intent to ratify, and with full knowledge of all the material circumstances, is a ratification." Town of Ansonia v. Cooper, 64 Conn. 536, 544, 30 Atl. 760, 762; Cyclone Fence Co. v. McAviney, 121 Conn. 656, 661, 186 Atl. 635. . . .

The plaintiff unconditionally accepted the two checks, and knew, or was charged with knowledge, that they were uncertified. Before entering "Paid" against the account, the bookkeeper must have looked at the checks to verify the amount at least. Certifications of checks are not hidden. Their very purpose requires that they be clearly so marked. The bookkeeper, as a reasonable person, could not fail to notice that the checks were not certified. Her knowledge was the knowledge of the plaintiff.

In Rathbun v. Citizens' Steamboat Co. of Troy, 76 N.Y. 376, at page 380, 32 Am. Rep. 321, upon facts essentially the same as those of the present case, the court decided that the "plaintiffs adopted and ratified the act of the carrier, by the unqualified acceptance of the check." In the present case, the trial court's conclusion to the same effect cannot be disturbed.

CASE NO. 8

Kirkpatrick v. Williams. 53 N.M. 477, 211 P. (2d) 506 (1949)

LUJAN, J. This is an action for damages alleged to have been sustained by the plaintiff on account of the breach of contract. The cause was tried before the court without a jury, resulting in a judgment for the defendant, and plaintiff appeals.

On Tuesday, December 23, 1947, Maurine Kirkpatrick, the plaintiff, called Velma Williams, the defendant, on the telephone and stated to her that she desired to take a beauty course in her school No. 2, located in the Rosenwald Building at Fourth and Central Avenue in Albuquerque. At that time she was advised by the defendant that she would be pleased to see and talk to her on the following Monday, December 29, . . . Although the plaintiff had been advised by the defendant that she could not interview her before December 29, she, nevertheless, went to School No. 2, on the afternoon of December 24, while the defendant was absent therefrom, and there told Mrs. Bernice Griego, defendant's daughter, that her mother had directed her to permit the plaintiff to register as a student in School No. 2, and then and there handed Mrs. Griego $125.00 in cash for the tuition. Relying upon the plaintiff's statement, the defendant's daughter furnished her with blank registration agreements, which the plaintiff filled out in her own handwriting. While Mrs. Jean Campbell, an instructor in School No. 2, was assisting students in their work, Mrs. Griego presented the agreement to her and requested that she sign it for the school as instructor, which she did, although she did not see or talk with the plaintiff. Mrs. Griego then kept the original thereof together with the money, and delivered a copy of the agreement to the plaintiff. Within a very short time thereafter, the defendant, upon learning that the plaintiff was a colored woman and a graduate from a beauty college, as well as a licensed operator and the owner of a beauty shop in Albuquerque, told her that she had no facilities in her school to give post-graduate work . . . and then and there tendered back the money, which the plaintiff refused to accept.

The court found, and such findings are supported by sufficient evidence, that there was no meeting of minds between Maurine Kirkpatrick and Velma Williams; that the alleged contract signed by Jean Campbell as instructor, was done without authority from the defendant, and therefore it was not valid or binding upon the defendant in any manner. The court further found that the defendant never ratified the act of her instructor, and that she offered and tendered a refund of the money paid out by the plaintiff to her daughter, but that it was refused. . . .

. . . plaintiff contends the defendant ratified the whole of her employee's contract. . . . The evidence does not sustain her contention. Before a principal can be held to have ratified the unauthorized act of an agent, or of an employee who assumes to act as such, it must appear, either expressly or by strong implication, that the principal intended to ratify the act, and, if such intention cannot be shown, there is no ratification. The defendant on learning that the plaintiff had already graduated from a beauty college and was a licensed operator under the laws of New Mexico as well as the owner of a beauty shop in Albuquerque, advised her that she had no facilities in her school to give post-graduate work or any instruction which she had not already received in her own beauty course, and then and there tendered back the money, which the plaintiff refused to accept. In Walls v. Erupcion Mining Co., 36 N.M. 15, 6 P. (2d) 1021, we said it is indispensable to ratification that the party held thereto shall have had full knowledge of all material facts. We have read the entire record and find the court's findings of fact supported by substantial evidence, and therefore they will not be disturbed.

CASE NO. 9

Sullivan v. Bennett. 261 Mich. 232, 246 N.W. 90, 87 A.L.R. 791 (1933)

FEAD, J., delivered the opinion of the court:

Plaintiff had judgment . . . for damages for failure of defendants, stockbrokers, to sell his stock at once on his orders given October 14 and 17, 1929.

Plaintiff had purchased various stocks through defendants, certain of which were held by the latter on margin account. Plaintiff testified that on October 14th he was in defendants' office; defendant Charles L. Smith told him his account would soon need more margin; he ordered all his stock sold and the account closed; Smith tried to dissuade him, but he insisted on sale, and Smith agreed to sell. Defendants deny that plaintiff ordered them to sell.

October 16th defendants wrote plaintiff for $4,000 margin. He knew this letter meant that his order to sell had not been carried out. He called at defendants' office on October 17th and left 10 more shares of stock, worth $670. He testified he ordered the 10 shares sold. Defendants claimed they were deposited as margin. Plaintiff said the reference was made at that time to the previous order to sell, and that Mr. Smith replied that, if prices had gone up instead of down, plaintiff would have thanked him for not selling. . . .

Smith testified it was agreed that certain specified stock should be sold to provide margins, but with the idea of continuing the account, if possible.

Plaintiff knew that sales of stock were followed by letters of notification to the customers. He received letters from defendants, dated October 17th and 18th, regarding sales of stock which Smith said was agreed to be first sold to cover margins; October 23d, demanding $2,500 on account of weakness of the market; October 24th, notice that defendants must hear from plaintiff the next morning in regard to his account; October 28th, two letters; October 29th, three letters; and October 31st, one letter, giving notice of sales of stock. The 10 shares deposited October 17th were sold October 29th. The letters covered all plaintiff's stock except 100 shares, apparently unsalable and still held for him by them.

The sales left plaintiff owing defendants slightly over $2,000, which was reduced some $200 by dividends in November. A friend of plaintiff had guaranteed his account to the amount of $2,000, and transfer was made November 22d, which closed the account except that defendants still had the 100 shares of unsalable stock. December 1st plaintiff received a statement for November, showing his account balanced, with the 100 shares of stock on hand. Later his attorneys consulted defendants, and this action was begun March 28, 1930. From October 17th until after December 1st plaintiff had no communication with defendants by way of protest, claim, inquiry, or otherwise. . . .

The general relationship of principal and agent, with its reciprocal incidents of good faith, candor, and confidence, the not unusual departure by agents from instructions to the benefit of their principals, and the sometime misunderstanding of directions, make it a reasonable rule that the acts of an agent shall be deemed ratified by the principal, unless repudiated by him within a reasonable time after knowledge of the departure. Story on Agency, § 258, succinctly states the rule:

". . . If the principal having received information, by a letter from his agent, or his acts, touching the business of his principal, does not, within a reasonable time, express his dissent to the agent, he is deemed to approve his acts, and his silence amounts to a ratification of them." . . .

As to stock transactions, Meyer, in the Law of Stock Brokers and Stock Exchanges, p. 410, says:

"The first principle of ratification in stock brokerage transactions is that a customer who wishes to take advantage of his broker's wrongful act must repudiate that act. If he does not he is deemed to have ratified it. He may not merely sit by and do nothing, but is bound at the risk of the loss of his claim affirmatively to indicate his repudiation. . . .

"This doctrine is not unfair, for the customers should not have the privilege of withholding approval or disapproval until the market has taken a turn for better or for worse, and then assuming the position which turns out the more profitable. To accord the customer that privilege would enable him to speculate at the broker's expense. Moreover, the broker should not be placed in a position where he does not know whether his act will be affirmed or disaffirmed, and therefore cannot act intelligently to minimize his own loss before the market has undergone too great a change. . . ."

Under the undisputed facts, and as

a matter of law, plaintiff ratified the failure of defendants to sell under the order of October 14th by failing to repudiate their conduct after knowledge of the breach of his instructions, and by the affirmative act of depositing more stock to the account, whether for sale or margin, thereby consenting to the continuance of the account as it was conducted. . . .

Both as a matter of law and of fact, we hold that plaintiff ratified defendants' conduct by failing to repudiate it. . . .

Review Questions

1. What distinguishes a servant from an agent?
2. List the various types of functions that to your knowledge are performed by agents.
3. Is a principal limited as to the acts that he may perform by the use of an agent?
4. May individuals who are legally incompetent to contract act as agents?
5. In what capacities may a banking institution act as an agent for others?
6. What formalities are necessary to the creation of an agency relationship?
7. May an agency relationship exist under an agreement unsupported by consideration?
8. Construct a fact situation illustrating an agency relationship by ratification.
9. What acts may constitute a ratification?
10. Illustrate an agency by estoppel.

Problems for Discussion

1. The Gulf Refining Company, defendant in the District Court, appeals from a judgment of $10,000 rendered at the suit of the administratrix of the estate of Percy Edward Brown upon the claim that he had come to his death by reason of the neglect of agents of the refining company, in that they had sold and delivered as kerosene oil a dangerous mixture of kerosene and gasoline which exploded when he made use of it for the purpose of kindling a fire in a wood stove. The refining company, however, does contend that if negligence was proved, it was not attributable to the defendant but rather to one P. S. Ford who sold and delivered the goods, it is claimed, as an independent contractor.

   The refining company also contends, as we have seen, that under its contract with P. S. Ford, and under the other facts relating to his employment and activities, he was an independent contractor, so that the company had no liability for his neglects or those of his employees. It is pointed out that the contract expressly imposes upon Ford the entire charge of the management and operation of the business, the furnishing of equipment and trucks, and the employment and payment of helpers, for whose actions, in the conduct of the business, the company should have no responsibility. However, the tank service station and petroleum products were the property of the refining company. Despite Ford's agreement to pay all license taxes, the refining company paid the annual tax for the privilege of operating three motor trucks, although the trucks belonged to Ford or a corporation which he controlled. It maintained a regular account in the bank at Danville in which Ford deposited the proceeds of sale, and Ford had no authority to check on this account. He kept a separate account in which he deposited his commissions and other personal funds and from which he paid the wages of his employees. The trucks used in making the delivery were painted an orange (Gulf) color and carried the company's emblem "Gulf Oil Products." Decide. (*Gulf Refining Co.* v. *Brown,* 93 F. (2d) 870 (1938)).

2. A employed B to sell automobiles. A did not know that B was an infant. Later A attempts to disaffirm a sale that B has made to C upon the basis of B's infancy. Will he succeed?
3. X, by telephone, authorizes Y to act as his agent for the sale of certain real property. Would you, upon the basis of this knowledge, be willing to accept a contract from Y signed by him as agent for X?
4. A borrowed money from the X Finance Company and gave a chattel mortgage on his car as security. B, a former employee of X, having reason to believe that A was about to remove the mortgaged car from the state and knowing that A was in default of his payments, took it upon himself to take possession of the car, which he then tendered to X, who accepted possession. B had exercised considerable force in obtaining possession of the car and had inflicted a serious head injury upon A. A sued X to recover for the injury he had suffered. X's defense is that B was not in their employ and had received no authority to take the car from A. Result?
5. Defendant's son bought a retail meat business toward which defendant contributed $200. The son opened a checking account in the name of his mother, the defendant, and she let it stand that way without protest. The son conducted the business as his enterprise but had defendant sign the checks with which to pay creditors. The business failed, and plaintiff, who had been supplying meat, brought an action to recover an unpaid balance from defendant. Defendant contends that she is not liable as a principal since nothing had taken place between her and the son from which it could be implied that an agency relationship was ever intended. Decide. (*Plankington Packing Co.* v. *Berry,* 199 Mich. 212)
6. The judge before whom this action was tried found, as facts, that one Malcolm held a judgment against the plaintiff for upward of $2,000, and had told the plaintiff he would discharge it for $500, but the plaintiff had not accepted the offer; that the defendant (who was a stranger to the plaintiff), having learned of the willingness of Malcolm to discharge the judgment for that sum, applied to him, and by the false representation that he came from and was a friend of the plaintiff, induced Malcolm to assign the judgment to him, for which he paid $500, and the plaintiff now claims the benefit of this purchase. Defendant having assumed to act as the agent of the plaintiff, the latter could ratify the act and entitle himself to the benefits of it. Decide. (*Garvey* v. *Jarvis,* 46 N.Y. 310)
7. Without authority from Y but professing to act on his behalf, X sells Z a certain machine and warrants its performance. May Y ratify the contract without being bound by the warranty?
8. X agreed to purchase a stock of merchandise from Y. Being unable to obtain the funds necessary, he suggested to Z that he take over the transaction. Z informed Y that he was ratifying the transaction. Can Z enforce the contract?

9. Without authority from Y, X entered into a contract in Y's behalf. What is the liability of X upon the contract under the following circumstances:
   (a) before a ratification by Y?
   (b) after a ratification by Y?
10. X, as a promoter of the Y Corporation, entered into a contract in behalf of the proposed corporation. After the corporation came into existence, it adopted the contract. Does this relieve X from his liability under the contract in the event the corporation is unable to perform?

13 AGENCY:

RIGHTS AND LIABILITIES OF PRINCIPAL TO THIRD PARTY FOR ACTS OF AGENT

► I. AGENT'S AUTHORITY THE BASIS OF LIABILITY

As a matter of law, the authorized act of an agent is regarded as the act of the principal. The principal acquires rights and liabilities only from those acts performed by his agent in what the law regards as an authorized capacity.[1] The problem, then, of determining the principal's rights to and liabilities for an agent's acts is very largely one of determining the limits of the agent's right of action.

An agency relationship is one that from outward appearances is voluntarily assumed. Consequently, an agent's authority is that which the principal confers upon him either (1) actually, or (2) apparently. Agency powers cannot at all times be conferred with such explicit definiteness as to obviate all misunderstanding of an agent's powers to act. The duties of one appointed as a general manager of a business establishment cannot, for example, be defined in any great detail. It is a frequent practice under such circumstances to place the agent in charge without any documentary evidence of authority. If the agency is to serve some special objective rather than a general purpose, it is much more possible to define and limit the agent's freedom of action. Even then the agent's authority may possibly extend far beyond that expressed in the grant of powers and intended by the principal.

An agent's authority is that which is expressly conferred upon him by the principal and that which will under the circumstances be implied as existing regardless of the intent of the principal.

► II. EXPRESS AUTHORITY

In many instances, principals find it necessary to deny liability for the acts of their agents, asserting that the authority to act has been exceeded. Much friction and litigation results from differing interpretations of an agent's powers, although difficulties of this nature can usually be avoided by the use of a written document to circumscribe, as far as is possible or desirable under the circumstances, the authority of the agent. Such would seem desirable not only from the point of view of the principal, but also from that of the agent and of third parties with whom he deals. Where an agent exceeds his authority, he acquires a personal liability for his act. And, since persons dealing with an agent are legally bound to ascertain not

[1] Berkovitz v. Morton-Gregson Co., p. 360.

only the existence of the agency but also the extent of the agent's powers, they should not rely too heavily upon inference. For his own protection, a person dealing with an agent should ascertain the agent's express authority, which can be done most effectively by inquiry of the principal.

A. POWER OR LETTER OF ATTORNEY

Written authority may be conferred upon the agent by means of a writing called a *power* or *letter of attorney.* Until revoked by the principal, the power of attorney remains in possession of the agent as evidence of his authority to act. This instrument need take no particular form unless required by statute. Following is a specimen power of attorney:

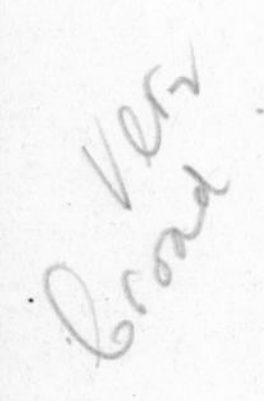

I, (the principal), of ______ County, ______, hereby constitute and appoint (the agent) of ______ County, ______, my true and lawful agent and attorney, for and in my name, place and stead to act as manager of the ______ ______ ______ located at ______, ______ County, ______.

I hereby grant unto my said agent and attorney full power and authority to do and perform all and every act and thing whatsoever necessary to be done as fully to all intents and purposes as I might or could do if personally present to accomplish the above designated purpose with the following exceptions, which powers I reserve unto myself:

1. Settle claims arising out of the conduct of the business,
2. Borrow money,
3. In any other way to pledge my credit other than for the purchase of merchandise used in the business,
4. Purchase of merchandise not nationally advertised.

In witness whereof, I have hereunto set my hand and seal this ______th day of ________, 19___.

____
The Principal

____
Witness

The agency thereby created is general in nature even though certain limitations of action are established. It still leaves unanswered questions as to whether the agent has authority to perform such acts as purchasing of equipment, hiring a hostess, installing telephones, contracting for various types of advertising, holding sales, or making express warranties. In addition, there is the problem of interpreting the contents of the instrument itself. What, for example, is meant by "nationally advertised"? Those powers, however, which are expressly conferred cannot be altered by implication or by oral evidence.[2, 3]

[2] Claflin v. Cont. Jersey Works, p. 362.

[3] Von Wedel v. McGrath, p. 362.

► III. IMPLIED OR APPARENT AUTHORITY

Every express grant of agency powers, whether general or special, carries with it, by implication, authority in addition to that conferred in so many words. Unless he makes specific limitations in the grant, the principal bestows upon the agent all powers that can be reasonably and logically understood as being necessary, proper, and usual to accomplish the purposes of the agency.[4, 5] It is also possible that the principal, by his intentional or negligent acts or conduct, will lead third persons to reasonably assume that certain authority exists. The principal is liable for the exercise of such apparent or assumed authority just as though it were expressly conferred. Following is a workable classification of an agent's possible implied or apparent authority.

A. INCIDENTAL AUTHORITY

An agent has the authority to do all acts that are incident and necessary to a fulfillment of the declared or understood objectives of the agency. What acts are necessary to a proper accomplishment of the principal's intentions and desires is entirely a question of fact.[6, 7, 8] It is conceivable that one installed as general manager of a retail selling establishment might have authority to contract, in the name of the principal, for advertising to a limited extent. Under competitive conditions, advertising is admittedly a necessary and proper mode of obtaining and retaining customers. However, it might be questioned whether such a selling agent would have the right to contract for billboard advertising. Very probably, the above agent would have the implied authority to make a reasonable commitment for holiday decorations in cooperation with a civic enterprise, upon the reasoning that such is necessary to retain the good will of the community. But would he have the right to contract for an elaborate Christmas display as an individual project?

It has been held that a selling agent who is in possession of the property has authority to make delivery and receive payment; that an agent authorized to deliver a deed has authority to affix and cancel revenue stamps where such are required to make the deed effective; and that a railway agent having authority to make contracts of shipment also has incidental authority to promise the time at which cars will be furnished the shipper. There is also precedent to the effect that a buying agent has the implied authority to purchase upon the principal's credit unless cash has been furnished him for this purpose. Usually, it cannot be implied that an agent who is authorized to sell real property also has authority to execute a contract of sale on behalf of his principal.[9] Usually his only authority is to find a purchaser who will take the property at a fixed price.

In a recent Wisconsin case, the court had this to say:

---

[4] Lumberman's Mut. Ins. Co. v. Slide Rule Co., p. 363.
[5] Cleveland, C. C. etc. Co. v. Green, p. 366.
[6] Lamm v. Charles Stores Co., p. 366.
[7] Silverstein v. Macy Co., p. 368.
[8] Law Reporting Co. v. Elwood Grain Co., p. 369.
[9] Payne v. Jennings, p. 370.

"While it is true that McCabe was not expressly authorized to employ any one to exterminate bedbugs from defendant's building, we think that, as defendant's rental agent, he was impliedly authorized so to do. . . . We entertain no doubt that a rental agent has implied authority to hire people to do such simple and inexpensive things as cleaning the premises, making them attractive and habitable by destroying vermin therein, or making small and necessary repairs to the premises." *Medley* v. *Trenton Inv. Co.,* 205 Wis. 30.

B. AUTHORITY BASED UPON CUSTOM AND USAGE

An agent's authority is subject to known custom and usage in the locality where he acts. The principal is deemed to have intended that his business should be conducted by his representative according to such customs and usages. Crystallized community practice may thus give an agent powers that otherwise might not be regarded as incidental to the authority granted. The reverse may as well be true. Established custom and practice in a community or market area may, for example, dictate that a certain type of selling agent does not have the right to warrant goods sold.[10] Yet, in the absence of such a custom, the right to warrant may be regarded as necessary to accomplish the purposes of the agency. The court in *Upton* v. *Suffolk County Mills,* 11 Cush. 586, said:

". . . When one authorizes another to sell goods, he is presumed to authorize him to sell in the usual manner, and only in the usual manner, in which goods or things of that sort are sold. . . . The usage of the business in which a general agent is employed furnishes the rule by which his authority is measured. Hence, a general selling agent has authority to sell on credit, and to warrant the soundness of the article sold, when such is the usage. But as stocks and goods sent to auction are not usually sold on credit, a stock broker or auctioneer has no authority so to sell them, unless he has the owner's express direction or consent. And it was said by Mr. Justice Thompson (9 Wheat. 647), that auctioneers have only authority to sell, and not to warrant, unless specially instructed so to do.

"As there is no evidence nor suggestion of a usage to sell flour with the hazardous warranty that it shall keep sweet during a sea voyage in which it must twice cross the equator, we deem it quite clear that nothing short of an express authority, conferred on Alcott by the defendants, would empower him to bind them by such a warranty."

C. AUTHORITY BY NECESSITY OR EMERGENCY POWERS

An emergency situation may serve to augment an agent's authority. Whenever a situation arises where immediate action is necessary to protect the interests of the principal and the principal cannot be looked to for instructions, action appropriate to that end may be taken by the agent.[11] Few indeed are the situations requiring such precipitous action that, with the availability of modern communication facili-

[10] Valley Shoe Corp. v. Stout, p. 372.
[11] Harris v. Railway Express Agency, p. 372.

ties, an agent has no time to get in touch with his principal for instructions. There is, of course, the possibility that the principal may be beyond reach of the agent.

Let us suppose that a general manager of a merchandising establishment is specifically prohibited from hiring help and entering into contracts of employment. A serious fire raging through the business block in which the business establishment is located would undoubtedly create such an emergency as to give the agent the right to contract for the removal of the merchandise. To illustrate:

In *Forrester* v. *Bordman*, 1 Story 43, it was held that an agent who was authorized to sell flour at a certain port for cash, upon finding the market glutted and the flour in danger of spoilage, had emergency authority to sell the flour elsewhere and upon credit.

D. AUTHORITY DERIVED FROM NATURE OF UNDERTAKING OR CONDUCT OF PRINCIPAL

> "By creating an agency the principal bestows upon the agent a certain character, and his authority in a given case is the attribute of this character." *Kilborn* v. *Prudential Ins. Co.*, 99 Minn. 176.

If a principal places an agent in a certain capacity, he thereby represents that the agent has authority in keeping with that capacity. By holding an agent out in a certain character, the principal leads others to believe that the agent possesses such authority as is ordinarily possessed by agents of such character. A person dealing with such an agent need not first determine the nature and extent of the agent's authority; he is justified, in the absence of knowledge to the contrary, in assuming that the authority that is apparent from the holding out exists and that the agent's duty is being properly discharged.[12, 13]

A principal cannot, for example, designate an agent as "manager" and at times leave him in sole charge of a business establishment and expect the world to understand that his authority has been limited to that of an office boy. Under such circumstances, a person of ordinary prudence, familiar with business practices, would logically and justifiably assume the agent to have authority sufficient to carry on the usual business affairs of the establishment. The principal would be bound by the apparent authority with which he has clothed the agent.

► IV. SECRET LIMITATIONS

A person dealing with an agent does so at his own risk. It is a rule of law that one dealing with an agent has the duty to ascertain the agent's authority. Such a person should inquire of the principal as to the extent of the authority expressly conferred or be certain that it can be reasonably understood, in the light of the surrounding circumstances, that the authority exists that the agent proposes to exercise.

Secret limitations or instructions issued to an agent are not part of his authority

---

[12] Heath v. Stoddard, p. 373.

[13] Oleson v. Albers, p. 374.

and consequently are not binding upon those who, without knowledge of their existence, deal with the agent.* The purpose of secret instructions is to guide the agent in the execution of his duties; the principal places reliance in the agent that the instructions will be followed but cannot use them to charge third parties with notice of a limitation of authority. This is succinctly stated in *Towle* v. *Leavitt,* 23 N.H. 360, where the court in speaking of a special agency said:

> "Where the authority is limited in a bona fide manner, and the limitation is to be disclosed by the agent, and is disclosed either with or without inquiry, any departure from such authority or instructions will not bind the principal; but where the authority or instructions given are in the nature of private instructions, and so designed to be, they will not be binding upon the parties dealing with the agent. And if the instructions are of such a nature that they would not be communicated if an inquiry was made (even though it be the duty of the person dealing with the agent to make the inquiry), it is not necessary that it should be made, for it would not be communicated if made."

Let us suppose that an agent has been authorized to lease coal barges with instructions from his principal not to take possession until they are properly insured. The lessor, having ascertained the authority to lease and take possession, is fully within his right to release the barges to the agent. The limitation to insure is obviously to govern the conduct of the agent and not a condition upon the right of the lessor to deliver possession. In the absence of custom and usage, under such circumstances, there is nothing charging the lessor with notice of the existence of such a limitation.

► V. LIABILITY FOR TORTS OF AGENT

It can be categorically and broadly stated that the principal is legally responsible for the torts of his agent—whether resulting from negligent or from intentional acts—committed while acting within the actual or apparent scope of his authority or employment. Thus, a principal becomes liable in tort where the agent procures a contract by means of fraudulent representations.

> "We conceive the true test in measuring the principal's responsibility to be whether the act of the agent was done in the prosecution of the business either impliedly or expressly intrusted to the agent. . . . If it was, the principal is responsible for the manner in which the agent executed his commission, even if he acted wantonly, recklessly, or against orders. . . . Of course, the moment the agent turns aside from the business of the principal . . . the principal is not liable." *Axman* v. *Washington Gaslight Co.,* 38 App. D.C. 150.

A determination of the principal's tort liability is, then, obviously very largely a question of fact and dependent entirely upon the circumstances in the particular case. It is quite impossible to categorize the manifold cases, since they are as varied in their factual aspects as are human relations.

* See Lumberman's Mut. Ins. Co. v. Slide Rule Co., p. 363.

► VI. AGENT ACTING FOR UNDISCLOSED PRINCIPAL

Usually the agent makes known the fact he is acting for another and reveals the identity of his principal. But sometimes a principal desires that his name be withheld in a transaction, or the agent may, for reasons best known to himself, hide the fact that he is representing another. Under such circumstances, individuals dealing with the agent do so upon the assumption that he is acting in a personal rather than a representative capacity. What, then, are the rights and liabilities of a principal in such a situation?

In relation to the acts performed by his agent, an undisclosed principal stands, with some exceptions, as will be later noted, in the same position as the principal would occupy had his identity been made known at the time of the agent's acts.[14] The principal may subsequently reveal himself as the real party in interest and avail himself of all rights that arose out of the transaction. Even though the third person dealt with the agent in his individual capacity, it should be of little or no consequence to him to whom he discharges the commitments he has made. From the purely objective and impersonal point of view, the important thing would seem to be the discharge of the obligation rather than performance to any specific person. This situation can be likened to the assignment of contractual rights. As will subsequently be seen, the third person, upon discovery of the principal, gains the advantage of having the right to look either to the agent or to the principal.

The fact that the agent entered into a written contract for the undisclosed principal in no way affects the rights of the latter against the person with whom the agent contracted. Parol evidence may be resorted to, if necessary, to establish either the rights or the liabilities of the principal. Such is not in violation of the parol evidence rule since the terms of the agreement are in no way contradicted or altered. The purpose is not to relieve the agent of his liability but to establish the agency relationship under which the contract came into being and thus establish the liability of the principal in addition to that of the agent.

A. EXCEPTIONS

The rights and liabilities of an undisclosed principal as established above are subject to the following qualifications:

1. *Contracts Under Seal*

Under the common law, one not appearing as a party to a contract under seal can neither sue nor be sued thereon. Consequently, under the common law rule, an undisclosed principal can acquire no rights or liabilities under such an instrument. There is some authority to the effect that the rule applies to all sealed instruments even though the seal is not required for the validity of the contract.

The effect of statutes abolishing common law seals cannot be stated with certainty. In some jurisdictions it has been held that such statutes did not change the

[14] White Tower Management Corp. v. Taglino, p. 376.

force and effect of sealed instruments and that the common law rule prevails; there is, however, authority to the contrary.

2. *Personal Agreements*

A person has the right to contract with another exclusively and the right to limit his liability to the person with whom he contracts. If a third person deals with the agent upon the express or implied condition that the agreement is to be between themselves only and to the exclusion of all others, the undisclosed principal acquires no right of action by virtue of the agreement. An undertaking that is personal to the agent would imply such a limitation.

3. *Negotiable Instruments*

Section 18 of the Negotiable Instruments Law reads:

"No person is liable on the instrument whose signature does not appear thereon except as herein otherwise provided."

This is a declaration of the common law rule that a principal is not liable upon the instrument unless he is properly identified thereon. Even though it is known at the time of the agent's signing that he is representing another, the principal cannot be held unless he is disclosed upon the instrument.

To illustrate the rule that an undisclosed principal cannot be held liable upon a negotiable instrument, let us suppose that A and B jointly undertook to purchase a patent. B was authorized to negotiate the purchase and to give his personal note without disclosing the copurchaser A. Upon discovery of the undisclosed principal A, the third person cannot hold him liable upon the note given by B. Let us realize, however, that A is responsible as an undisclosed principal upon the contract out of which the note and obligation arose.

4. *Settlement Between Principal and Agent*

It is the general rule that the third person cannot look to the undisclosed principal if, before his disclosure, the latter has settled with the agent in good faith.

> "As the third party contracted with the agent in his own name, or generally as an agent, without any knowledge of the principal, he has no right to look to the principal, if the principal, without any default upon his part would then be prejudiced by being made personally liable." *Yenni* v. *Ocean Nat. Bank,* 5 Daly (N.Y.) 421.

It can be argued that such a rule is fair to the party with whom the agent dealt, since the third party occupies just as good a position as he held before the principal was disclosed or discovered. There is, however, some authority to the effect—and what has been called the better rule—that the principal is not discharged unless the conduct of the third person led the principal to believe that settlement had been made with the agent.

▶ VII. RIGHTS OF THIRD PARTY

A. RIGHT OF ELECTION

The third party has the right to enforce the contract against either the agent or the discovered principal. If the third person has not gone so far as to have effected a settlement with the agent before the principal comes to light, he may elect the principal as the obligor. He must look to one or the other for satisfaction and, after having made his election, he must stand by his choice.

An *election* is a definite and unequivocally indicated intent by word or act to hold one of the two possible obligors. There is no agreement as to what acts are sufficiently indicative of an election. It is true, however, that to be regarded as an election an act must be of a most positive nature. Thus, commencement of suit against one of the parties, while evidence of an election, is in itself not conclusive and is generally held not to constitute an election. Nor would sending a statement of account be sufficiently presumptive to establish an election. And authority can be found holding that an unsatisfied judgment against one or the other is not a conclusive choice either, although the general rule is to the contrary. Accepting a note of the agent, on the other hand, has been held to be an election.

B. DEFENSES AVAILABLE TO THIRD PERSON

Whenever the third person deals with the agent *without knowledge* of the latter's representative capacity, he is entitled to avail himself against the undisclosed principal of any defenses, such as counterclaim or setoff, that would have been available to him against the agent. The undisclosed principal's rights to look to the third party are subject to all defenses that had accrued up to the time that the third party acquired knowledge of the existence of a principal. To illustrate:

Let us assume that A, the agent of P, is indebted to T to the extent of $500. A, acting in behalf of P, who is undisclosed, contracts to sell T $1,500 worth of merchandise. P's right to recover the $1,500 is subject to T's right of setoff for $500, which right he would have against A.

Constructive notice, as well as actual knowledge, of the representative capacity of the agent will prevent the operation of the above rule. The facts and circumstances surrounding the transaction may be of such a character as to charge the third party with notice of the fact that the person with whom he is dealing represents another. Let us suppose that a third party is negotiating for the purchase of certain property from an agent whose representative capacity was not disclosed. During the course of dealing, the third party discovers that the agent has neither possession of the property nor any evidence of title. Such facts have been held to be reasonable grounds to put the third party on inquiry and charge him with notice of the agent's true capacity.

Not infrequently a person will act for himself in an individual capacity and also for others in a representative capacity in respect to the same types of transactions. One dealing with such a dual character and having knowledge of his alternative capacities is charged with the duty to ascertain the capacity he occupies in the particular transaction.

CASES

CASE NO. 1

Berkovitz v. Morton-Gregson Co. 112 Neb. 154, 198 N.W. 868, 33 A.L.R. 85 (1924)

GOOD, J., delivered the opinion of the court:

Sam Berkovitz, the plaintiff, brought this action against Morton-Gregson Company, B. F. Kleeberger, and the State Bank of Omaha, to recover payments made in excess of amounts due on accounts of Morton-Gregson Company against plaintiff for merchandise. Trial was had to the court without a jury, resulting in a judgment for plaintiff as against Kleeberger, and in favor of defendants Morton-Gregson Company and State Bank of Omaha. Plaintiff appeals. The case presented in this court involves only the liability of Morton-Gregson Company to plaintiff.

At the time of the transactions out of which this controversy arises, plaintiff operated a retail meat market in Omaha, Nebraska, and Morton-Gregson Company was engaged in the meat-packing industry at Nebraska City, Nebraska. The packing company employed Kleeberger as its salesman and collector for the Omaha territory. In the course of his employment as salesman, Kleeberger called upon the plaintiff and took several orders each week for merchandise, which were forwarded to his principal at Nebraska City. These orders were filled and shipped to plaintiff, and an invoice for each order filled was mailed to plaintiff. The accounts for the merchandise thus sold were payable weekly. At the end of each week, Morton-Gregson Company prepared and sent to Kleeberger a statement of plaintiff's account. On the following Monday morning Kleeberger would call upon the plaintiff and collect the amount due. The amounts so collected were deposited in the Omaha National Bank to the credit of Morton-Gregson Company. This company had provided Kleeberger with a rubber stamp, as follows:

"Pay to Omaha National Bank, Omaha, Neb., or order. Morton-Gregson Co., Nebraska City, Neb., 208."

which he was required to stamp upon the back of the checks that were payable to Morton-Gregson Company. . . .

In January, 1918, Kleeberger began the practice of altering the statements of accounts against the plaintiff by changing the footings or totals of the accounts, so as to show a much larger amount than was actually due. Plaintiff did not check up these statements, but accepted them as correct and drew his checks therefor. When Kleeberger began this practice, he did not deposit these checks to the credit of Morton-Gregson Company in the Omaha National Bank, but indorsed on them the name of Morton-Gregson Company, per B. F. Kleeberger, and deposited them in his private account in the State Bank of Omaha. He would then draw a check upon his own account, payable to Morton-Gregson Company, for the amount actually due the company, and deposit this check in the Omaha National Bank to the credit of Morton-Gregson Company. . . .

Plaintiff contends that Morton-Gregson Company is liable to him for the excess collections upon two grounds: (1) That the acts of Kleeberger in presenting the altered and raised statements of account and in making the excess collections were within the apparent scope of his employment. . . .

Whether the acts of Kleeberger in altering and raising the statements of account and collecting excessive amounts, which he appropriated to his own use, can be said to be within the ostensible or apparent scope of his authority is a more serious question. While the statements of account were correctly made out at the home office and sent to Kleeberger for collection, the latter, when he presented the altered and raised statements of account to plaintiff, was certainly acting for and on behalf of his principal, and was within the line of his employment. So far as plaintiff was concerned, Kleeberger, to all appearances, stood as the agent and representative of Morton-Gregson Company, and was acting within the apparent scope of his authority. Morton-Gregson Company was without question a reputable business concern, and plaintiff, we think, was justified in the belief that its agent was reliable and trustworthy, and was warranted in the belief that the trusted agent of the Morton-Gregson Company was presenting accurate and true statements of his account. That he relied on the statements as being accurate and true was beyond question. We think he was justified in so acting. The fraud was perpetrated by Kleeberger while acting within the apparent scope of his authority.

In McFadden v. Lynn, 49 Ill. App. 166, it is held:

"A principal holding out an agent as having authority to represent him, and thereby asserting or impliedly admitting that the agent is worthy of trust and confidence, is bound by all his acts within the apparent scope of the employment. Hence, the principal may be held for the fraudulent acts of the agent."

In Commercial Union Assur. Co. v. State, 113 Ind. 331, 15 N.E. 518, it is held:

"An insurance company must bear a loss sustained by the misconduct or disobedience of its agent, acting within the scope of his authority, rather than the assured, who has dealt fairly with him as such, without notice."

This court has held in Bull v. Mitchell, 47 Neb. 647, 654, 66 N.W. 634:

"Where one of two innocent persons must suffer through the misfeasance of the agent of one, that one must suffer who has placed the agent in a position to perpetrate the fraud complained of."

In Adams v. Cole, 1 Daly, 147, it is said:

"A general agent or clerk employed to make sales of goods and require payment therefor, who obtains payment of false bills by fraud or deceit, held, as acting within the scope of his employment, and his principal is liable for the amount thus obtained. . ."

Birkett v. Postal Teleg.-Cable Co. 107 App. Div. 115, 94 N.Y. Supp. 918, is a case quite similar to the one under consideration. In that case plaintiff was accustomed to send telegrams through the Postal Telegraph Company, and at the end of each month to pay the agent of the company the amount due, as shown by the statements presented by the agent. The agent padded the statements and in the course of four years collected a large sum in excess of the true amount. The agent remitted the true amount to the company, as did Kleeberger in the case under consideration. The plaintiff in the Birkett Case had a list of the tariffs and charges of the company, and might have, from an examination thereof, ascertained the amount which should have been paid, but he relied upon the accuracy of the statements as presented. The court held in that case that the agent was acting within the scope of his agency in receiving the money for the benefit of defendant, and that the defendant company was liable for the fraud perpetrated by its agent.

Kleeberger was acting within the apparent scope of his authority, and his principal must be held responsible for his fraudulent conduct in raising and collecting excessive amounts from the plaintiff. . . .

CASE NO. 2

Claflin et al. v. Continental Jersey Works. 85 Ga. 27, 11 S.E. 721 (1890)

Plaintiffs are seeking to hold defendant liable for the acts of Lichtenstein as an agent who by authority of a written power of attorney carried on the defendant's business during his absence.

SIMMONS, J. . . . Where an agent's authority is conferred and defined in writing, the scope or extent of such authority is a question for determination by the court. . . . In requesting charges upon the extent and nature of a general agency, there seems to have been an attempt by the plaintiffs in error to enlarge the authority of Lichtenstein beyond the limits of his power, or at least to establish the construction that the instrument created a general agency. If there was any such effort, the court did not err in defeating it. It is not allowable, by the adduction of extrinsic oral evidence, to add to the powers expressly given in the writing. The authority must be proved by the instrument itself. The very purpose of a power of attorney is to prescribe and publish the limits within which the agent shall act, so as not to leave him to the uncertainty of memory, and those who deal with him to the risk of misrepresentation or misconception, as to the extent of his authority. To confer express authority is to withhold implied authority. There can be no parol enlargement of a written authority. Besides, the power of attorney was relied upon throughout the whole transaction. The plaintiffs in error believed Lichtenstein's acts to be within the letter of his authority, having taken the advice of counsel in reference thereto, so that they cannot claim to have been misled by any appearance of authority other than that which the writing gives.

Not true

CASE NO. 3

Von Wedel v. McGrath. 180 F. (2d) 716 (1950)

MC LAUGHLIN, C.J. This is an equity action under the provisions of Section 9(a) of the Trading with the Enemy Act, 40 Stat. 411, 50 U.S.C.A. Appendix, § 9(a). It sought the recovery of certain personal property vested in the Attorney General as successor to the Alien Property Custodian. The complaint was dismissed below on the ground that it appears on its face

> "that the plaintiff has no interest, right or title in the property within the meaning of Section 9(a) of the Act."

The complaint alleges: that plaintiff is a citizen of the United States, the wife of a German national; that on July 5, 1939, she and her husband left this country for a visit to Europe; that prior to departure, the husband, apprehensive that war might break out in Europe prior to their return to this country and that such condition might prevent him coming back to the United States, executed and delivered at New York City a general power of attorney to his friend and lawyer Pieter J. Kooiman; that an

> "express primary object of the giving of the power of attorney was to enable the disposal of all or part of the

property in the United States by gift to the plaintiff herein or otherwise, as the attorney in fact might deem best under all the circumstances"; that on September 1, 1939, while plaintiff and her husband were traveling in Germany, World War II started and the husband since then has been prevented, by causes beyond his control, from returning to the United States; that in 1940 Kooiman, as attorney in fact for the husband, transferred to plaintiff by way of absolute gift, property listed in a schedule attached to the complaint . . .

The all important question in the case is whether the power of attorney upon its face authorized a gift of the principal's property. The initial general language of the power appoints Kooiman

> ". . . to do any and all acts which I could do if personally present, hereby intending to give him the fullest power and not intending by anything hereinafter contained to limit or cut down such full power. . . ."

Specific powers are then stated, namely,

> "giving and granting unto him full power to demand, sue for, recover and receive all manner of goods, chattels, . . ."

and various other enumerated routine business powers. The instrument concludes by giving the attorney in fact

> "power and authority to do, execute and perform for me and in my name all and singular those things which he shall judge expedient or necessary in and about the premises, as fully as I, . . . , could do if personally present, . . ."

There is no real dispute about this last broad language as appellant in her reply brief concedes that its function is merely to round out the specified powers given by the document.

Among the carefully stated ordinary business powers set out in the instrument there is nothing which even implies that the attorney in fact is authorized to give his principal's property away. The authority within the instrument is to handle von Wedel's usual affairs. Under the settled law, that authority does not go beyond the specific subject

> ". . . even though it contains words in the most general terms extending the agent's authority." Brassert v. Clark, 2 Cir., 162 F. (2d) 967, 973.

Restatement on Agency, Section 37, says:

> "(1) Unless otherwise agreed, general expressions used in authorizing an agent are limited in application to acts done in connection with the act or business to which the authority primarily relates. (2) The specific authorization of particular acts tends to show that a more general authority is not intended."

In the absence of ambiguity or incompleteness, we must deal with the intent as actually expressed in the document itself. The power of attorney before us is neither ambiguous or incomplete. Under the settled law, the specific language governs. That language refers solely to von Wedel's ordinary business affairs. It contains nothing that can be reasonably construed as authority for the attorney in fact to make gifts of von Wedel's property . . . the command of the specific language must be pursued with legal strictness.

The judgment of the District Court will be affirmed. . . .

CASE NO. 4

Lumbermen's Mut. Ins. Co. v. Slide Rule & Scale Eng. Co. 177 F. (2d) 305 (1949)

LINDLEY, D.J. These three appeals grow out of a trial in the District Court wherein the controverted issue was whether Firemen's Fund Insurance Company, Citizens Insurance Company of New Jersey and Lumbermen's Mutual Insurance Company, hereinafter referred to, respectively, as Firemen, Citizens and Lumbermen, were liable as insurers to Slide Rule & Scale Engineering Company and its financial associate, General Credit Corporation, hereinafter termed, respectively, Slide Rule and General Credit, upon an alleged parol contract of insurance covering Slide Rule's inventory of goods, which, valued at $74,574.05, were destroyed by fire on February 8, 1947.

The District Court found that a valid parol contract of insurance had been made; . . . .

The District Court found that Edward Collins, an insurance agent duly licensed under the laws of Illinois, was at all times agent for the several companies; that, as such agent, he was authorized to solicit, receive and accept proposals for insurance, issue binders and issue and countersign policies; that from time to time he had issued policies in behalf of the companies and that he had previously written policies covering fire liability insurance for Slide Rule in the companies he represented.

The court found, further, that, for some time prior to December 27, 1946, Collins had solicited from Slide Rule purchase of fire insurance covering the latter's inventory of raw materials, those in process of manufacture and its finished product on hand, known as inventory insurance; that on December 27, 1946, Collins and one Anderson, the latter of whom represented Slide Rule and General Credit, met and discussed fire coverage on this inventory . . . that Anderson wrote Collins on January 10, 1947, saying that his people desired $75,000 insurance on monthly basis type policies suggested by Collins and asking that the insurance be made effective at once; that Collins immediately took steps to place such insurance with Lumbermen and later with the other companies; that Collins never advised Slide Rule or General Credit that any of the companies declined the insurance; that, likewise, he never told them the names of the companies with whom he had placed the insurance; that the evidence clearly disclosed an intention upon the part of Collins to bind each of the companies when and as they were designated by him. . . .

The court concluded as a matter of law that Collins had actual authority to bind all the companies; that he did bind each as he designated it in accord with his usual practice; that the parol contract was valid, as it included all the elements necessary to the making of a valid contract of insurance, including a proposal to insure, an agreement to insure, certainty of subject matter and a definite amount of insurance, the duration of the risk being understood to be the usual term, the rate the standard rate, and the policy, the agreed form of standard policy; that the amount of premium was ascertained and arranged for and credit extended. . . .

It is now settled law that insurance companies may enter into binding parol contracts to issue new policies, to renew existing policies or to transfer existing insurance from one location to another. (Cases cited) . . . The reason underlying the decisions is graphically expressed in Eames v. Home Ins. Co., 94 U.S. 621, 627, 24 L. Ed. 298, where the court said:

> "If parties could not be made secure until all the formal documents were executed and delivered, especially where the insuring company is situated in a different state, the beneficial effect of this benign contract of insurance would often be defeated and rendered unavailable. As said by Mr. Justice Field, in the case of Ins. Co. v.

Colt, 20 Wall. 560, 567, 22 L. Ed. 423, 425, 'It would be impracticable' (for a company) 'to carry on its business in other cities and states, or at least the business would be attended with great embarrassment and inconvenience, if such preliminary arrangements required for their validity and efficacy the formalities essential to the executed contract. . . . If no preliminary contract would be valid unless it specified minutely the terms to be contained in the policy to be issued, no such contract could ever be made or would ever be of any use. The very reason for sustaining such contracts is, that the parties may have the benefit of them during that incipient period when the papers are being perfected and transmitted.'" . . .

It is undisputed that Collins, as agent for the insurance companies, had blank policies in his possession which he was authorized to issue to his clients; that he did issue such contracts and collect the premiums therefor and that he had previously issued policies to Slide Rule and collected the premiums thereon. Such evidence, coupled with the other circumstances of record, we believe fully justify the finding of the court that Collins had actual authority to make contracts of insurance, either written or oral. Remembering that such actual authority may be implied from the facts, if they be of such character as to indicate an intention upon the insurer's part to create the agency, 2 C.J.S., Agency, § 23, pp. 1045, 1048 and 1050, it seems clear to us that Collins was the kind of agent who was authorized to make contracts of insurance and collect the premiums due thereon. The facts, it seems to us, are consistent only with actual authority upon his part to execute binding contracts of insurance in behalf of each of the insurance companies involved. Commissioned to make contracts of insurance, he had all the power and authority to do everything necessary to effectuate culmination of the undertaking. Restatement of Agency, §§ 35, 36, 43, 49, pp. 89, 90, 91, 103, 118, 119. We conclude, therefore, that the evidence amply sustains the finding that Collins had actual authority to make such a parol contract of insurance as is involved here. . . .

Much is said concerning communications from the insurance companies to Collins limiting the latter's authority. None of these was communicated to Slide Rule or General Credit and neither of them had any knowledge or notice of the same before the loss was incurred. Where one is clothed with actual authority to issue contracts, it matters not that his acts may have been in violation of private instructions or limitations upon his authority of which the person dealing with him has no actual or constructive knowledge. . . . 44 C.J.S., Insurance, § 149. . . . In Southern Life Ins. Co. v. McCain, 96 U.S. 84, 24 L. Ed. 653, the court said:

> ". . . The law is equally plain, that special instructions limiting the authority of a general agent, whose powers would otherwise be co-extensive with the business intrusted to him, must be communicated to the party with whom he deals, or the principal will be bound to the same extent as though such special instructions were not given."

It is said that the parties' minds did not meet upon the names of the companies to be bound. We think this wholly immaterial under the facts and circumstances of record. When the agent represents several companies and selects certain of them to be bound by the risk, he is contracting for undisclosed principals. Each of the companies he represents has intrusted him with the agency, and must be held to have given him authority as such agent to select it as the one to bear the risk. Such authority springs inevitably from his authority to make insurance contracts. The insured cannot be permitted to suffer because the agent fails to disclose at the time of making the contract which of several principals he binds. . . . Affirmed.

CASE NO. 5

Cleveland, C.C. & St. L.R.Co. v. Green. 126 Ohio St. 512, 186 N.E. 365, 87 A.L.R. 1268 (1933)

JONES, J., delivered the opinion of the court:

The authority of the claim agents to make the alleged oral agreement was put in issue by the general denial of the defendant. If such promises were made, the knowledge thereof was not brought home to the defendant's superior officers; therefore there could be no ratification. The plaintiff had pleaded that he was offered one of three jobs for life. He testified that he could select the position of firing a yard engine, the position of switchman, or a clerical position; he testified that he selected the higher paid position of firing a yard engine because it would lead to a promotion to the position of engineer. On the question of the agents' authority, the court charged the jury as follows:

> "Where a corporation or any individual holds out one as an agent to transact certain business for it, whether it be the settling of claims or other business, one dealing with that agent has a right to assume that the agent has authority to do the things necessary to carry out the transaction upon which he is engaged, provided that assumption is such a one as would be made by an ordinarily prudent person."

There was no direct proof of the claim agents' authority to make a promise guaranteeing a job for life. Did they have implied authority to make such promise?

The authority of claim agents to settle claims is special in character. While the authority of claim agents may comprehend the making of settlements for money damages, promises that may usurp the functions of superior officers in their management and control of their line of road and in their selection of its personnel cannot be said to fall within the usual scope of such special agents' authority. Public exigency, public safety, and public service are vital factors in a road's operation, and these factors should not be placed in the hands of subordinate agents, but should repose in charge of the executives who are in control of their several departments; and before a company can be held to such extraordinary promises the proof must establish that the proper officers either authorized such promises to be made or ratified them after knowledge that they had been made. . . .

CASE NO. 6

Lamm v. Charles Stores Company. 201 N.C. 134 (1931)

BROGDEN, J. Is a mercantile corporation liable in damages for the act of the general manager in issuing a warrant upon a forged check, supposed by him to have been given by a customer of the corporation?

. . . A correct application of the principles of law governing the transaction rests entirely upon whether Long, the general manager of defendant corporation, was acting wholly beyond the scope of his employment in writing the letter complained of and in procuring the warrant for the arrest of the plaintiff. Much has been written upon scope of employment, and the general outlines of the doctrine have been clearly marked. The term is elastic, and correct interpretation and application thereof must always depend upon the variability of given facts.

The plaintiff bases her right to recover upon three major facts: (a) That Long was general manager of the defendant, and therefore clothed with extensive discretion; (b) that many checks were taken by Long in payment of merchandise; (c) that the letter was written upon the stationery of defendant, and that, in writing the letter and issuing the warrant, the manager was thereby intending to benefit his employer and safeguard its rights.

In Kelly v. Shoe Co., 190 N.C. 406, Varser, J., said:

> "The designation manager implies general power, and permits a reasonable inference that he was invested with the general conduct and control of the defendants' business centered in and about their Wilmington store, and his acts are, when committed in the line of his duty and in the scope of his employment, those of the company."

Obviously, it is not the size of the job that the offending agent holds which determines liability, but the quality of the act done in the line of duty. This essential distinction was noted in Grier v. Grier, 192 N.C. 760, where it is written:

> "But liability in such cases is not ordinarily imposed upon the employer by reason of the extent of the authority of the agent, but rather upon the purpose of the act and whether it was done in the furtherance of the employer's business or was reasonably incident to the discharge of the duties intrusted to the employee."

. . . In the final analysis, the whole controversy reduces itself to the inquiry, was Long acting in the line of his duty when he wrote the letter forty-six days after the transaction, and procured the issuance of a warrant one hundred and nine days after the transaction? . . . There is no evidence that Long had ever collected an account from anybody or that any merchandise had ever been sold upon credit. Even if Long had authority to collect accounts, or such was within the line of his duty, resort to the criminal law by the agent, without the advice, counsel, or participation, knowledge, or ratification of the principal, was not incidental to such collection.

The plaintiff insists that she did not sign the check, and, furthermore, that she had never been in the store of defendant. . . . Hence it follows that the agent of defendant, without any justification, and without the sanction of any sort of business transaction, undertook to invoke the criminal law against the plaintiff either by reason of mistaken identity or by virtue of a reckless notion that she had committed a crime. All the authorities are in agreement that, if the agent, of his own notion, undertakes to set in motion the machinery of the criminal law to avenge an imagined wrong against his employer, such act does not impose liability upon the employer, unless such employer authorized or ratified the conduct of the employee. It is immaterial that the employee intended by such act to secure a benefit for the employer. This view is supported by the declaration of the court in Kelly v. Shoe Co. supra, as follows:

> "Liability does not flow from the employee's intent to benefit or serve the master, but it does flow from the acts of the servant or employee in attempting to do what he was employed to do; that is, the acts complained of must have been done in the line of his duty and within the scope of his employment."

Viewing the evidence from the

standpoint of plaintiff, her arrest and humiliation were wholly without warrant, and such conduct arouses a feeling of resentment and outrage. However, it was for this very reason that the wisdom of mankind has established courts of law for the purpose of giving to each citizen or litigant an abiding guaranty that his rights shall be determined, as far as humanly possible, in the cold neutrality of even and exact justice. The court is of the opinion that the judgment of nonsuit was properly entered.

Affirmed.

CASE NO. 7

Silverstein v. R. H. Macy & Co., Inc. 40 N.Y.S. (2d) 916 (1943)

CALLAGHAN, J. This is an action to recover damages for personal injuries suffered by the plaintiff while using a gymnastic device known as a "chinning bar" which he had purchased in defendant's department store. The complaint rested solely upon allegations of breach of warranty.

The device consisted of two metal tubes, one fitting within the other, with flattened ends in the nature of cups containing rubber rings, or washers. The device was to be fastened in a doorway of the user's home. It was to be tightened to fit the width of the doorway by turning the outer bar in one direction, which caused an internal screw to expand, thereby forcing the rubber-faced ends apart and against the door frame. Pressure, not suction, was claimed to be responsible for its firmness. . . .

In addition to the . . . directions stamped on the bar, and found in the pamphlet, the plaintiff testified that he was told by the salesman that the bar was a safe article to use for the purpose for which it was sold. Plaintiff further stated that the salesman directed him to use the bar in the manner specified in the pamphlets.

Plaintiff, who had purchased the bar in May, 1940, had used it in his home on numerous occasions during a period of about five months, or until October 5, 1940, without untoward result. On that day he had placed the bar in position in a doorway, tightened it as directed, and after seizing hold of it, swung his feet in pendulum fashion out and away from a point beneath the bar. Thereupon the bar fell from position, causing plaintiff to fall to the floor. He suffered serious injuries, for which he claims the right to recover damages.

Plaintiff weighed 170 pounds. He produced expert opinion evidence that the device was faulty in construction in that it provided no mechanism to check loosening of pressure when the outside bar was caused to turn by a person swinging on it.

The trial court dismissed the complaint upon the ground that the salesman was without authority to warrant the property sold. . .

The rule concerning the authority of a salesman in connection with a sale is stated in Burke v. Bonat, 255 N.Y. 226, 174 N.E. 635, as follows:

> "A salesman has implied authority in effectuating a sale to do whatever is necessary according to the usual course of procedure prevailing in the business. What that procedure is will commonly be a question of fact to be answered by a jury, unless the course of business is so notorious as to become a subject for judicial notice. . ."

The pamphlets above referred to were examined at the time of sale, and specifically discussed between plaintiff and the salesman. Respondent contends that any statements contained in the pamphlets as to the quality or fitness of the articles sold were representations of the manufacturer of the bar, and not binding on the defendant. We hold that the evidence would have warranted a finding that the defendant adopted the statements contained in these circulars.

Mechem in his work on Agency, 2d Ed., § 884, states the rule as follows:

"§ 884. Authority to warrant in accordance with descriptions furnished by principal. Where the principal furnishes the agent with written or printed circulars, or other descriptive matter relating to the goods to be sold, for the purpose of having these delivered or exhibited to prospective buyers, or otherwise used as a means of inducing sales, the agent would doubtless have implied authority to warrant the goods in accordance with any statements of fact contained in such circulars, provided such statements, if made under the same circumstances by the principal in person, would constitute warranties."

. . . reversed and a new trial ordered.

CASE NO. 8

Law Reporting Co. v. Elwood Grain Co.
135 Mo. App. 10, 115 S.W. 475 (1909)

BROADDUS, P.J. The plaintiff is a corporation organized under the laws of the state of New York. It is engaged in the business of copying and reporting proceedings and testimony of the Interstate Commerce Commission and other work of similar character. The defendant is a corporation of the state of Missouri, and operates a grain elevator near the city of St. Joseph . . . The plaintiff claims that in January, 1907, it contracted with the defendant to furnish to it the testimony and report in the hearing before the Interstate Commerce Commission in the investigation of the relation of railroad companies and grain and elevator companies, by which defendant agreed to pay to plaintiff for said work the sum of $486.90, and that it did furnish all of said testimony and delivered the same to defendant. . . . It was shown that plaintiff sent out a printed circular to the different grain and elevator companies calling their attention to its business, one of which was addressed to and received by defendant. After some correspondence, the following was addressed to the plaintiff:

"Jan. 1st. Law Reporting Company, 67 Wall St., New York City—Dear Sir: We acknowledge receipt of your letter of the 29th ultimo. You do not say in your letter how many folios there are in the grain investigation. Judging from your letter of December 17th, the amount cannot exceed 7,500 copies. If the number does not exceed 7,500, please send us a copy of the investigation as per terms outlined in your letter. Yours truly, Elwood Grain Co. By H."

In pursuance of the order contained in the foregoing letter, the plaintiff sent to defendant by express a copy of the investigation mentioned, which defendant refused to accept on the ground that the party making the order had no authority to do so. It was shown that the initial "H" attached to the order stood for W. H. Harroun, who was not an officer of the defendant company. It was shown, however, that he was the agent of the defendant, and did all its business in buying and selling grain. It was shown that Harroun was the proper party to receive and open all the correspondence addressed to the defendant, and whose duty it was to refer it to some one else or to dispose of it in some other manner; but a witness, one of defendant's officers, stated that he had no authority to make contracts for supplies for the office. . . . All the witnesses for defendant stated that the sole purpose of the organization was buying and selling grain. . . . The judgment was for plaintiff, from which defendant appealed.

The contention of defendant is that Harroun had no authority to make the contract. Therefore the only question before us is one of agency. Mechem on Agency, § 282, states the authority of an agent so far as it may affect the rights of third persons consists:

"First, and primarily, of the powers directly and intentionally conferred by the voluntary act of the principal; second, of those incidental powers which are reasonably necessary and proper to carry into effect the main powers conferred and which are not known to be prohibited; third, of those powers which usage and custom have added to the main powers and which the parties are to be deemed to have had in contemplation at the time of the creation of the agency, and which are not known to have been forbidden; fourth, of all such other powers as the principal has, by his direct act or by negligent omission or acquiescence caused or permitted persons dealing with the agent reasonably to believe that the principal had conferred; fifth, of all those other powers whose exercise by the agent the principal has subsequently, with full knowledge of the facts, ratified and confirmed."

In the first place, we are convinced that Harroun, when he made the contract in question, was exercising a power which was "reasonably necessary and proper to carry into effect" the main power conferred upon him as the sole agent of the corporation to buy and sell grain. It was important for him to be thoroughly informed as to all questions pertaining to the rates charged as such rates would affect the price to be paid for it. It is a well-known fact that the price of the commodity varies in different localities. Its price depends upon the distance from the great centers of trade; the rates of transportation varying according to the distance. The court takes judicial notice that the Interstate Commerce Commission under the law of its creation has much to do with the charges made by carriers for all kinds of products coming within the class known as interstate commerce. We can well understand that an agent intrusted by his principal with the sole power of buying and selling grain could obtain much information that would be useful to his principal in his business from the reports and proceedings of the Interstate Commerce Commission. The more complete the agent's knowledge of the business, the more efficient he would be as such, and anything that would increase his means of information materially and necessarily pertained to his authority.

Affirmed.

CASE NO. 9

Payne v. Jennings. 144 Va. 126, 131 S.E. 209, 48 A.L.R. 628 (1926)

WEST, J., delivered the opinion of the court:

On February 16, 1922, T. A. Jennings, appellee . . . listed his residence lot and three other adjoining lots for sale with Walker, Mosby & Calvert, Inc., real estate agents . . . the contract covering the residence lot read, in part, as follows:

"In consideration of your listing for sale and endeavoring to sell the real estate described, . . . I hereby authorize you to sell the same at the price of $12,000. Terms: $3,000, balance one, two and three years. Deferred payments to bear interest and be secured by a deed of trust upon the property."

The contract gave the agents the exclusive right to sell the property for six months, and provided further:

"Upon your securing a purchaser, ready, able, and willing to buy said property at said price and terms, or any other price and terms which I may hereafter accept, or agree to accept, I agree to pay you a commission on the gross price at which the same is sold or exchanged for other property of 5 per cent. on the first $10,000 and 2½ per cent. on the balance, and convey or cause to be conveyed with good title by general warranty deed, said property to any purchaser designated by you."

The clause touching the delivery of possession of the property read, "To be agreed."

On April 26, 1922, W. E. Graves, president of board of trustees of Marshall Lodge Memorial Hospital, Inc., agreed to purchase the property in his own name upon his own responsibility, at the price and upon the terms above stated, intending to turn his contract of purchase over to the hospital if it wanted the property.

At Graves's request, the contract of sale was made in the name of D. A. Payne. . . .

Upon learning that the agents had agreed to sell the property to D. A. Payne, Jennings refused to approve the contract, denied the authority of his agents to make it. . . .

. . . the court entered the decree complained of, canceling and annulling the contract of April 16, 1922, and directing that the same be surrendered to the complainant. . . .

A real estate agent is generally a special agent of limited powers, and those dealing with him deal at their peril. Usually his only authority is to secure a purchaser who will take the property at a price fixed by the owner. He cannot, unless expressly or impliedly authorized, execute a contract of sale on behalf of his principal. . . .

For authority to execute a contract of sale, binding on his principal, the agent must look to his agency contract. Authority simply to sell the property at a price named, leaving all the details of the transaction to be adjusted by the owner, does not include the power to execute a contract of sale. But, where the agency contract empowers the agent to sell the property at a price and upon terms set forth therein, and provides what if anything shall be done as to the examination of the title, what covenants the conveyance shall contain, when possession shall be delivered, and leaves no material detail unsettled to be thereafter adjusted between the owner and the vendee, the power to sell implies the power to execute a contract of sale in accordance with the terms of his agency contract, which will bind his principal. . . .

In Seergy v. Morris Realty Corp. 138 Va. 572, 579, 121 S.E. 903, Judge Sims, speaking for the court, said:

"This, of course does not mean that a real estate agent, may not be authorized by his principal to sign a contract of sale of real estate which will bind the principal, provided the terms of the authority are such that they, expressly or by necessary implication, definitely determine all the matters involved in the performance of the contract and are not left by the authority unsettled, to be adjusted by subsequent agreement of the owner with the purchaser."

We find nothing in the authorities relied on by the appellee in conflict with the views we have expressed herein. . . .

Since the terms of the agency contract left for the future determination of the owner the date of delivery of the possession of the property, which was a material detail in the execution of the contract of sale, we are of the opinion that the agent was not authorized to enter into the contract of sale with D.

A. Payne in the name of his principal, and that the principal is not bound thereby. . . .

For the reasons stated, the decree will be affirmed.

CASE NO. 10

Valley Shoe Corporation v. Stout. 98 F. (2d) 514 (1938)

SANBORN, C.J. This action at law was brought by the appellant, a corporation engaged in the manufacture of women's shoes, against the appellees, manufacturers of leather, to recover damages for an alleged breach of warranty that highly colored leather purchased by the appellant from the appellees in the year 1932 for the purpose of lining women's shoes, would not fade or crock.

. . . . .

Dealing generally with the contentions of the plaintiff with respect to rulings on evidence:

Its first complaint is that the court erred in admitting testimony of persons connected with the shoe and leather industry to the effect that all colored lining leathers would crock, that they had never heard of any which had fast colors, and that a guaranty of the fastness of the color of leather was unknown to the leather trade. This evidence was clearly admissible on the issue of the scope of Wills Engle's implied or apparent authority as a sales agent of the defendant.

. . . . .

CASE NO. 11

Harris v. Railway Express Agency. 178 F. (2d) 8 (1949)

HUXMAN, C.J. . . . The material facts of the complaint are that appellant procured the Railway Express Agency, Inc., the appellee, to deliver a trunk, weighing in excess of 230 pounds, to himself at 2115 Virginia Street, Topeka, Kansas; that around noon, September 14, 1946, one of appellee's trucks stopped in front of the above address with the trunk aboard; that because of the weight thereof, it was impossible for one man to unload it; that this appellee knew, or by the exercise of reasonable care should have known, at the time the trunk was dispatched; that the truck was not equipped with skids, pulleys, or with any other appliances to make it possible to unload, with safety to the persons unloading it; that upon arrival of the trunk at appellant's house, the driver, acting within the scope of his employment and for appellee's benefit, informed appellant that it would be impossible for him alone to unload the trunk, and asked appellant to assist him; that in response to such request, appellant started to assist appellee's driver, and in so doing was thrown to the ground by the weight of the trunk, causing him to slip and fall and to suffer severe injuries. The complaint alleged that appellee was negligent in failing to furnish skids, pulleys, or other appliances to enable the parties to unload the trunk with safety to themselves, and by failing to furnish a sufficient number of employees, including appellant, to perform the task of unloading the trunk, with safety.

Whether appellant was an emergency employee, is not free from doubt. Kansas has not dealt exhaustively nor clearly with the doctrine of an emergency employee. In Hockenberry v. Capital Iron Works, 96 Kan. 548, 152 Pac. 628, 629, reference is made to the Rule. The Rule as to what constitutes an emergency employee is well stated in 35 Am. Jur., Master and Servant, § 164, as follows:

> "While there is authority to the contrary, the prevailing view is that an employee who is confronted with

an unforeseen situation which constitutes an emergency, which rendered it necessary, in his employer's interest, that the employee have temporary assistance, is to be deemed to have had implied authority to procure necessary help and thus create between the employer and the emergency assistant the relationship of master and servant, which will engage responsibility on the part of the employer to the assistant for injuries chargeable to the neglect of the employer."

There is some divergence in the decisions as to the state of facts necessary to create an emergency so as to bring the rule into operation. No need exists, however, to discuss or analyze these cases in detail. For the purpose of the opinion, we will assume that there was an emergency warranting the servant of appellee to ask for assistance, and that appellant become an emergency employee.

The question then is, what acts of negligence were committed by appellee, after appellant became an emergency employee, upon which liability may be predicated. The only allegation of acts of negligence thereafter, upon which liability could possibly be predicated, is that appellee was negligent "in failing to furnish a sufficient number of employees, including plaintiff," to unload the trunk. In other words, the allegation is that appellee was negligent in furnishing only two employees to unload a trunk weighing 230 pounds. While appellant pled that the trunk "weighed in excess of 230 pounds," we think the fair inference is that the trunk weighed approximately 230 pounds. The weight of such a trunk, the amount of exertion required to lift it and move it to its storage place, is a simple fact concerning which all have common knowledge. We think that common knowledge of man's physical powers compels the conclusion that 230 pounds is not a great weight for two men to carry. . . .

CASE NO. 12

Heath v. Stoddard. 91 Me. 499

In an action to recover a piano which Spencer, a dealer in pianos, sold to the defendant the jury returned a verdict for the plaintiff.

WISWELL, J. . . . The piano was . . . the property of the plaintiff who intrusted it to one Spencer for the purpose of taking it to, and leaving it at, the house of the defendant, but without any authority, as the plaintiff claims and as has been found by the jury, to sell the piano or to make any contract for its sale; the arrangement being, as the plaintiff claims, that Spencer should merely take it to and leave it at the defendant's house and that a day or two later the plaintiff would go there and make a sale of it if he could.

Spencer had the piano taken to the defendant's house, but instead of simply leaving it so that the plaintiff might subsequently sell it, he assumed authority in himself to sell it to the defendant, who bought it and paid in cash and otherwise the full purchase price fixed by Spencer, without any knowledge of his want of authority.

Spencer was himself a dealer in pianos and musical instruments, and upon the very day when he made the arrangement with the plaintiff to take one of his (plaintiff's) pianos to the defendant's house, he had seen the defendant and attempted to sell him one of his pianos.

A principal is not only bound by the acts of his agent, whether general or special, within the authority which he has actually given him, but he is also bound by his agent's acts within the apparent authority which the principal himself knowingly permits his agent to assume, or which he holds the agent out to the public as possessing. . . .

Whether or not a principal is bound by the acts of his agent, when dealing with a third person who does not know the extent of his authority, depends, not so much upon the actual authority given or intended to be given by the principal, as upon the question, what did such third person, dealing with the agent, believe and have a right to believe as to the agent's authority, from the acts of the principal.

For instance, if a person should send a commodity to a store or warehouse where it is the ordinary business to sell articles of the same nature, would not a jury be justified in coming to the conclusion that, at least, the owner had by his own act invested the person with whom the article was intrusted, with an apparent authority which would protect an innocent purchaser?

. . . Spencer was a dealer in pianos. Immediately before this transaction he had been trying to sell a piano to the defendant. There was evidence tending to show that the plaintiff knew these facts. With this knowledge he intrusted the possession of this piano with Spencer for the purpose of its being taken by Spencer to the defendant's house with a view to its sale. Spencer was not acting merely as a bailee; he did not personally take the piano to the defendant's house, but had it done by a truckman or expressman; Spencer was employed for some other purpose. Whatever may have been the private arrangement between the plaintiff and Spencer, or the limit of authority given by the plaintiff, would not a jury have been warranted in coming to the conclusion that the purchaser was justified in believing . . . that Spencer had authority to sell, and that the plaintiff knowingly placed Spencer in a position where he could assume this apparent authority to the injury of the defendant? We think that a jury might have properly come to such a conclusion, and that consequently the instructions were inadequate in this respect, that it was nowhere explained to the jury that a principal might be bound by the acts of an agent, not within his actual authority, but within the apparent authority which the principal had knowingly and by his own acts permitted the agent to assume.

(Remanded to lower court for retrial.)

CASE NO. 13

Oleson v. Albers. 130 Neb. 823, 266 N.W. 632 (1936)

PAINE, J., delivered the opinion of the court:

This is an action at law to recover the purchase price of corn owned by the plaintiff and delivered to the defendant by a trucker, who collected the full purchase price from defendant, but did not pay the plaintiff, who is appellant in this court. . . .

It will be necessary to briefly review the evidence to determine the question submitted to this court. Plaintiff testified that he had known the defendant for 20 years, and that he was engaged in the business of feeding stock; that he had known George Worrell, who had been engaged in the trucking business, for two years previous to this transaction; that several days prior to this occurrence the trucker came to plaintiff and asked if he had any corn to sell, and said he had a man who wanted to buy corn, and plaintiff said that he would sell 800 or 900 bushels for 40 cents at his place. The trucker said he could then deliver the corn at 42 cents. Worrell said he would get in touch with his man and let plaintiff know. A few days later Worrell again asked him the price of corn, and plaintiff said there had been no change, and Worrell, the trucker, said that he had a man who would take the corn at 40 cents and pay Worrell two cents for delivering it. Plaintiff asked the name of the purchaser, because he did not want the corn delivered to a man who could not pay for it, and Worrell said it was Gus Albers. Worrell then hauled two loads on Saturday and the balance on Monday, making 843 bushels of corn in all. The trucker gave the plaintiff the weights, and plaintiff told Worrell to tell Albers to give plaintiff a check for his corn when it was convenient. A few days later plaintiff wrote a letter to Albers, asking for a check for the corn, and later Albers telephoned and said he had paid the trucker in full for the corn. . . . The corn was weighed at the elevator in Wisner, and when the trucker drove on the scales with the first load he was asked about the corn, and said, "Corn from Oleson to Albers," and that is the way it was put on all of the scale tickets. . . .

The burden was, of course, upon the plaintiff to establish that Worrell was the agent of the defendant by testifying to statements that Worrell had made to him. If the plaintiff had been able to produce the trucker, Worrell, on the witness-stand, such witness could have testified to facts and circumstances which might possibly have proved that he was the agent of the defendant, but the plaintiff's evidence lacks much of establishing that the trucker was the agent of the defendant, empowered by the defendant to purchase the corn of the plaintiff for the defendant. It may be admitted, as plaintiff claims, that the plaintiff did not seek out the trucker to sell his corn for him, but this does not make the trucker the agent of the defendant.

It is stated as the general rule, in the notes in 8 A.L.R. 203, that an agent authorized to sell commodities has no implied authority to receive or collect payment therefor (Ketelman v. Chicago Brush Co., 65 Neb. 429, 91 N.W. 282), but this rule is subject to several well-recognized exceptions. It is established by a long line of authorities that an agent, having possession of commodities which he is authorized to sell, has implied authority to receive or collect payment therefor. One of the earliest cases establishing this rule is that of Pickering v. Busk (1812), 15 East 38, 104 Eng. Repr. 758, wherein a broker sold hemp stored in a warehouse in his name for the benefit of an undisclosed principal, and it was held that a payment made to such broker bound the principal, although the agent proved unfaithful and did not account therefor to his employer.

Where a principal has, by his voluntary act, placed an agent in such a situation that a person of ordinary prudence, conversant with business usages and the nature of the particular business, is justified in presuming that such agent has authority to collect sums due to the principal, the debtor will be protected in case he relies upon the appearances of authority. It is undeniable that an agent to whom merchandise has been entrusted with authority to sell and deliver it is authorized to receive the price. . . .

In the case at bar the plaintiff gave the trucker possession of the corn knowing that it was being sold and delivered by the trucker to the defendant. Plaintiff made no inquiry of the defendant as to what the transaction was, although both parties had telephones on the same system. It was clearly the plaintiff who placed Worrell, the trucker, in a position such that an innocent purchaser of this corn had a right to assume that the trucker was authorized to sell and collect the purchase price of the corn, and while it is unfortunate that the plaintiff was deceived in the confidence that he placed in the trucker, yet the law has many times been laid down:

> "Whenever one of two innocent persons must suffer by the acts of a third, he who has enabled such third person to occasion the loss must sustain it." Broom's Legal Maxims (9th Ed.) 463. . . .

CASE NO. 14

White Tower Management Corp. v. Taglino 302 Mass. 453, 19 N.E. (2d) 700 (1939)

COX, J. . . . The plaintiff in this bill in equity seeks specific performance of a written agreement entered into by the defendants and one Taylor, admittedly acting as agent for the plaintiff, for the sale of a lot of land to Taylor by the male defendant. The agreement was assigned by Taylor to the plaintiff. The defendants, who are husband and wife, refused to carry out the agreement on the ground that they were induced to enter into it by false and fraudulent representations made by Taylor. . . . The judge found that there was inequitable conduct on the part of the agent of the plaintiff in negotiations leading to the execution of the agreement

> "in that he knew that the defendants would not enter into such an agreement if the purchaser were to be the White Tower Management Corporation, a corporation engaged in the restaurant business, and therefore concealed from the defendants the fact that he was agent for such corporation, and by misrepresentation led the defendants to believe that one or two individuals were to purchase the premises for the erection of a dwelling house thereon."

. . . The evidence as reported tends to show no mere concealment of the name of the purchaser. From the testimony of Taylor himself, as well as from that of the defendants, it appears that while Taylor did not affirmatively state that the plaintiff was not his principal, nevertheless he did represent that two individual buyers living in the Back Bay were the purchasers. Taylor admitted that the defendants asked him whom he represented. He was not bound to answer, but if he did, he was bound to tell the truth. . . . The affirmative statement that two people or a family consisting of two was the purchaser was, in the circumstances, a representation that the plaintiff was not the prospective purchaser. Taylor's answer could have been found to be a half truth, which in effect was a lie. . . .

It could have been found from the evidence that, if the defendants had known that the plaintiff was, in fact, the prospective purchaser, they would not have entered into the agreement. The plaintiff admittedly was engaged in the restaurant business, and there was evidence that the defendants would not sell . . . to "restaurant people," and so stated to Taylor. The representation by Taylor was material. . . The plaintiff does not contend that it is not bound by Taylor's misrepresentation. It ought not to be permitted to take the benefit of false and fraudulent misrepresentations made by its agent. . . .

We think that the evidence warrants findings (as in fact the judge appears to have found) that the fraudulent misrepresentations by Taylor as to a material matter were relied on by the defendants, and that not only is there no ground for specific performance, but that rescission would be warranted, and that the order for the return of the deposit is to be considered as restoring the plaintiff to its original position.

Review Questions

1. What is the basis of a principal's liability for the acts of his agent?
2. Indicate the nature of the problem of determining the extent of an agent's authority.
3. What is meant by the statement that third parties deal with an agent at their own peril?
4. What is a power of attorney?
5. What is meant by the phrase, "an agent's apparent authority"?
6. Define and illustrate incidental authority.
7. Illustrate the enlargement of an agent's express authority by custom and usage.
8. Illustrate an enlargement of an agent's express authority by necessity.
9. Construct a fact situation illustrating how an agent's express authority may be enlarged by the conduct of the principal.
10. To what extent are secret limitations binding upon those dealing with an agent?
11. What determines whether the principal is liable for the torts committed by the agent?
12. What is an undisclosed principal as distinguished from a disclosed principal?
13. The rule that the undisclosed principal can be held liable after his discovery is subject to what qualifications?
14. What constitutes an election to hold either the discovered principal or the agent liable?
15. Illustrate how an undisclosed principal's right of recovery may be defeated by a counterclaim that the third party has against the agent.

Problems for Discussion

1. A business establishment carries the name "Chrysler Sales Agency." Does this indicate an agency relationship?
2. X was employed by Y as a selling agent. Z had knowledge of the agency relationship but was not informed as to the extent of X's authority by other than X's representation that he had authority to act as both a buying and a selling agent. Upon the basis of this, X contracted with Z for the purchase of goods such as Y used in his business. Is Y liable upon this contract?
3. Through its agent, X, plaintiff sold defendant (the village of Stacy) a lighting plant. The agent selected the type of lighting plant, which he represented as being of sufficient size and capacity to meet defendant's needs. The plant proved to be inadequate and otherwise defective. In a suit for the purchase price, defendant sets up the defense of breach of warranty. Plaintiff established the fact that its agent had not been authorized to give warranties and had, in fact, been instructed not to warrant any plants sold. Decide.
4. A was employed by defendant to sell appliances and machines such as are used by dispensers of beauty. In attempting to sell plaintiff a permanent-wave machine, A undertook to give plaintiff a demonstration. The demonstration was so unskillfully accomplished that plaintiff ended, not with curls, but without any hair. A had no express authority to give demonstrations, and defendant

had established places at which buyers might get demonstrations at the hands of qualified operators. Can plaintiff recover?

5. X employed Y to sell and deliver merchandise and furnished him with a car for that purpose. Y sold the car to Z, and X brings an action to recover the car. Z contends that the car's being in Y's possession led him to believe that Y had authority to sell. Decide.
6. This action was instituted to recover the value of articles of food alleged to have been sold by the plaintiffs to the defendant. The plaintiffs were engaged in the meat and produce business in Bloomfield. The articles were purchased between August 1, 1918, and December 10, of the same year. They were ordered by one Roachman, who had been engaged about March 29, 1918, as manager of the club, and was known and is referred to in the testimony as the club manager or steward. Roachman was paid a salary of $200 a month, and also had the restaurant privilege of the club; that is, Roachman was to furnish the members with meals and refreshments to be supplied by him and for which they were to pay him, and the profit, if any, was to supplement his salary. Roachman was the steward during the entire period of the purchases from the plaintiffs. At the time of the first purchase, he introduced himself as the steward of the club. The goods ordered by Roachman were charged by the plaintiffs to the club, delivered to the clubhouse, accompanied by charge slips addressed to the club, with each order delivered. Bills were sent by mail monthly by the plaintiffs, addressed to the club. There was also evidence given by the plaintiff's bookkeeper that one or more checks of the club had been received and applied in part payment of the account. Decide. (*Heckel* v. *Cranford Country Club*, 97 N.J.L. 538, 117 Atl. 607)
7. X placed Y in charge of his grocery store as "general manager." Y, without authority, contracted with Z for advertising such as is ordinarily employed by like grocery stores. Is X liable?
8. Plaintiff was the owner of a valuable lot in the city of Pasadena referred to in the record as the Lake street property. She became acquainted with Arthur Palmer, a real estate agent in said city. The latter induced her to execute to him a general power of attorney. He borrowed $8,000 from the Mortgage Discount Company, giving as security a trust deed upon plaintiff's said lot, which he executed, together with a promissory note in the sum of $8,000, as attorney in fact of plaintiff, acting under said general power of attorney. This loan was handled through an escrow in the defendant United States National Bank. There was a prior incumbrance of $2,000 on said lot, which the bank paid, and after deducting escrow and other charges there was a net amount of $5,654.91 due out of the escrow, for which the defendant bank drew its check on its escrow account in favor of the plaintiff in her then name of Emma Martha Storz. This check was delivered to Palmer, who indorsed the same as follows: "Emma Martha Storz by Arthur Palmer, Attorney in Fact. Arthur Palmer." The check bearing said indorsement was presented by Palmer to the Bank of Italy in Pasadena. That bank, however, refused to accept or pay said check as thus indorsed. Palmer took the check out of the Bank of Italy at Pasadena and canceled the indorsements then on the check by drawing lines through the same, and represented the check to said bank with new indorsements thereon as follows:

"Pay to the order of Arthur Palmer Company

Emma Martha Storz"

And:

"Pay to the Order of Bank of Italy National Trust & Savings Ass'n.

Arthur Palmer Co."

Arthur Palmer Company was the name in which the said Arthur Palmer carried on his business. The name "Emma Martha Storz" in the new indorsement had been written by Arthur Palmer. In fact, her name to said indorsement had been traced on the back of said check by Palmer so as to simulate the true signature of Emma Martha Storz. The bank cashed said check and gave Palmer credit for the amount thereof and thereafter collected the same from the defendant bank upon which said check was drawn. This check was dated November 14, 1927, and was cashed by the defendant bank on the second day thereafter.

It is contended by appellant that the signing of her name by Palmer to the indorsement of said check was a forgery, and therefore the payment of said check under such an indorsement was unauthorized. Decide.

9. A, chauffeur of the defendant, in driving the defendant's car from Troy to Whitehall, broke down at Saratoga and procured the plaintiff to make temporary repairs thereon. In leaving the shop he told employees of the plaintiff to come and get the car if he broke down again, and to make all necessary repairs thereon to place it in first-class condition. He did so break down. He then sent a message to the plaintiff to come and get the car and repair it as above mentioned. The plaintiff took the car to his shop. Before repairing it he wrote the defendant several letters at his home address, telling him what he had done and asking if he should carry out the instructions of the chauffeur. He received no reply whatever. He then proceeded to repair the car. To what extent is defendant liable? (*Gage* v. *Callanan,* 109 N.Y.S. 844)
10. P engaged A to sell certain property with instructions not to make delivery unless payment was made by certified check payable to P. A sold certain of these goods to B for cash. A absconded with the proceeds, and P sues B to recover the purchase price. Result?
11. P engaged A to sell cars with instructions for him to sell only at the established retail price or at a price represented by the difference between the value of the buyer's trade-in as fixed by the Used Car Department and the retail price. To accomplish a sale to B, A allowed him $25 more than the Used Car Department had authorized him to allow on B's trade-in car. P refused to deliver the new car to B, who then sued for breach of contract. Result?
12. A was authorized by P to sell a quantity of corn at not less than 50 cents a bushel. A contracted to sell the corn to B for 49 cents a bushel. Is the contract binding upon P?
13. X was employed by Y as a collector of bills. X, while trying to collect from Z, engaged in an argument as to the amount due and as a result he viciously assaulted Z and broke his jaw. Is the principal, X, liable for this act?
14. B sold a horse to A without knowledge of the fact that A was representing P. B accepted A's 30-day promissory note, not being aware of the fact that A had been given cash with which to make the purchase. The note is unpaid at ma-

turity, and B, learning of P's interest in the transaction, sues to recover the purchase price. Result?

15. As an undisclosed principal, P authorized A to sell certain property to B upon credit. Subsequently P asserts his rights under the contract and seeks to collect the purchase price from B, who refuses to pay, since A, with whom he dealt, is indebted to him far in excess of the price of the goods. Can P recover? No

16. A contracted with X in behalf of an undisclosed principal, P. X, being in default of performance, was sued by A. During the pendency of the suit, X discovered that P was the real party in interest. X now contends that since A was acting as agent only, he cannot maintain the suit. Answer the contention.

undisclosed principal right of set off

14 AGENCY:

RIGHTS AND LIABILITIES AS BETWEEN AGENT AND THIRD PARTY

► I. LIABILITY OF AGENT ON AUTHORIZED CONTRACTS

By disclosing his representative capacity and the identity of his principal, an agent acquires no liability on authorized contracts entered into on behalf of his principal. Under such circumstances, the contract is that of the principal, and he alone can be called upon for satisfaction.

If, however, the agency or the identity of the principal is undisclosed, the agent becomes personally liable upon the contract.

> "If a person should be permitted to go through the form of entering into a contract as agent of a third person, and fail or refuse to disclose the name of his principal, the contract could not be enforced at all unless the agent could be held personally liable." *Tony* v. *McKissick,* 50 S.C. 218.

To avoid the possibility of being held personally liable, the agent should, in the execution of contracts, clearly disclose the principal and the fact that he is acting in a representative capacity only.[1, 2, 3] A contract signed "A, agent," without in any way indicating a principal to be bound, would be the obligation of A. Signing "A, agent of B" would not of itself assure A of being relieved of the obligation. The signature "B, by A, his agent," however, clearly establishes the representative capacity and the identity of the principal, relieving A of liability.

Let us take note of the sections of the Negotiable Instruments Law that bear upon this matter. Section 18 reads:

> "No person is liable on the instrument whose signature does not appear thereon, except as herein otherwise expressly provided."

Section 20 reads:

> "Where the instrument contains or a person adds to his signature words indicating that he signs for or on behalf of a principal, or in a representative capacity, he is not liable on the instrument if he was duly authorized; but the mere addition of words describing him as an agent, or as filling a representative character, without disclosing his principal, does not exempt him from personal liability."

Nothing will prevent an agent from voluntarily assuming a personal obligation upon the contract either exclusively or jointly with his principal. At times, such procedures may be necessary as an inducement to the third party to contract.

[1] Schwab v. Getty, p. 385.
[2] Shoenthal v. Bernstein, p. 387.
[3] Scire v. Am. Export Lines, p. 389.

Where such action is his apparent or expressed intent, he will be bound even though he signs the agreement in a representative capacity only. To illustrate:

In *Right Printing Co.* v. *Stevens,* 107 Vt. 359, the defendant contracted with the plaintiff for the printing of a legal brief to be used by the defendant in appealing a case for his client Robertson. The defendant requested the plaintiff to make out a bill for him to Robertson "so that it would aid him to collect his money." The court held that even though the plaintiff knew that the defendant was acting as attorney for Robertson he had, under the circumstances, personally bound himself to the contract. The court said:

> "Viewing the evidence in the light most favorable to the plaintiff, as we must, the language attributed to the defendant when he ordered the printing of the briefs is susceptible of the construction that the printing was to be done for himself, and that the credit of his client was not pledged. The fact that the plaintiff accepted the order upon the credit of the defendant is evidenced by the job tickets, the entry upon its books and subsequent statements sent to the latter; and his failure to protest and ask for a correction tends to show that the defendant so understood the situation and was content with it. The request of the defendant for a bill made out in the name of Mr. Robertson was not accompanied with a notice that the account should be so charged on the books. It was stated to be for the special purpose of enabling the defendant to collect his pay from his client."

► II. LIABILITY OF AGENT RESULTING FROM UNAUTHORIZED CONTRACTS

A. LIABILITY BASED ON CONTRACT

Whether a contract is authorized or unauthorized makes no difference in the liability of an agent who acts for an undisclosed principal. Regardless of authority, the agent acquires a personal obligation to the third person on the contract by failing or refusing to make known his employer. However, to say that an agent for a disclosed principal is personally liable upon an unauthorized contract would seem to be doing violence to the law of contracts, since at least apparent intent to be bound is essential.

B. LIABILITY BASED ON IMPLIED WARRANTY OF AUTHORITY

The law has well established that one professing to act in a representative capacity (for a disclosed principal) is presumed to impliedly warrant his authority. This presumption of an implied warranty may, however, be rebutted by the circumstances in the individual case. For example, if the agent expressly declares that he does not intend to warrant his authority, the presumption is entirely overcome. This is also true if the agent places all facts pertaining to his authority fairly and honestly before the third party, thus indicating that he is making no implied representation of authority. He thereby places the burden of ascertaining the limits of the authority upon the third party. As stated in *Newman* v. *Sylvester,* 42 Ind. 106:

> "It is material in such cases that the party complaining of a want of authority in the agent should be ignorant of the truth touching the agency. If he has a full knowledge of the facts, or of such facts as fairly and fully put him upon inquiry for them, and he fails to avail himself of such knowledge reasonably accessible to him, he cannot say that he was misled, simply on the ground that the party assumed to act as agent without authority."

Where the implied warranty of authority exists, the agent becomes liable to the third party for acting in excess of the actual or apparent authority.

► III. IMPLIED WARRANTY AS TO PRINCIPAL

The agent also impliedly warrants the source of his authority; he warrants that he is acting for an existing and competent principal. One dealing with an agent has the right to assume that the principal is legally conpetent to contract and that he exists. Should the principal be lacking in either of these respects, the agent is, as a general rule, personally bound to the third party. To illustrate:

(1) An agent representing a minor assumes a personal responsibility for performance of the contract.

(2) A promoter professing to contract for a corporation which is at the time in the process of formation can be held liable for breach of the implied warranty.

(3) An unincorporated association has no legal status and consequently is not capable of acting as a body. Only those members who give their assent to any action taken can be held legally. By professing to act for an unincorporated association, the agent warrants the existence of a nonexisting principal.

At least three qualifications to the application of this rule should be made.

(1) It does not apply where the third party is aware of the incompetency or nonexistence of the principal.

(2) Nor does it apply where it is understood that the agent is not to be bound —where the third party agrees to look exclusively to the principal for satisfaction.

(3) In the natural course of events it frequently transpires that an agent contracts without knowledge that his principal's death has taken place. In such an event, the warranty does not apply; the agent does not warrant that his principal will not die.

► IV. RIGHT OF THIRD PARTY TO RECOVER MONEY PAID TO AGENT

Whether the third party, who is entitled to recover money paid to the agent, also has the right of recovery against the agent depends upon the circumstances.

A. IN CASE OF DISCLOSED PRINCIPAL

If the basis for the third party's right to recover the money paid the agent is some wrongful act of the agent (as fraud) or mistake (as overpayment of an account), it may be recovered from the agent, *providing he has not made a settlement with the principal.* Thus, if an agent who is authorized only to solicit orders accepts payment, such is on his part a wrongful act—an act beyond his authority—and he would be held liable for return of the payment while the money remains in his possession. The agent cannot, however, absolve himself from liability by turning the money over to the principal after the third party has made claim upon him for its return.

Any payment made to the agent under circumstances other than those above indicated cannot be recovered from the agent even though he still retains the money. The court, in *Gulf City Construction Co.* v. *Louisville R. Co.,* 121 Ala. 621, said, in effect, that one receiving money as agent is not liable for its return to the payer in the absence of fraud or want of authority. To illustrate:

In the case of *Cooper* v. *Tim,* 38 N.Y.S. 67, the contract provided for the repayment to the third party of the price paid upon the happening of a certain event. The court held that such payment could not be recovered from the agent, although he had not paid it to the principal; that recovery could be obtained from the principal only.

B. IN CASE OF UNDISCLOSED AGENCY

Payments made to the agent by the third party without knowledge of the agency relationship can, under all circumstances, be recovered from the agent. This is true even though the agent has made payment to his undisclosed principal.

▶ V. AGENT'S TORT LIABILITY

An agent's representative character does not make him immune from liability for torts committed while acting for the principal. He does not lose his duty as an individual to observe the legal rights of others. If the tort is the result of his own negligence, he, as well as his principal, is liable to the injured party. And, in case the principal alone is forced to make good for the injury, he may look to the agent for redress. Liability for the injury ultimately resides with the negligent agent.

On the other hand, if the injury results not from the negligent conduct of the agent but rather from the performance of the act as authorized by the principal, the agent is nevertheless liable. Negligence is not an essential to liability. By the overwhelming weight of authority, an agent who innocently converts or trespasses upon property at the direction of the principal is liable to the owner.[4] The agent can, however, ultimately shift the liability to the principal by exercising his right to be indemnified.

---

[4] First Nat. Bank of Pipestone v. Siman, p. 390.

► VI. LIABILITY BASED ON FRAUD

An intentional misrepresentation of authority by an agent, made for the purpose of inducing the third person to act to his injury, would give the third person an election of one of the various remedies available for fraud.*

CASES

CASE NO. 1

Schwab v. Getty. 145 Wash. 66, 258 Pac. 1035, 54 A.L.R. 1382 (1927)

HOLCOMB, J., delivered the opinion of the court:

Appellant sued upon an instrument reading:

"Yakima, Washington, 3–2, 1923.
Yakima Ave. Near Third St.
Mr. Anton Schwab, Roslyn, Wash.—
Dear Friend Schwab: Referring to our talk at the depot yesterday, regarding the $1,000 worth of stock, Mr. Summers and I both agree to take back same January 1, 1924, if after that time you do not wish to keep it, providing you give us 15 days' notice.

"Yours very truly,
"Yakima Shoe Co.,
Geo. A. Getty, Pres.
P. S. Summers, Sec."

The evidence introduced on behalf of appellant shows that on and prior to February 28, 1923, respondent Getty and the decedent of the estate represented by the executrix, respondent herein, were the operating and controlling owners of the Yakima Shoe Company, a corporation. They desired more money to put into the business, and negotiated with appellant, already the owner of eleven shares, to put $1,000 more into the business, for which they agreed to sell him ten shares of the par value of $100 per share, and agreed with him that if he desired his money back after January 1, 1924, they would buy it back. It is an undisputed fact that appellant made demand for the repayment of the $1,000 about a year and a half after January 1, 1924, and it was not repaid.

The trial court found that the instrument above set out was the obligation of the corporation, Yakima Shoe Company, and not the individual obligations of Getty and Summers. The action was therefore dismissed.

The errors assigned may all be grouped into the contention that the court erred in construing the instrument in writing to be the obligation of the corporation and not of the individuals.

The court properly held that the written instrument fixed the liabilities of all the parties and its terms could not be altered by parol evidence. . . .

This instrument is a contract to take back certain stock of the Yakima Shoe Company, a corporation, after January 1, 1924, and repay the purchaser the sum of $1,000 paid for the stock. It is either a contract of the corporation, or of Summers and Getty personally. If it was intended to be a contract of the corporation of course, it is void, for a corporation cannot traffic in its own stock in this state. . . .

The cases, with great uniformity, hold that where the real principal is disclosed as the party to be obligated, and the only party, even though the signa-

* See p. 138.

tures may be irregular and defective, the principal will be held on the instrument. Sun Printing & Pub. Asso. v. Moore, 183 U.S. 642, 46 L. ed. 366, 22 Sup. Ct. 240. In that case a charter party was signed by one Lord, "for the Sun Printing & Publishing Association." Mr. Justice White, writing the opinion, said:

> "Clearly this was a disclosure of the principal, and an apt manner of expressing an intent to bind such principal" (citing cases).

Respondents rely strongly upon the Sun Printing & Pub. Asso. Case, supra, the Jacobs Case, supra, and other like cases, which hold, of course, that "I" and "we" used in instruments, or "we" or "our," or "we agree that we will take the stock back," if the instrument is signed by the corporation, does not change the signature. But in the Sun Printing & Pub. Asso. Case, supra, Judge White made it plain that where the signature was for and on behalf of the corporation it bound the latter, if the signer had the authority to make such a contract for his paper. He also went to some pains to show that the by-laws and resolutions of the corporation sufficiently authorized such a contract on behalf of the corporation to be made by the signer thereof. For that reason it was held to be the signature of and for the company and an obligation binding it, regardless, we apprehend, of whether it would have bound the signer individually, if unauthorized.

The writing before us, however, does not use the word "I," "we," or "our," as referred to in many of the cases cited by respondents, but uses the specific words, "Mr. Summers and I both agree to take back same after January 1, 1924," etc. These words are much more definite than the use of the word "I," "we," or "our," making it plain, in our opinion, that it was intended to make an agreement on the part of Summers and Getty that they would take back the stock at the time specified, and not the corporation.

The agreement in this case is more like that in the Gavazza Case, 53 Wash. 14, 42 L.R.A. (N.S.) 1, 101 Pac. 370, where the signer of the writing, Plummer, described himself as treasurer of the company in the instrument itself, but agreed for himself that he would, upon demand, accept a return of the stock and refund to the purchaser the money he had paid therefor. In that case the late Judge Morris, writing the opinion, said:

> "'It is too well settled to need any reference to authorities to show that an agent may, by the form of the promise and manner of his signature fix upon himself a personal liability.' Haverhill Mut. F. Ins. Co. v. Newhall, 1 Allen, 130.
>
> "The appellant has brought himself within this rule. The words of his undertaking, 'I will, upon demand, accept a return of his stock and refund to him the money he has paid,' would seem to indicate, irrespective of the application of the rule, that it was his purpose and intention to become personally bound, at least to lead respondent to infer (as respondent testified) that the obligation was personal. The addition of 'Treas.' to his signature neither adds to nor detracts from that obligation; it is simply, as the courts say, 'descriptio personae.'
>
> "If it is desired to escape personal liability in the contract of an agent or other representative, the intention so to do must be expressed in clear and explicit language; otherwise, a personal obligation arises."

While the instrument is novel, we are convinced that it was intended to be the personal contract of Getty and Summers individually, and not that of the company; that the contract contained apt words to bind them, even though they pretended to sign for and on behalf of the corporation.

The judgment of the lower court is therefore reversed.

CASE NO. 2

Shoenthal v. Bernstein. 93 N.Y.S. (2d) 187 (1949)

COHN, J. By letter dated September 14, 1946 and signed by defendant, plaintiff's assignor was engaged as manager of a retail store in Florence, Alabama, for a period of two years from January 1, 1947 at a salary of $10,000 per year, payable monthly, plus a percentage of the net profits as a bonus. . . . The store was owned by Ruth Shops, Inc., a corporation organized in February 1946 in Mississippi. . . .

Plaintiff's assignor assigned the cause of action for breach of the contract to his father, who brought this suit in this State against defendant to recover damages for alleged wrongful discharge. . . .

The letter on which plaintiff's cause of action is based reads in part as follows:

"Executive Office
Ruth Shops—Jean-Ann's—Libby's

Columbus, Mississippi

"Mr. Syd Shoenthal
Decatur, Illinois
Dear Mr. Shoenthal:

"This will acknowledge my visit to Decatur and our understanding for you to begin as manager of our Florence, Alabama store on January 1, 1947 and to take over the management of the Columbus Store as soon as it is completed.

"Your experience and background fit in nicely with our needs. We are comparatively new and are going to need all your co-operation and experience and we in turn, promise you our fullest cooperation. . . .

"Sincerely yours,
(sgd.) A. Bernstein"

Defendant claimed that he did not personally hire plaintiff's assignor; that in making the contract he acted as agent for a known principal to wit: Ruth Shops, Inc., . . . that plaintiff's assignor knew that he was being engaged by Ruth Shops, Inc. and that the letter of September 14, 1946 did not personally bind the defendant; that it was the intention of the parties that the contract was to be between plaintiff's assignor and Ruth Shops, Inc.

The sole issue in the case was whether defendant became personally liable to plaintiff's assignor or whether the corporation (which was not made a party to the action) alone was liable.

In directing a verdict for plaintiff for the full amount claimed, the trial judge held as a matter of law that by his letter defendant personally bound himself as employer and that the terms of such letter could not be varied or corrected by oral testimony. On this appeal, defendant urges that the court erroneously excluded parol evidence which was designed to show that at the time the agreement was entered into, plaintiff's assignor knew who the principal was; that from the very terms of the letter of employment it appears that defendant should not be personally bound, and that, at the very least, there was an obvious ambiguity in the contract itself with respect to whether it was the individual contract of defendant or a contract made solely for the principal, in which event parol evidence was admissible to show whose contract it was intended to be.

The writing upon which plaintiff relies, we are persuaded, is ambiguous as to the parties' intent to be bound. It does not clearly appear from the instrument itself that defendant intended to become personally liable. The writing at the very beginning shows a list of names indicating that it was sent from the executive offices of "Ruth Shops—Jean-Ann's—Libby's." In the body of the letter plaintiff's assignor is advised:

> "This will acknowledge my visit to Decatur and *our* understanding for you to begin as manager of *our* Florence, Alabama store." Later the writing states: "Your experience and background fit in nicely with *our* needs. *We* are comparatively new and are going to need all your co-operation." (Emphasis ours.)

The constant use of the plural in the letter and the notation of the various names by which the corporation was known at the top of the letter, together with knowledge on the part of plaintiff's assignor that Ruth Shops, Inc. was the real principal, would make it appear that defendant was acting for the corporation and not liable upon the contract. It was, therefore, proper for defendant to establish by parol evidence that plaintiff's assignor knew before September 14, 1946 that Ruth Shops, Inc. was the principal in the transaction. This, defendant . . . attempted to show by conversation which he had with plaintiff's assignor antedating the execution of the letter. Such testimony should not have been excluded. . . .

An agent acting for a disclosed principal may of course bind himself personally by a contract made in behalf of the principal if he so volunteers or if the other party requires it, Meyer v. Redmond, 205 N.Y. 478; 98 N.E. 906; 41 L.R.A.S. 675; Jones v. Gould, 200 N.Y. 18, 20; 92 N.E. 1071, 1072. If the other party to the contract elects to hold the signer thereof, parol evidence is, to be sure, not admissible to release him from the obligation he had voluntarily assumed, although it would be competent to bring in a third party not named, Gordon Malting Co. v. Bartels Brewing Co., 206 N.Y. 528, 537; 100 N.E. 457, 461. However, unless the contract clearly shows that it was intended to be the personal obligation of the agent of a known principal, the agent is not bound thereby individually and the party with whom he negotiates it, may look only to the principal for performance. Keskal v. Modrakowski, 249 N.Y. 406, 408; 164 N.E. 333. . . .

Where as here, the contract is ambiguous on its face as to whether it is the individual contract of the agent of a contract made for his principal although signed by the agent individually, parol evidence is admissible to show the intention of the parties. Hermadez v. Brookdale Mills Inc., 194 App. Div. 369. . . .

> "If the instrument is ambiguous as to parties, extrinsic evidence is admissible to prove that the parties intended to include or exclude either the principal or the agent."
>
> . . . "There is seldom any difficulty in applying the law, where the contract is made by an agent known to be acting in that capacity, who does not disclose the name of his principal for in such case the party dealing with the agent must necessarily rely on his credit, since he knows nothing concerning the responsibility of the undisclosed principal (Meyer v. Redmond, supra; Good v. Rumsey, 50 App. Div. 280, 63 N.Y.S. 981); but when the principal is known to the person dealing with the agent, and it is understood by both parties that the contract is negotiated for the principal, the courts should not close their eyes to the manner in which such contracts are constantly negotiated and by the application of an arbitrary rule hold that a contract in-

tended and understood to be that of the principal personally binds the agent, who had no intention of pledging his personal credit, the principal as well, so that the party dealing with him may look to whichever of them he finds to be the more responsible financially. It will not do, therefore, to hold that a contract negotiated by an agent for a known and disclosed principal becomes the contract of the agent, if in negotiating it verbally, or by writing not under seal, he signs his own name without taking the precaution to tell the person to whom he is writing that he is acting for his principal, which is already fully understood."

Upon the evidence received and upon such portions as were improperly excluded we think that there was an issue of facts as to whether plaintiff's assignor knew that defendant when signing the agreement, was acting as agent of Ruth Shops, Inc., and as to whether the contract itself, in the light of its ambiguity, and in the setting of this case, personally bound defendant to perform the terms of the contract.

Judgment unanimously reversed and a new trial ordered. . . .

CASE NO. 3

Scire v. American Export Lines. 93 N.Y.S. (2d) 457 (1949)

BASTOW, J. The plaintiffs, brother and sister, bring these actions to recover damages alleged to have been sustained by each when certain baggage owned by each was lost, destroyed or damaged while in the possession of the defendant.

. . . It was stipulated at the commencement of the trial that the defendant is engaged in the steamship transportation of passengers; that on May 2, 1947, the plaintiffs, residents of Utica, New York, boarded the S.S. Marine Perch—operated by the defendant—at Palermo, Italy to be transported to the United States; that each plaintiff had on board one large trunk and upon arrival at the point of destination each plaintiff demanded the delivery of said trunks and the defendant failed to deliver them. . . .

. . . They visited in Italy and on October 16, 1947 they purchased from the defendant for the sum of $342 a passenger ticket entitling them to be transported on the S.S. Marine Perch from Palermo, Italy to New York City. . . .

It was stipulated upon the trial that exhibit 2 is a facsimile of the ticket issued to the plaintiffs. This so-called ticket is printed on both sides of a sheet of paper approximately eight by twelve inches. At the top of the front page in bold type appear the words "American Export Lines—Inc—". underneath in somewhat smaller type is the word "agent." . . .

The defendant for a first separate and complete defense alleges in its answers that it was acting as a berth agent in the transportation of the person and property of the plaintiffs and that the passenger ticket purchased by plaintiffs was signed expressly for the master of the vessel involved by an agent of the United States and accordingly the ticket was a contract with the owner or charterer of the vessel and the defendant is under no personal liability. . . .

It has been stated that the word "agent" was printed underneath the defendant's name at the top of the ticket. At the end of the contract provisions appear the words "For the Master By American Export Lines, Inc. As agent for the Master By—." The blank space had no name inserted.

No proof was offered upon the trial that the defendant, or any one acting on its behalf, either in the formal contract, or otherwise, disclosed to the plaintiffs that the principal was the United States of America acting by and through the War Shipping Administration.

The rule is recognized that where a contract is made by an authorized agent in the name and on the account of a competent principal, the agent incurs no liability upon or with reference to the principal.

Mechem on Agency (2nd Ed.), Vol. 1, p. 999, § 1357.

This same author, however, states in Section 1169, page 850 that

"if, though disclosing the fact that he is an agent, he does not disclose who his principal is, but keeps the latter's identity concealed, the agent will ordinarily be personally liable unless he has clearly excluded such a result."

The general rule may be stated that where one party to a written contract is known to the other to be in fact acting as agent for some known principal, he does not become personally liable whether he signs individually or as agent. On the other hand, although known to be acting for an unknown principal, he is personally liable. Knowledge of the real principal is the test, and this means actual knowledge and not suspicion.

Restatement of the Law of Agency, § 321 provides:

"Unless otherwise agreed, a person purporting to make a contract with another for a partially disclosed principal is a party to the contract.

Comment:

"a. A principal is a partially disclosed principal when, at the time of making the contract in question, the other party thereto has notice that the agent is acting for a principal but has no notice of the principal's identity." . . .

If liability exists, the defendant may not escape it upon the ground that the undisclosed principal, the United States of America, is solely responsible to the plaintiffs for any damages they may have sustained. . . .

CASE NO. 4

First Nat. Bank of Pipestone v. Siman. 65 S.D. 514, 275 N.W. 347 (1937)

RUDOLPH, P.J. On December 22, 1934, one Harry Harms borrowed from the plaintiff bank $2,595.30, and to secure the payment thereof executed and delivered to the plaintiff a chattel mortgage covering certain sheep located in Moody county, S.D. This mortgage was duly filed with the register of deeds of Moody county. The mortgage provided that, if default be made in any of its terms, or if any attempt be made to remove, dispose of, or injure said property by the mortgagor or by any other person, then the mortgagee would be entitled to take immediate possession of the property covered by the mortgage for the purpose of realizing on its security. On February 7, 1935, while the mortgage was still in force and without the knowledge or consent of the plaintiff, the said Harms transported the sheep from Moody county to Sioux City, Iowa, and there delivered them to the defendants who were commission merchants operating in the Sioux City stockyards. The defendants sold the sheep and realized therefrom the sum of $1,870.76, out of which sum the defendants paid $44.25 as yardage and insurance, $32 commission to themselves, and $73.08 to the truckers for transporting the sheep from Moody county to Sioux City. The balance was paid over to Harms. The defendants had no actual knowledge of the indebtedness owing by Harms to the plaintiff, or of the chattel mortgage covering the said sheep, until some time after the entire transaction was completed, . . . The plaintiff in this action seeks to hold the defendants liable for the wrongful conversion of the said sheep. The trial court . . . held that the defendants were not liable to the plaintiff, . . .

. . . we are of the opinion that the question of notice or knowledge of the mortgage by these defendants is not decisive of their liability in this case. If the defendants were not purchasers of these sheep, and we agree with respondent that they were not, they were the agents of Harms in selling and disposing of the sheep to the packing company. By the great weight of authority an agent who assists his principal in converting property of a third person to the use of the principal or master is personally liable to the true owner for the loss thereby inflicted. . . . The defendants not only assisted in the sale, but actually conducted the sale, and thereafter disbursed the proceeds derived from such sale. Clearly, these defendants played an active and very important part in the conversion of these sheep. The only defense is that the defendants acted innocently and without knowledge or notice of plaintiff's mortgage. However, we are convinced that innocence or lack of notice or knowledge is no real defense. The applicable rule is well stated in the Restatement of the Law of Agency, § 349, as follows:

> "An agent who does acts which would otherwise constitute conversion of a chattel is not relieved from liability by the fact that he acts on account of his principal and reasonably, although mistakenly, believes that the principal is entitled to possession of the chattels."

. . . . .

The judgment appealed from is reversed.

Review Questions

1. Under what circumstances may an agent be liable upon authorized contracts?
2. How would you sign a contract when acting as an agent so as to avoid personal liability?
3. Is an agent personally liable upon an authorized contract entered into on behalf of an undisclosed principal?
4. Is an agent personally liable upon an unauthorized contract entered into on behalf of a disclosed principal?
5. How may an agent avoid the implied warranty that he has authority to act?
6. Upon what basis can an agent be held liable where he has contracted for a principal who has disaffirmed his contract upon the basis of mental incompetency?
7. Does an agent impliedly warrant that the principal for whom he is acting will be able and willing to perform the contract?
8. If a third party has made an overpayment to an agent, he may recover such from the principal. May he elect to recover it from the agent?
9. Can an agent avoid liability for an injury he has caused to another upon the basis that the principal had authorized the act from which the injury resulted?
10. What are the rights of a third party against the agent where the agent has intentionally misrepresented the extent of his authority?

Problems for Discussion

1. An agreement read, "Dear Friend Schwab: Referring to our talk . . . yesterday, regarding the $1,000 worth of stock, Mr. Summers and I both agree to take back same January 1, 1924, if after that time you give us 15 days' notice.

   "Yours very truly,

   Yakima Shoe Co.,
   Geo. A. Getty, Pres.
   P. S. Summers, Sec."

   Are Getty and Summers personally liable upon the above agreement?

2. The defendant corporation instructed its employee, Kartheiser, to take bids for a milling machine which had been advertised for sale. Kartheiser was offered $1,250 by plaintiff and accepted a check for that amount. Within a few hours the attempted sale was repudiated by defendant corporation and the check returned. Is the corporation liable to plaintiff? What will determine whether Kartheiser is liable? (*Moser* v. *Kyle Corporation,* 39 N.W. (2d) 587)

3. This case arose by Childs and Register, a partnership, hereinafter called the plaintiff, entering suit on a note against Henry G. Hampton, Jr., hereinafter called the defendant, before a Justice of the Peace. The stipulations are: "The whole case is to be decided on a few sentences of the note, and with the considerate cooperation of attorney for the defendant in error, this joint statement will save the Court much reading. The material parts of the note are as follows: 'Tifton, Georgia. May 6, 1947. On or before the 1st day of October, 1947, we promise to pay to the order of Childs and Register, the sum of one hundred sixty-two and 50/100 dollars, at Tifton, Georgia, for value received. . . (signed) E. Harold Hampton, by Henry G. Hampton, Jr.' The note was of printed form with space left for insertion of facts peculiar to each note, and the pronoun 'we' was inserted with pen and ink at the time of the execution of the note."

   The plaintiff contends that, since the pronoun "we" was inserted in the note, both E. Harold Hampton and Henry G. Hampton, Jr., the defendant, were severally and individually bound.

4. On June 17, 1946, John Howard, the manager of plaintiff, and defendant had a telephone conversation, which Howard, on direct examination, states was as follows: "Mr. Robinson called me over the telephone and ordered for a friend of his. I believe this gentleman was located in Sleepy Eye—ordered these tires 700 by 20, 10 ply and one 650 by 16, 4 ply Firestone tire. I took this order over the telephone recognizing Bob Robinson's voice, and he also told me who he was."

   On cross-examination, Howard testified that defendant told him that he was ordering the tires for a Mr. Peale of Sleepy Eye; that he (Howard) definitely knew at that time that defendant was not ordering them for himself; that defendant had no equipment upon which he could use the tires. Howard also testified that he was told by defendant at the time the tires were ordered that he, defendant, had Peale's check with him, but he was not told to whom it had been issued. In the course of the telephone conversation, defendant, according to Howard, said that he was using the Minnesota Poultry & Egg Company name, as he wanted that company's fleet discount.

The tires were delivered to the poultry company's plant the afternoon of June 17. Plaintiff's driver accepted the poultry company's check in payment and marked the bill "paid." The poultry company's fleet discount was given. The next day defendant gave Peale's check to the poultry company and later took the tires down to Peale. The check given by the poultry company was returned by the bank to plaintiff because of insufficient funds. Peale's check was deposited by the poultry company to its credit. A few days later, the poultry company filed a petition in bankruptcy. Plaintiff then brought this action against defendant. On the above facts, the trial court directed a verdict for defendant. Decide. (*Firestone Tire & Rubber Co.* v. *Robinson,* 31 N.W. (2d) 18)

5. The introductory part of a contract read: "Agreement between Horace Heard, Eli Sherman, and Newall Heard (the defendants), committee of the town of Wayland, on the one part, and William Simonds and John Chaplin on the other part." After a specific designation of the work to be done by Simonds and Chaplin, the agreement concluded: "Said committee are to pay the sum of $375 when said work is completed." The contract was signed by the defendants with their own names. Are they personally liable?
6. Assuming to act for B, A entered into a contract in B's name with C. B cannot be held upon the contract by reason of the fact that A had no authority to contract. Should A be personally held to performance of the contract?
7. Williams signed a promissory note in the following manner: "Williams, as agent." Can Williams successfully defend, in an action against him upon the note, by alleging that he acted as agent for Johns in executing the note?
8. X, acting as agent for P, sold Y a certain machine. Y insisted upon inserting a warranty of performance into the standard-form contract that X was authorized to use. X objected that he had no such authority but signed the contract saying, "I doubt if the boss will go for this." The machine did not perform in accordance with the warranty. What are Y's rights?
9. A contract was entered into between the "Cumberland Presbyterian Church of Abbott, by F. B. Wilkes, chairman of the building committee" and the Texas Seating Company. The Church being an unincorporated association, Wilkes was sued upon the contract as an individual. His defense was that he was acting as an agent for the church in an authorized capacity. Result?
10. Y owed P a sum of money. Y made payment to P's agent X but overpaid to the amount of $500. Y upon discovering the overpayment demanded a return of the money from X, who refused and turned the money over to his principal P. Before Y could get a return of the $500 from P, the latter became insolvent. Can Y look to X for repayment?
11. X contracted with Y without disclosing that he was in fact acting for his principal P. Can Y, after he discovers this fact, still hold X to the contract?
12. X, acting as the agent for P, contracted to sell Y certain store fixtures. P failed to carry out the contract. Can Y hold X for breach of contract?
13. At the direction of P, X sells merchandise that, unknown to X, belongs to Y and to which P has no right. Y sues X for the injury suffered and X defends upon the ground that he was acting in good faith at the direction of and for the benefit of P. Result?

15 AGENCY:

RIGHTS AND DUTIES AS BETWEEN PRINCIPAL AND AGENT

► I. DUTIES OF AGENT TO PRINCIPAL

An agent's duties to his principal are greater than those provided for by agreement. The law attaches legal rights and duties to many relationships, of which agency is one. The agent, in addition to being responsible for the substantial performance of those duties contained in the contract of agency, acquires certain other duties, which arise wholly out of the relationship itself. These duties are binding upon the agent even though he receives no compensation for his undertaking.

A. DUTY OF LOYALTY

An agent stands in the position of a fiduciary to his principal. In an agency relationship, the principal, in bestowing upon his agent certain actual and apparent powers, reposes in the agent trust and confidence that those powers will not be abused. Authority in the hands of an agent can be a dangerous and damaging force to the principal—a force that the principal is in no position to control. An agent could easily act for his own benefit or for the benefit of others in disregard of the principal's interests. Consequently, the agent has the duty to be loyal to his employer, being required to deal with such fairness and integrity as will fully protect the latter's interests and to do nothing that will be to his disadvantage.

Since an agency relationship is of a highly personal and confidential nature, the agent cannot delegate his duties to another if they call for the exercise of discretion, skill, or judgment. To allow a delegation of duties of this nature would be to defeat the principal's expectations which he bargained for upon the basis of the trust and confidence he reposed in the agent.[1, 2]

1. *Duty not to Profit or Obtain Personal Benefit*

The agent is, in loyalty to his principal, legally bound not to prosecute the agency for his own profit or to take advantage personally of information peculiar to the agency. Any advantages or profits so obtained by the agent are held by him in trust for the principal.[3] The principal can, upon reimbursing the agent for any expenditures made, require that such profits or advantages be transferred or made available to him. Therefore, any profits resulting from speculation by the agent with property of the principal belong to the latter, and the agent can be held to

[1] Barber Agency Co. v. Co-op. Barrel Co., p. 401.
[2] Kadota Fig Ass'n v. Case Swayne Co., p. 402.
[3] Quinn v. Phipps, p. 403.

account for them.[4] Nor is the agent entitled to a commission paid him by a third person with whom he might deal. It is at times difficult to distinguish between a gratuity and a commission arising out of the transaction. An agent who, through his efforts, is capable of making purchases below the market price cannot keep the difference for himself. And where the agent compromises a claim or settles a debt for a sum less than that furnished him by the principal for such purpose, he must return the balance to the principal.

2. *Duty not to Have or Represent Interest Adverse to That of Principal*

a. Sale or Purchase of Property. In loyalty to his principal, a selling agent cannot sell to himself or to an organization in which he has an interest without a full disclosure of such fact to the principal.[5] Unless the agent obtains the consent of the principal upon the basis of having acquainted him with all the facts, the principal can have the transaction set aside. To illustrate:

(1) In *Foss Inv. Co.* v. *Ater,* 49 Wash. 446, it was held that the principal could avoid a sale of real estate by the agent to a corporation in which the latter had a substantial interest.

(2) In *Steele* v. *Lawyer,* 47 Wash. 266, the agent employed to sell land represented to the principal that the property had been sold for taxes, and that the principal had no interest remaining. The agent knew that the tax sale was void but failed to so inform the principal. He then procured a quitclaim deed to the property from the principal for himself in the name of a third person. It was held that the deed was void at the election of the principal.

By the same token, an agent empowered to buy for his principal cannot sell the principal his own property unless the principal knows the facts and consents.

b. Investment of Funds. Likewise, an agent who is authorized to invest funds for his principal has the duty, in loyalty to his principal, not to invest the funds with himself or in any enterprise in which he has an interest. For example:

In *Sterling* v. *Smith,* 97 Cal. 343, the agent invested the principal's money in a corporation of which the agent was a stockholder. He failed to disclose to the principal the fact of membership and the fact that the corporation had a large indebtedness. It was held that even though the agent had no wrongful intent, he failed in his duty to the principal and therefore made himself personally liable.

c. Acting as Agent for Both Parties. The duty of loyalty prevents an agent from representing both parties in the same transaction.[6] Opposing interests can hardly be best served by the same agent. The possibilities are great that under such circumstances the interests of one or the other would be sacrificed. The court in *British America Assurance Co.* v. *Cooper,* 6 Colo. App. 25, pointed out that the best to be hoped of an agent acting in a dual capacity in a transaction is impartiality. However, this qualification is inconsistent with the concept of agency, since the agent is chosen by the principal to be a partisan and not an impartial arbitrator.

---

[4] Eagle Indemnity Co. v. Cherry, p. 404.

[5] Myers v. Ellison, p. 405.

[6] Quest v. Barge, p. 406.

d. Duty not to Engage in Rival Business. Unless it is clearly understood between the principal and agent, the latter has no right to engage in any business or dealings of his own that are of a similar nature or adverse to those of the principal.[7, 8] Should the agent violate this rule, he makes himself liable to the principal for any profits or advantages that he has gained.

Likewise, if an agent agrees to serve the principal exclusively, he cannot serve others at the same time. Thus, if an agent obtains the exclusive right to sell the principal's products in a designated area, he cannot undertake to represent a competing manufacturer. The extent to which an agent may represent others at the same time is dependent upon the understanding between him and his principal. To illustrate:

In *Randall* v. *Peerless Car Co.,* 212 Mass. 352, the agent had agreed to devote "his best energies" to his principal. It was held that this did not bind the agent to serve his principal exclusively.

B. DUTY TO INFORM PRINCIPAL

By employing an agent, the principal extends his personality to the degree that the eyes and ears of the agent are those of the principal for the purposes of the agency. The law imputes to the principal knowledge of all material facts possessed by the agent—such facts as are material to the purposes of the agency. The modern weight of authority undoubtedly is that this rule also applies to knowledge pertinent to the business of the agency that was acquired prior to the formation of the agency.

> "It is, however, only when the knowledge acquired by an agent in a previous transaction is legally presumed or clearly shown by circumstances, or other evidence, to have been in his mind at the time of the subsequent transaction, that it can be imputed to his principal therein." *Guaranty Trust Co.* v. *Koehler,* 195 Fed. 669.

This rule that *notice to the agent is notice to the principal* is frequently said to find its basis in the legal duty of the agent to inform his principal of all knowledge pertaining to matters over which his authority extends.[9] By failing to comply with this duty, the agent subjects himself to liability to his principal for any injury resulting from such a failure. To illustrate:

(1) An agent who discovers an unrecorded lien upon property that he is authorized to purchase has the duty of informing his principal of this fact. Should he act without imparting this knowledge to the principal, the latter is, nevertheless, charged with notice of the lien and acquires the property subject to it. Notice of the lien to the agent is imputed to the principal. And the agent, by failing in his duty, is responsible to the principal for the loss suffered.

(2) Similarly, knowledge by the agent of defects in property that he is authorized to sell—such as the worthlessness of securities—charges the principal with

---

[7] Colonell v. Goodman, p. 408.

[8] First Nat. Bank of Mandan v. Larsson, p. 410.

[9] Nissen v. Nissen Trampoline Co., p. 411.

notice of such facts. The agent should, to discharge his duty, convey such information to the principal.

(3) And if an agent, authorized to sell property for a definite price, has knowledge that the property has a much greater value than is thought by the principal, the agent is bound to impart such information to his principal.

C. DUTY TO OBEY INSTRUCTIONS

The agent has the duty of obediently carrying out and observing all instructions and limitations given to him by the principal.[10] Where the instructions are positive and unequivocal in meaning, the agent has no discretion in their observance. By his failure to adhere faithfully to instructions and limitations, the agent forfeits his right to commissions or compensation, subjects himself to discharge by the principal, and makes himself liable for any loss suffered by the principal. A deviation from the limits of the agency as established by the principal cannot be justified by laudability of motive. An agent instructed to buy goods of a given brand cannot, after purchasing goods of another brand, defend his actions upon the grounds that it was his conviction that the brand purchased was a "better buy" and consequently to the advantage of his employer. To illustrate:

In *Comley* v. *Dazian,* 114 N.Y. 161, the agent was entrusted to sell property for the principal at a price to be approved by the principal. The agent, by selling without approval, failed to obey instructions and made himself liable to the principal for the value of the property.

1. *Qualification of Rule*

The principal cannot expect the agent to follow instructions if to do so would be in violation of a positive rule of law or in disregard of the legal rights of others. The right and duty of an agent to exercise emergency powers further limits the application of the rule. Should an emergency situation arise, requiring immediate action for the protection of the principal's interests, the agent would not only be justified in disregarding instructions but might be required to take action appropriate to that end. To illustrate:

In *Bernard* v. *Maury,* 20 Gratt. (61 Va.) 434, the agent was instructed to buy certain bonds for the principal. Before the agent received the funds with which to buy, there had been a substantial and unexpected rise in the price of the bonds. It was held that the agent was justified in not carrying out the instructions to buy and in asking for further instructions, although a loss was occasioned by the delay.

D. DUTY TO ACCOUNT

The agent has the duty to hold himself accountable to his principal for all property, profits, and proceeds coming into his possession by virtue of the agency. This requires the agent to keep a record of his agency transactions, and such record must be of sufficient adequacy as to make it possible for the agent to comply with his duty of accountability. The principal can make reasonable demands upon the

---

[10] Mair v. S. Minn. Broadcasting Co., p. 412.

agent for statements and other evidence, such as receipts or vouchers, which would be necessary to show the true status of the agency's affairs.

A proper accounting for the principal's property demands that the agent refrain from commingling it with property of his own.[11] Intermingling of property makes the agent personally responsible for any loss of the principal's property. By depositing funds of the principal in his own personal account or in his own name without properly identifying the deposit as being that of his principal, the agent becomes liable for any loss, such as might, for example, result from insolvency of a bank.[12] By earmarking the funds as belonging to the principal, the agent has fully discharged his duty, providing he exercised proper care in selecting the depository.

It is also the agent's duty to surrender to the principal the latter's property upon demand. A wrongful withholding or misappropriation of the property by the agent would give the principal legal recourse against the agent to recover either the specific property or its value. Money held by the agent could not, however, be recovered by the principal unless he could identify the fund as belonging to him. In the event of being unable to make a specific identification, the principal would stand as a general creditor in respect to money in the hands of the agent.

E. DUTY NOT TO BE NEGLIGENT

An agent, upon undertaking performance of a task for another, gratuitously or for a compensation, assumes the legal obligation of doing it in a proper manner. A failure to perform the task in a proper manner is designated as negligence. Negligence in performance of duties consists of doing something that should not have been done or in omitting to do something that should have been done. More specifically, negligence would be a failure to exercise ordinary and reasonable care, skill, and diligence—the test being that care, skill, or diligence which a person of ordinary skill and prudence would exercise under like or similar circumstances.[13]

An agent authorized to sell on credit, while not guaranteeing that all accounts will prove good, would be responsible for losses due to extending credit indiscriminately. He has the duty to exercise such care, skill, and diligence in ascertaining whether the individual case merits the giving of credit as should be exercised by a person of ordinary skill and prudence engaged in a similar undertaking and in a like capacity.

The same problem arises when an agent is authorized either to buy or sell but no price is specified by the principal. In this case, the agent is again required to exercise proper care in determining what is a reasonable price. An agent would make himself liable to the principal if, for example, he contracted to sell the principal's products at a price that makes it impossible for the principal to perform.

It has also been generally held by the courts that the agent is negligent if he does not sell at the best price obtainable, even though he has been authorized to sell at a lower price.

[11] Rotzin v. Miller, p. 414.
[12] Hibbard v. Furlong, p. 415.
[13] Shatz Realty Co. v. King, p. 417.

► II. DUTIES OF PRINCIPAL TO AGENT

A. DUTY TO COMPENSATE

The duty of the employer to compensate the agent for his services arises from either an express or implied promise to pay.[14] If, in the absence of an express agreement, services are rendered under circumstances that exclude a gratuity, a promise to pay will be implied. Unless the amount of compensation has been agreed upon, the measure of the obligation is the reasonable value of the services.

The problems arising in respect to an agent's right to compensation are numerous. A few of the more general considerations under which they arise are as follows:

(1) The right to compensation is dependent upon adequacy of performance. As in most contracts, in accordance with the general rule, substantial performance is sufficient. Only if the contract is severable will the agent be entitled to compensation for partial performance.

(2) It can be said that by failing to discharge any of his various legal duties to the principal, the agent generally forfeits his rights to compensation.[15, 16, 17]

(3) If the principal wrongfully revokes the agency before the expiration of the contract, the agent cannot stand by in expectation of being compensated for the unexpired term. Like most other parties injured by a breach of contract, the agent has, under the general and better rule, the duty to mitigate damages—he has the duty to make a reasonable effort to find employment of a like or similar nature. The courts say that to hold otherwise would be an encouragement to idleness, which, as a matter of public policy, is to be discouraged.

B. DUTY TO REIMBURSE

It is implied from an agency relationship that the principal will reimburse the agent for all necessary and proper expenditures made in the conduct of the principal's affairs. The right of reimbursement is contingent upon the fact that the expenditures have been made within the limits of the agent's authority. An agent cannot take it upon himself to pay the principal's debts without authority to do so. Such voluntary payments will not entitle him to reimbursement. An agent employed to manage properties would have the right to be reimbursed for expenditures necessary to preserve and protect the properties from ordinary wear and tear; expenditures made for permanent improvements or for the reconstruction of buildings destroyed could not be charged to the principal. Likewise, a failure to obey instructions will bar the agent from exercising the right of reimbursement. Should an agent who is authorized to purchase 500 shares of stock purchase 100 shares only, he could not hold the principal liable for any money advanced on the purchase. A lack of proper accounts and records of expenditures made by the agent may prevent him from establishing his right to reimbursement.

---

[14] Harry H. Rosen Co. v. Eksterowicz, p. 418.

[15] Faultersack v. Clintonville Sales Corp., p. 420.

[16] Raymond v. Davis, p. 421.

[17] Wold v. Patterson, p. 422.

C. DUTY TO INDEMNIFY

It is also implied from an agency relationship that the principal will indemnify the agent for any losses or liabilities incurred as a consequence of performing his agency duties. There is every reason why the principal should assume the responsibilities for his own acts performed by the agent. Providing that he properly discharges his duties while acting in good faith, the agent has recourse against the principal to be indemnified for any losses suffered or liabilities imposed upon him as a result of his performance. By contracting for an undisclosed principal, an agent subjects himself to personal liability to those with whom he deals. Any liability for a failure of performance would ultimately repose in the principal. Likewise, if the agent, at the direction of the principal, deals with property in disregard of another's legal or equitable interest, the agent personally becomes liable for the conversion. However, if his actions were performed in good faith, without notice of such interest, he can look to his principal for indemnity in the event that liability for the conversion is imposed upon him. To illustrate:

(1) If an agent sells property at the direction of the principal which belongs to another, he thereby makes himself liable to the true owner. If he has acted in good faith, he can recover any loss he suffers from the principal.

(2) In *Horrabin* v. *Des Moines,* 198 Iowa 549, the plaintiff, under the direction of the City Engineer of Des Moines, entered upon property belonging to the Central Ice Co. and constructed a bridge approach, without knowledge of the fact that the city had no right to so use the land. The plaintiff had to pay a judgment, obtained by the Central Ice Co., for the damages resulting from the trespass. He then sued to recover from the defendant for whom the work was done. The court said:

> ". . . Where one is employed or directed by another to do an act not manifestly wrong, the law implies a promise of indemnity by the principal for damages resulting proximately from the good-faith execution of the agency. . . . While as between himself and the owner of the property, he was a trespasser, and liable as such, as between himself and the city, he was but acting in fulfillment of his duty and under the direction of the properly constituted authority of an officer of the city. . . . As between himself and the city, the wrong was the wrong of the city. . . ."

► III. AGENT'S RIGHT OF LIEN

To secure the agent for unsatisfied claims against the principal that arise out of the right to compensation, reimbursement, or indemnity, the law gives the agent a lien upon the principal's property in the agent's possession. The lien is dependent upon the agent's having and retaining possession of the principal's property. The agent's right of lien is merely the right of retention; redress, unless governed by statutory provision, has to be obtained through equitable proceedings.

CASES

CASE NO. 1

Barber Agency Co. v. Co-Operative Barrel Co. 133 Minn. 207, 158 N.W. 38 (1916)

TAYLOR, C. Plaintiff appealed from an order sustaining a demurrer to its complaint.

The complaint sets forth that W. H. Barber was a broker and maintained an organization for the sale of commercial products; that he made a contract with defendant to have the exclusive sale, at a stated commission, for a term of years, of all the butter tubs manufactured by defendant; that after performing such contract for more than four years and establishing a large and lucrative business in the sale of such tubs, he organized the plaintiff corporation which took over all his business and his organization, and has ever since continued the same without any change in the personnel or management thereof; that defendant refused to permit the plaintiff corporation to perform the remainder of Barber's contract for the sale of its tubs; and that plaintiff has been damaged thereby in the amount of the commissions which it could have earned during the remainder of the term.

The sole question presented and argued is whether Barber could transfer his contract to the plaintiff corporation without the consent of the defendant.

Barber was defendant's sales agent, and the case is controlled by the rules governing agency, and not by the rules which apply in the case of assignments of choses in action or of executory contracts creating rights of a different nature. The powers conferred upon an agent are based upon the confidence which the principal has in the agent's ability and integrity; and it is the universal rule that an agent cannot transfer to another powers calling for the exercise of discretion, skill, or judgment. . . . It is held that, where a principal has authorized a partnership to act as his agent, the subsequent dissolution of the partnership terminates the agency, and that a partner who takes over the business cannot continue to act as such agent unless the principal authorizes him to do so. . . .

In Wheaton v. Cadillac Automobile Co., 143 Mich. 21, 106 N.W. 399, the New Jersey Automobile Company, a partnership composed of two members, was defendant's selling agent in the state of New Jersey. One of the partners withdrew from the firm and assigned all his interest in the business to the other. The court held that this gave defendant the right to abrogate the contract.

In the present case, defendant made Barber its agent. He assumed to transfer to a corporation the powers conferred upon him personally. The corporation is a separate entity controlled by a board of at least three directors, and its stockholders and officers are subject to change at any time. If it acquired Barber's rights under his contract with defendant, it would retain such rights even if Barber should entirely sever his connection with it. To permit a person, employed as an agent, to transfer his duties and powers to a corporation without the consent of his principal would involve a more radical violation of the rules governing the relation of principal and agent than to permit a partnership, employed as an agent, to devolve its powers and duties upon one of its members. Barber could no more substitute plaintiff for himself as defendant's agent, without defendant's consent, than he could so substitute any other corporation or individual.

Order affirmed.

CASE NO. 2

Kadota Fig Ass'n v. Case-Swayne Co. 73 Calif. (2d) 815, 167 P. (2d) 523 (1946)

This case involves the validity of a surety bond executed under the following circumstances:

One J. J. Fluetsch was authorized as agent of the Glens Falls Indemnity Co. to execute and issue surety bonds in its behalf. The bond in question was executed by Fluetsch but before signing he went to Los Angeles and then remembered the bond was to be issued that day. He called Judge Shaffer by telephone and directed him to sign the bond in Fluetsch's name, as agent for the company, which was done.

The trial court held the surety bond to be void since not personally signed by the agent.

THOMPSON, J. . . . The record clearly indicates, without conflict, that no authority or discretion was attempted to be delegated by the agent, J. J. Fluetsch, to Judge Shaffer, to determine whether the bond should be executed or to pass upon the terms and conditions thereof. That was previously done by the agent himself. Judge Shaffer merely acted as the amanuensis for the duly authorized agent of the company, and signed his name at the agent's request. A signature to an instrument may be attached by (1) the hand of a party thereto, (2) by the hand of another, at the request of a party, or (3) by means of the mark of a party when he is unable to write his name. . . . It may be written, printed, stamped, typewritten, engraved or photographed. 58 C.J. 729, § 17. . . . In 17 C.J.S., Contracts § 62, subsec. c, p. 413, it is said that

> "One may be bound by an agreement to which his signature is affixed by procuration, adoption, or ratification, as well as though it had been written by his own hand."

While, in the absence of specific authority so to do, an agent may not delegate power to another to pass upon the terms of a contract or to bind the principal by its unauthorized execution, the agent may nevertheless delegate to another the power to perform purely mechanical acts with relation thereto. . . .

. . . (Sayre v. Nichols, 7 Cal. 535) the court uses the following pertinent language:

> "An agent cannot delegate any portion of his power requiring the exercise of *discretion or judgment;* it is otherwise, however, as to powers or duties merely *mechanical* in their nature. Hence, if empowered to bind his principal by an accommodation acceptance, he may direct another to write it, having first determined the propriety of the act himself; and it will bind the principal, though naming the delegate and not the agent, as the one exercising the power."

The foregoing language applies to the present case, in which there was no attempt to delegate authority to the amanuensis to exercise discretion with respect to the provisions of the bond, but merely authorized him to sign the agent's name to the document. It is not necessary that such authorization to merely sign the name of an agent to a surety bond shall be in writing. A multitude of authorities hold that an oral request to perform the mere mechanical act of signing another person's name to an instrument is valid and binding, even though the instrument is required to be in writing. . . .

We are of the opinion the signature is valid and binding when the authorization to sign the instrument is conveyed directly to the amanuensis by telephone, as it was in this case. . . .

CASE NO. 3

Quinn v. Phipps. 93 Fla. 805, 113 So. 419, 54 A.L.R. 1173 (1927)

TERRELL, J., delivered the opinion of the court:

. . . John S. Phipps . . . filed his bill of complaint . . . praying that the option secured by Quinn from Mrs. Watson be decreed to be held in trust for the sole benefit of the complainant; . . .

. . . decree was entered as prayed. . . .

Stripped of all embellishing verbiage, it may be confidently asserted that every instance in which a confidential or fiduciary relation in fact is shown to exist will be interpreted as such. The relation and duties involved need not be legal; they may be moral, social, domestic or personal. If a relation of trust and confidence exists between the parties (that is to say, where confidence is reposed by one party and a trust accepted by the other, or where confidence has been acquired and abused), that is sufficient as a predicate for relief. The origin of the confidence is immaterial.

Now let us inspect the record and see what it reveals to establish a relation of trust and confidence between Quinn and Phipps. It is shown that Quinn was a real estate broker doing business in West Palm Beach; that McDonald was the agent of Phipps; that Quinn on his own initiative approached McDonald and told him that he had a price on Mrs. Watson's property and requested him (McDonald) to assist him in finding a purchaser for it; that McDonald immediately communicated this information to Phipps, who authorized him (McDonald) to submit to Mrs. Watson through Quinn a cash offer of $50,000 for the property. It is further shown that McDonald urged Quinn to submit the offer to Mrs. Watson by long-distance telephone, but Quinn refused, agreeing instead to go to Boston in person to negotiate the purchase for Phipps. Quinn proceeded at once to Boston in compliance with his agreement with McDonald, but, after interviewing Mrs. Watson, instead of purchasing for Phipps, he purchased the property for himself at $45,000, and made no mention of Phipps's offer. . . .

It is contended by Quinn that the mere breach of his promise or agreement to purchase for Phipps did not establish a constructive trust in favor of Phipps.

. . . the modern current of authority both in this country and in England is to the effect that, if an agent be employed to negotiate the purchase of land for his principal, and violates the principal's confidence by purchasing the land with his own money and taking a deed therefor to himself, he becomes a constructive trustee for the principal's benefit, upon payment of the purchase price. . . .

The real estate business is not an avenue by which one may practice the tricks of his trade or prey on the innocent and unsuspecting purchaser, nor is it a cloak to cover fraud and deception, or a means for designing persons to short-circuit those who would deal squarely and in good faith. It is indeed a highly respectable business or profession; its ethics are well defined and presumed to be known to those who patronize or engage in that business. No business known to modern society has a longer or more respectable history. Real estate is a primary security for credit in all the civilized countries of the earth, and the real estate broker in our times is, and long has been, the medium through which annually many millions of dollars in earnings and savings are secured or invested. He is the agent of his principal in every sense, and, when that relation is undertaken, a fiduciary relation is created which bars the agent from becoming interested in the business or property antagonistic to his principal without his knowledge or consent. Every man, in other words, to whom a business is intrusted by another, has a trust to perform; and every man is a trustee whose business is to advise concerning, or to operate, the business of another.

. . . the decree of the Chancellor was properly entered, and is hereby affirmed.

CASE NO. 4

Eagle Indemnity Co. v. Cherry. 182 F. (2d) 298 (1950)

MC CORD, C.J. This action was brought by George T. Cherry, Harry T. Hoag, E. B. Manthey, and Thomas C. Blaylock, who composed the partnership firm of Southwest Industrial Equipment Company, against the Eagle Indemnity Company, a corporation organized under the laws of the state of New York. This suit is on a fidelity bond in the principal sum of $10,000.00. The case was tried by the district court without a jury, and judgment was entered in favor of plaintiffs in the amount of $9,039.74, plus interest.

The principal question presented is whether there is substantial evidence to support the finding of the trial court that the actions of the general manager of the partnership firm in buying and selling steel at a personal profit, when such steel was purchased in the partnership name and on the strength of its reputation and standing in the trade, was such fraud or dishonesty as would constitute a breach of defendant's fidelity bond, and render it liable for damages thereunder. . . .

In order to insure the honest and faithful performance of the duties of Chandler and the other partnership employees, the defendant, Eagle Indemnity Company, issued to the members of the partnership a fidelity bond upon payment of an agreed premium. . . .

When the relevant and material evidence is dredged up from the voluminous record in this case, it reveals conclusively that on different occasions during the months of May and June, 1947, Chandler purchased in the name of Southwest Industrial Equipment Company, from National Steel Products Company of Houston, Texas, several carloads of sheet steel which aggregated 451,624 pounds; that instead of taking over these steel shipments for his company he permitted one Batson to accept delivery of the steel and dispose of it for a profit on the open market, after which the profit received was divided between Batson and Chandler; that Chandler used the name of the partnership firm for which he worked, its reputation and its facilities to procure this steel and thereafter, through Batson, he clandestinely and fraudulently diverted the steel shipments from the company of which he was general manager to other persons and companies at an increased price, for which he was paid a share of the profits amounting to thousands of dollars. . . .

It is fundamental law that an agent bears a fiduciary relationship to his principal, and owes him the duty of good faith and loyalty. . . . By virtue of this relationship, no agent is entitled to take any unfair advantage that his position may offer him to profit, at his employer's expense, beyond the agreed compensation for his services. He should not be allowed to speculate for his own private gain adversely to the interests of his employer, or to compete with his employer's business without his knowledge or consent. Here, when Chandler, as the general manager and trusted employee of Southwest Industrial Equipment Company, purchased steel in his company's name which he would have been unable to procure on his own account, and later diverted the steel through Batson to the open market at a secret personal profit, he manifestly breached the duty of good faith which he owed to his employers. We therefore conclude the evidence unerringly discloses fraudulent and dishonest conduct on the part of Chandler while the fidelity bond was in full force and effect, and that such constitutes a clear breach of the terms of the bond for which the defendant is liable. . . .

The cases cited and relied upon by appellant are readily distinguishable under their own facts, and are in nowise applicable or controlling here. They merely hold that an employee need not account to his employer for an outside profit derived from an independent business not connected in any way with the business of his employer. Manifestly, that rule does not apply here. . . .

CASE NO. 5

Myers et al. v. Ellison et al. 249 Ala. 367, 31 So. (2d) 353 (1947)

. . . . .

SIMPSON, J. G. H. Myers and wife are the plaintiffs in a bill in equity to set aside a deed of 370 acres of land which they made to Dodd and Ellison, a firm of real estate brokers of Jasper, Alabama. . . .

Plaintiffs, who owned the land, employed Ellison as agent to sell it and first quoted a price of $9,500. Ellison interested Crawford in the property and subsequently reported to Myers that Crawford would not pay the price, but that he would pay $8,000. . . . Myers first declined this latter offer but later told Ellison he would accept it if the commission would come from the purchaser, that is, Myers to receive $8,000 net for the property . . . the deed . . . was not made to Crawford at all, but Dodd and Ellison were named in the conveyance as the grantees. The Myerses executed the deed without reading it, claiming that they put dependence in Ellison that the transaction was being consummated in the manner agreed upon, that is, that Crawford was buying the property. . . .

The trial court found all issues in favor of defendants and dismissed the bill, probably on the theory that since the Myerses were getting the full price, as last quoted by them, they had no just complaint. . . .

An agent sustains a position of trust toward his principal and in all transactions affecting the subject of his agency, the law dictates that he must act in the utmost good faith and must make known to his principal each and all material facts within his knowledge which in any way affect the transaction and subject matter of his agency. Lauderdale v. Peace Baptist Church, 246 Ala. 178, 19 So. (2d) 538; . . . 3 C.J.S., Agency, § 138a, p. 6. . . .

Consonant with this duty of utmost loyalty and good faith, a selling agent may not himself directly or indirectly become the purchaser of the property entrusted to him for sale without the full knowledge and consent of his principal. The pertinent rule is thus stated in 3 C.J.S., Agency, § 144a, p. 20:

"In the absence of full knowledge or consent on the part of his principal, an agent authorized to sell or lease his principal's property may not, either directly or indirectly, himself become the purchaser or lessee. . . . Accordingly, without his principal's knowledge and consent, he must not become a partner or otherwise jointly interested in purchasing the property."

. . . The extent to which the law frowns on the undisclosed purchase by the agent of his principal's property is thus explained in 1 Mechem on Agency, § 1198, 2d Ed.:

"The law looks at the natural and legitimate tendency of such transactions, and not at the motive of the agent in any given case. This tendency is demoralizing, and the fact that in a certain case the agent's motive was honorable, or that the result is more beneficial to the principal, will make no difference if the latter chooses to repudiate it."

In the light of these settled principles, and the prima facie voidableness of the sale under the circumstances related, it must be held that Myers had a right to rescind the sale. . . .

CASE NO. 6

Quest v. Barge. 41 So. (2d) 158 (Fla.) (1949)

BARNS, J. The vendee plaintiff brought suit for specific performance of a contract to sell property which was defended upon the grounds hereinafter stated. From an adverse decree the vendee appealed.

The record discloses that a real estate agent, Hugh R. Neighbors, was commissioned by J. T. Bevins and J. W. Weavers, co-partners, operating the Harlem Bar, in Pensacola, Florida, to purchase a brick building owned by appellees, Silas B. Barge and his wife, Evannah Barge. This property was in the same block as the Harlem Bar but was not listed for sale at this time and Neighbor's assignment was to persuade Barge to sell the property at a price agreeable to Bevins and Weaver.

When Neighbors approached Barge, he represented that he was in contact with some out-of-town people who desired to purchase property either in Pensacola or Mobile. To induce Barge to make his decision quickly he also represented that these out-of-town people would buy in Mobile if no suitable place were found in Pensacola in a very short time. When questioned by Barge as to the type of business they desired to operate, Neighbors said he heard or thought it was to be a second-hand store. These representations were untrue and were known to be so by Neighbors. After several visits Barge consented to sell his property for $11,000. Thereupon the contract of sale was executed, Neighbors signing as vendee and a check representing earnest money passed to Barge. This check was drawn on the Cabannis Agency, the realtors by whom Neighbors was regularly employed. Within several days after the signing of the contract of sale, appellee Barge learned the identity of the undisclosed principals and refused to be bound by the contract. Some five weeks later Neighbors assigned all his rights and obligations under the contract of sale to H. F. Quest, an employee of Bevins and Weaver, and appellant here.

On the 24th day of June, 1947, Quest filed a bill of complaint for specific performance of the contract of sale.

Appellee Barge successfully defended this suit in the court below. . . .

In order to fully comprehend the merit of appellee's defense, it is necessary to set forth facts which provide a background against which to consider the facts in the negotiations referred to.

The property which is covered by the contract of sale is a brick building in the City of Pensacola. In one part of the building appellee Barge operates a cafe; the remainder is let out to other establishments. The cafe is licensed to sell beer and wines and has a clientele in that business. Appellee Barge has for some time been desirous of selling whiskey on the premises, but has been unable to do so because of an ordinance of the city which prohibits more than one whiskey license to the block. The Harlem Bar, owned and operated by Bevins and Weaver, the real parties in interest to the contract, is in the same block as Barge's cafe and has the only available license to sell whiskey. Barge, Weaver and Bevins are competitors in the beer and wine trade.

For some years prior to the negotiations for the purchase of Barge's property, Weaver and Bevins have rented the premises occupied by the Harlem Bar. Recently, however, landlord trouble developed for them and their rent was more than doubled. As a result, they conceived the idea that it would be to their advantage to purchase their own premises. With this object in mind, Bevins and Weaver commissioned Neighbors to buy Barge's building, and thus the negotiations were begun which resulted in the contract of sale here in litigation.

The facts of the case show that Neighbors acted in the capacity of agent for both these parties to the contract. Bevins and Weaver commissioned Neighbors to purchase the Barge property for them. They did not want their identity known, and, at some stage of the proceedings directed Neighbors to sign the contract as vendee. They sent Neighbors to Barge knowing, again at some undisclosed stage of the negotiations, that he would become and did become the agent of Barge to sell the property. This fact was known to Bevins and Weaver, for Bevins testified that he understood that Neighbors was to receive the regular realtor's commission for selling Barge's property. Appellee Barge, on the other hand, knew only that Neighbors was in contact with some people who were interested in buying his property. He was led to believe by Neighbors' misrepresentation that they were "out-of-town people." Barge knew nothing of the relations between Neighbors and Bevins and Weaver. There can be little doubt that such limited knowledge of the true status of the agent Neighbors was insufficient to charge Barge with a full knowledge and consent to the double agency.

When Neighbors approached Barge to pursuade him to sell the property and expecting to become his agent for such purpose, an expectation that was fulfilled, it was incumbent upon him to make a full disclosure of all the facts of his relation to the vendee. In my opinion, the only alternative to this disclosure was to remain the agent of the vendee only. This principle is well established in the law.

In the American Law Institute's Restatement of Agency the duty of the agent assuming to act as agent for both parties to a transaction is as follows:

> "An agent who acts for adverse principals in a transaction is subject to a duty to act with fairness to each, *and to disclose to each all facts which he knows or should know would reasonably affect the judgment of each in permitting such dual agency,* except as to a principal who has manifested that he knows of such facts or that he does not care to know of them." . . .

Mr. Mechem in his learned treatise on the law of Agency states:

> ". . . If *my* agent enters into *your* employment without your knowledge of and consent to the double agency, you may repudiate because you were entitled to have a free and unprejudiced agent. Similarly, if your agent enters into *my* employment without my knowledge of the double relation,

I may repudiate." 2 Mechem on Agency (2nd Ed. 1914), § 2139. . . .

Perhaps the best statement of the law applicable to the inquiry at bar is that found in Evans v. Brown, 1912, 33 Okla. 323, 125 Pac. 469, 470:

"No principle is better settled than that a man cannot be the agent of both the seller and the buyer in the same transaction, without the intelligent consent of both. Loyalty to his trust is the most important duty which the agent owes to his principal. Reliance upon his integrity, fidelity, and ability is the main consideration in the selection of agents; and so careful is the law in guarding this fiduciary relation that it will not allow an agent to act for himself and his principal, nor to act for two principals on opposite sides in the same transaction. In such cases the amount of consideration, the absence of undue advantage, and other like features are wholly immaterial. Nothing will defeat the principal's right of remedy, except his own confirmation, after full knowledge of all the facts. Actual injury is not the principle upon which the law holds such transactions voidable. The chief object of the principle is not to compel restitution where actual fraud has been committed, or unjust advantage gained, but it is to prevent the agent from putting himself in a position in which to be honest must be a strain on him, and to elevate him to a position where he cannot be tempted to betray his principal." . . .

The decree appealed is affirmed.

CASE NO. 7

Colonell v. Goodman. 78 F. Supp. 845 (1948)

KIRKPATRICK, D.J. The plaintiff brought this action upon a contract by which, as he alleges, he was promised, for services in connection with the sale of the business of Parkway Oil Company, one of the defendants, a commission of five per cent upon the sale price.

The case was tried to the Court with a jury. The verdict was for the plaintiff and against all the defendants. . . .

The following is the substance of the plaintiff's case:

From 1937 until 1945 he was in the employ of American Oil Company as sales manager in charge of sales for Pennsylvania and six other states.

In 1939 and 1940 Parkway Oil Company, which operated a number of service stations in Philadelphia, was under contract with American to buy all its oil and gasoline from the latter. It was not, however, an exclusive distributor.

The plaintiff, beginning in the early part of 1939, in pursuance of his duties as sales manager for American, had numerous contacts and interviews with Goodman, the president of Parkway, in the course of which he made a number of suggestions for the improvement of its business and gave advice and assistance. During 1939 and the early part of 1940, the possibility of the plaintiff's leaving American and becoming interested in Parkway, either as a part owner or as an employee, was discussed. There never was any definite agreement but the plaintiff had some reason to think that the talk would lead to one.

In February or March, 1940, the plaintiff told Goodman that if he was to become financially interested in Parkway he would want it to have an exclusive distributorship and suggested that the Texas Company, a competitor of American, was the logical concern to negotiate with. . . .

The plaintiff went to New York where he interviewed one of the Texas vice-presidents and learned from him that Texas would not give an exclusive distributorship. However, in view of what was said at the interview, he came to the conclusion that Texas might be interested in purchasing Parkway and, on his return to Philadelphia, so advised Goodman. He, however, pointed out to Goodman that if Texas should buy Parkway there would be no possibility of his obtaining an interest in or employment with Parkway, whereupon Goodman promised him that if a sale to Texas should be consummated he would receive a commission of five per cent. At the same time Goodman told the plaintiff that he, Goodman, would handle all future negotiations with the Texas Company. . . .

In June, 1945, the plaintiff learned through a third party that Parkway had been sold to Texas and went to see Goodman who confirmed the news and also told the plaintiff that he would not get any commission.

The foregoing facts, which represent the evidence in its most favorable light to the plaintiff, present the case of an important official of a corporation, entrusted particularly with the promotion and maintenance of sales, who, without his employer's knowledge, sets about detaching one of his employer's largest customers and endeavoring to give its business to one of his employer's competitors, his purpose being to improve the business position of the customer with which he hopes (though without any definite assurance) to associate himself. When it appears that the competitor may be interested in purchasing the customer's business outright, he informs the customer of that fact, makes a contract with the customer to receive a commission on the sale and thereafter continues to advise and consult with the customer in the negotiations until the sale is consummated.

As to the nature of the cause of action; the plaintiff, in his complaint and consistently throughout the trial, maintained that the action was by an agent to recover a commission, . . .

The plaintiff, as a managing official or executive of a corporation, owed it a fiduciary as well as a contractual duty.

It can hardly be asserted, nor could a jury find, that a promise by a third party to compensate a sales manager of a corporation for his services in taking a large customer away from his employer is not one that tends to induce a violation of his duty. . . .

It is true that, as stated in § 393(e), Restatement, Agency, that an employee who expects to terminate his employment may, before the close of employment, make certain arrangements to establish himself in a new business, even with a view toward competing with his employer.

> "He may not, however, before the termination of his employment, solicit customers for such rival business, nor may he do other similar acts in direct competition with the employer's business," Restatement, Agency, § 393(e).

I do not believe that the plaintiff in the present case, even during the time when he had some prospect of becoming associated with Parkway, was justified in working, without his employer's knowledge, to switch Parkway's business from his employer to a competitor. However, that question is really not in the case because when he concluded, after his first interview with the Texas people, that they would not give Parkway a distributorship and made up his mind to advise Parkway of a possible sale and to do what he could to promote the sale, he ceased to be an employee planning to terminate his employment and became an employee working for compensation against his employer's interests. . . .

CASE NO. 8

First Nat. Bank of Mandan v. Larsson. 67 N.D. 243, 271 N.W. 289 (1937)

MORRIS, J. This is an action on a promissory note which was tried before the court, a jury having been waived. The plaintiff appeals from a judgment of dismissal and demands a trial de novo. . . . The note, dated March 10, 1934, and upon which about $1,900 was due at the time of trial, is a renewal of an indebtedness which had been renewed from time to time for a number of years.

At the time of trial the plaintiff held for collection another note dated June 29, 1931, given by Anton P. Ness to the defendant in the sum of $1,617.71. . . . The witness, Hess, was president of the bank. . . .

. . . On January 18, 1932, Hess wrote to the defendant:

"I hope to be able to get some money from Ness by the end of the month to apply on your note, but you should arrange to pay something besides and if you can pay your note down to the amount of the Ness Note, we will endeavor to work that out of him."

During the time that these letters were written Ness was indebted to the plaintiff bank in excess of $12,000. This indebtedness was partially secured. In addition to sums realized from its security the plaintiff collected from Ness $1,700 in $100 payments, which were applied upon Ness's debt to the plaintiff. The defendant did not know of Ness's indebtedness to the bank nor of his payments upon this indebtedness. The defendant claims that the plaintiff, while acting as his agent for the purpose of collecting the Ness note, received from Ness sufficient cash to pay the same, and that in failing to inform the defendant of Ness's indebtedness to the bank and its collections from him, the bank failed in its duty to him as his agent, and that these acts amount to bad faith and a constructive fraud upon the defendant which entitle him to damages equal to the amount due on the Ness note, and since this amount exceeds the note upon which this suit is brought, he is entitled to a dismissal of the suit. The trial court found in favor of the defendant's contention, and ordered the suit dismissed.

The plaintiff contends that Hess was acting as the defendant's agent in his individual capacity and that the bank was not the defendant's agent for the purpose of collecting the note. . . .

During the time that the letters from which we have quoted were written, Hess was president of the plaintiff bank and continued as such until July, 1934. He wrote these letters upon the bank's letterheads bearing his name as president. Some were signed as president, others were not. The correspondence deals not only with the collection of the Ness note, but also with the defendant's indebtedness to the bank. We have no hesitancy in saying that in the transactions concerning the Ness note Hess acted as an officer of the bank, and that the bank and not Hess as an individual, became Larsson's agent for the purpose of collecting the Ness note.

Hess testified that the payments made by Ness were credited in accordance with the debtor's definite and affirmative instructions. This testimony is undisputed. A debtor making a voluntary payment to a creditor to whom he owes several obligations has a right to direct to which debt or debts the payments shall be applied. . . .

Although the plaintiff could not apply Ness's payments contrary to his direction, it nevertheless occupied a very delicate position due to the fact that it had sought and obtained Larsson's note against Ness for collection while it was a substantial creditor of the maker. The plaintiff, in soliciting and accepting the collection under these circumstances, assumed an agency which charged it with the duty of advising Larsson of its relationship with Ness. In failing to advise Larsson that it was a creditor of Ness and was receiving payments from him, the plaintiff was guilty of a breach of duty to Larsson. . . . If an agent has interests adverse to the principal as to matters within the scope of the agency, it is the agent's duty to reveal such interests to the principal. Restatement, Agency, § 381.

A breach of duty alone is not sufficient to warrant the recovery of substantial damages by a principal against his agent. The principal must show that he was, in fact, damaged by the breach of duty, the measure of damages being the actual loss sustained. . . .

. . . Since from the record in this case it appears to us that the defendant may have suffered damages for which competent proof is available, the judgment is reversed and the case is remanded for further proceedings.

CASE NO. 9

Nissen v. Nissen Trampoline Co. 241 Iowa 474, 39 N.W. (2d) 92 (1949)

WENNERSTRUM, J. Plaintiff sought in her action to have declared void and thereby set aside three deeds to properties in which she previously had an interest. These deeds had transferred her interest in certain properties to defendant corporation of which plaintiff's former husband was president and majority stockholder. The trial court held that the defendant corporation was not guilty of any fraud and dismissed plaintiff's petition. She has appealed. . . .

The appellee, Nissen Trampoline Company, was organized as a corporation in June 1946. Its purpose is to manufacture and sell athletic equipment and its particular product is an apparatus consisting of supports to which springs are attached which in turn hold a tight canvas. By means of the springs and canvas greater resiliency is obtained in athletic tumbling exhibitions. . . .

Nissen has been president of the corporation since its organization and was so acting at the time of the signing of the deeds. The appellant was secretary until January 23, 1947. The minutes of the corporation show that on that date she was removed as secretary and an office employee was named in her place. . . .

It is appellant's contention that on or about March 1, 1947, she signed certain blank instruments which were presented to her by George P. Nissen, it being explained to her by him that they were papers in connection with the operation of the corporation. It is developed by the evidence that on or about March 4th the corporation received from Nissen three separate warranty deeds covering the three properties here involved. These deeds were signed by George P. Nissen and the appellant and are dated March 4, 1947. . .

The liability of a principal for the acts of its agent growing out of the agent's knowledge of certain facts as well as the liability of a principal under certain circumstances, including the situation where the agent is the sole representative of the principal, is commented upon in 2 Am. Jur., Agency, 300, par. 380, where it is stated:

"A qualification of the rule that the knowledge of an agent engaged in an independent fraudulent act on his own account is not the knowledge of the principal has also been made where the agent, though engaged in perpetrating an independent fraudulent act on his own account, is the sole representative of the principal. It is held under such circumstances that the agent's knowledge is imputable to his principal, and that the case falls within the general rule imputing the agent's knowledge to the principal. This qualification to the exception has been applied in cases involving agents and officers of corporations as well as in cases involving agents and other principals."

From a consideration of the many authorities we find the rule to be that a person is bound by the knowledge of his agent. This is predicated on the theory that it is the agent's duty to disclose all material facts coming to his knowledge with respect to the subject matter of his agency and it is presumed that he has discharged that duty. . . .

Applying the evidence in the instant case, a part of which has been heretofore set forth, to the rules of law heretofore announced, it is our conclusion that the fraudulent acts of Nissen are imputed to the corporation through the knowledge of Nissen of his fraudulent acts. He was the sole participating agent of the corporation in the obtaining of the deeds from the appellant. It is our firm conviction that his acts in relation to the appellant in the obtaining of her signature to the deeds were fraudulent in character and have been proved by clear, satisfactory and convincing evidence. . . .

. . . It should be kept in mind that under the authorities heretofore set out the principal cannot accept the fruits of the fraud practiced by the agent, repudiate the agent and his knowledge and yet retain the benefit obtained from the fraudulent transaction. . . . This is what the corporation is endeavoring to do. We cannot give our approval to such a procedure under the authorities previously set forth.

. . . the decree of the trial court is reversed . . . and the case is remanded for a supplemental decree in conformity with our holding herein announced. . . .

CASE NO. 10

Mair v. Southern Minn. Broadcasting Co. 226 Minn. 137, 32 N.W. (2d) 177, 4 A.L.R. 273 (1948)

MAGNEY, J. Plaintiff sued defendant to recover $1,250, his agreed salary for two months, claiming that defendant had violated and breached its contract of employment with him. The court directed a verdict for plaintiff. Defendant appeals from the order denying its motion for a new trial.

Defendant owns and operates a radio broadcasting station with studios in Rochester and Owatonna, Minnesota. On August 1, 1945, defendant employed plaintiff as its general manager for a term of five years, at a fixed salary per year, with a bonus, depending upon the increased profits of the business. The contract is in writing. It states that the duties to be performed by the general manager are those which usually appertain to such employment. After more than a year's operation of the business under plaintiff's management, the board of directors of the company was dissatisfied. The net income had decreased. The directors felt that the operating expenses were too high and that the income from the business was less than it should have been. On September 26, 1946, plaintiff received the following written order from the management:

"To Lester A. Mair:

"The Board of Directors directs you to appoint Maxine Jacobs, Assistant Manager of the Southern Minnesota Broadcasting Company, immediately, and until further notice issue all orders through her and contract for no expenditures without her approval. You are further directed to post notice of her appointment and authority as to execution of your orders on the bulletin board forthwith.

"Mrs. G. P. Gentling,
Chairman, Board of Directors,
Southern Minnesota Broadcasting Co."

Upon receipt of this order, plaintiff refused to continue with his work as long as the order was in effect. Defendant thereupon discharged him.

The trial court held that as a matter of law the order was unreasonable and directed a verdict as stated. . . .

The rule relative to the duties of an employee is stated in Von Heyne v. Tompkins, 89 Minn. 77, 81, 93 N.W. 901, 903, 5 L.R.A., N.S., 524, as follows: "Concededly, the relation of master and servant which existed between these parties cast certain duties upon the plaintiff, as the servant, which he was bound to fulfil and discharge; and the principal one was that of obedience to all reasonable orders of the defendant, the master, not inconsistent with the contract. Disobedience of reasonable orders is a violation of law which justifies a rescission by the master of the contract of employment, and the peremptory discharge of the servant. . . .

"So, if the orders given by the defendant were reasonable, under the circumstances, the discharge was in accordance with law, and was justifiable. If, upon the other hand, the orders were unreasonable, the discharge was contrary to law, unjustifiable, and would not protect defendant in an action brought by plaintiff to recover the reasonable value of his services. The defendant, when contracting with plaintiff, did not abdicate his right to manage his own business; nor did he surrender his position as owner of the farm and of the personal property thereon. He still retained the right to control his own affairs in his own way and any behavior of his servant in opposition or in violation of his reasonable orders and commands amounted to insubordination, which has always been held sufficient ground for the discharge of a servant."

The question, then, for determination is whether the order given plaintiff on September 26, 1946, was a reasonable order. If reasonable, it was his duty to obey, and his refusal to do so would justify defendant in discharging him. If unreasonable and inconsistent with the contract, his refusal to obey would be no justification for discharge. The board of directors has the right to manage the corporation, and when it gives an order the general manager must obey if it is a reasonable order. . . .

Plaintiff was employed as general manager of the company. There were no restrictions placed on him at the time of employment. His authority and duties were the usual ones that go with the position of general manager. Taking away his authority to issue orders directly was certainly inconsistent with his contract of employment and his position as manager. The authority previously vested in him and his right to direct activities were taken away from him. The order in question was incompatible with his contract of employment. To the employees, to the public, and to defendant itself, he would be manager in name only.

In Cooper v. Stronge & Warner Co. 111 Minn. 177, 179, 126 N.W. 541, 27 L.R.A., N.S., 1011, 20 Ann. Cas. 663, where the manager of a sales department who had been employed as such was superseded by another, but she was requested to remain as a clerk at the same salary, the court said:

". . . we . . . have concluded that,

if the master deliberately enters into a contract providing for the employment of another as manager, the employee has a right to insist upon retaining that grade, in the absence of any showing which would justify the master in reducing the rank of the servant. The grade of the employment may have been the inducing cause for this contract."

In the instant case, plaintiff was permitted to retain the name of manager, but his authority and prestige were taken away from him. It is fair to assume that no one in the position of plaintiff would have accepted the employment with such restrictions. . . .

So in this case there is no issue of fact for the jury. As to the reasonableness of the order, reasonable minds can come to but one conclusion. If so, it was for the trial court to determine as a matter of law. In making the determination that the order in question was unreasonable, it is our opinion that the trial court was clearly right.

Order affirmed.

CASE NO. 11

Rotzin v. Miller. 133 Neb. 4, 274 N.W. 190 (1937)

ROSE, J. This is a suit in equity by Mrs. Beverly Elizabeth Thomas Rotzin, plaintiff, to require A. R. Miller, William H. Thomas and Thomas D. Thomas, defendants, to account to her for a trust fund of $5,000, which her grandfather, David Thomas, willed to her in their care as trustees during her minority. Defendants admitted receipt of the trust fund, pleaded faithful execution of the trust and a willingness to turn over to plaintiff alleged trust property in their hands, including a deed for land and some diversified securities in small amounts. Upon a trial of the cause, the district court found the issues in favor of defendants, charged plaintiff with an overdraft of $146.55, with $50 for services in excess of other claims for compensation, with $200 for attorney's fees for defending the suit, made the sum of the three charges, or $396.55, a lien on the trust property and entered a decree in favor of defendants. Plaintiff appealed.

. . . . .

Before this litigation ensued, an attorney for plaintiff importuned defendants in a courteous manner to settle this controversy according to recognized standards of equity and justice. They declined to do so and stood on their own standards of accountability and on what they had done. When required to account in a court of equity, they offered to deed to plaintiff a quarter-section of land in Antelope county as a credit of $4,000, to assign to her 30 diversified securities, and to surrender the remainder as shown by their own accounts, which they introduced in evidence.

This land was not a part of testator's real estate and proved to be a poor investment. When it was encumbered by a 4,000-dollar mortgage defendants bought the lien in the name of a corporation called "Miller Allied Securities Company," trustee, before they qualified as trustees. Mortgagors made default in payment of their debt and later deeded the land, subject to the mortgage, to the Miller Allied Securities Company, trustee, but not naming the beneficiary. The title never stood in the name of plaintiff nor in the name of defendants as trustees for her . . . defendants . . . kept the title in such a condition as to enable them to sell the land at a profit, if possible, and unload it on plaintiff, if of little or no value. Some of the other property listed in their account as belonging to the trust estate is in a similar situation. Defendants are in no better situation than that of trustees who mingle trust funds with their own. The rules of equity that determine the accountability of defendants on the undisputed facts of this case have been stated in definite terms as follows:

> "Unless otherwise agreed, an agent receiving or holding things on behalf of his principal is subject to a duty to the principal not to receive or deal with them so they will appear to be his own, and not so to mingle them with his own things as to destroy their identity." Restatement, Agency, 900, § 398.

> "Unless the circumstances indicate otherwise, it is inferred that an agent employed to act for the principal is to act in the principal's name, and is to have title to anything obtained for the principal vested in the principal's name. In re Estate of Boschulte." 130 Neb. 284, 264 N.W. 881, 882.

According to these wholesome rules of equity, defendants did not perform their duties as trustees, or transact the business of the trust in the manner provided by law, or keep proper accounts, or hold the corpus of the trust in the name of the beneficiary or in their own names as trustees for the beneficiary, or fully inform her of their fiduciary transactions or turn over to her the trust property within a reasonable time after she reached her majority. By breach of trust and neglect of duty, they brought on plaintiff the burdens of litigation. Consequently, they are not entitled to compensation for services or to expenses or to costs or to fees of attorneys for defending the suit. . . . Plaintiff is entitled to a judgment against defendants for $5,000 with interest thereon at the legal rate from October 25, 1929, less payments received by her, and to costs in both courts. . . .

CASE NO. 12

Hibberd v. Furlong. 269 Mich. 514, 257 N.W. 737, 96 A.L.R. 794 (1934)

SHARPE, CH.J., delivered the opinion of the court:

The defendants are agents and brokers, transacting business on various stock exchanges for their customers. On Saturday, February 11, 1933, . . . the plaintiff gave one of defendants' employees a verbal open order to purchase 30 shares of Detroit Edison stock at $68 per share. It was then selling around $68.50 or $69 a share. The order was accompanied by a check on the First National Bank in Detroit, payable to the order of the defendants, for $2,100, signed by the plaintiff, and for which he was given a receipt and the amount thereof credited to his account. Defendants indorsed the check and deposited it on the same day in the National Bank of Commerce in Detroit.

. . . Plaintiff's check was cleared through the Detroit clearing house . . . and the amount thereof credited to the defendants' account in the National Bank of Commerce. Soon thereafter, and before either of the banks was opened for business on that day, a bank holiday was declared by proclamation of the Governor of the state, under which the banks were kept closed, and neither of them has reopened. The $2,100 deposit of defendants was intact in the National Bank of Commerce at the time it closed. The defendants received a dividend thereon from the receiver, amounting to 40 per cent. of the deposit, which was turned over to the plaintiff.

This action was brought to recover the balance claimed to be due plaintiff on his $2,100 check and interest thereon. . . .

The defendants contend that in

their receipt of the check from plaintiff, the proceeds of which were to be used in the purchase of a stock when it reached a stated price, and their deposit of the same in their bank in the usual course of their business, they were acting as agents of the plaintiff and that the relationship of debtor and creditor was not established thereby. The plaintiff insists that the defendants, by depositing the check in their bank to their own credit and thus mingling its proceeds with their other moneys, treated it as their own, and that when it passed through the clearing house and was paid they thereby became his debtor to the amount thereof.

"It seems to be clearly established that, when an intending purchaser orders a broker to purchase a particular stock for him, the relationship is that of principal and agent." Trowbridge v. O'Neill, 243 Mich. 84, 88, 219 N.W. 681, 683.

The general rule applicable to the relationship of principal and agent is stated in Mechem on Agency, § 1335, as follows:

"It is the duty of the agent to keep the property and funds of his principal separate from his own. If, without necessity, he has so commingled the goods or funds of his principal with his own that he cannot discriminate between the two, the whole mass so undistinguishable must be held to belong to the principal. If, without authority, he commingles in his dealings the goods of his principal and of himself, the principal will have the first charge upon the proceeds. So if he mingles the funds of his principal with his own and the whole is lost, the loss must fall upon the agent.

"This rule is of frequent application in cases where the agent has deposited money of his principal in a bank. In case it becomes necessary to make such a deposit, the agent will escape personal liability if he deposits it in the name of his principal in a bank of good credit, or if he so distinguishes it on the books of the bank as to indicate in some way that it is the money of his principal. If on the contrary he deposits it in his own name, or with his own funds, he will, in case of a failure of the bank, be liable to the principal for his money. . . ."

This rule seems clearly established. But, as stated therein, it does not apply if the commingling of funds was by authority of the principal, or if it became necessary to do so in the performance of the duty imposed on the agent in carrying out the order of his principal. . . .

The authorities relied on by plaintiff are applicable to an agent who receives moneys for, and to be delivered to, his principal, and who mingles them without authority in his personal account. Under the agency here created, the defendants received plaintiff's check for a specific purpose and deposited it, as he expected them to do, in their own account, to be in readiness at all times to make the purchase of stock in compliance with his instructions. Had they kept the check in their possession until the purchase was made, it would then have been necessary for them to deposit it in their own account in order to avoid the publicity incident to the purchase, and, if they had not presented it within a reasonable time, the plaintiff would have been discharged from liability thereon to the extent of the loss caused by the delay. . . .

"As a general rule of law every grant of power implies and carries with it, as an incident, authority to do whatever acts, or use whatever means are reasonably necessary and proper to the accomplishment of the purpose for which the agency was created, unless the inference of such power is expressly excluded by the instrument creating the agency or by the circumstances of the business to which the agency relates. Such incidental authority includes all acts and things which are connected with and essential to the business in hand, it is measured by the nature and necessities of the purpose to be accomplished and is prima facie co-extensive with the business intrusted to the agent's care. The means adopted, however, should be such as are most usual, such means indeed as are ordinarily used by prudent persons in doing similar business. This rule applies both to general and special agent unless the manner of doing the particular act is prescribed by the power." 2 C.J., pp. 578, 579, 580.

The conclusion seems unavoidable that the defendants handled this check in just the way the plaintiff desired and intended they should handle it, and that the loss incident to the closing of the bank in which it was deposited must be borne by him and not by the defendants.

The judgment is reversed and set aside. . . .

CASE NO. 13

Shatz Realty Co. v. King. 225 Ky. 846, 10 S.W. (2d) 456, 60 A.L.R. 1374 (1928)

LOGAN, J., delivered the opinion of the court:

. . . Delia King . . . made an oral contract with appellant whereby he undertook to procure for her a suitable and proper tenant for her house and premises. He was to collect the rents and otherwise act as agent of appellee in leasing and renting the property. Soon after the making of this contract, she moved away from Kentucky to another state, where she and her husband resided for several months. When she returned to Louisville, she discovered that the property had been seriously damaged by the acts of a tenant that she claims was procured for her by the appellant while acting as her agent.

She instituted suit against appellant, in which she set out the foregoing facts, and, in addition, she alleged that appellant rented her property to a woman by the name of Frey, and that in so doing he rented the property and premises to an undesirable, unsuitable, and unfit tenant without making any investigation as to the character, standing, or reliability of such tenant, and that he was grossly negligent in making the rental contract with the Frey woman without making any investigation as to whether she was a fit and proper person as a tenant. . . . The damages consisted of broken lights, holes bored in the doors, window-panes broken, sections of pipe removed, window cords cut, escutcheon removed from front doors, carpets damaged and removed from floors, basement locked up so that egress and ingress were prevented, liquor stains on floors, doorbells and wiring torn out, lead pipe removed, heater injured and destroyed, protection strips torn from stairways, Brussels carpet gone, plumbing attachments and equipment broken and destroyed, and divers other injuries of a similar kind and nature. . . .

There was a trial before a jury, which resulted in a verdict in favor of appellee for $1,000. . . . It is the general rule that a real estate agent must act in compliance with the instructions of his principal, and in accordance with customs prevailing in the community where he carries on his business. He is bound to exercise reasonable skill and diligence in the transaction of the business which is intrusted to him, and he will be responsible to the owner of the property for any loss resulting from his failure to exercise ordinary care in obtaining a tenant. He is only held to the exercise of ordinary care, and this would require him to make a reasonable investigation as to the character of the person who desired to become a tenant of his principal's property. If he makes such a reasonable inquiry and investigation, he is not bound for any loss to his principal occasioned by the misuse of the property by the tenant. But if he should fail to make such a reasonable investigation, and as a result of his failure a tenant should enter the property who was not a fit person to occupy the property, and damage should result to the property by reason of the acts of such a tenant, the agent will be responsible for such damage as was occasioned by his negligence. He is not a guarantor that the tenant is a suitable person to occupy the property, and when he has made a reasonable investigation and has acted in good faith believing the tenant is a suitable person to occupy the property, he cannot be held for any damage to the property by reason of the wrongful acts of the tenant. The agent owes to his principal to use such skill as may be requisite to accomplish the object of his employment, and he must be faithful to the interest of his employer. If he omits to exercise reasonable diligence and judgment, and as the result of such failure his principal is damaged, he may be held responsible for such damage. He must exercise the same diligence and good faith that a reasonably prudent man would exercise in renting the property if it were his own.

It is admitted by the appellant in this action that he made no investigation as to the character, fitness, or reliability of the tenant. . . .

The evidence is convincing that the woman to whom the house and premises were rented was not a lawabiding citizen, and that she made the house a rendezvous for bootleggers and other lawless associates. She resided in the property for two or three weeks, and at the end of that period the place was raided by federal prohibition officers and she and her associates were arrested. She executed a bond immediately after her arrest, and, so far as the record discloses, she occupied the premises for the month for which she paid rent. . . .

On the question as to whether appellee made a contract with appellant to rent the property, the evidence is conflicting, as it is on the question as to whether appellee agreed to accept the tenant without investigation on the part of appellant, and as the jury accepted the version of appellee, rather than that of appellant and his witnesses, the points are concluded against the contention of appellant. . . .

The burden of real estate agents should not be made unduly heavy, but this is an extreme case where the agent admits that he made no investigation and had no reason to believe that the tenant was a suitable person to occupy the premises. In such a case, where the tenant turns out to be such as this one was, he should be made to respond in damages to his principal if the tenant misuses the property in such a way as to damage it.

Judgment affirmed.

CASE NO. 14

Harry H. Rosin Co. v. Eksterowicz. 73 A. (2d) 648 (Del.) (1950)

LAYTON, J. An examination of many of the decisions bearing upon the right of a real estate agent to recover commissions indicates that the apparent confusion among them is capable of being resolved into certain fairly definable trends. Thus, where the contract is for an *exclusive agency* only, the owner is free to sell his property himself without liability to the agent for commissions. . . . This is not so, however, where, when the owner makes the sale, the agent has produced a buyer in accordance with his contract or when the owner in bad faith has otherwise defeated the agent from making good his sale. . . .

Where the contract of agency grants the *exclusive right of sale* and the owner sells his property at a time when the agent has neither procured a buyer nor is then actively negotiating with a bona fide purchaser, the cases are in decided conflict. Most of the authorities hold that the agent has a right of action against the owner. There is substantial authority to the effect that, in such case, the agent may recover his full commissions under the contract. . . . Other cases preclude any recovery whatsoever. South Florida Farms Co. v. Stevenson, 84 Fla. 235, 93 So. 247; Beck v. Howard, 43 S.D. 179, 178 N.W. 579; Turner v. Baker, 225 Pa. 359, 74 Atl. 172. And at least one well reasoned decision seems to hold that the agent's right of recovery is limited to his out of pocket expenses and time spent in attempting to make a sale, together, perhaps, with damages as the result of being deprived of his right to effect a sale during the remainder of the contract period. Isern v. Gordon, 127 Kan. 296, 273 Pac. 435, 64 A.L.R. 391.

Where the contract is one for an exclusive right of sale and the agent produces a purchaser prior to a sale by the owner or the owner in bad faith defeats a sale by the agent, it goes without saying that the agent may recover his full commission. Tsangares v. Fugazzi, 54 App. D.C. 334, 298 Fed. 207; Popplewell v. Buchanan, Tex. Civ. App., 204 S.W. 874.

There is yet another class of agency contracts wherein an exclusive right to sell is coupled with an agreement by the owner that the agent shall be entitled to his full commission no matter who accomplishes the sale. This, we believe, is such a contract. Upon reconsideration of the whole agreement we are of the opinion that it is fairly susceptible of the interpretation that the agency granted is an exclusive right of sale. Not only does the agreement state that Rosin shall have the "sole right and privilege" to sell but the reservation that he shall be entitled to his commission in the event the property is sold by anyone else clearly indicates that the owner intended this result. The contract providing, as it does, that Rosin is entitled to his full commission even though it did not effect the sale, we conclude that not only did Defendants breach the agreement by selling their property themselves, but also that the measure of damages would be the full commission. Turner v. Baker, 225 Pa. 359, 74 Atl. 172. This result rests upon the fundamental maxim that the parties are bound by the terms of their own agreement.

The provisions of this agreement, however, are exceedingly one-sided. The agent quite evidently has taken great care to protect his commission against every possible contingency. He has provided that he shall have the exclusive right to the sale of the property which, under the law above cited, places him in a preferred position. He has stipulated that the seller shall pay his full commission regardless of who makes the sale. The burden of revoking the agent's authority at the expiration of 90 days is placed upon the owner who, if he should fail to notify the agent of an intention to terminate the agency, remains bound by its terms until he should give one month's notice, in writing, of its cancellation. The contract even goes so far as to provide that if within three months after its termination, the property should be sold by the owner to a buyer with whom he or the agent had been negotiating during the term of the agreement, then the full commission shall be payable to the agent. In return, the agent promises merely to use his "efforts" to make a sale, whatever that vague term may be taken to mean. The basic question whether or not agency agreements of this sort are supported by valid consideration is not open to consideration in this case because defendants did not, under Rule 8(c) of the Superior Court Rules, affirmatively set forth the defense of failure of consideration. We will say in passing, however, that substantial authority exists for the proposition that such expressions as "in consideration of our efforts to sell your property" will not furnish the necessary consideration to support a bilateral agreement. Bell v. Dimmerling, 149 Ohio St. 165, 78 N.E. (2d) 49; Restatement of Agency, Vol. 2 § 449(B) p. 1058; and compare Abbott v. Stephany Poultry Co., Del. Super., 62 A. (2d) 243. If consideration is lacking, the agreement would necessarily have to be construed as unilateral in character, that is to say, an offer revocable at the will of the offeror until the completion of the required act. In such event the more modern trend of the authorities is to require, not full performance, but an acceptance on the part of the agent to be inferred from his advertising the property and otherwise making bona fide attempts to sell it. This, again, would be a question of fact which, if proved, would justify the conclusion that the unilateral offer had been converted into a binding bilateral agreement. Hutchinson v. Dobson-Bainbridge Realty Co., Tenn. App., 217 S.W. (2d) 6; Bell v. Dimmerling and Abbott v. Stephany Poultry Co., supra.

For the reasons above stated, we regretfully conclude that we must uphold the agreement in this case. If persons choose to be so improvident as to enter into this one-sided sort of contract, they must be bound by its terms and Courts are powerless to relieve them from the effect of what later may appear to be a bad bargain. . . .

CASE NO. 15

Faultersack v. Clintonville Sales Corporation. 253 Wis. 432, 34 N.W. (2d) 682 (1948)

Action . . . by Walter Faultersack . . . against the Clintonville Sales Corporation, a Wisconsin corporation, to recover $625.00 which the plaintiffs claim the defendant wrongfully retains as commission. Judgment for defendant. . . . On March 18, 1946, the plaintiffs entered into a written contract with the defendant, a corporation which conducted auction sales . . . to sell the plaintiffs' farm and personal property . . . The farm was encumbered by a mortgage and other liens totaling approximately $6,250.00.

Prior to the auction Arthur Umland, president of the defendant corporation, arranged with one Frank Challoner to make a loan, . . . in an amount sufficient to enable Challoner to bid on the farm at the sale. . . . This fact was not disclosed by Umland to the plaintiffs at any time prior to or during the sale.

At the auction when the bids were slightly over $5,000.00, Umland acting as auctioneer took a recess from the bidding to talk the bids over with the plaintiffs. At that time plaintiff, Walter Faultersack, said that he would not have the place sold for a price that would not pay for the mortgage.

The farm was finally sold to Frank

Challoner for $6,250.00 in the presence of Walter Faultersack. . . .

FAIRCHILD, J. The difficulty with the judgment entered at the circuit is that it overlooks the rule that the auctioneer loses his right to compensation by assuming a position inconsistent with his fiduciary relation as agent of the seller.

The auctioneer is deemed to be the agent of the seller. . . . Until the hammer goes down, the auctioneer is exclusively the agent of the vendor is the way the authorities have generally stated the rule.

It is well recognized that an agent is in a fiduciary relation to his principal. 1 Restatement, Agency, § 13. This fiduciary relation raises a certain duty on the part of the agent to make full disclosure of all facts that have a material bearing on the subject of the agency. . . .

Especially is he bound to disclose acts that have a tendency to favor the other party as against the principal. Acts which may directly limit or chill a bid at an auction are within that category. Here the arrangement between Umland, the defendant's president, and one Challoner, the proposed bidder, certainly had a relation to the subject of the agency. It contained elements directly affecting the agent's attitude toward and activities in respect to the sale of the plaintiffs' farm.

. . . The circumstances were capable of exerting an influence to fix a price unsatisfactory to the plaintiffs and satisfactory to the bidder, Challoner. Evidently that was what happened.

. . . It may be that plaintiffs agreed to let the farm go at that price. But had they known all the circumstances connected with the bid there is good reason to conclude that they would have rejected it.

This failure to disclose facts on the part of the defendant's officers amounted to a breach of the fiduciary relationship existing between the defendant and the plaintiffs. In the absence of full disclosure of the facts to the principal he can refuse to pay the commission or recover a commission already paid. . . .

Judgment reversed. Cause remanded with directions to enter judgment in favor of plaintiffs in accordance with this opinion.

CASE NO. 16

Raymond v. Davies. 293 Mass. 117, 199 N.E. 321, 102 A.L.R. 1112 (1936)

CROSBY, J., delivered the opinion of the court:

This is an action of contract upon an account annexed to recover salary due and money loaned. The case was referred to an auditor under an order that his findings of fact were to be final by agreement of the parties. The plaintiff introduced in evidence the auditor's substitute report which was the only evidence before the court, and filed a motion that it be confirmed, and that judgment be entered for the plaintiff. . .

It appears from the facts found by the auditor that the plaintiff had been employed by the defendant as manager of her farm in Natick, known as Carver Hill Farm, in this Commonwealth; that he hired the employees and paid them and the bills generally; that he kept a bank account under the name of "Carver Hill Orchard," drew checks on the account, and made purchases of supplies for the farm, the checks being signed by him as manager; that at times he advanced his own money to pay bills, including the expense of spraying the orchards; that he rendered annually to the defendant a report which was "insufficient in detail;" that the funds were not sufficient to meet the expenses of carrying on the farm owing to the inability of the defendant to supply them, and they were taken care of in part by the plaintiff and his son who was one of the employees on the farm. The auditor further found as follows: There was evidence that the plaintiff had always left certain farm implements, including a mowing machine, harrow, a sprayer, a tractor, ladders, pitchforks and other implements, exposed to the weather. In September, 1933, Henry T. Raymond, Jr., a son of the plaintiff, doing business as Raymond Bros. & Sons Co., to whom money was due for merchandise he had sold to the Carver Hill Farm, received from the plaintiff about five hundred and fifteen boxes of apples which he placed in cold storage in the name of Raymond Bros. & Sons Co. In March, 1934, the apples were sold by the company for $500 and this amount was credited on the books of the company to the account of the farm. The plaintiff was a stockholder in the Farmer's Co-Operative Exchange, and made purchases of farm supplies from this exchange. By reason of these purchases he received as a bonus or commission seven shares of stock from the exchange which he did not disclose to the defendant. The defendant by letter sent to the plaintiff on March 26, 1934, complained of the inadequacy of his accounts, and notified him that he was discharged. The auditor further found that the plaintiff "had no right to the seven shares (of stock) which were a secret profit," and disallowed the sum of $175 of item No. 2 being "money loaned to pay Farmer's Co-Operative Exchange" $275. The auditor stated the account to be that the defendant was indebted to the plaintiff in the sum of $1,515.17 with interest thereon of $70.75, making a total of $1,585.92 due the plaintiff from the defendant.

As manager of the defendant's farm the plaintiff was bound to exercise the utmost good faith in his dealings with her.

> "If the agent does not conduct himself with entire fidelity towards his principal, but is guilty of taking a secret profit or commission in regard to the matter in which he is employed, he loses his right to compensation on the ground that he has taken a position wholly inconsistent with that of agent for his employer, and which gives his employer, upon discovering it, the right to treat him so far as compensation, at least, is concerned, as if no agency had existed. This may operate to give to the principal the benefit of valuable services rendered by the agent, but the agent has only himself to blame for that result." Little v. Phipps, 208 Mass. 331, 333, 334, 94 N.E. 260, 261, 34 L.R.A. (N.S.) 1046.

The auditor found that the plaintiff made purchases on behalf of the defendant from a corporation in which he was a stockholder, and that because of such purchases he received a commission of seven shares of stock from that corporation. He did not inform the defendant of the receipt of these shares of stock. They constituted a "secret" profit for which he never accounted to the defendant. As the plaintiff was guilty of taking a bonus in the form of shares of stock in a corporation in which he was a stockholder, by reason of his purchases from that corporation on behalf of his employer, he is barred from the recovery of salary or wages.

CASE NO. 17

Wold v. Patterson. 229 Minn. 36, 39 N.W. (2d) 162 (1949)

MAGNEY, J. Plaintiff, a real estate broker, brought action to recover a

$5,000 commission on a real estate listing agreement. . . .

. . . On August 27, 1947, defendant Patterson signed a written listing agreement employing plaintiff to sell the property. . . .

Plaintiff produced one Ralph F. Jerome, as a prospective buyer, who on October 24, 1947, signed an earnest money contract agreement in terms in part as follows:

> "Received of Ralph J. Jerome, . . . ($2500.00) as earnest money, and in part payment for the purchase of the following described property (description and terms of payment and taking possession follow).
>
> "It is especially understood and agreed that this sale is made subject to approval by the owner of said premises in writing, . . ."

This instrument was signed by plaintiff and Jerome. It, together with a check for $2,500, was presented to defendant Patterson on October 24 or October 25, 1947. Plaintiff advised her as to the terms of the earnest money contract. She refused to sign or accept the check, saying:

> ". . . Oh, why don't you skip it for sixty or ninety days; we are not interested in selling now." . . .

She gave no reason why they were refusing to consummate the deal. At the time the check was tendered, Jerome did not have the money in the bank to meet it . . . Jerome himself testified. . . .

> "The check was not given to the girls at the Gardner Hotel; it was given to Mr. Wold and he knew—I told him that I would have to make that check good and it would take a day or two, and he ought to go down and make the offer."

We are of the opinion that plaintiff is not entitled to recover a commission under the facts in this case. When defendant Patterson turned down the earnest money contract and refused to accept the $2,500 check without giving any reason, she was not in possession of all the existing facts. Plaintiff failed to inform her that the check was worthless and that Jerome had no money on deposit in the bank on which the check was drawn. . . . In Hare v. Bauer, 223 Minn. 285, 291, 26 N.W. (2d) 359, 362, where as a part of the down payment the agent accepted the buyer's worthless note for $200 without disclosing such fact to his principal, we said:

> ". . . The agent must have dealt fairly with his principal, and if he . . . fails to disclose . . . pertinent facts to his principal, he is guilty of fraud and bad faith and forfeits his right to compensation."

Drawing of a check upon a bank in which the drawer has no funds, and uttering it, is a fraud. It amounts to a false affirmation that the money is there to meet it. When another presents the check knowing the drawer has no funds in the bank to meet it, he becomes a party to the fraud of the drawer and he becomes a willing assistant therein. . . .

Plaintiff owed a duty of loyalty to his principals. That duty included the disclosure to them that the proffered check was worthless. . . . His conduct constitutes such breach of duty to his principals as to forfeit all right to compensation under the real estate listing agreement. . . .

Review Questions

1. Are an agent's duties to his principal greater than those provided for by contract between the parties?

2. What is meant by the statement that an agency is a fiduciary relationship?
3. Is an agent entitled to make personal profits from the conduct of his principal's affairs?
4. Construct a fact situation illustrating the breach of an agent's duty of loyalty to his principal.
5. Is it possible for an agent to represent both parties in the same transaction?
6. How can an agent protect himself where he sells his own property to his principal?
7. Construct a fact situation under which the agent would have the duty to inform his principal.
8. Can an agent, upon having failed to obey his principal's instructions, defend his actions upon the grounds that he was attempting to act in the best interests of the principal?
9. Construct a fact situation under which the agent might be justified in departing from his principal's instructions.
10. Why should the agent refrain from intermingling the principal's property with his own?
11. What is the practical aspect of the rule that a principal stands as a general creditor to his agent where the principal cannot identify his specific funds in the hands of the agent?
12. If an agent is authorized to sell property without having received any instructions as to the price, may he sell at any price?
13. What are the possible consequences of an agent's failure to discharge any of his legal duties to the principal?
14. What is the agent's right of reimbursement?
15. Construct a fact situation under which the agent would have the right to invoke his right of indemnity.
16. What is the nature of the agent's right of lien?

Problems for Discussion

1. A, as P's agent, was given $2,300, with which A was to discharge P's debt to X. A induced X to accept $2,000 as settlement in full. Is A entitled to retain the $300?
2. P Insurance Co. employed A as an adjuster of fire insurance losses. After A had effected an adjustment in a particular case, the X Insurance Co., which was also involved in the same case, adopted his adjustment plan and paid him a substantial sum of money. The P Insurance Co. contends that it is entitled to this money. Answer the contention.
3. P authorized A to purchase merchandise for him upon a commission basis. A made some purchases from a partnership in which he was a silent member. A had not revealed to P his interest in the partnership. Is P justified in refusing to pay A the promised commissions?
4. P appointed A to look after his property and to be in complete charge of the property during P's absence. A discovered that P was delinquent in his tax payments and that the property was subject to sale for tax arrears. The property was sold to A for the amount of the taxes and a tax deed was issued to him. Some

years later, when P learned of this, he brought an action to recover the title from A. Did he succeed?

5. A, who was the agent of P (a theater manager), acquired knowledge concerning the profits of the business, as a result of his position. Consequently, A secretly overbid his principal and acquired the lease of the theater for himself. What are P's rights?
6. A accepted the sole agency from P for a certain machine and agreed to render his best efforts in making sales. Subsequently he accepted the agency for a competing machine. After learning of this, would P be justified in refusing to pay A the promised commissions?
7. A was a stockholder and director in the X corporation. A recommended the stock of the X corporation as an investment to P. Thereupon, P authorized A to purchase fifty shares for him. After the shares had been transferred to P, he discovered that they had been the property of A at the time of the transaction. P brought an action to have the transaction set aside. Result?
8. The defendant was engaged by the plaintiff to act as broker in the sale of property. The defendant sold the property to a corporation of which he was president and manager and at the time of the sale acted as the sole representative of the buyer corporation. In an action to recover the commission paid, the defendant asserts that he acted in good faith, that the terms procured were the best obtainable, and that the wrong if any was unaccompanied by any damage to the plaintiff. Decide. (*Wendt* v. *Fischer,* 243 N.Y. 439)
9. Plaintiffs, in their petition, allege that defendants listed their property for sale with plaintiffs as agent; that pursuant to such listing, plaintiffs showed the premises to Oreweiler and Hubble, who purchased the property from defendants, and that by reason thereof, the defendants owe the plaintiffs the regular commission on the sale price. One Chivers, agent for Central Realty Company, plaintiff, in a conversation with J. Clinton Nagle, the owner of the property, secured an exclusive listing for thirty days. An agent of the Wm. P. Zinn Company, one James Arnold, a few days thereafter showed the property to Oreweiler and Hubble. Arnold testified that he did so with the knowledge and consent of Central Realty Company and that the two brokerage firms were acting in cooperation in securing a purchaser. Arnold priced the property at $12,500, which the purchasers were not willing to pay. One of the occupants of the property stated to Oreweiler and Hubble that the property could be purchased for $12,000. It was then agreed that Oreweiler and Hubble would pay Arnold for his services. There is evidence supporting the conclusion that the amount agreed upon was $200. Arnold thereupon withdrew, and the occupants of the property took Oreweiler and Hubble to the Nagles, where the sale was made for $12,000. Shortly after the sale was made, Nagle learned that Arnold had taken the two purchasers to the property. Nagle stated to the purchasers that he would not go through with the sale at $12,000 if he had to pay a commission. The purchasers stated they had agreed to pay for the services of Arnold. Nagle requested the purchasers to sign a written statement to that effect, which they executed and which was introduced into the evidence. Decide. (*Reef et al.* v. *Nagle et al.,* 88 N.E. (2d) 424)
10. Bowen's $43,000 note was held by the Commercial Bank. Donaldson and Baden,

officers of the bank, granted a renewal upon payment of a $3,800 "curtail" and a bonus of $4,300, which was usury. The note was then sold to the Mount Vernon Bank, of which Donaldson and Baden were directors. Donaldson and Baden were not present, however, at the time the purchase was approved by the Mount Vernon Bank. The Mount Vernon Bank now resists the penalty of usury upon the contention that it had no knowledge of the usury involved. Result?

11. A, an investment broker, agreed to invest P's funds without charging P a commission. P directed that the funds should be invested in securities that had an AA investment rating by a designated investment service. A failed to comply with this request and invested the funds in highly speculative securities with a resultant financial loss to P. When sued for the loss, A's defense was that he had no liability since he was acting as a gratuitous agent. Result?
12. In A's warehouse are goods belonging to P that A is authorized to sell. Upon learning of an impending flood that threatens to engulf the warehouse and damage the goods, A disposes of them contrary to P's instructions. Will A be liable to P for disobedience of orders?
13. Defendant, the agent of plaintiff, an insurance company, effected an insurance policy and informed plaintiff thereof, upon which plaintiff, being dissatisfied, directed defendant to return the policy at once, saying that the risk was a prohibited one. Defendant, believing plaintiff misinformed as to the risk, so wrote, and held the policy. Plaintiff again directed the policy returned, which defendant did, but before notifying the insured thereof, a loss by fire occurred which plaintiff was compelled to pay. Can plaintiff recover? (*Washington Fire & Marine Ins. Co.* v. *Chesebro,* 35 Fed. 477)
14. A was employed by P as a traveling salesman; their agreement provided that P was to pay all necessary traveling expenses. A submitted a claim to P for $1,506 as his traveling expenses for the year. P refused to pay unless A would submit an itemized account of these expenditures. A then sued to recover. Did he succeed?
15. Hicks was hired as a selling agent by Johns for a period of one year. Within the first month of his employment, Hicks is wrongfully discharged. What should Hicks do to protect his contractual rights against Johns?
16. A, acting as P's selling agent, was required by the purchasers to furnish affidavits attesting to the weight of the goods sold. Can A recover from P the cost of obtaining the affidavits?

16 AGENCY:

TERMINATION OF AGENCY RELATIONSHIP

The termination of an agency relationship may vitally affect the interests of the principal, the agent, and those with whom the latter deals. To these parties, a knowledge of the rules relating to termination of an agency seems most desirable. The principal should, for example, know how and when an agent's powers can effectively be brought to an end. The third party ought to know to what extent he deals with an agent at his own peril—to what extent he speculates that the representative capacity of the agent still exists. To an agent, the termination of the agency may mean a breach of his contract of employment.

The modes by which an agency can be effectively brought to an end may be classified under four headings: (1) termination according to the agreement; (2) termination implied from the nature of the undertaking; (3) termination resulting from subsequent acts of the parties; and (4) termination resulting from operation of law.

► I. BY AGREEMENT

Generally, the duration of an agency covers a period agreed upon by the parties. Such an agency will terminate upon the expiration of the term even though the purposes of the agency have not been accomplished. In that case, the rights and liabilities of the parties are determined as of the time fixed for termination. Circumstances may, however, give rise to the presumption of an implied intent that the agency is to continue beyond the period agreed upon. An uninterrupted continuation of the employment after expiration of the term *may* be interpreted as an assent by the parties to the continuation of the agency for a like period and upon the same terms as contained in the original contract. It may also be held that an agency continues beyond the established time limit if such is necessary to complete the tasks undertaken before the "deadline." By way of illustration, it was held that the authority of a selling agent continued in respect to collection of the proceeds of sales accomplished during the fixed term.

The agreement may provide for the continuation of the agency relationship for an indefinite period of time. It may provide, for example, that upon the return of a former employee (agent) from the armed forces, the employment is to cease.

The parties may, of course, by mutual agreement, terminate the employment relationship at any time. Such an agreement would be a mutual rescission of the agency contract and would be binding.*

* See page 317.

► II. IMPLIED FROM NATURE OF UNDERTAKING

In the absence of an agreement to the contrary, the life of an agency relationship created to accomplish a specific purpose is usually presumed to continue until the transaction is completed, or at least for such time as would reasonably be required for its accomplishment. The courts have held, however, that agency powers of this nature must be exercised within a reasonable time. The completion of the task assigned to the agent naturally terminates the relationship, and it would seem, on the other hand, that an unmistakable failure of the agent to accomplish the specific objectives should likewise effect a termination. It has been held that where an agent failed in arranging for a loan from a specified person, his agency powers were thereby brought to an end.

► III. TERMINATION RESULTING FROM ACTS OF PARTIES

A. AGENCY AT WILL

An agency employment arising out of a contract that contains no provision for its duration nor any indication that the agency is to continue for a certain time is known as an agency at will. Its period of existence is dependent upon the wills of the principal and the agent. Either may elect at any time to terminate the employment.[1] There are, however, a few exceptions to this rule, which will be discussed in the following section on irrevocable agencies.

B. AGENCY FOR PERIOD OF TIME

1. *Termination Without Cause*

The duty to honor a contract is not necessarily absolute; the power to break a contract can effectively be exercised when the remedy of specific performance or injunction is not available for its breach. And equity will not decree performance of contracts involving personal services or confidences. Consequently, the parties to an agency relationship can at any time, without cause, subject to the exceptions to be considered in the section on irrevocable agencies, repudiate and relieve themselves of performance of the contract of employment. However, the one who repudiates thereby subjects himself to an action by the injured party for damages for the wrongful termination of the contract.[2], [3]

2. *Termination for Cause*

Either the principal or the agent has the right to terminate the employment for cause. A termination for cause gives no right to damages. The agent is justified in renouncing the contract without prejudice to his rights when, for example, the principal has himself broken the contract or has subjected the agent to abuse.

---

1 Wood v. Hutchinson Coal Co., p. 431.

2 Farmers' Fertilizer Co. v. Lillie, p. 434.

3 Geyler v. Daily, p. 435.

The agent's failure to discharge any of his various agency duties gives the principal cause for termination of the agency. Conduct on the agent's part—for example, intoxication—that will prevent him from properly and effectively representing the principal is sufficient ground for revocation of his powers.

C. VOLUNTARY DISPOSITION OF SUBJECT MATTER BY PRINCIPAL

A voluntary disposition of the subject matter by the principal is inconsistent with the powers granted the agent in respect to such subject matter and must be considered as manifesting an intent that the agency has been terminated. In fact, it has been said by the courts that such an act is a revocation as a matter of law. Thus, if the principal executes a deed to property that the agent has been authorized to sell, the agency for that purpose is terminated.

D. ADVERSE INTEREST ACQUIRED BY AGENT

If the agent voluntarily or involuntarily acquires an interest adverse to that of the principal, the agency is terminated. For example, the courts have held that, upon his being appointed administrator of an estate, the agent of a creditor of the estate can no longer represent the principal. As previously pointed out, an agent cannot fulfill his duty of loyalty to his employer when his interests lie elsewhere.

► IV. TERMINATION RESULTING FROM OPERATION OF LAW

The happening of certain events will, as a matter of law, serve to terminate an agency relationship, regardless of the intent or consent of the parties. When, by operation of law, the principal is deprived of his interest in, or control over, the subject matter of the agency, the employment terminates. Probably the most common illustration of such an event is bankruptcy of the principal. A levy on property by virtue of an execution issued upon a judgment against the principal would likewise end an agency in respect to such property.

The death or insanity of either the principal or the agent will, as a matter of law, terminate the agency.[4] The effect of death in relation to notice to third persons is discussed in the following section.

► V. REQUIREMENT OF NOTICE OF TERMINATION

A. VOLUNTARY TERMINATION

To be effective in respect to third persons, the termination of an agency must meet the requirement of notice to such parties. Either third persons must have actual notice of termination, or the circumstances must be such as to charge third persons with notice of termination. Notice of termination from any source is sufficient.

[4] In re Garland's Will, p. 436.

Upon voluntarily terminating the employment, the principal, in order to prevent being further bound by acts of his agent, finds it necessary to give notice of the termination to third persons. He has the duty to actually notify those persons with whom the agent has dealt, unless, of course, they have received notice from some other source. This notice need take no particular form.

The only practical way in which a principal can give notice to those persons with whom the agent has had no dealings is by means of publication. The notice should be contained in a newspaper of general circulation in the community in which the agent exercised his authority. A notice of this character effectively charges the public with notice of the revocation of the agency.

> "Knowledge by third persons of an act committed by the principal which is inconsistent with the agent's authority, charges them with notice that the agency has been terminated. A knowledge of facts which would indicate to a reasonably prudent person that the agency has been terminated or which would put such a person on inquiry, is the equivalent of actual notice." *Williams* v. *Birbeck, Hoffm.* (N.Y.) 359.

B. INVOLUNTARY TERMINATION—BY OPERATION OF LAW

Third persons are charged with notice of the termination of an agency by operation of law. They are presumed to have knowledge of that which, as a matter of law, will terminate an agency.

The common law rule that the acts of an agent performed after the principal's death are not binding upon the principal's estate has been severely criticized. There seems little reason why the principal's estate should be given a preferred position over third parties who have dealt with the agent in good faith and in ignorance of the principal's death. It has been suggested that the ends of justice would be better served by holding the estate of the deceased principal responsible for acts resulting from the principal's extension of his personality until such a time when notice of the principal's death can be given.[5] A few states have provided to this effect by legislative enactment, and some few courts have arrived at this conclusion upon purely equitable considerations.

► VI. IRREVOCABLE AGENCIES

A. AGENCY COUPLED WITH AN INTEREST

If the agent has an interest of his own in the subject matter of the agency, he is said to have a power coupled with an interest. The interest given the agent in the subject matter entitles him to act in his own name. Consequently, the authority to act is irrevocable even by death of the principal. By acquiring an interest or estate in the subject matter, the agent no longer stands as a representative of another in relation to such subject matter. The legal or equitable interest gives the agent the right to act in his own name within the limits of the authority attached to the interest. A good illustration of an agency coupled with an interest is

[5] Glennan v. Rochester Trust Co., p. 437.

a provision contained in a mortgage authorizing the mortgagee to sell the property in event of default of payment. The mortgagee's equitable interest in the property, coupled with the authority to sell, makes the agency irrevocable.

Likewise, a power of attorney to confess judgment on a note is an irrevocable agency.*

► VII. AGENCIES IRREVOCABLE TO A DEGREE

A. AGENCY AS SECURITY

At times an agent is given authority to act for the purpose of securing a discharge of the principal's obligation to himself or others. An agent may, for example, be empowered to collect a debt for the purpose of reimbursing himself for an amount due and owing him from the principal. Or an agent may be given an interest in the proceeds of the agency to secure payment of his commission. It has been generally held that such agencies (where the agent has no actual interest in the subject matter) are irrevocable to the extent that the principal cannot terminate them during his lifetime, although they are terminated by his death. There is authority to the contrary. The *Restatement of the Law of Agency,* § 139, declares that death of the principal does not revoke the authority of the agent to act.

CASES

CASE NO. 1

Wood v. Hutchinson Coal Company. 176 F. (2d) 682, 12 A.L.R. (2d) 1352 (1949)

SOPER, C.J. Leighton S. Wood, a sales agent in the coal business, sues Hutchinson Coal Company, the owner of coal mines in Logan County, West Virginia, for commissions in the sum of $18,946 on sales of coal made by the company which he claims he should have been allowed to make under the contract between them. At the trial below the judge directed a verdict for the defendant. The question is whether the principal in a nonexclusive sales agency contract may compete with the agent so as to deprive him of commissions on sales which the principal makes without the agent's assistance to a customer to whom the agent has previously sold goods, on which he has been paid a commission.

Wood is an experienced and capable coal broker with offices in Chicago. Hutchinson has sales offices at Cleveland and Philadelphia. The whole contract of the parties is contained in the following passage in a letter of March 14, 1935, from Hutchinson to Wood:

> "This will confirm our verbal understandings and present working arrangements by which we will continue to pay you 10¢ per ton commission on coal sold by you direct to customers and accepted and shipped by our Logan County mines."

The company did not abolish its own sales force but made the agreement with Wood because it needed additional business and desired to take advantage of his contacts to attract new accounts, es-

---

* See page 456.

pecially from among some twenty coke by-product plants which were so located as to be able to buy Hutchinson coal, a product well suited to their needs. . . .

The parties operated under the contract for twelve years. . . . Between 1936 and 1942 he secured three customers for Hutchinson, and from 1942 until 1947, one customer, the Milwaukee Solvay Coke Company, in connection with whose business the present controversy arose. . . . In 1942, through his efforts, Milwaukee signed a five-year agreement to buy coal from Hutchinson in an amount not to exceed 100,000 tons per year. . . . Throughout the term of the contract, Wood negotiated the annual price tonnage and shipping schedules; and the extent of his duties in servicing the contract is indicated by the fact that in 1946 he spent sixteen days in Milwaukee and made fifty long distance telephone calls to the Milwaukee Company. During the five year term of the contract, 1942 until 1946, Wood received $44,000 in commissions on sales to Milwaukee.

The Milwaukee contract expired on November 30, 1946; and Wood made no effort to renew it. In his view there was no need for haste. The shipping season ran from May until November, and there would be time enough if a new basic contract were negotiated before the end of the year. . . .

In the meantime, Hutchinson had made up its mind to sell directly to Milwaukee in order to avoid payment of further commissions to Wood on sales to this customer, and accordingly, before the 1942–1946 contract expired, began negotiations with Milwaukee which resulted, in October, 1946, in a new five year contract. . . . Wood learned for the first time about these new agreements on February 8, 1947. He considered his relations with the defendant terminated, and made no further effort to sell the defendant's coal.

Wood claims a commission of 10 per cent on all coal sold or to be sold under this contract. . . .

The answer to the problem raised by this controversy is found in our opinion in the rules of law announced in Sections 448 and 449 of the Restatement of Agency as follows:

"§ 448. Compensation. Agent as Effective Cause. An agent whose compensation is conditional upon his accomplishment of a specified result is entitled to the agreed compensation if, and only if, he is the effective cause of accomplishing the result."

"§ 449. Compensation. When Principal Competes. The principal does not, by contracting to pay compensation contingent upon the agent's success in accomplishing a definite result, thereby promise that he will not compete either personally or through another agent."

. . . An attempt is made to meet the requirements of Section 448 by advancing the theory that Milwaukee was Wood's customer and hence Wood was entitled to commissions on all Milwaukee's purchases. This position, however, cannot be maintained. For obtaining the customer and making the first sale Wood was entitled to and was paid the agreed commissions, but that situation did not continue indefinitely. It is well established that the successful negotiation of a contract by an agent does not give him a right to commissions on a renewal, which he does not secure, in the absence of an express contract to that effect. . . . The contract did not provide that commissions would be paid on all purchases made by Milwaukee or any other particular customer as is sometimes provided in a broker's contract, but only on such sales as the agent would make. He did not actually make the sale in question.

The argument is made, however, that although all this may be true, it was not Wood's fault because it came about through the unfair behavior in withholding helpful sales data from Wood while secretly negotiating with Milwaukee for Hutchinson's benefit. This contention brings us to a consideration of § 449 of the Restatement which states that a principal does not promise that he will not compete with his agent by contracting to pay compensation to the agent for the accomplishment of a definite result. . . . It is sufficient to say that the terms of the contract did not forbid the principal from competition with the agent. . . .

It is strongly urged upon us that Hutchinson was under an obligation to terminate the agency agreement before selling to any customer of the agent; and that in the absence of an express provision in the contract, Wood was entitled to a reasonable notice of cancellation and to a reasonable opportunity to prevail upon "his customer" to buy elsewhere. We agree that an agent is entitled to reasonable notice of the termination of an agency under a contract like that in suit, and that under certain conditions, a principal may be required to pay compensation on business secured by the agent until notice is given. . . . Such conditions were described in Gilbert v. Quinlan, 59 Hun. 508, 13 N.Y.S. 671, upon which the appellant heavily relies. There was an agreement on the part of a stockbroker to pay the plaintiff one-half commissions for all customers that the plaintiff brought him. The plaintiff procured a customer whose transactions through the broker were in considerable amount. Subsequently, in obedience to a change in the rules of the Board of Trade, the defendant gave notice to the plaintiff that the splitting of commissions on the customer's business would be discontinued. The court held that the plaintiff was not entitled to share commissions in the business done after he received the notice. In the course of the opinion reversing a judgment for the plaintiff, the court said:

> "In the submission of the case to the jury, the court instructed the jury that this contract was one which could not last forever. It was one that was terminable at the election or option of either party; that it would have been proper for the plaintiff at any time to have taken his customer to another broker, and it was entirely competent for the broker at any time, on giving reasonable notice, to have said to him: 'The relation which existed heretofore between Miner, your customer, and myself is now severed, and hereafter it is terminated.' . . ."

We are in accord with this opinion insofar as it holds that a principal, who agrees to pay commissions on the business of a particular customer without express limitation of time, must continue to pay them until he gives a notice of the termination of the arrangement; but in the pending case the principal did not attempt to terminate the contract and hence there is no occasion to apply this rule. Moreover, under the contract in our case, commissions were to be paid on specific sales accepted by the principal and not on all the business of a specific customer for an indefinite time. Wood was of course entitled to commissions on the sales to Milwaukee of which he was the procuring cause, but he was not entitled to commissions on sales which he did not make. He labors under the mistaken belief that he possessed a certain proprietary interest in the one customer which he brought to

Hutchinson in 1942; but this is not so under § 449 of the Restatement. Prospective buyers of coal, whether or not they were prior customers of Hutchinson secured by Wood, were in the field of competition that was open to both parties during the existence of the nonexclusive agency contract. Hutchinson had the right to sell them without the assistance of Wood, and Wood had the right to sell them the coal of another mine if he desired to do so. . . .

Affirmed.

CASE NO. 2

Farmers' Fertilizer Co. v. Lillie. 18 F. (2d) 197, 52 A.L.R. 552 (1927)

KNAPPEN, C.J., delivered the opinion of the court:

This writ is brought to review a judgment rendered in favor of . . . plaintiff . . . for breach of a contract made between the parties. . . .

By the first paragraph of the contract the company in terms engaged plaintiff

> "for a period of five years from and after November 15, 1915, as its sole agent for the state of Michigan for the sale of its fertilizer, silos, lime, and feeding tankage"

—all inquiries to the company from Michigan to be referred to plaintiff.

. . . . .

During the first year of the contract, plaintiff's agents, approved by the company, sold a considerable amount of fertilizer and a number of silos, on which plaintiff's commissions aggregated $3,359.06. During the next year there were substantial delays in the company's approval of agency contracts, presumably contributing to the great reduction in sales for that year. In 1918 the company confined plaintiff's territory to the southern part of Michigan. In that year orders under contract were accepted and filled by defendant for about one-half of the amount of fertilizer sold the first year, although more than sold the second year. At the opening of the second year, the company advised plaintiff it would sell no silos that year, and refused his request for permission to sell silos of another manufacture. Until July 1, 1918, the monthly advances of $250 were made; refusal to continue the advances was made July 5, 1918; and no payment was thereafter made. The company refused to ship any fertilizers into Michigan during the years 1919 and 1920, or to approve contracts of plaintiff's local agents.

Defendant bases its claimed right to reversal upon the proposition that the contract did not obligate it to ship goods into Michigan to fill plaintiff's orders, unless its refusal to do so was made in bad faith; that is to say, if defendant was justified, in the exercise of good business judgment, and in the absence of bad faith toward plaintiff, in refusing shipment to and sale of its products in Michigan. This proposition was presented by appropriate motion to direct verdict for defendant, as well as by requested instruction to the jury.

We are unable to agree with this contention. The contract was not an ordinary brokerage contract, without term and without consideration. The term was definitely stated as "five years from and after November 15, 1915." We find no statement of limitation or reservation by the company as to this term, or any authority to exercise an option whether or not to terminate the contract before the end of the five-year period. Ample consideration for the company's promise is found in plaintiff's agreement to

> "sell exclusively the above-mentioned products to parties approved by the company and as offered in Michigan,"

and impliedly during the entire five-year period. Plaintiff thus agreed not to sell for any of the company's competitors for the Michigan trade, and there were several such. As already stated, defendant refused to allow plaintiff to buy silos of another manufacturer. Plaintiff's long and intimate connection with the trade in question presumably gave his promise substantial value. The terms of the contract, taken together—including the provisions for furnishing prices for the year ahead, for furnishing brands of fertilizers similar in analysis and price to those furnished and sold by the company's chief competitors, for brands licensed as "Lillie's Special Brands," for stationery, circular advertising letters, regular advertising matter, catalogues, and booklets, and the agreement to do everything reasonably possible to enable plaintiff to meet competition—repel the idea of an existing option in defendant to terminate the agreement before the end of the specified term. . . .

CASE NO. 3

Geyler v. Daily et us. 70 Ariz. 135, 217 P. (2d) 583 (1950)

PHELPS, J. Appellant was plaintiff and appellees defendants in the trial court and they will be thus designated in this opinion. The facts in the case are that at all times here involved plaintiff was a duly licensed real estate broker engaged in the business of selling real estate in Arizona.

On August 28, 1947, defendants Daily entered into a contract in writing with plaintiff giving to plaintiff the exclusive right until January 1, 1948, to sell an 80-acre ranch belonging to defendants for the sum of $32,000 payable in the manner provided in said contract and agreeing therein to pay a 5 per cent commission to plaintiff in the event of sale.

Thereafter on October 10, 1947, plaintiff procured a purchaser for the ranch at the price named and payable in the manner provided for in the contract. The proposed purchaser was ready, able and willing to perform each and all of the terms of purchase provided for in the contract and at the time tendered his check in the sum of $3,200 as earnest money. Defendants refused to sell the ranch to the purchaser and claimed as an excuse therefor that they had on the previous day, to wit, on October 9th revoked plaintiff's authority to sell the ranch.

Plaintiff brought an action in the superior court of Maricopa County to recover the sum of $1,600 as and for his commission as provided for in the contract. The cause was tried to a jury and a verdict and judgment was rendered in favor of defendants. . . .

There is no dispute in the evidence that plaintiff procured a purchaser for defendants' property who was ready, able and willing to take and pay for the property in question on the terms and conditions fixed by defendants in their contract with plaintiff. Under such circumstances we have consistently held that the broker is entitled to his commission.

Defendants agree with the above principle of law but assert that defendants had a right to terminate plaintiff's agency contract and did terminate the same before he produced a purchaser for defendants' property, therefore defendants are not liable to plaintiff for any commission whatsoever, citing the case of Blaisdell v. Steinfeld, 15 Ariz. 155, 137 Pac. 555, 566, in support of their position.

The established rule of law that a principal has the power to revoke the authority of his agent at will is predicted upon the principle that a contract of agency calls for personal services and like other contracts creating personal relations will not be specifically enforced thus leaving the principal in such cases to determine how long the relation of principal and agent shall continue. This power exists even where the contract fixes a definite period for its existence. Under such circumstances, however, the power to revoke and the right to revoke are not coincidental. It does not follow that because a principal has the power to revoke the authority of his agent at any time that he has the right to exercise such power without liability, regardless of his contract in the matter. As was said in Mechem on Agency, 1st ed., § 209:

> ". . . It is entirely consistent with the existence of the power that the principal may agree that for a definite period he will not exercise it, and for the violation of such agreement the principal is as much liable as for the breach of any other contract. . . ."

Where the agreement does not expressly or by implication fix a definite period during which his agency shall exist the power and the right of the principal to revoke the agency coincide and the exercise of the right entails no liability. In the instant case the agency was exclusive and existed for a definite period of time. . . .

. . . judgment . . . reversed and the cause remanded with instructions to enter judgment for the plaintiff . . . in the sum of $1,600.

CASE NO. 4

In re Garland's Will 97 N.Y.S. (2d) 442 (1950)

GRIFFITHS, S. The executrix instituted this discovery proceeding against a bank and three former employees of decedent to recover the proceeds of a check in the sum of $2,000 alleged to have been cashed after the death of decedent. . . . The answer interposed alleged affirmatively that prior to the death of decedent on December 8, 1949, respondent drew a check dated December 9, 1949, on a designated bank for the sum of $2,000.00, signed the same as attorney in fact for the decedent, and delivered it to another who, on December 9th, cashed the check and paid the proceeds to respondent, who thereupon, pursuant to instructions of the decedent, disbursed sums totaling $833.85 to himself and others for services rendered and for traveling and other expenses.

. . . Whether or not the check was in fact drawn before or after the date of death (December 8, 1949) is immaterial, since as admitted in the answer, the check was not presented for payment until December 9th, the day after decedent's death.

The authority of respondent as attorney in fact was revoked by the death of his principal. Even if it be assumed that the check was drawn by respondent prior to the death of decedent, the check would be void unless cashed before the decedent's death. . . . Thus, the collection of the check and the receipt of the proceeds thereof after the death of decedent would be unauthorized irrespective of whether or not respondent knew of the death of decedent prior to the receipt of such proceeds. The issues raised by respondent's answer did not involve any claim by petitioner against the bank which honored the check for collection but rather related to petitioner's rights against the person who admittedly received the proceeds of the check after the death of decedent. . . . It is accordingly determined that petitioner has established her title and right to possession of the sum of $2,000 from the answering respondent. . . .

CASE NO. 5

Glennan v. Rochester Trust & S.D. Co.
209 N.Y. 12, 102 N.E. 537 (1913)

CULLEN, CH.J., delivered the opinion of the court:

The action is brought by the plaintiff as administrator of a depositor in the defendant trust company to recover the amount of a deposit made by the intestate. The defense was payment and an assignment of the deposit by the intestate to a third party. The payment proved was that of a check drawn by the intestate, but not presented to or paid by the defendant until after the death of the former, of which the defendant claimed to be ignorant. . . .

It is singular that there should be such a paucity of judicial decisions on this question, as seems to be the case. In my search through the reports I have been able to find only one on the precise point, Rogerson v. Ladbroke, decided by the English common pleas in 1822, 1 Bing. 93, 7 J. B. Moore, 412, 1 L.J.C.P. 6, in which it was held that the payment or rather the charge of a check to a depositor's account made by the banker after the death of the depositor, but before the bank had received knowledge of that fact, was a valid payment, and that the banker was not liable for the amount. There is another case often cited to the same effect (Tate v. Hilbert, 2 Ves. Jr. 112, 2 Revised Rep. 175), where the lord chancellor expressed the opinion that if the holder of a check had collected the money from the banker after the death of the drawer, but before the banker had knowledge of death, no court would take the money away from her. . . . But, while there is this paucity of judicial decisions on the subject, there seems to be absolute unanimity in the rule as declared by the leading text writers . . . all assert that, while a bank should not pay a check after the death of the drawer, still a payment made in good faith, without knowledge of the death, or of facts sufficient to cause inquiry, is a valid payment, though the only authority usually cited is that of Tate v. Hilbert, supra.

For the appellant it is argued, first, that a check of itself is a mere order for the payment of money, not operating as an assignment of any part of the fund, the authority of the drawee or the banker to pay which may be revoked or countermanded by the drawer. This is the rule of law prevailing in England and in this country, . . .

That the death of the principal revokes the authority of the agent to collect the check in those jurisdictions where the check is considered a mere order must also be conceded. . . .

It is further true that the common-law doctrine that death revokes an agent's power, even as to third parties dealing with the agent in good faith without notice, is the general rule in this state. . . .

At this point we reach the very crux of this case, and the question is whether payment of checks by banks or bankers is an exception to the rule stated. I think it is. It must be first borne in mind that the rule itself is an exception to the still broader rule that revocation of the power of an agent does not affect third parties dealing with him in good faith without notice. This is the rule of the civil law even where the agency is revoked by death. The common-law rule in some states has been changed by statute, in others repudiated . . . while in others still greatly limited . . . there is a difference between the liability of banks to their depositors and that of ordinary debtors to their creditors, which justifies excepting the payment of checks from the rule. If an ordinary debtor refuses to pay his debt to the agent of his creditor, his liability is in no respect increased. It is not so with a bank. Its contract with the depositor is to pay his checks as long as his deposit is sufficient for the purpose, and for a failure to pay the checks the bank is liable for any injury to the credit of the drawer occasioned thereby. In the ordinary conduct of a bank but a minute fraction of its payments is made directly to its depositors. The others are made on checks in favor of third parties, usually, at least in large cities, presented through other banks or the clearing house. The number of depositors is often very great, many of them living at other places than where the bank is located. Of the death of those prominent, either by their public position, their business activities, or great wealth, the bank might be apprised; but of the great mass their deaths would pass unknown by the bank unless notice of the fact was given. It would be utterly impracticable for business to be done if, before the bank could safely pay checks, it must delay to find out whether the drawer is still living. . . .

The rule that denies protection to persons dealing with an agent after the death of the principal, though in good faith and without knowledge of that fact, is an inherited one. In the Wilson Case it was declared by this court to be a harsh one, but the court felt that it had been too firmly established in this state to be disturbed by judicial decision, though it recommended a change by the legislature, to place the law in harmony with the more enlightened views of the present time, and to promote the interests of justice. The same reason which there constrained the court to give effect to the rule, despite its disapproval of it, should also impel us to hold the rule inapplicable to bank checks. If there it appeared that the doctrine of the common law had prevailed too long to be disregarded, it also appears almost equally clear that the common-law doctrine has never prevailed as to checks; for a legal proposition may be nearly as well established by its general acceptance and the failure of anyone to question it, as it can be by a series of judicial decisions. Even if it should be assumed that the distinction sought to be drawn between the relation of a bank to its depositors, and that between ordinary debtors and their creditors, would not justify a distinction in the principle of law applicable to the respective cases, nevertheless a rule of conduct of a whole people long prevailing and acted upon should not be subordinated to mere consistency of legal principles. The law presents anomalies. They are to be regretted; but no one would maintain that merely to avoid inconsistency courts would be justified in disregarding rules of action long established by judicial decisions, especially when the exception is more just than the general rule.

Review Questions

1. By what methods may an agency relationship be brought to an end?
2. Does it necessarily follow that an agency will terminate upon the date specified in the agency contract?
3. Construct a fact situation under which the period of the agency is determined by the nature of the undertaking.
4. What is an *agency at will?*
5. Can it be said that either party to an agency relationship has the power to terminate the agency without cause?

6. Construct a fact situation under which the principal would have cause to terminate the agency.
7. What acts of the parties to an agency relationship will cause its termination?
8. What may cause the termination of an agency relationship by operation of law?
9. Why is it important for the principal to give notice of the termination of the agency relationship?
10. When is actual notice of termination required, and when is notice by publication sufficient?
11. What is an *irrevocable agency?*
12. What is the effect of the death of the principal upon an irrevocable agency?

Problems for Discussion

1. P employed A as his agent for a period of one year at a fixed salary, which was to be paid monthly. At the expiration of the year, nothing was said to A concerning the termination of the employment, and A continued to discharge his duties as previously. After two months, P informed A that his employment was at an end. A contends that he has a contract of employment for one year. Decide.
2. A contract provided that the agent was to be paid "at a salary of $2,500 per annum." Does this create an employment for a definite period of time?
3. On March 11, 1918, the defendants employed the plaintiff to sell the farm, and signed and delivered to him a written agreement in the following terms:

"CONTRACT

"Suffield, Conn., 3/11/1918

"This is to certify that on this date I have given to Morton S. Harris the exclusive sale of my property, *viz.:* Six acres land more or less with all standing buildings thereon, for the sum of $8,000 (8000.00) and do agree to pay the said M. S. Harris 5 per cent of the purchase price at transfer of deed.

"F. B. McPHERSON
MINNIETTA S. McPHERSON."

The contract contains no provision as to its duration. Was it in force when the sale was made by the owner on April 20, 1918? Decide. (*Harris* v. *McPherson,* 97 Conn. 164, 115 Atl. 723, 1922)

4. The contract provided that the agent would be employed for one year "if he could fill the place satisfactorily." Can the employer arbitrarily determine whether the agent is unsatisfactory?
5. P employed A to collect delinquent accounts, the employment to continue for one year. Within a month, A abandoned his employment upon the grounds that he could not resort to the tactics required of him by P for the collection of accounts. Is this just cause for termination of the employment?
6. Would the failure of the employer to pay the agent's salary for a period of two months be cause for terminating the employment?
7. Would a suspicion on the part of the agent that the employer was in financial difficulties be cause for terminating the employment?
8. P employed A to sell certain property to the XY partnership. During the course of the negotiations, A became a limited partner in the partnership by investing $5,000. Later the sale to the partnership was completed. When P learned these facts he brought action to have the sale set aside. Result?

9. P employed A as general business manager of his business establishment. After P fired the bookkeeper in a fit of anger, P demanded that A keep the books until another bookkeeper could be found. A refused and P discharged him. Did P have cause for terminating the employment?
10. P, living in Texas, authorized A, living in Ohio, to collect rents upon his property in Ohio. After P's death, X paid $1,200 in rent money to A, neither having knowledge of P's death. A never paid the money to P's estate and the administrator sues X to recover the $1,200. Result?
11. P employed A as his agent to purchase eggs and poultry. Dissatisfied with A's work, P discharged him and published a notice to that effect. Professing to act on behalf of P, A continued to make purchases from X, who had not seen the published notice. Can X recover from P?
12. P gave A a power of attorney to sell the produce from P's land. A's compensation for his services was to be one-half of the proceeds so realized. P died, and the administrator of his estate revoked the power of attorney. A sues for breach of contract, contending that the agency was coupled with an interest. Result?
13. A and B had a joint ownership interest in a patent. B died, and the executrix gave A a power of attorney to dispose of the patent. Is this an irrevocable agency?
14. P owed A $1,500 and, as a means of discharging the obligation, he appointed A as his agent to sell certain property, authorizing A to reimburse himself for the $1,500 obligation out of the proceeds of the sale. Is this an agency coupled with an interest?

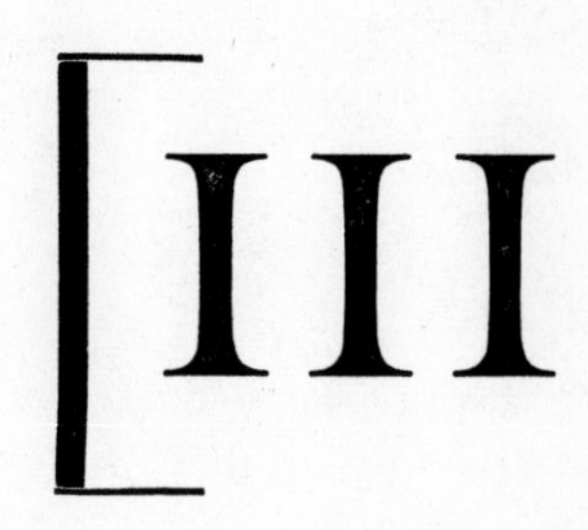

Negotiable Instruments

Chapter

17. INTRODUCTION TO LAW OF NEGOTIABLE INSTRUMENTS

18. REQUIREMENTS FOR NEGOTIABLE INSTRUMENTS

19. TRANSFER OF NEGOTIABLE INSTRUMENTS—NEGOTIATION

20. RIGHTS OF HOLDERS—HOLDERS IN DUE COURSE

21. LIABILITY OF PARTIES

22. PRESENTMENT, DISHONOR, PROTEST, AND NOTICE

23. CHECKS

24. DISCHARGE OF NEGOTIABLE INSTRUMENTS

17 NEGOTIABLE INSTRUMENTS:

INTRODUCTION TO LAW OF NEGOTIABLE INSTRUMENTS

"Negotiable papers . . . evidence not only a large part of the wealth of the country, but furnish the means and basis on which and by which the greater part of the commerce and business of the nation is conducted. There passes through the banking houses of the country and through the mails every day of the year, in this form, a merchandise that far 'outshines the wealth of Ormus and of Ind.' It has been truly said of them that they are 'couriers without luggage.'" *Gaston* v. *J. I. Campbell Co.,* 104 Tex. 576.

Few persons appreciate fully the extent to which the conduct of commercial affairs is expedited by the use of negotiable instruments. They are the well-oiled hubs upon which the wheels of business turn; it is by their use that credit is easily created and that credit is easily transferred.

Negotiable instruments represent contractual rights that are generally acceptable to businessmen in place of money.

► I. NEGOTIABLE INSTRUMENTS CLASSIFIED

There are two basic types of negotiable instruments, namely, (1) promissory notes and (2) bills of exchange.

A. PROMISSORY NOTES

Promissory notes are called *two-party paper,* the parties being the *maker,* the one who promises to pay, and the *payee,* to whom payment is promised. The Negotiable Instruments Law [1] defines a negotiable promissory note as being "an unconditional promise in writing made by one person to another, signed by the maker, engaging to pay on demand or at a fixed or determinable future time a sum certain in money to order or bearer." These requirements, which are necessary to have a negotiable contract, will be fully considered in the following chapter.

1. *Promissory Notes Classified*

Promissory notes obtain their names from the uses to which they are put. Following are the usual types of promissory notes encountered in the business world.

---

[1] The law pertaining to negotiable instruments has been codified by all the states and is substantially uniform. This legislation is cited as the Uniform Negotiable Instruments Law and in abbreviated form N.I.L., as it will be used in the following pages.

a. Mortgage Notes. The term *mortgage note* means that the maker's personal obligation to pay as represented by the promissory note has been secured by a collateral security contract, a mortgage. If the maker fails to meet his note obligation, the holder of the note can rely upon the mortgage contract for satisfaction; that is, he can look for payment to the property that was mortgaged.[2]

b. Conditional Sales Notes. A *conditional sales note* is given by a purchaser as evidence of his obligation for goods purchased under a conditional sales contract.[3] The conditional sales contract is a security contract giving the seller protection in the event the note is not paid.

c. Judgment Notes. A *judgment note* contains a provision whereby the maker consents to having judgment entered against him without trial in the event that the note is not paid when due.[4]

d. Bonds. *Bonds* are in the form of promissory notes and are generally negotiable. Bonds will be further discussed in the next chapter in relation to the requirements of negotiability.

$______ Due______ No.______

Ames, Iowa,______ ______

______days after date, for value received, I, we or either of us, promise to pay

______

or order______DOLLARS

at Ames, Iowa, with interest at the rate of______per cent per annum from date, payable semi-annually.

Principal and interest shall draw seven per cent semi-annual interest after due, and the principal shall be due and collectible at once if any interest is not paid when due. The makers, endorsers and guarantors of this note agree to pay a reasonable attorney's fee if suit is brought hereon, and consent that any Justice of the Peace may have jurisdiction to the amount of three hundred dollars, and hereby severally waive presentment for payment, notice of non-payment, protest, notice of protest, diligence in bringing suit against any party hereto and sureties consent that time of payment may be extended without notice thereof.

______

P. O.______ ______

PROMISSORY NOTE

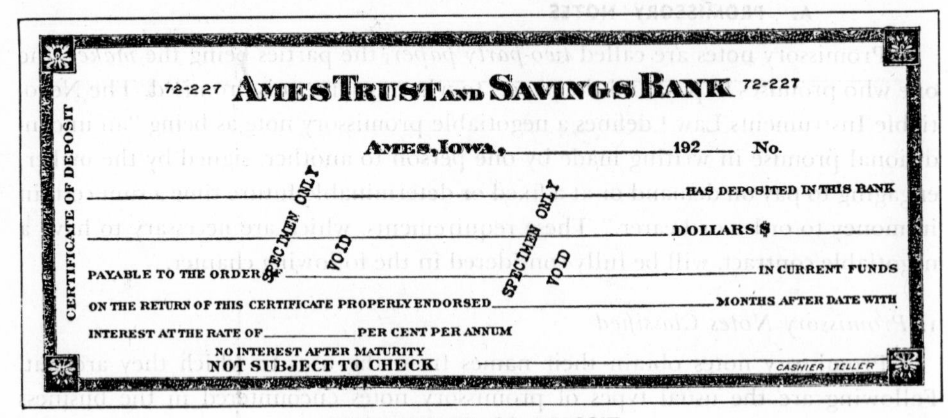

CERTIFICATE OF DEPOSIT

72-227 AMES TRUST AND SAVINGS BANK 72-227

AMES, IOWA, ______192___ No.

______HAS DEPOSITED IN THIS BANK

______DOLLARS $

PAYABLE TO THE ORDER OF______IN CURRENT FUNDS

ON THE RETURN OF THIS CERTIFICATE PROPERLY ENDORSED______MONTHS AFTER DATE WITH

INTEREST AT THE RATE OF______PER CENT PER ANNUM

NO INTEREST AFTER MATURITY

NOT SUBJECT TO CHECK

CASHIER TELLER

SPECIMEN ONLY VOID

SPECIMEN ONLY VOID

CERTIFICATE OF DEPOSIT

[2] See p. 720 for chattel mortgage contracts and p. 782 for real estate mortgages.
[3] See p. 725 for conditional sales contracts.
[4] See p. 456.

e. Certificates of Deposit. A *certificate of deposit* is a receipt (in the form of a promissory note) from a bank to a depositor. The ordinary deposit receipt that is received upon depositing money in a bank is not a certificate of deposit.

B. BILLS OF EXCHANGE

Bills of exchange (also called drafts) are *three-party paper,* the parties being: the *drawer* who orders the drawee to make payment to the *payee.* A bill of exchange arises usually upon the basis of a creditor-debtor relationship. The drawer (the creditor) draws upon the drawee (his debtor) to make payment to a third person. Thus, if A deposits money in the B bank, he has no specific funds in the bank, but becomes a creditor of the B bank to the amount of the deposit. It is upon the basis of this relationship that A draws checks—bills of exchange—upon B bank.

Section 126 of the N.I.L. defines a negotiable bill of exchange as being

> "an unconditional order in writing addressed by one person to another signed by the person giving it, requiring the person to whom it is addressed to pay on demand or at a fixed or determinable future time a sum certain in money to order or bearer."

These requirements will be fully considered in the next chapter.

1. *Checks*

Checks comprise the most common type of bills of exchange in use. Checks are specifically treated in Chapter 23.

2. *Bank Drafts*

A bank draft is, in effect, a check drawn by one bank upon another. There are many reasons for which bank drafts may be used. For example, a purchaser may submit a bank draft to the seller in payment of an obligation. The bank draft, carrying the bank's credit, may be more acceptaLle to the seller than the buyer's personal check.

CUSTOMER'S DRAFT

AMES TRUST & SAVINGS BANK 72-227

AMES, IOWA, ______ 19___

PAY TO THE ORDER OF ______ $______

______ DOLLARS

VALUE RECEIVED AND CHARGE TO THE ACCOUNT OF

TO ______

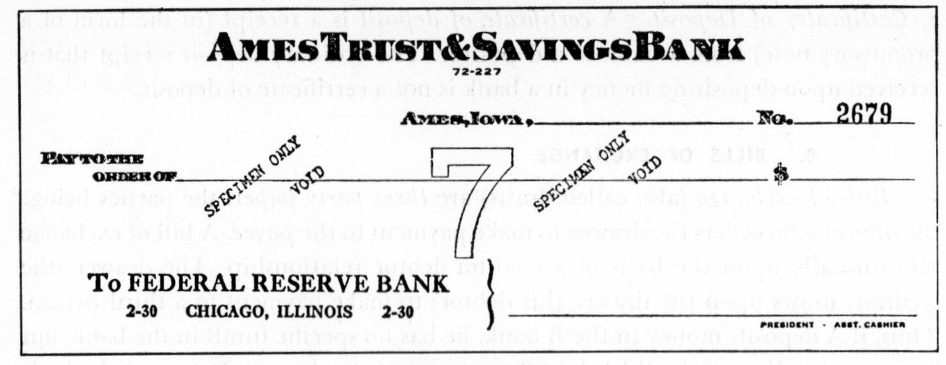
AMES TRUST & SAVINGS BANK
72-227
AMES, IOWA, ____________ No. 2679
PAY TO THE ORDER OF ____________ $ ______
SPECIMEN ONLY VOID
To FEDERAL RESERVE BANK
2-30 CHICAGO, ILLINOIS 2-30
PRESIDENT - ASST. CASHIER

BANK DRAFTS

3. *Trade Acceptance*

A *trade acceptance* is a bill of exchange drawn by a seller upon the buyer, payable to the seller at some future date. The trade acceptance is sent to the buyer for his acceptance and then returned to the seller. The advantage to the seller in extending credit to the buyer in this form, rather than upon open book account, is that he can sell (discount) the trade acceptance and thus realize upon it before the obligation is due.

The acceptor of a trade acceptance is in effect the maker of a promissory note.

Accepted ____________ 19____ (NAME OF CITY) (DATE)
Payable at ____________ (NAME OF BANK)
Signature ____________
Per ____________

$____________ TRADE ACCEPTANCE No.____________

____________ days after date pay to the order of OURSELVES

____________ Dollars

The obligation of the Acceptor of this bill arises out of the purchase of Merchandise from the Drawer.

To____________ ____________

TRADE ACCEPTANCE

4. *Banker's Acceptance*

A *banker's acceptance* is a bill of exchange used under circumstances similar to those in which a trade acceptance might be employed. Instead of being drawn upon the buyer, it is drawn upon the buyer's bank, with whom the buyer has made the necessary arrangements for its acceptance. The buyer may, for example, give the bank his own promissory note—with or without collateral security—to cover the amount of the instrument drawn upon the bank. Upon acceptance, the instrument drawn upon the bank carries the credit of the bank. Obviously, a banker's acceptance can be more easily sold (discounted) by the holder than can a trade acceptance.

► II. CREATION AND TRANSFER OF CREDIT BY USE OF NEGOTIABLE INSTRUMENTS ILLUSTRATED

Contractual rights to money may be evidenced either by simple contracts or by negotiable contracts, generally called *negotiable instruments.* Regardless of the nature of the transaction out of which a right to money arises, that right may be expressed in the form of a simple or nonnegotiable contract between the parties or in the form of a negotiable instrument. Let us suppose that A purchases an automobile from B on ninety days' credit. B undoubtedly will want some evidence of A's obligation to him. Instead of extending book credit, he has the alternatives of either a simple contract in writing or a negotiable instrument as evidence of the obligation. The type of negotiable instrument used under such circumstances could well be a promissory note.

Let us suppose, however, that the seller, B, demands immediate payment, which A is in no position to supply. Then A will call upon his banker to furnish the funds with which to make payment. The banker will require that his right to be repaid be evidenced by a writing in the form of a promissory note, probably supported by collateral security such as stocks or bonds. He could just as well accept a simple nonnegotiable contract, but, as will be made evident, such would not meet his needs.

It is very probable that A instead of actually accepting money from the bank, would accept deposit credit, exchanging his credit for that of the bank. He thus becomes a creditor of the bank because he has acquired a legal right to receive money upon his demand. Now A can transfer this right to receive money (credit) to B in either one of two ways. He could make an assignment—a simple contract—to B, but, in all probability, he would make the transfer by use of a check, which is a type of bill of exchange.

It is also possible that A, instead of purchasing deposit credit from the bank, would make arrangements whereby that bank would directly transfer its credit with some other bank to B in discharge of A's obligation. This transfer might be accomplished by an assignment but actually would be made by means of a bank draft, also a type of bill of exchange.

► III. CONSEQUENCES OF TRANSFER BY NEGOTIATION —ASSIGNMENT DISTINGUISHED

In the conduct of commercial affairs, the use of negotiable rather than simple contracts is explained by the fact that rights to money can be much more easily transferred when evidenced by negotiable instruments. Recall that the quality of a right cannot be improved when transferred by an assignment (which is the only method by which rights evidenced by a simple contract can be transferred); the assignee stands in no better position than his assignor—all defenses available against the original assignor are also available against the assignee or a subsequent assignee.[5] Because of the numerous risks involved, individuals are reluctant to accept rights to money by assignment.

In contrast, the quality of a right to money evidenced by a negotiable instrument may be improved by a transfer called a *negotiation.* A negotiation is accomplished by the indorsement and delivery—in some instances by delivery only—of a negotiable instrument. The holder of a right acquired by a negotiation may stand in a much better position than his transferor. The effect of a negotiation is to vest title in the holder *free of all personal defenses,* leaving available against the holder the *real defenses only*. Personal defenses are those which most ordinarily, and most frequently, arise—failure of consideration, fraud, undue influence, theft, and others—whereas the real defenses are few in number and less likely to arise.[6]

The following illustration will serve to emphasize further the advantages of a title to a right to money acquired by negotiation over one obtained by assignment:

A has contracted for the purchase of a bill of goods to the amount of $600 from B, payment to be made in ninety days. This right is one of B's current assets. Although evidenced by a simple contract, it is possible that it can be sold by B or used in payment of, or as security for, his obligations. Let us suppose that C, to whom the right has been transferred, upon attempting to collect, is met by A with a denial of liability based upon allegations that the agreement was tainted with fraud, that the implied warranty of fitness had been breached, that there was a failure of consideration, and that A has a counterclaim against B for the sum of $700, arising out of a transaction prior to the time that notice of the assignment had been given by C. Since an obligor can avail himself of all defenses against an assignee, it seems very likely that C's right to the $600 might be defeated.

Had the obligation, however, been evidenced by a negotiable promissory note and transferred by a negotiation to C as a holder in due course, the right to the $600 could not be defeated by these personal defenses. Whereas they would have been available to A against B, they are not available to A against C.

The further fact that with each successive negotiation the quality of a right is further improved by virtue of the liability of indorsers to the holder enhances the general acceptability of negotiable instruments in lieu of money. These special types of contracts have a high degree of negotiability and consequently are designated *negotiable instruments.* The philosophy underlying the law of negotiable instruments is that business transactions should be facilitated by making available evidences of rights to money that will pass freely from hand to hand.

Review Questions

1. How does a bill of exchange fundamentally differ from a promissory note?
2. What is a judgment note? Are judgment notes valid in your state?
3. Construct a fact situation illustrating the use of a bank draft.
4. What is the advantage of using a trade acceptance to evidence a credit transaction rather than to extend the credit upon open book account?

[5] See p. 252.
[6] See p. 509.

5. What could be the advantages of a banker's acceptance over a trade acceptance?
6. Can rights evidenced by a nonnegotiable contract be transferred from one person to another?
7. Explain the limitation to the use of contractual rights as evidenced by nonnegotiable contracts for credit purposes.
8. If your creditor were to offer you, in discharge of his obligation, either rights under a nonnegotiable contract by assignment or rights under a negotiable contract by negotiation, which would you accept? State your reasons.

Problems for Discussion

1. Without consideration, X gave Y a promissory note for $1,000. Upon maturity, Y brought an action against X to recover the $1,000. Can X successfully defend upon the grounds that there was no consideration given to support his promise to pay the $1,000?
2. Suppose that in the problem above, Y had negotiated the note to Z. Could Z recover from X, even though there was no consideration between X and Y?
3. X, the payee of a nonnegotiable note for $1,000 (which is a contractual obligation) made by A, discounts the note at the B bank. At maturity A refuses to pay, and the bank sues on the note. A sets up as a partial defense that X owes him $500, which debt arose before the assignment of the note to the bank, and further, as a complete defense, that X procured the note from A in payment of certain stock, in which transaction X had been guilty of fraud. Conceding the truth of the facts, and also conceding that the bank had no knowledge of them, are these defenses good against the bank?
4. A owed B $100. X owed Y $100. A contracted to sell M a horse for $100, which contract right A then assigned to B in full satisfaction of his debt to B. The horse died and A could not fulfill his contract with M. X contracted to sell N his car for $100, N giving X a certified bank check for that amount, which check X transferred to Y in full satisfaction of his debt to Y. The car burned and X could not fulfill his contract with N. Explain the relative positions of B and Y.
5. X wishes to discontinue extending book credit to Y because of the fact that Y procrastinates in the payment of his obligations, although he is fully able to pay. What course of procedure would you suggest to X?

18 NEGOTIABLE INSTRUMENTS:

REQUIREMENTS FOR NEGOTIABLE INSTRUMENTS

Negotiable instruments are contracts evidencing rights to receive money, which rights may be transferred by negotiation. But, whereas a simple contract may take any form of expression, the requirements for the creation of negotiable paper are most exacting—requirements that achieve the desirable elements of relative uniformity, simplicity, and certainty. Ability to judge whether an instrument possesses the characteristics of negotiability should, under most circumstances, be an accomplishment of all who engage in business affairs. One accepting rights under a nonnegotiable instrument stands in the position of an assignee, being required to give notice to the debtor for the protection of the assigned rights and also being subject to all personal defenses that exist between the debtor and the assignor. The acquirer of rights under a negotiable contract (by negotiation) need give no notice to the debtor, nor can the debtor use the personal defenses against him.*

Section 1 of the Uniform Negotiable Instruments Law provides that:

"An instrument to be negotiable must conform to the following requirements:

(1) It must be in writing and signed by the maker or drawer;

(2) Must contain an unconditional promise or order to pay a sum certain in money;

(3) Must be payable on demand, or at a fixed or determinable future time;

(4) Must be payable to order or to bearer; and,

(5) Where the instrument is addressed to a drawee, he must be named or otherwise indicated therein with reasonable certainty."

► I. WRITING AND SIGNATURE

A writing provides the necessary evidence whereby a right to money can flow freely in commercial channels. The method of writing is unimportant; it may be by pen, pencil, printing, or any other mode of making an impression or inscription durably. Business prudence demands that the writing be in some medium that cannot be altered easily.

A signature is generally thought of as an inscription in handwriting and in the true name of a person. For the purpose of creating a negotiable instrument,

---

* See p. 448.

however, the signature may be impressed or inscribed in any durable mode or in any form that the individual wishes to adopt as a signification of the assumption of the obligation. Printed signatures as well as those produced by means of rubber stamps have been held to be valid by the courts. An individual proprietor may personally bind himself by signing the business name of his establishment, and those who have never become burdened with the art of writing can sign by "X," their mark. One who signs an assumed name is equally as liable as though he had signed his own.

The signature need not appear in any certain place; [1] it can, for example, signify an intent to be bound equally well when contained in the body of the instrument as when appearing at the end. The practice is to place the signature at the lower right-hand corner of the instrument. While the N.I.L. makes no provision for the placing of the signature, Section 17 provides:

> "(6) Where a signature is so placed upon the instrument that it is not clear in what capacity the person making the same intended to sign, he is to be deemed an indorser."

This means that if the signature is not in the usual place, it will require proof to establish the liability of the signer in some capacity other than that of an indorser. As stated in 8 C.J. 108, "While the position of the signature is not fixed by any law, all departure from the usual place of the signature is liable to misconstruction and should be avoided."

► II. UNCONDITIONAL PROMISE OR ORDER

A. NATURE OF PROMISE OR ORDER

To be negotiable, a promissory note must contain a promise. The use of the term *promise* meets the requirements of the N.I.L. absolutely and with certainty. Any other language, however, which naturally implies a promise—an undertaking —to pay is sufficient. To illustrate:

The following expressions have been held by the courts to be the equivalent of a promise:

(1) This is to certify that I am to pay;
(2) obliges himself to pay;
(3) to be accountable for;
(4) to be delivered on call;
(5) I have borrowed.

An acknowledgment of a debt, such as an I.O.U., is not sufficient unless it is coupled with some expression that can be interpreted as a promise to pay.[2]

A bill of exchange to be negotiable must contain an order to pay. An order is a command or an imperative direction as distinguished from a mere request. Unless the term *order* is used in a bill of exchange, the language must clearly indicate a demand upon the drawee to pay.

---

[1] Field v. Lukowiak, p. 464.
[2] Bader v. Williams, p. 465.

B. PROMISE OR ORDER REQUIRED TO BE UNCONDITIONAL

A right—a promise or an order to pay money—that is to be evidenced by a negotiable instrument may not be made subject to conditions. A conditional right destroys the negotiable character of an otherwise negotiable contract.[3] *Nor can a nonnegotiable instrument become negotiable by a subsequent occurrence of the contingency upon which the right was conditioned.* The rule is "once nonnegotiable, always nonnegotiable." The right of money must exist with absolute certainty at the time of the creation of the instrument; it cannot be made dependent upon a contingency that may prevent its coming into existence or serve to terminate its existence. The fact that the right is absolute and cannot be defeated by a contingency greatly enhances its ability to pass freely from hand to hand.

Although conditions that prevent promises or orders from being absolute can be most heterogeneous, they usually arise out of provisions pertaining to either (1) the source from which payment is made, (2) the performance of the agreement out of which the obligation arose, or (3) the security of the obligation. It is not uncommon that a note is given as security for an obligation of the maker to the payee. Where such is indicated upon the instrument, the promise becomes conditional and the negotiable character of the note is destroyed. Such a provision is notice to any prospective acquirer that the promise to pay is not absolute and can be discharged by payment of the obligation it secures. Thus, where a note provides that it is to be returned to the maker when payment is made to the payee, it is a nonnegotiable instrument. Payment may be conditioned upon any imaginable extraneous event. An instrument would clearly be rendered nonnegotiable by a promise or order to pay conditioned upon the continued existence or the advent of a certain state of affairs during the life of the instrument. As an illustration, an instrument is not negotiable if payment is conditioned upon the event of a specified person's safe return from a journey or upon the event that the payee will continue in his present employment.

Section 3 of the N.I.L. reads:

> "An unqualified order or promise to pay is unconditional within the meaning of this act, though coupled with—
>
> (1) An indication of a particular fund out of which reimbursement is to be made, or a particular account to be debited with the amount; or
>
> (2) A statement of the transaction which gives rise to the instrument. But an order or promise to pay out of a particular fund is not unconditional."

1. *Reference to Source of Payment*

The negotiable character of an instrument is not necessarily affected if that instrument contains an expression indicating the source from which payment might be made or from which the obligor expects to reimburse himself. It is only when payment is conditioned upon the existence or sufficiency of a certain fund that negotiability is destroyed.[4] In such an event, the obligation is not the absolute

[3] Allison v. Hollenbeak, p. 465.

[4] Glendora Bank v. Davis, p. 466.

undertaking of the maker or the drawer—he assumes no personal responsibility—and if the fund fails, the obligation will also fail. The instrument would clearly be nonnegotiable in the case of a draft in which the order is to pay out of funds collected by the drawer or a note in which the maker promises to pay only out of the proceeds from a certain transaction or source. To illustrate:

(1) In *Scott City* v. *Advance-Rumley Thresher Co.*, 288 Fed. 739, it was held that County warrants * which specified that they were payable "out of any money in the treasury appropriated for road building" were nonnegotiable.

(2) In *Tomlin* v. *Neale*, 76 Cal. App. 726, a bill of exchange which provided for payment "to come out of my cotton returns" from a designated ranch was held to be a conditional obligation and nonnegotiable.

References in instruments to particular funds are in many instances undoubtedly intended for the purpose of identifying the instruments with the particular transactions out of which they arose or for the purpose of facilitating the keeping of accounts. Unless the reference to the fund clearly and unequivocally indicates an apparent intent that the fund alone shall be the source of payment, by far the majority of courts hold in favor of negotiability. The courts are most hesitant to establish conditions in credit instruments by implication. To illustrate:

In the case of *Van Tassel* v. *McGrail*, 93 Wash. 380, a note provided:

> "It is . . . agreed that the above note is to be paid from the proceeds from the sale of lots in the town of Vanors . . . and that ¼ of the proceeds . . . are to be applied to the payment of said note and interest and until the same is paid."

It was held that the promise was unconditional, this being a mere reference to the source out of which payment was expected to come, the note being in any event the absolute obligation of the maker. The moral to be derived from this illustration is that instruments with like or similar provisions may result in controversy and costly litigation.

2. *Reference to Transaction out of Which Instrument Arose*

An instrument is negotiable when it contains a mere reference to an extrinsic contract as the origin of, or the consideration for, the obligation. Its negotiability will not be destroyed by a mere recital of the transaction out of which the instrument arose.[5] The instrument is rendered nonnegotiable only if the obligation to pay is conditioned upon, or made subject to, the provisions of a collateral contract.[6] The courts will not, however, see fit to destroy the negotiability of an instrument unless its conditional character appears clearly and unquestionably upon its face.

a. As per Contract. By the overwhelming weight of authority, the appearance of the words "as per contract" upon an instrument in no way affects its negotiability. Such terminology is not generally interpreted as meaning that the obligation evidenced by the instrument is to be discharged in accordance with the provisions of

* A warrant is in the form of a bill of exchange drawn upon the treasurer of the drawer.

5 Rubio Sav. Bank v. Acme Farm Products Co., p. 466.

6 Westlake Mercantile Finance Corp. v. Merritt, p. 468.

the collateral contract. It is regarded as merely an identification of the transaction that occasioned the negotiable instrument. To illustrate:

In *Shawano Finance Corporation* v. *Julius,* 214 Wis. 637, a provision in a note read, "This note covers deferred installments under a conditional sale contract made this day between the payee and the maker hereof." This provision was held to be a mere reference to the origin of the note and therefore did not make the note subject to the terms of the sale contract.

b. Subject to Contract. An instrument which by its terminology is made subject to a collateral agreement is nonnegotiable—such a declaration is generally held to be a clear indication that the promise or order is not absolute but is conditioned upon the terms of the collateral agreement. Such a phrase as "subject to terms of a contract between the maker and the payee," or words of a similar nature, when found in a note, serve notice that the note is a nonnegotiable contract.

3. *Reference to Security Contract*

Frequently notes contain a recital to the effect that the obligation is secured by a collateral security contract, such as a mortgage. Since both a note and a mortgage arise out of, and are executed as a part of, the same transaction, there is some contention that by such a reference the mortgage becomes a part of the note and that the promise to pay is consequently conditioned upon the mortgage terms. By the weight of authority, however, such a note stands by itself, and its negotiability is not affected by provisions contained in the security contract to which it refers.[7]

A note that unequivocally declares, *"This note is secured by a mortgage and subject to the provisions of such mortgage,"* would undoubtedly be held nonnegotiable.

Special mention must be made of the situation relating to corporate bonds containing provisions of a "subject to" nature. Although there is much authority to the contrary, the modern tendency of the courts has been to conclude that such clauses as "subject to the provisions of a mortgage . . . to which . . . reference is made for . . . the rights of the holders . . . and terms and conditions upon which said bonds are issued, received, and held," and provisions of a similar and even more qualifying nature do not destroy the negotiability of the bonds in which they are contained. The justification for so holding has been that the reference does not relate to the rights to payment as evidenced by the bonds but rather to the rights of the holders concerning the security of payment.

► III. PAYABLE IN A SUM CERTAIN IN MONEY

The need for limiting payment of a negotiable instrument to money is obvious. To have a high degree of negotiability, an instrument must be made payable in a medium that has general acceptability, in a medium that lawfully circulates as money—a characteristic not possessed by merchandise or services. To perform

[7] Davis v. Union Planters Nat. Bank & Trust Co., p. 469.

properly the functions of money, an instrument must, of necessity, be capable of being transformed into money if the holder so wills.

A. PAYABLE IN PARTICULAR KIND OF CURRENT MONEY

In addition to providing that an instrument to be negotiable needs to be payable in money, Section 6 of the N.I.L. provides:

"The validity and negotiable character of an instrument are not affected by the fact that:

(5) It designates a particular kind of current money in which payment is to be made."

There is no agreement among the courts as to whether the terms "payable in currency" and "payable in current funds," when used to designate the medium of payment, make the instrument payable in money. Some courts interpret such expressions as including things other than money and hold nonnegotiable the instruments in which such terms appear. The modern and more general rule—and what is thought to be the better rule—is that such instruments are payable in money and are negotiable.

In a recent Iowa case which overruled former holdings that instruments "payable in current funds" are nonnegotiable, the court said:

"The phrase 'current funds' as used in the certificate of deposit in suit is the equivalent of 'current money' as used in the Negotiable Instruments Act. Both expressions mean whatever is receivable and current by law as money. . . . The great weight of authority also sustains this conclusion." *Feder* v. *Elliot,* 198 Iowa 447.

B. ACT IN ADDITION TO PAYMENT IN MONEY

Section 5 of the N.I.L. makes provision that:

"An instrument which contains an order or promise to do any act in addition to the payment of money is not negotiable."

The purpose of this provision is to prevent the introduction of contractual undertakings that would impede the free use of instruments in the place of money. Such a rule helps to retain simplicity of form, which, if an instrument is to pass freely from hand to hand, is absolutely necessary. Undertakings that have been held to destroy negotiability are, for example, commitments to keep machinery in repair, to hold property in trust, to pay taxes, and not to sell or mortgage property pledged as security.[8]

There is no uniformity of opinion among the courts as to the application of this provision of the N.I.L. to at least two types of undertakings that logically find their way into credit instruments: (1) a promise—distinguished from an option to be exercised upon demand—to deposit additional collateral should the collateral held to secure the obligation depreciate to a certain extent in value; and (2) a promise to insure property pledged as security for the obligation. The reasoning underlying the refusal of some of the courts to recognize the application of this

[8] International Harvester Co. v. Watkins, p. 471.

rule to undertakings of such a nature is well stated by Justice Carroll in *Finley v. Smith,* 165 Ky. 445, where he said:

"In many jurisdictions it has been held that a promise to furnish additional collateral, further to secure an instrument for the payment of money, should the collateral originally supplied depreciate in value, does not render the instrument nonnegotiable. . . . In other jurisdictions a contrary opinion has found support. . . . We take the view expressed in the group of decisions first above cited, that such a stipulation is not a promise to do an act 'in addition to the payment of money,' but a promise, rather, to do an act in aid of and incidental to, the payment of money. . . . If its real purpose is to aid the holder to secure the payment of money and protect him from the risks of insolvency, if it steadies the value of the note, and makes it circulate more readily, then it should not be fatal to negotiability. The promise to furnish more collateral is, it seems to me, such an incidental promise. It is not, strictly speaking, 'an order or promise to do an act in addition to the payment of money,' but is rather an order or promise to do an act that will better secure the promise to pay the money stipulated at the time fixed in the note."

1. *Acts not Affecting Negotiability*

Section 5 of the N.I.L. makes four exceptions to the provision considered above by further providing:

"But the negotiable character of an instrument otherwise negotiable is not affected by a provision which:

(1) Authorizes the sale of collateral securities in case the instrument be not paid at maturity; or

(2) Authorizes a confession of judgment if the instrument be not paid at maturity; [9] or

(3) Waives the benefit of any law intended for the advantage or protection of the obligor; or

(4) Gives the holder an election to require something to be done in lieu of payment of money."

a. Sale of Collateral Securities. Frequently the payee of a negotiable instrument will require the obligor to supply security in the form of stocks or bonds to be held by the payee. Very usually a note will provide that such collateral security may be sold by the holder in the event the note is not paid when provided for. Such does not destroy negotiability.

b. Confession of Judgment. A note containing a provision that authorizes the holder to obtain a confession of judgment is known as a *judgment note.*

An authorization to confess judgment is a provision whereby the obligor makes possible the entering of a judgment against himself without resort to the usual legal process. He thereby waives the right to notice and trial by a court of record and consents to judgment being confessed against him for the amount due on the

[9] Iglehart v. Farmers Nat. Bank, p. 472.

note. By such method the machinery of the law for the enforcement of a judgment can immediately be put into motion upon nonpayment at maturity of the note. It not only saves considerable expense but also saves time. A typical provision whereby such authority is given follows:

> "And to secure payment in event this note is not paid at maturity, I hereby authorize irrevocably, any attorney of any court to appear for me in such court, and to confess a judgment, without process, in favor of the holder of this note. . . ."

A majority of the states do not, however, sanction the use of such a short cut in procedure when contained in a note.

c. Waiver of Benefit of Law. Very common to negotiable instruments are provisions whereby secondary obligors waive the conditions, such as presentment, protest, notice of dishonor, and nonextension of time, upon which their liability is dependent. Obviously, provisions of this nature facilitate collection of, add greater security to, and consequently enhance acceptability of, instruments in which they appear. As a general rule, the courts hold that such provisions do not impair negotiability. A matter open to question is whether or not such benefits of law as the right to appeal, statute of limitations, and statutory property exemptions can be waived.

d. Act in Lieu of Payment of Money. The election to require something in lieu of payment of money must reside entirely with the holder. Providing he has the right to elect that payment shall be made in money or otherwise, the instrument is, within the meaning of the N.I.L., payable in money in every sense of the word. An illustration of the use of such an alternative payment provision is a situation where convertible bonds give the holder an option to receive money or other securities of the obligor corporation.

C. SUM CERTAIN

If credit paper is to serve as a substitute for money, it must carry a message of value upon its face; it must establish with certainty the amount of money it represents. To be negotiable, an instrument must during its lifetime—until its date of maturity arrives—show with certainty the amount to which the holder is entitled.

Section 2 of the N.I.L. declares:

> "The sum payable is a sum certain within the meaning of this act, although it is to be paid—
>
> (1) With interest;
>
> (2) Or by stated installments; or
>
> (3) By stated installments, with a provision that upon default in payment of any installment or of interest the whole shall become due; or
>
> (4) With exchange, whether at a fixed rate or at the current rate; or
>
> (5) With costs of collection or an attorney's fee, in case payment shall not be made at maturity."

A note payable with interest without providing for a definite rate of interest is not rendered nonnegotiable because of uncertainty of the sum payable. Where interest is provided for without specifying the rate, the legal rate will apply.

The usual practice is to provide that after maturity and during the period of default an instrument is to carry a higher rate of interest. Such a provision is held by a preponderance of the courts not to affect the negotiable character of an otherwise negotiable instrument. A provision of this nature comes into play only after maturity and, consequently, does not prevent the value of the instrument from being determined with certainty before maturity.

It is to an extent the practice that instruments will provide for a fixed discount if paid before maturity or before a fixed date. No general rule as to the effect of this type of provision can be stated. It has in some jurisdictions been held that such a provision renders the sum uncertain and destroys negotiability, while in other states a contrary conclusion has been arrived at. Thus, in *First National Bank of Iowa City* v. *Watson*, 56 Okla. 495, a note payable in installments provided for a discount of 6 per cent if paid within fifteen days from date. The court said:

> "He (the maker) could if he saw fit . . . discharge his debt at 94 per cent, or thereafter pay 100 per cent on the dollar. Under such conditions the sum payable was at the time of the execution of the instrument, clearly indefinite and uncertain."

Similar conclusions have been arrived at in Michigan, South Dakota, Tennessee, and Iowa. Contrary conclusions can be found in Minnesota, Nebraska, Texas, and Ohio. Instruments of this nature, unless the rule of the specific jurisdiction is known to favor certainty, should be avoided.

A provision that requires payment of costs of collection or an attorney's fee, or both, like a provision for a higher rate of interest upon default, does not prevent the determination of the value of the instrument prior to its maturity. It is only after maturity that it might become necessary to invoke the aid of such a provision. It cannot be denied that a provision of this character makes an instrument much more acceptable as a substitute for money. The usual practice is to provide for a reasonable attorney's fee rather than for a stated amount or fixed percentage of the face value of the instrument. Many courts will allow only a reasonable fee, even though the amount or percentage is fixed.

While not affecting the negotiable character of an instrument, provisions for attorney's fees are, as a matter of public policy, regarded as being invalid in some states. An inquiry into the local situation should be made.

► IV. CERTAINTY OF TIME OF PAYMENT

A. DATE OF INSTRUMENT

An instrument is not rendered invalid by the fact that it is issued undated. Section 17 (3) of the N.I.L. reads:

> "Where the instrument is not dated, it will be considered to be dated as of the time it was issued."

Section 13 authorizes the insertion of the true date in providing that:

"Where an instrument expressed to be payable at a fixed period after date is issued undated, or where the acceptance of an instrument payable at a fixed period after sight is undated, any holder may insert therein the true date of issue or acceptance, and the instrument shall be payable accordingly. The insertion of a wrong date does not void the instrument in the hands of a subsequent holder in due course; but as to him the date so inserted is to be regarded as the true date."

An instrument which carries no date is, as brought out in the following section, demand paper payable immediately.

1. *Antedating and Postdating*

The validity or negotiability of an instrument is not affected by the fact that it carries a date other than the day of its issue. Section 12 of the N.I.L. reads:

"The instrument is not invalid for the reason only that it is ante-dated or post-dated, provided that is not done for an illegal or fraudulent purpose. The person to whom an instrument so dated is delivered acquires the title thereto as of the date of delivery."

A postdated check can circulate as a negotiable instrument. The only effect of postdating a check is that the drawee bank may not honor it prior to the date appearing thereon. Paying prior to the date of the check would be in violation of the drawer's order to the bank and in breach of the contract between the parties. In *John Hancock Mutual Life Ins. Co.* v. *Mann,* 86 F. (2d) 783, the court said:

"In the execution of a post dated check . . . and its acceptance, there is no fraud or deceit. There is the necessary implication of extension of credit on the part of the payee to the maker of the check. There is also the inference that the maker has no funds in the bank with which to presently meet the sum named in the check, but that he will have the necessary money in the bank on the date of the post dated check. . . ."[10]

B. WHEN PAYABLE ON DEMAND

An instrument payable on demand meets the requirements of certainty of time of payment. Section 7 of the N.I.L. is explanatory of what as a matter of law is required to constitute demand paper. It reads:

"An instrument is payable on demand:

(1) Where it is expressed to be payable on demand, or at sight, or on presentation; or

(2) In which no time for payment is expressed.

Where an instrument is issued, accepted, or indorsed when overdue, it is, as regards the person so issuing, accepting, or indorsing it, payable on demand."

---

[10] John Hancock Mutual Life Ins. Co. v. Mann, p. 474.

C. WHEN PAYABLE AT FIXED OR DETERMINABLE FUTURE TIME

An instrument payable at a fixed time specifies the date of payment, as, "I promise to pay on January 3, 1947."

In explanation of the term *determinable future time,* the N.I.L. in Section 4 provides:

"An instrument is payable at a determinable future time, within the meaning of this act, which is expressed to be payable:

(1) At a fixed period after date or sight; or

(2) On or before a fixed or determinable future time specified therein; or

(3) On or at a fixed period after the occurrence of a special event, which is certain to happen though the time of happening be uncertain."

If the time of payment in an instrument is conditioned upon a contingency that may never happen, the instrument is nonnegotiable. Unless the time of payment is determinable within the meaning of the N.I.L., the promise or order to pay is conditional. The requirement of certainty of time would not be met by making payment contingent upon events such as the declaration of a dividend upon a specified stock or the marriage of certain persons. These events may never happen. The occurrence of the event by which the time of payment is to be determined will not serve to make a nonnegotiable instrument negotiable.

If, however, the time of payment in an instrument is determined by the happening of an event that must of necessity happen, the instrument is negotiable. The uncertainty of the time at which the event will happen is immaterial so long as the certainty of its happening exists. Therefore, an instrument that is payable "thirty days after the maker's death" meets the time requirement. To illustrate:

(1) In *West Texas Loan Co.* v. *Montgomery,* 27 N.M. 296, a note provided for an extension of the time of payment "until frost." It was held that the note was negotiable, being payable at a determinable future time.

(2) In *Specht* v. *Beindorf,* 56 Neb. 556, a note provided for payment "Six months after date . . . if elected county commissioner." It was held nonnegotiable, not being payable at a fixed or determinable future time.

(3) In *Scott* v. *Dagel,* 200 Iowa 1090, a note provided that it was payable upon the settlement of an estate. It was held to be nonnegotiable, being payable upon the happening of an event that might never happen.

D. PROVISIONS ACCELERATING TIME OF PAYMENT

A provision that gives the maker of a note an option to discharge his obligation prior to maturity does not render the time of payment uncertain and consequently does not affect negotiability [§ 4 (2)].[11] It is not uncommon for notes to be drawn so as to give the maker the privilege of paying part or all of the obligation at any time before the due date or at specified times before the due date.

---

[11] Barnwell v. Hanson, p. 475.

Many notes provide that for *certain reasons* the maker may be called upon for payment prior to the maturity date—provisions that accelerate the time of payment. The object of introducing an accelerating clause into an instrument is to give the holder greater protection against the possibilities of nonpayment, to give the holder greater security that payment can be realized.[12] The effect of accelerating clauses upon the negotiability of instruments cannot be dogmatically stated. The situation is rendered complex by the wide variety of accelerating provisions and by the disagreement among the courts as to their effect upon the negotiable character of instruments.

The more common accelerating clauses may be classified under the four types given below. This classification is based on the reasons for which the accelerating clauses may be exercised by the holder.

(1) *Making the instrument due and payable upon a failure by the maker to pay interest or an installment of the principal*

The negotiability of a note is not affected by a provision that, either automatically or at the option of the holder, speeds up the time of payment because of a failure to pay either interest or an installment. Acceleration clauses of this type are fully consistent with the concept of negotiability—they enhance the quality of acceptability of credit instruments. A failure to pay the interest or an installment may be, to the holder, the first indication of the financial disability of the obligor—it might be the signal to the holder that immediate action may be necessary for the protection of his interests.

(2) *Making the instrument due and payable upon a failure by the maker to carry out the terms of a collateral agreement*

There is no agreement among the courts as to whether an acceleration provision of such a nature destroys negotiability. This is true even when it relates to a default of the provisions of a collateral security contract such as a mortgage. It is not uncommon that a note will provide that, unless the terms contained in the accompanying mortgage are complied with by the maker of the note (the mortgagor), the note will become due and payable at once. By the terms of the mortgage, the maker is usually required to pay taxes and keep the buildings insured. Probably a majority of the courts hold that such accelerating provisions do not destroy negotiability. It cannot be denied that default by the maker to carry out the mortgage provisions might impair the security of payment and might justify immediate steps toward collection. There seems little reason why that which improves the quality of transferability should be held to destroy negotiability.

(3) *Making the instrument due and payable upon a failure by the maker to furnish additional collateral when the collateral held to secure the obligation depreciates in value*

If a provision gives the maker the alternative right of depositing additional collateral or allowing the maturity of the instrument to accelerate, this provision does not, by the more general and better rule, render the time of payment uncertain and, consequently, does not destroy negotiability. Such provisions are not to be

---

12 McCornick & Co., Bankers v. Gem State Oil & Products Co., p. 476.

confused with those containing an absolute promise or order to deposit additional collateral—provisions not calling for acceleration of payment.*

(4) *Making the instrument due and payable at the option of the holder whenever he deems himself insecure*

It is generally held that a note is nonnegotiable when it allows the holder to declare the instrument due and payable at his whim or fancy without any default on the part of the maker.

► V. PAYABLE TO ORDER OR BEARER

To be negotiable, an instrument must contain evidence that the parties apparently intended it to be such—it must contain what are usually called *words of negotiability*.[13] The almost universally used and accepted words of negotiability are *order* or *bearer,* which serve as an expression of consent that the instrument may be transferred. These particular words need not be used. Section 10 of the N.I.L. reads:

> "The instrument need not follow the language of this act, but any terms are sufficient which clearly indicate an intention to conform to the requirements hereof."

The court in *Raymond* v. *Middleton,* 29 Pa. 529, had this to say:

> "So commonly are the terms 'or order,' 'or bearer,' employed in commercial instruments, that we are apt to suppose them essential to negotiability. It is otherwise. Words are but the signs; thought is chiefly valuable; and when for a sufficient consideration, the minds of the parties have concurred in an agreement, that is a contract, and it must be executed as they intended, unless forbidden by law. 'Order' or 'bearer' are convenient and expressive, but clearly not the only words which will communicate the quality of negotiability. . . . The concession therefore may be made, that if the makers of this note having omitted the usual words to express negotiability, had said, 'This note is, and shall be negotiable,' it would have been negotiable."

A. WHEN PAYABLE TO ORDER

Section 8 of the N.I.L. provides:

> "The instrument is payable to order where it is drawn payable to the order of a specified person or to him or his order. It may be drawn payable to the order of:
>
> (1) A payee who is not maker, drawer, or drawee; or
> (2) The drawer or maker; or
> (3) The drawee; or
> (4) Two or more payees jointly; or
> (5) One or some of several payees; or
> (6) The holder of an office for the time being."

* See p. 455.

[13] Haggard v. Mutual Oil & Refining Co., p. 478.

B. WHEN PAYABLE TO BEARER

Section 9 of the N.I.L. provides that under the five following circumstances an instrument is payable to bearer.

(1) *"When it is expressed to be so payable"*

An instrument payable to a specific bearer, as "pay to A, the bearer," would not be negotiable. It is not payable to the bearer, which means any bearer.

(2) *"When it is payable to a person named therein or bearer"*

Thus, an instrument that reads, "Pay to A or bearer," would be negotiable.

(3) *"When it is payable to the order of a fictitious or nonexisting person, and such fact was known to the person making it so payable"*

An instrument knowingly made payable to the order of a fictitious or nonexisting payee is regarded as payable to bearer because of the theory that, since such a payee is not capable of indorsing, the maker or drawer must have intended the instrument to be transferred by delivery.

In contemplation of law, whether a payee is fictitious or nonexisting is entirely dependent upon whether the person executing the instrument intended the payee to be fictitious or whether such person had knowledge of the fact that the payee as designated was nonexistent.[14] The maker of a note or the drawer of a bill of exchange must have knowledge of the fact that the payee as designated is either (1) the name of a person who is to have no interest in the instrument or (2) the name of a person who is nonexistent. To illustrate:

(a) A real person is a fictitious payee if the maker or drawer of the instrument intended that the payee was to have no interest in the instrument. Thus, in *Snyder* v. *Corn Exchange Nat. Bank,* 221 Pa. 599, a clerk with authority to draw checks upon his employer's account fraudulently drew checks payable to the order of "Jones," an existing person. The clerk, intending that "Jones" was never to have any interest in the checks, indorsed the name of "Jones" thereon and obtained the money for his own purposes. The question arose whether the indorsement was a forgery and consequently whether the holder had title. The court held the instrument to be bearer paper—payable to a fictitious payee—and the indorsement was not necessary to a transfer of title.

(b) An instrument payable to the order of a nonexisting payee may be order paper. Thus, an instrument that is payable to the order of a deceased person is not payable to bearer (order of a nonexisting payee) unless the fact of death is known "to the person making it so payable."

(c) A misdescription of the payee does not in itself constitute a fictitious or nonexisting payee. An instrument made payable to the order of "Clearmount Storage Co." in payment of an indebtedness to the Claremont Storage Warehouse, Inc., was held not to be payable to bearer, as the maker did not intend a fictitious payee and did not have knowledge of the nonexistence of such a payee.*

---

* Section 43 of the N.I.L. reads: "Where the name of a payee or indorsee is wrongly designated or misspelled, he may indorse the instrument as therein described, adding, if he thinks fit, his proper signature."

[14] Hillman v. Kropp Forge Co., p. 479.

(4) *"When the name of the payee does not purport to be the name of any person"*

A check drawn payable to the *order* of One Load of Hay, Cash, Accounts Payable, or any other impersonal payee is a bearer instrument and can be negotiated by delivery only. It is presumed that the maker or drawer of an instrument, by using an impersonal payee, intends the instrument to be payable to the bearer. An instrument with a blank space for the name of the payee would, until a name is inserted,* circulate as bearer paper. It has been held, however, that by drawing a line through the space for the name of a payee, the maker thereby indicates his intent that no payee, impersonal or otherwise, is to be inserted and that the instrument is not payable to bearer.

(5) *"When the only or last indorsement is an indorsement in blank"*

Thus, if an instrument that on its face reads "Pay to the order of A" is indorsed "A," it is indorsed in blank and has become a bearer instrument that can be negotiated by delivery only. Section 40 of the N.I.L. reads:

> "Where an instrument, payable to bearer, is indorsed specially, it may nevertheless be further negotiated by delivery."

CASES

CASE NO. 1

Field v. Lukowiak. 114 N.J.L. 268, 176 Atl. 319 (1935)

LLOYD, J. The action was on an irregularly signed promissory note, and resulted in a verdict being directed for the plaintiffs. The defendants appeal, and claim that motions for nonsuit and for direction were improperly refused. . . .

. . . The defendants' signatures on the note in question were in the upper left-hand corner of an ordinary printed form. The note read as follows:

> August 15th, 1931
>
> $1,600
>
> Edward Lukowiak, Jos. M. Lukowiak,
> Anna Lukowiak, Helen Lukowiak
>
> On Demand after date promise to pay to the order of E. J. Field, Sixteen Hundred Dollars at 5%
>
> Payable to E. J. Field, personally.
>
> Value received. Sixteen Hundred Dollars.
>
> No. 1, Due on Demand.

The grounds of the motions for nonsuit and direction were that the signatures were so irregular as to constitute the signers indorsers rather than makers under Section 63 of the Negotiable Instruments Act, which provides that

> "a person placing his signature upon an instrument otherwise than as maker, drawer or acceptor is deemed to be an indorser, unless he clearly indicates by appropriate words his intention to be bound in some other capacity,"

* See § 14 of the N.I.L., which authorizes filling in blanks.

and that, the note being payable on demand, as indorsers the defendants were entitled to notice of dishonor within a reasonable time after the note was drawn.

. . . The position of the signature on the paper is immaterial if it clearly appears to have been intended as such. While the signatures in the present instance are at the top rather than at the lower right-hand corner of the paper, as is usually the case, it clearly imports an intention to be bound thereby, and it is equally clear that it must have been as makers; otherwise there are no makers and consequently no indorsers. They were the persons primarily liable and absolutely required to pay the note. They were neither indorsers nor drawers, and therefore not entitled to demand for payment or notice of nonpayment.

. . . the learned judge was right in refusing to nonsuit the plaintiffs and in directing the verdict for the plaintiffs.

CASE NO. 2

Bader v. Williams. D. of C., 61 A. (2d) 637 (1948)

CLAGETT, A.J. Appellant sued appellee for the full amount of an "I.O.U." signed by appellee and her husband on account of money previously advanced as part of the purchase price of a restaurant business to be conducted as a joint enterprise by the husband and appellant. The case was tried to a jury but at the close of the evidence the trial court directed a verdict for appellee. This appeal is from the judgment entered on such directed verdict.

The "I.O.U." sued upon follows:

"Glenn E. Bader
April 12, 1947
I.O.U. 2165.55 for
Business Expense at
4408 Arkansas Ave.
(Sgn.) Carl N. Williams
(Sgn.) Frances H. Williams" . . .

Appellant urges, first, that the instrument sued on was a negotiable promissory instruments so as to make applicable the provision of the Uniform Negotiable Instruments Law providing that such an instrument is deemed prima facie to have been issued for a valuable consideration. We can not agree with this contention. The Code requires that a negotiable promissory instrument contain an unconditional promise or order to pay a certain sum in money on demand or at a fixed or determinable future time to order or to bearer. . . . As the instrument here in question does not comply with these requirements, none of the statutory presumptions of the Negotiable Instruments Acts, such as that of valuable consideration urged by appellant, are applicable in this case. . . .

CASE NO. 3

Allison v. Hollenbeak. 138 Iowa 480 (1908)

MC CLAIN, J. On September 4, 1903, one Henry Principal executed and delivered to the defendant a promissory note for $3,500, payable on or before April 1, 1906. The note was payable by its terms to the order of defendant, and was in the usual form of negotiable promissory notes, save that on the back were written at the time of its execution these words:

"This note is secured by purchase money mortgage on one hundred and sixty acres of land in Guthrie County, Iowa, and payee herein agrees to look to mortgage security for payment of this note."

. . . defendant indorsed the note in blank and delivered it to the firm of Osgood, Allison & Son, and by that firm it was subsequently transferred to plaintiff. On February 27, 1905, at a sale on foreclosure under the mortgage, the sum of $2,500 was realized from the property, which amount was credited on the note, and this action is to recover the balance with interest.

The stipulation written on the back of the note at the time of its execution became a part of it. . . . The instrument was thereby rendered nonnegotiable. Nevertheless by the indorsement thereof defendant assumed an obligation to his indorsee or any subsequent holder to pay the amount due as provided in the instrument, according to its tenor. . . . As against the maker, plaintiff could have no relief, save that afforded by resort to the mortgage security. . . . And the same stipulation, made a part of the note, which thus limited the liability of the maker, also constituted a limitation on the liability of defendant as indorser. . . .

CASE NO. 4

Glendora Bank v. Davis, et al. 204 Cal. 220, 267 Pac. 311 (1928)

The negotiability of a promissory note containing the following provision is in issue:

"This note is given in payment of merchandise and is to be liquidated by payments received on account of sale of such merchandise."

SHENK, J. . . . It is clear that the last clause of the note, above quoted, is susceptible of no other reasonable interpretation than that payment of the note or any part thereof was to be made out of receipts from the sale of the merchandise for which the note was given, and that this provision is "a promise to pay out of a particular fund," the existence of which depended on the contingency of the sale of the merchandise which might not take place at all or might take place to some, but to an uncertain extent. These factors were fatal to the negotiability of the note. . . .

CASE NO. 5

Rubio Savings Bank v. Acme Farm Products Co. 240 Iowa 547, 37 N.W. (2d) 16, 9 A.L.R. (2d) 459 (1949)

OLIVER, J. Defendant Acme Farm Products Company is a partnership composed of defendants Paul M. Ross and Hannah J. Ross, husband and wife, of Chicago, Illinois, at which place the partnership is engaged in the produce business. Weisz Produce was a trade name under which Maurice Weisz operated a produce business at Brighton, Washington County, Iowa. Early in 1947 Weisz Produce made a number of sales and shipments of eggs and poultry to Acme Farm Products Company. The checks received in payment were deposited by Weisz Produce in its account in plaintiff Rubio Savings Bank, of Brighton. The two checks in suit, for $6,500 and $5,000, respectively, were made to Weisz Produce by Acme, April 1, and April 3. Weisz Produce indorsed them, deposited them in its account in plaintiff bank and received credit for the amounts thereof.

Plaintiff forwarded the checks for collection, through channels. Before they were presented to the Chicago bank upon which they were drawn, Acme ordered payment stopped:

"Reason: Merchandise for which these vouchers were advanced was diverted to other outlets (dealers)."

In the meantime Weisz Produce had withdrawn from its account in plaintiff bank the amounts of these checks. . . . Weisz disappeared and was adjudicated a bankrupt. Thereafter plaintiff brought this action for $11,500. . . .

Defendants' answer alleged the checks were without consideration and were procured by fraud. In reply plaintiff alleged it was a holder in due course. . . . There was a verdict and judgment for plaintiff. . . .

. . . In considering whether this form of instrument is sufficient to deprive others of their rights as holders in due course, it will, of course, be construed most strongly against Acme, because Acme prepared it.

On the face of the checks is printed: "Endorsement: Guarantee delivery in good order, weight and count merchandise listed opposite side." Defendants contend this language makes payment conditional upon the delivery of the merchandise. We disagree. Paper non-negotiable by reason of its conditional character is commonly distinctly conditional in form with language such as—on condition that—if—in the event, etc. 10 C.J.S., Bills and Notes, § 86a, p. 525. See Home State Bank v. Martin, 196 Iowa 1029, 195 N.W. 977. Defendants do not point to any specific language as expressly or impliedly supporting their contention. They argue merely that this is the tenor of these instruments. A like argument would be equally applicable to any check which refers to an executory consideration. The absence of any language in the instruments indicating payment was conditional upon delivery of the merchandise requires a conclusion to the contrary.

A mere reference in the instrument to an extrinsic agreement or a statement of the origin of the transaction does not impair negotiability. . . .

The memoranda on checks describing the funds and the source from which they come or the payment intended by the checks do not act as a notification to one discounting them of any facts which he is bound to investigate. Bost v. Block, 195 Okla. 198, 156 P. (2d) 610. Knowledge that an instrument was given for the sale of goods warranted or guaranteed by the seller does not deprive an indorsee of his status as a holder in due course, if the warranty or guaranty is breached, where the holder had no knowledge of the breach prior to taking the instrument. . . .

Various decisions in analogous cases support this conclusion. Some of them are Coffin v. May, 104 N.J.L. 347, 140 Atl. 331, 333, 61 A.L.R. 819, "This trade acceptance covers 222 radio cabinets and benches which are absolutely guaranteed and are to be replaced . . . if found damaged. . . ." Critcher v. Ballard, 180 N.C. 111, 104 S.E. 134, "This note is for the purchase of stallion, and said Ames warrants him. . . ." First Bank of Marianna v. Havana Canning Co., 142 Fla. 554, 195 So. 188. Check made June 7. "For berries to be delivered to us June 8th." . . .

Weisz Produce deposited the two checks in plaintiff bank April 2 and 5, respectively. Each was indorsed to plaintiff bank "for deposit only." In accordance with the customary conduct of these parties, the amounts of the checks were credited to the Weisz Produce account and it was permitted to check against and withdraw those credits. Defendants contend the indorsement made plaintiff bank merely a trustee for Weisz Produce and not a holder in due course.

Although decisions from some jurisdictions support this view it has been sharply criticized by various writers. See Ogden on Negotiable Instruments, 1947, p. 199; Brannon's Negotiable Instrument Law, 5th Ed. 437. Plaintiff cites, as holding to the contrary: Atlantic City National Bank v. Commercial Lumber Co., 107 N.J.L. 492, 155 Atl. 762, 75 A.L.R. 1413; Security Bank of Minnesota v. Northwestern Fuel Co., 58 Minn. 141, 59 N.W. 987; Blatz Brewing Co. v. Richardson & Richardson, Inc., 245 Wis. 567, 15 N.W. (2d) 819. Moreover, it is not the rule in this state. . . . Goeman v.

Livestock National Bank, 238 Iowa 1088, 29 N.W. (2d) 528, held instruments thus indorsed, where credit was given the depositor, passed title to the bank to which they were thus indorsed. . .

We are not prepared to overrule these holdings. It is our conclusion the indorsement "for deposit only" did not prevent plaintiff bank being a holder in due course. . .

CASE NO. 6

Westlake Mercantile Finance Corp. v. Merritt. 204 Cal. 673, 269 Pac. 620, 61 A.L.R. 811 (1928)

PRESTON, J., delivered the opinion of the court:

On April 30, 1925, under the trade-name of Aristocrat Distributing Company, one J. B. Vallen entered into a contract in writing with Charles A. Merritt and Charles A. Parlier, a copartnership doing business under the name of Merritt & Parlier, with reference to the sale and delivery by the former to the latter of a certain number of dishwashing machines. . . At the time of the making of the contract, and as a part of the transaction, Merritt & Parlier accepted two drafts or trade acceptances drawn by the Aristocrat Distributing Company, payable to themselves. . . . The material part of the earliest of these acceptances is here set forth:

Plaintiff, alleging itself to be a holder in due course of these instruments, sued the defendants as acceptors thereof for the amounts specified therein. Defendant copartnership, pleading the non-negotiability of said instruments, introduced and proved an uncontradicted defense to said obligations unless plaintiff can be said to be an innocent purchaser thereof for value. . . . The whole question turns upon the negotiability or non-negotiability of said drafts, and this question must be determined from the face of the instruments themselves. . . . The question is further refined by the construction to be placed upon the above clause, reading:

"The obligation of the acceptor hereof arises out of the purchase of goods from the drawer, maturity being in conformity with original terms of purchase."

In other words, is said clause the expression of a contingency as to the maturity of the acceptances, or does it merely refer to the consideration for which they were given? Particularly, does the expression, "maturity being in conformity with original terms of purchase," refer to the date set up in the body of the trade acceptances, or does it refer to the underlying contract between the parties? It will be observed that these acceptances were made payable to the drawers themselves. The question

> No. —. Los Angeles, Calif., 4/30, 1925, date of sale. $420 to Merritt & Parlier, San Jose, Calif., on June 30th, 1925. Pay to the order of ourselves at Los Angeles, Calif., the sum of four hundred twenty and 00/100 dollars. The obligation of the acceptor hereof arises out of the purchase of goods from the drawer, maturity being in conformity with original terms of purchase. Accepted at San Jose, Cal., dealer's town, on 4/30, 1925, date of order. Payable through Security State Bank, San Jose, Cal., dealer's bank.
>
> Merritt & Parlier, Trade Name of Acceptor.
> By Chas. A. Merritt, Authorized Acceptor.
>
> Aristocrat Distributing Co.,
> J. B. Vallen.

further arises: For what reason were these paragraphs inserted? Without them the instruments are perfect trade acceptances, negotiable in form in every respect. If these paragraphs were not intended to make the collateral agreement a part of the instruments, then they are a fraud upon the acceptors, who had a right to believe that they would mature only as in said contract provided.

We are fortunately not without assistance in the proper construction of these instruments, for the identical question was presented to the highest courts in both the states of Minnesota and Texas. It seems that the representatives of this patented article, the Aristo dish-washing machine, have in other states been long on promises, short on performances, and quick on negotiations of the obligations executed by the credulous and unwary merchants. In Minnesota, in the case of Heller v. Cuddy, 172 Minn. 126, 214 N.W. 924, the court held the above paragraph to be "a statement of the transaction which gives rise to the instrument". . .

. . . As above intimated, we are of the opinion that the said paragraph does make the underlying contract a part of said instruments for the purpose of determining the maturity date thereof, which may be different from that set forth in said instruments themselves. In this connection we are constrained to disagree with the opinion announced in the above-quoted case. We are in accord, however, with the reasoning set forth in Lane Co. v. Crum, (Tex.) 291 S.W. 1084, which is also a case involving the identical language here under consideration. In that case there was in the court of civil appeals (284 S.W. 980), a majority opinion in accord with the Minnesota holding, to which there was a dissenting opinion by Mr. Justice Stanford. The supreme court, however, adopted the reasoning of Mr. Justice Stanford, in the following language:

". . . In our opinion the clause has effect to render the trade acceptances nonnegotiable under the law merchant as well as under the Negotiable Instruments Act. . . . The obligation of the acceptor, according to the terms of said clause, arises, not from the instruments themselves, but from a collateral transaction. For an instrument to be negotiable, the obligation of the maker must arise exclusively from the instrument. No obligation arising from a collateral transaction can be imported into the terms of the instrument without destroying the negotiability of the instrument. 8 C.J. pp. 113, 114. A negotiable instrument has been termed 'a courier without luggage,' whose countenance is its passport. This apt metaphor does not fit these trade acceptances, for the reason they are laden with the equipment of a wayfarer who does not travel under safe conduct. By their express terms, these instruments bear burdens whose nature must be sought for beyond the four corners of the instruments themselves. . . . The legal effect of the clause is to render the paper subject to all the rights and equities of the parties to the collateral transaction from which the obligation of the acceptor arises. . . ."

The judgment is affirmed.

CASE NO. 7

Davis et ux. v. Union Planters National Bank & Trust Co. et al. 171 Tenn. 383, 103 S.W. (2d) 579 (1937)

Plaintiffs executed their promissory note (which note was secured by a deed of trust on plaintiffs' home) to Turley. The agreement was that Turley was to sell the note and turn the proceeds over to plaintiffs. The note (with mortgage) was negotiated to the defendant and

Turley used the proceeds for his own purposes. This action is to enjoin the foreclosing of the deed of trust.

MC KINNEY, J. The question before us is whether a certain note is negotiable. If not, the assignee thereof takes it subject to all equities and defenses available between the original parties.

Plaintiffs insist that the following provision in the note destroys its negotiability:

"Upon breach of any promise made in this note or in the deed of trust securing it, at the option of the holder the entire indebtedness hereby evidenced shall become due then or thereafter as the holder may elect regardless of the date of maturity. Notice of the exercise of such option is hereby expressly waived." . . .

The weight of authority, as well as the better-reasoned cases, holds that the form of the note determines its negotiability. The note alone must be looked to in considering its negotiability. The annotator of 75 A.L.R., p. 1211, upon this question says:

"The weight of authority supports the doctrine of the reported case that, notwithstanding the rule that two or more instruments executed by the same parties at the same time and referring to each other must be construed together, the form of a note or bond may alone be considered in determining its negotiability, although it is secured by a mortgage or trust agreement, and that, unless the terms of the latter are referred to in a way to incorporate their provisions into the note or bond, the mortgage or trust agreement is but an incident thereto and is to be regarded as a security only, the provisions of which will not render the bond or note non-negotiable if it is otherwise a negotiable instrument." . . .

Counsel for plaintiffs have referred us to a number of cases supporting the well-recognized rule clearly and succinctly stated in 3 R.C.L. 883, 884, as follows:

"It may be stated as the general rule that wherever a bill of exchange or promissory note contains a reference to some extrinsic contract, as distinguished from a reference importing merely that the extrinsic agreement was the origin of the transaction, or constitutes the consideration of the bill or note, the negotiability of the paper is destroyed."

There is considerable conflict in the authorities as to whether the presence of words in a note "as per contract of even date herewith" would be sufficient to render the paper non-negotiable.

As illustrative of the foregoing text, in American Exchange Bank v. Blanchard, 7 Allen (Mass.) 333, it was held that the note was non-negotiable because it was payable "subject to the policy."

The Court of Appeals of New York, in Enoch v. Brandon, makes this very clear statement of the rule invoked by plaintiffs:

"If in the bond or note anything appears requiring reference to another document to determine whether in fact the unconditional promise to pay a fixed sum at a future date is modified or subject to some contingency, then the promise is no longer unconditional. What that document may provide is immaterial. . . ."

The note in question contains no such reference and does not provide that it is subject to the deed of trust. The holder is at liberty to examine the deed of trust to see what promise, if breached, would authorize him to accelerate the maturity of the note. Or he can ignore the acceleration clause and defer action until the due date of the note.

In 9 C.J. 49, it is said:

"But where a bond contains special stipulations and its payment is subject to contingencies not within the control of the holder, it is deprived of the character of a negotiable instrument and becomes exposed to any defense existing thereto, as between the original parties to the instrument."

The payment of the note in controversy is subject to no contingencies not within the control of the maker, which distinguishes this cause from those cited by plaintiffs. There is no uncertainty as to the amount or the time of payment; hence it is unnecessary to refer to any other instrument to ascertain these facts.

This is a case where one of two innocent parties must suffer, and the loss will have to be borne by plaintiffs, due to their misplaced confidence in Mr. Turley. . . .

CASE NO. 8

International Harvester Co. v. Watkins. 127 Kan. 50, 272 Pac. 139, 61 A.L.R. 687 (1928)

HUTCHISON, J., delivered the opinion of the court:

. . . The plaintiff had sued upon the six notes given by the defendant to local dealers for the tractor and harvester thresher and assigned before maturity to the plaintiff harvester company. The answer admitted the execution of the notes and for defense alleged . . . that the notes were not negotiable, . . .

Appellant insists that the notes are not negotiable, because they contain orders and promises to do acts in addition to the payment of money. The face of each note contains the following paragraph . . . :

"This note . . . is given for McCormick-Deering tractor No. T.G. 38,413 and I hereby agree that title thereto, and to all repairs and extra parts furnished therefor, shall remain in the payee, owner or holder of this note until this and all other notes given therefor shall have been paid in money, and if at any time he shall deem himself insecure, he may take possession of said property and hold the same until all of said notes and the expenses of such repossession shall have been paid, and if default is made in the payment of this or any other of such notes, or if said property or any part thereof is levied upon, or the undersigned attempts to sell or remove the same, then the owner or holder thereof may declare this and every other such note due, and may take or retain possession of said property, and sell the same at public or private sale, with or without notice, pay all expenses incurred thereby, including expense for repossessing, storing, reconditioning and reselling the same, and apply the net proceeds on this and other notes given for the purchase price thereof. I further agree in consideration of the use of said property to pay any balance remaining unpaid on this or any other such note after the net proceeds of such sale are applied, and that if said property, or any part thereof, shall be lost, damaged or destroyed before full payment of the purchase price, I shall not on that account be entitled to a rescission of this contract or abatement in price."

Is there anything in this long statement included in the face of the notes that amounts to a promise on the part of the maker to do anything in addition to the payment of money to meet the obligations of the notes? He authorizes the payee or holder to deduct from the proceeds derived from the sale of the property held as security the expense for repossessing, storing, reconditioning, and reselling the property and to credit the net proceeds on the note, and then promises to pay the balance remaining unpaid. Is this not substantially the same as saying that, in case the property is taken and sold to pay these notes, I further agree to pay all expense of reconditioning, storing, repossessing, and reselling the same? These may be proper and usual obligations in a chattel mortgage, but they are none the less promises to do some additional act. . . .

In Killam v. Schoeps, 26 Kan. 310, 313, 40 Am. Rep. 313, it was said by Justice Brewer under similar circumstances:

> "The additional stipulation is not in reference to the payment of money, but a matter entirely foreign and distinct. There might as well be included in one agreement a contract for the lease of real estate, or the hiring of chattels, or the performance of labor with an absolute promise to pay a sum certain at a certain time, and then affirm that by reason of this absolute promise the entire contract is a negotiable instrument."

Whatever may be said as to necessary costs and expenses incidental to the collection from the sale of the property, it certainly cannot be expanded to include "reconditioning" and a further promise as to and for the use of the property. . . .

> "The Negotiable Instruments Law was adopted for the purpose of establishing uniformity in the law pertaining to negotiable instruments. First State Bank v. Williams, 164 Ky. 143, 175 S.W. 10. The purpose of the law, among others, is to establish definite rules by which persons dealing in bills and notes may, by examining an instrument, know whether or not it is a negotiable instrument. Perhaps some of the rules respecting negotiable instruments are arbitrary (Killam v. Schoeps, supra), but they should be followed, for to hold otherwise would make the law of no force." Foley v. Hardy, 122 Kan. 616, 618, 50 A.L.R. 422, 253 Pac. 239. . . .

CASE NO. 9

Iglehart v. Farmers Nat. Bank. 197 Atl. 133, 200 Atl. 833, 117 A.L.R. 667 (Md.) (1938)

MITCHELL, J., delivered the opinion of the court:

. . . Except as to variance in date and amount, the two notes upon which the judgment was entered are similar in form, as follows:

> "Joint and several note. Annapolis, Md., ——— 192—. On demand after date, for value received, we jointly and severally promise to pay to the Farmers National Bank of Annapolis, or order ——— dollars, negotiable and payable at said bank; . . . And whenever, in the judgment of the holder of this note, it may become necessary, for his or its protection, we authorize entry of judgment against us at any time before maturity of this note."

Each of these notes was signed by Phillips L. Goldsborough, Jr., on the face thereof, and each of them was indorsed on the back in blank by the appellant and Mr. Goldsborough, in the order named. . . .

. . . the appellant . . filed a petition in the nature of a motion to vacate and annul the judgment as against him, in substance setting forth: . . . (2) that no notice of dishonor of either of said notes was given to him as indorser; . . .

No contention is made that the judgment was not properly entered against Goldsborough; and hence the sole question before us is whether the authorization for the entry of the judgment, under the facts as shown, was binding upon Iglehart. In the solution of that question, it is apparent that it is necessary to first determine the status of the appellant with reference to his original transaction with the bank. Stated differently: (1) Was the appellant a joint maker, or was he an indorser of the notes? and (2) Was the obligation which he signed a negotiable or nonnegotiable instrument? There is nothing in the record to indicate other than that the appellant placed his signature upon the notes in question at their inception and prior to transfer to the bank. . . .

In Good v. Martin, 95 U.S. 90, 97, 24 L. Ed. 341, 342, it is said:

> "In the case of a note not negotiable, if any party writes his name on the back of the note, at or sufficiently near the time it is made, his signature binds him in the same way as if it was written on the face of the note and below that of the maker; that is to say, he is held as a joint maker, or as a joint and several maker, according to the form of the note."

The Negotiable Instruments Act, Code, art. 13, § 82, provides:

> "A person placing his signature upon an instrument otherwise than as maker, drawer, or acceptor is deemed to be an indorser, unless he clearly indicates by appropriate words his intention to be bound in some other capacity."

Inasmuch as it was not necessary for the appellant to place his signature upon the notes in order to effect their negotiability, his indorsement was irregular: this, however, in itself would not deprive him of the right to have notice of demand and dishonor in accordance with the statute, if the instruments before us are held to be negotiable. The main question, therefore, resolves itself into the determination of the character of the instruments upon which the judgment was entered; because, if they are nonnegotiable, the status of the appellant is that of a joint maker. . . .

Under the Negotiable Instruments Act, however, section 82, above quoted, limits the liability of such person to that of an indorser, unless he adds words to indicate otherwise. Section 108 of said act provides that notice of dishonor by nonpayment must be given to each indorser, with some exceptions not involved in this case, and that every indorser not so notified is discharged.

. . . as stated in 7 Am. Jur. p. 892, § 184:

> "Where judgment can be obtained, and execution immediately issued thereupon at any time after a note is made, it is not due at a fixed and determinable period at all, unless it be treated as due from and after delivery; the time of payment depends on the whim or caprice of the holder, and is absolutely uncertain. This prevents the note from being negotiable. For it is essential to negotiability that the instrument be payable at a fixed and determinable future time. The Uniform Act provides that the negotiable character of an instrument is not affected by a provision authorizing a confession of judgment, if the instrument is not paid at maturity. Upon familiar principles of statutory construction, this provision renders nonnegotiable an instrument authorizing judgment to be entered before maturity."

Applying these principles to the notes in the instant case, the natural query arises as to the meaning of the words,

> "and whenever in the judgment of the holder of this note, it may become necessary, for his or its protection, we

authorize entry of judgment against us at any time before maturity of this note."

It seems to us that there is no ambiguity in their meaning, and that their effect is to leave to the discretion of the holder the determination of the time at which the judgment might be entered, thereby making it possible that the judgment could have been entered on the notes, upon the authority of the warrant of attorney, at any time either before or after the maturity thereof. Characterized as they are by the uncertainty as to the time at which judgment could have been entered upon them, we therefore hold that they are nonnegotiable instruments, and, as such, not governed by the statute.

. . . the notes were nonnegotiable; and, being nonnegotiable, the status of the appellant was that of a joint maker; and it must follow that, as such, he is bound as though he had signed the notes on the face thereof, with Goldsborough. The position of the signature of the maker is not controlling. In other words, he is bound by the terms of the contract on which the bank loaned the money; one of which terms, as an inducement or condition to the granting of the loan, was the power to enter judgment by confession. . . .

Judgment affirmed with costs.

CASE NO. 10

John Hancock Mut. L. Ins. Co. v. Mann. *86 F. (2d) 783 (1936)*

EVANS, C.J., delivered the opinion of the court:

Appellant assails a judgment for $53,387.10 recovered by appellee, the beneficiary named in a life insurance policy issued by appellant, on the ground that the policy had lapsed for non-payment of premium. The controversy turns upon whether payment was made when insured gave to the insurer's general agents a post dated check which was subsequently dishonored because of insufficient funds. Shortly afterwards the insured committed suicide.

The material facts are:

A check for $612.50 (the amount of the quarterly premium which was due July 16th) was given by insured to, and made payable to, insurer's general agents, Joseph and Sherman Strong, on August 14, 1930, post dated September 5, 1930.

The insured's bank balance on the morning of September 5 was $231.29 and at the end of the day was $155.65, . . .

The general agents notified the home office of the payment (the manner of payment not being specified), an entry was made on the books of the company showing payment, and the agent was given credit therefor. . . .

Upon receipt of the dishonored check from the bank, the general agent sent it to the home office, which wrote the insured a letter on September 29 returning the dishonored check and stating the policy had lapsed and giving the conditions upon which reinstatement might be made. . . .

Counsel agree that had insurer accepted insured's note, the dates being the same, such acceptance of the note would have been payment of the premium. . . .

We may therefore narrow our inquiry to the differences and similarities between the insurer's acceptance of a post dated check instead of a note and the authority of general agents of an insurance company to extend credit to an insured.

In approaching this question, it is necessary to keep in mind that the payment of a premium on a life insurance policy is optional with the insured, who always has the privilege of terminating his insurance by not paying the premium. The consideration of a note by him given for the amount of the premium is the payment of said premium and the continuance of the life insurance policy. Inasmuch as the execution of a note creates a liability on the part of the insured which did not previously exist, it constitutes the consideration for the payment and satisfaction of the premium. Wherein does the execution and acceptance of a post dated check permit of a different conclusion?

Prior to the issuance of the post dated check there was no liability on the part of the insured to pay the premium. Upon the delivery of the check there arose a legal liability on his part. If the check were a presently due check the consideration would arise, but acceptance of such a check would be upon the hypothesis of money in the bank with which to pay the check. If there were no funds in the bank, it would be optional with the insurer to retain the check and enforce the liability or repudiate the effect of its acceptance because of fraud. . . .

In the execution of a post dated check, however, and its acceptance, there is no fraud or deceit. There is the necessary implication of extension of credit on the part of the payee to the maker of the check. There is also the inference that the maker has no funds in the bank with which to presently meet the sum named in the check, but that he will have the necessary money in the bank on the date of the post dated check. . . .

There existed no valid reason why the agents would not have loaned the money to insured. By so doing they, of course, obligated themselves to the insurer. This, we think, was the effect of the transaction. Having extended the credit to the insured, the premium was paid and the agents became (as was recorded on the books of the company) liable to the insurer for the amount of the premium. The effect of the entire transaction being a payment of the premium, it could not be nullified by the death of the insured nor by the discovery of the fact that the credit was unwisely extended. . . .

The judgment is affirmed.

CASE NO. 11

Barnwell v. Hanson. 80 Ga. App. 738, 57 S.E. (2d) 348 (1950)

GARDNER, J. Under the pleadings and the evidence, the controlling question involved is whether the suit was brought within the statute of limitations. The note sued on was under seal. Actions upon bonds or other instruments under seal shall be brought within 20 years after the right of action shall have accrued. . . .

Upon default by the maker in the payment of the semi-annual interest on this note on February 28, 1927, did the principal of the note become instantly due and payable, under the clause in the note that immediately upon such default the entire principal "shall become instantly due and payable"? It is to be noted that the clause in this note, unlike the acceleration clause in many notes, does not provide that upon default in the payment of the interest the entire principal shall, at the option of the holder, become immediately due and payable. In such a case, the holder of the instrument would have to exercise the option in order for the note to become due and payable. . . .

. . . the settled rule in this State is that where the acceleration clause in a note or other instrument for the payment of money is absolute in its terms and not optional with the holder, then upon default in the payment of the interest installment the entire debt "automatically and ipso facto" becomes due and payable, that is, the debt matures, without regard to any affirmative action on the part of the holder to declare same due, or to enforce such provision or insist thereon, which is necessary when the acceleration clause is optional and not absolute.

The plaintiff holder urges, however, that the defendant maker can not interpose, as to her, the plea of the statute of limitations because she was, under the facts, presumed to be a holder in due course of the note. The plaintiff relies on the principle that she being a holder in due course, without notice of any defects in the note, could not be defeated in her attempt to collect this note because she had a right to rely upon the apparent fact that the note would not mature and become payable until two years after its date. . . .

The note sued on is a negotiable instrument. The inclusion therein of a provision whereby the entire principal became due on failure of the maker to pay the semi-annual interest did not change the note to a non-negotiable one. According to the weight of authority, a promissory note otherwise negotiable is not rendered non-negotiable by a provision therein that, upon default by the maker in the performance of certain agreements, the note is to become due and payable. . . .

. . . It follows that the holder in due course, acquiring such a note, would acquire same subject to this provision in the note. Such a provision in the note is sufficient to put the holder in due course upon inquiry as to whether or not there has been a default in the payment of this interest by the maker. The exercise of any diligence in this regard by the person acquiring the note, would disclose whether the maturity of the note has been accelerated by a default, causing the statute of limitations to commence. . . .

Judgment (for defendant) affirmed.

CASE NO. 12

McCornick & Co., Bankers, v. Gem State Oil & Products Co. 38 Idaho 470, 222 Pac. 286 (1923)

ADAIR, D.J. The plaintiff instituted this action against the defendant and appellant upon three certain written instruments known as trade acceptances. . . .

On the margin of each instrument appears the following:

"Trade Acceptance.

The obligation of the acceptor of this bill arises out of the purchase of goods from the drawer. Upon the acceptor hereof suspending payment, giving a chattel mortgage, suffering a fire loss, disposing of his business or failing to meet at maturity any prior trade acceptance, this trade acceptance, at the option of the holder, shall immediately become due and payable."

There is no controversy as to the facts in the case. It appears that on May 4, 1920, the Utah Rubber Company, for a valuable consideration, sold and delivered all three of these trade acceptances to the respondent bank. The instrument involved in this appeal was duly indorsed by said Utah Rubber Company, but the other two were not so indorsed. After selling these instruments to the respondent bank the appellant gave back to the drawer, as payment in full thereof, the goods for which the bills were originally given. This was done on June 1, 1920, and without notice of the assignment of said instruments to the respondent. The first notice which appellant ever received of the transfer of said instruments was about June 24, 1920. After maturity of these bills respondent instituted this suit to recover thereon from the appellant. Appellant pleaded payment, and, after the submission of testimony, which was undisputed, the court directed a verdict in favor of the respondent and against appellant on the instrument which had been indorsed, and against the respondent and in favor of the appellant on the two instruments not indorsed. The appellant appealed from the judgment entered against it upon the verdict thus rendered. . . .

If the instrument is non-negotiable, the appellant could set up the defense of payment against the assignee thereof, the respondent herein, and, since the payment and discharge of the instrument was made without notice of its assignment, and before maturity, it would be a valid and complete defense to said action. . . .

We are concerned, therefore, only with the one question as to the negotiability of said instrument. Aside from the printed matter on the margin, the paper is purely an ordinary bill of exchange, properly drawn and accepted, and complying in all respects with the requirements of the statute and the law merchant as to negotiable paper. There is obviously no doubt but that it would be negotiable, except for such marginal matter, and to that, and that alone, we will direct our attention.

The law of bills and notes and other means of trade, like all other substantive law, is the creature of growth. Founded on the custom and needs of merchants it is the combined result of reason and experience, and should keep pace with and respond to commercial usage.

In the modern commercial world, trade acceptances are fast becoming an important form of contract, ranking with notes, checks, drafts, and other mediums of trade. The matter contained therein, aside from the direct order to pay money, is often valuable and intended to facilitate its transfer, and an option similar to that inserted in the margin of the instrument in question might tend to assist the holder in its transfer or sale to another. The fact that it does contain matter other than an order for the payment of money does not in itself render it nonnegotiable.

The paper involved here provides for the acceleration of the time of payment upon the happening of any one of five events, four of which, viz., suspending payment, giving a chattel mortgage, disposing of his business, or failing to meet at maturity any prior trade acceptance, are wholly within the control of the acceptor or maker, and the other contingency, that is, suffering a fire loss, is an event over which no party to the paper has any control. None of the contingencies named are within the control of the holder. . . .

The overwhelming trend of modern authority is to the effect that, where an instrument is made payable on a definite day, and also contains a conditional promise to pay at an earlier date, the instrument is not necessarily rendered nonnegotiable by such acceleration clause.

The most common cases involving this principle which have arisen are those which provide for accelerating the due date, at the option of the holder, for default in the payment of interest, and those where several notes maturing at different times belong to a single transaction and form a connective series; the negotiability thereof is not affected by a provision that, on the failure of the maker to pay any one of the series, the rest shall become due and payable at the option of the holder.

The general rule is that, where instruments are payable at a day certain, or sooner, if some specific event shall happen, they shall be construed to be due at all events at the day limited, and to be negotiable. 8 C.J. 138. . . .

In the case of Utah State National

Bank v. Smith, 180 Cal. 1, 179 Pac. 160, the California court held that, under the Negotiable Instruments Act of that state, providing that an instrument to be negotiable must be payable at a determinable future time, when a note is so payable, and it further provides that, if interest is not paid when due, both principal and interest shall become due at the option of the holder, such a note is negotiable; "determinable" meaning what may be determined, found out, definitely decided upon or settled.

In the late case of Nickell v. Bradshaw, 94 Ore. 580, 183 Pac. 12, 11 A.L.R. 623, the court held that a note otherwise negotiable, but containing the clause "due if ranch is sold or mortgaged," is not rendered nonnegotiable by the quoted words.

In each of these last-mentioned cases a very exhaustive and well-considered opinion is written, reviewing the modern decision on the question of the effect of such acceleration clauses. In these opinions the writers point out the difficulty and impossibility of laying down any hard and fast rule which could govern each individual case that might arise. In Nickell v. Bradshaw, supra, Judge Harris quotes with approval from the opinion in Ernst v. Steckman, 74 Pa. 13, 15 Am. Rep. 542, as follows:

"The principle to be deduced from the authorities is this: To constitute a negotiable promissory note, the time, or the event, for its ultimate payment, must be fixed and certain; yet it may be made subject to contingencies, upon the happening of which, prior to the time of its absolute payment, it shall become due. The contingency depends upon some act done or omitted to be done by the maker, or upon the occurrence of some event indicated in the note; and not upon any act of the payee or holder, whereby the note may become due at an earlier day."

We think this general rule should be, and the same is, adopted in this state, and, applying it to the paper here in question, we hold that the same is negotiable. None of the conditions in the acceleration clause depend upon any act of the holder, nor are they within his control, but all of such contingencies depend either upon some act or omission of the maker, upon an event indicated in the paper not within the control of either party.

The judgment is affirmed, with costs to respondent.

CASE NO. 13

Haggard v. Mutual Oil & Refining Co.
204 Ky. 209, 263 S.W. 745 (1924)

CLARKE, J. The single question presented by this appeal is whether or not the following check is a negotiable instrument:

$2,500.00. Winchester, Ky., July 10, 1920.
The Winchester Bank, of Winchester, Ky.:
Pay to Arco Refinery Construction Company twenty-five hundred and no/100 dollars, for . . .

Mutual Oil & Refining Co.,
By C. L. Bell, Pres.

. . . the Negotiable Instruments Act (Acts 1913, p. 213), § 1, provides that:

"An instrument to be negotiable must conform to the following requirements: . . .

(4) Must be payable to the order of a specified person or to bearer."

Since, as the check itself shows, and as is admittedly true, the maker, in issuing the check, drew a line through the printed words "or bearer," we need only to examine it to ascertain whether or not it was "payable to the order of a specified person," for unless so, it lacked one of the essentials prescribed for negotiability.

Section 8 of the act . . . defines when an instrument is payable to order as follows:

"The instrument is payable to order where it is drawn payable to the order of a specified person or to him or his order."

It will be noticed that the above check is not payable to the order of the payee, nor to the payee or its order, but is payable simply to the payee. It therefore seems to us too clear for dispute that this check is not payable to order, and is therefore, as the lower court held, not negotiable.

In other words, we think it is clear that subsection 8 means, as it says, that the instrument must be payable either (1) to the order of the payee, or (2) to the payee or order, and that it does not permit of the construction that the instrument may be payable (1) to the order of the payee, (2) or to the payee, or (3) to his order. . . .

CASE NO. 14

Hillman v. Kropp Forge Co. 340 Ill. App. 606 (1950)

FEINBERG, J., delivered the opinion of the court: Plaintiffs (for convenience hereinafter referred to as the currency exchange) brought suit upon a check issued by defendant (hereinafter referred to as Kropp) . . . payable to Tolabeag Engineers (hereinafter referred to as Tolabeag), upon which defendant stopped payment. . . .

. . . Defendant had in its employ one Thomas J. Lane, who was superintendent of defendant's machine shop from 1940 until 1944, when he was promoted to superintendent of maintenance. He had authority to prepare and submit to defendant's purchasing department purchase requisitions for material and parts needed for defendant's business. Defendant's purchasing agent from time to time received suggestions and recommendations from Lane as to suppliers of the materials requisitioned by him. Lane entered into a conspiracy with his wife, also a former employee of defendant, to defraud defendant. The scheme involved the creation of the fictitious name "Tolabeag Engineers," a combination of letters of the names of Lane and his wife. To carry out the object of the conspiracy, the wife went to Cleveland, Ohio, rented office space in the name of Tolabeag Engineers, and opened a bank account in that name in a Cleveland bank. In the established routine of defendant's business, Lane, in the performance of his duties, prepared requisitions, which were submitted to the "works manager" and then in turn to the purchasing agent. The name Tolabeag Engineers appearing in such requisitions was furnished by Lane to the works manager. . . . These requisitions in question, furnished to the purchasing agent by Lane, were signed by Lane on a line intended for his signature, and thereafter the purchasing agent inserted the name Tolabeag Engineers in the several requisitions involved. . . . Purchase orders were then prepared by the purchasing department and approved by the officers in authority, in accordance with the established procedure. These purchase orders bearing the name Tolabeag were mailed to Cleveland at the address furnished by Lane and appearing in the requisitions. . . .

The next step in the established procedure of defendant was to receive invoices for alleged deliveries called for by the purchase orders. Pursuant to the conspiracy, Lane had his wife send invoices from Cleveland in the name of Tolabeag. . . . By some trick or device, Lane falsely recorded, upon the receiving records of defendant, receipt of the material from Tolabeag . . . to correspond to the purchase orders, and induced defendant's receiving clerk to approve the receiving record with the false entries made by Lane. In the next successive step of established routine the documents—namely, requisition, purchase order, receiving record and invoice—were transmitted to the proper department, where these records were then checked, and checks were issued to the order of Tolabeag, and either mailed to Cleveland, or, in some instances, handed to Lane on his representation that John Tolabeag was in town and wanted Lane to pick up his check for him. . . .

The four checks in question were all endorsed by Lane in the name of the payee and cashed by Lane, as already indicated. . . . Tolabeag Engineers is a fictitious concern, existing in name only and created for the purpose of carrying out the conspiracy. . . . Lane had cashed all of his salary and bonus checks, issued by Kropp, at the currency exchange over a period of several years, and had established his identity with the latter and developed their confidence.

The controlling question presented upon this appeal is whether the statute, ch. 98, par. 29, § 9, subpar. (3), Ill. Rev. Stat. 1949 is applicable to the instant facts, which would make the checks in question "bearer" checks. The section reads in part as follows:

> "The instrument is payable to bearer: . . .
>
> "3. When it is payable to the order of a fictitious or non-existent or living person not intended to have any interest in it, and such fact was known to the person making it so payable, or known to his employee or other agent who supplies the name of such payee."

It is earnestly argued by defendant that the proper construction to be placed upon this statute would require that the "employee or other agent who supplies the name of such payee" should be one who has some authority in the preparation, execution or issuance of the check as distinguished from an employee such as Lane, whose duties were confined to the shop, as already outlined.

The amendment passed by the legislature July 2, 1931, added to the section as it previously existed "or known to his employee or other agent who *supplies* the name of such payee." (Italics ours.) This amendment followed the decision in United States Cold Storage Co. v. Central Manufacturing District Bank, 343 Ill. 503, and was intended to overcome the conclusion reached in the case cited. This court substantially said so in Houghton Mifflin Co. v. Continental Illinois Nat. Bank & Trust Co. of Chicago, 293 Ill. App. 423, which was decided after the 1931 amendment to the statute, where we reversed a judgment in favor of the drawer of the check against the bank which cashed it, and where the checks were made payable to living persons not intended to have any interest in them, and whose endorsements were forged by an employee of the drawer. We there said:

> "The purpose of the amendment is to place the responsibility upon the drawer of an instrument for the acts

of his agent who names a fictitious payee without the drawer's knowledge. This is accomplished by treating such instrument as bearer paper transferable by delivery."

There, too, the contention was raised that even under the amendment it is still the intention of the duly authorized officers which controls, and the dishonesty of the defrauding clerk does not supersede the intention of the company's duly authorized agents. In disposing of this contention, we said:

"There is no language in the statute from which such limitation on its meaning can be inferred."

New York, which has no corresponding statute as the amendment in question, nevertheless in Swift & Co. v. Bankers Trust Co., 280 N.Y. 135, 19 N.E. (2d) 992, followed the law of Illinois, which was held applicable to the transaction, and concluded that the amendment controlled. It was there, too, observed that the amendment in Illinois was passed after the decision of the United States Cold Storage Co. case, *supra*.

The question here presented has been ably argued by both sides, and the numerous cases in this State and elsewhere, cited by them, we have carefully reviewed. We feel the construction of this amendment contended for by defendant is too narrow and would unduly restrict what we regard as the intention of the legislature to protect those who in good faith cash such checks. It is conceded here by defendant that, if these checks can be properly regarded as bearer checks, liability exists.

Upon the facts submitted, we conclude that Tolabeag was a fictitious person, and that the name was supplied by Lane, an employee within the meaning of the amendment, since he was an integral part of the required procedure established by defendant, which ultimately led to the issuance of the checks in question. The fact that his duties did not call upon him to prepare, execute or issue the checks in question would not take it out of the amendment. . . .

It follows that the trial court erred in entering judgment for defendant. . . . Accordingly, it is reversed and judgment is here entered for plaintiffs. . . .

Review Questions

1. What are the requirements for a negotiable instrument?
2. What constitutes a valid signature for the creation of a negotiable instrument?
3. Would a promissory note that was written on the side of a barn be negotiable?
4. What is the logic in requiring an unconditional promise or order for the creation of a negotiable instrument?
5. Construct an instrument in which the order is subject to a condition that defeats its negotiability.
6. Would the happening of the event upon which the promise to pay is conditioned render the instrument negotiable?
7. What determines whether an instrument in which a fund has been indicated as the source of payment is negotiable or not?
8. Construct a promissory note in which the promise to pay is made subject to a collateral contract.
9. Why should a promise to perform an act in addition to the payment of money destroy the negotiability of the instrument in which it is contained?

10. Construct a credit instrument that provides for the doing of an act in addition to the payment of money, which additional act renders the instrument non-negotiable.
11. Construct a credit instrument that provides for the doing of an act in addition to the payment of money, which additional act, however, has no effect upon the negotiability of the instrument.
12. An instrument is made payable in either money or diamonds—at the election of the holder. Is it negotiable?
13. An instrument provides for the payment of interest but fails to specify the interest rate. Does this affect negotiability?
14. When is an instrument payable on demand?
15. What is the meaning of the term *determinable future time?*
16. Construct a promissory note that provides for payment upon the happening of an event that is certain to happen, although the time of its happening is uncertain.
17. Is an instrument that is payable on or before a certain date negotiable?
18. What is an *accelerating clause* in a credit instrument?
19. What are the various reasons for which it may be desirable to provide for the acceleration of the time of payment in a promissory note?
20. Is an instrument invalid by virtue of the fact that it has been issued undated?
21. Is a postdated check negotiable?
22. Distinguish *order* instruments from *bearer* instruments.
23. Construct an instrument which is payable to the order of a fictitious payee.
24. What is the effect of a blank indorsement appearing upon an instrument which is of the order variety upon its face.

Problems for Discussion

1. Briggs is the holder of the following instrument, which was in the handwriting of Simms:

   On March 1, 1947, I, Otha Simms, promise to pay to John Briggs or order the sum of $100.

   Can Simms successfully resist payment upon the contention that the instrument is not signed?
2. Is the following a negotiable instrument?

   T. W. Shearer, Waterville, Kans.: I owe you $4,683.34, money advanced on Shearer College Camp.

   Mrs. Rena Shearer

   (*In re Linkman's Estate*, 191 Wis. 353)
3. Is the following a negotiable instrument?

> This is to certify that I have received of A $1,000, which is to be returned when called for by the bearer of this instrument.
>
> B.

4. A note recited:

   "Payable on April 21, 1947, if I receive the position with the X Corporation for which I have made application."

   The maker did receive the position. Is the instrument negotiable?

5. A note contained a provision to the effect that it was secured by a trust deed and was payable in biweekly installments as set out in the deed and as prescribed by the constitution and by-laws of the payee association. Negotiable or nonnegotiable?

6. Is the following negotiable?

> 120 Dover, Oct. 27th, 1893
>
> Piscataquis Savings Bank
>
> Pay James Lawlor, or order, One Hundred and Twenty Dollars and charge same to my account on Book No. . . . .
>
> (Signed) J. N. CUSHING
>
> Witness:
>
> The bank book of the depositor must accompany this order.

(*White* v. *Cushing*, 88 Me. 339, 24 Atl. 164)

7. The note sued on was as follows:

> 500.00.
>
> Omaha, Nebr., October 15, 1890.
>
> Six months after date, we or either of us promise to pay to W. R. Vaughan, or order, the sum of five hundred dollars, for value received, payable at the Nebraska National Bank, Omaha, Nebraska, with interest at the rate of ten per cent. per annum from date until paid. And, in case of a suit brought to collect this note, I will also pay the plaintiff therein a reasonable sum, not exceeding ten per cent., to be fixed by the court as attorney's fees, if elected county commissioner.
>
> GEORGE E. TIMME

(*Specht* v. *Beindorf*, 56 Neb. 553)

   Is it negotiable?

8. Is a note upon which the following appears negotiable or nonnegotiable?

> The tolls collected under lease dated Feb. 17, 1922. will be credited on the face of this note until paid.

(*Jones* v. *Green*, 173 Ark. 862)

9. Is the following instrument negotiable?

> Cleveland, Ohio, January 2, 1924
>
> I borrowed money from Petros Shemonia, the sum of five hundred dollars ($500.00) with 4 per cent interest. The borrowed money ought to be paid within four months from the above date.
>
> Vassili Malik Verda

(*Shemonia* v. *Verda,* 24 Ohio App. 246, 157 N.E. 717)

10. A promissory note provided that it was to be paid out of the first money received from the sale of certain lots and that, if sufficient was not received by the time the note matured, a new note was to be given for the unpaid balance. Was this note negotiable?
11. In an action by plaintiff, C. V. McClenathan, upon the following instrument the question before the court was whether the instrument was negotiable:

> For value received I promise to pay Elizabeth Gamble, or order, the sum of fifteen hundred dollars in twelve months after I shall become the legal owner of one hundred and fifteen acres of land conveyed to me by my father, H. V. Davis, reserving to him, H. V. Davis, a life estate in said land, by which at his death I am to become possessed of and the owner in fee of said one fifteen acres, situated in the southeast corner of section 30, in township 18 north, range 11 east of the third P.M., Champaign county, Illinois.
>
> Emmons Davis

(*McClenathan* v. *Davis,* 243 Ill. 87, 90 N.E. 265)

Decide.

12. A promissory note provided: ". . . this note is collateral to a stock subscription of even date herewith." Is the note negotiable or nonnegotiable?
13. The plaintiff, Garon, loaned $1,000 to the five defendants whose names were inscribed on the back of the following note:

> 1000.00 Mount Holly, N.J. Feb. 24, 1931
>
> Three months after date we promise to pay to the order of Richard D. Garon at The Union National Bank and Trust Company at Mount Holly One Thousand & 00/100 Dollars without defalcation for value received.

The following signatures appeared on the back of the note:

"James G. Becker
H. J. Wagner
Theo. J. Bozarth
Dallas R. Jobes
W. H. Bryant"

(*Garon* v. *Becker,* 118 N.J.L. 98, 191 Atl. 546)

The lower court held the defendants to be liable as indorsers. Decide.

14. A promissory note provides that in the event the collateral deposited as security depreciates in value the maker agrees to deposit additional collateral to the extent of the depreciation. The maker, when sued upon the instrument, contends that the note is nonnegotiable. Decide.
15. A note provided for the payment of $1,000 and the delivery of 500 bushels of wheat. Was this a negotiable instrument?
16. A promissory note provides that the holder may confess judgment if at any time he feels insecure. Does this impair its negotiability?
17. A note provides that the holder shall have the option of receiving $1,000 in cash or property of such value. Is it negotiable?
18. A note contained a promise to pay "in successive semiannual payments of not less than One Thousand Dollars each for a period of eight years from date, and the balance then due to be payable on demand thereafter, with interest on the principal unpaid at the rate of six per cent per annum, payable semiannually, together with all taxes assessed upon said sum against said payee or the holder of this note."

    (*Persky* v. *Bank of Am. Nat. Assoc.,* 261 N.Y. 212, 185 N.E. 77)

    Is it negotiable?
19. The case turns upon the question whether the note is negotiable. It reads as follows:

> $4,500.00. No._____ Kansas City, Mo., Sept. 18th, 19___ Due_____ Six months _______ after date for value received _________ I promise to pay to the order of Merchants' Refrigerating Company, Kansas City, Missouri, _______ forty-five hundred and no/100 _______ dollars at the office of the Merchants' Refrigerating Company, Kansas City, Mo., with interest from maturity until paid at the rate of six per cent per annum. To secure the payment of this note and of any and all other indebtedness which ______ I ______ now owe to the holder hereof, or may owe him at any time before the payment of this note ______ I have hereto attached, as collateral security the following: (Collateral described.)
>
> The above collateral has a market value of $6,250.00. If, in the judgment of the holder of this note, said collateral depreciates in value, the undersigned agrees to deliver when demanded additional security to the satisfaction of said holder; otherwise this note shall mature at once. Any assignment or transfer of this note, or obligations herein provided for, shall carry with it the said collateral securities and all rights under this agreement. And I hereby authorize the holder hereof on default of this note, or any part thereof, according to the terms hereof, to sell said collateral or any part thereof, at public or private sale and with or without notice, and by such sale the pledgor's right of redemption shall be extinguished.
>
> C. B. Hoffman

(*Holliday State Bank* v. *Hoffman,* 116 Pac. 239)

Decide.

20. Is the following instrument negotiable?

> Miami, Florida, March 16, 1925
>
> On or before eighteen months after date, for value received, I promise to pay to the order of Shoreland Company $2,187.50, at its office in Miami, Florida, with interest thereon at the rate of eight per cent per annum from date until fully paid. Interest payable semiannually. The maker and endorser of this note further agree to waive demand, notice of nonpayment and protest; and in case suit shall be brought for the collection hereof, or the same has to be collected upon demand of an attorney, to pay reasonable attorney's fees for making such collection. Deferred payments are to bear interest from maturity at ten per cent per annum semiannually.

(*First Nat'l Bank* v. *Bosler*, 297 Pa. 353, 147 Atl. 74)

21. Does an instrument that provides for payment "at the option of the holder" meet the time of payment requirement necessary for a negotiable instrument?
22. Is the following note negotiable, when signed by the maker?

    I promise to pay to the University of X $500 upon its seventy-fifth anniversary.

23. Does the following provision affect the negotiability of a ninety-day note?

    This note to be due and payable at once upon breach of any promise made in this note or in the deed of trust securing it.

24. A provision in a note conferred on the payee or holder a security title to an automobile owned by the maker and provided that the payee or holder of the note could at any time he deemed himself insecure take possession of the automobile, sell the same, and apply the proceeds in discharge of the debt evidenced by the note. Is the note negotiable?
25. A note provides for the payment of $1,000 on September 15, 1946, "or before if my crop shall be sold at a price in excess of $1,000." Is the note negotiable?
26. On January 3, 1947, X executed a promissory note, which he delivered to Y. The note provided "thirty days from date I promise to pay, etc." but was not dated. Y inserted the date of December 10, 1946. Can he collect the note from X thirty days after the date so inserted?
27. Suppose that in the preceding problem, Y transferred the note to Z after he inserted the date of December 10, 1946. What are Z's rights against X?
28. An instrument reads: "Pay to X or to whomever he may direct." Is it negotiable?
29. Smith, as general manager of Brown's business establishment, was authorized to draw checks. Smith drew a check payable to the order of Day, who was a creditor of Brown, but Smith did not intend that Day should get the check. In fact, Smith intended to defraud his employer by having Ross cash the check. Ross indorsed the check with Day's name and received payment from the drawee bank. Brown protests that the check cannot be charged to his account because of the forged indorsement. Decide.

19 NEGOTIABLE INSTRUMENTS:

TRANSFER OF NEGOTIABLE INSTRUMENTS—NEGOTIATION

A negotiation is the transfer of a negotiable instrument made in such a manner as to give the new holder a better title than that possessed by the transferor. Recall that acquiring title to a right to money by an assignment subjects the acquirer to the same defenses as are available to the obligor against the transferor, whereas a transfer by negotiation in due course cuts off all personal defenses existing against the transferor.* Section 30 of the N.I.L. provides that the negotiation of an instrument, if payable to bearer, may be accomplished by delivery, and if payable to order, by indorsement and delivery by the holder.

► I. TRANSFER OF ORDER PAPER WITHOUT INDORSEMENT

Section 49 of the N.I.L. reads:

"Where the holder of an instrument payable to his order transfers it for value without indorsing it, the transfer vests in the transferee such title as the transferor had therein, and the transferee acquires, in addition, the right to have the indorsement of the transferor. But for the purpose of determining whether the transferee is a holder in due course, the negotiation takes effect as of the time when the indorsement is actually made."

A transferee of an unindorsed order instrument, while holding the instrument in its unindorsed form, stands in the same position as an assignee of a right evidenced by a simple contract.[1] The quality of the title is not improved by a transfer without indorsement. Such a transferee, however, may acquire an improved position by exercising his right to have the instrument indorsed by the transferor. Should the transferee within the intervening time acquire knowledge of any defenses available against his transferor, his title would be defective to that extent. To illustrate:

Let us suppose that A has taken a check from the payee B by a transfer without an indorsement. And let us further suppose that, while holding the check, A acquires knowledge that:

(1) the check was not given for any consideration, or

(2) it was the result of a fraud practiced by the payee upon the drawer, or

(3) the obligation evidenced by the check had been discharged by the drawer to the payee.

A subsequent indorsement of the instrument by the order payee would not

---

* See p. 447.

[1] Drzewieki v. Stempowski, p. 492.

free A's title of these defects. Had he in the first instance, without knowledge of such defenses, taken the instrument by indorsement and delivery, his position would have been that of a holder in due course and his title free of such defects.

► II. NEGOTIATON OF ORDER PAPER

A. INDORSEMENT AND DELIVERY

A negotiable instrument that is payable to order requires for its negotiation not only an indorsement by the holder to whose order it is payable but also a delivery.[2] Usually an indorsement consists of the name of the transferor written upon the instrument.[3] Section 31 of the N.I.L. provides:

"The indorsement must be written on the instrument itself or upon a paper attached thereto."

The writing may take any form. Indorsements by means of a typewriter or rubber stamp have been held to be sufficient.

Section 32 of the N.I.L. reads:

"The indorsement must be . . . of the entire instrument. An indorsement, which purports to transfer to the indorsee a part only of the amount payable, . . . does not operate as a negotiation of the instrument."

To illustrate:

In *Barkley* v. *Muller,* 164 App. Div. 351, the indorsement on a note transferred to the plaintiff, the indorsee, a one-half interest. The indorsement was held invalid and the plaintiff acquired no right to bring an action on the instrument.

Section 32 further provides that:

"An indorsement . . . which purports to transfer the instrument to two or more indorsees severally, does not operate as a negotiation of the instrument."

Section 32 further provides that:

". . . where the instrument has been paid in part, it may be indorsed as to the residue."

The indorsement of an order instrument serves two separate and distinct functions. In the first place, it is the means by which title to the instrument is transferred, and in the second place, it stands as evidence of the extent of the indorser's undertaking in respect to the instrument.

Although the signature of the indorser is sufficient as an indorsement, additional words may be added, words that modify the rights of the holder or the liabilities of the indorser. Indorsements containing such words are classified as either *special, restrictive, qualified,* or *conditional,* as distinguished from an *indorsement in blank.* A discussion of these various types of indorsement follows.

[2] Cartwright v. Coppersmith, p. 494.

[3] Markey v. Corey, p. 495.

B. INDORSEMENT IN BLANK

Section 34 of the N.I.L. reads:

". . . An indorsement in blank specifies no indorsee, and an instrument so indorsed is payable to bearer and may be negotiated by delivery."

The blank indorsement is the form most commonly used. It usually consists of the name of the transferor only. Where the last or only indorsement of an order instrument is in blank, it has the legal effect of converting the instrument to the bearer variety. By failing to specify to whom payment should be made, the indorser leaves the instrument payable to any holder. One who acquires an instrument so indorsed must realize that, should it fall into the hands of others, it could be converted to their own use. A thief, for example, could negotiate the instrument by delivery or present it for payment and thereby defeat the title of the rightful owner. The holder of an instrument so indorsed may, by virtue of Section 35 of the N.I.L., convert the blank indorsement into a special indorsement and thereby prevent either payment to another or a further negotiation without his indorsement. To accomplish this effect, the holder need only write over the signature of the indorser in blank "Pay to (name of the holder)."

C. SPECIAL INDORSEMENT

Section 34 of the N.I.L. reads:

"A special indorsement specifies the person to whom, or to whose order, the instrument is to be payable; and the indorsement of such indorsee is necessary to the further negotiation of the instrument."

Illustrations of special indorsements would be "Pay to John Doe" and "Pay to the order of John Doe." Either form requires the indorsement of the indorsee, John Doe, to further negotiate the instrument.

D. RESTRICTIVE INDORSEMENT

By adding appropriate words to his signature, an indorser can restrict, or even entirely prevent, the further negotiation of an instrument. An indorser can, by his indorsement, serve notice to all prospective acquirers of the instrument that the indorsee's rights to deal with the instrument are limited, that the indorsee has a restricted title sufficient only to accomplish the indorser's specified purpose.[4] A restrictive indorsee, in any event, holds the legal title and can sue upon the instrument; the restriction upon the title usually means that the indorser reserves the beneficial interest to himself or another. In such a way, an indorser can safeguard his interests whenever he finds it necessary to entrust negotiable paper to another.

Section 36 of the N.I.L. reads:

"An indorsement is restrictive, which either—

(1) Prohibits the further negotiation of the instrument; or

(2) Constitutes the indorsee the agent of the indorser; or

[4] First Nat. Bank of Sioux City v. John Morrell & Co., p. 495; See Rubio Savings Bank v. Acme Farm Products Co., p. 466.

(3) Vests the title in the indorsee in trust for or to the use of some other person."

An illustration of a restrictive indorsement that would prohibit the further negotiation of the instrument would be "Pay A only." The indorser need not indicate his reason or purpose for restricting negotiation of the instrument. The more commonly used restrictive indorsements carry the message that the indorsee is the indorser's agent for the purpose of either collecting the instrument or receiving it for deposit to the indorser's account. Illustrations of such restrictive indorsements would be "Pay A for Collection" and "Pay A for Deposit."

In forwarding negotiable paper for collection, banks customarily use, as a form of indorsement, "Pay to any bank or banker. All previous indorsements guaranteed." By the weight of authority, this type of indorsement is not restrictive and does not prevent a holder from acquiring an unlimited title. In those states which have enacted the Bank Collection Code, this form of indorsement is restrictive.

E. QUALIFIED INDORSEMENT

By adding appropriate qualifying words to his signature, an indorser can limit his liability as an indorser. Section 38 of the N.I.L. provides that:

"A qualified indorsement constitutes the indorser a mere assignor of the title to the instrument."

A qualified indorser can be held liable only for a failure of the implied warranties usually given by an assignor, which warranties are enumerated in Section 65 of the N.I.L. The fundamental difference in the liability of the unqualified indorser (one who makes either a blank or special indorsement) and the qualified indorser is that the latter does not undertake to pay the instrument in event of its dishonor—in the event it is not paid by the primary obligor.*

The words commonly used to qualify an indorsement are "without recourse." It should be noted that it is generally held that such terminology as "I hereby sell, transfer, and assign the within note" added to the indorser's signature constitutes an unqualified indorsement and is not an assignment.

A qualified indorsement in no way affects the negotiability of an instrument upon which it appears.

F. CONDITIONAL INDORSEMENT

An indorser may add words to his signature directing that payment be made to the indorsee only upon the happening of a specified event. The indorser can thereby pass a conditional title to the indorsee, a title conditioned upon fulfillment of the event specified in the indorsement. Any holder subsequent to a conditional indorsement holds the instrument or the proceeds from its collection subject to the right of the indorser to have the condition met. To illustrate:

Let us suppose that A has executed a promissory note payable to B, who by special indorsement has negotiated the instrument to C. Now let us suppose that

* See p. 541.

C has, in payment for a house, transferred the note to D by means of the following indorsement: "Pay to D upon condition that D will furnish me an abstract of title to Lot 4, Block 8, College Heights Addition, Ames, Iowa, showing a good merchantable title. (signed) C." C, the indorser, retains his right to the instrument or the proceeds realized from its collection against D and all subsequent holders until such time as the condition is satisfied.

Obligors upon the instrument prior to the conditional indorsement need not ascertain whether the condition has been fulfilled before they make payment to the holder. Section 39 of the N.I.L. provides:

> "Where an indorsement is conditional, a party required to pay the instrument may disregard the condition, and make payment to the indorsee or his transferee, whether the condition has been fulfilled or not."

In our illustration above, the maker A and the payee indorser B can, in disregard of the conditional indorsement, discharge the instrument by payment.

G. INDORSEMENT BY IMPROPERLY DESIGNATED PAYEE

Section 43 of the N.I.L. reads:

> "Where the name of a payee or indorsee is wrongly designated or misspelled, he may indorse the instrument as therein described, adding, if he thinks fit, his proper signature."

► III. NEGOTIATION OF BEARER PAPER

A bearer instrument can be negotiated by a mere delivery. It is a common practice, however, to indorse bearer paper whenever it is transferred; the indorsement usually is in blank. While such is not necessary to accomplish the negotiation, it in no way impairs negotiation. The indorsement merely serves to add the security of the indorser to the instrument.

An instrument that is originally, on its face, of the bearer variety remains such during the course of its existence. A special indorsement will not change its character, and it may still be further negotiated by delivery. On the other hand, it is thought that when an instrument is payable to bearer because the last or only indorsement is in blank (such an instrument being order on its face), the instrument can again be converted to order paper by a special indorsement. After that an indorsement and delivery are necessary for its further negotiation.

► IV. SURRENDER TO DRAWEE DISTINGUISHED FROM NEGOTIATION

A bill of exchange presupposes a debtor-creditor relationship between the drawee and drawer; the drawee has a contractual obligation to pay the instrument as ordered by the drawer. The delivery of an instrument to the drawee upon payment is not a negotiation.[5] For example, the holder of a check upon presenting it

[5] Kuhns v. Live Stock Nat. Bank, p. 497.

to the drawee bank for payment is not transferring title to the instrument but is merely requiring the drawee to discharge his contractual obligation to the drawer, thereby discharging the drawer's obligation to the holder. By paying the check, the drawee extinguishes it as a credit instrument and does not become a holder of it. Consequently, upon the surrender of the instrument for payment, an indorsement by the holder is not necessary and cannot be required of him. A refusal by the drawee to honor the instrument would be a breach of the contract between the drawer and the drawee.

It seems to be an invariable practice for the holder, upon receiving payment from the drawee, to place his signature upon the back of the instrument. Such a signature serves no other purpose than that of evidence that payment has been received. The holder does not thereby assume any liability as an indorser to the drawee.

It should be realized, however, that the drawee of an instrument may acquire title to it by a negotiation before the date of its maturity. Under such circumstances the drawee, if necessary, could take action against the drawer and indorsers to force payment at maturity.

CASES

CASE NO. 1

Drzewiecki v. Stempowski. 232 Wis. 447, 287 N.W. 747 (1939)

This action was begun on May 13, 1938 by Frank Drzewiecki and Mary Drzewiecki, his wife, plaintiffs, against Nepomocyna Stempowski, Strozyk-Zalewski Company, a corporation, and John S. Strozyk, defendants, to secure partial satisfaction and discharge of a certain note and mortgage given by plaintiffs. There was a trial, the court found for the plaintiffs and held that the mortgage should be satisfied . . . and judgment was entered on the 9th day of December, 1938. The defendant Stempowski appeals. . . .

ROSENBERRY, CH.J. On the 12th day of June, 1923, the plaintiffs were the owners of certain premises in the city and county of Milwaukee and on that day they executed to the Strozyk-Zalewski Company, a corporation, a negotiable promissory note in the amount of $2,500 with interest thereon at the rate of 6 per cent per annum, payable three years after date. To secure the payment thereof they executed a mortgage upon real estate, which was duly recorded on June 22, 1923, and on the 2d day of July, 1923, the Strozyk-Zalewski Company duly assigned and delivered the note and mortgage for value to the defendant Stempowski, which assignment was recorded on June 4, 1930. . . . On January 22, 1925, the Strozyk-Zalewski Company was voluntarily dissolved and ever since has been out of business. The plaintiffs in ignorance of the fact that the note and mortgage had been assigned, made . . . payments to John S. Strozyk, who was the former president of the Strozyk-Zalewski Company. . . .

It further appears that when the note and mortgage were assigned, the note was not indorsed by the Strozyk-Zalewski Company.

It is to be noted that all the payments were made after the note became due. The note not having been indorsed by the payee, the defendant Stempowski was not a holder in due course. Being payable to the Company or order, it could be negotiated only by indorsement. . . .

The transfer for value of the instrument payable to order without indorsement vests in the transferee such title as the transferrer had therein, subject to defenses available against the transferrer. Although the transferee may require an indorsement, he does not become a holder in due course until the time of the actual making of the indorsement. . . .

Where an instrument, negotiable only by indorsement, has been transferred by assignment or by delivery, payment to the original holder without notice of the transfer is a defense against the assignee. . . .

The defendant Stempowski being an assignee and not an indorsee, the law relating to payment to original creditors applies. It is the undoubted law of this state that payment by a debtor to his original creditor protects him against an assignee of the debt unless he has notice of the assignment. . . .

The question therefore arises, Was payment to Strozyk payment to the Strozyk-Zalewski Company which was in process of dissolution? Chapter 181 makes provision for dissolution of corporations. Section 181.-02 provides:

> "All corporations whose term of existence shall expire by their own limitation, or which shall be dissolved, shall nevertheless continue to be bodies corporate for three years thereafter for the purpose of prosecuting and defending actions, and of enabling them to settle and close up their business, dispose of and convey their property and divide their assets and for no other purpose. . . ."

The resolution dissolving the company having been filed in the office of the Secretary of State on January 22, 1925, the corporation had no existence on June 14, 1928, when the plaintiffs paid . . . Strozyk. It is considered therefore that that payment did not operate as a discharge . . . of the note in question. . . .

We have carefully examined the record in this case. From that examination it appears without dispute that the plaintiffs dealt with Strozyk personally and with no one else. All the notices were sent in the name of Strozyk, all the receipts were issued in his name. He never pretended to act for and on behalf of the Strozyk-Zalewski Company or anyone else but himself. . . .

While this case presents a very difficult situation in this that both the plaintiffs and the defendant Stempowski trusted Strozyk and now one of two innocent parties must suffer a loss due to his misconduct, nevertheless that does not operate to change the rule of law. Upon the facts of this case we find no ground on which it can be said that payment to Strozyk was a payment to the Strozyk-Zalewski Company. While it may be that plaintiffs in this case because of inability to read the English language and unfamiliarity with business transactions may not have been aware of the legal consequences of what they did, nevertheless the rule applied is that they were charged with knowledge or notice of such facts as would be brought home to an ordinarily prudent man. Applying this rule, plaintiffs must be charged with notice of the fact that they were making payments to Strozyk and were dealing with him individually. . . .

Judgment appealed from is reversed. . . .

CASE NO. 2

Cartwright v. Coppersmith. 222 N.C. 573, 24 S.E. (2d) 246 (1943)

This case involved the question of ownership of 4 promissory notes executed by defendant Coppersmith to Sarah E. Elliott, deceased. One Mrs. Lydia Mae Whitehurst claims title by endorsement of the notes to her. The trial court held the notes to be the property of the estate of the deceased.

DEVIN, J. The appellant, Mrs. Whitehurst, assigns error in the ruling of the court below in the exclusion of portions of the testimony of defendant W. B. Coppersmith. . . .

Mr. Coppersmith, in the absence of the jury, was examined as to the circumstances of the transaction and communications between him and the deceased. Upon this evidence alone Mrs. Whitehurst relied to make out her case. The pertinent portions of the excluded testimony tended to show that while the witness was on a visit to Sarah E. Elliott, in 1937, she asked him to assign the Coppersmith notes to Mrs. Whitehurst.

> "She wanted her to have those notes after her death. The only thing she wanted was the interest as long as she lived, and she wanted me to pay the notes to Mrs. Whitehurst."

Witness advised her the only way she could do that without making a will was to endorse the notes and make them payable to Mrs. Whitehurst. The notes were kept in an envelope in the possession of Sarah E. Elliott, and she went and got them and brought them to a little table in the room near the door. Not having a pen convenient, the witness wrote with pencil on each note "Pay within note to Lydia Mae Whitehurst without recourse," and Sarah E. Elliott signed the endorsement on each note and retained possession of the notes. That was July 10, 1937. Mrs. Whitehurst was there, standing in the door. Witness further stated that he paid the interest on the notes afterwards; that he saw the notes some six or twelve months before her death (in 1940) in possession of Sarah E. Elliott at her home, and the endorsements were still on them. Afterward, he or his son paid the interest "in the office there," and when witness saw them the endorsements had been erased, but the notes showed dimly the endorsements and date. Witness did not make the erasures and did not know who did. Sarah E. Elliott never said anything to him about it.

. . . After defendants rested plaintiff Cartwright testified that he was one of the executors of Sarah E. Elliott and that he first came into possession of these notes in November 1939; that Sarah E. Elliott had possession of them before they came into his possession; that at the time the notes came into his possession there were no endorsements on them, but he could see that there had been endorsements thereon which had been erased. . . .

The burden of proof was upon Mrs. Whitehurst to show not only the endorsement of the notes by Sarah E. Elliott, but also that the intention to give or assign them to her was completed by delivery, actual or constructive. In this we think she has failed, even if the entire evidence of Mr. Coppersmith had been admitted.

. . . To constitute delivery there must be a parting with the possession and with power and control over it by the maker or endorser for the benefit of the payee or endorsee. To constitute delivery it must be put out of possession of the endorser. . . . An actual delivery, however, is not essential, and a constructive delivery will be held sufficient if made with the intention of transferring the title, but there must be some unequivocal act, more than the mere expression of an intention or desire. . . .

It is true the fact of retention of possession by the endorser is not always fatal to a claim of constructive delivery. It is said in 10 C.J.S., Bills and Notes, § 78, p. 513:

> "There may be a delivery notwithstanding the maker keeps the note in his possession, where it is apparent that he intended to hold it for the benefit and as the agent of the payee."

. . .

But here the proffered testimony falls short of coming within that principle. . . . The notes were retained in possession by the endorser, after signing the endorsement, without any declaration of agency or purpose other than that she wished the endorsee to have them after her death. The notes continued in her exclusive possession until some two years later when they came into the possession of J. M. Cartwright for her, with the endorsements erased. There was no parting of control over them either to the endorsee or to any other person for her benefit. The expressed intention did not contemplate a present transfer but a prospective donation. The intention not having been completed by delivery, title did not vest in the endorsee. . . .

CASE NO. 3

Markey v. Corey. 108 Mich. 184, 66 N.W. 493, 36 L.R.A. 117 (1895)

The question before the court was whether the defendant was liable as an indorser upon the following writing upon the back of the note being sued upon: "I hereby assign the within note to Matthew M. Markey." Signed by Corey.

LONG, J. The usual mode of transfer of a promissory note is by simply writing the indorser's name upon the back, or by writing also over it the direction to pay the indorsee named, or order, or to him or bearer. An indorsement, however, may be made in more enlarged terms, and the indorser be held liable as such. In Sands v. Wood, 1 Iowa 263, the indorsement was, "I assign the within note to Mrs. Sarah Coffin." In Sears v. Lantz, 47 Iowa 658, the indorsement on the note was, "I hereby assign all my right and title to Louis Meekley." And in each case the party so assigning was held as indorser, the court in the latter case saying of Sands v. Wood:

> "He used no words that, in and of themselves indicated that he had bound or made himself liable in case the maker, after demand, failed to pay the note. But it was held the law, as a legal conclusion, attached to the words used the liability that follows the indorsement of a promissory note."

The language used in the assignment to the note in suit does not negative the implication of the legal liability of the assignor as indorser, and as the words are to be construed, as strongly as their sense will allow, against the assignor, he must be held as indorser.

It must be held, therefore, that the memorandum on the note did not relieve Corey from his liability as indorser.*

CASE NO. 4

First Nat. Bank of Sioux City, Iowa v. John Morrell & Co. 53 S.D. 496, 221 N.W. 95, 60 A.L.R. 863 (1928)

BROWN, J. Defendant conducts a pack-

* AUTHOR'S NOTE: This case presents the overwhelming weight of authority. See Brannon, *Negotiable Instruments Law*, 6th Ed., p. 472.

ing plant industry in Sioux Falls and sells its products in different parts of the United States, receiving in payments checks from its customers on banks in their respective localities. It deposited those checks in Sioux Falls National Bank, indorsed as follows:

"Pay to the order of Sioux Falls National Bank, for deposit only.

John Morrell & Co."

By agreement with the bank defendant was credited conditionally in its checking account with the amount of the checks, but the bank was at all times to retain a minimum balance of $20,000, to take care of what was known as "the float," being checks in process of collection, which might not be paid. Between plaintiff and Sioux Falls National Bank, mutual accounts had been maintained for a number of years. In the early part of January, 1924, defendant deposited in Sioux Falls National Bank 20 checks, aggregating about $3,900, all bearing the indorsement hereinbefore quoted, receiving credit for such checks under the agreement already referred to. The Sioux Falls National Bank, on January 8th, 9th, and 10th, transmitted these checks to plaintiff at Sioux City, indorsed:

"Pay to the order of the First National Bank of Sioux City, Iowa. Sioux Falls National Bank 98—1. Thomas A. Wadden, Vice President and Cashier."

And each was transmitted in a letter reading:

"We inclose herewith for collection and return items as listed below—followed by a list of the checks inclosed."

Plaintiff, in accordance with a custom between it and the Sioux Falls Bank, credited the latter conditionally with the amount of the checks, and forwarded them for collection to banks in the localities on which they were drawn. On the morning of January 11th the Sioux Falls Bank failed to open, and was taken over by the Comptroller of the Currency for liquidation.

The vice president of the John Morrell & Co., who was also a director of Sioux Falls National Bank, telegraphed to the various makers of the checks and had payment of them stopped, and the makers of the checks thereafter paid the accounts represented by the checks direct to defendant. The dishonored checks were returned to plaintiff, and plaintiff brings this action, claiming that defendant is liable to it as indorser of the checks. The action was tried by the court without a jury, and from judgment on a decision in favor of defendant, and an order denying a new trial, plaintiff appeals.

Appellant contends that, because defendant received credit in his account in the Sioux Falls National Bank for the amount of the checks, the relation of debtor and creditor existed between defendant and the bank; that the bank became the owner of the checks, and that, by its indorsement of them to plaintiff, plaintiff became the owner of the checks, with a right of recourse, in the event of their dishonor, against any prior indorser. But this contention entirely ignores the contract between defendant and the Sioux Falls bank, created by the indorsement on the checks. The indorsement "for deposit only" is a restrictive indorsement and clearly vests title in the indorsee in trust for the indorser. Such an indorsement confers upon the indorsee the right to transfer its rights as indorsee, because the indorsement authorized payment "to the order of Sioux Falls National Bank"; but the subsequent indorsee (in this case, plaintiff) acquires only the title of the first indorsee under the restrictive indorsement, and, irrespective of the directions contained in the letters of transmittal, plaintiff could only have the

the rights of an agent or trustee for the defendant, clothed with authority to collect the checks. Appellant says that:

> "It is frankly conceded that the sole and only purpose of stopping payment of these checks was to enable defendant to reduce its balance in the Sioux Falls bank when the same closed, and, by collection of the items through other channels, thus to realize 100 cents on the dollar, instead of taking the proportion of loss, if any, which other depositors may sustain through failure of the bank."

But this is just what defendant had a lawful right to do. It had a right at any time to revoke the agency of plaintiff for collection of the checks, and to avoid loss by collecting through other channels the accounts due from the makers of the checks. Had the checks been collected through the medium of the banks, and the money had reached the Sioux Falls National, the relation of debtor and creditor between the bank and defendant would then, and not until then, have arisen.

The right of an indorsee under a restrictive indorsement . . . is not the right to recover from the indorser on dishonor of the instrument.

The judgment and order appealed from are affirmed.

CASE NO. 5

Kuhns v. Live Stock Nat. Bank. 289 N.W. 893 (Iowa) (1940)

PAINE, J. This is an action at law, in which Barton H. Kuhns, plaintiff-appellant, as trustee in bankruptcy of Central Bridge & Construction Company, a bankrupt corporation, seeks to recover from the Live Stock National Bank of Omaha the sum of $15,000, being the amount of funds of the said construction company which Elmer G. Risk, its president, transferred to said bank in payment of his personal notes. . . .

Plaintiff further alleged that on January 12, 1937, the Central Bridge & Construction Company deposited with the defendant bank $19,215.39 of its own funds, which defendant bank placed to the credit of the Central Bridge & Construction Company in its open checking account; that the next day, January 13, 1937, Elmer G. Risk and M. E. Carman did wrongfully and unlawfully, and without the authority of the Central Bridge & Construction Company or its board of directors, withdraw and divert from the corporate funds so deposited the sum of $15,000, which on said day the said Elmer G. Risk turned over to the defendant bank in payment of a personal debt which he owed the said bank, which debt had not yet become due. . . .

For . . . answer, said defendant bank alleges that . . . the board of directors of said depositor corporation adopted a resolution, which is set out in full as exhibit A, . . . which duly authorized the three officers of said corporation [E. G. Risk, president, W. G. Johnson, vice-president, and M. E. Carman, secretary] . . . or either of them, to discount bills of exchange, sign and deliver checks and drafts of the corporation upon said bank, and, quoting from the last paragraph of exhibit A,

> "said Live Stock National Bank is authorized to honor and pay checks or drafts so signed or drawn by them, or either of them, including drafts or checks to their own order, and said bank shall not be responsible or liable in any event for application of funds paid or withdrawn thereon." . . .

Appellee . . . contends that in regard to this check, first, there was some transaction between the corporation and Risk, and that appellee was not required to inquire into that because of the corporate resolution authorizing and directing the bank to honor checks payable to an officer of that corporation, regardless of how they were applied. The check having validly got into the hands of Risk, it operated as an assignment of the corporate funds held by the bank for the corporation. Thereafter the bank stood on the same footing as any other third party who might have purchased this check from Risk. Again, the bank in its reply brief says:

> "Not being required to look into how or why this was done, the bank then, like any other innocent third party, could buy this check."

These contentions of the bank imply that the bank contends that it was a holder in due course, but remember, the bank was the drawee, and when it pays a check drawn upon it, then it cannot be a holder in due course.

The payment of a check by the drawee bank is not a negotiation and does not make the bank a holder within sec. 30. The check is extinguished and cannot be put in circulation again so as to bind the drawer or indorsers. . . .

This same question has been before this court in the case of National Bank of Commerce v. Farmers' & Merchants' Bank. 87 Neb. 841, 128 N.W. 522, 523, in which section 30 of the negotiable instruments law is discussed. The question of what is meant by negotiating an instrument is explained:

> "If A. gives B. a check on C. Bank, and B. presents the check at the counter of C., no negotiation is necessary or had. He simply demands and receives payment; but, if B. goes to D. store and buys a bill of goods, and tenders the indorsed check in payment, he negotiates the check. The difference is clear and well defined. The presentation by defendant of the check in controversy for payment was not a 'negotiation' of the check within the meaning of the statute quoted.

> "If a depositor seeks to pay his own debts to a bank by an appropriation of funds to his credit in a fiduciary capacity, the bank acting as depositary of the trust funds is charged with knowledge of the character of the appropriation and will be compelled to refund, as the bank, in honoring the checks payable to itself out of the trust account, participates in . . . committing a breach of trust." People ex rel. Barrett v. State Bank of Herrick, 290 Ill. App. 130, 8 N.E. (2d) 71, 73. . . .

The resolution, doubtless furnished by the bank, and adopted by the board of directors of the corporation, was designed to, and would, protect the bank in each and all of the transactions between the corporation and the bank, with perhaps a single exception. In a clear case, such as this, of loss to the corporation and benefit to the bank in the payment in full of its own notes, which were signed by the president of the corporation in his individual capacity, in our opinion the resolution was insufficient to protect the bank. The resolution authorized the bank to pay checks drawn to the order of certain officers of the bank, including the president. But when the president of the bank received that letter inclosing a corporation check, being used by the president of the corporation to pay his private notes to that bank, it would be perfectly clear that money was being taken out of the corporation's deposit for personal use. We find nothing in the resolution which authorizes this to be done.

Review Questions

1. What is the meaning of the term *negotiation?*
2. If you had an election as to whether you would acquire contractual rights by negotiation or by assignment, which would you prefer, and why?
3. By what method is the negotiation of an instrument payable to bearer accomplished as distinguished from the method required for the negotiation of an instrument payable to order?
4. What is the position of the holder of unindorsed order paper?
5. What is the effect of indorsing an order instrument in blank?
6. How can the holder of an order instrument that is indorsed in blank protect himself against loss by theft or by loss of the instrument?
7. For what reasons are restrictive indorsements generally used?
8. What terminology is commonly used in effecting a qualified indorsement?
9. Is an indorser who transfers an instrument by means of a qualified indorsement relieved from all liability upon the instrument?
10. What parties to an instrument are bound by a conditional indorsement?
11. An instrument that is payable to bearer contains a special indorsement. Does this indorsement make it an order instrument?
12. How may paper that is order on its face be transformed into bearer paper?
13. Is an indorsement of a check payable to the order of the holder necessary upon presentment of the check to the drawee bank for payment?

Problems for Discussion

1. A contracted with the B correspondence school for a course in horticulture, giving B his $300 negotiable promissory note in payment of the tuition. The note was transferred by B to X, who sues upon it at maturity. A's defense is that he was induced to contract for the correspondence course by fraudulent representations made by B. Is this a good defense?
2. Brown received the following unindorsed check from Black:

   "Pay to the order of Black $500

   White."

   When Brown presented the check to the drawee bank, payment was refused because the check had not been indorsed by Black. Brown was also informed by the bank that White had ordered the bank not to pay the check, since Black obtained it from White by fraud. Brown then obtained Black's indorsement upon the check. What are his rights?
3. Brown, living in New York, sent Black, living in California, a check which was payable to the order of Brown but which Brown had failed to indorse. Black wishes to obtain the necessary indorsement without again relinquishing the check to Brown. What is your advice?
4. McNeil was the payee on a $1,000 promissory note of which Alley was the maker. McNeil owed Paul $750 and in discharge of this obligation he indorsed the note to the extent of $750 to Paul. Can Paul, upon maturity of the instrument, force Alley to pay him $750?
5. An order instrument contained the indorsement "Pay to Cook only." Cook

gave the instrument to his nephew. Upon maturity the maker refuses to pay the nephew, contending he is obligated to pay no one other than Cook. Answer the contention.

6. A note payable to John Hull or bearer is indorsed as follows: "Pay to the order of Jim Taff. (Signed) John Hull." Is an indorsement of this instrument required for its further negotiation?
7. An instrument is made payable to the order of John Hull and indorsed as follows: "John Hull." How can this instrument be negotiated?
8. A promissory note is made payable to Jones or bearer. Jones executes an assignment of the note to Smith and delivers both the assignment and the note to Smith. Does Smith stand as an assignee or as the holder of rights acquired by negotiation?
9. A check payable to the order of A is deposited with the X bank with the following indorsement: "For collection, A." While the check is in the possession of the X bank, its doors are closed because of insolvency. The receiver for the bank collects the check and deposits it to A's account and then pays him 50 cents on the dollar, which is all that is available for the bank's creditors. A sues to recover the balance. Should he succeed?
10. An order instrument is transferred by the payee to A by the following indorsement: "I hereby assign all my right, title, interest in and to this instrument to A." Is this a good negotiation?
11. A, who is the holder of a check indorsed in blank, writes over the blank indorsement: "Pay to the order of A." May he do this?
12. A drew a check payable to B or bearer and delivered it to B, who then lost it. The check was found by X, who signed B's name upon the back and delivered the check to Y. When Y tendered the check to the drawee bank, payment was refused, A having stopped payment. Y then sued A on the check. Did he recover?

20 NEGOTIABLE INSTRUMENTS:

RIGHTS OF HOLDERS—HOLDERS IN DUE COURSE

► I. HOLDERS DISTINGUISHED

Unless a holder of a right to money evidenced by a negotiable instrument can qualify either (1) *as a holder in due course* or (2) *as a holder who acquired his title to the right through a holder in due course,* he stands in the position of an assignee. Section 58 of the N.I.L. reads:

> "In the hands of any holder other than a holder in due course, a negotiable instrument is subject to the same defenses as if it were nonnegotiable. But a holder who derives his title through a holder in due course, and who is not himself a party to any fraud or illegality affecting the instrument, has all the rights of such former holder in respect to all parties prior to the latter."

Whereas an assignee acquires a contractual right subject to all defenses that the obligor has against the party with whom he contracted, a holder in due course acquires a contractual right free of all personal defenses that exist in the obligor's favor. The transfer of the rights to the holder in due course by negotiation is said to cut off all personal defenses. To illustrate:

A is the maker of a promissory note upon which B's name appears as payee. B has now transferred to C this right to money, as evidenced by the note. When C makes claim against A for payment, A sets up the defense that he has never received the consideration (a car) for which the note was given to B. Nevertheless, if C stands as a holder in due course, he will be able to recover from A. However, if C stands as an assignee, he cannot recover upon the note.

► II. RIGHTS OF HOLDER THROUGH HOLDER IN DUE COURSE

A holder who derives his title to an instrument through a holder in due course acquires the title of the latter. The right of a holder in due course to enforce the instrument free of all personal defenses is not impaired by a transfer to a holder who has knowledge that such defenses exist against the paper. Such a holder need not meet the requirements of a holder in due course, since he acquires the title of his transferor. Only if the holder is himself a party to any fraud or illegality affecting the instrument will his right to recover on the instrument be impaired. Thus, in the last illustration, C as a holder in due course could transfer his protected title to D, even though the latter has knowledge of the fact that B gave no consideration for the note. Likewise, if D should transfer the instrument to E the latter would also derive his title through a holder in due course and would also stand in the same protected position.

The above rule is founded upon the theory that a holder in due course should be able to use the instrument as he sees fit and to his best advantage. He should be able to bestow his title upon another as a gift, even though the donee has notice of defenses against the obligation evidenced by the instrument. Likewise, a holder in due course should be able to sell his protected title to whom he pleases. As the courts have said, the whole world should be his market.

Therefore, it is a matter of importance to be able to determine when a holder is a holder in due course.

► III. WHAT CONSTITUTES A HOLDER IN DUE COURSE

Section 52 of the N.I.L. requires that, to qualify as a holder in due course, one must have taken the instrument under the following conditions.

"(1) That it is complete and regular upon its face;

(2) That he became the holder of it before it was overdue, and without notice that it had been previously dishonored, if such was the fact;

(3) That he took it in good faith and for value;

(4) That at the time it was negotiated to him he had no notice of any infirmity in the instrument or defect in the title of the person negotiating it."

Some explanation of the least obvious requirements follows.

A. COMPLETE AND REGULAR INSTRUMENT

It seems that, to be complete within the meaning of Section 52 (1), an instrument must carry upon its face all the requirements of negotiable paper. Although by virtue of Sections 13 and 14, the holder is authorized to fill in any blanks and omissions, he cannot stand as a holder in due course by accepting such an instrument. An instrument containing blanks has been held to be incomplete and irregular.[1]

Any obvious alteration appearing upon an instrument, regardless of the purpose for which it was made, prevents the instrument from being complete and regular. Such a fact should arouse the suspicion of any prospective acquirer.[2] To illustrate:

(1) In the case of In re *Philpott's Estate,* 169 Iowa 555, the acquirer of a note payable "on or before four ——— after date" was not a holder in due course, the instrument being incomplete.

(2) In *General Motors Acceptance Corp.* v. *Talbott,* 39 Idaho 707, the acquirer of a note upon which the date had been obviously altered and upon which the cancellation dates of revenue stamps were prior to the date of the note was held not to be a holder in due course. The instrument was not complete and regular upon its face.

---

[1] Moore v. Vaughn, p. 515.

[2] W. W. Marshall & Co. v. Kirschbraun & Sons, p. 516.

(3) In *Balliet* v. *Wollersheim,* 241 Wis. 536, the court in concluding that the holder of a promissory note was not a holder in due course said:

> "The note on its face appears to carry two rates of interest and at the very least, this produces an irregularity of form and an uncertainty as to the amount of interest due upon the note. . . . As we read the note, it creates the appearance that the parties either originally stipulated for interest at the rate of 1% per annum and that the note was altered by writing in the arabic figure '6' or that the note was originally to bear interest at the rate of 6 per cent and that it had been changed to 1 per cent by somebody who neglected to strike out the arabic figure '6.' In any event, it contains irreconcilable provisions as to payment, is uncertain as to amount and hence is either nonnegotiable or irregular in form, two terms which probably mean the same thing in this situation and certainly have the same effect.
>
> "We are unable to escape the conclusion that the note is not fair and regular on its face because of the conflicting rates of interest apparently stipulated for, and the resulting uncertainty as to the amount payable upon it. In view of these conclusions, we hold that the Appleton State Bank was not a holder in due course, and that plaintiff as its transferree is subject to the defense of alteration."

B. TAKING INSTRUMENT BEFORE MATURITY

Ordinary business prudence demands that an instrument circulating after its maturity be looked upon with suspicion.

> "But where a negotiable note is found in circulation after it is due, it carries suspicion on the face of it. The question instantly arises, why is it in circulation,—why is it not paid? Here is something wrong. Therefore, although it does not give the indorsee notice of any specific matter of defense . . . yet it puts him on inquiry; he takes only such title as the indorser himself has, and subject to any defense which would be made, if the suit were brought by the indorser." *Fischer* v. *Leland,* 4 Cush. (Mass.) 456.

Although one who takes an instrument after maturity cannot be a holder in due course, nevertheless, by virtue of Section 58 of the N.I.L., he is protected against personal defenses, *providing he acquires title through a holder in due course.* By taking an instrument after maturity, the indorsee acquires only such title as his indorser had and is subject only to such defenses as would be available against his indorser. If his indorser is a holder in due course or if his indorser has taken title from a holder in due course, he is fully protected. To illustrate:

A promissory note, which was due January 2, 1952, was executed by A to B. On December 4, 1950, B indorsed the note to C, who qualified as a holder in due course, and consequently any personal defense which A might have had against B was cut off by the negotiation to C. On January 4, 1952—after maturity—C indorsed and delivered the note to D. Although D took the instrument after maturity, he acquired the title of C, a holder in due course, and is as fully protected, providing he himself was not a "party to any fraud or illegality affecting the instrument."

1. *Maturity of Demand Paper*

Section 53 of the N.I.L. reads:

> "Where an instrument payable on demand is negotiated an unreasonable length of time after its issue, the holder is not deemed a holder in due course."

Section 193 of the N.I.L. reads:

> "In determining what is a "reasonable time" or an "unreasonable time," regard must be had to the nature of the instrument, the usage of trade or business (if any) with respect to such instruments, and the facts of the particular case."

a. Checks. The drawer of a check expects that it will be presented for payment within a relatively short time after it is drawn. A check is not used to obtain credit as is a note but rather to presently discharge an obligation. Checks are not intended to circulate for any considerable time after their issue. Obviously, in view of the provisions of Section 193, it cannot be stated arbitrarily or even with reasonable certainty when a check is overdue for the purpose of its negotiation. Cases in which this has been in issue have held that periods of two, four, eleven, and even twenty-four days have not been so unreasonable as to prevent the acquirer from occupying the position of a holder in due course. The court in *Cowing* v. *Altman*, 71 N.Y. 435, observed:

> "The retention of a check by the holder for a considerable time without presentment, where no defense exists to it, is unusual, and this circumstance is sufficient to put a party taking it upon inquiry, and a check dated, as in this case, several months before its transfer, which might have been presented at or soon after its date, will, in the absence of explanation, be treated as overdue."

b. Demand Notes. It can be said that, in general, the period of time before a demand note becomes overdue is somewhat longer than it is in the case of a check. Usually a note is given as evidence of an extension of credit, which would in itself imply that demand for payment is not to be made presently. It has been held that a demand note taken two years after issue was not overdue, but, on the other hand, courts have declared notes overdue after three months and even lesser intervals after the date of issue. What constitutes a reasonable time in any given instance would be dependent upon the peculiar facts and circumstances involved. For example, such matters as (1) the practice of the banking community in dealing with demand notes and (2) the question of whether or not the parties have made provision for interest payments would be factors bearing upon the issue.

C. TAKING IN GOOD FAITH

The element of good faith as required of a holder in due course is not easily defined. Broadly speaking, it can be said that to be a holder in due course one must, in acquiring the instrument, have dealt honestly and fairly in respect to the rights of all prior parties.[3] The lack of good faith on the part of the acquirer, as put by the court in *Gerseta Corp.* v. *Wessex-Campbell Silk Co.*, 3 F. (2d) 236:

> "means that he must have knowledge of facts which render it dishonest for him to take the particular piece of negotiable paper under discussion. Knowledge, not surmise, suspicion, or fear, is necessary; not knowledge of the exact truth, but knowledge of some truth that would prevent action by those commercially honest men for whom law is made."

The purchaser of negotiable paper has no duty to make inquiry concerning its quality. To impose such a duty would greatly restrict the transferability of credit instruments.[4] If, however, the purchaser has knowledge of facts that make him suspicious or that ought to make him suspicious that all is not well, a failure to make inquiry will amount to bad faith.[5] Nor does the law impose upon the purchaser a duty to exercise due care (not to be negligent) in respect to discovering infirmities in the instrument or defects in the title of his indorser. The test of good faith of a purchaser is not whether he might have known, but rather whether he did have knowledge of some fact that, according to the standards of honest and fair-minded men, would deter acquisition of the instrument.[6]

> "Good faith implies honest intent. It is consistent with negligence, even gross negligence. A blundering fool may therefore be found to have acted in good faith, though under like circumstances a shrewd businessman might be deemed to have acted in bad faith." *Schintz* v. *American Trust and Savings Bank*, 152 Ill. App. 76.

To illustrate:

(1) In *Bergheim* v. *McRae*, 190 Minn. 571, a bank cashier had embezzled funds, of which fact the defendant was aware. The defendant, to protect the cashier from prosecution, advanced him sufficient funds to cover the amount wrongfully taken from the bank. As security the defendant acquired a note from the cashier, which note the cashier had been holding in trust for the plaintiff. It was held that the defendant was not a holder in due course. He was not acting in good faith when he accepted the note from the cashier with the knowledge of the cashier's dishonesty. The court said in effect that knowledge of these facts should have put defendant on inquiry and a failure to inquire amounted to commercial bad faith.

(2) It is generally held that the mere fact that an instrument was purchased at a large discount does not in itself indicate a lack of good faith. Thus, in *Ham* v. *Merritt*, 150 Ky. 11, the plaintiff had paid only $100 for a $300 note. It was held that this fact in itself does not prevent good faith.

(3) In *Title Guarantee etc. Co.* v. *Pam*, 232 N.Y. 441, it was held that a holder who had taken a note with knowledge that the amount due was a matter of dispute between the maker and payee was not a good faith holder.

(4) In *Jenkins* v. *Planters' Bank*, 34 Okla. 607, a check contained the state-

[3] Bonnette v. Ponthieux, p. 517.
[4] Quanah, Acme, & P.R. Co. v. Wichita State Bank, p. 518.
[5] New Port Richey v. Fidelity Co., p. 520.
[6] Merchants' Nat. Bank v. Detroit Trust Co., p. 522.

ment, "Submitted with bid on H.S.D. Bldg." It was held that the acquirer of the check was not a good faith holder. Such words on an instrument indicate that it is held only as security, being returnable if the bid is not accepted, and put an acquirer on notice as to the right to negotiate the instrument.

(5) In *Taylor* v. *Atlas Sec. Co.,* 213 Mo. App. 282, the holder purchased a note from the payee with knowledge that it had been given on the purchase of an automobile which was worth less than half of the amount of the note. It was held that he had not taken the note in good faith.

D. TAKING FOR VALUE

A holder in due course is one who has given value for the instrument. Value is, in Section 25 of the N.I.L., declared to be:

". . . any consideration sufficient to support a simple contract. An antecedent or pre-existing debt constitutes value."

An antecedent or pre-existing debt, being past consideration, would not support a promise evidenced by a simple contract.* There is a very real need for making a past debt *value,* so that a promise evidenced by a negotiable instrument will be enforceable. Many are the instruments that come into being for the purpose of discharging or securing a past obligation, and it is a common occurrence that after their issue negotiable instruments are transferred to a holder to pay or to secure a debt.

1. *Holder for Value to a Limited Extent*

If the holder of an instrument has paid less than its face value, this fact does not ordinarily prevent a recovery of the full amount. Payment by the purchaser of a sum substantially less than the face value, however, may be evidence of bad faith —it may indicate that the purchaser harbored a suspicion that something was wrong with the instrument. There are two situations under which a holder may recover to a limited extent only and not for the face value of the instrument.

a. Holder to Extent of Lien. As previously seen, if an instrument is given to secure an obligation, the holder is a holder for value. Section 27 of the N.I.L. limits the rights of a lien holder by providing:

> "Where the holder has a lien on the instrument, arising either from contract or by implication of law, he is deemed a holder for value to the extent of his lien."

This provision does not prevent the holder from recovering the face value of the instrument when the obligor has no available defenses. If the instrument is enforceable between the original parties, the lien holder can recover the full amount. Upon recovery, the holder does, however, occupy the position of a trustee in respect to the funds over and above the amount due him. It is only when the obligor on the instrument has a defense that would be available against the original holder that the lien holder will be limited to recovering only the amount of the obligation for which the instrument stands as security.

---

* See p. 89.

b. Holder to Extent of Payment Made. Section 54 of the N.I.L. reads:

"Where the transferee receives notice of any infirmity in the instrument or defect in the title of the person negotiating the same before he has paid the full amount agreed to be paid therefor, he will be deemed a holder in due course only to the extent of the amount theretofore paid by him."

Although Section 25 of the N.I.L. provides that value is any consideration sufficient to support a simple contract, it appears from this section that an unexecuted promise is not value. A holder, in order to be a holder in due course to the full extent of the face value of the instrument, must have given in full that which he promised as the purchase price. To illustrate:

By acquiring a $600 promissory note from Y, the payee, in consideration of his promise to pay $500, does not become a holder in due course. The promise to pay is consideration, making the agreement binding between Y and X, but it is not value such as is required of a holder in due course. Should the holder X learn that the maker has a defense against the payee, he cannot, by making payment as promised, become a holder in due course and defeat the right of the maker to assert his defense. The holder will, however, stand as a holder in due course to the extent of payment actually made prior to the time that notice of the defense was acquired. If the holder has paid only $100 prior to such notice, he can enforce the note against the maker to that extent only.

c. Credit as Value. It would seem that if the consideration for an instrument is credit rather than a promise to pay, the extension of the credit should constitute value. After extending credit to the transferor as the agreed purchase price, the holder certainly has fully given the consideration bargained for. This problem of whether credit is value arises especially when banks discount negotiable instruments and give the sellers deposit credit in payment rather than cash. The question is: Are such banks holders for value and thus holders in due course?

By far the majority of the courts have not seen fit to accept the point of view presented above and hold that a bank is not giving value by giving deposit credit. It is held that only after the depositor has drawn upon the credit does the bank become a holder for value and then only to the extent of the withdrawals. Not until the credit has been completely exhausted does the bank, as a general rule, become a holder in due course for the full face value of the instrument upon which deposit credit was given. In determining whether the deposit has been drawn against, the rule is that the first money deposited is the first money taken out.[7]

There is, however, some modern authority to the effect that deposit credit constitutes value within the meaning of Section 25. Such is the rule in England.

► IV. PAYEE AS HOLDER IN DUE COURSE

Usually the payee whose name appears upon an instrument deals directly with the maker or the drawer of the instrument, and, consequently, cannot qualify as a holder in due course. Standing in such a relationship to the original obligor, the

[7] First Nat. Bank of Appleton v. Court, p. 523.

payee must have knowledge of any existing defenses. It is possible, however, that the payee may not have dealt directly with the original obligor, that he acquired the instrument from an intermediary and not as a result of any transaction with the maker or drawer. To illustrate:

The case of *Drumm Construction Co.* v. *Forbes,* 305 Ill. 303, presented the following facts: Lamberton, an automobile salesman, owed Forbes $950, which he was unable to pay. Lamberton represented to Drumm that a car could be purchased from Forbes for $950. Drumm executed a check for such amount payable to Forbes, but gave it to Lamberton for the purpose of making the purchase. Lamberton delivered the check to Forbes in payment of his personal obligation. Forbes, having no knowledge of the arrangement between Drumm and Lamberton, was held to be a holder in due course. While this represents the weight of authority, considerable opinion to the contrary can be found.

► V. DEFENSES

A. RIGHTS OF HOLDER AGAINST IMMEDIATE PARTY

In a consideration of the rights of a holder of a negotiable instrument against the parties who have obligated themselves, it is necessary in the first instance to have in mind the distinction between *immediate* and *remote* parties. It should be remembered that the holder's rights against the party from whom he received the instrument are subject to all defenses available to the latter. A payee who accepts a note directly from the maker is not a holder in due course; he must of necessity have actual knowledge of any defenses that the maker has. The payee must know: (1) whether there has been a lack of consideration or a failure to give the consideration promised; (2) whether the signing of the instrument was induced by fraud, undue influence, or duress; (3) whether the instrument has never been delivered to the payee; or (4) whether the instrument has been paid before maturity. An indorsee holder stands in the same relationship to his indorser. The rights of the holder of a negotiable instrument against the immediate prior party are subject to the same defenses as though the contract were nonnegotiable. The holder stands in the same position as an assignee.

B. RIGHTS OF HOLDER AGAINST REMOTE PARTIES

One who obligates himself by putting his name upon a negotiable instrument should be aware of the possible extent of his obligation. An obligor, whether primary (as a maker, drawer, or drawee upon acceptance), or secondary (as an indorser) should fully realize that, although he may have a defense by which he could avoid making payment to the party with whom he dealt, this right may be defeated by a subsequent transfer of the instrument to a remote party. An instrument in the hands of a holder in due course or a holder who has derived his title through a holder in due course is not subject to personal defenses—such defenses as arise out of the transaction between the immediate parties. The right of such a holder to receive payment can be defeated only by the so-called *real* or *absolute* defenses. A consideration of the more common and important real and personal defenses follows.

C. REAL DEFENSES

A party who is charged with liability upon a negotiable instrument can successfully defend for the reasons that (1) no contractual obligation to pay ever existed, (2) the holder has no title to the instrument, or (3) as a matter of public policy the obligation should not be enforced even in favor of a holder in due course. One of the above reasons will be found to underlie each of the six specific real defenses considered in the following paragraphs.

1. *Forgery*

Section 23 of the N.I.L. declares that:

> "Where a signature is forged or made without the authority of the person whose signature it purports to be, it is wholly inoperative. . . ."

The possibility that the instrument carries a forged name is one of the risks that a holder of necessity must assume. In event of his inability to collect on the instrument because of forgery, the holder's recourse is against his transferor, who warrants that the instrument is genuine and that his title is good. A holder of negotiable paper must, and as a practice does, rely to no small extent upon the responsibility of the party from whom the instrument is received. In such a way, the burden is ultimately shifted to the person who accepted the instrument from the forger.

a. Payment by Party Whose Name Has Been Forged. If one whose name has been forged to an instrument makes payment to a bona fide holder, such payment cannot be recovered. Certainly an individual should know what obligations he has assumed even if he is unable to recognize his own signature. Payment of a forged instrument constitutes gross negligence, the consequences of which will have to be taken by the payer rather than by the innocent holder of the forged instrument.

b. Payment of Forged Instrument by Drawee. If the drawer's name has been forged to an instrument and payment is made by the drawee to a bona fide holder, such payment cannot be recovered. It is presumed that the drawee is acquainted with the signature of the drawer and certainly is in a better position to ascertain whether it is genuine than is the holder. Banks, of course, carry records of the signatures of those who draw upon them. The loss will obviously fall upon the drawee (and not the drawer) since the drawee can charge the drawer's account only when authorized by the drawer to do so.[8]

2. *Material Alteration*

A material alteration of a negotiable instrument is any change that will have the effect of altering the contractual obligation or the legal relationships as originally evidenced by the instrument. A material alteration is defined by Section 125 of the N.I.L. as being:

[8] U.S. Fidelity & Guaranty Co. v. First Nat. Bank of Omaha, p. 525.

"Any alteration that changes:

(1) The date;

(2) The sum payable, either for the principal or interest;

(3) The time or place of payment;

(4) The number or the relations of the parties;

(5) The medium or currency in which payment is to be made;

Or which adds a place of payment where no place of payment is specified, or any other change or addition which alters the effect of the instrument in any respect, is a material alteration."

Illustrations of material alterations not made so obvious by Section 125 would be:

(1) A substitution of the holder's name for that of the payee;

(2) The addition of the word "surety" after the name of a comaker;

(3) The removal of contract terms or conditions from the instrument, such, for example, as are contained in a conditional sales note;

(4) A substitution of the word "bearer" for "order";

(5) The transforming of a qualified indorsement into a general indorsement by a removal of the words "without recourse."

a. Alteration as Defense against Holder in Due Course. An altered instrument in the hands of a holder in due course is not completely invalid. The defense of material alteration is available against a holder in due course only to the extent of the alteration. Section 124 of the N.I.L. reads:

"But when an instrument has been materially altered and is in the hands of a holder in due course, not a party to the alteration, he may enforce payment thereof according to its original tenor."

If the payee of a $10 check should raise the figure to read $100 and then indorse it to H, a holder in due course, H could collect from the drawer to the extent of $10 only. The defense of material alteration is available against the holder in due course only to those parties who acquire their obligations upon the instrument prior to the alteration. Those who indorse an instrument subsequent to the alteration acquire a liability to the full extent of the instrument in its altered form. An indorser warrants that the instrument is genuine and in all respects what it purports to be. In the illustration above, the payee, by virtue of his undertaking as evidenced by his indorsement, can be looked to by H for payment of the $90, providing H has realized $10, the original tenor of the check, from the drawer.

b. Payment of Raised Instrument by Drawee. There is considerable conflict among the authorities as to whether the drawee who pays a raised instrument must stand the loss or whether it can be charged to the drawer. The more generally accepted rule seems to be that the paying drawee makes payment at his own risk, and this is true even though the drawer has by his own negligence made the alteration possible.[9]

[9] Glasscock *v.* First Nat. Bank, p. 526.

3. *Want of Execution and Delivery*

Section 15 of the N.I.L. provides that:

> "Where an incomplete instrument has not been delivered it will not, if completed and negotiated, without authority, be a valid contract in the hands of any holder as against any person whose signature was placed thereon before delivery."

Certainly an undelivered instrument that is incomplete in some material respect or that contains only a signature cannot be said to evidence a contractual obligation. The fact that such an instrument is completed after falling into the hands of a thief who negotiated it to a holder in due course does not commit the signer to a contractual undertaking.

4. *Fraud as to Nature of Instrument*

The Wisconsin N.I.L. (§ 1676–25) departs from the uniform act (§ 55) by providing:

> ". . . and the title of such person is absolutely void when such instrument or signature was so procured from a person who did not know the nature of the instrument and could not have obtained such knowledge by the use of ordinary care."

This is an enactment of the generally accepted common law rule that fraud can be asserted as a real defense and thus bar recovery, if it is used for the purpose of inducing a person to sign a negotiable instrument that he reasonably believes is an instrument of an entirely different nature. It has been suggested that, since the framers of the N.I.L. omitted the inclusion of this special type of fraud as a real defense, the intent was, and the result has been, to abrogate the common law rule and make fraud, regardless of its nature, a personal defense not available against a holder in due course. Since the enactment of the N.I.L., some cases have adhered to the common law doctrine that such fraud is in essence a forgery and, consequently, a real defense. Other cases have taken a contrary view.

It should be noted, however, that even in those jurisdictions where such a fraud is regarded as a real defense, the defrauded party will not be protected against a holder in due course if his own negligence made the perpetration of the fraud possible. Between two innocent parties, the loss will be made to fall upon him who was negligent.

5. *Illegality*

Depending upon the circumstances, illegality may be either a personal or a real defense.

> "The authorities justify the statement that a defendant may insist upon the illegality of the contract or consideration, notwithstanding the note is in the hands of an innocent holder for value, in all those cases in which he can point to an express declaration of the Legislature that the illegality insisted upon shall make the security, whether contract, bill or note, void. But unless

the Legislature has so declared, no matter how illegal or immoral the consideration may be, a commercial note in the hands of an innocent holder for value will be held valid and enforceable." *Sondheim* v. *Gilbert,* 117 Ind. 71.

Unless the statute expressly or by implication clearly makes an instrument void, the courts are hesitant to deny the right of a holder in due course to recover. The effect of illegality as a defense against a holder in due course resolves itself very largely into a consideration of the intent and wording of the particular statute involved. In by far the majority of instances, illegality is only a personal defense, which cannot be set up against a holder in due course.

6. *Incapacity*

a. Infancy. A minor may avoid his contractual obligation at his election or he may disaffirm his indorsement and recover the instrument from a holder in due course. The law makes no distinction between the status of an infant under a negotiable contract and the status of an infant under a simple contract. In either case, the infant is given protection as a matter of public policy.

b. Insanity. As a general rule, insanity can be set up as a defense even against a holder in due course. There are decisions, however, that hold that insanity cannot be asserted as a defense if the holder has no knowledge of the lunacy.

c. Intoxication. Intoxication to a degree "so as to suspend the reason and create impotence of mind at the time of entering into the contract" constitutes contractual incompetency. Consequently, one who has signed a negotiable instrument while in such a condition may within a reasonable time after his return to sobriety avoid his contractual undertaking. A failure to disaffirm within a reasonable time will be interpreted as an affirmance of the contract.

As a general rule, intoxication as a defense is not available against a holder in due course. Although there is some authority to the contrary, contractual disability due to intoxication is generally held to be only an equitable defense, which is cut off by a subsequent negotiation. Wisconsin is one of the notable exceptions that holds intoxication to be a real defense.

D. PERSONAL DEFENSES

Some of the more important defenses that are cut off by a negotiation of a negotiable instrument—defenses of which an obligor cannot avail himself against a holder in due course or against a holder who has derived his title through a holder in due course—are as follows:

1. *Lack or Failure of Consideration*

To be enforceable between the immediate parties, a negotiable contract, like a simple contract, must be supported by consideration. A payee cannot enforce a promissory note against a maker from whom it was received as a gratuity. Nor could X, a payee, recover on a note given him in consideration for a car that he never delivered. The same would be true as between immediate indorsers and indorsees.

An instrument in the hands of a holder in due course or one who derives his title through a holder in due course is not subject to the defense of lack or failure of consideration. The acceptability of negotiable instruments would be greatly restricted if prospective purchasers were burdened with the need of determining whether such instruments are supported by consideration.

2. *Illegality of Consideration*

If a negotiable instrument is based upon an illegal consideration, this fact will not defeat the right of a holder in due course to collect. If the illegality merely affects the consideration of the contract, it is only a personal defense, which is cut off by a negotiation. If the instrument is declared by statute to be rendered void by the illegal transaction out of which it arose, illegality is a real defense and as such is available against all holders.[10]

3. *Fraud*

Recall that, if the nature of the instrument to be executed is misrepresented, fraud may possibly be a real defense. It is more usual, however that fraud partakes of a different nature. Generally the misrepresentation does not relate to the character of the instrument being signed, but rather to some facts that induced the execution and delivery of a writing that the signer knows is a negotiable instrument. Fraud of this nature is merely a personal defense and as such cannot be used by the defrauded primary obligor as a defense against a holder in due course. The same rule holds true if an indorser has been induced by fraud to negotiate an instrument that is subsequently negotiated to a holder in due course. Should the defrauded indorser be called upon to pay, the defense of fraud would not be available to him.

4. *Lack of Delivery*

Section 16 of the N.I.L. provides that:

"Every contract on a negotiable instrument is incomplete and revocable until delivery of the instrument for the purpose of giving effect thereto."

This provision applies to immediate parties and to remote parties who are not holders in due course. As to holders in due course, Section 16 further provides:

"But where the instrument is in the hands of a holder in due course, a valid delivery thereof by all parties prior to him so as to make them liable to him is conclusively presumed."

Lack of delivery of a completed instrument is a personal defense, which is cut off by a negotiation of the instrument to a holder in due course. Bearer instruments, of course, get more easily into circulation without a delivery than order instruments, which require an indorsement for negotiation. An instrument payable to bearer can readily be negotiated by a thief or finder since an indorsement is not required. However, it is entirely possible that an order instrument may, without a delivery, fall into the hands of the designated payee or indorsee, who could then indorse and transfer possession of the instrument to a holder in due course. The

---

[10] Sabine v. Paine, p. 528.

instrument in the hands of a holder in due course creates a conclusive presumption that a valid delivery had been made to all prior parties.

a. Conditional Delivery. This section finds its application especially where an instrument has been delivered conditionally—where it has been agreed that the instrument is not to be effective until or unless a specified condition has been met. Within the meaning of Section 16, there would be no "delivery of the instrument for the purpose of giving effect thereto" until the condition had been met. The conditional transferee could assert no rights under the contract until there had been compliance with the condition.[11] But should the instrument be negotiated in breach of faith to a holder in due course, a delivery would be conclusively presumed, and the defense of lack of delivery or conditional delivery would not be available against the holder. To illustrate:

An insurance agent A, realizing the effectiveness of the technique of a sale on trial as a means of overcoming sales resistance, induced B to accept a policy upon the understanding that it could be returned by B within thirty days from the date of its issue. At the same time, A accepted B's promissory note for the amount of the first premium charge with the understanding that the note was to be returned to B if he should elect within the thirty-day period not to retain the policy. This note was conditionally delivered to A and does not effectively represent an obligation on the part of B until the condition has been removed. There is nothing, however, other than A's own conscience that would prevent him from negotiating the note to H, a holder in due course. In H's hands the note would represent a valid obligation of B, since a delivery from B to A would be conclusively presumed.

5. *Material Alteration*

Section 124 of the N.I.L. reads:

> "Where a negotiable instrument is materially altered without the assent of all parties liable thereon, it is avoided, except as against a party who has himself made, authorized or assented to the alteration."

Any person who takes it upon himself to alter materially a negotiable instrument or makes himself a party to a material alteration thereby deprives himself of the right to recover.[12, 13] An instrument that has been altered is not completely void in the hands of a holder in due course. As has been previously pointed out, a holder in due course can recover to the extent of the original tenor of the instrument. If the payee on a promissory note should raise the figure of $100 to read $1,000, the maker would have a complete defense in an action upon the instrument by the payee. The instrument in the hands of a holder in due course could be enforced to the extent of the original figure, $100.

a. Innocent Alteration. Section 124 of the N.I.L. makes no distinction as to whether the alteration was the result of fraudulent design or of an unintentional

[11] Gilbert v. Pioneer Nat. Bank of Duluth, p. 529.
[12] Perry v. Manufacturers Nat. Bank of Lynn, p. 530.
[13] Columbia Grocery Co. v. Marshall, p. 531.

wrong-doing. But the majority of the courts take the view that, unless the alteration was fraudulently made, the instrument is not void and that a holder who innocently made the alteration can recover upon the instrument as it stood before the alteration. Other courts have arrived at the conclusion that even an innocent alteration avoids the instrument completely but that recovery can be had upon the original obligation for which the instrument was given.

6. *Discharge Before Maturity*

If an instrument is discharged—as by payment—before maturity, good business practice demands that steps be taken to prevent its further circulation. Should a discharged instrument come into the hands of a holder in due course, it again represents a binding contract, and the obligor can again be called upon to pay. Discharge of an instrument before maturity is a personal defense, which is cut off by a negotiation to a holder in due course. Consequently, at the time of discharging the instrument, the obligor should make certain that the instrument is surrendered to him bearing unmistakable evidence that the obligation has been satisfied. Destruction of the instrument is the most certain method of preventing recirculation.

CASES

CASE NO. 1

Moore v. Vaughn et al. 167 Miss. 758, 150 So. 372 (1933)

The plaintiff, Moore, brought action to recover upon the following instrument:

$50.00 September 16th, 1931

February 1st, 1932, after date ________ promise to pay to the order ________ Fifty ________ Dollars. For value received with interest at the rate of ________ per cent per annum from ________ and if the interest be not paid annually to become as principal, and bear the same rate of interest. This note is negotiable and payable without defalcation or discount and without any relief or benefit whatever from stay, valuation, appraisement or homestead exemption laws.

D. F. Vaughn

No. 4. Due ________

The note contained several endorsements and Moore had purchased it for value. The maker, Vaughn, set up the defense of failure of consideration.

MC GOWEN, J. The appellant, Moore, contends that he is the holder, for value, in due course, of said notes, that the notes with the blanks therein were delivered to Anderson with implied authority to fill in the blanks, and that the words "This note is negotiable" render the notes bearer notes and negotiable instruments; and that therefore any evidence offered as a defense on behalf of the maker of the notes is incompetent. . . .

The defense of failure of consideration is not available where the instrument is in the hands of a holder in due course. Of course, however, if a person seeking a recovery is not a holder in due course, the instrument is subject to the same defenses as if it were a non-negotiable instrument. . . .

In disposing of the contention that the recital in the instruments, "This note is negotiable," cures the defects, we will say that such recital does not render the notes negotiable. . . . For illustration, if A undertakes to sell B a horse, and puts a label on a cow reading, "This is a horse," such label does not change the character, or name, of the animal. . . . The contract here to the effect that the notes were negotiable did not supply the requirement mandatorily fixed by the statute, and does not avail to render them complete and regular on their face, so that Moore can now be declared to be a holder in due course.

We are therefore clearly of the opinion that Moore, the appellant here, took the notes with the infirmity thereon, and was put upon inquiry of Anderson, who sold them to him. If Anderson, to whom the notes were delivered by the maker, had filled in the blanks, and Moore had paid value therefor, without notice, the defense here probably could not have interposed.

We are not unmindful of the great value to the commercial world of removing obstacles in order to facilitate the transfer of negotiable instruments. Ninety per cent of the great volume of the business of this country is conducted by the medium of negotiable instruments. Negotiable instruments, of one kind or another, are absolutely essential, in this day, to business of all kinds; but, where a person buys paper with patent defects thereon, with unfilled blanks, and his transferor does not fill same, nor does he do so himself, he stands charged with knowledge of such defects and irregularities apparent on the face of the paper, and he is not a holder in due course. . . .

CASE NO. 2

W. W. Marshall & Co. v. Kirschbraun & Sons. 100 Neb. 876, 161 N.W. 577 (1917)

DEAN, J. . . . The defendant company is an Omaha concern engaged in the manufacture of creamery butter, having many cream stations in this and other states. On April 12, 1913, and for a few months prior thereto, F. M. Woods was the agent of defendant in charge of its station at Niobrara. On that date the market price of the cream product called butter fat was 30 cents a pound at Niobrara, and Mr. Woods purchased about 600 pounds, giving checks therefor representing a price paid of $2.01 a pound. . . . When the checks were presented to defendant payment was refused on the ground that the agent exceeded his authority in purchasing the cream at a figure so greatly in excess of its market value. . . .

On April 12th, there were four cream stations at Niobrara. A rivalry arose among three of the agents with respect to the purchase price of cream. In the morning the market price was 30 cents a pound or thereabouts, but at noon the buyers were paying 70 cents. In the afternoon one buyer paid $1 a pound, and shortly thereafter another paid $2, and before night Mr. Woods and one or more of his rivals were paying $2.01 a pound. . . . But it is not without significance that before the day closed Woods was the only agent who had on hand any of the cream bought that day at more than $2 a pound; all of the other agents by some means having contrived to dispose of their respective purchases to the unsuspecting agent of defendant. . . .

Marshall & Co., appearing as plaintiffs herein, are merchants who sue to recover $37.98 as innocent purchasers of a check for that amount issued to G. Summers for cream on April 12, 1913, at $2.01 a pound. The check, properly filled in and with the name "F. M. Woods" appended thereto over the word "operator," was introduced in evidence . . . a line was drawn through the words, "This check for cream only. Not good for more than $15." The words beneath the line are plainly discernible. The check in question is in such condition as to put the purchaser on inquiry, and he could not be an innocent purchaser. It contained two limitations: First, it was by its printed terms good for only $15; second, the $15 limitation was defaced. There is no testimony as to the time when, nor by whom the Marshall & Co. check was changed. . . . From all the facts in evidence we conclude that Marshall & Co., even if they did not have actual knowledge, were put upon inquiry as to the validity of the check on which they brought suit, and as to them they are only entitled to recover the same as the other defendants, namely, 30 cents a pound for the cream that was sold to Agent Woods by G. Summers, from whom Marshall & Co. purchased the check in suit. . . .

CASE NO. 3

Bonnette v. Ponthieux. 41 So. (2d) 127 (La.) (1949)

HARDY, J. This is a suit in which plaintiff, claiming to be the holder in due course of a check in the sum of $525.00, seeks to recover said amount from defendant as the maker of said instrument.

On or about January 15, 1948, defendant and A. B. Bonnette, plaintiff's brother, were negotiating with respect to the sale by Bonnette to defendant of a second-hand school bus. Defendant contends that he reached an agreement with Bonnette on the sale price of $525.00, and that he agreed to consummate the purchase upon making a "trial run" of the vehicle, to New Orleans and return, in order to determine whether or not the vehicle would serve his purpose. . . . Ponthieux, on or about the said date of January 15, 1948, made and delivered to A. B. Bonnette a check in the sum of $525.00 drawn on Planters Trust & Savings Bank of Opelousas.

In any event, a few days after the stated transaction, defendant and an employee set forth for New Orleans in the ex-school bus. Their journey was fraught with inconvenience, trouble and difficulty. Tires blew out, the radiator hose and water pump gave way, necessitating replacement on arrival in New Orleans, and the motor consumed 17 quarts of oil on the round trip, according to their testimony. Immediately upon the return to Marksville defendant sent word to A. B. Bonnette that he refused to purchase the bus. Bonnette, in response to defendant's message, went to Ponthieux's dwelling that same evening, at which time the parties heatedly discussed the matter. . . .

A short time after this interview, despite Ponthieux's request for the return of his check and rescission of the conditional agreement, A. B. Bonnette tendered the check in question to the Union Bank at Marksville, where, upon his endorsement, he received the sum $525.00 in cash, and the bank transmitted the check for collection through its usual banking channels. Ponthieux, failing to receive the return of the check, became suspicious, called the bank, and was advised by the cashier, Mr. Gremillion, that the check had been cashed upon receipt of which information Ponthieux advised the said official of the bank that the check was no good, that he had no account with the Planter's Bank of Opelousas, and that, assuredly, it would be returned unpaid.

In turn Mr. Gremillion contacted Mr. A. B. Bonnette and advised that he would be required to make good to the bank the amount he received.

At this point, for the first time in this rather involved sequence of events, the plaintiff in this suit, Cyprien Bonnette, brother of A. B. Bonnette, appears as an actor in this comedy of errors. For it was at this stage that A. B. Bonnette contacted his brother, Cyprien, explained that he had spent the money he received from the bank, which he would have to make good, and asked his brother to make this amount good to the bank for him. Cyprien, obviously a model of brotherly devotion, immediately agreed, and produced the sum of $525.00 which he transmitted to Mr. Gremillion, cashier. . . . Gremillion, at and upon receipt of the dishonored check, covered the amount with the sum furnished by Cyprien Bonnette, and delivered the check to Cyprien. Some time later Cyprien returned to the bank in person and tendered the check for collection. Despite Mr. Gremillion's reminder that Ponthieux had no account with the drawee bank, Cyprien Bonnette insisted that the effort be made, and, on advice of Gremillion, deposited the check with the understanding that it would be charged to his account when it was returned unpaid. This event took place in due course, whereupon, after demand and refusal of payment by defendant, this suit was instituted.

The defense is based upon two very obvious grounds, first, that plaintiff was not a holder in due course, in good faith, and without knowledge of existing equities between defendant and A. B. Bonnette, the payee of the check, and, second, that the mechanical defects in the motor vehicle were of such a degree and extent as to make the same unacceptable to defendant. . . .

After trial there was judgment in favor of plaintiff in the sum of $462.73, representing the amount sued for, less certain credits for repairs. In his judgment our learned brother of the District Court took occasion to observe that "plaintiff was not a holder in good faith and in due course of the check forming the basis of his suit." . . .

Beyond any question of a doubt plaintiff was not a holder in good faith and in due course of the check which serves as the basis for this action, and accordingly, he is bound by any and all equities existing between this defendant and A. B. Bonnette, the original payee of the check.

It matters not that the seller made no express warranty of the vehicle, for it is well established in this State that a seller warrants the thing sold as being fit for the intended purpose, unless such warranty is expressly waived. . . .

We think it is definitely established in the instant case by almost uncontroverted testimony that the bus in question was so afflicted with vices and defects of various kinds that this defendant, the buyer, would not have purchased the vehicle with knowledge of such defects.

The evidence further preponderated in favor of defendant's contention that his purchase was conditioned upon the trial trip.

. . . judgment in favor of defendant.

CASE NO. 4

Quanah, Acme, & P.R. Co. v. Wichita State Bank & T. Co. 127 Tex. 407, 93 S.W. (2d) 701 (1936)

CRITZ, J., delivered the opinion of the court:

The court of Civil Appeals has made a very fair and comprehensive statement of the issues in this case. It is as follows:

". . . Appellant is a railroad corporation. . . . From 1909 until about September, 1931, it had in its employment one T. K. Hawkins as its treasurer and auditor whose duty was to collect and deposit all moneys and revenues arising from such business to plaintiff's credit in its depository bank at Quanah, . . . the Security National Bank of Quanah. It was alleged, in substance: that much of the outbound freight moved on other roads and that the delivering carrier collected the revenues and distributed same among the carriers participating in the haul in accordance with the proportion earned by each. That the said T. K. Hawkins would draw a draft against the collecting carriers for the proportional amount of freight coming to appellant and deposit same in the said Security National Bank of Quanah. That about March, 1925, "the said T. K. Hawkins began the practice of withholding from deposit one or more of the drafts above described, for which he would request the Security National Bank to issue to him bills of exchange payable to him as treasurer . . . for varying amounts . . . and at his request said depository bank issued to said T. K. Hawkins many bills of exchange drawn against other banks . . . and which practice occurred practically every month from March, 1925, to August, 1931. That up to about the month of April, 1931, such bills of exchange were payable to T. K. Hawkins, Treas. . . . But after said date said bills of exchange were made payable to T. K. Hawkins, Treas., Q. A. & P. Ry. Co."

"It is further averred that such bills of exchange were indorsed 'T. K. Hawkins, Treas.;' that all of these bills of exchange were paid for by drafts drawn by T. K. Hawkins for freight as aforesaid and were each and all the property of appellant; that T. K. Hawkins embezzled, with the aid of appellee, Wichita Bank & Trust Company, the proceeds of bills of exchange between March, 1925, to September, 1931, in amounts which aggregated the sum of $63,054.65; that the scheme used by Hawkins was to indorse and deliver such bills of exchange to appellee, some of them personally and some of them by mail, each of them to be credited and were credited to his personal account and that all of the funds so deposited were withdrawn on the individual check of Hawkins; that the bank knew, by virtue of the form and contents of said bills of exchange and that T. K. Hawkins had indorsed same, that such bills of exchange were the property of appellant; . . .

"This petition in fact, specifically alleges knowledge on the part of appellee of said misappropriations and embezzlements but it seems to have been agreed in the trial court and acquiesced in by all parties in oral argument before this court, that it had only such knowledge as might be visited upon it by all the facts and circumstances connected with and surrounding the transactions leading to the acquisition of the funds aforesaid."

It is not controverted that the bills of exchange involved in this suit were negotiable instruments. Furthermore, it is the settled law that the bank had a perfect right to purchase such bills from Hawkins in his trust capacity, provided it did not act in bad faith in doing so. In this connection it is the settled law of this state that the ordinary rule of notice does not apply to the purchaser of a negotiable instrument for a valuable consideration before maturity. The test in negotiable instrument cases is good faith, and not diligence or negligence. Unless the purchaser has actual knowledge of facts and circumstances that would render the paper noncollectible, or has knowledge of such facts as that a purchase of the instrument would amount to bad faith, it is immaterial that he has notice of such facts as would put a reasonably prudent person on inquiry, and that such inquiry would lead to discovery. . . .

Ordinarily, one in possession of a negotiable instrument has the power to dispose of it. Certainly, where the one in possession is the payee on the face of the instrument, even in a trust capacity, he has the right in such capacity to negotiate it. Also, it is the law that a negotiable instrument passes as a species of currency without inquiry. If the buyer pays a valuable consideration and acts in good faith, his title cannot be impugned. . . .

From what has been said, it is evident that we hold that these bills of exchange were negotiated to this bank under circumstances that made it a good-faith purchaser thereof.

From the above, it is evident that we must answer the following question in order to decide this case:

If a person negotiates to a bank a bill of exchange payable on its face to the person negotiating it in a trust capacity, and the purchasing bank, in the very transaction by which it acquires the instrument, passes its proceeds to the individual checking credit of the trustee on its books, and thereafter allows him to check out such proceeds on his individual checks, and as a result of such transactions the fund is lost to the true owner, is the bank liable for such loss to such true owner? . . .

In our opinion, the above question should be answered in the negative. In this connection, we think the great weight of and better authority is to the effect that it is not deemed a breach of trust, or such a suspicious circumstance as to put a duty on the bank to investigate, for a trustee to carry trust credits in his personal bank account, and this even though such fact is known to the bank. In this connection, it is generally held that the bank is entitled to believe that the trustee will check the trust credit out of his personal account for proper trust purposes. The main reasons for this rule are that to require the bank to investigate such transactions would put a burden on the bank for which it is not paid by the trust, and would clog the handling of commercial paper in a way that would be to the disadvantage generally of trust business, and also to business in general.

CASE NO. 5

New Port Richey v. Fidelity & D. Co.
105 F. (2d) 348, 123 A.L.R. 1352 (1939)

SIBLEY, C.J., delivered the opinion of the court:

The City of New Port Richey . . . on June 1, 1930, signed by its officers and its corporate seal twenty-six bonds payable to bearer. . . . The bonds were duly validated, but they were never issued or agreed to be issued to anyone, but were deposited for safe-keeping in a lock box of the city in the vault of a bank. Bank robbers drilled into the vault and stole the bonds. On October 24, 1935, thirteen of them were acquired, with all coupons attached, by Suwanee Life Insurance Company, and sold by it to Pierce-Biese Corporation, a bond dealer, who sold them to F. M. Blount, Inc. These are each alleged to have taken the bonds in due course for value and without notice of any infirmity in the title. Pierce-Biese Corporation reacquired the bonds and attempted to resell them, but it was discovered that the city claimed they were stolen. Pierce-Biese Corporation had a policy of insurance against loss by stolen bonds, issued by Fidelity & Deposit Company of Maryland, and the latter, having indemnified its insured, acquired the bonds. The City of New Port Richey is now engaged in refunding its indebtedness and will not recognize these bonds. They cannot be sued on for they are not due till 1950. A declaratory judgment affirming the validity of bonds and coupons as obligations of the City was sought and on stipulated facts obtained. The City appeals.

The main questions presented are: Were the bonds ever negotiable instruments, since they had never been delivered? Were they negotiated to a holder in due course so as to prevent enquiry thereabout? What effect had the presence of ten overdue coupons attached to each bond?

. . . As between the immediate parties and all others not holders in due course, delivery is essential to the existence of the instrument as a legal obligation. Until put in operation by delivery, the original instrument and indorsements of it are, as to such parties, incomplete and revocable, and a delivery may be shown to have been conditional or for a special purpose. . . . One who fully completes a negotiable paper, withholding delivery, assumes the risk of its getting out of his possession into the hands of a holder in due course. He must care for it much as he would for his paper money. . . .

The case then turns on whether a holder in due course is here involved. Fidelity and Deposit Company is not such, for it took the bonds after full knowledge of the defense to them. But it acquired the rights of any former holder in due course, for such rights are transmitted and not destroyed by a transfer after notice to a third party. . . . The petition alleged Suwanee Life Ins. Co., Pierce-Biese Corporation, and F. M. Blount, Inc., each to be a holder in due course. The answer categorically denied each was such. On that issue it was stipulated as to each that it in October, 1935 (presumably in Florida),

> "in the ordinary course of business, without knowledge or notice of any illegality thereof or any infirmity in the title thereto, for value"

bought the bonds. It was also stipulated that at each transfer all the coupons, ten on each bond being past due, were annexed to the bonds. . . . Each bond and coupon was regular and complete on its face. The stipulation is that they were taken for value and without notice of infirmity in the instrument or defect in the title. But the stipulation does not admit they were taken in good faith, or that there was no notice of previous dishonor, and it is admitted that coupons No's. 1 to 10, inclusive, on each bond were overdue, the earliest by nearly five years. We are faced by the question, What effect in law or fact do these overdue coupons have?

It has been said that unsevered coupons add nothing to a bond which itself promises to pay interest, and they may be disregarded. This is hardly true in the present case, for each coupon is in form a complete promissory note payable to bearer, and the bond's only promise as to interest is to pay

> "upon the presentation and surrender of the annexed interest coupons as the same respectively mature."

The coupons are the promise to pay interest, and their non-surrender at maturity shows the interest has not been paid. . . . It seems to us as to the coupons which were overdue in October, 1935, when the first negotiation happened, no taker could be a holder in due course, and the City's defense would in any case be good against them.

The overdue coupons have also a bearing upon the negotiation of the bonds and immature coupons. They inform the taker that for some reason the City has, from the beginning and during nearly five years, never paid a dime of interest. . . . It is generally held that default in an instalment of principal known to the indorsee prevents his taking the paper as to unmatured instalments free from defenses. 8 Am. Jur., Bills and Notes, § 432. Some courts have thought that a known default in paying interest stands on a like basis. . . . Still others have thought the known nonpayment of interest, though not in law notice of dishonor, is a fact to be considered with all other circumstances on the question of the bona fides of the taking. . . .

We take the view last stated as the true one. . . .

We therefore hold that while overdue interest coupons do not as a matter of law defeat the claim of holder in due course of an unmatured bond, that bona fides in taking it is open to question as a matter of fact and that all the circumstances of the purchase, including the number of past due interest coupons, the price paid for the bond, and the reliability of the seller, are to be considered in determining the question. That fact question has not been determined in this case. The judgment is set aside and a new trial awarded, to be in accordance with the opinions herein expressed.

Reversed.

CASE NO. 6

Merchants' Nat. Bank v. Detroit Trust Co. 258 Mich. 526, 242 N.W. 739 (1932)

MC DONALD, J. The defendant has appealed from a judgment in an action of replevin for the recovery of certain corporate bonds which were stolen. . . .

Was defendant a holder in due course?

Section 52(4) defines a holder in due course as one who has taken the instrument under certain conditions, one which is:

> "Fourth, That at the time it was negotiated to him he had no notice of any infirmity in the instrument or defect in the title of the person negotiating it."

Section 56 provides:

> "To constitute notice of an infirmity in the instrument, or defect in the title of the person negotiating the same, the person to whom it is negotiated must have had actual knowledge of the infirmity or defect, or knowledge of such facts that his action in taking the instrument amounted to bad faith."

In this case, the plaintiff having shown that the bonds were stolen, the burden was then upon the defendant to prove that it was a holder in due course.

It is claimed by the plaintiff that within ten days after the theft of the bonds it mailed written notices containing a description of them to all of the principal banks and trust companies of the middle west including the defendant company. The defendant denies having received such a notice. . . . According to the defendant's custom, mail addressed to the Detroit Trust Company and not to any particular person or department was opened by one of the mail clerks and sent to the person in charge of the business to which it related. Following this custom, the plaintiff's notice, if received at the mailing department, would be sent to Mr. Butler, vice president in charge of the financial department, then to Mr. Miller, assistant treasurer, and finally to Mrs. Irving, collateral loan teller. All of these officers had a part in the loan for which the bonds were accepted as collateral. We have no reason to doubt their testimony that they did not see or receive the notice. But, assuming that it was received, that they saw it and forgot about it or carelessly mislaid it so that it was not in their minds at the time they acquired the bonds, or assuming that it was received but through the carelessness of the mailing clerk it was not brought to the attention of the officers, how would these facts affect the company's title as holder in due course?

In Toledo, Saginaw & Muskegon Railway Company v. Peters, 177 Mich. 76, 143 N.W. 18, 24, this court adopted the following rule stated in section 200, Jones on Corporate Bonds and Mortgages (3d Ed.):

"A purchaser of negotiable bonds before due, for a valuable consideration, in good faith and without actual knowledge or notice of any defect of title, holds them by a title valid as against every other person. Even gross negligence at the time of purchase does not alone defeat the purchaser's title. A purchaser may have had a suspicion of a defect of title, or knowledge of circumstances which would excite such suspicion in the mind of a prudent man; or he may have disregarded notices of stolen bonds; and yet, if he had purchased for value in good faith, his title cannot be impeached. Such suspicion, or ground of suspicion, or of knowledge on his part, may be evidence of bad faith; but before his title can be impeached his bad faith must be established. It must be shown that he did not purchase honestly."

In the instant case, if the defendant did not acquire the bonds honestly, it was because it had notice that they were stolen. The plaintiff claims it had actual notice. We think there was no evidence to overcome the presumption that the notice mailed by the plaintiff was delivered to the defendant's mailing department; but neither was there any evidence in contradiction of the officers that they did not see the notice or acquire knowledge of its contents. . . .

. . . it has been held that one is not required to examine such notices or, if examined, charge his mind with them or cumber his files with them. . . .

In Toledo, Saginaw & Muskegon Railway Company v. Peters, supra, it was said that one may disregard notice of stolen bonds and yet be a purchaser in good faith. In saying that one may disregard the notice, it was not meant that he may willfully close his eyes to it. He may not resort to trick or artifice to avoid knowledge of its contents, or he may not purposely forget it. He must act in good faith. Such notice may be evidence of bad faith, but it is not conclusive. In the instant case, the notice was received by the mailing clerk, but the three officers of the trust company deny that they received it or were made acquainted with its contents. We know of no reason why we should doubt their testimony. The record shows that they acted in good faith.

As the bonds in question were acquired before maturity, for value, and in good faith, the defendant is a holder in due course. . . .

The judgment is reversed. . . .

CASE NO. 7

First Nat. Bank of Appleton v. Court.
183 Wis. 203, 197 N.W. 798 (1924)

DOERFLER, J. . . . On the 16th day of August, 1921, Havorka & Co., sold a small block of stock to the defendant, and took from him his promissory note payable to it, for the sum of $1,000, . . . Havorka & Co. . . . indorsed this note to the N. Simon Cheese Company, a corporation, without recourse. . . . On August 19, 1921, being three days after the execution of the said note, the cheese company indorsed the note to the plaintiff, and the plaintiff thereupon gave the cheese company credit on its open checking account. On the date of the indorsement of the note to the plaintiff, the cheese company at the opening of business on that day had to its credit in its account with the plaintiff bank a balance of $20,739.23. On the same day the bank honored and paid checks of the cheese company aggregating $90,959.50, leaving a balance at the close of business on that day to the credit of the cheese company of $14,289.20. This would indicate that on said last-named date the cheese company had made sufficient deposits to the credit of its account in the bank to account for such balance at the close of such day. . . .

In his answer the defendant alleges that the sale of the shares of stock to the defendant by Havorka & Co. was induced by various alleged false and fraudulent representations . . . and that the bank had . . . not become the holder of the note in due course. . . .

A vital, concrete proposition here presented is whether a bank in discounting a note of one of its depositors, and crediting the amount to the checking account of such depositor, becomes the bona fide owner of such note for value, where it appears from the evidence that on the date of the discount the depositor added largely to his balance by additional deposits, but withdrew from his account by checks actually paid an amount sufficiently large so as to leave to his credit at the close of business on that day a sum considerably less than the amount to his credit at the opening of business on that day, but leaving a balance at the close of business largely in excess of the amount credited by the discount of the note.

It has been firmly established in this state and throughout the country that a bank is not a holder in due course of a negotiable instrument in its possession, unless it has honored and paid checks of the depositor, or has given value for the note, or has assumed an obligation of the depositor on account of the discount of the note. Under such circumstances the mere relationship of debtor and creditor is created between the bank and the depositor, and so long as that relation continues, and the deposit is not drawn out, the bank is held subject to the equities of the prior parties, notwithstanding the note was taken before maturity and without notice of any infirmity therein.

In Mann v. Second Nat. Bank, 30 Kan. 412, 1 Pac. 579, the court said:

> "The proposition rests on the plainest principles of justice. . . . Whenever the holder is a bona fide holder, he has the right to claim protection, but protection only to the extent he has lost or been injured by the acquisition of the paper. If he has parted with value, either by a cash payment or the cancellation of a debt, or giving time on the debt, or in any other manner, to that extent he has a right to claim protection; but when he has parted with nothing, there is nothing to protect. A mere promise to pay is no payment. He may rightfully say to the party from whom he purchased: 'The paper you have given me is valueless, and therefore, I am under no obligations to pay;' and if the paper be in fact valueless, payment cannot be compelled. . . ."

There is thus raised the question in this case whether, after the discount of a note, the amount being placed to the credit of the depositor in his checking account in the bank, and he subsequently withdraws from such checking account an amount equal to his credit at the time of the deposit, and including the amount of the discounted note, the bank becomes a bona fide holder for value of the note, notwithstanding there may remain thereafter at all times between the date of the discount of the note and the maturity of the note a balance in excess of the amount of the note.

We have examined the cases, the textbooks, and the reference books upon this subject, and we find the rule firmly established by overwhelming authority, that in such case the bank becomes a holder for value of the note. Under such circumstances the authorities hold that the doctrine of the presumption of the application of payments applies; the maxim being stated as follows: "The first money in is the first money out." . . .

Where a note is executed to a depositor, and the note is indorsed to a bank, and the amount credited to the depositor's account, the rights of the maker are referable to the amount so credited, and vanish when the bank honors the checks of the depositor whereby the amount is withdrawn. . . .

In the instant case plaintiff . . . proved that it gave value for the note, ...

CASE NO. 8

United States Fidelity & Guaranty Co. v. First Nat. Bank of Omaha. 129 Neb. 102, 260 N.W. 798 (1935)

PAINE, J. The United States Fidelity and Guaranty Company, plaintiff and appellee, brought action to recover $500 from the First National Bank of Omaha, defendant and appellant, on the ground that it had paid to the defendant $500 upon proof of loss under the terms of its bond protecting said defendant bank against loss on payment of forged instruments, whereas it had been fully reimbursed for said loss, which fact it concealed from the plaintiff.

In the petition it is alleged . . . That on October 9, 1928, defendant filed written proof of loss with plaintiff for a forged check, dated October 5, 1928, that was drawn upon the account of the Jerpe Commission Company of Omaha, payable at the First National Bank of Omaha, and bearing the forged signatures of its treasurer and president, said check being payable to Joe Fernald, and by him indorsed in blank, and . . . that indemnity or reimbursement on account of the forgery has not been received, . . . That the defendant bank filed its amended answer, admitting that it paid a forged check of the Jerpe Commission Company purporting to be signed by G. C. Swanson and M. Olander, officers of said company, and gave due notice under the terms of its bond to the plaintiff company, and that plaintiff's agent requested defendant to attempt recovery of the amount paid on said check from the indorser thereon, and that defendant bank sent said check back to the Omaha National Bank, which bank returned it to the First National Bank of Lincoln, and the First National Bank of Lincoln collected $500 from the first indorser [Shostak], but that said indorser had later demanded a return of the payment made from the First National Bank of Omaha, claiming that he had not known that said bank had actually paid the check, and thereupon the First National Bank of Omaha paid back to said indorser the amount of the check, and defendant bank denies that it was ever reimbursed or indemnified in any other manner, and asks that plaintiff's petition be dismissed. . . .

. . . the court entered judgment for the plaintiff for $683.50, with interest at 7 per cent. . . .

When a check has been paid and canceled by the drawee bank, and the amount is charged to the drawer's account, and credit given the account of the bank presenting the check, and the drawee bank fails to return the check to the presenting bank within the time allowed by the clearing house rules, it is considered paid for all purposes. This is because the drawee bank is deemed the place of final settlement, where all prior mistakes and forgeries shall be corrected and settled once for all, and if the forgery is overlooked and payment is made, it must be deemed final. The rule seems to be well established that a drawee bank which pays a forged check to a bona fide holder for value and without fault, cannot recover the payment from him. 5 Michie, Banks and Banking, § 269. It has been held that, although the rules of the clearing house provided that drawee banks might return checks at any time before 3 p. m., a bank can only do so where it has at no time debited the amount of the check against the account of the drawer. First Nat. Bank of Philadelphia v. National Park Bank of New York, 100 Misc. 31, 165 N.Y.S. 15.

The first National Bank of Omaha, drawee, having actually accepted and paid the forged check and canceled it, suffered the loss thereof. Shostak's voluntary payment of $500 was one he was not required in law to make, having made such payment by mistake, without knowing that the check had actually been paid and canceled by the drawee bank.

As a general rule, payment under a mistake of fact, which the payer was under no legal obligation to make, may be recovered back. 48 C.J. 759; . . .

We therefore hold that the payment made by Shostak was under a mistake of fact, and that he was legally entitled to recover the amount from the First National Bank of Omaha, which bank had the right to recognize this liability and repay the amount to Shostak, without suit.

This question being settled, it is plain that the defendant bank, having paid a forged check and suffered a direct loss thereon, was entitled, under its blanket bond, to recover the amount of its loss from plaintiff, United States Fidelity and Guaranty Company. . . .

Reversed and dismissed.

CASE NO. 9

Glasscock v. First Nat. Bank. 114 Tex. 207, 266 S.W. 393, 26 A.L.R. 320 (1924)

GREENWOOD, J., delivered the opinion of the court:

The facts are that on October 12 and on October 13, 1916, there was on deposit in appellee bank in the name of Mrs. W. A. Glasscock, subject to her check, a sum exceeding $500. On October 12th she directed her son-in-law, M. J. Rose, to draw a check, payable to his order, for $5. He drew said check in lead pencil, and she signed the same. As drawn the check read:

> San Angelo, Tex., 9/12, 1916. No. .
> The First National Bank: Pay to M. J. Rose or order $5.00 five dollars.
> (Signed) Mrs. W. A. Glasscock

A blank space was left between the words "five" and "dollars," as above indicated, no line being drawn through said space.

The following day Rose presented this check to appellee, and when so presented the figures "$5" had been changed to "$500," and the blank space between the words "five" and "dollars" had been filled in by Rose with lead pencil, so that the same then read:

San Angelo, Tex., 9/12, 1916. No. .
The First National Bank: Pay to M. J. Rose or order $500.00 five hundred dollars, for loan six months.
(Signed) Mrs. W. A. Glasscock

The appellee, without any knowledge that the check had been altered, paid Rose on same $500, and charged that amount to the account of Mrs. Glasscock. Appellant sued the appellee bank to recover this amount, less $5 for which the check was drawn. . . .

We think the sounder principles underlie the cases denying the drawer's liability on a forged instrument which was complete when it left the drawer's hands, though it contained a blank space which made it easier for a forger to raise the instrument.

We see no escape from the conclusion announced by the circuit court of appeals, through Judge Sanborn, in Exchange Nat. Bank v. Bank of Little Rock, 22 L.R.A. 686, 7 C.C.A. Ill., 19 U.S. App. 152, 58 Fed. 140, in the following language:

"When the drawer has issued a draft or note complete in itself, but in such a form as to be easily altered without attracting attention, and it is afterwards fraudulently raised by a third person, without his knowledge or authority, and then bought by an innocent purchaser, it is not his negligence, but the crime of the forger, that is the proximate cause of the loss. Forgery and consequent loss cannot be said to be the natural or probable consequence of issuing a draft inartificially drawn. The presumption is that dealers in commercial paper are honest men, and not forgers, and that such paper will not be changed. It will not do to say that everyone whose negligence invites another to commit a crime is liable to a third party for the loss the latter sustains thereby. One who, by carelessly leaving a pile of shavings near his house, invites another to commit the crime of arson that results in the burning of his neighbor's buildings, is not liable to his neighbor for that loss. The farmer who negligently turns his horse into the highway, and thereby invites a thief to steal it, does not thereby lose title to his horse when an innocent purchaser has bought him of the thief. Nor is there, in our opinion, any sound reason why the liability of the maker of a promissory note or bill of exchange, complete in itself when issued, but subsequently . . . raised without his knowledge or authority, should be measured by the facility with which a third person has committed the crime of forgery upon it, or why he should be held liable for the loss resulting from such a forgery. The altered contract is not his contract. His representation was not that the forged contract was his, but that the original contract was his, and the rule caveat emptor makes it the duty of the purchaser when he buys it, and not of the maker, to then see that it is genuine."

The supreme court of Iowa goes to the heart of the matter in asking:

"But could it be anticipated that

> such negligence would cause another to commit a crime, and can it be said a person is negligent who does not anticipate and provide against the thousand ways through or by which crime is committed?" Knoxville Nat. Bank v. Clark, 51 Iowa, 264, 33 Am. Rep. 135, 1 N.W. 491. . . .

In the instant case, the payee of the check entirely erased the figures "$5" and substituted therefor the figures "$500," and then utterly perverted the scope, purpose, and intent of the check by inserting the word "hundred" in the blank after the written word "five." It is quite too plain for argument that he had no implied authority to do anything he did, and that what he did was utterly beyond the contemplation of the maker of the check; and, we think, she cannot be considered bound by his acts under sound rules of the law of agency, negligence, or estoppel.

The justice of the rule to which we adhere appears to have become generally recognized throughout the United States. All the States, save about four, have adopted a substantially uniform negotiable instruments law, whereby it seems that the material alteration of negotiable paper relieves all parties thereto from liability thereon who have not made, authorized, or approved the alteration, provided that a bona fide holder may nevertheless enforce payment of the paper as it stood prior to its alteration.

We answer that the loss, under the facts certified, must fall on the bank instead of the drawer of the check.

CASE NO. 10

Sabine v. Paine. 223 N.Y. 401, 119 N.E. 849 (1918)

COLLIN, J. . . . The action is upon a promissory note in the sum of $2,100 made by the defendant and owned by the plaintiff. . . . Under the evidence and the decision of the Appellate Division, this appeal presents the single question, Is a usurious promissory note enforceable by a holder in due course? . . .

When the Negotiable Instruments Law was enacted, it was an established rule of law in this state and many other jurisdictions that a holder of a note void by virtue of a statutory declaration because of usury, who became such before the maturity of the note for value and without notice of the usury, could not enforce the note. The rule is an exception to the general principle that a negotiable instrument, in the hands of an innocent holder, who had received it in good faith in the ordinary course of business, for value, and without notice of a defense, is not invalid and is enforceable by the holder. . . .

The rule, constituting an exception to it, rests upon the legislative intention and enactment. An instrument which a statute, expressly or through necessary implication, declares void, . . . is without legal efficacy. It cannot obligate a party or support a right. In Claflin v. Boorum, 122 N.Y. 385, 388, 25 N.E. 360, 361, we said:

> "A note void in its inception for usury continues void forever, whatever its subsequent history may be. It is as void in the hands of those who made the usurious contract. No vitality can be given to it by sale or exchange, because that which the statute has declared void cannot be made valid by passing through the channels of trade. . . ."

The statutes of this state fix the rate of interest upon the loan or forbearance of money at $6 upon $100 for one year, and . . . provide:

> "All bonds, bills, notes, . . . whereupon or whereby there shall be reserved or taken, . . . any greater sum,

or greater value, for the loan or forbearance of any money, goods or other things in action, than is above prescribed, shall be void. Whenever it shall satisfactorily appear by the admissions of the defendant, or by proof, that any bond, bill, note, assurance, pledge, conveyance, contract, security or any evidence of debt, has been taken or received in violation of the foregoing provisions, the court shall declare the same to be void, and enjoin any prosecution thereon, and order the same to be surrendered and canceled." General Business Law (Cons. Laws, c. 20) subsec. 370, 371, 373.

The statute is peremptory and unequivocal in enacting that a usurious obligation is absolutely void.

The Legislature did not by enacting Section 96 of the Negotiable Instruments Law intend to abrogate the rule we have stated. The statute declaring the usurious instrument void is not repealed expressly or through implication. . . .

CASE NO. 11

Gilbert v. Pioneer Nat. Bank of Duluth. 206 Minn. 213, 288 N.W. 153 (1939)

PETERSON, J. One Paquin submitted a bid to sell coal to the city of Duluth. The bid was accompanied by Paquin's check for $1,500 payable to the City of Duluth, which was in lieu of bond as security for making and executing a contract if his bid were accepted. The defendant, having first taken security from Paquin, certified the check under an agreement that Paquin was to deposit the check as security for his bid, and, if his bid were rejected, to return and surrender the check to it, whereupon the bank was to cancel and release the security. The city rejected Paquin's bid and held the check subject to his order. Ten days were to elapse between the opening and awarding or rejection of bids. During this period the Pittsburgh Coal Company, a judgment creditor of Paquin, garnished the check. Plaintiff was appointed receiver of the check in the garnishment proceedings and brings this action as such receiver.

The court below permitted defendant to show the contract between it and Paquin relative to the use to be made of the check. It held that the check was certified and deposited under the special contract between the defendant and Paquin, that Paquin had no right to the check and that plaintiff, standing in the shoes of Paquin's judgment creditor, acquired by the garnishment proceedings no different or greater right than Paquin had. Judgment was ordered for defendant. . . .

As between the immediate parties and as regards a remote party other than a holder in due course, delivery of a negotiable instrument may be for a special purpose only and not for the purpose of transferring the property in the instrument. . . . Where the delivery is for a special purpose only, the taking of security by a party liable on the instrument does not change the nature or effect of the transaction. . . . Since a certified check is in effect an accepted bill of exchange, . . . it may be delivered for a special purpose under the rule.

Plaintiff claims as a holder in due course and cites and relies on National Mechanics' Bank v. Schmelz Nat. Bank, 136 Va. 33, 116 S.E. 380, and similar cases holding that a holder in due course of a certified check takes free from defenses as between the certifying bank and other immediate parties. But plaintiff was not a holder in due course, and the rule relied on does not help him. Whatever rights plaintiff had to the check were acquired in the garnishment proceeding. . . .

. . . . .

Paquin had no right to the check against defendant because of the contract under which the check was delivered. Plaintiff acquired no right against the bank by the garnishment, because there was none, Paquin being without any, to be acquired. Nor did the garnishment enlarge plaintiff's right to those of a holder in due course. . . .

Defendant was not liable to Paquin on the check, nor was it liable to plaintiff standing in his shoes.

Affirmed.

CASE NO. 12

Perry v. Manufacturers Nat. Bank of Lynn. 25 N.E. (2d) 730, 127 A.L.R. 339 (Mass.) (1940)

COX, J., delivered the opinion of the court:

This is an action for the conversion of shares of stock. The answer alleges, among other things, that the stock in question was pledged as collateral for the plaintiff's debt; that the debt being unpaid, the defendant rightfully sold the collateral and applied the proceeds to the payment thereof. . . . The plaintiff excepted to the allowance of the defendant's motion that a verdict be directed for it. The bill of exceptions alleges that

> "The plaintiff's claim that the stock was converted depends upon the plaintiff's claim that prior to the time when the defendant took the stock the notes for which the stock stood as collateral had been avoided by a material alteration."

. . . The stock in question was pledged as collateral for the notes which, as written, bore interest at the rate of five per cent per annum the figure "5" being inserted in the appropriate spaces. It is undisputed that about January 2, 1932, the defendant's note teller drew a pencil line through the figure "5" on the face of each note and inserted in pencil the figure "6". . . . After the figures were changed, the plaintiff paid four quarterly installments of interest at the rate of six per cent. . . . On January 20, 1933 . . . demand was made for payment of the notes. . . . The plaintiff did not pay, and the defendant caused the collateral to be transferred to its name on May 15, 1933, when it purported to sell the collateral to itself, crediting the plaintiff's account with the value thereof computed on the basis of the highest quotation for that date on the New York Stock Exchange. It advised the plaintiff of this, stating that

> " 'from sales today to the Manufacturers National Bank' it had received a total of $45,135.06. . . ."

On October 17, 1935, the defendant sold the securities through its brokers for $66,146.44, and at that time the plaintiff's indebtedness to the bank, with interest computed at five per cent, was $68,178.91. No question is raised as to the accuracy of the figures hereinbefore stated. The principal contention of the plaintiff is that the notes were materially altered without the plaintiff's authority or assent, that they were thereby avoided, and that the sale of the stock was a conversion. . . . The defendant contends . . . that the changes or notations were not material, being in the nature of memoranda. . . .

. . . Section 148, among other things, provides:

> "Any alteration which changes . . . 2. The sum payable, either for principal or interest; . . . is a material alteration."

We are of opinion that there was a material alteration of the notes in question. . . .

Although the material alteration, unassented to by the plaintiff, would avoid the note as to him nevertheless, unless the alteration was fraudulent, it would not presumptively cancel or extinguish the debt for which the note was given, and would not deprive the defendant of the benefit of any security that it may have taken. . . . This rule finds support in other jurisdictions. . . . There was evidence for the jury upon the question whether the alterations were fraudulently made . . . purpose of indicating to its officers and employees the amount of interest that the plaintiff would be expected to pay upon his notes; . . . This evidence was to be weighed by the jury with the fact of the alteration itself. . . .

We, therefore, have a case where (1) there are material alterations of the notes in question; (2) the plaintiff may have assented to them; (3) they may have been made without fraudulent intent, the plaintiff not assenting; (4) they may have been made with fraudulent intent, the plaintiff assenting; and (5) they may have been made with fraudulent intent the plaintiff not assenting. Except for the question of the alterations being material, all the other issues involved were for the jury, and it follows that a verdict could not have been directed for the plaintiff, and also that there was error in directing a verdict for the defendant. . . .

CASE NO. 13

Columbia Grocery Co. v. Marshall. 131 Tenn. 270, 174 S.W. 1108 (1915)

FANCHER, J. The case was brought to collect on an open account, notes which had been executed by defendant covering the account but materially altered by complainants. The case involves the question as to whether suit can be maintained on the original account.

The Columbia Grocery Company is a partnership composed of Mose and Ben Lazarous, doing a wholesale grocery business at Columbia, Tenn. Defendant, O. M. Marshall, was a retail merchant at Campbell's Station, in Maury county, and for several years had purchased goods of the complainants, and a running account had existed for considerable time. Complainants sold this business and desired to close out their accounts. They urged defendant to pay his indebtedness, and he disputed a large part of the account. After some considerable dispute about this, he finally agreed to give his interest-bearing notes, which he did, covering the account. . . . The notes were eleven in number. . . . One note fell due each two months during the years 1914 and 1915. . . .

Ben Lazarous discovered that the bookkeeper had left out a clause they usually inserted in serial notes of this character, and they had it filled in with a typewriter on each note; the first being as follows:

> "This is note 1 of a series of 11, default in payment of any note of this series all notes become due and payable."

Defendant's attention was not called to this alteration. . . . The defendant resists a recovery on the grounds:

First. That the notes were intended and did extinguish the original indebtedness, being taken in settlement and closing out of the account; and that, the notes being void because of the alteration, no recovery can be had.

Second. That, the alteration being fraudulently made, no recovery can be had, regardless of whether the original account was extinguished.

From a review of the authorities,

we are of the opinion that the weight of authority is as follows:

That the taking of a promissory note of a debtor does not extinguish the original debt, nor operate as a payment, unless so intended or agreed between the parties, though it may extend the time of payment, and if for any reason without fraud the creditor loses his right to sue on the note, he is at liberty to sue on the original indebtedness. . . .

It does not clearly appear in the present case that there was an intention, at the time these notes were executed, that they were to settle and extinguish the original demand for goods, wares, and merchandise sold and delivered. And the modern rule being that this intention must appear or else the creditor can sue upon the original debt when he loses his right innocently or without fraud, we reach the conclusion that the case must turn alone on whether the complainants have lost that right on account of their own wrongs.

The question in the case then is: What is the degree of the wrong or the effect of the material alteration made in each of these notes? . . .

If the alteration of a written instrument is made by the holder with a design and intent to defraud the maker, it extinguishes the debt. This rule is founded on public policy, and in order to preserve the integrity of valid legal instruments, by providing a punishment for the wrong, and to deter the holder from tampering with it. If, however, the alteration is without fraudulent intent, while it will destroy the instrument, it will not destroy the right to recover on the original consideration, of which the instrument is a mere evidence. . . .

There is some authority that although the alteration be material and fraudulent, since a bill or note suspends and is not absolute payment of the debt for which it was given, such alteration only extinguishes the security, and the original consideration remains, but this is not sound doctrine. . . .

. . . this act of the complainants . . . was not made in an innocent effort to conform the instrument to the true intention and agreement of the parties or through ignorance, or any other simple, guileless motive. It was a secret and stealthy attempt to gain an advantage. The defendant says that he would not have executed the papers with stipulations that, in the event of default of one, all would become due and payable, and it is reasonable to believe he would not. He was attempting to get a breathing spell between payments so he could meet them, one by one, through a period of two years. His wife had been sick in the hospital, and he was embarrassed financially. His debts were pressing him. These insertions in the notes destroyed the whole advantage he had gained by losing the account and substituting time notes, if he should be so unfortunate as to fail in one small payment. . . .

Affirmed for defendant.

Review Questions

1. What is the importance of acquiring rights evidenced by a negotiable instrument either as a holder in due course or through a holder in due course?
2. Upon what reasoning is it held that a holder who derives his title through a holder in due course acquires as good a title as that possessed by the holder in due course?
3. What requirements must the holder of an instrument meet before he can occupy the preferred position of a holder in due course?

4. Can the acquirer of an instrument "payable thirty days from date," upon which no date appears, assert the position of a holder in due course?
5. Does it necessarily follow that one who has acquired an instrument after its maturity is subject to all the defenses existing against the instrument?
6. When is a demand instrument overdue?
7. What is the test of bad faith such as would prevent a holder from becoming a holder in due course?
8. Why should the fact that a note has been purchased at a substantial discount not be accepted in itself as conclusive evidence of bad faith?
9. How does the requirement of value differ from consideration?
10. To what extent can a lien holder of a negotiable instrument recover upon it?
11. Does a bank become a holder in due course of an instrument for which it gave the holder deposit credit rather than cash?
12. Construct a fact situation under which the payee named in the instrument would be a holder in due course.
13. What is the difference between immediate and remote parties to negotiable instruments?
14. When may the drawer of a check assert any of the personal defenses against the holder of the check?
15. Are the real defenses available against all holders of negotiable instruments?
16. Can a person who has paid an instrument to which his name has been forged recover the payment?
17. Can a drawee bank who has made payment upon a forged check recover the payment?
18. When is an alteration of an instrument material?
19. Is an instrument that has been materially altered completely invalid in the hands of a holder in due course?
20. Explain the defense of want of execution and delivery.
21. Is illegality a real or a personal defense?
22. May a minor disaffirm his obligation upon a note that he has executed and that is in the hands of a holder in due course?
23. Enumerate some of the more important personal defenses that are cut off by a negotiation of an instrument.
24. When will delivery of an instrument be conclusively presumed?
25. Is it possible that an instrument, unsupported by consideration at the time of its issue, can become enforceable against the promisor?
26. Construct a fact situation illustrating a conditional delivery of a negotiable instrument.
27. To what extent is a material alteration a personal defense only?
28. Will a party who innocently altered an instrument be denied recovery?
29. Why should the maker of a promissory note demand its surrender from the holder at the time he makes payment?

Problems for Discussion

1. After having been duly executed, bearer bonds of the X City were stolen from the city's lock box. The thief sold them to Brown, who qualified as a holder in due course. The Y Bank, with knowledge that the bonds had been stolen, ac-

cepted the bonds from Brown as collateral to secure a loan. What is the position of the Y Bank as holder of the bonds against the X City?

2. A trade acceptance which was dated August 1, 1919, provided for payment December 1. Was this instrument complete and regular upon its face? (*United Ry.* v. *Siberian Comm. Co.*, 117 Wash. 347)
3. The defendant, for the accommodation of the maker, indorsed a promissory note. After the indorsement and without the knowledge of the defendant, the maker added the words "with interest" to the face of the note. Can the plaintiff, who is a holder in due course, recover? (*McGrath* v. *Clark*, 56 N.Y. 34)
4. X purchased a $1,000 note from Y, the payee, for the sum of $500. Should this evidence be accepted as conclusive of bad faith?
5. X employed Y to present a check to the drawee bank for payment. The bank dishonored the check without stating any reason for its refusal to pay. The fact was that the drawer of the check, Brown, had exhausted his credit with the bank. Y then accepted the check from X in payment for services rendered to X. Does Y stand as a holder in due course of the check?
6. Why did Brown, the owner of a retail establishment, issue instructions to his employees not to accept checks when presented ten days after the date of issue?
7. M accepted an instrument payable to the X Corporation from P, one of its officers, in discharge of a personal obligation from P to M. Is M to be regarded as a holder in due course?
8. X accepted a negotiable instrument from Y by special indorsement. X had knowledge of the fact that five years previously Y had been guilty of fraud in accepting negotiable paper in exchange for worthless securities. Does this prevent X from being a good faith holder of the instrument?
9. The appellants Clark are the owners of certain real property in the city of Seattle on which they constructed a dwelling. At the time the house was in process of construction, Fraser was the manager of the Enterprise Plumbing Company, and as such manager contracted with the Clarks to furnish the necessary materials and to do certain plumbing required by the plans of the house. After he had partially performed his contract, he informed the appellants that the balance of the material to complete the work would cost between $65 and $70, and that he did not have such materials and could not obtain them on credit, but that they could be procured from the plaintiff. The appellant Charles Clark thereupon made out a check for the sum of $70, payable to the plaintiff, and delivered it to Fraser with the request that he get the necessary materials from the plaintiff and deliver the check to it in payment. Fraser took the check and delivered it to the plaintiff as directed, but requested it at the time he did so to credit $36.71 thereof to a certain account which he had theretofore purchased for the Clark dwelling and for which he had not paid, to credit $18.29 thereof to his general account, and to pay him the balance of $15 in cash. The plaintiff cashed the check and made disposition of the money as thus requested. Later on Fraser obtained from the plaintiff plumbing supplies of the value of $68.74, which were delivered at the house of the appellants and actually used by Fraser in completing his plumbing contract with them. During all this time the appellants and the plaintiff were strangers, having had no direct dealings with each other of any kind whatsoever. Was plaintiff a holder in due course? (*Bowles Co.* v. *Fraser*, 109 Pac. 812)

10. X and Y were business partners. X executed his promissory note to Brown as evidence of X's obligation to Brown for the installation of a furnace in the residence of X. Brown, being in need of money, sold the note to Y. When X learned that Y was the holder of the note, he assured Y that he would never pay the note, since the furnace failed to perform as Brown had guaranteed it would. X contends that Y, by failing to make inquiry of him before purchasing the note, was not acting in good faith and consequently was not a holder in due course. Decide.
11. The payee of a negotiable instrument negotiated it to his creditor in payment of a debt. The creditor sues the maker, who establishes the fact that the payee had never given the promised consideration for the note. Can the creditor recover from the maker?
12. D has a balance of $1,000 in the X bank. He deposits a check for $500 and then draws out $750. Is the bank a holder in due course of the check representing the deposit?
13. On July 20, 1909, plaintiff signed his name to a blank check. Thereafter David Ryckoff and Benjamin Silberman stole the check, filled in the name of F. A. Mann as payee and the sum of $147.87 as the amount thereof, and presented it to the State Bank, where plaintiff kept his account, and procured it to be certified. Thereafter they indorsed said check with the name of F. A. Mann and passed it to defendant for value, who collected the amount thereof from the said bank. Plaintiff, having taken up said check from the bank, now sues defendant as for money had and received for the amount of the check. Decide. (*Linick* v. *A. J. Nutting & Co.*, 125 N.Y. Supp. 93)
14. Brown indorses a $1,000 promissory note, upon which Brown is the payee, to Black as security for a $500 debt which Brown owes Black. Upon maturity of the instrument, what are Black's rights against the maker White under the following conditions:
    (a) White has a counterclaim of $800 against Brown?
    (b) White has no defenses or claims against Brown?
15. Brown, a holder in due course, presented a promissory note, upon which White's name appeared as maker, at White's office for payment. White's cashier paid the note. It was then discovered that the note was a forgery. Can White recover the amount paid to Brown?
16. X signed a blank check and left it on his desk for his secretary to complete after securing the necessary information. Y, the office boy, falls to temptation and appropriates the instrument. He writes in the amount of $100 and makes it payable to himself. C, a holder in due course, acquires the instrument and sues A for the amount. Can he recover?
17. X's negotiable bearer bond, which he acquired directly from the obligor, was stolen from him after maturity. The thief sold the bond to Y, an innocent purchaser. Upon discovering the bond in Y's possession, X brings an action of replevin. Result?
18. Suit to recover from B. T. Lanier and W. R. Miller the amount of a promissory note. Said note was executed by Lanier and delivered by him to W. R. Miller, and afterwards, before maturity, in due course of trade, for a valuable consideration they became the owners of said paper. The defendant Lanier filed his sworn plea of non est factum, the particular vice in said note sought to be

reached by the plea being that the note had been fraudulently altered after its delivery to Miller by erasing therefrom the following memorandum: "The consideration of this note to be paid by four lots in Bunkley's addition to the town of Stamford." Plaintiffs replied that, if such alteration had been made, they had no notice of the same, and that said note was by defendant Lanier so carelessly drawn and made that such change, if any, did not and does not show or evidence itself to plaintiffs or any other prudent person, whereby the defendant is estopped to deny the execution of the note as sued on. Decide. (*Lanier* v. *Clarke,* 133 S.W. 1093)

19. Pioneer Bank issued its cashier's negotiable certificate for $300 to V. L. Norrell, who subsequently indorsed and delivered it to P. A. King in payment of a gambling debt. Thereafter, King indorsed and delivered the check to complainant, operating Winecoff Hotel, in due course for full consideration, without notice of the gambling transaction.

    Meanwhile, however, Norrell, the payee, had notified the maker bank not to pay the check, and the bank refusing payment upon presentation, the Hotel company brought this suit. Decide. (*Winecoff Operating Co. Inc.* v. *Pioneer Bank,* 165, S.W. (2d) 585)

21 NEGOTIABLE INSTRUMENTS:

LIABILITY OF PARTIES

► I. PRIMARY AND SECONDARY PARTIES DISTINGUISHED

Parties whose names appear on negotiable instruments have either a *primary* or a *secondary* liability to pay.

A. PRIMARY LIABILITY

A *primary* liability is an absolute and unconditional liability, a liability that attaches in accordance with the terms of the instrument as soon as the name is placed upon the instrument. Parties possessing a primary liability are (1) makers of promissory notes; (2) acceptors of bills of exchange.

B. SECONDARY LIABILITY

A *secondary* liability is, as the term suggests, a conditional liability, a liability that attaches only when the primary party has failed in his undertaking and the holder has complied with certain conditions. A secondary party is one, who, by his signature, gives an assurance that he will pay if (1) the instrument is properly presented to the primary party for payment or acceptance; (2) the instrument is dishonored; (3) the instrument is protested when necessary; and (4) he is properly notified of such dishonor. These conditions need not be complied with if they have been waived by the terms of the instrument. Parties possessing a secondary liability are (1) drawers of bills of exchange including checks; (2) indorsers.

► II. CONTRACTUAL UNDERTAKINGS OF PRIMARY PARTIES

A. THE MAKER

In addition to expressly undertaking to pay the note in accordance with its terms, the maker of a promissory note also impliedly makes certain admissions, for which he will be held responsible. Section 60 of the N.I.L. declares:

> "The maker of a negotiable instrument by making it engages that he will pay it according to its tenor, and admits the existence of the payee and his then capacity to indorse."

1. *Admission of Existence of Payee*

By executing a note, a maker impliedly represents that the payee as named in the instrument is existing. He cannot thereafter deny his liability upon the grounds that no such payee exists in fact. Consequently, a nonexistent corporate payee can enforce a note against the maker. The maker will not be heard to deny the corporate existence of the payee.

In *Engle System Co.* v. *Norris,* 132 Tenn. 472, a note payable to "The Ingle System Co.," a nonexistent corporation, was held to be enforceable by the plaintiff, to whom it was given by the maker, without the need of proving that the payee was in fact a corporation. By the execution of the note, the maker admitted the existence of the corporation, although in fact it was nonexistent.

2. *Admission of Payee's Capacity to Indorse*

By executing a note, the maker also impliedly represents to the world that the payee named has the capacity to indorse at the time of the execution of the instrument. He represents that the payee can transfer a good and valid title to the instrument by indorsement. The result follows that the maker cannot deny the holder's title or the holder's right to enforce the note even though the payee is an infant, a bankrupt, a thief who inserted his own name as payee, a corporation who acted beyond its corporate powers, or any person legally incompetent or legally denied the right to act.

This principle has been applied most frequently to instruments made payable to unlicensed foreign corporations. Although by virtue of its failure to meet the statutory requirements to do business such a corporation is denied the right to enforce the contract, nevertheless, in the hands of a holder in due course the instrument is enforceable against the maker. By the execution of the instrument, the maker admits the capacity of the unlicensed corporation to transfer a valid title by indorsement.

B. DRAWEE AS ACCEPTOR

1. *Liability to Pay Based on Acceptance*

Negotiable instruments are payable either immediately or at some future time. If a bill of exchange is immediately payable, it will be presented to the drawee for payment; on the other hand, if payable at some future time, the bill of exchange will be presented to the drawee for his acceptance. The drawee of a bill of exchange has no liability on the instrument unless and until he signifies his assent to honor the order of the drawer. By obtaining an acceptance prior to the maturity of the bill, the holder can add the drawee's credit to the instrument. The drawee's assent to be bound by the instrument must be in writing and signed by the drawee. The usual method of indicating the acceptance of the drawer's order is for the drawee to write the word *accepted* upon the face of the instrument, with the date and his signature, thus:

"Accepted
11/14/46
(*Signature of Drawee*)"

Thereupon the drawee acquires a primary liability to pay the instrument. As it is expressed by Section 62 of the N.I.L.,

"The acceptor by accepting the instrument engages that he will pay it according to the tenor of his acceptance."

a. Modes of Acceptance. Section 133 of the N.I.L. provides that:

"The holder of a bill presenting the same for acceptance may require that the acceptance be written on the bill, and, if such request is refused, may treat the bill as dishonored."

No special words need be written on the instrument to constitute a valid acceptance. In fact, the mere signature of the drawee stands as an acceptance of the obligation by him. An acceptance may be written upon a separate piece of paper such as a letter or a telegram. Section 134 of the N.I.L. reads:

"Where an acceptance is written on paper other than the bill itself, it does not bind the acceptor except in favor of a person to whom it is shown and who, on the faith thereof, receives the bill for value."

The writing must, however, unequivocally indicate that an acceptance was intended.[1] To illustrate:

(1) Such expressions by the drawee as "We will honor," "Will pay the draft," "Forward your checks. They will undoubtedly be taken care of . . . when presented," and "We will protect this check," have been held to be unconditional acceptances.

(2) On the other hand, such expressions as "The draft is good," and "Have funds with which to pay the draft" have been held not to be acceptances.

A promise to accept a bill may be the equivalent of an acceptance. Section 135 reads:

"An unconditional promise in writing to accept a bill before it is drawn is deemed an actual acceptance in favor of every person who, upon the faith thereof, receives the bill for value."

Section 137 deals with situations under which an acceptance will be implied. Although Section 136 gives the drawee twenty-four hours within which to decide whether or not to accept the bill, he has no right to retain the bill should the owner demand its return. A failure to return the instrument is interpreted as constituting an acceptance. Section 137 provides:

"Where a drawee to whom a bill is delivered for acceptance destroys the same, or refuses within twenty-four hours after such delivery, or within such other period as the holder may allow, to return the bill accepted or nonaccepted to the holder, he will be deemed to have accepted the same."

2. *Liability upon Raised Instruments*

That part of Section 62 which is quoted above has created some doubt as to the extent of the liability of an acceptor of a raised instrument. Prior to the passage of the N.I.L., an acceptor was held liable only for the amount ordered paid by the drawer. For example, by accepting a bill raised from $10 to $100, a drawee was liable only for the amount ordered paid by the drawer, namely, $10. It would seem that this common law rule has been abrogated by the passage of the N.I.L. Un-

[1] Night & Day Bank v. First Nat. Bank of Shreveport, p. 543.

equivocally Section 62 reads that the acceptor engages to pay according to the tenor of his acceptance. The tenor of the drawer's acceptance of a raised instrument is certainly the amount as it appears upon the instrument. Some courts have accepted this meaning and have held the acceptor liable to the extent of the raised figure. However, this seems far from being the accepted rule at the present time.

3. *Implied Admissions*

In addition to his primary liability to pay, the drawee admits upon acceptance (Section 62 of the N.I.L):

> "(1) The existence of the drawer, the genuineness of his signature, and his capacity and authority to draw the instrument; and
>
> (2) The existence of the payee and his then capacity to indorse."

Problems similar to those already considered in connection with the admissions of a maker of a promissory note are raised by the admissions pertaining to the existence of the drawer and his capacity and authority to draw the instrument. This is also true as to admissions pertaining to the existence of the payee and his then capacity to indorse the instrument.[2]

By virtue of his relationship with the drawer, the drawee is presumed to know the latter's signature. Usually the drawee is in such a position that the genuineness of the drawer's signature can be ascertained. This is especially true in the case of a drawee bank. Consequently, when an instrument in the hands of a holder in due course is accepted by the drawee, he acknowledges that the drawer's signature is genuine, and he accepts the responsibility to pay the instrument even though the signature is forged.

► III. CONTRACTUAL UNDERTAKING OF SECONDARY PARTIES

A. THE DRAWER

The liability of the drawer of a bill of exchange—exclusive of a check—to pay the instrument is conditional. He engages to pay the bill only in the event of compliance with certain conditions. Section 61 of the N.I.L. declares that:

> "The drawer by drawing the instrument . . . engages that on due presentment the instrument will be accepted or paid, or both, according to its tenor, and that if it be dishonored, and the necessary proceedings on dishonor be duly taken, he will pay the amount thereof to the holder, or to any subsequent indorser who may be compelled to pay it. . . ."

The drawer of a bill of exchange, like the maker of a promissory note, as provided by Section 61 of the N.I.L., ". . . admits the existence of the payee and his then capacity to indorse. . . ."

---

[2] Nat. City Bank of Chicago v. Nat. Bank of Republic, p. 544.

B. INDORSERS

The liability of an indorser on a negotiable instrument is dependent upon the nature of his indorsement; it is dependent upon whether he indorsed with or without qualifications.

1. *Qualified Indorsers*

A qualified indorser—one who indorses "without recourse"—does not undertake to pay the instrument in the event of its dishonor. The purpose of a qualified indorsement is to pass title to the instrument without incurring liability for its payment. Like an assignor, the qualified indorser gives no assurance that the primary parties will or can pay the instrument.

Although the qualified indorser does not undertake to pay the instrument, he does, by virtue of his indorsement, make certain implied warranties pertaining to the instrument. Section 65 of the N.I.L. declares:

> "Every person negotiating an instrument by delivery or by a qualified indorsement, warrants:
>
> (1) That the instrument is genuine and in all respects what it purports to be;
>
> (2) That he has a good title to it;
>
> (3) That all prior parties had capacity to contract;
>
> (4) That he has no knowledge of any fact which would impair the validity of the instrument or render it valueless."

Should there be a failure of these warranties, the indorser will be held absolutely responsible for any loss occasioned the holder. For example, a qualified indorser would be liable to the holder of a note where the name of the maker has been forged or where the infant maker has disaffirmed his contractual undertaking. The holder of an instrument secured by collateral that he knows has become impaired may for that very reason be prompted to negotiate the instrument *without recourse.* Nevertheless, in the event that the instrument is not paid, a subsequent holder may look to the qualified indorser for breach of the implied warranty that he had no knowledge of any fact that would render the instrument valueless.[3, 4]

Let it be noted that the liability of a transferor of bearer paper is the same as that of a qualified indorser. Whereas a qualified indorser (like an unqualified indorser) is liable to all subsequent parties, the transferor of bearer paper is liable only to his immediate transferee. Section 65 of the N.I.L. reads:

> "But when the negotiation is by delivery only, the warranty extends in favor of no holder other than the immediate transferee."

2. *Unqualified Indorsers*

An unqualified indorser assumes a conditional liability to pay the instrument in the event of its dishonor. Like the drawer of a bill of exchange, he engages to

[3] Leekley v. Short, p. 545.
[4] State Bank of Lehr v. Lehr Auto & Machine Co., p. 546.

pay upon the conditions that the instrument has been duly presented, has been dishonored, and that the proper proceedings on dishonor have been taken. Such proper proceedings are:

(1) Protest of the instrument if necessary; and

(2) Notice of dishonor to the indorser.

The holder of an instrument should recognize that if he wishes to preserve his recourse for payment against an indorser, he must meet the following requirements:

(1) The instrument must be presented for payment or acceptance as provided by law;

(2) In the event of dishonor, the instrument, if a foreign bill, must be protested; and

(3) Proper notice of the dishonor must be given the indorsers.

A failure to meet any of these requirements will discharge the indorser from any further liability for the instrument.

In addition to the unqualified indorser's conditional liability to pay the instrument, he impliedly warrants the instrument in certain respects. Section 66 of the N.I.L. declares:

> "Every indorser who indorses without qualification, warrants to all subsequent holders in due course:
>
> (1) The matters and things mentioned in subdivisions one, two, and three of the next preceding section; and,
>
> (2) That the instrument is at the time of his indorsement valid and subsisting." [5]

Thus, if an instrument is unenforceable against the primary obligor because of illegality, the indorser stands responsible.

► IV. ACCOMMODATION PARTIES

Frequently, persons lend their names upon negotiable paper for the purpose of giving the holder greater security. For example, a person may indorse an instrument without having any interest in the instrument itself, for the purpose of standing as security in event that the instrument is not paid and thereby giving the instrument greater acceptability. Section 29 of the N.I.L. defines an accommodation party as being:

> ". . . one who has signed the instrument as maker, drawer, acceptor, or indorser, without receiving value therefor, and for the purpose of lending his name to some other person."

Section 29 establishes the liability of an accommodation party in these words:

> "Such a person is liable on the instrument to a holder for value, notwithstanding such holder at the time of taking the instrument knew him to be only an accommodation party."

Any person who lends his name to another upon negotiable paper should be fully cognizant of the fact that he acquires the same responsibility as a regular party

[5] Wachova Bank & T. Co. v. Crafton, p. 547.

to the paper.[6, 7] In general it can be said that an accommodation party is liable to all parties on the instrument subsequent to the party accommodated. However, the party for whose accommodation the instrument was signed cannot look to the accommodation party for satisfaction. For example, if the payee of a note should induce Mr. X to indorse the instrument for accommodation, the indorser X would not be liable to the payee even though the instrument was indorsed prior to the delivery of the note to the payee.

CASES

CASE NO. 1

Night & Day Bank v. First National Bank of Shreveport. 150 La. 954, 91 So. 405, 26 A.L.R. 310 (1922)

PROVOSTY, CH.J., delivered the opinion of the court:

The plaintiff, a bank of St. Louis, Missouri, sues the defendant, a bank of Shreveport, Louisiana, upon a check payment of which was refused for want of funds to the credit of the drawer. The question is whether two certain telegrams sent by the defendant bank, on the faith of which the check was cashed by plaintiff, amounted to an acceptance of the check or a promise to pay it on presentation. The check was to the order of W. J. Burroughs, who sent the following telegram to defendant: "Is check of E. O. Shad Harper for $220 good?"

Defendant's telegram in answer was: "We have funds to pay check E. O. Shad Harper for $220."

The check and these telegrams being presented to the plaintiff bank, it sent to the defendant the following telegram:

"Confirm your wire of to-day to W. J. Burroughs that you will honor $220 check E. O. Shad Harper."

Defendant telegraphed back:

"This confirms our telegram to W. J. Burroughs that we have funds to pay draft E. O. Shad Harper for $220."

These telegrams of defendant simply imparted the information that the balance of the drawer was sufficient to meet the check, and did not import an acceptance of the check or a promise to pay it. They seem to have been carefully worded for guarding against acceptance of promise to pay. In fact, the person who sent them testified that he took this wording from the code of the American Bankers' Association, where for saying exactly what was said in these telegrams the word "lounging" is to be used, and for accepting or promising to pay a check the word "lovebird" is to be used.

The law as to whether a wording such as that of these telegrams imports acceptance or promise to pay is stated in a note in 8 L.R.A. (N.S.) 1148, as follows:

"It seems to be a well-settled rule of law that the drawee of a check will not be liable to the holder thereof upon a claimed contract of acceptance external to the check, where the alleged agreement upon the part of the drawee is based upon its statement that the check is 'good,' or 'all right,' or words of like import."

The complaint of plaintiff is that it was misled to its prejudice by these telegrams. If so, plaintiff has but itself to

[6] Elkhorn Production Credit Assoc. v. Johnson, p. 548.
[7] Leonard v. Woodward, p. 549.

blame for not having known better the import of language. Moreover, plaintiff, at the time it cashed this check, was a member of the American Bankers' Association, and should have known that the said telegrams used the formula of that association for simply advising of the present condition of a depositor's balance. . . .

CASE NO. 2

National City Bank of Chicago v. National Bank of the Republic of Chicago. 300 Ill. 103, 132 N.E. 832, 1153 (1921)

THOMPSON, J., delivered the opinion of the court:

On January 4, 1915, the Jackes-Evans Manufacturing Company of St. Louis purchased a draft for $629.80 from the Broadway Savings Trust Company of St. Louis, drawn on the National City Bank of Chicago and payable to the order of the American Sheet & Tin Plate Company of Pittsburgh. On the same day the St. Louis company inclosed the draft in a letter addressed to the Pittsburgh company, and deposited the letter in a mail box. Andrew H. Manning rifled this mail box and stole the draft. He substituted his name for the name of the American Sheet & Tin Plate company. The alteration of the draft was done with such skill that it could not be detected by inspection. January 9, Manning appeared at Barnett Brothers' jewelry store, in Chicago, and selected and agreed to purchase certain diamonds for $600. In payment of the purchase price Manning tendered to P. Barnett the altered draft for $629.80. Manning, in the presence of Barnett, indorsed the draft in blank, and Barnett, with the consent of Manning, took the draft to the drawee, the National City Bank of Chicago, and personally presented it to that bank for acceptance. The bank accepted the draft by writing across the face of the draft these words and figures:

"Accepted, payable through Chicago clearing house 55,055, Jan. 9, '15 —The National City Bank of Chicago. per G. D. Grim, Paying Teller." . . .

. . . Thereafter Barnett indorsed the draft to the order of the National Bank of the Republic, and January 11, 1915, deposited the draft to the credit of his account with said bank. January 12, 1915, the National City Bank, the drawee, through the Chicago clearing house, paid the National Bank of the Republic the sum of $629.80 in payment of the draft. February 4, 1915, the National City Bank returned to its customer, the Broadway Savings Company, this draft, along with other canceled paper for January. The draft was received in St. Louis the following day, and the St. Louis bank at once notified its Chicago correspondent, the drawee, that the draft had been altered by changing the name of the payee, and asked that its account be credited with the amount of the draft. The drawee in turn notified the National Bank of the Republic of the alteration, and asked for reimbursement, which was refused. The drawee voluntarily credited the account of the St. Louis bank with the amount of the draft, and brought suit in the circuit court of Cook county against the National Bank of the Republic to recover the amount paid on this draft. Judgment was rendered in favor of the drawee, and that judgment was affirmed, on appeal, by the appellate court for the first district. . . .

In its last analysis the question presented for decision is the liability of the accepter of a negotiable instrument under § 62 of the Negotiable Instruments Law . . . which provides:

"The accepter by accepting the instrument engages that he will pay it according to the tenor of his acceptance, and admits:

1. The existence of the drawer, the genuineness of his signature, and his capacity and authority to draw the instrument; and

2. The existence of the payee and his then capacity to indorse."

The instrument which appellee accepted was payable "to the order of Andrew H. Manning." By its acceptance it admitted that Andrew H. Manning was in existence, and that Andrew H. Manning at the time of acceptance was not suffering any legal disability which would affect his ability to pass title to the instrument accepted by means of indorsement. According to the plain language of this section, appellee, by its general acceptance, bound itself to pay a draft for $629.80, payable to the order of Andrew H. Manning. After the draft was accepted by appellee the drawer was discharged from liability thereon. . . . This construction of § 62 is in accordance with that sound principle which declares that where one of two innocent parties must suffer a loss the law will leave the loss where it finds it.

The judgments of the Appellate and Circuit Courts are reversed.

CASE NO. 3

Leekley v. Short. 216 Iowa 376, 249 N.W. 363 (1933)

An action in equity to foreclose a real-estate mortgage and for judgment upon the note against the makers and against an indorser "without recourse" under implied warranties claimed to exist under section 9525 of the 1931 Code. A motion to dismiss the petition was sustained and an order and judgment of dismissal entered. Plaintiff appeals.

ANDERSON, J. . . . plaintiff's petition is in the ordinary form of a suit in foreclosure, and alleges that on the fifth day of June, 1931, the defendants I. E. and Erma Short executed and delivered to Ella B. Ward a promissory note for $10,000 due March 1, 1936; that said note was secured by mortgage upon 270 acres of farm land in Butler County, Iowa; . . . that on or about the first day of August, 1931, the plaintiff purchased from Ella B. Ward the said note and mortgage and paid therefor in property reasonably worth $10,000, and $208 in cash. Ella B. Ward indorsing the said note as follows: "Without recourse on me pay to the order of ——." At the same time . . . Ella B. Ward executed a written assignment to the plaintiff, assigning the note and mortgage; said written assignment being made "without recourse" . . . interest and the taxes due September 1, 1931, had become delinquent and remained unpaid; . . . and by reason of said delinquencies, the plaintiff elected to declare the whole amount of said mortgage and note due and payable. The petition further alleges that the said real estate is not worth the sum of $10,000 and is not worth more than $6,500; . . . that the defendants I. E. and Erma Short are insolvent and were insolvent at the time the note and mortgage were executed.

The . . . claim is that even though a note is transferred by a qualified indorsement, if the indorser knew that the note was of no value and that the person could not collect it, such indorser thereby perpetrated fraud upon the purchaser and obtained the money upon false pretense. The appellant contends in argument that the appellee knew she was selling a worthless note to the plaintiff. . . . The plaintiff's petition is a complete answer to this contention. The petition alleging that this particular note was not worth more than $6,500 and "will not sell at sheriff's sale for an amount in excess of $6,500." The conclusion necessarily follows that the note was not valueless and that the defendant had "no knowledge of any fact which would impair the validity of the instrument or render it valueless." It also follows that there was no breach of an implied warranty that the note was not "valueless." The fact that the note was not worth par does not render it valueless or impair its validity.

The warranties implied by the statute, accompanying an indorsement without recourse, do not include the solvency of the maker, but are restricted to matters affecting the legal enforceability of the paper; and, without an allegation of fraud or deceit, there can be no recovery thereon based upon the insolvency of the maker or his inability to pay. . . .

CASE NO. 4

State Bank of Lehr v. Lehr Auto & Machine Co. 54 N.D. 608, 210 N.W. 89 (1926)

CHRISTIANSON, C.J. . . . Briefly stated the controlling facts alleged in the complaint are: That on or about May 9, 1919, one Ed Sukut executed and delivered to the defendant, the Lehr Auto & Machine Company, a promissory note in the sum of $1,750, payable October 1, 1919, . . . That on or about September 26, 1919, . . .

> "the defendant did then and there indorse, sell, and set over the above-described note to this plaintiff by a qualified indorsement without recourse . . ."

The complaint further alleges that said note was executed and delivered to the defendant by said Sukut in consideration of a gas tractor and a set of plows which were sold by the defendant to Sukut upon an express warranty as to the workmanship, material used, general construction, and adaptability to perform the work for which they were purchased; that said machinery failed to comply with the warranty in any respect, and that such machinery was tendered back to the defendant by said Sukut, who at the time of the tender demanded a return of his note; that this all occurred before the defendant sold the note to the plaintiff; and that the defendant had knowledge of such breach of warranty prior to September 20, 1919, but that all of such facts were unknown to the plaintiff at and prior to the time that it purchased the note from the defendant. . . .

The cause of action before us is predicated upon . . . section 65, Uniform Negotiable Instruments Law . . .

The question presented for determination is: Do the facts set forth in the complaint in this case constitute a cause of action for a breach of warranty under this section? In our opinion this question must be answered in the affirmative. By the express language of this section every person who negotiates an instrument by a qualified indorsement enters into a contract with the person to whom the instrument is negotiated to the effect that he warrants, among other things, that

> "he has no knowledge of any fact which will impair the validity of the instrument or render it valueless."

This contract is as explicit and as binding as if the provisions of the section were written out in full over the signature of the indorser on the back of the note.

If a person desires to qualify or limit the contract which the law in effect writes over his signature when he places his name under a qualified indorsement on the back of a negotiable instrument, he ought to do so by appropriate recital to that effect. In this case the defendant merely indorsed the note without recourse. The result was that it entered into a contract with the plaintiff to the effect that the defendant warranted to the plaintiff that it had no knowledge of any fact which would impair the validity of the instrument or render it valueless. . . . According to the allegations of the complaint, at the time the defendant negotiated the note to the plaintiff the maker of the note had a complete defense thereto as against the defendant or any holder thereof other than a holder in due course, and these facts were all known to the defendant, but were unknown to the plaintiff who purchased the instrument in reliance upon the warranties given by the defendant as a part of the transaction incident to the negotiation of the note. The negotiation by the defendant of the promissory note, without recourse, in these circumstances renders it liable to the indorsee for damages resulting from a breach of the warranty on the part of the defendant that it had no knowledge of any fact which would impair the validity of the instrument or render it valueless. . . .

CASE NO. 5

Wachova Bank & T. Co. v. Crafton. 181 N.C. 404, 107 S.E. 316, 16 A.L.R. 1375 (1921)

Statement by HOKE, J. . . . The action is brought by an indorsee and holder in due course of a promissory note given by one J. M. Carver to J. W. Crafton, defendant, for money won by defendant in a game of cards, and indorsed by the defendant, the payee of the note in due course and for value to plaintiff bank. There was denial of liability, the defendant, the indorser, alleging that the note in question was for an amount won in a gambling transaction. . . .

HOKE, J., delivered the opinion of the court:

Our statute applicable to the note in question . . . renders this and all notes and contracts in like cases void, and it is urged in support of his Honor's ruling that, this being true, no action thereon can be sustained. The position as stated is undoubtedly the law in this jurisdiction, and is in accord with well-considered authorities elsewhere. . . .

This principle, however, is allowed to prevail only where the action is on the note to enforce its obligations, and does not affect or extend to suits by an innocent indorsee for value and holder in due course, against the indorser on his contract of indorsement. It is very generally held—uniformly, as far as examined—that this contract of indorsement is a substantive contract, separable and independent of the instrument on which it appears, and, where it has been made without qualification and for value, it guarantees to a holder in due course, among other things, that the instrument, at the time of the indorsement, is a valid and subsisting obligation. It is so expressly provided in our statutes on negotiable instruments . . . and the statute in this respect, as in so many of its other features, is but a codification of the general principles of this branch of the mercantile law, as established in the better-considered decisions on the subject. . . .

And in Norton on Bills & Notes it is said that

> "every indorser who indorses without qualification warrants to his indorsee and to all subsequent holders," among other things, "that the bill or note is a valid and subsisting obligation."

In applying these principles, the cases hold that, on breach of the contract of indorsement, a recovery by a holder in due course will be sustained against the indorser, though the instrument is rendered void by the statute law. . . .

On both reason and authority,

therefore, the defendant should be held liable for breach of his own contract of indorsement, and under the facts established by the verdict, there should be judgment for plaintiff.

CASE NO. 6

Elkhorn Production Credit Assoc. v. Johnson. 251 Wis. 280, 29 N.W. (2d) 64, 2 A.L.R. (2d) 256 (1947)

FRITZ, J. In the case at bar the material matters of fact are to the following effect: The respondent signed the note as an accommodation maker for his son, with the knowledge of plaintiff, the payee and holder thereof, and in connection with and as security for the note, the son gave plaintiff as security for the note a chattel mortgage on certain farm machinery. . . . Subsequently, plaintiff without respondent's knowledge agreed with the son to release the lien of the mortgage on the tractor, and upon respondent's being advised that the son sold the tractor, respondent immediately conferred with plaintiff and objected to its releasing said lien thereon and informed the plaintiff that respondent would assume no further obligation on the note. But plaintiff released said lien over respondent's objection and without his knowledge. When the note became due the son defaulted in the payment thereof. . . .

The court stated . . . that respondent

"in the execution of the note of April 16, 1945, payable to the plaintiff, as an accommodation maker was a surety and secondarily liable on the note." . . .

. . . The respondent was primarily —and not merely secondarily—liable to the plaintiff, even though it knew him to be only an accommodation party. The following provisions in § 117.38 (42), Stats. are not applicable to the facts:

"A person secondarily liable on the instrument is discharged: . . . By giving up or applying to other purposes collateral security applicable to the debt, or, there being in the holder's hands or within his control the means of complete or partial satisfaction, the same are applied to other purposes."

In Bosworth v. Greiling, 213 Wis. 443, 250 N.W. 856, the action was to recover on a note signed by the defendant Greiling as an accommodation maker. His second contention was:

"that it should be held that the note was discharged, since the defendant was an accommodation maker, and the bank from time to time, as the company deposited moneys with it, had within its control the means of complete satisfaction of the note."

In relation to that contention this court said, 213 Wis. at page 449, 250 N.W. at p. 858:

"The difficulty with defendant's second contention is that, while he was an accommodation maker, his liability to the bank was primary. . . . The contention that defendant was discharged because the bank at various times had within its control the means of complete or partial satisfaction of the note is based upon section 117.38 (42). (Supra) . . . That section is obviously not applicable to the facts here, since the defendant was primarily, not secondarily, liable to the bank. We think defendant's second contention without merit." . . .

. . . Consequently, as the respondent herein is primarily instead of secondarily liable on the negotiable instrument in question, there are not applicable to him the provisions in subsec. (42) of § 117.38, Stats.

The judgment appealed from is reversed and cause remanded with directions to enter judgment for plaintiff's recovery from respondent of the amount owing on the note. . . .

CASE NO. 7

Leonard v. Woodward. 25 N.E. (2d) 705, 127 A.L.R. 999 (Mass.) (1940)

QUA, J., delivered the opinion of the court:

This action is upon a promissory note for $1,500, payable on demand to the plaintiff's intestate and signed on its face, apparently as joint makers, by the defendant and one Emery. At the trial and at the argument before us the defendant took the position that he signed the note for the accommodation of the plaintiff's intestate, and that as to him the note was without consideration. . . .

Evidence favoring the plaintiff tended to show that the plaintiff found the note in her intestate's safe deposit box; that on the day of the date of the note her intestate lent $1,500 to Emery by giving him a check for that amount; and that Emery was the defendant's father-in-law. The defendant testified that he signed the note for the accommodation of the plaintiff's intestate and received nothing of value for so doing; that he was acquainted with the plaintiff's intestate but was not related to him; that Emery asked him to sign as an accommodation to the plaintiff's intestate, as the latter wanted a note with joint makers, so that he could discount it at the bank if he wished to do so; that when the note was signed both the plaintiff's intestate and Emery understood that the defendant was not to be held responsible by either of them; and that the defendant never authorized or consented to the check for $1,500 being made payable to Emery.

Of course the defendant would not be liable to a party for whose accommodation he signed. . . . But the jury were not obliged to find that the defendant signed for the accommodation of the plaintiff. They could think it more probable that the defendant signed at the request of his father-in-law, Emery, for the accommodation of Emery in order that Emery might get the loan of $1,500 from the plaintiff's intestate. On this record it was for the jury to say for whose accommodation the defendant signed. . . . If the defendant signed for the accommodation of Emery, in order that Emery might receive the $1,500, the defendant would be liable to the plaintiff's intestate and to the plaintiff. An accommodation party

> "is liable on the instrument to a holder in due course, notwithstanding such holder at the time of taking the instrument knew him to be only an accommodation party." G.L. (Ter. Ed.) c. 107, § 52; . . .

The plaintiff's intestate was "prima facie" a holder in due course. . . . A payee may be a holder in due course. . . .

Evidence that the plaintiff's intestate and Emery "understood" that the defendant would not be held responsible did not disclose a separate ground of defense, and except for its bearing upon consideration and accommodation, would have been inadmissible, as it tended to vary the written contract embodied in the note. . . .

What has been said indicates that there was evidence warranting a verdict for the plaintiff, and that there was no error in refusing to direct a verdict for the defendant or in refusing to rule as matter of law that there was no consideration for the note. . . .

Review Questions

1. How does a *primary liability* differ from a *secondary liability?*
2. Upon what conditions is a secondary party to a negotiable instrument liable?
3. What parties to a negotiable instrument have
   (a) A primary liability?
   (b) A secondary liability?
4. What are the express and the implied contractual undertakings of parties who are primarily liable upon a negotiable instrument?
5. When does the drawee become liable upon a bill of exchange?
6. Does an oral promise by the drawee that he will accept the bill when presented bind the drawee?
7. What is the effect of the drawee's failure to return a bill to the holder within twenty-four hours after it has been presented for acceptance?
8. Can the drawee, after acceptance, be held liable upon an instrument to which the drawer's signature has been forged?
9. To what extent does a qualified indorser limit his liability?
10. What implied warranties does the qualified indorser make?
11. To what parties to a negotiable instrument are the following parties liable?
    (a) An unqualified indorser?
    (b) A qualified indorser?
    (c) One who transfers bearer paper by delivery?
12. In what respect does the liability of an unqualified indorser differ from that of a qualified indorser?
13. What is an accommodation party?
14. Does the liability of an accommodation indorser differ from the liability of a regular unqualified indorser?

Problems for Discussion

1. Phillips executed a promissory note that he intended to be payable to his creditor Carns. Not knowing the full name of the intended payee (Carns), Phillips entrusted the note to his agent with instructions to ascertain the name of the intended payee, to insert the name in the note, and to deliver the note to Carns. The agent failed in his trust and inserted his own name and negotiated the note to Ryan, a holder in due course. When Phillips was confronted with the note for payment, he denied liability upon the contention that the agent never had title to the note and consequently could not pass title to Ryan. Is Phillips liable?
2. X drew a bill of exchange payable in thirty days from date upon his creditor Y and delivered it to Z. Upon the expiration of the thirty days, Y refused to pay and Z sues him for payment. Can he recover?
3. A presents a bill of exchange to B, the drawee, for acceptance. In a rage, B tears the bill into four pieces, which he throws into the wastebasket. Can A hold B liable as a primary obligor even though B has clearly indicated it is not his wish to be bound on the instrument?

4. A, who is the holder of a bill of exchange drawn by B, wires the drawee: "Will you accept B's bill drawn on you for $100?" The drawee wires back: "B is good. Send on your paper." Is this an acceptance?
5. Monroe forged the name of the Central State Bank as drawer upon a sixty-day draft drawn upon the Midland National Bank. When presented to the Midland National Bank, it was accepted, and Monroe then negotiated the bill to Willisma, a holder in due course. When the bill is presented for payment, can the Midland National avoid paying, since the name of the drawer was forged?
6. Defendant indorsed a note to plaintiff "without recourse," knowing that the maker was insolvent and that installments shown upon the instrument as having been paid were in fact not paid. The note is not paid by the maker, and defendant contends that his qualified indorsement absolves him from liability. Decide.
7. A forged B's name to a check which A made payable to himself. A indorsed the check to C, who in turn indorsed it "without recourse" to D. The check is dishonored, and D looks to C for payment. Can he recover?
8. X, the payee on a note, is an infant. He indorses the note to A, who then indorses the note to B "without recourse." B indorses the note to C and C indorses the note to D. The note is not paid by the maker at maturity because of insolvency and X, the minor, disaffirms the contract. Can the holder D look to A for satisfaction?
9. X negotiates a note to A by blank indorsement, and A then transfers the note to B by delivery. B indorses the note to C, who then indorses the note to D. Which of the indorsers are liable to D?
10. The president of the X bank negotiated a note "without recourse" to Y. The note was secured by a chattel mortgage upon certain cattle, and the bank president knew that the maker of the note had no mortgageable interest in the cattle. The maker defaulted and Y looked to the X bank for satisfaction. Result?
11. Morse executed a promissory note to the order of Cain, who indorsed it without qualification to James, a holder in due course. James found it impossible to enforce the note against the maker, Morse, because of illegality. Is Cain liable to James?
12. A induced B to become an accommodation comaker of a note evidencing a $500 loan from the X bank to A. Upon maturity, the note is dishonored by A, and suit is brought against B. His defense is that his promise is not enforceable, since he personally received nothing for his signature. Result?
13. Long obtained acceptance of a bill of exchange drawn upon Bell by letter. White purchased the bill from Long after being told that Bell had accepted. White, however, was never shown Bell's letter of acceptance. Can White hold Bell as an acceptor after Long gives him the letter of acceptance?
14. Brown was the drawee upon a sight draft. When the instrument was presented for acceptance, Brown merely wrote his name across the face of the draft. Is this a sufficient acceptance?
15. The Commercial Credit Company claims of the defendant Ward & Son Auto Company $250 damages upon the allegation that J. D. Stanley executed to the defendant a negotiable promissory note for $435.75, dated May 21, 1923, payable in monthly installments of $36.12 per month, beginning on May 21, 1923,

and continuing each month for 12 months. Stanley was a minor, under 21 years of age, at the time the note was executed by him, and was, therefore, without legal capacity to execute the note and bind himself thereby, and the defendant indorsed the note to plaintiff without recourse, and Stanley has failed or refused to pay the note. Decide. (*Commercial Credit Co.* v. *Ward & Son Auto Co.*, 215 Ala. 34)

22 NEGOTIABLE INSTRUMENTS:

PRESENTMENT, DISHONOR, PROTEST, AND NOTICE

► I. CONDITIONS PRECEDENT TO LIABILITY OF SECONDARY PARTIES

The holder of a negotiable instrument need take no formal steps to establish the liability of a primary obligor to pay the instrument. However, it is necessary that the holder meet certain legal requirements in order to establish the liability of secondary parties.* The conditions precedent to such liability on the part of secondary parties to the holder are:

(1) That the holder will have properly presented the instrument for payment or acceptance as the case may require;

(2) That the instrument will have been dishonored by the primary party (payment or acceptance cannot be obtained or is refused);

(3) That the instrument will have been protested if required;

(4) That notice of dishonor will have been given to the secondary parties.

Unless the holder complies with these requirements, he cannot look to the secondary parties upon the instrument for payment. The detailed requirements, as set out in the N.I.L. to meet the conditions upon which the liability of secondary parties is dependent, follow.

► II. PRESENTMENT FOR PAYMENT

A. PRIMARY PARTIES

As a matter of good business practice, credit instruments are and should be presented to the primary obligors for payment at the time of their maturity. In fact, it is not uncommon that such obligors will be given reasonable notice of the holder's expectation that the obligation will be met when due. However, a failure to make a presentment for payment will not have the effect of discharging a primary party from his obligations under the instrument. A presentment for payment is not a prerequisite to the continued liability of those who are primarily liable upon negotiable paper. Section 70 of the N.I.L. unequivocally declares:

"Presentment for payment is not necessary in order to charge the person primarily liable on the instrument."

Although the primary party is not discharged from making payment by a failure of presentment, he will, upon the basis of his readiness, willingness, and ability

---

* See p. 537 for basic concept of primary and secondary liability.

to meet payment at the time and place specified in the instrument, be excused from paying interest or costs of collection. The primary party's readiness, willingness, and ability to pay are the equivalent of a tender.*

1. *Notes Payable at Bank*

Section 87 of the N.I.L. reads:

"Where the instrument is made payable at a bank it is equivalent to an order to the bank to pay the same for the account of the principal debtor thereon."

Promissory notes frequently designate a particular bank at which they are payable. Such a provision serves as an authorization to the bank to make payment on behalf of the maker. A failure, however, to make presentment to the designated bank for payment will not discharge the maker, the primary obligor.[1]

B. SECONDARY PARTIES

Section 70 of the N.I.L. states:

"But except as herein otherwise provided, presentment for payment is necessary in order to charge the drawer and indorsers."

1. *Time of Presentment—Day*

The requirements as to the time at which presentment of a negotiable instrument must be made are stated in Section 71 of the N.I.L.:

"Where the instrument is not payable on demand, presentment must be made on the day it falls due. Where it is payable on demand, presentment must be made within a reasonable time after its issue, except that in the case of a bill of exchange, presentment for payment will be sufficient if made within a reasonable time after the last negotiation thereof."

a. Instruments Payable at Fixed or Determinable Future Time. An instrument payable at a fixed or determinable future time must be presented for payment on the day it falls due. A presentment made prior to the maturity date is as ineffective to charge secondary parties with liability as is one made after maturity. The rules for determining the due date should, therefore, be fully comprehended.

Section 86 of the N.I.L. provides for the computation of the time of maturity as follows:

"Where the instrument is payable at a fixed period after date, after sight, or after the happening of a specified event, the time of payment is determined by excluding the day from which the time is to begin to run, and by including the date of payment."

It is not in keeping with commercial practice for instruments to be presented for payment upon Sundays or holidays. Consequently, Section 85 of the N.I.L. provides:

---

* See effect of tender, p. 319.

[1] Binghamton Pharmacy v. First Nat. Bank, p. 567.

"When the day of maturity falls upon Sunday, or a holiday, the instrument is payable on the next succeeding business day. Instruments falling due on Saturday are to be presented for payment on the next succeeding business day, except that instruments payable on demand may, at the option of the holder, be presented for payment before twelve o'clock noon on Saturday when that entire day is not a holiday."

b. Demand Notes. As indicated above, Section 71 requires that demand notes must be presented for payment within a reasonable time after their issue in order to charge secondary parties with liability. There is no categorical answer to the question, "What is a reasonable time?" The problem is similar to that involved in determining when demand notes are overdue; the answer depends upon the circumstances of the particular case. What may be regarded as a reasonable time under one set of facts may be far from reasonable under others. Such factors as the usage in the community in respect to the particular type of paper, or contract terms indicating an intent that it is to be a continuing obligation would have an important bearing in determining reasonableness of time. It has been held in particular cases that delays in presentment ranging from as high as ten years down to twenty-five days have been unreasonably long. Section 193 of the N.I.L. must be considered in connection with this problem. However, some states have established a statutory period of time within which demand notes must be presented for payment.

c. Demand Bills of Exchange Exclusive of Checks. Section 71 of the N.I.L. states:

". . . that in the case of a bill of exchange, presentment for payment will be sufficient if made within a reasonable time after the last negotiation thereof."

Therefore, the liability of the drawer and of the indorsers of a bill of exchange can be preserved for the period of the statute of limitations in jurisdictions that hold that the statute begins to run from the date of issue. This provision does not require that the instrument be negotiated within a reasonable time, but only that it be presented within a reasonable time after the last negotiation.[2] It would seem that a holder who has delayed an unreasonable length of time in making a presentment may negotiate the bill to another holder. He would thus revive the liability of the secondary parties, which had expired while the instrument was in the holder's hands. It is to be doubted whether such a result was intended.

A demand bill of exchange is looked upon as a credit instrument used to accomplish an immediate purpose; it is not regarded as evidencing an extension of credit for any considerable period of time. Consequently, the time within which it must be presented for payment by the holder is relatively short in comparison with the time allowed for demand notes. Time is usually measured in units of days and only occasionally in weeks.

d. Checks. Section 185 defines a check as being a "bill of exchange drawn on a bank payable on demand." Thus, Section 71, which requires that a demand bill

[2] Columbian Banking Co. v. Bowen, p. 569.

of exchange need be presented for payment only within a reasonable time after the last negotiation thereof, also applies to checks. However, this provision applies only to indorsers of checks, since Section 186 makes this qualification in respect to drawers:

> "A check must be presented for payment within a reasonable time after its issue, or the drawer will be discharged from all liability thereon to the extent of the loss caused by delay."

An unreasonable delay in presenting a check for payment will, then, operate to discharge indorsers absolutely, whereas the drawer will be held liable to the full extent less any loss that he has suffered as a result of the delay in presenting the check for payment within a reasonable time after its issue.

A check, by its very nature, suggests that it be promptly presented to the drawee for payment. Checks are not intended to be continuing obligations and should be presented for payment with dispatch.[3]

2. *Hour of Presentment*

To be sufficient, a presentment must also be made at the proper hour of the day. Section 72 states, "At a reasonable hour on a business day."

If the presentment is made at a place of residence, it must be done before the hours of rest. It has been held that a presentment at the maker's residence at nine o'clock at night, even though the maker had retired, was sufficient to charge the indorsers with liability. A presentment shortly before twelve o'clock at night has been held an improper presentment.

A presentment at a place of business must be made within the accepted hours of business. Section 75 makes a specific provision in instances where presentment is required to be made at a bank. It reads:

> "Where the instrument is payable at a bank, presentment for payment must be made during banking hours, unless the person to make payment has no funds there to meet it at any time during the day, in which case presentment at any hour before the bank is closed on that day is sufficient."

In some states it is held that the maker has the right to provide funds for a discharge of the note at any time before the bank closes and that a presentment of a note without its being left until the bank's closing hour is not sufficient. Under this rule, a note cannot be regarded as dishonored until after the regular closing hour of the bank. A notice of dishonor made prior to that time would be premature and of no avail. In other states, a presentment at any time during the banking day with a refusal of payment at that time constitutes an immediate dishonoring of the note. The safe practice is to leave the note with the bank for the entire banking day.

The courts have not been arbitrary in applying the rule that presentment must be made during the usual and customary banking hours. In a number of instances, obtaining admission after banking hours and finding an agent of the bank who would be authorized to make payment has been held to constitute a sufficient presentment to hold secondary parties liable on the instrument.

---

[3] Viles v. S. D. Warren Co., p. 571.

3. *Place of Presentment*

The rules governing the place where presentment must be made are set out in Section 73:

"Presentment for payment is made at the proper place—

(1) Where a place for payment is specified in the instrument and it is there presented;

(2) Where no place of payment is specified, but the address of the person to make payment is given in the instrument and it is there presented;

(3) Where no place of payment is specified and no address is given and the instrument is presented at the usual place of business or residence of the person to make payment;

(4) In any other case if presented to the person to make payment wherever he can be found, or if presented at his last known place of business or residence."

4. *Manner of Presentment*

The requirement of presentment must be literally met—the demand for payment must be accompanied by the actual production and exhibition of the instrument.[4, 5] Section 74 reads:

"The instrument must be exhibited to the person from whom payment is demanded, and when it is paid must be delivered up to the party paying it."

A demand by telephone, even though encountered by a refusal to pay, will not excuse the actual exhibiting of the instrument. Ordinarily a presentment is not accomplished by mailing the instrument to the primary obligor with a demand for payment. However, where it is the established custom to send drafts or checks drawn on a bank to the drawee by mail, such has been held a sufficient presentment.

5. *Presentment Excused*

Certain exceptions to the rule that actual presentment is required must be noted.[6] The following sections of the N.I.L. pertain to situations under which presentment is not required or is excused.

Section 79:

"Presentment for payment is not required in order to charge the drawer where he has no right to expect or require that the drawee or acceptor will pay the instrument."

Thus, presentment of a check upon which the drawer has ordered payment stopped is not necessary to charge the drawer with liability.

Section 81:

"Delay in making presentment for payment is excused when the delay is caused by circumstances beyond the control of the holder, and not imputable

---

4 Gilpin v. Savage, p. 573.

5 Commercial Trust Co. v. New England Macaroni Mfg. Co., p. 574.

6 O'Neal v. Clark, p. 575.

to his default, misconduct, or negligence. When the cause of delay ceases to operate, presentment must be made with reasonable diligence."

Section 82:

"Presentment for payment is dispensed with:

(1) Where after the exercise of reasonable diligence presentment as required by this Act cannot be made;

(2) Where the drawee is a fictitious person;

(3) By waiver of presentment, express or implied."

By virtue of Section 111 of the N.I.L., a waiver of protest is made to include a waiver of presentment.

6. *Presentment to Other than Principal Debtor*

In general, the holder of the instrument or an authorized agent must make the presentment to the party primarily liable, providing he can be found. The holder of the instrument need do no more toward actually finding the obligor than to comply with the requirements as to the place where presentment must be made. Special situations are governed by the following sections of the N.I.L.:

Section 76:

"Where the person primarily liable on the instrument is dead, and no place of payment is specified, presentment for payment must be made to his personal representative if such there be, and if, with the exercise of reasonable diligence, he can be found."

Section 77:

"Where the persons primarily liable on the instrument are liable as partners, and no place of payment is specified, presentment for payment may be made to any one of them, even though there has been a dissolution of the firm."

Section 78:

"Where there are several persons, not partners, primarily liable on the instrument, and no place of payment is specified, presentment must be made to them all."

► III. PRESENTMENT FOR ACCEPTANCE

A. WHEN REQUIRED

All bills of exchange need not be presented to the drawee for acceptance as a prerequisite to charging secondary parties with liability. In many instances, the holder may elect to present the instrument for payment at maturity without obtaining a prior acceptance. The acceptance of the drawee, however, is desirable in that it lends the credit and security of the drawee to the instrument. The holder of a bill has the right to present the bill for acceptance at any time before its maturity. The drawee's refusal to accept constitutes a dishonor, and the holder must treat it as such and give notice to the drawer and indorsers. It should be noted that the drawee, by virtue of Section 136 of the N.I.L., has twenty-four hours within which to decide whether or not he will accept the bill.* Therefore, unless a refusal is unequivocally given, notice should not be given before the twenty-four hours have expired.

Instances in which a presentment is a legal requirement are set out in Section 143 of the N.I.L.:

"(1) Where the bill is payable after sight, or in any other case, where presentment for acceptance is necessary in order to fix the maturity of the instrument; or

(2) Where the bill expressly stipulates that it shall be presented for acceptance; or

(3) Where the bill is drawn payable elsewhere than at the residence or place of business of the drawee."

B. TIME FOR PRESENTMENT

Section 144 gives the holder of a bill that must be presented for acceptance the alternatives of either presenting it or negotiating it within a reasonable time. A failure to do so will discharge the drawer and all indorsers. As indicated before, a reasonable time in relation to bills of exchange is usually a matter of days.

As in the case of presentment for payment, a reasonable hour of a business day before the instrument is overdue is required. Sections 72 and 85 of the N.I.L. apply to a determination of the time when a bill must be presented for acceptance as well as the time when it must be presented for payment.

C. CONDITIONS EXCUSING PRESENTMENT

Section 148 of the N.I.L. provides for situations under which presentment for acceptance is excused and, unless it is accepted without a presentment, the instrument may be treated as dishonored. It reads:

"Presentment for acceptance is excused, and a bill may be treated as dishonored by nonacceptance, in either of the following cases:

(1) Where the drawee is dead, or has absconded, or is a fictitious person or a person not having capacity to contract by bill;

(2) Where, after the exercise of reasonable diligence, presentment cannot be made;

(3) Where, although presentment has been irregular, acceptance has been refused on some other ground."

► IV. NOTICE OF DISHONOR

A dishonor results from the failure of a party to accept or pay the instrument, as the case demands, after the requirements of presentment have been met. Upon dishonor of the instrument the holder must meet the further requirement of giving

* See p. 539.

notice of the dishonor as a prerequisite to holding secondary parties liable.* Section 89 of the N.I.L. provides for this in the following words:

"Except as herein otherwise provided, when a negotiable instrument has been dishonored by nonacceptance or nonpayment, notice of dishonor must be given to the drawer and to each indorser, and any drawer or indorser to whom such notice is not given is discharged."

A. FORM OF NOTICE

It is not necessary for the notice of dishonor to follow any particular form. Section 96 of the N.I.L. provides:

"The notice may be in writing or merely oral and may be given in any terms which sufficiently identify the instrument, and indicate that it has been dishonored by nonacceptance or nonpayment. It may in all cases be given by delivering it personally or through the mails."

Section 97 further attests to the unimportance of the form of the notice. It reads:

"Notice of dishonor may be given either to the party himself or to his agent in that behalf."

Although the notice can take any form, meeting the legal requirements of notice is imperative. For example, the holder cannot rely upon the fact that a drawer has actual knowledge of the dishonor. It is the notice from the holder to the secondary parties that informs them that they will be looked to for payment. Upon the basis of the notice, they will prepare to meet the claim. In *Jagger* v. *National German-American Bank,* 53 Minn. 386, the court characterized the requirements of notice as follows:

"Mere knowledge of the dishonor of paper is not notice. Notice signifies more. It must come from one who is entitled to look to the party for payment, and must inform him (1) that the note has been duly presented for payment; (2) that it has been dishonored; (3) that the holder looks to him for payment. Although, probably, if the notice comes from the proper party, and contains the first two of these requisites, the third would be implied."

It cannot be denied that the best practice is to use a written notice signed by the holder. A copy of the notice should be retained as evidence of the fact that notice was given.

B. TIME WITHIN WHICH NOTICE MUST BE GIVEN

The time within which notice of dishonor must be given to secondary parties is governed by the following rules:

Section 102:

"Notice may be given as soon as the instrument is dishonored; and unless delay is excused as hereinafter provided, must be given within the times fixed by this Act."

Section 103:

* See O'Neal v. Clark, p. 575.

"Where the person giving and the person to receive notice reside in the same place, notice must be given within the following times:

(1) If given at the place of business of the person to receive notice, it must be given before the close of business hours on the day following;

(2) If given at his residence, it must be given before the usual hours of rest on the day following;

(3) If sent by mail, it must be deposited in the post office in time to reach him in usual course on the day following."

Section 104:

"Where the person giving and the person to receive notice reside in different places, the notice must be given within the following times:

(1) If sent by mail, it must be deposited in the post office in time to go by mail the day following the day of dishonor, or if there be no mail at a convenient hour on that day, by the next mail thereafter.

(2) If given otherwise than through the post office, then within the time that notice would have been received in due course of mail, if it had been deposited in the post office within the time specified in the last subdivision."

C. MANNER OF GIVING NOTICE—MAILING

As already indicated, a notice may be given by any manner or means. Section 105 of the N.I.L. creates a conclusive presumption of notice where the notice was properly mailed. It reads:

"Where notice of dishonor is duly addressed and deposited in the post office, the sender is deemed to have given due notice, notwithstanding any miscarriage in the mails."

A failure to receive the notice is evidence which has a bearing upon whether or not the notice was ever mailed. It is well for the holder to have some proof of the mailing.[7]

Section 106 establishes what meets the requirements of depositing a notice in the post office thus:

"Notice is deemed to have been deposited in the post office when deposited in any branch post office or in any letter box under the control of the post office department."

D. REQUIRED PLACE OF SENDING NOTICE

The place to which the notice of dishonor must be sent is governed by the rules set out in Section 108 of the N.I.L.:

"Where a party has added an address to his signature, notice of dishonor must be sent to that address; but if he has not given such address, then the notice must be sent as follows:

(1) Either to the post office nearest to his place of residence, or to the post office where he is accustomed to receive his letters; or

[7] State Bank of East Moline v. Standaert, p. 577.

(2) If he lives in one place, and has his place of business in another, notice may be sent to either place; or

(3) If he is sojourning in another place, notice may be sent to the place where he is so sojourning.

But where the notice is actually received by the party within the time specified in this act, it will be sufficient, though not sent in accordance with the requirements of this section."

E. THOSE ENTITLED TO GIVE NOTICE

As a matter of practice, the holder of the instrument or his agent (as a collecting bank) will give notice of the dishonor. Section 94 of the N.I.L. gives the agent to whom the dishonor was made the alternative rights of giving notice to his principal or to the parties to be charged with liability. The section provides:

"Where the instrument has been dishonored in the hands of an agent, he may either himself give notice to the parties liable thereon, or he may give notice to his principal. If he gives notice to his principal, he must do so within the same time as if he were the holder, and the principal upon the receipt of such notice has himself the same time for giving notice as if the agent had been an independent holder."

Section 90 of the N.I.L. also bestows authority to give notice upon those parties to the instrument who might be compelled to pay the holder and who would thus acquire rights against all prior parties. It reads:

"The notice may be given . . . by or on behalf of any party to the instrument who might be compelled to pay it to the holder, and who, upon taking it up, would have a right to reimbursement from the party to whom the notice is given."

F. NOTICE BY SECONDARY PARTIES

Upon receiving notice of dishonor, a secondary party must realize that in the event that he is called upon to pay, his ability to look to prior parties upon the instrument is dependent upon their having received notice of the dishonor. If the holder of the instrument has given notice, it will inure to the benefit of the secondary party who paid the instrument. Upon receiving notice of dishonor, an indorser should give notice of dishonor to all prior parties upon the instrument to whom he may have to look for payment. He should not take the chance that the holder has given notice to all prior parties. The time within which a secondary party must give notice is provided for by Section 107 of the N.I.L. thus:

"Where a party receives notice of dishonor, he has, after the receipt of such notice, the same time for giving notice to antecedent parties that the holder has after the dishonor."

G. TO WHOM NOTICE MAY BE GIVEN

Section 97 reads:

"Notice of dishonor may be given either to the party himself or to his agent in that behalf."

Notice, of course, must be given to *all* parties to whom the holder might wish to look for satisfaction. And notice to an agent without authority to receive notice is a nullity. Before notice is served upon an agent of the party sought to be charged with liability on the instrument, it should be ascertained whether the agent has authority to receive such notice. A notice given to a mere clerk or bookkeeper would probably not be sufficient. In serving notice upon a corporation, care must be exercised in determining who is in authority to receive the notice. Where there is any doubt, a notice by mail is the best method.

Section 98 provides for notice when a party is dead and such fact is known to the holder. As is to be expected, it says:

> ". . . the notice must be given to a personal representative, if there be one, and if with reasonable diligence he can be found. If there be no personal representative, notice may be sent to the last residence or last place of business of the deceased."

As a precautionary measure, it is wise to send a notice by mail even though there is a personal representative of a deceased partner. Such will forestall any difficulty in the event (1) that the personal representative lacks authority to act, or (2) that he has not yet been duly appointed.

Section 99 provides for notice to partners. As in other partnership relations, notice to one partner is notice to all, since partners stand as agents for one another. Even though there has been a dissolution of the firm, notice to one of the former partners is sufficient. This applies, of course, only to partnership obligations.

Where the secondary party has been adjudged a bankrupt or an insolvent, or where he has made an assignment for the benefit of his creditors, notice made as provided by Section 101 may be given either to the party or to his trustee or assignee. There can be no harm in giving notice to both.

H. NOTICE NOT REQUIRED OR DELAY EXCUSED

1. *Reasonable Diligence Required*

Although there are circumstances under which notice can be dispensed with as a prerequisite to charging secondary parties with liability, it is wise to give notice whenever possible. In any event, a reasonable effort to give notice must be made. Section 112 of the N.I.L. provides:

> "Notice of dishonor is dispensed with when, after the exercise of reasonable diligence, it cannot be given to or does not reach the parties sought to be charged."

2. *Delay Excused*

Section 113 provides:

> "Delay in giving notice of dishonor is excused when the delay is caused by circumstances beyond the control of the holder, and not imputable to his default, misconduct, or negligence. When the cause of delay ceases to operate, notice must be given with reasonable diligence."

3. *Drawer not Required to Be Notified*

Section 114 of the N.I.L. enumerates the situations under which no notice of dishonor need be given the drawer of the instrument. They are:

"(1) Where the drawer and drawee are the same person;

(2) When the drawee is a fictitious person or a person not having capacity to contract;

(3) When the drawer is the person to whom the instrument is presented for payment;

(4) Where the drawer has no right to expect or require that the drawee or acceptor will honor the instrument;

(5) Where the drawer has countermanded payment."

4. *Indorser not Required to Be Notified*

Section 115 enumerates the following situations under which notice to an indorser can be dispensed with:

> "(1) Where the drawee is a fictitious person or a person not having capacity to contract, and the indorser was aware of the fact at the time he indorsed the instrument.
>
> (2) Where the indorser is the person to whom the instrument is presented for payment.
>
> (3) Where the instrument was made or accepted for his accommodation."

5. *Waiver of Notice*

The parties to an instrument may waive their legal right of notice either before or after the time for giving notice.[8] This waiver of notice may be either expressly made or implied from the circumstances. A waiver of presentment is presumed to carry with it a waiver of notice of dishonor. Expressions on the part of the obligor that he will take care of the matter or that he cannot meet the obligation have been held to imply a waiver of notice. It should be noted that (by virtue of Section 111 of the N.I.L.) a waiver of protest is also a waiver of presentment and of notice of dishonor.

Instruments frequently carry waiver provisions upon their face. These are binding upon all parties to the paper. Section 110 of the N.I.L. reads:

> "Where the waiver is embodied in the instrument itself, it is binding upon all parties; but where it is written above the signature of an indorser, it binds him only."

► V. PROTEST

A. MEANING AND PURPOSE OF PROTEST

> "It is true that technically speaking the word "protest" only applies to and covers the formal writing and declaration made by the officer, who is ordinarily

[8] Toole v. Crafts, p. 579.

a notary, stating that the bill or note was duly and regularly presented in accordance with the laws governing commercial paper, and that payment was refused, and that he thereby formally protests the same for nonpayment. This, however, does not cover the meaning of the word as generally used in commercial transactions and as it is commonly understood in the business world. In its popular sense it includes all the steps necessary to fix the liability of the indorser and this necessarily includes demand of payment, refusal to pay, and notice." *Montpelier Bank* v. *Montpelier Lumber Co.,* 16 Idaho 730.

The procedure of protesting an instrument is *for the purpose of establishing documentary evidence that there has been compliance with the requirements of presentment, dishonor, and notice.* As a matter of business practice, the protest is accomplished by a notary public, although Section 154 of the N.I.L. also authorizes the making of a protest, in the presence of two or more creditable witnesses, by any respectable resident of the place where the bill is dishonored. The notary, after having presented the instrument and its having been dishonored, will execute a formal document which meets the requirements as set forth in Section 153 of the N.I.L. It reads:

"The protest must be annexed to the bill, or must contain a copy thereof, and must be under the hand and seal of the notary making it, and must specify:

(1) The time and place of presentment;

(2) The fact that presentment was made and the manner thereof;

(3) The cause or reason for protesting the bill;

(4) The demand made and the answer given, if any, or the fact that the drawee or acceptor could not be found."

This document is generally called the *certificate* or *manifest of protest.*

The protesting of an instrument also accomplishes the giving of notices to the secondary parties by the notary, and the certificate stands as proof of the fact that notices have been given. Following is a specimen copy of the notice of protest sent to secondary parties.

To _____: You will please take notice that on _____, 19___, a check (or note) for ________ dollars, signed by ________, and payable at ________, and indorsed by you, and due this day, is protested for nonpayment, and that the holders look to you for the payment thereof; payment of same having been demanded and refused.

____________________, Notary Public

Let it be noted that the protesting of an instrument will not of itself fix the liability of secondary parties. Notice of dishonor is not dispensed with by the act of protesting.

Certificate of Protest

STATE OF IOWA, ... COUNTY, ss.

BE IT REMEMBERED, That on the .... day of .... in the year of our Lord, Nineteen Hundred and .... at the request of ....
.... holder of the original .... which is hereto attached, I, ..., a Notary Public in and for the County aforesaid, duly commissioned and qualified, and residing at .... in said County, did present the said .... to ....
.... and demanded .... thereof, which was refused
....
Whereupon I, the said Notary, at the request aforesaid, did PROTEST, and do by these presents most solemnly and publicly protest, as well against the maker and endorser of the said .... as against all others whom it doth or may concern, for exchange, re-exchange and all costs, charges, damages, and interest already incurred and hereafter to be incurred for want of .... of the said ....

AND I FURTHER CERTIFY, That on the .... day of ...., A. D. 19 . due notice of the presentment and protest of the said .... (by notice partly written and partly printed, by me signed) was given by me to the .... endorser of the said .... by depositing notice in the Post Office at .... (prepaying the postage thereon) for the following persons, to-wit:

Notice for ....
" " ....
" " ....
" " ....
" " ....
" " ....
" "

Each of the above named places being the reputed place of residence of the persons to whom the said notice was directed, respectively, and the nearest post office thereto, and that the postage thereon was prepaid.

IN TESTIMONY WHEREOF, I have hereunto set my hand and affixed my Notarial Seal, the day and year aforesaid.

....

Notary Public.

Recorded in Book .... at folio ....

Fees, Etc. { Protest, $..........
Notice, $..........
Postage, $..........
$..........

B. REQUIRED TIME OF PROTEST

Section 155 of the N.I.L. specifies that the protest must be made on the day of its dishonor. It does make provision, however, that, if the instrument has been duly noted for protest, the certificate of protest may be subsequently executed and dated the day of dishonor and noting.

Noting an instrument for protest, as the term implies, consists of making an informal record of the necessary information upon the basis of which a formal protest can subsequently be executed. The notation of the necessary information is usually entered upon the instrument itself. Noting is resorted to where it is impossible or inconvenient to execute immediately the formal document of protest.

C. CONDITIONS REQUIRING PROTEST

Protest is required only in the case of foreign bills of exchange. However, other instruments may be protested. Section 118 of the N.I.L. provides:

"Where any negotiable instrument has been dishonored it may be protested for nonacceptance or nonpayment, as the case may be; but protest is not required except in the case of foreign bills of exchange."

This is further amplified by Section 152, which reads:

"Where a foreign bill, appearing on its face to be such is dishonored by nonacceptance, it must be duly protested for nonacceptance, and where such a bill which has not previously been dishonored by nonacceptance is dishonored by nonpayment, it must be duly protested for nonpayment. If it is not so protested, the drawer and indorsers are discharged. Where a bill does not appear on its face to be a foreign bill, protest thereof in case of dishonor is unnecessary."

A *foreign bill of exchange* is one which is drawn in one state and payable in another, or drawn in one country and payable in another, which fact is indicated upon the face of the instrument. The reason for requiring a protest of this type of instrument is to furnish the drawer, who is in another jurisdiction, with reliable evidence that the instrument was dishonored. In the event of suit against secondary parties, the certificate of protest serves as acceptable proof of compliance with the necessary conditions. It is because of this fact that instruments other than foreign bills of exchange are commonly protested for nonpayment or nonacceptance.

CASES

CASE NO. 1

Binghamton Pharmacy v. First Nat. Bank. 131 Tenn. 711, 176 S.W. 1038, 2 A.L.R. 1377 (1915)

GREEN, J., delivered the opinion of the court:

The defendants below, the Binghamton Pharmacy and Kilpatrick Brothers, W. A. Kilpatrick and L. H. Kilpatrick, executed a note payable to the order of "ourselves," which they indorsed in blank and discounted at the Chickasaw Bank & Trust Company. The note was due December 29, 1912, and was payable at the said Chickasaw Bank & Trust Company.

Prior to its maturity this note was rediscounted by the Chickasaw Bank & Trust Company at the First National Bank of Memphis. It was not presented for payment at the Chickasaw Bank & Trust Company when it matured. . . .

On January 7, 1913, the Chickasaw Bank & Trust Company failed.

Later the First National Bank demanded payment of the note from its makers, which they declined, on the ground that they had sufficient funds on deposit in the failed bank to meet the note at its maturity, and . . . that they are discharged from liability on the note on account of the omission of the First National Bank to present it for payment at the Chickasaw Bank & Trust Company, where the note was made payable, when it fell due.

The lower courts rendered judgment in favor of the First National Bank, . . .

The defense is based on § 87 of the Negotiable Instruments Act . . . as follows:

> "Instrument Payable at Bank Equivalent to What.—Where the instrument is made payable at a bank, it is equivalent to an order to the bank to pay the same for the account of the principal debtor thereon."

It is contended that under the provisions of the section quoted it became the duty of the holder of this note to present it for payment at the bank, where it was payable, upon maturity, and that for neglect of this duty the holder must respond to the makers for the damage suffered by them in consequence of this neglect of duty.

The argument is that § 87 of the Act of 1899, making any instrument payable at a bank, the equivalent of an order on the bank, puts upon the holder of a note payable at a bank the same duties as rest upon the holder of an ordinary check. Quite a plausible brief is offered in support of this contention, to which we might assent, were it not for § 70 of the Act of 1899, which contains this language:

> "Presentment for payment is not necessary in order to charge the person primarily liable on the instrument;" . . .

The difference between the drawer of a check and the maker of a note is that the latter is primarily liable on the instrument, while the former is not. The maker of a note, "by the terms of the instrument, is absolutely required to pay the same." That is to say, he is primarily liable on the instrument. § 192. The drawer of a check or bill of exchange is not primarily liable, but he engages that if the instrument be dishonored he will pay the amount thereof to the holder or subsequent indorser, who may be compelled to pay it. § 61.

The provisions of § 70 therefore, which we have quoted above, do not apply to the drawer of a check or bill of exchange, while they do apply to the maker of a note.

By § 186 of the Act of 1899, it is made the duty of the holder of a check to present the same for payment

> "within a reasonable time after its issue, or the drawer will be discharged from liability thereon to the extent of the loss caused by the delay."

There is, therefore, an absolute duty resting upon the holder of a check to present the instrument for payment at the place where it is payable, within a reasonable time. If he breaches this duty, the drawer is discharged from liability to the extent he is damaged by the breach. . . .

The obligation of the maker of a note is not a conditional promise to pay only at a specified place, but is a promise to pay generally, even though a place of payment is named. . . .

We think that § 87, declaring an instrument payable at a bank the equivalent of an order on the bank, was only intended to settle the vexed question of the bank's right, without specific authority, to pay such an instrument and charge same to the account of the principal debtor. Prior to the Act of 1899, in Tennessee and elsewhere, the fact that a note was made payable at a bank did not, without more, confer authority upon the bank to pay the note, when presented there at maturity by the holder, out of funds standing on deposit to the credit of the maker. A contrary rule obtained in many states.

Section 87 authorizes a bank, at which an instrument is made payable, to pay same for the account of the principal debtor. To that extent, all instruments payable at a bank are orders on the bank designated. The language used in this section, however, must not be so expanded as to destroy other provisions of the act.

Our attention has not been called to any decision of the question here determined in a jurisdiction where the Negotiable Instruments Law has been enacted. Prior to the compilation of this law, there were authorities to the contrary. . . .

CASE NO. 2

Columbian Banking Co. v. Bowen. 134 Wis. 218, 114 N.W. 451 (1908)

June 10, 1903, the banking firm known as the Farmers' & Merchants' Bank, of Bangor, Wis., sold to the defendant a $400 draft, drawn in the usual form, dated on that day, payable to defendant's order, and drawn by such firm on the National Bank of North America, at Chicago, Ill. The draft was sent to the defendant at Barron, Wis., and was indorsed by him to A. R. Tabbert, to whom it was forwarded by mail, at Spokane, Wash., June 16, 1903, and was there received by him June 20th thereafter. He was at Spokane temporarily and was on his way to the city of San Francisco, Cal. July 14, 1903, he indorsed the draft and sold the same to the plaintiff at such city, receiving $400 therefor. On that day, in due course, plaintiff sent the draft by mail to the Bankers' National Bank, of Chicago, Ill., by which it was received July 18th thereafter, and was then, as requested, duly presented to the drawee for payment, which was refused, whereupon it was duly protested for nonpayment by a duly authorized notary public, who forwarded a manifest thereof with notices of protest. . . . Plaintiff upon receipt of the manifest and notices duly sent the one for defendant to him at Barron, Wis., by whom it was duly received, . . .

The case was tried by the court resulting in findings of fact in accordance with the statement, and a conclusion of law that plaintiff became the owner of the draft in due course, and was entitled to judgment for $210, with costs. . . .

MARSHALL, J. . . . Counsel for appellant have presented quite an extended argument, referring to many authorities, as to the law antedating and independently of the negotiable instrument statute . . . to support the proposition, that appellant was released from liability on the instrument in question, because of the period intervening between his parting therewith and the presentation thereof to the drawee for payment. . . .

The primary question discussed by appellant's counsel, it is believed, is fully covered by the negotiable instrument law. There are a multitude of decisions regarding the character of a bill of exchange and that of a check, as those terms are used in business transactions, and to what extent the incidents of one are identical with those of the other, which decisions are so variant in their phrasing of the matter as to produce more or less confusion in respect thereto with many apparent, and some real, conflicts, to remedy which was one of the principal objects of the law.

To that end it was provided in section 1680:

"A bill of exchange is an uncondi-

> tional order in writing addressed by one person to another, signed by the person giving it, requiring the person to whom it is addressed to pay on demand or at a fixed or determinable future time a sum certain in money to order or bearer,"

and it was further provided in section 1684-1, "A check is a bill of exchange drawn on a bank, payable on demand."

As to whether the incidents of the species of bills of exchange last mentioned are the same as those of bills of exchange generally, it was further provided in the section last referred to,

> "Except as herein otherwise provided, the provisions of this act applicable to a bill of exchange payable on demand apply to a check."

The only exception referred to material to this case is contained in section 1684-2, in these words:

> "A check must be presented for payment within a reasonable time after its issue or the drawer will be discharged from liability thereon to the extent of the loss caused by the delay."

Keeping in mind that the discharge from liability above referred to because of unreasonable delay after the issuance of a check in presenting it for payment, is of the drawer only, and that this action is against the payee who indorsed the instrument in question without qualification and put it in circulation, we turn to section 1678-1, which provides, as to a bill of exchange payable on demand, which from the foregoing obviously includes a check or draft on a bank of the character of the one in question,

> "presentment for payment will be sufficient if made within a reasonable time after the last negotiation thereof."

From the foregoing it seems plain that as regards the payee of such an instrument as we have here, who puts the same in circulation with his unqualified indorsement thereon, and all subsequent parties thereto so indorsing the same, presentment for payment is sufficient, as regards their liability, if made within a reasonable time after the last negotiation. A bill of exchange payable on demand, regardless of its character, put in circulation, so long as its circulating character is preserved may be outstanding without impairing the liability of indorsers thereof. Formerly the length of time within which a bill of exchange might circulate without impairing such liability was more or less uncertain, rendering it very difficult to determine any one case by the decision in another. That difficulty was removed, so far as practicable, by the provision that only the time need be considered intervening between the last negotiation and the presentment. . . .

. . . . .

Applying the law as aforesaid to the facts of this case, it is readily seen that the delay in presenting the paper for payment between its date and the negotiation to the bank at San Francisco is immaterial. Appellant unqualifiedly indorsed the paper and put it in circulation by sending it to Tabbert at a distant part of the country, probably knowing that he was a traveler. Tabbert received the paper while journeying with the intention of going to San Francisco and held it till he arrived there and then negotiated it. It was promptly presented for payment thereafter and so in time, as regards that circumstance, to preserve the liability of appellant. . . .

The point is made that the instrument was not presented to the drawee for payment during banking hours. The negotiable instrument law at section 1678-2 provides that

> "Presentment for payment to be sufficient, must be made: . . . at a

reasonable hour on a business day. . . ."

The evidence shows that the paper, after taking its course through the clearing house, was presented to the drawee for payment on the afternoon of the same day between the hours of 3 and 6 o'clock. The proof is to the effect that such was the customary way of doing such business in Chicago, where the drawee was located. That is, as we understand it, that the business day of the bank continued after the closing of the clearing house transactions so as to enable banks holding paper for collection, refused recognition in such transactions, to be presented for payment as was done in this case. That satisfies the statute. What constitutes business hours of a bank, within the meaning of the statute, has reference to the general custom at the place of the particular transaction in question. In case of a transaction occurring in a foreign jurisdiction, as in the instance in question, the court cannot take judicial notice of what constitutes reasonable hours on a business day. Daniel on Negotiable Instruments (5th Ed.) § 601. It is a matter of proof, though in case of the notarial certificate of the transaction, as here, being regular so as to furnish prima facie proof that the paper was duly presented for payment, that raises the presumption that the presentment was made at a proper time. . . .

Judgment affirmed.

CASE NO. 3

Viles v. S. D. Warren Co. 132 Me. 277, 170 Atl. 501 (1934)

PATTANGALL, J. . . . Plaintiff admits receiving check, which it is agreed was not paid by reason of the insolvency of the bank on which it was drawn. Defendant's position is that, had the check been presented for payment within a reasonable time, plaintiff would have received his money. . . .

It appears that defendant was indebted to plaintiff; that their places of business were some sixty miles apart; that defendant mailed a check, payable to plaintiff's order, to plaintiff, for the full amount of the debt, with a voucher attached bearing the indorsement, "Account poplar contract, $2,000"; and that it was received at plaintiff's office on the following day. The next morning the check was taken from the envelope by plaintiff's bookkeeper, who prepared a deposit slip to accompany it when banked, and set the documents aside for plaintiff's attention. Plaintiff was not at his office on the day the check arrived nor on the following day until after banking hours, when he first learned of its arrival. He then indorsed it, and the next morning it was deposited in the local bank and forwarded in the regular course of business, arriving at the bank on which it was drawn one day too late to be cashed on account of the closing of that bank. Defendant had, at all times, a sufficient deposit to meet the check. . . .

The general rule governing the question of reasonable time for presentation of checks for payment is well established. If the bank on which the check is drawn and the payee are in the same place, the check should be presented during banking hours of the first secular day following its receipt; if in different places, it should be deposited in the mail in like time. Special circumstances may excuse delay in either case, but in their absence the rule is absolute. . . .

Plaintiff admits the rule, but contends that, under the circumstances existing in this case, the delay of one day beyond the time fixed by it was not unreasonable. The points relied on are: (1) That plaintiff did not personally receive the check until the day after it came to his office and had no reason to anticipate it at that particular time; (2) that, the check being accompanied by a voucher, the acceptance of it automatically receipted in full the account for which it was given, so that it required his personal attention and could not properly have been looked after by his bookkeeper; (3) that his absence from his office was occasioned by his being engaged in important public business in connection with the state Senate, of which he was a member.

These reasons for delay beyond the time fixed as reasonable under normal conditions are urged as sufficient to take the case out of the general rule. We cannot agree with that conclusion. . . .

The authorities are agreed that certain circumstances of a general nature excuse delay. These are listed by Story, Parsons, Randolph, and Daniels, and quoted in many legal opinions substantially as follows:

> "(1) Inevitable accident or overwhelming calamity; (2) prevalence of a malignant disease which suspends the ordinary operations of business; (3) the presence of political circumstances amounting to a virtual interruption and an obstruction of the ordinary negotiations of trade; (4) the breaking out of war between the country of the maker and that of the holder; (5) the occupation of the country where the parties live, or where the note is payable, by a public enemy, which suspends commercial intercourse; (6) public and positive interdictions and prohibitions of the state which obstruct or suspend commerce and intercourse; (7) the utter impracticability of finding the maker or ascertaining his place of residence."

. . .

In Barker v. Parker, 6 Pick. (Mass.) 80, the court saw no excuse in the fact that on the day when presentment should have been made there was a heavy rainstorm and the plaintiff lived twenty miles distant, saying that,

> "if it had appeared that a violent tempest had so broken up or destroyed the roads, or obstructed them that they were impassable, perhaps it might have been considered a providential interception, on account of which the plaintiff would not have been charged with negligence."

Somewhat similar circumstances failed to excuse in McDonald v. Mosher, 23 Ill. App. 206. Here the jury found against the drawer of the check. The court reversed its finding, saying:

> "It does not appear it was physically impossible for appellee to have traveled the distance of two miles to the village on that day. While the law does not require it should be made manifest it was absolutely impossible so to do, yet it does require it should be shown it was actually and reasonably impossible to do so.
>
> . . . One may be willing to sacrifice a sum of money, large or small, rather than take a cold, disagreeable, and difficult walk or ride, and yet this fact affords no just cause for the conclusion that it was reasonably a physical impossibility for him to make such trip."

In Wilson, Executrix v. Senier, 14 Wis. 411, the court said . . .

> "Illness, in order to constitute a sufficient excuse, must be that of the holder or his agent and of such a character as to prevent due presentment by the exercise of due diligence. And where an endorser was called from home in consequence of the dangerous illness of his wife and left his house in care of a lad without authority to open letters, it was held that he had lost recourse against his prior endorsers by the consequent de-

lay in giving notice. He should have left some one in charge with authority to open letters." . . .

The foregoing cases are fairly illustrative of the position generally taken in jurisdictions where the question has arisen. . . .

By the great weight of authority, the holder of a check is held to a high degree of care in protecting the maker from loss by reason of the closing of the bank against which the check is drawn. The rule appears to be based on sound grounds from every standpoint—legal, equitable, and moral. . . .

In the instant case, plaintiff, in the exercise of the degree of care which the law demands, should either have visited his office during some period of the day when his legislative duties permitted or have arranged with his bookkeeper to act in his stead. His office was in the state capitol and accessible to the state house by telephone. If plaintiff's agent was negligent in not communicating with his principal, and if that negligence caused the loss, plaintiff is responsible. . . .

Judgment for defendant.

CASE NO. 4

Gilpin v. Savage. 201 N.Y. 167, 94 N.E. 656 (1911)

CULLEN, C.J. The action is brought against the indorser of a promissory note, made payable at a particular place designated by street and number, which was the residence of the maker. The only question in the case is whether the presentment to the maker was sufficient to charge the indorser. At the maturity of the note it was in the hands of the Columbia National Bank, which was located about two miles from the maker's residence, in Buffalo. After some delays the cashier of the bank succeeded in calling up the maker at his place of residence. He stated to him that the bank held the note, and the further conversation between the parties we will assume to be sufficient to establish a demand for its payment and refusal or statement of inability on the part of the maker to comply with the demand. The cashier had the note in his possession when the demand was made, and the maker made no request to see it or for its production, but stated he would call at the bank, which he did a short time subsequently. . . .

By section 116 of the Negotiable Instruments Law an indorser engages that on due presentment a note or bill will be paid, and that if it be dishonored, and if the necessary proceedings on dishonor be duly taken, he will pay the amount thereof to the holder; by section 130 presentment for payment is necessary in order to charge the indorser; by section 132 presentment, to be sufficient, must be made at a proper place as defined in the act; and by section 133 presentment is made at a proper place where a place of payment is specified in the instrument, and it is there presented. These statutory provisions seem to be a mere re-enactment of the common law as it has hitherto obtained in this state, with the possible exception that they may have altered the rule that, where no possible damage could occur to the indorser by the failure to make proper presentment, he was not discharged by such failure, which exception, however, was of the most limited character, mere insolvency of a party primarily liable on the instrument not being sufficient to create it. Smith v. Miller, 52 N.Y. 545.

It seems to us entirely clear that no proper presentment of the note was made. Presentment of a note and demand of payment must be made by actual exhibition of the instrument itself, or at least the demand should be accompanied by some clear indication that the instrument is at hand, ready to be delivered, and such must really be the case. Daniel on Negotiable Instruments, § 654. Although it may not be necessary actually to produce the note, if the maker refuses to pay it, it must be there at the place for presentment; otherwise, the presentment is insufficient. . . .

So necessary is it that the demand be made at the place specified in the instrument, in order that the indorser may be charged, that the addition to a promissory note payable generally, of words specifying a particular place of payment is held to be a material alteration of a contract, which of itself discharges the indorser.

The counsel for the respondent seeks to sustain the judgment below on two propositions: First, that a demand over the telephone on the maker, at the place specified in the note, is the same as a demand at that place by ordinary speech; second, that the possession of the note by the cashier was sufficient to make the demand a proper one. The truth of the first proposition as a general rule may be conceded; but the argument ignores the fact that a valid presentment, as hitherto pointed out, consists of something more than mere demand. It requires personal attendance at the place of demand with the note, in readiness to exhibit it if required, and to receive payment and surrender it if the debtor is willing to pay. The counsel cites several cases in which it is said that the possession of the instrument by the person making the demand is sufficient although it is not actually exhibited. These statements were entirely accurate when made, before the general use of the telephone. When demand is made by ordinary human vocal power, unaided by mechanical device, it is plain that the person making the demand is necessarily present at the place at which the demand is made, and if the instrument is in his possession the presence of the instrument is equally clear. The statement, if now inaccurate, is so by the use of the telephone. If the theory on which the decisions of the courts below have proceeded is to prevail, it is difficult to see why a valid presentment of a note payable in Buffalo might not be made over the telephone from New York; or, if that is to be deemed too great a distance, where shall the line between a sufficient and insufficient demand and presentment be drawn? Will a demand for payment of an instrument payable in Buffalo be good if made at Batavia, and bad if made at Rochester? . . .

CASE NO. 5

Commercial Trust Co. v. New England Macaroni Mfg. Co. 247 Mass. 366, 141 N.E. 285 (1924)

CARROLL, J. This is an action on a promissory note in the sum of $2,000, dated April 24, 1920, and payable in 90 days to the plaintiff at its place of business. The maker is the New England Macaroni Manufacturing Company, and the other defendants are indorsers.

Although the note in suit was payable to the plaintiff at its place of business the record does not show that the note was in the plaintiff's possession or at its banking house at maturity. Before the enactment of the Negotiable Instruments Law, it was settled that the plaintiff, being the payee of the note payable at its bank, in case the maker did not appear on the due date with funds for payment, was not required to make formal presentment or demand. It was presumed, in the absence of proof to the contrary, that the note was at the banking house on the day of maturity. . . .

The more difficult question is whether this presumption survives under the Negotiable Instruments Law. Section 74 provides that

"the instrument must be exhibited to the person from whom payment is demanded,"

and by section 72 presentment for payment to be sufficient must be made by the holder, or by some person authorized to receive payment on his behalf, at a reasonable hour of a business day, at a proper place, to a person primarily liable on the instrument, or, if he is absent or inaccessible, to any person found at the place where presentment is made.

By section 87 of the statute, when the instrument is payable at a bank, it is equivalent to an order to the bank to pay the same for the account of the principal debtor thereon. Section 75 provides, when an instrument is payable at a bank, presentment must be made during banking hours unless the person to make payment has no funds there to meet it,

"in which case presentment at any hour before the bank is closed on that day is sufficient."

A strict construction would seem to require that the plaintiff should make formal presentment and demand of the note at its maturity. The Negotiable Instruments Act, however, did not in our opinion change the rule previously established, that a note payable to a bank at its place of business was presumed, in the absence of evidence to the contrary, to be at its maturity at the bank. Evidence of formal presentment and demand was not required. And it was not intended, by the Negotiable Instruments Act, to do away with this presumption or change the well-established rule in reference to the evidence required to show due presentment when the instrument was payable to a bank at its banking house. It was recognized in Union Trust Co. v. McGinty, 212 Mass. 205, 98 N.E. 679, Ann. Cas. 1913C 525, that the Negotiable Instruments Act did not cover the whole field of negotiable instrument law. In the absence of an express provision to the contrary, we must assume that the presumption in favor of the plaintiff continues. . . .

CASE NO. 6

O'Neal v. Clark. 229 Ala. 127, 155 So. 562, 94 A.L.R. 589 (1934)

. . . . .

BOULDIN, J., delivered the opinion of the court:

The questions presented on this appeal concern the liability of indorsers on a certificate of deposit issued by a bank.

Indorsers claim a discharge for want of presentment and notice of dishonor. . . .

On January 1, 1932, the Andalusia National Bank issued to Dr. Franklin A. Clark, plaintiff, a certificate of deposit for $12,000 in usual form

"payable to the order of himself 12 months after date on the return of this certificate properly endorsed. Interest at 4% payable quarterly."

As part of the transaction, and before the delivery of such certificate of deposit, R. N. McLeod, C. A. O'Neal, L. M. Milligan, T. E. Henderson, and C. S. O'Neal, officers, directors, or stockholders of the bank, indorsed the same on the back in blank.

Dr. Clark was, at the time, a depositor of the bank, having on general deposit a sum greater than the amount of the certificate, and, on execution of the certificate, drew his check in favor of the bank for like amount, and same was charged against his checking account.

Without question the indorsers were original parties to the instrument, given in consideration of his leaving the money in the bank, just as if he had made a time deposit in the first instance on the security of such indorsement.

On October 3, 1932, before the maturity of the certificate of deposit, the bank failed, closed its doors, and a receiver took charge for liquidation under the national banking laws. He occupied the same offices, kept regular hours for the business of liquidation up to and including the date of maturity, January 1, 1933.

The instrument was not presented for payment at maturity. It was, prior to maturity, filed with the receiver as a claim against the closed bank, and there remained at date of maturity. . . .

A certificate of deposit, such as here involved, having all the requirements of negotiability defined by law, is a negotiable instrument. In effect, it is a promissory note. . . .

Without question, therefore, this instrument is subject to the requirements of law touching presentment for payment and notice of dishonor.

The Negotiable Instruments Law is quite inclusive, apt, and concise in terms, designed to advise all parties to commercial paper of their legal rights and duties.

Touching presentment for payment, the statute declares:

> ". . . Except as herein otherwise provided, presentment for payment is necessary in order to charge the . . . indorsers." Code, § 9096.

The statute further declares:

> "Presentment for payment is dispensed with: (1) Where after the exercise of reasonable diligence presentment as required by this chapter cannot be made." § 9108, Code.

What are the requirements of the chapter as to presentment in this case?

The instrument was payable at a bank, the issuing bank, which was also the maker, the party due to make payment.

> "Where the instrument is payable at a bank, presentment for payment must be made during banking hours, unless the person to make payment has no funds there to meet it at any time during the day, in which case presentment at any hour before the bank is closed on that day is sufficient." § 9101, Code.

This contemplates, as of course, an open going bank, functioning as a bank, with whom people can do the business to be done at a bank. . . .

The fact that the receiver winding up the affairs of the closed bank was at the banking place on the day of maturity can make no difference. He had no connection whatever with honoring or dishonoring paper presented for payment. Neither he nor any one else could act for the bank in making payment. As a bank, it had ceased to exist. It was not a mere question of inability to pay as in case of insolvency or bankruptcy, but want of lawful authority to function with regard to the presentation of paper for the purpose of binding indorsers.

We hold, under the law, presentment was dispensed with or excused in the case at bar. . . .

Notice of dishonor is made a condition to the liability of an indorser, a law-made condition, written into the contract. It is not a question of knowledge of dishonor, otherwise acquired, nor of injury to the indorser from want of notice. The law takes these issues out of such transactions. . . .

The mere fact that presentment cannot be made to the maker, and is therefore excused, by no means dispenses with the necessity to give notice of dishonor to the indorser. . . .

Code, § 9135, defines other cases in which notice of dishonor is not required to be given to an indorser. The only one claimed to have bearing on this case is: "(3) Where the instrument was made or accepted for his accommodation." . . .

The fact that the indorsers were officers or stockholders of the banking corporation, lending their credit to the bank in forwarding a banking business in which they had an interest, does not render them accommodated indorsers. . . .

By the great weight of authority the interest of a stockholder or officer in the corporation whose paper he indorses does not render the instrument one made for the indorser's accommodation. . . .

We are of opinion, therefore, that nothing shown in the instant case excused the giving of notice of dishonor to these indorsers, and a failure to give same resulted in their discharge. . . .

CASE NO. 7

State Bank of East Moline v. Standaert. 335 Ill. App. 519 (1948)

BRISTOW, J., delivered the opinion of the court:

In a proceeding instituted by the plaintiff, State Bank of East Moline, to recover payment on a note from the defendants Alfons and Lena Standaert, and Alois and Anna De Vos, makers and indorsers respectively, the circuit court of Rock Island county, in a trial without jury, entered a judgment in favor of the plaintiff, from which the defendant indorser, Anna De Vos, appeals. . . .

The sole issue presented herein is whether the plaintiff bank gave the defendant indorser notice of dishonor as required under the terms of the Negotiable Instruments Law. . . .

From the record it appears that on February 28, 1920, defendants Alfons Standaert and Lena Standaert made and delivered their promissory note to the defendants Alois De Vos and Anna De Vos. . . .

Before maturity the defendants Alois and Anna De Vos sold the note and mortgage to the plaintiff bank. The note was not paid at maturity. . . .

At the trial the plaintiff bank contended that, when the note in controversy was not paid on the due date, notice of its dishonor was sent to the defendant indorsers.

In support thereof plaintiff offered the testimony of Leota Baker who was employed as teller-bookkeeper in 1925, and charged with the duty of attending to maturing notes. She stated that it was the unswerving custom of the bank to send to the parties, 10 days prior to the due date of a note, a notice describing the note and specifying its maturity date. If the note was not paid at maturity, this same form of notice with the added notation that it had not been paid by the maker, and that the indorser should make payment thereon, was mailed by the bank at the close of the day on which the note was due.

She further testified that she did not recall preparing or sending out the particular notice of dishonor to the defendant indorsers, Alois and Anna De Vos, on February 28, 1925, when the Standaerts failed to pay the obligation, but that during her seven years of service to the bank she knew of no instance where the bank failed to give notice of dishonor. . . . B. H. Ryan, who was assistant cashier . . . reiterated the custom of the bank respecting notices of dishonor, and explained that some of the records of the bank pertaining to such notices, including the records in the instant case, were destroyed after 10 years. . . .

The defendant, Anna De Vos, contends in this proceeding that she should not be charged with the payment of the note on the ground that she did not receive notice that the instrument had been dishonored, and therefore, under the Negotiable Instruments Law she was discharged. She maintains that she did not know that the note was not paid until suit was filed in 1932, some seven years after the obligation was due. In fact, the plaintiff bank loaned her some $19,000 in 1928 and 1929 without any reference to the note in controversy, or her liability thereon. . . .

The Negotiable Instruments Law provides that when a negotiable instrument has been dishonored by nonpayment, notice of dishonor must be given to the indorser, otherwise he is discharged. (Ill. Rev. Stat. 1947, ch. 98, par. 110 (Jones Ill. Stats. Ann. 89.110)) Such notice may be given by mail, and where it is duly addressed and deposited in a post office, the sender is deemed to have given due notice, notwithstanding any miscarriage in the mails. . . .

This requirement of addressing and depositing the notice in the post office does not prescribe the precise testimony to be introduced in a cause, but rather sets forth the ultimate facts to be established by the evidence. In other words, to charge an indorser with the payment of a note, the plaintiff must establish that the notice of dishonor was addressed and actually mailed . . . and these facts may be proven by direct or circumstantial evidence as any other fact in the case.

In the case at bar the only evidence of plaintiff's compliance with the statutory requirement of giving notice of dishonor to the indorser was the testimony of Leota Baker that it was the custom of the bank at the close of the business day on which a note was due and unpaid to send a notice. . . .

Although Leota Baker was charged with preparing these notices, she did not recall preparing or sending any particular notice of dishonor to the defendant, Anna De Vos, on February 28, 1925. Moreover, she did not know who was charged with posting the bank's mail on that date. She stated that perhaps Emma Callewaert did it, since the post office was on her way home, or perhaps even she, herself, posted the mail. Emma Callewaert, however, was not in the employ of the bank on the due date of the note, and there is no certainty as to who posted the mail, or whether, in fact, any mail was posted on that date. Therefore, other than the description of the general custom of the bank of notifying indorsers, the only evidence tending to prove, even circumstantially, that notice of dishonor was prepared and mailed to the defendant was the inference from Leota Baker's self-serving declaration that she always did her duty and never failed to send out a notice of dishonor.

The courts have taken cognizance of the intricacies and expansion of business enterprises, and the cases reveal a liberalizing tendency with reference to the proof required to establish the posting of a letter. (Ponder v. Jefferson Standard Life Ins. Co., 6 F. (2d) 300; Peirson-Lathrop Grain Co. v. Barker (Mo. App.), 223 S.W. 941; 86 A.L.R. 539 et seq.) From a review of the cases, however, it is evident that while courts may not require the person mailing the letter for a large concern to have a distinct recollection of the particular letter, there must be some evidence on the part of the person whose general practice it was to post the mail that the custom was complied with on the date in question. (25 A.L.R. 9, 13; 86 A.L.R. 539, 541; 31 C.J.S. 781; Peirson-Lathrop Grain Co. v. Barker, supra; Cook v. Phillips, 109 N.J.L. 371, 162 Atl. 732. . .

In Cook v. Phillips, supra, the court stated:

"We do not think that the mere

dictation or writing of a letter coupled with evidence of an office custom with reference to the mailing of letters is sufficient to constitute proof of mailing the same, in the absence of some proof or corroborating circumstances sufficient to establish the fact that the custom in the particular instance had in fact been followed."

In the instant case there was not even evidence of the dictation or writing of the particular notice of dishonor.

This prevailing judicial opinion, moreover, has been followed by the Illinois courts. In Meyer v. Krug, 298 Ill. App. 625, the court held that the evidence was insufficient to establish a presumption of mailing where the plaintiff merely showed a general business practice with reference to mailing letters, but did not offer evidence by the person charged with the duty of mailing the letters on the particular date, that the custom was followed.

. . . in the instant case there is no evidence that the particular notice was prepared, or put in an envelope, or addressed, or even deposited in a place where it would ordinarily be taken up by an employee charged with the duty of posting the bank's mail, as in the cases cited by plaintiff. Plaintiff offered no copies of the notice, or records of any kind indicating that the notice was mailed herein. Therefore, even under the most liberal interpretation of the law, plaintiff's evidence is insufficient (Prudential Trust Co. v. Hayes, 247 Mass. 311, 142 N.E. 73). . . .

It is the opinion of this court, in the light of the foregoing analysis, that plaintiff failed to establish, either by direct or circumstantial evidence, that it mailed the notice of dishonor to the defendant indorser, Anna De Vos, . . . therefore, under the terms of the Negotiable Instruments Law, the defendant indorser was discharged. . . .

CASE NO. 8

Toole v. Crafts et al. 193 Mass. 110, 78 N.E. 775, 118 Am. St. Rep. 455 (1906)

Suit upon a promissory note signed by the defendant Howard A. Crafts and indorsed before delivery by Linus D. Crafts who alone defends. No demand for payment sufficient to charge the indorser was ever made upon the maker of the note. After the time for making a demand had expired the indorser Linus D. Crafts during the course of a conversation with one Ally, the attorney for the plaintiff, signed a waiver of "demand, notice and protest," which the attorney wrote upon the note.

HAMMOND, J. The defendant contended that at the time he signed the waiver he was not aware that he had been freed from his liability, but the court rightly ruled that if he knew the facts which released him, his ignorance as to their legal effect would not save him from the consequences of the waiver.

Defendant offered to show by his own testimony that at the time he signed the waiver he did not know that he had been relieved from liability on the note. This evidence was excluded. While, as above stated, it was not admissible to relieve him from the consequences of his waiver in the absence of fraud, yet upon the question of whether the representations of Ally were the real and effective inducement to his action it was admissible. It might well be that a man believing himself to be liable upon a note could be more easily influenced to sign such a waiver than one who believed himself free from liability.

. . . judgment reversed and remanded for a new trial.

Review Questions

1. What steps must be taken to fix the liability of secondary parties to negotiable instruments?
2. What is the effect upon the liability of secondary parties if there has been a failure to present an instrument for payment at the time and place specified?
3. What steps are required of the holder of an instrument as a condition to holding the primary party liable?
4. What is the effect of a provision in a promissory note that makes it payable at a designated bank?
5. What is the rule for determining the due date of an instrument that is payable a fixed number of days after date?
6. What is the importance of complying with the above rule?
7. What is the requirement as to the time for presentment for payment of demand notes? Of demand bills of exchange?
8. Since the rule is that a demand bill of exchange must be presented for payment within a reasonable time after the last negotiation thereof, for what period of time can the liability of the secondary parties be preserved?
9. In what respect does the liability of a drawer of a check differ from that of a drawer of any other type of demand bill of exchange if the instrument is not presented for payment within a reasonable time after its issue?
10. At what hour of the day must presentment for payment be made?
11. Where should an instrument be presented for payment when the instrument fails to specify a place for presentment?
12. Is a demand by telephone for payment of an instrument sufficient presentment?
13. Under what circumstances will presentment for payment be excused?
14. To whom should an instrument, upon which various individuals are liable as partners, be presented for payment?
15. What is a foreign bill of exchange?
16. Are the requirements as to time for presentment of a bill of exchange for acceptance different from the requirements for presentment for payment?
17. Under what circumstances is a presentment for acceptance required?
18. Within what period of time must the notice of dishonor be given?
19. If the notice of dishonor is not actually given to the party for whom it is intended, how should it be sent?
20. Is a secondary party to an instrument authorized to give notice of its dishonor?
21. In what various ways may a waiver of notice by a secondary party be accomplished?
22. What are the mechanics of protesting an instrument for dishonor?
23. When is the protest of an instrument required as a matter of law?
24. Does protesting an instrument dispense with the need of giving notice to secondary parties?
25. What does *noting an instrument for protest* consist of?

Problems for Discussion

1. Horn is the maker of a promissory note held by Burrell. The morning of the day the note is due, Horn calls Burrell and tells him to present the note at the

X bank, where he has left funds for its payment. One week later Burrell has not yet presented the note. Does this discharge Horn?

2. A, the payee holder of a draft payable on sight, negotiated it to B. B held the draft for nine months and then transferred it to C, who immediately presented it to the drawee for payment. The draft was dishonored, and A was looked to for payment. It was his contention that presentment had been delayed too long and that as a consequence he was discharged. Decide.
3. A, the drawer of a check payable to B, contends that B's failure to present the check for payment until four days after issue of the check discharged him from liability on the instrument. The drawer, drawee, and payee all resided in the same banking locality. Answer the contention.
4. A promissory note is dated July 25, 1947, and is payable three months from date. It is presented for payment on October 26, 1947. Is this a proper presentment?
5. A promissory note is due August 5, 1947. The holder presented it for payment on August 4 at 5 P.M. Is this a proper presentment?
6. A was a holder in due course of a bill of exchange drawn upon B. Some days before maturity, A wrote to B, informing him that the bill was due and payment was expected of him. A also set out a copy of the bill of exchange in his letter. This letter reached B on the day the bill fell due. B did not remit payment, and A sued him to recover. Result?
7. An instrument payable ninety days after its date falls due on a Saturday. The holder finds it inconvenient to make presentment on that day, so he waits until the next Monday. Is this a sufficient presentment?
8. An instrument was payable in three months from its date. The due date fell on Saturday and the holder made presentment on that day. The instrument was dishonored and the indorsers refused to pay upon the contention that they were discharged. Decide.
9. A promissory note provided for payment at the Merchants National Bank. At maturity the holder presented the note for payment at the maker's place of business and the note was dishonored. Are the indorsers liable?
10. An instrument was made payable at the X bank, which was in receivership at the time the instrument was due. No presentment was made, and Jones, an indorser, resists payment, claiming that the failure to present the instrument discharged him. Decide.
11. A note was made payable at the X bank. The holder of the note indorsed it to the X bank "for collection" two days prior to its maturity date. Was the fact that the note was at the X bank on the due date a sufficient presentment for payment?
12. A bill of exchange provides for payment on September 29, 1947. Must this instrument be presented to the drawee for acceptance as a condition to holding secondary parties liable?
13. A draft payable in thirty days from date drawn upon John Dill provided for payment at the Pioneer State Bank. The holder, upon the maturity date, presented the draft to the bank for payment and it was dishonored. Can he hold the drawer liable?
14. If you were the holder of a bill of exchange payable at a certain future time, why would you present it to the drawee for acceptance?
15. The holder of a thirty-day sight draft presents it to the drawee for acceptance

one year after its issue. The draft is dishonored and the holder looks to the drawer for payment. Will he succeed?

16. A draft payable sixty days after sight is sent to the drawee bank for acceptance. Three days later the holder calls at the bank for a return of the draft. The draft had been mislaid and the cashier of the bank represented that it had never been received. One week later the draft is discovered and returned to the holder unaccepted.
    (a) Can the holder recover from the drawee bank at maturity?
    (b) Should the holder treat the draft as dishonored after it is returned unaccepted?
17. Gibbs presented a draft to the drawee Carl for acceptance. Carl, wishing to communicate with the drawer, holds the draft and suggests that Gibbs call for it later. Two days later Gibbs demands a return of the draft and Carl refuses. Gibbs immediately notifies the drawer of dishonor. Can Gibbs expect to recover from the drawer upon the basis of the instrument's being dishonored by nonacceptance?
18. The holder of a bill of exchange demands payment from the drawer three days after the bill was dishonored by nonpayment. What will determine whether the holder can recover from the drawer?
19. The holder of a dishonored note, unable to find the indorser, delivered notice of the dishonor to the indorser's wife at his (the indorser's) store. Is this a sufficient notice?
20. A, the holder of a dishonored instrument, mailed B, an indorser, a properly addressed notice of dishonor within the time required under Section 104 of the N.I.L. The letter, however, carried insufficient postage and was returned to the sender A. He remailed the notice the following day, and it was received by B in due course. Is this a sufficient notice?
21. The holder of a dishonored note mailed a notice to the indorser as required by Section 104 of the N.I.L. The notice was lost in the mails. Can the indorser avoid payment upon the ground that he was never given notice of dishonor?
22. Jones, the holder of a promissory note, placed it in the hands of his agent for collection. The agent presented the note for payment upon the due date and payment was refused. The next day the agent notified Jones of the dishonor and Jones, on the following day, served notice upon Willis, an indorser upon the note. Jones and Willis were fellow townsmen. Willis refused to pay upon the contention that notice as required by Section 103 of the N.I.L. was not given. Decide.
23. The following names appear as indorsers upon a dishonored note: Bass, Crane, Bull. The holder has given the required notice to the last indorser, Bull. What may Bull do for his protection?
24. X was the holder of a draft drawn in the state of Maine, which fact, however, did not appear upon its face. The draft was payable at Louisville, Kentucky, and when presented for payment it was dishonored. The holder failed to protest the draft but served notice of dishonor upon the indorsers. Are the indorsers liable upon the draft?

23 NEGOTIABLE INSTRUMENTS: CHECKS

► I. NATURE OF CHECKS

Section 185 of the N.I.L. declares a check to be "a bill of exchange drawn on a bank payable on demand," and it further declares that "except as herein otherwise provided, the provisions of this act applicable to a bill of exchange payable on demand apply to a check." Substantially the same rules of law apply to checks as apply to other forms of bills. The main points of difference will be brought out in the following discussion.

► II. RELATIONSHIP BETWEEN DRAWER AND DRAWEE BANK

Every bill of exchange presupposes a creditor-debtor relationship existing between the drawer and drawee. Such a relationship arises when one deposits funds in a bank—the bank becomes the debtor of the depositor, who stands in the position of a general creditor. Where the deposit is held in a checking account, the bank also agrees with the depositor to pay as he orders by his checks, if these are properly presented. The drawee bank has a contractual obligation to honor the orders of the drawer as evidenced by the checks to which he has affixed his signature.

► III. DRAWEE'S OBLIGATIONS

A. TO HOLDER AND DRAWER

The drawee bank has no obligation to the holder of a check. A check does not represent an assignment of funds held by the bank so as to give the holder a present right to the money. It is merely an order from the drawer to the drawee bank directing the bank to discharge its contractual obligation. The bank's only obligation is to the drawer. Should it fail to honor a check without just cause, it would make itself liable to the drawer for damages caused by injury to his credit or any special damages that could be proved.[1]

B. STOP-PAYMENT ORDERS

The drawee bank is as much under a contractual obligation to honor the drawer's stop-payment orders as it is to honor his orders to pay. At any time before a check has been honored, the drawer can countermand the order to pay by order-

[1] State Bank of Siloam Springs v. Marshall, p. 586.

ing the bank not to pay.[2] Unless the bank observes the stop order, it makes itself liable to the drawer for any *injury* caused him by payment of the check.*

A stop-payment order in no way alters the rights between the drawer and the holder of the check. If the check represents a valid contractual obligation, it is enforceable against the drawer. To illustrate:

(1) Let us suppose that A gives B a check in payment for a car. Upon discovering the car to be quite the contrary to B's representations, A immediately stops payment upon the check. The check in the hands of B is not an enforceable obligation, since A has available the defense of fraud. In the event, however, that B has negotiated the check to C, a holder in due course, the stop-payment order will be of no avail. The personal defense of fraud will not be available against the holder in due course, C. Although the stop order will prevent him from cashing the check, he has the right of action for its collection against the drawer.

(2) "A check is essentially commercial paper, possessing the attributes of a contract and certain characteristics of property and it is equivalent to a promise to pay upon the part of the drawer. It is executory in its nature.

"The case of *Dowling et al.* v. *Parker et al.,* 221 Ala. 63, 127 So. 813, 814, is particularly applicable to the instant case. In the Dowling case, a mortgagor, still in possession of a mortgaged mule, negotiated a sale of the mule. By mutual agreement the purchaser made the check for the price payable to the mortgagee. The purchaser took possession of the mule, and when it died, within a few days, he stopped payment on the check. The Supreme Court declared:

" 'Defendant gains nothing by the fact that a check is deemed a conditional payment—conditioned on its being cashed. It expresses a contract of the drawer to pay, and, if not cashed because of his countermand or other cause not the fault of the payee, a suit lies as on a promissory note or other bill of exchange.' " *Scott* v. *State,* 33 So. (2d) 390 (Ala.)

► IV. CERTIFICATION OF CHECKS

Section 189 of the N.I.L. reads:

"A check of itself does not operate as an assignment of any part of the funds to the credit of the drawer with the bank, and the bank is not liable to the holder, unless and until it accepts or certifies the check."

The act of certification of a check is characterized in *Meads* v. *Merchants' Bank,* 25 N.Y. 143, as follows:

"The certification of a check by the bank upon which it is drawn is analogous to the acceptance of a bill of exchange. The check itself is, when presented to the banker and accepted by him, an appropriation of so much of the funds of the drawer in favor of the holder. It produces a complete novation in respect of the amount named in it; the holder is substituted in the place of the drawer

[2] Keller v. Fredericktown Sav. Inst., p. 587.

* See Speroff v. First Central Trust Co., p. 101.

as the creditor of the bank; the bank charges the amount of the check against the drawer on his account, and becomes primarily liable to the holder."

Section 187 of the N.I.L. provides that the certification of a check is equivalent to an acceptance; that is, the certifying bank makes the same promises and admissions as those made by an acceptor of a bill of exchange.

However, the certification of a check differs fundamentally in one respect from an acceptance. Section 188 of the N.I.L. provides:

> "Where the holder of a check procures it to be accepted or certified the drawer and all indorsers are discharged from liability thereon." [3]

The acceptance of a bill of exchange has no such effect; the holder can still look to all parties for satisfaction. From the point of view of the drawer and indorsers, a certification is a payment of the instrument. In effect, the certifying bank has discharged the existing instrument and by the certification has issued an entirely different instrument to the holder, an instrument more in the nature of a certificate of deposit.

When the certification is obtained by the drawer, as is frequently the case, he is not relieved of liability upon the instrument. The certification merely gives the assurance that the funds are available and that the instrument will be honored upon a proper presentment. As such, it lends considerable security to the instrument. The drawer could be looked to for satisfaction, however, as a party secondarily liable if the check should be dishonored for some reason.[4]

► V. DRAWER'S LIABILITY

The liability of a drawer of a check differs somewhat from that of a drawer of an ordinary bill of exchange. As noted previously, the drawer of a check is not absolutely discharged by the failure of the holder to present the instrument for payment within the required time. He is discharged only to the extent of the loss caused by the delay. Thus, if a check is retained an unreasonable length of time after its issue and the drawee bank closes its doors because of insolvency before it is presented for payment, the loss will fall upon the holder of the check. He will be able to realize that amount which the bank can pay upon its obligations. For example, if the check is for $50 and the bank is 50 per cent solvent, the holder will realize $25 and absorb the balance as the loss caused by his delay. Federal deposit insurance has greatly lessened the risk to a holder of a check.

The drawer of a check (unlike the drawer of a bill of exchange) impliedly represents that funds are available to meet the obligation represented by the check. Consequently, where a check is dishonored for a lack of funds, the drawer has made himself liable to the holder for fraud. Penal statutes are provided to discourage the fraudulent drawing of checks when no funds are available to meet the obligation.

[3] Linsky v. U.S., p. 588.
[4] Welch v. Bank of Manhatten Co., p. 589.

CASES

CASE NO. 1

State Bank of Siloam Springs v. Marshall. 163 Ark. 566, 260 S.W. 431, 34 A.L.R. 202 (1924)

HART, J. At the time the plaintiff drew the checks in question on the defendant bank she had on deposit there a sum subject to her check which was greater than the amount of the four checks drawn by her upon which the bank refused payment. The ground upon which the bank dishonored the checks was that it had applied the deposit of the plaintiff towards the payment of a debt which she owed the bank, but which was not then due. It was also shown by the plaintiff that she was not at the time insolvent, and that the bank had no lien on her deposit.

The general rule is that a bank is bound to honor checks drawn on it by a depositor, if it has sufficient funds belonging to the depositor when the check is presented, and the funds are not subject to any lien or claim; and for its refusal or neglect to do so it is liable in an action by the depositor. This rule is so well settled in this state as well as elsewhere that a citation of authorities in support of it is not necessary.

In McCall v. First National Bank, 138 Ark. 370, 211 S.W. 919, 4 A.L.R. 940, and First National Bank v. McFall & Co., 144 Ark. 149, 222 S.W. 40, this court held that, in case a bank wrongfully dishonors, through mistake or otherwise, a merchant or trader's check, injury to his credit may be inferred from the fact that he is a merchant or trader, and substantial damages may be awarded upon proof of that fact without anything more.

The reason is that the act of the banker in refusing to honor the check imputes insolvency or bad faith to the drawer of the check, and has the effect of slandering the merchant or trader in his business. The refusal to pay the check injures the credit of the merchant or trader, and because this element of damages is difficult to prove and estimate, temperate damages are allowed. They are more than nominal damages, and are such as would be a reasonable compensation for the injury to the credit of the merchant or trader.

Subsequent to the rendition of these decisions the Legislature of 1921 passed act 496, whereby the act of the General Assembly of 1913 creating the state bank department was amended. Section 10 of the act reads as follows:

> "A depositor, whether a merchant or trader or otherwise, may recover from any bank doing business in this state for or on account of its wrongful dishonor of his check only upon allegation and proof of such special damages as have approximately resulted to him thereform." General Acts of 1921, p. 514 at 524.

The evident purpose of the section quoted was to change the rule announced in the decisions referred to above, and to require depositors in all cases to prove the amount of damages they have suffered by reason of the bank's refusing to pay their checks before they can recover more than nominal damages. In short, merchants and traders must prove actual loss to their credit before they can recover damages from a bank for refusing to pay their checks.

The plaintiff, not being a merchant or trader, was not entitled to recover more than nominal damages under the proof made. Her testimony that she suffered damages to her credit in business was not sufficient to allow her to recover more than nominal damages. She must show the facts or circumstances which occasioned the damages and the amount thereof. At most she only showed in the present case that her checks were dishonored by the bank, and that she suffered some inconvenience thereby. It is not shown that she suffered any loss of patronage to her rooming and boarding house, or that she was prevented from supplying her guests with food or other articles necessary for their use and comfort. It is shown that one of the merchants in question refused to extend her credit any further, but she continued to buy from him for cash.

It follows that the judgment must be reversed, and the cause remanded for a new trial.

CASE NO. 2

Keller v. Fredericktown Sav. Inst. 66 A. (2d) 924, 10 A.L.R. (2d) 423 (Md.) (1949)

GRASON, J. On September 20, 1947, Mrs. Keller (appellant) was a depositor with the Fredericktown Savings Institution. . . . On that day she drew a check for $5,000.00 on said bank to the order of the Allied Realty Corporation. . . . On September 23, 1947, she signed and delivered to a bank official an order to stop payment on this check. The check was thereafter paid by the bank. She instituted suit against the bank, which was tried in the Circuit Court for Frederick County before a judge, without the aid of a jury. A verdict was rendered for the bank and judgment being entered thereon, the case comes to this court on appeal.

On the morning of September 23, 1947, at nine o'clock, Mr. Albaugh, treasurer of appellee, received in the mail from the Bank of Bethesda, Bethesda, Maryland, the check in question, together with the following instructions in writing from that bank:

> "Check by Miriam Strouse Keller payable Allied Realty Corp. Upon receipt, please wire if paid or if not paid—collect."

The payee named in the check had deposited it in the Bank of Bethesda. Mr. Albaugh called Mr. Bogley, President of the Bank of Bethesda, by telephone and told him the check was good, and he was "remitting for it." He deducted two dollars for service charge, drew a draft on the Riggs National Bank of Washington for $4,998.00,

> "placed it in an envelope, sealed it and placed a 3-cent stamp on it and put it in the mail basket for delivery to the Post Office when the clerk went to the Post Office the next time."

At that time

> "the draft was recorded on the draft register, which is our book where we record all drafts we issue on any of our correspondent banks. . . . A credit slip was made to the Riggs National Bank of Washington for $4,998, crediting the Riggs National Bank for the amount of the draft we had drawn on them. . . . Mrs. Keller's account had not been charged on the ledger of the bank at the time the order to stop payment was given."

Mrs. Keller says she called at the bank between eleven and eleven fifteen that morning and saw Mr. Griffin, vice president of appellee, with whom she had transacted business for years . . . the check was at the bank at that time. He procured for her a form to stop payment on this check, which he filled out and Mrs. Keller signed. Even though the check on which she gave a written order on the bank to stop payment was in the bank at that time, which he knew, he seemed to think that what Mr. Albaugh had done in the matter might prevent Mrs. Keller from stopping payment on the check, and he says he took the stop payment order conditionally. Of course, the order was either effective or futile. He had no authority or right to accept the order conditionally. These are the facts in the case, and present the single question: Did the bank have a right to pay the check to the Bethesda Bank and charge the same to appellant's account, under the circumstances in this case?

It may be said generally that the relation of a bank and a depositor is that of debtor and creditor; the money deposited in it is regarded as a loan to the bank by the depositor, with the right of the depositor to draw on it to the extent of the deposit. A check drawn by the depositor for a given sum of money to a person named therein is not an assignment, because the bank owns the money deposited, subject to the right of the depositor to draw on it.

Acceptance of a check must be in writing. . . . A telephone conversation by the payor bank to the payee bank that a check will be accepted for payment is not in law an acceptance. The payee bank could not successfully sue the appellee in this case if the check in question had not been paid to it, because there was no acceptance in writing of the check by the appellee. . . .

If a check is cashed at the window of the bank upon which it is drawn, of course the check is dead. If a check is sent through the mail by a bank, for collection or payment to the bank on which it is drawn, and that bank charges the check on its books to the account of the drawer of the check or gives credit for it on its books to the account of the payee bank, this is equivalent to payment and the check is dead. 9 C.J.S., Banks and Banking, § 245, p. 502.

In this case, at the time the order to stop payment on the check was given the appellee had not accepted it for payment nor paid the check. It would be strange, under these circumstances, if the appellant could not stop payment on this check when no parties to the transaction would be harmed. By stopping this check the holder would be relegated to a suit at law against Mrs. Keller, and her responsibility thereon would be decided at the trial of the case.

We conclude that the learned judge below was in error in holding that the bank was not liable to Mrs. Keller, and the judgment appealed from is reversed.

Judgment reversed, and judgment entered for appellant for $5,000.00, with interest from September 23, 1947, and costs.

CASE NO. 3

Linsky v. United States. 6 F. (2d) 869 (1925)

JOHNSON, C.J. . . . Defendant gave an order for merchandise and a check for its price to the Board of Survey of the United States government on February 8, 1921. On February 10, 1921, the Board of Survey caused the check to be certified by the Tremont Trust Company, upon which it was drawn. On February 15, 1921, the goods for which the check was drawn were delivered, and on February 17, 1921, the Tremont Trust Company was closed at the end of that business day by order of the bank commissioner of the commonwealth of Massachusetts. The plaintiff deposited this check in the Federal Reserve Bank at Boston on the same day that the Tremont Trust Company was closed, and the following day the check was returned because of its closing. The defendant at all times had sufficient funds deposited in the Tremont Trust Company to cover this check, and upon its certification the Trust Company deducted and charged the defendant's account with the amount of the check. . . . The check has always been retained by the plaintiff, and it has not in any way attempted to effect the collection of the said check, other than by this suit. . . .

Under General Laws of Massachusetts, c. 107, §§ 210, 211, if the holder of a check procures it to be accepted or certified, the drawer and all indorsers are discharged from liability thereon.

In Minor v. Russ, 156 Mass. 458, 31 N.E. 489, . . . it was held that, if the drawer of a check gets it certified for his own benefit, and then delivers it to the payee, he is not discharged; but if the payee, for his own benefit, gets it certified, instead of getting it paid, then the drawer is discharged. In its opinion, at page 460 (31 N.E. 490), the court said:

> "When a check payable to another person than the drawer is presented by the drawer to the bank for certification, the bank knows that it has not been negotiated, and that it is not presented for payment, but that the drawer wishes the obligation of the bank to pay it to the holder when it is negotiated, in addition to his own obligation. But when the payee or holder of a check presents it for certification, the bank knows that this is done for the convenience or security of the holder."

All of the decided cases are to the same effect. . . .

The acceptance of the check by the Tremont Trust Company at the request of the payee, charging the same to the account of the drawer and retaining the funds, was equivalent to a redeposit of them by the payee. . . .

The debt for which the check was given was therefore extinguished, and there could be no recovery, either upon the check or upon a count for the value of the goods. . . .

CASE NO. 4

Welch v. Bank of Manhatten Co. 35 N.Y.S. (2d) 894 (1942)

Ernest J. Pirman drew two checks totaling $2,750 on defendant bank payable to the order of plaintiff and had them certified by the defendant bank. The checks were delivered by Pirman to plaintiff as part payment for the purchase and sale of a parcel of real estate. When the checks were presented to the bank, the bank refused payment. The refusal was at the request of Pirman who claimed that plaintiff had breached the contract of purchase and sale and had committed serious waste on the property. The defendant admitted it held the money and made a motion that Pirman be added as a party defendant and that the court determine which party was entitled to the money, plaintiff or Pirman.

Where, as in the instant case, the certification was at the request of the drawer, the drawer was not discharged from liability. The certification merely operated as an assurance that the check is genuine and that the certifying bank becomes bound with the drawer. Under the circumstances, defendant should be permitted to interplead Pirman as a party-defendant so that he may interpose a defense based upon his claim of fraud and waste and thereby compel plaintiff and Pirman to litigate on the trial which of the two is entitled to the moneys set aside and being held by the bank for the payment of the checks. It is only where a check is certified at the request of the payee or holder that a bank may not resist the enforcement of its contract of certification in order to make a set-off or counterclaim available to its depositor. Obviously the reason for this is that under such circumstances the drawer is discharged from any further liability on the check since the certification is equivalent to an acceptance and a complete novation occurs, creating the relation of debtor and creditor between the payee or holder and the bank.

Review Questions and Problems

1. What relationship exists between the drawer of a check and the drawee bank?
2. What forms the basis of the drawee bank's duty to honor a check when it is presented for payment?
3. As the payee of a check, A presents it to the drawee bank for payment. The check is dishonored. A sues the drawee bank. Can he recover?
4. The payee of a check that contains the following statement, "This check represents an assignment of funds," presents it to the drawee bank for payment. The bank dishonors the check without cause. Does this give the holder a right of action against the bank?
5. Will a stop-payment order be entirely effective against a holder in due course?
6. What is the procedure for certifying a check?
7. How does the certification of a check differ from an acceptance of a bill of exchange?
8. What determines whether a certification discharges the drawer from further liability?
9. How does the liability of the drawer of a check differ fundamentally from the liability of the drawer of an ordinary bill of exchange?
10. Plaintiff drew two checks upon the defendant drawee bank, which checks were each for less than the plaintiff's balance but in the aggregate were more. Both checks reached the drawee bank at the same time and the bank refused to pay either. Is the bank liable to the plaintiff? (*Castaline* v. *Nat. City Bank,* 224 Mass. 416)
11. Plaintiff seeks an injunction to prevent the defendant bank from making payment of a check given under the following circumstances:

    "The history of the check in question is as follows: Plaintiff, a married lady, lives in the suburbs of the city of Sioux City, and on December 27, 1919, was so fortunate as to have a comfortable balance to her credit in the Mid-West Bank in that city. On the day named one Noltze, also known in the record as John Doe, appeared at plaintiff's home and professed to sell her 15 gallons of whisky for $1,000, for which sum she gave him the check. The check, though given December 27, 1919, was dated January 15, 1920. On receiving it Noltze took it to the bank at once, and at his request an officer of the bank certified it. On or before January 1st following, and 15 days before the check was payable, the plaintiff, who modestly admits she is 'a judge of whisky,' appears to have sampled the stuff, and to her disgust discovered that it 'had no kick in it'; that it was not whisky at all, but was 'water.' As was natural in one having the Missouri river flowing at her feet, and offering her its limpid and sparkling waters without money and without price, she concluded that John Doe (alias Noltze) had swindled her, and at once called up the bank by telephone and notified it not to honor the check. On January 19, 1920, the check was presented for payment by or in behalf of one Ray Dale." (*Wilson* v. *Midwest State Bank,* 193 Iowa 311) Decide.
12. Is the drawee bank liable to the drawer for its failure to honor a stop-payment order when the check is in the hands of a holder in due course?

24 NEGOTIABLE INSTRUMENTS:

DISCHARGE OF NEGOTIABLE INSTRUMENTS

► I. DISCHARGE OF INSTRUMENTS

A discharge of a negotiable instrument means its extinguishment as a contract. A discharge of the instrument serves to relieve all parties to the instrument from further liability. Section 119 of the N.I.L. enumerates five methods by which a discharge may be effected. It reads:

"(1) By payment in due course by or on behalf of the principal debtor;

(2) By payment in due course by the party accommodated, where the instrument is made or accepted for accommodation;

(3) By the intentional cancellation thereof by the holder;

(4) By any other act which will discharge a simple contract for the payment of money;

(5) When the principal debtor becomes the holder of the instrument at or after maturity in his own right."

A. PAYMENT IN DUE COURSE

In the ordinary course of business events, negotiable instruments are usually discharged by payment upon maturity or shortly thereafter. This constitutes payment in due course. Section 88 of the N.I.L. states that:

"Payment is made in due course when it is made at or after maturity of the instrument to the holder thereof in good faith and without notice that his title is defective."

It is to be observed that payment before maturity does not discharge the instrument. As previously noted, such payment is a personal defense only, and should the instrument remain in circulation it would represent a valid obligation in the hands of a holder in due course.

The payment must be made by or on behalf of the principal debtor; otherwise, the instrument continues as evidence of an obligation to pay. Thus, if an indorser pays the instrument at maturity, not on behalf of the principal debtor but in discharge of his own liability, he becomes the holder of the instrument which represents a continuing obligation against the primary party. This is provided for in Section 121 of the N.I.L. thus:

"Where the instrument is paid by a party secondarily liable thereon, it is not discharged; but the party so paying it is remitted to his former rights as regards all prior parties, and he may strike out his own and all subsequent indorsements, and again negotiate the instrument except:—

(1) Where it is payable to the order of a third person, and has been paid by the drawer; and

(2) Where it has been made or accepted for accommodation, and has been paid by the party accommodated."

To illustrate:

(1) Payment by the Drawer

Suppose that Jones, the payee upon a bill, upon presenting the bill to the drawee (acceptor) is refused payment. The drawer then pays Jones who indorses the bill to the drawer. The drawer cannot further negotiate the bill. To allow the drawer to further negotiate the bill would have the effect of continuing the liability of the payee indorser Jones. The drawer may, however, look to the drawee (acceptor) for payment.

(2) Payment by the Party Accommodated

Suppose that Allen has executed a promissory note for the benefit and accommodation of Boots. After Boots pays the instrument, he should not be allowed to negotiate it and continue the liability of Allen. Boots is the one who must, in any event, ultimately pay, and after he does pay the instrument is discharged. Payment by him is recognized as a discharge of the primary obligor.

1. *Payment by Means of Negotiable Paper*

An instrument is discharged when the holder receives payment of the money or when he accepts something other than money in payment. A holder may agree to accept goods, services, or negotiable paper as payment in lieu of money. However, the mere acceptance of negotiable paper usually is not regarded as an acceptance of payment in discharge of the instrument.[1]

It is very common for a check or draft to be tendered as a means of paying an obligation evidenced by a note. If, by agreement, such a check or draft is received as payment, it will effectively discharge the instrument. Ordinarily, however, checks and drafts are not payment until they themselves are paid.* The holder is not obligated to surrender the note until he has received payment on the check or draft given him.

Many instruments are not paid at maturity but are renewed. The question frequently arises as to whether the renewal instrument stands as a discharge of the obligation evidenced by the matured instrument. Where it is agreed by the holder to accept the new instrument in payment, a discharge, of course, is effected. Although it is held in some states that the renewal instrument is payment, the majority rule is to the contrary.

B. INTENTIONAL CANCELLATION

Cancellation of an instrument is accomplished by some act of the holder in relation to the instrument showing that the instrument has been discharged. It

---

* See Maryatt v. Hubbard, p. 205.

[1] Industrial Bank of Commerce v. Shapiro, p. 595.

may consist of impressing the instrument with unmistakable evidence that the obligation has been satisfied, of mutilating or completely destroying it, or of surrendering it to the obligor. An intentional cancellation by the holder discharges the instrument regardless of whether or not it has been paid. An unintentional cancellation is not binding upon the holder. Section 123 of the N.I.L. reads:

> "A cancellation made unintentionally, or under a mistake, or without the authority of the holder, is inoperative; but where an instrument or any signature thereon appears to have been cancelled the burden of proof lies on the party who alleges that the cancellation was made unintentionally, or under a mistake or without authority."

C. ACTS DISCHARGING SIMPLE CONTRACT

Negotiable instruments are contracts and as such may be discharged by any means which will discharge a simple contract for the payment of money. Thus an obligation as evidenced by a negotiable instrument will be discharged by the expiration of time as specified by a statute of limitations and by bankruptcy proceedings.

D. DISCHARGE BY RENUNCIATION

Section 122 of the N.I.L. provides that the holder may effect a discharge of the instrument by a renunciation of his rights. This section reads:

> "The holder may expressly renounce his rights against any party to the instrument, before, at, or after its maturity. An absolute and unconditional renunciation of his rights against the principal debtor made at or after the maturity of the instrument discharges the instrument. But a renunciation does not affect the rights of a holder in due course without notice. A renunciation must be in writing, unless the instrument is delivered up to the person primarily liable thereon."

Renunciation as a method of discharge is peculiar to negotiable contracts.[2] A simple contract cannot be discharged in this manner. It will also be recalled that the agreement of a creditor to release his debtor is not binding unless it is supported by a consideration, and it will be remembered that the payment of a sum less than that due and owing is not consideration.

E. MATERIAL ALTERATION

The effect of a material alteration upon an instrument has been fully discussed elsewhere. The circumstances under which a negotiable instrument will be discharged by material alteration should be ascertained by reference to the treatment accorded this title under real and personal defenses.*

---

* See Perry v. Manufacturers Nat. Bank of Lynn, p. 530; Columbia Grocery Co. v. Marshall, p. 531.

[2] Northern Drug Co. v. Abbett, p. 596.

► II. DISCHARGE OF SECONDARY PARTIES

A. UNDER RULES OF SURETYSHIP

A secondary party upon a negotiable instrument stands in the relationship of a surety to the primary party, who upon the face of the instrument appears to be the principal debtor. Consequently, any act that under the law of suretyship would release a surety from further obligation, would also serve to release a secondary party upon a negotiable instrument. Acts on the part of the creditor (the holder of the instrument) that will effect the discharge of a surety (a secondary party upon the instrument) are:

(1) The release of the principal debtor;

(2) An extension of time to the principal debtor;

(3) An alteration in the nature of the contractual obligation for which the surety stands liable; and

(4) A handling of the collateral pledged by the principal debtor as security in a way not consistent with the contract.

Where the principal debtor upon an instrument is given his release by the holder or where the holder consents to an extension of time without the consent of the parties secondarily liable, the liability of the secondary parties can be preserved by the simple expedient of reserving all rights against them. Unless such a reservation is provided for at the time of the release or extension of time of payment, all parties to the contract are discharged. Section 120 of the N.I.L. provides that a person secondarily liable on the instrument is discharged:

> "(5) By a release of the principal debtor, unless the holder's right of recourse against the party secondarily liable is expressly reserved.
>
> (6) By any agreement binding upon the holder to extend the time of payment, or to postpone the holder's right to enforce the instrument, unless made with the assent of the party secondarily liable, or unless the right of recourse against such party is expressly reserved."

B. METHODS PECULIAR TO NEGOTIABLE INSTRUMENTS

Section 120 of the N.I.L. provides as follows:

> "A person secondarily liable on the instrument is discharged:
>
> (1) By any act which discharges the instrument;
>
> (2) By the intentional cancellation of his signature by the holder;
>
> (3) By the discharge of a prior party;
>
> (4) By a valid tender of payment made by a prior party."

C. STRIKING OUT INDORSEMENT

Section 48 of the N.I.L. reads:

> "The holder may at any time strike out any indorsement which is not necessary to his title. The indorser whose indorsement is struck out, and all indorsers subsequent to him, are thereby relieved from liability on the instrument."

CASES

CASE NO. 1

Industrial Bank of Commerce v. Shapiro. 94 *N.Y.S.* (2d) 437 (1950)

VAN VOORHIS, J. On August 9, 1946, one Ernest E. Altman borrowed $900 from plaintiff bank, for which he gave his note and chattel mortgage on his 1942 Packard sedan. The chattel mortgage was duly filed in the office of the clerk of the county of Sullivan, New York, where Altman resided. By November 20, 1946, Altman had reduced this loan to $675 and was made another loan by plaintiff on a new note of $1,056, of which $675 was credited in payment of the former note and the balance, less discount, delivered to Altman. A new chattel mortgage securing this note was given on the same automobile, but the original chattel mortgage was not released nor discharged of record. The first note was stamped paid. But before the second note and mortgage were given, and on October 28, 1946, Altman sold and delivered said Packard automobile to defendant Chester Shapiro, who brought it to New York City. Plaintiff knew nothing of this sale, nor did Shapiro have actual (although he had constructive) notice of the chattel mortgage filed in Sullivan County. On April 21, 1947, Altman gave to plaintiff a further note for $1,056 and a third chattel mortgage upon the same automobile. By then the second note had been reduced to $704 and the excess was paid to Altman, less the discount. The balance due on the last note is $880.

Plaintiff sues defendant in conversion. Plaintiff claims against defendant the amount of its alleged special property in the automobile by reason of these transactions. There was a conversion when defendant, having constructive notice of this chattel mortgage, bought and removed the automobile from Sullivan County in violation of the terms of the chattel mortgage without plaintiff's consent, provided that the original chattel mortgage was still a lien at that time.

The complaint has been dismissed upon the ground that Altman no longer owned the automobile when he gave the last two chattel mortgages thereon to plaintiff, and that the note secured by the first chattel mortgage has been paid out of the avails of the second note, with the consequence that the first chattel mortgage, although never released, no longer secures anything and its lien has been extinguished. We take another view.

A promissory note is delivered and accepted as evidence of a debt rather than in payment thereof, unless there be an agreement that the note is received in payment of the debt. . . .

When the first note given by Altman was marked paid, it was merely renewed. The fact that the second note was larger in amount does not prevent its being a renewal to the amount of the prior note. Only the excess over the previous note was paid in cash to Altman; the rest was just a bookkeeping transaction. The original debt was not extinguished. Marking the first note paid signified that the first negotiable instrument which evidenced the debt had been cancelled and superseded *pro tanto* by another. It is well established that a second chattel mortgage upon the same property covered by a former chattel mortgage, to secure the same debt, is not of itself a cancellation of such first mortgage, even though the second has been given to secure a larger loan. . . .

In this case, the first chattel mortgage, on which alone defendant is liable, stated that it was given to secure the first note, which meant presumptively that it was given to secure the debt for which the note was given. When the first note was later renewed, the debt was not thereby extinguished. Defendant is liable for the unpaid amount of the debt which was secured by the first chattel mortgage that was in existence at the time when defendant converted the automobile. . . .

CASE NO. 2

Northern Drug Co. v. Abbett. 205 Minn. 65, 284 N.W. 881, 121 A.L.R. 1349 (1939)

PETERSON, J., delivered the opinion of the court:

On June 15, 1935, the William A. Abbett Drug Company, a corporation, executed and delivered to plaintiff its promissory note in the sum of $900 due on August 15, 1935, which defendant endorsed. On August 30, 1935, the Abbett corporation filed a voluntary petition in bankruptcy. On September 13, 1935, plaintiff filed a claim against it in bankruptcy for $900 based on the note, reciting that the consideration therefor was goods and merchandise sold by the claimant to the bankrupt. In the bankruptcy proceedings, which are not set out in full in the record, the Abbett corporation made an offer of composition which was accepted by its creditors and confirmed by the court. Plaintiff refused to assent to the acceptance of the composition offer, but on November 13, 1935, it received a dividend of $225 by check from the referee in bankruptcy for which it gave a receipt that it was 25 per cent of "and in full settlement of" its claim allowed in the composition proceedings. This action is brought by the plaintiff as payee to recover from defendant as endorser the amount of the note with interest, less the amount of the dividend paid to it in the composition in bankruptcy. Many defenses were interposed by the defendant of which we shall consider only the one that the defendant was discharged as endorser by plaintiff's renunciation of its rights against the defendant, since that defense, if it is sustained, is decisive of the case.

. . . The discharge in bankruptcy affects the remedy but not the right. It destroys the remedy by enabling the debtor to plead the discharge in bar as a defense personal to himself. It does not pay or extinguish the debt. . . . In Zavelo v. Reeves, 227 U.S. 625, the court held that a discharge, while releasing the bankrupt from legal liability to pay a debt that was provable in bankruptcy, leaves him under a moral obligation that is sufficient to support a new promise to pay the debt. The court said . . . :

> "The theory is that the discharge destroys the remedy, but not the indebtedness. . . ."

. . . However much the authorities may differ as to the attributes of the right and the theory of the remedy, all agree that the debt survives and that there remains a real but unenforceable duty on the part of the bankrupt to pay.

While the nature of the bankrupt's obligation after discharge is not determined by express provision of the bankruptcy act and is arrived at by the process of construction, the statute is explicit as to the liability of the bankrupt's endorsers and others similarly liable. Section 16 of the Bankruptcy Act, 11 U.S.C.A. § 34, provides that the liability of a person who is a codebtor with, or guarantor, or in any manner a surety for the bankrupt shall not be "altered" by the discharge of the bankrupt. The statute prevents the discharge in bankruptcy of the maker of a negotiable instrument from discharging an endorser. . . .

The debt evidenced by the note was extinguished by plaintiff's renunciation of the same in the receipt which it gave for the dividend in the composition proceedings. Mason Minn. St. 1927, § 7165, provides that the holder in the manner therein provided may expressly renounce his rights against the parties liable on a negotiable instrument and that the renunciation of the holder's rights against the principal debtor at or after maturity discharges the instrument. Renunciation may be with or without consideration. Where the holder does not receive a consideration the renunciation amounts to a gratuitous release. . . . Where the holder renounces his rights under a promissory note the debt evidenced by the note is extinguished. . . . The so-called receipt was also a full settlement of plaintiff's claim. It was a release in full. . . . In the ordinary meaning of language, "full settlement" in a release means payment or satisfaction extinguishing the claim. . . . Although the release was without consideration, since plaintiff was entitled to the dividend as its share of the consideration paid by the bankrupt for the composition, . . . plaintiff signed the instrument voluntarily. . . . Plaintiff had a right to object to the exaction of the release as part of the receipt as being in excess of the authority of the referee acting as the distributing agent of the bankruptcy court, . . . but did not see fit to assert that right. The giving up of its rights under the note was a renunciation. . . . Where a debt is extinguished by act of the parties as by payment, accord and satisfaction, or voluntary release, it ceases to have existence for any purpose. . . . The duty is not only rendered unenforceable, it is discharged. The discharged debt will not even support a new promise. . . . By renouncing its rights under the note, plaintiff discharged and released all parties including defendant.

Review Questions and Problems

1. Enumerate the methods by which a negotiable instrument may be completely discharged.
2. Hill is the maker of a promissory note that is payable on or before March 15, 1948. On March 13, 1948, Hill makes payment of the note to the holder, Long, who assures Hill that the note will be delivered to him as soon as Long can get it from his safety deposit box in an adjoining town. Instead of returning the note to Hill, Long negotiates it to Brill, a holder in due course. Brill gives the note to his nephew on March 20, 1948. By virtue of Section 58 of the N.I.L., what are the rights of the nephew against the maker Hill?
3. X is the indorser of a note that has been dishonored by the maker. X pays the amount of the note to the holder. Does this discharge the note?
4. A note is due and the maker gives the holder a draft drawn upon a third party. Does this discharge the note?
5. A owes B upon an open book account. B, feeling generous, writes A that he will compromise for one half the full amount. A accepts B's generous offer and makes a tender of such an amount. Can B now recover the full amount?
6. Suppose the same facts as in Question 5, but assume that the obligation from A to B is evidenced by a promissory note.

7. What are the requirements for an effective renunciation of rights under a negotiable instrument?
8. An instrument contains the following indorsements: Abe Black; John Jones; H. Prugh. The holder wishes to release Black from his obligation and therefore strikes out Black's name. Can he now look to Jones and Prugh for payment?
9. A holds B's promissory note, upon which X is an indorser. B cannot pay at maturity, and A wishes to give him an extension of time. How can this be done without discharging X from his liability as a secondary party?
10. The owner of a note and mortgage told the mortgagor that he considered them paid and intended to give them to the mortgagor. After the death of the owner, his legal representative seeks to collect on the note from the mortgagor. Result?
11. The following indorsement appeared upon a note: "If the holder (payee) of this note does not survive the maker, then this note is not to be paid, but is to be canceled and surrendered." The holder died before the maker. In your opinion, is this provision a renunciation as required by Section 122 of the N.I.L.
12. Wilson, the holder of a promissory note, wrote to the maker: "In view of your financial reverses, it is my intent not to collect on your note, which I will return to you as soon as I can get it from the bank." The note is never returned to the maker and upon its due date is presented to the maker for payment by Hobbs, a holder in due course. Is the maker obligated to pay?

Personal Property and Related Topics

Chapter

25. PERSONAL PROPERTY

26. THE LAW OF SALES

27. BAILMENTS

28. SECURITY INTERESTS IN PERSONAL PROPERTY

25 PERSONAL PROPERTY AND RELATED TOPICS:

PERSONAL PROPERTY

► I. PROPERTY IN GENERAL

One of the fundamental characteristics of our economic society is the institution of private property. Man's economic activity revolves about property. The business student can readily visualize the vital role that property plays in the satisfaction of human wants. Economists speak of economics as the science of wealth. All wealth is owned by someone—it is property.

The institution of private property consists of the rights, privileges, and powers of individuals or groups of individuals to acquire, use, enjoy, and dispose of things tangible or intangible to such an extent as is compatible with social objectives.

"As industrial and economic and social conditions change, and indeed as public sentiment changes, the idea of property changes. . . . In general it may be said that as population becomes more dense and concentrated in very large cities, with the corresponding increase in complexity of organization made necessary to support so large a population in so small an area . . . individual property rights, in many cases, have to be correspondingly diminished and curtailed in the public interest." *People* v. *La Fetra,* 185 N.Y.S. 632

A. PROPERTY AS INTANGIBLE CONCEPT

In its technical legal sense the term *property* is an intangible concept, signifying those rights, privileges, and powers which the law confers upon individuals in relation to things tangible or intangible as distinguished from the things themselves. This can be called *ownership*. Such is the concept of our institution of private property. Property, for example, determines where the benefits—income—derived from a house reside. Correspondingly, the owner of a secret formula, a trade-mark, or good will is the individual who has the law-protected rights to its undisturbed use and disposition.[1, 2]

B. POPULAR MEANING OF TERM PROPERTY

In its popular sense the term *property* has reference to things that may be the subject of ownership. It is used to designate the subject matter to which the various property rights, privileges, and powers may attach. This includes not only physical objects capable of being reduced to physical possession, but also things intangible in nature—things existing only in contemplation, such as a formula or the good will of a business.

---

1 Pro-Phy-Lac-Tic Brush Co. v. Hudson Products, p. 613.

2 Safier's Inc. v. Bialer, p. 615.

► II. PERSONAL PROPERTY DISTINGUISHED FROM REAL PROPERTY

The importance of distinguishing between real and personal property can be made apparent by the following partial enumeration of the different legal incidents that attach to real and to personal property:

(1) Whereas real property must be conveyed by a formally executed instrument which for the protection of the grantee must be recorded in a public office, personal property may be transferred by delivery only or by a simple informal writing.

(2) Under the Statute of Frauds the requirements for the enforceability of a contract pertaining to real property differ from those for the enforceability of a contract for the sale of personal property.

(3) Usually only real property is subject to the right of dower.

(4) Judgments are liens only upon real property.

(5) Real property and personal property are subject to different tax laws.

For our purposes it is both practical and sufficient to classify property as either *personal* or *real*. Personal property cannot be defined by inclusion; therefore, it may be said that all property that is not real is personal. For the present it will be adequate to regard real property as land or anything that is permanently attached as part of the land. The term *real property,* when used to designate ownership interest in land, is limited to an estate of freehold, which is either an estate of inheritance or an estate for life. Any other interests in land and things thereto permanently attached are classified as personal property.

A. PERMANENT ATTACHMENT

By annexation to land, personal property can become a fixture, a part of the realty. The cases are legion in which the issue has been whether personal property has been converted to the status of real property by annexation. Cases of this nature are constantly coming before the courts. This results in large measure from man's ever-changing modes and practices and the multifarious activities in which he uses property attached to realty in varying degrees and for varying purposes. The court *In re Trevey,* 14 L.T. Rep. N.S. 193, speaks of the lack of harmony among the decisions thus:

> "Perhaps there are no subjects in law more difficult to deal with than the question raised as to fixtures . . . each new case seems only the more to disturb any fixed or certain rule that seemed deducible from former cases, and, indeed, on most questions on this subject, a court can easily give precedents that seem to uphold the doctrine it arrives at or is anxious to arrive at."

The three basic factors taken into consideration by the courts in testing whether personalty has become realty by annexation are: (1) the intention of the person making the annexation; (2) the mode of annexation; and (3) the adaption of the thing annexed to the purpose for which the realty is used.

1. *Intention Test*

The first and primary consideration of the courts seems to be the intention with which the annexation was made; not the secret intention, but the intention as it is evident from the circumstances in any given case.[3]

> "The law presumes that because the interest of a tenant in the land is temporary . . . it permits annexations made by him to be detached during his term, if done without injury to the freehold. The law presumes that because the interest of the vendor of real estate, who is the owner of it, has been permanent, that he has made annexations . . . with a view to a lasting enjoyment of his estate, and for its continued enhancement in value. So the mortgagor of land is the owner of it, and has a permanent interest therein and the law presumes that improvements which he makes thereon, by annexation of chattels, he makes for himself, for prolonged enjoyment, and to enhance permanently the value of his estate. . . ." *Tifft* v. *Horton,* 53 N.Y. 377

2. *Mode of Annexation Test*

Since the forms of annexation may be of varying degree and character, annexation of itself can be no absolute test of conversion to realty under all circumstances. Not infrequently have articles not physically attached been held to be realty, and yet at times property physically attached has been held not to have taken on the character of realty. Annexation is a factor to be considered in conjunction with the other factors. In some instances, of course, articles are so united with realty as to leave no doubt, as when their removal would be injurious to the realty.[4]

> "To make it a fixture, it must not merely be essential to the business of the structure, but it must be attached to it in some way, or, at least, it must be mechanically fitted so as, in ordinary understanding, to constitute a part of the structure itself." *Wolford* v. *Baxter,* 33 Minn. 12

3. *Use Test*

Seats placed in a theater are adapted to the purpose of the undertaking to which the realty is devoted; machinery introduced into a plant may be very appropriate and essential to the conduct of the manufacturing enterprise; electric fans affixed in hotel rooms enhance the usefulness of the premises as a hostelry. The courts regard such relationships as strongly indicating that the articles were intended by annexation to become a permanent part of the realty.[5]

It is no simple task for the courts to make a distinction at all times between realty and personalty. As previously stated, the rights of adverse claimants are frequently dependent upon whether the property in issue is real or personal. There is no denying that in many cases the conclusion has been made to fit the needs of the particular situation.

---

3 Kent Storage Co. v. Grand Rapids Lumber Co., p. 617.

4 Dermer v. Faunce, p. 618.

5 Smyth Sales Corp. v. Norfolk Bldg. & Loan Assoc., p. 619.

B. CONVERSION OF REALTY TO PERSONALTY BY SEVERANCE

By severance, any part of real property may be converted into personal property when such is the intention. Upon becoming detached, property does not necessarily become personalty; it remains realty until the owner has indicated his intention to treat it otherwise.

There is some authority to the effect that the severance need not be actual, that an unequivocal intention to remove a part of the realty is sufficient. The selecting, marking, and selling of growing trees and the sale of a house with the understanding that it is to be removed have been held to constitute conversions to personalty without actual severance.

C. STATUS OF CROPS

The term *crops* in its broadest sense includes products of the soil produced by annual planting, cultivation, and labor as well as those annual products from perennial plants which require an expenditure of labor by man, such as fruits grown for the market. Crops are technically known as *fructus industriales* to distinguish them from *fructus naturales,* those products of the soil which are not dependent upon the labor of man. The perennial plants from which fruits are grown without the use of human labor and grass that is not planted or cultivated are illustrations of the latter.

The following extract taken from *Bagley* v. *Columbus Southern Ry. Co.,* 98 Ga. 626 (1896) well expressed the state of the law as to whether growing crops are real or personal property:

> ". . . Indeed, we are free to confess that about the only deduction we have been able to draw therefrom (a review of various decisions and expressions of writers) is that a growing crop is a sort of legal species of chameleon, constantly changing color to meet the emergency of each peculiar class of cases in which the question arises whether it is to be considered as personalty or as realty. . . ."

A review of the most recent decisions bears this opinion out. In some jurisdictions crops are regarded as realty and in others as personalty. Some states hold that growing crops are realty until matured and ready for harvest. It seems to be a general rule that between grantor and grantee growing crops are regarded as realty unless reserved as personalty in the deed. In many jurisdictions, various acts, such as a sale or an adjudication in bankruptcy, serve as a constructive severance and a conversion to personalty. Arkansas has made the distinction that growing crops planted by an owner are realty, while those planted by a tenant are personalty as regards the owners but realty as regards all others. Generally, under the Statute of Frauds crops are regarded as being personal property.*

---

* See Rankin v. Ridge, p. 195.

► III. PERSONAL PROPERTY CLASSIFIED

The term *chattels* is generally used to designate personal property, which can be classified as chattels real and chattels personal. *Chattels real* are those interests in land that are less than a freehold estate, such as a lease for a period of years. All other personal property comes under the heading of *chattels personal.*

Personal property, both chattels real and chattels personal, can further be classified as being *personal in possession* or *personal in action.* Property in occupation, use, and enjoyment by the rightful owner is said to be *personal in possession.*

Property personal in action is the right to reduce a thing to occupation, use, and enjoyment, by legal action if necessary. To illustrate:

X has contracted to sell Y his pedigreed dog. X now refuses to perform. Since the dog is unique in many ways, Y has a right of action to get possession of the dog. If the dog were not unique, Y would have the right to obtain a sum of money in lieu of performance. Or let us suppose that Y gave X his promissory note in payment for the dog. The note is evidence of the legal right which X has to the amount of money specified therein. It may become necessary for X to take legal action to reduce the specified sum to his possession. A right of action to reduce a thing to possession is called a *chose in action.*

► IV. PROCESSES OF ACQUIRING TITLE TO PERSONAL PROPERTY

A. ACQUIRING TITLE TO PROPERTY NOT OWNED

Existing property is either owned or not owned. Property not owned consists of (1) things that have never been reduced to the exclusive possession of man, such as things in their native state, as wild animals, and (2) things whose ownership has been intentionally abandoned. The person who first takes possession of unowned property acquires title to the same. This is known as *acquiring title by occupation.*

B. TITLE BY CREATION

Man's daily mental and physical efforts produce many items of personal property. It is the accepted rule that the creative producer acquires title to the results of his exertions. The painter acquires title to the sunset produced by his skill; the brain child of the inventor belongs exclusively to him, which he may protect by a patent; and the discoverer of the elixir of life would be able to reap his fortune. The individual may, of course, bargain away the title to the products of his future efforts by contract. For example, the discoveries of most industrial research men inure to the benefit of their employers.

The Constitution of the United States declares that Congress shall have power

> "to promote the progress of science and useful arts, by securing for limited times, to authors and inventors, the exclusive right to their respective writings and discoveries."

This provision forms the basis for our copyright and patent laws.

1. *Copyright*

a. Nature of Federal Copyright Statute. The creator of an intellectual or artistic product has the common law right that the product shall not be used by others. If the work is released to the public by general publication, this common law right is relinquished and the public has the right of duplication. The creator can obtain for himself, however, the exclusive right of duplication and distribution to the public by obtaining a statutory copyright. Our federal copyright statute gives the authors and artists the exclusive right to publish, multiply, and sell their intellectual and artistic productions for a period of twenty-eight years, with the right of renewal for a like period.

b. Subject Matter of Copyright. The federal copyright statute provides that the following classification of subjects may be copyrighted:

(1) Books, including composite and cyclopedic works, directories, gazeteers, and other compilations
(2) Periodicals, including newspapers
(3) Lectures, sermons, and addresses to be delivered orally
(4) Dramatic or dramatic-musical compositions
(5) Musical compositions
(6) Maps
(7) Works of art; models or designs for works of art
(8) Reproductions of a work of art
(9) Drawings or plastic works of a scientific or technical character
(10) Photographs
(11) Prints and pictorial illustrations
(12) Motion-picture photoplays
(13) Motion pictures other than photoplays

The statute further provides that the subject matter of copyright is not limited to the above enumeration. In general, any *original* intellectual production may be protected by copyright.

> "It would be difficult to define, comprehensively, what character of writing is copyrightable, and what is not. . . . Generally speaking, authorship implies that there has been put into the production something meritorious from the author's own mind; that the product embodies the thought of the author, as well as the thought of others; and would not have found existence in the form presented, but for the distinctive individuality of mind from which it sprang. A mere annal, on the contrary, is the reduction to copy of an event that others, in a like situation, would have observed; and its statement in the substantial form that people generally would have adopted. A catalogue, or a table of statistics, or business publications generally, may thus belong to either one or the other of these classes. If, in their makeup, there is evinced some peculiar mental endowment—the grasp of mind, say in a table of statistics, that can gather in all that is needful, the discrimination that adjusts their proportions—there may be authorship within the meaning of the copyright

grant as interpreted by the courts. But if, on the contrary, such writings are a mere notation of the figures at which stocks or cereals have sold, or of the result of a horse race, or base-ball game, they cannot be said to bear the impress of individuality, and fail, therefore, to rise to the plane of authorship. In authorship, the product has some likeness to the mind underneath it; in a work of mere notation, the mind is guide only to the fingers that make the notation. One is the product of originality; the other the product of opportunity." *National Tel. News Co.* v. *Western Union Tel. Co.,* 119 Fed. 294

*c. Steps Necessary to Secure Copyright.** Obtaining a copyright is accomplished by meeting the following three requirements: (1) publication; (2) inscribing the thing published with the statutory form of copyright notice; [6] and (3) depositing two copies in the copyright office, or placing two copies in the mail addressed to the register of copyrights, accompanying the copies by a claim of copyright. Upon having met these requirements, if the subject matter is copyrightable, the owner's claim is registered and his exclusive right is established.

Publication consists of the production being "placed on sale, sold, or publicly distributed." Publication without immediately meeting the other two requirements will prevent the author from obtaining a copyright subsequently. As the courts have said, "Works already in the public domain are not the subject of copyright."

d. Infringement. Infringement upon a copyright consists of someone else's doing that which is exclusively reserved to the owner of the copyright without his consent. A necessary element of infringement is that the original production has been copied.

"The true test of piracy (infringement) . . . is not whether a composition is copied in the same language or the exact words of the original, but whether, in substance, it is reproduced; not whether the whole, but a material part, is taken." [7] *Maxwell* v. *Goodwin,* 93 Fed. 665.

Copyright does not prevent others from using ideas, facts, theories, arts, or systems set forth or expounded in a published work. Copyright extends only to the arrangement of composition as used in the original work.[8] To illustrate:

(1) In *Baker* v. *Selden,* 101 U.S. 99, it was held that a system of bookkeeping was not protected by the copyright of a book describing it. The court said:

"But there is a clear distinction between the book, as such, and the art which it is intended to illustrate. . . . The same distinction may be predicated of every other art. . . . A treatise on the composition and use of medicines, be they old or new; on the construction and use of ploughs, or watches, or churns; or on the mixture and application of colors for painting or dyeing . . . would be the subject of copyright; but no one would contend that the copyright of the treatise would give the exclusive right to the art or manufacture described therein."

* For detailed requirements, see Copyright Office *Bulletin.*

[6] Leigh v. Gerber, p. 622.

[7] Verney Corp. v. Rose Fabric Converters Corp., p. 623.

[8] Dorsey v. Old Surety L. Ins. Co., p. 624.

(2) The reason for this rule was stated in *Holmes* v. *Hurst,* 174 U.S. 82, thus:

"The object of copyright is to promote science and the useful arts. If an author, by originating a new arrangement and form of expression of certain ideas or conceptions, could withdraw these ideas or conceptions from the stock of materials to be used by other authors, each copyright would narrow the field of thought open for development and exploitation, and science, poetry, narrative, and dramatic fiction and other branches of literature would be hindered by copyright, instead of being promoted. A poem consists of words, expressing conceptions of words or lines of thoughts; but copyright in the poem gives no monopoly in the separate words, or in the ideas, conception, or facts expressed or described by the words. A copyright extends only to the arrangement of the words. A copyright does not give a monopoly in any incident in a play. Other authors have a right to exploit the facts, experiences, field of thought and general ideas, provided they do not substantially copy a concrete form, in which the circumstances and ideas have been developed, arranged, and put into shape."

2. *Patent*

a. Nature of Patent. The federal patent statute gives to inventors the exclusive (monopoly) right to make and sell their inventions for a period of seventeen years. A patent, unlike a copyright, cannot be renewed. After the expiration of the seventeen-year period, the public is free to duplicate and sell the article on which the patent has expired.

b. Subject Matter of Patent. The statute reads:

"Any person who has invented or discovered any new and useful art, machine, manufacture, or composition of matter, or any new and useful improvement thereof, not known or used by others in this country, before his invention or discovery thereof, and not patented or described in any printed publication in this or any foreign country, before his invention or discovery thereof, or more than one year prior to his application, and not in public use or on sale in this country for more than one year prior to his application, unless the same is proved to have been abandoned, may, upon the payment of fees required by law, and other due proceedings had, obtain a patent therefor."

To be patentable, a thing must be either a physical object, such as a machine, or a process that is capable of producing a physical result. The courts have said: "A mere abstraction is not an art or process such as can be patented." To illustrate:

(1) In *American Chemical Paint Co.* v. *C. R. Wilson Body Co.,* 298 Fed. 310, it was held that a method of treating steel, before painting, with a mixture of alcohol and phosphoric acid, is patentable as an art or process.

(2) In *David E. Kennedy, Inc.* v. *Beaver Tile Co.,* 232 Fed. 477, it was held that the method of making a floor by applying tiles under pressure was an art or process which could be patented.

(3) In *Berardini* v. *Tocci,* 190 Fed. 329, it was held that a system for code messages was a mere abstraction and not patentable.

c. Elements of Patentability. A patent will not be granted unless the elements of (1) invention, and (2) utility, are present.[9, 10, 11] Invention has been defined as:

> "That intuitive faculty of the mind put forth in the search for new results, or new methods, creating what had not before existed, or bringing to light what lay hidden from vision." *Hollister* v. *Benedict etc. Mfg. Co.,* 113 U.S. 59

The cases are many in which the courts have held that a product of mere mechanical skill is not patentable.

> "It cannot be considered invention to produce a machine or formulate a method which any successful mechanic would produce when required to effectuate a given result." *Wirebounds Patents Co.* v. *H. R. Gibbons Box Co.,* 25 F. (2d) 363

It has been held that the following do not involve invention and are not patentable:

(1) Placing sheets of flypaper face to face

(2) Putting wheels under a roadbuilding machine to make it portable

(3) Changing a machine to increase speed of production

(4) Broadening the flange of a mailbag and increasing the number of rivets used in attaching it to the bag

(5) Widening an automobile bumper

To be patentable, the statute provides that an invention or discovery must have utility.

> "All that the law requires is that the invention should not be frivolous or injurious to the well-being, good policy, or sound morals of society." *Lowell* v. *Lewis,* 1 Mason 302

d. Steps Necessary to Secure Patent. The procedure for obtaining a patent is outlined by the federal patent statute and by rules as issued by the Patent Office. In essence, the following steps are required:

(1) Written application must be made to the commissioner of patents, which should be signed by the inventor and two witnesses.

(2) The application must describe (*a*) the invention, (*b*) a practical method of carrying it into effect, and (*c*) some practical use.

(3) The application must contain a specific claim of the part, improvement, or combination which is regarded as the invention or discovery. In *Knight Soda Fountain Co.* v. *Walrus Mfg. Co.,* 258 Fed. 929, the court said:

> "What is not claimed distinctly in the invention, the public possesses. A patent is sustained, not for what the inventor may have done in effect, but what is pointed out clearly and distinctly."

(4) Drawings must be submitted with the application "whenever the nature of the case admits of it." The drawings, like the application, must be signed by the inventor and two witnesses.

---

[9] Gilman v. Kestral Corp., p. 626.

[10] Funk Bros. Co. v. Kalo Co., p. 627.

[11] Harley C. Loney Co. v Nelson, p. 628.

(5) The commissioner may require the applicant to submit a model of convenient size.

(6) If the invention is a composition of matter, the commissioner may require specimens of ingredients in quantities sufficient for experiment.

C. TITLE BY TRANSFER

Transfer of title means the passing of property rights from *one individual to another.* A transfer of title may be accomplished either voluntarily—with the consent of the owner—or involuntarily—by operation of law. Voluntary transfers may be effected by contract (by sale and assignment), by gift,[12] and by will.

Transfers by operation of law are those which take place by virtue of legal process or judicial decree. A *decree of specific performance* is an involuntary transfer of title by court order. Judicial sales, in which the court in effect is the vendor, are transfers of title by operation of law. Illustrations of such are sales under mortgage foreclosure, tax sales, sales by trustees in bankruptcy, and sheriff's sales to realize proceeds to satisfy judgments of record. A man who dies without a will allows the legislature to make a will for him; as a result of intestacy, property is passed in accordance with the laws that have been provided regardless of any expressed intention of distribution by the deceased.

D. TITLE BY ACCESSION

When building a water tank for his horses, X mistakenly used some of Y's lumber. The question arises as to who has ownership of the finished product. The solution lies in the *doctrine of title by accession,* under which the owner of property may acquire the right to that which is united with his property. Stated otherwise: If the property of two persons becomes joined in such a manner as to form a whole, one or the other may acquire title to the whole. The addition may consist of either material things or labor.[13]

The more important rules governing the acquiring of title by accession can be stated with some certainty, although there is some difference of opinion as to their applicability. The following tests must be qualified by the principle that only an unintentional trespasser—one who acts in good faith under a belief of right—can acquire title by accession. An intentional wrongdoer cannot deprive the true owner of his property under the doctrine of accession.

1. *Change of Species Test*

One of the older tests employed by the courts in determining whether an innocent converter has acquired title to the property has been the *change of species test.* In *Potter* v. *Marde,* 74 N.C. 36, the rule was stated thus:

"It seems to be generally agreed that if the person who bestows his labor on the property of another thereby changes it into another species of article . . . the owner of the original material cannot recover the article in its altered

---

[12] Sinclair v. Travis, p. 630.

[13] Bozeman Mortuary Assoc. v. Fairchild, p. 631.

condition, but must content himself with the value of the article in the shape in which it was taken from him.

"In *Lampton* v. *Preston,* 24 Ky. (1 J. J. Marsh) 454, the court declared a change of species as being the conversion of property 'into something specifically different in the inherent and characteristic qualities, which identify it.' By way of illustration, the court said, 'Such is the conversion of corn into meal, of grapes into wine, . . . Here, although the meal possesses no quality which the corn did not, yet it not only does not possess all the same qualities, but there is difference in the name, character, the solidity, and every attribute which distinguishes one species from another. Meal and corn are different, as lime and rock, or rye and whiskey.

" 'It seems to have been an established doctrine of the common law, as early as the year books, that no change of mere form could divest the right of the owner of the material, as leather made into shoes, cloth into a coat, timber into plank, blocks or shingles; in all of which cases the material is not altered in its qualities or kind, and can be easily identified.' "

2. *Relative Value Test*

The change in species test has been modified by the *relative value test.* The modern courts seem to take into consideration the degree in the change in value to a greater extent than mere physical change. The court, in *Wetherbee* v. *Green,* 22 Mich. 311, said:

"No test which satisfies the reason of the law can be applied in the adjustment of questions of title to chattels by accession, unless it keeps in view the circumstance of relative values. When we bear in mind the fact that what the law aims at is the accomplishment of substantial equity, we shall readily perceive that the fact of the value of the materials having been increased a hundred-fold, is of more importance in the adjustment than any chemical change, or mechanical transformation, which, however radical, neither is expensive to the party making it, nor adds materially to the value."

Upon the basis of this, the rule has been applied by the courts that if the labor or material added to the property of another has given the finished product its *substantial value,* title has been acquired by accession by the one who contributed the great increase in value. This increase in value must be so substantial as to be grossly out of proportion to the original value of the property. Even when the original property can be identified, under these circumstances, the acquiring of title by accession will not be prevented. This rule is based upon the equitable consideration that to allow the original owner the right to the property would be unjust to the innocent converter.

To illustrate:

(1) In *Lewis* v. *Courtright,* 77 Iowa 190, the defendant was an innocent converter in cutting grass belonging to the defendant. The court, in holding that title to the cut grass was held by the defendant, said:

". . . The question we are called upon to determine is whether, under the facts of the case, the title to the hay vested in the defendant. It is shown that the value of the grass before it was cut was small; some of the evidence tending to show that it was but 8 to 10 cents an acre. Each acre yielded from 1 to 1½ tons of hay, which was worth in stack from $2 to $3 per ton. Under these facts, we think it would be manifestly unjust to hold that the ownership by the plaintiff of the grass gave him title to the hay. It is true the hay in stack is the grass which belonged to plaintiff, cut and cured, and preserved for use; but the labor of defendant, rendered in good faith, under a claim of right, gave to the hay substantially all its value."

(2) In *Wetherbee* v. *Green,* 22 Mich. 311, timber valued at $25 was converted into hoops whose value was $700. The court held that title had passed to the innocent converter.

(3) In *Eaton* v. *Langley,* 65 Ark. 448, it was held that the innocent converter did not acquire title by producing crossties worth 12½ cents per tie from timber worth 2 cents per tie. The difference in value was not sufficiently great.

3. *Principal and Accessory Test*

In those cases where an accessory part has been added to a principal part in such a manner that the parts cannot be disunited without injury to the whole, the owner of the principal part acquires title to the accessory part by accession. The owner of the accessory part is entitled to the reasonable value of his part.

To illustrate:

(1) In *Eaton* v. *Monroe,* 52 Me. 63, the plaintiff furnished the canvas, at a cost of $40.63, out of which Hall had a sail made at a labor and additional material cost of about $18. In deciding whether the plaintiff had title to the sail, the court said:

> "In *Pulsifer* v. *Page,* 32 Me. 404, this court held that a right of property, by accession, may occur when materials belonging to several persons are united by labor into a single article; and that the ownership of an article, so formed, is in the party . . . to whom the principal part of the materials belonged. In respect to the sail, it is clear the canvas formed the principal part of it, and the plaintiff being the owner of the canvas, he would, within the authority of this case, be the owner of the sail when it was completed."

(2) In *Wetherbee* v. *Green,* 22 Mich. 311, the court said:

> "It may often happen that no difficulty will be experienced in determining the identity of a piece of timber which has been taken and built into a house; but no one disputes that the right of the original owner is gone in such a case."

(3) In *Bozeman Mortuary Assoc.* v. *Fairchild,* 253 Ky. 74, where a battery, tires and various other accessories had been added to a stolen automobile the court said:

> "The removal of these accessories . . . would destroy the machine's usefulness until the owner should replace them. It may be said, then, that these accessories were united to the principal thing so as to constitute an integral part of it and the owner of the greater acquired title to the lesser articles. The

installation of these items is not far removed from repairs to a chattel, and it is the rule that ordinary repairs become a part of the thing repaired by accession."

E. ACQUIRING TITLE TO PROPERTY FOUND

A finder does not acquire title to property by virtue of the finding. It can be said that the finder of property acquires a better right to that property as against all others except the true owner. Statutes should be consulted for the procedure whereby finders may acquire title. It is the purpose of these statutes to effect, if possible, a return of the property to the true owner.

▶ V. JOINT OWNERSHIP OF PROPERTY

Property may be owned jointly by two or more persons. Joint ownership means that the various owners hold an *undivided interest in* the whole. Property may be owned jointly by either of two methods: *tenancy in common* or *joint tenancy*.

The right of survivorship is the basic distinguishing characteristic between these two methods of joint ownership. In *joint tenancy,* upon the death of one of the joint owners, his interest passes to the surviving owner or owners; whereas in *tenancy in common,* upon the death of one of the joint owners, his interest passes to his heirs. Ownership as joint tenants avoids the need of probating an estate, and such avoidance is highly desirable in certain instances, as between husband and wife, inasmuch as probating an estate is not only time-consuming and troublesome, but also expensive.

The common law right of joint tenancy has been variously affected by statutory enactments; nevertheless, survivorship can usually be accomplished by a declaration of intention to that effect in the instrument that creates the joint tenancy. As an illustration, Pennsylvania has by statute abolished survivorship as an incident of joint tenancy but does not prevent the *creation* of the right of survivorship.* The terminology frequently employed to accomplish a joint tenancy is: *A and B as joint tenants with the right of survivorship and not as tenants in common.* Real estate, bank accounts, and corporate securities are properties in relation to which joint tenancy is commonly used.[14, 15]

CASES

CASE NO. 1

Pro-Phy-Lac-Tic Brush Co. v. Hudson Products. 86 F. Supp. 859 (1949)

MEANEY, D.J. This is an action alleging infringement of plaintiff's trade-mark "Perma-Grip" brought under the Trade-mark Act of 1905, 15 U.S.C.A. § 96 (now revised 15 U.S.C.A. § 1114 et seq.) . . . .

Defendant uses "Poli-Grip" as a trade-mark for a denture cream for holding false teeth. . . .

* See Lafayette v. Brinham, 69 A. (2d) 130.

[14] Union Properties v. Cleveland Trust Co., p. 634; see also Short v. Milby, p. 770.

[15] In the Matter of the Estate of Ernest G. Wilson, p. 636.

Plaintiff's "Perma-Grip" is a powder contained in a can and packaged in an orange, white and red cardboard carton. Defendant's "Poli-Grip" is a cream contained in a metal tube and packaged in a brown, white and tan cardboard carton. "Perma-Grip" is printed in thin black lettering on an orange background. "Poli-Grip" is printed on its package in large bold tan letters on a white background.

The name "Poli-Grip" was adopted by the defendant subsequent to its use of the term "Polident" for a powder manufactured by defendant and advertised extensively since 1936, as a cleansing powder for false teeth. . . .

Plaintiff's salesman, Cloud, conducted a survey in several southern states calling on druggists. After identifying himself as representing the Pro-Phy-Lac-Tic Brush Company he would usually ask, "Do you carry our denture powder?" Cloud testified that on many occasions he was handed a package of defendant's product "Poli-Grip" or the druggist pointed to a package of "Poli-Grip" on a shelf with the response "Is this yours?"

Jules Lennard, Sales Administrator of the Block Drug Company, a firm affiliated with defendant, conducted a survey in some of the same states covered by plaintiff's salesman Cloud making purchases of "Perma-Grip" and "Poli-Grip." Lennard testified that on no occasion was he handed one when the other was asked for.

. . . The pertinent provisions of the Act, 15 U.S.C.A. § 96, are:

> ". . . Any person who shall, without the consent of the owner thereof, reproduce, counterfeit, copy, or colorably imitate any such trade-mark . . . in connection with the sale of merchandise of substantially the same descriptive properties . . . shall be liable to an action for damages. . . ."

Plaintiff argues that its mark is infringed because:

1. Each mark is composed of two parts which are separated by a hyphen or its equivalent.

2. The first word or part of each mark has two syllables.

3. Each mark begins with the letter "P."

4. The accent is on the first syllable in each case, so that there is a rhythmic identity.

These statements are true, but they do not solve the problem; they tend to show similarity but the ultimate question is whether the similarity is likely to cause confusion. . . .

In determining whether the similarity is sufficient to require restraint the court must inquire whether the ordinary purchaser in the exercise of ordinary care and caution would be misled or deceived. . . .

. . . In the final analysis the decision becomes a matter of the application of such general principles to the factual situation actually obtaining in the instant case. The court among other things is called on to ascertain what it believes would be the reaction of that mythical being "the ordinary purchaser." It does not seem likely that such a purchaser, using the ordinary attention displayed by even the casual buyer of merchandise, would become so confused as not to be able to distinguish between the bisyllabics "Poli" and "Perma." Auricularly they are sharply distinct, despite the fact that they begin with the same lene consonant, the voiceless labial mute, P.

The sole inference of colorable imitation is directed to the general similarity of aural representation, as the packaging, printing, and package hues are in no wise alike. True, the suffixes of the marks are identical; but the word "grip" is descriptive of the qualities of the products and hence is not to be regarded as the dominant portion of either mark. . . .

The trade-marks "Perma-Grip" and "Poli-Grip" are not so alike in sound or appearance as to cause purchasers or prospective purchasers to be confused.

Defendant has not colorably imitated plaintiff's trade-mark within the meaning of the Trade Mark Act. . . .

CASE NO. 2

Safier's Inc. v. Bialer. 93 N.E. (2d) 734 (Ohio) (1950)

BLYTHIN, J. For about three years prior to May, 1950, the defendant Jack P. Bialer was a salesman for A. D. Goodman-Golden Company, a corporation. The Company was engaged in a general cigarette, tobacco and candy jobbing business and it was defendant's duty to make weekly or periodical calls on 95 of his employer's customers. He operated under an employment contract which, among other things, provided that in the event that he left the company's employ he would not engage in the same line of business directly or indirectly as a salesman in Cuyohaga County for a period of one year thereafter, if such involved customers of the employers.

About the first of May, 1950, the A. D. Goodman-Golden Company entered upon negotiations looking to the sale of all of its assets. It is clear that this became known or was made known to the defendant. He, the defendant, concerned himself about his own welfare to the extent of entering into a new employment agreement, in writing (Plaintiff's Exhibit 1), with his employer . . . This agreement does not appear to be substantially different from the one under which the parties had amicably and successfully operated in the past. It was perhaps a little more formal and verbose than the former and original agreement, and it is claimed that it was negotiated and entered into, at least in part, for the protection of defendant Bialer in case of a sale being consummated; in other words, Bialer was then thinking of his employment situation and the possible danger to it involved in a possible sale of the business of his employer. Whatever may have been in the minds of the parties at the time it seems quite clear that Bialer voluntarily entered into the agreement and then knew that one of the changes embodied in it from the original agreement was that it—the new—was between A. D. Goodman-Golden Company *"their successors and assigns"* while the original contract was purely personal and contained no reference to "successors or assigns." . . .

The employer A. D. Goodman-Golden Company sold all its assets and business to Safier's, Inc. . . . by a written contract between the parties . . . dated May 10, 1950, which contract included the following:

> "7. Seller agrees to assign to the Buyer all contracts of employment held by Seller with certain of its employees; Seller also agrees not to employ those indicated herein and Buyer agrees to retain them on terms indicated in contracts of employment referred herein. Such employees are Jack Bialer, Otto Broz, and Jack Epstein."

The employment contract with Bialer was transferred by assignment thereon as follows, and delivery thereof was made to the purchaser of the business, Safier's Inc.

> "May 10, 1950. Pursuant to a contract of sale entered into this date between ourselves and Safier's, Inc., we hereby assign the foregoing contract between ourselves and one Jack Bialer to said Safier's, Inc. . . ."

It is not claimed that defendant Jack Bialer or his services should be bought or sold in the market without his consent and we are not here concerned with that question. The real issue is that of whether or not a restrictive covenant of the kind mentioned is an asset of a business transferable with such business and enforceable by the new owner.

The transfer took effect between the 10th and 15th days of May. It is undisputed that Bialer, defendant herein, visited the new owner on May 13 (Saturday) and that he was informed that such owner would welcome his continuance in the employment on the basis of his written agreement with the previous owner. There was no term of employment prescribed in the agreement of employment. Either party could terminate it at any time. The record discloses that Bialer, on May 13, said to Safier's, Inc., that he would continue and would be on the job Monday morning (May 15). Preparatory to action he selected or took some sample or give-away materials from the stock of Safier's, Inc. After leaving the place of business on Saturday, May 13, and before Monday, May 15, rolled around, Bialer changed his mind and ended his employment. He immediately proceeded to solicit the customers of his former employer, A. D. Goodman-Golden Company, on behalf of a new employer engaged in the same and identical line of business, and is still doing so. . . .

Based upon the above, and bearing in mind that it is conceded that the restrictive covenant is reasonable and would be enforceable by A. D. Goodman-Golden Company against Bialer if he had voluntarily left its employment, we are called upon to answer one simple but very sharp question:

Is a restrictive covenant of the kind here in issue, when for the benefit of successors and assigns, an asset of the employer in its business, and one which may be effectively transferred by it as a part of a sale of all its assets? . . .

Seeking answer to our first question we find no difficulty in holding that the "good will" of a business is a very valuable asset. That "good will" is reflected in good customers and, indeed, those customers can very well be the sum and substance of a very valuable business. The right to sell as a part of a business the "good will" developed over a period of years cannot be questioned and that "good will" must in a case such as this include the trade built up over the years with particular tradesmen. Having those tradesmen as customers and having at its own risk and expense furnished to Bialer as a paid employee free access to them and association with them, it must follow that A. D. Goodman-Golden Company had a perfect right to protect that "good will" under reasonable conditions and for a reasonable period of time against a raid by Jack Bialer, and, as between the company and Jack Bialer the good will, under the conditions stated, was the *property* of the company to the extent that it could contractually be protected. . . . Reason, common sense and fair dealing dictate that one who, as an employee, has dealt for his employer with his employer's customers, can properly contract to grant to the employer a reasonable limit of protection in those customers as a "good will" asset. The Court has no difficulty whatever in concluding that the restrictive covenant is a transferable asset where, as in this case, the benefits are to the employer, "its successors and assigns" and that, in the instant case, the employment contract was properly sold and assigned. That the employment ceased by the voluntary act of Bialer, and he then acting within his rights, does not vitiate the restrictive covenant but, on the contrary, gives it life. . . .

CASE NO. 3

Kent Storage Co. v. Grand Rapids Lumber Co. 239 Mich. 161, 214 N.W. 111, 113 (1927)

WIEST, J. . . . Plaintiff sued to recover the value of pipes in a steam heating system in a building situated on premises purchased of defendant, and removed by defendant after sale to plaintiff. Defendant removed the pipes and sold them as junk. Defendant claims the pipes were reserved, under the terms of sale, with right of removal. We quote the reservation relied on and its context:

> "All that certain piece and parcel of land . . . consisting of the buildings and real estate . . . including the boilers, power plant, sprinkler equipment . . . reserving therefrom the cupola on top of mill, and pipe running from said cupola to the coal bin, and the stoker apparatus in the boiler room, all of which is the property of C. B. Newcomb, also the balance of the machinery, belting, shafting, and equipment in said mill. . . ."

. . . The building covered by the contract had been used by defendant for a considerable period of time, prior to the sale, for the manufacture of finished lumber and millwork, and the circuit judge found that the heating system was installed as a permanent fixture to the freehold and with no intent that it was to remain personal property. It may clarify thought on the subject to recall that the term "fixture" necessarily implies something having a possible existence apart from realty, but which may, by annexation, be assimilated into realty. Whether it retains the character of a chattel fixture or loses such and becomes realty depends upon the application of principles of law to particular facts. In considering legal principles applicable to this case, it should be kept in mind that the heating system was installed by the owner of the building. This has a direct bearing upon the subject of intention for it will be presumed the owner intended the heating system as an accessory to the realty and a lasting benefit thereto, and it will not be presumed that the owner of the fee intended the heating system as a mere temporary improvement to be removed as a chattel in case of sale of the land. . . . It is a salutary rule that whatever is affixed to a building by an owner in complement, to facilitate its use and occupation in general, becomes a part of the realty, though capable of removal without injury to the building. The act of an owner of a building in annexing a fixture manifests his intention of whether it is to remain a chattel or become an accession to the realty and not his secret undisclosed intention. . . .

Clearly, under the contract of sale, right to remove "the balance of the machinery, belting, shafting, and equipment" related solely to chattels and not to the heating system. Cases involving machinery and trade fixtures are of little help. The heating system was installed and used by the owner as an outfit of the building and complement of the real property.

In Quinby v. Manhattan Cloth & Paper Co., 24 N.J. Eq. 260, it was held that steam piping, used for heating purposes in the manufacturing business carried on for many years in the premises, with some of the piping resting on pieces of wood along the floor and the remainder along the walls and partitions and supported by iron rests, or brackets, nailed upon pieces of wood, firmly nailed to the walls, were fixtures and a part of the realty. . . .

The judgment for plaintiff is affirmed.

CASE NO. 4

Dermer v. Faunce. 62 A. (2d) 304, 582, 10 A.L.R. (2d) 203 (Md.) (1948)

HENDERSON, J. The appellees in this case, the owners of a store and residence at 2301 Edmondson Ave., in Baltimore City, entered into a contract on February 15, 1946, with one Gerald Golden, as general contractor, for improvements to the property for the sum of $8,000. The appellant, a registered plumber, entered into a subcontract dated March 15, 1946, with Golden to furnish materials and labor in the installation of plumbing and a complete heating system on the premises for the sum of $1,500, payable in installments as specified work was completed. There were no contractual relations between the owners and the subcontractor. Golden was to complete all the work by April 15, 1946, but failed to do so. On May 15, 1946, the owners cancelled their contract with Golden and ordered Dermer off the premises. Dermer thereupon brought an action of replevin against the owners for five radiators, two unit heaters, one Teco hot water heater and certain loose pipes and fittings placed on the premises by Dermer. . . . Upon trial of the case the Court submitted special issues to the jury, and the jury found that on May 15, 1946, four of the radiators were "physically attached to the permanent piping in said house," but could be removed without damage to the building, and that the two unit heaters were not physically attached. The undisputed testimony showed that none of the other material had been attached. The radiators, which were not new, were of standard type, not especially adapted to the premises. It was undisputed that Dermer had not been paid for any of the material in question by Golden or Faunce, and that the plant was not in operable condition. . . . Dermer testified that he paid for all of the material in question and ordered it sent to the premises, but denied that he had attached the radiators or authorized anyone to do so; when he went to the premises with the Sheriff he found that four of the radiators had been attached "hand tight" to the piping. Faunce testified that he saw Dermer "hook up" the four radiators. The issue of fact as to who attached the radiators was not resolved by the jury's findings. The court found a verdict in favor of the defendants, . . . and entered judgment in favor of the defendants for a return of the goods or their value.

In an opinion filed in the case, the court took the view that title to all of the material passed to the owners, or to the general contractor, upon delivery to the premises, ...

. . . In the case at bar there was no sale of material to Golden or consignment to him, nor was he obligated to pay for the material until it had been properly installed in the building. Rule 2, section 37 of Article 83 of the Code, § 19, Uniform Sales Act provides:

> "Where there is a contract to sell specific goods and the seller is bound to do something to the goods for the purpose of putting them into a deliverable state, the property does not pass until such thing be done."

It has been held, under the corresponding section of the Uniform Sales Act, that title to machinery delivered to the buyer's premises under a contract to install, did not pass to the buyer. Sliter v. Creek View Cheese Factory, 172 Wis. 639, 179 N.W. 745. See also Williston, Sales, Rev. Ed. § 265. We are unable to find anything in the contract between Dermer and Golden to indicate that the parties intended title to pass by mere delivery of material to the premises, or by anything short of physical annexation.

The appellees contend, however, that regardless of the intention of the parties to the installation contract, and in the absence of any contractual relation between Dermer and the landowners, the latter acquired title to all the material in question by operation of the law of fixtures, i.e., by annexation or constructive annexation. The rigors of the common law rules as to fixtures have been generally abated in the case of landlord and tenant or trade fixtures. On the other hand, as between vendor and vendee, or mortgagor and mortgagee, they have been applied (Schofer v. Hoffman, 182 Md. 270, 34 A. (2d) 350, and cases there cited), and even extended to include accessories, not physically attached but essential to the operation of the principal machinery in a manufacturing plant, which are said to pass by constructive annexation. . . . In such cases the most important test is the intention of the parties, as gathered from the agreement, the nature of the subject matter and the conduct of the parties. The fact that particular articles are readily detachable without damage to the realty and may be used elsewhere are factors to be considered, although not controlling. . . .

In Dame v. Wood, 75 N.H. 38, 70 Atl. 1081, 1082, there was a contract to install a heating plant, but the building was destroyed by fire before the work was completed. In holding that the landowner was liable to the contractor for the labor and materials put into the work, the court found that both parties understood

> "at the time the contract was made and thereafter, that from day to day as the work progressed, as fast as any portion of the boiler, piping, and radiators had been set up and connected in its proper place, it was not thereafter to be removed."

In Munroe v. Armstrong, 179 Mass. 165, 60 N.E. 475, where a subcontractor removed partially installed plumbing, after default of the general contractor, this was held to be a tortious act, but it was held that he was within his rights in removing unattached material delivered to the premises. See also note 69 L.R.A. 892.

In the case at bar we think the doctrine of constructive annexation is not applicable, and cannot effect a conversion of the unattached materials into realty. It is conceded that the built-in portions of the plant lost their character as personal property. The four radiators that were attached "hand tight" present a more difficult question. If they were attached by someone other than Dermer or his authorized agent, it seems clear that Dermer would not thereby lose his right to possession. See Tiffany, Real Property, 3d Ed., § 606, p. 559. While the testimony as to who made the connection is conflicting, we think the undisputed testimony that they were not tightened with a wrench, and were not connected to the boiler, indicates that they had not yet lost their character as personal property. Something remained to be done by Dermer before they were in operable condition and ready for acceptance by the landowners.

Judgment reversed and entered in favor of the plaintiff for the property replevied or its value. . . .

CASE NO. 5

Smyth Sales Corp. v. Norfolk Bldg. & Loan Assoc. 116 N.J.L. 293, 184 Atl. 204, 111 A.L.R. 357 (1936)

CASE, J. . . . Plaintiff sued in replevin to recover possession of certain portions of an oil burner equipment which, in its entirety, had been sold to the owner of the premises upon a filed conditional sale contract. The trial judge, sitting without a jury upon an agreed state of facts, found for the plaintiff. . . .

La Ferra, as owner, was building a four-family house with a single heating plant. On August 25, 1930, he entered into a written contract with Smyth Sales Corporation whereby the latter undertook to install an oil burner, tank, and the additional equipment incident thereto, including a pump, the same to be and remain the personal property of the seller, notwithstanding the manner in which the property might be attached to the premises, until the entire purchase price should have been paid. . . . The tank was buried three feet under ground. It was connected with the pump and burner by piping (a part of the equipment) which passed through the foundation wall of the house, was otherwise attached, and also, for approximately twenty feet, was so incased that its removal would require the breaking of the concrete cellar floor. Plaintiff's suit is directed against the burner, the tank, and the pump. If any of such articles are removed, no heat can be generated unless other appliances are installed in their stead.

On September 9, 1930, La Ferra executed a mortgage, recorded October 3, 1930, to defendant, Norfolk Building & Loan Association, in the amount of $16,000 covering the premises. On April 24, 1931, one Scrocco obtained a judgment against La Ferra on mechanic's lien and defendant purchased the premises at the execution sale held thereunder. Defendant thus acquired and still holds record title. . . .

The case turns upon the construction to be given section 7 of the Uniform Conditional Sales act. . . . For present discussion, the statutory provisions may be thus restated: An attempted reservation of title to goods so affixed to the realty that they are not severable without material injury to the freehold is void as against any person who has not expressly assented to the reservation; . . .

In determining whether the removal of the replevined goods would result in material injury to the freehold, we do not weigh the destructive effect of the breaking up of the concrete floor of the cellar incident to the removal of an essential part of the equipment because we reach our conclusion on broader grounds, but we note that the physical affixation of the equipment to the realty here clearly appears. Many years ago our courts stated a principle that has more recently become known as the institution doctrine. . . . Our late Chief Justice Gummere, in writing the opinion for this court in Knickerbocker Trust Company v. Penn Cordage Company, 66 N.J. Eq. 305, 58 Atl. 409, 410, 105 Am. St. Rep. 640, said:

"The rule laid down in Feder. v. Van Winkle, and followed in Temple Company v. Penn Mutual Life Insurance Co., states the true principle to be applied in the determination of the question when it is presented. Whenever chattels have been placed in and annexed to a building by their owner as a part of the means by which to carry out the purposes for which the building was erected or to which it has been adapted, and with the intention of permanently increasing its value for the use to which it is devoted, they become, as between the owner and his mortgagee, fixtures, and as much a part of the realty as the building itself; and this is true, notwithstanding that such chattels may be severed from and taken out of the building in which they are located, without doing any injury either to them or to it, and advantageously used elsewhere, and notwithstanding that the building itself may thereafter readily be devoted to a use entirely different from that which was contemplated when the annexation was made."

Those adjudications were between owner and mortgagee, but they enunciate a principle of wider application.

Let us consider the property presently in litigation. Advancing needs of society and marked refinements in living and working conditions and in the design and function of buildings to meet those conditions have made necessary a development of the conception of what really constitutes a building as contrasted with furnishings or severable fixtures—speaking broadly, of what is land as contrasted with chattels. It is logical that the legal conception of what we refer to, with varying shades of meaning, as "building," or "realty," or "freehold" should keep pace with actual changes in the substance which the conception represents. Particularly is this so with regard to houses, and more particularly apartment houses, and with respect to certain living facilities which must be provided by the owner as, essentially, parts of the structure. Formerly tenants took their own stoves to and from the leased premises; so, too, oil lamps, ice boxes, bathing vessels, and the like. Those ways are now largely outmoded, particularly in the cities; not only outmoded but to a degree eliminated, necessarily so in many of the habitations provided for the multiple housing of tenants. In this climate conditions of habitation must include the means of heat in the winter and of refrigeration in the summer. In our case the building is a dwelling, housing four families, built for year-round occupancy and heated by a system wherein the heat is generated in the cellar by a single oil burning equipment. The structure cannot function for the purpose, and the only purpose, for which it was built unless it has a heating system. . . . It is a part of the house. . . . It is something that must be in and of the building instituted as an apartment dwelling house, before the structure so instituted can, as a structure, properly function. The removal of it would be, pro tanto, a disintegration of the structure. With as little physical disturbance doors could be lifted from their hinges, windows from their frames, radiators from their pipes, chandeliers and brackets from the ceilings and walls, bathtubs from their settings, and numerous other accessories, personalty in their manufacture but by attachment and function part of the completed house could be taken out. If dwelling houses consisted simply of floors and roof with supporting walls masoned into the ground, the extent of physical disruption incident to the severance of an object would perhaps furnish a satisfactory and workable rule as to whether that object could be removed without injury to the freehold. But that type of construction does not prevail and that test is wholly inadequate. . . . In such a situation the degree of affixation is less important than the indispensability of that which is affixed. . . .

It is clear from the stipulated facts that the articles which respondent sought to recover are indispensable parts of the heating system which is itself an essential part of a building designed for use as an apartment house . . . It follows that . . . by the terms of the statute, the attempted reservation of title was void as against the appellant who did not assent to the reservation.

The judgment below will be reversed.

CASE NO. 6

Leigh v. Gerber. 86 F. Supp. 320 (1949)

RIFKIND, D.J. . . . suit for infringement of two copyrights, one for a painting and the other for a reproduction thereof. . . .

The complaint alleges that the plaintiff created a painting which he entitled "Struggle for Existence," and duly secured a certificate of registration of copyright therefore; that plaintiff authorized the magazine "Parade" to publish a reproduction thereof; that the magazine published a reproduction of the painting in an edition which it copyrighted; that plaintiff is the assignee of Parade's interest in the copyright of the reproduction and of any cause of action for infringement thereof which "Parade" has; and that defendants published a picture which infringed the copyright of the painting and the copyright of the reproduction. The answer alleges that the complaint fails to state a claim; admits that the answering defendants published and circulated the allegedly infringing picture . . . alleges that the photograph in the magazine did not bear the required copyright notice, wherefore the picture was placed in the public domain. . . .

It is not seriously denied by the defendants that the plaintiff created the painting; secured a copyright registration in 1948; and authorized "Parade" to publish a reproduction of the painting. It further appears . . . that on the reproduction, as published in the magazine, no copyright notice appears; that the edition of the magazine in question was copyrighted and properly marked; that "Parade" assigned to the plaintiff, after publication, all its rights and interests in the copyright of the reproduction published in the magazine and all causes of action arising from infringement thereof. . . .

Reproductions of a work of art constitute a distinct class of copyrightable material. 17 U.S.C.A. § 5. By publishing a reproduction of plaintiff's painting in a copyrighted edition of its magazine, did "Parade" secure a copyright in the reproduction . . . when it did not own the author's rights in the original? . . .

Does the authorized publication of a reproduction of a copyrighted work of art, in a copyrighted periodical, with notice of the copyright of the periodical, but omitting notice of the copyright of the work of art, constitute failure to comply with the notice requirements of the copyright laws and result in dedication to the public of the work of art?

Since one who innocently copies from an infringing copy is liable as an infringer to the owner whose unpublished work was infringed . . . it would seem to follow that one who copies from a licensed and copyrighted published reproduction is liable to the copyright owner of the original. But over 45 years ago, in the Mifflin case, the Supreme Court held that the author of a copyrighted novel lost his copyright when his licensee published a serialization of the novel in a copyrighted edition of a periodical but failed to give notice of the author's copyright. Mifflin v. Dutton, 1903, 190 U.S. 265, 23 Sup. Ct. 771, 47 L. Ed. 1043. . . .

Six years after the Mifflin decisions, the copyright law was completely revised, and in Section 3 of the Copyright Act of 1909 it was provided:

"The copyright provided by this title shall protect all the copyrightable component parts of the work copyrighted, and all matter therein in which copyright is already subsisting, but without extending the duration or scope of such copyright. The copyright upon composite works or periodicals shall give to the proprietor thereof all the rights in respect thereto which he would have if each part were individually copyrighted under this title." 17 U.S.C.A. § 3.

That it was the intention of the Congress thereby to effect a change in the law is made clear by the statement of the House Committee reporting the bill, that

"Section 3 does away with the necessity of taking a copyright on the contributions of different persons included in a single publication, but in express terms we provide that it shall not extend the duration or scope of any copyright nor do we intend to make copyrightable anything which has fallen into the public domain." H.R. Rep. No. 2222, 60th Cong., 2nd Sess., February 22, 1909, p. 8. . . .

CASE NO. 7

Verney Corporation v. Rose Fabric Converters Corporation et al. 87 F. Supp. 802 (1949)

. . . . . .

COXE, D.J. These are motions (1) by plaintiff for a preliminary injunction restraining the defendants from alleged infringement of a copyright, and (2) by defendant Rose Fabric Converters Corporation to dismiss the action for failure to state a claim upon which relief can be granted. . . .

The complaint . . . alleges that on April 16, 1947 plaintiff copyrighted a design for use upon textiles and textile prints. The design and the certificate of registration, copies of which are annexed to the complaint, show that the registration was in Class K, on Form KK, of a

"claim to copyright in a print or label used for article of merchandise, viz., chrysanthemum print . . . for textile and textile print."

It was thus a commercial print or label. The complaint then alleges that, after notice by plaintiff, the defendants have infringed the copyright in the following manner, viz.: Rose Fabric by delivering uncolored fabrics to the defendant Raytex Dyers and Printers, Inc., with instructions to imprint thereon, in various color combinations, a copy of plaintiff's design; Raytex by imprinting plaintiff's design upon the uncolored fabrics and delivering the same to Rose Fabric and to the defendants Cindy Frocks, Inc. and Helene Lynne; Rose Fabric by selling such imprinted fabrics to Cindy Frocks and Helene Lynne; and Cindy Frocks and Helene Lynne by manufacturing such imprinted fabrics into women's dresses and selling the same to the public.

. . . Plaintiff's design is not an artistic reproduction of a single chrysanthemum, but an artistic reproduction of several curly chrysanthemums, each surrounded by similar curly lines, so that they all blend into a harmonious whole. It appears from the affidavits submitted, and from an inspection of the dresses exhibited on the argument, that the design is printed in a continuous running form, repeating the design over and over, in distinctive colors, upon the fabric from which the dresses are made, and also that the fabric itself is in the distinctive colors. There is no showing by plaintiff that there was any copyright notice upon each repetition of the design. Defendants contend not only that the copyright is invalid but also that, if it is valid, copyright protection has been lost through publication without a proper copyright notice.

The Copyright Act of 1909, 17 U.S.C.A., classified in Section 5 the works entitled to copyright protection. Subsection (k) provided for "Prints and pictorial illustrations." In Kemp &

Beatley v. Hirsch, D.C.E.D.N.Y., 34 F. (2d) 291, 292, it was held that dress patterns were not copyrightable under the Act. Cf. Millinery Creators' Guild v. Federal Trade Commission, 2 Cir., 109 F. (2d) 175, 177 (affirmed without discussion of the point in 312 U.S. 469, 61 Sup. Ct. 708, 85 L. Ed. 955), where the court said that

> "What passes in the trade for an original design of a hat or a dress cannot be patented or copyrighted."

The lack of statutory copyright protection for dress designers has been repeatedly pointed out by the Court of Appeals in this Circuit. Nat Lewis Purses v. Carole Bags, 2 Cir., 83 F. (2d) 475, 476; White v. Leanore Frocks, 2 Cir., 120 F. (2d) 113, 114–115; Belding Heminway Co. v. Future Fashions, 2 Cir., 143 F. (2d) 216, 218.

Section 2 of the Act of July 31, 1939, 53 Stat. 1142, Ch. 396, amended Section 5(k) by adding the words "including prints or labels used for articles of merchandise," so that the question here is whether plaintiff's design is a print or label used for an article of merchandise. Clearly it is not a label. The word "print" was defined by the Copyright Office in its Circular No. 46, dated March 18, 1941, as follows:

> "The term 'print' as used in the said Act, may be defined as an artistic work with or without accompanying text matter published in a periodical or separately, used in connection with the sale or advertisement of an article or articles of merchandise."

While the design may have been properly registered as a print for an article of merchandise, plaintiff, by printing it on the fabric from which the dresses are manufactured, uses the design as a part of the article of merchandise itself. It is obviously not used in connection with a sale or an advertisement of either the fabric or the dresses, but is an attempt by plaintiff to obtain a monopoly of the design in the manufacture of dress fabrics and dresses, to which it is not entitled. Cf. Adelman v. Sonner's & Gordon, Inc., D.C.S.D.N.Y., 21 U.S. Pat. Q. 218. Plaintiff's use of the design in an advertisement of its fabrics and the products of Royal Frocks, as shown in an exhibit submitted by it in support of its motion, is a proper use of the design, and the use contemplated by the statute. See Ball on the Law of Copyright and Literary Property (1944), § 183.

But, even if there were doubt as to the invalidity of the copyrighted design when so used on fabrics and dresses, which I do not entertain, still plaintiff's copyright on the design has been lost by failure to publish on the fabric and the dresses, in connection with the design, the proper copyright notice.

> "Every reproduction of a copyrighted work must bear the statutory notice." DeJonge & Co. v. Breuker & Kessler Co., 235 U.S. 33, 36, 35 Sup. Ct. 6, 59 L. Ed. 113.

. . . Plaintiff's motion for a preliminary injunction is accordingly denied, and the motion of the defendant Rose Fabric Converters Corporation to dismiss the action is granted.

CASE NO. 8

Dorsey v. Old Surety L. Ins. Co. 98 F. (2d) 872, 119 A.L.R. 1250 (1938)

PHILLIPS, C.J. . . . Dorsey brought this suit against Old Surety Life Insurance Company, hereinafter called Insurance Company, for alleged infringement of copyrights on three forms of life insurance policies, seeking an injunction against future infringements and damages for alleged past infringements.

In his bill Dorsey alleged that he is the originator and author of three types of insurance policies, denominated "Family, Group Life Insurance Policy," "Family Group Policy," and "Reserve Loan Life Insurance Co. Policy Family Group"; that copyrights covering such policies were duly granted to him in October, 1927, November, 1928 and September, 1930, respectively, and that he is now the owner of such copyrights; that such policies were composed, edited, prepared, arranged, and compiled by him at great expense after extended research and as a result of more than thirty years of actuarial and sales experience in the life insurance field; that such publications are of the value of $100,000; that commencing on a date unknown to him and continuing until on or about July 28, 1936, the Insurance Company had without license, leave, right, or authority knowingly published, issued, and sold certain insurance policies denominated "Family Group Policy" which infringed vital portions of Dorsey's copyrighted publications. . . .

The trial court sustained a motion to dismiss the bill and entered its decree dismissing the suit. Dorsey has appealed.

The right secured by a copyright is not the right to the use of certain words, nor the right to employ ideas expressed thereby. Rather it is the right to that arrangement of words which the author has selected to express his ideas.

In Kaeser & Blair, Inc. v. Merchants' Ass'n, Inc., 6 Cir., 64 F. (2d) 575, 577, the court said:

"It has been frequently held that the copyright law does not afford protection against the use of an idea, but only as to the means by which the idea is expressed."

It follows that Dorsey's copyrights in no wise restricted the right of the Insurance Company to use the plans of insurance embraced in the copyrighted policies. They only restricted the use or copying of the means of expression selected by Dorsey to the extent that such means were original with Dorsey.

To be copyrightable, a work must be original in that the author has created it by his own skill, labor, and judgment. . . .

The copyrighted forms here involved in the main are an aggregation of . . . standard provisions including those required by statute. As to those provisions it is clear that there is no infringement. One work does not violate the copyright in another simply because there is a similarity between the two, if the similarity results from the fact that both works deal with the same subject or have the same common source. . . . The provisions dealing specifically with the family group are alleged to be new and original. The copyrights if valid at all must be limited to those particular provisions and to the particular means employed by Dorsey to express the contractual terms thereof. The provisions in the policies of the Insurance Company dealing particularly with the family group are neither an exact nor a substantial copy of the family group provisions in the copyrighted policies. There is no more similarity than might naturally be expected in policies embracing the same plan of insurance and incorporating like contractual provisions. There can be no doubt that the Insurance Company is free to make contracts embracing like contractual provisions as those included in the copyrighted policies and to use suitable words to express the provisions of such contracts so long as it does not copy the particular means of expression originated by Dorsey.

. . . Necessarily, where the same contractual provision is to be expressed there will be similarity of language. To constitute infringement in such cases a showing of appropriation in the exact form or substantially so of the copyrighted material should be required.

Hence, we think the trial court was fully warranted in holding upon the face of the bill that the policies of the Insurance Company did not infringe Dorsey's copyrighted forms.

The decree is affirmed.

CASE NO. 9

Gilman v. Kestral Corporation. 86 F. Supp. 765 (1949)

SWEENEY, CH.J. The plaintiff is the owner of United States Patent No. 2,449,935 issued on September 21, 1948, and, as such, brings this action against the defendant charging infringement seeking damages therefor, and an injunction against further infringement. The defendant denies infringement and asserts the invalidity of the patent and, in a counterclaim, seeks a declaratory judgment to the effect that the patent is invalid for want of invention.

The defendant's device does not differ radically from the plaintiff's, and I do not doubt seriously that a charge of infringement properly lies if the plaintiff's patent is valid. We therefore address ourselves entirely to the question of the validity of the plaintiff's patent. The patent covers a football dummy. . . . Its principal utility lies in the fact that children can use it as though it were a regulation football dummy, but without injuring themselves because it is light and resilient. The article covered by the patent consists of a self-erecting dummy, which is of relatively large size and light weight. It is a hollow, inflated, resilient figure with a weighted bottom which, when the figure is set upon the ground, tends to keep it erect and, when knocked over, tends to bring it again to an erect position. The claims which are in suit when analyzed cover four elements: (1) the body portion or outer surface of the article is made of inflatable material; (2) the article is "frustro-conical" in shape, that is, in the shape of a cone with its pointed top cut off; (3) the article has a rounded base, and (4) the base of the article has a non-rigid container attached to the interior of the bottom into which sand, or some other weighty material, may be introduced.

. . . As early as 1915 a catalog of F. A. O. Schwartz, one of the largest toy sales companies, contained a description of a self-erecting doll, called a "roly-poly," with a rounded bottom. Beach balls and water toys composed entirely of an inflatable bladder had been in conspicuous production and use for more than a year prior to the date plaintiff filed the patent claims in suit, December 10, 1947. Furthermore, during the war the defendant was engaged in manufacturing a device for distilling fresh from salt water. This device was made entirely of a vinylite plastic bladder which floated in the water and which was kept erect by water ballast in its base. Patent No. 1,677,450 to Max Wilhelm Iden, on July 17, 1928, discloses the use of a flexible ballast container as a weight to make an inflatable device self-erecting. Therefore, the only new mechanical expedient to which plaintiff resorted was to secure the weight to the inside of the bottom of the bladder.

It is elementary that however new and useful, or even revolutionary and beneficial, an idea may be, it is not in and of itself patentable. . . . The real problem involved was not a mechanical problem at all but consisted of so positioning the weight in the bladder as to produce a self-erecting device. The technique by which this was done was well known to the defendant and others long before the plaintiff found occasion to use it. It is impossible to dignify the obvious application of this technique to this problem with the name invention. Hence, I find as a fact that there was no invention in the plaintiff's patent. . . .

CASE NO. 10

Funk Bros. Co. v. Kalo Co. 92 L. Ed. 414 (1948)

DOUGLAS, J., delivered the opinion of the court:

This is a patent infringement suit brought by respondent. . . The District Court held the product claims invalid for want of invention and dismissed the complaint. . . The Circuit Court of Appeals reversed, holding that the product claims were valid and infringed . . . The question of validity is the only question presented by this petition . . .

It was the general practice, prior to the Bond patent, to manufacture and sell inoculants containing only one species of root-nodule bacteria. The inoculant could therefore be used successfully only in plants of the particular cross-inoculation group corresponding to this species. Thus if a farmer had crops of clover, alfalfa, and soy beans he would have to use three separate inoculants. There had been a few mixed cultures for field legumes. But they had proved generally unsatisfactory because the different species of the Rhizobia bacteria produced an inhibitory effect on each other when mixed in a common base, with the result that their efficiency was reduced. Hence it had been assumed that the different species were mutually inhibitive. Bond discovered that there are strains of each species of root-nodule bacteria which do not exert a mutually inhibitive effect on each other. He also ascertained that those mutually non-inhibitive strains can, by certain methods of selection and testing, be isolated and used in mixed cultures. . . .

We do not have presented the question whether the methods of selecting and testing the non-inhibitive strains are patentable. We have here only product claims. Bond does not create a state of inhibition or of non-inhibition in the bacteria. Their qualities are the work of nature. Those qualities are of course not patentable. For patents cannot issue for the discovery of the phenomena of nature. See LeRoy v. Tatham, 14 How. (U.S.) 156, 175, 14 L. Ed. 367, 375. The qualities of these bacteria, like the heat of the sun, electricity, or the qualities of metals, are part of the storehouse of knowledge of all men. They are manifestations of laws of nature, free to all men and reserved exclusively to none. He who discovers a hitherto unknown phenomenon of nature has no claim to a monopoly of it which the law recognizes. If there is to be invention from such a discovery, it must come from the application of the law of nature to a new and useful end. . . . Mackay Radio & Teleg. Co. v. Radio Corp. of America, 306 U.S. 86, 94, 83 L. Ed. 506, 510, 59 Sup. Ct. 427 . . . The Circuit Court of Appeals thought that Bond did much more than discover a law of nature, since he made a new and different composition of non-inhibitive strains which contributed utility and economy to the manufacture and distribution of commercial inoculants.

But we think that that aggregation of species fell short of invention within the meaning of the patent statutes.

Discovery of the fact that certain strains of each species of these bacteria can be mixed without harmful effect to the properties of either is a discovery of their qualities of non-inhibition. It is no more than the discovery of some of the handiwork of nature and hence is not patentable. . . . Each of the species of root-nodule bacteria contained in the package infects the same group of leguminous plants which it always infected. No species acquires a different use. The combination of species produces no new bacteria, no change in the six species of bacteria, and no enlargement of the range of their utility. . . .

There is, of course, an advantage in the combination. The farmer need not buy six different packages for six different crops. He can buy one package and use it for any or all of his crops of leguminous plants. And, as respondent says, the packages of mixed inoculants also hold advantages for the dealers and manufacturers by reducing inventory problems and the like. But a product must be more than new and useful to be patented; it must also satisfy the requirements of invention or discovery. . . .

CASE NO. 11

Harley C. Loney Co. v. Nelson. 81 F. Supp. 965 (1948)

. . . . .

REEVES, CH.J. The sole question for decision in this case is whether Patent No. 2,036,757 issued to James W. Hume, Jackson, Michigan, is valid.

The patent was applied for on December 3, 1932. It related to an improvement in the balancing of vehicle wheels provided with pneumatic tires. The reasons back of the invention as recited in the patent were, that

> "the increasing speed at which motor vehicles are driven has resulted in the necessity of dynamically balancing the wheels."

To achieve a good result it was necessary to balance the entire assembly, which would include the wheel, the rim, and the tire; these constituted the complete unit.

Some of the factors requiring a balancing means were: The circumstance that the shifting of the rim during the rolling action resulted in variation of the thickness of the flanges; the welding of the rims; the variation in tire construction; and the concentrated weight of the valve stem of the inner tube. These all tended to cause an unbalanced condition of the wheel.

There was a further recitation that previously the attempts to remedy conditions of unbalance on motor vehicle wheels were cumbrous, expensive and ineffective and the means employed lacked "flexibility and ease of installation." The object of the invention, as specified by the patentee, was

> "to provide a balancing mass for vehicle wheels of the pneumatic tire type, which is inexpensive, effective and may be readily and adjustably positioned along the flange of the wheel rim to balance the wheel, rim, and tire assembly."

The attaching portion or means was either by set screws or the equivalent, which was construed to include the spring clip type of attachment.

It is the contention of the defendant, among other things, that the patent was invalid by reason of anticipation, and, moreover, that it involved no more than mere mechanical skill. The defendant was reinforced in this contention by a decision of the Court of Appeals, Seventh Circuit, styled Harley C. Loney Co. v. Revenscroft, 162 F. (2d) 703. From the facts before that court it was held that the patent and the claims thereof were invalid in the light of the prior art, and, moreover, the invention did not involve discovery but merely the exercise of mechanical skill. . . . It is a matter of common knowledge, and the evidence so shows, that the speed of automobiles was greatly increased upon the highways approximately after the year 1920. The result was that unbalance of the tire structure or unit became a problem to automotive engineers and others. With increasing speed of motor vehicles the problem increased and automobile engineers were perplexed, nonplussed and confused as to how the problem might be solved.

Many and unavailing efforts were made to solve the problem. It was then that plaintiff appeared with his proposed device as above described. It was promptly commercially successful. It was recognized by automotive engineers and others as great progress toward, if not a complete solution of the vexing problem. After much study and inquiry and after four years, the patent office granted the patent. Apparently the problem confronting the patent office was whether the device or means proposed by the applicant was anticipated and well known in the prior art. The question urged there, and here, was that conditions of unbalance had been previously experienced in pulleys, fly wheels, etc., and that test weights to be attached for experimental purposes had employed identical means of attachment, such as set screws and spring clips, as in this case; and neither then, nor now, did those who studied the device consider that it was a device used in combination with other elements and factors and that the device standing alone was not the sole object of the invention.

As indicated, the only serious question in this case is whether the patentee discovered a new and useful art or any new and useful improvement thereof. In the case of Montgomery Ward & Co. v. Clair, 8 Cir., 123 F. (2d) 878, loc. cit. 881, the Court of Appeals of this Circuit said:

> "The law is that whoever finally perfects and improves a device and renders it capable of practical, useful and effective operation is entitled to a patent although others had the idea and made experiments toward putting it into practice."

This rule is universal and is a sound postulate for a decision in this case. That the patentee in this case perfected a device in such way as to make it capable of practical, useful and effective operation cannot be denied. It was a new problem and there was no prior art.

The demand for the product was enormous. Even the defendant or her principal was successfully using the device and has strenuously resisted this action, not upon the ground that there was no infringement but upon the sole ground that it was not a patentable device and therefore the patent was void. The devices of the defendant or her employer were not substantially different from that of the plaintiff either in the result attained, the means of attaining that result, or the manner in which its different parts operate and cooperate to produce said result.

. . . The contention of the plaintiff as well as the contents of the patent and its obvious usefulness all bring it within the doctrine of General Electric Supply Corporation v. Maytag Co., 8 Cir., 100 F. (2d) 218, loc. cit. 221, where the court said:

> "A new combination of old elements whereby a new and useful result is produced, or an old result is obtained in a more facile, economical, and efficient way, is protected by a patent."

. . . Plaintiff is entitled to a decree as prayed. Counsel for plaintiff will submit a proposed decree.

CASE NO. 12

Sinclair v. Travis. 231 N.C. 345, 57 S.E. (2d) 394 (1950)

Civil action brought against defendant Effie S. Travis to recover on two certain promissory notes given by her to N. A. Sinclair. . . . Ruth Travis and Dorothy Travis were later made defendants. . . .

Plaintiff is a resident of Franklin County, State of North Carolina, and is the duly appointed, qualified and acting executrix of, and the sole devisee and legatee under the last will and testament of N. A. Sinclair, deceased.

. . . defendants make these averments:

That . . . on March 28, 1938, defendant Effie S. Travis duly received a letter from her father, N. A. Sinclair, written from the Hotel Sir Walter in the city of Raleigh, North Carolina, reading as follows:

"Dear Effie:

"I have been very far from well since I wrote you last. I enclose note for you to sign and return to me at Fayetteville. Your last note was Jany 26, 1937—since then I have loaned you 14 payments of $80—which amounts to $1120—and $150 for taxes—totalling $1270— Understand that I am not charging you anything that I have sent you for your self or the children—but only my payments on the property—and I have and do will to Ruth and Dorothy your indebtedness and notes to me, so in case I die before you do—or they do—these notes will be the property of the children and no one else will have any interest in them.

"With love to you & Dorothy

"N. A. Sinclair

"Keep this letter carefully as it will protect the children after my death if any question should arise about my will.

"Dad"

That by reason of the agreements aforesaid between defendant Effie S. Travis and her father, her said children became, and are now, the owners in their own right of both of the said notes. . . .

WINBORNE, J. While there are extensive allegations of fact in support of the position taken by defendants in this action, the evidence pivots around the letter of March 28, 1938, from N. A. Sinclair, plaintiff's deceased husband, and testator, to his daughter, the defendant Mrs. Effie S. Travis. Hence, decision on this appeal is determinable, in the main, upon proper construction as to the meaning of this letter. Defendants allege and contend that the defendants, Ruth Travis and Dorothy Travis, granddaughters of N. A. Sinclair, are the owners of the two notes on which this action is based—for that the letter created a gift *inter vivos* from N. A. Sinclair to them. . . .

The subject of gifts *inter vivos* has been under consideration, and treated by this Court, and pertinent authorities cited and assembled, in several recent decisions. . . .

In 226 N.C. 313, 38 S.E. (2d) 224, Buffaloe v. Barnes, preferred stock in a corporation was the subject of the alleged gift *inter vivos*. Devin, J., writing the opinion for this Court, summarizes the law in this manner:

"To constitute a gift there must be an intention to give, and the intention must be consummated by a delivery of, and loss of dominion over, the property given, on the part of the donor. . . . To constitute delivery of shares of stock as the consummation of a valid gift *inter vivos* the donor must divest himself of all right and title to the stock and of all dominion over it. . . . The transaction must show a completely executed transfer to the donee of the present right of property and the possession. . . ."

Applying these principles to the case in hand, the letter fails to show facts sufficient to constitute a gift *inter vivos*. The language used fails to show an intention to give, and then the delivery, which are elements essential to the making of a gift *inter vivos*. Rather, the language used is more of testamentary character,—and being in the handwriting of N. A. Sinclair, nothing else appearing, it might have taken effect as a codicil to his will. But, as such, it was subject to be revoked (1) by the affirmative written declaration of N. A. Sinclair and, in his will which was probated, he did revoke all other wills and testaments theretofore made by him, and (2) by operation of law, upon the subsequent marriage of the testator, G.S. § 31-6, and he subsequently married. . . .

Hence, we hold that, on this record, defendants have failed to show ownership of the notes, and plaintiff was entitled . . . to judgment in accordance with this opinion.

Reversed.

CASE NO. 13

Bozeman Mortuary Asso. v. Fairchild. 253 Ky. 74, 68, S.W. (2d) 756, 92 A.L.R. 419 (1934)

STANLEY, C. . . . The amount involved in this case is small, but the principal is important.

The appellant, a corporation, engaged in the business of a funeral director, in Bozeman, Mont., had a seven-passenger Buick automobile stolen in that city on July 26, 1931. On August 9th following, one Phillips was arrested in Rockcastle county, Ky., while in possession of that machine and its custody was taken over by the sheriff, N. J. Tipton. The arresting officer testified that Phillips was arrested for "shooting up a filling station." The jailer testified that he was charged with "stealing an automobile." The county judge testified that no criminal charge against Phillips appeared on his docket. For some reason not expressly disclosed by the record before us, Phillips was not tried, but was released in about three weeks. On December 1st the sheriff, Tipton, as an individual, filed suit against Phillips in the Rockcastle quarterly court on a claim for "a loan of money and garage bill" for $152, and an attachment was levied on the machine. Without either Phillips or the owner of the stolen machine being brought before the court in any way, judgment was rendered six days after the suit was filed, the attachment sustained, and the car ordered sold. The sheriff, officially, sold the machine to himself, personally, for $100. The date is not disclosed in this record, but a few months later, according to the appellee Fairchild, the sheriff's son-in-law, he traded him another machine for that automobile.

When the owner, the appellant, sought afterward to recover its automobile, it could not do so amicably. It then brought this suit against Fairchild and Mrs. Lillie Tipton, widow of the former sheriff, to recover the machine or its value, and for $300 damages for its wrongful detention. Every allegation of the petition was denied and a counterclaim asserted for $130.48 for a battery, muffler, tires, and a few minor parts, and oil and grease furnished the car, also repairs and storage. . . .

After the evidence was introduced before a jury, the court discharged the jury and rendered a judgment to the effect that the plaintiff was entitled to the possession of the automobile, but that the defendant Fairchild, having placed upon the machine what the court determined to be "necessary improvements" or accessories at a cost of $81.18, was entitled to a judgment on his counterclaim for that sum. A lien was adjudged him therefor, and the machine ordered sold to satisfy that lien. . . .

The law of accession, or acquisition of property by addition, had its origin in the civil law or Code of Justinian. From the beginning it has been regarded as the common law of England and so was transplanted into our jurisprudence. With the changing conceptions of justice and the growth of modern conditions, the original arbitrary rule has been ameliorated and made more varied in its meaning and application. This applicability to complex conditions renders hazardous any attempt to give a comprehensive definition.

A pioneer and perhaps the leading case in America is Chief Justice Robertson's opinion in Lampton's Ex'rs v. Preston's Ex'rs, 24 Ky. (1 J. J. Marsh.) 454, 19 Am. Dec. 104. The facts were that when Preston recovered possession from Lampton of a certain lot there was in the yard a quantity of unburnt and burnt bricks. The perplexing question was as to whom the bricks belonged, whether to Lampton, who did not own the soil out of which they were made but of which he was possessed at the time when he made the bricks, or to Preston, who was the true owner of the soil but who had no hand in making the bricks. After an exhaustive consideration of the principles and authorities, the final decision was reached. It was held that the unburnt brick belonged to Preston as the owner of the clay on payment for the molding, for although in the form of brick, and strictly speaking they could not be called clay, yet the material was still clay and might be combined in the common mass and constitute again a substratum for the soil, possessing all its previous qualities, so that the owner of the soil could identify the clay in the artificial form of soft brick and could recover it. But the burnt brick were held to belong to the manufacturer, Lampton, personally, because there had been an essential and radical change in the quality of the native clay through his labors. While the facts of that case are not in analogy to those of the case at bar, we may look to the opinion for the principles to be applied. We draw from it the division of cases of this nature into two classifications. Says the opinion:

"When the authorities speak of rights by accession of other materials as well as skill or labor; as in the case of the cloth manufactured out of the wool of a stranger, and of the manufacturer. Here the fabric would belong to the manufacturer; because the several parcels of wool could not be identified and separated. . . .

"Right by 'specification' can only be acquired when, without the accession of any other material, that of another person, which has been used by the operator innocently, has been converted by him into something specifically different in the inherent and characteristic qualities, which identify it. Such is the conversion of corn into meal, of grapes into wine, etc. Here, although the meal possess no quality which the corn did not, yet it not only does not possess all the same qualities, but there is difference in the name, the character, the solidity, and every attribute which distinguishes one species from another. Meal and corn are different, as lime and rock, or rye and whiskey."

The facts of the present case obviously place it under the classification where the rights are designated as by accession as distinguished from rights by specification, for there was no change in the form or transmutation in the species of the subject-matter. The consideration of relative values of the original and the new, which often has an important bearing in the adjustment of the title to chattels by accession, also supports this conclusion. . . .

The new battery, tires, and other accessories put upon the automobile in substitution of those worn out—either by the defendants or others who had it after it was stolen—could yet be identified and be removed, which fact creates some difficulty and takes the case out of that line where there was such confusion or intermingling of properties as to make them inseparable. We do have some cases of this character, at least in respect to separability, to be noticed. Where the automobile or other chattel is subject to a conditional sale contract or mortgage, with respect to accessions the general rule is that title to the accessories will not pass with the principal chattel when reclaimed by the conditional vendor or on foreclosure of the mortgage where they can be readily identified and detached without injury to it. Blackwood Tire & Vulcanizing Company v. Auto Storage Company, 133 Tenn. 515, 182 S.W. 576, L.R.A. 1916E, 254, Ann. Cas. 1917C, 1168; note 68 A.L.R. 1242. In those annotations are digested cases holding property to pass by accession and cases holding the contrary, the different conclusions depending upon whether the seller of the accessories (including specifically automobile tires and the like) had retained title to them. Berry, in his work on Automobiles, section 1806, shows that distinction, but couples with the matter of identity the important consideration of whether the accessory may be detached without injury to the principal chattel. The removal of these accessories . . . would destroy the machine's usefulness until the owner should replace them. It may be said, then, that these accessories were united to the principal thing so as to constitute an integral part of it and the owner of the greater acquired title to the lesser articles . . . The installation of these items is not far removed from repairs to a chattel, and it is the rule that ordinary repairs become a part of the thing repaired by accession. . . .

But our decision in this case may not rest wholly upon any conclusion in respect to the nature of the accessions, for the relation of the parties always has a controlling influence.

Upon the principle that a party can obtain no right by nor derive any advantage from his own wrong, the willful trespasser, as against the owner, can never acquire title to the thing itself and will never be allowed to reclaim the articles he has put upon it or commingled with it, or to receive their value, however great or small the change wrought in the original article may be, or however much or little the enhancement in value may be. . . .

The second class of claimants, that is, those who come into possession of another's property innocently or under color of title and alter or add to it, are commonly referred to as unintentional trespassers. Their rights and the limitations upon those rights upon the authority of a number of cases, including those we have cited, are thus stated in a general way in 1 C.J. 385:

> "One, although technically a trespasser, may, if he has acted under a mistake of right and without wrongful intent, acquire a right of property by accession. It is not, however, the policy of the law to offer any encouragement to trespassers, to put a pre-

mium upon carelessness in regard to the rights of others, or to make one person suffer for the mistake of another; and ordinarily a trespasser, although acting under a mistake or right, cannot acquire title to property by accession, as against the owner, where its identity is not lost and it has not been so increased in value as to make it obviously inequitable for the original owner to reclaim it. . . ."

We are now led to the inquiry whether the defendant Fairchild is to be regarded as a willful or unintentional trespasser. He testified that he had no knowledge of the source of title to the machine of his father-in-law, the sheriff, and consequently did not know that it was stolen property. There is no express evidence to the contrary, although we have the circumstances staring us in the face. We suppose we must give verity to the defendant's declarations of innocence and accept them. At any rate, we shall do so for the opinion. Even so, he stands, stript of any right to the property or the accessories he placed upon it, for the innocent purchaser from a willful trespasser or thief acquires no greater right than he. An owner is never divested of his property by theft, and therefore a sale by a thief, or by any person claiming under a thief, does not vest title in the purchaser as against the owner though the sale was made in good faith and in the ordinary course of trade. Title to personal property, like a stream, cannot rise higher than its source. An owner may follow his property and reclaim it wherever he may find it, whether the person who has it came into possession innocently or otherwise, for a thief cannot confer title even upon a bona fide purchaser. That defect in title will continue to exist in all subsequent sales. . . .

Public welfare and public policy will not allow one to assert any rights to stolen property or to anything he spends or puts on it as against the owner. To hold otherwise would be to encourage the nefarious business of handling stolen automobiles which has grown to such amazing and alarming proportions.

Further pursuit of the subject would be merely to repeat the substance of the opinions, general and specific, in other and less impressive language. The conclusion of the whole case is that accessories put upon the stolen machine went with it to the owner, and that the plaintiff was entitled to have his claim for damages for the wrongful detention and the depreciation of his property given consideration by the court.

Wherefore the judgment is reversed and case remanded for a new trial consistent with this opinion.

CASE NO. 14

Union Properties v. Cleveland Trust Co. 152 Ohio 484, 89 N.E. (2d) 638 (1949)

. . . in October, 1941, Union Properties, Inc., obtained a default judgment for $800.45 against one John Allen in the Municipal Court of Cleveland.

. . . an order in aid of execution was issued against the Cleveland Trust Company as the debtor of Allen. . . .

The Cleveland Trust Company did not comply with the order and an action was thereafter brought against it in the Municipal Court by Union Properties, Inc., to recover the sum of $792 with interest and costs. In an order of interpleader, entered at the instance of the Cleveland Trust Company, it, the trust company, was directed to pay to the clerk of the Municipal Court the sum of $795.37 and John Allen and his wife, Needa Allen, also known as Nellie Allen, were made parties defendant to the action with the right to "set up their claims to the said funds." In the separate answer and cross-petition of Needa Allen, she averred among other things:

> "That at all of said times the said sum of $792 in the possession of the defendant, The Cleveland Trust Company, was held by said trust company on a savings account, payable to the order of either of said Needa Allen or of said John Allen, or the survivor of them. That at all of said times said money in said bank, and credit from said bank for same, was the sole separate property of this new defendant, Needa Allen, and that said defendant John Allen had no right, claim, title or interest therein or thereto." . . .

Both John and Needa Allen testified that the original deposit of $100 and all other money subsequently deposited belonged exclusively to Needa; that the original $100 deposit represented the repayment of money which she, Needa, had loaned; and that the account was opened in the name of John Allen because Needa Allen by reason of an injury was prevented from going to the bank. . . .

A finding and judgment was entered by the Municipal Court in favor of Needa Allen on the ground

> "that it is her money, and is not subject to payment of the judgment against her husband John Allen." . . .

A motion for a new trial was filed and overruled and on appeal on questions of law to the Court of Appeals, that court, without a written opinion, affirmed the judgment below. . . .

ZIMMERMAN, J. In the case of Cleveland Trust Co. v. Scobie, Admr., 114 Ohio St. 241, 151 N.E. 373, 48 A.L.R. 182, this court laid down the rule, since adhered to in principle, that where one opens a savings account in a bank to the joint credit of himself and another, payable to either or the survivor, and it is apparent that the depositor intended to transfer to the person, to whom he made the account jointly payable, a present joint interest therein equal to his own, the person to whom the account is made jointly payable is entitled to the balance of the money in the account upon the death of the depositor as against the claim thereto of the depositor's personal representative.

Section 710-120, General Code, enacted solely for the benefit and protection of banks, provides:

> "When a deposit has been made, or shall hereafter be made in any bank or trust company transacting business in this state in the name of two or more persons, payable to either, or the survivor, such deposit or any part thereof, or any interest or dividend thereon, may be paid to either of said persons whether the other be living or not; and the receipt or acquittance of the person so paid shall be a valid and sufficient release and discharge to the bank for any payments so made."

Basing its argument upon the holding in the Scobie case, supra, language used in the opinion in that case, other cited cases and Section 710-120 General Code, Union Properties, Inc., contends that under the contract of deposit, John Allen was invested with a present joint and equal interest in the deposit which would have enabled him to withdraw all the funds at any time, hence, Union Properties, Inc., pursuant to its judgment against John Allen and the order in aid of execution issued thereon, can compel the appropriation of the funds in the account to itself in the right of John Allen.

Most of the cases decided by this court relating to so-called joint and survivorship bank accounts dealt with the status and rights of the survivor. Under those decisions, the survivor has been held entitled to the balance in the account because he ostensibly acquired a joint and equal interest in the funds under the contract of deposit and nothing transpired during the lives of the depositors to indicate that the intention was different from that expressed in such contract. See Berberick v. Courtade, 137 Ohio St. 297, 28 N.E. (2d) 636, and the cases cited therein.

However, no question of a survivor's rights is involved in the present controversy. Neither do we have a situation where a bank complied with an order in aid of execution and paid the deposit to the judgment creditor of one of the depositors. Here, we are concerned wholly with a subsisting deposit intact and the rights, intention and attitude of the depositors with respect thereto during their joint lives.

In our opinion, in controversies like the present one involving the deposit and arising during the joint lives of the depositors, the form of the deposit should not be treated as conclusive on the subject of joint ownership and the door should be opened to evidence that the deposit was in truth made and maintained on a different basis. In other words, the "realities of ownership" may be shown. The leading case in the United States supporting this rule is Moskowitz et al., Exrs. v. Marrow, 251 N.Y. 380, 167 N.E. 506, 66 A.L.R. 870, concurring opinion by Chief Judge Cardozo, approved by five of the associate judges. Compare Buckley v. Buckley, 301 Mass. 530, 17 N.E. (2d) 887; People's Savings Bank in Providence v. Rynn, 57 R.I. 411, 417, 190 Atl. 440, 443.

This court does not weigh evidence. Both the lower courts found, in effect, upon evidence of sufficient probative force that, notwithstanding the form of the account in the bank, the money on deposit was in reality the sole property of Needa Allen and that in opening the account and subsequently it was not the intention that John Allen should have a joint and equal interest therein. This being so, it followed that Union Properties, Inc., could not appropriate the money in the account to satisfy the judgment it held against John Allen alone. . . .

Judgment affirmed.

CASE NO. 15

In the Matter of the Estate of Ernest G. Wilson, Deceased. 404 Ill. 207 (1949)

GUNN, J., delivered the opinion of the court:

On March 10, 1943, Dr. Ernest G. Wilson and Mary Aldah Wilson rented two safety-deposit boxes in the First Trust & Savings Bank of Kankakee . . . and in addition to the printed lease card signed by Dr. and Mrs. Wilson and left with the bank, there was stamped on said card the following: "As joint tenants with the right of survivorship and not as tenants in common." There was also a joint checking account in said bank, and the signature card signed by both Dr. and Mrs. Wilson authorized either to draw funds from said account. Also stamped on this signature card were the words, "As joint tenants with the right of survivorship and not as tenants in common." All of these cards were left with the bank, and were produced by an officer of the bank. Wilson died September 24, 1946. When the boxes were opened, No. 371 contained $36,-896 in currency. Admittedly Dr. Wilson made the money that was found in the box. Also in this box was a paper in the handwriting of Dr. Wilson, as follows:

> "There is $37,000 in this box and it is a joint tenancy between my wife, Mary Aldah Wilson, and myself, E. G. Wilson, M.D., 6-11-46." . . .

The joint checking account had in it

$1,837.52 at the time of Dr. Wilson's death.

Dr. Wilson left a last will devising his property, one half to his wife, Mary Aldah Wilson, and the other half to two children of his former wife, equally. The wife was made executrix of the will, and as such failed to inventory any of the property contained in the safety-deposit boxes, or in the bank account. A petition was filed in the county court of Kankakee County to require the executrix to inventory such property, but Mary Aldah Wilson answered that she owned it individually by reason of being the survivor of a joint tenancy in the contents of the boxes and of the bank account. The county and circuit courts of Kankakee County agreed with her contention. The Appellate Court held that Mrs. Wilson was not entitled to the contents of the boxes as the survivor of a joint tenancy in their contents, but that the money in the bank account was properly held to be hers by virtue of the contract of deposit . . . in our opinion the correct solution is to be found in properly applying the provisions of section 2 of the statute on joint rights and obligations. (Ill. Rev. Stat. 1947, chap. 76, par. 2) The part of this statute applying to the contents in the safety-deposit boxes reads as follows:

> "Except as to executors and trustees, and except also whereby will or other instrument in writing expressing an intention to create a joint tenancy in personal property with the right of survivorship, the right or incident of survivorship as between joint tenants or owners of personal property is hereby abolished, and all such joint tenancies or ownerships shall, to all intents and purposes, be deemed tenancies in common." . . .

. . . the person claiming personal property as the survivor of a joint tenancy has the burden of showing he comes within the exceptions where the incident of survivorship is permitted. Let us therefore look at the requirements of the statute which would allow the survivor of joint renters of a safety-deposit box to claim ownership of its contents by reason thereof.

First, the instrument must be a writing, as the statute recites

> "whereby will or other *instrument in writing* expressing an intention to create a joint tenancy in personal property," etc.

Appellant substantially contends that any writing, regardless of form, complies with the statute, but aside from the fact that the statute carries an inference that the writing should have the general requirements of a will as to description of property, parties, and certainty of its objects, it should at least be something similar to the requirements of law relating to the conveyance of goods and chattels upon consideration not deemed valuable in law. This statute provides transfers of goods and chattels without valuable consideration must be by will or by deed, as in the case of real estate, or by possession remaining *bona fide* in the donee. . . . The public policy manifested by both acts is directed against secret transfers and as an aid to creditors, so it would seem reasonable to believe the General Assembly intended the instrument in writing mentioned, to describe the personal property intended to pass to a survivor of joint box renters, and not leave it to an ambiguous document which conveyed nothing presently, but would operate prospectively at the time of death, whether soon or remote, on any personal property in the box.

Further, the instrument in writing must express an intention to create a joint tenancy in *personal property* with the right of *survivorship.* Appellant claims the rental receipt expresses the intention of creating a survivorship in personal property found in the safety-deposit box. If it be conceded the stamped words, "joint tenancy with right of survivorship," indicated something was to be taken by a survivor, the subject matter is left to conjecture, as no chattel property is described or even mentioned. The box contract does not purport to convey anything, but merely acknowledges the lease or rent of an empty box. Moreover, this exhibit was not a contract between Dr. and Mrs. Wilson, but one between the Wilsons, on one part, and the bank, on the other. So, while the subject matter was an empty box, the parties, *viz.,* the bank and the Wilsons, mutually agreed it was rented jointly and with right of survivorship, which contract by ordinary rules of construction could only apply to the subject matter of the contract, *viz.,* the use of a safety-deposit box. No property is described, and nothing purports to transfer goods or chattels from one party to another. To support the contention of appellant we must hold that a writing, delivered to the bank as the other party to the contract, conveyed, as between the husband and wife, all contents then or thereafter found by the survivor in the leased box.

To do this we must reform the contract by adding something the parties did not put in it. We think the statute authorizes personal property to be held in joint tenancy with the right of survivorship only as an exception to the general provision abolishing survivorship in personal property in such cases. To create the incident of survivorship the parties must comply with the statute. There must be a transfer to the joint tenants of personal property. It must be identified and described. The transfer must be by written instrument specifying such to be the purpose, and finally, if the property transferred is money or currency, the amount must be specified at the time title passes to the joint tenants. There is no principle of which we are aware which permits the transfer of undefined amounts of money, varying from time to time, by the mere designating of one party to a contract of renting as "joint tenants with right of survivorship." The legislature never intended the words "instrument in writing" to be other than what is ordinarily required for the purpose. The means used in the present case to rent a safety-deposit box from a bank by a contract between it and its lessees, cannot be considered as a transfer of ownership or title to its contents merely because the parties have had stamped on the contract that the lessees are joint tenants with right of survivorship as one of the contracting parties.

. . . The precise question discussed has not been previously decided by this court, but reason and logic require us to hold there has been no transfer of the title of the money and bearer bonds in box No. 371, in a manner conformable to statute, to enable appellant to claim same as survivor. The courts of other jurisdictions have also decided that renting a lockbox in a bank in the name of two or more persons, as joint tenants with the right of survivorship, does not on the death of one vest the personal property in the box in the survivor. (Mercantile Safe Deposit Co. v. Huntington, 35 N.Y. S. 390; Gilkinson v. Third Ave. R. Co. 63 N.Y.S. 792; In re Brown, 149 N.W. Supp. 138, affirmed 217 N.Y. 621, 111 N.E. 1085; Black v. Black, 199 Ark. 609, 135 S.W. (2d) 837; In re Estate of Wohleber, 320 Pa. 83, 181 Atl. 479) We are in accord.

. . . Inherent in the general type of cases involved here is the desire upon the part of a living person to have the benefit of testamentary disposition of his chattel property without a will, and at the same time retain dominion during his lifetime. We hold that the currency and bearer bonds in the safety-deposit boxes should have been inventoried by the executrix. . . .

The deposit account is governed by a different part of the statute, which reads:

> "provided, that when a deposit in any bank or trust company transacting business in this State has been made or shall hereafter be made in the names of two or more persons payable to them when the account is opened or thereafter, such deposit . . . may be paid to any one of said persons whether the other or others be living or not, and when an agreement permitting such payment is signed by all said persons at the time the account is opened or thereafter the receipt or acquittance of the person so paid shall be valid and sufficient discharge from all parties to the bank for any payments so made." (Ill. Rev. Stat. 1947, chap. 76, par. 2)

The joint contract with the bank was signed by both Dr. and Mrs. Wilson, and was in accord with the requirement of the statute, and in addition bore thereon the words: "as joint tenants with the right of survivorship and not as tenants in common." This, under many authorities, constituted an agreement between the bank and the depositors by which the survivor took title by contract and not by gift at death of either. Under this statute, before amendment, when the language was not substantially different, we have held such deposit was properly paid to the survivor. . . .

Judgment affirmed.

Review Questions

1. How does the legal concept of the term *property* differ from its popular meaning?
2. Enumerate some of the limitations that society places upon the individual in the use of his belongings.
3. Distinguish real property from personal property.
4. Indicate how the requirements for the transfer of real property differ from the requirements for the transfer of personal property.
5. Is a judgment a lien against personal property?
6. Does personal property upon being annexed to real property become part of the realty?
7. May personal property annexed by a tenant become real property?
8. Construct fact situations under which a tenant (a) would have the right, and (b) would not have the right, to remove personal property that he has annexed to the realty.
9. The owner of a factory building introduces machinery for use in the manufacturing enterprise. Would you regard this as being real or personal property?
10. Are growing crops held to be realty or personalty in your state?
11. Enumerate the various methods by which title may be acquired to personal property.
12. How does a patent differ fundamentally from a copyright?
13. May a production be copyrighted after it has been published?
14. What is the test of infringement upon a copyright?
15. For what period of time is a production protected by a copyright?
16. For what period of time is an invention protected by a patent?

17. What are the elements of patentability?
18. By what methods may a voluntary transfer of title to personal property be accomplished?
19. Can an intentional wrongdoer acquire title to personal property by accession?
20. In determining whether title to property has passed by accession, would you favor the change of species test or the relative value test? Why?
21. What are the rights of the owner of an accessory part that has been added to a principal part?
22. In what respect does ownership in joint tenancy differ from ownership in tenancy in common?

Problems for Discussion

1. The plaintiff leased space from the defendant for the purpose of operating a tonsorial parlor. Before expiration of the plaintiff's lease, defendant wishing to remodel the building agreed that the plaintiff was during the period of remodeling to have occupancy of another room rent free. The plaintiff accepted this offer and signed the following agreement: "The undersigned hereby agrees to hold the insurance company [defendant] harmless from all liability for damages to the person or property of the undersigned." The plaintiff sued to recover for damages resulting from a loss of business. He contends the word property referred to his tools and equipment; to visible tangible things capable of physical custody. He contends the contract had no reference to his business or trade and therefor did not release the defendant for damages to such. Decide. (*Wood* v. *Sec. Mut. Life Ins. Co.*, 112 Neb. 66)
2. The terms *goods* and *choses in action* are used in the personal property section of the Statute of Frauds. Explain the meaning of these terms.
3. Which of the following would you regard as being fixtures?
   (a) Iceboxes furnished tenants in an apartment building
   (b) An outdoor brick fireplace constructed by a tenant
   (c) A brick garage and concrete sidewalks constructed by a tenant who leased the premises for fifteen years
   (d) Loose planking in an upper floor of a gin house upon which it was the practice to spread cottonseed
   (e) Individual hog houses used by a tenant, which houses are on skids so that they can be easily shifted about
   (f) A church bell before it is placed in the church tower
4. Plaintiff sold Whittier a planer and secured the purchase price by a chattel mortgage. Whittier installed it in his sawmill, located upon land that was mortgaged to defendant. The machine was bolted to the mill floor, connected to the blower system, and integrated with the mill by means of belts, shafts, and pulleys. Defendant acquired the property by foreclosure, and plaintiff asserts his chattel mortgage rights against the planer. Result?
5. A, a tenant restaurateur, installed booths, lights, refrigerators, soda fountain, and bar upon the leased premises. Their removal would necessitate some injury to the building such as removal of portions of the floor. The owner of the premises contends that these items of property are part and parcel of the realty and cannot be removed by the tenant upon expiration of the lease. Result?

6. Is growing nursery stock personalty or realty?
7. A sells his farm to B and orally reserves the right to all growing crops. B disregards his oral agreement and harvests and sells the crops. A brings an action of trover for the alleged conversion of his property. Will he succeed?
8. Almost two years after the death of the intestate mother, daughter Mary Ann Bradshaw found three bags containing $950 sewed in a blanket which was in a trunk of linens, blankets, and other materials which had belonged to deceased.

   This sum of money the administrator claims as part of the estate.

   From the evidence it appears that the daughter Mary was the youngest child of the deceased and unmarried at the time of her mother's death.

   That for sometime prior to her death she had designated this trunk as the "hope chest" for this daughter in which she placed materials from time to time, including the blanket in question, which she explicitly stated her daughter was to have.

   The trunk or chest, as it was called, eventually came into the possession of this daughter sometime after the death of the mother, still containing the blanket.

   The testimony bears out the fact that this trunk or chest was called and considered Mary's "hope chest." Decide. (*In re Tardibone's Estate,* 94 N.Y.S. (2d) 724)
9. Would a professor's lectures to his class constitute publication so as to prevent subsequent copyright?
10. Dill has his picture taken by the Acme Portrait Studio. He orders six prints of a certain proof. May he reproduce his picture from the prints?
11. Would an architectural plan for the building of a house be patentable?
12. Would a process for the reinforcing of hollow trees be patentable?
13. Would a device that could be used only for gambling be patentable?
14. Lampton, as an innocent converter, took clay belonging to Preston and made bricks. The clay was worth approximately $20 and the finished bricks approximately $5,000. By an application of what tests might it be concluded that title had been acquired by Lampton?
15. X steals Y's walnut log and makes gunstocks. May Y recover the gunstocks?
16. X and Y are joint owners of certain property. Who will acquire Y's interest in such property upon his death?

26 PERSONAL PROPERTY AND RELATED TOPICS:

THE LAW OF SALES

The law pertaining to sales transactions, which provides the legal foundation for the conduct of many commercial affairs, is exceedingly broad. The term *sales transaction* refers to an actual or contemplated transfer of title to personal property by means of contract. A sales contract under which title to the property has passed to the buyer is designated as a *contract of sale.* A contract under which title is to pass to the buyer at some future time is called a *contract to sell.*

Every sales transaction has as its basis a contract, which to be valid must contain all the essentials requisite for an enforceable contract. A contract either of sale or to sell need take no special form. It may be written or oral; however, it is subject to the provisions of the Statute of Frauds.*

To achieve uniformity in the law of sales, most states have enacted the Uniform Sales Act as it was prepared by the Commissioners on Uniform Laws. The Uniform Sales Act is a codification of what were thought to be the most acceptable common law rules.†

► I. SUBJECT MATTER

A. CONTRACT TO SELL

The validity of a contract is not dependent upon the abilities of the parties to perform their undertakings. In fact, the purpose of a contract is to give redress if one of the parties fails for some reason not excused by law to perform his promise. Obviously, then, a contract to sell is not dependent upon an existing subject matter. Within the limits of the law, an individual may undertake to sell anything he pleases. The subject matter need not be in existence or owned by the seller.

B. CONTRACT OF SALE

Logically, it would seem that to have a present transfer of title, the subject matter of the transaction must be in existence and properly *identified.* Under the early common law, this was the accepted rule; property not actually in existence could not be sold or mortgaged. Reasoning that such a restriction unduly hampered commercial transactions, there was introduced into the law the doctrine that potentially existing property could be the subject matter of a contract of sale. This view is denied by the Uniform Sales Act. Section 5(3) reads:

---

* See p. 190.

† The Uniform Sales Act has to date been adopted by about thirty-four states, Alaska, Hawaii, and the District of Columbia. Its purpose is to achieve uniformity in the law of sales by a codification of what are thought to be the most acceptable rules.

"Where the parties purport to effect a present sale of future goods, the agreement operates as a contract to sell the goods."

Potentially existing property is that which will come into existence in the natural course of events from property owned by the seller or in which he has a present interest. It is property existing not actually but only in possibility, such as a growing crop. Under this doctrine, title to the property vests in the buyer upon its coming into existence without need of identification or appropriation of the goods to the contract.*

► II. TIME OF PASSING OF TITLE

The time of passing of title in a sales transaction can be a very important consideration. To illustrate:

(1) Risk of loss usually follows the title. Thus in the event the property in respect to which the parties are dealing is destroyed, the time of passing of title will determine whether the loss falls upon the seller or buyer.

(2) Let us suppose that the seller becomes bankrupt and that both the buyer and trustee in bankruptcy claim the goods. The buyer's right to the goods is dependent upon whether title passed prior to the bankruptcy.

A. INTENTION OF PARTIES

The cardinal rule with reference to the time of passing of title in a sales transaction is that *title will pass when the parties intend it to pass.* Title will pass according to the intention as expressed in the agreement or as it is apparent under the circumstances. Section 18(2) of the Uniform Sales Act reads:

"For the purpose of ascertaining the intention of the parties, regard shall be had to the terms of the contract, the conduct of the parties, usages of trade, and the circumstances of the case." [1]

1. *Limitation upon Rule of Intention*

The above principle must be qualified by the rule that, regardless of the intention of the parties, the title will not pass at least until the subject matter of the transaction is known and properly identified. Logically, title cannot pass to a buyer before the subject matter to which the right of property relates is reduced to a certainty. Section 17 of the Uniform Sales Act states this rule thus:

"Where there is a contract to sell unascertained goods, no property in the goods is transferred to the buyer unless and until the goods are ascertained."

Section 5(3) provides that:

"Where the parties purport to effect a present sale of future goods, the agreement operates as a contract to sell the goods."

The buyer and seller can, of course, provide for either the present or the future transfer of title to goods that are ascertained at the time of the agreement.

---

* See Low v. Pew, 108 Mass. 347.

[1] Warner Bros. & Co. v. Israel, p. 662.

B. RULES GOVERNING TIME OF PASSING TITLE IN ABSENCE OF INTENTION

In probably the majority of sales transactions, the buyers and sellers fail to indicate any positive intention as to when title is to pass. As a result, the courts have formulated rules by which the time of passing of title is determined in the absence of a declared or determinable intention—rules that create a presumptive intention on the part of the buyer and seller. These rules govern unless they can be overcome by sufficient evidence of the express or implied intention of the buyer and seller that title is to pass at some other time.

1. *Ascertained Goods*

As previously indicated, *ascertained goods* are such as are known and identified at the time of agreement.[2] The rule pertaining to ascertained goods as codified in the Uniform Sales Act, Section 19, reads:

> "Rule 1. Where there is an unconditional contract to sell specific goods, in a deliverable state, the property in the goods passes to the buyer when the contract is made and it is immaterial whether the time of payment, or the time of delivery, or both, be postponed."

Rule 1 is amplified by the following qualification contained in Rule 2 of the same section:

> "Rule 2. Where . . . . the seller is bound to do something to the goods, for the purpose of putting them into a deliverable state, the property does not pass until such be done."

To illustrate:

In *Hamilton* v. *Gordon,* 22 Ore. 557, the plaintiff brought action to obtain possession of wheat, which he contends he had purchased from the defendant. In other words, the plaintiff's contention was that title had passed to him. The agreement between the plaintiff and defendant specified that the defendant "hereby sells and agrees to deliver to (plaintiff) all the grain harvested . . . sacked in good merchantable sacks." The court said:

> "As between the parties, it [passing of title] is generally considered a question of intention. And it may often happen that the parties have expressed their intention in a manner that leaves no room for doubt. Where, however, they have not done so in express terms, the intention must be collected from the agreement, and the courts have adopted certain rules for that purpose. As a general rule, where, by the agreement, the vendor is to do anything with the property, for the purpose of putting it in a deliverable condition, or into that state in which the purchaser is bound to accept it, the performance of these things, in the absence of circumstances showing a contrary intention, is taken to be a condition precedent to the vesting of the property in the buyer, and also when the goods are sold by weight or measure, and anything remains to be done for the purpose of ascertaining the quantity, in the absence of any-

[2] B. A. Griffen v. Northwestern Fish Co., p. 663.

thing showing a different intention, the title does not pass until the goods are weighed or measured.

"By the terms of the agreement in this case, the grain was to be harvested and sacked 'in good merchantable sacks' by the vendor, in order to put it in a deliverable condition. . . . The contract is only a contract for the sale of a certain crop of grain, and if defendant has violated his agreement, by delivering only a part of the grain, and refusing to deliver the remainder, plaintiffs, if damaged, have their remedy, but not by an action to recover possession of the property."

2. *Fungible Goods*

Section 76 of the Uniform Sales Act defines *fungible goods* as being:

". . . goods of which any unit is from its nature or by merchantile usage treated as the equivalent of any other unit."

Illustrations of fungible goods would be: grain in bulk or in sacks of uniform size; like units of lumber, coal, and oil.

Unless a contrary intention is evident in an agreement for the sale and purchase of fungible goods, title passes at the time of the agreement, providing the mass from which the goods are to come has been ascertained. Only the mass from which a specified amount of goods is to be taken needs be determined and agreed upon.

Although it is not universally followed, this rule is contained in the Uniform Sales Act, Section 6(2), which reads:

"In the case of fungible goods, there may be a sale of an undivided share of a specific mass, though the seller purports to sell and the buyer to buy a definite number, weight, or measure of the goods in the mass, and though the number, weight, or measure of the goods in the mass is undetermined."

To illustrate:

In *O'Keefe* v. *Leistikow,* 14 N.D. 355, the defendant had agreed to purchase seventy bushels of flax at $2 a bushel, which flax was part of a larger mass. The plaintiff's right to recover the purchase price was dependent upon whether title had passed to the defendant. The court said:

"It is an undisputed fact that the flax was all of one quality and grade, and fit for seeding purpose. Was a separation from the mass, or the measuring of 70 bushels, a condition precedent to the passing of the title to the defendant? We agree that it was not. . . . The flax was in bulk, but its separation is not necessarily a condition precedent to the passing of title. . . . It seems to be generally held that, if the property sold is mixed with other property not like in quality or size and a certain grade or quality only is sold, then the separation and selection is presumptively a condition precedent to the passing of title. It is also held in many cases that, if there must be measuring or selection of certain kinds of property from a mass before the price can be ascertained, then no title presumptively passes. These rules are always subject to the intention of the parties. In this case the property was identified and ascertained. The subject-matter of the contract was specified as 70 bushels of flax on the Ops farm. The price was fixed. . . . Nothing was undetermined, or dependent upon measuring or weighing of the flax. The mere fact that the 70 bushels were mingled with other flax is not of controlling importance. . . . The buyer and seller became tenants in common of the flax, each having a right to take his share therefrom."

3. *Unascertained Goods*

A contract relating to unascertained goods, other than fungible goods, is a contract to sell. There can be no passing of title until the specific subject matter of the contract has been agreed upon. Rule 4(1) of Section 19 of the Uniform Sales Act is a codification of the common law rule that applies (in the absence of a determinable intention on the part of buyer and seller) in fixing the time of passing of title under a *contract to sell* unascertained goods. It reads:

"Where there is a contract to sell unascertained or future goods by description and goods of that description, and in a deliverable state are unconditionally appropriated to the contract, either by the seller with the assent of the buyer, or by the buyer with the assent of the seller, the property in the goods thereupon passes to the buyer. Such assent may be expressed or implied, and may be given either before or after the appropriation is made."

Let us note that this rule makes the passing of title to unascertained goods entirely dependent upon a subsequent act of appropriation *with the assent of both parties.* It is frequently the case that the buyer impliedly gives his previous assent to the seller for the latter to make the appropriation. Such is the case when goods are ordered. An appropriation that will satisfy the requirements of the rule is any act which unequivocally indicates an intention that certain goods of the kind and quality specified have been assigned to the performance of the contract to sell. It is an act that earmarks certain goods as being the subject matter of the contract.[3] Clearly, the question of what constitutes a sufficient allocation to effect a passing of title is one of fact. It has been held that setting the goods aside and marking them for the buyer, pointing out the goods to the buyer, or putting the goods into the buyer's receptacles have been sufficient acts of appropriation. Delivery to a carrier for transmission to the buyer would, in any event, be an appropriation. Rule 4(2) of section 11 creates such a presumption:

"Where, in pursuance of a contract to sell, the seller delivers the goods to the buyer, or to a carrier or other bailee (whether named by the buyer or not) for the purpose of transmission to or holding for the buyer, he is presumed to have unconditionally appropriated the goods to the contract, except in the cases provided for in the next rule and in section 20. This presumption is applicable, although by the terms of the contract the buyer is to pay the price before receiving delivery of the goods, and the goods are marked with the words 'collect on delivery' or their equivalents."

This rule does not, however, prevent some prior act from constituting a sufficient appropriation.

[3] Calif. Animal Products Co. v. Lappin, p. 665.

4. *Goods Delivered or Freight Paid by Seller*

Rule 5 of Section 19 of the Uniform Sales Act creates this rather logical presumption:

> "If the contract to sell requires the seller to deliver the goods to the buyer, or at a particular place, or to pay the freight or cost of transportation to the buyer, or to a particular place, the property does not pass until the goods have been delivered to the buyer or reached the place agreed upon."

5. *Sale on Trial and Agreement of Sale or Return*

A sale on trial or approval is a sales technique designed to overcome sales resistance. It is an agreement whereby the seller gives the buyer possession of goods in the hope that they will meet his requirements or gain his approval. It is in the nature of an option to purchase. Title does not pass to the buyer unless he expressly or impliedly indicates his satisfaction with and his acceptance of the goods.[4] A failure to voice disapproval or a failure to return the goods within the time specified for trial in the agreement will be interpreted as an approval and acceptance. If no time is specified, the period of trial is a reasonable time. During the period of trial the prospective buyer holds the goods as a bailee.

An *agreement of sale or return* is a somewhat similar selling technique. It is in the nature of a present sale with an option to return the goods. In most jurisdictions title vests in the buyer and remains with him until he elects to return the goods to the seller. The election must be exercised within the time agreed upon or, in the absence of any specified time, within a reasonable time. To illustrate:

(1) In *Hunt* v. *Wyman*, 100 Mass. 198, the defendant agreed to buy the plaintiff's horse upon the understanding that "If he (the plaintiff) would let him take the horse and try it, if he did not like it he would return it . . . the night of the day he got it." The horse, while in the defendant's possession, was injured and the plaintiff brought action to recover the purchase price. The court held that this was a sale on approval and that title and risk remained in the plaintiff.

(2) Agreements in which the buyer is given the right "to return goods if they are not satisfactory" are interpreted as being contracts of sale or return under which title rests in the buyer, rather than options to purchase.

C. BILL OF SALE

A bill of sale is the document executed for the purpose of serving as evidence of the transfer of title. It is not essential to the passing of title unless the contract agreement is that a bill of sale is to be given. A bill of sale as evidence is a protection to the buyer, especially if the goods are to remain temporarily in possession of the seller. And, if the bill of sale has been acknowledged at the time of its execution, it can be placed of record in order to protect the rights of the buyer against claims of third parties.

There are circumstances under which the possessor of property may be re-

[4] Gottlieb v. Rinaldo, p. 666.

quired to submit evidence of ownership. For example, it is generally required that before an automobile can be registered by a new owner a bill of sale must be submitted.

Following is a specimen copy of a bill of sale:

KNOW ALL MEN BY THESE PRESENTS:

That I, Andrew Thomas of the city of Ames , State of Iowa , in consideration of the sum of Five Hundred Dollars , to me paid by John Carney , of the city of Ames , the receipt whereof is hereby acknowledged, have bargained, sold, granted, and conveyed, and by these presents do bargain, sell, grant, and convey unto the said John Carney his executors, administrators, and assigns one Fordson Tractor, Model H, No. 06-543. To have and to hold the same unto the said John Carney his executors, administrators, and assigns forever. And I for myself and for my heirs, executors and administrators, do hereby covenant with the said John Carney , his executors, administrators, and assigns, that I am the true and lawful owner of said described goods hereby sold, and have full power to sell and convey the same; that the title, so conveyed, is clear, free, and unincumbered; and further, that I do warrant and will defend the same against all claim or claims of all persons whomsoever.

IN WITNESS WHEREOF, I have hereunto set my hand this fourteenth day of May 1951.

SIGNED AND DELIVERED IN PRESENCE OF:

(Signed) Andrew Thomas

(Signed) Mary Adams

(Signed) H. J. Rohlf

D. SECURING PAYMENT IN RELATION TO PASSING OF TITLE

All buyers do not merit credit, nor are all sellers in a position to extend credit. Consequently, the seller will at times find it necessary to make some provision to secure payment of the purchase price before control of the goods is relinquished to the buyer. Following is a presentation of some of the commercial practices by which the seller can assure himself of payment before the buyer can obtain possession of the goods.

1. *C.O.D. Shipments*

A *C.O.D.* (*cash on delivery*) shipment is a device by which the seller of goods appoints the delivering carrier as his agent to collect the purchase price as a condition to delivery of the goods to the buyer. As a general rule, delivery of the goods to the carrier presumptively passes title to the buyer. This rule is contained in Rule 4(2) of Section 19 of the Uniform Sales Act. The seller merely retains the right of possession to secure payment. In some jurisdictions it is held, however, that C.O.D. makes payment by the buyer and delivery to him a condition precedent to the passing of title.

2. *Order Bill of Lading Shipments*

A *bill of lading* is a contract between shipper and carrier for the transportation of goods. It also serves as a receipt for goods delivered to the carrier. Bills of lading, as used in commercial transactions, are usually either *straight* or *order*. A *straight bill of lading* provides for delivery of the goods to a designated person, the consignee. In making delivery of the goods under such a bill, the carrier need be concerned only with the identity of the consignee specified in the document. The designated consignee can, with qualification, be the only lawful claimant, and the bill of lading need not be surrendered to the carrier. Under a straight bill of lading, delivery of goods to the carrier is an unconditional appropriation of the goods to the contract and presumes a passing of title to the consignee unless there are facts to overcome this presumption.

An *order bill of lading* requires the delivery of the goods to a designated person *or his order*. It is a negotiable document of title, representing title to the goods in transit. Upon its surrender a holder of this document properly endorsed is entitled to receive the goods from the carrier. A seller can retain control of the goods in transit by the simple expedient of shipping to his own order or to the order of an agent. In this way, the buyer cannot get the goods from the carrier until such time as the seller or his agent makes available to the buyer the bill of lading properly endorsed.

When the seller takes the bill of lading to his own order without any qualifying circumstances, it is strong presumptive evidence that his intention is to retain title to the goods while in transit. Such a presumption will entirely overcome the presumptive intention that delivery of goods to the carrier is an unconditional appropriation of the goods to the contract.*

Very frequently the purpose of the seller in retaining control of the goods by use of an order bill of lading is to assure himself of payment. This can be accomplished by attaching a draft to the bill of lading; the latter is then forwarded to an agent of the seller, usually a bank, for the purpose of obtaining payment or acceptance of the draft by the buyer. Upon payment or acceptance, whichever is required, the bill of lading, properly endorsed, is delivered to the buyer. Some courts hold that under such an arrangement, unless a contrary intent can be shown, title and ownership of the goods remain with the seller. It has been said that this is almost conclusive evidence of such an intention.

A different conclusion is arrived at under the Uniform Sales Act. By virtue of Section 20(2), if the seller retains control of the goods under a bill of lading for the limited *purpose of security*, he retains only a security interest in the goods, all other rights of ownership passing to the buyer upon delivery of the goods to the carrier. The rule reads:

> "Where goods are shipped, and by the bill of lading the goods are deliverable to the seller or his agent, or to the order of the seller or of his agent, the seller thereby reserves the property in the goods. But if, except for the form

* See p. 646, for Section 19 Rule 4 (2) of the Uniform Sales Act.

of the bill of lading, the property would have passed to the buyer on shipment of the goods, the seller's property in the goods shall be deemed to be only for the purpose of securing performance by the buyer of his obligations under the contract."

E. IMPORTANCE OF POSSESSION OF GOODS *

As previously observed, possession of the goods *need not be transferred* to the buyer as a condition to the passing of title. A delivery is, however, necessary to give the buyer protection against the creditors of, or subsequent purchasers from, the seller. Unless a delivery to the buyer has been effected, such claimants to the goods will have a priority. In the absence of notice that title has passed, leaving goods in the possession of the seller is basis for a justifiable belief that the seller continues as owner. The change of possession must be sufficient in character to indicate that ownership has changed or must at least induce third parties to inquire about the ownership. As a general rule, some actual visible change of possession is required. However, if an actual manual change is not practical, the courts have found that some inconsiderable act is sufficient to constitute a change of possession.

► III. WARRANTIES

Warranties in sales transactions can be likened to relatives in that they are ever-present appendages. Warranties play a most important role in the field of buying and selling. They are the means by which the buyer can obtain a degree of protection against a seller who has not achieved the qualifications of an Utopian.

A *warranty* is in the nature of an assurance from the seller to the buyer in respect to the character, quality, and/or title of the goods. It is regarded as a *promissory* representation † either voluntarily undertaken by the seller—an *express warranty*—or imputed to him by law—an *implied warranty*. The seller assumes the responsibility that the facts be as they are or were represented either expressly or impliedly, thus insuring the buyer against a failure of such facts. In the language of the layman, the seller guarantees the goods in certain respects.

A. EXPRESS WARRANTIES

The uniform Sales Act, Section 12, defines an express warranty as being:

> "Any affirmation of fact or any promise by the seller relating to the goods . . . if the natural tendency of such affirmation or promise is to induce the buyer to purchase the goods, and if the buyer purchases the goods relying thereon. No affirmation of the value of the goods, nor any statement purporting to be a statement of the seller's opinion only shall be construed as a warranty."

* See Section 70 (c) of the Federal Bankruptcy Act.

† This is to be distinguished from misrepresentation which forms the basis of fraud. A warranty may amount to a false representation with intent to defraud the buyer, thereby giving him also his remedy in tort for fraud and deceit.

1. *Affirmation of Fact*

The act embodies the modern rule that an affirmation of fact may amount to a warranty. It is a demonstration of the modern trend to give the buyer greater protection—a limitation on the scope of the doctrine of *caveat emptor* (let the buyer beware).

No special words or forms of expression such as "warrant," "guarantee," "represent," "assert," or "promise" are essential as an element of a warranty. A bare statement of facts may be sufficient from which to infer that the buyer warrants the facts to be as states. Any positive and definite statement of facts in respect to the goods that reasonably appears to have been made for the purpose of inducing the buyer to act, is a warranty. In many instances, sellers acquaint buyers with the character, quality, and quantity of their products by affirmation of such facts printed upon the containers. Such affirmations of fact printed upon a seed bag constitute a warranty without need of any formal words or declarations of warranty. It can be reasonably supposed that such statements are meant to induce sales; the seller intends them as statements upon which the buyers can rely. To illustrate:

In *Baumgartner* v. *Glesener,* 171 Minn. 289, the defendant published an advertisement offering seed corn for sale in which he stated that the seed was graded, had a germinating test of 95 per cent, and was acclimated to the community. The court held this affirmation of fact to be a warranty, it having been made with the intent to induce the plaintiff to make a purchase.[5]

2. *Sales Talk*

Our competitive system has produced and fostered high-pressure salesmanship. During the course of years, sellers have evolved various techniques and practices designed to overcome the buyers' sane judgment of their needs. So-called *dealer's talk, puffing,* and *opinions* are most effective weapons in the hands of professional sellers in overcoming sales resistance. The law attaches no responsibility to sales talk, words of commendation and praise, or statements of opinion. Buyers are aware of the accepted practice and must learn to discount such extravagant statements as "good as gold," "best buy in town," "wear like iron," "will sell like hot cakes," and "nearly as good as new." Only such statements as reasonable persons would rely upon qualify as warranties.*

3. *Extent of Express Warranty*

The doctrine of *caveat emptor* does not apply to such facts as are contained in an express warranty. The warranty applies to both obvious and hidden defects. The buyer may absolutely rely upon the facts as represented and has no duty to make an inspection of the goods or take steps to ascertain the correctness of the facts. It is held as a general rule that even an inspection by the buyer will not preclude the operation of a warranty upon which the buyer relies. However, should the buyer be aware of a defect, it will not be covered by a warranty. An inspection of the goods

* See p. 138.

[5] Baumgartner v. Glesener, p. 667.

by the buyer may raise the question as to whether or not the buyer relied upon or waived the warranty.

B. IMPLIED WARRANTIES

By means of attaching implied warranties to sales contracts, the law has greatly limited the rule of *caveat emptor*. There is a tendency for the courts to extend rather than to restrict the scope of implied warranties. Depending upon the circumstances, sellers are charged with responsibility for the existence of certain facts. An implied warranty is based upon the presumed intention of the parties and cannot be assumed if it *clearly* appears from the contract that the buyer and seller intended otherwise; a warranty contrary to the intention of the parties will not be implied. Following are the well-defined circumstances under which warranties are implied.

1. *Implied Warranty of Title*

The early common law rule was that a purchaser of goods assumed the risk of his vendor's having title—the law implied no warranty of title on the part of the seller. The exceptions to this rule became so numerous that one of the English judges found occasion to remark that they "well nigh eat up the rule." The exceptions have feasted well and have consumed the rule in its entirety. The present-day rule that a sale of goods is accompanied by an implied warranty of title has been firmly ingrafted upon our law.

2. *Sale by Sample and or Description*

In many instances it is necessary when purchasing goods to rely upon a sample and/or description of the goods to determine their nature and quality. If a sale is made by sample, there is an implied warranty that the goods will correspond in every material respect to the sample that served as an inducement to buy.[6, 7] Similarly, if goods are sold by a description upon which the buyer places reliance, the seller impliedly warrants that the goods will correspond to the description. This suggests a strong resemblance to an express warranty based upon an affirmation of fact. If the purchase of goods is induced by sample and description, the goods must correspond with both sample and description.

3. *Implied Warranty of Merchantability*

The implied warranty of merchantability is applied to two distinct types of cases: (1) to situations where goods are purchased for the purpose of resale (in this connection the term *merchantability* means that the goods sold are as marketable and fit for resale as goods of like nature ordinarily would be; (2) to situations where goods are purchased for general use (in this connection *merchantability* means that the goods sold are fit for the use to which goods of like nature would ordinarily be put). To illustrate:

(1) In *Keenan* v. *Cherry and Webb*, 47 R.I. 125, the plaintiff had purchased a

---

[6] Pauls Valley Milling Co. v. Gabbert, p. 668.

[7] Lindsey v. Stalder, p. 669.

fur coat from the defendant. Upon the first occasion it was worn, the coat split down the back and thereafter continued to display a like propensity. The court said:

"The warranty of merchantability was that the coat was fit to wear, not for any particular length of time or satisfactorily to the buyer, but to wear as an article of apparel."

(2) In *Gardiner* v. *Gray,* 4 Camp 144, the defendant had contracted to sell the plaintiff "waste silk." The product furnished by the defendant was of such a nature that it had no commercial value. The court, in holding that there was a breach of the implied warranty of merchantability, said:

"The intention of both parties must be taken to be that it (the subject matter of the contract) shall be salable in the market under the denomination mentioned in the contract. . . . The purchaser cannot be supposed to buy goods to lay them on the dung heap."

Section 15(2) of the Uniform Sales Act has stated the rule illustrated above thus:

"Where the goods are bought by description from a seller who deals in goods of that description (whether he be the grower or manufacturer or not), there is an implied warranty that the goods shall be of merchantable quality."

4. *Implied Warranty of Fitness For A Particular Purpose*

Ordinarily a buyer has no recourse against the seller if goods purchased fail to meet his expectations. There is no general implied warranty that goods will reasonably meet the particular requirements of the buyer; in this respect the rule of *caveat emptor* reigns. However, if the buyer acquaints the seller with the particular purpose for which the goods are to be employed and relies upon the skill and judgment of the seller in making a selection of goods to meet his needs, the law implies a warranty that the goods will reasonably fit the particular purpose.[8, 9, 10] The elements necessary to create such a warranty are: (1) the buyer's making known his purpose to the seller; (2) the buyer's relying upon the seller in making a selection; and (3) the seller's acceptance of the commission to make a selection. Obviously, if the buyer limits the seller in any manner in making his choice—for instance, if the buyer should specify goods by a trade name—this warranty will not apply.[11]

Section 15(1) of the Uniform Sales Act expresses the general present-day rule that the implied warranty of fitness applies to sellers without distinction and not only to manufacturers or producers, as was usually held before the adoption of the Act.

5. *Warranty of Food Products*

From very early times the law has held vendors of articles for human consumption responsible for the wholesomeness of their products. In a very early English

---

[8] Bekkevold v. Potts, p. 673.

[9] Beaman v. Testori, p. 674.

[10] Ladd v. Reed, p. 675.

[11] Iron Fireman Coal Stoker Co. v. Brown, p. 676.

case (22 Henry VII, 91) the court remarked: "No man can justify selling corrupt victual. . . ." In holding vendors of foods and beverages accountable, one of the basic considerations, as a matter of public policy, has been the preservation of human life and health. Aside from any implied warranties that might arise, the law imposes a duty upon those who sell articles of food to exercise reasonable care to insure consumers from injury. A failure to exercise the required care is negligence, which gives rise to a tort liability for any resultant injury.

a. Responsibility of Retailer to Consumer. A sale by a retailer of foods and beverages for immediate consumption is, with few exceptions, held to carry with it an implied warranty of fitness for human use. The elements of an implied warranty of fitness for a particular purpose are usually present in a sale of food products. In some states, the warranty is applied even to canned and packaged goods, but in a few well-considered cases this has been denied upon the reasoning that the dealer is in no better position to know the contents than the purchaser. However, the dealer is liable in tort for any negligence in selling such goods.

b. Responsibility of Restaurateur. Operators of public eating places are universally held liable for serving patrons food that does not meet standards for human consumption. Some courts place the liability upon an implied warranty; others limit the warranty to food that is self-prepared; and some take the view that a sale of food products to patrons is not a sale of goods but the rendition of a service.[12] Regardless of such diversity of reasoning, a liability exists on the grounds of either an implied warranty of fitness or negligence in vending harmful food products.

c. Responsibility of Manufacturer, Packer, or Bottler. Manufacturers, packers, and bottlers are directly liable to the consumer for injury resulting from the sale and use of unwholesome articles of food or beverages, even though the goods have passed through intermediate hands. Their liability is based either upon the theory of an implied warranty or upon the theory of negligence.

► IV. RIGHTS AND REMEDIES OF SELLER

A. RIGHTS OF SELLER FOR BREACH OF CONTRACT

1. *After Passing of Title*

In general, the legal rights of the seller against the buyer for a breach of contract are dependent upon whether title to the goods has passed. If the title to the goods has passed, the seller may sue the buyer for the purchase price. This rule is declared in Section 63(1) of the Uniform Sales Act thus:

> "Where, under a contract to sell or a sale, the property in the goods has passed to the buyer, and the buyer wrongfully neglects or refuses to pay for the goods according to the terms of the contract or the sale, the seller may maintain an action against him for the price of the goods."

Before the buyer has a right of action, he must, however, have substantially

[12] Cliett v. Lauderdale Biltmore Corp., p. 677.

performed the contract or tendered a performance. Since delivery and payment are concurrent conditions, the seller must be ready, willing, and able to make delivery to the buyer in accordance with the terms of the agreement.

2. *Before Passing of Title*

As a general rule, if title to the goods has not passed and the buyer refuses to accept them, the seller can recover only damages for the breach of the contract. The measure of damages in such a case is the difference between the contract price and the market value of the goods at the approximate time provided in the contract for delivery. This rule of damages, of course, presupposes that the seller has control of the goods so as to be able to dispose of them on the market.

Under special circumstances, it is possible for the seller to recover the whole of the purchase price even though title to the goods has not passed to the buyer. Section 63 of the Uniform Sales Act provides:

> "(2) Where, under a contract to sell or a sale, the price is payable on a day certain, irrespective of delivery or of transfer of title, and the buyer wrongfully neglects or refuses to pay such price, the seller may maintain an action for the price, although the property in the goods has not passed, and the goods have not been appropriated to the contract. . . .
>
> "(3) Although the property in the goods has not passed, if they cannot readily be resold for a reasonable price . . . the seller may offer to deliver the goods to the buyer, and, if the buyer refuses to receive them, may notify the buyer that the goods are thereafter held by the seller as bailee for the buyer. Thereafter the seller may treat the goods as the buyer's and may maintain an action for the price."

3. *Right to Retain Purchase Price*

The buyer cannot recover any payments made on the purchase price in the event he is in breach of his contract. The seller may retain such payments regardless of whether he has suffered any damages.[13]

B. RIGHTS OF UNPAID SELLER AGAINST GOODS

1. *Unpaid Seller's Lien*

An unpaid seller has the right to retain possession and exercise the right of lien over the goods until payment or a tender of payment of the purchase price is made. Section 54 of the Uniform Sales Act is a recognition of this common law right of lien, which exists in favor of an unpaid seller. The situations under which the right of lien arises are, in Section 54, declared to be:

(a) where the goods have been sold without any stipulation as to credit;

(b) where the goods have been sold on credit, but the term of credit has expired;

(c) where the buyer becomes insolvent.[14]

---

[13] Bisner v. Mantell, p. 678.

[14] Rock-Ola Mfg. Corp. v. Leopold, p. 680.

The right of the unpaid seller to a security interest in the property is, as in the case of all common law liens, dependent upon possession of the property. A loss of possession or of the right of possession is a loss of the lien. While the goods are in the seller's possession, his security claim is paramount to claims of purchasers from, and creditors of, the buyer. However, a qualified delivery of the goods to the buyer will not defeat the seller's right of lien.

2. *Stoppage in Transitu*

The seller's right of stoppage *in transitu* is in effect an extension of his right of lien. Upon discovery that the buyer is insolvent, the seller has the right to reclaim possession of the goods while they are still in the course of transit. As a general rule, the time at which the insolvency arose is immaterial so long as it was unknown to the seller. It may, in fact, have existed for some time prior to the delivery of the goods to the transportation agency.

At times it is no easy problem to determine when the transit of goods has terminated. There can, of course, be no question where the goods have come into the physical possession of the buyer, his agent, or one claiming under him, as, for example, a purchaser. Some courts have taken the view that transit does not end until physical possession of the goods is actually obtained. The majority rule as found in the Uniform Sales Act is, however, that transit ends after the arrival of the goods at their destination and the acknowledgment of the carrier or other bailee to the buyer that the goods are being held for him. The rules as to when goods are or are not considered as being in transit are explicitly stated in Section 58 of the Uniform Sales Act.

The requirements that the seller must meet to effectively exercise his right of stoppage in transitu are set out in Section 59 of the Uniform Sales Act as follows:

"(1) The unpaid seller may exercise his right of stoppage in transitu either by obtaining actual possession of the goods or by giving notice of his claim to the carrier or other bailee in whose possession the goods are. Such notice may be given either to the person in actual possession of the goods or to his principal. In the latter case the notice, to be effectual, must be given at such time and under such circumstances that the principal, by the exercise of reasonable diligence, may prevent a delivery to the buyer.

"(2) When notice of stoppage in transitu is given by the seller to the carrier, or other bailee in possession of the goods, he must redeliver the goods to, or according to the directions of, the seller. The expenses of such delivery must be borne by the seller. If, however, a negotiable document of title representing the goods has been issued by the carrier or other bailee, he shall not be obliged to deliver or justify in delivering the goods to the seller unless such document is first surrendered for cancellation."

The exercise of the right of stoppage in transitu may be defeated where the goods are represented by a negotiable document of title as an order bill of lading. Section 62 of the Uniform Sales Act reads:

"If, however, a negotiable document of title has been issued for goods, no seller's lien or right of stoppage in transitu shall defeat the right of any purchaser for value in good faith to whom such document has been negotiated, whether such negotiation be prior or subsequent to the notification to the carrier, or other bailee who issued such document, of the seller's claim to a lien or right of stoppage in transitu."

This same view is found incorporated in Section 42 of the Uniform Bills of Lading Act.

3. *Right of Resale*

A seller who is rightfully in possession of the goods has the right to resell the goods if the buyer refuses to accept them or pay for them. He is likewise entitled to resell them if he has repossessed them by virtue of the right of stoppage in transitu. The seller is not responsible to the buyer for any profit made on the resale, but he can look to the buyer for any loss suffered, which would be the difference between the contract price and the price at which the goods were sold. The resale can be made either privately or publicly, as best suits the seller. He is, however, required to conduct the sale in such a manner as to protect the interests of the original buyer, i.e., in such a manner as would be calculated to bring a fair price. This duty is based upon the theory that the seller is acting as the agent of the buyer who is in default.

There is no agreement among authorities as to whether the seller is obligated to notify the buyer of the resale. The Uniform Sales Act provides that notice of an intention to resell is not necessary. Under all circumstances, it would seem to be a wise precaution to notify the buyer of an intent to resell. However, if the goods were of a highly perishable nature, such a course of procedure might be impracticable and consequently excused.

The seller should wait a reasonable time before the goods are resold, yet it is his duty to resell them within a reasonable time. A reasonable time before resale would not be the same as a reasonable time within which the goods must be sold.

4. *Right of Rescission*

Instead of reselling the property, the seller may rescind the transfer of title to the buyer, thus reacquiring title to the goods. The seller would then have recourse against the buyer for any damages he has suffered by virtue of the breach of contract. Section 61(2) of the Uniform Sales Act provides:

> "The transfer of title shall not be held to have been rescinded by an unpaid seller until he has manifested by notice to the buyer or some overt act an intention to rescind."

► V. RIGHTS AND REMEDIES OF BUYER

A. FOR BREACH OF CONTRACT

If the title to the goods has not passed to the buyer and the seller fails to deliver the goods as required by the contract, the buyer has a right of action for damages for breach of contract. The measure of damages will generally be the difference between the contract price and the market value of the goods at the time and place specified in the contract for delivery.

If the seller withholds delivery of the goods after the title has been vested in the buyer, the latter may treat it as a conversion. This would entitle him either to recover the goods by an action of replevin or to recover any damages he has suffered.

B. FOR BREACH OF WARRANTY

The alternative rights of the buyer for a breach of warranty by the seller are enumerated in Section 69 of the Uniform Sales Act as follows:

"(a) Accept or keep the goods and set up against the seller, the breach of warranty by way of recoupment in diminution or extinction of the price;

(b) Accept or keep the goods and maintain an action against the seller for damages for the breach of warranty;

(c) Refuse to accept the goods, if the property therein has not passed, and maintain an action against the seller for damages for the breach of warranty;

(d) Rescind the contract to sell or the sale and refuse to receive the goods, or, if the goods have already been received, return them or offer to return them to the seller and recover the price or any part thereof which has been paid."

It should be noted that a breach of warranty is treated as either a breach of contract or a breach of a condition, as the buyer is given the right either to bring an action for damages or to rescind the agreement and get a return of the purchase price.[15]

In no event can the buyer rescind where he knew of the breach of warranty when he accepted the goods. As conditions precedent to exercising the right of rescission, the buyer must (1) notify the seller of his election to pursue this course and (2) return or offer to return the goods in substantially the same condition as that in which they were when title was transferred to him.

C. RIGHT OF INSPECTION

The buyer has the right that he be afforded an opportunity to inspect the goods before he accepts them. Section 47 of the Uniform Sales Act declares the common law right of inspection to be:

"(1) Where goods are delivered to the buyer, which he has not previously examined, he is not deemed to have accepted them unless and until he has had a reasonable opportunity of examining them for the purpose of ascertaining whether they are in conformity with the contract.

"(2) Unless otherwise agreed, when the seller tenders delivery of goods to the buyer, he is bound, on request, to afford the buyer a reasonable opportunity of examining the goods for the purpose of ascertaining whether they are in conformity with the contract."

This inspection must be accomplished with reasonable promptness, and the

---

[15] Reno Sales Co. v. Pritchard Industries, p. 681.

seller must be notified promptly of an election to reject the goods. A failure to act with dispatch will be interpreted as an acceptance of the goods by the buyer and will prevent him from rescinding the contract. As previously mentioned, an acceptance will not, however, bar him from a recovery for damages suffered due to the breach of contract.

In those instances where the buyer agrees to pay for the goods before delivery by the carrier, such as when goods are shipped C.O.D. or "cash against bill of lading," it is generally held that he waives his right of inspection. He may, however, after accepting delivery of the goods, return them to the seller, if they do not meet the requirements of the contract, and demand a return of the purchase price.

► VI. BILLS OF LADING AND WAREHOUSE RECEIPTS AS NEGOTIABLE DOCUMENTS OF TITLE

A. DEFINED AND CHARACTERIZED

Section 27 of the Uniform Sales Act defines a negotiable document of title thus:

> "A document of title in which it is stated that the goods referred to therein will be delivered to the bearer, or to the order of any person named in such document is a negotiable document of title."

CAPITAL STOCK $100,000.00 BONDED FOR $5,000.00

EAST TEXAS COMPRESS & WAREHOUSE CO.

A Public Warehouse

NEGOTIABLE COTTON RECEIPT

Issued at Tenaha, Texas,............................19....

Received for storage from.............................. for account of..............................

ONE BALE COTTON CANCELED Weight..........

Good
Bad Order Gin No.............. Class.................. Compress No..........

On the presentation and return of this receipt to the above named warehouse and the payment of all charges and Insurance (if carried by warehouse) said cotton will be delivered immediately to Bearer. We do not insure cotton unless requested by owner in writing.

Countersigned and Weighed by: EAST TEXAS COMPRESS & WAREHOUSE CO.

.... ASHFORD JONES, President.

NEGOTIABLE WAREHOUSE RECEIPT

Documents of title originate when goods are placed in the hands of a bailee, usually for the purpose of transportation or storage. In the first instance, the document will be a bill of lading, and in the latter, a warehouse receipt. These documents, which evidence the fact that the bailee has the goods in his possession, may be either nonnegotiable or negotiable in form. A nonnegotiable document obligates the bailee to make delivery of the goods to a specified person only, whereas a negotiable document may provide for delivery to the bearer or to the order of the person named in the instrument. In this manner, title to the goods can be transferred by a mere transfer or negotiation of the document, which is symbolic of the title. If the document is in bearer form, it may be negotiated by delivery only; but if it is in order form, both endorsement and delivery of the document will be required.

B. CONSEQUENCES OF NEGOTIABILITY

The chief characteristic of a negotiable instrument is that the holder is able to transfer a better title to it than that which he possesses. If A sells B a horse, A can transfer a title to the animal which would be no better than that which he himself has. Therefore, in the event that the horse is stolen property, the true owner would not be deprived of his title. A thief or finder can, however, pass a good title to a bearer form of negotiable instrument. Let us suppose that A has induced B, through fraudulent representations, to sell him a horse for future delivery, and that later A assigns his right to the horse to C. The defense of fraud is available to B, should C seek to obtain satisfaction on the right he acquired from A. In contrast, the transfer of a negotiable document of title, even though it was acquired by fraud, gives the purchaser a good title to the goods which would be free from the defense of fraud. The quality of the title to a negotiable document of title can be improved by a transfer to a bona fide purchaser—a purchaser who acquires the document in good faith and for value.[16] It is because of these legal consequences which attach to negotiable documents of title that order bills of lading are generally referred to as "yellow perils." (This designation has partly been coined because the order bills of lading are printed on yellow paper to distinguish them from straight nonnegotiable bills, which are on white paper.)

Documents of title were not generally regarded as having the attributes of negotiability by the common law courts. This character of negotiability has been derived very largely from legislation. Under the Uniform Bills of Lading Act, which has been enacted in a slight majority of the states, there is no limitation as to who can transfer a good title to a negotiable bill of lading. A negotiable bill of lading is as truly negotiable as a negotiable bill of exchange or note. A finder or a thief can transfer a good title to an innocent purchaser if the instrument is properly indorsed or is in bearer form. Under the Warehouse Receipts Act, which is in force in practically all the states, the negotiability of the warehouse receipt has been somewhat restricted. It provides, in essence, that a valid transfer of title can be accomplished only by the owner or by someone to whom the receipt has been entrusted by the owner. For example, A could not transfer good title by a transfer of a warehouse receipt representing grain that he had stolen from B. The same provision is made in the Uniform Sales Act in Section 32:

"A negotiable document of title may be negotiated:

(a) By the owner thereof, or

(b) By any person to whom the possession or custody of the document has been entrusted by the owner, if, by the terms of the document, the bailee issuing the document undertakes to deliver the goods to the order of the person to whom the possession or custody of the document has been entrusted, or if

[16] Southern Pac. Co. v. Bank of America, p. 683.

at the time of such entrusting the document is in such form that it may be negotiated by delivery."

C. RESPONSIBILITY OF BAILEE

Since a negotiable document of title is representative of the title to the goods, the bailee will require that the document be surrendered before the goods can be obtained. Unless the bailee obtains the document, he may later be called upon to deliver goods as represented by the instrument. The only safe course of procedure for the bailee is either to require a surrender of the document of title or to secure indemnity against possible future loss resulting to him by virtue of the outstanding document.

The bailee who issues a document of title without first having received possession of the goods may find himself responsible to an innocent purchaser of the document. It is generally held—and so provided by the Uniform Bills of Lading Act—that a carrier is responsible when an agent fraudulently issues a negotiable bill of lading without having received the goods or when the goods are not as represented in the bill of lading.

D. LIABILITY OF INDORSERS

Indorsers of negotiable documents of title do not stand as sureties for the performance of the agreement; they are not responsible for a failure of the bailee to deliver the goods as the document requires. An indorser can be held liable only for the breach of certain warranties, which are implied from his indorsement. Section 36 of the Uniform Sales Act states these warranties as follows:

"A person who for value negotiates or transfers a document of title by indorsement or delivery, including one who assigns for value a claim secured by a document of title unless a contrary intention appears, warrants:

(a) That the document is genuine;

(b) That he has a legal right to negotiate or transfer it;

(c) That he has knowledge of no fact which would impair the validity or worth of the document; and

(d) That he has a right to transfer the title to the goods and that the goods are merchantable or fit for a particular purpose, whenever such warranties would have been implied if the contract of the parties had been to transfer without a document of title the goods represented thereby."

Similar provisions are contained in the Uniform Bills of Lading Act and in the Uniform Warehouse Receipts Act.

CASES

CASE NO. 1

Warner Bros. & Co. v. Israel. 101 F. (2d) 59 (1939)

CHASE, C.J. . . . The plaintiff, a British corporation, has sued to recover the unpaid remainder of the purchase price of four lots of sugar it sold to the defendant, a New York citizen residing in the City of New York. Jurisdiction based upon diversity of citizenship with the required amount in controversy was made to appear . . .

The basis of the dispute between the parties is not factual but is centered upon the meaning as a matter of law of a written contract they entered into at New York on April 19, 1934 for the purchase by the defendant from the plaintiff of one thousand tons of Philippine Islands centrifugal sugar. The sugar was then in the Philippines. The contract bore the heading "Philippines—C.I.F. Terms"—and the decision upon this appeal turns upon whether it was what is known as a c.i.f. contract with the well-known legal incidents of such an undertaking or whether the duty rested upon the seller to make actual delivery of the sugar before it was entitled to be paid the purchase price in full.

The seller, acting pursuant to the provisions of the contract, shipped the sugar from the Philippines to the buyer in New York City on the S.S. Belgium Maru on May 10, 1934, under a bill of lading; obtained insurance for the benefit of the buyer; and sent a draft with the documents attached for 95 per cent of the purchase price less freight to a bank in New York City at which the buyer had established an irrevocable credit. The draft was duly honored. Afterwards the ship entered New York harbor with the sugar which was in all respects in the quantity and condition called for by the contract. Before the ship arrived at New York, however, the Jones-Costigan Act, 7 U.S.C.A.S. 608 et seq., became effective and the sugar became subject to its provisions. The sugar quota, fixed for the Philippine Islands for the year 1934, was filled before this sugar arrived and it was placed in a bonded warehouse by the defendant where it remained until later released. The defendant not only denies its liability for the remainder of the purchase price on the ground that the plaintiff breached the contract by failing to deliver the sugar but has filed a counterclaim for damages it suffered because of a drop in the price of the sugar while it was held in bond.

The appellant rightly insists that the nature of the contract into which the parties entered is not to be determined alone upon what they saw fit to call it but from the substance of the agreement they made. . . .

Under a c.i.f. contract the seller receives a purchase price payable as the parties agree and for that consideration is bound to arrange for the carriage of the goods to their agreed destination, for insurance upon them for the benefit of the buyer, and either to pay the cost of the carriage and insurance or allow it on the purchase price. When this has been done the seller has fully performed and is entitled to be paid upon delivery of the documents to the seller regardless of whether the goods themselves have arrived at their destination or ever will. . . . It has been said that a c.i.f. contract is one for the sale of documents relating to goods rather than a sale of the goods. . . . This, though perhaps an unduly broad generalization, serves to emphasize the distinctive character of such a contract. As the goods which constitute the subject matter are really the substantial part of the transaction it seems more realistic to treat such a contract as one under which the title to the goods passes to the buyer upon the delivery of documents alone; and that is so because the requisite antecedent acts of the seller are, when followed by delivery of the documents, a complete performance of the contract by the seller. . . .

For the moment we will accept the buyer's contention that there was no delivery of the sugar to him at the point of destination and confine the inquiry to whether or not delivery was necessary, not as a matter of performance by the carrier of its contract, but as a matter of performance by the seller of the contract of sale upon which it has sued. In order to become entitled to payment of the purchase price under the ordinary c.i.f. contract, of course, such delivery of the goods would not be a condition precedent to be performed at the risk of the seller. Nor is it made so merely because the obligation to contract for the carriage is expressed in the form of delivery of the goods at a designated place. . . . Conversely, if the parties agreed that payment in full for the sugar should be made if the sugar was duly shipped as the contract of purchase required and it failed to arrive at destination for any cause after shipment, potent evidence that the contract was intended to be the c.i.f. contract it was labelled would be afforded. And this contract did contain such an agreement as follows:

"In the event of non-arrival of this sugar arising from loss of vessel or any other cause after shipment has been made in conformity with contract stiplations: payment for any remaining balance of invoice account, not previously drawn against under letter of credit, to be made on the scheduled, or original approximate, due date of arrival of steamer(s) at discharging port—based on shipping weights and tests. . . ."

This specific provision making payment due regardless of the arrival of the sugar at destination shows plainly that the parties did not intend to, and did not, make actual delivery of the sugar to the buyer a condition upon the seller's right to be paid the purchase price in full. Consequently, it must be held that the seller made full performance by shipping the sugar and delivering the documents as required by the terms of the contract of sale; that the contract was in substance as well as in name a c.i.f. contract which passed the title to the buyer without delivery to him of the sugar itself; and that the actual receipt of the sugar was thereafter at the risk of the buyer.

CASE NO. 2

B. A. Griffin Co. v. Northwestern Fish & Seafood Co. 226 Minn. 497, 33 N.W. (2d) 838 (1948)

MAGNEY, J. Defendant appeals from a judgment entered upon findings in plaintiff's favor.

Plaintiff is a wholesaler of fish, with offices in Milwaukee. Defendant is also a wholesale dealer in fish, with its place of business in Minneapolis. . . . On and prior to December 12, 1943, plaintiff was the owner of 2,060 ten-pound boxes of frozen so-called Lake Superior herring, which fish was in the cold storage warehouse of the Dormer Company. . . . On or about said date, defendant orally agreed to purchase from plaintiff this lot of fish at 12¼ cents per pound. . . .

As defendant was short of storage

space, it did not want the fish shipped to it, but desired to have it remain in the warehouse. . . . Plaintiff made arrangements with the Dormer Company for the continued storage of the fish. Under date of December 31, 1943, an invoice was mailed to defendant. It stated net cash seven days. . . .

Plaintiff at that time wrote the Dormer Company requesting that the fish be placed in the name of defendant and that a warehouse receipt be made out to defendant and mailed to it. Plaintiff stated: "They want it to be put into their name as of the last expiration date. . . ."

On January 4, 1944, in response to plaintiff's letter, the Dormer Company opened up a ledger account in the name of defendant, transferring the account from plaintiff to defendant. A letter from the Dormer Company to plaintiff of that date reads in part:

> ". . . we have today transferred to the account of . . . Northwestern Fisheries Minneapolis, Minn. 2060 10# boxes herring.
>
> . . . . .
>
> "You will find enclosed warehouse receipts and also invoice for storage charges which you can kindly forward to the respective parties."

The Dormer Company made out an invoice to defendant for storage charges from December 23, 1943, to January 23, 1944, and also made out what its manager in a letter of transmittal called a warehouse receipt, but which in fact was merely a transfer or delivery slip and was so designated. These were mailed, not to defendant, but to plaintiff. . . . On January 18, 1944, the invoice for the storage charges made out in defendant's name was forwarded by plaintiff to defendant, with a letter which informed defendant that the fish was in defendant's name at the Dormer Company. . . .

. . . The Dormer Company on January 31, 1944, mailed direct to defendant another bill for storage from January 23 to February 23, 1944, covering the same fish. On or about February 2, 1944, plaintiff demanded payment for the fish. On or about the same day, defendant returned the invoice of December 31, 1943, and informed plaintiff that its order was cancelled because it had never received a warehouse receipt for the fish and did not have title to the merchandise. . . .

The price on frozen herring started to slip the middle of January. It was a falling market. The fish was held in storage for some time and processed to prevent spoilage. It was finally sold for animal food at a very low price. . . . This action was brought to recover the difference between the invoice value and the sum finally received as salvage, plus storage and processing charges. It was tried before the court without a jury, and the findings favored plaintiff. . . .

Defendant also claims that title did not pass to it because it had received no delivery of the fish, since the Dormer Company at no time acknowledged to it that it held the fish on defendant's behalf as required by M.S.A. § 512.43 (3), a part of the Uniform Sales Act, which reads:

> "Where the goods at the time of sale are in the possession of a third person, the seller has not fulfilled his obligation to deliver to the buyer *unless and until such third person acknowledges to the buyer that he holds the goods on the buyer's behalf;* but as against all others than the seller the buyer shall be regarded as having received delivery from the time when such third person first has notice of the sale." . . .

. . . It seems to us under the facts here that the statute has been complied with . . . Here, the Dormer Company knew that plaintiff was the owner of the fish in storage at its plant; that on December 31, 1943, plaintiff asked it to put this fish in the name of defendant; and that it did put the fish in the name of defendant on or before January 4, 1944. Two invoices for storage of this fish had been made out to defendant by the Dormer Company, both of which it received. In our opinion, the Dormer Company thus acknowledged to defendant, the buyer, that it held the goods on the buyer's behalf, and that as a result plaintiff had fulfilled its obligation to deliver the fish. . . .

M.S.A. § 512.18 provides:

"(1) Where there is a contract to sell specific or ascertained goods, the property in them is transferred to the buyer at such time as the parties to the contract intend it to be transferred.

"(2) For the purpose of ascertaining the intention of the parties, regard shall be had to the terms of the contract, the conduct of the parties, usages of trade and the circumstances of the case."

Section 512.19 provides rules for ascertaining intention, Rule 1 of which reads:

"Where there is an unconditional contract to sell specific goods, in a deliverable state, the property in the goods passes to the buyer when the contract is made and it is immaterial whether the time of payment, or the time of delivery, or both, be postponed."

The goods in the instant case were specific goods. They were in a deliverable state. Plaintiff was the owner of the goods, which were in storage at the Dormer Company. Defendant wanted the goods to remain in storage with the Dormer Company, as it was short of storage space. Plaintiff made the necessary arrangements with the Dormer Company to keep the goods in storage for defendant and had the account transferred on the books from plaintiff to defendant. The sale was completed. The Dormer Company issued invoices for storage to defendant, which it received.

In E. L. Welch Co. v. Lahart Elev. Co., 122 Minn. 432, 436, 142 N.W. 828, 830, the court stated the rule:

". . . In case of sale of specific goods—that is, goods that are specified at the time the contract is made —the title passes at the time the parties intend that it shall pass. The presumption is that it passes at the time the contract is made, and it will pass at that time unless some facts are shown that indicate a contrary intention. This is true, although neither payment nor delivery are then made. . . ."

There are no facts in this case indicating an intention that title should not pass at the time the contract was made for this specific merchandise. . . .

Judgment affirmed.

CASE NO. 3

California Animal Products Co. v. Lappin et al. 54 R.I. 75, 170 Atl. 71 (1934)

RATHBUN, J. . . . On or about December 20, 1930, plaintiff accepted from the defendants an order for 110 cases of Calo Dog Food Products. On or about January 15, 1931, the brokers mailed to the defendants an invoice of the goods together with an order on the warehouse in Boston, where they were stored, to deliver them to the defendants. The 110 cases were part of a larger mass stored in the same warehouse. The warehouse company had issued to the plaintiff a warehouse receipt for the entire lot and none of the parties notified said company of the agreement to sell a portion of the goods. On January 31, 1931, before any separation had been made, a fire damaged the entire lot of goods. . . .

It should be borne in mind that this is an action to recover the purchase price and not an action for breach of contract. It is therefore necessary to consider whether title to the goods passed from the plaintiff to the defendants.

It is clear that no portion of the large number of cases was set aside from the common mass or marked for identification as constituting the 110 cases necessary to fulfill the contract, and the warehouse company never agreed to hold any goods for the defendants.

Section 1, c. 306, Gen. Laws 1923, provides as follows:

> "Where there is a contract to sell unascertained goods no property in the goods is transferred to the buyer unless and until the goods are ascertained, but property in an undivided share of ascertained goods may be transferred as provided in section six of chapter three hundred and five."

Said section 6 (chapter 305) provides in part as follows:

> "There may be a contract to sell or a sale of an undivided share of goods. If the parties intend to effect a present sale, the buyer, by force of the agreement, becomes an owner in common with the owner or owners of the remaining shares."

There is no evidence tending to show that the parties intended that the buyer become an owner in common with the seller. No part of the common mass was set aside or selected to fill the order; and the warehouse company did not agree to hold any of the goods for the benefit of the purchaser or for the common benefit of the purchaser and seller. It is well settled that in such circumstances title does not pass . . . To constitute a sale the parties must intend to transfer immediate ownership in some specific article or articles.

Judgment for plaintiff reversed.

CASE NO. 4

Gottlieb v. Rinaldo. 78 Ark. 123, 93 S.W. 750, 6 L.R.A. (N.S.) 273 (1906)

MC CULLOCH, J. . . . The plaintiff, David M. Rinaldo, brought this suit against the defendants, B. Gottlieb and the Pacific Express Company, to recover $372, the value of two diamond rings. It is alleged in the complaint that the plaintiff is a merchant doing business in the city of Hot Springs, dealing in watches, diamonds, jewelry, etc.; that defendant Gottlieb is a merchant engaged in like business in the city of Pine Bluff, and defendant Pacific Express Company is a common carrier; that the plaintiff delivered said rings to defendant Gottlieb,

> "with the agreement and understanding that if she (defendant) was pleased with same she should keep them and account to the plaintiff at the above value, and, if not pleased, would, within a reasonable time, return them to plaintiff at said city of Hot Springs."

It is further alleged that the rings were never returned, and judgment is prayed in the sum of their aggregate value. Defendant Pacific Express Company paid to plaintiff the sum of $300, and the action, as to that defendant, was dismissed.

The other defendant, Gottlieb, filed her separate answer, as follows:

> ". . . That she has done all in her power to return said rings to the plaintiff, but she is informed and so charges that the said package has been lost by the said express company, without fault or negligence on her part."

The court sustained a demurrer to the answer, and, the defendant declining to plead further, judgment against her in the sum of $72 was rendered in favor of the plaintiff.

It is argued in support of the decision of the court below that the contract set forth in the pleadings amounted in effect to what is known in trade language as an agreement for "sale or return" of the articles named. Under such a contract the title passes to the purchaser subject to the right to return the articles within the specified time; and if, before the expiration of such time, the property is destroyed, either by inevitable accident or by the negligent act or omission of the purchaser, he is responsible for the price. Such, however, is not the effect of the contract set forth in the pleadings. The complaint alleges that the rings were delivered to the defendant

> "with the agreement and understanding that, if she was pleased with the same, she should keep them and account to the plaintiff at the above value, and, if not pleased, would, within a reasonable time, return them to plaintiff at said city of Hot Springs."

The answer states the contract in the same language, and the same does not constitute a contract of "sale or return." Under the contract stated, the title remained in the seller, and any loss or damage sustained from any cause except negligence of the purchaser fell upon the seller. . . . The distinction between the two classes of contracts is concisely stated by the supreme court of Massachusetts in Hunt v. Wyman, 100 Mass. 198, as follows:

> "An option to purchase if he liked is essentially different from an option to return a purchase if he should not like. In one case the title will not pass until the option is determined; in the other the property passes at once, subject to the right to rescind and return."

But, in whatever light the contract in this case may be viewed, whether as a contract for "sale or return," or as an agreement to purchase if satisfied with the article, we think that the defendant, in stating in her answer that she delivered the rings to the carrier for transportation, showed performance of her contract to return them to the plaintiff. The delivery to a responsible carrier properly consigned to the plaintiff was a delivery to the plaintiff. . . .

We see no reason why the same rule applicable to delivery to carriers of goods sold should not apply to an agreement to return articles sent for inspection. Where the mode of transportation in return is agreed upon, or where no mode is agreed upon, and the party under obligation to return adopts a mode of transportation justified by the usages of trade, the delivery is complete when the goods are placed in the hands of the carrier properly consigned.

CASE NO. 5

Baumgartner v. Glesener. 171 Minn. 289, 214 N.W. 27 (1927)

LEES, C. . . . In March and April, 1925, appellant published an advertisement in Renville county newspapers offering for sale yellow Murdock 1923 seed corn, and representing that the corn was graded, well acclimated to Renville county, and that its germinating test was 95 per cent. Respondent saw the advertisement, called on appellant, purchased some of the corn and planted it in a field of 30 acres, of which 4 acres were planted with seed corn respondent had grown and 26 acres with the corn sold by appellant.

Appellant testified that, prior to the date of the sale, he discovered the in some instances only 80 per cent of the corn germinated, that he did not change his advertisement but told those who came to buy that it tested as above stated, and that he gave respondent this information. This was flatly denied by respondent. The corn with which respondent planted 4 acres of the field was also of the Murdock variety, and it had a germinating test of 85 per cent. The soil of the 30-acre field was of the same quality, and the whole field was prepared for planting and planted in the same manner and on the same day. The whole field was cultivated alike and all the corn received the same care. The portion of the field planted with the seed purchased from appellant had a poor stand. Much of the seed failed to germinate, and the field was about half as much per acre as the yield from the remainder of the field and from a larger field adjoining, which was also planted with respondent's seed corn.

The evidence showed that seed corn having a germinating test of much less than 95 per cent would have produced a much better stand and yield than respondent obtained. From land planted with his own seed corn he had a yield of 44 bushels an acre, while from similar land planted with the seed purchased from appellant the yield did not exceed 22 bushels an acre. . . .

The advertisement contained a positive affirmation as to the quality of the seed. It was made for the purpose of selling the corn, and was relied on by respondent. Appellant's testimony concerning the alleged conversation showed nothing more than a modification of the warranty contained in the advertisement, reducing the percentage ascertained by the germinating tests from 95 to 80.

According to the weight of authority, in the sale of seed necessarily intended for planting, a warranty will ordinarily be implied that the seed is reasonably fertile, and will germinate if properly planted. . . .

The complaint alleges an express warranty, and, as a general rule such a warranty excludes one by implication; but since the adoption of the Uniform Sales Act, although an express warranty of quality be given, one not inconsistent with it may also be implied. Section 15, Uniform Sales Act. . . .

There was both an express and an implied warranty of the seed corn.

Order affirmed.

CASE NO. 6

Pauls Valley Milling Co. v. Gabbert. 82 Okla. 500, 78 P. (2d) 685, 117 A.L.R. 466 (1938)

PHELPS, J. . . . The trial judge, without a jury, gave plaintiff judgment for damages sustained on account of producing a smaller crop of oats from seed bought from defendant than he would have produced if defendant had delivered him the character or kind of seed oats which he ordered, and the defendant appeals. . . .

The plaintiff operated a farm near Pauls Valley, in which city the defendant operated a seed store. Two or three weeks before sowing time the plaintiff visited the defendant's store in Pauls Valley, and there in a small box on the desk of defendant's representative he saw some oats which he, the plaintiff, testified were "Texas Red Rust Proof Seed Oats." There is no evidence of any express oral or written representation having been made to plaintiff, but, according to his testimony, he ordered 20 bushels of seed oats by that sample, at 80 cents a bushel, to be delivered in two weeks. He paid for them several days before delivery.

In due time defendant's truck driver delivered the oats to plaintiff at a country store near plaintiff's farm, and plaintiff was present at the point of delivery. At that time and place he opened the sacks containing the oats and inspected them. According to his own testimony he knew immediately that they were not the kind of oats he had ordered; nevertheless, he said nothing to the defendant about it, and went ahead and planted them. The following is his testimony on that question:

> "They were just little old black slick oats, very common stock . . . and so when I seen them—opened them, I noticed they were not what I had bought at all, but I went ahead and sowed them." . . .

As stated, he made no effort to communicate with the nearby defendant. . . .

The only complaint of plaintiff, and the theory upon which the case was tried, is that the seed were not the kind ordered by him; that he ordered the red rust-proof and he received just ordinary oats. As stated by plaintiff in his brief, "they could not sell a horse and deliver a mule."

On a sale by sample, such as this was, a warranty exists that the goods shall be according to sample. . . .

The question whether inspection, acceptance, and retention of goods waives a warranty, or, as sometimes put, whether the warranty survives acceptance, is one over which there has been much argument and, at least in states not having the Uniform Sales Act * . . . a question on which there appears to be a great difference of opinion . . . The authorities in many states are so greatly at odds that the law approaches that state of flexibility whereunder it is sometimes said that each case depends on its own facts and circumstances. . . .

We believe that both in legal theory and by the precepts of common justice the defendant should not be held in damages for the crop which would have been plaintiff's had he but simply spoken. It cannot be said that plaintiff owed no duty at all to the defendant. He could have avoided these damages by disclosing the facts to the seller; a very simple task. It should be borne in mind that this is an action on contract, not tort. Defendant's delivery of the wrong kind of oats, or its misconception of plaintiff's original order, could easily have been an innocent mistake. We do not hold that it is not liable for its innocent mistakes to the extent that those mistakes themselves may prejudice another. But when such a mistake is discovered by the buyer in ample time to avoid injury, and when it is an easy and simple matter for the buyer to so avoid it, and he fails to do so, then he himself is, in effect, voluntarily producing his own injury, and we refuse to inflict the consequences of such conduct upon the defendant. Good conscience will not permit such an unwarranted extension of the doctrine. . . .

The judgment is reversed, and the cause is remanded, with directions to enter judgment for the defendant.

CASE NO. 7

Lindsey v. Stalder. 120 Colo. 58, 208 P. (2d) 83, 12 A.L.R. (2d) 519 (1949)

MOORE, J. Defendant was a dealer in lumber and building material. Plain-

* Section 49. In the absence of express or implied agreement of the parties, acceptance of the goods by the buyer shall not discharge the seller from liability in damages or other legal remedy for breach of any promise or warranty in the contract to sell or the sale. But if, after acceptance of the goods, the buyer fails to give notice to the seller of the breach of any promise or warranty within a reasonable time after the buyer knows, or ought to know, of such breach the seller shall not be liable therefor.

tiffs were engaged in the building and construction business and operated a wood products mill in which the millwork items required by their operations were produced.

On March 5, 1946, plaintiffs ordered from defendant a carload of lumber. The said order was in writing and described the lumber ordered as follows: "No. 2 Common & Btr rough green Alder, with Maple developing." . . .

Forthwith upon receipt of plaintiffs' order defendant ordered the lumber from the Morton Lumber Company of Seattle, Washington. The plaintiffs paid to defendant the sum of $1,132.04 prior to the delivery of any lumber which sum was the full amount due defendant on account of said purchase. Plaintiffs paid additional sums to Oregon business firms for milling, transit and drying charges. The lumber, as thus worked upon at plaintiffs' cost, did not arrive in Denver until November 14, 1946. Plaintiffs then inspected the lumber and refused to accept it, claiming that it was inferior to the quality and grade of lumber specified in their order, and unfit for the uses for which it was purchased. Thereupon the lumber was sold to the Davis Furniture Company of Denver for the sum of $1,595.11. . . .

Upon plaintiffs' refusal to accept the lumber when it arrived in Denver, defendant inspected the shipment and one of the plaintiffs testified that defendant made the statement that

> "It was terrible, he had seen better lumber than that burned, it just wasn't on grade, wasn't what it was supposed to be."

Referring to the statement of the defendant at the time of inspection by him, plaintiff Walter J. Stalder, Jr., further testified that the defendant said that

> "it wasn't what we ordered, that the grade wasn't No. 2 common, and wasn't what the invoice stated."

Thereafter the defendant protested the quality of the lumber to the Morton Lumber Company and, in the presence and at the solicitation of plaintiffs, defendant wrote the Morton Lumber Company stating in substance that Mr. Stalder had suffered a loss, "Due to the poor grades and badly milled lumber." . . .

Prior to the placing of the order by plaintiffs a small sample of alder wood was shown by defendant to one of the plaintiffs and the defendant stated, "Here's what it looks like."

The trial court found the issues in favor of the plaintiffs and against defendant and entered judgment for the sum of $472.60 and costs, which was the difference between the total expenditures made by plaintiffs and the sum received upon the resale of the lumber.

Defendant contends that plaintiffs failed to meet the burden of proof resting upon them to establish that the lumber which was delivered at Denver after being kiln-dried, resawed and milled in Oregon, was not in conformity with plaintiffs' original order for "No. 2 common & btr rough green alder." The defendant further contends that by working upon, milling and kiln-drying the lumber, its character was so changed that it was impossible to determine in Denver whether or not it was properly graded as "No. 2 common & btr rough green alder," before being processed in Oregon.

Plaintiffs assert that the judgment should be affirmed upon three grounds, namely, (1) that there was a breach of an implied warranty that the bulk should correspond with the sample submitted as to quality; (2) that since the defendant knew the particular purpose for which the lumber was required there was shown a breach of an implied warranty that the lumber should be reasonably fit for such purpose; and (3) that the transaction amounts to a sale of goods by description and that there was shown in the evidence a breach of the implied warranty that the lumber would correspond to the description.

Questions to Be Determined

First: *Does the fact that defendant exhibited a small piece of alder wood and made the statement, "Here's what it looks like," give the transaction the characteristics of a "sale by sample," carrying with it a warranty that the bulk shall correspond with the sample in quality?*

This question must be answered in the negative. It is clear from the evidence that the purchasers did not rely on any representations of the defendant concerning the quality of the lumber. They knew that defendant had never handled any alder wood and was not at all familiar therewith. The record discloses that the chief reliance of plaintiffs in ordering the "rough, green alder," was the recommendation of their own employees. There is nothing in the record to indicate that the small sample exhibited was "rough, green, alder," but every indication is that such sample was not in the rough, green state. Thus it is apparent that the sample exhibited was not even the kind of material ordered by plaintiffs. The burden of proof was upon them to establish that the sample shown them was exhibited as a fair representation of the bulk of what they ordered; that they relied thereon; and that the sample induced the sale. There is no evidence tending to show these essentials of a sale by sample. In 46 Am. Juris. at page 552, is the statement:

"If the contract of sale is connected by the circumstances attending the sale with the sample, and refers to it, and the sample is exhibited as the inducement to the contract, the contract of sale may be a contract of sale by sample, with the consequence that the seller warrants the bulk of the goods to correspond with the specimen exhibited as a sample. However, the mere circumstance that the seller exhibits a sample at the time of the sale does not of itself make it a sale by sample, so as to subject the seller to liability on a promise of warranty as to the nature and quality of the goods, because it may be exhibited not as a promise or warranty that the bulk corresponds to it, but merely to enable the purchaser to form a judgment on its kind and quality."

In Weston v. Barnicoat, 175 Mass. 454, 56 N.E. 619, 49 L.R.A. 612, it was held that a sample of granite sent by a seller did not become a part of a subsequent contract for delivery of a monument. The court said:

". . . the letter made the test of performance conformity to the words of description used, not conformity to the piece of stone previously shown."

So in the case at bar, the test of defendant's performance was conformity to the words of description used, namely, "rough green alder," and not conformity with the piece of finished wood exhibited.

Second: *Is there here present a breach on the part of the defendant of an implied warranty that the lumber ordered would be reasonably fit for the particular purpose for which the same was purchased by plaintiffs?*

This question is answered in the negative. Sec. 15(1), chapter 228, Session Laws 1941, provides:

"Where the buyer, expressly or by implication, makes known to the seller the particular purpose for which the goods are required, and it appears that the buyer relies on the seller's skill or judgment (whether he be the grower or manufacturer or not), there is an implied warranty that the goods shall be reasonably fit for such purpose."

The essential elements set forth in the statute which give rise to the implied warranty under discussion are wholly absent in this case. There is no evidence that defendant was informed concerning the "particular purpose for which the goods (were) required." There is no evidence that plaintiffs relied "on the seller's skill or judgment" concerning the uses to which alder might be put. It affirmatively appears, however, that plaintiffs did not place reliance upon the "skill or judgment" of defendant, because they were fully advised that he had no experience with alder wood.

Third: *Does the transaction between the parties amount to a "sale by description" in which there is an implied warranty that the lumber will correspond to the description; and, if so, is any breach of such warranty shown?*

It is clear that the parties consummated a "sale of goods by description" as those words are used in section 14, chapter 228, Session Laws 1941, which provides inter alia that:

> "Where there is a contract to sell or a sale of goods by description, there is an implied warranty that the goods shall correspond with the description . . ."

The description given in the contract was a quantity of "No. 2 Common & Btr rough green Alder, with Maple developing." The test of defendant's performance is whether or not there was conformity to the words of description used. The plaintiffs had the burden of establishing this lack of conformity. If there is competent evidence to sustain such lack of conformity, the judgment of the trial court should not be disturbed. If there is an absence of such evidence the judgment cannot be permitted to stand. Accordingly, we review the evidence.

Plaintiffs, having ordered "No. 2 . . . rough, green Alder," and intending to change the character thereof by resawing to smaller dimensions, machining and kiln-drying the lumber at their expense before delivery, are confronted with the difficulty of establishing lack of conformity to the description in the contract, by witnesses who at no time saw the lumber in the "rough, green" stage. The time to correctly grade lumber as "No. 2 rough, green" or otherwise would certainly appear to be when the lumber was still in the "rough, green" state. It may be true that the finished product as delivered to plaintiffs in some form other than "rough, green" was not what either the plaintiffs or defendant expected; however, this fact does not necessarily prove that plaintiffs did not get what they ordered.

Plaintiffs offered in evidence, and the court admitted, Exhibit M, which was a letter from the Morton Lumber Company in response to the complaint of the defendant concerning the quality of the lumber. This letter, signed by H. P. Caldwell, contains the following:

> "Alder is graded on National Hardwood Lumber Association grades, plus some that OPA had added, and generally speaking Alder is graded at the originating mill as follows, in brief: #2 Com. Minimum cutting 3″ × 24″, each board to yield 50% Clear One Face cuttings. No particular attention is paid to defects. It is the cuttings that are left that determine the grade. . . ."

This is the only specific statement in the record concerning the method of grading the lumber in question. The deposition of Mr. Caldwell contains the following:

"Q. Did you see the lumber when it was in stock or loading? A. Yes, when it was in stock and when it was loading.

"Q. Was there any difference between the lumber ordered and the lumber shipped? A. No."

Herbert Hast, an expert witness of long experience in the lumber business, was called by defendant and testified that No. 2 common rough, green alder could only be graded as such at the original sawmill, and before it was further worked upon. . . .

"Q. If an order is given for No. 2 rough green alder, that would mean in the rough? A. Yes, that is the way it would be graded.

"Q. After it is milled and kiln dried you couldn't tell what its grade was in the original state? A. No, you could not."

The witness Caldwell, having stated that there was no difference between the lumber order and that delivered, and the foregoing testimony of the witness Hast being undisputed in any way, the question is whether there is any evidence to support the judgment. All that appears is the fact that plaintiffs were displeased with the shipment, and that defendant thought the lumber inferior and in order to keep good will endeavored to satisfy his customer. Under the uncontradicted testimony of Hast, neither plaintiffs nor defendant could say whether the shipment was properly graded No. 2 common or better rough green alder at the time it was so graded.

There being no competent evidence to establish that No. 2 common or better rough green alder was not supplied as called for by the plaintiffs' order, and for the further reasons hereinabove assigned, the judgment is reversed.

CASE NO. 8

Bekkevold v. Potts et al. 173 Minn. 87, 216 N.W. 790 (1927)

WILSON, C.J. . . . The action is to recover money paid upon the purchase price of a Fordson tractor, a two-wheel truck used as a trailer, a connecting hitch, and a hydraulic hoist for unloading.

The contract of sale contained a printed provision:

"No warranties have been made in reference to said motor vehicle by the seller to the buyer unless expressly written hereon at the date of purchase."

None were written thereon.

The proofs, received over the objection that it was in violation of the parol evidence rule, showed that the seller knew the particular purpose for which the outfit was to be used and that the buyer relied upon the seller's judgment that it was suitable. There was, therefore, an implied warranty, unless excluded by the said language of the contract, that the machinery was reasonably fit for such purpose. . . .

It is only when an implied warranty is inconsistent with an express provision of the contract that all implied warranties are merged in, or superseded by, the express provisions of the contract. In other words, warranties are not implied in conflict with the express terms of the contract. It has always been competent for the parties to put their entire agreement in writing and to expressly stipulate that no obligation arising out of an oral agreement imposition of law, or otherwise, shall rest upon either, save as defined by their written agreement. If the parties wish to avoid the implied warranty, they must in form, or in substance contract against it.

An implied warranty is not one of the contractual elements of an agreement. It is not one of the essential elements to be stated in the contract, nor does its application or effective existence rest or depend upon the affirmative intention of the parties. It is a child of the law. It, because of the acts of the parties is imposed by the law. It arises independently and outside of the contract. The law annexes it to the contract. It writes it, by implication, into the contract which the parties have made. Its origin and use are to promote high standards in business and to discourage sharp dealings. It rests upon the principle that "honesty is the best policy," and it contemplates business transactions in which both parties may profit. Defendants' claim does not commend itself to us as consistent with the honesty of purpose with which they are entitled to be credited in their dealings with their customers. The doctrine of implied warranty should be extended rather than restricted. . . .

We are of the opinion that the parties intended to say that no contractual warranties had been made; that the seller had not spoken or written any warranty in reference to the outfit. There was no other way by which such warranties could have been "made." No action of the parties was necessary to "make" that implied warranty which the law writes into it. We must conclude that the parties did not intend to exclude the implied warranty which could easily have been done in unmistakable terms had they so chosen. Hence there was no error in receiving the evidence to prove the breach thereof. . . .

CASE NO. 9

Beaman v. Testori. 333 Mich. 194, 35 N.W. (2d) 155 (1948)

DETHMERS, J. Plaintiffs sue for an amount due on contract for the manufacture and delivery to defendants of a mold. Defendants seek recoupment for damages occasioned by plaintiffs' alleged failure to manufacture the mold in accord with the terms of the agreement. From judgment for plaintiffs defendants appeal.

Defendant Testori testified that he submitted a working model coil cleaner to plaintiff Yeager and asked if he could make a mold or die for the manufacture thereof which would work; that Yeager said he could; that plaintiffs quoted a price of $1,600 in writing and that defendants gave plaintiffs a written order therefor on that basis; that upon delivery the mold was defective and would not work, as a result of which defendants suffered damage.

Plaintiff Yeager testified that he had agreed to and that plaintiffs did build a mold in accord with designs and specifications submitted by defendants but that he had not guaranteed that it would work. . . .

Defendants also claim an implied warranty that the mold would work. They rely on . . . Dunn Road Machinery Co. v. Charlevoix, etc., Co., 247 Mich. 398, 225 N.W. 592, 593, 64 A.L.R. 947, in which this court held that, under the statute and the common law as well, there was an implied warranty of fitness of a machine for a particular purpose when the purchaser had made known to the manufacturer-seller the purpose for which the machine was desired and had trusted to the latter's skill and judgment to furnish a machine for that purpose. The inapplicability of the statute and the Dunn case is readily apparent from the fact that the defendants here did not rely upon plaintiffs' judgment and skill to produce a mold which would work, but relied upon them only to build one in accord with the designs and specifications furnished by defendants. The undisputed testimony is that plaintiffs did build it in accord therewith. In the Dunn case this court said:

"It is well stated by Mr. Mechem as follows:

" 'The implied warranty of fitness is not to be extended to cases which lack the necessary conditions upon which it depends. The essence of the rule is, that the contract is executory; that the particular article is not designated by the buyer; that only his need is known; that he does not undertake or is not able to determine what will best supply his needs, and therefore necessarily leaves the seller to make the determination and take the risk; and if these elements are wanting, the rule does not apply. If a known, described and defined article is agreed upon and that known, described or defined article is furnished, there is no implied warranty of fitness, even though the seller is the manufacturer, and the buyer disclosed to him the purpose for which the article was purchased.' 2 Mechem, Sales, § 1347."

The trial court properly rejected defendants' theory of an implied warranty. . . .

CASE NO. 10

Ladd v. Reed. 320 Mich. 167, 30 N.W. (2d) 822 (1948)

BUSHNELL, CH.J. Ladd, a combustion engineer, doing business as W. C. Ladd Company, at Grand Rapids, Michigan, sought recovery of a balance of $400 due him for work, labor, and materials furnished to defendant. On January 22, 1945, Reed addressed three letters to Ladd. In the first, plaintiff was authorized to furnish

"all necessary labor for the completion and erection of stack and installing grates and other necessary equipment for the boiler"

at defendant's plant at Athens, Michigan, for the sum of $625. Overtime work was to be paid for not to exceed $150, and the work was to be completed within 30 days. In the second letter, plaintiff was authorized

"to install a new stack to be 60 ft. by 26 in. in diameter to replace the present stack"

for the sum of $500. In the third letter he was authorized

"to furnish and install the necessary brick work and chute and grates to replace the Dutch oven for the sum of $500."

. . . the trial judge said:

". . . Defendant in his answer does not claim that the work was not performed according to the written orders or contract, but sets up a notice or plea of recoupment in which he claims that plaintiff represented or warranted that the finished job would produce certain results, which he contends that it does not do, and that there is a breach of warranty. However, there is no such warranty included in the written orders for said construction work, sued upon; and no warranty is implied as in the case of sales of merchandise under the Uniform Sales Act."

The contracts were not for the sale of combustion equipment as argued by Reed, but were for services and material to be provided by Ladd in his capacity as a combustion engineer. Such contracts do not fall within the provisions of the Uniform Sales Act, . . . and therefore there was no implied warranty of quality or fitness for a particular purpose. . . .

CASE NO. 11

Iron Fireman Coal Stoker Co. v. Brown et ux. 182 Minn. 399, 234 N.W. 685 (1931)

WILSON, C.J. . . . Defendants H. Rowatt and Frances M. Brown appealed from an order denying their motion for a new trial.

The action is to foreclose a mechanic's lien based on the installation of an iron fireman coal stoker. The court found, as defendants claimed, that it would not do the work for which it was sold and purchased, though reasonable efforts had been made to have it do so. The court later granted plaintiff's motion to amend the findings so as to give plaintiff the relief sought. This was upon the theory that an article was sold under a trade-name within G.S. 1923, subd. 4, and hence without an implied warranty.

G.S. 1923, 8390, subd. 4 (Uniform Sales Act, Section 15(4)) reads:

"In the case of a contract to sell or a sale of a specified article under its patent or other trade name, there is no implied warranty as to its fitness for any particular purpose."

If a person requests a dealer to deliver to him a specifically designated article, known to the buyer and the trade by its trade-name, and it is done, it is obvious that the article would be sold under its trade-name within the meaning of the statute. Such negotiation indicates that the article is known by both parties and the buyer has designated just what he wants. He knows what he wants. The theory of the statute is that, since he knows what he wants, and gets it, after having so designated it, it must be supposed that the trade-name carries such qualities as to cause the purchase. . . .

This provision of the statute is merely a restatement of the common-law rule that, where there is a sale of a known, described, and defined article, and if that article is in fact supplied, there is no implied warranty. But we think the rule at common law and now under such a statute means articles known in the market, and among those familiar with that kind of trade, by that description.

In this case it would seem that the "Iron Fireman" was not known to defendants. They were entirely ignorant as to its ability or capacity or the work which it would do. Plaintiff was in possession of all the facts. Defendants did not even know it had a trade-name. It then had a limited use in their community. Plaintiff sought to sell them the equipment, and assured them that they would not have to go to the furnace room the last thing at night nor the first thing in the morning. They were willing to buy something that would accomplish that purpose. They had no knowledge of the "Iron Fireman" by reputation or otherwise. They made their desires known to plaintiff. One of the reasons that caused them to buy was that plaintiff repeatedly told them they would take the equipment out if not satisfactory. Defendants unsuccessfully attempted to make it work. Plaintiff knew defendants had no knowledge of the equipment or its operation.

Defendants' reliance upon plaintiff's judgment as to the suitability of the equipment to meet their requirements is evident from all the circumstances. . . .

The fact that the article has a trade-name does not do away with the implied warranty arising out of the circumstances indicated. . . .

Under the circumstances, we are

of the opinion that under this subdivision of the statute there was an implied warranty that the equipment was reasonably fit for the purpose for which it was sold.

The doctrine of implied warranty is to be liberally construed. The rule is an equitable one.

Reversed.

CASE NO. 12

Cliett v. Lauderdale Biltmore Corporation, Inc. 39 So. (2d) 476 (Fla.) (1949)

SEBRING, J. The appellee, the proprietor of a hotel and dining room, served a meal containing unwholesome food to the appellant, a paying guest, who became ill as the result of its impurity. . . .

The sole question for determination on the pleading is whether the proprietor of a public restaurant or dining room who serves a meal containing unwholesome food to a paying guest for immediate consumption on the premises is under an absolute liability for the damages proximately resulting from the impurities, on the theory of an implied warranty of fitness.

The question is one of first impression in this jurisdiction. In other states where the issue has been presented the courts have been in sharp division on the matter. Some courts have held that in the absence of statute a victualer serving food for immediate consumption on the premises may not be held liable for food deleterious to health, without proof that he was guilty of negligence; while others have determined that aside from any question of negligence such a purveyor of foods for a valuable consideration is under an absolute liability for unwholesome food served by him, on the theory of an implied warranty of fitness. . . .

In our opinion the implied warranty theory of liability comports with the general trend of the better reasoned cases and is supported, on principle at least, by decisions from our own jurisdiction.

In Blanton v. Cudahy Packing Co., 154 Fla. 872, 19 So. (2d) 313, this court held that a manufacturer and packer of tinned meat products was liable for injuries sustained by a buyer who became sick from eating the product which had been purchased in the original tin from a retail grocer, on the theory that the transaction involved a sale out of which there arose an implied warranty as between the manufacturer and the ultimate consumer that the food was wholesome and fit for human consumption. In Smith v. Burdine's, Inc., 144 Fla. 500, 198 So. 223, 131 A.L.R. 115, it was decided that a retailer of lipstick which contained poisonous substances was liable for injuries sustained by the purchaser as the result of its use, on the theory that the transaction involved a sale out of which there arose an implied warranty as between the retailer and the purchaser that the article was harmless and not deleterious to health when properly used.

These cases establish the principle that as to items of foods or other products in the original package which are offered for sale for human consumption or use generally, a person who purchases such items in reliance upon the express or implied condition or assurance that they are wholesome and fit for the uses or purposes for which they are advertised or sold, and who is injured as the result of unwholesome or deleterious substances therein which are unknown to the buyer, may hold either the manufacturer or the retailer liable in damages for injuries sustained by him, on the theory of an implied warranty of wholesomeness or fitness of such article or product for the purposes for which it was offered to the public.

The appellee maintains that the principle of implied warranty established by the Florida cases has no bearing on the facts of the case at bar, for the reason that the purchase of a meal in a restaurant does not involve the "sale" of the items of food ordered but only the purchase of a "service" of which the food is but an incidental part, and hence that the doctrine of implied warranty is not applicable.

The contention advanced by the appellee is supported by some of the decisions from other jurisdictions. And, though we express no opinion on the point, the principle may have some application to meals served "boarding house style," where the guests have no voice in the selection of the items of food to be prepared for their use and no real ownership in the victuals placed before them but only the right to consume such as they need and take no more. But we cannot see its soundness where the transaction is with respect to a table d'hote meal or one by the a la carte method of choosing each item the guest desires. To say that when one selects his soup, entree, vegetables, dessert and beverage individually from a wide variety of items listed on a menu, only a "service," and not a "sale" of the meal purchased, is involved, and that because of that fact the restaurant keeper may escape liability for unwholesome or poisonous food served to a paying guest unless the latter can point to specific acts of negligence in its care or preparation, seems basically unsound.

We can perceive no substantial basis for holding a restaurant keeper who serves food for immediate consumption on the premises to a less degree of responsibility than that imposed upon a retailer who sells food for immediate consumption off the premises. Whether such a transaction be termed a service or a sale every argument for implying a warranty in the ordinary sale of food over the grocery counter for consumption off the premises would seem to be applicable with as great a degree of force to the purchase of a meal for consumption in a hotel dining room or restaurant.

> "The basis of implied warranty is justifiable reliance on the judgment or skill of the warrantor, and to charge the seller of an unopened can of food for the consequences of the inferiority of the contents of the can, and to hold free from liability a restaurant-keeper who opens the can on his premises and serves its contents to a customer, would be a strange inconsistency." Cushing v. Rodman, 65 App. D.C. 258, 82 F. (2d) 864, 868, 104 A.L.R. 1023.

We hold, therefore, that with respect to the guest of a hotel dining room or restaurant who receives, eats and pays for victuals delivered to him on his order, the proprietor must be held to the same degree of duty as regards the wholesomeness of such food as the law imposes upon a retailer of foods and other like products for consumption away from the premises.

. . . The judgment appealed from is reversed and the cause is remanded for further proceedings in accordance with law.

CASE NO. 13

Bisner v. Mantell. 92 N.Y.S. (2d) 825 (1949)

RASMUSSEN, J. Plaintiff seeks to recover in this action on two causes of action. First, a breach of contract and second, for moneys had and received. At the completion of his case, he elected to proceed on the theory of quasi contract for moneys had and received in the amount of Three Hundred Seventy ($370.00) Dollars.

On April 22, 1948, plaintiff and his wife entered defendant's store and selected from defendant's merchandise one (1) Singer three-piece living room suite at an agreed price of Three Hundred Fifty Nine ($359.00) Dollars, one (1) American bedroom suite at an agreed price of Three Hundred Nineteen ($319.00) Dollars, and one (1) Daystrom breakfast set at an agreed price of Sixty Nine and 95/100 ($69.95) Dollars or a total of Seven Hundred Forty Seven and 95/100 ($747.95) Dollars. Plaintiff paid a deposit of Twenty ($20.00) Dollars on the above date and subsequently made weekly or bi-weekly payments at the store until November 11, 1948, when the total amount paid in was Three Hundred Seventy ($370.00) Dollars. On November 17, 1948, defendant's agent forwarded a letter to the plaintiff's wife which reads as follows:

"Mrs. Robert Bisner
14 113th Street
Troy, New York

"Dear Mrs. Bisner:

"Reviewing your account, we find that since August you have paid approximately $5.00 each week instead of the agreed amount of $15.00.

"We must have your remittance of $95.00 to place your account on a current basis and the agreed installment per week in order to continue your account.

"Thanking you for your attention, I remain,

"Yours truly,
(signed) Mrs. Delores Finn . . ."

Apparently the above furniture was purchased on what is commonly known as a "lay away" plan. The particular items of furniture were to be stored in defendant's warehouse until such a time as plaintiff would secure an apartment. It is undisputed that the furniture was placed in defendant's warehouse, ear-marked for the plaintiff and still remains there. It is undisputed that plaintiff never demanded delivery of the furniture. Plaintiff has never demanded the furniture nor has he offered to pay the balance of Three Hundred Seventy Seven and 95/100 ($377.95) Dollars due thereon, and he seeks in this action to recover the amount paid in by him. The defense contends that there was a breach of contract which prevents plaintiff's recovery.

There was no fraud on the part of the defendant and mistake on the part of the plaintiff proven, nor was there any evidence of mutual mistake.

I find that the "lay away" feature of this transaction did not affect or change a valid sale. There was at least an executory contract which was breached by the plaintiff, and I have searched in vain to find any cases in this State affecting the rule that a vendee who has made a payment on an executory contract, who has causelessly breached the contract which has been fully performed by the vendor, cannot recover back the amount paid.

It is the settled law that payments upon an executory contract of sale may not be recovered back by the purchaser who has breached the contract. Beveridge v. West Side Construction Co., 130 App. Div. 139, 114 N.Y.S. 521: In Lawrence v. Miller, 86 N.Y. 131; the defendant contracted to sell and the plaintiff to buy a tract of land; plaintiff made a part payment and afterwards failed to carry out the contract. The Court held that he could not maintain an action to recover back the money paid, although its retention by the defendant would more than compensate him for the damages sustained by the plaintiff's failure to fulfill the contract.

The case of Nelson v. Landesman, 118 Misc. 832, 193 N.Y.S. 574, was an action for money had and received. The plaintiff, the vendee, similarly breached his contract and sought to recover Five Hundred ($500.00) Dollars paid as part payment of the purchase price. In that case, as in the one at bar, there was a completed contract and the court denied recovery of the part payment.

The law is well settled that the only time that a recovery is allowed is when the money paid in was in the nature of a deposit and not where it was made as part payment. There can be no question but what the money paid in by the plaintiff was part payment for the merchandise.

Judgment for the defendant of no cause of action with costs.

CASE NO. 14

Rock-Ola Mfg. Corp. v. Leopold. 98 F. (2d) 196, 117 A.L.R. 1101 (1938)

HOLMES, C.J., delivered the opinion of the court: . . .

On April 2, 1937, appellee ordered from appellant one hundred coin-operated personal weighing scales for immediate delivery, terms $1,500 down, balance in three and six months, notes for unpaid balance to be given. . . . On receipt of the order and appellee's check for $1,500, appellant wired its acceptance thereof, advising that the scales could not be shipped for three weeks. The check was deposited in Chicago for collection, but was dishonored by the bank in Jackson upon which it was drawn, and was returned to appellant with an endorsement showing insufficient funds. At appellee's request, the check was re-deposited, and was paid and cancelled on April 15th. . . . appellant's credit manager made a new investigation of appellee's financial condition. This investigation revealed . . . that there were ten judgments against him enrolled as having been rendered from June 4, 1934, to March 26, 1937, for a total of $681.56, all unsatisfied.

On April 21st, appellant wired appellee as follows: "New credit angle to straighten out writing fully." On the same day, it wrote a letter advising appellant that it would not be justified in making the sale on a credit, because of the number of judgments outstanding, but hoped appellee would proceed with the sale on a cash basis. On April 30th, appellee wrote appellant replying to its letter and telegram, protesting its refusal to sell except for cash, insisting that his credit was good . . . that, unless the machines were shipped at once, they would be bought elsewhere and an action would be brought for breach of contract; and that all other orders from appellee to appellant should be cancelled.

On May 3rd, appellant advised appellee that, in accordance with his request, the order for scales had been cancelled, and inclosed its check for $1,500 as a refund of the amount paid, . . . suit by attachment was instituted by appellee against appellant . . . for breach of the contract of sale in the amount of $7,500, the difference in the contract price and the price alleged to have been paid for similar scales bought elsewhere. . . .

On the trial of the case, the court declined to permit appellant to introduce evidence tending to show the insolvency of appellee at the time agreed upon for shipment of the goods, or at later dates; would not admit evidence of the judgments rendered against appellant, and that they remained unsatisfied; and, at the close of the evidence showing the order and correspondence above referred to and the purchase of other scales at $75 each, instructed the jury to find for appellee, leaving for its determination only the amount of damages to be assessed. An exception to each of these rulings was duly taken. Verdict was rendered for appellee in the amount of $3,000, and this appeal is from the judgment entered thereon.

Under applicable decisions, it is well established that a seller of goods on credit, upon learning of his buyer's insolvency, may refuse to deliver except for cash. This right, which is related to the lien of the seller and the right of stoppage in transitu, is not qualified or diminished by a payment of a part of the purchase price, nor is it affected by the terms of the credit agreed upon or the security contemplated. . . .

Appellee contends that appellant did not refuse performance unless the consideration were paid in cash, and that its letter did not so state. We think the words,

> "we would not be at all justified in extending credit on the number of scales requested by you because of the number of judgments reported as remaining outstanding and unsatisfied," and "we hope you can see your way clear to handling this on a cash basis,"

made it clear that appellant refused to ship the scales unless the price was paid in cash. Moreover, the letter from appellee to appellant, under date of April 30th, must be construed as a refusal to pay cash. In it, appellee advised appellant that, if the scales were not shipped under the terms stipulated in the order, he would buy elsewhere and sue for the difference. Under the circumstances, appellant was fully justified in treating the contract as at an end and refunding the amount already paid.

. . . The allegation of insolvency of the buyer presented the principal issue in the case, and this issue was for the jury to determine. . . .

. . . The judgment of the District Court is reversed, and the cause remanded for further proceedings not inconsistent with this opinion.

CASE NO. 15

Reno Sales Co. v. Pritchard Industries. 178 F. (2d) 279 (1949)

DUFFY, C.J. Plaintiff brought this action to recover $12,050.56, the alleged unpaid balance of the purchase price of a quantity of wastebaskets sold to defendant. In its answer defendant admitted receipt of the baskets, but denied liability for the unpaid purchase price, claiming that the baskets did not conform to sample and were of inferior quality and workmanship, and that it had offered to return all of said baskets to plaintiff. Defendant also interposed a counterclaim demanding $25,833.56, the amount which it had paid on its account for said baskets, plus $1,374.86 freight charges, again alleging that the waste baskets shipped by the plaintiff were of poor workmanship and were not merchantable, and that it had offered to return all of said baskets to plaintiff.

. . . The court dismissed the counterclaim and entered judgment for the plaintiff, from which judgment this appeal is taken. . . .

Both parties seem to agree that, in order to establish a prima facie case, it was incumbent upon defendant to prove four necessary elements: (1) that the contract of sale was by sample; (2) that there was a breach of warranty; (3) that the rescission was made within a reasonable time; and (4) that defendant had a right to rescind the contract in part and affirm it in part. Plaintiff contends that the defendant was unable to rescind in toto, and had waived any right it might have had to rescind.

The first element was not in dispute, and the district court held that the sale was by sample. As to the second element, the trial court found:

". . . The evidence indicates that, so far as the defendant-counterclaimant has made any inspection of the merchandise, it does not conform to sample and is therefore a violation of one of the implied warranties under the Uniform Sales Act, ..."

The parties are in dispute over whether the attempted rescission was timely. What constitutes a reasonable time must be determined after considering all of the attendant circumstances. Defendant was a wholesaler and retailer of office equipment. The baskets shipped to it in large quantity were in individual sealed cartons. Plaintiff knew that such baskets were to be resold and reshipped in said cartons to customers of defendant. . . . Defendant offered evidence to show that instead of plywood panel ends being evenly machined and glued in the recesses, as in the sample, metal fasteners had been used, which, being driven across the grain of the center ply, had a tendency to split it thus causing the baskets to be split at the end. Although sometime in October, 1946, defendant had received a complaint about one or more baskets shipped to a customer, it concluded that the damage had occurred in shipment because the carton itself was damaged. It was not until December 3, 1946, that defendant had actual knowledge of the latent defects of the baskets. Immediately defendant checked other baskets in stock and finding some that were unsatisfactory consulted its attorney. The reasonable time in which a purchaser of chattels must rescind the contract runs only from the time the purchaser had knowledge of or is chargeable with knowledge of the breach of warranty. . . . We conclude that the attempted rescission by defendant was timely.

We must now focus our attention on the conflicting contentions pertaining to the fourth element. Under the circumstances of this case, is a partial rescission of the contract permissible? The trial court said:

". . . and by selling several thousand of the wastebaskets, (defendant) has exercised a right of ownership inconsistent with that of the seller and cannot restore the seller to the status quo by a return of the goods. Rescission cannot be partial. . . ."

Defendant contends that at the time of the trial, it had on hand 16,750 baskets; that it had the right to return not only the six separate shipments sued on by plaintiff which totaled 11,134 baskets, but also the shipments of August 2nd, 9th and 15th, 1946, which totaled 5,179 baskets. Stated differently, defendant insists that, having 16,750 baskets in its possession, it had the right to rescind the nine shipments from August 2 to October 24, 1946, inclusive, which totaled 16,313 baskets, and to pay for the three shipments that it is unable to return.

Defendant admits that it is a well settled rule of law that a purchaser is not permitted to affirm a contract in part and rescind as to the residue, but argues that this rule does not apply to severable contracts. . . .

Under the Uniform Sales Act of Illinois, defendant had a choice of alternative defenses. It could have kept the baskets and set up the breach of warranty in diminution or extinction of the sales price; it could have kept the baskets and sued the plaintiff for damages for breach of warranty; or it could have rescinded the contract and offered to return the baskets. Defendant elected the last of these alternatives, and tried the case on the theory of rescission, offering no evidence as to damages.

Rescission implies renunciation of the sale and disclaimer of the ownership of the goods. Here the defendant continued to offer for sale and to sell baskets long after the discovery of the defective baskets—in fact, right up to the time of the trial. Defendant, recognizing that such a course of sales does not square with its present theory of rescission, now makes claim that the contract was severable, and that baskets sold, or offered for sale, by it came from the 3,000 baskets as to which no rescission is attempted.

. . . The transaction here was one sale of one type of waste basket, each at the same price, as evidenced by one purchase order. We hold that the contract of sale was an entire contract. . . .

Finding no error, the judgment of the trial court is affirmed.

CASE NO. 16

Southern Pac. Co. v. Bank of America. *23 F. (2d) 939 (1928)*

LINDLEY, D.J. Ono & Co., of San Francisco, shipped to Chicago certain crab meat, imported from Japan, taking a bill of lading from plaintiff, Southern Pacific Railway Company, for the delivery of the merchandise in Chicago, to the order of the shipper, vendee to be notified. The consignor sold and assigned the bill of lading, and sight draft for $37,000 on its Chicago vendee accompanying same, to the Pacific National Bank, who forwarded it to a bank in Chicago for collection, with instructions to surrender the bill of lading upon payment of the draft. Upon presentation, the vendee said that the goods had not arrived, and that it would not honor the draft until their arrival.

Immediately thereafter, however, vendee, discovering the goods in Chicago in possession of plaintiff's delivering carrier, fraudulently procured their delivery by the railroad without production of the bill of lading, and in violation of its provisions that the merchandise should not be delivered until the bills should be surrendered, and at once deposited the goods in a public warehouse, taking negotiable warehouse receipts therefor. Defendant, Bank of America, without notice of any infirmity in the vendee's title, at the latter's request, loaned it $34,000, taking the receipts, duly assigned, as security. The Pacific National Bank, discovering the facts with regard to the wrongful procuration by the vendee, demanded that the plaintiff recognize that it, through its agent, had wrongfully, though innocently, delivered the goods, and it pay therefor. This the plaintiff did, taking an assignment of the bill of lading and draft for $37,000.

Armed with these muniments of title, plaintiff demanded of defendant the surrender of the merchandise, and, that being refused, instituted this replevin suit. Plaintiff claims that the original vendor's title has never passed to defendant, either by its consent or by estoppel, and that as successor to that title plaintiff is the present owner as against the fraudulent vendee and the defendant, even though the latter made its advancement in good faith upon the warehouse receipts. Defendant asserts that plaintiff, having by its agent's wrongful delivery made possible the negotiation of the warehouse receipts, is estopped to assert its title as against defendant, for the reason that, where one of two innocent persons must lose, he who made the loss possible should suffer.

The first question presented is as to the position of defendant. Section 58 of the Uniform Warehouse Receipts Act, in force in Illinois . . . provides that "to purchase includes to take as mortgagee or as pledgee"; "Value is any consideration sufficient to support a simple contract;" and "a thing is done 'in good faith,' within the meaning of this act, when it is in fact done honestly, whether it be done negligently or not."

Defendant had no knowledge whatever of the outstanding order bill of lading, or of any other facts or circumstances affecting the invalidity of the title of the original vendee. It relied upon the apparent title of the warehouse receipts, and upon that reliance advanced the sum of $34,000. The fact that the borrower was then heavily indebted to the bank is not important, in view of the fact that the loan was made upon the goods, and not the credit of the borrower.

In Commercial National Bank v. Canal-Louisiana Bank, 239 U. S. 520, 36 Sup. Ct. 194, 60 L. Ed. 417, the court said:

"The negotiation of the receipt to a purchaser for value without notice is not impaired by the fact that it is a breach of duty or that the owner of the receipt was induced 'by fraud, mistake or duress' to intrust the receipt to the person who negotiated it. And, under section 41 . . . one to whom the negotiable receipt has been duly negotiated acquires such title to the goods as the person negotiating the receipt to him, or the depositor or person to whose order the goods were deliverable by the terms of the receipt, either had or 'had ability to convey to a purchaser in good faith for value.' The clear import of these provisions is that if the owner of the goods permits another to have the possession or custody of negotiable warehouse receipts running to the order of the latter, or to bearer, it is a representation of title upon which bona fide purchasers for value are entitled to rely, despite breaches of trust or violations of agreement on the part of the apparent owner."

Defendant, therefore, should be treated as a bona fide purchaser for value of the warehouse receipts, without notice of infirmity.

Plaintiff succeeded to the title of the Pacific National Bank under the bill of lading. It did so, however, after its agent had wrongfully delivered the goods to the vendee, and the latter had assigned the warehouse receipts to defendant for value, and with full knowledge of those facts. It now contends that its title, thus acquired, is superior to that of the defendant. No owner of merchandise may be deprived of the title thereto, except by his consent, or by the existence of such facts as will create an estoppel against him to assert his title. A thief can convey no title to a bona fide purchaser, nor can a trespasser, or other tortious taker of merchandise, convey a good title thereto. However, one who secures title to property by fraudulent representations may convey good title to a bona fide purchaser. The vendor is there estopped to assert its rights.

Here, by its fraudulent representations, the vendee persuaded the delivering carrier to surrender the goods. That delivery was a conscious, voluntary delivery, induced by fraud, true it is, but none the less a delivery consciously and voluntarily made, a delivery within the apparent scope of the plaintiff's agent's authority. The goods were not stolen; they were not received by the vendee as a result of a trespass, but consent to delivery was fraudulently procured. It follows that the purchaser from the vendee stands in the position of the purchaser from any fraudulent vendee, whose rights by virtue of the doctrine of estoppel are well recognized as being superior to those of the vendor or parties in privity with him. In this situation it would be contrary to the established law to allow the plaintiff, who has purchased its title with full knowledge of the facts, to prevail against the bona fide purchaser, for its act, through its agent, made possible the procurement of the negotiable warehouse receipts and the sale thereof by the vendee. . . .

The court, therefore, finds the issues for the defendant. Judgment shall be entered for the return of the property, or, in the alternative, that the plaintiff shall pay the defendant the amount for which the same is now rightfully held as security by the defendant, ...

Review Questions

1. For what reasons might it become necessary to determine whether a sales transaction is a contract of sale or a contract to sell?
2. What is potentially existing property? What is the status of a contract for the sale of potentially existing property under the Uniform Sales Act?
3. Is the execution of a bill of sale necessary to the passing of title to goods to the buyer?
4. What is the basic test for determining at what time title to goods passes to the buyer?
5. What rules govern the time of passing of title in a sale where there is no determinable intention on the part of the buyer and seller as to the time when title is to pass?
6. What are ascertained goods?
7. What are fungible goods?
8. Must there be an appropriation of fungible goods to effect a passing of title to the buyer?
9. A sales contract provides f.o.b. point of destination. What bearing would this have upon determining the time of passing of title?
10. With whom does the risk of loss reside under a sale on trial? Under an agreement on sale and return?
11. When does title pass if the goods are shipped C.O.D. to the buyer?
12. How does the order bill of lading differ from the straight bill of lading?
13. How can the order bill of lading be used very effectively by the seller of goods for the purpose of assuring payment from the buyer?
14. Is the risk of loss to goods in transit under an order bill of lading upon the buyer or seller?
15. What may be the consequences of the buyer's leaving the seller in possession of the goods?
16. How does fraud differ from a breach of warranty?
17. May a mere statement of facts constitute an express warranty?
18. Does an express warranty apply to both obvious and hidden defects in the goods warranted?
19. May the buyer and seller avoid implied warranties by contractual agreement?
20. Illustrate the implied warranty of merchantability.
21. What circumstances give rise to the implied warranty of fitness for a particular purpose?
22. Under what circumstances may a seller of goods recover the agreed purchase price for a breach of performance by the buyer even though title to the goods has not passed to the buyer?

23. Under what circumstances does the unpaid seller have a right of lien upon the goods sold?
24. What is the right of stoppage in transitu?
25. What fact would prevent the seller from exercising the right of stoppage in transitu when the goods are being shipped under an order bill of lading?
26. What are the buyer's remedies for a breach of warranty?
27. Can the buyer demand the right of inspection of goods shipped C.O.D. before he makes payment to the carrier?
28. What is a negotiable document of title?
29. Can a finder or a thief transfer title to a properly indorsed order bill of lading?
30. Can a finder or a thief transfer title to a properly indorsed negotiable warehouse receipt?
31. Indorsing a negotiable document of title in blank is a dangerous practice. Why?
32. What is the liability of an indorser of a negotiable document of title?

Problems for Discussion

1. Pugh contracts to purchase certain specified lumber from Morse, the agreement providing for payment of cash upon delivery. Before delivery was made the lumber was carried away by flood waters. Upon whom is the loss?
2. The Alabama Legislature passed sales tax legislation which became effective March 1, 1937. On October 26, 1936, one Blair ordered mill work from the McPhillips Mfg. Co. The order was accepted and it provided, "All millwork will be delivered f.o.b. trucks, job site. All doors will be delivered f.o.b. cars Birmingham." The State Tax Commission is seeking to collect the tax on millwork delivered to Blair after March 1, 1937. Decide. (*McPhillips Mfg. Co.* v. *Curry,* 2 So. (2d) 600)
3. Defendants were copartners who, on January 16, 1930, contracted with plaintiff for the purchase of 400 calendars, upon which, according to the contract, certain indicated advertising of defendants and their business was to be printed. After that printing was done, but before delivery of the calendars "f.o.b. cars, St. Paul," as the contract required, defendants attempted to repudiate. Their one defense now is that, while they might be liable for damages for breach of contract, they are not so for the contract price, their assertion being that, when repudiated, the contract was wholly executory, that the goods had not been appropriated to the contract, and so title had not passed. Decide. (*Louis F. Dow Co.* v. *Bittner,* 187 Minn. 143)
4. On April 14, 1925, defendant gave one of plaintiff's traveling salesmen a written order for a quantity of gloves, describing them by number, size, and name. The salesman made a memorandum, stating that the gloves were to be shipped over the Chicago & Northwestern Railway in August, and were to be paid for in November. The order was accepted and defendant notified thereof. Plaintiff had the gloves in stock, selected those ordered, packed them ready for shipment, set them aside in its warehouse, and attached shipping tags bearing defendant's name and address. Thereafter and on June 30, defendant countermanded the order and requested plaintiff to cancel it, but plaintiff refused. On August 12 the gloves were shipped to defendant and an invoice mailed. On receipt of the invoice, defendant notified plaintiff that it would refuse to receive the gloves.

They were tendered to defendant by the railroad company, were refused, and have remained in the hands of the railroad company ever since. Plaintiff's salesmen did not carry or attempt to sell gloves after June 30. They are goods usually sold by wholesalers for the fall trade and are not readily salable after June.

The trial court held that these facts fell short of showing that the property in the gloves had passed to the defendant before the order was countermanded, and that plaintiff could not recover the purchase price. Decide. (*Western Hat & Mfg. Co.* v. *Berkner,* 172 Minn. 4)

5. Plaintiff sold defendant fifty cases of Chateau Yquem of the vintage of 1901, which at the time of the transaction was part of a larger mass in the cellars of Schroeder and Schyler in Bordeaux, France. Defendant contends that the passing of title to him was dependent upon a segregation of fifty cases from the larger mass. Answer this contention. (*Gourd* v. *Healy,* 206 N.Y. 423)
6. This is an action in replevin to recover a quantity of corn held by the defendant sheriff by virtue of a levy of a writ of attachment. The plaintiff prevailed, and the defendants appeal.

   The evidence is meager, but the record discloses that February 28, 1908, Clyde Merryman owned 2,000 bushels of shelled corn contained in several bins in his granary. Upon that date Merryman sold to the plaintiff 2,000 bushels of corn, received a check for approximately one half of the purchase price, and agreed to deliver the grain at the plaintiff's elevator in Axtell. The same day Merryman sold in like manner 2,000 bushels of corn to the Hayes-Eames Elevator Company, and received a check for half of the purchase price. Merryman then prepared two bills of sale purporting to convey to each of his vendees "one thousand bushels of shelled corn now located in the N.W. 1/4 of section #28, township 7, range #16, Kearney county, Nebraska." These documents were given by Merryman to his brother-in-law, a Mr. Wells, with directions to deliver the corn to the respective vendees. Merryman negotiated the checks, paid Wells for delivering the corn, and then absconded. In the forenoon of March 2 Wells filed the bills of sale with the county clerk, informed the vendees of the transaction, and delivered 348 bushels of the corn to the plaintiff. The corn was accepted, but the plaintiff directed his banker not to pay said check. Subsequently, but before the check was presented, the order was rescinded, and the check thereafter paid upon presentation. At 7:00 P.M. on March 2 the Farmers' & Merchants' Bank of Axtell caused an attachment to be levied on all of the undelivered corn. Decide. (*Seldomridge* v. *Farmers' & Merchants' Bank et al.* 127 N.W. 871)
7. "Sold to Muscoda Mfg. Co., the power plant formerly used by the City of Bocobel, consisting of two boilers, two engines, two steam pumps. Muscoda Mfg. Co. agrees to pay the sum of $1,800 for the outfit, to be paid $200 cash and the balance, $1,600, to be paid before taking out the plant, and plant to be taken out before June 1, 1920." Upon whom is the risk of loss before the removal of the plant?
8. The evidence discloses that appellant during 1920, 1921, and 1922 was a retail jewelry dealer and appellee's intestate was an "exchange manager" in charge of one of the eight exchanges at Camp Grant. Hobert Hooker was an employee of appellant and looked after the merchandise at the Camp which appellant had there for sale. He testified that on May 14, 1921, deceased examined some dia-

monds which appellant had there, selected a 1⅛ carat stone and a ring mounting which he liked, and in accordance with his request the diamond was mounted and the ring made to fit his finger. The following day he called and received the ring, signing at that time a "sales ticket," and, in reply to the question of deceased as to what the ring was going to cost him, appellant told deceased $550. Hooker further testified that deceased said "he was going to try and sell the ring and when he sold it he would pay for it and if he did not sell it he would return it, as he wanted to purchase a larger stone and intended to buy a larger one as soon as he sold and paid for this one," to which arrangement appellant assented. Edward E. Allen, another salesman of appellant, testified to substantially the same as Hooker. It further appeared from their testimony that although appellant was to receive therefor only $550 and the deceased was to have all over that amount he could get, the actual retail price of the ring was $650; that Sutton never sold the ring but wore it himself, never paid for it, and that his widow had it after his death, which occurred on September 19, 1922.

It is the contention of appellee that the transaction as disclosed by the foregoing facts constituted a bailment or consignment for sale; that no title to the ring ever passed to Sutton and that appellant has misconceived his appropriate remedy of replevin. Decide. (*Bolender* v. *Pearce,* 238 Ill. App. 137)

9. At an auction sale of plaintiff's stock and farm produce, certain hay in a mow was offered, with an announcement that it would be sold in five-ton lots, with the privilege to the successful bidder for any lot of taking a larger quantity at the same price, if he should see fit. Under this arrangement defendant was the successful bidder for the first lot, and announced his election to take all of the hay offered at the same price. Some question was raised as to how the quantity should be ascertained, and it was agreed that it might be weighed, as taken away, on a neighbor's scales, and, further, that the buyer might allow it to remain in plaintiff's mow until the same was needed for the storing of the next crop. The buyer paid a portion of the purchase price in cash, and by the terms of the sale he was to have time for payment of the balance. Before any of the hay was removed it was destroyed by accidental fire, without any fault on the part of plaintiff. Under these facts, the simple question was whether the title of the hay had passed, so that the defendant as purchaser became liable for the price. Decide. (*Allen* v. *Elmore,* 121 Iowa 241)
10. Following is a letter from plaintiff to defendant confirming the sale of a carload of corn to defendant: "This confirms our telephone conversation resulting in the sale to you of one car of Yellow Ear Corn. This car sold to you at $1.28 a bushel of 70 lbs. delivered to New Philadelphia via B. & O. Railroad." The corn arrived in damaged condition. Upon whom was the risk of loss?
11. X sold cows to Y with the understanding that the purchase price was to be paid in full on the day delivery was made. At the time of the delivery, X agreed that the buyer Y was to have a few days to pay. Should the seller's judgment-creditors be entitled to attach the cows?
12. Betts, a radio dealer, induced Hall to take a radio on "ten days' trial." Who has the risk of loss during the ten-day period?
13. Uline purchased photographic equipment from Day with the understanding that Uline could, within two months, return any item purchased that did not

prove satisfactory. During the two months' period, the equipment was damaged by vandals. Day seeks to recover the purchase price. Will he succeed?

14. Patterson ordered goods C.O.D. from Filmore. The goods were destroyed by an act of God while in transit. Who will suffer the loss: the carrier, the buyer, or the seller?
15. X is the designated consignee upon a straight bill of lading. The carrier refuses to deliver the goods to X unless he surrenders the bill of lading. Is the carrier within its rights?
16. Johnson purchased an electric motor from Nelson. One week later, when Johnson complained that the motor was not operating as it should, Nelson said, "I will guarantee that the motor is in perfect condition." The motor proves to be defective. Can Johnson hold Nelson for breach of an express warranty?
17. X purchased a bottle of elixir from the Y Drug Company, which bottle was labeled "The Tonic of Spring." The label further stated, "Will put spring into your step, sparkle into your eyes, and color into your cheeks." The elixir failed to produce such results for X and he sues for breach of express warranty. Result?
18. Dunbar sold a book to Lahr, having forgotten that he had borrowed the book from Fritz some years before. Fritz recovered his book from Lahr. Upon what basis is Dunbar liable to Lahr?
19. The appeal in this case is from a judgment for $2,550 recovered by the appellee against the appellants in a suit for an alleged breach of warranty of a Seitz motor truck sold by the latter to the former in May, 1913. The regular market price of the truck was $3,600, but, as the one in question had been used for demonstration purposes, a reduction of $350 was made for that reason, and the price paid by the appellee was $3,250. It is averred in the declaration that the appellee bought the truck upon the warranty that it "was a first-class car, was as good as new and was in sound and first-class condition; and, that, if it was not abused but handled with care, it would last the plaintiff at least four years."

    A fundamental theory of the defense was that the statements attributed to the vendors by the declaration were not shown to have been made as warranties or otherwise than as a mere expression of belief in the high quality and utility of the motor truck offered for sale. Decide. (*Rittenhouse-Winterson Auto Co.* v. *Kissner,* 129 Md. 102)
20. The Hyde Construction Co. contracted for the purchase from Stevenson of gravel which it intended to use on a certain construction job. It is subsequently discovered that the gravel contracted for is not suitable for the intended use. What facts would be necessary to substantiate the company's contention that an implied warranty of fitness had not been met?
21. Heard purchased an automobile from Wiley for the sum of $400 under an agreement whereby title passed to Heard at the time of the transaction. Later Wiley in exercising his right as an unpaid seller resold the automobile to Perry for the sum of $500. Heard contends he is entitled to the difference of $100. Is he right?
22. A sold ascertained property to B upon the understanding that payment was to be made upon delivery. Before delivery had been made, B sold the property to C, who paid cash. A then delivered the property to B's business establishment, where it was deposited, while A accompanied B to the bank to receive payment.

The bank refused to extend B credit and it was A's intention to repossess himself of the property. In the meantime, C had appeared at B's place of business and had taken possession of the property. A institutes an action to enforce a seller's lien upon the property. Will he succeed?

23. Walker purchased a quantity of seed from Gold. The title to the seed had passed to Walker but possession remained with Gold, who then refused to make delivery to Walker unless the latter tendered cash instead of a check. What was the basis of Gold's refusal?

24. Ray sold and shipped goods to Nixon under an order bill of lading. The bill of lading, properly indorsed, was sent to Nixon. While the goods were in transit, Ray discovered that Nixon was insolvent and, not wanting to take a chance upon receiving payment, he ordered the carrier to return the goods to him.
    (a) What will the carrier require before it will comply with Ray's order?
    (b) Suppose that Nixon has sold the goods and has transferred the bill of lading to Hughes. What would be the position of Hughes?

25. Quincy contracts to have Wright make him a farming implement of special and unique design. After the implement is completed, Quincy refuses to accept it. May Wright recover the agreed purchase price or must he be content with recovering damages for breach of contract?

26. Dewart sold goods to Butts, which he warranted to be of a specified grade. After the goods had been delivered, Butts determined that the goods were not as warranted. What are his rights?

27. Berry sold goods to Marlin, the agreement providing for payment upon delivery of the bill of lading. Marlin refuses to accept the bill of lading until he is given an opportunity to inspect the goods. Berry treats this as a breach of contract and sues. Result?

28. The agent of the S. W. and M. Ry. Co. issued a bill of lading describing the goods as being "10 boxes of 1,000 bayberry candles each." The bill of lading is transferred to an innocent purchaser who, upon receipt of the goods, discovers the shipment to be not bayberry candles, but candles of a lesser value. What are the rights of the holder of the bill of lading?

29. X had a warehouse receipt, which provided for delivery of the goods to the bearer, stolen from his office safe. The thief transferred the receipt to Y, an innocent purchaser. Does Y hold a good title?

30. Defendant purchased a machine of plaintiff under the trade name of a "Huelsdonk Concentrator." There was evidence that plaintiff had full knowledge of defendant's requirements and that plaintiff prevailed upon defendant to buy the machine, stating, "It is the thing you want for your job." Did the sale under the circumstances carry the implied warranty of fitness? (*Drumar Mining Co.* v. *Morris Revine Mining Co.*, 33 Calif. App. (2d) 492)

27 PERSONAL PROPERTY AND RELATED TOPICS:

BAILMENTS

► I. NATURE OF BAILMENTS

In man's everyday personal and commercial affairs there are few, if any, more commonplace transactions than those in which temporary possession—as distinguished from title—of personal property is transferred from one person to another for a specific purpose. The following illustrations indicate the wide range of uses for this type of transaction: A places his automobile in the possession of B garage for repairs or storage; C deposits his securities with the D bank for safekeeping; E delivers his corn to F's grist mill to be ground; G rents H's pleasure boat for a week-end outing; I delivers his silverware to his neighbor J for safekeeping; K borrows L's car to take his mother-in-law to the station; and M, as a favor to his friend N, agrees to deliver a valuable parcel to a third party; O takes delivery of merchandise from P agreeing to sell it for P; Q, a public officer acting in his official capacity, takes custody of R's property.

Transactions like these are known as *relations of bailment,* and the person transferring the property is called the *bailor,* as distinguished from the *bailee,* the person who takes possession of the property for some temporary purpose.

► II. DISTINGUISHING CHARACTERISTICS

A bailment is a delivery and acceptance of personal property under an express or implied agreement between the bailor and bailee. The characteristic elements of a bailment are as follows:

(1) A delivery and acceptance of personal property under an express or implied agreement between the bailor and bailee that

(2) the transfer of possession is without intent to pass title to the bailee;

(3) possession is to be for some temporary purpose;

(4) possession is to revert to the bailor or someone entitled to possession either upon the fulfillment of the purpose of the bailment, at the expiration of a period of time, upon the happening of a specified event, or at the bailor's demand if so agreed.

A. DELIVERY AND ACCEPTANCE

Ordinarily there can be no bailment relation unless there is a delivery and acceptance of the subject matter by the bailor to the bailee. The acceptance may consist of either (1) actually taking physical possession of the property, or (2) taking control over the property without actual physical possession—constructive possession.[1, 2, 3] The following illustrates a constructive delivery:

An innkeeper stands as a bailee in respect to the property of his guests, although the innkeeper does not have actual possession. It is sufficient that the guests' property is upon the premises and therefore under the implied care and control of the innkeeper.

B. CONSTRUCTIVE BAILMENTS

The law may recognize the existence of a bailment relation even though there has been no delivery and acceptance of property from one to another. The element that forms the basis of the bailment is possession.

> ". . . The typical instance of such a constructive bailment is where one sells a chattel to another, who pays the price thereof, and the vendor refuses to deliver it to the vendee. Here the law implies the contract of bailment, and holds the vendor answerable as bailee. In such a case it is apparent that there has been no delivery by the bailor to the bailee, and yet the bailment exists constructively. All the other examples of constructive bailment which are given in the books, as in the case of a finder, of a captor or salvor, of an attaching officer, are cases where the person having possession of the chattel is held to be a bailee, although there has never been either an actual or a constructive delivery of the chattels to the bailee by the bailor. In other words, the essential fact of legal significance in all these cases is possession. It certainly is not delivery, for, in none of these cases of constructive bailment is there either an actual or a constructive delivery." *Wentworth* v. *Riggs,* 143 N.Y.S. 955

C. SALE OR EXCHANGE DISTINGUISHED

The distinguishing feature of a sale is the passing of title to the transferee. In a contract of bailment, the transferee acquires mere possession, with the title remaining in the owner, who is usually the bailor.[4] Since risk of loss follows title, it becomes important at times to determine whether a given transaction was one of sale or of bailment. A determination of where ownership resides may also become necessary when creditors of either the transferor or the transferee lay claim to the property as a means of obtaining satisfaction of their demands.

Let us suppose that A delivers his grain to a mill for the purpose of having it ground into flour. Does title remain in A? The answer depends upon whether A is to receive the flour produced from his own grain or is merely to be paid in flour equivalent to the grain he left.

> "Thus, where logs are delivered to be sawed into boards, or leather to be made into shoes, rags into paper, olives into oil, grapes into wine, wheat into flour, if the product of the identical articles delivered is to be returned to the original owner in a new form, it is said to be a bailment, and the title never

[1] Malone v. Santora, p. 698.
[2] Theobald v. Satterthwaite, p. 700.
[3] Marsh v. Am. Locker Co., Inc., p. 702.
[4] Ginsberg v. Kugler, p. 703.

vests in the manufacturer. If, on the other hand, the manufacturer is not bound to return the same wheat or flour or paper, but may deliver any other of equal value, it is said to be a sale or a loan, and the title to the thing delivered vests in the manufacturer." *Laflin etc. Powder Co.* v. *Burkhardt*, 97 U.S. 110

D. STORAGE OF GRAIN IN WAREHOUSE

The concept of a bailment has assumed a somewhat altered form in its application to the relationship created by the storage or deposit of grain with a warehouseman. This represents one instance in which the law recognizes a bailment relationship even though the identical article delivered is not to be returned to the bailor in its original or altered form. It is well established that a bailment relationship exists when grain is deposited in an elevator with other like grain with the understanding that the various depositors have the right to a return of the amount of their deposits. And it has been held that the transaction is a bailment although the depositor has an option either to demand a return of grain or to elect payment in money.

E. CONSIGNMENTS FOR SALE

A bailment relationship is created by the modern practice of consigning goods to a retailer as an agent and bestowing upon him the authority to sell the goods on behalf of the principal. While the goods are in the possession of the consignee, he holds them as the property and at the risk of the consignor. Consignments for sale are used for varying reasons. For example, the owner of the goods to be sold may regard the retailer as a poor credit risk and deliver the goods to the retailer on consignment. He thereby retains title in himself as security while making the retailer responsible as a trustee for the proceeds of the sale. Or it might be that the retailer, although financially responsible, chooses not to accept the business risks of the middleman. He might prefer to sell the goods as an agent-bailee on a commission basis, leaving title and its attendant inventory risks with the consignor-bailor.

This type of bailment relationship departs from the orthodox bailment in that upon a sale of goods the agent-bailee is authorized to deliver possession to the buyer. Possession of goods not sold and of proceeds from those sold reverts to the principal-bailor.

Parties entering into a consignment agreement should realize the necessity of clearly defining the relationship and above all of avoiding contractual provisions that are at variance with the characteristics of this type of bailment. A considerable number of cases have come before the courts which involve transactions partaking of the character of both sales and consignments for sale.[5] Upon occasion the courts have found it necessary to hold that certain contracts are sales, although possessed of agency characteristics; on the other hand, contracts have been held to constitute consignments for sale, even though containing provisions suggestive of a sales transaction. The incidents of ownership cannot be bestowed upon the transferee

[5] Greenlease-Lied Motors v. Sadler, p. 704.

without creating the possibility that the question will be raised as to whether ownership in fact resides in the transferee even though the contract contains a declaration to the contrary. The right of the consignor to demand payment for any unsold goods would seem to establish conclusively the existence of a sales transaction rather than a consignment for sale. It would be suggestive of a sale if the consignee were given the right to determine the terms and conditions under which the goods are to be sold.

► III. CLASSIFICATION OF BAILMENTS

In order to establish the duties of bailees, bailments can conveniently be classified as follows:

(1) Bailments for the sole benefit of the bailor. This type is characterized by the fact that the bailee has possession of the property without compensation or benefit to himself. The bailee may act, for example, as a gratuitous depository for the bailor.

(2) Bailments for the sole benefit of the bailee. Representative of this type is a gratuitous loan of property for the use of the bailee.

(3) Bailments for the mutual benefit of bailor and bailee. This class of bailments is of prime commercial importance. Illustrations are: contract arrangements by which the bailee accepts possession of the property, for a compensation, for the purposes of repairing, transporting, storing, or safekeeping; delivery of possession of property to the bailee as security for a debt, which property is usually in negotiable form, such as notes, stocks, or bonds; and, where the bailee rents, leases, or hires property from the bailor.

► IV. DUTIES OF BAILEE

A. TO CARE FOR PROPERTY

1. *Liability Under Contract*

The contract of bailment may fix the duties of the bailee in respect to the care and use of the property. The bailee is liable for any loss to the bailor when he violates any of the contract provisions.

2. *Liability for Negligence*

Generally the parties to a bailment relation have not agreed upon what care the bailee is to take of the property. In these instances, the law requires that the bailee exercise what as a matter of law is regarded as proper care of the property. Stated otherwise: the bailee becomes liable to the bailor for any loss or damage to the property resulting from the bailee's negligence—his failure to exercise proper care. This arbitrarily imposed liability is founded upon the element of possession of the property by the bailee.

In seeking to establish the standard of conduct required of a bailee in relation to the property in his possession, it is often futilely asserted that: (1) in a bailment for the benefit of the bailor, only slight care is required; (2) that in a bailment for mutual benefit, ordinary care must be exercised; and (3) that in a bailment for the sole benefit of the bailee, extraordinary care must be taken of the property. In establishing for the lay mind standards of conduct for a bailee, there is little help in the additional statements that: (1) ordinary care is such care as the individual usually exercises over his own property; (2) that slight care is care of a lower degree; and (3) that extraordinary care is of a higher degree. Unfortunately, care cannot be measured quantitatively. Under certain circumstances, a gratuitous bailee may, in fact, be required to exercise a higher degree of care than a bailee under a mutual benefit bailment. Certainly a gratuitous bailee would be expected to exercise a higher degree of care over a valuable piece of jewelry than would be required of a bailee for hire in relation to a decrepit lawn mower.

As a practical matter, the standard to be observed by the bailee is that of reasonableness. He cannot be expected to do more in protection of a bailor's interest in the property than that which a reasonable and prudent man would do under like or similar circumstances. Whenever the conduct of the bailee is in issue, proper care is that care which the jury—the fact-finding body—regards as being proper care by an application of the above test.

B. NOT TO EXCEED HIS AUTHORITY

A bailee has the duty not to depart from the contract of bailment. He makes himself absolutely liable for the property when used for an unauthorized purpose or in an unauthorized way. Thus, if by agreement the bailee is to have custody of the property for safekeeping only, his use of the property would make him liable for damage or loss, regardless of cause.

C. CARE REQUIRED OF COMMON CARRIER BAILEES

Common carriers, as distinguished from private-contract carriers, are those carriers who hold themselves out to supply the public with transportation services. A common carrier is one that has dedicated himself to serve the public generally, that is, to serve indiscriminately all who apply. On the other hand, a private-contract carrier is one who has not dedicated himself to give a public service; he is free to choose for whom and at what time he will carry.

One who has established himself as a common carrier is engaged in a public calling and is required by law to carry continuously, without discrimination and to the full extent of his facilities, and at such charges as have been sanctioned by public authority. Another legal consequence of the public nature of the common carrier's undertaking is the carrier's peculiar responsibility as a bailee of the goods while they are in his possession. Whereas a private-contract carrier is liable for loss or damage to goods resulting only from his own negligence, the basic rule is that a common carrier is liable as an absolute insurer of the goods. Regardless of the cause of the loss or damage—whether due to the negligence of the carrier or not—the shipper can look to the carrier for satisfaction. The law recognizes, however, certain exceptions to this extraordinary bailee liability. When the loss or damage to the goods is due *exclusively* to any of the following causes, the carrier is not responsible. Should the negligence of the carrier contribute to the loss or damage, he will not be relieved of liability.[6]

1. *Exceptions to Liability*

a. Act of God. The term *act of God* as here used has a limited meaning. Some comprehension of the limits of its meaning can be gathered from the following excerpt taken from *Nugent* v. *Smith,* 1 C.P.D. 423:

> "The rain which fertilizes the earth and the wind which enables the ship to navigate the ocean are as much within the term 'Act of God' as the rainfall which causes a river to burst its banks and carry destruction over a whole district or as the cyclone that drives a ship against a rock or sends it to the bottom. Yet the carrier who, by the rule, is entitled to protection in the latter case, would clearly not be able to claim it in case of damage occurring in the former."

An accident due to an act of God is conceived as resulting entirely and directly from natural causes that could not reasonably have been foreseen or expected and so could not have been prevented. High tide would not be regarded as an act of God unless extraordinarily high. Fire is usually the result of human agency and not the result entirely of natural forces. Consequently, in *Merchants' Despatch Co.* v. *Smith,* 76 Ill. 542, it was held that the great Chicago fire was not an act of God such as to relieve carriers of their liability. Fire caused by lightning would be an accident caused by act of God as defined above.

b. Act of Public Enemy. The term *public enemy* as here used is not to be taken as having reference to the popular concept as established by the activities of J. Edgar Hoover's G-men. It means rather an armed force operating against the government. Carriers cannot be expected to guard against such a contingency.

c. Inherent Nature of Goods. In the absence of negligence on his part, a carrier incurs no liability for loss or deterioration of goods resulting entirely from their peculiar inherent characteristics. For example, if a horse dies as a result of his refusal to eat, or of fright, or of any inherent debility, the loss occasioned by the death will fall upon the owner and not the carrier.

d. Act of Shipper. Examples of this would be damage caused by improper packing by the shipper or resulting from carrying out shipping instructions of the shipper. Thus, if a shipper elects to ship perishables without icing in the expectation of cool weather, the carrier is not responsible for any spoilage resulting from a change in weather conditions.

e. Exercise of Public Authority. The carrier is protected when goods are taken from him through proper processes of the law. The carrier is helpless against such acts as a seizure of goods by an officer of the law under a writ of attachment or in compliance with quarantine regulations.

[6] Ry. Express Agency v. Schoen, p. 706.

"The reason for such a rule is at once apparent; for to hold that a railroad company is bound to resist the lawful authority in protecting the goods of a shipper would be to lay down a doctrine dangerously approaching anarchy." *Southern R. Co.* v. *Heymann,* 118 Ga. 616

f. Delays Resulting from Causes beyond Carrier's Control. A common carrier does not have a law-imposed liability as an insurer to the extent of being responsible for delays in the delivery of goods. When there is loss or damage due to delay caused by factors beyond his control, such loss falls upon the owner of the property. The carrier will be held responsible only when the delay can be traced to his negligence.

"In the absence of special contract there is no absolute duty resting upon a railroad carrier to deliver the goods intrusted to it within what, under ordinary circumstances, would be a reasonable time. Not only storms and floods and other natural causes may excuse delay, but the conduct of men may also do so." *Geisner* v. *Lake Shore etc. R.,* 102 N.Y. 563

► V. LIMITATION OF LIABILITY BY CONTRACT

Many bailment contracts contain the stipulation that the goods are held by the bailee at the owner's risk. In some states, by contract with the bailor, a bailee may limit or entirely avoid liability that he would otherwise have.[7] The bailor can choose not to enter into the bailment relationship if he finds it desirable not to accept the bailee's limited liability.

The limitation of a bailee's liability is dependent upon an understanding to that effect between the bailor and bailee. Thus, it has been held that the mere posting of a notice denying liability for loss of a car by fire is not binding upon the bailor unless there was proof that he saw the notice.

A. LIMITATION OF LIABILITY BY CARRIERS

Common carriers have a limited right to contract away their law-imposed bailee liability. It is the generally accepted rule that a carrier may not avoid liability for loss or damage that results from its own negligence. However, liability for loss or damage due to other causes may be effectively limited or avoided by a contract between the shipper and carrier. Some states have enacted statutes or adopted constitutional provisions prohibiting carriers, or at least certain classes of carriers, from contracting away their extraordinary liability. As an example the Iowa statutes provide the following:

"Section 8042. No contract, receipt, rule, or regulation shall exempt any railway corporation engaged in transporting persons or property from the liability of a common carrier . . . which would exist had no contract, receipt, rule, or regulation been made or entered into."

[7] Kolt v. Cleveland Trust Co., p. 708; see also Malone v. Santora, p. 698.

1. *Limitation of Liability to Agreed Value*

In the majority of states, and by virtue of a federal statute, a carrier may, with exceptions, limit his liability to an agreed valuation. It is recognized that risk of loss is a factor determining the cost of transportation. Consequently, transportation charges will vary with the value of the article. The rate on a horse declared to have a $1,000 value would be higher than the rate on a mere $25 horse. If the risk of loss is greater, the compensation should also be greater. As the courts have said, where the agreed valuation is fair and reasonable and made for the purpose of furnishing a basis for the carrier's liability, it is conclusive and binding. It would tend to encourage dishonesty to allow the shipper to recover the true and actual value when a lesser valuation had been agreed upon.

CASES

CASE NO. 1

Malone v. Santora. 135 Conn. 286, 64 A. (2d) 51 (1949)

BROWN, J. The plaintiff in each of these cases sued the defendant to recover for damage to the plaintiff's automobile consequent upon its being stolen from the defendant's parking lot, where the plaintiff owner had left it and paid the required parking charge. In each case judgment was rendered for the plaintiff and the defendant has appealed.

The essential facts are undisputed and may be thus summarized: The plaintiff Johnson's car was stolen on the evening of November 22, 1946, and that of the plaintiff Malone on the evening of November 29, 1946. Each was subsequently recovered in damaged condition. . . . About 8 P.M. on November 22 the plaintiff Johnson drove her car into the lot, paid the defendant or one of his attendants the customary twenty-five-cent charge and left the car with him in response to his statement, "Leave your keys, I'll park the car." She left her keys in the car and he parked it. For the purpose of identification she was given a ticket, a detached part of which he placed on the car. On it was printed:

"Liability. Management assumes no responsibility of any kind. Charges are for use of Parking space until 11 P.M. Not responsible for cars left open after 11 P.M. You may lock your car."

She left and when she returned for her car shortly before 11 P.M. it could not be found. It had been stolen meantime. Upon her return the defendant and two attendants were there on duty. In accepting this car as he did, the defendant acted in the ordinary course of his business as a parking lot operator and in accord with his practice as to the car of the plaintiff and as to those of many others, not only upon that evening but upon other occasions also. It was his policy to insist that no one claiming a car should be allowed to drive it off the lot without first presenting the identifying ticket, unless the claimant was known to the defendant or his employees.

About 7 P.M. on November 29 the plaintiff Malone drove his car onto the parking lot, turned it over to one of the defendant's employees, paid the twenty-five-cent charge and received a ticket from the attendant, who placed the detached part of it on the car. The printing on the ticket was of the same purport as recited above. Malone put the ticket in his pocket without reading it and left. The attendant parked the car, leaving the key in the switch. Shortly before 10 P.M. Malone returned, presented the ticket to the attendant and demanded his car. It could not be found. Meantime a person had entered the lot and stated to one of the attendants that his brother was the owner of the car and that he had requested him to get the car for him. Malone had authorized no one to call for the car and the person making the request was an impostor and a thief. One of the attendants delivered the car to him and he drove it away. On that evening at least three attendants were on duty.

In each case the court concluded: There was a bailor and bailee relationship between the plaintiff and defendant; the wording on the ticket and sign did not bar the plaintiff's right of recovery; on the ground of public policy the bailment was not subject to the limitation on liability therein set forth; the defendant was negligent in the discharge of his duty as bailee; the plaintiff is entitled to recover for the damage accruing to his car, that of the plaintiff Johnson being $168 and that of the plaintiff Malone $400. Whether these conclusions are justified is the question determinative of these appeals.

In recent years there have been many decisions concerning the liability of operators of parking lots for cars parked thereon by customers. As has been well observed, cases of this nature may be divided into

> "two types: first, those where the attendant merely collects the fee and designates the area in which to park, the driver himself doing the parking and retaining complete control over the car, locking it or not as he wishes; and second, those lots, usually enclosed, where the attendants take complete charge of the car at the entrance, park it, retain the keys and move the car about as necessary, giving the driver a check or ticket, upon presentation of which they deliver the car to him." 27 Geo. L.J. 162, 163.

As this article goes on to point out, situations of the second type have usually been held to give rise to liability on the ground that the transaction is a bailment, while liability has been denied in those of the first, the courts holding that the lack of the essential element of possession in the lot operator renders the relationship one of a license or of a privilege to park rather than of bailment. . . .

Whether a car owner merely hires a place to put his car or has turned its possession over to the care and custody of the lot operator depends on the place, the conditions and the nature of the transaction. . . . Among the significant facts in each of the instant cases were these: The lot was inclosed, the defendant's attendants were present to attend to cars brought in to be parked; the plaintiff paid the parking charge to the attendant who gave him his claim ticket; the plaintiff left the switch key in the car at the request of the attendant who then took the car and parked it; no particular space for placing the car was either mentioned or contemplated. Under the principles which we have stated, it is clear that in each case these facts, without more, warranted, if in fact they did not require, the conclusion that the relationship between the plaintiff and the defendant was that of bailor and bailee. . . .

The defendant has assigned error in the court's conclusion that recovery was not barred by any limitation of liability in the ticket's provision or the wording of the sign. In so far as the Malone case is concerned, the fact that the plaintiff had no knowledge of the content of either shows that he did not assent to and could not have been bound by any such agreement. Maynard v. James, 109 Conn. 365, 370, 146 Atl. 614, 65 A.L.R. 427. In the Johnson case also there is good reason for concluding that one purpose for which the ticket was given and accepted was to afford a means of identification for the plaintiff in claiming her car and that it did not constitute a contract exempting the defendant from liability. The language of the ticket suggests that the defendant was charging the plaintiff only rental of space and assumed no responsibility of any kind. Since the plaintiff read the ticket she knew its terms. Had she herself parked the car on the lot, left it here and paid the charge, the transaction might have been regarded as constituting a case of the first type referred to above, with consequent immunity of the defendant from liability for theft of the car. Even so, the court's conclusion that the defendant was responsible under a bailor and bailee relationship was not necessarily unwarranted. An existing contract may be modified or abrogated by a new contract arising by implication from the conduct of the parties. 4 Page, Contracts (2d Ed.) § 2471. So here the defendant's subsequent assumption of control of the car, acquiesced in by the plaintiff, was totally inconsistent with an agreement of the first type and afforded reason for concluding that the contract actually made was one of bailment of which the provision exculpating the defendant from responsibility was no part. Actions may be held to speak louder than words, and the defendant's assumption of control of the car may be held to have negativated any intent by either party that an agreement for a license upon the terms indicated by the ticket should in fact arise. Upon the facts, what was in form such a contract lacked that intent to make it effective without which no true contract could come into existence. Davis v. Davis, 119 Conn. 194, 201, 175 Atl. 574.

We must regard the transaction in the Johnson case as giving rise to a bailment, and the provision against liability printed on the ticket could not avail the defendant to bar recovery by the plaintiff. This is so because of

> "the well-recognized rule that the right of a bailee to limit his liability by special contract does not go to the extent of relieving him against his own negligence." (Cases cited). . . .

The reason is that such a provision is

> "revolting to the moral sense, and contrary alike to the salutary principles of law and a sound public policy." Welch v. Boston & A.R. Co., 41 Conn, at page 342. . . .

There is no error in either case. . . .

CASE NO. 2

Theobald v. Satterthwaite. 30 Wash. (2d) 92, 190 P. (2d) 714, 1 A.L.R. 799 (1948)

MALLERY, CH.J. From a judgment in favor of the plaintiffs, the defendants appeal. Appellants Satterthwaite run a barber shop and beauty shop in the city of Tacoma under the name of the Crystal Palace Barber and Beauty Shop. It consists of a suite of three rooms, the back room being the barber shop, the middle room being the operating room of the beauty shop and the room facing the outside being a reception room.

No attendant was kept in the reception room and the interior of it was visible to outsiders through a glass door. Outsiders could not see into the operating room, nor could persons in the operating room see into the reception room. There was a sign in a conspicuous place in the shop which read: "Not responsible for hats, coats and purses."

The respondent Mae Theobald had patronized the beauty shop on a number of occasions previous to the day in question and knew the arrangement of the rooms. On a previous occasion she had inquired of appellant Helen Satterthwaite if the reception room was a safe place to leave her coat and had been assured that it was safe. Nothing had been stolen from the reception room in twenty years of operation and the hooks in that room were the only places provided for customers on which to hang their wraps. There was no bell or warning device on the door that sounded when it was opened. A thief could see into the reception room and if a garment hung there could open the door, take it off the hook and leave without being seen from the operating room.

On December 24, 1946, the respondent Mae Theobald came into the beauty shop by appointment to get a permanent wave. She sat in the reception room with her fur coat on until the appellant Helen Satterthwaite invited her into the operating room. Whereupon, she removed her coat as was natural and expected for the period while receiving her permanent wave. She hung it on a hook provided for wraps in the reception room. Neither of the appellants was aware that she had worn her fur coat on that day. When appellant Helen Satterthwaite had finished the work on respondent's hair, respondent went into the reception room to get her coat and found that it had been stolen. An alarm was given and the police were called but to no avail. She valued the coat at $300 for which amount the lower court gave her judgment upon the theory that the apellants were bailees of the coat and had been negligent in caring for it because of having furnished an unsafe place to leave it.

The appellants contend that they are not liable because there was no bailment. Respondent contends that there was a bailment and relies upon the rule in Bunnell v. Stern, 122 N.Y. 539, 25 N.E. 910, 911, 10 L.R.A. 481, 19 Am. St. Rep. 519. In that case a lady had gone to a clothing store to buy a cloak. In order to try on a new garment she took off her cloak and laid it down in the presence of store attendants some distance away from the mirror she used in her fitting. Of this the store employees had knowledge. After her fitting she returned for her coat and found it gone. The court said:

> "Under these circumstances we think that it became their duty to exercise some care for the plaintiff's cloak, because she had laid it aside upon their invitation, and *with their knowledge*, and, without question or notice from them, had put it in the only place that she could."

One of the cases discussed by the court in Bunnell v. Stern, supra, is Carpenter v. Taylor, 1 Hill, N.Y., 193, which the court said was not in point and distinguished it in this language:

> "In Carpenter v. Taylor, the plaintiff entered the saloon of a hotel to get refreshments between 12 and 1 o'clock at night, and when he went out the place was being closed. He left his opera glass behind, but it did not appear where, and the next morning when he called for it, it could not be found. As it did not appear that the defendant, or any of his servants ever received, or even saw, the glass, it was properly held that he was not responsible for its loss."

Thus in the case relied on by respondent, knowledge of the bailee's possession was held to be an essential factor to the existence of a bailment. Since in the instant case the appellants were unaware of the presence of the fur coat this element of knowledge brings them under the rule of Carpenter v. Taylor, supra, rather than under that of Bunnell v. Stern upon which respondent relies.

However we think there is another and better ground upon which the appellant must prevail. That is that there was no change of possession or delivery in this case. In defining bailment, 6 Am. Jur. 140 says:

> "In its broadest sense it has been said to include any *delivery* of personal property in trust for a lawful purpose."

While we are not inclined to view the element of delivery in any technical sense, still we think there can be no delivery unless there is a change of possession of an article from one person to another. Where property is stolen the loss will lie where it falls unless the owner can prove that it was due to the negligent act of another who had a duty of care with regard to it. The duty of care falls upon the bailee because he possesses the article and has the power of custody or control over it. This situation will not arise unless the owner parts with control over the article as a result of the bailee coming into possession of it. One who takes off a garment and deposits it in his own presence, as one would do in a restaurant, retains the power of surveillance and control in himself and the burden of care is not transferred with regard to such an article because the operators of the restaurant have not knowingly received the exclusive possession, and dominion over it. In the instant case the respondent may not have had an adequate opportunity for surveillance, nevertheless she had not transferred control of it to the appellants by a delivery and they were unaware that a valuable fur coat had been left in the reception room.

We therefore agree with appellants' contention that there was no bailment in this case because there was no change of possession of the coat and hence no delivery. It follows that, in the absence of a bailment, the appellants owed the respondent no duty or care and were not negligent in failing to guard it effectively.

The judgment is reversed.

CASE NO. 3

Marsh et al. v. American Locker Co., Inc. 7 N.J. Supra. 81, 72 A. (2d) 343 (1950)

JACOBS, S.J.A.D. This is an appeal from a judgment of dismissal entered in the Law Division at the close of the plaintiffs' case.

Mr. Irving Marsh was the only witness. He testified that he . . . had purchased costume jewelry in New York City invoiced at $2,743.70. The jewelry was in a package which he carried to the Pennsylvania Railroad Station, intending to take a train to Newark. . . . He saw a vacant locker in the large open space between the main waiting room and the outgoing trains, placed his package in the locker, and, after inserting a dime and turning the key, tried the door to see that it was locked and removed the key. Having used the lockers on earlier occasions he was familiar with their operation and, although he denied that he had read the contents, he knew that the front of the lockers bore directions as to the amount to be inserted and other written material. He had lunch, returned to obtain his package, inserted his key and found that the package was gone. He went to the Railroad baggage room and advised of his loss. . . . He thereafter filed a formal claim and was offered the sum of $10 which was refused. . . .

. . . the appellants rely mainly upon the contention that there was a common law bailment. . . .

Although conflicting views have been expressed by the authorities as to whether common law bailments necessarily arise out of contract they all recognize the need that there be possession of the property by the bailee. See 4 Williston, Contracts (Rev. Ed. 1936). . . . Determination as to where possession lies is ordinarily not difficult where exclusive physical control has been transferred to and assumed by the bailee. . . . However, it becomes troublesome as situations arise involving facts and considerations which depart from the traditional ones presented in the earlier cases . . . when dealing with the safe deposit cases, Professor Williston stresses that although the depositor is given a key

> "the box is left in a place which is wholly within the possession and control of the other party and not accessible to the depositor without the former's consent." Williston, supra, p. 2923 . . .

In Cornelius v. Berinstein, 183 N.Y. Misc. 685, 50 N.Y.S. (2d) 186 (Sup. Ct. 1944) Justice Searl in nonsuiting the plaintiff expressly applied the foregoing to support his conclusion that there was no bailment where the evidence indicated that the missing property had been placed by the plaintiff in his locker at the defendant's bowling center. The plaintiff had a key to the locker and the defendant had a master key which fit all of the several hundred lockers in the premises. . . .

The foregoing may be contrasted with the transaction before us. No human being acting on the defendant's behalf participated or received possession of the plaintiffs' property. The defendant had no means of knowing whether a package had been placed in the locker, whether Mr. Marsh had properly locked it or whether he had removed a package which he had placed therein. Through his exclusive operation of the locker and possession of the key, Mr. Marsh, rather than the defendant, retained primary physical control of the package. Although the defendant also had access for the purpose of removing property remaining more than twenty-four hours, this was not intended to and did not in fact operate to withdraw the primary control afforded to Mr. Marsh during his proper occupancy of the locker. . . .

We have reached the conclusion that the plaintiffs did not establish a common law bailment sufficient to withstand the defendant's motion of dismissal without any affirmative showing of negligence or other proof of contractual relationship between the parties. It seems to us that a contrary view would afford greater protection to those who choose to avail themselves of the automatic facilities at nominal charge than they ought reasonably anticipate and would subject the legitimate business operations of the defendant to claims of unlimited amount without knowledge of the facts or substantial opportunity of denial. . . .

CASE NO. 4

Ginsberg v. Kugler. 174 N.Y. Supp. 143 (1919)

BIJUR, J. Plaintiff delivered certain silk to defendant for manufacture into waists. While the silk was in defendant's possession, his premises were burglarized and the silk stolen. This action was brought to recover its value.

The sole question presented is whether the arrangement under which the silk was delivered constituted a bailment or a sale. It is conceded that, if the contract was of bailment, defendant is not liable, but that, if it was a sale, the judgment was right, and should be affirmed.

I think that upon plaintiff's own testimony the contract was one of bailment. He testified that he brought the defendant some silk and asked if he (defendant) "could manufacture some waists for me"; that the price fixed was $39 a dozen waists; that he "was supposed to sell" defendant the silk at $1.25 a yard; and that the price of the silk was to be credited against the contract price of the waists. The goods were sent to defendant with a memorandum, upon which appeared the words: "Sent to Alco Waist & Dress Co. for my use only, H. Kugler." And plaintiff further testified that the waists were to be manufactured for his use only, and delivered in two weeks.

From these facts it is quite clear that the defendant was bound under his contract to use the particular material delivered to him by the plaintiff for the latter's exclusive use, and to return it in the form of finished silk waists. The arrangement between the parties presents the familiar situation of a delivery of specific goods or property by one party to another for the performance of work thereon, with the obligation to return it in changed or improved form, which has always been held to constitute the party receiving it a bailee, as distinguished from a purchaser. The essential nature of the relation between the parties was not changed by the fact that the goods, as a matter of bookkeeping, were formally charged to defendant. . . .

CASE NO. 5

Greenlease-Lied Motors v. Sadler. 216 Iowa 302, 249 N.W. 383 (1933)

KINTZINGER, J. The plaintiff was engaged in the sale and distribution of Oldsmobile automobiles at Omaha, Neb. One Clayton Crowley was an automobile dealer at Council Bluffs, under the name of "Crowley Motors." One of Crowley's selling agents was one W. Johnson.

On the 11th of April, 1931, Mr. Johnson arranged for the sale of the Oldsmobile car on a cash basis, to the defendant John J. Sadler of Council Bluffs. Crowley did not have the model Sadler wanted, so on April 12 he went to the Greenlease-Lied Motors Company's salesrooms in Omaha for the purpose of getting possession of the kind of a car Sadler wanted . . . but with the specific understanding that he return the car or the cash received from the sale of it by 4 o'clock the same day.

When Crowley called on the plaintiff to get possession of the car, he told them that he had practically made a sale of this car for cash in Council Bluffs; that if they would allow him to take it out he would sell it and come back and pay them the cash or return the car by 4 o'clock that afternoon. . . .

Crowley then drove the car to Council Bluffs, and turned it over to Johnson to close the sale with Sadler on a cash basis with an allowance of $100 for a Dodge used car. . . .

. . . Johnson delivered the car, the registered assignment, and the license plates to defendant. Thereupon Sadler gave Johnson the Dodge car, a check for $177.90, and an assignment of an old judgment against Crowley which Sadler had secured from Carl M. Huber, for the balance.

Johnson then took the check, the

assigned judgment, the Dodge car, and a copy of the bill of sale, marked "Paid," to Crowley. Mr. Crowley never authorized Johnson to sell on that basis, and immediately after learning of the unauthorized sale he called at the defendant's store, returned the papers he had received from Johnson, and told Sadler he could not accept anything but cash for the car, as it belonged to the Greenlease-Lied Motors Company of Omaha. Appellant contends the transaction amounted to a conditional sale, that the agreement was not recorded, and therefore not binding on defendant, and that the sale vested title in defendant.

Appellee contends that the title in the car remained in the plaintiff: (1) Because the transaction between the plaintiff and Crowley made Crowley plaintiff's agent, and the title of the car was in the plaintiff, and that Crowley was only authorized to sell for cash; and (2) that the title of the car never, in fact, passed to the defendant because neither Crowley nor his agent Johnson had any authority to sell the car upon any other terms than on a cash basis. . . .

The lower court found from the evidence as a matter of fact that the plaintiff company did not intend to part with the title of the car in any manner unless and until they received the cash therefor, that the title of the car never did pass to Crowley, and that Crowley in effect became and was the agent of the plaintiff for the purpose of sale, and that he had no authority to sell except on a cash basis. . . .

The definition of a "conditional sales contract" and an agreement creating a "bailment and agency" is set out in the case of Donnelly v. Mitchell, 119 Iowa 432, 93 N.W. 369, 371. In that case, speaking through McClain, J., we said:

"To constitute a conditional sale within the terms of the statute, there must be a delivery of possession to the purchaser, with the intention of passing immediate ownership . . . subject only to the reservation of title to the seller as security for the purchase money. . . . If the contract is conditional as to the transfer ownership to the vendee, so that on his failure to perform the condition no right as owner has passed to him, and no definite obligation to pay the purchase price has accrued, then, instead of the transaction being a conditional sale, such as is contemplated by the statute, the delivery of possession constitutes a bailment only, with a right of purchase. In such a case the vendee has only an executory and conditional agreement for purchase, and until he exercise his right under such agreement he remains merely a bailee."

In the case at bar there was no binding agreement on the part of Crowley to pay for the automobile. The facts in this case show that the car in question was delivered to him for the purpose of sale to a prospective purchaser, and that he, out of the proceeds of the sale, was to pay the plaintiff the cash proceeds of the sale, less his commission. If there was no such sale made the car was to be returned to the plaintiff by 4 o'clock the same day.

We believe that under the peculiar nature of the transaction between plaintiff and Crowley, the question of whether the transaction amounted to a conditional sale, or created an agency and bailment, was for the jury. . . .

"The primary test as to the character of a contract, as to whether it constitutes a contract of sale or one of agency, is the intention of the parties gathered from the whole scope and effect of the language employed, and in doubtful cases the question must be determined upon a review of all that passed between the parties, before and contemporaneously with the dealings under consideration, and is generally a question of fact to be determined by a jury." 52 C.J. 43. . . .

We believe that was sufficient evidence to warrant a jury in finding that Crowley was plaintiff's agent in the transaction. . . .

. . . judgment . . . affirmed.

CASE NO. 6

Railway Express Agency v. Schoen. 70 Ariz. 87, 216 P. (2d) 420 (1950)

UDALL, J. J. Schoen, as plaintiff (appellee), brought suit against the A.T. & S.F. Railway Company and the Railway Express Agency to recover damages in the sum of $2,009 alleged to have been suffered by him in connection with a shipment of some twenty cartons of merchandise (principally costume jewelry) weighing approximately 1,200 pounds. The amended complaint alleged that the shipment arrived at Holbrook, Arizona

"in such a damaged condition as to be wholly valueless, and many items of said shipment were missing" and that this was caused "as a result of the careless and negligent handling by the defendants."

The case was tried to the court sitting without a jury. The trial court held the plaintiff had not established his claim as to the articles alleged to be missing but had established the damaged condition of the shipment. Judgment was thereupon entered for the plaintiff against (1) the Santa Fe for the sum of $120.40 (which award was based upon the declared value of the shipment) . . . and (2) against the Railway Express Agency for the sum of $1,028.88. This appeal is by the latter defendant only. . . .

The evidence, stated in the light most favorable to a sustaining of the judgment shows that about May 1, 1946, the plaintiff delivered to defendant (appellant) at Bergenfield, New Jersey, the shipment in question for transportation by it to Dallas, Texas. The goods were consigned to the shipper in care of defendant with instructions to hold the same at Dallas until called for. The goods arrived at that destination safely and were thereafter stored by defendant as a warehouseman in its "on hand department." . . . Stored in this department are all the goods received by defendant which are not to be delivered in Dallas. As this department was then stored to its approximate capacity with goods, two cartons, out of the twenty containing plaintiff's shipment, were placed on the floor as there was not sufficient storage space in the bins provided for that purpose.

The record further shows that during the night of May 28–29, 1946, there occurred a tremendous and unprecedented storm in Dallas. There were 6.22 inches of rainfall during a 24-hour period and 4.27 inches of this fell within a 2-hour period. This was the heaviest rainfall experienced in Dallas since the establishment of the weather bureau there in 1913. By reason of the downpour, water seeped into the basement through the doors and windows. The wind reached a velocity of 47 miles per hour and as a result of the storm the electric power for lighting and other purposes failed and was not restored until 8 A.M. the following morning. The basement used by defendant is so constructed that artificial lighting is required at all times. With the power failure defendant's employees were unable to carry on their duties.

The next morning the two cartons of plaintiff's shipment that were on the basement floor were thoroughly watersoaked. They were taken to another room, the contents removed, dried, and repacked, and there is no claim this salvage operation was not promptly and skillfully done.

Early in September, 1946, in accordance with plaintiff's instructions, his stored goods were shipped via freight to him at Holbrook, Arizona. The shipment arrived in a somewhat dilapidated condition and the owner, seeing for the first time the damage to his goods, commenced this litigation with the result heretofore stated.

. . . The defendant contends the sole and only cause of the damage sustained was the torrential storm which could not have been foreseen or provided against by defendant. The law controlling in such a situation is well stated in the case of H. A. Johnson & Co. v. Springfield Ice & Refrigerating Co., 143 Mo. App. 441, 127 S.W. 692, 697:

> "The defendant cannot escape the consequences of its negligence because the flood was an act of God. It is a well-settled principle that, if the defendant's negligence commingled with and operated as a contributive element proximate to the injury, it is liable even though such injury was due to an act of God. In order for the defendant to escape liability under the exemption afforded by law, the act of God *must be the sole* and only cause of the injury, and this, too, unmixed with the negligence of the defendant, for if the defendant's negligence commingled with it in the loss as an active and co-operative element, and the loss is proximate thereto, or, in other words, is a reasonable consequence of the negligent act, it is regarded in law as the act of the defendant rather than as the act of God. . . ." (Emphasis supplied)

See also 67 C.J., Warehouseman and Safe Depositaries, § 84.

During the period of nearly four months that defendant held plaintiff's goods stored in its warehouse in Dallas it held them as a warehouseman, not as a carrier, and hence its liability must be determined under the law of bailments.

A warehouseman is not an "insurer" but is a bailee for hire, and is held to that degree of care which a reasonably careful man would exercise in regards to similar goods of his own. In other words he is bound to exercise only ordinary diligence or a "reasonable" degree of prudence in caring for the goods stored.

Applying these principles of law to the facts in the instant case it is apparent that the plaintiff has wholly failed to establish negligence on the part of the defendant unless it can be said that leaving two of plaintiff's cartons on the floor constituted negligence per se. There is not a scintilla of evidence as to any other act that might be termed negligence on defendant's part. . . .

The testimony in this case, wholly uncontradicted, shows one of the most violent and extraordinary rainstorms ever known in Dallas. The evidence further shows that the storm was wholly unanticipated. There was no evidence that water had ever entered the storage basement before or that defendant had any reason to foresee that water would get into the basement or cause damage to goods resting upon the floor of the warehouse. There is no showing that there was anything unusual or improper in permitting stored goods to remain on the floor rather than to be placed in bins, or that any loss had ever been sustained previously by such practice. This significant statement appears in the United Produce Co. case, supra (279 Ky. 519, 131 S.W. (2d) 472):

> "Men are not called upon to guard against every risk that they may conceive as possible but only against what they can forecast as probable."

We hold that inasmuch as there was no contrariety in the facts as to so-called acts of negligence by defendant, but one reasonable legal conclusion can be drawn therefrom, i.e., that the plaintiff failed to prove his case.

As there is nothing in the record to indicate that defendant failed to exercise that degree of care with respect to the storage of plaintiff's goods that a reasonably prudent owner would have exercised under like circumstances, the judgment is reversed with directions to enter judgment for the defendant Railway Express Agency. . . .

CASE NO. 7

Kolt v. Cleveland Trust Co. 93 N.E. (2d) 788 (Ohio) (1950)

SKEEL, J. This appeal comes to this court on questions of law from a judgment for the plaintiffs entered upon the verdict of a jury in the Court of Common Pleas of Cuyahoga County. The plaintiff's action was for the recovery of money which he alleged he had placed in the night depository or vault of the Superior and East 123rd Street branch office of the defendant, and when called for was not returned because it could not be found.

The plaintiff, a retail meat dealer, by virtue of a contract with defendant had been accustomed to using the night depository facilities of defendant at its East 123 and Superior Avenue branch to make deposits of money and checks after banking hours, the deposits being made usually on Saturday night and on nights just preceding holidays.

For the purpose of receiving night deposits, the bank had installed a night depository vault. There was a small metal door placed in the outer wall of the East 123rd Street side of the banking rooms. This door was fitted with a locking device which could be opened only by the use of a key but which could be locked shut simply by completely closing the door. On the inside of this opening there was a metal chute about three feet long which led into a safe within the banking rooms. The top of this chute located just inside the outer metal door above described had a swinging door placed horizontally across the top constructed very much like the receiving door of a package or parcel mail box used by the United States Post Office Department.

The manner in which the night depositor would make his deposit was by first opening the outside door by the use of a key furnished by the bank. He would then pull down the swinging inner door at the top of the chute which would bring up a shelf completely closing the end of the chute. He would then put his deposit on such shelf and release the inner door which would swing up, closing the chute and drop the shelf down so that when the door was closed the deposit would fall through the chute and into the vault or safe.

Entrance to the safe or vault was controlled by a combination lock which could only be used after it was unlocked by a key. The duty of unlocking this safe or vault at a specified time was delegated to two employees—one who had the key, and the other who was given the combination, both of whom were required to be present at all times when the vault door was opened.

The right to use the night depository facilities was controlled by contract. The plaintiff entered into a written contract with the defendant on Jan. 16, 1946, whereby for a consideration of twenty-five cents for each "sack placed in the night chute" with a minimum charge of $1.00 per month, the plaintiff was given the right to make use of the night deposit facilities of defendant at East 123 and Superior Avenue branch.

. . . The contract in part provided:

"The undersigned hereby agrees to use the Night Depository Facilities only for overnight keeping of sacks, which sacks shall contain nothing other than currency or commercial paper, or both, and further agrees that a person authorized by the undersigned will call at the bank to receive and receipt for said sack(s) on the first banking day following each placing by or on behalf of the undersigned of any sack in the Night Chute. Bank shall have no duty or obligation whatsoever to see that the contents or and part thereof of any sack is tendered for deposit for credit to any account with Bank, nor to ascertain the contents or disposition of contents of any sack receipted for by any authorized person.

"The undersigned expressly understands and agrees that each use or attempted use by the undersigned of the Night Depository Facilities shall be at the undersigned's sole risk at all times and further expressly understands and agrees that the relationship of debtor and creditor between Bank and undersigned shall not arise out of any use or attempted use of the Night Depository Facilities, each separate use by the undersigned of the Night Depository Facilities being deemed to have been completed each time any sack hereinabove listed found in the Night Receptacle by Bank is receipted for by any authorized person."

The contract also provided who should call at the bank the next business day after the night deposit had been made and take possession of the deposit bag or sack. David T. Kolt and Alfred Rafal, in addition to Aaron A. Kolt were so designated.

The sacks provided under the contract were provided with a padlock, the depositor holding the only key. The depositor would place his deposit in the sack, lock it and then with the use of the key to the night chute, deposit it as above described. When the bank opened the next business day, the employees designated would open the night deposit vault in the presence of each other and one would take out the sacks and the other would make a record of the number of each bag or sack thus found in the night vault and the bag or sack would then be taken to the cashier's cage of the one holding the key to the night vault, there to await being called for by the several depositors.

The plaintiff's petition alleges that on the night of March 15, 1947, he, with Alfred Rafal, placed a deposit of money and checks, totaling $1,772.00 . . . together with Rafal's deposit of a smaller amount and together they went to the bank, unlocked the outer door, opened the chute, placed the sack which was then wrapped in a paper bag, on the shelf of the inner door, shut the inner door so that the sack would fall into the vault below and then locked the outer door and departed.

On March 17, 1947, at about 10 o'clock A.M. Rafal called at the bank to get the sack but it was not to be found nor was there any record of Sack No. 29 being found with the other night deposits.

Upon trial, the court charged the jury that the only question for their consideration is whether or not the plaintiff had established by a preponderance of the evidence that he had placed the deposit in the night deposit vault.

It is defendant's contention that . . . by the contract (in part above quoted) deposits made thereunder were to be at the depositor's risk. . . .

Of necessity, no one representing the bank is present when a night deposit is made. Whether such deposit has actually been made must be established in every event by the evidence of the depositor. It would therefore be a very natural position of the bank to take that until the sack is actually accounted for by the bank's clerks in the ordinary procedure of accounting for night deposits sacks, such deposits should be at the risk of the depositor. Such a contract is not void as against public policy. . . .

Where the circumstances are such that the possession of another's property is attended with unusual risks, the parties dealing at arm's length as free agents may lawfully make any reasonable provision therefor as the circumstances justify.

Contracts relieving the promisor from liability even for his negligence have been upheld on the broad grounds of freedom of contract guaranteed by the federal and state constitutions. For example, as between landlord and tenant, it has been held that the relationship is not a matter of public interest but relates exclusively to the private affairs of the parties concerned and that the two parties stand upon equal terms. 175 A.L.R. 87, par. 46, Perry v. Payne, 217 Pa. 252, 66 Atl. 553, 11 L.R.A., N.S., 1173, 10 Ann. Cas. 589; Kirshenbaum v. General Outdoor Adv. Co., 258 N.Y. 489, 180 N.E. 245, 247, 84 A.L.R. 645

The right of the bank to immunity from whatever cause except its wilful wrongdoing in furnishing night deposit services under the terms of an exculpatory agreement is supported in theory at least by the almost universal rule that a common carrier (railroad) may by contract relieve itself from liability even for its negligence or that of its servants or employees in the construction and use of private sidings and spur tracks.

The case law of bailment supports the same principles of law. Again quoting from 175 A.L.R. p. 110, par. 55 the author says:

"The modern development of the law of bailments and its extension to many new and varied transactions as a result of the increasing complexity of today's commercial relationships is reflected accurately in the position the courts take in regard to the exculpatory clauses found so frequently in bailment contracts. While the right of the ordinary bailee to make a contract exempting him from liability due to his negligence or the negligence of his employees is recognized with practical unanimity, *a strong tendency to hold such contracts void as violative of public policy is noticeable in the decisions of the courts which deal with contracts of bailment for hire entered into by the bailee in the course of a general dealing with the public; and this tendency becomes more pronounced the more recent the decisions,* although there is still respectable authority for the view that such provision may be valid against all but gross negligence. Bailees of the second type as this term is understood here, are persons who make it their principal business to act as bailee and who deal with the public on a uniform and not an individual basis as evidenced by the fact that their contracts as a rule are printed on identification tokens or are posted in their place of business. The chief representatives of this type of bailees are owners of parcel checkrooms, owners of parking places, garagemen and warehousemen." . . .

The method devised by the defendant for safeguarding deposit sacks properly placed in the night deposit chute exemplified a high degree of care and protection for the property of depositors, and the manner in which these precautions were carried out in the first business day after the claimed use of the night deposit facilities by the plaintiff is not refuted by the plaintiff except by his claim that the deposit sack was put in the chute.

The plaintiff's action is upon the contract, the terms of which places the risk upon him until actually receipted for. As indicated, the manner in which night deposits must of necessity be made, should permit the defendant to protect itself within reasonable limits.

We conclude, therefore, that the court's charge entirely eliminating the contract from the consideration of the jury, was in error. . . .

Review Questions

1. What are the elements of a bailment?
2. Construct a fact situation illustrating a bailment where there has been no actual delivery of the property by the bailor to the bailee.
3. Illustrate a bailment where the bailee does not in fact take possession of the property.
4. What is the basic distinction between a bailment and a sale?
5. How do bailments in respect to grain differ from the basic concept of a bailment transaction?
6. Is a consignment for sale a bailment?
7. Under what circumstances might it be desirable to employ a contract of consignment?
8. Illustrate (a) a bailment for the sole benefit of the bailor, (b) a bailment for the sole benefit of the bailee, and (c) a bailment for mutual benefit of the bailor and the bailee.
9. To what extent is a bailee liable for injury to the property when he has exceeded his authority to deal with the property?
10. What is the test of a common carrier?
11. In what respect does the liability of a common carrier bailee differ from that of a contract carrier bailee?
12. What are the exceptions to a common carrier's extraordinary liability?
13. Can an ordinary bailee limit his liability by contract with his bailor?
14. To what extent may common carrier bailees limit their liability by contract?

Problems for Discussion

1. X rented a safety deposit box of the Y bank, in which he placed his securities. Is the Y bank a bailee?
2. Plaintiff's property disappeared from a locker which he had rented for the season from the defendant bowling alley operator. Plaintiff seeks to hold defendant liable as a bailee. Decide. (*Cornelius* v. *Berinstein,* 50 N.Y.S. (2d) 186)
3. Plaintiff while inspecting the fit of a pair of trousers which he was contemplating purchasing left his trousers in a dressing booth which was provided by the defendant for such purpose. A valuable diamond ring disappeared from the fob pocket of plaintiff's trousers while they were in the dressing room. Is the defendant liable as a bailee? (*Hunter* v. *Reed,* 12 Pa. Super. 112)
4. A merchant provides a parking lot for the convenience of his customers. Is he a bailee of the cars parked there?

5. The defendant, a resident of Midland, made a special agreement with the plaintiff, a hotel-keeper, to board at his hotel for a certain sum per day. He remained there about 10 months, paying at the agreed rate. A few days before leaving, his overcoat was stolen from his room by a person who was not in the employ of the plaintiff. The plaintiff brought an action to recover $40.00, the balance due by the defendant for board and lodging, and the defendant counterclaimed to the same amount for damages for loss of his coat. Decide. (*Katz* v. *Noland,* 50 C.L.J. [Eng.] 193)
6. The plaintiff while trying on hats at the defendant's store placed her handbag under her own hat upon the store counter. Later when she picked up her hat the handbag was gone. There was no evidence that the clerk knew that the plaintiff had a handbag. Is the defendant liable as a bailee? (*Powers* v. *O'Neil,* 34 N.Y.S. 1007)
7. Plaintiff, a manufacturer, received an order for goods to be delivered to the defendant's place of business. X, an unknown person, and not the defendant, had placed the order. After the goods had been delivered to the defendant, he received a telephone call to the effect that the goods had been sent to the wrong address and would be called for. X called for the goods, professing to be acting in behalf of the plaintiff. Is the defendant liable as a bailee? (*Krumsky* v. *Loeser,* 37 Misc. 504)
8. As a neighborly gesture, A volunteered to gratuitously keep and care for B's valuable pedigreed dog during B's absence. A disregarded B's feeding instructions, and as a result the dog died. Is A liable to B.
9. Hanson "contracted" to sell Jensen twenty-five tires and, as he had only ten tires on hand, he "borrowed" fifteen from Overton, agreeing to return fifteen like tires upon receipt of his next tire shipment. After receiving his next shipment of tires but before returning any tires to Overton, Hanson was forced into bankruptcy. Overton claims fifteen tires under a contract of bailment. Decide.
10. During her lifetime A let B have 200 shares of corporate stock which B needed as collateral to secure his personal obligation at a bank. A written memorandum described the transaction thus: "I have this day let B have 200 shares of X stock which he needs as collateral." B resists a return of 200 shares to the estate of A upon the contention that the transaction was a debt and not a loan of specific property, since the certificates were indorsed in blank and a return of the specific certificates was never contemplated. Decide.
11. The defendant kept a garage. In other words, he occupied a building in which he rented space for the storage of automobiles. Some of the storage was "dead"; that is, cars not in use were deposited there, put away sometimes for the season. Other storage was "live"; that is, the storage of cars in active daily use. The plaintiff was a "live storage" customer. In the case of live storage, the customer could put his car in and take it out daily at will, at any hour of the day or night. Each customer was given a key, and after the garage was locked up at midnight he could open the door to put his car in or take it out. The patrons of the garage all knew this and knew that it was the custom of the establishment. Several patrons were physicians, and it was virtually essential for them to have unrestricted access to the garage; otherwise they could not patronize the place. Is this a bailment? (*Hogan* v. *O'Brien,* 206 N.Y.S. 831)

12. A garage owned and operated by defendant in the city of Grand Junction was destroyed by fire January 22, 1918. Plaintiff owned an automobile which was destroyed in this fire. In an action for damages therefor he obtained a verdict and judgment.

    The garage in question was heated by a furnace located under the center of the main floor. That portion of the floor directly over the furnace, and there constituting the ceiling of the furnace room, was of wood. Upon it cars were stored, and it was more or less oil soaked. Within five feet of the furnace door was a wooden post extending from the floor of the furnace room to the ceiling. The night was cold and there was a good fire in the furnace. The "night man" or "watchman" who had charge of the furnace was a high-school boy who slept in the repair shop. Ashes had been raked out of the furnace that night and allowed to remain about the post above mentioned. From them the fire started, climbed this post to the main floor, and first broke through the roof directly above.

    No other reasonable theory of the origin of the fire can be formulated from the evidence. If this evidence was believed by the jury, it was sufficient to make it fairly certain that the fire was caused by the negligence of defendants or their employees. It rebuts the probability that the fire originated in any other manner.

    Defendants pleaded, and offered to prove, release of liability by contract consisting of a sign two feet square posted over the repair room in the garage, which sign stated that they would not be liable for loss by fire. Decide. (*Parris* v. *Jaquith,* 70 Colo. 63)
13. Rowe borrowed Ware's car to take his wife to the station. At the station he met his friend Nodland and invited him to take a ride. While enroute to a tavern, Rowe was stopped by armed bandits and the car was taken from him. What is his liability to Ware?
14. A delivers grain to the B elevator under an agreement that he is to have the option of later taking delivery of a like amount of grain or accepting the market price. Before he exercises the option, the elevator burns. What are A's rights?
15. In *Hyde* v. *Cookson,* 21 Barb. 92, there was a written agreement between the plaintiffs and one Osborn in relation to tanning a quantity of hides. The hides were to be furnished by the plaintiffs on a commission of 5 per cent for buying, and 6 per cent for selling, the leather. Osborn was to take the hides to his tannery, manufacture them into hemlock sole leather, and return it to the plaintiffs, who were to sell it in their discretion. When sold, the account was to be made up and the net proceeds of the sales, after deducting the costs of hides, commissions, interest, insurance, and other expenses, were to be the profit or loss to accrue to Osborn in full for tanning the hides. Does Osborn have title to the hides while in his possession?
16. A shipped fruit over the B railroad in late summer. The fruit was damaged by frost which was unusually early. Is the B railroad liable?
17. A tendered a shipment of goods to a common carrier giving detailed routing instructions. Due to the negligence of one of the carrier's employees, the instructions were not followed. The goods were destroyed while en route by an unprecedented flood. Is the carrier liable to A for the value of the goods?

28 PERSONAL PROPERTY AND RELATED TOPICS:

SECURITY INTERESTS IN PERSONAL PROPERTY

It is a fact of common knowledge that for varying reasons obligors will not or cannot at times meet their personal obligations. To compensate for this aggravating human deficiency and to aid business transactions, various legal and commercial devices have been developed whereby personal property can be charged with the obligation in the event that the obligor fails to discharge his personal debt. The creditor's right to obtain satisfaction of his claim from the personal property of the debtor may arise either by operation of law or by contract arrangement.

These security interests in personal property are, broadly speaking, designated as *liens* or *encumbrances*. However, in the restricted and technically legal sense of the word, liens are such security rights as are bestowed under certain circumstances upon the creditor by law rather than by any arrangements he has entered into with his debtor or with the owner of the property. The commercially important devices whereby a security interest is created by contract are (1) the pledge or pawn contract, (2) the chattel mortgage, (3) the conditional sales contract, and (4) the relatively modern device of the trust receipt.

► I. LIENS

A. NATURE OF LIENS

Although the subject matter of liens is today quite thoroughly covered by statutory enactment, the lien originated and developed as a common law security device. Modern lien statutes are not only a general declaration of the common law but also serve in many instances to change the common law concept of a lien as well as to extend greatly the application of the principle of lien security.

The common law concept of a lien is the right of certain classes of bailees to *retain* possession of the bailed property as security for an obligation. The common law lien has three basic characteristics: (1) it applies to personal property only; (2) it is dependent upon possession and the retention of possession; (3) it consists of the right of retention only until the obligation is discharged.

It should be recognized that the bailee may waive his rights of lien.[1]

B. TYPES OF PROPERTY SUBJECT TO LIEN

Whereas common law liens arise only in relation to personal property, many statutory enactments have extended the right of lien to real property as well. Il-

[1] Wilson v. Malenock, p. 731.

lustrative of such is the *mechanic's lien,** which gives persons who have furnished materials or labor for the improvement of real property a claim upon such property as a security for payment.

C. REQUIREMENT OF POSSESSION

Like many statutory liens, a common law lien is dependent upon the continued possession of the property by the claimant.[2] The lien is in effect the mere right to retain the property in possession until the obligation is discharged and a voluntary surrender of possession cancels the lien. By virtue of modern statutes, a creditor may, in certain instances, retain his right of lien even though he has surrendered possession of the property. To protect his claim upon the property, however, he must file notice of the lien in the public records. Some statutes make provision for the attaching of a lien without the need of the property ever to have been in the possession of the creditor. An illustration of this is the statutory *landlord's lien* to secure the payment of rent. The lien attaches to all property used or kept upon the premises and, in the case of agricultural lands, upon all crops grown.

D. ENFORCEMENT OF LIEN

A common law lien consists of the mere right to retain possession of the property until the obligation is discharged. In the absence of an agreement, the creditor does not have the right to sell the property and apply the proceeds to the satisfaction of the debt—to do so without the consent of the owner would constitute a conversion of the property. The lien holder's only recourse is to resort to the proper legal procedure for the satisfaction of his claim. For example, he can reduce the claim to a judgment and then levy upon the property held so that it can be sold by judicial proceedings. Holders of statutory liens are generally given the right to sell the property that has been impressed with a lien. There is such a diversity of statutory procedure for the enforcement of liens that a generalization should not be relied upon.

E. CLASSIFICATION OF COMMON LAW LIENS

Under common law, certain classes of bailees have the right to retain possession of chattels as security for an obligation due them. These common law liens are of two types, either special or general. *Special liens* are those under which the creditor has the right of possession as security for the compensation due under the contract of bailment and not for general balances due. The *general lien* gives the creditor a claim upon the property for all obligations due him—past, present, or those that may arise in the future.

1. *Special Liens*

a. Bailees Engaged in Public Callings. Historically the right of the common law lien was first recognized as existing only for those engaged in a public calling—

---

* See p. 824.

[2] Clarksburg Casket Co. v. Valley Undertaking Co., p. 732.

common carriers, warehousemen, and innkeepers * who had dedicated themselves to serve the general public. It was logically reasoned that, since those engaged in rendering public services were not free to choose with whom they could deal and since they were required to serve all to the full extent of their facilities, they should have the right to retain the subject matter of the contract of bailment in their possession as security for their compensation.

> "It cannot be denied that the innkeeper's liability for the loss of goods of his guest is extraordinary and exceptional. Compelled to afford entertainment to whomsoever may apply and behave with decency, the law, as an indemnity for the extraordinary liabilities which it imposes, has clothed the innkeeper with extraordinary privileges. It gives him, as a security for unpaid charges, a lien upon the property of his guest, and upon goods put by the guest into his possession." *Cook* v. *Kane,* 13 Ore. 482

b. Artisans' Liens.

> "It may now be laid down as a general rule, that every bailee for hire who by his labor and skill has imparted an additional value to the goods, has a lien upon the property for his reasonable charges. This includes all such mechanics, tradesmen and laborers as receive property for the purpose of repairing, or otherwise improving its condition." *Grinnell* v. *Cook,* 3 Hill (N.Y.) 485

The common law lien does not extend to bailees who do not enhance the value of the property in their possession by their services. Thus, a bailee for storage has no common law lien, and an accountant would have no lien upon books placed in his possession for examination.[3]

2. *General Liens*

A general lien consists of the right to retain possession of the property of a creditor to secure the total obligation due, regardless of whether the obligation arose in relation to the property. The right of general lien exists as a matter of common law only in favor of attorneys-at-law, bankers, doctors, brokers, and wharfingers.

F. SCOPE OF STATUTORY LIENS

The right of lien has been greatly extended by legislative enactment.[4] Little value can be derived from an enumeration of any of the many special liens created by statute. The statutes of the particular jurisdiction should be consulted. It is suggested that, if possible, the nature of the liens existing in a predominantly industrial and commercial state be compared with those in a typical agricultural state. Such would clearly demonstrate that the particular needs of the individual community are the factors motivating legislation.

---

* Local statutes should be consulted as to the rights and duties of innkeepers.

[3] Graben Motor Co. v. Brown Garage Co., p. 732.

[4] State ex rel. McConnell v. People's Bank & T. Co., p. 733.

▶ II. PLEDGES

A. NATURE OF PLEDGE

The *pledge* or *pawn* is a bailment whereby the bailee, for the express purpose of securing a debt or obligation due him, receives possession of personal property belonging either to the debtor or another. Although the term *pawn* has the same legal significance as *pledge,* through common usage it has taken on a restricted meaning. To the American public, a pawn has come to mean a method of raising cash by "hocking" tangible personal effects, usually in a pawnshop. These transactions are in essence no different from the securing of a debt by pledging stocks, bonds, insurance policies, pass books, negotiable documents of title such as bills of lading and warehouse receipts, or various other negotiable instruments. Apart from the pawnshop trade, tangible property is little used in the commercial world as a basis for pledges. Because of the impracticability of taking and retaining possession of tangible property as security for commercial transactions, the chattel mortgage is usually employed as a means of establishing a security right in this type of property. The use of intangibles—choses in action—as collateral security is indispensable to trade and industry.

B. NECESSARY ELEMENTS

A contract of pledge exists if the following elements are present:

(1) The pledgee must have possession of the property;

(2) the purpose of the possession must be to secure the payment of a debt or the performance of an obligation due the pledgee;

(3) the legal title must remain with the pledgor; and

(4) the pledgor must have a right to redeem the property.

1. *Possession*

Just as under the common law lien, the right of security under a pledge agreement is dependent upon the pledgee having and retaining continuous possession of the property. A voluntary release of the property by the pledgee operates as a release of his security interest in the property and makes it possible for creditors of the pledgor to levy upon it. Placing the pledgor even temporarily in possession of the property makes possible a sale or pledge to an innocent purchaser; such a sale would effectively defeat the right of the creditor to look to the property for satisfaction.

Not every release of possession will nullify the security interest in the property. The courts recognize that a surrender of possession to the pledgor under special circumstances does not defeat the pledgee's security right. It has been held that the pledgee's security title in the property is not destroyed by a surrender of the pledged property to the pledgor for repair purposes or for the purpose of having it sold for the benefit of the pledgee. Likewise, if the pledgor acts as the agent of the pledgee in taking collateral security for purposes of collection, the pledgee's security interest is not defeated by the surrender of possession.

C. DEBT OR OBLIGATION SECURED

As a rule, the contract of pledge is evidenced by the terms of a negotiable instrument, usually a promissory note. Generally such a note is also evidence of the obligation that the pledge agreement secures. Unless otherwise provided, the pledged property secures only the obligation evidenced by the note. The commercial practice, however, is to make the pledge all inclusive, so that it serves as security for all existing obligations as well as those that might arise in the future.

1. *Transfer of Debt*

Whether or not it is evidenced by a negotiable or nonnegotiable contract, a claim to money and the property given as security can be transferred by the pledgee to a third person. This is generally known as the *pledgee's right to repledge the property.* Unless the pledgor and pledgee have agreed to the contrary, the security will follow the obligation.

It depends upon the terms of the pledge agreement whether an all-inclusive pledge—one covering both existing and future obligations—will operate in favor of the transferee. If the pledge provision in a note reads that the pledged property is to cover future obligations to the *payee,* the provision will not extend to a subsequent holder of the instrument. However (as is usually the case), if the note provides that this right is to rest with the holder or the owner of the instrument, the right operates for the benefit of all subsequent transferees. Such a note generally reads:

> ". . . having deposited with said bank and pledged as collateral security for the payment hereof and of all other debts and liabilities to *the owner hereof* due or to become due."

D. RIGHTS AND DUTIES OF PLEDGEE

1. *Duty as Bailee*

As a bailee of the property, the pledgee is required by law to exercise the proper care against loss or damage. He is liable only for any loss or damage resulting from his negligent conduct. The pledgee has no duty to the pledgor to see that the value of the property is preserved. He may stand by idly and witness the collateral decline in value, and this is true even if the agreement gives the pledgee the right to sell in the event that the collateral declines in value to a certain extent. The power to sell is said to be a right and not a duty.[5]

If the security is in the form of negotiable paper, the pledgee, however, is obligated to take such steps as are necessary to preserve the liability of the obligors whose names appear upon the paper. Thus, upon maturity, presentment for payment would be the pledgee's duty, and in the event of dishonor he would be required to give notice to parties having a secondary liability. And it would likewise devolve upon the pledgee to take legal action for the enforcement of the paper before the period of limitations expires.

[5] First Nat. Bank v. Hattaway, p. 734.

2. *Right to Income from Property*

As a general rule, it can be asserted that the pledgee has the right to the income from, or the natural increase of, the property held in pledge. The pledgee takes such derivative property as part of the pledge and is held accountable for it to the pledgor to the same extent as for the property that originally constituted the pledge. Thus, a pledgee would acquire additional security by a biological multiplication of pledged livestock or the cashing of interest coupons on a bond held as security. Whenever an assignment of a stock certificate is accompanied by a power of attorney as a means of accomplishing a transfer upon the books of the corporation, there is no question about the pledgee's right to the dividends.

3. *Right of Reimbursement*

At times a pledgee finds it necessary to make essential expenditures in connection with the pledged property. The pledgee has the right to be reimbursed for all expenses that are reasonably necessary for the care and preservation of the property held as security. Illustrations of essential expenditures are necessary repairs to tangible property, payment of taxes and assessments, payment of an installment due on corporate stock, and payment of the premium to preserve the insurance policy pledged.

4. *Pledgee's Rights upon Default*

a. Before Maturity. The pledgee has no right to sell the property before maturity of the obligation unless such has been agreed to between the parties. In many instances where the pledge consists of collateral securities, the pledgee is authorized to sell before maturity if certain contingencies happen, for example, depreciation of collateral to a specified extent.

b. After Maturity. If the pledgor fails to discharge his obligation and does not redeem the property at maturity, the pledgee has alternative rights of proceeding to satisfy his claim. He may reduce the obligation to a judgment and levy upon the property for sale by judicial proceedings, or he may file a bill in equity for foreclosure of the pledge. This latter course might be necessary if the pledgor has wrongfully taken the property from the pledgee and other claimants are asserting a priority right. Upon being satisfied of the pledgee's security interest in the property, a court of equity will order the property sold at judicial sale for the benefit of the pledgee.

c. Right of Sale. The pledgee's most direct and effective course of procedure in satisfying his claim is to exercise his right to sell the pledged property at public auction without resort to judicial proceedings. The prerequisites to sale at public auction are: (1) a demand for payment must have been made upon the pledgor; and (2) the pledgor must have been given reasonable notice of the time and place at which the sale is to be held. Although the parties have agreed that the property may be sold at public or private sale without notice, it has been held that a demand of payment is necessary. The demand for payment and the notice of sale are separate and distinct.

It is characteristic for commercial pledge agreements to provide for the right of resale at private or public sale without notice to, or demand upon, the pledgor. In any event, it is the duty of the pledgee to act in good faith and to make a reasonable effort to obtain a fair price.

The requirements of notice to the pledgor are usually fixed by statute law. For example, Iowa requires ten days' written notice addressed to the pledgor by registered mail. What constitutes reasonable notice in the absence of statutory declaration is dependent entirely upon the circumstances surrounding the individual case.

It should be noted that when property is sold at public auction, notice of such must be publicly given. This is required even where the agreement provides for sale without notice. From the point of view of the law, public notice is of the essence of a public sale. Generally the mode of giving notice is prescribed by statute, but in the absence of such the usual and customary manner is acceptable.

d. Disposition of Proceeds. The pledgee has the right to apply the proceeds from the sale exclusively to a discharge of the obligation and to reimbursement for necessary expenditures. Any balance remaining from the proceeds of the sale are the property of the pledgor, and until they are placed in his possession the pledgee holds them in the capacity of a trustee. Of course, if the proceeds from the sale are insufficient to discharge the debt completely, the pledgor remains responsible for the deficit.

▶ III. CHATTEL MORTGAGES

A. NATURE OF CHATTEL MORTGAGES

Chattel mortgages are extensively used in the commercial world for the purpose of securing personal obligations. A *chattel mortgage* presents a device whereby the creditor acquires an interest in specific personal property as a protection against the possibility that the debtor will fail to meet his obligation when due. This type of security contract differs fundamentally from the pledge in that possession of the property may remain with the obligor. Possession by the creditor is not essential to the validity of his security right.

The chattel mortgage is used extensively to secure loans, although it may be used to secure the payment of the purchase price of the mortgaged property.

B. DESCRIPTION OF PROPERTY MORTGAGED

The validity of a chattel mortgage is dependent upon a sufficient description of the property covered by the mortgage. In *Farmers' etc. Bank* v. *Stockdale,* 121 Iowa 748, the Iowa court said that no property is mortgaged

> "by a sweeping statement to the effect that the instrument . . . is intended as a conveyance of all the property the mortgagor has, and all that he ever expects to have." The mortgagee can acquire no security interest in property as against

innocent third parties unless the mortgage so describes it that third parties can identify it "with the aid of such inquiry as the mortgage would suggest." [6]

"Descriptions do not identify of themselves; they only furnish the means of identification. They give us certain marks or characteristics,—perhaps historical data or incidents,—by the aid of which we may single out the thing intended from all others." *Willey* v. *Snyder,* 34 Mich. 60

To illustrate:

(1) It is generally held that a general description is sufficient if the location of the property is stated. Thus in *Bank of Shelbyville* v. *Hartford,* 268 Ky. 138, a mortgage upon bowling alleys and accessories used by mortgagors in operation of the business *in a designated building* was held a sufficient description.

(2) In *Hart County Deposit Bank* v. *Hatfield,* 236 Ky. 725, a description of "mules, cattle, farming tools, corn, tobacco and hay" was held to be insufficient in the absence of reference to present ownership, source of title, present physical possession, usual location or other means whereby the property could be identified.

C. NATURE OF MORTGAGEE'S INTEREST

It is generally recognized that the mortgagee (the creditor) has only a security interest in the mortgaged property and not a legal title. This interest of the mortgagee ceases to exist upon a discharge of the obligation by the mortgagor (the debtor). Consequently, the mortgagee has no right to possession of the mortgaged property unless such is provided for in the mortgage contract or by state statute. Many states give the mortgagee the right of possession. Witness the contents of Section 10014 of the 1939 Iowa Code, which reads:

"In the absence of stipulation in the mortgage, the mortgagee of personal property is entitled to the possession thereof, but the title shall remain in the mortgagor until divested by sale as provided by law."

D. FILING OR RECORDING REQUIRED

Whenever the mortgagor retains possession of the mortgaged property (as is usually the case), *the mortgagee,* to protect his security interest in the property, must take steps to notify the public of his interest in the property. The chattel mortgage statutes of the various states provide that unless the mortgage is either filed in, or spread upon, the records of a designated public office—usually that of the county recorder—it will not be valid against certain classes of claimants. Unless the mortgagee meets the requirements of notice, he may find that his right to security in the property has been defeated by

(1) a subsequent mortgagee who has filed or recorded his mortgage;

(2) a creditor of the mortgagor who has attached or levied upon the property; or

(3) a subsequent purchaser who had no notice of the mortgagee's interest.

The need to give public notice is therefore imperative. The requirements for notice in a particular jurisdiction should be ascertained.

---

[6] Stewart v. Clemens, p. 735.

The purpose of filing or recording instruments in a public office is to give constructive notice of their contents to the world at large. Everyone is presumed to know all that appears of public record or filing. Consequently, if a person who deals with personal property has reason to question the honesty or integrity of the possessor, that person should avail himself of the opportunity to search the public records for any possible encumbrances. In many localities, private or mutual benefit agencies (such as credit bureaus) make daily or weekly reports available showing the encumbrances against property that are shown by the public records.

E. STATUS OF MORTGAGES ON AFTER-ACQUIRED PROPERTY

1. *As Between Mortgagor and Mortgagee*

It is not unusual that mortgages are executed on property that is not owned by the mortgagor. This is done upon the supposition that the mortgagor expects or hopes to acquire the property in the future. Generally a mortgage upon property not owned by the mortgagor contains an *after-acquired clause.* Between the mortgagor and the mortgagee such a mortgage or mortgage provision is valid. The security interest of the mortgagee attaches at the time the property is acquired by the mortgagor. Prior to that time, the agreement stands as a contract whereby the mortgagor has promised that the creditor shall have a security interest in the property upon its acquisition.

2. *As Against Third Parties*

It is the common law rule (although some exceptions will be subsequently noted) that a mortgage must relate to property that is presently or potentially owned by the mortgagor at the time of the execution of the mortgage if it is to be valid against subsequent purchasers from, or attaching creditors of, the mortgagor. It is possible, however, for the mortgagee to establish a priority by taking possession of the property at the time of its acquisition by the mortgagor. As against third parties who had actual knowledge, as distinguished from public notice, of the mortgagee's contract for future security, the mortgagee will prevail.

3. *Future Crops*

After a crop is planted, it becomes potential property and as such can be the subject matter of a mortgage that will effectively protect the mortgagee against future claimants if the requirements of notice have been met. The status of mortgages upon crops to be grown in the future is not so certain. In probably the majority of our states, crops to be grown in the future can effectively be mortgaged so as to give the mortgagee a security interest paramount to the claims of creditors or purchasers. However, it should be recognized that the security interest of the mortgagee is taken upon the contingency that the crop will be grown and—what is more important—that the mortgagor will retain his interest in the land so that the growing of the crop will be possible.[7]

In a considerable number of the states, crops must be at least potentially in

[7] Steele v. Brooks, p. 737.

existence before the mortgagee can get a security interest that cannot be defeated by creditors or subsequent purchasers. Let it be remembered, however, that between the mortgagor and mortgagee, a mortgage covering future property is binding and becomes enforceable upon the property's coming into existence.

4. *Merchandise to be Acquired*

A mortgage on a stock of merchandise held for resale presents a unique situation. Obviously the mortgagor cannot be denied the right of resale, and yet the mortgagee would be unwilling to extend credit unless given a security right in future acquired merchandise. Therefore, it is usually provided that the mortgagor is required to keep a stock of merchandise that will be substantially equal to that on hand at the time of the execution of the mortgage and that such stock of goods shall stand as security for the mortgagee's claim. By the very nature of the transaction, the mortgagee gives his consent to a resale of the merchandise, thereby waiving his right of security against bona fide purchasers. The mortgagee's interest thus stands as security only against claimants other than purchasers in course of trade.*

In what is probably a minority of the states, it is held that such a mortgage is as valid as one upon existing property. However, the majority rule is that such a mortgage provision is not binding upon third parties who obtain an interest in or claim upon the newly acquired property, unless those claimants have actual knowledge of the mortgage provision. An attachment or levy by good-faith creditors will defeat the mortgagee's right. Under such circumstances, the mortgagee's only protection would be either actual notice to other claimants of his right, or taking possession of the property before other creditors can assert their claims and before the mortgagor has effected a sale.

F. RIGHTS AND DUTIES OF MORTGAGOR

1. *Care of Property*

The mortgagor has the duty not to defeat the interest of the mortgagee in the property. He subjects himself to liability for acts that adversely affect the security position of the mortgagee or are inconsistent with his rights in the property. Waste, destruction, substantial change in form, or sale in denial of the encumbrance constitute acts regarded as detrimental to the position of the mortgagee.

Most states provide penal statutes as an incentive to the mortgagor to respect the interest of the mortgagee. These statutes are not only for the protection of the mortgagee but also for the protection of prospective purchasers. Section 13037 of the Iowa Code serves as an illustration of these statutory provisions, although the gravity of the offense and the penalty will vary in the various states. This section reads:

> "If any mortgagor of personal property or purchaser under a conditional bill of sale, while the mortgage or conditional bill of sale upon it remains unsatisfied, willfully and with intent to defraud, destroys, conceals, sells, or in any manner disposes of the property . . . without the written consent of the

* See Gibson Oil Co. v. Hayes Equipment Mfg. Co., p. 739.

then holder of such mortgage or conditional bill of sale, he shall be guilty of larceny and punished accordingly."

2. *Right to Proceeds in Event of Sale*

The mortgagee's consent to sale of the property constitutes a waiver of his security right, and the purchaser takes an absolute title free of the encumbrance. Moreover, it is a general rule that the mortgage does not attach to the proceeds of the sale. This is true even if it is agreed between the mortgagor and the mortgagee that the proceeds are to be applied to the mortgage indebtedness. Before this could be accomplished, creditors of the mortgagor could take appropriate steps to avail themselves of the funds for the satisfaction of their claims. To assure that the proceeds of the sale will not go astray, the mortgagee's procedure is either (1) to make provision that payment will be made directly to him, or (2) to have the property sold in his name and on his behalf by the mortgagor as his agent.

G. FORECLOSURE

In the event that the mortgagor fails to pay his obligation at maturity, the mortgagee may take steps to avail himself of the mortgaged property as a means of satisfying his claim. Almost invariably, chattel mortgages will reserve in the mortgagee the power of sale upon default. This gives the mortgagee the right to take possession of the property and to sell it publicly or privately, without notice unless notice is provided for in the contract. However, he is under a duty to act in good faith and to sell as advantageously as possible. In some states, statutes regulate the execution of the reserved power of sale, for example, requiring a public sale with notice and a subsequent accounting to the mortgagor.

The mortgagee has available at all times the equitable right of *foreclosure* of the mortgage. Upon being satisfied as to the mortgagee's right to foreclose, the court will order the property sold at judicial sale for the benefit of the mortgagee.

While most states have provided statutory procedure for the enforcement of chattel mortgages, this is not the exclusive method that can be employed. For example, Iowa provides for public sale with notice without need of resorting to judicial process. The mortgagee may either avail himself of this course of procedure or exercise his right of sale if provided for in the contract, or take court action to obtain a decree of foreclosure. In some states, the statutory procedure is the exclusive method by which the mortgagee can avail himself of the mortgage security.

1. *Disposition of Proceeds*

The proceeds from the foreclosure sale can be applied only to a discharge of the mortgage obligation. Since the amount of the debt is the mortgagee's only interest in the property, the mortgagor is entitled to any surplus. Of course, if the proceeds from the sale are insufficient to discharge fully the mortgagor's personal obligation, he remains responsible for the deficit.

► IV. CONDITIONAL SALES

A. NATURE OF CONDITIONAL SALES

An exceedingly important commercial credit device is the conditional sale contract. As the term suggests, a *conditional sale* is a sale only upon the fulfillment of a specified condition. In other words, the seller of personal property retains the title to the goods until the condition agreed upon has been fully complied with by the buyer. The condition that the buyer must fulfill is almost invariably the payment of the purchase price. Possession of the property is surrendered to the purchaser, who acquires all incidents of ownership subject to the security title retained by the seller.[8] The buyer has the right to the use and enjoyment of the property and with him resides the risk of loss.

The retention of the title by the seller is the feature that distinguishes the conditional sale from an *absolute* sale, by which complete title is presently transferred to the purchaser. No particular form is required for the creation of a conditional sale contract. The important feature to be observed is the reservation of title in the seller. Unless such is the reasonably apparent intention of the parties, the transaction may by the courts be construed as an absolute sale (with a passing of title) and a mortgage back to secure the purchase price.

B. SECURITY POSITION OF VENDOR

1. *Under Recording Acts*

Modern recording statutes, as found in most of the states, make the common law rule of *caveat emptor* no longer applicable to those persons dealing with property subject to a conditional vendor's title if they have no notice of the vendor's interest. The burden of protecting his title is placed upon the vendor.[9] Like a chattel mortgage, the conditional vendor, to protect his interest in the property, is obligated to take steps to notify the public of the buyer's limited right to the goods in his possession. The statutes of the various states provide that, unless a copy of the conditional sales contract is either filed in or spread upon the records of a designated public office (usually that of the county recorder), the contract will not be valid against creditors of or purchasers from the buyer who have had no actual notice of the seller's security title. Unless the mortgagee meets the requirements of notice, his title to the property may become inferior to the claims of a subsequent purchaser, donee, mortgagee, pledgee, or creditor. Thus the modern doctrine is "Let the conditional vendor beware." The requirements for notice in a particular jurisdiction should be ascertained.

Of course it is imperative for those who purchase or extend credit upon the basis of personal property to take note of what the public records contain. Actual knowledge of the existence of a conditional sales contract is, however, effective.[10]

---

[8] Hansen v. Kuhn, p. 737.

[9] Spencer v. Staines, p. 739.

[10] Gibson Oil Co. v. Hayes Equipment Mfg. Co., p. 739.

2. *Sale of Goods to be Resold*

Obviously a conditional vendor who sells goods to a buyer for the purpose of resale cannot preserve his security title against subsequent purchasers. By the very nature of the transaction, the conditional buyer is authorized to sell in the ordinary course of trade, and of necessity the conditional seller waives his security title against subsequent purchasers. It is from the funds derived from a resale of the goods that the conditional vendor hopes to get satisfaction of his claim. Purchasers have the right to assume that, if one is in possession of property for the express purpose of satisfying the demands and whims of the buying public, he has the consent of all interested parties that it may be sold.

There is no reason why the conditional vendor's title should not be valid against other claimants, such as attaching or levying creditors; in fact, this is the general rule.

C. RIGHTS AND DUTIES OF BUYER

1. *Use and Enjoyment*

The buyer who has purchased under a conditional sales contract is entitled to the possession, use, and enjoyment of the property as long as he meets the conditions of the contract. It is only upon the buyer's default that the seller can deprive him of his beneficial ownership in the goods.

The conditional buyer's interest in the property is regarded as being sufficiently substantial for the courts as a general rule to allow him to maintain legal action against either the seller or third persons who have wrongfully deprived him of possession of the property.

2. *Duty to Respect Vendor's Title*

The buyer has the duty not to commit any acts that might be inconsistent with the vendor's security title. Committing the property to waste, destruction, or change in form would give the conditional vendor the right of action for conversion. In the absence of an agreement to the contrary, the buyer has no duty to the vendor to retain his beneficial interest in the property. He may sell or assign his beneficial ownership in a bona fide transaction—a transaction that is not intended as a means of depriving the conditional vendor of his security position.

Most states have statutory enactments providing for punishment of a conditional vendee who acts with intent to render the vendor's security position ineffective. These statutes are for the protection of third parties as well as for the protection of the conditional seller.

3. *Right to Obtain Absolute Title*

The conditional vendor cannot prevent the vendee from ultimately obtaining absolute title to the property. The passing of a title is dependent not upon the will of the seller but rather upon the buyer's performance of the contract conditions. Title will vest in the buyer automatically as a matter of law at the time the terms of the contract are fully performed. Should the vendor refuse to accept performance, a tender of performance is equally effective. For example, if the condition is payment of the purchase price, a tender of payment, although refused, will vest title irrevocably in the buyer.

The acceptance of a note as evidence of the purchase price is not regarded as a payment that would divest the conditional vendor of his title. In such a note, it is usually the practice to provide that title is reserved until the note is paid. The note's transfer carries with it the security title to the property and vests it in the holder.

D. WAIVER OF TITLE BY VENDOR

In the course of a sales transaction, title will pass when the parties intend it should pass. A conditional vendor may waive his reserved title at any time and so vest absolute title in the vendee. Any acts on the part of the vendor that would be inconsistent with his retention of the title would be interpreted as being a waiver of his title to the property. To illustrate:

(1) In a majority of the states, the vendor waives his security title by commencing an action to recover the purchase price of the goods. The courts reason that a suit for the purchase price must be brought upon the theory that the vendor treats the title as being in the buyer. Under this rule, the buyer, upon commencing a suit for the purchase price, gives up his right to retake the property.

(2) In many states the vendor's act of accepting a chattel mortgage upon the property is interpreted as a waiver of his right of repossession of the property under the conditional sales contract. In the case of *In re A. E. Richardson Co.*, 294 Fed. 451, the court said:

"It is manifestly inconsistent that title shall remain in the vendor, and also that the purchaser shall execute and deliver a chattel mortgage."

E. RIGHTS OF VENDOR UPON DEFAULT

1. *Right to Sue for Purchase Price*

At the time of a default by the vendee, a conditional vendor may choose to bring a suit for the recovery of the unpaid purchase price. In some jurisdictions, such a course of procedure would exclude the conditional vendor from subsequently exercising his right of security under the conditional sales contract; other jurisdictions deny that he has thereby forfeited his right to retake the property.

2. *Right to Retake Property*

After the vendee's default, the logical counterpart of the retention of title is the right of the conditional vendor to repossess himself of the property. It is indeed rare that this right is not declared in the contract. As a precautionary measure and with a view to exercising his right of repossession, the vendor's course of procedure should be to declare the purchase price due and payable and make a demand that the property be surrendered to him. In the event of a refusal, he may proceed to take possession by whatever peaceable means he has at his command. Some courts have even held that the use of reasonable force is not to be condemned. However, in no event is a breach of the peace permissible. Should the vendor fail in his personal efforts to reduce the property to his possession, he may invoke the aid of a court and recover the property by an action of replevin.

3. *Rights After Repossession*

Without giving consideration to unusual contractual provisions and the few instances of legislative control which will subsequently be presented, the rights of the conditional vendor after repossession may be summarized as follows:

(1) He has the right to retain or to resell the property repossessed, keeping all payments that have been made by the vendee.

(2) In the absence of a contractual provision providing otherwise, the seller has no further right of recovery against the buyer. Thus, if a deficit exists after a resale or if the value of the property is not sufficient to equal the unpaid purchase price, the loss falls upon the seller.

(3) Consequently, it is common practice to insert a provision in the agreement to the effect that any deficit upon resale will be an obligation of the buyer.

(4) However, any surplus value is the property of the seller. It is most unusual for the conditional sales contract to provide for a return of the surplus to the defaulting buyer.

4. *Limitations upon Right of Repossession*

Some states have come to recognize the obvious disadvantage under which the vendee is placed by becoming a party to the typical conditional sales contract. There is little justice in a commercial practice whereby a buyer, for reasons entirely beyond his control, may lose not only the property purchased but also a substantial portion of the purchase price. This is especially true if the loss would unjustly enrich the seller. In some instances the buyer has been afforded protection by judicial declaration and in others by legislation. The trend in this direction should be accelerated.

A few courts take the position that a repossession by the seller is in the nature of a rescission of the contract. The seller is required to account to the buyer for the payments he has made less an amount sufficient to care for the depreciation and to compensate for the use and enjoyment of the property while in the buyer's possession.

In those few states where a conditional sale is viewed as an absolute transfer of title with a security interest back to the vendor—a chattel mortgage—the buyer is also protected. In such a case, a sale is required, with the surplus going to the mortgagor (the buyer).

The Uniform Conditional Sales Act, as it has been adopted in all too few states, affords the buyer protection against such unduly harsh consequences; at the same time it amply protects the seller's interests. Sections 16 to 26 inclusive should be consulted.

► V. TRUST RECEIPTS

A. NATURE OF TRUST RECEIPTS

The trust receipt, which is well known to the import trade, has come into general use in recent years as a device to secure the repayment of loans made to retailers for the purchase of merchandise. At the present time, financial institutions especially favor its use for the purpose of securing advances to automobile dealers for the purchase of their stock in trade.

While there is considerable variation in the procedure by which a trust receipt agreement may evolve, the basic mechanics are as follows: Upon advancing money or its credit to a customer for the purpose of purchasing goods, a bank or other financial institution (such as a finance company) will take the bill of lading to the goods in its own name. The bill of lading will then be surrendered to the customer under a trust receipt agreement, which usually authorizes the sale of the goods in the ordinary course of trade. The trust receipt usually provides that the merchant will hold in trust for the lender:

(1) the bill of lading;

(2) the goods after possession is taken from the carrier;

(3) the proceeds from a sale of the goods; and

(4) contractual rights, such as promissory notes, resulting from sales upon credit.

Thus, the lender has a continuing security, which will still be in effect after completion of the transaction.

In some instances the trust receipt will provide that payment to a specified extent must be made to the lender, whereupon the borrower can obtain a release together with authority to dispose of the goods.

The following facts will illustrate the typical procedural steps in a trust receipt transaction:

Cook, a retail dealer, wishing to provide himself with a stock of goods and not having sufficient funds to meet the purchase price, will arrange with a financial agency—in this instance the Security Bank—for credit sufficient to discharge the purchase price obligation to the seller. Thereby Cook obligates himself to pay the bank the same amount as the bank pays, or promises to pay in the future, to the seller. However, the bank will not assume the obligation to pay or advance any funds to the seller until its resultant claim against Cook is secured.

This is accomplished by arranging for the bill of lading (endorsed either in blank or to the order of the bank), with draft attached, to be sent directly to the bank. Upon paying or accepting the draft, whichever the case requires, the bank becomes entitled to possession of the bill of lading; this is equivalent to possession of the goods. The bill of lading will then be surrendered to Cook, the retailer, under a trust receipt agreement.

B. LEGAL STATUS

In its contemplated operation, the trust receipt agreement gives the lender a security position superior to that which could have been obtained by means of a conditional sale or a chattel mortgage contract. Moreover, this is accomplished without need of giving public notice. The theory is that the purchased property is owned by the lender, and anything which the borrower accepts in lieu of the original goods remains the property of the lender; the borrower holds it merely in trust for him. Consequently, no claims to the property can be asserted by creditors of the borrower or by purchasers who acquired the goods in violation of the trust receipt agreement. In theory the trust receipt is a security contract, valid without being filed or recorded.

There is no legal doubt as to the effectiveness of the lender's security position against the borrower. However, considerable disagreement exists among the courts as to the exact nature and operation of this type of security contract as it affects third parties.[11]

Commercial convenience and *necessity,* it is contended, are the justifications for the trust receipt form of security relation. A considerable number of the state courts are not convinced, however, that such a secret security position is necessary to the orderly and expeditious conduct of commercial affairs. Their attitude has been that if this need and necessity exists it should be given legislative recognition. These courts have been impressed with the fact that the chief purpose of using this type of security device is to avoid the statutory requirements for the protection of a security position and therefore have held that these transactions are either conditional sales or chattel mortgages. In *Ohio Savings Bank* v. *Schneider,* 202 Iowa 938, the court said:

> "The trust receipt was in the nature of a conditional sale, and doubtless came under the operation of our statute which requires such an agreement to be recorded to impart constructive notice."

The federal as well as some state courts have given recognition to the trust receipt theory of security position. They hold that purchasers who do not acquire goods in the ordinary course of trade and in compliance with the terms of the trust receipt agreement take the property subject to the title of the lender, although no constructive notice by filing or recording has been given. The rights of attaching and levying creditors of the borrower are likewise held to be subject to the rights of the lender as evidenced by the trust receipt.

At the present time approximately one fourth of the states have enacted the Uniform Trust Receipt Act, which gives legislative recognition to this recent type of security device. Although the act does not require a filing or recording of the trust receipt by the lender for his protection against subsequent claimants, it does provide for a limited type of constructive notice. It requires that a specimen copy of the contract under which the parties operate must be filed with the Secretary of State within thirty days after the loan has been made. By meeting this require-

[11] Handy v. C.I.T. Corp., p. 741.

ment, the security rights of the lender will be protected for a period of one year, after which a refiling will be required.

CASES

CASE NO. 1

Wilson v. Malenock. 138 Pa. Super. 544, 194 Atl. 508 (1937)

CUNNINGHAM, J. The dispute in this case was whether the defendant, an autobody repairman who rebuilt plaintiff's car, had a common-law lien for the cost of the repairs, or, by contract, waived his lien and was therefore liable to plaintiff in an action of trespass for converting the car through refusing to deliver it to him until the repair bill was paid.

The back of plaintiff's 1930 Chevrolet car was damaged on April 14, 1936, as the result of a collision with a car owned by one Brock. Brock promised plaintiff to pay for the repairs to plaintiff's car, and, through his wife, told plaintiff to take the damaged car to defendant's garage; plaintiff did so on April 18th although he had not known defendant previously. . . .

Plaintiff subsequently brought this action of trespass based on the theory of a conversion of his car by defendant. The court below . . . found for plaintiff for the value of the car, as repaired, at the time of defendant's refusal to deliver, namely $106. The basis for the decision of the court below was its finding of fact

"that Malenock agreed to repair Wilson's car, the understanding being that the cost of the repairs was to be paid solely by Brock."

The trial court concluded that defendant had no common-law lien because

"there were no contractual relations between the owner of the property and the person claiming the lien out of which the implication of (the) existence of (a) common-law lien (might arise)." . . .

It is plain in this state that, in absence of circumstances showing a contrary intention, a person who repairs a chattel at the instance of the owner, or his authorized agent, has a common-law lien or right to retain possession of the chattel until paid. . . .

It is equally well settled that the parties to the bailment may enter into a contract expressly providing that no lien for repairs shall arise; or, if the contract between the parties be inconsistent with a lien, the lien does not exist. . . .

. . . when the testimony is considered as a whole in the light of the circumstances surrounding plaintiff's delivery of his car to defendant, and particularly the fact that defendant went ahead with the repairs only after receiving a phone call from "Scotty" (a third party presumably calling in behalf of Brock), it supports a finding that Malenock knew, or at least gave plaintiff the impression he knew, that "Scotty" had authority from Brock in this matter. Defendant, speaking of his conversation with plaintiff at the time of the delivery, stated:

"He said, 'Well, has anybody been here?' I said, 'No.' Well he mentioned a name—I think it was Brock—and he said, 'He wrecked my car, and told me to come here and have it repaired and he would pay for it.'" . . .

We cannot say that this evidence, together with the other facts presented, did not justify the findings that Malenock either knew or assumed that

"Scotty" was acting for Brock, and that, by repairing on "Scotty's" word, he undertook to look solely to Brock for payment. The conclusion of law that Malenock waived his lien for the value of the repairs naturally follows.

Judgment affirmed.

CASE NO. 2

Clarksburg Casket Co. v. Valley Undertaking Co. 81 W.Va. 212, 94 S.E. 549, 3 A.L.R. 660 (1917)

POFFENBARGER, J., delivered the opinion of the court: . . .

So much of the decree as allows to Weimar and Reynolds a lien for a meritorious claim amounting to $120 will have to be reversed, for they have no shadow of a lien for the claim. It is for storage of the vehicles of the corporation, while used by it in its business. Necessarily the company had possession and control of them when used in the conduct of funerals, wherefore they were frequently out of the possession of the claimants of the lien. In such cases the common law gave no lien. . . . A garage keeper has no lien on an automobile for storage, if the owner is permitted periodically to take it out and use it. . . . The rule requiring continuous and unbroken possession in the establishment of a common-law lien, such as that of a warehouseman, is very strict. Without it, such a lien is impossible, and, where there is one, it is lost the moment the possession is broken. . . .

CASE NO. 3

Graben Motor Co. v. Brown Garage Co. 197 Iowa 453, 195 N.W. 752, 31 A.L.R. 832 (1923)

STEVENS, J., delivered the opinion of the court:

Appellee, a corporation, brings this action in replevin to recover the possession of an automobile from the defendant, a corporation engaged in the business of keeping a garage. The automobile was purchased by one Miller from appellee, and a purchase-money mortgage given to secure the unpaid portion of the purchase price. On or about October 1, 1921, Miller placed the car in appellant's garage for storage at the agreed price of $10 per month. It remained in storage until this action was commenced in August, 1922. Appellee based its right to the possession of the automobile upon its purchase-money mortgage, which had been breached by Miller; appellant defended upon the theory that it has a common-law lien, which is superior to the mortgage lien of appellee. . . .

Appellant relies wholly upon a common-law lien. The business of a garage keeper is, in some respects, similar to that of a livery-stable keeper, in which carriages are kept for hire. No lien existed at common law in favor of livery-stable keepers. . . . So far, however, as the decisions in other jurisdictions have been brought to our attention, statutes creating a lien in favor of livery-stable keepers have been construed as having no application to garage keepers. . . .

Section 3137 of the Code makes the lien of livery-stable keepers subject to prior liens of record, so that, if the court were to hold that this statute is applicable to garage keepers, it would not avail appellant, as the mortgage in question was recorded prior to October 1, 1921. Appellant argues that the case comes within the rule of the common law, which permitted a lien for repairs upon personal property. Liens for repairs were allowed at common law upon the theory that an additional value was imported thereto. Preservation of automobiles by storage is quite different from value added by the skill of the artisan in making repairs thereon. Liens existed at common law in favor of innkeepers, farriers, common carriers, and warehousemen, who were bound by law to serve the public in these occupations. Appellant does not claim a lien as a warehouseman, which is now regulated by statute, but relies entirely upon an assumed common-law lien. None of the liens allowed at common law exist in favor of appellant, and the legislature of this state has not seen fit to enact legislation specifically creating a lien for storage or hire in favor of a garage keeper. . . .

CASE NO. 4

State ex rel. McConnell v. People's Bank & T. Co. 155 Tenn. 519, 296 S.W. 12 (1927)

CHAMBLISS, J., delivered the opinion of the court:

This appeal is from a decree granting the cashier and assistant cashier of an insolvent bank a preferential lien on the assets in the hands of the receiver for salaries earned within ninety days of the appointment of the receiver, pursuant to the provision in Shannon's Code, § 3564, for such a preferential lien in favor of "all employees and laborers of any corporation," . . .

. . . it is . . . insisted that a cashier and assistant cashier of a bank do not properly come within the term "employees," as used in this legislation; that it was not the intention of the legislature to provide for a preference in favor of these bank officers in case of insolvency. We have no reported case deciding this precise question. . . .

In Baldwin's Century edition of Bouvier's Law Dictionary, under "employee," while it is said that the term is one of rather broad significance, the learned author adds:

"It is not usually applied to higher officers of corporations, or to domestic servants, but to clerks, workmen, and laborers collectively."

In 20 C.J. pp. 1242–1244, it is said that the context and the connection in which the term "employee" is used must largely determine whether, in a particular case, the term includes a certain person, and that "it rarely refers to the higher officers of a corporation or government, or to domestic servants, and is usually distinguished from an official or officer, or one employed in a position of some authority." This text is supported by a number of citations, and the note quotes from one of the cases cited the following:

"The officers of the company are its representatives, and, it may be said, are the official masters who direct and control the servants and employees. The former are appointed and elected, and are trustees; . . . the latter are hired and are the subordinates of the former."

And in the same note we find the following:

"While the word 'employee' is not to be read with full generic force, it has been adjudicated to embrace more than the words 'operative' and 'laborer.' It may be said generally that the term 'employee' includes persons employed by the corporation in comparatively subordinate positions, which cannot correctly be described as either 'operatives' or 'laborers.' Hopkins v. Cromwell, 89 App. Div. 481, 85 N.Y. Supp. 840. . . ."

. . . because of the apparent unwisdom of rewarding the higher officers in control of a business, which has been so conducted as to reduce it to insolvency, by the granting of a preference in favor of such claims as they may assert, we are constrained to the conclusion that it was not the intention of the Legislature to include the managing officers of a bank within the provisions of the statute under consideration. This conclusion is supported by the construction given Shannon's Code, § 3540, providing for a lien in favor of journeymen or "other person employed" by a contractor, denying the lien to one employed to superintend the work, . . .

The decree of the Chancellor is reversed.

CASE NO. 5

First Nat. Bank v. Hattaway. 172 Ga. 731, 158 S.E. 565, 77 A.L.R. 375 (1931)

BECK, P.J., delivered the opinion of the court:

J. F. Hattaway brought suit against First National Bank of Blakely, alleging in substance as follows: Defendant has damaged petitioner in the sum of $10,000, by reason of the following facts: In the fall of 1920 petitioner delivered to defendant fifty bales of cotton to secure certain indebtedness due by the plaintiff to defendant. . . . Each of the notes has the following stipulation:

"I represent that I am sole and lawful owner, and have full power and authority to pledge such collateral, and I hereby constitute the president, vice-president, and cashier of said corporation, jointly and severally, my attorney or attorneys to collect, sell, or otherwise dispose of the whole or any portion of said collateral, either at public or private sale, and without notice (to) me of an intention to sell, in case of the non-performance of this contract, applying the proceeds to the payment of this note, including interest, and accounting to me for the surplus, if any; and at any such sales or sale the said corporation or any officer or agent thereof may be the purchaser in whole or in part. In case of deficiency, I hereby promise to pay to said bank the amount thereof forthwith, after such sale, with interest at the same rate as above named."

After maturity of the notes, defendant was by plaintiff instructed to sell the cotton pledged whenever the price thereof would pay the notes in question, but this it failed to do; . . . It is alleged that the defendant's failure, refusal, and omission to sell the cotton under the conditions stated was wrongful, negligent, and injurious to petitioner, whereby he sustained loss in the sum aforesaid; that defendant did not exercise ordinary diligence in making a sale of said cotton when authorized, and was grossly negligent in omitting to sell the cotton for a period of at least a year and a half, after the request to do so and while the same was declining in price; that the cotton was finally sold without notice to petitioner; that the defendant has not, though requested so to do, accounted to petitioner for the proceeds thereof; and that defendant should account to petitioner, not only for the funds received, but for the value of the cotton as alleged. . . .

Neither at common law nor under the statutes of this state, in the absence of contract, is the holder of collateral bound to sell it, though he may have the right to sell it, under certain conditions, by giving notice as required by the statute. As a matter of law, a pledge of chattels is a mere security for the obligation that the pledgor would pay the debt. The pledgee may sell the collateral in order to protect himself, if he deems it wise to do so, after compliance with the statute as to notice, etc., or in the exercise of special contractual power. But he is not obliged to sell the collateral to satisfy the debt in whole or in part, even upon the demand of the pledgor. The pledgee may look solely to the promisor, and may proceed against him on his promise, without exhausting the collateral. The creditor may sue on the note and obtain an ordinary common-law judgment, without exhausting the security. The property pledged, the chattel in the present case, is merely security for the debt. Where the creditor holds a promissory note given him by his debtor and holds other promissory notes or other collateral for the principal obligation, he is bound to use ordinary diligence in collecting the collateral; but as regards other pledges, such as cotton, stocks of corporations, and the like, the obligation of the creditor is to exercise ordinary care in the preservation of the collateral, to the end that it may be delivered to the debtor when he pays the debt in substantially as good a condition as it was in when received. The doctrine is thus stated in 21 R.C.L. 689, § 49:

> "It is the well-settled general rule that a pledgee, though entitled to do so, is not bound to sell the pledge at the maturity of the debt, but may sell or not at his option, and in the absence of any agreement requiring the pledgee of property to sell it on the maturity of the debt he cannot be held liable for a depreciation in the value of the property occurring after the maturity of the debt secured by the pledge. The pledgor having the right of redemption, he must redeem and sell the pledged property himself if he wishes to avoid loss by depreciation."

And the rule has also been stated in this language:

> "Where there is no contract varying the powers and duties of the parties, as a general rule the pledgor cannot make it the duty of the pledgee to sell by directing or requesting him to do so. 49 C.J. 997, and cit."

Judgment reversed.

CASE NO. 6

Stewart v. Clemens. 220 Ala. 224, 124 So. 863, 66 A.L.R. 1454 (1929)

BROWN, J., delivered the opinion of the court:

Action of detinue by appellant against appellee to recover the possession of

> "two bay mare mules, ten or twelve years old, and being the T. C. Montgomery mules, or mules gotten by said defendant from said T. C. Montgomery," . . .

The plaintiff claims title to the property and the right to immediate possession under a mortgage. . . . The defendant claims through purchase from Montgomery. . . .

The language of plaintiff's mortgage in so far as it undertakes to describe the mortgaged property is:

> "all my, or our live stock and personal property of every kind now in my or our possession, and owned by me or us, and all live stock and personal property hereafter acquired, including horses, mules, colts, cows, yearlings, hogs, wagons, buggies, farming implements and household goods. . . ."

. . . so far as the blanket description relates to after-acquired property, it is without efficacy to confer right or title that would authorize plaintiff to recover in this action. Its only effect is its tendency to confuse and render more uncertain, especially as to third persons, that part of the description supposed to cover the mules in controversy:

> "all of my or our live stock and personal property of every kind now in my or our possession and owned by me or us."

Our decisions, which are in accord with the great weight of judicial opinion, have been very liberal in allowing parol testimony to identify and make certain indefinite descriptions of property in chattel mortgages, and especially so where the mortgage was on crops to be grown in the future on land in which the mortgagor, at the time of the execution of the mortgage, had a present interest. . . .

Still it has been held that a mortgage of "my entire crop of every description" is too indefinite to be enforced. . . . On the other hand, when the property was described as "my entire crop of cotton and corn," when aided by evidence showing that the mortgagor at the time of the execution of the mortgage owned a farm in Blount county and of the quantity of crops grown therein, during the year the mortgage was given, the uncertainty was "reasonably removed," showing the intention of the parties that the mortgage should cover the entire crop of cotton and corn raised by the mortgagor on his farm during the year the mortgage was given. . . .

Justification of this liberal rule allowing parol proof to aid a general and meager description in a crop mortgage, though neither the situs of the property nor the residence of the mortgagor is stated, is in a measure found in the fact that such property is not susceptible of any other but a general description, and, of necessity, during the period of its development and growth, it has a fixed and permanent situs. It must be the product of lands in which the mortgagor has a present interest when the mortgage was given. . . .

But as to movable chattels that may be easily described with particularity, the general rule sustained by the great weight of authority is that a mortgage which neither sufficiently describes the property nor states where it is situated, nor gives the place, county, or state where the mortgagor resides, is insufficient. . . .

The importance of requiring the mortgage under such circumstances to state the location of the property was recognized and well stated in Hurt v. Redd, 64 Ala. 85, where it was observed:

"The mortgage is of 'fourteen mules, now' (at the time or date of executing the mortgage) 'on my' (the mortgagor's) 'plantation in Russell county, Alabama.' It was sufficiently specific and certain. The number of the mules is stated, and the place at which they would be found. Parol evidence that the mortgagor had but one plantation in Russell county, and had there only fourteen mules, rendered the property, on which the mortgage was to operate, definite and certain, capable of positive identification. . . ."

But where a mortgage designed to cover specific chattels does not describe any particular property or furnish data which will direct the attention of those reading it "to some source of information beyond the words of the parties to it," its recordation is not constructive notice to third persons, and parol evidence is not admissible to aid the description so as to charge them with notice. . . .

The description of the property in the case at bar is a mere net or catchall, indefinite in its statement as to ownership, does not show the location of the property, nor the residence of the mortgagor. It is not limited to property owned by the mortgagor at the time, but it refers to the property of others, as well as that to be after acquired, and as to third persons is too indefinite to be aided by parol testimony, or charge such third persons with notice. . . .

CASE NO. 7

Steele v. Brooks. 34 Ala. App. 584, 42 So. (2d) 63 (1949)

HARWOOD, J. . . . The complaint . . . charged defendant with the destruction of a lien held by the plaintiff, appellee here, on a bale of cotton, and is in words and figures as follows:

"The plaintiff claims of the defendant the sum of $121.48, as damages; on September 3, 1947, one, John Sartin, Jr. who was then residing in DeKalb County, Alabama, executed to the plaintiff a certain mortgage, covering, among other things, the entire crops of produce and all rents accruing to the said John Sartin, Jr. during the year, 1947, in the County in which he then resided. . . . Plaintiff avers that thereafter and during the month of October, 1947, said mortgage being still unpaid, there accrued to the said John Sartin, Jr. from produce raised by him in said County and rents accruing to him from crops grown by him in DeKalb County, Alabama, on the farm of Mrs. Mary Koger, one bale of cotton, gin #486, . . . and plaintiff avers that the defendant, Munford C. Steele, so took possession of said bale of cotton and disposed of same, that by reason thereof plaintiff's mortgage lien on said bale of cotton was destroyed and made of no effect, to the plaintiff's damage in the sum as aforesaid." . . .

Since the lien allegedly destroyed was attached to property whose description in the mortgage was uncertain to the extent that it could not be pointed out by reference to such description, the burden was on the plaintiff to show, not only that the bale of cotton described was raised by the mortgagor Sartin in DeKalb County, but that it was the product of lands in which the mortgagor had a present interest at the time he gave the mortgage. For while the thing itself need not have identity, or separate entity, yet it must be the product or growth, or increase of property, which has at the time a corporate existence, and in which the mortgagor has a present interest, not a mere belief, hope or expectation, that he will in future acquire such an interest. . . .

In the trial below the plaintiff testified that at the time Sartin executed the mortgage to him, on which plaintiff's lien depends, Sartin was living on Mrs. Mary Koger's farm, where he was farming; that Sartin grew cotton and corn, and he, plaintiff, knew of "two and a piece" bales of cotton that Sartin made.

This was all of the evidence that could in anywise be construed as tending to establish the identity of the bale of cotton described in the complaint, the identity of which is necessary to establish plaintiff's lien.

This evidence is obviously insufficient in tending to show that the bale of cotton described . . . was raised by Sartin, the mortgagor, in DeKalb County on land in which he had a present interest at the time he gave the mortgage. It results that the plaintiff thus failed to establish the existence of the lien he alleges was destroyed by the defendant. . . .

CASE NO. 8

Hansen v. Kuhn. 226 Iowa 794, 285 N.W. 249 (1939)

BLISS, J. The controlling question in this case is whether the appellee, Van Druff, as the assignee from the vendor in a conditional sales contract of a motor truck to Kuhn, the vendee, was the "owner," under paragraph 8 of Section 4863, of the Code of 1935, so as to be liable, under Section 5026, to one injured by Kuhn in the operation of said truck. . . .

On November 13, 1935, the Quick Motors sold Kuhn a Ford truck for $494.52, of which he paid $75 then, and executed his promissory note for the balance, payable in twelve, equal, monthly installments. Title to the truck was reserved in the seller for the purpose of securing to him the payment of the purchase price. For default in any payment, or for depreciation in value, or whenever the seller or assignee felt unsafe, he might take possession of the truck, and upon notice sell it at public auction and apply the proceeds on the debt, with any excess going to the vendee. . . . The contract was recorded. The truck was registered in the office of the county treasurer of Pottawattamie County, in the name of Kuhn, . . . On December 5, 1935, the defendant Kuhn while driving the truck on a highway some miles east of Council Bluffs collided with another truck, thereby severely injuring the appellant who claimed he was riding in the defendant's truck. . . .

At the close of the appellant's testimony, the appellee moved for a directed verdict in his favor upon several grounds, but all were bottomed on the fact that he was not the owner of the truck. This motion was sustained generally, and judgment for the appellee was entered thereon. . . .

Paragraph 8 of Section 4863 is in the words following:

> " 'Owner' shall include any person having the lawful ownership, use or control, or the right to the use or control, of a motor vehicle, under a lease or otherwise, for a period of ten or more successive days."

Section 5026 provides:

> "In all cases where damage is done by any car driven by . . . consent of the owner, by reason of negligence of the driver, the owner of the car shall be liable for such damage."

Paragraph 8 of Section 4863 does not purport to define the term "owner". . . .

To have been included therein the appellee must have had, either the "lawful ownership, use or control" of the truck under his contract, or he must have had "the right to the use or control" of the truck under his contract. In our judgment he was in neither status.

The transaction between the Quick Motors and Kuhn was undoubtedly a conditional sale. It was not a contract of bailment, nor was it a lease in the ordinarily accepted meaning of that term. Kuhn bought the truck. The only matter held in abeyance was the completed payment. He became the beneficial owner, the equitable owner, the substantial owner, immediately upon the execution of the contract. Only the naked title remained in the seller, subject to being completely divested, upon the receipt of the final deferred installment of the purchase price. Other than the matter of payment, such a sale transaction is in nowise different from an absolute sale. The New Hampshire court, in Mercier v. Nashua Buick Co., 84 N.H. 59, 146 Atl. 165, 168, spoke of it thus:

> "In its structure and contemplation a conditional sale is no different from any other completed sale. The property sold remains security for the debt, but the transaction of sale itself is a concluded one. The agreement divides itself into two separate parts, one of a fully effected sale and one of provision for securing payment. In this respect it is in full analogy with a sale in which the price is secured by a mortgage of the property sold."

If, under the contract, the possessor is clearly obligated to pay for the article sold, it is a conditional sales contract, even though the words "sell," "sold," or "sale" be absent from the writing. . . .

Under the above stated test, the writing in this case was a conditional sale contract.

Having concluded that the contract was one of conditional sale, it must be determined what were the respective rights and obligations of the appellee and the defendant, pertaining to the truck, under the contract. Necessarily the naked title remained in the seller, until transferred to the assignee. Such retention is an essential of a conditional sale contract. . . . But such title is retained solely for the purpose of security. The other attributes of ownership, such as possession, use, control, or the right thereto, under such a contract, pass to the purchasing vendee. It is true there is, ordinarily, in the vendor or his assignee, a limited right of restriction in some of these matters, but save, as so limited, these rights of the vendee are absolute. . . .

We will not further extend this opinion with citation of authority from other jurisdictions, in view of the definite holdings of this court. But wherever the question has come up for decision, the courts have quite uniformly held that the purchaser under the contract was the owner. . . .

The judgment . . . is affirmed.

CASE NO. 9

Spencer v. Staines. 291 N.W. 51 (Mich.) (1940)

CHANDLER, J. On September 26, 1934, defendant Staines sold, by conditional sales contract, a stock of merchandise for resale to one Leo P. Meagher, who took possession thereof on the same day. The contract was never recorded as required by 2 Comp. Laws 1929, § 9550 (Stat. Ann. § 19.381). . . .

The vendee defaulted in the terms and conditions of the agreement and on December 28, 1937, surrendered to the vendor that portion of the stock covered by the conditional sale contract which had not been sold by him. On January 7, 1938, Staines resold the stock to defendant Jacobson. Subsequent to December 28, 1937, and prior to the sale to Jacobson, Meagher filed a voluntary petition in bankruptcy and was adjudicated a bankrupt thereon.

The bill of complaint herein was filed by the trustee in bankruptcy, seeking a return of the merchandise or the value thereof. The trial court entered a decree ordering defendant Staines forthwith to pay to plaintiff the sum of $600 and costs, said sum being the value of the merchandise as found by him.

The statute requiring filing of the conditional sales contract in order for the reservation of title to be effective, except as between the vendor and vendee, was obviously intended for the protection of creditors, extending credit during the period the instrument was not on file, and subsequent mortgagees and purchasers in good faith. . . .

The decree should be modified, permitting a return of the merchandise as recommended by the commissioner, with the further provision that if return is not made within 30 days from the date of the filing of this opinion, the decree of the trial court shall stand affirmed, with costs to appellee. If the goods are returned within the time limited, appellant shall recover costs.

CASE NO. 10

Gibson Oil Co. v. Hayes Equipment Mfg. Co. 163 Okla. 134, 21 P. (2d) 17, 88 A.L.R. 104 (933)

BUSBY, J., delivered the opinion of the court:

This is a replevin action wherein

the Hayes Equipment Manufacturing Company seeks to recover from the Gibson Oil Company eight gasoline pumps. These pumps were sold by the Hayes Equipment Manufacturing Company to one S. L. Martin, under a conditional contract executed on August 24, 1927, by the terms of which title was retained in the vendor, until the purchase price should be paid in full. $220 was paid on the purchase price and the unpaid portion thereon at the time of trial was approximately $754.84, plus interest. On the same date Martin agreed to transfer these pumps to the Gibson Oil Company for a consideration of $960, $268 in cash and the balance in credit on a pre-existing indebtedness owing by Martin to the Gibson Oil Company. . . . The conditional sales contract executed by Martin was not recorded until September 7, 1927. . . . the court rendered judgment for the plaintiff for the possession of the property, or in lieu thereof its value and fixed the value at $900. . . .

The next question that presents itself is whether or not the defendant was a purchaser for value without notice, actual or constructive, of the existence of the conditional sales contract. At the time the defendant purchased the gasoline pump from Martin the conditional sales contract was not of record and it was therefore not charged with constructive knowledge thereof. The plaintiff urges in support of the judgment of the trial court that the defendant had actual knowledge of the existence of the conditional sales contract imputed to it through one of its agents, a Mr. Deathridge. If this is true, the recording of the contract was immaterial. . . .

The witness S. L. Martin testified that at the time that the conditional sales contract was executed by himself to the plaintiff, Mr. Deathridge was present in his office both while the negotiations were going on for the purchase of the pumps from the plaintiff by Mr. Martin and when the conditional sales contract was finally signed. . . . It is a generally recognized rule of law that the knowledge of the agent is imputed to the principal in connection with any transaction conducted by, or participated in by, the agent in behalf of the principal. . . . We . . . conclude that defendant through its agent Deathridge was charged with the actual knowledge of the existence of the conditional sales contract, upon which the plaintiff predicated its right to recover. The contention of the defendant to the effect that the plaintiff consented to the transfer and thereby waived its rights to recover under the conditional sales contract is based upon the general doctrine that where the vendee in the conditional sales contract expressly or impliedly consents to the sale of the property by the vendee, he waives the lien and the purchaser takes the title freed of any claim on the part of the vendor. This rule finds support in the authorities. . . .

It is analogous to the rule applied by our courts in connection with chattel mortgages to the effect that where the mortgagee consents to a sale of the mortgaged property by the mortgagor the purchaser receives the property free of any lien. . . .

However, this doctrine is not inconsistent with a right of the vendor or mortgagor to retain his lien against or interest in the property in the hands of the purchaser or transferee provided it is the intention of the parties that such interest be retained and the intention is communicated to the transferee or purchaser. The rule appears in 11 C.J. page 625, in the following language:

> "When a mortgagee's consent to a sale by the mortgagor is given on condition, the condition must be per-

formed in order to render the consent a waiver of the mortgage lien as between the parties, or as against a purchaser who was a party to the condition or had knowledge thereof."

This doctrine may be properly applied to the case under consideration. The record discloses by the testimony of Mr. Phillips the agent for the plaintiff who acted for the plaintiff in the sale of the pumps to Martin and by the testimony of Mr. Martin, that at the time the conditional sale contract was executed, Phillips was advised that Mr. Martin intended to transfer the pumps to the defendant. The testimony of Martin also is to the effect that Mr. Deathridge the agent of the defendant was there at the time these negotiations were had and these statements were made. Notwithstanding the fact that such transfer was contemplated, the conditional sales contract retaining a lien by the plaintiff was executed; from which the logical conclusion may be drawn that it was the intention of all the parties that the vendor in the conditional sales contract intended to retain a lien upon the property in the hands of the transferee, until the purchase price thereof was paid. This being a logical deduction from the evidence it is in support of the judgment and finding of the trial court.

The Supreme Court of Washington had a similar problem before it in the case of Allis-Chalmers Mfg. Co. v. City of Ellensburg, 108 Wash. 533, 185 Pac. 811. In that case a contractor made the contract with the city to equip a power plant. He purchased certain machinery under a conditional sales contract from plaintiff with intention of installing it in the power plant of the city and did so install it. In an action to recover this machinery from the city by the vendor under the conditional sales contract, the city urged that the vendor at the time the contract was executed knew the purpose for which the machinery was to be used and consented thereto and was thereby barred from recovery of the property. The court held that the plaintiff could recover for the reason that the city had actual notice of the conditional sales contract and the conditions thereof, before any of the equipment of the machinery went into its plant.

In connection with the case at bar it is obvious that the consent, if any, to the transfer and the execution of the conditional sales contract herein were simultaneous acts; in fact, the evidence indicates that the consent to the transfer was agreed upon before the conditional sales contract was actually executed.

If plaintiff intended to relinquish its title by consenting to the transfer by the vendee, it probably would never have executed a contract. At least such is the reasonable inference.

. . . judgment . . . affirmed.

CASE NO. 11

Handy v. C.I.T. Corp. 291 Mass. 157, 197 N.E. 64, 101 A.L.R. 447 (1935)

RUGG, CH.J., delivered the opinion of the court:

This is an action of tort for conversion of an automobile. The trial judge directed a verdict for the defendant. The relevant facts disclosed by the plaintiffs' bill of exceptions are these:

The defendant, a finance company, had a general business arrangement, followed in the instant case, with one Stiles, a retail dealer in automobiles. An automobile would first be received by the distributor in Boston from the factory. Stiles would go to Boston to take possession of the automobile. The distributor would make out a bill of sale to the defendant;

eighty-five to ninety per cent. of the purchase price would be paid by the defendant and the balance by the dealer; Stiles would sign an instrument termed a "trust receipt" acknowledging receipt of the automobile from the defendant and agreeing to hold it, or, if sold, its proceeds, as the defendant's property. That so-called "trust receipt" would be taken by the defendant. The automobile would then be driven off by Stiles and with the defendant's knowledge displayed for sale in his garage without any indication that the defendant had any claim upon it. The so-called "trust receipt" contained Stiles' agreement to return the automobile

> "on demand in good order and unused but with liberty to us to exhibit and if the written consent of C.I.T. has first been obtained to sell the same for its account for cash for not less than $915.00," and it provided that "C.I.T. may at any time cancel this trust and repossess itself of said motor vehicle or the proceeds thereof."

The defendant knew that it was customary for Stiles to sell such automobile to the public, that the trust receipt was not recorded in any place and that no member of the public had means of knowing that the defendant had any claim on the automobile. The defendant was aware that Stiles was selling automobiles thus obtained by him to the public and that they were displayed for sale and that no method was used by the defendant to notify anybody that the defendant had a claim on such automobiles.

The automobile here in question, so held by Stiles, was sold by him to the plaintiffs, who are father and son, without written consent of the defendant. . . . The plaintiffs neglected to register the automobile but kept dealer plates of Stiles on it. It was sometimes kept in Stiles' garage, and sometimes at the plaintiffs' home. The plaintiffs took general care of the automobile though Stiles often borrowed it for use for display purposes. It cannot be inferred that they had knowledge of the defendant's claim. Stiles assigned the conditional sales agreement and note to the Greenfield Loan & Acceptance Corporation, and never paid the defendant anything on the automobile. On August 26, 1931, the defendant repossessed the automobile from Stiles and refused a demand from the plaintiffs that it be returned to them. The plaintiffs continued to make payments to the Greenfield Loan & Acceptance Corporation on their note, and on October 27, 1931, paid the balance due on it. . . .

In order to prevail the plaintiffs must prove that at the time of the conversion they had a complete property either general or special in the automobile, and the right to its immediate possession. . . . The defendant contends that under the instrument signed by Stiles it had legal title to the automobile all the time and a right to repossess it at any time, since no payments were made to the defendant, and that the plaintiffs had no title to the automobile or right to its possession. . . .

An owner's rights in his chattel are protected to every reasonable extent. . . . There are equitable considerations in favor of a bona fide purchaser of such property intrusted by the holder of its legal title to the possession of another with authority to sell. . . .

The contention of the defendant is that the dealer, Stiles, was not a factor or agent, but merely one in possession of the automobile under the provisions of the so-called trust receipt. When examined at large, the authorities are not in accord as to the legal consequences of such an instrument as was signed by Stiles and held by the defendant. All are in agreement that it creates no trust, because by its terms the finance company for which the automobile is held "in trust" retains legal title, which in a true trust vests in the trustee. It is not often spoken of as creating the relation of pledgor and pledgee, since the essence of the transaction is to place the possession of the automobile in the dealer and not in the finance company. It is more like a conditional sale, but the dealer is not seeking a position in which he will ever become sole owner. It is evident that the contract is one of financing rather than of sale. . . . Because of a natural and inherent disinclination toward such concealed ownership of chattels intended to be exposed for sale, some courts have treated the trust receipt as equivalent to a chattel mortgage and required it to be a matter of public record. General Motors Acceptance Corporation v. Berry, 86 N.H. 280, 167 A. 553; McLeod-Nash Motors, Inc., v. Commercial Credit Trust, 187 Minn. 452, 246 N.W. 17, 87 A.L.R. 290. That hardly seems a logical position for these reasons: Where the finance company secured its legal title from the wholesale automobile distributor, the dealer's position under a trust receipt cannot be that of a mortgagor for he never had legal title and never conveyed it to the so-called mortgagee. Moreover, the mortgagee may regain possession only on default, whereas the trust receipt permits repossession of the car at any time. This is also contrary to the theory on which has been developed the law of trust receipts in their original field as governing the relation of an importer of goods to his banker who buys from the foreign seller and takes title to himself. . . . The evidence in the case at bar warrants the conclusion that the contractual relationship between the defendant and Stiles under the instrument signed by the latter is to some extent that of principal and agent. The defendant, as owner, authorizes the sale of the automobile on certain conditions and leaves possession of the automobile in the hands of Stiles as its agent. The sale by the dealer is made by him as agent of an undisclosed principal. The fact that the principal does not enjoy all the gains or suffer the losses of ownership, such as any profit or loss realized upon the sale as compared with the purchase price, does not destroy the agency relationship but merely defines its limits. The finance company and the dealer each has manifested its consent that the dealer, on behalf and subject to the control of the finance company, take possession of the automobile and sell it. . . .

NOTE: Massachusetts passed the Uniform Trust Receipt Act in 1936; St. Mass. 1936, C. 264.

Review Questions

1. In what fundamental respect does a lien differ from a pledge?
2. What are the basic characteristics of the common law lien?
3. How does the mechanics' lien differ from the common law type of lien?
4. What is required under some modern lien statutes in lieu of retention of possession of the property to make the lien effective?
5. How does the method of enforcement of a lien under common law differ from the procedure generally provided by lien statutes?
6. Distinguish special liens and general liens. What is the extent of an attorney's lien upon the property of his client?

7. What special liens have been created by statute in your state which are not recognized under the common law?
8. What type of property plays the most important role in the commercial use of the pledge transaction?
9. What elements characterize the pledge?
10. Will a conditional surrender of the pledged property to the pledgor defeat the creditors' right of pledge?
11. Construct a fact situation under which a surrender of possession of the pledged property will not affect the pledge security.
12. May a pledge be made to cover future obligations?
13. Does the pledgee have the right to repledge the property?
14. What determines whether the future-obligations provision of a pledge agreement operates in favor of a transferee?
15. Enumerate the rights and duties of the pledgee in relation to the pledged property.
16. In the event of the pledgor's default, may the pledgee retain the property in satisfaction of the obligation?
17. Does the pledgee have the right to retain the proceeds derived from a sale that are in excess of the obligation secured?
18. Who is entitled to possession of property under a chattel mortgage?
19. Upon which of the parties to a chattel mortgage do the recording statutes place the burden of recording the mortgage?
20. To what extent is a chattel mortgage upon future property, exclusive of crops, effective?
21. How can the mortgagee make his security interest in future property, exclusive of crops, effective against third parties?
22. Is a mortgage upon a potentially existing crop valid?
23. What problem is presented by a chattel mortgage upon property held for resale? To what extent is such a mortgage valid against claimants other than purchasers in the course of trade?
24. Does the mortgagee acquire a security interest in the proceeds resulting from the sale of the mortgaged property?
25. What is the usual method of foreclosing a chattel mortgage? What statutory regulations are found in your state pertaining to a chattel mortgage foreclosure?
26. In what fundamental respect does the conditional sales contract differ from the chattel mortgage?
27. What is the purpose of filing or recording a conditional sales contract?
28. Where does the risk of loss of property sold under a conditional sales contract reside?
29. What are the conditional vendee's duties in respect to the property purchased under a conditional sales agreement?
30. Does the acceptance of additional security by the conditional vendor constitute a waiver of his rights under his conditional sales contract?
31. What is the effect, under the Uniform Conditional Sales Act, of an action by the vendor to recover the purchase price?
32. Summarize the possible rights of the conditional vendor upon default of the buyer.

33. In what two fields is the trust receipt primarily used?
34. Illustrate the use of a trust receipt as a security device.
35. Indicate the varying attitudes of the courts in respect to the nature of the trust receipt relationship.
36. Which of the above theories of the trust receipt relationship do you favor? State your reasons.
37. What is the status of the security position of the trust receipt holder under the Uniform Trust Receipt Act?

Problems for Discussion

1. The Lewis Garage refused to release Gray's car until a repair bill of $129 was paid. Three months later Gray tendered the $129 but, since he was unable to pay $15 demanded by the garage for storage, the garage retained possession of the car. Gray brought an action to recover the car upon the basis of his tender. Did he succeed?
2. O'Brien owned an iceboat, which was stored with Buxton, who also served as its sailing master. The question arose whether Buxton was entitled to a common law lien for his services as sailing master. Decide. (*O'Brien* v. *Buxton,* 9 N.J. Misc. 876)
3. X contracted to do certain printing for Y, who furnished the type. X claims a lien upon the type in his possession. How would you decide in the absence of a controlling statute?
4. X deposited goods with Y, a warehouseman, for storage. Y refuses to surrender the goods until he has been paid the storage charges. Assuming that warehousemen are given no statutory lien, can X recover the goods from Y without first making payment for the storage service?
5. X spent a month at the Y hotel. Being unable to pay his bill, the hotel claims a lien upon X's car, which was kept in the hotel garage. Does the hotel have a lien against the car for all claims?
6. Stark had pledged certain stocks and bonds with the Security Bank as collateral to secure a loan. The bank temporarily released the stocks and bonds to the auditors who were going over Stark's books. While the stocks and bonds were in the possession of the auditors, they came into the hand of Stark, who pledged them with the National Bank. Can the Security Bank recover the stocks and bonds from the National Bank?
7. A obligated himself to B for $500, giving B a stock certificate endorsed in blank as security. B transferred the $500 claim against A to C and also surrendered to C the security. C sold the stock certificate for $1,500 one day after A's $500 obligation had matured without having demanded payment from A. Is either B or C liable to A for a conversion of the pledged property?
8. The X bank holds securities pledged by A to secure a loan. The creditors of A claim the right to the income from the pledged securities. Result?
9. Plaintiff borrowed money from Hamaker and pledged a diamond ring as security. The pledge agreement (promissory note) read, "As collateral security for the payment of this and any other liability of mine to Hamaker or other holder thereof, due or to become due." Hamaker sold the note and delivered the security to defendant. Plaintiff was indebted to defendant for services

rendered in obtaining a divorce for plaintiff. Defendant contends the pledge stands as security for this obligation as well as for the amount of the loan. Plaintiff tendered the amount of the loan and brought an action to recover the ring. Result? (*Foster* v. *Abrahams*, 241 Pac. 274)

10. The X bank holds a $1,000 promissory note, in which A is the payee, as security for the latter's $200 loan. The bank fails to take the proper steps—presentment and notice—necessary to fix liability of an indorser upon the instrument. The maker of the note is unable to pay, and the indorser cannot be held. The bank sues A for the amount of the loan, and A resists payment upon the contention that the bank failed in its duty respecting the pledged property. It is the bank's contention that it was not its duty to preserve the value of the security. Result?
11. Turner uses a radio, which he holds as a pledge, to entertain his friends. While the radio was in use, the house was struck by lightning and the radio was practically ruined. Is Turner liable to the pledgor?
12. Todd had pledged a bond with Cline to secure a $500 obligation. After the obligation was due, Cline made demand for payment and notified Todd that, unless the obligation was paid, the bond would be sold. Two weeks later Todd had not paid, and Cline made a private sale of the bond for $525, the amount of the obligation plus interest. What will determine whether Todd has legal recourse against Cline?
13. The sufficiency of the following descriptions of mortgaged property was questioned:

    (a) 3,000 boxes of Winesaps and Rome Beauty apples located in the Bryant warehouse at Zillah, Washington.

    (b) One walnut sofa, four straight walnut chairs, two bedroom rockers, and other items belonging to the mortgagor.

    (c) One Packard coupe automobile, color dark brown, 1939 model. What is your opinion?
14. X gave Y a mortgage upon ten acres of sugar beets growing upon a described tract. The tract consisted of 41.36 acres of sugar beets. Is this a sufficient description?
15. X mortgaged his truck to Y, who failed to record the mortgage contract. X contends the mortgage is invalid because of this fact. Answer the contention.
16. Hawkins executed a mortgage to Brand upon a specified lot of leather, which mortgage was properly recorded. Without the consent of Brand, Hawkins made the leather into belts and sold them to Donhowe. Has Brand lost his security interest in the leather?
17. A mortgaged his manufacturing equipment to B, the mortgage containing an after-acquired clause. The mortgage was properly recorded. A subsequently acquired additional equipment, which he mortgaged to C, who was unaware of B's mortgage. C claims a superior right to the new equipment. Result? Would your conclusion have been the same if the facts were that C had personal knowledge of the existing mortgage between A and B?
18. Contemplating renting a farm, A borrowed money from B in January, 1940, with which to launch upon the venture. As security, A executed a chattel mortgage to B, which was made to cover the crops to be grown by A in the future. In February of that same year, A found a farm that satisfied him. In 1942, A

made an assignment for the benefit of his creditors. The question then arose whether the creditors or B were entitled to the 1942 crops. Decide.

19. A chattel mortgagee A authorizes B, the mortgagor, to sell the mortgaged property; it was understood that the obligation to A is to be satisfied out of the proceeds. Before payment is made to A, a creditor of B's levies upon the money. A claims a lien upon the money under his chattel mortgage. Result?
20. A sold B a threshing outfit on credit; it was understood that B was not to place any encumbrances upon it and that A was to have a lien upon all proceeds earned by use of the machine until such time as it would be paid for. However, B borrowed money from C, who accepted a chattel mortgage upon the property involved as security. Assuming that the agreement between A and B had been placed of record and that C had no notice of A's rights and had properly recorded his mortgage, who has the prior right to the threshing outfit?
21. Defendant purchased certain machinery from plaintiff under a conditional sales contract. Defendant defaulted in payment and plaintiff took possession of the machinery and sold it for $1,450. He then sued defendant for $550, that being the difference between $1,450 and the unpaid purchase price. Did he recover?
22. A sold B an automobile under a conditional sales contract. B failed to meet the condition of payment, and A commenced an action to recover the purchase price. Before the conclusion of the suit, B sold the car to C. A then commenced an action against C to recover the car. Will A succeed?
23. M sold F two sectional metal corncribs under a conditional sales contract for use upon F's farm. The cribs were firmly embedded in a concrete base at the time of their erection. F became insolvent, and the question arose whether M, the conditional vendor, or O, the holder of the real estate mortgage, had the prior right to the cribs. Decide.
24. Clinton had purchased an automobile under a conditional sales contract. He failed to pay the last installment of $100 and the automobile was repossessed by the vendor, who sold it for $750. What are Clinton's rights?

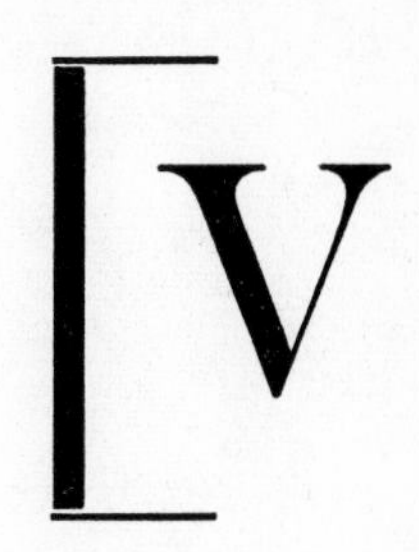

Real Property and Related Topics

Chapter

29. REAL PROPERTY

30. REAL ESTATE MORTGAGES

31. LANDLORD AND TENANT

32. LIENS UPON REAL PROPERTY

29 REAL PROPERTY AND RELATED TOPICS:

REAL PROPERTY

► I. OWNERSHIP INTERESTS CLASSIFIED

In Chapter 25 it was established that, in general terms, real property is land or anything that is permanently attached as a part of the land. When, on the other hand, the term *real property* is used to designate ownership interest in land, it is limited to an estate of freehold, which is either an estate of inheritance or an estate for life. Easements, however, are, properly speaking, not ownership interests in land and will be treated separately.

A. ESTATES OF INHERITANCE

An *estate of inheritance* is, as the term suggests, such an ownership interest as would, upon the owner's death, descend to his heirs.

1. *Estates in Fee Simple*

The purchaser of real property wants title in fee simple, which can be transferred to him by the seller providing the latter has an estate in fee simple. An *estate in fee simple* is the highest degree of ownership recognized by law. It has been said to be "an estate to a man and his heirs forever" and "a full and absolute estate beyond and outside of which there is no other interest, or even shadow of right." It is absolute ownership, giving the proprietor the unqualified right of use and enjoyment, together with the unlimited right of disposition during his lifetime. In addition, it has the characteristic of descending to the owner's heirs generally should he die without a will. To illustrate:

In the case of *State Bank of Jansen* v. *Thiessen,* 9 Neb. S.C.J. 343, the instrument transferring title read:

> "To my son Earnest Ackmann . . . without any power or right . . . to sell, mortgage, or otherwise encumber said land, I give, devise and bequeath . . . to the said Earnest Ackmann and his heirs forever."

The court held that the phrase "and his heirs forever" was controlling and transferred a title in fee simple:

> "It is a fundamental rule that when an estate in fee simple is devised that an attempt by the testator to prevent alienation is ineffective and void."

The above concept of ownership in fee simple needs to be qualified. The incidents of fee simple are subject to at least the following limitations:

(1) The owner's right of use and enjoyment is subject to the rights of other members of society. The property can be used to such an extent and only in such ways as are compatible with social objectives.

(2) It is subject to the right of eminent domain, the police power of the state, and taxation.

(3) It is subject to the rights of creditors (exclusive of the right of homestead).

(4) The right of dower or courtesy presents a limitation to its disposition.

(5) It may be subservient to easements in favor of others.

(6) Its use and enjoyment may be subject to restrictive covenants contained in the grant. It is common, for example, that property is restricted in its use to residential purposes or that it shall not be occupied by members of designated races.[1, 2]

2. *Fees in Expectancy*

Fees in expectancy are nonpossessory ownership interests in real property. They consist of the rights to the future enjoyment of the fee simple interest in land that is temporarily in the use and enjoyment of another. Such interests exist where a life estate ownership has been created. One having a *life estate in land* has, as the term suggests, the right to the benefits of the land for the duration of a designated life, which is usually that of the life tenant. During the period of the life estate, the fee simple is held in abeyance as a *fee in expectancy*. Upon termination of the life estate, the fee in expectancy becomes a possessory fee simple. Fees in expectancy are classified as being either *reversions* or *remainders*.

a. Reversions. If A, who owns property in fee simple, grants B a life estate (use and enjoyment for life), he thereby creates a noninheritable life ownership interest in the property, retaining for himself that which he originally had, less the life estate. A has thus created a situation whereby he has no right of possession to the property that he owns but to which he will acquire the right of possession in the future. The interest in the property that resides in A during this period is known as an *estate in reversion*. It is an inheritable interest which can pass to A's heirs upon his decease.

b. Remainders. If, upon the creation of the life estate, A conveys to a third person C that ownership interest which remains, the latter has an *estate in remainder*. That which remains upon the termination of the life estate will go to C and in this instance will be a fee simple.

3. *Easements*

a. Nature of Easements

"A pure easement is one where the land of one person, which land is denominated the 'servient tenement,' is subjected to some use or burden for the benefit of the lands of another person, whose lands are termed the 'dominant tenement.'" *Patterson* v. *Chambers' Power Co.*, 81 Ore. 328

A and B own adjoining land. A acquires the right to cross B's land for the purpose of making available a highway to "himself and his heirs." This is an *easement*. The right of way constitutes a burden upon B's estate; this burden is not for the benefit of A personally but for the benefit of the land he owns. The right of way

---

1 Norris v. Williams, p. 761.

2 Shelley v. Kraemer, p. 762.

attaches to A's estate and will pass with the estate to subsequent owners, thus continuing as a charge upon B's estate forever, unless terminated.[3]

The true easement, as characterized above, is to be distinguished from a personal right in the nature of an easement, which is designated by the courts as an *easement in gross*. For example, A may acquire the right to cross B's land for his personal benefit and not for the benefit of an estate in adjoining land. According to the weight of authority, this privilege, being personal, cannot extend beyond the life of the grantee A. The majority of the courts say that such a personal right is "not assignable or inheritable; nor can it be made so by any term in the grant." The contrary view is expressed in *Poull* v. *Mockley,* 33 Wis. 482, where the court said, "we cannot see any substantial reason for holding that an easement in gross cannot be assigned or transferred, especially when the language of the grant shows unmistakably that the intention was that it should be enjoyed by the grantee, 'his heirs and assigns.' "

b. Creation

(1) By Grant, Express and Implied. Easements come into being either by grant (by deed) or by prescription. An easement by deed may be created by a reservation in the deed conveying the property to which it is to attach or by a separate deed that operates to convey the easement interest only. To illustrate an easement by reservation: A, in conveying land to B, reserves the right to pipe water to his adjacent land from a spring located upon the land being conveyed.

At times the circumstances surrounding the conveyance of real property are such as to give rise to an *implied easement,* circumstances that make it appear that the grantor and grantee intended that the grant should include an easement. Such an easement is generally designated as one *by necessity*. It is based upon the theory that if one conveys property he also conveys whatever is necessary for its beneficial use and enjoyment, and if one conveys a part of his property, he reserves that which is strictly necessary for the use and enjoyment of the portion retained. To illustrate an implied easement by grant:

A sells one half of his 360-acre farm to B, and that half which B acquires is not adjacent to a highway. The facts are that B's most direct and convenient egress and ingress to a public road is over the land retained by A. Under these circumstances, it will be implied that an easement of right of way over A's land was intended, since it is necessary to the beneficial use and enjoyment of the land conveyed.

After the conveyance described in the above facts, if the grantor, A, were found in the position of B, it would be implied that a reservation of a right of way was intended.

(2) By Prescription. Acquiring an easement by prescription means that the easement has been acquired by the right of long usage. Thus, if a person uses another's land for a statutory period of time as a benefit to his own estate, he thereby creates a permanent easement.[4, 5] This statutory period of time is the same as the time

---

[3] Penn Bowling Recreation Center v. Hot Shoppes, p. 765.

[4] Engleman v. Kalamazoo, p. 767.

[5] Wilson v. Waters, p. 768.

within which an action must be brought to recover an interest in real property. Usually this period of time is twenty years, but in some jurisdictions it is only five. The requisites for acquiring an easement by use (by prescription) are:

(1) The use must be open and notorious;

(2) it must be exercised under some color (as an invalid deed) or claim of right;

(3) it must be continuous and adverse to the true owner.

B. LIFE ESTATES

1. *By Grant or Will*

Life estates are created either by operation of law or voluntarily by the owner of the fee simple estate. A voluntary life estate comes into being by virtue of a grant by deed or by a provision in a will. For example, A may provide in his will that B, his surviving spouse, is to have the use and enjoyment of the property for the period of her life, with the remainder to go to his sons C and D.

2. *Curtesy*

At common law, by virtue of marriage the husband acquired the right to the income and profits derived from the real property owned by the wife. This right was dependent upon the continuation of the marital relationship and did not extend beyond the period of the wife's life. However, if a child was born alive to the union, the husband thereby became vested with a life estate in the whole of the wife's property, an estate that could then be enjoyed by the husband after the wife's death for the period of his natural days. This is known as an *estate by curtesy.*

Although most of the states have abolished the estate by curtesy, some states have only modified it.

3. *Dower*

Common law dower is the estate in the property of the husband of which the wife becomes possessed upon his death. The common law right of dower consists of the wife's life estate in one third of all the real property owned by the husband during the coverture. Like curtesy, dower presents an absolute limitation upon the disposition of real property by the titleholder. Unless the wife joins in the deed of conveyance, her dower interest remains outstanding. For this reason both husband and wife are required to join in the execution of the real estate contract and the deed.

Today the right of dower is regulated by statute in the various states. In some states the common law right of dower has been abolished; in other states it has been modified; and in still others, statutes are declaratory of the right as it exists under common law. Some states have given husband and wife identical interests in each other's property; the Iowa statute is an illustration of this—the provision being a modification of the common law right of dower. This provides that the surviving husband or wife will acquire a fee simple title to one third of all the estate owned by the deceased during the period of marriage.

4. *Rights of Life Tenant*

The ownership interest of the life tenant may be assigned or mortgaged; in that event, the assignee or mortgagee acquires the same rights possessed by the life tenant. The remainderman may, for example, wish to acquire the estate of the life tenant and thereby obtain an unqualified fee, which would entitle him to immediate possession. The value of the life estate is determined by the life expectancy of the person for whose life the estate exists and by the annual income value of the property. It should be recognized that the remainderman may be paying a substantial price for the right of possession, which, due to the uncertainty of life, he might presently have acquired. This risk can, to a certain extent, be offset by insuring the life upon which the life estate is based.

The right of use and enjoyment of the property by a life tenant is much more limited in scope than is that of an owner in fee simple.[6] As long as he remains within the bounds of the law, the owner in fee simple can do as he chooses with the property. He can destroy the buildings or deplete the natural resources. The life tenant, on the other hand, is entitled only to the income and profits and has the duty to preserve the premises for the holder of the remainder or the reversion. For example, a life tenant may work to exhaustion a mine, well, or quarry that was opened before the creation of the life estate, but a life tenant may not exploit those resources of the property which are not in evidence at the time his estate vests.

► II. JOINT ESTATES

Estates in real property may be owned by more than one individual. The following are the various species of joint ownership with their legal incidents.

A. ESTATES IN JOINT TENANCY AND TENANCY IN COMMON

The right of survivorship is the basic distinguishing characteristic between these two capacities of joint ownership. In joint tenancy, upon the death of one of the joint owners, that owner's interest passes to the surviving owner or owners, whereas in tenancy in common, upon the death of one of the joint owners, his interest passes to the heirs of the deceased. Consequently, ownership in joint tenancy avoids the need of probating an estate, which avoidance in certain instances, as between husband and wife, is very desirable. Probating an estate is not only time consuming and troublesome but also expensive.

The common law right of joint tenancy has been variously affected by statutory enactments; nevertheless, survivorship can usually be accomplished by a declaration of that intention in the instrument which creates the joint tenancy.[7] The terminology frequently employed to accomplish a joint tenancy is: *A and B as joint tenants with the right of survivorship and not as tenants in common.*

There is no assurance or certainty that a joint tenancy will continue in existence until the death of one of the joint tenants. Its continued existence is dependent

[6] Barker v. Barker, p. 770.
[7] Short v. Milby, p. 770.

upon the will of the joint tenants, and certain of their actions may destroy the relationship. For example, if A and B hold an estate as joint tenants and B conveys his interest by deed to C, the joint tenancy is terminated. A and C then hold the estate as tenants in common.

B. ESTATES BY ENTIRETY

"An estate by the entirety is held by husband and wife as one person under one title, the grant, gift or devise which created the estate operating in such manner as to give each the whole." *Maitlen* v. *Barley,* 174 Ind. 620

Tenancies by entirety resemble joint tenancies in that they also have the characteristic of survivorship. Like joint tenancies, they are used as a means of avoiding administration of a decedent's estate and facilitating the disposition of the property by the surviving spouse. A tenancy by entirety differs fundamentally from a joint tenancy in that it cannot be destroyed by the action of any of the tenants. Its destruction requires the joint action of the various owners.

C. COMMUNITY PROPERTY

Some states provide for a community system of matrimonial gains between husband and wife. In essence, all property that is acquired by the parties during the period of marriage is jointly owned, share and share alike, but is under the control and management of the husband. Property that is separate and not subject to community rights is that property which belonged to either spouse at the time of the marriage or which has been acquired during the marriage period by gift, descent, or in exchange for property owned prior to the marriage.[8]

► III. METHODS OF ACQUIRING TITLE

The proprietary rights to an estate are designated as the *title to the property.* Title to real property is ordinarily acquired by means of a voluntary transfer by deed or by descent.

A. VOLUNTARY TRANSFER BY DEED

The most usual method of acquiring title to real property is by means of a deed executed voluntarily by the owner in discharge of a contractual obligation to a buyer. A *deed* is an instrument formally executed by the grantor to the grantee, which upon delivery to the grantee invests him with the grantor's proprietary rights in the property.

1. *Warranty Deeds*

It is usual that a conveyance of title to real property is accomplished by use of a *warranty deed* as distinguished from a quitclaim deed. The virtue of a warranty deed is that the grantor thereby makes the following warranties to the grantee: (1)

[8] Intermountain Realty Co. v. Allen, p. 771.

that he has a title in fee simple and the right to convey; (2) that the property is free from all encumbrances except as noted; and (3) that he, his heirs, executors, and administrators will defend the title for the benefit of the grantee, his heirs, and assigns against all lawful claimants.

In many states, statutes authorize the use of words of warranty without the need of reciting the above-enumerated covenants in the deed. Usually the clause "conveys and warrants" is used to incorporate the covenants of warranty without enumeration.

2. *Quitclaim Deeds*

A transfer of title by quitclaim deed is a transfer without warranty. The grantor merely relinquishes to the grantee all his interest in the property, whatever that interest might be. A quitclaim deed is used under circumstances where the grantor has no desire to make warranties in respect to the title that is being conveyed. For example, a wife, having failed to join the husband in the execution of the deed, may be called upon to release her dower interest in the property. A quitclaim deed would be the appropriate instrument for accomplishing this purpose. Quitclaim deeds are probably used chiefly for the purpose of correcting defective titles to property as they appear of public record.

B. INVOLUNTARY TRANSFER

Under certain circumstances, transfers of title to property take place by operation of law without the consent of the owner. Transfers by operation of law are those that take place by virtue of legal process or judicial decree. A decree of specific performance is an involuntary transfer of title by court order. Judicial sales, in which the court in effect is the vendor, are transfers of title by operation of law. Illustrations of such are sales under mortgage foreclosure, tax sales, sales by trustees in bankruptcy, and sheriff's sales to realize proceeds to satisfy judgments of record.

C. TITLE BY DESCENT OR WILL

Subject to the rights of creditors and the dower or curtesy interest of the spouse, the law gives everyone the right to dispose of his property upon his death by a properly executed will. Whenever a decedent has failed, during his lifetime, to make provision for the disposition of his property upon his death, in effect he has extended that privilege to the state legislature. In the absence of a will, title to property passes to the heirs of the deceased as provided by legislative enactment.

D. TITLE BY ADVERSE POSSESSION

By exercising the rights of ownership over another's property for a certain period of time, a person acquires title by the doctrine of adverse possession. This doctrine is based primarily upon the public policy of favoring and protecting long, uninterrupted possession of land. This doctrine is invoked, as one court stated it, "as a matter of public policy, to promote the repose of society, and to put down litigation." The law goes so far as to protect the adverse possessor against all claimants to right of possession other than the true owner.

The prerequisites to title by adverse possession are: (1) actual, open, and notorious possession under some claim of title, which is (2) adverse to the true owner and (3) continuous for the requisite period of time.[9] The length of occupancy required is determined by the various states' statutory periods for the bringing of actions to recover interests in real property. Usually this period is twenty years, but in many of the states it is much less. Local statutes should be consulted.

(1) In *Merrill* v. *Tobin,* 30 Fed. 738, the court said:

> "It will ordinarily be sufficient evidence of actual possession if the person claiming title puts the premises to the use which they are naturally fitted for; or, in other words, such a use as the actual owner would ordinarily put them to."

(2) In *Paducah Cooperage Co.* v. *Paducah Veneer Co.,* 135 Ky. 53, the plaintiff and the defendant were owners of adjoining land. The plaintiff had for fifteen years claimed a strip of land which the defendant contended was his. The court held that the plaintiff, in the absence of actual inclosure or occupancy of the strip, did not acquire title.

(3) In *McCullough* v. *Wall,* 38 S.C.L. 68, it was held that occupation of property for five or six weeks annually as a fishing place is not a possession and use sufficient to acquire title.

(4) In *Folley* v. *Thomas,* 46 Ind. App. 559, it was said that the protection of wild lands from trespassers was such an act of ownership as to give a title by prescription.

► IV. STEPS IN A REAL ESTATE TRANSACTION

A. PRELIMINARY CONTRACT

By reason of the Statute of Frauds, a contract to transfer any interest in real property must be in writing if it is to be enforceable. A writing is all the more necessary since the closing of a real estate deal cannot be accomplished without the lapse of some time. Above all, the purchaser is interested in acquiring a good title to the property, *a title in fee simple,* against which there are no claims. Consequently, before accepting a deed to the property, the purchaser will exercise some diligence in determining the extent and the condition of the seller's proprietary interest. The buyer could rely upon the seller's possession as evidence of his title and upon the warranties in the deed for his protection. However, such is not the modern or desirable practice. Unless the title is insured or is transferred by a Torrens Certificate,* the purchaser will require assurance that the public records show a good title in the seller, free of liens and encumbrances.

---

* See *The Principles of Real Estate Law,* by Nathan William MacChesney, pp. 665–673, for a brief yet adequate treatment of the Torrens system of land registration.

[9] Walthall v. Yohn et al., p. 773.

B. RECORD TITLE

Under the common law, a grantee had to do nothing to protect his title to the property conveyed. A subsequent conveyance by the same grantor could in no way affect the first grantee's title, even though the subsequent purchaser had no notice of the prior conveyance. The first grantee's title, which he held as a matter of fact, protected him not only against subsequent purchasers but also against the creditors of his grantor. He stood secure in his title, which he held as a matter of fact.

The same thing was true under the common law in respect to those who held a security interest in real property. A mortgagee, for example, was secure in the fact that he held a mortgage upon the property. All persons dealing with the property were bound by that fact, and a purchaser, although without notice of the encumbrance, nevertheless took title subject to it.

Under modern recording statutes, those who hold an interest in real property are, for their own protection, required to give notice of their interest by recording the instrument that created their interest. Such recording is to be made in the public records of the county where the land is located. Third parties no longer deal with the property at their own peril. They can and should rely upon the facts as they are established by the records. In the absence of actual notice of facts to the contrary, such as actual possession of the property, the title and the encumbrances as they appear in the public records can be conclusively relied upon.[10] For example, if A determines that the record title of certain realty is in B, A can, in reliance upon the records, safely take title to, or a security interest in, the property. The fact that B has previously conveyed or mortgaged the property to X, which fact does not appear of record, can in no way affect A's position. By recording his instrument, A would effectively defeat the rights of X.

The public records will also show such matters as tax liens, mechanics' liens, and judgment liens against the property, as well as derivative title by will or descent.

C. ABSTRACTS OF TITLE

Ordinarily the purchaser, through his attorney, determines by means of an abstract of the title, as that title appears in the records, whether the seller's title is acceptable. A real estate contract will characteristically provide that the seller agrees to furnish the purchaser with an abstract of title showing a good and merchantable title.

An abstract of title is a history of the record title from its origin to date. In it are set forth the operative facts of all matters appearing of record which in any way pertain to or affect the title to the property. Abstracts are prepared upon order by private agencies, usually designated as *title* or *abstract companies.* Generally the seller is in possession of an abstract to the property, having acquired it from his grantor. In such an event, the abstract is continued to date; that is, the abstracter will show all matters of public record since the last date on the abstract. An ab-

[10] Schell v. Kneedler, p. 774.

stract is a valuable adjunct to real property and should be adequately protected against loss or destruction.

Let it be understood, however, that an abstract of title furnished by the seller is no assurance of a good title. The abstracter does not attempt to pass upon the validity of the title; he merely undertakes to show in abstracted form those things which are found in the records. His only responsibility is to set forth faithfully and accurately the findings of his search of the records. In his certificate, which is an essential feature of an abstract, the abstracter certifies that this has been done. The condition of the title is established by an examination of the abstract. It is desirable that this examination be accomplished by an attorney of proved ability.

1. *Examination of Abstracts*

The purpose of the examination by a competent attorney is to determine whether the requirement of a merchantable title has been satisfied. In the event that the abstract does not show a good title, the seller will be required to take the steps necessary to make the title good.

A merchantable title is a record title such as a person of reasonable prudence will accept. It need not be perfect in every technical detail. It is also a record title that will stand as prima facie proof of the owner's proprietary interest in the property, such proof as will make it unnecessary to establish facts not evidenced by the records.

Some of the more common title defects, limitations, and restrictions for which the examiner will search are: (1) misdescriptions of the property; (2) improperly executed deeds; (3) discrepancies in names; (4) unreleased or improperly released mortgages; (5) failure of a spouse to join in the execution of a deed for the purpose of releasing dower; (6) restrictive covenants in deeds limiting the use of the property; (7) judgments against titleholders; (8) mechanics' liens; (9) tax liens; (10) improper legal proceedings in which a disposition of the title is made, such as in foreclosure of mortgages and probate proceedings by which the title is vested in the heirs or devisees.

D. EXECUTION AND DELIVERY OF DEEDS

The various states have statutory requirements for the execution of deeds. It is usual that at the time of execution the deed is required to be acknowledged by the grantor. In some states, this is a prerequisite to the recording of the instrument; in other states, it is also required that the execution be witnessed. In many states, a deed, to be effective, must contain a seal or that which answers for a seal.

Delivery of the deed is essential to an effective conveyance of title to real property. The deed is inoperative as an instrument of conveyance until the grantor by some act has placed the deed beyond his control and authority.[11] Placing the deed in the hands of the grantee is a most effective method of delivery. And a delivery to a third person is as effective as a delivery to the grantee himself.

A delivery in escrow is made by placing the deed in the possession of a third

---

[11] Costello v. Costello, p. 775.

person with instructions that the deed be delivered to the grantee upon the fulfillment of a condition, which is usually payment of the purchase price.[12] This procedure is applicable especially to the purchase of realty on the installment plan. In the event of failure of performance by the purchaser, the deed will be returned to the seller; on the other hand, if the purchaser completes his payments, the deed will be delivered to him by the escrow holder.

CASES

CASE NO. 1

Norris v. Williams. 189 Md. 73, 54 A. (2d) 331, 4 A.L.R. (2d) 1106 (1947)

DELAPLAINE, J. This suit for specific performance was brought by T. Bayard Williams and William G. Lynch, trustees of the estate of John T. Grace, deceased, to compel George R. Norris and A. Margaret Norris, his wife, to comply with their agreements to purchase certain real estate in Dundalk.

The contract of sale, executed on June 23, 1946, recites that the trustees bargain and sell to Norris and his wife the parcel of about one acre of land at the southwest Corner of Dundalk and Baltimore Avenues for the sum of $45,000; that the purchasers made a partial payment of $2,500; and that the balance will be paid in cash within 30 days therefrom. The contract contains a proviso that in the event this property is not zoned for commercial use, or cannot be used as such for any other reason, then the contract shall be void and the deposit shall be refunded to the purchasers.

The record shows that Grace devised his estate to the trustees with direction to pay the income to his widow for life, and with power to sell and invest the principal. On the land is the house in which he resided until his death in 1921. His widow continued to live there for 25 years, and after her death the trustees found no one interested in buying the place for a residence. The land has been zoned by the Zoning Board of Baltimore County for commercial use. But the purchasers refused to settle on account of the fact that the deed executed by Grace and his wife on February 14, 1917, conveying to the Eastern Land Company all of their 50-acre tract of farm land except the parcel now in question, contains a covenant that for the period of 50 years the parcel excepted shall be used for residential purposes only.

It was shown that the property is now located in the business section of Dundalk, and that the restriction cannot benefit any one. The chancellor accordingly ordered the purchasers to pay the balance of $42,500, with interest from the date of the decree, upon receiving a deed from the trustees conveying the property free and clear of the restriction. The appeal is from that decree.

The law is clear that where a grantor imposes a restriction upon land conveyed for the benefit of land which he retains, it will be binding upon the grantee and his successors in title; and likewise where a grantor imposes a restriction upon land retained for the benefit of land which he conveys, the restriction will be binding upon himself, his heirs and assigns. . . .

. . . However, restrictions upon

[12] Gross v. Housner, p. 777.

the use of land are in derogation of the natural right which an owner possesses to use and enjoy his property, and are repugnant to trade and commerce. Consequently restrictive covenants are construed strictly against their establishment and effect, and liberally in support of the unrestricted use of the land. . . .

The land purchased by the Eastern Land Company from Grace was one of the tracts acquired during the First World War for the Dundalk Company to provide building sites for homes for war workers, particularly those employed at the plant of the Bethlehem Steel Company at Sparrows Point. The record shows that about 1,000 acres of land were acquired for the Dundalk Company at a cost of about $200,000. By 1918 this truck farm section was transformed into a thriving community. One of the most common forms of creating building restrictions is by the establishment of a general building plan covering a tract divided into a number of lots. In this case, however, it is conceded that, if the Dundalk Company ever adopted any definite building plan for the development of the 49 acres acquired from Grace, such plan was soon abandoned on the west side of Dundalk Avenue. Within a short time Grace's home on the west side was in the midst of the business district. . . .

Under the circumstances now existing, the covenant made by Grace and his wife in 1917 is no longer effective for the purpose for which it was imposed. It is evident that the purpose of the restriction was to make the locality a suitable one for residences; but, owing to the general growth of the town, and the development of the neighborhood west of the avenue as a business district, this purpose can no longer be accomplished.

Usually the duration of a restriction upon the use of land is not expressly limited. In the case before us the duration of the restriction was definitely limited to 50 years, from February 14, 1917, to February 14, 1967. Thus more than 30 years of the life of the covenant have elapsed. We now hold that, even though the duration of a restrictive covenant is expressly limited, equity will not enforce the covenant where a considerable part of the life of the covenant has elapsed and where, owing to a change in the character of the neighborhood, not resulting from a breach of the covenant, the reason for enforcement of the covenant no longer exists, and such enforcement would merely encumber the land and injure or harass the covenantor without benefiting the covenantee. For example, in a case arising in New York City, where the owner of the lot on the southwest corner of 145th Street and St. Nicholas Avenue entered into a covenant in 1886 that he would not erect any apartment house thereon within the period of 25 years, the Court of Appeals of New York in 1905 held that, although only 19 of the 25 years had elapsed, the covenant was nevertheless unenforceable, because its purpose had been defeated by the unexpected action of others in erecting apartment houses in the immediate vicinity. McClure v. Leaycraft, 183 N.Y. 36, 75 N.E. 961, 5 Ann. Cas. 45.

In view of the fact that the restriction imposed upon the property in this case is no longer effective and enforceable, the decree of the chancellor will be affirmed. . . .

CASE NO. 2

Shelley v. Kraemer. 334 U.S. 1, 92 L. Ed. (Adv. 845), 68 Sup. Ct. 836, 3 A.L.R. (2d) 441 (1948)

VINSON, CH.J., delivered the opinion of the court:

These cases present for our consideration questions relating to the validity of court enforcement of private agreements, generally described as restrictive covenants, which have as their purpose the exclusion of persons of designated race or color from the ownership or occupancy of real property. Basic constitutional issues of obvious importance have been raised.

. . . On February 16, 1911, thirty out of a total of thirty-nine owners of property fronting both sides of Labadie Avenue between Taylor Avenue and Cora Avenue in the city of St. Louis, signed an agreement, which was subsequently recorded, providing in part:

> ". . . the said property is hereby restricted to the use and occupancy for the term of Fifty (50) years from this date, so that it shall be a condition all the time . . . and shall attach to the land, as a condition precedent to the sale of the same, that hereafter no part of said property or any portion thereof shall be, for said term of Fifty years, occupied by any person not of the Caucasian race, . . ."

The entire district described in the agreement included fifty-seven parcels of land. The thirty owners who signed the agreement held title to forty-seven parcels, including the particular parcel involved in this case. . . .

On August 11, 1945, pursuant to a contract of sale, petitioners Shelley, who are Negroes, for valuable consideration received from one Fitzgerald a warranty deed to the parcel in question. The trial court found that petitioners had no actual knowledge of the restrictive agreement at the time of the purchase.

On October 9, 1945, respondents, as owners of other property subject to the terms of the restrictive covenant, brought suit in the Circuit Court of the city of St. Louis praying that petitioners Shelley be restrained from taking possession of the property and that judgment be entered divesting title out of petitioners Shelley and revesting title in the immediate grantor or in such other person as the court should direct. The trial court denied the requested relief on the ground that the restrictive agreement, upon which respondents based their action, had never become final and complete because it was the intention of the parties to that agreement that it was not to become effective until signed by all property owners in the district, and signatures of all the owners had never been obtained. The Supreme Court of Missouri sitting en banc reversed and directed the trial court to grant the relief for which respondents had prayed. That court held the agreement . . . violated no rights guaranteed to petitioners by the Federal Constitution. . . .

The second of the cases under consideration comes to this Court from the Supreme Court of Michigan. The circumstances presented do not differ materially from the Missouri case. . . .

Petitioners have placed primary reliance on their contentions, first raised in the state courts, that judicial enforcement of the restrictive agreements in these cases has violated rights guaranteed to petitioners by the Fourteenth Amendment of the Federal Constitution and Acts of Congress passed pursuant to that Amendment. Specifically, petitioners urge that they have been denied the equal protection of the laws, deprived of property without due process of law, and have been denied privileges and immunities of citizens of the United States. We pass to a consideration of those issues.

Whether the equal protection clause of the Fourteenth Amendment inhibits judicial enforcement by state courts of restrictive covenants based on race or color is a question which this

Court has not heretofore been called upon to consider. . . .

It should be observed that these covenants do not seek to prescribe any particular use of the affected properties. Use of the properties for residential occupancy, as such, is not forbidden. The restrictions of these agreements, rather, are directed toward a designated class of persons and seek to determine who may and who may not own or make use of the properties for residential purposes. The excluded class is defined wholly in terms of race or color: . . .

It cannot be doubted that among the civil rights intended to be protected from discriminatory state action by the Fourteenth Amendment are the rights to acquire, enjoy, own and dispose of property. Equality in the enjoyment of property rights was regarded by the framers of that Amendment as an essential precondition to the realization of other basic civil rights and liberties which the Amendment was intended to guarantee. . . .

Since the decision of this Court in the Civil Rights Cases, 109 U.S. 3, 27 L. Ed. 835, 3 Sup. Ct. 18 (1883), the principle has become firmly embedded in our constitutional law that the action inhibited by the first section of the Fourteenth Amendment is only such action as may fairly be said to be that of the States. That Amendment erects no shield against merely private conduct, however discriminatory or wrongful.

We conclude, therefore, that the restrictive agreements standing alone cannot be regarded as a violation of any rights guaranteed to petitioners by the Fourteenth Amendment. So long as the purposes of those agreements are effectuated by voluntary adherence to their terms, it would appear clear that there had been no action by the State and the provisions of the Amendment have not been violated. Cf. Corrigan v. Buckley, 271 U.S. 323. . . .

But here there was more. These are cases in which the purposes of the agreements were secured only by judicial enforcement by state courts of the restrictive terms of the agreements. The respondents urge that judicial enforcement of private agreement does not amount to state action. . . .

The short of the matter is that from the time of the adoption of the Fourteenth Amendment until the present, it has been the consistent ruling of this Court that the action of the States to which the Amendment has reference, includes action of state courts and state judicial officials. Although, in construing the terms of the Fourteenth Amendment, differences have from time to time been expressed as to whether particular types of state action may be said to offend the Amendment's prohibitory provisions, it has never been suggested that state court action is immunized from the operation of those provisions simply because the act is that of the judicial branch of the state government. . . .

These are not cases, as has been suggested, in which the States have merely abstained from action, leaving private individuals free to impose such discriminations as they see fit. Rather, these are cases in which the States have made available to such individuals the full coercive power of government to deny to petitioners, on the grounds of race or color, the enjoyment of property rights in premises which petitioners are willing and financially able to acquire and which the grantors are willing to sell. The difference between judicial enforcement and nonenforcement of the restrictive covenants is the difference to petitioners between being denied rights of property available to other members of the community and being accorded full enjoyment of those rights on an equal footing. . . .

We hold that in granting judicial enforcement of the restrictive agreements in these cases, the States have denied petitioners the equal protection of the laws and that, therefore, the action of the state courts cannot stand.

CASE NO. 3

Penn Bowling Recreation Center v. Hot Shoppes. 179 F. (2d) 64 (1949)

MC ALLISTER, C.J. In 1939, the Norment Estate conveyed a portion of its real property to appellee, Hot Shoppes, Inc., and subjected a part thereof to a sixteen-foot right of way for ingress and egress. This resulted in an easement for the benefit of the balance of the unconveyed property, adjacent thereto, which was retained by the Estate, and which, by virtue of the easement, became the dominant tenement. A part of this dominant estate came into ownership of appellant, Penn Bowling Recreation Center, Inc., . . . two years after the creation of the right of way.

On February 5, 1948, appellee, Hot Shoppes, erected a barrier of iron posts and cement concrete blocks within the right of way and alongside of it, interfering with the full enjoyment of the easement by Penn Bowling; and shortly thereafter, appellant filed its complaint to enjoin appellee from maintaining the structure within the right of way and interfering with the use thereof. Appellee, in its answer denied that appellant was entitled to the use of the right of way, and asked for a permanent injunction against such use by appellant, as well as for judgment declaring it to be permanently forfeited and extinguished by abandonment. . . . The district court granted appellee's motion for summary judgment as prayed; and from such judgment, the Penn Bowling Recreation Center appeals.

The arguments that appellee addressed to the district court on the hearing on the motion for summary judgment embraced the contentions that appellant, as owner of the dominant tenement, had forfeited and extinguished the right of way by abandonment, as the result of subjecting the servient tenement to an additional and enlarged use or servitude in connection with other premises to which the easement was not appurtenant; that it had been guilty of the misuse of the easement of the right of way by reason of having used it for the parking of motor vehicles; and that, by certain masonry constructions, appellant had, in any event, made it impossible to use the right of way for egress and ingress.

With regard to the claim that appellant had subjected the servient tenement to a burden in excess of that imposed by the original easement, it appears that after the creation of the right of way for the benefit of the dominant tenement, appellant purchased not only that tenement but other real property adjacent thereto, the latter property not being entitled to the enjoyment of the easement. Appellant than constructed a building occupying a part of the dominant tenement, as well as the additional property adjacent thereto. Not all of the dominant tenement is occupied by the building. In fact, the total of the area of that portion of the dominant tenement, together with the non-dominant property over which the building is constructed, is a smaller area than the area of the original dominant tenement. The building, thus constructed, houses a large bowling alley and restaurant. Appellant in the past has been using the right of way to bring fuel oil, food, equipment, and supplies to the building, and removing trash, garbage, and other material therefrom.

It is contended by appellant that since the area of the dominant and non-dominant land served by the easement is less than the original area of the dominant tenement, the use made by appellant of the right of way to serve the building located on the lesser area is not materially increased or excessive. It is true that where the nature and extent of the use of an easement is, by its terms, unrestricted, the use by the dominant tenement may be increased or enlarged. . . . But the owner of the dominant tenement may not subject the servient tenement to use or servitude in connection with other premises to which the easement is not appurtenant. . . . Appellant, therefore, may not use the easement to serve both the dominant and non-dominant property, even though the area thereof is less than the original area of the dominant tenement.

The disposition of the foregoing issue brings us to the principal legal question in the case: whether appellant's use of the right of way resulted in the forfeiture and extinguishment of the easement by abandonment, and thereby entitled appellee, on a motion for summary judgment, to a decree permanently enjoining appellant from using the right of way.

Misuse of an easement right is not sufficient to constitute a forfeiture, waiver, or abandonment of such right. The right to an easement is not lost by using it in an unauthorized manner or to an unauthorized extent, unless it is impossible to sever the increased burden so as to preserve to the owner of the dominant tenement that to which he is entitled, and impose on the servient tenement only that burden which was originally imposed upon it. . . .

From the record before us, we are unable to ascertain what the total additional burden is that has been cast upon the servient tenement as the result of appellant's use of the right of way for ingress to, and egress from, the building which was located on part of the dominant and the non-dominant property. As has been mentioned, the building houses a bowling alley and restaurant. From affidavits on file, it appears that a soda fountain and luncheonette used in connection with the restaurant are located in that part of the building situate on the non-dominant real estate, which, of course, is not entitled to enjoyment of the easement; and it further appears that the right of way is used for the purpose of bringing supplies for the fountain and luncheonette and removing trash and garbage therefrom. . . . But it is declared on the part of Penn Bowling that if the right of way were barred to appellant, a great hardship would result in the operation of the building housing the bowling alley and other facilities, and would necessitate large and expensive alterations of its building. Appellant may well be obliged to remodel its structure in order to operate, but it would appear that this can be done and, consequently, appellee is not entitled to a decree extinguishing the easement or to a permanent injunction on the pleadings and proofs before us. Furthermore, appellant's building fronts on a public thoroughfare and changes conceivably could be made so that the non-dominant property could be served from the street.

In accordance with the foregoing, the judgment is set aside and the case remanded to the district court for further proceedings consonant with this opinion, with the reservation of right to the appellee to apply for a temporary injunction pending final decision of the court.

CASE NO. 4

Engleman v. Kalamazoo. 229 Mich. 603, 201 N.W. 880 (1925)

BIRD, J. Defendant city gave plaintiff notice to remove, within thirty days, a stairway leading from the street to the basement of his business block situated at the corner of Burdick and Water Streets. Plaintiff responded by filing this bill to restrain defendant from enforcing its order. From an adverse decree, plaintiff appeals. . . .

Plaintiff's contention is that he has a prescriptive right to maintain and use the stairway; that Nicholas Baumann constructed it in 1870, and maintained it until 1895; and that such right being appurtenant to the land conveyed passed to plaintiff in 1899.

The defendant denies that any such right exists, or is vested in plaintiff. It insists that stairways into basements in the business district were permitted in the early history of Kalamazoo; that they have been suffered to remain by the city until such times as the density of traffic made it necessary to remove them; . . .

The testimony tends to show that the use of the stairway has been continued and uninterrupted for half a century. . . .

That Nicholas Baumann, during his life, claimed this right appears from the fact that he controlled it, repaired it, and he and his tenants used it. Without its use the two business places in the basement could not have been utilized. So far as the record shows, he recognized no equal or superior right in the city, and paid tribute to no one for the right to use it. . . .

. . . it is claimed by counsel for the city that the right to occupy the street for the stairway began and has continued by permission, and therefore the length of time it has been used would not ripen into a vested right. . . . We are unable to see the value of this argument, as it conceded that the record is barren of any evidence as to how the use began. . . . As there is no proof as to how the right began, we do not think these presumptions are very important in view of the fact that, after the right has been exercised for practically a half century, it is conclusively presumed that it had its beginning in a grant. In the case of Berkey & Gay Furniture Co. v. Valley City Milling Co., 194 Mich. 234, 160 N.W. 648, in discussing that question, it was said:

> "It has been held that the open, notorious, continuous, and adverse use across the land of another from a residence or place of business to a public road for more than twenty years affords a conclusive presumption of a written grant of such way; and that, when the passway has been used for something like half a century, it is unnecessary to show by positive testimony that the use was claimed as a matter of right, but that after such use the burden is on the plaintiff to show that the use was only permissive."

If that rule be applied to the facts in this case, it undoubtedly settles the contention of the parties in favor of the plaintiff. . . .

This use was not a mere temporary or transient use, as is illustrated by the use of the street for a fruit stand, which this court passed upon in Pastorino v. Detroit, 182 Mich. 5, 148 N.W. 231, but it is a construction of a permanent character. . . . The character of the right claimed, its construction, whether of a permanent nature, and its visibility are influential in determining whether the right has accrued. In the present case the permanent character of the structure of brick, stone, and iron, all in full view of the public, and its use in connection with the operation of the building, were ample notice to the public authorities that plaintiff and his vendor were claiming rights therein. . . .

The decree of the trial court is reversed, and one made which will be in accord with these views. . . .

CASE NO. 5

Wilson v. Waters. 64 A. (2d) 135 (Md.) (1949)

DELAPLAINE, J. The record in this case contains three appeals taken by Elsie Wilson from three judgments entered against her in the Circuit Court for Howard County. The judgments were recovered by plaintiffs in three suits for damages for barricading a road over land from plaintiffs' four houses to Cissell Avenue in the village of North Laurel. . . .

Plaintiffs alleged in the three suits that for more than twenty years they had used the road along the northern line of defendant's land as a means of access to the rear of their houses, but on April 15, 1946, defendant erected a fence along the northern line, and also a gate across the road at the intersection of Cissell Avenue, and locked the gate, and subsequently removed the gate and extended the fence across the road, thereby depriving them of its use. The three suits were consolidated and tried together. After the trial court denied defendant's motions for directed verdicts, the jury awarded a verdict in favor of plaintiffs for the sum of $5 in each case.

Plaintiffs did not claim an easement in the land by grant. They claimed a right of way by prescription. It has always been the law in Maryland that no person who has a right of entry into any land shall enter thereinto but within twenty years after his right of entry accrued. This rule was embodied in the Statute of 21 James I, ch. 16, enacted by Parliament in 1623. 2 Alexander's British Statutes, Coe's Ed., 599. It is now in force in Maryland by virtue of Article 5 of the Maryland Declaration of Rights, which proclaims that the inhabitants of Maryland are entitled to the Common Law of England and also to the benefit of such of the English statutes as existed on July 4, 1776, and which

> "have been found applicable to their local and other circumstances, and have been introduced, used and practiced by the Courts of Law or Equity." Safe Deposit & Trust Co. of Baltimore v. Marburg, 110 Md. 410, 414, 72 Atl. 839.

But it is well settled that adverse possession sufficient to give marketable title to land must be open and notorious, continuous and exclusive. . . .

In this case the testimony concerning the location and width of the road, which plaintiffs swore positively they had used more than twenty years, was sufficiently definite to warrant submission of the case to the jury. Waters, age seventy-four, testified that the road was there when he moved to "Four Block" thirty-five years ago, and that he had used it continuously until it was barricaded by defendant. Kenneth Burley, age forty-four, testified that there had been a dirt road there ever since he was "big enough to know." He swore that he had used it ever since 1926, when he bought his first automobile. Elmer F. Warner, who had driven over the road to deliver feed, paint and other supplies from a store in Laurel, testified that the road was there when he started to school more than a quarter of a century ago. He described the road as a country lane between 18 and 20 feet wide.

Defendant's main contention is that there was no legally sufficient evidence that plaintiffs' use of the road was exclusive. She claims that when she bought her lot in 1934, it was unenclosed and unimproved, and that there was no road on the lot until one was made for hauling building materials when she built her house; and that any use of the road by plaintiffs was merely in connection with permissive use by the general public. It may be stated as a general rule that when a person has used a roadway over the land of another openly and continuously and without objection for twenty years, it will be presumed that the use has been adverse under a claim of right, unless it appears to have been by permission. To prevent a prescriptive easement from arising from such use, the owner of the land has the burden of showing that the use of the way was by license inconsistent with a claim of right. Cox v. Forrest, 60 Md. 74, 80; Condry v. Laurie, 184 Md. 317, 41 A. (2d) 66. On the other hand, where the land has been used by the general public by implied license, it will be presumed that the use of the land by a neighboring landowner was not adverse, but permissive, unless there was some distinct act indicating an exclusive use under a claim of right and distinguishable from the general use. Pirman v. Confer, 273 N.Y. 357, 7 N.E. (2d) 262, 111 A.L.R. 216. In applying this rule in a Massachusetts case, Chief Justice Shaw said:

"A regularly formed and wrought way across the ground, paved, macadamized, or graveled and fitted for use as a way, from his own estate to the highway, indicating a use distinct from any use to be made of it by the proprietors, would, in our opinion, be evidence of such exclusive use and claim of right. So would be any plain, unequivocal act, indicating a peculiar and exclusive claim, open and ostensible, and distinguishable from that of others." Kilburn v. Adams, 7 Metc., Mass., 33, 39 Am. Dec. 754, 756

Plaintiffs admitted that no one was denied use of the road. Tradesmen used it in delivering coal, fuel oil, wood and ice, paint, feed and other supplies. Hogs were driven down the road to the pen in the back yard. L. Edwin Carr, while acting as deputy sheriff over twenty years ago, went over the road to search for dogs without license tags. Ridgely Selby, an undertaker, used the road in moving the dead. He swore that the road was the same in recent years as it was in his youth, when he hauled coal over the road from the coal yard. It is evident that the road became very useful for the occupants of the four houses. However, we do not consider the tradesmen, the deputy sheriff, and the undertaker as the general public exercising an implied license. They were visitors whose right of passage was based upon the claim of right of the owners of the houses. Jean v. Arseneault, 85 N.H. 72, 153 Atl. 819

Moreover, no effort was made to establish the status of the narrow dirt road as a public street. It was not contended that the authorities of Howard County ever recognized the road as a highway. We adopt the rule that if a road led at its start only to the premises of the persons using it, such circumstance is sufficient to prove their user under a claim of exclusive right, in the absence of proof to the contrary. If a road, which was started in such a manner as to make the user adverse and exclusive, is afterwards enjoyed in common with the public, the user does not lose its exclusive character as the result of the joinder of the public therein. . . . Since plaintiffs testified that they had used the road in this case without objection for more than twenty years, we think the jury had the right to determine that defendant and her predecessors in title would not have acquiesced in the use of the road for so long a period, when it would have been to their interest to have stopped it, unless they believed that the parties using it had a right of way, of which they should not be deprived. The right of way cannot prejudice anyone except the present owner, who waited many years before she barricaded the road. An easement over her land by prescription is sanctioned by public policy.

We hold that the trial court ruled correctly in denying defendant's motions for directed verdicts. The three judgments entered upon the verdicts of the jury will therefore be affirmed. . . .

CASE NO. 6

Barker v. Barker et al. 249 Ala. 322, 31 So. (2d) 357 (1947)

FOSTER, J. . . . Counsel for both parties treat the interest of Sarah M. Barker after her husband's death as a life estate, with remainder to his children. While in possession under such right, she kept the interest on the Bice mortgage paid. This was her duty, since she was entitled to receive the rents and profits during that time. . . .

Before she died she sold the timber on the land for $700, and used $400 of that money in paying the balance of the principal of the mortgage debt. The balance of $300 has not been accounted for, and is not involved in the contentions in this case. She had no right to sell the standing timber to make merchandise for her personal benefit, such as this occurrence was shown to be. . . . Her right to cut and dispose of standing timber is limited and does not extend that far 33 Am. Jur. 820

CASE NO. 7

Short v. Milby. 64 A. (2d) 36 (Del.) (1949)

HARRINGTON, C. By deed dated April 11, 1934, John J. Yoder and Mary A. Yoder, his wife, conveyed a tract of land, consisting of approximately eighty (80) acres, in Kent County, to Willard M. Short, single man, and Emma Short, single woman, "their Heirs and Assigns." But the habendum clause stated that the lands and premises bargained and sold to the parties of the second part "their Heirs and Assigns" were for their use "jointly and not as common tenants their Heirs and Assigns, forever." This provision limits the general granting clause and is the important provision of the deed in determining what estate was conveyed to the grantees. 16 Am. Jur. § 239, p. 573; . . .

Willard M. Short died intestate and unmarried on the fourteenth day of August, 1946, leaving to survive him, as his only heirs at law, four sisters, Emma Short, the plaintiff, Addie Gooden, Brenda Murray and Ella Baxter; three brothers, Abram Short, H. Ole Short and Joseph Short; and seven nephews and nieces, Roland Unruh, Paul Unruh, Ruth Unruh Devlin, Beulah Unruh Robinson, Clarence Taylor, Reba Taylor Meeks and Emma Taylor Crossley. All of these heirs are parties to this proceeding.

On the twenty-first day of April, 1948, Emma Short, the plaintiff, entered into a contract in writing, whereby she agreed to sell, and Charles R. Milby and Amy E. Milby, his wife, agreed to purchase the said eighty acre tract of land for $6,500. The purchase price was to be paid on or before June 1, 1948

> "upon the execution and delivery of a good and sufficient deed, conveying the said farm by a good, marketable

title in fee simple, free and clear of all liens and encumbrances."

The defendants, Charles R. Milby and Amy E. Milby, his wife, refused to comply with their contract on the ground that Emma Short did not have absolute title to the property.

The question, therefore, is whether the Yoder deed of April 11, 1934, conveyed an estate in joint tenancy to Willard M. Short and Emma Short.

When such an estate is created, the right of the survivor to take on the death of the other tenant is an incident of the estate. Tiff. Real Property, 2d ed. 627, 635; 1 Pomeroy Eq. Jur., 5th Ed., § 408

Section 3734 of the Revised Code of 1935 provides:

"Sec. 1. Estate in Joint Tenancy; Created Only by Express Words; Exception of Estates Granted to Executors or Trustees:—No estate, in joint tenancy, in lands, tenements, or hereditaments, shall be held, or claimed, by, or under any grant, devise, or conveyance made to any persons, other than to executors or trustees, unless the premises therein mentioned shall be expressly granted, devised, or conveyed to such persons, to be held as joint tenants and not as tenants in common."

The language of the statute reflects the modern rule and clearly shows that joint tenancies are not favored and can only be created by clear and definite language not reasonably capable of any different construction. . . . It may be safer to use the words of the statute, but that is not absolutely essential if the grantor's intent to create a joint tenancy clearly appears from the language used. The conveyance to Willard M. Short and Emma Short "jointly and not as common tenants their Heirs and Assigns, forever" clearly indicates the grantor's intent to create a joint tenancy. . . in Davis v. Smith, 4 Harr. 68, the court held that a devise to the testator's two grandsons "jointly" did not necessarily mean in joint tenancy as tenants in common would also hold an estate jointly until severance.

But here other words are added which clearly negative any intent to create a tenancy in common. The use of the words "their Heirs and Assigns, forever" is not inconsistent with this conclusion. . . .

A decree will be entered compelling the defendants Charles R. Milby and Amy E. Milby to perform their contract.

CASE NO. 8

Intermountain Realty Co. v. Allen. 60 Idaho 228, 90 P. (2d) 704, 122 A.L.R. 647 (1939)

AILSHIE, CH.J., delivered the opinion of the court:

This is an action for cancellation of a written lease and agreement and for recovery of possession of the real property involved therein and for damages for the retention thereof.

Appellant Realty Company, a Montana corporation, duly licensed to do business in this state as a foreign corporation, was the owner of the Hotel Whitman Building in Pocatello. August 18, 1937, a certain lease and agreement was entered into between appellant and E. L. Allen, one of the respondents herein, by the terms of which space in the hotel building, to be used as a café, was "leased and let" to Allen for a term of five years, at a specified rental of 7 per cent of the gross sales made by respondent, or a minimum rental of $150 per month. About November 7th Allen took possession of the restaurant property and delivered to appellant his promissory note for $1,716.16, with interest at 6 per cent per annum, payable in installments and secured by a chattel mortgage. Respondent thereafter defaulted in the payments due. April 14, 1938, the parties entered into a written modification of the lease and agreement, whereby the lease should expire and terminate August 15th following. Although respondent was a married man, his wife, Lillian Allen, one of the respondents herein, did not sign or acknowledge the original lease and agreement nor the modification thereof. July 29, 1938, respondent repudiated the written modification and refused to vacate and surrender possession of the property. September 8th this action was instituted and the cause was heard before the court October 17th following. Judgment of dismissal was entered from which this appeal has been taken. The trial court held that the alteration and modification of the lease was void because of the failure of Allen's wife to sign and acknowledge the same as required by sec. 31—913, I.C.A.

Section 31—913, to which the question refers, reads as follows:

> "The husband has the management and control of the community property, except the earnings of the wife for her personal services and the rents and profits of her separate estate. But he can not sell, convey or encumber the community real estate unless the wife join with him in executing and acknowledging the deed or other instrument of conveyance, by which the real estate is sold, conveyed or encumbered."

Appellant urges that:

> "At common law the interest created by a lease for a specified period, whether for a number of weeks, months, or years, was a 'chattel real,' and, as such, personal property"

and in support thereof cites a great many authorities. . . .

In the very outset it must be observed that the courts of this state are committed to the proposition that:

> "A written lease of community property for a term of years is a conveyance and an incumbrance within the provisions of C.S. § 4666 (31—913, I.C.A.), and is void unless the wife joins with the husband in the execution and acknowledgment thereof." Fargo v. Bennett, 35 Idaho 359, 206 Pac. 692. . . .

Now it is contended in the present case that, while a lease of real property, in order to be binding upon the lessor, must be executed by both husband and wife (if the lessor is a married man), nevertheless, as to the lessee who recieves such a lease, it is only a "chattel real" and is not "community real estate" within the purview and meaning of sec. 31—913, supra; and that the lessee, although a married man, may dispose of it without the consent of his wife.

The term "chattels real" originated under the feudal system of the common law and was intended primarily to designate any and all interests in real estate of lesser dignity than a freehold estate, and which lesser estates or interest descended under the rules for devolution of personal property and not as freehold or fee simple estates. . . .

11 C.J., p. 385, defines chattels real thus:

> "Chattels real are interests which are annexed to or concern real estate, as estates for years, at will, by sufferance, from year to year, and various interests of uncertain duration. Chattels real are to be distinguished from a freehold, which is realty. A freehold is an estate for life or in fee; a chattel real, for a less estate. Any estate in

lands which does not amount to a freehold is, however, a chattel real. Strictly speaking, a chattel real is not a term applicable to chattels which are not attached to, or issue out of, realty."

Having in mind the foregoing, it will be seen that simply calling this property right a "chattel real" and therefore personal property does not satisfy the issue we are confronted with because this so-called "chattel real" is nevertheless still an interest in and right of possession to real estate and no one seems to deny that in the case at bar whatever it may be called, real, personal or mixed, it is community property. When respondent Allen secured a lease on the restaurant rooms in the Whitman Hotel, he acquired something which at once became the property and asset of the marital community composed of himself and his wife. . . . According to the provisions of the instrument known as a lease, by which this property right was acquired, he and his wife became entitled to and took possession of real property. An action to eject them or quiet title against them involves the right to possession of real property, and whatever its technical legal name, it will still be an interest in real property or, to be more exact, the right of possession and use of real property.

Moreover, had respondent's creditor obtained a judgment against him and caused an execution to be levied on this leasehold estate, under the provisions of sec. 8—310, I.C.A., it would have been sold as real estate; and if the leasehold had more than two years unexpired term to run, the sale would have been subject to redemption under the statutes providing for execution sales of real estate. . . .

The judgment is affirmed. . . .

CASE NO. 9

Walthall v. Yohn et al. 252 Ala. 262, 40 So. (2d) 705 (1949)

SIMPSON, J. Statutory bill (by appellant) to quiet title to some twenty acres of wild, wooded, uncultivated land. The appellant is the owner of the legal title and the appellees (defendants below) rely on adverse possession under color of title to defeat recovery. This color of title of appellees consists of a deed from the State of Alabama to them under date of July 20, 1932, based on a purported tax sale had in 1929. There is no question but that this deed from the State was void, and it is not contended otherwise, since the tax sale through which it came was the result of a double assessment, the taxes having been paid on one assessment by the owner thereof through whom appellant claims title.

. . . As we interpret the testimony, the appellees did pay the taxes on the land each and every year from the time they received the deed from the State up to the time of the filing of the suit in 1946. The appellant, however, or his predecessors in title, paid the taxes continuously through 1929; in 1931 the land, with other land, was sold for the 1930 taxes and bought in by the State, but in 1937 appellant redeemed this particular land, paying all taxes due during this period (years 1930 to 1936, inclusive); he has paid taxes on the land continuously since that time. Thus is his legal title traced directly back to a common source and is unaffected by the tax sale under the double assessment unless appellees' title has been perfected by adverse possession. It is to be noticed here that appellees' reliance for title is rested on the prior sale in 1929, culminating in a deed from the State to them in 1932, and not the sale for 1930 taxes from which appellant later made a redemption.

Aside from the payment of taxes and an occasional visit by one of them to look at the land, appellees' actual possession consisted entirely of posting a couple of signs on the land at the time of the purchase from the State and granting some rights of way across it. As for appellant's acts of possession, in addition to payment of the taxes as before indicated, there was evidence that he at various times placed signs on the land, cut and sold timber therefrom, and repaired fences partially across the tract in an effort to stop the dumping of trash thereon. Just when all these various acts were performed is left to uncertainty, but some definite and open acts of ownership were shown to have been asserted by appellant just prior to the institution of the suit—repairing of fences, erection of signs, employment of a watchman. According to appellant's testimony, there were no indicia of an adverse claim at the time he filed the suit. Indeed, the testimony of one of the appellees is to the effect that the signs he testified he erected on the land soon disappeared.

. . . Appellant having proven ownership of the legal title and having made out a prima facie case of peaceable possession, it was then the burden of the appellees, claiming only by adverse possession under color of title, to show actual adverse possession. In the recent case of Tensaw Land & Timber Co. v. Rivers, 244 Ala. 657, 15 So. (2d) 411, this court held in effect that rare and widely separated acts, no matter how clearly they have indicated a purpose to claim title, do not show a possession of wild land sufficient to establish title by adverse possession. Further, in said case it was held that mere casual acts of ownership do not constitute adverse possession.

As against the legal title, to work a divesture thereof, we pointed out in Turnipseed v. Moseley, 248 Ala. 340, 344, 27 So. (2d) 483, 485, 170 A.L.R. 882, that

> "there must have been actual occupancy, clear, definite, positive, notorious, continuous, adverse and exclusive for the requisite period, under claim of right (by claimants), of a definite tract, and the burden was on them to establish this by clear and convincing evidence."

. . . the appellant was entitled to the relief prayed, that is, the quieting of his title to the land. . . . It results that the decree appealed from will be reversed and one here entered in his favor.

CASE NO. 10

Schell v. Kneedler. 359 Pa. 424, 59 A. (2d) 91, 2 A.L.R. (2d) 854 (1948)

LINN, J. The plaintiff, a widow suing in her own right and as executrix of her husband's estate, filed this bill to enforce a secret trust against six defendants: the Bradys (plaintiff's daughter and son-in-law), Kneedler and Grammes, to whom the Bradys conveyed, and the Arners (husband and wife) to whom Kneedler and Grammes conveyed. Defendants filed preliminary objections. The court sustained them as to all the defendants except the Bradys and directed that the bill be dismissed as against Kneedler, Grammes and the Arners. The plaintiff appeals.

The bill avers that plaintiff and her husband, being the owners of certain real estate in South Whitehall Township, Lehigh County, subject to a mortgage in default, conveyed it in 1935 to the mortgagee, Home Building Association. The residence was occupied by the plaintiff and the Bradys. . . . She alleges that they bought it back from the building association in October, 1941, for $4,850 but took title in the names of the Bradys "who" in the words of the bill, "were to hold said title in trust for Complainant and her husband and orally agreed so to do." This deed was promptly recorded. On October 23, 1946, the Bradys conveyed the property to Harry O. Kneedler and Lloyd E. Grammes by a deed recorded. On November 6, 1946, they conveyed to the Arners by deed recorded. The plaintiff avers that after the Bradys conveyed to Kneedler and Grammes, but before Kneedler and Grammes conveyed to the Arners, plaintiff advised Kneedler and Grammes and the Arners "that the Bradys had no legal right to convey said premises to any one but to the complainant and her husband." She also avers that none of the grantees made any inquiry of her concerning her title. She prayed that the Arners be restrained from disposing of or encumbering the premises; that they be conveyed to plaintiff; and for an accounting by Kneedler and Grammes. . . .

The deed to the Bradys was recorded and they were in possession; that fact makes it immaterial for present purposes that plaintiff and her husband also lived in the same house with the Bradys. Neither Kneedler nor Grammes, when they bought from the Bradys, had any knowledge, actual or constructive, of the secret trust; they were bound by the recorded title and could rely on possession by the Bradys. Finding title and possession in one person relieved them from further inquiry on the premises. Indeed, this conclusion is but an application of the general principle that, in the absence of proof to the contrary, actual possession is presumed to be in him who has the record title. It would be intolerable to require an intending purchaser or encumbrancer to ask every person living in a property, be they many or few, whether or not he has a better title than the record owner, who is also in possession. This would be to shift the burden of clear proof of notice from him whose neglect to record his deed has caused the trouble to him who has been guilty of no neglect, and would reverse the rule that the possession of one holding under an unrecorded deed, in order to be effective as against a subsequent purchaser, must be open, notorious, distinct, and unequivocal. . . .

In the circumstances, plaintiff has shown no right to enforce the secret trust against the defendants against whom the bill was dismissed. . . .

CASE NO. 11

Costello v. Costello. 136 Conn. 611, 73 A. (2d) 333 (1950)

BROWN, C.J. In this action the plaintiff, as administratrix of her deceased husband's estate, sought a decree setting aside a deed of real estate executed by him purporting to convey an undivided two-thirds interest therein to their son and the remaining undivided one-third to his brother. The jury in answer to an interrogatory rendered a special verdict that the deceased by this deed intended to make a testamentary disposition of the property described in the deed. . . .

The court . . . rendered judgment for the plaintiff decreeing the deed null and void, cancelling it and setting it aside as an attempt to make a testamentary disposition of the property. . . .

. . . James R. Costello died on August 19, 1946, without leaving a will. . . . On April 1, 1941, James R. Costello signed a quitclaim deed purporting, "for the consideration of love and affection received to my full satisfaction," to convey to his son an undivided two-thirds interest and to his brother John an undivided one-third interest in the property. . . . On September 4, 1946, this deed was recorded. From the date James signed the deed until his death he continued in possession of the property. . . .

. . . The deed was prepared by and executed in the office of Attorney O'Brien, who had acted as attorney for James for many years and so continued to act to the time of James's death on August 19, 1946. Shortly after James' death the attorney took the deed from a folder containing other papers relating to the affairs of the intestate which was kept in a filing cabinet in his office and showed it to James, Jr.; after the attorney had communicated with the defendant John, it was recorded. The deed at that time had been reinforced by four pieces of scotch tape where the paper had apparently started to break along the three lines where it had been creased in folding. In 1941, subsequent to the execution of the deed, and in 1942 and 1943, the intestate in making return of his taxable property upon a form which provided for the signature of either the owner or agent signed as and swore that he was the owner of the real estate in question. On April 24, 1941, the intestate executed a fifteen-year lease of a portion of the premises which expressly reserved in him as lessor the right to sell the property during the term. This instrument was prepared by and executed before Attorney O'Brien. The claims of the parties were in sharp conflict as to the intestate's intent in executing the deed and as to who had possession and control of it after execution.

Section 6951 of the General Statutes, which provides that "no will or codicil shall be valid to pass any estate" unless it is made and executed in accordance with certain requirements therein detailed, is prohibitive and exhaustive with relation to one's power "to dispose of his property after death by will—that is, by bequest or devise." . . . Nevertheless,

"One may transfer property in such a way that interests in it will arise only at his death, and he may transfer it in contemplation of his death, in lieu of making a will; but to be valid such transfers must convey a present interest. . . . One may not make a valid transfer of property where the intent is not to convey a present interest, but solely to create interests which will arise at death, except in compliance with the requirements of the Statute of Wills; and any such attempted transfer is void. . . . If this were not so it would lie in the power of any person at any time, by making conveyances of property, to circumvent the statute. The intent of the testator, whether to convey a present interest or to make a disposition of his property to take effect only at his death, is the controlling element in determining the validity of a transfer. . . ." Bowen v. Morgillo, 127 Conn. 161

By reason of these principles, the defendant could prevail in this case only upon the basis of a conditional delivery.

"But it is an essential characteristic and an indispensable feature of every delivery, whether absolute or conditional, that there must be a parting with the possession of the deed, and with all power and control over it, by the grantor for the benefit of the grantee *at the time of delivery*. . . . To constitute a delivery, the grantor must part with the legal possession of the deed and of all right to retain it. The present and future domination over the deed must pass from the grantor. And all this must happen in the grantor's lifetime." Porter v. Woodhouse, supra.

What the intestate's intent was, and whether or not he had possession or control of the deed upon or after its delivery to Attorney O'Brien on April 1, 1941, presented questions of fact for the determination of the jury. . . .

The answer depends in large measure upon the appraisal by the jury of the testimony of the defendant's witnesses, Attorney O'Brien, who stated among other pertinent facts that the intestate handed the deed to him after executing it and instructed him to keep it and to deliver it to the grantees upon the intestate's death, and that he had never relinquished possession of it to the intestate. It is unnecessary to refer to the evidence in detail. Suffice it to say that the jury could properly have found upon all of the evidence that the intestate, in leaving the deed with his attorney upon its execution, did not intend to convey a present interest to the grantees but instead intended to have the deed become operative upon his death, and then only if he had not meantime made or provided for other disposition of the property; that the deed did not remain in the attorney's possession during all of the time until the intestate's death; that the intestate continued to have power and control over it during this entire interval; and that he at no time made delivery of it with intent to vest title in the grantees. We mention but one bit of testimony which affords strong corroboration for our conclusion. The defendant James, Jr., who was a witness for the plaintiff, testified:

"My father told me he had left a deed with a lawyer . . . and . . . it is just as good as a will and has the same effect . . . it has all the effect of a deed and it avoids all the fees encountered in probate court."

Whether this indicated an intent by the intestate that no interest should vest under the deed until his death was for the jury to determine in the light of all the circumstances and under the court's unchallenged instructions, which must be deemed to have been correct.

There is no error. . . .

CASE NO. 12

Gross v. Housner. 322 Mich. 448, 34 N.W. (2d) 38 (1948)

REID, J. The bill of complaint was filed in this case by plaintiffs for specific performance of an escrow agreement and for other relief. . . . From a decree for plaintiffs, defendant administrator appeals. . . .

On April 12, 1946, plaintiffs, Robert F. Gross and Elaine Gross, his wife, went with said Benjamin Robinson, a man of then 80 years of age, to the office of Walter O. Estes, attorney. A quit claim deed was drawn wherein Benjamin Robinson . . . conveyed lots 100 and 101 of Parkview Land Company's Addition to the city of Lansing . . . to plaintiffs. Mr. Robinson deposited said deed in the hands of Walter O. Estes, attorney, as escrow agent, without reserving any right to recall or control but with instructions to deliver the same for record only upon his (Mr. Robinson's) death. The escrow agreement . . . is as follows:

"It is hereby agreed by and between Ben Robinson, as first party, and Robert F. Gross and Elaine Marie Gross, as second parties, that the certain quit claim deed executed by the first party to the second parties be and hereby is deposited with Walter O. Estes, in escrow to be delivered subject to this escrow agreement between the parties.

"The purpose of this escrow is to guarantee the care and support of the first party by the second parties during first party's lifetime, and the payment by the second parties of the first party's burial expenses. . . ."

On April 16, 1946, a disagreement arose between Mr. Robinson and the Grosses because plaintiffs, following doctor's orders, refused to give Mr. Robinson money to buy beer or whiskey. Mr. Robinson, having obtained intoxicants from some other source, had become unruly and was found by Mr. Gross lying in the street. . . .

Mr. Robinson did not want to return to his own house until he had removed the Grosses therefrom, due to the disagreement he had had with the Grosses. . . . He died April 30, 1946.

On April 22, 1946, Clarence Patrick had accompanied decedent Robinson to the office of the escrow agent where it is claimed that Robert F. Gross asked the escrow papers be destroyed. (Mr. Gross testified that he did not ask to have the escrow papers destroyed.) Decedent Robinson requested destruction of the papers and the escrow agent Estes destroyed the deed in the presence of decedent Robinson and Clarence Patrick (but not in the presence of Gross) and made some notations on the escrow agreement. . . .

Defendants claim that the escrow agreement of April 12, 1946, is not valid and binding, and that the plaintiffs did not fully perform the agreement, and further claim that the plaintiffs are estopped from claiming title under the escrow agreement by their conduct in rescinding the agreement. Plaintiff Gross denies that he consented to the cancellation of the deed and denies rescinding the contract.

The trial judge found that the agreement was valid. . . .

A careful review of all the testimony convinces us of the correctness of the above findings on the part of the trial court. . . .

In Cook v. Sadler, 214 Mich. 582, at page 586, 183 N.W. 82, at page 83, we said:

"On the question of depositing deeds in escrow it is observed by Gates on Real Property that:

" 'When a deed which has been duly executed has been put into the hands of a third person, to be by him delivered to the grantee at a future time, or upon the performance of certain conditions, or the happening of some event, it is said to be delivered "in escrow," and the deed will not be effective unless the condition be performed or the event happens, and the Michigan courts have consistently held that, where a grantor makes a deed to another and deposits the deed with a third party, to be held by such third party until the grantor's death, and to be delivered to the grantee named in the deed, the grantor reserving no dominion or control over the deed during his lifetime, a valid delivery is thereby made, and an immediate estate is invested in the grantee, subject to a life estate in the grantor.' "

In the case at bar, the conditions set forth in the escrow agreement were either fully performed by the grantees or the grantees were prevented from making a full performance either by the actions of the grantor or by the administrator of the grantor's estate following the grantor's death.

Review Questions

1. What distinguishes real property from personal property?
2. What is an estate in fee simple, and how does it differ from a fee in expectancy?

3. How does an estate in remainder differ from a reversion?
4. How does a pure easement differ from the so-called easement in gross?
5. Construct a fact situation illustrating the creation of an easement by prescription.
6. In what ways may a life estate be created?
7. How do the common law rights of dower and curtesy differ from those provided by statute in your state?
8. Can a life tenant convey his ownership interest to another?
9. Why is it important to distinguish joint tenancy of property from tenancy in common?
10. How does a tenancy in the entirety differ from a joint tenancy?
11. Distinguish a warranty deed from a quit claim deed.
12. Construct a fact situation illustrating an involuntary transfer of title to real property.
13. Can the owner of real property defeat the dower right of the surviving spouse by providing for the disposition of the property to others in his will?
14. What happens to a deceased owner's property when he has failed to make disposition of it by will?
15. What are the requirements in your state for the execution of a valid will?
16. Explain the meaning of title by adverse possession.
17. Why is a preliminary written contract desirable when purchasing real estate?
18. What is an abstract of title and what function does it perform in a real estate transaction?
19. Explain the difference between a title of record and a title as a matter of fact.
20. What is the test of a merchantable title?
21. Why should the grantee record his deed without delay?
22. Construct a fact situation illustrating delivery of a deed.

Problems for Discussion

1. A conveyance clause in a deed reads: "To A and his Heirs." What kind of an ownership interest does it create?
2. A conveys a life estate interest in certain lands to B by deed. Where does the outstanding ownership interest reside?
3. A and B were owners of adjoining property, and A gave B permission to use a right of way over his land. B did use the right of way for twenty-five years and then sold his land to C. A refused C the use of the right of way. C contends the use by B ripened into an easement for the benefit of the land he purchased from B. Is C's contention tenable?
4. This is an appeal from a judgment in favor of plaintiff. The action involves a dispute as to the boundary line between the northeast quarter of section 17, township 115, range 40, in Yellow Medicine county, owned by plaintiff, and the northwest quarter of the same section, owned by defendant.

   The trial court found that ever since 1920 defendant has been in possession and actual occupation of the northwest quarter as tenant or owner, and that during all of that time, as tenant or owner, he has farmed the strip of land here involved.

   It is the contention of defendant that the court's finding that the defendant, as tenant or owner, has been in possession and actual occupation of the northwest quarter of the section involved, and as tenant or owner has *farmed* the strip of land here involved, compels a conclusion that defendant has acquired title to the strip by adverse possession. Decide. (*Johnson* v. *Raddohl,* 32 N.W. (2d) 860)

5. A owned adjoining lots 1 and 2, upon which he built separate two-story structures which have a party wall between them. The upper floors are reached by a stairway contained entirely within the building located on lot 2. A conveyed lot 2 to B without making any reservation for the use of the stairway. B refuses A the right to use the stairway. What, if any, are A's rights?
6. Not being versed in real estate matters, A purchased a tract of land from B without inquiring into the latter's title. In fact, the record title to the property was in X. A did file for record, however, the quitclaim deed that he accepted from B. A took occupancy of the land and operated it as a truck farm for twenty-one years. Then the true owner X appeared and brought an action to oust A. Will he succeed?
7. Winn sold his place of dwelling to Forbes, who, after obtaining the deed, mailed it to the County Recorder for recording. The deed was lost in the mails and before it was recovered Gowan recorded a deed to the same property, which deed he had obtained from Winn in satisfaction of a long-standing debt. Gowan had no knowledge of the deed to Forbes. Who has title to the property?
8. Throckmorten conveys an estate to West "for the life of West's wife." West dies before his wife. Has the life estate terminated?
9. Johnson's wife becomes the owner of a farm by inheritance. What are Johnson's ownership interests in the farm?
10. Boyer conveyed property to Anderson by quitclaim deed. Subsequently, it was established that the property belonged to Boyer's brother and it was taken from Anderson. What are his rights against Boyer?
11. A and B are joint owners of a parcel of real estate. B dies intestate. What disposition will be made of his interest in the property?
12. A clause in a will provided: "First: I give, bequeath and devise my Old Homestead . . . to my son, James Mulvanity, and my sister, Mary Nute, as joint tenants. It is my desire that my son and sister shall have the right and privilege to occupy the premises during their lifetime, and upon decease of one, the title to vest in survivor."

    In an action for partition by the son, the question arose whether a joint tenancy or a joint life estate with contingent remainder to the survivor had been created. (*Mulvanity* v. *Nute,* 68 A. (2d) 536)
13. A and B acquired title to certain realty as joint tenants with the right of survivorship. B then mortgaged his interest, which C acquired through foreclosure proceedings. A died, and C claims A's interest by right of survivorship. Result?
14. As the owner of certain realty, A provides in his will that B—the surviving spouse—shall have one fourth of the income from the property for a period of ten years. Would it be to B's advantage to refuse to take possession under the will?
15. A and B, husband and wife, acquired title to land with the deed reading "A and B tenants by the entirety." B then conveyed her interest by deed to her

sister C. Upon the death of B, both A and C lay claim to B's interest in the property. Who will prevail?

16. The purchaser of real property is furnished an abstract of title by the seller. Does this assure the purchaser of obtaining a good title to the property?
17. Harper purchased real property from Miller. Harper accepted the deed from Miller without ever having the abstract of title examined. Later it was discovered that there was a $700 special assessment against the property, which Harper was required to pay. The abstracter had certified in the abstract that there were no special assessments against the property. Will Harper be able to hold the abstracter liable?
18. Before leaving on a hazardous ocean voyage, A executed a deed to his real property in favor of his wife B. He placed this deed in the hands of his banker with instructions that upon his death it should be delivered to B. Some years later A died and the deed was delivered to B. The heirs of A now contend that the deed was void since there had been no delivery during A's lifetime. Decide.
19. This was an action by plaintiff against defendant to forfeit the latter's life estate upon the basis of alleged waste. Defendant had taken possession of the land under a deed which was not recorded. Subsequently she was named in the will of her grantor (her mother) as life tenant of the property in question. Plaintiff had purchased the interest of the remaindermen. Decide. (*Taylor* v. *Perdue,* 58 S.E. (2d) 902)

30 REAL PROPERTY AND RELATED TOPICS:

REAL ESTATE MORTGAGES

► I. NATURE OF REAL ESTATE MORTGAGES

A mortgage is a contract whereby a creditor—the mortgagee—acquires an interest in the land of the debtor or another—the mortgagor—for the purpose of securing the debtor's personal obligation. It is a collateral security contract given for the purpose of securing a debtor's personal obligation to his creditor. Upon payment of the obligation, the mortgagee's interest in the mortgaged property is terminated, while upon a default of payment, the mortgaged property may be charged with payment of the debt. To illustrate:

A agrees to lend B $10,000 upon the condition that B will, in addition to his personal credit, give A a security interest in his farm. To accomplish this, B will (1) execute his promissory note to A, which note represents B's personal obligation to A, and (2) execute a mortgage, which secures B's personal obligation to A. Then, if B defaults in his personal obligation, the mortgage contract gives A the right to look to the farm as a means of satisfying the debt.

► II. NATURE OF MORTGAGEE'S INTEREST

There are two views as to the nature of the interest acquired by a mortgagee; these are generally designated as the *title and lien theories of mortgages.* Under the title theory, the mortgagee acquires the legal title to the property mortgaged, whereas under the lien theory, the mortgagee acquires not an estate in the property but a security interest only, with the title remaining in the mortgagor. As a practical matter, under present laws, there is little difference between these two theories; the distinction is more historical than practical. From the point of view of the mortgagee's position, present-day laws make little distinction.

A. TITLE THEORY

In early common law, the view was held that the mortgagor conveyed the legal title to the mortgagee. However, this was upon the condition that, should the mortgagor discharge his obligation as required by the mortgage contract, the property was to be reconveyed to him. Subject only to the limitation of reconveyance to the mortgagor, the mortgagee, in the absence of other provisions in the contract, could claim the benefits incident to ownership. He was entitled to possession and to the income from the property. And upon default by the mortgagor, the mortgagee's title automatically became absolute.

This made possible the extremely unjust enrichment of the mortgagee. A default, however slight or innocent, by the mortgagor effected a forfeiture of the lands. This was abhorrent to the conscience of the courts of equity, who came to the view that in reality the object of the relationship was to secure a personal obligation. They insisted therefore that the debtor should be given a reasonable opportunity after default to discharge the debt and so redeem the property. This right to redeem is called the mortgagor's *equity of redemption.*[1]

Many of the states, but not a majority, still adhere to the doctrine that a mortgage conveys the legal title to the mortgagee subject to the right of redemption (that is, the right to discharge the mortgage encumbrance in accordance with the defeasance clause). The mortgagor's *right* of redemption is to be distinguished from his *equity of redemption.* Statutes of a number of states provide that the mortgagee cannot take possession of the property until default, but other states give him a right of possession at any time. At the time of redemption from foreclosure after the mortgagee has had possession, he must account to the mortgagor for the income derived from the property while it was in his possession. Usually the mortgagee has little interest in taking possession if the security is adequate and is not being impaired.

B. LIEN THEORY

The lien theory of mortgages, which is in force in the majority of the states, is an adoption of the view taken by the courts of equity. This theory recognizes that the mortgage relationship is for the purpose of securing an obligation. Consequently, the mortgagee gets a bare security interest in the property, with the legal title remaining in the mortgagor. Although the mortgagee has no right of possession under this theory, he can effectively protect himself against impairment of the security by petitioning a court of equity for the appointment of a receiver. As the court said in *Totten* v. *Harlowe,* 90 Fed. (2d) 377:

> "In the District of Columbia the rule is that where the mortgagor is permitted to remain in possession of the property he is entitled to take the rents even after default and even though the land, when sold, should be insufficient to pay the debt. . . . This rule . . . grows out of the fact that it is only the property itself, and not the rents and profits, which is pledged. But . . . courts of equity always have the power, when the debtor is insolvent, and the mortgaged property is insufficient security for the debt and there is good cause to believe that it will be wasted or deteriorated in the hands of the mortgagor, as by cutting of timber, suffering dilapidation, etc., to take charge of the property by means of a receiver, and preserve not only the corpus but the rents and profits for the satisfaction of the debt. . . ."

► III. FORM, EXECUTION, AND RECORDING

As attested by the wide variety of mortgage forms in use, a mortgage need take no particular form. Many states provided statutory forms, which may be used at

---

[1] Hoyd v. Citizens Bank of Albany Co., p. 790.

the election of the parties. The safest procedure is to adhere to the use of local mortgage forms. In title-theory states, the instrument will contain the same words of conveyance and warranty as a deed. For example:

> "The Mortgagor has hereby granted, bargained, and sold to the said Mortgagee, his heirs, and assigns forever, the following described land . . . and the mortgagor does hereby fully warrant the title to said land, and will defend the same against the lawful claims of all persons whomsoever."

Or the instrument may merely state, "conveys and warrants," or some other short form authorized by statute.

In lien-theory states, words of conveyance are generally used in the creation of a mortgage interest, although words of conveyance are not essential since legal title does not pass to the mortgagee. Terminology indicating the creation of a mortgage relationship is sufficient.

Peculiar to the mortgage is the *defeasance clause,* which makes the conveyance to the mortgagee conditional. It provides that upon the fulfillment of certain conditions—usually payment of a debt—which conditions may or may not be set forth in the mortgage, the conveyance is to be void and of no effect. In some states the use of the phrase "the mortgagor mortgages to the mortgagee" is sufficient to create the security interest, and, by implication, without need of a defeasance clause, the security interest ceases to exist upon payment of the obligation secured.

Almost without exception, the execution of a mortgage must meet the same requirements as are essential for the execution of a deed.

Under present-day recording statutes, the mortgagee is, for his own protection, obligated to have the mortgage recorded in the county where the land is located. Unless the mortgagee thus gives public notice of his interest in the property, it may be defeated (1) by a subsequent sale to a bona fide purchaser, or (2) by a subsequent mortgage or other lien established as a matter of record.

A. ORDINARY DEEDS AS MORTGAGES—EQUITABLE MORTGAGES

Courts of equity are not concerned with the form of the instrument but rather with its purpose as intended by the parties.[2, 3] A deed which on its face is an absolute conveyance without a defeasance clause nevertheless will be regarded as a mortgage where such was the purpose of the instrument. Parol evidence can be used to show that the conveyance was intended merely to secure a loan. Cases are numerous in which the courts have declared the principle that, regardless of the camouflage or disguise, a mortgage relationship existing in fact will be treated as such. For example, A may make an absolute conveyance of his land to B for a recited consideration of $10,000. If it can be established, either by a written instrument or by oral evidence, that the $10,000 represented a loan from B to A with the conveyance made as security for its repayment, the transaction will be treated as a mortgage relationship.

---

[2] Henderson Baker Lbr. Co. v. Headley, p. 791.
[3] Ashbrook v. Briner, p. 792.

B. CONVEYANCE WITH RIGHT TO REPURCHASE

Closely resembling mortgages are agreements giving the grantor the right to repurchase the property within a certain time. Let us suppose that in the illustration in the preceding paragraph, A and B have entered into a separate agreement giving A the right to repurchase for $10,000 within a stated period. Whether this would make the transaction a mortgage or a conditional sale is dependent upon whether A and B regard the $10,000, recited as consideration in the conveyance, as a loan. If B has the right to collect the $10,000 by legal means, a mortgage would be conclusively indicated. However, if the repayment is entirely optional with the grantor A, a conditional sale must be assumed. In that case, the grantor would have no equity of redemption. A contract showing a great difference between the value of the property and the repurchase price would support the contention that a mortgage was intended.

C. TRUST DEEDS AS MORTGAGES

The X Corporation sells a $1,000,000 bond issue to the public, pledging its real property as security for repayment of the loan. Let us suppose that in this instance there are a thousand purchasers of the bonds. It would be impossible for the borrower to execute a separate and distinct mortgage upon its property for the security of each individual bondholder. Instead, the individual obligations are secured by the execution of a single instrument, known as a *trust deed.*

As a security device, the trust deed presents the simple expedient of a conveyance of the property by the borrower to a trustee, who holds the property as security for the various creditors. If the borrower defaults in payment, the trust deed may be foreclosed for the purpose of satisfying the obligations. The trustee will make a reconveyance of the property to the borrower upon payment of the obligation secured.

► IV. TRANSFER OF MORTGAGED PROPERTY

Without the consent of the mortgagee, a mortgagor may transfer his interest in the mortgaged property; the transferee thereby acquires the same rights as those possessed by the mortgagor. The mortgagor may likewise make disposition of the property by will, gift, or sale. In any event, the transferee will take the property subject to the security interest of the mortgagee. If the debt due the mortgagee is not paid at maturity, he may foreclose the mortgage and subject the property to payment of the obligation.

A. POSITION OF PURCHASER OF MORTGAGED PROPERTY

Unless the purchaser of mortgaged property buys it clear and free of a mortgage encumbrance, he will pay his grantor the value of the property less the amount of the mortgage encumbrance. By paying the mortgage debt at its maturity, he will then have paid full value for the property. To illustrate:

A agrees to purchase B's farm, upon which A and B have placed a value of $10,000. B's equity in the property is, however, only $5,000, since M holds a $5,000 mortgage upon the premises. Therefore, A will pay B $5,000, the value of his actual interest. Whether B has an obligation or an option to pay the $5,000 mortgage debt at maturity depends upon whether he promised his grantor to pay or whether he merely took the property subject to the mortgage.

Commonly, upon buying the mortgaged property, a purchaser will *assume* and *agree to pay* the mortgage indebtedness as *part of the purchase price,* and such agreement will be contained in the real estate contract as well as in the deed of conveyance. The purchaser thereby acquires a personal obligation to pay the mortgage debt to the mortgagee. The agreement between the purchaser and the mortgagor operates as a third-party beneficiary contract of the creditor type in favor of the mortgagee. By this contract, the mortgagor delegates his duty to pay the debt to the purchaser, who thereby becomes the principal debtor with the mortgagor his surety. The delegation of the duty to pay does not operate to release the mortgagor from his obligation to pay.

On the other hand, unless the purchaser agrees with the mortgagor that he will pay the mortgage debt, he acquires no personal obligation for its discharge. He merely holds the property subject to the mortgage lien. He recognizes that the mortgage debt is an encumbrance upon the title and that it must be paid to give him a clear title.

There is a practical distinction between the position of a grantee who purchases the property *subject to* the mortgage and one who purchases and *assumes* the mortgage obligation. This distinction can be summarized thus:

(1) By assuming the mortgage, the purchaser becomes personally liable to pay the debt. Although the property has declined in value to less than the mortgage indebtedness, the purchaser is obligated to pay. Upon foreclosure, if the property is sold for less than the mortgage debt, a deficiency judgment will be entered against the purchaser who assumed the mortgage.

(2) By taking the property *subject to* the mortgage, the purchaser does not personally agree to pay the mortgage debt. At the maturity of the mortgage obligation, if the value of the property is less than the amount of the mortgage, the purchaser can choose not to pay and thus forfeit the property. He cannot be held for any deficit resulting from a foreclosure sale. Whether a purchaser has personally obligated himself to pay the mortgage indebtedness is dependent upon the intent of the contracting parties and not necessarily upon the language employed.[4]

► V. TRANSFER OF MORTGAGEE'S INTEREST

Let us recall that a mortgage is a collateral security contract given to secure a personal obligation that usually is evidenced by a promissory note. This right to money may be transferred by the mortgagee by an assignment or a negotiation if the instrument is negotiable in form. The transfer of the right carries with it the

[4] Flynn v. Kenrick, p. 793.

mortgage security. The debt is the principal thing—the security is attached as an accessory. Unless the holder of the security interest also holds the obligation that it secures, he has nothing. He is regarded as holding the mortgage right in trust for the owner of the right to the money.

The purchaser of the obligation and of the mortgage security should notify the mortgagor of the transfer. It is also imperative that an assignment of the mortgage be recorded. Such will forestall a subsequent assignment by the mortgagee.

► VI. PAYMENT AND RELEASE OF MORTGAGE

The mortgagee need not accept payment of the obligation before its maturity date. He cannot be forced to liquidate his investment before the time at which he has agreed to accept payment. However, many mortgage contracts do extend to the mortgagor the right of payment before the due date.

A. PAYMENT OR TENDER AT MATURITY

The mortgage will be extinguished by payment or a tender of payment at such time as is authorized by the mortgage contract. Whatever security interest is held by the mortgagee automatically reverts back to the mortgagor. The mortgagee's right to the property, whether a legal title or a security interest, is nullified by the operation of the defeasance provision of the contract. The effect of a tender, however, is not to discharge the obligation; it serves only to discharge the mortgage lien and to end further interest payment.*

B. PAYMENT OR TENDER AFTER MATURITY

Under the lien theory of mortgages, a release of the mortgage lien is accomplished by a tender of payment or payment after maturity of the amount due on the mortgage. Under the title theory, payment will not discharge the mortgage lien. By virtue of the default by the mortgagor, title vests absolutely in the mortgagee. To release the mortgage, a reconveyance of the property from the mortgagee to the mortgagor is required.

C. RELEASE OF RECORD

Although a mortgage may be actually extinguished as between the mortgagor and the mortgagee, it may still appear in the public records as a claim against the property. To be assured of a clear record title, the mortgagor should request the mortgagee to release the mortgage upon the records. Usually this may be accomplished either by a marginal notation upon the record of the mortgage or by the execution and recording of an instrument of release. Statutes usually provide a penalty for a failure on the part of the mortgagee to clear the record within a specified time after being requested to do so in writing. The mortgagor may invoke the aid of an equity court should the mortgagee fail to discharge voluntarily the mortgage lien.

---

* See p. 319.

► VII. FORECLOSURE PROCEEDINGS

The term *foreclosure* as it is here used has reference to the proceedings instituted by the mortgagee upon a default by the mortgagor, such proceedings being for the purpose of charging the mortgaged property with payment of the defaulted obligation. Although possible, it is unusual for a mortgage to secure an obligation other than one for the payment of money. This gives us license to say that the mortgagor's failure to pay his debt when due gives rise to the mortgagee's right to avail himself of the mortgaged property as a means of obtaining satisfaction. A mortgage contract usually provides for acceleration of the due date upon a failure of the mortgagor to perform any of the covenants contained in the mortgage. For example, the mortgagee will have the right to declare the whole debt due and payable at once should the mortgagor fail to pay taxes upon the property, to pay interest, to meet any installment where the principal is so payable, or to keep the property insured.

A. TYPES OF FORECLOSURE PROCEEDINGS

Statutes in the various states govern the course that the mortgagee must or may pursue in getting at the mortgaged property as the source from which his claim is to be satisfied. In many jurisdictions, the mortgagee is given optional methods of procedure, whereas in others there is only one exclusive course that can be pursued. For example, in Iowa the only method of foreclosure is action in court by equitable proceedings. The method or methods available in any particular jurisdiction should be determined individually. Following is a brief description of the more common foreclosure practices.

1. *By Suit in Equity*

The most generally used practice is foreclosure by equitable proceedings. A court of equity will direct that the property be sold, after ascertaining the rights of the mortgagee and the extent of the mortgage lien. The sale is accomplished strictly under the jurisdiction and direction of the court, thus insuring protection to the interests of both the mortgagor and the mortgagee. The proceeds of the sale are applied to payment of costs of the proceedings and to the discharge of the mortgage debt. Any surplus is credited to the mortgagor. If there is a deficit, it becomes a deficiency judgment against the mortgagor.

Usually the mortgagor is given a statutory period—one year in Iowa—within which he may redeem the property sold. The purchaser will not be given his deed to the property until this period of redemption has expired.

2. *By Suit at Law (Scire Facias)*

In a few jurisdictions, notice may be served on the defendant to show cause why a judgment should not be entered for the amount due by virtue of the mortgage. Recovery is by a judgment in a court of law, not by decree as under equitable proceedings. The judgment is enforced by the issuing of a special execution upon the mortgaged property. This type of proceeding is limited to situations where there are no conflicting claimants.

3. *By Exercise of Power of Sale*

The majority of the states provide that a mortgage may be foreclosed by the exercise of a power of sale given the mortgagee or trustee in the security contract. Following is such a provision taken from a mortgage contract:

> "Upon any default in the performance of the foregoing conditions, the mortgagee, his executors, administrators, successors, or assigns may sell the mortgaged premises . . . by public auction on or near the premises . . . complying with the terms of the mortgage and with the statutes relating to the foreclosure of mortgages by the exercise of a power of sale, and may convey the same by proper deed to the purchaser in fee simple; and the mortgagor and all persons claiming under him shall forever be barred from all right and interest in the mortgaged premises."

In this way the mortgagee can obtain satisfaction of his claim without resorting to judicial processes. The proceeds of the sale are applied to the satisfaction of the debt, with any surplus being given to the mortgagor. It is a simple, cheap, and expeditious method of effecting a settlement out of court. And in those states which provide a period of redemption after sale, the mortgagor is as fully protected as under any other mode of foreclosure.

The power of sale gives the mortgagee the right to act as the mortgagor's agent and to sell the property on his behalf. In this role, the mortgagee has the duty to act in the best interests of the mortgagor. Often the mortgage will provide that the mortgagee may be a purchaser at the sale.

Most states which sanction foreclosure by exercise of a power of sale have statutes regulating the sale. To protect the mortgagor's interests and to prevent an abuse of power, it is usually required that the sale must be publicly held after proper notice has been given. Some statutes require the mortgagee to file an accounting of the sale.

4. *By Entry and Possession*

Taking possession of the mortgaged property and continuing in its possession for a prescribed period of time is sufficient to accomplish a foreclosure in a few jurisdictions. Unless the mortgagor redeems the property within such time, title to the property vests irrevocably in the mortgagee. The statutes should be examined to ascertain the procedure required to effect entry either by peaceable means or under process of law.

5. *Strict Foreclosure*

Strict foreclosure is a proceeding whereby the mortgagor's equity of redemption is completely cut off. In effect, the mortgagor's equity of redemption is being foreclosed. The court fixes a time for payment, and unless the mortgagor complies, title will vest absolutely in the mortgagee free of all liens and encumbrances and without need of sale.

This type of procedure is prohibited in some states and, on the whole, is used sparingly. Only under unusual circumstances will it be allowed. A reason for its use might be afforded by a situation in which the value of the property is clearly insufficient to meet the mortgage indebtedness.

B. MORTGAGOR'S RIGHT TO REDEEM AFTER DEFAULT

In accordance with the view of the early equity courts, which granted the mortgagor the right to redeem his property within a reasonable time after default (failure to pay the debt), statutes in the various states give the mortgagor a similar right of redemption.

> "The sole object of the statute in giving this right of redemption was to afford protection to those whose rights would otherwise be cut off and lost by a foreclosure, and of course to prevent purchasers . . . from acquiring an indefeasible title for a substantially inadequate price." *Whiteman* v. *Taber,* 205 Ala. 319

The period of time within which the mortgagor may redeem is dependent entirely upon the statutory provision. It is common that the equity of redemption continues for one year after the sale of the property. The Uniform Mortgage Act so provides.

CASES

CASE NO. 1

Hoyd v. Citizens Bank of Albany Co.
89 F. (2d) 105 (1937)

ALLEN, C.J. This is an appeal from an order of the District Court dissolving a restraining order issued in a proceeding filed under section 75 (a) to (r) of the Bankruptcy Act, 47 Stat. 1470.* An action had previously been filed in the state court to foreclose a mortgage upon some 226 acres of farm land and a foreclosure decree had been entered in favor of appellee (the mortgagee), and sale had been ordered. Appellee bought in the property at the foreclosure sale. Before confirmation of sale by the state court, appellant (the mortgagor) filed his debtor's petition in the district Court. . . .

Appellee urges (1) that the debtor cannot avail himself of the privileges of the act because he has no "property," . . .

The term "property" is not defined in the enactment. It is unlimited by any qualifying phrase, and doubtless was used in its ordinary sense as interpreted in the various decisions of the federal and state courts. Property is a nomen generalissimum and extends to every species of valuable right and interest, including real and personal property, easements, franchises, and other incorporeal hereditaments. . . .

Since the land is situated in Ohio, the Ohio statutes and decisions control.

* Section 75(a) to (r) is that part of the Bankruptcy Act which provides for agricultural compositions and extensions.

Whatever interest appellant had in these premises at the time of filing his petition must be determined in light of the fact that the sale had not then been confirmed and his right to redeem had not been barred. . . . Appellant claims that this interest is an equity of redemption and constitutes a substantial estate in the land. On behalf of appellee it is urged that whatever right appellant has is a personal right only, carrying with it none of the incidents of property. Such a right, called the "statutory right of redemption," arises after completion of sale on foreclosure. Its inception, its duration and its exercise depend entirely on the terms of the statute which creates it.

The common law right to redeem, recognized by section 11690, General Code, differs essentially from the statutory right to redeem. This statutory right, which in certain states is held to be personal only, is in addition to the right to redeem which is inherent in and an accompaniment of the equity of redemption considered as an estate. The Ohio statute does not extend the common law equity of redemption into a statutory right of redemption. No additional time is given after completion of the sale, in which the mortgagor may redeem. The statute merely sets the time of confirmation of sale as the point at which the equity of redemption is cut off.

The Ohio courts have repeatedly recognized that the equity of redemption includes both the right to redeem and the substantial estate of the mortgagor. . . .

A sale in Ohio is not complete until valid confirmation . . . appellant at the time he filed his petition had an equity of redemption consisting of an estate and not of a mere right to redeem. Under Ohio law this constitutes property.

The equity of redemption in Ohio is a substantial estate subject to dower . . . to conveyance and judicial sale . . . and descendible to the heirs upon the death of the mortgagor. . . . It constitutes a real and beneficial estate descendible by inheritance and only alienable by deed . . . and is an insurable interest in land. . . .

We conclude that as the sale had not been confirmed at the time of filing the petition, appellant's equity of redemption had not been barred, and that it constituted "property" . . . .

CASE NO. 2

Henderson Baker Lumber Co. v. Headley. 42 So. (2d) 821 (Ala.) (1949)

SIMPSON J. . . . The present appeal is by Henderson Baker Lumber Company, hereinafter to be referred to as Baker, . . .

Baker's bill sought injunctive relief against Headley . . . from further cutting of timber on lands allegedly owned by Baker and the removal of logs stacked along the highway, which were in part the product of such cutting. . . .

The substance of Headley's cross bill, after denying the contentions made by Baker . . . exhibits the following: . . . that in the year 1937 the plaintiff corporation, through its president, Henderson Baker, proposed to Headley that if he would agree to log in part the plaintiff's Myrtlewood sawmill, plaintiff would advance all sums necessary for the purchase of timber and lands as requested by Headley, the title to be taken in the name of the plaintiff as security for the purchase price thus advanced, and that a percentage of all the timber cut in the form of the stumpage value thereof would be credited against such purchase price, and when all of said funds had been repaid out of the stumpage take-outs, the plaintiff corporation would by appropriate instrument reconvey the lands to Headley in fee simple; in compliance with this understanding and agreement, the lands described were so purchased by Headley with the money thus loaned to him, and the title thereto taken in the name of the plaintiff corporation as security for such advances; that Headley fully complied with this agreement, has fully repaid the amount of his indebtedness owing to Baker, has a full and exclusive right to the possession and enjoyment of said lands and in equity is entitled to specific performance by having the plaintiff corporation convey to him the fee simple title as was agreed in the 1937 agreement.

The cross bill further alleged that in the particular territory where the property is located, it was a general custom among sawmill operators and log contractors (Headley being a log contractor) for the mill operators to operate in the manner so alleged and to advance the costs of timber and land, the title to be taken as security for such advances in the name of the sawmill company, and that when the cost of the purchase price had been fully paid and the debt satisfied by logs or cash, the operators then would reconvey the remaining land and timber to the logging contractor by appropriate instrument; and that Headley's agreement with the plaintiff was pursuant to this general logging and sawmill custom.

. . . The controlling principles of law applicable to the cross bill and the proven facts in support thereof can best be stated by quoting the following from the opinion on the first appeal:

"... Speaking of this character of relief, the Court in O'Rear v. O'Rear, 220 Ala. 85, 123 So. 895, 896, said: 'When one person makes a loan to another with which to purchase lands, and by mutual agreement a deed is made directly from the vendor to the lender as security for the loan, the transaction partakes of the nature both of a resulting trust and a mortgage. A resulting trust, because the money loaned becomes that of the borrower, and the title acquired with his money is taken in the name of another; a mortgage, because it is given as security for the debt due from lender to borrower.' "

. . . The impartial mind could not but be impressed that the evidence strongly preponderated to sustain the cross bill. In addition to the testimony of Headley's witnesses, the correspondence between Baker and Headley, as well as Baker's own records, as we interpret them, tend strongly to corroborate Headley's contention of what was the contract between the parties. His whole course of dealings with Baker and Baker's attitude in regard thereto, including payment by Headley of considerable of his own money for taxes on the lands and furnishing some logs to the mill from timber cut from his own and other lands in order to liquidate his debt to Baker, all tend to support his claim that the money advanced to him was a continuing binding debt on his part, which he was attempting to pay in order to acquire the title to the lands.

. . . Affirmed.

CASE NO. 3

Ashbrook v. Briner. 137 Neb. 104, 288 N.W. 374 (1939)

KROGER, D.J. This is an action to quiet title to 1,600 acres of land in Sioux county, Nebraska, and from an order dismissing plaintiff's action against two of the defendants, this appeal is prosecuted.

The record discloses the following

facts: On March 20, 1925, Burwell R. Price was the owner of the real estate in question and on said date executed and delivered to his father, James W. Price, a warranty deed conveying said real estate to said James W. Price. On the same date, and as a part of the same transaction, a defeasance contract was executed and acknowledged by the same parties, wherein it was stated that the conveyance was as security for a loan of $7,000, which was to be due and payable in five years, with interest at 6 per cent, and that upon the payment of said loan said James W. Price was to reconvey said premises to Burwell R. Price, or to any other person whom he might, in writing, designate.

The loan of $7,000 had not been repaid when, on December 12, 1933, James W. Price died testate, a resident of Jefferson county, Iowa. . . .

On November 15, 1934, Burwell R. Price entered into a written contract for the sale of the land in controversy to Harry H. Ashbrook, plaintiff in this action, and on February 6, 1935, executed and delivered a warranty deed to said premises in favor of plaintiff. . . .

It is the theory of the plaintiff that the conveyance of March 20, 1925, was a mortgage in fact, and that legal title to the premises did not pass to James W. Price by such conveyance, and that Burwell R. Price was still the owner of the legal title to said premises, which title was conveyed to the plaintiff by the deed executed and delivered February 6, 1935; that the interest of James W. Price in said premises was a chattel interest, or personal property, and that upon his death it became the absolute property of Mary A. Price, his widow.

It is the contention of the defendants that the conveyance of March 20, 1925, did pass the legal title to James W. Price, and that upon his death title passed to his devisees under the provisions of his will. . . .

Here we have two instruments executed as a part of the same transaction, to wit, a warranty deed and a contract of defeasance, and it has been held that, where two instruments are made at the same time with reference to the same transaction and to effectuate the same purpose, they will be construed together to the same extent as though made in one instrument. . . .

It is a well-settled principle that a court of equity will consider the substance and not the form, and that the particular form or words of a conveyance are unimportant if the intention of the parties can be ascertained.

In this state the usual form of mortgage differs but slightly from the wording of the two instruments executed in this case, if the same are construed together and treated as one instrument; and so construing them, it is apparent that the parties intended the conveyance as a mortgage and not as a transfer of the legal title with the right of redemption. . . .

We therefore hold that the deed and defeasance contract executed March 20, 1925, are to be construed together and, when so construed together, they constitute a mortgage given as security for the payment of a debt, and and that the legal title did not pass to James W. Price; . . .

CASE NO. 4

Flynn et al. v. Kenrick et al. 285 Mass. 446, 189 N.W. 207 (1934)

Plaintiff sold real property, encumbered by a mortgage, to defendant, the contract providing as follows:

"Said premises are to be conveyed on or before September 1, 1930, by good and sufficient warranty deed of the party of the first part, conveying a good and clear title to the same, free from all incumbrances except a first mortgage of $5,000 . . . and for such deed and conveyance the party of the second part is to pay the sum of $6,500 of which $100 has been paid this day, balance above mortgage, is to be paid in cash upon delivery of said deed."

The property was deeded to defendant, the deed reciting "subject to the mortgage." The mortgage indebtedness was not paid and upon foreclosure the property was sold for $4,500 and a deficiency judgment was paid by the plaintiff, the mortgagor. The plaintiff is seeking to recover the payment from defendant upon the theory that the mortgage had been assumed.

CROSBY, J. It has long held in this commonwealth that where land is conveyed subject to a mortgage the grantee does not become bound by mere acceptance of a deed to pay the mortgage debt. In the absence of other evidence, the deed shows that the grantee merely purchased the equity of redemption. If a deed contains stipulation that the land is subject to a mortgage which the grantee assumes or agrees to pay, by his acceptance of the deed the law implies a promise to perform his promise. The contention of the defendants that they purchased merely the plaintiffs' equity of redemption and did not assume and agree to pay the mortgage cannot be sustained in view of the agreement, the deed, and the agreed facts. The agreement recites that the defendants for such conveyance are to pay

"the sum of Sixty-five Hundred dollars—of which One hundred dollars have been paid this day—balance above mortgage, is to be paid in cash upon delivery of said deed."

It thus appears that for the deed and conveyance the defendants agreed to pay the sum of $6,500; that $100 was paid on the date of the agreement, and on delivery of the deed the sum of $1,400 was to be paid. The words "balance above mortgage" properly construed mean that the defendants having paid $100 obligated themselves to assume and pay the mortgage, and that the balance above the mortgage of $1,400 is to be paid upon the delivery of the deed.

The words of the deed "for consideration paid" interpreted in the light of the agreement mean that the defendants under the terms of the agreement are to pay $6,500 as the entire consideration. This seems to have been the construction put upon the agreement and the deed by the parties, as it is agreed that after the defendants entered into possession of the property they paid the interest installments on the mortgage until July 7, 1932. The agreement of the defendants to pay $6,500 for the property is equivalent to a stipulation that they assumed or agreed to pay the mortgage. . . .

Review Questions

1. What is the purpose of a mortgage contract?
2. What is the lien theory of mortgages? Which mortgage theory is accepted in your state?
3. What is the defeasance clause in a mortgage?
4. Why is it incumbent upon the mortgagee to record the mortgage?
5. May an ordinary deed of conveyance be construed as a mortgage?
6. What determines whether a conveyance of property with the right of repurchase is a mortgage?

7. What is a trust deed and under what circumstances is it usually employed?
8. May the mortgagee transfer his security interest in the mortgaged property without the consent of the mortgagor?
9. What is the position of the purchaser of mortgaged property in regard to the mortgage indebtedness?
10. As a purchaser of mortgaged property, would you prefer to assume the mortgage or purchase subject to the mortgage?
11. What step should the assignee of a mortgage take for his protection?
12. Can the mortgagee be forced to accept payment of the mortgage debt before its maturity date?
13. What is required to effectively release a mortgage?
14. What is meant by the term foreclosure?
15. What is the nature of the mortgagee's equity of redemption?
16. By what possible means may a mortgage be foreclosed in your state?
17. Distinguish between a mortgagor's right to redeem and his equity of redemption.

Problems for Discussion

1. A, who was indebted to B, executed a mortgage upon his land in favor of B for the purpose of securing the indebtedness. B insists he has the right to take possession of the mortgaged property. Decide.
2. Harrison mortgaged his property to Camp to secure a $5,000 obligation. Camp failed to record his mortgage until some time after a deed to the property from Harrison to Hurst had been recorded. What effect does this have upon Camp's security position?
3. A gave B an absolute deed to a tract of land in consideration of the sum of $5,000. It was agreed between A and B by a collateral writing that A was to have the right to repurchase the land for $5,400 one year from the date of the conveyance. A failed to exercise this right, and even though the agreement provided that time was of the essence he brought an action in equity to redeem the land. Will he succeed?
4. A executed an absolute deed to B for the purpose of securing an indebtedness; it was orally agreed that A could redeem the land by a repayment of the obligation. B recorded the deed and executed a deed to the property in favor of his wife. He placed it in escrow with instructions it should be delivered to his wife upon his death. B died, and the deed was delivered as directed. A now brings a bill in equity to redeem the land from what he contends was a mortgage. Decide.
5. Wills purchased a farm from Burton upon which Ryan held a $10,000 mortgage. In the agreement of purchase, Wills undertook to "assume the mortgage obligation." The property was sold at foreclosure sale for $9,000. What are the rights of Ryan to recover the deficit?
6. Assume in the previous question that Wills had purchased the property "subject to the mortgage."
7. Bacon, the mortgagor, tendered the correct amount of the mortgage obligation to Kirkland, the mortgagee, upon the due date. Kirkland, believing the amount tendered to be incorrect, refused to accept it. Immediately thereafter all of

Bacon's property was taken over by a receiver under bankruptcy proceedings. Kirkland contends he has a priority upon the mortgaged property. Decide.

8. The mortgagee refuses to record a mortgage satisfaction, much to the embarrassment of the mortgagor. What can the mortgagor do?
9. A purchased B's farm for $4,000 cash. C held a $5,000 mortgage upon the land, which mortgage was properly recorded. The conveyance from B to A made no mention concerning the mortgage indebtedness. A and B both died, and the mortgage debt became due. The mortgage was foreclosed and the property sold in a depressed real estate market for $4,000. B's estate paid the deficiency of $1,000 and brought action against A's estate to recover the amount, upon the theory that A had assumed the mortgage indebtedness. What will you take into consideration in deciding whether this contention should be sustained?

31 REAL PROPERTY AND RELATED TOPICS:

LANDLORD AND TENANT

"The law concerning landlord and tenant is as old as civilization itself. It came into existence in the infancy of civilization, and has come, by gradual accretion of new rights, privileges, and principles during the centuries of its development, to be considered as one of the most momentous, extensive, and far-reaching branches of the law." *Minneapolis Iron Stove Co.* v. *Branum,* 36 N.D. 355

The leasing of property plays a very important role in the economic life of the nation. Those who rent their places of abode far outnumber those who are home owners. Likewise, business properties are more frequently leased than owned.

► I. NATURE OF RELATIONSHIP

A landlord and tenant relation arises out of a contract that is either express or implied. It is based upon the intent of the parties to have such a relationship exist, that intent being evidenced either by their expressions or conduct.

The elements that determine a landlord and tenant relation are:

(1) Occupation of the premises by the tenant, the *lessee,* with the assent of the landlord, the *lessor.*

(2) Occupation by the tenant in subordination to the landlord's title and rights. Unless the one who occupies the premises does so in recognition of the other's superior title, he cannot stand as a tenant. Thus, if A is given possession of land by consent of the owner B, he cannot occupy the position and exercise the rights of a tenant if he himself claims ownership of the land.

(3) There must be a reversionary interest in the leased premises remaining in the landlord. This means that upon the termination of the tenant's interest in the premises there must be an ownership interest remaining in the landlord. Conveying one's entire interest in a given property is an *assignment* rather than a lease.

(4) The tenant must have the *right* to possession and control of the premises. Under the early common law it was necessary for the tenant to take possession as an essential to the existence of the relation. This is no longer required—a lease becomes effective upon its execution, unless otherwise specified, and an entry upon the premises by the tenant is not required.

(5) The creation of an interest in the land—an estate—in the tenant. This distinguishes a tenant from a licensee. A tenant is given exclusive possession of the premises "as against all the world including the owner," whereas a licensee has a temporary privilege in the use of the property.[1] A license, as distinguished from a

[1] Halpern v. Silver, p. 807.

lease, is a personal right which can be exercised only by the person to whom it is granted. Consequently, a licensee cannot assign his right to another, as can a lessee. Also, a license, being a personal right, terminates upon the death of either of the parties.

► II. THE LEASE

The term *lease* in its everyday usage refers to the contract creating the landlord tenant relation. Usually the lease need not be in any particular form and is enforceable in oral form providing it does not exceed the period of time specified in the Statute of Frauds. The Iowa Statute of Frauds, for example, specifies that leases for a term not exceeding one year need not be in writing to be enforceable.* Local statutes should be consulted for special requirements. Some states, for example, require leases exceeding a specified term to be acknowledged at the time of execution.

The reader should recognize that if either of the parties concerned wishes to record (place of public record) the lease, it is generally required that the lease be acknowledged at the time of its execution.†

► III. TENANCIES CLASSIFIED

Tenancies are classified upon the basis of the duration of the tenants' leasehold interests.

A. TENANCY FOR YEARS

A lease for years is one which is to endure for a *definite and ascertained period of time,* whether the period of time is for more or less than a year. The term *years* is used to indicate that the tenant's leasehold interest is fixed as to duration. Thus, leases for a fixed number of days, weeks, months, or for a period of one or more years are tenancies for years.

Unless limited by constitutional or statutory provisions, a lease may be for any length of time which the parties agree upon. Long-term leases are used under circumstances where the tenant plans to make substantial improvements upon the premises, which will revert to the landlord upon the termination of the lease.

As an illustration of constitutional limitation upon the duration of leases, the constitution of the State of New York provides that leases for agricultural lands may not exceed twelve years.

B. PERIODIC TENANCIES—FROM YEAR TO YEAR OR FROM MONTH TO MONTH

A periodic tenancy is one which will continue for another period equal to the one that has expired, and will continue indefinitely thereafter for like periods unless terminated by the giving of notice by either of the parties.[2, 3] Thus, if a tenant

---

* See p. 189.
† See p. 192.
[2] Spiritwood Grain Co. v. Northern Pac. Ry. Co., p. 808.
[3] Welk v. Bidwell, p. 811.

has a lease for a period of one year, and after the expiration of the year he stays in possession with the consent of the landlord, it is implied that a tenancy for another year certain exists, coupled with the possibility of an indefinite number of years thereafter. Unless either of the parties gives the necessary notice during the current year of the lease, the tenancy will continue for another year after the expiration of the current year. This is known as a *tenancy from year to year*. In the same way, the holding over by the tenant under a lease for a month creates a *tenancy from month to month*.

A tenancy from year to year or month to month may also be created by agreement of the parties.

C. TENANCY AT WILL

The distinguishing characteristic of a tenancy at will is that it may be terminated at the pleasure of either party.

> "All general and undefined tenancies, whether they originate simply by permission of the owner, or where the tenant has entered under a void lease or been let in pending . . . a purchase, or wherever there has been no express agreement between the parties as to the terms of the occupancy, provided the entry was a lawful one or with the consent of the owner, are now held to be tenancies at will." *Den* v. *Drake,* 14 N.J.L. 523

► IV. TERMINATION OF TENANCIES

A. TERMINATION OF TENANCY BY EXPIRATION OF PERIOD

A *lease for years* terminates coincident with the expiration of the period as fixed by the lease. Termination of a lease of this type is not dependent upon notice being given by the landlord to the tenant to quit the premises, unless the lease provides for the giving of notice. Even then courts have held that, where a statute provides that no notice is necessary to bring about the termination of a lease for a specified time, a provision in the lease for notice is void.

B. TERMINATION OF TENANCY BY DESTRUCTION OF, OR INJURY TO, LEASED PREMISES

A destruction of the *subject matter* of the lease to such a degree that it makes the premises untenantable terminates the lease. For instance, if a tenant has leased only the building and *not the land upon which it rests,* or even a part of a building, such as an apartment, a destruction of the premises will release him from further payment of rent. In the case of *McMillan* v. *Solomon,* 42 Ala. 356, the court said:

> "Where there is a lease of apartments in a house and those apartments are destroyed, the thing rented is gone. . . . It would be shocking to our sense of justice to compel a tenant to pay the rent of a room in a house for twenty years which had been destroyed within the first twenty-four hours. The rent in this case should be apportioned to the time of occupation before the fire."

Where the lease covers the building and also the land upon which it is situated, a destruction of the building does not, under the common law, terminate the lease and the tenant is not relieved from the payment of rent. In *Nashville, etc. Ry. Co.* v. *Herkens,* 112 Tenn. 378, the court said:

> "Where a building is rented without any language indicating that only the building itself is leased . . . both the building and the land pass under the lease, and a destruction of the building will not end the lease."

In those states where this common law rule has not been changed by statute the tenant may find it desirable to introduce a proper provision into the lease for his protection. This can be done by specifying that a destruction of or injury to the building will terminate the lease. Or it could be specified that the landlord shall repair the premises within a certain time and his failure to do so will cause the lease to terminate and relieve the tenant of further liability.

C. TERMINATION OF TENANCY BY USE OF PREMISES BECOMING UNLAWFUL

A lease for premises to be used for an undertaking that is subsequently prohibited by law is thereby terminated without further liability on the part of the lessee. When, however, the lease contemplates the use of the premises for more than one purpose, a prohibition of one of the purposes—providing it is not the primary or principal purpose—will not terminate the lease. To illustrate:

(1) In *Adler* v. *Miles,* 126 N.Y.S. 135, the lease provided that the premises were to be used and occupied "for the exhibition of moving pictures and no other purposes whatsoever." It was held that the enactment of an ordinance prohibiting the use of premises for such a purpose terminated the lease.

(2) In the case of *In re Bradley,* 225 Fed. 307, the lease provided that the premises were to be used as "a saloon and for no other purpose." It was held that the enactment of a law prohibiting the sale of intoxicating liquors did not terminate the lease since the word "saloon" applies also to a place in which nonintoxicants are sold.

(3) In *McCullough Realty Co.* v. *Laemmle Film Service,* 181 Iowa 594, the lease provided that the premises were to be used "for film exchange and film and theater supply purposes only." An ordinance was subsequently passed prohibiting the use of nonfireproof premises for the keeping, storing, handling, or repairing of inflammable motion-picture films. It was held that this prevented the primary use of the premises and terminated the lease. The court said that the handling of theater supplies was shown to include only those minor incidentals which are kept by a film exchange for the accommodation of the trade but necessary to the conduct of the primary purpose of the business.

D. TERMINATION OF TENANCY BY FORFEITURE

1. *Provision in Lease*

It is a common practice for leases to provide for their termination by the landlord if the tenant should fail to meet specified conditions. The right of forfeiture by the landlord is commonly based upon such things as

(1) failure of the tenant to pay rent or taxes;
(2) failure of the tenant to keep the premises insured;
(3) subletting or assigning the lease by the tenant;
(4) use of the premises for unlawful or other specified purposes;
(5) in the event of the bankruptcy or insolvency of the tenant.

2. *Statutory Provision*

Many states have enacted statutes that give the landlord the right of forfeiture upon various grounds, including the unlawful use of the premises, nonpayment of rent, and breach of the agreement not to assign or sublet. Local statutes should be consulted in this respect. Provision in the lease for forfeiture is not necessary to permit the exercise of the right of termination upon statutory grounds.

E. TERMINATION OF TENANCY BY NOTICE TO QUIT

1. *Periodic Tenancies*

Tenancies from year to year or month to month are most ordinarily terminated by a notice to quit, given either by the landlord or by the tenant, one to the other. State statutes usually specify the time within which the notice must be given. Local statutes must be consulted, as a failure to give notice within the specified period prior to the expiration of the current term has the effect of extending the lease for another term. In those states where the statute does not provide for the giving of notice, the common law rules of six months' notice for a tenancy from year to year and of one month's notice for a tenancy from month to month will apply. Some few states without statutory provision have followed the rule that notice must be given a reasonable time before the expiration of the current term of the lease.

By agreement the parties may fix any period of notice that they see fit. Such an agreement is binding regardless of statutory provisions or of the common law rule.

2. *Tenancies at Will*

Under common law, notice is not required to terminate a tenancy at will. Any act indicating the will of either of the parties to terminate the relationship is sufficient, such as a demand of possession by the landlord. However, in many states it has been provided by statute that notice to quit is necessary for the termination of a tenancy at will. Therefore, local statutes should be consulted.

F. TENANT'S RIGHT TO REMOVE CROPS

The tenant's right to remove annual crops that mature after the termination of the lease is known as the *right to emblements.* Whether the tenant has the right to reap the fruits of his efforts after the lease has terminated is dependent upon the circumstances.

1. *Under a Fixed Term—Tenancy for Years*

The common law rule is that the tenant does not have the right to emblements under a tenancy for a fixed term. Consequently, the growing crop reverts to the landlord upon the termination of the lease unless the right of removal has been acquired by the tenant either by (1) a provision in the lease or (2) a general custom in the neighborhood.

2. *Under an Uncertain Term*

If the time of termination is determined by the landlord—as under a tenancy from year to year or a tenancy at will—the tenant has the right to remove the growing crops. Many statutes that fix the period of notice to terminate a tenancy from year to year set the time of notice so as to terminate the lease after the crops are harvested.

3. *Upon Surrender or Forfeiture by Tenant*

If the tenant abandons the lease, he is not entitled to growing crops as emblements. Likewise, if the tenant causes a forfeiture of the lease, the growing crops revert to the landlord as part of the leased premises. Thus, where a tenant fails to pay rent and the landlord under the terms of the lease re-enters and takes possession, the tenant's right to the growing crops is lost.

► V. RIGHTS AND LIABILITIES OF PARTIES

A. POSSESSION OF PREMISES

The tenant has the right to obtain possession of the premises in accordance with the terms of the lease. The landlord has no right to withhold possession unless (1) the lease was obtained from him by fraud or (2) the tenant has failed to comply with a condition precedent to the vesting of the leasehold interest in the tenant.

Therefore, the landlord cannot refuse to give the tenant possession upon the basis of a mere failure of performance of a term of the lease. To illustrate:

(1) In *South Congregational Meetinghouse* v. *Hilton,* 11 Gray (Mass.) 407, the lease provided that the tenant was to build a new front according to certain plans and specifications. It was held that this was not a condition precedent to the vesting of the leasehold interest in the tenant and the failure of the tenant to comply did not entitle the landlord to withhold possession.

(2) In *Blanc's Cafe* v. *Corey,* 118 Wash. 10, it was held that a deterioration of the tenant's financial condition after the execution of the lease did not justify withholding of possession by the landlord.

The remedies available to the tenant for the landlord's failure to give possession are (1) money damages and (2) an action to obtain possession. The tenant need not take less than he bargained for, but he has the election to do so and to recover damages for that which he failed to get.

B. USE OF PREMISES

1. *Purpose and Manner of Use*

A tenant has the right to put the leased premises to such use as the parties have agreed upon, and, in the absence of any agreement restricting the use, it is his right to use the premises as he sees fit,[4, 5] subject to the following restrictions:

(1) The use may not differ materially from that to which the premises are ordinarily put or to which they are adapted. To illustrate:

(a) In *Lovett* v. *U.S.,* 9 Ct. Cl. 479, it was held that premises intended to be used as a hospital could appropriately be used by the tenant as a smallpox hospital but that its use as a burial ground was a misuse.

(b) In *Nave* v. *Berry,* 22 Ala. 382, it was held that a house built for use as a hotel could, in the absence of any stipulation in the lease, be employed as a seminary for young ladies.

(c) In *Leominster Fuel Co.* v. *Scanlon,* 243 Mass. 126, it was held that the tenant of a room could decorate it to his own taste as long as he did no injury to the premises.

(d) In *Dellwo* v. *Edwards,* 73 Ore. 316, it was held that a lease of land for agricultural purposes did not entitle the tenant to sell water to others.

(2) The use must be in a proper and tenantlike manner so that it will not amount to a waste or destruction of the premises. The tenant makes himself liable for any permanent injury to the premises that is an injury above ordinary wear and tear. To illustrate:

(a) In *Chalmers* v. *Smith,* 152 Mass. 561, the tenant was held liable for having put excessive weight into a building and thereby causing it to collapse.

(b) Such acts as: tilling a farm contrary to the established practice of crop rotation, removing shade trees, allowing the pasture to become overgrown with brush, removing sand and gravel, cutting timber for purposes other than to obtain necessary fuel or lumber for making repairs to the premises—all of these have been held to constitute waste by the tenant.

2. *Landlord's Right of Entry*

In the absence of any agreement with the tenant, the landlord has only a limited right of entry upon the premises during the term of the lease. The tenant is in effect the owner of the premises and is entitled to their use and enjoyment without interference by the landlord. Reasons that give the landlord the right of entry are: (1) to demand payment of rent when due; (2) to prevent waste; (3) to perform acts necessary to avoid liability—such as making the premises safe for passers-by; and (4) to execute orders given by a public authority, as an order from the board of health. If the landlord makes an entry for other purposes without the consent of the tenant, or without authority for such entry being given in the lease, he makes himself liable to the tenant as a trespasser.

3. *Eviction by Landlord*

An eviction consists of (1) the expulsion of the tenant by the landlord from the use and enjoyment of at least a material part of the premises, or (2) the abandon-

[4] Carbon Fuel Co. v. Gregory, p. 813.
[5] Boyd H. Wood Co. v. Finkelstein, p. 814.

ment of the premises by the tenant when the conduct of the landlord has materially deprived him of the use and enjoyment of the premises. The right of the tenant to abandon the premises is dependent upon an act of some seriousness on the part of the landlord—an act that indicates the intent of the landlord to deprive the tenant of the use and enjoyment of the premises. A mere trespass by the landlord does not justify abandonment. The courts have said that acts of the landlord that are sufficient to sustain an eviction must be of a grave and permanent character and must have been done with the intention of depriving the tenant of the use of the premises in an important rather than a trivial matter.[6]

> "It must consist of an invasion of a material character, tending to make further occupation attendant with serious consequences or continuing discomfort." *Saunders* v. *Fox,* 178 Ill. App. 309

To illustrate:

(1) In *Kimball* v. *Grand Lodge of Masons,* 131 Mass. 59, it was held that the removal of articles of furniture did not constitute the basis of an eviction.

(2) In *Lounsbery* v. *Snyder,* 31 N.Y. 514, it was held that the piling of firewood upon the leased premises after notice by the tenant to discontinue the practice did not constitute the basis of an eviction.

(3) In *Lumiansky* v. *Tessier,* 213 Mass. 182, it was held that an interference with the person of the tenant is a mere trespass. There the landlord violently expelled the tenant from the premises for the sole purpose of preventing him from conversing with an official inspector.

(4) In *Dimmods* v. *Daly,* 9 Mo. App. 354, it was held that the piling of bricks over a cellar grating located in an alley did not constitute an act of eviction even though such rendered the cellar damp and unwholesome.

(5) In *Meyers* v. *Bernstein,* 104 N.Y.S. 384, it was held that failure to furnish adequate power as required by the lease was an act of eviction.

(6) In *Donovan* v. *Koehler,* 103 N.Y.S. 935, the opening of a bowling alley beneath a leased flat constituted such a nuisance as to be an act of eviction.

(7) It has been held that the presence of vermin such as rats or bedbugs constitutes a constructive eviction. This is especially true when the landlord has agreed in the lease to keep the premises free of vermin.

(8) A failure to supply hot water and adequate heat may be regarded as a basis for eviction.

The tenant has a reasonable time within which to exercise his right to abandon the premises. If the tenant does not abandon the premises within a reasonable time, he has waived his right and can no longer assert an eviction. After abandonment, the tenant is no longer obligated to pay rent and he may recover damages from the landlord.

4. *Landlord's Responsibility for Condition of Premises*

The landlord makes no implied warranty as to the condition of the premises or that the premises will be fit for any particular use or purpose; it is the duty of

[6] Texas Co. v. Christian, p. 815.

the tenant to determine for himself the condition of the premises or whether the premises are suitable for his purpose.[7] It is only when the landlord is guilty of fraud (as when he conceals the condition of the premises or fails to disclose facts not readily available to the tenant) that the tenant may abandon the premises because they are not fit for the intended purpose. To illustrate:

(1) In *Scheffler Press* v. *Perlman,* 115 N.Y.S. 40, it was held that there was no implied warranty on the part of the landlord that the floors in the leased building had the necessary carrying capacity for the installation of printing presses.

(2) In *Coulson* v. *Whiting,* 12 Daly (N.Y.) 408, it was held that the landlord was not under duty to disclose the fact that the premises were possessed of noxious smells since such fact was obvious and subject to disclosure by the tenant's examination.

(3) In *Leech* v. *Husbands,* 152 Atl. 729 (Del.), it was said that ordinarily there is no implied warranty that the premises are free from vermin, bugs, or disease germs. However, it is the duty of the landlord to disclose conditions known to him if such knowledge is not readily available to the tenant by a reasonable examination. Thus, in *Minor* v. *Sharon,* 112 Mass. 477, it was held that the landlord's failure to disclose his knowledge that the premises were infected with smallpox constituted fraud.

(4) In *Stovall* v. *Newell,* 75 P. (2d) 346, it was held that the landlord's statement to the effect that the premises were in "first-class shape" was not a warranty as to the condition of the premises. The court said that such general words of commendation are regarded as mere "sales talk" and the expression of a personal judgment.

C. REPAIRS

Care should be exercised by the parties to a lease in fixing the responsibility of making repairs to the premises. In the absence of any agreement or statutory provision, the landlord has no obligation to make ordinary repairs.[8] As the court said in *Smith* v. *Chappell,* 25 Pa. Super. 81: "A tenant is bound not only to commit no waste but to make fair and tenantable repairs, necessary to prevent waste and decay of the premises." In accordance with this, it has been held that a tenant has an obligation to repair a street sidewalk, while a landlord is not obligated to restore fences destroyed by rains. Some courts have gone so far as to hold that, even though the repairs are required by a public authority, it is the obligation of the tenant rather than the landlord to make such repairs.

When parts of the premises are used in common by various tenants, the landlord has the duty to keep such parts in repair. Therefore, the landlord of an apartment building is required to keep the stairways, halls, roof, and foundation of the building in repair.[9]

"When . . . a building . . . is divided among several tenants, . . . and

---

[7] Luedtke v. Phillips, p. 816.
[8] Edwards v. Ollen Restaurant Corp., p. 817.
[9] State of Maryland v. Manor Real Estate & Trust Co., p. 818.

none of them rent the entire building, the rule must then be applied so as to make each tenant responsible only for so much as his lease includes, leaving the landlord liable for every part of the building not included in the actual holding of any one tenant." *O'Connor* v. *Andrews,* 81 Tex. 28

Local statutes bearing upon the duty to repair the premises should be consulted. Some states have, by statute, placed the burden entirely upon the landlord. A North Dakota statute, for example, requires the landlord, in the absence of an agreement to the contrary, to put the premises in a condition fit for human habitation and to repair subsequent "dilapidations." Under a Georgia statute, the landlord has the duty to make ordinary repairs, but not repairs that were obviously necessary at the time the lease was entered into.

D. IMPROVEMENTS

Tenants frequently make improvements to the leased premises, improvements that are necessary to their full use and enjoyment of the premises. As a general rule, the tenant has a right to remove such "trade fixtures" upon the termination of the lease. However, there is the possibility that the improvement will be regarded as a permanent part of the realty and the tenant will not be allowed to remove it unless the lease includes a definite provision for its removal. It has been held that the following improvements may not be removed by the tenant: a hanging floor in a business house; a baker's oven; fences; windmills; and a store front.

At the same time, the landlord cannot be held liable for the value of the improvements unless he agrees to pay for them. If improvements are to be made by the tenant, it is desirable that the lease should provide for the following: (1) the right of removal by the tenant or the obligation of the landlord to make compensation; (2) the time period within which the tenant has the right to remove the improvements. In some jurisdictions, the tenant has no right of removal after the expiration of the lease unless the lease has given him that specific right. Local statutes should be consulted.

► VI. RENT

Rent is the consideration given by the tenant for the use of the premises and it may be in money, services, or property, as crops. Even though the tenant does not agree to pay a specific amount, it will be implied that he has agreed to pay a reasonable rent for the use of the premises.

A. WHEN PAYABLE

Usually the lease will specify the time at which the rent is payable. In those instances where no time of payment has been agreed upon, the general rule is that the rent is not payable until the term of the lease has expired. However, this rule is subject to the following exceptions:

(1) The statutes of some states fix the time of payment if the parties have failed to agree upon a time.

(2) The established custom existing in a community may determine the time of the rent payment.

(3) The courts have held that when the tenant agrees to pay in products of the soil, the rent is payable within a reasonable time after the maturity of the crops.

B. LANDLORD'S LIEN FOR RENT

In many states the landlord is given a lien upon the property of the tenant for rent that is past due. Since the statutes in the various states vary greatly as to what property is subject to lien and as to what type of obligations entitle the landlord to a lien, local statutes should be consulted. For example, the Iowa landlord's lien provision as contained in the 1939 Code follows.

> "Section 10261. *Nature of landlord's lien.* A landlord shall have a lien for his rent upon all crops grown upon the leased premises, and upon any other personal property of the tenant which has been used or kept thereon during the term and which is not exempt from execution.
>
> "Section 10262. *Duration of lien.* Such lien shall continue for the period of one year after a year's rent, or the rent of a shorter period, falls due. But in no case shall such lien continue more than six months after the expiration of the term."

CASES

CASE NO. 1

Halpern v. Silver. 65 N.Y.S. (2d) 336 (1946)

BONEPARTH, J. . . . plaintiff alleges the following:

On or about December 6, 1945, he and one David Newmark, entered into "an agreement of lease." . . . Newmark was at the time the owner of a certain building. By said agreement Newmark, described therein as the landlord, granted "permission" to the plaintiff to install and maintain a coin metered washing machine, for a period of three years from the date of installation. The equipment was to remain the property of the plaintiff, and the plaintiff was granted access to the equipment, the landlord to furnish the "space, power and facilities for the operation of said equipment . . ." for which plaintiff agreed to pay $4 per month.

The complaint further alleges that subsequently, Newmark sold the premises to the defendants, who, in March, 1946, disconnected the washing machine, and in other respects refused to comply with the agreement made with Newmark, and "evicted the plaintiff from his said premises." . . .

The agreement in question does not create the relationship of landlord and tenant. By all the tests laid down in analogous cases, it cannot be construed as a lease.

In Tips et al. v. U.S., 5 Cir., 70 F. (2d) 525, an action for rent was based on an agreement, made by the Secretary of War, whereby in consideration of a "monthly rental," he "leased" for one year to defendant "3,101 square feet of (floor) space . . . to be designated by the commanding officer" of the Air Depot, for the storage of crated aeroplane engines. The circuit Court held the agreement did not create the relation of landlord and tenant, saying at pages 526, 527:

> "... A tenancy involves an interest in the land passed to the tenant and a possession exclusive even of the landlord except as the lease permits his entry, and saving always the landlord's right to enter to demand rent and to make repairs. A mere permission to use land, dominion over it remaining in the owner and no interest in or exclusive possession of it being given, is but a license. 35 C.J. Landlord & Tenant, § 10 . . ."

In United Merchants' Realty & Improvement Co. v. New York Hippodrome, 133 App. Div. 582, 118 N.Y.S. 128, 130, affirmed 201 N.Y. 601, 95 N.E. 1140, plaintiff agreed to let and defendant agreed to take "all of the roof . . . space" on a certain building for a term of two years to be used solely for displaying advertising, and to pay a yearly rental.

The Court held this was not a lease, saying, 133 App. Div. at pages 584, 585, 118 N.Y.S. at page 130:

> "... There was no specific property leased, but what seems to have been intended was a right to use the roof to erect upon it an advertising sign . . . no possession of the premises was given, except for the purpose of maintaining the sign. It is quite clear that the defendant was not given exclusive possession of the premises at any time. . . ."

Defendants contend that the agreement created a mere license.

A license in respect to real property is defined as

> ". . . authority to do a particular act or series of acts upon the land of another without possessing any interest or estate in such land. . . ." 37 C.J. Sec. 173 p. 279

The chief distinction between a license and an easement lies in the fact that an easement implies an interest in the land, while a license does not. 33 Am. Jur. pp. 398, 399; 37 C.J. p. 280

In the instant case, there is no language in the agreement which indicates an intention to burden or incumber the land with an easement. It provides in substance that the plaintiff is granted "permission" to "install and maintain" the washing machine in the premises, with the right of "access to the said equipment." Of course, the parties could have by a proper instrument, in plain language, however, created rights in the plaintiff which would have constituted an incumbrance on the land.

Accordingly, it must be held that the agreement, upon which the instant complaint is based, gives a license merely, does not create an easement, and is not a lease, and defendants are not bound by the agreement with Newmark.

The license given by the agreement was revoked by the conveyance of the premises by Newmark to the defendants. . . .

CASE NO. 2

Spiritwood Grain Co. v. Northern Pac. Ry. Co. 179 F. (2d) 338 (1950)

THOMAS, C.J. The Spiritwood Grain Company owned a grain elevator located on ground leased from the Northern Pacific Railway Company at its station at Spiritwood, North Dakota. The elevator and its contents were destroyed by fire on September 26, 1948. The property destroyed was insured by Millers National Insurance Company. Suit was brought by the Grain Company against the Railway Company to recover the loss on the ground that the fire was negligently spread by one of the Railway Company's steam locomotives. The Insurance Company having paid the loss joined as party plaintiff under its right of subrogation.

In its answer the Railway Company . . . alleged exemption from liability by reason of an exemption clause in the lease.

At the conclusion of plaintiffs' testimony the defendant moved for directed verdict. . . .

The motion for a directed verdict was sustained by the court and judgment was entered dismissing the action on the merits with costs against the plaintiffs, and the plaintiffs have appealed.

The appellants contend in this court, as they did in the district court: That the exemption from the liability clause in the lease was nullified by a statute of North Dakota. . . .

The lease originally entered into . . . was executed August 27, 1938, "effective as of August 1, 1937." . . .

On June 22, 1942, the Russell-Miller Milling Co., lessee, assigned to Dunwell Brothers; written consent thereto was given by the Railway Company on April 19, 1944.

On June 4, 1945, Dunwell Brothers assigned the lease to the appellant, Spiritwood Grain Company, and the written consent of the Railway Company was given thereto on July 10, 1945.

The written lease fixed no date for its termination. But paragraph 11 provided that "The Railway Company may also, without assigning any reason therefor terminate this lease at any time upon six months' written notice. . . ." And paragraph 14 provided that "The lessee may terminate this lease by giving thirty days' notice in writing. . . ." It was provided further that as annual rental the lessee would pay in advance $15, and all general taxes and special assessments. . . .

Paragraph 7 states the right of exemption from liability relied upon by the Railway Company. It reads:

"7. It is understood by the parties that the leased premises are in dangerous proximity to the tracks of the Railway Company, and that persons and property on the leased premises will be in danger of injury or destruction by fire or other causes incident to the operation of a railway, and the lessee accepts this lease subject to such dangers. It is therefore agreed, as one of the material considerations of this lease without which the same would not be granted, that the lessee assumes . . . all risk of loss, damage or destruction to buildings or contents or to any other property brought upon or in proximity to the leased premises by the lessee, or by any person with the consent or knowledge of the lessee, without regard to whether such loss be occasioned by fire or sparks from locomotive engines or other causes incident to or arising from the movement of locomotives . . or to whether such loss or damage be the result of negligence or misconduct of any person in the employ or service of the Railway Company, or of defective appliances, engines or machinery. And the lessee shall save and hold harmless the Railway Company from all such damage, claims and losses."

Unless in violation of a controlling statute of public policy it is generally held that a railroad company may by contract exempt itself from liability for damages to buildings or structures upon its right of way due to fires, even though such fires are due to its own negligence. . . .

The statute which appellants contend nullifies the exemption clause of the lease is a part of Chapter 49-16 of the Revised Code of North Dakota 1943. The two material sections following the heading "Liability of Railroads for Negligence" read:

"49-1601. Liability of Railroad for Damages from Fire. All railroad corporations operating or running cars or engines over roads in this state shall be liable to any party aggrieved for all damages resulting from fire escaping or scattered or thrown from any such car or engine. . . .

"49-1605. Contract Exempting Railroad from Liability Void. Any contract, rule, regulation, or device whatsoever the purpose or intent of which shall be to enable any railroad corporation to exempt itself from any liability created by this chapter to that extent shall be void. . . ."

The important contention of the Railway Company is that it has a vested right in the lease involved, including the exemptions from liability expressed in paragraph 7 thereof, supra, and that sections 49-1601 and 49-1605, supra, do not affect that right retroactively.

In support of this contention the Railway Company relies upon section 1-0230 of the Revised Code of 1943, which reads:

"Vested Rights Protected. No provision contained in this code shall be so construed as to impair any vested right or valid obligation existing when it takes effect."

And section 1-0210 of the same code which reads:

"Code Not Retroactive Unless So Declared. No part of this code is retroactive unless it is expressly declared to be so."

Attention is directed to the fact that the lease in question was made in 1938, and the Railway Company contends that, therefore, it was a valid existing contract obligation in 1943 when the 1943 code was adopted and that it still is an existing obligation.

The appellants' reply to the foregoing argument is that the lease of 1938 created a tenancy at will since the tenancy by the terms of the lease was of indefinite duration; that the attempted assignment of such a lease is void and results only in bringing the tenancy to an end; that when the Railway Company in this case permitted the assignee to occupy the premises on the same terms a new tenancy at will arose which was in no respect a continuance of the former tenancy. Therefore, the appellants argue, the assignment to the Grain Company of June 4, 1945, became effective by the approval of the Railway Company on July 10, 1945, and a new lease was thereby created subsequent to the operative date of the Revised Code of 1943 under which the exemption clause of the lease was void.

The Railway Company replies that the lease does not create a tenancy at will.

The statutes of North Dakota do not define a tenancy, or an estate, at will, but they require a thirty-day notice to terminate such an estate, section 47-1701, and no decision of any court of North Dakota involving such tenancy or estate has been called to our attention, and we have found none. We assume, therefore, that when such a case arises there the courts will accept and follow the weight of authority of the courts of this country.

In this country tenancies at will have been generally recognized. Such a tenancy is one made at the will of the lessor and held at the will of the lessee for an indefinite period. A statute requiring a notice to quit or a provision of the lease requiring notice of termination does not change its character. Such a lease is not assignable, but if the lessee attempts to assign it and the owner or lessee recognizes the transferee as tenant a new tenancy at will is thereby created. The transfer in such a case is effective as against the transferor. 32 Am. Jur., Landlord and Tenant, § 321, p. 294; 51 C.J.S., Landlord and Tenant, § 156 et seq.

Although under the lease in this case the duration of the tenancy is indefinite, it does not create a pure tenancy at will. Paragraph 1 provides that "As annual rental the lessee shall pay in advance the sum of fifteen and no/100 ($15.00) dollars." Such a lease creates a tenancy from year to year, which is defined as follows:

> "A tenancy from year to year is a form or species of tenancy at will, which also possesses many of the qualities and incidents of a term for years. It is indeterminate as to duration and may be assigned or demised." 51 C.J.S., Landlord & Tenant, § 131, p. 728.

It may be created by contract, as in the present case, or by implication of law as when a tenant for years holds over after the expiration of the term. "A tenancy from year to year," however created, "is comprehended in the term 'estates at will.'" Hunter v. Frost, 47 Minn. 1, 49 N.W. 327 . . . .

We are interested here, then, in the incidents of a lease from year to year, particularly in whether the payment of rent each year renews and extends the old lease for another year or whether it brings into existence a new lease. The lease in question was effective by its terms August 1, 1937. The annual rental was, therefore, payable in advance on August first for each succeeding year. The assignment to the Grain Company was approved by the Railway Company on July 10, 1945. If on payment of the annual rent on August 1, 1945, a new lease came into existence the exemption clause was void under the statute then in effect.

The question thus presented has been before the courts frequently. Most of the cases which we have found involving the question fall into one of two classes: first, cases like the present one where the tenancy is created by a written lease for an indefinite term but reserving an annual rental and providing in most such cases for termination upon notice by either party. The notice to terminate may be provided by statute. The second class of cases includes those year to year leases arising by implication of law. They usually arise where a lease is for a fixed period of time reserving annual rentals, and the tenant, with the acquiescence of the landlord, holds over after the expiration of the fixed term. In such case the tenancy is for year to year and may be terminated by notice at the end of any year.

Beginning at an early date in this country the tenancy in the first class of cases has been held to be continuous, and in the second the courts have held that a new lease comes into existence at the beginning of each year.

We think that the weight of authority supports the conclusion expressed above although there are cases to the contrary. We hold, therefore, that the original lease is a continuing contract and a new lease did not come into existence at the beginning of each new year. It follows that the exemption clause in the lease was not rendered void by sections 49-1601 and 49-1605 of the Code of 1943. . . .

CASE NO. 3

Welk v. Bidwell. 136 Conn. 603, 73 A. (2d) 295 (1950)

INGLIS, J. The question raised by the plaintiff's appeal in this action is whether in the case of a month-to-month tenancy the tenant, by holding over after the landlord has notified him of an increase of rent, becomes obligated to pay that increase in spite of his protest. . . .

The facts found may be summarized as follows: The plaintiff was the owner of a farm in Glastonbury upon which stood a tobacco barn. The defendant owned and occupied property directly across the highway and was engaged not only in farming but also in the sale and exchange of new and used farm machinery and equipment. In January, 1946, the defendant leased from the plaintiff his entire tobacco barn, with the stipulation that the defendant should have the "right of way thereto and entry guaranteed to premises," on a month-to-month basis for a monthly rental of $10. Thereafter, the defendant stored in the barn a large quantity of farm machinery, tractors, grain, small tools and other items and, to protect that property, he put hasps and padlocks on the barn doors.

About May 1, 1946, the plaintiff notified the defendant that he should either remove his property or thereafter pay $125 per month rent. The defendant refused to pay such a sum, saying that it was an outrageous price. Thereafter, the defendant continued to occupy the premises and periodically tendered to the plaintiff the rent at the rate of $10 per month. He has at no time either expressly or impliedly agreed to pay $125 per month rent but, on the contrary, has at all times claimed the right of occupancy at the rate of $10 per month. . . .

The trial court concluded . . . the defendant . . . was liable to the plaintiff for rent at the rate of $10 per month from May 1, 1946, to the date of trial, a total of thirty-six months. . . .

There is a sharp conflict of authorities whether a landlord may obligate the tenant to pay an increased rent under circumstances as related above. About half of the jurisdictions in which the question has been passed upon hold that he may and the other half hold that he may not. 32 Am. Jur. 800; note, 109 A.L.R. 197, 203, 205. The reasoning by which some of the courts reach the conclusion that the tenant becomes bound to pay the increased rent is, in substance, that a tenant has no right to occupy the property except upon the terms fixed by the landlord and if those terms are not acceptable the tenant is free to vacate. Abraham v. Gheens, 205 Ky. 289, 282, 265 S.W. 778, 40 A.L.R. 186. The answer to that line of reasoning is that, where, as in this state, provision is made for the ousting of a tenant by summary process on the expiration of a lease, the landlord is as free to oust the tenant as the tenant is to vacate, if the terms upon which the tenant proposes to hold over are not acceptable to the landlord.

The crux of the matter lies in the fact that a lease is a contract. In the case of a rental on a month-to-month basis the tenancy is not regarded as a continuous one. The tenancy for each month is one separate from that of every other month. . . . For each new month, therefore, there must be a new contract of leasing. Where there has been no meeting of the minds there is no contract. If a landlord insists on one rate of rental and the tenant insists on another, there is no meeting of the minds.

Our statute, General Statutes, § 7106, provides:

> "No holding over by any lessee, after the expiration of the term of his lease, shall be evidence of any agreement for a further lease. . . ."

The fact that the defendant in this case held over in possession of the property after the expiration of his lease for the month of April, 1946, did not in itself create a lease for the subsequent month. The parties were free to make a contract for the future occupancy of the property.

If there had been no dispute between them as to the terms of the future occupancy, the holding over by the tenant and the acquiescence therein by the landlord would have raised such a contract by implication. . . . But if there had actually been no meeting of the minds either because of ambiguity or uncertainty in negotiations or because the negotiations had not been completed, then, of course, there could have been no contract. . . .

It is clear that the plaintiff could not, by merely giving notice to the defendant that he should either remove his property from the premises or thereafter pay $125 a month rent, impose upon the defendant a lease for the ensuing months at that rental. The defendant's flat refusal to agree to pay that rent left the parties without any contract with reference to the occupancy of the property. The question, therefore, arises as to what was the nature of the defendant's tenancy after May 1, 1946. He was not a trespasser, because he had entered into possession of the property prior to that time under a lease which gave him the right of possession. The plaintiff could have revoked that right and recovered the right of possession by peaceable entry or by way of summary process. . . . This he did not do. The defendant was not a tenant at will, because such a tenancy exists only when the occupation of the property is with the landowner's consent, continuing during the tenancy. . . . Obviously, here, the plaintiff was not consenting to the defendant's continued possession. A tenancy at sufferance arises when a person who came into possession of land rightfully continues in possession wrongfully after his right thereto has terminated. Restatement, 1 Property § 22. . . . That is the situation in this case. The defendant, prior to May 1, 1946, was rightfully in possession of the property. After that date he held over without a lease and was in wrongful possession. Accordingly, he was after that date a tenant at sufferance. . . .

As a tenant at sufferance, the defendant was not liable for any stipulated rent. He was not obligated to pay the $125 per month demanded by the plaintiff. Nor was his obligation fixed at the rate of $10 per month which he had been paying. His obligation was to pay the reasonable rental value of the property which he occupied. . . . The trial court made no finding as to the reasonable rental value of the property but instead assessed damages on the basis of the former rent of $10 per month. This was error. . . .

CASE NO. 4

Carbon Fuel Co. v. Gregory. 131 W. Va. 494, 48 S.E. (2d) 338, 2 A.L.R. (2d) 1143 (1948)

FOX, J. The facts are simple and are not in dispute. The record discloses that on November 3, 1942, the Carbon Fuel Company leased to Oliver Gregory, as an incident of his employment as a miner, and in connection with plaintiff's coal operation, a certain tenement house, then known as number 95, upon the premises of the plaintiff, and at a rental of $10.50 per month. It was provided in the lease that same might be terminated at any time, by either party, by giving to the other five days' notice of the intent to terminate the same. But, it seems to be conceded by all concerned that the enactment of the Federal Rent Control Act nullified, in effect, this five day provision, and that the right to terminate on the part of the landlord could only be invoked for cause. The lease also contains this provision:

"It being understood that said premises are intended solely for the occupancy of employees of the party of the first part, and that the proper conduct of the business of the party of the first part requires that none but his employees and their families shall occupy the same."

There is no provision in the lease which specifically limits the use of the leased premises. . . .

The lessee, the defendant herein, continued to occupy said premises until the 12th of March, 1947, on which date the Carbon Fuel Company, the lessor, plaintiff herein, wrote to the lessee as follows:

"It has been brought to my attention that you are selling ice cream and other items in and about your house. This house was leased to you for tenement purposes only and you are, hereby, notified to discontinue the above selling of merchandise of any nature."

The lessee replied to this letter on March 17, to which, on the same date, the lessor made his reply insisting on the discontinuance of the activities referred to in its first letter. On March 22, the lessee again wrote to the lessor insisting upon his right to sell ice cream, whereupon, on March 26, 1947, the lessor notified the lessee to vacate the said premises on or before April 3, 1947

"for the reason that you have violated a substantial obligation of your tenancy, as provided in Section 6 (a) (3) (i) of the Rent Regulation for Housing pursuant to which this notice is given." . . .

The sole question here presented is the interpretation to be given to the lease under which the lessee occupies the tenement involved. There is nothing in the lease which in direct terms, places any restrictions whatever upon the use of the leased premises. Under settled law, the lease should be construed most strongly against the lessor, who, it is assumed, prepared the same, and who had it in its power to incorporate therein restrictions on the use of the leased premises and failed to do so. The general rule is that

"A lessee of real property is entitled to the exclusive use of the demised premises for any purpose not prohibited by the lease, not amounting to waste or destruction of the subject-matter," and "Where doubt exists as to the meaning of lease restrictions as to the use of property, such provisions are to be resolved in favor of lessee and against lessor." Oakwood Smokeless Coal Corporation v. Meadows, 184 Va. 168, 34 S.E. (2d) 392, 396.

The case in which these holdings were made was not one involving the tenancy of residence property, but we know of no reason why the general rule there announced should not be applied to the case at bar. We can well understand why a coal mining company, furnishing houses for its employees, should contemplate that its tenants would use such houses for residence only; but this supposition on the part of the mining company is, in our opinion, insufficient on which to base a positive restriction of the use of such premises for other than residential purposes. In our opinion, we are not justified in giving to it a different meaning than that expressed by the lease itself, unless upon some clear implication to the contrary, which we think does not exist in this case.

Affirmed.

CASE NO. 5

Boyd H. Wood Co. v. Finkelstein. 84 N.Y.S. (2d) 459 (1948)

FROESSEL, J. Application for an order reviewing the action of the respondents, the Temporary City Housing Rent Commission, in denying petitioner's application for a certificate of eviction.

Petitioner's application to the respondents was based on the claim that the tenant was violating a substantial obligation of the tenancy, in that the apartment was being occupied by more persons than had been contemplated by the landlord, when he originally let the apartment. The facts are as follows:

(1) Petitioner rented the apartment to the tenant on December 1, 1936, allegedly on the understanding that it would be occupied by the tenant and her son, who was then about sixteen years of age. They both occupied the apartment until the son was inducted into the military service in March, 1943. Thereafter the mother continued to reside there alone. While in the military service and in October, 1944 the son married. Upon his separation from the service in February, 1946, he returned to the home he had left bringing with him his wife. Thereafter and in December, 1946, a child was born to them. The mother is employed as a domestic and returns home every weekend. The petitioner appears to have collected rent under these circumstances for well over a year before applying to the Commission for a certificate.

Certainly these facts do not spell out a substantial violation of the tenancy. Matter of Park East Land Corp., 83 N.Y.S. (2d) 165. This was the son's home, as well as his mother's, for thus it was rented. His absence in the military service made it nonetheless so. It is inconceivable that marriage required him to give up his home, or that a child born of the marriage would have the same consequences. Indeed, the public policy of this state may be found in the Penal Law which makes it a misdemeanor to refuse to rent to a person merely because he has a child or children (§ 2041) or to provide in a lease that during the term thereof "the tenant shall remain childless or shall not bear children" (§ 2042). . . .

CASE NO. 6

Texas Co. v. Christian. 177 F. (2d) 759 (1949)

HUTCHESON, C.J. Appellee, plaintiff below, lessee and operator of a gasoline filling station leased from appellant . . . put forward for recovery three separate and distinct claims. . . .

The third was that in response to his repeated complaints, defendant removed the leaking tanks from plaintiff's premises and replaced them with other tanks, but failed and refused to reinstall in the pumps the computers and meters, thereby rendering the leased premises unfit for occupancy, and in effect evicting plaintiff therefrom. . . .

On the constructive eviction counts, appellant's point is that, taking the plaintiff's evidence most favorably for him, it did not show such an eviction. For instead of showing acts of a grave and serious nature, done with the intent of depriving the tenant of the beneficial use of the property, and having permanently injurious effects, it shows quite the contrary. Insisting that the undisputed evidence shows merely a condition of small and temporary inconvenience, which could have been easily and promptly remedied by a very small expenditure, the meters and computers being on the premises and capable of being easily installed, appellant urges upon us that the duty to make these small installations and save himself from the heavy losses plaintiff claims to have suffered was imposed on him, by the terms of his lease, requiring him to maintain the premises in repair, and by the principles of fair dealing, requiring him to take reasonable steps to prevent or minimize damages. . . .

. . . The evidence is undisputed that the computers and meters were on the leased premises, and completely available to plaintiff, and that they could have been installed for a very small sum and a very short time. In view of these facts, the fact that large damages are claimed by plaintiff for defendant's failure to install them, and the further fact that in Alabama as generally elsewhere, it is the duty of one claiming to have been wronged to take reasonable steps to prevent or minimize damages therefrom, we are of the opinion that the claim of plaintiff, that the mere failure of the defendant to make these simple installations constituted a constructive eviction, staggers credulity, and it is difficult for us to see how reasonable minds could have concluded, as the jury did, that the complained of failure was such an eviction. . . .

CASE NO. 7

Luedtke v. Phillips. 190 Va. 207, 56 S.E. (2d) 80 (1949)

BUCHANAN, J. The plaintiff below, Mrs. Luedtke, plaintiff in error here, recovered a verdict against the defendant, Phillips, for injuries sustained when a wall cabinet full of dishes fell and struck her in the kitchen of an apartment rented by her from Phillips. The court set aside this verdict and entered judgment for the defendant. This is the error assigned.

. . . Phillips bought a wooden cabinet weighing about fifteen pounds and took it to the apartment in his car. A plumber was there, an employee of the Spiers firm, engaged in installing heating and plumbing in the new kitchen. Phillips left the cabinet there and told the plumber he would get somebody to put it up. Later the plumber, having some spare time while waiting for the heating system to drain, on his own initiative attached the cabinet to the wall above the sink, which Mrs. Luedtke said was the only suitable place for it. This was done by means of inserting screws above two and one-half inches long through holes at the back of the cabinet for that purpose. When Phillips came back and found the cabinet installed, he took hold of it, shook it and it seemed to be all right; so he thanked the plumber for his good work.

. . . She occupied and used the apartment from that time until the accident happened in September, 1946, five or six months after she moved into the apartment, and about a year after the cabinet had been installed. . . .

The law as thus stated in Caudill v. Gibson Fuel Co., 185 Va. 233, 38 S.E. (2d) 465, is applicable to the facts, and is controlling:

> ". . . Where the right of possession and enjoyment of the leased premises passes to the lessee, the cases are practically agreed that, in the absence of concealment or fraud by the landlord as to some defect in the premises, known to him and unknown to the tenant, the tenant takes the premises in whatever condition they may be in, thus assuming all risk of personal injury from defects therein. . . ."
>
> "The logical conclusion from the principle that the landlord is under no implied obligation as to the condition of the demised premises or as to the repair of defects therein is that the landlord is not responsible to the tenant for injuries to person or property caused by defects in the demised premises where the landlord has not made any warranty or contract as to the condition of the demised premises or as to the repair of defects and is guilty of no wilful wrong or fraud. . . ." 32 Am. Jur., Landlord and Tenant, § 662, pp. 526–7, and cases cited. . . .

The evidence in this case affords no ground for a recovery by the plaintiff and the judgment of the trial court is accordingly . . . affirmed.

CASE NO. 8

Edwards v. Ollen Restaurant Corporation. 98 N.Y.S. (2d) 815 (1950)

FEIDEN, J. This is a summary proceeding brought by the landlord to recover possession of the "store and basement" of premises 16 Howard Avenue, Brooklyn, New York City, occupied by the tenant as a restaurant and bar and grill. Both sides concede that the tenant occupies the premises as a statutory tenant, the lease running from April 1st, 1945, to March 31st, 1948, having terminated. It is the claim of the landlord that the tenant has violated substantial obligations of the lease. There are two floors above the leased premises.

The pertinent provisions of the lease are as follows:

"That the Tenant shall take good care of the premises and shall, at the Tenant's own cost and expense make all repairs on the demised premises, and at the end or other expiration of the term, shall deliver up the demised premises in good order or condition, damages by the elements excepted.

"The landlord shall supply the Tenant with thirty (30) tons of coal per annum, for the purpose of heating the demised premises. In the event that more than thirty (30) tons are required, the Tenant shall then supply the deficiency. The Tenant further agrees to tend to the furnace which supplies the heat to the demised premises and if necessary to hire a janitor at its own cost and expense for such purpose."

The furnace referred to in the lease supplies heat to the entire building. In November, 1948, the furnace broke down. When no heat was supplied, due to the breakdown, for over a year, the tenant of the upper floors instituted proceedings in the Magistrates' Court against the landlord. The case was thereafter, in the usual course, referred to the Court of Special Sessions of the City of New York. By registered letter, dated January 6, 1950, which according to the return receipt was received by the tenant on January 7, 1950, the landlord called the tenant's attention to its failure to repair the heating system and to provide heat. The letter stated that if the landlord was required to make the repairs, proceedings would be instituted to recover possession of the leased premises. The landlord gave the tenant until 8:00 A.M. on January 9, 1950, and referred to previous demands for compliance with the terms and conditions of the lease. At the conclusion of the case in the Court of Special Sessions some time in January, 1950, the landlord replaced the furnace. Two or three weeks thereafter, the heating system broke down again. The tenant asked the landlord if he would contribute towards fixing the furnace. However, the landlord himself had the furnace repaired on the tenant's promise to pay half the cost. After the furnace was repaired, the tenant refused to pay its share. The furnace broke down once again and has not been repaired, with the result that since February, 1950, up to the time of the trial during the month of May, 1950, no heat was supplied to the building. . . .

Neither counsel nor the court has been able to discover any New York case dealing with the obligation of a tenant with respect to furnaces located in demised premises. This precise question of law however has been the subject of adjudication in other jurisdictions. These cases held that under a covenant by a lessee to keep premises in repair, the replacement of a worn-out, useless furnace or a boiler by a new one is a repair which the tenant is obligated to make. Bell House v. Wilkins, 34 Ga. App. 285, 129 S.E. 797; Peck v. Scoville Mfg. Co., 43 Ill. App. 360; Arnold Evans Co. v. Hardung, 132 Wash. 426, 232 Pac. 290, 45 A.L.R. 9, 45 A.L.R. 52

In the absence of a covenant to the contrary the lessor is under no obligation to repair the demised premises. A lessee assumes all the risks arising from the condition of the premises unless there is an express agreement on the part of the lessor in relation thereto, and, an express covenant will not be enlarged by construction. . . .

Where, as in this case, the exclusive control of the basement was in the tenant, there can be no question that the obligation to keep and maintain that portion of the premises including the furnace devolved upon the tenant. . . .

The tenant was required on the expiration of the term to deliver up the demised premises "in good order or condition, damages by the elements excepted" and was required during the term of the lease to "take good care of the premises . . . and at the Tenant's own cost and expense make all repairs." The term "damages by the elements excepted," covers destruction by fire, without the fault or neglect of the lessee, and includes all injury by wind, rain, snow, frosts, and heat, as well as ordinary decay from natural causes, 51 C.J.S., Landlord and Tenant, § 368, p. 1102. The provision requiring the tenant to surrender up the premises in good order, damages by the elements excepted, and that requiring the tenant to take good care of the premises must be read together. They imposed on the tenant the obligation to keep and maintain the furnace in good, workable condition. . . .

CASE NO. 9

State of Maryland v. Manor Real Estate & Trust Co. 176 F. (2d) 414 (1949)

SOPER, C.J. This is a suit under the Federal Tort Claims Act, 28 U.S.C.A. §§ 1346, 2671 et seq., and the Maryland Wrongful Death statute, Code Md. 1939, art. 67, § 1 et seq., brought in behalf of the widow of Evered W. Anderson to recover damages for his death. The defendants are . . . the United States of America. The complaint charged that Anderson died of endemic typhus, a disease transmitted by means of the bite of a flea from an infected rat, which in this case was caused by the negligence of the defendants in failing to take adequate measures to exterminate the rats on the premises of an aggregation of apartment houses in which Anderson was a tenant. The District Judge dismissed the complaint, holding that although negligence was proved, the evidence did not sufficiently establish that Anderson's death was caused thereby. . . .

The house in which Anderson lived was one of twenty-two three-story row dwellings, one hundred and twenty-five years old, located in the 600 and 700 blocks of North Calvert Street in Baltimore City. The Railroad Company purchased them more than thirty years ago as a site for a freight terminal, but the project was abandoned and most of the houses, including No. 619 in which Anderson lived, had been vacant for many years. In June, 1943, they were leased to the Federal Public Housing Authority for a nominal rental to aid the government in the pressing need for housing for defense workers in the Baltimore area during the war. . . .

During the period of government control the wooden floors of the cellars were honeycombed with rat burrows and the garbage from the apartments frequently overflowed the dilapidated uncovered containers furnished by the landlord to the tenants, and spilled upon the floor. Only one janitor and a helper were employed to service the more than twenty houses in the 600 and 700 blocks; the helper worked full time but the janitor was present only three or four hours a day in the winter. . . . As a result of this deplorable situation, many large and bold rats, often four or five at a time, were observed in the cellars each time the tenants descended to dispose of their garbage and trash. Mrs. Anderson and the tenants generally complained to the agent, but to no avail.

. . . The dismissal of the complaint as to the Housing Authority cannot be sustained. The Authority transformed the sixteen houses in the 600 block into a large number of apartments, agreed to supply the tenants with heat, furnished containers in the cellars, one for each house, for the reception of garbage, and provided janitor service. There can be no question under these circumstances as to the responsibility of the Housing Authority for the condition of the basements, and its liability for the consequences of its neglect. It is true that there was no covenant on its part in the lease in this case to keep the property in repair, and that under the law of Mayland the general doctrine is that there is no implied covenant requiring the landlord to make repairs, and no implied warranty that the house shall be fit for habitation; but the landlord's obligations are different in the case of multiple unit dwellings for "where he leases separate portions of the same building to different tenants, and reserves under his control the halls, stairways, and other portions of the building used in common by all of the tenants as means of access to their respective rooms or apartments, he is under an obligation to use reasonable diligence to keep the portions so retained under his control of the building in a safe condition and free from improper obstructions. . . . This obligation of the landlord to the tenants of different parts of the same building in reference to the halls, stairways, doors, etc., of which he has kept possession for their common use, has been held not to result from the implied covenant for quiet enjoyment incident to the leases of the several portions of the building, but to be of the same character as that of any other owner of real estate, who permits or invites others to use it for a particular purpose, to keep it safe for those using it within the scope of the invitation. . . . 32 Am. Jur., Landlord & Tenant, § 688

. . . The judgment of the District Court is . . . reversed and the case is remanded to the District Court with directions to assess the plaintiff's damages.

Review Questions

1. By what elements is a landlord and tenant relation determined?
2. To what extent is an oral lease enforceable?
3. What are the characteristics of a tenancy for years?
4. What are the characteristics of a tenancy from year to year?
5. What is a tenancy at will?
6. Will the destruction of a building necessarily terminate the lease under which the building was rented?

7. What is a forfeiture provision in a lease?
8. Is it necessary to give notice to quit to terminate a tenancy at will?
9. Of what does a tenant's right of emblements consist?
10. Does the tenant have the remedy of specific performance for a failure of the landlord to give possession of the leased premises?
11. What are the limitations upon a tenant's right to use the leased premises?
12. Illustrate an act of eviction by the landlord.
13. In the absence of contractual agreement is the landlord responsible if the leased premises are not suitable for the tenant's intended purposes?
14. Who is responsible for repairs to the leased premises?
15. What is the tenant's right to remove permanent improvements that he has made upon the leased premises?
16. Is the landlord obligated to pay for permanent improvements made by the tenant?
17. May rent be payable in something other than money?
18. What is the landlord's right of lien in your state?

Problems for Discussion

1. By contract, Morgan acquired the right to remove sand and gravel from Gilpin's land, for which right Morgan agreed to pay $2,500 a year and agreed further that he would not remove more than a stated maximum. Morgan failed to pay and Gilpin seeks to exercise a landlord's lien over loading equipment that Morgan had moved upon the premises. Result?
2. X agrees to let Y use a part of his premises as a right of way for a consideration of $100 a year. Does this create a landlord-tenant relation?
3. It appears that plaintiff is the owner of the premises; that she acquired title thereto by purchase from a former owner who had heretofore entered into a contract by which he leased the premises to the defendant at an agreed monthly rent of $22; and plaintiff's title is subject to all rights that became vested in defendant thereby. The lease contained the following stipulation: "To have and to hold the above rented premises unto the said party of the second part (the tenant) for the full term of which he shall wish to live in Albert Lea from and after the first day of December 1904." The only question involved under the stipulation is the construction of its provisions of the lease. Defendant has at all times paid the rent as it became due; plaintiff contends that the lease created either a tenancy at will, at sufferance, or from month to month, and that plaintiff could terminate the same at any time by proper notice. The trial court held in harmony with the defendant's contention that the contract created a life estate in defendant terminable only at his death or removal from Albert Lea. Decide. (*Thompson* v. *Baxter,* 107 Minn. 122)
4. Jacobs and Schwartz entered into an oral lease for a period of five years. Is this a tenancy at will?
5. X leases from Y for a period of five years at an annual rental of $1,200. Is this a tenancy from year to year?
6. Snyder leased a dwelling from Coons for a period of one year at a rental of $75 a month. After the termination of the year, Snyder remained in possession of the premises against the wishes of Coons. At the end of the first month,

Snyder tendered $75 to Coons, who accepted it with the statement that he expected Snyder to vacate the premises immediately. Snyder contends that he has another lease for a period of one year. Decide.

7. Dakin leased a building to Joseph for an indefinite period of time at $25 a month "to be paid at Joseph's convenience." What kind of tenancy is this?
8. Suppose that, in Question 7, six months after the agreement was entered into Joseph paid Dakin $150 and it was agreed that Joseph was to continue in possession of the premises upon payment of a like rental every six months thereafter. Does this change the nature of the original lease?
9. X agreed to lease certain premises to Y "until the premises are sold." What type of tenancy was created?
10. Johnson leased a dwelling from Briggs for a period of one year. At the end of the year, Johnson quit the premises. Briggs contends that Johnson's failure to give notice to quit continued the lease for another year. Decide.
11. Gleason rented a farm from Draper for a period of three years. One month after he took occupancy all the buildings were destroyed by a cyclone. Does this release Gleason from the obligation to continue to pay rent?
12. The transfer of the landlord's reversionary interest to the tenant terminates the lease. Illustrate.
13. Brook leased certain premises from Crawford at an annual rental of $600, the lease not specifying the time at which the rent was payable. The day that Brook was to take possession, Crawford heard a rumor that Brook's credit was not good. May he demand payment of the rent as a condition to giving possession of the premises?
14. X rented land from Y for agricultural purposes. X discovered gravel upon the premises and proceeds to sell gravel to others. Is he within his rights?
15. The defendant resisted payment of the rent, on the ground that his lease had been broken by the plaintiff by a partial eviction. It appears that plaintiff was the owner of the adjoining premises, No. 469 Lincoln Avenue, and across the rear of both lots stood a barn, the second story of which plaintiff began to remodel into a living apartment soon after defendant took possession. The defendant is a plumber, and occupied the lower floor of the barn as a shop. An outside stairway was constructed to permit access to the apartment, and the tenants of the apartment were permitted by plaintiff to pass to the street over defendant's lot. As a result of the remodeling, defendant's back yard was filled with building materials and rubbish. The defendant claims that by reason of these acts he was deprived of the use and enjoyment of a portion of the premises, and to such extent he was evicted. Decide. (*Kuschinsky* v. *Flanigan,* 170 Mich. 245)
16. Can the landlord dictate to the tenant what crops are to be grown upon the leased premises?
17. Jepsen leased a building from Emery for the purpose of operating a drugstore. The lease provided that Emery was to put new locks upon the doors and to erect one partition as required by Jepsen. After Jepsen took possession, Emery refused to do these things. Jepsen vacates the premises contending an eviction. Decide.
18. Action by plaintiff tenant for property damage arising from the collapse on May 8, 1945, of the first floor of the building numbered 5 and 6 Fulton Place,

Boston. This floor was equipped as a refrigerator room, 37 feet by 20 feet in area and 9 feet in height, and was supplied with the necessary brine from pipes of the Quincy Market Cold Storage and Warehouse Company. The floor of the room was of wood planking supported by timbers 13 inches by 12 inches, placed 10 inches apart. Although the building was about 150 years old, it did not appear how long the first floor had been fitted up for refrigeration. The property had been purchased by the defendants Harry Weiner and his wife Alice H. Weiner in 1942, and the first floor was rented by them to the National Creamery Company, a corporation, as tenant at will, in 1944, to be used for the storage of pickled herring in barrels. Four hundred fifteen barrels, each weighing from 330 to 340 pounds, were therein put in storage by the creamery company. On May 8, 1945, the floor of this refrigerator room collapsed and many of the 365 barrels which at that time remained in storage fell into the cellar. There was evidence that the floor timbers had become rotted where they joined the walls in the rear of the building. Decide. (*Gade* v. *National Creamery Co.,* 10 A.L.R. 1009)

19. Buelo leased a building, which, as the lease specified, he was to use as a cardboard-box factory. When Buelo started to install his machinery, he discovered that the building was too small for the intended purpose. May he avoid the lease?
20. After the commencement of a lease for one year of certain rooms and cellars of a storehouse in a town, for the purpose of trade, the building was destroyed by fire, not attributed to the fault of any person. Before the expiration of the term, the lessor entered upon the premises without the consent of the lessee and commenced the erection of a new building upon the locality of that which had been consumed and retained possession until the end of the term. In a charge to the jury, in a suit on the note given for the rent, the court below asserted the proposition that this entry was an eviction of the lessee, and the plaintiff could not recover. Decide. (*McMillan* v. *Solomon,* 42 Ala. 356)

32 REAL PROPERTY AND RELATED TOPICS:

LIENS UPON REAL PROPERTY

► I. JUDGMENT LIENS[1]

A. IN GENERAL

Statutes in the various states provide that a judgment is a lien against the real property of the defendant. The requirements of local statutes should be ascertained. In general, the lien applies to all real property (not exempt) * that is located within the territorial jurisdiction of the court in which the judgment was obtained. Usually the judgment may be imposed as a lien on real property located elsewhere, by having the judgment recorded at a designated office in the county where the property is found. It is also generally required that a judgment obtained in an inferior court (as a justice of the peace court) must, to become a lien against real property, be filed and recorded in a designated superior court.

1. *Judgment as Lien upon Property in Another State*

The full faith and credit clause of the Constitution of the United States makes it easy to obtain a judgment in one state and to impose that judgment as a lien against realty in another state. Article IV, Section 1 reads: "Full Faith and Credit shall be given in each State to the public Acts, Records, and judicial Proceedings of every other State." As a consequence, a judgment, for example, may be obtained in Ohio upon a judgment rendered in Illinois without examination of the merits upon which the judgment was given in Illinois. Ohio will give full faith and credit to the Illinois judgment.

2. *Purchasers and Lenders Subject to Lien*

Purchasers of real property take the property subject to all existing judgment liens. Consequently, a prospective purchaser of real property, before he accepts a deed to the property, will determine whether it is free of judgment liens. Likewise, one who accepts a security interest in real property (as a mortgagee) takes it subject to existing judgment liens.

3. *Doctrine of Lis Pendens*

Under the doctrine of *lis pendens,* one who acquires an interest in real property that is in some way involved in litigation takes the property subject to the outcome of the litigation.

---

* Property is said to be exempt from execution when it cannot be taken to satisfy a judgment debt. As an illustration, the individual's home may not be taken for this purpose without his consent. This particular exemption is called the "right of homestead." Local statutes should be consulted.

[1] M. & J. Finance Corp. v. Hodges, p. 829.

"The theory of the doctrine of lis pendens is to preserve the situation as it is when the original litigation is commenced until the termination, so that the successful party may then take the fruits of it without interruption from another who may have, during its pendency, sought to obtain some right to the property in controversy." *Hovey* v. *Elliott,* 118 N.Y. 124

The types of legal actions that may involve real property are:

(1) actions to recover real property;
(2) foreclosure or enforcement of liens (such as mechanics' or tax liens);
(3) actions to quiet title;
(4) specific performance;
(5) divorce proceedings;
(6) probate proceedings;
(7) eminent domain proceedings; and
(8) injunctions.

B. EXEMPT PROPERTY

All real property cannot be taken to satisfy a judgment obligation. Constitutional or statutory provisions in the various states provide that the homestead is exempt from liability for the debts of the owner.

"A man's homestead must be his place of residence; the place where he lives; . . . where he surrounds himself with the ordinary insignia of home, and where he may enjoy its immunities and privacy." *Philleo* v. *Smalley,* 23 Tex. 499.

The extent to which real property is considered a homestead varies greatly. For example, Iowa provides (subject to exceptions) that if in the country (a farm), a home may not exceed forty acres, and otherwise it may not exceed one half of a block.

C. ENFORCEMENT OF LIEN

A judgment lien may be enforced by a seizure of the property and sale as provided by statute. However, the judgment debtor is given the right to redeem the property within a prescribed time after the sale. Unless he does redeem within the allowed period of time, the sale becomes absolute and the purchaser gets title.

► II. MECHANICS' LIENS

A. NATURE OF MECHANICS' LIENS AND UNDERLYING THEORY

Mechanics' liens, statutory in origin, make it possible for those who have contributed to the improvement of real property to obtain security for the compensation to which they are entitled.

In common law there was no lien available to those who furnished their labor or materials for the improvement of real property like that available to artisans in relation to personal property.* The courts have found considerable justification

* See p. 714.

for the statutes in the various states that provide for a lien of this nature—a lien upon the real property in favor of those who contributed to the improvement.[2]

> "This is based on the principle that the material used or the labor performed upon a specific property has enhanced its value, and that it is right that the person furnishing material may follow his material into the structure of which it became a part, or that the laborer should pursue the result of his toil in order to secure his just compensation because the structure is the result of the material furnished or the labor done." *Lamb* v. *Goldfield Mining Co.*, 37 Nev. 9

Although there is considerable variation in details, the various statutes giving the right of mechanics' liens are substantially alike in their operation and effect. In this discussion the basic features of mechanics' lien legislation will be indicated. Local statutory provisions must be consulted for specific requirements.

B. PERSONS ENTITLED TO LIEN

The designation *mechanic* has come to have a broad meaning in connection with liens upon real property. Although the early statutes were limited in their scope of application, it is the modern tendency to give protection to all persons who contribute to the improvement of real property by furnishing material or labor.[3] Section 10271 of the 1939 Iowa Code is illustrative:

> "Every person who shall furnish any material for or perform any labor upon any building, including those engaged in the construction or repair of any work of internal improvement and those engaged in grading any land or lot, by virtue of any contract with the owner, his agent, trustee, contractor, or subcontractor shall have a lien upon such building and upon the land belonging to such owner on which the same is situated, or upon the land or lot so graded, to secure payment for material furnished or the labor performed."

The statute in the particular jurisdiction will designate what class or classes of persons are entitled to protection.

1. *Contractors and Subcontractors*

It should be noted that, in order to qualify for a lien, one need not contract directly with the owner of the property. It is customary for principal contractors—or original contractors, as they are at times designated—to sublet portions of the contract to subcontractors. The right of lien is possessed by these subcontractors as well as by the original contractor. Thus, if A contracts to erect a house for the owner of the property and sublets the contract for installation of the heating plant to B, who in turn sublets the contract for the sheet-metal work to C, all three parties would have a right of lien.

2. *Materialmen and Laborers*

Likewise, materialmen and laborers contracting directly with the owner or with a principal contractor or a subcontractor are eligible for a lien. A materialman

[2] Cutler-Hammer Inc. v. Wayne, p. 829.
[3] Breeding v. Melson, p. 830.

who furnishes materials to another materialman has been held not to be included within a mechanics' lien statute. To extend protection to such a point would be impractical and a burden upon the owner.

One who qualifies as a materialman under a contractor or subcontractor must have furnished the material for the improvement of the specific property and not upon the general credit of the purchaser. To illustrate:

A, who is a building contractor, purchased a large quantity of cement from B without reference to any particular building projects and stored it in his own warehouse. Some of the cement was subsequently used for the improvement of C's property, but this fact does not give B a right of mechanic's lien for the unpaid purchase price of the cement used. The cement was not furnished by B for the improvement of that specific property. Under these circumstances, title passed directly to the contractor A, and he became his own materialman.

C. PROPERTY AND INTERESTS SUBJECT TO LIEN

A mechanic's lien attaches not only to that portion of the land upon which the improvement is effected or upon which the improvement is placed but also upon the whole of the realty deriving the benefit from the improvement.[4] If the improvement is upon what is identified and recognized as a lot, tract, or parcel of land, the lien ordinarily attaches to the whole. In any event, the lien will include such an area of ground as is necessary for the convenient and proper use of the building or improvement.

A mechanic's lien may attach to any interest in real property that can be assigned, transferred, mortgaged, or sold under execution. If an owner in fee simple contracts for the improvement of property, any resultant liens will attach to the fee. If a lessee contracts for the improvement of leased premises, any mechanic's lien will attach to the lessee's interest only, unless the owner of the property gave his express or implied consent to the improvement. In that event the lien would attach to the whole ownership interest.

D. TIME WHEN LIEN ATTACHES

The point of time at which a lien attaches to the property becomes important when it is necessary to determine priority between conflicting claimants. As a general proposition, a mechanic's lien holder stands in priority to encumbrancers and purchasers subsequent to the time the lien attached.

Under a majority of statutes, a mechanic's lien probably attaches and is made effective as of the time the claimant first began to perform the work or to deliver the materials upon the premises. The latter are presumed to have contributed to the improvement, and the materialman need not prove that they were actually used. In other jurisdictions the lien is said to attach as of the time that the improvement project was begun, regardless of the time when the work was completed or when the materials were furnished. And in some states it has been held that a lien relates back to the time of entrance into the contract.

[4] Mansfield Lbr. Co. v. First State Bank of Vian, p. 831.

As a general rule, the claimants of mechanics' liens upon the same property stand in equal rights. If the property is not sufficient to pay all claims in full, they share the amount realized pro rata. In some jurisdictions a priority is given according to the times of filing the claims for record, while in others a priority is given in the order of the time at which the lien originally attached. Some states give certain classes of claimants, such as laborers, a priority over claimants of other classes.

E. PRESERVING OR CONTINUING LIEN

In states where a lien attaches prior to, and without need of, filing it for record, the lien continues effective as a secret lien for a certain period of time. Usually a lien claimant is under no obligation to take steps to notify third persons of his right of lien until the period of time as provided in the statute has expired. For this reason, the examiner of a title will advise the purchaser to take note of the possibility that mechanics' liens may not appear of record when the liens resulted from recent or present improvements effected upon the property. One who accepts a mortgage upon premises is bound to exercise like care.

Mechanics' liens statutes usually provide that, to preserve and continue his lien, a lien claimant must file a statement containing certain information within a specified time. The period is in most cases 60, 90, and 120 days after the right of lien attaches or the last of the material or labor was furnished or the contract is completed.[5] This statement must be filed with a public official, such as the clerk of court. The Iowa statute, for example, provides that a verified statement must be filed with the clerk of the district court, that a contractor must file within ninety days, and that a subcontractor must file within sixty days from the date on which the last of the material was furnished or the last of the labor was performed.

F. OWNER'S LIABILITY

Before the owner of the improved property makes payment of the contract price to his contractor, he must satisfy himself that he will not be held responsible for obligations due to subcontractors or materialmen. Not infrequently the owner will complete his contract payments in reliance upon the integrity or ability of his contractor to meet the obligations due to subcontractors, materialmen, and employees who contributed to the improvement, only to find that liens are subsequently filed against the property. To illustrate:

A, the owner of improved property, made the final payment on the contract price upon completion of the work. The principal contractor, being insolvent, failed to pay the architect his $2,500 fee; the architect thereupon filed a lien against the property. A was obligated to pay the $2,500.

Section 10282 of the 1939 Iowa Code makes the following provision for the protection of the owner:

> "No owner of any building upon which a mechanics' lien of a subcontractor may be filed, shall be required to pay the original contractor for com-

[5] Electric Contracting Co. v. Brown, p. 832.

pensation for work done or material furnished for said building until the expiration of sixty days from the completion of said building, unless the original contractor shall furnish to the owner:

(1) Receipts and waivers of claims for mechanics' liens, signed by all persons who furnished any material or performed any labor for said building, or

(2) A good and sufficient bond to be approved by said owner, conditioned that said owner shall be held harmless from any loss which he may sustain by reason of filing of mechanics' liens by subcontractors."

In some states the owner can, before making payment, require the contractor to furnish him with a sworn statement containing a schedule of the amounts due or to become due to all who have contributed or are contributing to the improvement. The owner can then govern his actions upon the basis of the sworn statements and make payment without fear of mechanics' liens, providing none have been filed of record. It is his duty to retain sufficient funds to pay all such indicated claims.

G. EXTENT OF LIEN

Let us suppose that A contracts with B for a $5,000 improvement to A's real property and that, upon completion of the work, mechanics' liens are claimed upon the property to the extent of $6,000. The question arises as to what extent the property can be charged with payment of these claims. According to the general rule, liens are available only to the extent of the contract price. In this instance, the various claimants would generally share pro rata in the $5,000 fund available. This is in conformity with the so-called *New York system* of liens.

A few jurisdictions have enacted the so-called *Pennsylvania* or *absolute system* of liens. Under these lien laws the property is chargeable to the full extent of the lien claims, irrespective of the contract.

H. WAIVER OF LIEN

The owner may protect himself to some extent by including a waiver of mechanics' liens in the contract with his contractor. Some courts have held that a waiver of all liens by the principal contractor is also effective against those who deal with or through him. On the other hand, there is authority to the effect that in his contract with the owner a principal contractor cannot bind others by a stipulation of waiver of lien.

► III. TAX LIENS

Delinquent taxes assessed against real property are usually made a lien upon the property by statute or constitutional provision. Anyone acquiring an interest in real property takes it subject to such lien. A tax lien is enforced by the sale of the property.

CASES

CASE NO. 1

M. & J. Finance Corporation v. Hodges. 230 N.C. 580, 55 S.E. (2d) 201 (1949)

BARNHILL, J. The plaintiff's chattel mortgage was executed 30 September 1948 but was not registered until 26 October 1948. The automobile was seized under execution on defendant's judgment 22 October 1948. Thus on the date of seizure under execution, plaintiff's mortgage was not of record. Which party holds the prior lien? This is the one question posed by this appeal. Our decisions answer in favor of defendants. . . .

Unregistered mortgages are of no validity whatsoever as against creditors and purchasers for value unless they are registered. They take effect as against such interested third parties from and after registration just as if they had been executed then and there. . . .

Even so, it is not every creditor who is protected against unrecorded mortgages. A creditor has no claim to the personal estate of his debtor until he has first fastened a lien upon it in some manner sanctioned by law. . . .

While a judgment constitutes no lien upon the personal estate of the judgment debtor, seizure thereof by an officer under authority of an execution creates a special property therein and a lien thereon for the purpose of satisfying the execution. It is the levy under execution that creates the lien in favor of the judgment creditor. . . .

At the time of the seizure under execution by defendant sheriff, plaintiff's mortgage was not of record. . . .

As the defendants acquired an effective lien upon the automobile prior to the registration of plaintiff's mortgage their lien is superior. Therefore, the judgment entered must be

Reversed.

CASE NO. 2

Cutler-Hammer, Inc. v. Wayne. 101 F. (2d) 823 (1939)

HUTCHESON, C.J. Appellant is one of a number of materialmen and laborers who, before the bankruptcy of Clare & Company, furnished it, as a contractor, material and labor for use on a building job. Bankruptcy supervening before the job was finished, and there being ample funds to complete it, the trustee finished the job. On its completion, the owner, under an agreement with the trustee, the lien claimants and all others concerned, agreed that he and his building should be released, and that all the claims should be transferred to and made against the deposited funds, deposited in the bankruptcy court . . . a sum sufficient to pay all lien claims in full. Appellant and others, in accordance with the agreement, duly claimed, on statutory and equitable grounds, liens on the deposited funds.

Appellee opposed their allowance on the ground that, dependent for their validity upon strict compliance with the Georgia lien statutes, Secs. 67-2001, 67-2002, the third requirement of which was the commencement of an action for the recovery of the amount of their claims within twelve months from the time the same became due, the claims to liens were invalid because claimants had not commenced such action, and bankruptcy having supervened, they could not now do so. . . .

The purpose of the lien statutes in every state is, in substance, the same;

this is, to give the furnisher of labor and material a claim upon the owner, to compel him at his peril to withhold final payment until he has received assurance from the contractor that he has paid all material and labor claims, which are or which may be perfected into liens. Bankruptcy does not discharge valid liens any more when, though inchoate and in the process of completion, they are in good standing when bankruptcy comes, than when every required step has already been taken. When it supervenes, it does not take from laborers and materialmen funds devoted to their claims, to appropriate them to the general creditors, merely because some step in the procedure, which there is still time to take, has not been taken. . . .

We think the authorities do not admit of any other view than that, when, as here, the owner deposits in the bankruptcy court the unexpended balance of the contract price, he deposits it to the extent necessary to discharge the liens, not as money of the estate, but as money of the lien claimants. . . .

The judgment is reversed, and the cause is remanded, with directions to allow the lien claims.

CASE NO. 3

Breeding v. Melson. 34 Del. 9, 143 Atl. 23, 60 A.L.R. 1252 (1927)

RICHARDS, J., delivered the opinion of the court:

A claim in a mechanic's lien proceeding was filed in the Superior Court in and for Sussex County, on July 27, 1922, by John T. Melson, the plaintiff below, for work done and materials furnished in connection with the building of a moving picture theater . . .

A motion for binding instructions, on the ground that it was not shown that the plaintiff was a contractor within the meaning of the law, was refused.

This refusal of the court to instruct the jury at the close of all the testimony taken in the case to find a verdict for the defendant, is the sole assignment of error.

Under the statute of this state providing for the filing of mechanics' liens, a contractor must file his statement within 30 days after the expiration of 90 days from the completion of the building, house or structure contracted for by him and upon which he desires to secure a lien. 29 Laws of Delaware, 725.

The courts of this state have decided that a contractor, within the meaning of the statute, is one who furnishes both labor and materials for the erection of any building, house or structure. . . .

The greatest part of the claim filed in this case was for superintending the work of building the theater, and it was contended on behalf of the plaintiff in error that this was not labor of such a character as would entitle the plaintiff to file a claim in mechanics' lien proceeding.

Williams v. Alcorn Electric Light Co. 98 Miss. 468, 53 So. 958, Ann. Cas. 1913B, 137, is the only authority cited in support of this contention. It holds that the word "laborer," when used in its ordinary and usual acceptation, carries with it the idea of actual physical and manual exertion or toil, and did not include superintending the construction of a building. This decision is not supported, however, by the weight of authority in this country, which is to the effect that mechanic's lien statutes such as ours, providing that

> "it shall and may be lawful for any person or persons having performed or furnished work and labor or material, or both, to an amount exceeding

twenty-five dollars in or for the erection, alteration, or repair of any house, building, or structure, in pursuance of any contract, express or implied, . . . to obtain a lien upon such building, house, or structure," include all persons who perform labor in the construction or reparation of a building, irrespective of the grade of their employment, or the particular kind of service.

No distinction is made between skilled and unskilled labor, or between mere manual labor and the labor of one who supervises and directs. . . .

CASE NO. 4

Mansfield Lumber Co. v. First State Bank of Vian. 147 Okla. 8, 293 Pac. 1079, 79 A.L.R. 958 (1930)

HERR, C., filed the following opinion:

One C. L. Hill was the owner of lots 8 and 9 in block 25, in the town of Vian, Okla., and the First State Bank of Vian, defendant, was the owner of part of lot 7, in said block, on which there was located a one-story brick building, in which said bank was conducting its business. Mr. Hill decided to build a two-story brick building on his lots. He discussed the construction thereof with one Allen Scott, vice president of defendant bank, in which discussion it was suggested by Mr. Hill that the construction of his building would make defendant's building look rather odd unless it placed an additional story thereon. Following this discussion, an agreement was reached between Scott and Hill that Hill should construct an additional story on the bank building, in connection with his building, and, in consideration therefor, he was to have the rentals arising from the additional story for a period of 10 years from the completion thereof. . . .

In accordance with this contract, Hill, in connection with the construction of his building, erected an additional story on the building belonging to the bank, and, in the course of constructing these buildings, he purchased material from the plaintiff, Mansfield Lumber Company, which material was used in the building and construction thereof. At the completion of the buildings, there remained due and owing plaintiff the sum of $1,158.40, of which amount material to the value of $635.63 remaining unpaid was used in the construction of the bank building.

Plaintiff, in due course, filed its materialman's liens against these buildings. This suit is to foreclose the lien on the bank building. . . . The trial was to the court, resulting in judgment in favor of plaintiff against Hill for the sum of $1,158.40, and decreeing a lien against his leasehold in and to the bank building in the sum of $635.63, and a denial of the lien against the interest of the defendant bank. Plaintiff appeals.

The main assignment is that the judgment is contrary to law. In our opinion, this assignment is well taken. The contention of plaintiff is that, by the written lease contract, defendant bank made and constituted Hill its agent for the purchase of the material and the construction of the building. With this contention we agree. The building was constructed for the sole use and benefit of the defendant, and not for the accommodation or convenience of Hill. The bank, under the contract, was obligated to reimburse Hill for the construction of the building out of the rents arising therefrom. The building was to be constructed under the directions of the bank, and Hill was required to execute a bond guaranteeing the construction thereof in a workmanlike manner and as provided by the contract, and indemnifying the bank against lien claims. This, undoubtedly, constituted Hill the agent of the bank.

In volume 27 Cyc. at page 58, the following rule is announced:

> "It is usually held that where a lease contains a provision authorizing the lessee to make repairs or improvements at the cost of the lessor, either generally, or by deducting the cost from the rent, or where part of the consideration for the lease is the making by the lessee of improvements which become a part of the realty, or that improvements made by the lessee shall revert to the lessor, a mechanic's lien may attach to the property for work done or materials furnished pursuant to a contract with the lessee. . . ."

Defendant relies upon the cases of Hudson-Houston Lumber Co. v. Parks, 91 Okla. 46, 215 Pac. 1072; Antrim Lumber Co. v. Mendlik, 110 Okla. 76, 236 Pac. 422. These cases are not applicable to the situation here presented. Therein improvements were made by tenants in possession for their own use and benefit, and the lessor was under no obligation to reimburse them for the expense thereof in any manner whatsoever. . . .

It follows from what has been said that the court erred in denying plaintiff a lien against the interest of the bank in and to the premises in question. . . .

CASE NO. 5

Electric Contracting Co. v. Brown. 39 So. (2d) 100 (La.) (1949)

KENNON, J. Alleging that it had furnished labor and materials of the value of $251.70 for the construction of a frame dwelling on a lot owned by defendants, James F. Brown and wife, in the City of Alexandria, Louisiana, during the period February 5 to April 25, 1947, and that on June 13, 1947, it had filed a lien against this property after the contractors had failed to pay its account after demand, plaintiff filed suit praying for judgment against defendant Brown and his wife, and for recognition of its recorded lien.

Plaintiff began the electrical work on the Brown house on February 5, 1947, and completed same ready for use on March 10, 1947. Two employees of the company returned on April 25, 1947 for the purpose of installing a Kraus-Hines ground clamp which was required by the ordinance of the City of Alexandria. Plaintiff's witness explained that this type of ground clamp was not available when the work on the Brown house was completed on March 10th and that plaintiff had, with permission of the city electrical inspector, installed a different (but effective) type of clamp. On the day the clamp was changed, plaintiff's employees also discussed with Mr. Brown his complaint that certain of the inside receptacles or plugs would not work satisfactorily, but no work was done on these receptacles and Mr. Brown seems to have been satisfied with the electrician's explanation that the receptacles installed were the best available.

Plaintiff's contention is that its contract to do the labor and furnish the materials for defendants' house was not completed until the Kraus-Hines clamp was installed on April 25th and that the lien filed on June 13th was within the sixty day period required by the applicable statute. . . .

The defendants, who apparently paid the contractor for the labor and materials furnished by plaintiff, resist on the ground that the statutory time period of sixty days had expired before plaintiff's lien was filed.

Under these circumstances, we think the holding of the Court in the case of Hortman-Salmen Company, Inc., v. White, 168 La. 1067, 123 So. 715, is applicable, and, as stated by the Court in that case, the last labor is done and the last service or material is furnished, within contemplation of the lien statute, when the building is treated as completed and the correcting of defects which may appear from time to time in the work after the building is considered and treated as completed, is not to be considered or deemed as part of the labor contemplated by the statute in fixing the time. Otherwise, as the Court in that case observed, the time within which to record liens might linger indefinitely and the rank of mortgages and other claims against the property might be displaced unreasonably.

The above case was cited with approval in the more recent case of Hicks v. Tate, La. App., 7 So. (2d) 737. In that case, the Court of Appeal for the First Circuit held that the installation of a drain cock some sixty days after the other work was completed did not permit the renewal of the sixty day period in which a lien might be filed.

Plaintiff has argued in brief that the *quantity* of material last delivered or the *amount* of labor last performed are not controlling and cited the case of Shreveport Long Leaf Lumber Company, Inc. v. Spurlock, 9 La. App. 224, 120 So. 126, in which the delivery of a single additional yard of gravel nearly ninety days after the job was otherwise completed, had the effect of renewing the lien period.

In the case before us, no additional materials were furnished on April 25th. The cost of the ground clamp was approximately $1.00 and there is no testimony that the clamp first installed was of less value than the replacement clamp installed in April. Plaintiff has cited the Shreveport Long Leaf Lumber Company case, supra, holding that where a city ordinance requires inspection and approval, there can be no last delivery or last performance as respects time for recording liens until after such inspection and approval. This point is not relevant in the case before us as there is no testimony in the record that approval by the City of Alexandria was delayed until after the installation of the new clamp on April 25th.

Plaintiff is claiming the benefit of a lien by virtue of a statute. The burden of showing that his claim comes within the statute is upon the plaintiff. We believe this burden has not been met. . . .

Review Questions

1. Is a judgment a lien upon all real property owned by the judgment debtor?
2. What property is exempt from execution in your state?
3. What is the relationship of the full faith and credit clause of the Federal Constitution to judgment liens?
4. What is the doctrine of lis pendens?
5. How is a judgment lien enforced?
6. What is the scope of modern mechanics' lien laws?
7. May one acquire a lien upon real property without having contracted for the improvement of the property with the owner?
8. Is a lessee's interest in real property subject to a mechanics' lien?
9. Why may it be important to determine the date upon which a mechanics' lien attached?
10. What is the lien claimant usually required to do for the purpose of preserving and continuing his lien? What is the requirement in your state?
11. What can the owner of property do before discharging his contractual obliga-

tion for the improvement of the property to prevent liability upon a mechanic's lien?

12. Is the property chargeable to the full extent of the liens filed against it?
13. How may the purchaser of real property assure himself that there are no mechanics' liens against the property?

Problems for Discussion

1. Orson obtained a judgment of $2,700 against Green. Subsequently, Green conveyed certain of his real property to Mallory, who had failed to take note of the judgment. Mallory then mortgaged the property to Roberts, who knew of the judgment against Green but failed to recognize that the judgment was entered against Green at the time of his ownership of the property. What are the rights of the various parties in relation to the real property?
2. Simmons obtains a judgment against Cooper in the state of Maine. Being unable to get the judgment satisfied, Simmons would like to levy upon certain real property that Cooper owns in the state of Vermont. How can he accomplish this?
3. A was under contract to construct a dwelling. He contracted for the necessary lumber from the Acme Lumber Co. The Acme Lumber Co. purchased part of the lumber from the Ideal Lumber Co. Does this entitle the Ideal Lumber Co. to a mechanic's lien?
4. Bunte contracted to paint Dickson's house, the agreement providing that Dickson was to furnish the paint and other necessary materials. Dickson authorized Bunte to make the necessary purchases from the Acme Paint Co. and advanced him funds for this purpose. Bunte, in making the purchases, had them charged to himself and used the money advanced by Dickson to purchase interior decorations for himself. What are the rights of the Acme Paint Co.?
5. Shelhorn, a building contractor, purchased fifty water softeners from the Puritan Corp. He stored these softeners in his central depot out of which he took materials as they were needed and out of which he also sold materials to the public. Shelhorn installed twenty-five of the softeners in houses which he built for purposes of resale. The Puritan Corp. seeks to obtain mechanics' liens upon the twenty-five properties upon which the softeners were placed. Should the corporation succeed?
6. X contracted to buy certain real property from Y. An examination of the abstract of title revealed no mechanics' liens against the property appearing of record. Does this give X assurance that he will take the property free of possible mechanics' liens?

Business Organizations

Chapter

33. DISTINGUISHING FEATURES AND FORMATION OF THE PARTNERSHIP

34. RELATIONS OF PARTNERS TO THIRD PERSONS; THEIR POWERS AND LIABILITIES

35. RELATIONS OF PARTNERS TO ONE ANOTHER; THEIR RIGHTS AND DUTIES

36. DISSOLUTION AND TERMINATION OF PARTNERSHIP

37. CHARACTER AND FORMATION OF BUSINESS CORPORATIONS

38. POWERS, DURATION, AND TERMINATION OF CORPORATIONS

39. STOCKHOLDERS' POSITION

40. CORPORATION MANAGEMENT AND CONTROL

	Partnerships	Corporation
origin	Contract	chartered by state
liability	unlimited	limited
tax	none	corp. tax.
existence	life of partners or shorter	perpetual or shorter

33 BUSINESS ORGANIZATIONS:

DISTINGUISHING FEATURES AND FORMATION OF PARTNERSHIP

The widespread use of the corporation and the advent of various other statutory and common law forms of business organization have greatly diminished the use of the general partnership as an organization device in man's quest for business profits. Nevertheless, the general partnership is still of prime importance as a form of business unit and is used very prominently in the conduct of small-scale commercial enterprises and the professions.

No attempt will be made here to evaluate the advantages or disadvantages of this form of organization over other types. It is not the province of this work to determine by what standards the choice is made of a form of organization for the conduct of a business enterprise. Many factors must be taken into consideration in selecting the form best suited to the needs of the individual situation. However, an understanding and an appreciation of the legal aspects of the various types of business units are of a certainty prerequisites to an intelligent choice. Such understanding and appreciation are no less necessary to an intelligent conduct of the business enterprise after the type of business organization has been selected. A knowledge of the legal principles under which an organization is formed, is operated, and is dissolved should, therefore, prove to be a considerable aid to the associated members in the discharge of their responsibilities and the protection of their interests.

► I. ESSENTIAL ELEMENTS

A partnership is defined by the Uniform Partnership Act, Section 6, as being: "An association of two or more persons to carry on as co-owners a business for profit." Therein are found the various elements which, in combination, constitute a partnership.

A. AN ASSOCIATION

The general partnership is a common law form of organization. The authority for its creation exists in the common law right of voluntary association. It comes into being and exists by virtue of the assent of the participating parties. The basic requirement, then, for the existence of a partnership between individuals is contractual assent. There can be no partnership relation between persons unless there is present an intention that a partnership shall exist.[1, 2, 3] The contract of partner-

[1] In re Ganaposki, p. 846.
[2] Coens v. Marousis, p. 847.
[3] Phillips v. Phillips, p. 848.

ship may be express, or it may be implied from the circumstances in the individual case. An express intention in combination with the other elements of a partnership will, without question, constitute a partnership. Where the other elements of a partnership are present, the intent will be implied upon the basis of existing facts.

B. A JOINT VENTURE

Individuals cannot create a partnership merely by expressing their intent that a partnership relation shall exist between them. To create a partnership, the contract must relate to a joint venture that is possessed of those characteristics incident to the conduct of a business for profit. The intent that a partnership shall exist can be implied from a factual situation that consists of a joint venture composed of the requisite elements of a partnership, even though the parties express an intent to the contrary.

In *Malvern Nat. Bank* v. *Halliday*, 195 Iowa 734, the court observed that the salient features of the ordinary partnership are: (1) a community of interest in capital employed; (2) a community of power of administration; and (3) a community of interest in profits and losses. The court said, "These are the primary tests and constitute the indicia of the existence of a partnership." These are the incidents of co-owners conducting a business for profit.

1. *Interest in Capital Employed*

As a matter of practice, property engaged in the conduct of a partnership enterprise is owned jointly by the partners. *Joint ownership of property is not, however, an essential to the existence of a partnership relation.* Joint ownership may be indicative of the existence of the relationship but is of itself no test. It is recognized that a partner need have no actual ownership interest in the property or capital employed. The property or capital used for partnership purposes may belong exclusively and entirely to one partner. To illustrate:

Let us suppose that A and B form a partnership toward which A contributes $500 in cash and certain real estate, and toward which B contributes only his skills and services. Under these circumstances, B acquires no actual conveyable ownership interest in the property contributed by A. Ownership of the physical property will, in the absence of an agreement to the contrary, continue to reside with A. Upon a cessation of the partnership, B can claim no part of the assets contributed by A any more than A can claim the continued benefits of B's services. A's contribution was the use of the property rather than the property itself. To hold that A's contribution is partnership property would require a clear indication that A intended to make it such.

A partnership relation does, however, possess the characteristic that the members have an interest in the property, both tangible and intangible, which has been dedicated to the joint enterprise to the extent that such property shall be used exclusively for the benefit of the members of the firm. The joint use of property, while not conclusive, is evidence that a partnership relation exists. A community of interest in the capital employed, to the extent indicated above, is one of the essentials to the existence of a partnership. Joint ownership would clearly establish a community of interest.

2. *Power of Administration*

Every member of a partnership has the implied right to take part in the management of the firm's affairs. Consequently, an active participation in the conduct of a joint business venture may, in conjunction with other circumstances, lead to the conclusion that a partnership exists. However, taking part in the management of a concern is not in itself a sufficient test of a partnership relation. It is not uncommon that a business concern will employ an individual for the express purpose of having him exercise his managerial ability. This still leaves him far removed from being a partner in the firm. On the other hand, absence of the right of management will not prevent one from occupying the capacity of a partner. Frequently the members of a partnership will, by agreement, vest the function of management in one or various members of their group. The fact that one of the partners waives his right of management will not prevent the undertaking from retaining the character of a partnership.

3. *Interest in Profits and Losses*

A joint venture that does not contemplate a quest for mutual profit cannot qualify as a partnership. Many joint undertakings in which the profit motive is not present are in daily operation. For example, (1) there are associations motivated by the desire to mutually benefit the members in social, educational, or religious ways; (2) labor organizations exist for the primary purpose of mutually benefiting their members by working to protect their interests; and (3) there are many types of business associations, such as credit associations, whose objects are the dissemination of business information and the rendering of business aids to their members. In all these cases, and in others, the absence of the profit motive will conclusively overcome an allegation that a partnership exists.

While there can be no partnership without the sharing of profits, a sharing of profits is not a conclusive test that a partnership exists.[4] It is merely potential evidence that the parties' intention was to create a partnership. Some states hold that the sharing of profits is prima facie evidence to this effect. This evidence may be overcome by a showing that the profits were received for some reason other than a share in the joint venture. Section 7(4) of the Uniform Partnership Act indicates the reasons for which an individual may be given an interest in the profits of a partnership without participating as a partner. It reads:

"The receipt by a person of a share of the profits of a business is prima facie evidence that he is a partner in the business, but no such inference shall be drawn if such profits were received in payment:

(*a*) As a debt by instalments or otherwise,

(*b*) As wages of an employee or rent to a landlord,

(*c*) As an annuity to a widow or representative of a deceased partner,

[4] Aetna Ins. Co. v. Murray, p. 849.

(*d*) As interest on a loan, though the amount of payment vary with the profits of the business,

(*e*) As the consideration for the sale of the goodwill of a business or other property by instalments or otherwise."

The prevailing view is that the sharing of losses is one of the essentials to the existence of a partnership relation. The sharing of losses need not be expressly provided for but will be inferred from the sharing of profits. It is reasonable to presume that a joint venture that contemplates the sharing of profits also contemplates, in the absence of a showing to the contrary, the sharing of losses. However, a participation in the risks of an enterprise does not of itself indicate a partnership.

In conclusion it can be said that an agreement to share profits and losses is strong evidence that a partnership is in being. It is not, however, conclusive evidence to that effect. For example, arrangements are common whereby a landlord will furnish a farm to be operated by the tenant upon the agreement that expenses and profits of the operation are to be shared in a certain proportion.

To illustrate:

In *Merrall* v. *Dobbins,* 169 Pa. St. 480, Dobbins and Griffin entered into what they called a "contract of lease" by which Dobbins leased a hotel to Griffin for $20,000. The contract further provided that: (1) Griffin was to give his undivided attention to the promotion of the business; (2) Dobbins was to have the right of free access to the premises; (3) Dobbins was to have 80 per cent of the net profits of business done on the premises; (4) Dobbins was to appoint a bookkeeper and cashier and receive all money and make all payments; (5) Dobbins was not to be liable for business done or debts contracted by Griffin.

The court, in holding this arrangement to be a partnership, said:

". . . The enumerated terms in the lease are not the characteristics of a lease but of a partnership. The business to be carried on is not spoken of as a business of Griffin. . . . It is to 'the business done on the premises' that Griffin is to give his whole attention; of it, that the bookkeeper is to take charge, an account to be stated and the net profits ascertained; and from it that he is to be paid, and the parties to receive, the one 80 per cent, and the other 20 per cent. The business of which the agreement speaks and of which an account is to be kept, a statement made, and the profits divided is the business of a distinct entity—a partnership, in which the partners are joint owners and which they share as proprietors."

► II. CONTRACT OF PARTNERSHIP

As has been seen, a partnership agreement need take no particular form. It may be predicated upon the most informal understanding of the parties or may arise from their conduct alone.[5] Only insofar as a partnership agreement falls within the provisions of the Statute of Frauds is there a need for a writing. Some courts have held that a contract of partnership for a period exceeding one year falls

[5] Eckhard v. Comm. of Internal Revenue, p. 850.

within the statute unless provision is made that the partnership may be dissolved within the year by the consent of the partners.

The prudent procedure in the formation of a partnership is to execute a written agreement, even though such is not legally required. A writing that adequately establishes the rights and duties of the partners will go far toward preventing future frictions and misunderstandings. While types of partnership contracts vary considerably to meet the requirements of individual cases, typical provisions pertain to:

(1) the names of the partners;
(2) the name of the partnership;
(3) the period of its duration;
(4) the nature of the business undertaking;
(5) the capital contributions of the various partners;
(6) in what proportions profits are to be shared and at what times they are to be divided;
(7) the sharing of losses;
(8) a definition of the powers of the individual partners—for example, a division of management;
(9) the rights and duties of the partners to each other;
(10) causes and methods of dissolution;
(11) how the partnership property is to be divided upon dissolution.

► III. PARTNERSHIP NAME

A partnership name is not a legal necessity, although in practice it is highly desirable. Unless prohibited by statute, the partners are almost unlimited as to a choice of a name by which the organization will be known. It may consist of the names of the partners, or be purely fictitious, or may contain the designation "Company," making it suggestive of a corporation. A partnership name is at most a convenient substitute for the names of the individual partners. Contracts executed either in the firm name or in the individual names of all partners are equally binding upon the partnership.

Local statutes should be consulted for possible limitations upon the use of a partnership name. For example, some jurisdictions prohibit the use of terminology that would lead to the belief that the organization is a corporation; other states provide that the partnership name must disclose the names of the various partners. Of course, a name that is an infringement upon a name already in use by others cannot be adopted.

► IV. PARTNERSHIP AS LEGAL ENTITY

As a general rule, unlike a corporation a partnership is not regarded as being a legal entity existing separate and apart from the partners composing it.[6, 7] Conse-

---

[6] Dunbar v. Farnum, p. 852.
[7] Reed v. Ind. Acci. Com., p. 853.

quently a partnership has no powers of action in its own right, as does a corporation. While this is the general rule, expressions to the contrary can be found in the cases, and there are many instances in which the legal entity theory has been applied to partnerships for certain purposes, as witness the following expressions:

> "In respect of rights of contract and interests otherwise and contests between a firm and its member or members, as well as in respect of the rights of creditors of a firm, the distinctiveness of the firm as an entity from the member or members is recognized in this jurisdiction." *Williams* v. *Wilson,* 205 Ala. 119
>
> "It has been often pointed out that a partnership cannot properly be regarded as a legal entity separate and distinct from the several partners therein. For certain purposes this fiction may be very properly indulged. In keeping partnership accounts and in marshaling the assets of an insolvent or liquidating firm this is constantly done." *Jones* v. *Blum,* 145 N.Y. 33
>
> "The well established rule which excludes creditors of the several partners from the partnership property until that has paid the debts of the partnership, is derived from the acknowledgment that a partnership is a body by itself." *Menagh* v. *Whitwell,* 52 N.Y. 146

The entity theory is recognized under statutes that permit a partnership to sue or to be sued in the firm name and authorize the partnership as a firm to acquire, hold, and transfer real property. Section 8(3) of the Uniform Partnership Act reads:

> "Any estate in real property may be acquired in the partnership name. Title so acquired can be conveyed only in the partnership name."

In further recognition that a partnership is to some extent a legal entity, it is not questioned that a partnership, irrespective of its members, may enter a contract of suretyship, may act as an agent, may mortgage its property, and may be a member of another partnership.

► V. PARTNERSHIP PROPERTY

Partnership property is that property used for partnership purposes in which the partners have a joint ownership interest. The test of partnership property is not whether it is being used for the mutual benefit of the partners but rather whether it was contributed to, or subsequently acquired on account of, the partnership.[8] The distinction must be made between property whose *use only* has been dedicated to the joint enterprise and property whose *corpus* has been dedicated to partnership purposes.*

The legal incidents of partnership property make it important to recognize the distinction between the property owned by the partnership and that which is owned by the partners individually and is used in the conduct of the business.[9] For example:

(1) Surplus partnership property is, upon dissolution of the firm, subject to

* See illustration on p. 838.

[8] Azevedo v. Sequeria, p. 854.

[9] Dixon v. Koplar, p. 855.

division among the partners either equally or in prearranged proportions. Because of this partners should establish with some care the nature of the property used.

(2) Upon distribution, partnership creditors have a priority on partnership property, and individual creditors have a priority on the property individually owned by the partners even though it has been used in the conduct of the business.

(3) The partnership (rather than its members) is considered the owner of partnership property for purposes of taxation. Thus in *U.S.* v. *Westbrook-Thompson Holding Corp.*, 94 F. (2d) 532, it was held that a transfer of partnership property to the individual partners was taxable as a transfer under a revenue statute. The court said:

> "It is argued that a partnership is not a separate entity from its members, as a corporation is separate from its stockholders, and that such a partition of the partnership property does not really change its ownership or title or effect any transfer. To this we do not agree. The title to the stock of the partnership was joint. In case of insolvency, partnership property must go first to partnership debts. In case of a partner's death, the survivor would take and administer it. A partner desiring individually to borrow on or sell his interest in the stock standing in the partnership name would be embarrassed. When his share in it is put into his own name, all this is changed. He no longer owns a half interest in each share, but owns severally and entirely his proportion of the shares. He may be no richer, but his title in each share has been altered. By the partition each partner transfers to the other his title in each share which goes to the other, and when the new certificates are issued, as was done here, the legal title to every share has been changed from joint ownership to separate and individual ownerships. . . ."

Whether the several items of property that are contributed by the various partners for the conduct of the business become assets of the partnership or continue in the ownership of the contributors is a question of fact to be determined from the circumstances in each particular case. This point should be established with certainty in the partnership agreement. Property acquired with firm funds is presumed to be partnership property, as are all things manufactured or produced by the partnership. And all property and rights that are acquired in connection with the operations of the business, such as profits and good will, belong to the firm.

A. TITLE TO PARTNERSHIP PROPERTY

A partnership cannot hold legal title to real property since, as a general rule, it is not regarded as a legal entity. Therefore, title must be held in the joint names of the various partners, or by one or more of the partners in trust for all. In some jurisdictions there is statutory authority for a partnership's holding and conveying title in the firm name.

With respect to personal property, business practice and usage has firmly established the right of the partnership to deal in the firm name.

> "A partnership as such, can at law be the vendor in a bill of sale or other conveyance of personal property. The custom of the country teaches us that

this is so. . . . Vast quantities of personal property of all kinds are contracted for, bought and sold by such firms under their firm names each year, and their right to thus buy and sell goes unchallenged." *Hendren* v. *Wing,* 60 Ark. 561

► VI. INSTANCES OF PARTNERSHIP LIABILITY WITHOUT EXISTENCE OF PARTNERSHIP IN FACT

A. BY ESTOPPEL

A person who in fact is not a partner may, by his expressions or conduct, lead others to believe justifiably that he is apparently a partner (1) in an existing partnership, (2) of another person, or (3) of persons who are not in fact associated as a partnership. Under the doctrine of estoppel, a partnership liability will be imposed upon such a person in favor of those who have extended credit to the actual or apparent partnership in reliance upon the representations made.*

Similarly a person will be held liable as a partner when he consents to another's making like representations. By the weight of authority, and as is provided for in the Uniform Partnership Act (Section 16), an express or implied assent to the representation of partnership is necessary to impose the unlimited liability of a partner.

The general rule is that assent to and not mere knowledge of the fact that one is being represented as a partner is essential. However, some courts have held that, where a person has knowledge of the fact that another is holding him out as a partner, he becomes liable as a partner unless he takes steps to prevent such representations.

To illustrate:

(1) In *Look* v. *Watson,* 118 Me. 339, the defendant X allowed the plaintiff to deal with the firm of X and Sons without informing him of the fact that it was a corporation and not a partnership as the name implied. The court held that by allowing the use of his name in this manner, X became liable as a partner.

(2) In *Munton* v. *Rutherford,* 121 Mich. 418, one Beckwith published in a newspaper the statement that he had formed a partnership with Mrs. Rutherford, which statement was false. The question presented to the court was whether the defendant Mrs. Rutherford was liable as a partner by estoppel. The court said:

> ". . . Mrs. Rutherford was under no legal or moral obligation to publish a denial of this newspaper story. Any one who saw fit to deal with Mr. Beckwith, relying on this item, did so at his peril. If she had been shown the article, and assented to it and credit had been given on the strength of such assent, the rule of estoppel would have applied. There being no evidence that she authorized or assented to it, there is no room for the application of the rule."

B. DEFECTIVE INCORPORATION

A corporation exists either de jure or de facto. A corporation de jure is one that has complied fully or substantially with the statutory requirements for its

* In re Ganaposki, p. 846.

creation. A de facto corporation is an organization operating as a corporation as a matter of fact, although it has no existence as a corporation as a matter of law. It is an organization that has made a good-faith attempt to organize under the enabling statute but has failed in some substantial respect. As said in *Finnegan* v. *The Knights of Labor Building Assoc.*, 52 Minn. 239:

> " 'Color of apparent organization under some charter or enabling act' does not mean that there shall have been a full compliance with what the law requires to be done nor a substantial compliance. A substantial compliance will make a corporation de jure, but there must be an apparent attempt to perfect an organization under law."

A de facto corporation and its stockholders are accorded the same status and the same protection against third parties as are a de jure corporation and its members. It can carry on its affairs without interference as effectively as it could have if all requirements had been met. It is only the state that can challenge its right to operate and to exist as a business unit. Unless an organization qualifies at least as a de facto corporation, its members cannot claim limited liability. The nature of their liability has presented somewhat of a problem to the courts. As a general rule, it is held that the liability of the members of such an organization is that of partners. It is reasoned that, since there is no legally recognized organization that is intermediate between partnership and corporation, the defective corporation must be a partnership. Some few jurisdictions have held, however, that, since the intent was to have a corporation with the consequent limited liability of its members, no unlimited partnership liability can be imposed. This is especially true in regard to the liability existing between the members of the organization.

► VII. LIMITED PARTNERSHIP DISTINGUISHED

The salient feature of a limited partnership is that one or more of the partners can enjoy a limited liability and that one or more of the partners must have an unlimited liability, as do partners in a general partnership. Their liability (like that of stockholders in a corporation) is limited to the amount of their contributions to the business enterprise. Limited partners are in reality only contributors of capital —capital upon which they agree to take a return in the form of speculative profits rather than at a fixed rate. Being mere contributors of capital, they have no voice in the management and conduct of the business venture. Taking part in the management of the partnership will subject them to unlimited liability.

Unlike a general partnership, a limited partnership is not a common law form of organization. The authority for its existence is derived from legislative enactment.* Like a general partnership, the limited partnership has its origin in a partnership contract, but before it is given legal recognition, the requirements of the enabling statute must be satisfied. The basic requirement of such statutes is the proper execution and filing of a certificate containing certain detailed information.

*Most states have enacted the Uniform Limited Partnership Act. Some variations have been made. Local statutes should be consulted for requirements.

A failure to comply with the requirements of the statute will give the organization the status of a general partnership, with all members having unlimited liability. Such an organization has the legal status of a limited partnership only within the state of its formation. Elsewhere it will be regarded as a general partnership.

CASES

CASE NO. 1

In re Ganaposki et al. 27 F. Supp. 41 (1939)

JOHNSON, D.J. An involuntary petition in bankruptcy was filed on June 15, 1938, against William Ganaposki, and Louis C. Ganaposki, trading as the Pittston Tire Company. On June 30, 1938, William Ganaposki filed an answer denying that he was a partner in the company, and asking that the creditors' petition be dismissed as to him.

The issues raised by the petition and answer were referred to David Rosenthal, referee in bankruptcy, to take testimony and make a report thereon. On September 28, 1938, the referee filed his report, in which he finds that William Ganaposki and Louis Ganaposki were partners in the Pittston Tire Company, and that the partnership is insolvent. The report concludes with a recommendation that William Ganaposki be adjudged a bankrupt as a partner in the company.

William Ganaposki has filed exceptions to this report, raising the question whether the facts before the referee warrant the conclusion that he was a partner.

The referee held numerous hearings, and took much testimony from which he has found that the name William Ganny, which was sometimes used by William Ganaposki, appeared on various checks, drafts, and financial statements of the Pittston Tire Company, and that one of these financial statements was made in the handwriting of William Ganaposki. From these facts the referee concludes that the name William Ganny was held out to the trade as a partner, and that consequently William Ganaposki was a partner within the purview of the Bankruptcy Act, 11 U.S.C.A. § 1 et seq.

The referee was in error in this conclusion. To justify an adjudication, the evidence must show that a partnership in fact existed between the alleged partners. Buffalo Milling Co. v. Lewisburg Dairy Co., D.C., 159 Fed. 319; Fahey v. Sapio, 5 Cir., 30 F. (2d) 330, certiorari denied 279 U.S. 871, 49 Sup. Ct. 512, 73 L. Ed. 1007. The mere holding out of William Ganaposki as a partner is not sufficient to create this relationship. In re Evans, D.C., 161 Fed. 590; In re Kaplan, 7 Cir., 234 Fed. 866; In re Kuntz, D.C., 33 F. (2d) 198. Third persons who are misled by such holding out, and act to their detriment have rights against such individual so holding out based upon the doctrine of estoppel. Section 16, Uniform Partnership Act. . . . However, the doctrine of estoppel is not sufficient to create a partnership as between the alleged partners, or as to third persons who have not in fact been misled.

There is no evidence in the present case of any partnership agreement between the Ganaposkies. There is no evidence that William Ganaposki made any contribution to the capital, shared in the profits, or had any control over the management of the business. In short, the referee's conclusion is based solely upon the "holding out" of William Ganaposki as a partner. Under the foregoing authorities this is not sufficient, and consequently the exceptions to the referee's report must be sustained. . . .

CASE NO. 2

Coens v. Marousis. 275 Pa. 478, 119 Atl. 549 (1932)

KEPHART, J. Plaintiff brought this action to recover the value of his services as manager of a shoeshine parlor. Defendant, having secured rooms in New Castle, Pa., equipped them with furniture and a stock of goods suitable for conducting such business. He then solicited Coens, the plaintiff, to manage it under an agreement that, after the receipts from the business should repay the cost of the original investment, maintenance, and the board and room of plaintiff and defendant, plaintiff, who was to receive no compensation for his services meanwhile other than board and room, was to be given a half interest in the business. Coens conducted the place under this arrangement for a period of 20 months, when defendant requested him to take charge of another business for a brief time. Thereafter defendant was repeatedly requested to make settlement. This he failed to do; no adjustment of plaintiff's claim was ever reached, and he was refused the interest that had been agreed upon. He now claims compensation in quantum meruit for the services performed. The court below, after hearing plaintiff's case, directed a nonsuit for the reason that the cause of action concerned the relations of partners. . . .

Whether a partnership existed must be found from the terms of the agreement. A partnership relation may be created where one gives money or effects and the other labor or skill, under an agreement for a proportionate division of profits and losses (cases cited); but, where the agreement contemplates the formation of a partnership at some future time, as in this case, and the entire capital is contributed by one of the parties, the other furnishing his services free until such time as the former is reimbursed from the profits, when the latter is to be given an interest in the business, it is evident no partnership is intended until these events occur. Persons who have entered into a contract to become partners at some future time, or upon the happening of some future contingency, do not become partners until the agreed time has arrived, or the contingency has happened. . . . A mere agreement to form one does not of itself create a partnership, nor does the advancement by one party of his agreed share of the capital. The entire agreement must be considered with all the attending circumstances. . . . Appellee's citations are instances where the partnership existed prior to the happening of the event, or where the condition lapsed into partnership without any further act of either party.

Not only is there here a mere intention to form a partnership in the future, but it could only become one if the venture was successful, and the interest duly given. Plaintiff was not ipso facto to become a partner—it required an affirmative act; defendant was to give him a half interest in the business. It is for the breach of this covenant the action is predicated. Defendant repudiated the agreement by refusing after the accumulated profits had reimbursed him for his investment, to give plaintiff the interest therein stipulated.

The court below was in error in holding the facts evidenced a partnership relation.

CASE NO. 3

Phillips v. Phillips. 49 Ill. 437 (1863)

CATON, C.J. Over 20 years ago John Phillips emigrated from Scotland and settled in Chicago with his family, consisting of a wife and four sons and two daughters. He was then very poor. He was a wood turner by trade, and commenced that business in a very small way with a foot lathe. He was frugal, industrious, and honest, and prospered as but few men, even in this country, prosper. He labored hard with his own hands, and as his sons grew up they joined their work to his. . . . In the meantime the business had grown from the smallest beginning, with a single foot lathe, to a large manufactory, with extensive machinery propelled by steam. . . .

The business had always been conducted, as it was begun, in the name of John Phillips, the father, although in a few instances bills were made out to John Phillips & Sons by persons with but a superficial acquaintance with them, which were paid without eliciting remark or particular attention. The books were all kept in the name of John Phillips, with the exception of a few entries made by a bookkeeper in the name of John Phillips & Sons. Indeed, there is, and can be, no question that, if there was a copartnership embracing the father and sons, the firm name adopted was John Phillips.

The complainant, to show a copartnership, proves that the sons all devoted their time and attention to the business after they attained their majority, without regular salaries as laborers or servants; that funds which they drew from the concern for their support were charged to each one separately, while neither received a credit for labor or services; that the father, upon one or two occasions, stated to third persons that his sons were interested in the business; and he also relies upon the appearances to the outside public and the interest which all took in the success of the business.

For the defense it is claimed that, following the habits and customs of their forefathers in Scotland, the sons continued to serve the father in the same relation and with the same fidelity after attaining their majority as before, under the distinct and often declared understanding that all should belong to the father during his life, and at his death the business and property should be left by him to his children, as he should think proper. . . . If such was the understanding and purpose of the parties, then there was no partnership. Originally, undoubtedly, the entire concern belonged to the father, and it so continued, unless by the agreement of the father the sons were admitted into the concern as partners; for as before intimated, we know of no means by which the sons could become partners with the father, and thus acquire a title to his property without his knowledge or consent. Did the father ever consent that his sons, or either of them, should be admitted as partners with him? Did he ever agree that they should be part owners of this property? On repeated occasions the subject of a copartnership with his sons was presented to him, both in the presence of the complainant and his brothers, and he ever repudiated the suggestion in the most emphatic terms. The very suggestion even seemed to excite his indignation. Upon one occasion he expressed himself in this characteristic phrase: "Na, Na! I will ha' nae sons for partners as long as I live. Damn them! They would put me out of the door."

. . . Had there been ever any agreement, express or implied, that there should be a partnership, they, as parties to it, must have been aware of it. If not expressed in words, there must have been at least the mental intention and tacit understanding on the part of the father that they should be admitted as partners, and on their part to assume the benefits and liabilities of partners, and this could not be without their knowledge. Others might be deceived by appearances. Others, ignorant of the customs and traditions of their forefathers, which are so fondly cherished by emigrants from the old country, and particularly from Scotland, might draw erroneous conclusions as to the true relation existing between them as a family, by seeing men in middle life zealously bending their energies under the guidance of their father to the promotion of the success of the business. Whoever should apply customs prevalent among native Americans to this state of facts would unhesitatingly conclude that all were in partnership. And so, no doubt, many were deceived; nor was it deemed necessary by any of the parties, on all occasions, to undeceive them by a full explanation of this family arrangement.

But the question here is, what was the actual fact? and not what observers supposed was the fact from appearances. It is the internal truth we are seeking, and these external appearances are only important as they may enable us to arrive at this truth; and when we so find the truth by indubitable proof in a different direction than that indicated by these external appearances, then these must go for naught. Here we have the positive testimony of every living man who has the absolute knowledge of the facts, including the complainant himself, all testifying most unqualifiedly that there was no partnership.

Decree is reversed, and the bill dismissed.

CASE NO. 4

Aetna Ins. Co. v. Murray. 66 F. (2d) 289 (1933)

MC DERMOTT, C.J. The defendant below appeals from a judgment rendered on a verdict of a jury in a suit on a fire insurance policy covering a stock of shoes. The fire destroyed part of the stock and damaged the balance. . . .

It is contended that the evidence disclosed that plaintiff was not the sole and unconditional owner of the property insured. The only support in the record for this defense is the testimony of plaintiff that he had arranged with two of his employees to pay them for their services a percentage of the net earnings of the business, in addition to their salaries; and the testimony of one of his employees that she

> "did not have any interest in the business but would have had a 25 per cent bonus in addition to her salary when Mr. Murray was paid back his $11,-000.00 with interest, then she would have a 25 per cent interest."

From all the testimony, a finding was warranted that the arrangement was simply to compensate employees for services by supplementing their salaries by a percentage of net earnings. Such a profit-sharing arrangement does not give the employees any title to the properties of the employer. London Assurance Corp. v. Drennen, 116 U.S. 461, 6 Sup. Ct. 442, 29 L. Ed. 688; Brown v. Franklin Fire Ins. Co., 178 Cal. 302, 173 Pac. 403; Martin Co. v. O'Connor, 120 Okla. 92,250 Pac. 529. A participation in the profits as compensation for services rendered, does not create a partnership. Berthold v. Goldsmith, 24 How. 536, 543, 16 L. Ed. 762; Meehan v. Valentine, 145 U.S. 611, 619, 12 Sup. Ct. 972, 36 L. Ed. 835. In an exhaustive note to the case of Cudahy Packing Co. v.

Hibou, 18 L.R.A. (N.S.) 1032, decisions from forty jurisdictions are cited in support of this statement and none to the contrary. . . .

CASE NO. 5

Eckhard v. Commissioner of Internal Revenue. 182 F. (2d) 547 (1950)

MURRAH, C.J. The first question presented by this appeal is whether the petitioner taxpayer and his wife were business partners for income tax purposes during the taxable year 1943. The Commissioner determined that they were not, and the Tax Court affirmed. . . .

The primary facts are not in dispute. The taxpayer graduated from the University of Nebraska in 1924. While in school, he married his present wife, whose legal education was interrupted by their marriage and the birth of a baby. The taxpayer earned from $40 to $175 per month at various jobs. To supplement the family income, the wife secured a job at a bank, beginning at $85 per month. She soon became secretary to the president of the bank, in which capacity she checked loans, passed upon collateral, and transacted other important banking matters. Her salary increased from $85 to $150 a month. She invested her savings in a home and stock in an oil company. The husband and wife had discussed the possibility of getting into some kind of business together. In 1941, while the husband was employed as a salesman for the General Tires, Inc., he heard of an opportunity to buy a tire agency at Oklahoma City. After he and his wife came to Oklahoma City and investigated the business, they decided to sell their home and the stock in the oil company, and invest the proceeds in the tire business.

Accordingly, they sold the home for approximately $3,500, and the stock in the oil company for about $4,000. They purchased 50 of the 147 shares of the corporation owning the tire business, paying $2,500 in cash and giving a joint note for $2,500. The shares of stock were taken in the name of the taxpayer-husband, because the parent corporation refused to do business with a woman. Under the petitioner's contract with the corporation, he agreed to purchase the remaining shares of the corporation for a stipulated sum. It was also agreed that he would receive a salary of not to exceed $350 per month, and all of the profits of the business after deducting 6 per cent dividends on the outstanding stock and sound reserve for taxes.

The remainder of the proceeds of the sale of the home and oil stock were invested in the business, the parties moved to Oklahoma City and established a home; and the wife and husband worked together in the operation of the retail and wholesale tire business. The wife looked after the administrative details, the hiring and firing of help, keeping books, and running the office. The husband devoted most of his time traveling and overseeing the outside work.

Through the joint efforts of the taxpayer and his wife, the business prospered, and in January 1943, the taxpayer purchased the remaining outstanding stock for $10,657.50. . . . In the following February, he dissolved the corporation, and thereafter operated the business as a sole proprietorship. The wife drew no salary—as a matter of fact, neither actually drew a salary, but drew on the business for living expenses. The remainder of the profits were invested in real estate and other properties in the joint name of husband and wife. The parties never had any formal partnership agreement, the wife stating that when it became necessary to have a written agreement with her husband, she would not be living with him. No partnership accounts were set up showing the interest of each, and no partnership returns were ever filed. In fact, the business was conducted in the name of H. A. Eckhard, either as president of the corporation, or as owner of the business. . . .

The Tax Court's conclusions are based upon a number of considerations, among which was the total lack of any written agreement or of any other books or records indicating an intention to conduct the business as a partnership. Nor did the court think that there was a positive oral agreement between the husband and wife. These facts, while not conclusive, coupled with the conduct of the business in the name of the taxpayer as the sole proprietor, led the court to conclude that while the wife did contribute capital originating with her, along with skill and services in the conduct of the business, such contributions were those of a wife to a husband's business, and not as a business partner. And, while a husband and wife may engage in business as partners, we will scrutinize the family arrangement to determine whether in the last analysis, the parties really intended in good faith to join together their money, labor and skill for the purpose of carrying on the business as a bona fide partnership. Each case must rest upon its own facts, but in determining the intent of the parties, the court will look at what the parties actually did to effectuate their avowed intentions. While investment of capital, skill and labor are essential attributes, they are not conclusive. In short, taxation being a practical matter, we should look through the form to the substance of their transactions.

. . . The Fourth Circuit in Ritter v. Commissioner, 174 F. (2d) 377, held that a gift of a father to a son as a contribution to the partnership, who contributed no other capital or services during the time involved, did not create a partnership for tax purposes, in the face of a written agreement. The court thought that the partnership lacked economic reality.

In Trapp v. United States, supra, we denied an asserted partnership between husband and wife for income from the production of oil, the leases of which were purchased by the husband, and operated by him without any outward evidence of a partnership with his wife, although the wife did have a small estate when they were married many years before, which the husband used in his bond business, and which later ripened into the oil ventures.

The Second Circuit, in Morrison v. Commissioner, 177 F. (2d) 351, denied an asserted partnership between the taxpayer, his wife and minor sons, based upon gifts of interests in the business to the wife and sons. The court sustained the findings of the Tax Court to the effect that the taxpayer was in reality a sole proprietor.

But the facts here are quite different from those cases. Nor are they like Earp v. Jones, 10 Cir., 131 F. (2d) 292; Grant v. Commissioner, 10 Cir., 150 F. (2d) 915; and Bradshaw v. Commissioner, 10 Cir., 150 F. (2d) 918, where the husband transferred a half interest in his business to his wife, and entered into a formal written partnership agreement, but continued to control and operate the business as before. In those cases, the courts rightly looked beyond the formal arrangements to the substance of the transaction, and held that the husband remained "monarch of all he surveyed."

The facts in our case fall more nearly within Graber v. Commissioner, 10 Cir., 171 F. (2d) 32. In both cases, the wife contributed capital originating with her, and used her skill and business judgment in the joint conduct of the business. In neither case did the parties have a formal agreement. In both cases, the partnership was obscured either by collateral partnerships or corporate entities. But the facts in both cases carry with them the conviction that the parties did, in good faith, intend to engage in business as partners. The absence of a formal agreement, and the failure to set up the books as partners, is certainly not conclusive. When judged in the light of realities, we think the evidence conclusively establishes a bona fide business partnership. . . .

The case is reversed and remanded with directions to determine the petitioner's tax liability in accordance with the views herein expressed.

CASE NO. 6

Dunbar v. Farnum. 109 Vt. 313, 196 Atl. 237, 114 A.L.R. 996 (1937)

POWERS, CH.J. . . . This is an action of contract to recover damages for the breach of an executory contract for the sale of a water system in the town of Lyndon. It was tried by jury in the court below, and, at the close of the evidence, a verdict was ordered for the defendants. The plaintiff excepted.

The defendants are husband and wife. They owned and operated the water system in question and thereby supplied their customers with domestic water at scheduled rates. They carried on this and other business, ostensibly as partners, under the firm name and style of Scott M. Farnum & Wife. They regarded and conducted themselves as partners, and so registered in the secretary of the state's office. The title to the water system and other real estate was held by them in their trade name. Mr. Farnum was the active and managing partner, while Mrs. Farnum made collections, did the banking, and kept the company books.

There was evidence warranting findings of the following facts:

The plaintiff negotiated with the defendants for the purchase of the water system, and on November 24, 1934, he and Farnum went to St. Johnsbury, and had a contract drawn by an attorney. The contract is captioned "Memo. of Agreement between Scott M. Farnum and Wife and Harold Dunbar, all of Lyndon, Vermont," and is signed by the plaintiff and Scott M. Farnum. The name of Nellie M. Farnum is attached to it, but it is not denied that this name was written by Farnum. . . .

The defendants are sued as partners. To establish the contract sued on, the writing above referred to was received in evidence. As we have seen, this contract was not signed by the partnership and does not profess to be executed as a partnership agreement. Rather, it purports to be the joint contract of the individual Farnums. . . .

There is a spirited disagreement among the authorities as to whether a partnership is a legal entity, separate and apart from the individuals composing it. Some say that it has no such separate existence, basing their conclusions upon what is said to be the theory of the common law. Others hold that it has such separate existence and that it stands before the law the same as a person or corporation does. Still others maintain that it is so far personified as to be treated as an entity in most of its relations, though it does not have all the attributes of a person. The business world has always regarded a partnership as a person, and there is a growing tendency on the part of the courts to adopt the commercial view. . . .

Judge Learned Hand, now an eminent member of the Circuit Court of Appeals, Second Circuit, said in Re Samuels & Lesser, D.C., 207 F. 195, 198, that

> "The whole subject of partnership has undoubtedly always been exceedingly confused, simply because our law has failed to recognize that partners are not merely joint debtors. It could be straightened out into great simplicity, and in accordance with business usages and business understanding, if the entity of the firm, though a fiction, were consistently recognized and enforced. Like the concept of a corporation, it is for many purposes a device of the utmost value in clarifying ideas and in making easy the solution of legal relations."

This court has long been committed to this entity theory.

It is frequently said that a partner, acting for his firm, stands as a principal as to his own interest and as an agent as to the interest of his partners. But under this entity theory, a more accurate conception of the transaction is that a partner, so acting, acts in the single capacity of agent of the firm, the individuality of the partners being merged therein. . . .

It necessarily follows that when a firm is sued, a partnership undertaking must be established to warrant a recovery. The issue is one of partnership liability, alone. Individual liability is not at all within the issue to be tried, though such a liability may result from a plaintiff's verdict.

So it was that we said in the original opinion that the suit broke down when it appeared that the contract sued on was not a partnership engagement.

CASE NO. 7

Reed v. Industrial Acci. Com. 10 Cal. (2d) 191, 73 P. (2d) 1212, 114 A.L.R. 720 (1937)

LANGDON, J., delivered the opinion of the court:

This is a petition to review an award of the Industrial Accident Commission. The facts are simple and undisputed.

On March 11, 1935, W. B. Mellott, a building contractor, obtained a policy of workmen's compensation insurance from Hartford Accident & Indemnity Company, for the period of one year. The insured was designated therein as "W. B. Mellott . . . Individual." Thereafter Mellott became associated with Irwin G. Gordon, another contractor, and they conducted the building contract business as "W. B. Mellott and Irwin G. Gordon, doing business as Gordon and Mellott." The policy remained unchanged. The record does not disclose whether the insurance company had knowledge of the association.

On March 5, 1936, while the policy was in force, George Reed, an employee, sustained a compensable injury, and filed his application with the commission. . . . The position of said respondent is, in brief, that the policy insured W. B. Mellott, an individual, and not the partnership of Gordon & Mellott; that Reed was employed by the firm of Gordon & Mellott, and not by W. B. Mellott; and that consequently, the policy did not cover the injury, because Reed's employer, the partnership, was not insured. This position is unsound on principle and contrary to prior decisions in this state.

The underlying fallacy in respondent's argument is the assumption that the partnership is a distinct unit, separate from the members thereof. Occasional suggestions of this "entity" theory of partnership are found in statutes or decisions, but, apart from exceptional situations, a partnership is not considered an entity, but an association of individuals. . . . In consonance with this view, an employee of a partnership is an employee of each of the partners, and no individual partner may escape liability to such employee on the ground that only the partnership and not the individuals composing it can be held. . . . The result is that W. B. Mellott, a partner in the firm of Gordon & Mellott, was an employer of petitioner Reed, and was undoubtedly liable to Reed for workmen's compensation. Since W. B. Mellott procured insurance with respondent company to cover such liability, and paid the required premium therefor, the company must perform its obligation by paying the award. . . .

CASE NO. 8

Azevedo v. Sequeria. 132 Cal. App. 439, 22 P. (2d) 745 (1933)

THOMPSON, J. In 1914 a partnership was organized in the name of A. J. Azevedo & Co., consisting of seven members including the plaintiffs and defendants to this suit. . . . A. J. Azevedo testified that he purchased with partnership funds six shares of the capital stock of the Gustine Creamery, Inc., a corporation, "for the company." He afterwards purchased one additional share of stock. Without the knowledge of the defendants these shares were issued in the name of A. J. Azevedo & Co. . . .

Mr. Sequeria testified that seven shares of the creamery stock were purchased so that each of the original seven partners might separately own one share. . . . Azevedo was the manager of the dairy business. There is evidence to indicate that he acted as the agent for the respective members of the partnership in the purchase of the stock, and that the purchase price of the stock was originally taken from the proceeds of the business and subsequently charged to each in the final accounting. Sequeria testified that in a subsequent conversation A. J. Azevedo

> "told me I would get my share without any trouble, . . . that he knew it was mine." . . .

This evidence is sufficient to support the findings of court to the effect that the original stock was purchased by A. J. Azevedo as the agent of each individual member of the original partnership for their private ownership, and that he wrongfully procured the issuing of the stock in the name of the partnership; that each member owned one share of the stock which earned by means of stock dividends two additional shares, and that the defendants Sequeria, Avila, and Pereira are the owners of three shares each of said stock. The judgment is therefore amply supported by the evidence.

It is true that,

> "unless the contrary intention appears property acquired with partnership funds is partnership property."

Almost any kind of property may be acquired and owned as partnership property. The intention with which the property is acquired and used will usually determine the question as to whether it is partnership or individual property. The intention of the parties with respect to the ownership of property acquired at the time of the organization of the partnership or subsequently may be determined by the acts or oral declarations of the parties. 20 R.C.L. 855, § 62. In the absence of evidence to the contrary, it will be presumed from the fact that if the stock is purchased in the name of the partnership and with its funds that it belongs to the partnership, and that the interest of each member therein extends jointly and not separately to the whole thereof. 20 R.C.L. 870 § 81. But it is not unusual that real or personal property may be acquired and used for the benefit of the partnership and still be owned individually by one or more of the partners. Indeed, in the present case the plaintiffs are contending that the very stock which is involved in this suit is their individual property and not that of the partnership to which they succeeded in association with other members. From the fact that this stock was purchased from the funds of the partnership business in the name of the firm, there is a presumption that it belongs to the partnership. But that presumption has been dispelled by substantial evidence that it was the intention of the parties that the creamery stock was to be purchased and owned individually by the respective partners in equal shares. The fact that one additional share was subsequently purchased so that each of the seven members might own a share is a strong circumstance supporting the finding of the court that it was the intention of the partners that the stock should become their individual property. . . .

CASE NO. 9

Dixon v. Koplar. 102 F. (2d) 295 (1939)

VAN VALKENBURGH, C.J. October 27, 1937, I. H. Koplar and M. Horwitz, copartners, doing business at St. Louis, Missouri, under the style and trade name of the St. Louis Wholesale Grocery Company, were adjudicated bankrupts, both as a partnership and as individuals, in the Eastern Division of the Eastern Judicial District of Missouri. Previously a voluntary petition for relief under Section 74 of the Bankruptcy Act of 1898, as amended, 11 U.S.C.A. § 202, had been filed, and the bankrupts had made an offer of composition in said proceedings, but were unable to secure a requisite number of acceptances. Thereupon, on October 27, 1937, they voluntarily consented to adjudications in bankruptcy. In due course, Joseph F. Dixon, appellant herein, was duly appointed and qualified as trustee of the partnership estate and of the individual estates of the bankrupt partners. The partnership assets are insufficient to pay the partnership debts. Both Horwitz and Koplar are married men, heads of families, and residents of the State of Missouri. Section 1163 of the Revised Statutes of Missouri, 1929, . . . provides as follows:

> "Each head of a family, at his election, in lieu of the property mentioned in the first and second subdivision(s) of section 1160 may select and hold, exempt from execution, any other property, real, personal or mixed, or debts and wages, not exceeding the value of the amount of three hundred dollars, except ten per cent of any debt, income, salary, or wages due such head of a family. . . ."

. . . Horwitz . . . claimed as exempt, out of the partnership property, an automobile truck of the value of $150, and, in addition thereto, certain canned goods of the total value of $136.71, which added to the $13.29 claimed as exempt out of the individual estate would make up the $300 claimed by him under said Section 1163. In like manner Koplar claimed as exempt, out of the partnership property, certain canned goods, soap, and other merchandise, of the total value of $279.89, which added to the $20.11 claimed and allowed out of his individual estate would make for him a total of $300, claimed under the provisions of said Section 1163. . . .

The trustee filed his report of exempt property in which he held that the individual parties were not entitled to receive any exemptions out of the partnership assets. Exceptions were filed to this report, which were by the referee overruled, and the trustee's report was sustained on the ground that the individual bankrupts could not, under the law of Missouri, claim exemptions out of the bankrupt partnership estate. . . .

The general law, as declared by the overwhelming weight of authority, is that where the state law does not allow an exemption to individual partners out of the partnership property, such exemption cannot be allowed in bankruptcy. . . .

There is no individual ownership of partnership property until, at least, the partnership has ceased activity and all its debts have been paid. . . . Under the Bankruptcy Act, 11 U.S.C.A. § 1 et seq., a partnership is a distinct entity, a person separate from the partners who compose it. . . .

Review Questions

1. How does the Uniform Partnership Act define a partnership?
2. Is the partnership a common law form of business organization?
3. Is it necessary to the existence of a partnership that the partners jointly own the property used in the partnership business?
4. Is joint ownership of property a conclusive test of the existence of a partnership?
5. Can there be a partnership without a sharing of profits?
6. Is an agreement to share losses a conclusive test of the existence of a partnership?
7. Are there any limitations upon the choice of a partnership name in your state?
8. Indicate some instances in which the entity theory of a partnership has been recognized.
9. What is the concept of partnership property?
10. Indicate the importance of distinguishing between property owned by the partnership and property that is owned by the individual partners but is being used for partnership purposes.
11. Construct a fact situation illustrating a partnership by estoppel.
12. What are the characteristics of a limited partnership?
13. Is the limited partnership a common law form of organization?
14. What is the effect of a limited partner's taking part in the management of the partnership affairs?
15. What is the status of a limited partnership in states other than the state in which it was formed?

Problems for Discussion

1. Action was brought by Harvey against Childs and Potter, to recover $158.40, for seventeen hogs sold by Harvey to Potter.

   Potter is in default. Childs denies his liability. His liability is claimed solely on the ground that he was a partner of Potter in the adventure for which the hogs were purchased.

   The partnership claimed rests on the following state of facts: Potter went to Childs and told him that he had contracted for about two carloads of hogs, to be delivered at Loudonville the next day, and had not the money to pay for them. He asked Childs to advance the money and take an interest in the hogs. Childs refused. Thereupon, Potter proposed that if he would let him have the money to enable him to pay for the hogs he had bought, and others he might have to buy to make the two carloads, he (Childs) should take possession of the hogs, at Loudonville, as security for the money, take them to Pittsburgh, sell them, and take his pay from the proceeds of the sale; that he might have one half the net profits of the venture and that in no event should Childs sustain any loss, but the money advanced by him should be fully paid by Potter in case the amount realized from the sale of the hogs was insufficient. Childs accepted the proposition and, it being agreed that $2,500 would be enough to pay for the two carloads, advanced that sum to Potter. Afterward, without the knowledge of Childs, Potter bought the hogs in question of Harvey, on his own credit, and they made part of the two carloads of hogs which were taken possession of by Childs, sold in Pittsburgh, and the avails of the sale appropriated in payment of the money advanced by him. No profits were made. The avails of the sale were insufficient to pay the amount advanced by Childs, and Potter paid him the deficiency and for his time and expenses in the transaction. Decide. (*Harvey* v. *Childs,* 28 Ohio St. 319)

2. A worked for B as a clerk in the latter's hotel. It was agreed that A was to share the profits of the enterprise equally with B as compensation for his services. Is B liable as a partner?
3. A and B were sued as partners for the debts created by a Masonic lodge of which they were members. Can such an allegation be sustained? (*Ash* v. *Glue,* 97 Pa. 493)
4. The object and purpose of the mutual relations of Halliday and Judson are fairly well defined in the written contract in evidence. It was a contract of lease, as well as a contract for the joint operation and management of the farm. It defined the name of the business, what each member was to do in furnishing his share of the necessary capital and labor which went into the business, how the business was to be conducted, and how the property and the proceeds were to be divided and disposed of after all expenses were paid. It was stipulated in the contract that the firm should be known as Judson & Halliday. Certain paragraphs read as follows:

   Division of Receipts and Expenses. The renter furnishes the labor against the landowner's land, the productive livestock is furnished by the firm, and the net farm receipts are divided equally between the landowner and the renter.

   Hogs. The firm will furnish approximately 25 brood sows. It is the intention to make hogs one of the principal sources of income.

   Cattle. The firm will furnish about —— milk cows to be kept on the farm. Receipts of dairy products sold belong to the firm. If milk and cream are sold to a creamery, the value of the butter used by the landowner and the renter is to be taken out of their respective shares. The renter and the landowner are to have all the necessary milk and cream to use in the home.

   Other Kinds of Livestock. Other kinds of livestock, such as feeding cattle, hogs, and sheep, will be furnished by the firm, and all the expenses and receipts will be divided equally.

Marketing. The renter agrees to deliver to the local market, without charge to the landowner, all crops, livestock, or livestock products, and the proceeds shall be deposited to the credit of the firm.

Accounts, Inventories. A detailed inventory of all firm property shall be made on the first of March each year during the life of this contract, and the renter shall keep an accurate account of all firm business.

Final Settlement. If the parties cannot agree upon final settlement, one to buy the other's interest in the firm property, said property shall be sold on the market and the proceeds divided. Did this create a partnership? (*Malvern Nat. Bank* v. *Halliday,* 195 Iowa 734)

5. It was agreed between the partners of an insolvent partnership and its creditors that the business was to be continued under a management designated by the creditors until their claims were fully paid out of profits. Are the creditors partners in the enterprise?
6. X and Y are the sole partners in two different partnerships, one of which is engaged in the automotive business and the other in the sale and servicing of household equipment. Both partnerships are insolvent and are declared bankrupt. The first partnership has assets sufficient to discharge 20 per cent of the creditors' claims and the second partnership has assets sufficient to discharge 85 per cent of its creditors' claims. The creditors of the first partnership contend that the assets of both partnerships should be pooled for the benefit of all creditors. What do you think?
7. A published a newspaper notice to the effect that he had formed a copartnership with B. This was not true, as B had merely advanced funds for A's business venture. B did nothing to deny the allegation made by A. X sold goods to A on credit and now sues B as a partner, contending that the credit was extended entirely upon the fact that the newspaper notice gave him reason to believe that a partnership had been formed. Decide.

34 BUSINESS ORGANIZATIONS:

RELATIONS OF PARTNERS TO THIRD PERSONS; THEIR POWERS AND LIABILITIES

► I. AGENCY CHARACTER OF PARTNERSHIP

One of the consequences of a partnership relation is the mutual agency relationship existing between the partners. In a partnership, each member is an agent of all partners and, in effect, a coprincipal. It has been said that the real basis of individual liability of partners is the fact that they occupy the status of principals in all partnership transactions.

As an agent, a partner has the authority to bind the partnership in respect to all transactions that are legitimately within the scope of the firm's business.[1] Persons dealing with a partner who professes to be acting on behalf of the partnership have the right to assume, in the absence of knowledge to the contrary, that he has the usual agency authority to represent the firm in transactions such as are reasonably necessary and incidental to the business. For example, a partner in a firm of undertakers could, without consulting his copartners, make a contractual commitment for a reasonable number of caskets, which would be binding upon the partnership. However, he could not create a partnership liability upon a contract for the purchase of a pleasure boat. Such implements of leisure are not necessary, incidental, or usual to the conduct of an undertaking establishment, and it cannot be implied that such authority exists.

To illustrate:

In *F. F. Beasley Lumber Co.* v. *Sparks,* 169 Ark. 640, the court held that it was not within the apparent scope of authority of partners engaged in the business of selling building material to contract for the construction of a building.

A. IMPLIED POWERS IN TRADING AND NONTRADING PARTNERSHIPS

1. *Distinction Between Trading and Nontrading Partnerships*

A more realistic appreciation of the extent of a partner's implied powers to bind the partnership can be obtained by giving consideration to the two generally recognized types of partnerships, namely:

(1) trading or commercial, and

(2) nontrading or noncommercial.

A *trading* partnership has as its distinctive feature the fact that its primary object and function is the buying and selling of commodities. A *nontrading* partner-

[1] Delta Asbestos Co. v. Sanders, p. 866.

ship has as its primary purpose not the buying and selling of commodities, but rather the production of commodities or the rendering of services. For example, partnerships engaged in agricultural or manufacturing pursuits and those engaged in selling legal, financial, accounting, engineering, and other types of services would classify as nontrading.

2. *Implied Powers in Trading Partnerships*

The reason for making this distinction between trading and nontrading firms is that the implied powers of trading partners are much broader than those of non-trading partners.[2] In fact, it is recognized that *as a matter of law* partners of all trading partnerships have certain identical implied powers—that is, powers that as a matter of law are attributed to the partners. The following are some of the more common powers thus attributed to all partners in trading partnerships.

a. Power to Buy and Sell. Naturally and logically, every partner in a trading partnership has an apparent authority to accomplish the major purpose for which the organization exists. Common to all members of commercial partnerships is the implied power to buy and to sell commodities in which the firm deals and in such quantities as are reasonably within the scope of the business undertaking. The power to sell carries with it the power to make the usual warranties.

b. Power to Borrow Money. The borrowing of money is a necessary requirement for the conduct of a commercial enterprise. Consequently, the law presumes that all members of a trading partnership have the implied agency authority to borrow money for the firm.[3] If the loan is reasonably within the requirements of the particular business, the firm will be bound even though the partner who negotiated the loan converted the proceeds to his personal use.

In conjunction with the power to borrow money goes the power to give security for the debt. Thus, if a partner borrows money for the firm, he also has the power to pledge any or all of the firm's personal profits as security for the obligation.

c. Power to Deal with Negotiable Paper. Commercial concerns find it not only convenient but also necessary to use and to accept negotiable instruments in the conduct of their affairs. This practice is common to all trading partnerships. As a result, the various partners have the implied authority to issue, accept, and indorse commercial paper where such function appears to be within the scope of the business undertaking. However, to bind the firm, a partner must use the firm name or the names of the various partners.

d. Power to Make Collections, Settlements, and Payments. Partners in a trading partnership have the implied power to make collections of firm debts and to make payment of firm obligations. They have the right to compromise doubtful or disputed claims and to execute releases to debtors of the firm. These are all necessary to the conduct of a business enterprise.

---

[2] Gordon v. Marburger, p. 866.
[3] Higgins v. Beauchamp, p. 868.

e. Power to Employ and to Discharge. Partners have the implied power to engage such employees and agents as are necessary to carry on the business operations of the firm. Likewise they have the implied authority to discharge those in the employ of the partnership.

3. *Powers in Nontrading Partnerships*

In the case of nontrading partnerships, it is not presumed as a matter of law that the copartners are entrusted with general authority in partnership affairs. As in an ordinary agency relationship, the authority must be established as a matter of fact. It is not presumed that all members of noncommercial partnerships have certain common powers. Individual considerations in each particular case are the controlling factors as to whether authority to act exists.

"The principle governing a non-trading partnership is well settled. There are three classes of cases where each partner connected with such associations may lawfully bind the firm; the burden in each case, being on the plaintiff to prove the facts by which such authority is established, or from which it may be implied: (1) Where he has express authority to do so; (2) where the contract made, or thing done, is necessary in order to carry on the business of the partnership; (3) and where it is usually or customarily incident to other partnerships of like nature." *Woodruff* v. *Scaife,* 83 Ala. 152

The moral to be drawn from this situation is that one dealing with a partner of a nontrading partnership cannot assume that certain authority exists but must satisfy himself that the authority to be exercised can be established as a matter of fact. One cannot, for example, assume that nontrading partners have the universal right to borrow money. Individual circumstances may, however, lead one to conclude reasonably that such authority does exist in fact. To illustrate:

In *Alley* v. *Bowen-Merrill Co.,* 76 Ark. 4, it was held that a partner in a law firm had the power to bind the partnership on a contract for the purchase of lawbooks. The court said:

". . . the act of one partner in a firm of lawyers in the scope of its business is the act of all. It is generally held that nontrading firms have no power to borrow money and sign negotiable paper, and that one member of such firm has no power to bind the other members by signing the firm name to such paper. . . . This is because such transactions are not generally within the legitimate scope of the business of such firms. There is no reason why such firms should not be bound by the acts of their members within the scope of their business . . . there is no reason why a firm of lawyers should not be bound by the act of one of its members in buying such lawbooks as may be reasonably necessary for carrying on the business. Such an act is certainly within the scope of the business of such a partnership. It is impossible to practice law successfully in these times without some lawbooks. As Mr. Bates (1 Bates, Part. Sec. 343) says: 'It is difficult to conceive of a partnership which does not require some purchases to be made in the usual course of its business.' In nontrading firms this is certainly necessary. He instances the case of lawyers purchasing their lawbooks. . . . The purchase of lawbooks reasonably necessary in the business is a responsibility and liability incident to a partnership for the practice of law, and when lawyers come together for that business they are presumed to repose in one another the trust and confidence necessary to attend to the duty of purchasing lawbooks for the firm, and to clothe each with authority to bind the other."

B. LIMITATIONS UPON PARTNERS' IMPLIED POWERS

Partners frequently agree among themselves to limit their authority. Arrangements may be made to divide authority among the various partners or to limit the authority of one or several of the partners. Such arrangements are in the nature of secret limitations and are not binding upon third persons unless they have knowledge of such. In the absence of knowledge to the contrary, third persons dealing with a partner have the right to assume that he possesses such authority as is apparent under the circumstances. Thus, even though Jones and Smith, who are engaged as partners in a mercantile enterprise, agree that Smith is to have no authority to make purchases for the firm, nevertheless contracts for purchases by Smith would be binding upon the partnership unless this limitation was known to those from whom the purchases were made.

C. ENLARGEMENT OF PARTNERS' IMPLIED AUTHORITY

1. *By Agreement*

A partner's implied powers may, of course, be enlarged by an agreement among the partners. Authority may be expressly conferred in the articles of partnership or in a collateral understanding.

2. *By Ratification*

Unauthorized acts of a partner may be ratified by his copartners and thus may be made binding upon the partnership. The requirements for the ratification of a partner's unauthorized conduct are established by the law of agency.

3. *By Estoppel*

The rules of estoppel apply to partnership relationships with the equal force and effect with which they apply to other agency relationships. To illustrate:

In *Salinas* v. *Bennett,* 33 S.C. 285, one of two partners, X, without authority, mortgaged the partnership realty to secure a loan, which was then with the knowledge of the other partner, Y, used for partnership purposes. The court held that Y, having accepted the benefit of the loan, was at the time of foreclosure of the mortgage estopped from denying X's authority to execute the mortgage.

D. ACTION REQUIRING UNANIMOUS CONSENT

It is recognized as a matter of law that certain acts require the unanimous consent of the partners. Section 9(3) of the Uniform Partnership Act gives expression to, and application of, this principle in the following words:

"Unless authorized by the other partners or unless they have abandoned the business, one or more but less than all the partners have no authority to:

(*a*) Assign the partnership property in trust for creditors or on the assignee's promise to pay the debts of the partnership.

(*b*) Dispose of the good will of the business.

(*c*) Do any other act which would make it impossible to carry on the ordinary business of a partnership.

(*d*) Confess a judgment.

(*e*) Submit a partnership claim or liability to arbitration or reference."

These limitations may, of course, be removed by agreement among the partners. One or more of the partners may be delegated by the group as a whole to perform any or all of the above functions.

E. NOTICE TO ONE PARTNER AS NOTICE TO ALL

As in other agency relationships, if one of the partners, while acting within his authority and scope of the partnership business, acquires notice or knowledge in respect to partnership affairs, such knowledge is imputed to all members of the partnership. Partners are not charged with notice of information that was acquired by one of their number while not representing the firm. The conclusive presumption of knowledge on the part of all partners arises only when the partner who acquires the knowledge is acting as a partnership representative and thus acquires a duty to communicate the facts to the other members with whom he is associated. To illustrate:

In *Renfro* v. *Adams,* 62 Ala. 302, it was held that notice to one partner to record a satisfaction of a mortgage held by the partnership was notice to all partners. The failure to record the satisfaction as required by statute made all of the partners subject to the penalty provided by the statute.

► II. EXTENT AND NATURE OF PARTNERS' LIABILITY

A. ON CONTRACT—JOINT LIABILITY

The common law provides that partners are jointly liable upon partnership contracts. A joint contractual obligation is based upon one promise only—the promise of the joint obligors as a group. Consequently, partners can be considered bound as if they were a single person. A joint contractual undertaking carries with it three important legal consequences, a discussion of which follows.

1. *Joint Suit Against Partners*

In the absence of statutory provision to the contrary, suit upon a partnership obligation must be brought against all the partners. One partner cannot be sued individually unless he has assumed a personal liability for the partnership obligation. And unless such a several liability exists, the partners must be sued as a group and a judgment obtained against the partners as a group. A partnership judgment creditor may, however, look to the individual property of any or all of the partners after the firm property has become exhausted.

The above common law rules have been greatly changed and modified in many of the states by statutes.[4] Many states have, for example, completely abolished common law joint obligations by providing that all joint obligations are also several. Section 10975 of the 1939 Iowa Code is a typical provision. It reads:

> "*Joint and several obligations.* Where two or more persons are bound by contract or by judgment, decree, or statute, whether jointly only, or jointly and severally, or severally only, including the parties to negotiable paper, common orders, and checks, and sureties on the same or separate instruments, or by any liability growing out of the same, the action thereon may, at the plaintiff's option, be brought against any or all of them."

Section 10983 is made to apply specifically to partnerships by providing:

> "*Partnership.* Actions may be brought by or against a partnership as such, or against all or either of the individual members thereof, or against it and all or any of the members thereof; and a judgment against the firm as such may be enforced against the partnership property, or that of such members as have appeared or been served with notice. A new action may be brought against the members not made parties, on the original cause of action."

2. *Release of One Partner a Release of All*

Since a joint obligation is based upon but one right, a release of one of the joint obligors extinguishes the right and, consequently, releases the other obligors too. A release of one partner from a partnership obligation will serve as a release of all partners. It should be pointed out that one joint obligor can be released without effecting a release of the other obligors if the release specifically reserves the right against the other obligors. Unless such a reservation of rights is provided for, a release to one will be a release to all.

3. *Survivorship*

One of the common law consequences of joint liability is that, in the event of the death of one of the joint obligors, the obligation survives only to the remaining obligors. The estate of the deceased obligor is not liable upon the joint obligation as it would be were the obligation joint and several. The rule of survivorship has, however, been abolished by legislative enactment in some of the states. By way of illustration, Section 10975 of the 1939 Iowa Code, cited above, further reads:

> "When any of those so bound (jointly only, or jointly and severally, or severally only) are dead, the action may be brought against any or all of the survivors, with any or all of the representatives of the decedents, or against any or all such representatives."

B. TORT LIABILITY

The nature and extent of a partner's tort liability is well stated by the court in *Boston Foundry Company* v. *Whiteman*, 31 R.I. 88, when it said:

---

[4] Day v. Power, p. 868.

"By the great weight of authority, it is well settled that all the members of a firm are liable for fraud committed by one of them in the ordinary conduct of the firm's business, although the others do not participate in the fraud and have no knowledge of it. It is well established in the law of agency that a principal is civilly liable for the tortious or fraudulent act, whether criminal or not criminal, of his agent, not only when he has previously authorized or subsequently ratified the act, but even though he may have expressly forbidden it, if it has been committed by the agent in the course and as a part of his employment. Applying these principles of agency, therefore, a firm is liable for any loss or injury caused to any person not a member of the firm, or for any penalty incurred by any wrongful act or omission of a partner, acting in the ordinary course of the business of the firm, or with the authority of his copartner. . . . For torts committed by a partner, or by an agent for whose misconduct the partnership is liable, the injured party may, at his election, sue all the partners, or any one or more of them. Supposing a tort to be imputable to a firm, an action in respect of it may be brought against all or any of the partners. If some of them only are sued, they cannot insist upon the other partners being joined as defendants, and this rule applies even where the tort in question is committed by an agent or servant of the firm and not otherwise with the firm itself." [5]

To illustrate:

In *Lockwood* v. *Bartlett,* 130 N.Y. 340, the facts were that a partner, in the conduct of the firm's business, refused to return the plaintiff's property. The court held all of the partners liable for the conversion.

► III. LIABILITY OF INCOMING PARTNER

One who acquires the status of a partner in an existing partnership has no personal responsibility for the existing partnership obligations unless he voluntarily agrees, by word or act, to become personally bound.[6] The incoming partner's interest in the business enterprise is subject, of course, to the satisfaction of all claims against the partnership, including those existing at the time he becomes a member of the firm.

Section 17 of the Uniform Partnership Act reads:

"A person admitted as a partner into an existing partnership is liable for all the obligations of the partnership arising before his admission as though he had been a partner when such obligations were incurred, except that this liability shall be satisfied only out of partnership property."

---

[5] Polis v. Heizmann, p. 869.

[6] Stephens v. Neely, p. 870.

CASES

CASE NO. 1

Delta Asbestos Co. v. Sanders. 259 Mich. 317, 243 N.W. 16 (1932)

WIEST, J. Defendants Wells and Sanders are brother and sister and conducted a storage and trucking business under the name of Security Storage & Transfer Company, with Wells as active and managing partner. Wells, in the name of the company, signed an order for a liquid roof preservative, sold by plaintiff, and the product was billed to and received by the company. This suit was brought to recover the contract price of the product, was tried without a jury, and defendants had judgment.

The court found the matter was outside the scope of the company and defendant Sanders, not having authorized or ratified the transaction, was not liable and defendant Wells was induced to sign the contract by false and fraudulent representations, and was not liable. The name "Security Storage & Transfer Company" plainly indicated the scope of the business carried on. Storage in a warehouse and carriage by trucks was, and for many years had been, the sole business of the company. Defendant Wells could not depart from the scope of the partnership without authorization and bind his copartner by a wholly foreign contract. . . .

It must have been manifest to plaintiff's agent that the purchase was not one, apparently, for carrying on the business of the partnership in the usual way, unless it was to make deliveries of orders procured by plaintiff.

We find no assent by defendant Sanders, no acts of ratification by her, and no evidence justifying application of the doctrine of estoppel. As soon as defendant Sanders discovered the transaction, she repudiated it and refused to be bound thereby and so notified plaintiff. . . .

CASE NO. 2

Gordon v. Marburger. 109 Wash. 496, 187 Pac. 354, 9 A.L.R. 369 (1920)

PARKER, J., delivered the opinion of the court:

The plaintiff, Gordon, commenced this action in the superior court for Yakima county against the defendant Marburger, seeking an accounting of their partnership affairs and the appointment of a receiver to take charge of their partnership property, pending the settlement of their differences. The Growers' Service Company was made a defendant, because the remaining partnership property, consisting of potatoes, was stored in its warehouse. Arthur Karr was by the court appointed receiver, and by order of the court sold the potatoes stored in the service company's warehouse. The proceeds of the sale, after paying the storage charges and the expenses of the sale, amounted to $525. In the meantime W. J. Aumiller filed in the receivership proceedings his complaint in intervention, seeking to have his claim, amounting to $300, established as a claim against the potatoes and the proceeds of the sale thereof. The case came on for trial upon the merits as to the accounting controversy between Gordon and Marburger, and also as to the claim of lien made by Aumiller against the potatoes and the proceeds thereof. Judgment was rendered, decreeing Gordon to be entitled to the whole of the proceeds of the sale of the potatoes, after the payment of the receivership expenses, by reason of Marburger's appropriation of other property of the partnership. It was also adjudged that the relief prayed for by Aumiller be denied, and his complaint in intervention be dismissed. From this disposition of the cause, Aumiller has appealed to this court. . . .

On April 10, 1917, Marburger and Gordon entered into a partnership agreement, looking to the raising of potatoes during the crop season of 1917. . . . Marburger was to do the work and superintend it, in so far as labor was concerned, while Gordon was to furnish all money necessary for seed, for carrying on the work, for harvesting the potatoes, and for marketing the same. . . .

On June 12, 1917, Marburger borrowed from Aumiller $150, executing and delivering to Aumiller his note therefor, payable January 1, 1918. He at the same time executed and delivered to Aumiller a chattel mortgage upon the growing crop of potatoes, to secure the payment of this note. This was done by Marburger individually in his own name. Thereafter, on November 1st, Marburger again borrowed from Aumiller $50, executing his promissory note therefor, payable thirty days after date. No written security was given accompanying this note, but it was orally agreed between them that it be treated as being secured by the chattel mortgage already given. Thereafter, on January 12, 1918, Marburger again borrowed from Aumiller $100, no written evidence of any security accompanying this note, but Marburger promising that he would deliver to Aumiller the receipts issued by the Growers' Service Company, evidencing the storage of the potatoes in its warehouse. A few days thereafter Marburger delivered four of such receipts to Aumiller, but without any indorsement thereon of any nature.

No contention is here made against the judgment of the trial court, in so far as it awards the proceeds of the sale of the potatoes here involved to Gordon as against Marburger, so we proceed upon the assumption that the fund is the property of Gordon, as between those two. It is conceded that the business relation between them was that of a nontrading partnership, and that Marburger's power to contract debts and encumber the partnership property was limited accordingly. In Snively v. Matheson, 12 Wash. 88, 50 Am. St. Rep. 877, 40 Pac. 628, Judge Dunbar . . . said:

"The presumption is that one partner has no power to bind the other partners. Hence, before recovery can be obtained upon a contract entered into by one partner in a nontrading partnership against the other partners, it must be affirmatively shown by the party attempting to bind the noncontracting partners either that the authority to bind was conferred by the articles of incorporation, or that authority had been specially conferred, or that it had been the custom of such partnership to recognize this right to such an extent as would give innocent dealers a right to rely upon the custom."

It was also recognized as the law in that decision that, in the doing of acts ordinarily necessary to be done by one partner, in the performance of partnership duties assigned to such partner, he can bind the other partners and their interest in the partnership property. It is plain, however, that in this partnership Marburger had no duties to perform in the partnership business rendering it at all necessary for him to borrow money to further the partnership interests, nor was there any custom of dealing by either of the partners, touching the partnership business, in the least suggesting that Marburger was authorized to borrow money for the partnership, or encumber its property. The contentions of counsel for Marburger are rested upon the theory that Gordon was a silent or dormant partner, and that Aumiller was warranted in dealing with Marburger upon the assumption that he was the sole owner of the potatoes. . . . It is hard to believe that Aumiller was wholly ignorant of Gordon's interest in the potatoes, in view of the fact that Aumiller prepared the rent receipt evidencing the leasing of the land to both Marburger and Gordon for the raising of these potatoes. . . . This significant fact . . . and the fact that this was purely a nontrading partnership, we think, compels the conclusion that in no event can Aumiller at this time be heard to say, as against the rights of Gordon, that he was led to believe that Marburger was the sole owner of the potatoes, with absolute right to borrow money and secure the payment of the same by encumbering them. . . .

CASE NO. 3

Higgins v. Beauchamp. Kings Bench, 3 K.B. 1192 (1914)

HORRIDGE, J. This is an action to recover two sums of money which had been borrowed from the plaintiff by one Milles upon the representation that the money was to be used for the purposes of the business of a firm in which the defendant and Milles were partners, and of which Milles was the manager. The partnership deed expressly negatived the power of any one partner without the consent of the others to borrow money so as to bind the partnership. There being no express authority to borrow, the question is whether there was any implied authority . . . the managing partner of a common trading partnership has implied authority to borrow money for partnership purposes, and in so borrowing he may bind the other partners although he may wrongfully apply it to other than partnership purposes. But was this a common trading partnership in the sense in which that term is used in the cases? For that we must look at the partnership deed. It provides that the business of the firm shall be that

> "of proprietors and managers of picture palaces, cinematographic theatres and exhibitions, variety entertainments, concerts, theatrical performances, and all other forms of entertainment."

I do not think that that is a trading business of the kind from which authority to the managing partner to borrow money or accept bills of exchange is to be implied. The judge in the court below does not seem to have applied his mind to this question, but to have proceeded upon the assumption that the defendant by allowing Milles to hold himself out as manager of the business, irrespective of the nature of the business, rendered himself liable for Milles' unauthorized borrowing in the absence of negligence on the part of the borrower, and that is a proposition which clearly cannot be sustained. The appeal must be allowed.

CASE NO. 4

Day v. Power. 219 Iowa 138, 257 N.W. 187 (1934)

CLAUSSEN, J. The Bank of Pulaski was conducted by a partnership. It became insolvent. Plaintiff was appointed its temporary receiver. An order was made by the court directing him to bring suit against the defendants, who were members of the partnership, for "their liability to the depositors of said Bank as partners of the same." The validity of such order is not in question. Thereupon this suit was commenced. The petition alleged that the Bank of Pulaski was operated by a partnership; that defendants were included in the list of partners; that plaintiff was the duly appointed, qualified, and acting receiver of said partnership; that, at the time of filing the petition, $125,891.08 was due depositors of the bank; and that the defendants were primarily liable for all the liabilities of the bank and were then owing said receiver the full amount of the indebtedness of the bank. The petition asked judgment for the amount of the deposits of the bank, namely, $125,-891.08.

In this situation defendants filed a motion for a more specific statement asking that plaintiff state whether persons other than defendants were partners and the names of such others, if any; . . .

. . . the motion . . . was overruled by the trial court, and of such action defendants complain.

It is well settled that every partner is individually liable for partnership debts. In this situation it is entirely immaterial whether or not there were partners in the bank other than defendants. Either partner could be sued alone for the partnership debts. . . .

We find no error in the record, and as a consequence the orders appealed from are affirmed.

CASE NO. 5

Polis v. Heizmann. 276 Pa. 315, 120 Atl. 269, 27 A.L.R. 948 (1923)

WALLING, J., delivered the opinion of the court:

In the summer of 1917 Frederick Polis, the plaintiff, was the owner of a small farm in an outlying district of Philadelphia, a part of which he leased as a piggery to the defendants, Frederick Heizmann and Ernest Heizmann, brothers, and partners in the business. Later, however, the city authorities prevented the use of the place for such purpose. Thereupon Frederick Heizmann went to the premises to remove some lumber, and, in an altercation over his right to do so, wilfully and intentionally struck and injured the plaintiff, who brought this suit against both defendants for the injury so sustained. Ernest Heizmann was not present at the assault, and neither authorized nor ratified it; for which reason the trial judge granted a compulsory non-suit, and the refusal to take it off forms the basis of this appeal by plaintiff.

The action of the court below was right. Where two are charged jointly with a tort there must be a recovery against both or neither. . . .

We cannot sustain plaintiff's contention that the absent partner was liable for the tort committed by the other; that would be so in some cases, but not in this. The injury here is charged and shown to have been maliciously and wantonly inflicted by wilful and intentional violence, in extent and character such as would constitute the crime of aggravated assault and battery. A partnership relation in a lawful enterprise will not render one partner liable for the intentional criminal act of another. The liability of the absent partner is based on the theory of agency; but an agent's wanton criminal act will not bind his principal. The true rule is that "a tort committed by one partner will not bind the partnership or the other copartner, unless it be either authorized or adopted by the firm, or be within the proper scope and business of the partnership." 38 Cyc. 481

Knocking a man down, as in this case, with the fist and then again with an automobile, both done wilfully, cannot be said to come within the scope of the business of raising pigs. The principle is well stated in Rowley's Modern

Law of Partnership, Vol. 1, § 512, as follows:

"A somewhat peculiar situation arises when the torts complained of are wilful and malicious on the part of the offending partner. It will be remembered that the wrongful act, in order to give the party injured a right of action on account of partnership relation, must have been done . . . within the scope of the partnership authority, or, at least, apparent authority. Hence, as wilful and malicious torts are not within the usual scope of partnership authority, partners will usually be relieved from liability for such acts by their copartner. . . ."

While here the act of the offending partner in going for the lumber was within the scope of the firm's business, the vicious assault committed by him was not, and for that he alone was liable. . . . The case is different where the master or partner sought to be charged was present at the assault, and failed to protest. See Williams v. F. & W. Grand Five, Ten & Twenty-Five Cent Stores, 273 Pa. 131, 116 Atl. 652. . . .

The judgment is affirmed.

CASE NO. 6

Stephens v. Neely. 161 Ark. 114, 255 S.W. 562, 45 A.L.R. 1236 (1923)

HART, J. It seems that the main purpose of the action in the circuit court was to charge M. Neely as a partner with Jack McDonald, on the promissory note which the firm of McDonald Bros. had executed to Mrs. Helena Hanks in the sum of $10,000 on March 27, 1914. It appears that certain payments were made on the note by Jack McDonald from time to time until the 2nd day of April, 1918, and that this suit was instituted on September 27, 1921, to recover the balance due

It is insisted that the court erred in giving the following instruction:

"If you find from the evidence that Neely was not a partner when the note was executed, but that he afterwards became a partner, and, by special promise or agreement, assumed liability for the debt evidenced by the note, then the court charges you as a matter of law that he is liable only on such special promise or agreement. . . ."

We cannot agree with counsel for the plaintiffs in this contention. There is no presumption that an incoming partner of an existing partnership assumes liability for the previous debts of the concern. He is not bound for such debts unless he makes himself so by express agreement or by such conduct as will raise the presumption of a special promise. Ringo v. Wing, 49 Ark. 457, 5 S.W. 787. The promissory note signed by McDonald Bros. is the basis of this action. The law of partnership is but a branch of the law of principal and agent. The ground of liability of one partner for the acts of the other is that of implied agency within the scope of the partnership. If Neely was bound by the fact that McDonald had made payments on the note after he became a member of the firm, then he could not even show that he had not assumed the debts of the old firm. The credit of a new member of a firm does not enter into the consideration of the creditors of the old firm, and it would be manifestly unjust to hold the new partner liable unless he, by an express or implied agreement, assumed the debts of the old firm. Hence, if Neely is liable at all in the present case, it is upon an express or implied agreement to pay the debts of the old firm. If his liability depends upon making such an agreement, he has the right to plead the statute of limitations in regard thereto, and his plea of the statute in bar of his liability could not be defeated by showing that his partner had made a payment on the old indebtedness since the time it is claimed he became liable therefor. In such cases it will be presumed that the partner made the payment in discharge of his own obligation, and the burden of proof would still be upon the creditor to show that the incoming partner has assumed the debts of the old firm. Hence this assignment of error is not well taken.

We find no reversible error in the record, and the judgment for defendant will be affirmed.

Review Questions

1. To what extent can a partner bind the partnership by his acts?
2. Construct a fact situation under which an act of an individual partner would not be binding upon the partnership.
3. What is a trading partnership as distinguished from a nontrading partnership?
4. In what respect do the powers of partners in a trading partnership differ from the powers of those in a nontrading partnership?
5. To what extent are contractual limitations of a partner's usual powers binding upon third persons with whom he deals?
6. When is unanimous consent of the partners required?
7. What is the effect of releasing one partner from a partnership obligation?
8. What is the extent of a partnership's tort liability for the acts of the individual partners?
9. Construct a fact situation under which a partnership would be liable for the tort of an individual partner.

Problems for Discussion

1. The complainant sued the defendants as partners composing the firm of J. M. Mason & Co. to recover $5,505.57 overdraft, together with accrued interest, making the sum of $6,585.54. A judgment was rendered for the latter sum. Defendant Hoover appealed.

   It appears that the defendants were partners in the mercantile business at Bellbuckle. About October, 1912, they fell in debt to the bank by overdraft in the sum of about $3,000. Hoover was the moneyed man of the firm, but did not stay in the store or give any attention to the business, its conduct being confided wholly to Mason, in whom Hoover had the greatest confidence. When the knowledge of the overdraft was brought to the attention of Hoover, he promised to pay it off, but stated to the cashier Shoffner that it must never occur again; that Mason's checks must not be paid unless there should be money in the bank to the credit of the firm to meet them. During the next year the firm checks drawn by Mason were from time to time honored until there was an overdraft of the amount sued for. Decide. (*Bank of Bellbuckle* v. *Mason*, 139 Tenn. 659)
2. Tom, Dick, and Harry were engaged in the practice of medicine under a partnership agreement. They had agreed that all purchases made on behalf of the firm exceeding $50 would require unanimous approval. Dick purchased adhesive tape, various drugs, and surgical instruments on behalf of the partner-

ship from the Acme Supply Co. without having obtained the required approval. Is this binding upon the partnership?

3. X, a member of a partnership engaged in farming, employed Y, a physician, to render medical services (whenever needed) to the farm laborers. Is this contract of employment binding on the partnership?
4. A, B, and C operated a department store as partners. Anticipating an improvement in the firm's business, A ordered two new delivery trucks from X. A's optimism is not justified and B and C deny that the partnership is bound by A's act. Decide.
5. Stratton, Stray, and Strutt were associated as partners in the practice of law. The firm had represented Twill in a lawsuit, for which he was charged a fee of $150. Without authority, Strutt agreed to accept a radio worth approximately $75 in discharge of the obligation. Is this binding upon the partnership?
6. Pooley, Barnum & Co. sued Edwin Whitmore & Co. on two promissory notes for $185 each, made by W. A. Whitmore, payable at six and nine months respectively, to the order of "Whitmore Brothers" and indorsed in that name. Whitmore Brothers, a firm composed of Edwin Whitmore and the said W. A. Whitmore, were partners in publishing the *Public Ledger,* a newspaper in the city of Memphis, and also conducted a general job-printing office in that city. The notes in suit, however, were drawn and indorsed by W. A. Whitmore in discharge of a private debt that he owed to one Cannon. Edwin Whitmore is the surviving partner of the firm and puts in a special plea of *non est factum,* and insists that the firm is not bound to pay on the ground that it is not a partnership debt. Defendants in error reply that they are bona fide purchasers for value of the note in due course of trade and therefore are entitled to recover, notwithstanding the wrong or fraud of W. A. Whitmore in using the partnership name in a personal transaction.

   The court below instructed the jury that ". . . as a general rule, one partner is not liable for the act of another partner not within the scope of the partnership business. That if one partner sign a promissory note or other negotiable paper in the firm name, without the knowledge or consent of the other partner, and for a matter not within the scope of the partnership business, the other partner will not be liable unless he ratify the act or unless the paper gets into the hands of some purchaser before maturity, who had no knowledge or notice of the consideration between the original parties, and who paid a valuable consideration for the paper. That such a person would be an innocent holder for value, and without notice."

   Is this an accurate statement of the law? (*Pooley* v. *Whitmore,* 57 Tenn. 629)
7. X and Y were partners engaged in retail selling. A check payable to the partnership was indorsed by X and cashed at the Z bank. X used the proceeds for his own personal use and Y brought an action against the Z bank to recover. It is Y's contention that, since X had never been given authority to indorse checks, the bank was not justified in honoring the indorsement. Decide.
8. X, Y, and Z were associated as partners in a mercantile business. The partnership was indebted to P, who, when X called upon him requesting his indulgence in the matter, threatened to bring suit immediately unless given a sixty-

day judgment note. X executed such a note in the name of the partnership. Is his act binding?

9. A statute provides that unless the mortgagee records a satisfaction of the mortgage within thirty days after being requested to do so by the mortgagor, he shall forfeit $50 to the mortgagor. After X had discharged his mortgage obligation to the mortgagee (a partnership), X requested A, one of the partners, to enter a satisfaction of the mortgage. The satisfaction was not recorded within the thirty-day period. A had never communicated the request to the other partners. Is the partnership subject to the forfeiture provision of the statute?
10. Lamm and Hisey were associated as partners in buying old furniture and selling antiques. They maintained business establishments at Milwaukee, Wisconsin, and Hot Springs, Arkansas. A creditor obtained a judgment against the firm in Arkansas and the partnership assets in that state were not sufficient to satisfy the judgment. Can the creditor avail himself of the partnership property in Wisconsin?
11. Tolley and Hobbs were associated as partners in the conduct of a grocery business. Hobbs used the truck belonging to the partnership for the purpose of taking his family and neighbors to a picnic. On the side of the truck was painted: "Tolley and Hobbs, Dealers in Fancy Groceries." While returning home from the picnic, Hobbs negligently ran into Gayer's car. In settlement, Hobbs gave Gayer a thirty-day promissory note for $200 to which he signed the partnership name. Is this act binding upon the partnership?
12. Z was admitted to the partnership consisting of Z and Y. Shortly thereafter the partnership was dissolved by bankruptcy. The partnership creditors consist of A, whose claim antedates the admission of Z as a partner, and B, whose claim arose subsequent to Z's admission. To what extent is Z personally responsible to A and B?

35 BUSINESS ORGANIZATIONS:

RELATIONS OF PARTNERS TO ONE ANOTHER; THEIR RIGHTS AND DUTIES

► I. RIGHTS AND DUTIES ESTABLISHED BY PARTNERSHIP AGREEMENT

A partnership results from an express or implied contract. It is desirable that this contract be in written form and that it cover the various matters outlined in a previous chapter. This contract basically determines the respective rights and duties of each partner to the other. The members of a partnership have it within their power to define the relationship existing between them. In the absence of any agreement to the contrary, the rules of law as set forth in this chapter apply in determining what the rights and duties of the partners are to one another —rights and duties that arise as a matter of law from the nature of the relationship.

Since the relation existing between partners is basically that of principal and agent, the rights and duties existing between the partners are essentially those existing between a principal and agent. There are, however, certain other rights and duties, which arise out of the joint enterprise aspect of the business undertaking—rights and duties not peculiar to the ordinary agency relationship.

► II. FIDUCIARY CHARACTER OF RELATIONSHIP

Partnership is a fiduciary relationship, a relation of trust and confidence. Aside from the mutual agency aspects, it entails numerous other personal and confidential contacts.

> "There is no stronger fiduciary relation known to the law than that of a copartnership, where one man's property and property rights are subject to a large extent to the control and administration of another." *Salkinger* v. *Salkinger,* 56 Wash. 134.

As a result, the law imposes the duty of utmost good faith upon the partners toward each other in respect to partnership affairs. Partners have the duty to take not the slightest advantage of one another in their mutual relations. The attitude of the courts is well expressed in *Stein* v. *Warren,* 161 N.Y.S. 247, where the court said:

> "The authorities unanimously agree that there is scarcely any relation in life which calls for more absolute good faith than the relationship of partners."

To illustrate:

(1) In *Johnson* v. *Peckham,* 132 Tex. 148, the facts were that plaintiff (Johnson) and defendant (Peckham) were partners operating oil and gas leases. The de-

fendant contracted to purchase the plaintiff's interest in the partnership for $1,500. Shortly thereafter the defendant sold the property which had been held by the partnership to a third party for $10,500. Negotiations for this sale were begun prior to the time that the defendant contracted to purchase the plaintiff's interest.

In sustaining a $3,750 judgment for the plaintiff, the court said:

> ". . . The applicable principle which seems to meet with general acceptation is thus stated in 20 R.C.L. p. 879: 'Since each is the confidential agent of the other, each has a right to know all that the others know, and each is required to make full disclosure of all material facts within his knowledge in any way relating to the partnership affairs. This necessity for good faith and the making of a full disclosure of all important information applies in the case of sale by one partner to another of his interest in the partnership. Such a sale will be sustained only when it is made in good faith, for a fair consideration and on a full and complete disclosure of all important information as to value. . . .' . . . The absolute duty to disclose was upon Peckham."

(2) In *Gianuso* v. *Weis,* 195 N.Y.S. 279, the facts were that a partner had entered into a contract on behalf of the partnership with a corporation of which he was the principal stockholder and president. The contract being disadvantageous to the partnership, it was set aside by the court. Under the circumstances, the contracting partner had not exercised the requirement of good faith toward the partnership. A partner may not derive a personal profit out of the transactions of the firm.

(3) If a partner engages in an enterprise which is in competition with the partnership, he can be compelled to account for the profits made. Such profits would belong to the partnership.

Some courts have gone so far as to declare that the relationship of partners is that of trustees to one another, and statutes can be found to this effect. The Uniform Partnership Act recognizes the status of a partner as that of a trustee to a limited extent by providing in Section 21 that:

> "Every partner must account to the partnership for any benefit, and hold as trustee for it any profits derived by him without the consent of the other partners from any transaction connected with the formation, conduct, or liquidation of the partnership or from any use by him of its property. . . ."

Being able to have partnership profits declared as being trust property when in the hands of a partner makes it possible for the partnership to recover the specific property from the partner in the event of his insolvency. Otherwise it might be contended that the partnership occupies the position of a creditor only; as such it would have no preference to the profits.

► III. RIGHT OF PARTICIPATION IN MANAGEMENT

Partners have an equal voice in the management of the partnership unless they have agreed otherwise. The partnership agreement may provide that management shall be shared equally and that all matters pertaining to the partnership business shall be the subject of mutual consultation and agreement. Or the partnership agreement may delegate complete management to one partner or certain phases of management to the individual partners. The conduct of the partners may imply a delegation of the management function. To illustrate:

In *Miller* v. *Ashley,* (Ore.) 271 Pac. 596, the court observed that the fact that one partner almost exclusively attended to the financial affairs of the firm for a number of years is very convincing evidence that the other partners had agreed to such right of control.

In the conduct of the ordinary business and commercial affairs of a partnership, the majority opinion of the partners is controlling. A two-man partnership should therefore make provision for a method of breaking deadlocks resulting from differences of opinion; otherwise the dissolution of the partnership may be the only alternative. Of course, the possibility of a deadlock exists in any partnership composed of an even number of partners. Action such as changing the capitalization, undertaking business ventures not originally contemplated, the admission of new partners, and any other action that is not consistent with the terms of the partnership agreement requires the consent of all partners.* Unless a partner waives the contractual rights that he has acquired from the partnership agreement, these rights cannot be denied him.[1]

Disproportionate contributions of capital by the partners in no way vary the rule of equal management unless the partners have agreed to the contrary.

► IV. RIGHT TO INFORMATION

The right to information is essential to a proper and intelligent exercise of the right of management. Excluding a partner from information would, in effect, be excluding him from control of the business. Every partner has the right to be fully informed of all matters pertaining to the affairs of the partnership. Consequently, it is the duty of every partner to inform his copartners fully of all facts that are material to the affairs of the firm.

The right to information includes a right to inspect the books and files of the partnership.[2] Section 19 of the Uniform Partnership Act provides:

> "The partnership books shall be kept, subject to any agreement between the partners, at the principal place of business of the partnership, and every partner shall at all times have access to and may inspect and copy any of them."

Unless the partners come to a different understanding, the law imposes upon them individually the duty of keeping or seeing that proper partnership accounts are kept. If one of the partners is the general manager of the firm, the duty rests upon him. It devolves upon the partners to supply the keeper of the books with the necessary information.

* See p. 862.

1 Katz v. Brewington, p. 881.

2 Sanderson v. Cooke, p. 882.

► V. RIGHT TO AN ACCOUNTING

At times it becomes necessary for partners to come to a mutual understanding regarding their respective property rights in the joint enterprise.[3, 4] If the partners cannot arrive at a settlement by mutual agreement, equity makes available the remedy of accounting for the purpose of establishing their respective interests in the firm. However, a partner cannot invoke the aid of equity for purely arbitrary reasons. Before a court of equity will order that an accounting be made, it must be satisfied that such is necessary.

A. UPON DISSOLUTION

Should a partnership cease to exist as a going concern, it may become necessary to petition a court of equity for an accounting with a view to a final adjustment of the partnership affairs. At times, partnership affairs become so complex and complicated that no voluntary agreement can be arrived at as to the partners' respective interests at the time of dissolution.

B. WITHOUT DISSOLUTION

> "While a forced accounting without a dissolution is not impossible, it is by no means a matter of course, for facts must be alleged and proved showing that it is essential to the continuance of the business, or that some special and unusual reason exists to make it necessary." *Lord* v. *Hull,* 178 N.Y. 9

The reasons for the reluctance of courts to make available an accounting without dissolution, where there is only slight provocation, are well stated in *Lord* v. *Hull, supra.* The court continued:

> "Aside from the inconvenience of constant interference, as litigation is apt to breed hard feelings, easy appeals to the court to settle the differences of a going concern would tend to do away with mutual forbearance, foment discord, and lead to dissolution. It is to the interest of the law of partnership that frequent resort to the courts by copartners should not be encouraged, and they should realize that, as a rule, they must settle their own differences, or go out of business."

While it is impossible to establish all the specific reasons for which this remedy may be made available, some of the underlying causes can be noted. Those specifically provided for in Section 22 of the Uniform Partnership Act are:

(1) where a partner is wrongfully excluded from the partnership business or of possession of its property by his copartners;

(2) where the right exists by the terms of an agreement;

(3) where profits are being withheld which rightfully belong to the partnership.

---

[3] Pugh v. Newburn, p. 883.
[4] Wilson v. Moline, p. 884.

▶ VI. RIGHT OF REIMBURSEMENT AND CONTRIBUTION

In the absence of an agreement to the contrary, a partnership has the obligation to reimburse the individual partner for the following items:

(1) For the capital contributed to the enterprise;

(2) for any advances beyond the capital commitments with interest; and

(3) the partnership must indemnify every partner in respect of payments made and personal liabilities reasonably incurred by him in the ordinary and proper conduct of its business, or for the preservation of its business or property. (As Section 18 [*b*] of the Uniform Act provides.)

It is entirely a question of fact whether an expenditure made or liability incurred by a partner falls within the above. The right of reimbursement would clearly exist where a partner has paid taxes upon firm property, paid attorney fees necessitated by defending a suit against the partnership, or paid traveling expenses while acting on behalf of and in the interests of the partnership.

When partnership assets are insufficient to discharge these obligations, they stand as partnership losses to be shared equally by the partners. Consequently, the partner who has contributed more than his ratable share has the right of contribution against those partners who are in a solvent condition. Let us suppose that partner A has expended $600 in behalf of the partnership. If the partnership assets are not sufficient to reimburse him, he would have the right of contribution to the extent of $400 against his copartners B and C.

▶ VII. RIGHT TO RECEIVE COMPENSATION FOR SERVICES

Partners can well afford to have an understanding of some certainty relative to (1) the extent and nature of services each is to contribute to the partnership business, and (2) the circumstances, if any, under which they are to receive compensation for services.

In the absence of any agreement the following rules apply:

(1) The partners have the legal obligation to devote such of their time and energy as are reasonably necessary to a proper conduct of the enterprise.

(2) The partners are not entitled to compensation for their services other than their share of the profits.

(3) A partner who renders extraordinary services—services disproportionate to those of the other partners—has no right to compensation unless the circumstances are most unusual and are such that from them an agreement to compensate him can be implied.* To illustrate:

(a) In *Cole* v. *Cole,* 119 Ark. 48, it was held that a partner conducting the entire business during the illness of his copartner had no right to receive com-

* See Williams v. Pedersen, p. 887.

pensation for the greater services. The court said that the illness of a partner is one of the risks incident to the partnership form of business unit.

By the same token, a partner would have no claim for compensation if the neglect of his copartner forced him to render greater services. The recourse of the aggrieved partner would be to obtain a dissolution of the partnership.

(b) In *Rains* v. *Weiler,* 101 Kan. 294, the court said:

"A case where an active and managing partner devotes his whole time and attention to a partnership business at the instance of other partners, who are attending to their individual businesses and giving no time or attention to the business of the firm, presents unusual conditions which take the case out of the general rule as to compensation and warrants the implication of an agreement to pay compensation."

(4) The Uniform Partnership Act, Section 19, provides that "no partner is entitled to remuneration for acting in the partnership business, except that a surviving partner is entitled to a reasonable compensation for his services in winding up the partnership affairs." Many states deny the partner the right of compensation for services rendered as a surviving partner.

► VIII. RIGHTS IN RESPECT TO PARTNERSHIP PROPERTY

Partners have no individual ownership interest in the firm's property. Section 25(1) of the Uniform Partnership Act declares that, with his partners, a partner is a co-owner of specific partnership property as a *tenant in partnership.* The legal incidents of tenancy in partnership are dissimilar from those of other types of joint ownership. To meet the needs of the relationship, the rights of tenancy in partnership are greatly restricted. Some of the more important negative and positive incidents are as follows.

A. OWNERSHIP NONTRANSFERABLE

If A and B own property as *tenants in common,* either, without the consent of the other, can transfer his ownership interest to a third person, who thereupon becomes a joint owner. In this respect, a partner's ownership interest is dissimilar. Section 25(2)(*b*) of the Uniform Act provides:

"A partner's right in specific property is not assignable except in connection with the assignment of the rights of all the partners in the same property."

A partnership is a personal relationship, a relationship of trust and confidence. To allow a partner to substitute another in his place by a transfer of his ownership interest would not be compatible with such. Since ownership carries with it the rights of management and control, the new owner would in effect become a partner.

The reasons for preventing a partner from making a voluntary transfer of his ownership apply equally well to involuntary transfers. The consequences of an involuntary transfer would be the same—the introduction of a new partner into the enterprise. Section 25(2) makes provision against involuntary transfers. It reads:

"(*c*) A partner's right in specific partnership property is not subject to attachment or execution, except on a claim against the partnership. . . .

"(*d*) On the death of a partner his right in specific partnership property vests in the surviving partner or partners, except where the deceased was the last surviving partner, when his right in such property vests in his legal representative."

Other incidents of tenancy in partnership that are not common to ordinary joint ownership are that a partner's interest is not subject to dower, to allowances to widows, heirs, or next of kin.[5]

B. PARTNER'S BENEFICIAL INTEREST TRANSFERABLE

The two most important positive incidents of tenancy in partnership are (1) the individual partner's right to share in the management and conduct of the enterprise, and (2) the individual's beneficial interest in the partnership. The nature of a partner's beneficial interest in the partnership is described by Section 26 of the Uniform Act to be "his share of the profits and surplus, and the same is personal property."

This beneficial interest—this right to share in profits and surplus—is subject to either voluntary or involuntary transfer. It may be assigned by the partner, attached, or levied upon by the partner's creditors, and at the time of the death of the partner it will devolve to his heirs or pass as he directs.

In the event of an *assignment* of this beneficial interest by a partner, the legal consequences are provided for in Section 27 of the Uniform Act:

"(1) A conveyance by a partner of his interest in the partnership does not of itself dissolve the partnership, nor, as against the other partners in the absence of agreement, entitle the assignee, during the continuance of the partnership, to interfere in the management or administration of the partnership business or affairs, or to require any information or account of partnership transactions, or to inspect the partnership books; but it merely entitles the assignee to receive in accordance with his contract the profits to which the assigning partner would otherwise be entitled.

"(2) In case of a dissolution of the partnership, the assignee is entitled to receive his assignor's interest and may require an account from the date only of the last account agreed to by all the partners."

► IX. PROFITS, SURPLUS, AND LOSSES

The articles of partnership usually provide for the extent to which the various partners, upon dissolution, will share in the business profits and the surplus assets, as well as the extent to which they will share the losses. It is only in the absence of an agreement respecting profits, losses, and surplus that the following rules apply.

Profits will be shared equally by the partners, irrespective of disproportionate

[5] Woodward-Holmes Co. v. Nudd, p. 885.

capital contributions or services rendered.[6] Even though partner A has contributed $5,000 to the enterprise, and partner B has contributed $10,000, nevertheless the profits will be divided equally between them, unless they have agreed otherwise.

Surplus is that partnership property which remains after all partnership liabilities have been discharged, including the return of the capital contributions to the partners. Unless agreed otherwise, capital contributions are regarded as obligations of the partnership to the contributing partners.[7] In the absence of a contrary agreement, surplus, like profits, will be shared equally among the partners. Let us suppose that, in the illustration given above, upon dissolution the total partnership assets are $50,000 and the firm's liabilities to outside creditors are $15,000. Distribution would be made as follows: $15,000 to outside creditors; a return of the partners' capital contributions—$5,000 to A, and $10,000 to B; the balance (surplus) of $20,000 to A and B equally.

Partners are presumed to undertake the sharing of *losses* in equal proportion to the sharing of profits. Unless agreed otherwise, partners who share profits equally will be required to contribute equally to the losses incurred. Continuing the illustration above, let us suppose that upon dissolution the partnership assets are $25,000. After outside creditors have been paid, the balance would be $10,000 with which to pay the partners' capital contributions. This represents a capital loss of $5,000. Since profits are shared equally, this capital loss must be borne equally by A and B, that is, $2,500 each. Under these circumstances, final settlement would result in a distribution of $2,500 to A and of $7,500 to B. Now let us suppose that upon dissolution the partnership assets are $15,000. After this has been distributed to the creditors, there would be a capital loss of $15,000 (A's contribution of $5,000 and B's of $10,000). In order to share this loss equally, A would be required to make a contribution of $2,500 to B.

CASES

CASE NO. 1

Katz v. Brewington. 71 Md. 79, 20 Atl. 139 (1889)

Bill to wind up the affairs of the firm of L. Katz and Co.. Brewington claimed that Katz had taken possession of the books and assets of the firm and excluded him from all participation in the firm's business.

BRYAN, J. Each partner has an equal right to take part in the management of the business of the firm. Although one of them may have an interest only in the profits, and not in the capital, yet his rights are involved in the proper conduct of the affairs of the firm, so that profits may be made. So each partner has an equal right to information about the partnership affairs, and to free access to its books. The complainant had a right to learn from the books whether there were profits, and whether there were debts. If he were denied this information, as charged in his bill of complaint, a sufficient reason appears for not

[6] Williams v. Pedersen, p. 887.

[7] Glenn v. Weill, p. 887.

alleging that profits had been earned, and that debts existed. In Const. v. Harris, 1 Turn. & R., 496, Lord Eldon said:

> "The most prominent point, in which the court acts, in appointing a receiver of a partnership concern, is the circumstance of one partner having taken upon himself the power to exclude another partner from as full a share in the management of the partnership as he who assumes that power himself enjoys."

This principle seems to be universally approved by the authorities. It is decisive of the present question. The order must be affirmed. Order affirmed, with costs; and cause remanded.

CASE NO. 2

Sanderson v. Cooke. 256 N.Y. 73, 175 N.E. 518 (1931)

CRANE, J. Charles D. Barney & Co. is an old established brokerage house with which the plaintiff became connected in 1911. . . . the firm continued until December 31, 1918, at which time, either by agreement dated that day, or January 1, 1919, the firm was dissolved and a new firm formed, in which the plaintiff and J. Horace Harding became special partners. This special partnership was continued by agreements dated December 23, 1919, and June 29, 1920, and terminated by agreement in writing dated the 14th day of January, 1921.

As a special partner, Mr. Sanderson's rights were limited to a return of his capital contribution, and a fixed percentage thereon. These he received upon retirement. . . .

This litigation arises out of a supposed property right which the plaintiff claims to have in the old books of account. The various partnerships, beginning with 1911, and continuing down to the 28th day of February, 1921, were a continuation of the business of Charles D. Barney & Co. without interruption.

In 1926, Mr. Sanderson asked to see and examine the books of the old firms, which were then in the possession of Charles D. Barney & Co., and was afforded the opportunity, not only of inspecting the books personally, but of having them examined by public accountants, . . . Private or family accounts were kept by the senior member of the firm, J. Horace Harding. The defendants were willing to have the plaintiff inspect these personally, but refused to permit him to make and take copies of them. . . .

The general rule regarding business partnerships is that books should be kept, open to the inspection of any partner at all reasonable times, even after dissolution, subject, however, to special ageement. Even under these broad statements of the law, a partner's rights are not absolute. He may be restrained from using the information gathered from inspection for other than partnership purposes. The employment of an agent to make an inspection does not authorize the selection of anybody he may choose for the purpose. The agent employed must be a person to whom no reasonable objection can be taken, and the purpose for which he seeks to use the right of inspection must be one consistent with the main purposes and the well-being of the whole partnership. . . .

We are not treating here, however, with a partnership in existence, a going concern, nor with an action for a partnership accounting and the inspection incident thereto, nor with joint partnership property left on dissolution, for safekeeping, in the custody of the other partner or partners. We have much more than this. Whatever may be the property right of a partner in the partnership books, he may transfer and dispose of it like his right to any other bit of property by express, or necessarily implied, agreement. This is succinctly and forcibly stated in a short opinion by Mr. Justice Albert Cardozo, in Platt v. Platt, 61 Barb. 52, page 53. Writing of a former partner, whose executors claimed a right to inspect partnership books, the justice said:

"Nathan C. Platt had parted with his interests in the partnership, and conveyed it to the defendant. While that sale stands, the plaintiffs have no rights in the property. While that sale stands, the books belong to no one but the defendant; and while they belong exclusively to him, no one else has the right to a general inspection of them."

We find expressions running through all these various partnership agreements clearly indicating that it was the intention that every succeeding firm continuing the business of Charles D. Barney & Co. should take as its property the books, records, files, and office chattels used by the preceding firm.

The court holds that the old books of account are the property of the partnership.

CASE NO. 3

Pugh v. Newbern. 193 N.C. 258, 136 S.E. 707, 58 A.L.R. 617 (1927)

BROGDEN, J., delivered the opinion of the court:

The question of law presented is this: Has one partner the right to have the other partner arrested for an alleged wrongful conversion of partnership funds in a civil action brought for an accounting?

The general rule is that one partner cannot sue another partner at law until there has been a complete settlement of the partnership affairs and a balance struck. . . .

This general rule is supported by the decided weight of authority. Many of the leading authorities are collected in a valuable note found in 21 A.L.R. 12.

There are, however, well-established exceptions to the general rule. A partner may maintain an action at law against his copartner upon claims growing out of the following state of facts:

(1) Claims not connected with the partnership.

(2) Claims for an agreed final balance.

(3) Claims upon express personal contracts between the partners.

(4) Failure to comply with an agreement constituting a condition precedent to the formation of the partnership.

(5) Where the partnership is terminated, all debts paid, and the partnership affairs otherwise adjusted, with nothing remaining to be done but to pay over the amount due by one to the other, such amount involving no complicated reckoning.

(6) Where the partnership is for a single venture or special purpose which has been accomplished, and nothing remains to be done except to pay over the claimant's share.

(7) When the joint property has been wrongfully destroyed or converted.

(8) When one partner has been guilty of fraud in contracting the debt or in incurring the obligation or by concealing the property or by other device defeating the rights of the complaining party. . . .

In the case now under consideration . . it clearly appears from the pleadings that there are serious disputes of fact between the parties, the settlement of which will require a more or less complicated reckoning. . . .

Hence, it cannot be ascertained

what portion of the money in controversy belongs to each of the parties, or whether, indeed, any part thereof would belong to the plaintiff.

Therefore we are of the opinion that the arrest of the defendant was improvidently granted and that the trial judge was in error in refusing to vacate the order of arrest made in the cause.

CASE NO. 4

Wilson v. Moline. 229 Minn. 164, 38 N.W. (2d) 201 (1949)

LORING, CH.J. This is an action for the accounting of profits derived from a partnership formed to raise turkeys during 1945 near Isanti, Minnesota. The trial was before the court, which concluded that plaintiff had been overpaid in the sum of $198.50. Plaintiff appeals from an order denying his motion for new trial.

May 8, 1945, the parties entered into a written partnership agreement for the raising of turkeys, under which plaintiff, A. J. Wilson, contributed $5,000 to apply on the purchase of baby turkeys and other expenses. Clinton Moline, defendant, agreed to furnish grounds, buildings, and equipment for the raising of approximately 12,000 turkeys. It was agreed that Wilson was to have a drawing account of $130 a month; that the partnership accounts were to be kept accessible to the parties; and that the partnership was to terminate at the end of the season of 1945, whereupon Wilson was to be reimbursed for the sum of $5,000 advanced by him and to receive all the profits from the sale of one-fourth of all turkeys raised and marketed by the partnership during the 1945 season "as shown on the account books of this partnership." It was further provided that upon receipt of the sum of $5,000 and profits by Wilson "this partnership shall be wholly terminated."

Some 10,711 turkeys were raised and marketed. At the close of the 1945 season, $5,000 was paid to Wilson, and, in addition to the monthly drawing account, the sum of $2,378.86 was paid on account of the profits of the partnership. In his complaint, plaintiff alleged that his interest and share in the profits from the partnership greatly exceeded the sum of $2,378.86. He further alleged that the books of the partnership were kept entirely by Moline, to which Wilson was not given complete access for examination, and that there was no accounting of the partnership between the parties.

It appears that Wilson was in charge of the operation of the farm in so far as the feeding, raising, and care of the turkeys was concerned. Moline was in entire charge of the account books and finances of the partnership. Moline also operated another turkey farm and a separate company under the style of Moline Feed Company, which sold turkey feed, commercial mash, corn, and oats. The partnership "books" were kept in the office of the feed business at Isanti, Minnesota, and not at the farm. The "records" of the partnership were kept in the same account book as Moline kept the records for a different turkey farm partnership, called the Berglof partnership, the feed business, and his personal affairs. This account book was a mere check register. It made no distinction between transactions for maintenance of buildings between the two turkey partnerships nor the amounts of feed allocated thereto. The chief supporting vouchers were unsigned weight slips and a few bills of lading for carload lots of feed. It appeared that when the season was ended in October 1945 the books of the partnership were not in a current condition. . . .

Defendant was selling the same commercial mash, corn, oats and grain in a retail feed business to other customers than the partnerships. He would haul commercial mash from the Wilson partnership farm in very substantial amounts to other places in a large area around Isanti. He testified that he did this on a half dozen occasions. There was no record of these occasions, of how many sacks were taken, or of what was done with the accounting charged to the farm in connection with those sacks. . . .

The strongest reasons why defendant should not be permitted to profit from any irregularities or inaccuracies in his accounting system are based on the fiduciary relations which Moline undertook by his partnership contract with Wilson. The situation is not that of a vendor of feed establishing his claim to recover for goods sold and delivered. Here, a fiduciary has mingled the trust res with his own property, and, indeed, with property of a business adverse to the partnership.

Under the facts of the case at bar, defendant was deriving profits from the sale of feed to the turkey-raising partnership, at least to the extent that it was not being delivered to the Wilson-Moline farm and was being used in the feed company business or for the Berglof-Moline partnership. Plaintiff is entitled to an accurate account. Defendant cannot produce such an account. He has kept inadequate books. The burden of proof is on defendant, as trustee, to show that he is entitled to the credits he claims for the feed sold by his personal feed business to the partnership.

Reversed and new trial granted consistent with the rule set forth in this opinion.

CASE NO. 5

Woodward-Holmes Co. v. Nudd. 58 Minn. 236, 59 N.W. 1010 (1894)

MITCHELL, J. The effect of the findings of the trial court is that the real estate which is the subject of this action was formerly the property of a manufacturing copartnership composed of defendant's husband and one Holmes, having been purchased, paid for, and used by the firm as a site for its manufacturing plant, the title being taken in the individual names of the partners; that, in an action brought by one partner against his copartner to dissolve the partnership and wind up its affairs, the property was ordered sold as one parcel, the proceeds to be applied in payment of the firm debts, and the surplus, if any, divided between the partners according to their respective rights; that at such sale it was sold to plaintiff's grantor for an amount somewhat in excess of the sum required to pay the debts of the firm; that this surplus was distributed between the partners, no part of it being paid to defendant; that defendant was not a party to the action, and has never joined in any conveyance of the property. The defendant, as wife of one of the partners, claimed an inchoate interest in an undivided half of the premises, and this action was brought to determine this adverse claim.

It is now held with practical unanimity by the American courts that, if partnership capital be invested in land for the benefit of the company, all the incidents attached to it which belong to any other stock, so far as consistent with the statute of frauds and the technical rules of conveyancing, and that it will be treated as personal estate until it has performed all its functions to the partnership, and thereby ceases to be any longer partnership property, and until then it is not subject to either dower or inheritance, but that, after all the purposes of the partnership have been thus accomplished, whatever land remains in specie will be regarded as real estate. The question is, at what precise moment is it reconverted into real estate, or, to speak more accurately, does it resume all the attributes and incidents of real property? We think the answer is, the moment the partnership is terminated and wound up by judgment or agreement, and it is determined that it no longer forms a part of the partnership stock, and is not required for its purposes. When a partnership is dissolved, and its affairs wound up and completely ended, and any land remains in specie, unconverted, this must be deemed a determination that it is no longer a part of the copartnership stock, and an election to hold it thereafter, individually, as real estate. During the continuance of the partnership the partners can convey or mortgage it, in the course of their business, whenever they see fit, without their wives joining in the conveyance or mortgage, and the wives would have no dower or other interest in it. This is one of the very objects of treating partnership real estate as personal property; for otherwise the business of the firm might be stopped, and the partners unable to realize on the assets of the firm, by reason of the wife of one of them refusing to join in the conveyance or mortgage. They have the same power of disposition over it for the purposes of a dissolution of the partnership, the payment of its debts, and the distribution or division of the capital among themselves; for until that is done the property has not fulfilled its functions as personalty, or ceased to be partnership property. And what the partners may thus do voluntarily the court may do for them, in an action brought to dissolve the partnership and wind up its affairs. As the defendant was not a party to the former action, she is, of course, not estopped by it, nor is it evidence against her of anything except of the fact of its own rendition. But the material fact remains that in the process of the dissolution of the firm, and the winding up of its affairs, in an action for that purpose, the land was sold and converted into money, and the money distributed among the creditors and partners according to law. Upon these facts, under the rules already announced, the land in the hands of the purchaser is not subject to any inchoate interest of the wives of the partners. The error which lies at the foundation of the whole argument of defendants' counsel is in the assumption that, at the time of the purchase of this property, it became the individual real estate of the husband, and that the inchoate right of the wife under the statute immediately attached, subject only to a lien for the payment of partnership debts. This is not correct, and none of the authorities that we have found so hold. The fact is that only so much of it becomes the individual real estate of the partner as remains in specie, unconverted, after all the purposes of the partnership have been entirely fulfilled, and it is only to such of it that any inchoate interest of the wife ever attaches. If counsel's contention is correct the partners could never, even during the active life of the copartnership, convey perfect title to partnership land without their wives joining, except to the extent actually necessary to pay existing debts of the firm. This would practically involve, in every case where one of the wives refused to join in a conveyance, the necessity of a suit to which she is made a party, in order to determine whether the sale was necessary to pay debts. Any such rule would hamper the business of the firm to an extent that might practically defeat the purposes of the partnership. . . .

Upon the facts found, judgment ought to have been ordered in favor of the plaintiff, ...

CASE NO. 6

Williams v. Pedersen. 47 Wash. 472, 92 Pac. 287 (1907)

HADLEY, CH.J., delivered the opinion of the court:

This is an action between partners for an accounting, settlement, and dissolution. . . .

It is contended that the court erred in its findings. This contention arises chiefly from appellant's claim that respondent was away much of the time while the Pedersen and Williams logs were being cut, and appellant urges that respondent is not entitled to share in logs cut while he was away. The evidence sharply conflicts as to the amount of time respondent was absent in person. His testimony was to the effect that he was there practically all the time, and that when he was away his brother worked in his place. Nothing in the record indicates that the court should not have accepted respondent's testimony as true, and, if true, he reasonably did his share of the work, or caused it to be done. The partnership had not been dissolved, and its work continued, even under appellant's theory, at such times as respondent was present and assisted therein. Appellant seems, however, to adopt the view that the partnership work was so intermittently done that it ceased when respondent was away, and that appellant then cut logs at the same place on his own account, and not that of the partnership. We think the evidence does not justify the appellant's position. The partnership undertook to cut the timber, and there had been no agreed cessation of its work as such. The partnership operations therefore continued, although respondent was for a time away from the work. Even if it be true that appellant did the greater amount of work about the firm's business, still no agreement between the partners is shown that one was to receive a greater share of the partnership earnings for his services by reason of the absence of the other. In the absence of such an agreement, one partner is not entitled to recover from the other by reason of inequality of services. In Wisner v. Field, 11 N.D. 257, 91 N.W. 67, the court said:

> "We find no case in which it has been held that a mere inequality of services by partners is alone ground for compensating the one doing the greater part of the work, in the absence of an agreement, express or implied." . . .

There are instances where the course of dealing of the partners is such, and also where the services rendered are of such an extraordinary character, that the law implies a contract to pay one partner for extra services; but such facts are not established by the evidence here. The findings are sustained by the evidence in the record, and we see no reason for disturbing them.

The judgment is affirmed.

CASE NO. 7

Glenn v. Weill. 319 Pa. 380, 179 Atl. 563 (1935)

KEPHART, J. D. Gleich & Co., a partnership formed April 14, 1928, was composed of Glenn, Weill, and Gleich, Prior to that date, Gleich was the sole proprietor of the business. By the terms of the partnership agreement Gleich sold to Glenn and Weill each a "one-third interest in said business." Gleich was to receive a salary of $6,000 a year, and Weill a salary of $5,000 a year, while Glenn, who was not required to give his time to the business, was to receive $2,500 a year against his share of the net profits. The partnership was dissolved on December 31, 1931, by the expulsion of Glenn and Weill from the partnership place of business. As stated by the court below, Gleich "forced his partners out of the business." Thereupon Glenn filed a bill for an accounting, and the court below, after hearing, directed an account to be filed.

In the account filed, each of the partners was credited with a one-third interest, or $12,207.59, in the original capital of the concern—$36,622.77. Glenn filed exceptions to the account, of which only the fifth, which was directed to this set-up, was sustained. The court below found this feature of the account to be improper, and ordered that the capital should be allocated according to the amounts contributed by the various partners: Gleich $1,622.77, Glenn $25,000, and Weill $10,000. The result of this adjudication is that Gleich owes the partnership some $14,000 instead of $3,800 as initially stated, that there is due to Glenn approximately $9,000 instead of some $3,600 due from him, and that there is owed Weill approximately $5,000 instead of $7,000. From the final decree and account filed thereunder, Gleich takes this appeal.

The only question before us is whether the capital contributed should be distributed in dissolution equally or in proportion to the amounts contributed by each partner. The agreement of partnership contains nothing as to capital contributions, but appellee averred in his bill that $35,000 of the initial capital shown on the partnership books was made up of $25,000 paid in by Glenn and $10,000 paid in by Weill. Gleich did not deny this averment, and the court below was amply warranted in finding that Gleich's contention, that the amounts put in the business by the other two partners were not contributions to the joint capital but were payments for an interest in his business, was without merit. The court states:

> "It was always carried on the books as partnership capital and appears in the account as partnership capital, and we find as a fact that the sum of Thirty-Five Thousand Dollars was capital contributed to the partnership property by Glenn and Weill."

Under these circumstances, the one-third interest in the business mentioned in the agreement was undoubtedly a one-third interest in the profits and losses, and in any surplus after paying all the debts.

It is firmly settled that upon dissolution of a partnership the assets are to be devoted, after the payment of debts, to the repayment to the partners of their contributions to the firm capital. . . .

From the above discussion, it necessarily follows that where, as here, the books of a partnership show an unequal contribution of capital and there is nothing in the partnership agreement to show that the capital should not be returned in proportion to the amounts contributed, that return will be governed by the ordinary rule of law, which is that the distribution of capital upon dissolution of a partnership is in the same proportion in which such capital was furnished.

The decree of the court below is affirmed at the cost of the appellant.

Review Questions

1. What is meant by the statement that a partnership is a fiduciary relationship?
2. Does the majority rule apply to all partnership matters?
3. What does a partner's right to an accounting consist of?
4. Construct a fact situation under which a partner would be entitled to an accounting without dissolution.
5. Construct a fact situation under which a partner would have the right of reimbursement.
6. Does a partner have a right to recover compensation for his services to the partnership if no such provision is contained in the partnership agreement?
7. Does a partner have the right to be compensated for extraordinary services to the partnership?
8. What is the nature of a partner's ownership interest in the partnership property?
9. Upon the death of a partner, do his heirs acquire an interest in the partnership property?
10. What is meant by saying that "a partner's interest in the partnership is not subject to dower"?
11. Characterize a partner's beneficial interest in the partnership.
12. Does a transfer of a partner's beneficial interest in the partnership cause a dissolution of the partnership?
13. What determines the proportion in which partners share in the profits and in the losses?
14. In what proportions will partners share in partnership surplus?
15. Are the capital contributions of partners a partnership liability?

Problems for Discussion

1. Codding and Potdorf were associated as partners. Strayer agreed to pay Codding 10 per cent commission upon all goods purchased by the partnership from the Novelty Manufacturing Co. During the course of the year, Codding collected $2,342.80 in commissions, which fact was not known to Potdorf. When Potdorf discovered this fact, he brought action for the purpose of having the commissions declared as being partnership profits. Did he succeed?
2. A, B, and C were members of a profitable partnership. While A was away, recovering from a nervous breakdown, B and C sold the business, including the good will. Can A have the transaction set aside?
3. A, B, and C are members of a partnership organized for the purpose of operating a retail sales establishment. A and B propose that the partnership venture into the wholesale field, for which the partnership has sufficient capital. Is C subject to the will of the majority?
4. This is a bill in equity by Whitcomb to compel contribution by his former copartners to the losses incurred by the partnership. The articles of partnership provided:

   "J. C. Converse to contribute $25,000; to receive interest on the same at

7 per cent, and devote such time as he may be able to give; to receive 25 per cent of net profits.

"J. M. Whitcomb to contribute $50,000, receive 7 per cent interest on the same; to give all his time to the business, and receive 25 per cent of the net profits.

"E. R. Blagden to contribute all his time to the business, and receive 25 per cent of the net profits.

"Walter Stanton to contribute all his time to the business, and receive 25 per cent of the net profits."

Upon termination and settlement of the firm by mutual consent, a loss of about $25,000 was disclosed. Blagden is insolvent. Decide. (*Whitcomb* v. *Converse,* 119 Mass. 38)

5. X is associated with four other partners. X contributed $50,000 and the other partners $25,000 each. X contends that this fact alone entitles him to two votes in deciding partnership policy. Decide.
6. The partnership agreement between A and B provided that B was to keep accounts and books. B kept the books in such a fashion that the true state of affairs could not be determined without his explanations. As a result, differences arose between A and B as to the amount of the partnership profits. Would this entitle A to an accounting without dissolution?
7. Kiner was a surviving partner and he spent considerable time in winding up the affairs of the partnership. He filed a bill against the partnership for compensation for the service he had rendered. Decide.
8. Jim's partner, Joe, entered a dancing marathon over the protests of Jim. As a result, the whole burden of conducting their business fell upon Jim's shoulders for a period of three weeks. Can Jim collect compensation for this extraordinary service?
9. Suppose that a partner contributes the use of a $50,000 building to the partnership enterprise, retaining title to the building in himself. Would destruction of the building be a partnership loss toward which the other partners would be required to contribute?
10. This is a bill in equity in which the plaintiffs claim an interest in letters patent issued to the defendant John R. Whittemore for inventions made by him. When the inventions were made and the letters patent issued, the parties were copartners in the business of manufacturing and selling agricultural implements, and in the foundry business, and the patents were for improvements in agricultural implements. The inventing and patenting of new and improved machines was no part of the business of manufacturing and selling them, and did not come within the scope of the partnership business. By the articles of copartnership, each partner was to give his time to the business of the firm and not to engage in any other speculation or business in his own name and on his own account to the detriment of the firm; Whittemore used his time, and labor and materials belonging to the firm, in making improvements in machines manufactured and sold by it. Decide. (*Belcher* v. *Whittemore,* 134 Mass. 330)
11. A owns a one-fourth interest in a partnership that by the partnership agreement is to continue for a ten-year period. A sells his interest in the partner-

ship to B before the expiration of the ten-year period. The acquisition of this interest entitles B to what rights?

12. A and B were partners in the operation of a farm. A was indebted to X, who obtained a judgment against A. Thereupon, a levy was made upon certain personal property belonging to the partnership for the purpose of satisfying A's personal obligation. Can the partnership prevent the sheriff from making a sale of this property?
13. X and Y, partners, had contributed $20,000 and $10,000 respectively to the partnership. The partnership was declared bankrupt and all of the partnership assets were taken to satisfy its creditors. What adjustment will be made between X and Y?
14. Under a partnership agreement, A contributed $50,000; B, $25,000; and C, his skill and services. It was agreed that profits were to be shared equally, but nothing was said as to losses. An accounting upon dissolution revealed that the operation of the partnership had resulted in a $30,000 loss, leaving $45,000 of the original capital for distribution. How will A, B, and C fare upon the final settlement?

36 BUSINESS ORGANIZATIONS:

DISSOLUTION AND TERMINATION OF PARTNERSHIP

► I. DISSOLUTION DISTINGUISHED

The uncertainty of a continued existence is one of the serious disadvantages attributed to the partnership form of business organization. A partnership has far more possibilities of dissolution and possible consequent termination as a going concern than does any other form of business unit.

A dissolution is a disruption of the contractual relationship existing between the partners. When for any reason the partners cease to be associated in the carrying on of the business enterprise, a dissolution has taken place. A dissolution is of itself not a termination of the partnership but rather the basis upon which the partnership may be brought to a conclusion as a business enterprise. After a dissolution has transpired, to effect a termination requires the additional steps of winding up the firm's affairs—including liquidation of its assets—and distribution of the available funds to the firm's creditors and the partners. Commonly, after a dissolution, some of the partners will make settlement with the disassociating partner or partners, or with those who represent their interests, while as a new firm they will continue the business operations without disruption.

► II. CAUSES OF DISSOLUTION

A termination of the contractual relationship existing between partners is brought about either (1) by operation of the partnership agreement, (2) by act of one, some, or all partners, (3) by operation of law, or (4) by court decree.

A. BY OPERATION OF PARTNERSHIP AGREEMENT

1. *Expiration of Fixed or Determinable Term*

The partnership agreement may either expressly or impliedly fix the period of time for which the partnership enterprise is to endure. Where the agreement expressly provides for a fixed or determinable period of time for which the business is to be carried on, the expiration of such period will effect a dissolution of the partnership.

a. Expiration of Implied Term. Many partnerships are organized for the accomplishment of a specified purpose. In such instances it is logically implied that the term of the partnership will be that time which is necessary fully to complete the business venture. Consequently the partnership ceases to exist when the specified undertaking has been fully accomplished. Other circumstances may imply the intent of the partners to continue the partnership for a fixed or determinable period of time. To illustrate:

In *Zimmerman* v. *Harding,* 227 U.S. 489, the court held that a partnership for the operation of a leased hotel was by implication to continue for the period of the lease.

B. BY ACT OF PARTNERS

1. *Under Partnership at Will*

A partnership at will exists if no fixed term has been agreed upon and a term cannot be implied from the nature of the undertaking. It is the right of every partner to terminate such a partnership whenever he so chooses, either for arbitrary reasons or for no reasons at all. This is the general rule and is embodied in Section 31 of the Uniform Partnership Act. All a partner needs to do to effect a dissolution is to notify his copartners of his withdrawal. In the event that he cannot arrive at an amicable financial settlement with his copartners, he may resort to his equitable remedy of an accounting.

2. *In Breach of Partnership Agreement*

Section 21(2) of the Uniform Act reads:

> "Dissolution is caused in contravention of the agreement between the partners . . . by the express will of any partner at any time."

While this is not the universal rule, it is supported by the weight of authority. The rule is a recognition of a contracting party's power arbitrarily and effectively to break the contract, where the remedy of specific performance or injunction is not available. Therefore, in violation of the contract terms, a partner may withdraw from the partnership and effect a dissolution. The courts will not force the continuation of a relationship as personal as that obtaining between partners.

Of course, where a partner terminates the relationship without cause and in violation of the partnership agreement, he subjects himself to an action for any damages resulting to his copartners. Although he has the power to break the contract, it is in violation of his legal duty to do so. To illustrate:

In *McCollum* v. *McCollum,* (Tex.) 67 S.W. (2d) 1055, the plaintiff, upon receiving notice that he was no longer a member of the partnership, brought an action to obtain a temporary mandatory injunction to restore him to his position as a partner. The court in denying him the injunction said:

> "This injunction, in effect, attempts to prevent the dissolution of a partnership. Under the law a partnership calling for the personal services of the partners can always be dissolved, even though it constitutes a breach of contract. The right to dissolve may not exist but the power to dissolve always exists; there may be a suit for damages for the breach, but the power to dissolve nevertheless exists. There can be no such thing as an indissoluble partnership."

The partnership agreement may contain a provision that gives a partner the right to terminate the relationship upon the happening of a certain event, or it may give him the right to do so arbitrarily.

3. *By Mutual Agreement*

As is true of all contracts, a partnership agreement, regardless of any provisions it contains, may be terminated by the mutual consent of the contracting parties. A mutual rescission need not be expressed in so many words but may be implied from the conduct of the partners. The sale of all partnership property with the consent of all partners may readily lead to the conclusion that the termination of the partnership was intended.

4. *Expulsion of Partner*

Section 31(1*d*) of the Uniform Act makes provision that, in accordance with the terms of an agreement between the partners, an expulsion of a partner from the business will cause a dissolution. However, the right of expulsion must have been exercised in good faith and not merely for the purpose of ridding the firm of the partner.

C. BY OPERATION OF LAW

As a matter of law, the happening of certain events is held to effect the dissolution of a partnership. Among them are the following:

1. *Death of Any Partner*

The death of a partner disrupts the personal relationship that the law regards as vital to the continuation of the partnership.

> "The personal qualities of each member of a firm enter largely into the inducements which lead parties to form a copartnership; and if the abilities and skill, or the character and credit, of any one are withdrawn, the contract between them is terminated and the copartnership is dissolved." *Martlett* v. *Jackman,* 3 Allen (Mass.) 287

This does not mean that of necessity the business enterprise must be liquidated upon the decease of one of the partners. As a matter of fact, the surviving partners may discharge the interest of the deceased partner to his legal representatives and continue the business undertaking as a new firm. It is also possible that the continuity of the business may be preserved by admitting as new partners the person or persons to whom the interest of the deceased partner passes. In realization of the undesirability of having the business disrupted by death, partners at times will make provision designed to forestall an immediate liquidation.[1]

The partnership agreement may contain a provision that the partnership is not to dissolve upon the death of one of its members. For example, the agreement may provide for a continuation of the business for the period of time originally contemplated by the partners or for a specified period after the date of death. Where such is provided, it is contemplated that the representatives or heirs would occupy

1 Hale v. Wilmarth, p. 902.

the position of the deceased partner. Such an agreement is not only binding upon the surviving partners, but is also a contractual obligation surviving to the deceased partner's estate. The failure of the decedent's legal representative or heirs to carry out the legal obligation not to liquidate the business may subject them to damages for breach of contract.

A contractual provision to the effect that the partnership business *shall* continue is to be distinguished from an agreement that the partnership business *may* continue by the admission of the legal representatives, heirs, or assigns of the deceased partner. The latter type of agreement is binding neither upon the surviving partners nor upon those to whom the deceased partner's interest has passed; the continuation of the partnership business is entirely at their option.

Another method by which the continuation of the partnership business can be assured after the death of a partner is to provide that the deceased partner's interest is to remain in the employ of the partnership for a fixed period of time, or to provide that such interest is to be paid out in installments over a period of time. Such a provision in effect creates a new partnership, consisting of the surviving partners. The estate of the deceased partner occupies the position of a creditor to the new firm and has no liability to new creditors. However, the estate retains its liability to the creditors of the old firm, who also become creditors of the new firm.

2. *Bankruptcy*

Bankruptcy is that unfortunate state of affairs which exists when a person has been given judicial recognition of his inability fully to meet his obligations. One of the legal consequences of such a judicial pronouncement is to vest control over the bankrupt's property in the offices of the court for the purposes of liquidation and distribution to the bankrupt's creditors. Consequently, the bankruptcy of a partnership or that of one or more partners will cause a dissolution of the partnership. It is the adjudication of bankruptcy and not the insolvency that causes the dissolution.

3. *Illegality*

When the continuation of the partnership venture becomes contrary to statutory declaration or public policy, as a matter of law, the partnership is regarded as dissolved. A law prohibiting the sale of certain commodities would effect the dissolution of all partnerships dealing exclusively in such commodities. The adoption of the Eighteenth Amendment to the Federal Constitution, which provided for liquor prohibition, is a case in point.

A law partnership was declared dissolved when one of the members suffered the good fortune of being the public's choice for judge. The continuation of the partnership under the circumstances would not have been in the best interest of society. Public policy requires the removal of even the slightest possibility of abuse of a public office.

D. BY COURT DECREE

A court of equity has jurisdiction to decree the dissolution of a partnership under circumstances that would make its continuation unjust and inequitable. Obviously, no exact limits of a court's rights to exercise this function can be established. Some of the recognized causes for which a court of equity will, upon application, grant an order of dissolution follow.

1. *Incapacity of Partner*

Whenever a partner becomes incapacitated to such an extent as to prevent him from substantially discharging his duties as contemplated by the partnership agreement, dissolution will be decreed. The incapacity must be of more than a temporary character. It must be of such a nature as to indicate reasonably that a recovery cannot be effected in time to allow the partner to substantially discharge his obligations to the firm. For example, it was held that an illness from which the partner was recovering at the time of the hearing was not sufficient cause for a dissolution.

Mental impairment of a partner may warrant a dissolution, and, almost without exception, a decree of dissolution will be granted upon the basis of a judicial pronouncement of insanity. It is the general rule, however, that a finding of insanity will not of itself bring about a dissolution of the partnership, but it will serve as the basis upon which a decree of dissolution will be made available.

2. *Misconduct of Partner*

A partner's conduct that seriously interferes with or prevents the accomplishing of partnership purposes or conduct that is prejudicial or harmful to the copartners will serve as cause for a dissolution by court decree. A dissolution would unquestionably be warranted by such practices as the willful and persistent violation of the partnership agreement, the misappropriation of partnership property or funds, or deceit in respect to partnership affairs. A partner's personal conduct and affairs, if below the accepted standards of the community, may be very prejudicial or injurious to the partnership. To illustrate:

(1) In *Nichols* v. *Mumford,* 213 Mich. 201, plaintiff and defendant were engaged as partners in feeding livestock for market. The court granted a dissolution of the partnership upon the basis of the defendant's dishonesty in representing to the plaintiff that cattle were being shipped to Buffalo when in fact the defendant was shipping them to Chicago.

(2) In *Abbot* v. *Johnson,* 32 N.H. 9, it was said that a partnership may be dissolved where one partner in violation of the partnership agreement sold spiritous liquors.

(3) In *Young* v. *McKenney,* 197 Ky. 768, the court said, "A partner's failure or refusal to comply with the terms of the partnership agreement as to contributing capital or services . . . is one ground for dissolution."

(4) In *Cottle* v. *Leitch,* 35 Cal. 434, it was held that a partnership could be dis-

solved because one partner made false entries in the partnership books, thus depriving his copartners of their share of the profits.

3. *Dissension among Partners*

Like all personal relationships, the personal contacts of partners at times are productive of misunderstandings and disagreements. Fortunately these are usually of a temporary and fleeting character. However, when they have been indulged in to such an extent as to have destroyed the mutual confidence requisite to the proper functioning of a partnership enterprise, equity will grant dissolution. Equitable relief is contingent upon a showing that the circumstances render a continuation of the partnership impracticable or impossible.[2]

> "It is not for every act of misconduct on the part of one partner that a court of equity . . . will dissolve the partnership and close up the affairs of the company. The court will require a strong case to be made, and it is laid down . . . that a court has no jurisdiction to make a separation between partners for trifling causes or temporary grievances involving no permanent mischiefs. 3 Kent, 60." *Cash* v. *Earnshaw,* 66 Ill. 402

> "Of course where there are constant quarrels, irreconcilable differences and personal ill-will which makes cooperation impossible, equity will administer relief." *Josephthal* v. *Gold,* 171 N.Y.S. 1041

4. *Business Unprofitable*

A partnership seeks to make profits, and when its business becomes unprofitable there is no reason for its continuation. Consequently, if it can be shown that the partnership enterprise is unprofitable and can be carried on only at a loss, equity will lend its aid to bring the business to a conclusion. The Uniform Partnership Act, Section 32, provides to this effect. To illustrate:

In *Thomson* v. *Langton,* 51 Cal. App. 142, dissolution of the partnership was granted because of a fire loss in excess of one half of the partnership assets. It was apparent that the business could be conducted only at a loss unless additional capital was obtained. The court said:

> "A partner cannot be forced to make a contribution of additional capital, and it necessarily follows that he could not be compelled to join in raising money by borrowing. . . ."

5. *Procedure*

Upon granting an order of dissolution, the court ordinarily will appoint a receiver to assume control over the partnership assets. However, this step will be taken only if it appears necessary as a protection of the interests of the partners. By decreeing the dissolution of a partnership, a court assumes jurisdiction over the accounting and final settlement of the firm's affairs.

---

2 Potter v. Brown, p. 903.

▶ III. STATUS OF PARTNERSHIP AND PARTNERS AFTER DISSOLUTION

A. LIMITED EXISTENCE OF PARTNERSHIP

Dissolution of a partnership is not synonymous with complete cessation of all partnership affairs. Although dissolution actually terminates a partnership, its continued existence is recognized for limited purposes. After dissolution it is necessary that numerous acts be performed with a view to a final settlement of the firm's affairs: (1) Existing contractual obligations must be discharged; (2) satisfaction must be obtained on partnership claims against others; and (3) the firm's debts must be paid. A conversion of the firm's assets into cash is usually brought about in order to pay creditors and to distribute the balance, if any, among the partners or their representatives.[3]

1. *Extent of Partners' Authority*

The dissolution of a partnership terminates the general agency relationship existing between the partners. A partner or certain of the partners may remain in authority for the purposes above indicated, and no partner has authority to act for the partnership after its dissolution for any other purposes. Subject to qualifications that will be subsequently made, it can be said that after dissolution an unauthorized act by a partner is not binding upon the other partners. The responsibility for the act rests entirely with the partner who failed to take heed of the revocation of his general authority by the dissolution.

> "The legal rule is fixed on this subject. If the survivors of a partnership carry on the concern, and enter into new transactions with the partnership funds, they do so at their own peril, and the representative of the deceased (partner) may elect to call on them for the capital, with a share of the profits, or with interest. If no profits are made, or even if a loss is incurred, they must be charged with interest on the funds they use, and the whole loss will be theirs." *Brown's Appeal,* 89 Pa. 139

2. *Right of Liquidation*

In the event of a dissolution by the death, bankruptcy, or wrongful act of one of the partners, the right to extinguish the dying partnership embers rests with the remaining partner or partners.[4] Where the dissolution resulted from other causes, all partners have the right to participate equally in the winding-up process. Of course, the partners can agree otherwise; they may, for example, provide in the partnership articles or at the time of dissolution that one of the partners shall have the sole right of bringing the partnership affairs to an end.

In some states, the right of liquidation is controlled by statute. For example, in the State of Washington it is provided that the liquidation of the partnership shall be accomplished by an administrator appointed by the court. The surviving

[3] Froess v. Froess, p. 905.

[4] In re Vitelli's Estate, p. 906.

partner or partners are given five days within which to apply for the position of administrator.

B. PARTNERSHIP LIABILITY FOR UNAUTHORIZED ACTS SUBSEQUENT TO DISSOLUTION

1. *Termination of Liability Dependent upon Notice*

Although the dissolution of a partnership serves as a revocation of the partners' general authority as agents, it does not follow that the partners will be automatically absolved of possible future liability for acts not essential to the winding-up process. As to third persons, it is presumed that the partnership continues as a going concern until they have notice or are charged by law with notice to the contrary. Until such has taken place, the partnership stands responsible for the acts of its partners the same as though there had been no dissolution.[5] The term *notice* as above used does not mean in any sense of the word that third parties must have actual knowledge of the dissolution imparted to them. It means, rather, that a certain factual situation exists—such as a dissolution because of illegality—or that certain steps have been taken after which the partners can no longer be held liable. The legal requirements of notice follow.

a. Notice as a Matter of Law. In some instances the partners are not required to take any active steps in making known the dissolution of the firm. It is the common law rule that, where a dissolution has been effected by operation of law or by court decree, notice of such is attributed to third parties. A dissolution by operation of law and court decree is said to be open, notorious, and public, because everyone is bound to take notice. It should be noted that in many instances this common law rule has been modified by statute, specifically by the Uniform Act. The latter requires that notice of dissolution be given by the partners or their legal representatives in all instances except as provided by Section 35(3):

> "The partnership is in no case bound by any act of a partner after dissolution (a) where the partnership is dissolved because it is unlawful to carry on the business . . . or (b) where the partner has become bankrupt. . . ."

b. Notice by Acts of Partner or Partners. Two steps are required in those instances in which the burden of making known the dissolution of the partnership falls upon the partners themselves if they wish to avoid further liability.

(1) It is necessary to give actual notice to all persons who have had credit dealings with the partnership.

(2) For the benefit of those who have had no credit dealings with the partnership but who have knowledge of its existence, it is necessary to make known publicly the fact of dissolution.

Actual Notice. As a general rule, it is required that actual or personal notice of dissolution need be given only to those who have had business transactions involving the extension of credit with the firm in the past. This rule is incorporated in the Uniform Partnership Act in Section 35, which reads:

[5] Mulkey v. Anglin, p. 907.

"(1) After dissolution a partner can bind the partnership. . . . (*b*) By any transaction which would bind the partnership if dissolution had not taken place, provided the other party to the transaction

(1) Had extended credit to the partnership prior to dissolution and had no knowledge or notice of the dissolution."

In some jurisdictions it has been held that all persons who have had past dealings with the firm are entitled to actual notice, regardless of whether credit was involved. The requirements of notice in the particular jurisdiction should be ascertained.

No particular mode of giving notice is required. The imparting of actual knowledge of the dissolution is, of course, most certain when accomplished by a written notice, which will serve as evidence. Under the Uniform Act it seems that notice can be less than actual notice; Section 3(2) reads:

"A person has 'notice' of a fact within the meaning of this Act when the person who claims the benefit of the notice (a) states the fact to such person, or (b) delivers through the mail, or by other means of communication, a written statement of the fact to such person or to a proper person at his place of business or residence."

Public Notice. While the courts have recognized various methods of giving constructive notice, the generally recognized mode is by newspaper advertising. The provision made in Section 35 of the Uniform Act is for advertisement.

". . . in a newspaper of general circulation in the place at which the partnership business was regularly carried on, and in the legal periodical, if any, designated by rule of court in such place or places for the publication of legal notices."

The need for giving notice of dissolution is of paramount importance to a partner who withdraws from a firm whose business will be continued. Unless the requirements of actual and public notice are met, a retiring partner may be held liable for the obligations of the new firm.[6]

C. LIABILITY OF INDIVIDUAL PARTNERS FOR ACTS AFTER DISSOLUTION

In the event that the partnership is held liable for acts subsequent to dissolution, it does not necessarily follow that such liability will be equally borne by the partners. The acting partner may be required to assume the entire responsibility for his act, or the burden may fall upon the partners equally.

1. *Under Common Law*

The common law rule seems to be that unless the acting partner has knowledge of the dissolution or is by law charged with notice of the dissolution, the liability for his act must be borne by the various partners. Therefore, if a partner acts for the partnership with knowledge of its dissolution or under circumstances where the law attributes such knowledge to him, he alone is held responsible and he has

[6] Marquette Cloak & Suit Co. v. Netter & Meyer, p. 908.

no right of contribution from the other partners. This means that in those instances where a dissolution is caused by operation of law and by court decree, the partners as well as the public generally are bound to take notice of that fact. For example, should a partner make a contractual commitment in ignorance of the death of one of his copartners, he alone would be bound.

2. *Under Legislative Enactment*

The above situation has been considerably changed by legislative enactment because of the obvious unfairness to the acting partner. The Uniform Partnership Act makes provision that, in some instances of dissolution by operation of law, the acting partner is not individually liable unless he had knowledge of the dissolution. Section 34 reads:

"Where the dissolution is caused by the act, death, or bankruptcy of a partner, each partner is liable to his copartners for his share of any liability created by any partner acting for the partnership as if the partnership had not been dissolved unless

(*a*) The dissolution being by act of any partner, the partner acting for the partnership had knowledge of the dissolution, or

(*b*) The dissolution being by the death or bankruptcy of a partner, the partner acting for the partnership had knowledge or notice of the death or bankruptcy."

D. DISTRIBUTION OF ASSETS

After the assets and liabilities of a dissolved partnership have been ascertained by an accounting, the next step is the distribution of the assets to the various claimants. This usually requires the conversion of the partnership property into cash. In any event, sufficient cash must be made available to discharge the obligations to partnership creditors. The partners may agree to a distribution of any surplus property *in specie,* and in some instances the courts have granted a partition of the property among the partners. Where such is impracticable the only solution is a conversion of the property into cash. Under Section 38 of the Uniform Partnership Act, a partner in a dissolved partnership is given the right to have the distribution made to the partners in cash rather than in kind.

1. *Order of Distribution*

The order of distribution of the partnership assets is as stated in Section 40 of the Uniform Act. It provides:

"(*b*) The liabilities of the partnership shall rank in order of payment, as follows:

I. Those owing to creditors other than partners,

II. Those owing to partners other than for capital and profits,

III. Those owing to partners in respect to capital,[7]

IV. Those owing to partners in respect to profits."

[7] Baum v. McBride, p. 910.

2. Contribution in Event of Insufficient Firm Assets

In the event that the partnership assets are insufficient to satisfy the partnership obligations, those partners who are solvent and are available will be called upon to contribute sufficient funds to discharge the liabilities. Contributions will be shared by the partners in the same proportion as they shared profits.

3. Firm Creditors against Personal Creditors—Marshaling of Assets

The doctrine of marshaling of assets is defined in the case of *Farmers' T. and T. Co.* v. *Kip*, 192 N.Y. 266, as being

> ". . . a rule which courts of equity sometimes invoke to compel a creditor who has the right to make his debt out of either of two funds, to resort to that one of them which will not interfere with or defeat the rights of another creditor who has recourse to only one of these funds."

Such a situation arises if the partnership assets are insufficient to discharge the partnership obligations and the assets of the individual partners are insufficient to discharge both the firm's creditors and the individual partners' creditors. It is the general rule that under such circumstances the firm's creditors have priority on partnership assets and the creditor of a partner has priority upon the property of the partner. To illustrate:

A partnership consisting of X and Y has assets of $50,000 and liabilities of $60,000. X has no personal creditors and no personal assets. Y has personal assets of $15,000 and claims against him by personal creditors to the extent of $12,000. Under the circumstances, the partnership creditors have the legal right to look to both the partnership assets and the assets of the individual partners for satisfaction, whereas the creditors of the individual partner can look only to the partner's assets. By applying the above rule, the creditors of Y can first look to Y's personal assets for satisfaction. The balance of Y's personal assets will then go to the satisfaction of the partnership creditors.

CASES

CASE NO. 1

Hale v. Wilmarth. 274 Mass. 186, 174 N.E. 232, 73 A.L.R. 980 (1931)

CARROLL, J., delivered the opinion of the court:

In this suit in equity the plaintiff, the executor of the will of Mrs. Blackinton, a deceased member of a partnership, seeks to have declared void a provision in the partnership agreement between the testatrix and the defendants, that upon her death her interest in the partnership should become the property of the defendants. . . .

The partnership agreement was duly executed in June, 1917. It provided that on the death of Mrs. Blackinton her interest in the firm should become the property of the defendants, that the profits of the business should be divided, one quarter payable to Mrs. Blackinton. She died in December, 1922. In her will she stated,

"I have purposely omitted Harry S. Wilmarth and Edwin Robinson Wilmarth (the defendants), as I have amply provided for them during my lifetime, by giving them an interest in the V. H. Blackinton & Co."

The main contention of the plaintiff is that the words in the partnership agreement, to the effect that on the death of Mrs. Blackinton her interest in the partnership should become the property of the defendants, are testamentary in nature and therefore inoperative and void under the statute of wills. . . . In Murphy v. Murphy, 217 Mass. 233, 104 N.E. 466, it was held that partnership agreements providing for the disposition of the interest of partners in partnership property after the death of one or more of the parties are frequent; that when fairly made without intent to evade the statute of wills they are valid and open to no objection. There are sound reasons, as stated in the opinion at page 236 of 217 Mass., 104 N.E. 466, 467,

"why a fair agreement entered into by partners, as to the disposition of partnership property in the event of the death of one or more of the partners, should be sustained. The terms of such an agreement made by those most familiar with the real character and value of the property are quite as likely to be just as an arrangement made after the decease."

. . . Mrs. Blackinton could provide, if she so desired, that her interest should be sold to the surviving partners at a fixed price, or contract for the disposition of her interest on her death, as stated in the partnership agreement. . . .

Mrs. Blackinton did not make a gift; she made a contract with the defendants, supported by a consideration. . . . As a part of this transaction, she was to transfer half her interest in the partnership and retain as long as she lived the remaining half, each partner reserving the right to terminate the partnership on thirty days' notice, and upon her death her interest in the business was to cease. The land was conveyed, the agreement was reduced to writing, and the stipulation inserted that upon the decease of Emma W. Blackinton her interest in the firm "shall become the property" of the defendants. This written agreement was under seal. By its terms the defendants were to bear three-fourths of any loss. The salary of each defendant was fixed at $1,500. Mrs. Blackinton was exempt from any attention to or care of the business. . . .

CASE NO. 2

Potter v. Brown. 328 Pa. 554, 195 Atl. 901, 118 A.L.R. 1415 (1938)

BARNES, J., delivered the opinion of the court:

The dissolution of a partnership is sought in this proceeding, where it is charged that the wrongful conduct of three of the ten members of the firm affects prejudicially the carrying on of its business and renders impracticable the continuance of the partnership.

The parties to this litigation have been conducting a general insurance business in Philadelphia since January 1, 1934, under the firm name of Henry W. Brown & Co. This long-established business has been a prosperous one. It was founded in 1871 by Henry W. Brown, the father of defendant Henry I. Brown, Sr., and has continued through various successor partnerships until the formation of the present firm in 1934.

The present partnership was formed in 1934, when the parties entered into a written agreement of partnership for a term of five years from

January 1, 1934. While the agreement expressly vests in all partners the right to be acquainted with, vote upon, and participate in firm business, it confers unlimited control over the business of the firm upon Henry I. Brown, Sr. The only right reserved to the majority in number of the firm members, rather than in interest, was to vote for admission of partners into the firm, or to terminate the interest of any partner other than Henry I. Brown, Sr.

From the record it appears that the net profits of the business after payment of partners' salaries (other than Henry I. Brown, Sr.) amounted to $80,484.52 for the year 1936, nor did the prosperity of the business decline after the institution of this proceeding, . . . The amounts received by the plaintiffs, as salaries, shares of profits, and bonuses from the business were substantial, . . . A portion of the payments to the plaintiffs consisting of personal bonuses was distributed by Henry I. Brown, Sr. out of his individual share of the profits. It was also Mr. Brown's practice to pay similar bonuses to employees of the business in recognition of meritorious services. . . .

The partnership differences giving rise to the present litigation concerned the proposed admission into the partnership of Charles H. Moore, who had been the accountant for the firm for several years. At the regular monthly partnership meeting held November 30, 1936, Henry I. Brown, Sr. proposed to his associates that new articles of partnership for a ten-year period be executed, giving to him complete control over partnership affairs without any limitation whatsoever, and that Moore be admitted into the firm as a partner. Both proposals were rejected by the plaintiffs. . . . The admission of Moore into the firm was defeated by a vote of seven to three, all seven plaintiffs voting against the motion, and the three defendants voting in its favor. The plaintiffs deny any animosity toward Moore, but assert that membership in the firm should be limited to insurance men.

Thereafter Mr. Brown called a special meeting of partners which was held on December 8, 1936, to reconsider the vote taken at the prior meeting, but again the result was the rejection by the same vote of the motion to admit Moore into the partnership. Then in order to compel his partners to submit to his wishes, the senior partner called another special meeting for the following day for the purpose of acting on a motion to reduce salaries. He introduced at this meeting and had passed a resolution to reduce the plaintiffs' salaries to an unspecified amount. On December 15, 1936, the plaintiffs received checks representing a 50 per centum reduction of the amount of the salaries then due them.

Subsequently Mr. Brown abandoned his intention of coercing his partners, and while the resolution of December 9, 1936, reducing salaries has not been formally rescinded, checks in the full amount of their salaries were delivered shortly thereafter to plaintiffs, and on each due date since that time they were given checks for all salary due. However, the plaintiffs refused to attend any meetings of the firm subsequent to December 9, 1936, upon the ground that Mr. Brown's conduct had breached the partnership agreement.

The present bill was filed by plaintiffs thereafter, praying for a decree of dissolution of the partnership and that they be granted the right to continue the business under the name of Henry W. Brown & Co. until the expiration date of the partnership agreement. The court below after hearing reached the conclusion that the defendants had willfully and persistently violated the partnership agreement and had so conducted themselves that it was not reasonably practicable to carry on the business in partnership with them. It entered an order dissolving the partnership, enjoining the three defendants from interfering with the affairs of the partnership, and decreeing that plaintiffs should continue the business during the remainder of the partnership period under the name of Henry W. Brown & Co.

Few, if any, reasons upon which ordinarily the dissolution of a partnership will be decreed are present in this case. There is neither allegation nor proof of fraudulent or dishonest practices and conduct upon which a dissolution would be granted. While it is well settled, as we said in Herman v. Pepper, 311 Pa. 104, at page 108, 166 Atl. 587, 588, that

> "the exclusion of one partner by another from the management of the partnership business or possession of the partnership property is undoubtedly ground for dissolution by a court of equity,"

we are of opinion that the plaintiffs have failed to show that they were denied their proper share of participation in the management of the business. The rights of the partners among themselves are regulated by the articles of partnership. Where, as in this case, the partnership articles provide for the vesting of exclusive control in one partner, such stipulation will be strictly enforced. . . .

The ill-advised and almost immediately abandoned attempt to reduce the salaries of the plaintiffs does not, in our opinion, under the particular circumstances, constitute such gross misconduct on the part of Brown, Sr. and the two partners who supported him, as to require their expulsion from the business. It is not apparent from the evidence that the occurrence has in any way interfered with the success of the partnership. The contention of the plaintiffs that the continuance of the partnership with the defendants is impractical is so manifestly inconsistent with the success of the business that the absence of merit therein is obvious. Differences and discord should be settled by the partners themselves by the application of mutual forbearance rather than by bills in equity for dissolution. Equity is not a referee of partnership quarrels. A going and prosperous business will not be dissolved merely because of friction among the partners; it will not interfere to determine which contending faction is more at fault.

The case is ruled by the principle as stated in Story on Partnership, § 287, where it is said: "It is proper to observe that it is not for every trivial departure from duty or violation of the articles of partnership, or for every trifling fault or misconduct that courts of equity will interfere and decree a dissolution. . . ."

. . . the decree of the court below is reversed, and it is ordered that the bill be dismissed.

CASE NO. 3

Froess v. Froess. 284 Pa. 369, 131 Atl. 276 (1925)

SADLER, J. Philip J. and Jacob Froess were equal partners, engaged in the sale of pianos and other musical instruments, and had been so jointly interested for many years. The first named died on January 29, 1920, and the copartner continued the business as survivor for some time thereafter. Letters of administration upon the estate of the decedent were granted to the widow, and negotiations looking to the payment of her husband's share of the assets, based on a valuation of the partnership property made immediately after his death, followed, but no satisfactory arrangement as to payment could be agreed on. No consent to the continuance of the firm business was given, but the same was managed by Jacob, who took exclusive possession of the assets. The firm's affairs were not settled within a reasonable time, and a bill was filed on August 3, 1921, asking for the appointment of a receiver, an accounting by the liquidating partner, and for a decree that the share found due be paid to plaintiff. After answer and hearing, a decree was entered on October 26, 1921, granting the relief prayed for. . . . During the pendency of the hearing . . . notice was given of the purpose of the administratrix to demand her husband's share of the assets, with interest on the value thereof from the time of dissolution, rather than a share of any profits, and subsequently a formal election to so claim was filed in writing. This . . . left undetermined only the value of the property as of the date of Philip's death.

. . . the total was fixed at $91,-977.71, each partner being entitled to one-half thereof, or $45,988.85. This finding of fact by the court is assigned for error, as is the final decree based thereon. . . .

. . . two months after the filing of conclusions of fact and law by the court and the entry of the decree . . . leave to amend the answer was asked, so as to set forth the legal claim that the value of the assets must be determined by the sale price at the time of actual liquidation, and not based on the audit or computation from the books as of the date of dissolution, which would result in a deduction from the amount found payable. The request was properly refused as too late. It may also be noted that it proposed to consider a calculation upon an improper basis. . . .

The interest of the decedent is fixed by a valuation as of the time of the dissolution, and all members of the firm are entitled to a part of the surplus of assets over the amount necessary to pay the creditors of the firm. . . .

"The legal rule is fixed on this subject. If the survivors of a partnership carry on the concern, and enter into new transactions with the partnership funds, they do so at their peril, and the representatives of the deceased may elect to call on them for the capital, with a share of the profits, or with interest. If no profits are made, or even if a loss is incurred, they must be charged with interest on the funds they use, and the whole loss will be theirs." Brown's Appeal, 89 Pa. 139, 147. . . .

Following the recognized rule, the right to so choose was expressly provided in the Uniform Partnership Act (§ 42); . . .

Decree is affirmed.

CASE NO. 4

In re Vitelli's Estate. 92 N.Y.S. (2d) 322 (1949)

HENDERSON, S. The sole issue to be determined in this accounting proceeding is whether or not the claim of the objectant, Theresa Borelli, should be allowed.

The decedent and one Francesco Borelli were partners in the jewelry business in New York City. Such partnership continued until the death of Francesco Borelli in Italy on July 18, 1937. Thereupon the decedent herein, the surviving partner, through an accountant, without a formal dissolution, determined that as of December 31, 1937, the sum of $1,229.22 was the interest of Francesco Borelli in the partnership. This sum was set up as a liability in favor of Francesco Borelli in the books of the business which the decedent continued to operate until his death on January 21, 1941.

No consent to the continuance of the firm business was given nor were there ever any negotiations looking to the payment of the interest of Francesco Borelli.

Thereafter, in the year 1945 the claimant, the wife of Francesco Borelli, arrived in the United States from Italy. Upon her arrival, Mrs. Borelli promptly communicated with the attorney for the estate of the decedent concerning the interest of Francesco Borelli in the partnership of Borelli and Vitelli.

On April 2, 1949, a formal claim for the sum of $1,229.22 was presented. Interest on said sum from December 31, 1937 is also requested.

In respect to this claim, it is conceded that the objectant is the sole beneficiary under the will of Francesco Borelli.

. . . Upon the death of Francesco Borelli, the partnership was dissolved. It became the duty of the survivor to settle the partnership affairs and remit the deceased partner's share to his representative. If the survivor carries on the business without an agreement, the representative of the deceased partner is entitled at his option to receive the profits attributable to the use of his rights in the property of the dissolved partnership or in lieu thereof, interest may be demanded on the value of the deceased partner's interest ascertained as of the date of dissolution. . . .

The claimant by reason of her right to elect between interest and profits could obviously conduct an inquiry as to which would be the more advantageous. An accounting of the partnership assets therefore might be compelled. The right to compel such an accounting would continue until barred by the ten year statute of limitations. Sec. 53, Civil Practice Act, Smith v. Maine, 145 Misc. 521, at p. 540, 260 N.Y.S. 409, 425, at p. 433. It necessarily follows therefore that her time to make a choice would continue for the same duration.

The claimant herein has chosen to take the interest at the legal rate on the value of the interest of Francesco Borelli in the assets of the partnership as fixed by the decedent herein. This choice having been made within the period of time given to her, the claim is allowed in accordance with her request. . . .

CASE NO. 5

Mulkey v. Anglin. 166 Okla. 8, 25 Pac. (2d) 778, 89 A.L.R. 980 (1933)

WELCH, J., delivered the opinion of the court:

. . . W. T. Anglin, Alfred Stevenson, and Forrest M. Darrough, a partnership doing business as the Holdenville Finance Company, as plaintiffs, sued the defendants, Jas. H. Mulkey and R. D. Howell, as partners, doing business as the Mulkey Motor Company, for the balance due on each of thirty-eight promissory notes which were originally executed and made payable to "Mulkey Motor Company," and were sold to plaintiffs, and in each instance conveyed by general indorsement, "Mulkey Motor Company by Jas. H. Mulkey, Member of the Firm." The notes were sold and indorsed to plaintiffs at various dates between June, 1927, and January, 1928.

The defendants contend that the Mulkey Motor Company was not a partnership at that time, while admitting that the Mulkey Motor Company was a partnership composed of said two partners for several months or a year prior to June, 1927. They contend that on June 6, 1927, the Mulkey Motor Company was incorporated with Jas. H.

Mulkey, R. D. Howell, and Mrs. R. D. Howell, as stockholders, and that, at all of the times of assignment and indorsement involved in this action, the Mulkey Motor Company was a corporation and engaged in business as such, and that the defendants are therefore not personally liable.

The plaintiffs contend, . . . the defendants did not . . operate or conduct their business as a corporation, but, on the contrary, continued to conduct their business in the exact and identical manner as before, and held themselves out to the public and to the plaintiffs as continuing to be partners, that defendants took no steps whatever to dissolve their partnership, and that they permitted the plaintiffs to believe and rely upon the fact that the partnership continued to exist. . . .

As to most . . . facts there was conflict of evidence, but the evidence is sufficient to sustain the finding of fact that after June 6, 1927, the defendants continued to conduct and operate their business as a partnership, and to hold themselves out as partners, and to such an extent as to permit the plaintiffs to believe and rely upon the fact of the continuance of the partnership.

In fact, there was no effort made by the defendants whatever to legally dissolve their partnership. They were admittedly partners prior to June, 1927, and prior thereto had dealt with the plaintiffs in the same manner as they did deal with them after said date, and, if it was the intention of the defendants to incorporate their business, and to dissolve their partnership in June, 1927, they made no effort whatever to dissolve their partnership in the manner provided by law. . . .

The Supreme Court of Arizona, in passing upon this very question in the case of Overlock v. Hazzard, 12 Ariz. 142, 100 P. 447, in the body of the opinion says:

"It is well settled that, where there has been a change in the membership of a partnership, to relieve a retiring partner from any liability for the debts of the partnership in the future, reasonable notice must be given to persons dealing with the partnership of such change. Gilbough v. Stahl Building Company, 16 Tex. Civ. App. 448, 41 S.W. 535. What will be deemed sufficient notice will depend upon circumstances. There is no difference in principle between the case where a corporation succeeds to the business of a partnership, and the case where a change has been made in the membership of a partnership, with regard to the duty of imparting notice of such change. Ordinarily a change from a partnership to a corporation is attended with such change of name and frequently with such other changes as not to require personal notice of such change. Where, as in the present case, there is no change of name or place of business or other change which might reasonably be presumed to impart notice, some kind of notice reasonably adapted for that purpose ought to be given. The question whether personal notice is reasonably required must be determined from the circumstances of each case. . . ."

. . . judgment of the trial court is . . . affirmed.

CASE NO. 6

Marquette Cloak & Suit Co. v. Netter & Myer. 151 So. 820 (La. App.) (1934)

The partnership of Netter and Meyer was formed prior to 1923. On June 14, 1923, Meyer died and his widow and three sons succeeded to his interest. December 1, 1930, Mrs. Meyer transferred her interest to Sylvan G. Meyer. The other two sons had withdrawn from the partnership prior to this time. The plaintiff sued the partnership and Mrs. Meyer to recover for goods sold and delivered during October, November and December, 1931, and January, 1932. Mrs. Meyer claimed she had withdrawn from the firm prior to the sale and delivery of the goods and was not liable.

TALIAFERRO, J. In this court, while plaintiff does not concede that Mrs. Meyer ceased to be a member of the firm of Netter & Meyer after December 1, 1930, yet discussion in brief is restricted almost entirely to the question of her responsibility to plaintiff because, on December 1, 1930, plaintiff was a creditor of the firm and was never notified thereafter of Mrs. Meyer's withdrawal therefrom; and, therefore, continued to extend credit to it, as had previously been the rule, largely, if not entirely, under the belief that she was still a member thereof and responsible for its obligations.

It is shown beyond any question, notwithstanding denial thereof by Mrs. Meyer and her son, Sylvan, that on December 1, 1930, Netter & Meyer was due plaintiff over $500 on account. This indebtedness was liquidated by giving of firm notes on February 14, 1931. These notes were paid as they matured. Therefore, in view of these established facts, plaintiff was entitled to have actual notice of Mrs. Meyer's retirement from the firm as a member. So long as they were in ignorance of the change, in view of past business relationship of the two firms, plaintiff had the right to assume that Mrs. Meyer's interest in and membership of the firm continued, and, acting upon that assumption, to extend credit to the partnership with the assurance that it could hold her responsible for partnership obligations. . . .

There was an abortive effort by defendants to prove that notice was given plaintiff by mail of Mrs. Meyer's withdrawal from defendant firm. They did not produce a copy of such notice and it is shown that the change in the firm's membership was not published in the newspapers in the city of Alexandria, where it carried on its business. It is not shown that the change in its membership personnel was generally known in the community there. In fact, it is not disclosed that any one had knowledge of the change, except defendants.

We are impelled to the conclusion that Mrs. Meyer's retirement from this firm was designedly guarded from public knowledge. No knowledge of the shift reached Bradstreet's Agency prior to September 14, 1931. A report of that date, and several prior by that agency, state the firm to be composed of Mrs. Meyer and Emile Netter. Plaintiff's salesman, who lived in the city of Alexandria, knew nothing of the change until informed by Sylvan Meyer about April 1, 1932. This information was imparted to him by Mr. Meyer during a conversation between them at the company's place of business, at which time the salesman was endeavoring to collect a check of the firm which had been dishonored. Meyer stated that plaintiff could not "get anything from the firm," and, being reminded that his mother was responsible as one of its members, replied that she had nothing to do with the firm. This salesman often went to this store, took orders for merchandise, and had frequent contact with Netter and Sylvan Meyer. He transmitted to plaintiff the information given him in April, 1932, about Mrs. Meyer's retirement from the business in December, 1930, and his letter to his principal was the first intelligence received by them on the subject.

Judgment for plaintiff affirmed.

CASE NO. 7

Baum v. McBride. 152 *Neb.* 152, 40 *N.W.* (2d) 649 (1950)

WENKE, J. This is an appeal by Theodore Baum, plaintiff, from an order of the district court for Scotts Bluff County establishing the rights of the partners to the assets of the partnership of the McBride Potato Company. . . .

The evidence establishes that the partnership began about September 1, 1939. Baum testified: "He (McBride) said that we would put everything we had together and start in the potato deal." Baum had no property to put in the partnership but was to secure sufficient financial backing to enable it to carry on its business. This he did through his father.

The record contains no evidence that any agreement was ever made or understanding had between these parties, at the time they entered into this partnership, of how the capital furnished by each of the partners should be distributed in case of a dissolution of the partnership. Under this factual situation we find the following principles applicable to the capital furnished to the partnership by McBride at the time of the formation thereof: . . .

As stated in Adams v. Hubbard, 221 Pa. 511, 70 Atl. 835, 837, in quoting from 22 Am. & Eng. Ency. of Law (2d ed.), pp. 86 and 87, as follows:

> " 'Where a partnership is dissolved and its affairs are wound up, there must be a return of the firm capital to the partners contributing it, in order that there may be a distribution of the profits. Each partner's contribution is regarded as a firm debt to such partner, which must be repaid before there are any profits to be divided. Where one partner has advanced capital in excess of another, the amount advanced is a preferred claim upon the property of the firm. The distribution of capital upon dissolution is in the same proportion in which such capital was furnished.' "

. . .

The evidence establishes that on September 1, 1939, when the partnership began, it took over and operated under the name of "McBride Potato Company," which trade name had previously been used by McBride in connection with his business. When the partnership started operating it took over that account in the bank. McBride then had on deposit therein the sum of $86.60. The partnership also took over and used certain personal property of McBride. . . . The personal property so taken over consisted of two potato graders worth $250 each and office and warehouse equipment, which included several sets of scales, two typewriters, two desks, chairs, filing cabinets, etc., reasonably worth $250. The partnership also took over from McBride 21 bales of printed bags worth $62.35 per thousand and 50 pounds of twine worth 30 cents per pound. . . . These bags were worth $1,309.35 and the twine $15.

Prior to September 1, 1939, McBride had entered into contracts for the delivery of potato bags in the total of 249,000. . . . These contracts were turned over to the partnership. At that time the market value had gone up and there is evidence that at the time they were turned over to the partnership the bags had increased an average of $24 per thousand. . . . The increase in the market value of these bags at the time the contracts therefor were turned over to the partnership belonged to McBride and he is entitled to the same as capital invested in the partnership. This amount we find to be in the sum of $5,976.

The evidence establishes that Mc-

Bride invested $8,136.95 of capital in the partnership at the time of its organization and that he is entitled to a credit for that sum. . . .

. . . we find that from the time the partnership started doing business until about April 13, 1942, when Baum was ousted therefrom, Baum received $7,252.58 therefrom, and McBride $14,300.42. . . .

When McBride ousted Baum and took over the partnership assets he caused to be removed from the Mitchell warehouse some 61,962 potato bags of various sizes. These potato bags were mostly new. The evidence establishes they were reasonably worth $7,968.98, with which amount McBride should be charged. McBride thereafter used $431.01 of the funds of the partnership. He also stayed in possession of the warehouses of the partnership . . . during the potato season of 1942–1943, ... We find the reasonable value of the use of this property for the period McBride so used it to be $4,500. . . . The evidence also establishes that after April 13, 1942, there not being sufficient funds of the partnership available, McBride paid $1,045.52 of partnership obligations. . . .

A summation of these items shows that McBride has received sufficient of the assets of the partnership to return to him the capital he invested therein and an amount in the sum of $10,765.36 in excess of that received from the partnership by Baum. Baum, in order to adjust this excess received by McBride, is entitled to half of that amount from McBride. . . .

. . . the decree of the trial court is reversed with directions to enter decree in accordance herewith.

Review Questions

1. Does it necessarily follow that the dissolution of a partnership will result in its termination as a business enterprise?
2. Construct a fact situation illustrating a partnership for an implied term.
3. What is a partnership at will?
4. Can a partner bring about the dissolution of the partnership in violation of his partnership contract?
5. What is meant by the phrase "dissolution of a partnership by operation of law"?
6. Does the death of one partner necessarily mean a discontinuance of the partnership?
7. Does the bankruptcy of one of the partners cause a dissolution of the partnership?
8. For what reasons may a court of equity decree the dissolution of a partnership?
9. Is illness of a partner sufficient basis for a dissolution of the partnership?
10. Is disagreement among partners a sufficient basis for a dissolution of the partnership?
11. For what purposes does a partnership continue after its dissolution?
12. With whom does the right to liquidate the partnership rest?
13. What steps should a partnership take upon its dissolution to prevent further partnership liability?
14. What is the usual mode of giving notice to the general public that the partnership has ceased to exist?

15. To whom should actual or personal notice of dissolution of a partnership be given?
16. Is a partner who contracts in behalf of the partnership after its dissolution solely liable upon the contract?
17. What is the order of distribution of the assets of a liquidating partnership?
18. How does the insolvency of one or some of the partners affect the solvent partners at the time of liquidation, if the partnership assets are not sufficient to pay creditors?
19. Define marshaling of assets. How may it apply in the liquidation of a partnership?

Problems for Discussion

1. A and B formed a partnership under which it was agreed that A was to be on the lookout for farms that could be bought and then sold at a profit. B was to advance the capital, and the profits, after B's advances had been returned to him, were to be divided equally. B brought an action for an accounting upon his election to terminate the partnership. A resists the action, contending that B has no right to terminate the partnership since no farms had as yet been bought or sold as the agreement contemplated. Decide.
2. X and Y have associated themselves in a partnership venture, which they agree is to continue for five years. One year later, X withdraws and takes with him the property he had contributed. What are Y's rights against X?
3. Lawson assigns his interest in a partnership to his creditor, Coffman. Does this cause a dissolution of the partnership?
4. Radke and Foil were associated as partners. They provided in the partnership agreement that in the event of the death of either, the decedent's heir (a son) was to be given the election to continue as a partner in the enterprise. Radke died and his seventeen-year-old son, being the heir, elects to become a partner. Not wishing to be associated in business with an adolescent, Foil desires to liquidate the business. Can the heir prevent this?
5. This bill is brought to procure a dissolution and winding up of the affairs of a partnership entered into between the parties under a written agreement for the canning of fish and the manufacture of pomace and fish guano, and to continue for the term of five years from July 1, 1881. The copartnership agreement provides that the plaintiffs shall furnish the capital with which to carry on the business, and shall furnish, also, all materials at cost; that the defendants shall have charge of and superintend the manufacturing department at the factory in Gloucester, keep correct books, and submit weekly statements of the business to the plaintiffs, make good and marketable goods, at the lowest possible cost, in such quantities as the plaintiffs should deem advisable. The grounds upon which the dissolution is asked for are the willful and persistent neglect of the defendants to comply with the terms of the written agreement and that the business is being conducted at a great loss. Decide. (*Rosenstein* v. *Burns*, 41 Fed. 841)
6. This is a suit upon a note dated January 1, 1880, signed by "B. Callender & Co." It was signed and delivered to the plaintiff by B. Callender, and at that time the only parties composing the firm were the said Callender and the de-

fendants Bolles and Wilde. The defendant Hall, who was formerly a partner, had withdrawn from the firm on July 2, 1877, and notice of the dissolution was given by publication in the *Boston Daily Advertiser,* but no personal notice was given to the plaintiff. The note in suit was given in renewal of a former note which the plaintiff held at the time of the dissolution.

It further appears that the defendant Hall, in December, 1877, filed his petition in bankruptcy, was adjudicated a bankrupt, and thereupon, in June, 1878, received his discharge. Is Hall liable as a partner? (*Eustis* v. *Bolles,* 146 Mass. 413)

7. A and B are partners in a profitable business venture. Partner A reflects his prosperity by the purchase of a new car, a new home, and by sending his son to college. B objects to such a display of economic status, contending it will create resentment in the community and thus injure the business. A fails to share B's views, and relations between the two become strained. B brings an action to dissolve the partnership. Should he succeed?
8. At the time that Wormley and Davenport were negotiating for the formation of a partnership, Davenport stated that he was a better than average accountant and could supervise the accounting aspects of the business. After the formation of the partnership, Wormley discovers that Davenport could not distinguish a debit from a credit. Can he have the partnership dissolved?
9. Partners X and Y had agreed not to sell to anyone at a discount. Y, in violation of the partnership contract, persistently continued to sell to certain of his friends at less than the established retail price. What are X's remedies?
10. A partnership suffered a substantial loss during the last accounting period. Can one of the partners obtain a decree of dissolution upon the basis of this?
11. A and B operated a mercantile business as a partnership. In liquidating the partnership upon the death of B, A conveyed the partnership realty to a creditor in satisfaction of a partnership obligation. B's legal representative objects, contending that A has no authority to dispose of the real property of the partnership. Decide.
12. B, who was the liquidating partner of a dissolved partnership, accepted a bill of exchange drawn upon the partnership for the purpose of compromising a doubtful claim against the partnership. Does the accepted bill evidence a valid claim against the partnership?
13. A, B, and C had been partners for twenty years when A decided to retire. He sold his interest to B and C, who continued the enterprise. Neither he nor the partnership gave any notice of the withdrawal other than was carried as a news item in the local paper. Some time after the withdrawal, B and C overextended themselves on a purchase of merchandise and were faced with insolvency. The partnership was forced into bankruptcy and A was looked to for satisfaction since he alone had any personal assets. Can he be held?
14. As a retiring partner, A sent notices of his withdrawal to all past and present creditors of the partnership by mail. The notice addressed to X was never received by him. Can A be held upon a partnership obligation to X that was acquired subsequent to the time of his withdrawal?
15. The principal question in the case is, whether Loveland had notice of the dissolution of the firm of Dillon, Beebe & Co., which occurred March 29, 1869, prior to August 31, 1869, when the note upon which the action was brought

was made. The firm was engaged in the business of the purchase, shipment and sale of lumber, and its principal office was at Toledo, in the state of Ohio. Loveland was employed to purchase lumber in the western states and in Canada, and resided at Detroit. Notice of dissolution was published in the newspapers at Toledo, and a copy was mailed to him, addressed to him at Detroit.

Loveland, on his direct examination, testified positively that he never received a notice. On his cross-examination, he stated that he had no recollection of receiving or seeing the notice, and that, if he had seen it, he thought he should have remembered it. The judge submitted it to the jury to find whether the plaintiff received the notice. The defendants' counsel excepted to the submission of the question to the jury, on the ground that the mailing of the notice was all that the defendant was required to do to protect him from liability for Loveland's subsequent services. Decide. (*Austin* v. *Holland,* 69 N.Y. 571)

37 BUSINESS ORGANIZATIONS:

CHARACTER AND FORMATION OF BUSINESS CORPORATIONS

"Persons also are divided by the law into either natural persons or artificial. Natural persons are such as the God of Nature formed us. Artificial are such as are created and devised by human laws, for the purposes of society and government, which are called corporations." I *Blackstone Commentaries,* 123

"President Nicholas Murray Butler of Columbia University recently said: 'I weigh my words when I say that in my judgment the limited liability corporation is the greatest single discovery of modern times, whether you judge it by its social, by its ethical, by its industrial, or, in the long run,—after we understand it and know how to use it,—by its political, effects. Even steam and electricity are far less important than the limited liability corporation, and they would be reduced to comparative impotence without it. . . . It substitutes co-operation on a large scale for individual, cut-throat, parochial competition. It makes possible huge economy in production and in trading. It means the modern provision of industrial insurance, of care for disability, old age and widowhood. It means—the only possible engine for carrying on international trade on a scale commensurate with modern needs and opportunities.'" *Fletcher's Cyclopedia of the Law of Corporations,* Vol. 1, Sec. 21 (1st ed.)

The corporation is the predominant form of business organization today. Its use in the conduct of large-scale business enterprise is almost universal. Because of the fact that it is peculiarly adapted to the raising of large amounts of capital from numerous contributors and to the placing of that capital under a single management, the corporation has made large-scale commercial ventures possible. The corporation's popularity as a vehicle for capital investment—or speculation, as some will choose to call it—is explained by the feature of limited liability of the contributors. The corporation is usually identified in the public mind with large business enterprises. Let it be recognized, however, that the corporation has likewise a definite place in the conduct of small business undertakings. The majority of the approximately half-million American corporations are, in fact, relatively small. In many instances the capital contributions come exclusively from the management. As an organization device for the conduct of these many small business ventures, the use of the corporation is largely motivated by the limitation of risk, a limitation that is not enjoyed by the members of a partnership or an unincorporated association.[1, 2] Other advantages possessed by the corporation over other

[1] Lamm v. Stoen, p. 930.

[2] Petrovich v. Felco Chemical Corp., p. 931.

forms of business organizations will be indicated in the following pages; the most important of these advantages undoubtedly is the corporation's right of succession. The continuity of a business enterprise that operates under the corporate form is highly certain; its existence is not dependent upon the continued existence of the same membership.

▶ I. CLASSIFICATION OF CORPORATIONS

A. PRIVATE CORPORATIONS

1. *Private Stock Corporations*

Corporations are used for many purposes other than the conduct of business undertakings. The type of corporation employed in the pursuit of business profits is generally designated as the *private stock corporation.* Its distinguishing feature is that it employs a capital stock, which is divided into shares. The membership consists of the holders of these shares of stock, and the corporation is authorized to distribute dividends to the stockholders.

Corporations engaged in rendering public services (public utilities) such as light, water, heat, and transportation, although being private in the true sense of the word, are known as *quasi-public corporations.* Such corporations employ private capital and are motivated by profits as is any other private business undertaking. Because of the nature of the services they render—services that are regarded as of vital importance to the public welfare—the public has taken upon itself the right to limit the return from the capital employed and to set up rules and regulations under which these public services shall be rendered.

> "Thus, all bank, bridge, turnpike, railroad, and canal companies are private corporations. In these and other similar cases the uses may, in a certain sense, be called public, but the corporations are private, as much so as if the franchises were vested in a single person. The state, by virtue of its right of eminent domain, may take private property for public purposes upon making compensation. It may delegate this power to a private corporation by reason of the benefit to accrue to the public from the use of the improvements to be constructed by the corporation." *Rundle* v. *Delaware etc. Canal,* 21 F. Cas. No. 12,139

> "A public service or quasi public corporation is one private in its ownership but having an appropriate franchise from the State to provide for a necessity or convenience of the general public incapable of being furnished through the ordinary channels of private competitive business and dependent for its exercise upon eminent domain or some agency of government." *Attorney-General* v. *Haverhill Gas Light Co.,* 215 Mass. 394

2. *Nonstock Corporations*

State statutes make provision for the chartering of private corporations "not for pecuniary profit." Such corporations can be employed for the establishment and conduct of (quoting from Section 8582 of the 1946 Iowa Code) "churches, colleges, seminaries, lyceums, libraries, fraternal lodges or societies, temperance societies, trades' unions or other labor organizations, commercial clubs, associations of business men, agricultural societies, farmers' granges, or organizations of a benevolent, charitable, scientific, political, athletic, military or religious character."

Corporations of this kind have no capital stock and issue no shares. Membership is determined by the rules and regulations set up by the organization. At times certificates of membership are issued to the members as evidence of their affiliation, but such a certificate is in no sense of the word a share of stock. Only upon dissolution can a nonstock corporation make a distribution of dividends or property to its members.

B. PUBLIC CORPORATIONS

"Strictly speaking, public corporations are such only as are founded by the government, for public purposes, where the whole interests belong also to the government." *Dartmouth College* v. *Woodward,* 4 Wheat. (U.S.) 518

Public corporations are chartered and exist to discharge governmental functions. Those units of local government which are subordinate to the state operate as and possess the attributes of a corporation. Illustrations of such are county, city, town and village governmental units. In addition to these, there are many local subdivisions of government—public bodies such as school districts, drainage districts, water districts, and various boards and commissions—whose purposes are the discharging of various public functions. A state university is also an illustration of a public corporation.

► II. LEGAL CONCEPTS OF CORPORATIONS

The various and varied definitions of a corporation establish two different basic concepts of this form of business unit. Usually the corporation is designated (1) as a legal entity (a person, in the eyes of the law), and not infrequently it is regarded (2) as an association of individuals. This Jekyll and Hyde complex that the law has attributed to the corporation is not only convenient but is at times necessary. Sometimes there must be a disregard of the generally accepted theory that a corporation is a legal person in its own right, and recognition must be given the fact that a corporation is composed of a membership. The corporation is recognized as an entity only insofar as it is necessary to have a form of business unit with which legitimate activities can be carried on with ease and convenience.

A. THE CORPORATION AS LEGAL ENTITY

Most representative of the many definitions stressing the entity concept of a corporation is that of Chief Justice Marshall; this definition is to be found in his opinion in the famous *Dartmouth College* case. Writers have come to call this definition a classic. Chief Justice Marshall there wrote:

"A corporation is an artificial being, invisible, intangible, and existing only in contemplation of law. Being the mere creature of law, it possesses only those properties which the charter of its creation confers upon it, either expressly or as incidental to its very existence. These are such as are supposed best calculated to effect the object for which it was created. Among the most important are immortality, and, if the expression may be allowed, individuality; properties by which a perpetual succession of many persons are considered as the same, and may act as a single individual. They enable a corporation to manage its own affairs, and to hold property without the perplexing intricacies, the hazardous and endless necessity, of perpetual conveyances for the purpose of transmitting it from hand to hand. It is chiefly for the purpose of clothing bodies of men, in succession, with these qualities and capacities that corporations were invented, and are in use. By these means, a perpetual succession of individuals are capable of acting for the promotion of the particular object, like one immortal being."

1. *Legal Incidents of Entity Concept*

Certain definite legal consequences are carried with the legal concept that a corporation is, for most purposes, an artificial being, a person existing in the eyes of the law separate and apart from its stockholders.

a. Continuous Succession. Since a corporation as a legal person is not identified with its membership, its life is not dependent upon the continuance of the membership that originally composed it. A corporation can have continuous succession even though its membership is constantly changing. One of the fundamental characteristics of a corporation is said to be its capacity of continuous succession without limit of time. Unless, as is the present-day practice, the life of a corporation is limited by its articles of incorporation or by statutory or constitutional provision, it may continue indefinitely until it is legally dissolved.

b. Property Ownership. All property, real and personal, acquired by a corporation is owned exclusively by the corporation. It is the corporation that holds legal title to such property, and it is only the corporation that can subsequently convey or mortgage that property. The stockholders have a mere beneficial interest in the corporate assets. To illustrate:

(1) In *Humphrey* v. *McKissock,* 140 U.S. 304, the court in passing upon the right of stockholders to convey corporation property without corporate action said:

"The property of a corporation is not subject to the control of individual members, whether acting separately or jointly. They can neither encumber nor transfer that property, nor authorize others to do so. The corporation—the artificial being created—holds the property and alone can mortgage or transfer it; and the corporation acts only through its officers, subject to the conditions prescribed by law."

(2) An illustration of what is probably an extreme application of this principle is found in *People's Pleasure Park Co.* v. *Rohleder,* 109 Va. 439. The court there

held that a conveyance of land to a corporation composed of colored persons was not in violation of a restrictive covenant which provided that title to the land was never to vest in colored persons. The court recognized the corporation as a legal entity holding the title as a person separate and apart from its members. It is to be questioned whether such a conclusion is in keeping with the spirit and the intent of the restrictive covenant. It is likely that some courts under such circumstances might submerge the entity concept and recognize the corporation as being in fact an association of its members.

(3) In *Exchange Bank* v. *Macon Construction Co.*, 97 Ga. 1, the facts were that the A Construction Co. contracted with the B Railway Co. for the construction of a railroad, the contract providing that all of the stock of the B Railway Co. was, upon completion of the contract, to become the property of the A Construction Co. The railroad was, upon completion, operated by the A Construction Co., which borrowed money from the C Bank for the purposes of paying employees engaged in operating the railroad and paying for railroad equipment purchased by the A Construction Company. The C Bank held the notes of the construction company as evidence of the obligations. Upon being unable to collect from the construction company, the bank contended that it was in fact a creditor of the railway company and should be allowed to share in its assets.

In denying the bank this position, the court said:

> "Every corporation is a person—artificial, it is true, but nevertheless a distinct legal entity. Neither a portion nor all of the natural persons who compose a corporation, or who own its stock and control its affairs, is the corporation itself; and when a single individual composes a corporation, he is not himself the corporation. In such case the man is one person, created by the Almighty, and the corporation is another person, created by the law. It makes no difference in principle whether the sole owner of the stock of a corporation is a man or another corporation. The corporation owning such stock is as distinct from the corporation whose stock is so owned as the man is from the corporation of which he is the sole member. . . . The construction company and the railroad company being, therefore, distinct corporations, and the bank being a creditor of the former only, and not of the latter, it is clear that the bank has no lien upon the property of the railroad company."

c. Corporate Liabilities and Rights. The stockholders have no personal responsibility for the debts or other liabilities of the corporation. It is only the corporation that can be looked to for satisfaction. Contracts entered into by a corporation confer no rights or liabilities upon the stockholders. Likewise, the stockholders are not liable for the corporation's torts committed through its representatives. A stockholder, unlike a member of a general partnership, risks only his equitable interest (in effect, the value of the stock he holds) in the corporation. It is only the corporation that can sue and be sued. In many respects the legal rights of a corporation are identical with those of a natural person.[3]

[3] N.Y. Society for S.V. v. MacFadden Pub., p. 931.

d. Members Not Agents. A corporation acts not through its members but through its duly selected representatives, its management. The stockholders are not agents of the corporation and cannot represent it in the conduct of its affairs. Only at corporate meetings when the stockholders are exercising their right of management are their actions binding upon the corporation. It is recognized that in such instances the corporation is more than a fiction, that it is in fact an association of individuals.

e. The Corporation as Resident, Person, and Citizen under Statutory and Constitutional Provisions. A corporation is regarded as being a resident or inhabitant for certain limited purposes. For example, statutes that define the jurisdiction of courts and the authority to tax upon the basis of residence are held to apply, generally, to corporations as well as to natural persons. Whether corporations are to be regarded as included is dependent upon the purpose of the statute and the need for, or desirability of, including corporations.

These same considerations hold where statutes or constitutional provisions relate to *persons* or *citizens*. The corporation is regarded as a person within the meaning of the due process clause of the Fourteenth Amendment to the Federal Constitution. Corporations as well as natural persons are entitled to the constitutional protection afforded by that part of the Fourteenth Amendment which reads:

> ". . . nor shall any state deprive any person of life, liberty, or property without due process of law, nor deny to any person within its jurisdiction the equal protection of the laws."

The due process clause in the Fifth Amendment to the Constitution of the United States applies to corporations as well as to natural persons. The courts recognize that to deprive a corporation of its property or to burden it unduly would in fact be depriving the corporation of its property.

The Constitution of the United States provides that diversity of citizenship of litigants shall give the federal courts jurisdiction. Within the meaning of this provision, corporations are regarded as having citizenship in the state of their incorporation. There is little reason why the federal courts should not be given jurisdiction over cases involving corporations. However, the courts have been reluctant to recognize the corporation itself as a citizen. In the past this reluctance resulted in the spurious reasoning that all the stockholders of the corporation are conclusively presumed to be citizens of the state of incorporation. Such a fiction is no longer indulged in, and the corporation itself is accepted as a citizen of the state of its incorporation for the purpose of suits in the federal courts.

However, it is denied that a corporation can be a citizen within the meaning of that clause of Article IV, Section 2, of the Federal Constitution which provides:

> ". . . the citizens of each state shall be entitled to all privileges and immunities of citizens in the several states."

As here used, the term *citizens* has reference only to natural persons, members of the body politic, and not to fictitious beings created for limited purposes only. To hold that corporations are citizens within the contemplation of the above clause would mean that the various states could impose no restrictions upon foreign corporations doing business within their borders. As a result, corporations could transact business in all states as freely as in the state that granted them the right and power to act as corporations.

Likewise, a corporation is not regarded as a citizen under that part of the Fourteenth Amendment to the United States Constitution which provides:

> "No state shall make or enforce any law which shall abridge the privileges or immunities of citizens of the United States."

A corporation cannot obtain a United States citizenship and hence has no protection under this provision.

B. THE CORPORATION AS AN ASSOCIATION OF INDIVIDUALS

The association idea of a corporation is given prominence in many of the numerous definitions. This concept is well expressed by Justice Field in *Kansas Pac. R. Co.* v. *Atchison R. Co.,* 112 U.S. 414, when he said:

> "A private corporation is, in fact, but an association of individuals united for a lawful purpose and permitted to use a common name in their business, and to have a change of members without dissolution."

1. *Legal Incidents of Association Concept*

> "The general proposition that a corporation is to be regarded as a legal entity, existing separate and apart from the natural persons composing it, is not disputed; but that the statement is a mere fiction existing only in idea, is well understood, and not controverted by any one who pretends to accurate knowledge on the subject. It has been introduced for the convenience of the company in making contracts, in acquiring property for corporate purposes, in suing and being sued, and to preserve the limited liability of the stockholders, by distinguishing between the corporate debts and property of the company, and of the stockholders in their capacity as individuals. All fictions of law have been introduced for the purpose of convenience and to subserve the ends of justice. . . . But, when they are urged to an intent and purpose not within the reason and policy of the fiction, they have always been disregarded by the courts." *State* v. *Standard Oil Co.,* 49 Ohio St. 137

a. Protection of Stockholders' Rights. The fact that stockholders' rights are protected by courts of equity is a recognition that the corporation is in reality composed of an association of individuals. The corporation is regarded as an entity only insofar as it is necessary to carry on the business enterprise for the benefit of the stockholders. Despite the fact that the corporation has the legal right to sue in respect to corporate affairs, courts of equity will recognize the right of the stockholders to take appropriate action whenever the corporation refuses or cannot take steps necessary for the protection of the stockholders' interests.

> "If the directors are false to their duty, and there is danger that they will, from corrupt motives or blind obstinacy, abandon, neglect, or sacrifice the interests of the shareholders committed to their charge, then the courts of equity will permit stockholders to intervene for their own protection, and to

seek and obtain the aid of the court. . . . The questions in every case are: Is the complaining stockholder remediless unless he represents his own interest? Is there danger of the commission of a flagrant wrong? If these questions be answered in the affirmative, he will be allowed to intervene, notwithstanding that the remedy is an extreme one, and should not be permitted without hesitation and caution." *General Electric Co.* v. *West Asheville Impr. Co.*, 73 Fed. 386, 387

To illustrate:

In *Weidenfeld* v. *Sugar Run R. Co.*, 48 Fed. 615, a stockholder was granted the right to obtain an injunction when the officers of the corporation failed to resist the appropriation of the corporation's property by the defendant.

b. Fraud or Illegal Acts. Incorporators cannot shield themselves against the consequences of their fraudulent or illegal acts by hiding behind the artificiality of a corporation. If the corporation is being used as a means of accomplishing that which is fraudulent or illegal, the courts will always accept the acts of the corporation as those of the stockholders.[4] To illustrate:

(1) In *D. I. Felsenthal Co.* v. *Northern Assurance Co.*, 284 Ill. 343, 1 A.L.R. 602, the court said:

"It is true as contended by appellant that the general rule of law is that the wilful burning of property by a stockholder in a corporation is not a defense against the collection of the insurance by the corporation, and that the corporation cannot be prevented from collecting the insurance because its agents wilfully set fire to the property without the participation of authority of the corporation or all of the stockholders of the corporation. When, however, the beneficial owner of practically all of the stock in a corporation, and who has the absolute management and control of its affairs and property and is the president and a director, sets fire to the property of a corporation, or causes it to be done, there is no sound reason to support the contention of appellant that the corporation should be allowed to recover on a policy for the destruction of corporate property by a fire so occasioned."

(2) In *Moore & Handley Hdwe. Co.* v. *Towers*, 87 Ala. 206, it was pointed out that if the members of a partnership sell their business and agree not to compete with the purchaser, and then organize as a corporation with the intent of avoiding their contractual obligation not to compete, the corporation as an entity will be disregarded.

Conversely, an action by the stockholders that is contrary to the reasons and purposes of the incorporation will be attributed to the corporation. The corporation will be regarded as an association of individuals.

c. When Purely a Subsidiary Instrumentality. Another class of cases in which the courts will not allow the interposing of the corporate fiction as a shield is that of corporations performing acts through and by means of subsidiary corporations

---

[4] Rudin v. Steinbugler, p. 932.

wholly under their dominance and control. It is reasoned that the subsidiary corporation is in fact an extension of the personality of the parent company, which stands responsible for the acts of its agent.[5, 6]

► III. FORMATION

A. AUTHORITY FOR FORMATION

A corporation, unlike a partnership, cannot come into being by the mere will of the associating members. A corporation is a creation of the state, existing only because the state has given sanction through its legislative body.

> "We must bear in mind that a corporation is purely a creature of the law and can exist only by permission of the state, that in all of the states of this country the state legislative department is the only department of government empowered to form corporations or authorize their formation, or prescribe or extend their term of existence, and that, except insofar as it is limited by constitutional provision, the power of the legislature in this regard is absolute." *Boca Mill Co.* v. *Curry,* 154 Cal. 326

1. *Right of States to Create Corporations*

The power of the various states of the Union to create corporations is derived from the Tenth Amendment to the Federal Constitution, which reads:

> "The powers not delegated to the United States by the Constitution nor prohibited by it to the States, are reserved to the States respectively or to the people."

It is upon this basis that the legislatures of the various states have the right (subject to any state constitutional limitations) to

(1) determine the method by which corporations shall come into being;
(2) determine the purposes for which corporations may be created; and
(3) determine the rights and powers corporations may exercise.

Virtually all the corporations engaged in business have been created under the laws of the various states.

2. *Right of Federal Government to Create Corporations*

Congress has the implied power to create corporations for various purposes. This power of incorporation is derived from Article I, Section 8, of the Federal Constitution, which declares:

> "The Congress shall have power . . . To make all Laws which shall be necessary and proper for the carrying into Execution the foregoing Powers, . . ."

In *McCulloch* v. *Maryland,* 4 Wheat. 407, the U.S. Supreme Court said:

> "Although among the enumerated powers of Government we do not find the word 'bank' or 'incorporation,' we find the great powers to lay and

[5] Charles E. Austin Inc. v. Kelly, p. 934.
[6] Ohio Edison Co. v. Warner Coal Corp., p. 935.

collect taxes, to borrow money, to regulate commerce, to declare and conduct a war, and to raise and support armies and navies. The sword and the purse, all the external relations, and no inconsiderable portion of the industry of the Nation, are intrusted to its Government. It can never be pretended that these vast powers draw after them others of inferior importance merely because they are inferior. Such an idea can never be advanced. But it may with great reason be contended that a government intrusted with such ample powers, on the due execution of which the happiness and prosperity of the Nation so vitally depend, must also be intrusted with ample means for their execution."

It is under this authority that the Congress may charter national banks as well as corporations engaged in interstate commerce, such as telegraph companies, railroads, and bridge companies operating over a stream between two states.

B. METHOD OF CREATING CORPORATIONS

The original method of acquiring the right of corporate existence was that of special legislative enactment. This required sovereign authority, in the true sense of the word, for the creation of a corporation. Whether the petitioners would be granted authority to operate in the corporate form was subject entirely to the collective will of the legislative body. The present-day widespread use of the corporate form of business organization can be, in no small degree, attributed to the abolition of this discriminatory, cumbersome, graft-producing, and time-consuming method of incorporation. The granting of special corporation privileges was at times all too dependent upon the influence that could be exerted upon individuals of the legislative body.

The result was the adoption of incorporation by means of general enabling statutes, and this method is generally employed today. No longer is there need for formally petitioning for the right to operate under the corporate form. Anyone who can meet the standards and requirements set forth in the corporation law is entitled to a grant of corporate powers. A corporation is in fact brought into being by the voluntary action of the incorporators, by which they meet the provisions of the enabling statute and secure the recognition by the state that the requirements have been met. It is this recognition that constitutes the grant of authority.

Many state constitutions make provision for incorporation by general incorporation laws, thus limiting the legislative right to grant corporate powers by special act. The following provisions taken from the Constitution of the State of Iowa are characteristic:

"Article VIII. Corporations. Section 1. No Corporation shall be created by special laws: but the General Assembly shall provide, by general laws, for the organization of all corporations hereafter to be created, except as hereinafter provided.

"Section 12. Subject to the provisions of this article, the General Assembly shall have power to amend or repeal all laws for the organization or creation of corporations, or granting of special or exclusive privileges or immunities, by a vote of two-thirds of each branch of the General Assembly; and no exclusive privileges, except as in this article provided, shall ever be granted."

C. PROCEDURE

The following steps are probably most typical of the procedure required in the formation of a corporation:

(1) The incorporators, having met the requirements as to number and citizenship, will prepare or have prepared articles of incorporation, in which is set forth the detailed information required by the enabling statute.

(2) Upon being properly executed, the articles, accompanied by the necessary fees, will be submitted to the Secretary of State.

(3) Upon being satisfied that the articles are in proper form, that they meet the requirements of law, and that their object is lawful and not against public policy, the Secretary of State will file the articles in the proper state records and issue to the incorporators a certificate of incorporation.

(4) The articles of incorporation are then placed on public record, usually in the records of the County Recorder's office of the county in which the corporation's principal place of business is located. This is usually the responsibility of the Secretary of State.

(5) The incorporators and directors hold their first meetings for the purpose of taking the necessary steps for the completion of the organization, such as acceptance of the charter, adoption of by-laws, and election of officers.

(6) It is usually required that the incorporators give public notice of the incorporation by newspaper publication and submit proof of having given notice to the Secretary of State.

D. COMMENCEMENT OF CORPORATE LIFE

The time at which an organization takes on the character of a corporation is dependent upon the particular statute under which it is organized.[7] The diversity of procedural requirements for incorporation under the various enabling statutes results in a diversity of operative facts that produce corporate existence. As a general rule, it can be said that corporate existence is dependent upon the incorporators' having complied with all the conditions set forth in the statute. Thus, under some statutes, a corporation comes into being upon the filing of the articles of incorporation with the proper state official.

Other acts that may ignite the torch of corporate life are:

(1) the filing of the articles in the proper state records after their official approval, or

(2) the completion of the organization (election of officers, etc.) after official approval of the articles has been obtained, or

(3) the issuing of a certificate of incorporation by the proper state officer.

Illustrative of the latter is the provision contained in Section 8359 of the 1939 Iowa Code, which reads:

---

[7] Whiting & Sons Co. v. Barton, p. 936.

"The corporation may commence business as soon as the certificate is issued by the secretary of state, and its acts shall be valid if the publication (notice of incorporation) is made within three months from the date of such certificate."

All statutes are not this explicit in designating when corporate life is to begin.

E. THE CHARTER

The granting of the corporate charter can be regarded as that act which breathes life into a corporation. It is symbolic of the grant of authority to an association of individuals to operate under that preferred status known as a corporation. The charter confers the right to be a corporation and the right to exercise corporate powers within the limits defined by the articles of incorporation and the laws of the state of incorporation.[8]

"The charter of a corporation found under the general incorporation act, does not consist of its articles of association alone, but of such articles taken in connection with the law under which the organization takes place. The provisions of the law enter into and form a part of the charter." *Danville v. Danville Water Co.,* 178 Ill. 299

Ever since the famous *Dartmouth College* case, 3 Wheat. 518 (1819), the charter of a corporation has been accepted as a contract between the corporation, the state, and the stockholders. The charter is in fact as the court said in *Garey v. St. Joe Min. Co.,* 32 Utah 497:

"The basis of three distinct contracts. The charter is a contract between the state and the corporation . . . between the corporation and the stockholders . . . between the stockholders and the state."

F. THE CORPORATE NAME

An identifying name is one of the essentials to the existence of a corporation. A corporation, like an individual, must have a name in which it can do the various things concerning the enterprise.

The various states have statutory provisions regulating the adoption and use of the corporate name. These statutes are in general designed to accomplish the following purposes:

(1) The selection and use of a name which clearly indicates to the public that the enterprise is incorporated. Usually the name must carry more than the word "Company," since this term is very commonly used to designate a partnership. To illustrate: In *American Cigar Lighter Co.,* 138 N.Y.S. 455, the court held that the name "Electric Cigar Lighter Company," without benefit of "abbreviation, affix or prefix thereto" did not legally and necessarily import "corporation." Under the Ohio statute the addition of the prefix "The" to the above name would be sufficient. The practice in New York State is to require, when the term "Company" is used, the affix of "Inc." The requirements of the statute in the particular state should be ascertained.

---

[8] Warren v. 536 Broad St. Corp., p. 937.

(2) The selection and use of a name which is not the same or similar to one already in use.[9, 10]

G. CORPORATIONS DE JURE AND DE FACTO

A corporation exists either de jure or de facto. A *corporation de jure* is one that has complied fully or substantially with the statutory requirements for its creation. A *de facto corporation* is an organization operating as a corporation as a matter of fact, although it has no existence as a corporation as a matter of law; it is an organization that has made a good-faith attempt to organize under the enabling statute but has failed in some respect. As said in *Finnegan* v. *The Knights of Labor Building Assoc.*, 52 Minn. 239:

> " 'Color of apparent organization under some charter or enabling act' does not mean that there shall have been a full compliance with what the law requires to be done, nor a substantial compliance. A substantial compliance will make a corporation de jure, but there must be an apparent attempt to perfect an organization under law."

A de facto corporation and its stockholders are accorded the same status and the same protection against third parties as are a de jure corporation and its members. It can carry on its affairs without interference as effectively as it could have if all requirements had been met. It is the state alone that can challenge a corporation's right to operate and to exist as a business unit. Unless an organization qualifies at least as a de facto corporation, its members cannot claim limited liability.[11] The nature of their liability has presented somewhat of a problem to the courts. As a general rule, it is held that the liability of the members of such an organization is that of partners. It is reasoned that, since there is no legally recognized organization that is intermediate between partnership and corporation, the defective corporation must be a partnership. However, some few jurisdictions have held that, since the intent was to have a corporation with the consequent limited liability of its members, no unlimited partnership liability can be imposed, at least as between the members of the organization.

► IV. STEPS PRELIMINARY TO CORPORATE EXISTENCE—PROMOTION

A. PROMOTER DEFINED

> "In a comprehensive sense 'promoter' includes those who undertake to form a corporation and to procure for it the rights, instrumentalities and capital by which it is to carry out the purposes set forth in its charter, and to establish it as fully able to do its business. Their work may begin long before the organization of the corporation, in seeking the opening for a venture and projecting a plan for its development, and may continue after the incorporation by attracting the investment of capital in its securities and providing it

[9] Meridian Yellow Cab Co. v. City Yellow Cabs, p. 938.

[10] Grand Rapids Trust Co. v. Haney School Fur. Co., p. 939.

[11] Hughes Co. v. Farmers' Union Produce Co., p. 940.

with the commercial breath of life." *Old Dominion Copper Mining etc. Co.* v. *Bigelow,* 203 Mass. 159

B. RIGHTS AND LIABILITIES OF CORPORATION FOR ACTS OF PROMOTER

1. *Contracts*

A promoter of a corporation is not an agent of the proposed corporation, since there is no principal for whom the promoter could act. Consequently, a corporation acquires no rights or liabilities from the promoter's contracts unless the corporation, upon coming into existence, adopts the contracts as its own or unless it is provided in the corporate charter or statute that the contracts of the promoter are those of the corporation.[12] To illustrate:

In *Hladovec* v. *Paul,* 222 Ill. 254, it was held that a contract of the promoter limiting the number of shares which could be issued to any one person was not binding upon the corporation.

2. *Torts*

A corporation cannot be held liable for torts of the promoter committed prior to the creation of the corporation. Thus a corporation is not liable for a fraudulent prospectus that has induced others to invest in the proposed corporation. The tort liability is solely that of the promoter.

C. LIABILITY OF PROMOTER

1. *Contracts*

A promoter's liability upon contracts that have been entered into preliminary to the creation of the corporation is dependent entirely upon the circumstances and the application of the following rules:

(1) If the promoter has personally entered into the contract, he is liable even though the contract is entirely for the benefit of the intended corporation.[13]

(2) The adoption of the contract by the corporation will not of itself release the promoter from his contractual liability.

(3) A promoter is relieved of his contractual liability where a *contract of novation* has been entered into between the corporation and the party with whom the promoter has contracted. Under a contract of novation, the contracting party agrees to release the promoter and to accept the corporation in his place. An adoption of a contract by a corporation is not a contract of novation.

(4) On the other hand, if the promoter has contracted not personally but in the name and upon the credit of the proposed corporation, he is not liable. Thus, if it is clearly understood between the promoter and the other contracting party that the latter will not look to the promoter but will take his chances that the corporation will be brought into existence and that the contract will then be adopted, the promoter will have no liability upon the contract.

---

12 Meyers v. Wells, p. 942.

13 King Features Syndicate v. Courrier, p. 943.

D. RELATION OF PROMOTER TO CORPORATION AND STOCKHOLDERS

1. *Duties as Fiduciary*

A promoter occupies the position of a fiduciary toward the prospective corporation and its stockholders. The law imposes upon him the duty of good faith in his dealings in behalf of and with the corporation. It is upon this basis that a promoter is denied the right to reap any secret profits out of his promotional efforts.

> "Hence, if any of them has a secret contract for the purchase of property, . . . or an agreement that he shall have stock in the corporation without paying therefor, any advantage which he thereby obtains is a fraud on the other shareholders and upon the corporation, and he will not be permitted to retain it." *Wills* v. *Nehalem Coal Co.,* 52 Ore. 70

> "If a promoter has a property to sell to the company, it is quite open to him to do so; but upon him, as upon any other person in a fiduciary position, it is incumbent to make full and fair disclosure of his interest and position with respect to that property." *New Sombrero Phosphate Co.* v. *Erlanger,* 5 Ch.D. 73

To illustrate:

In *Hayward* v. *Leeson,* 176 Mass. 310, the promoters, after the creation of the corporation but while they were the sole stockholders, voted themselves stock as payment for their services in obtaining options for the purchase of land. The court in holding that the corporation had the right to recover the stock said:

> "Payment to promoters of remuneration for their services is not made valid by a vote passed by the corporation, when the corporation is in the sole control of the promoters before the capital has been issued to the public. The persons to whom the promoters owe the duty which they owe by reason of their fiduciary relation are the persons who put their money into the enterprise at the invitation of the promoters, that is to say, the future stockholders."

2. *Right to Recover for Services*

It is generally recognized that a promoter has no right to recover for his expenditures or services performed in bringing the corporation into being unless (1) such is provided for by statute or by the corporate charter, or unless (2) the corporation, after its formation, agrees to pay him. In some states, however, it is held that the promoter may recover for such services and expenditures as are reasonably necessary to the formation of the corporation upon the theory that the corporation should pay for the benefit it receives. If the promoter intended his services as a gratuity, he cannot recover. To illustrate:

In *Powell* v. *Georgia etc. Ry. Co.,* 121 Ga. 803, it was held that, since the promoters had agreed among themselves that their services would be rendered without compensation, a promoter could not recover for his services upon the theory that the corporation had received the benefit.

CASES

CASE NO. 1

Lamm v. Stoen. 226 Iowa 622, 284 N.W. 465 (1939)

OLIVER, J. Norske Selskab (the Norwegian Society) was a sixty-year-old unincorporated literary and social club at Decorah, Iowa, consisting of more than 100 members of Scandinavian blood. The society had a constitution and bylaws, elected officers, held regular meetings, kept records, charged $3 annual dues, and appears to have been a solvent and well conducted institution.

In 1925, it leased club rooms from one Higgins by written lease executed in the name of the society by its president. . . .

Later the society desired additional room and authorized its officers to again negotiate with Higgins. Resulting from these negotiations was the termination of the former lease and the making of the lease in controversy executed in the name of the society by its president for the term beginning August 1, 1927, and ending August 1, 1937. . . .

The lease also contained the following recitations: . . .

"No individual member of the party of the second part shall be liable for rents or repairs in connection with this lease. . . ."

Before the lease terminated in 1937, the society notified appellant that it had decided to exercise its option for a 10 year extension. Appellant refused to consent to this, . . . She refused to accept rent from the society which was tendered as it fell due and which tenders were thereafter maintained. In September, 1932, appellant instituted this suit in equity to quiet title to the real estate. The defendants named were four individuals as officers and members of Norske Selskab, an unincorporated society, in their representative capacity for the entire membership of said society. . . . The decree of the trial court dismissed the petition for want of equity and adjudicated the lease to be valid and to give the society the right to occupy the premises thereunder until August 1, 1947, with right to redecorate and deduct the reasonable expense thereof from the rents. From this decree plaintiff has appealed.

Appellant contended in the trial court, and now urges that since the society was an unincorporated association and because of the clause in the lease exonerating the individual members from liability for payment of rent, the lease was lacking mutuality both of liability and of remedy and was, therefore, invalid and of no legal effect. It is true that, strictly speaking, a voluntary unincorporated association of this nature has no right to contract and cannot maintain a suit in the name of such voluntary unincorporated association alone. . . .

We have also held that the individual who contracts in the name of a voluntary unincorporated association is personally liable thereon, in the absence of an agreement with the other party releasing him from personal liability, and that such other members of said association as authorize, consent to or ratify such undertaking are also personally liable, in the absence of an agreement exempting them. . . .

The personal liability of representatives and members of a voluntary unincorporated association appears to be based upon principles of agency. The person making the contract for the association has been held liable upon the theory that he was in fact a principal or held himself out as agent for a principal who had no legal status. Other members who authorize or ratify such contract are liable because it was made by their agent. . . .

Conversely one who contracts with an association as a legal entity and capable of transacting business and receives money or other valuable consideration therefrom may not deny the validity of the contract on the ground that the association has no legal existence. . . .

Does the clause, no individual member shall be liable for rents or repairs, destroy the obligation or the remedy? The assets of the association, including the effects specifically mortgaged to the landlord, were not thereby exempted from the obligation. As above noted, the individual members had no severable interest in such assets but only the right to jointly enjoy the same while they were members. Therefore, exempting the members from liability did not exempt the assets of the association. The assets were liable for the obligations of the lease and such obligations could be legally enforced against said assets. . . .

Wherefore, the decree is affirmed.

CASE NO. 2

Petrovich v. Felco Chemical Corporation. 86 N.Y.S. (2d) 327 (1949)

COLDEN, J. An action for damages for personal injuries sustained by the plaintiffs, as a result of the explosion of a steel drum containing liquid soap, which was manufactured by the corporate defendant and sold to the plaintiffs' employer. The sole incorporators, stockholders, officers and directors were joined as party defendants, upon the theory that in truth and fact they were copartners in the business of the corporation and were conducting said business under the guise of the corporate form. The individual defendants now move to dismiss the complaint for legal insufficiency.

A corporation must be judged "as a single body, and not as a congregation of individuals," Matter of Vannier v. Anti-Saloon League of New York, 238 N.Y. 457. . . . The test for justifying the disregard of the corporate entity is fraud or illegality; it is invoked where to preserve the corporate fiction, would work inequity or injustice. . . . Nothing of this character is alleged in the complaint or even claimed in the brief.

We have here a case involving an accident which has resulted in personal injuries for which a cause of action is clearly stated against the corporate defendant. The disregard of the corporate entity is attempted solely upon the basis of dominance and control by individuals who incorporated, and now manage and control said corporation through ownership of stock. This of itself does not justify the disregard of the corporate fiction in an action of this character. As was stated in Elenkrieg v. Siebrecht, 238 N.Y. 254, at page 262, 144 N.E. 519, at page 521, 34 A.L.R. 592:

"Many a man incorporates his business or his property . . . for the very purpose of escaping personal liability, and he may do so as a cover if in fact the corporation really exists—is doing business as permitted by the laws of this state or the state of its incorporation; in other words, is a person recognized by the law." . . .

CASE NO. 3

New York Soc. for S.V. v. MacFadden Publications. 260 N.Y. 167, 183 N.E. 284, 86 A.L.R. 440 (1932)

HUBBS, J., delivered the opinion of the court:

The plaintiff is a domestic corporation organized under an act of the Legislature (Laws 1873, c. 527) to enforce

> "the laws for the suppression of the trade in and circulation of obscene literature . . . and articles of indecent and immoral use."

The act authorized it to take and hold real and personal property. It is dependent upon voluntary contributions for its support.

The defendant corporation, MacFadden Publications, Inc., is the publisher of the newspaper, the New York Evening Graphic, and the individual defendant is the president of that corporation in personal charge and control. Articles were published in that paper which charged the plaintiff with crimes and highly improper and reprehensible conduct. The articles were libelous upon their face.

In this action to recover a judgment for damages against the defendants growing out of the publication of these articles, the trial court directed a judgment for the plaintiff for $10,000, and stated that the articles are libelous, false, and defamatory. . . .

It is clearly settled in this jurisdiction by controlling authority that a corporation may maintain an action for libel without proof of special damage in case a false publication

> "is defamatory and injurious and directly affects its credit or the management of its business and necessarily causes pecuniary loss.
>
> "The same rule is applicable to a corporation as to individuals. Where the latter may recover without proof of special damage, a corporation may also. . . ."

Corporations engaged in charitable, social welfare, benevolent and religious work, have the right to acquire and hold property which may produce a profit or income. Indeed, the statute under which plaintiff was organized expressly grants that power to it. Many such corporations own and control very valuable properties, and in their management such corporations establish a reputation, rights and interests similar to the reputation, rights and interests acquired by individuals and corporations engaged in business for profit. To decide that such corporations have no reputation acquired in the management of their affairs and property which can be injured or destroyed by a malicious libel, unless special damage is proved, would constitute a reflection upon the administration of justice. Benevolent, religious, and other like corporations have interests connected with property and its management which should have the same protection and rights in courts in case of injury as corporations engaged in business for profit.

Their usefulness depends largely upon their reputation for honesty, fair dealing and altruistic effort to improve social conditions. . . .

The judgment should be affirmed, with costs.

CASE NO. 4

Rudin v. Steinbugler. 103 F. (2d) 323 (1939)

SWAN, C.J. On January 31, 1938, George E. Steinbugler, an attorney at law, was adjudicated bankrupt upon his voluntary petition. His trustee in bankruptcy brought suit in the district court to set aside transfers of property to the bankrupt's wife which were alleged to be fraudulent as to creditors. The bankrupt, his wife and Park Equine Amusement Corporation were named as defendants. They have appealed from a decree in favor of the plaintiff.

The questions raised are chiefly questions of fact. The first is whether the bankrupt was insolvent on December 20, 1936, on which date he claims to have made a gift to his wife of all the stock of said Amusement Corporation by delivering to her unendorsed stock certificates. We may assume that the fact of non-endorsement of the certificates would not prevent the transfer from being an effective gift. . . . But since the transfer was without consideration it was presumptively fraudulent as to existing creditors. . . . That presumption was not repelled; on the contrary, the district court found that the bankrupt was insolvent on the critical date. It is admitted that his debts were $16,800 and his assets, exclusive of three disputed items, only $10,724. With those items included, assets would have exceeded admitted liabilities by $2,400. . . .

The appellants further contend that the plaintiff failed to prove that the stock of the Amusement Corporation had any value at the time of its transfer. The record refutes this contention. The corporation was organized in the summer of 1935 to operate a pony track and riding school in Prospect Park, Brooklyn. In December of that year the bankrupt purchased 50 per cent. of its stock for $850, thus becoming the sole stockholder. During the year 1936 the pony track business conducted in the name of the corporation, netted the bankrupt about $3,000, and a like sum in 1937 for, despite the alleged gift of the stock to his wife, he continued to take the receipts and pay from his personal account the expenses of the business. If the corporation is to be treated as a juristic person separate and apart from its sole stockholder (and the appellants so treat it), their contention is futile that stock of a corporation yielding such net returns was worthless.

The second transaction which the decree set aside was a purported transfer from the Amusement Corporation to the bankrupt's wife of all its ponies and equipment in consideration of her agreement to pay certain debts of the bankrupt and of the corporation. This transaction took place on January 10, 1938—the very day on which Hashagen, a former client of the bankrupt, obtained a judgment against him for some $8,600. The district court found that this transfer was made by the bankrupt with the intent to defraud his creditors and that his wife participated in such intent. This finding is amply supported by the record and is not challenged by the appellants, their contention being that the property transferred belonged to the corporation, not to the bankrupt, and therefore can not be reached for the benefit of his creditors. But this contention is based on a fallacious premise, for the district court expressly found that the ponies and equipment were really the bankrupt's property; that he disregarded the corporation and carefully omitted all formalities necessarily attendant upon the preservation of the corporate entity; and that he recognized the corporation as a mere dummy and "a department for his own activities." This conclusion is fully justified. No corporate stock records or books of account were kept; no income tax or other tax reports were filed; no elections or corporate meetings held, except the one directors' meeting which purported to authorize the transfer of January 10, 1938; no dividends were declared, although the bankrupt received the net income of the business; and on November 20, 1936, he executed in the name of the corporation a chattel mortgage as security for his individual debt. Under the circumstances disclosed by the record the corporate entity was properly disregarded by the district court. . . .

Decree affirmed.

CASE NO. 5

Charles E. Austin, Inc. v. Kelly. 321 Mich. 426, 32 N.W. (2d) 694 (1948)

BOYLES, J. Plaintiff, a Michigan corporation, filed this bill of complaint in the circuit court for Wayne county in chancery to enjoin the secretary of State from levying upon any of plaintiff's property for the purpose of collecting any gasoline taxes, ...

The case results from an audit by the secretary of State's office of the plaintiff's records for the period from September 1, 1939, to October 31, 1940. . . . The plaintiff Charles E. Austin, Inc., is a Michigan corporation with an authorized capital of $10,000. The sole shareholder is Margret P. Austin, the wife of Charles E. Austin, who holds all of the stock as trustee for her children. She is also president and secretary of the company. It is engaged in the wholesale gasoline business in the city of Detroit. As a wholesale distributor, it is required to secure a wholesale distributor's license each year from the secretary of State under the State Gasoline Tax Act. . . .

The plaintiff during said period filed monthly reports with the secretary of State and paid the gasoline taxes due according to such reports. As a wholesale distributor of gasoline, it also operated a "boat terminal transfer" within the meaning of said Gasoline Tax Act, as well as a "bulk storage plant." This plant consisted of four storage tanks. . . . The real estate and tanks were owned by Margret P. Austin and the tanks were leased by her to Charles E. Austin, Inc. Tank No. 1 was qualified as a "boat terminal transfer." Tank No. 3 was a "bulk storage tank." Tanks Nos. 2 and 4 were leased to the Joy Oil Company, Ltd., by Margret P. Austin during the navigation season and were used by that company for the storage of gasoline pending transshipment to Canada. The said Joy Oil Company, Ltd., is a corporation organized under Canadian law. Margret P. Austin is also the president and secretary of this company, and also owns all of its shares. It carries on no operations within the State of Michigan except that during the period here involved it stored gasoline in tanks Nos. 2 and 4, and possibly on one occasion in tank No. 3, pending transshipment by boat to Canada. It is not authorized to do business in Michigan. Plaintiff concedes that to some extent there was a commingling of its gasoline with that of the Joy Oil Company, Ltd., in the four tanks. The Joy Oil Company, Ltd., obtains gasoline from suppliers in Michigan and also by railroad tank cars from outside the State of Michigan. When the gasoline was shipped by rail to Detroit it was stored in the tanks leased by it from Margret P. Austin pending transshipment by boat to Canada. . . .

We are not impressed with any merit in plaintiff's claim that under the circumstances of this case the gasoline stored in the tanks pending transshipment to Canada is not liable for the gasoline tax, interest and penalties imposed by the State. Tax-exempt gasoline and taxable gasoline was commingled by the plaintiff and Joy Oil Company, Ltd., and there was a break in the continuity of transportation of the gasoline in interstate and foreign commerce, for the convenience and benefit of the plaintiff. . . .

Nor is there merit in plaintiff's claim that Charles E. Austin, Inc., a separate corporation, is not liable for the gasoline tax on gasoline transshipped by Joy Oil Company, Ltd. . . . the separate existence of the two corporations will be ignored and both will be regarded as one where they are so organized and carried on that one is a mere instrumentality or agent or adjunct of the other. . . .

CASE NO. 6

Ohio Edison Co. v. Warner Coal Corporation. 79 Ohio App. 437, 72 N.E. (2d) 487 (1946)

PER CURIAM. . . . In this action the plaintiff is seeking to charge the W. H. Warner & Co., Inc., with responsibility for debts ostensibly incurred by The Warner Coal Corporation—a distinct legal entity.

A reading of the record discloses that for a considerable period before the happening out of which this law suit arose, the W. H. Warner & Company acted as selling agent for certain West Virginia coal mines and as such selling agent sold coal to the plaintiff . . . the owners of the mines desired to sell them. The plaintiff was interested in preserving a source of coal supply and the W. H. Warner & Company, Inc., was interested in continuing its relation as selling agent for the mines. They set themselves to the task of devising some plan to accomplish their respective desires . . . the plan was devised and executed whereby the Warner Coal Corporation was organized. Its entire capital stock of $50,000 was subscribed and paid for by W. H. Warner & Company, Inc., and the plaintiff advanced $100,000 as a pre-payment on coal to be delivered. . . .

After The Warner Coal Corporation was duly organized it entered into a contract with the W. H. Warner & Company, Inc., to act as selling agent and perform most of the management of the corporate affairs.

It is clear from the record that the purpose of the W. H. Warner & Company, Inc., was to continue the relation of selling agent for the coal mines, and not to become the owner thereof with its attendant responsibilities—and this purpose must have been fully understood by the plaintiff. There is no doubt that all the forms of law were complied with at all times, to accomplish this purpose unless the fact that The W. H. Warner & Company, Inc., owned all the stock of The Warner Coal Corporation and the two corporations had the same officers defeats that purpose.

While it is claimed that The W. H. Warner & Company, Inc., usurped complete control of all the corporate functions of The Warner Coal Corporation, we find that in the contract between the two corporations the ultimate authority of the board of directors of The Warner Coal Corporation was expressly stipulated.

This is not a case of a mere mask behind which W. H. Warner & Company was conducting its own business. The Warner Coal Corporation had title to the mines. . . . It operated the business of mining the coal and had a substantial capital reasonably regarded as adequate to enable it to operate its business and pay its debts as they matured. Various unforeseen economic factors intervened to defeat the expectation.

It is undoubted law that a corporation may be formed, and usually is, for the specific purpose of avoiding liability and loss beyond the contribution to its capital.

That is not a fraudulent intent. On the contrary, the law recognizes it as a purpose in conformity to sound public policy. In the case at bar, no other intent is disclosed and that intent was fully understood by the plaintiff at the time.

Of course, if the record disclosed facts showing that through this parent corporation and wholly owned subsidiary The W. H. Warner & Company, Inc., was in fact the lessee of the mines and was operating them and that the wholly owned subsidiary was simply its agent in the ostensible ownership and operation of the mines and that The W. H. Warner & Company, Inc., was the undisclosed principal, a case of liability would be presented even in the absence of any other consideration. But no such case is presented here. The existence of the two corporations as distinct entities was preserved at all times. Nor were their properties, capital, or business commingled.

As the law authorized the creation of corporations for the purpose of limiting liability and The Warner Coal Corporation was organized and conducted in conformity to such laws, we are of the opinion that the common pleas court was correct in holding that no case was presented for the disregard of the corporate entity and holding The W. H. Warner & Company, Inc., liable for the debts of The Warner Coal Corporation. . . .

CASE NO. 7

Whiting & Sons Co. v. Barton. 204 Mass. 169, 90 N.E. 528 (1910)

KNOWLTON, C.J. This is an action of replevin to recover certain merchandise of the assignee holding under a conveyance of the White-Gates Paint and Varnish Co. for the benefit of its creditors. This corporation is now in bankruptcy, and the action is defended by the trustee. . . . The White-Gates Co. was organized under the laws of this state, and its agreement of association and the proceedings under it were filed with the Commissioner of Corporations on September 10, 1907, and its certificate of incorporation was issued by the Secretary of the Commonwealth on the same day. In July, 1907, White and Gates, two of the subsequent incorporators, were at the plaintiff's factory, and . . . gave an order for a large number of brushes, stating that they, with one Philbrick, were to form a corporation, and these brushes were to be made for and delivered to the new corporation, on or before September 1, 1907.

. . . on September 5, 1907, a meeting was held by White and Gates and two men of the name of Curry, and an agreement of association in the usual form was signed, containing a waiver of the notice of the time and place of holding the first meeting for the organization of the corporation, and appointing September 9, 1907, as the time for holding this meeting.

On September 7, Gates called at the plaintiff's factory and had a talk with Whiting, the treasurer of the plaintiff company, and handed him a printed card of the White-Gates Paint and Varnish Co. which had been prepared in anticipation of the organization of the corporation. A place of business in Boston, which had been hired beforehand, was designated, on this card. He told Whiting that the company was formed, and to go right ahead and deliver the goods. The goods described in the writ were accordingly delivered at the designated place of business of the supposed new corporation, on the morning of September 9, and at the same time were charged as goods sold to this corporation on a credit of four months from November 1, 1907. The corporation made an assignment for the benefit of its creditors on January 31, 1908, and afterwards was adjudged a bankrupt. . . . The replevied goods were taken by the corporation after its organization, and credited as bought of the plaintiff.

The first question is whether the title to the merchandise passed by the supposed sale and delivery on the morning of September 9. We think it plain that it did not. There was then no such corporation as the plaintiff supposed it was dealing with. By the terms of the statute of 1903 (St. 1903, p. 425, c. 437, § 12) the language of the certificate to be issued by the Secretary of the Commonwealth is that the persons named as subscribers "are hereby made an existing corporation"; and "the certificate shall have the force and effect of a special charter," . . . By the same section it is provided that "the existence of every corporation which is not created by special law shall begin upon the filing of the articles of organization in the office of the Secretary of the Commonwealth." As the certificate, which has the effect of a special charter, is to be issued forthwith, it is assumed by the statute that the filing of the articles and the making of the certificate will take place at substantially the same time. Until there was a corporation, there was no party with which the contract in this case could be made, or to which the title could pass. There is no doubt, therefore, that, after the delivery plaintiff could have replevied the property from anyone in whose possession it was found. . . .

CASE NO. 8

Warren v. 536 Broad St. Corporation. 6 N.J. Super. 170, 70 A. (2d) 782 (1950)

DONGES, J.A.D. This is an appeal from a judgment of the Superior Court, Chancery Division.

Plaintiff a minority shareholder of the defendant 536 Broad Street Corporation complains of a proposed special meeting of the company's stockholders and of the action contemplated to be taken thereat. The special meeting was called for the purpose of considering and acting upon a resolution, the object of which is to amend the corporate charter so as to delete therefrom Article Seventh which reads as follows:

"Seventh: No real estate owned by the corporation may be leased, mortgaged, sold, or exchanged, unless the Board of Directors shall, at a properly called meeting, adopt a resolution authorizing the officers to make such sale, lease, mortgage, or exchange of the real estate of the corporation, and unless and until such resolution of the Board of Directors receives the approval in writing of the holders of not less than seventy-five per cent (75%) of the stock of the company issued and outstanding at the time such resolution is adopted." . . .

The main question presented for our determination is whether the Charter of 536 Broad Street Corporation may be amended so as to delete Article Seventh, if such amendment is accomplished in a manner consonant with the General Corporation Act.

Plaintiff contends that every corporate charter is a binding contract between the corporation and its stockholder and by the stockholders *inter sese*. That proposition of law is well settled and is amply supported by the decisions of our State. However, it must also be remembered that the law existing at the time the charter is granted is as much a part of that charter as though that law were fully and explicitly stated in the charter, and every stockholder is presumed to have purchased his stock, subject to the charter as so expanded. . . .

The 536 Broad Street Corporation was incorporated under the provisions of the General Corporation Act of New Jersey, P.L. 1896, Chap. 185 as amended and supplemented, down to February 2, 1927. Section 27 of the said General Corporation Act . . . provides in part as follows:

"Every corporation organized under this act may . . . alter or amend existing provisions for the regulation of the management and affairs of the corporation, and make such other amendment, change or alteration as may be desired, in manner following: The board of directors shall pass a resolution declaring that such amendment, change or alteration is advisable and calling a meeting of the stockholders to take action thereon. The meeting shall be held upon such notice as the by-laws provide, and in the absence of such provision, upon ten days' notice, given personally or by mail; if two-thirds in interest of each class of the stockholders having voting powers shall vote in favor of such amendment, change or alteration, the corporation shall make a certificate thereof under its seal and the hands of its president or vice-president and its secretary or assistant secretary, which certificate shall be acknowledged or proved as in the case of deeds of real estate, and such certificate shall be filed in the office of the Secretary of State, and upon the filing of the same, the certificate of incorporation shall be deemed to be amended accordingly." . . .

These provisions of the General Corporation Act, which is part of the charter of the 536 Broad Street Corporation, are broad enough to permit the amendment contemplated, provided, the required number of votes are secured and the proper procedure followed. . . .

CASE NO. 9

Meridian Yellow Cab Co. v. City Yellow Cabs. 206 Miss. 812, 41 So. (2d) 14 (1949)

SMITH, J. Appellant filed its original bill of complaint in the Chancery Court of Lauderdale County, praying that

". . . the defendant, City Yellow Cabs, be permanently enjoined from using the corporate name, City Yellow Cabs or any corporate name containing the words 'Yellow Cabs' or any corporate name similar to the corporate name of complainant";

and for general relief.

The suit was predicated upon the claimed protection of appellant by Section 5322, Code of 1942, as follows:

"No corporation shall be created under the laws of this state with the name of any existing corporation of this state nor with the name of any company or corporation for profit incorporated under or by virtue of the laws of any government, or of any other state or territory, now or hereafter doing business in this state which has heretofore filed or may hereafter file in the office of the secretary of state of Mississippi a copy of its charter or articles of incorporation or certificate of incorporation, as required by the laws of this state, or with a name so similar thereto as to be misleading."

The facts, as developed in the record before us, are that both appellant and appellee are chartered under the laws of Mississippi, domiciled at Meridian, and doing a similar taxicab business in said city. The corporate name of appellant is "Meridian Yellow Cab Co., Inc." and that of appellant is "City Yellow Cabs." On the sides of the cabs of both companies under their respective names in small lettering are the words "Yellow Cab" in large letters. The cabs of appellant are yellow all over except the tires, and those of appellee are yellow all over except for the hood, fenders and tires. . . .

American Jurisprudence lays down the practice to be that

"The inquiries when equitable relief is sought must be whether it is likely that the public will be misled and whether the complaining corporation is likely to be injured. Experience, not in the particular case, but in other cases, must be employed in determining the fact. Mere conjecture is not sufficient. Moreover, whether the court will interfere in a particular case must depend upon circumstances; the identity or similarity of the names; the identity of the business of the respective corporation; how far the name is a true description of the kind and quality of the articles manufactured or the business carried on; the extent of the confusion which may be created or apprehended; and other circumstances which might justly influence the judgment of the judge in granting or withholding the remedy." 13 Am. Jur., par. 137, p. 274

The Supreme Court of Oregon observed that the authorities justified the conclusion that primarily it is not the name which is protected, but the business. . . . Since we have decided that the name "City Yellow Cabs" is so similar to that of "Meridian Yellow Cab Company, Inc.," as to be misleading, this statute was transgressed to that extent, and, therefore, appellee could not lawfully operate under its misleading name in the City of Meridian, and environs, in competition with appellant in a manner that confused the public by the misleading nomenclature. We are not to be considered as holding, by what we have just said, that appellee could not operate elsewhere under its chartered name, "City Yellow Cabs," beyond the competitive sphere of the two taxicab companies, as shown in the record.

Therefore, we reverse the decree of the Chancery Court, and enter a decree here restraining appellee from operating its taxicab business in the City of Meridian under its name "City Yellow Cabs," and from utilizing the words "Yellow Cab or Cabs" upon its cabs, or otherwise, in its said business in the City of Meridian, or environs, so long as appellant, "Meridian Yellow Cab Company, Inc." is also engaged in the taxicab business in said area. . . .

CASE NO. 10

Grand Rapids Trust Co. v. Haney School Furniture Co. 221 Mich. 487, 191 N.W. 196, 27 A.L.R. 1020 (1922)

WIEST, J., delivered the opinion of the court:

Bill to restrain defendant company and its incorporators from doing business under the same name as the defunct corporation of which plaintiff is receiver, and from receiving any mail addressed to the Haney School Furniture Company.

The defendants, by answer, set up the dissolution of the old corporation, asserted the right to take the name because there was no existing corporation of such name, . . . a temporary injunction was granted, ...

The injunction cannot stand unless it can be held that the right to the corporate name as representative of an existing good will is an asset in the hands of the receiver and capable of being sold.

The corporation was a creature of the law, and when it finished the course fixed by law its name was no longer that of an existing corporation. The bill shows no exclusive products to which the name has attached a trade meaning. Defendants have a right to manufacture the same products at will.

The purpose of defendants in taking the name is immaterial if they have kept within the law.

It is said the defendants have seized the name to fool the public. If so, that fact is of no concern to the receiver, unless it interferes with something he can sell and pass to others.

The receiver cannot carry on the business of the old corporation, and therefore it is inconceivable that defendants' use of the name will result in unfair competition as against plaintiff as receiver.

To invoke redress there must be an existing corporation with invaded rights, or with rights of creditors to be worked out in the process of dissolution. . . .

The protection of a tradename extends only to the party entitled to use it in the trade.

In Mayer Fertilizer & Junk Co. v. Virginia-Carolina Chemical Co. 35 App. D.C. 425, it was said:

> "The terms 'good will' and 'business' are not synonymous. Good will, like a trademark, is but an incident to, and can have no existence apart from, the business in which it had its origin. 'It is tangible only as an incident, as connected with a going concern or business having locality or name, and is not susceptible of being disposed of independently.' Metropolitan Nat. Bank v. St. Louis Dispatch Co. 149 U.S. 436, . . . In this case the Southern Fertilizing Company wound up its affairs and abandoned its business. Necessarily, its good will became extinct. There was nothing tangible to which it might attach. . . ."

We recognize the value of good will to a going business, and its value as an asset in case of sale of such a business; but we cannot extend the holdings with reference to such recognized value to a business terminated by operation of law.

The injunction restrained defendant company from receiving any mail addressed to the Haney School Furniture Company, and ordered such mail to be delivered to the plaintiff. Defendant is within its rights in the use of the name, and it has a right to receive mail addressed to it; but mail received, if any, for the receiver, must be turned where it belongs. . . .

The temporary injunction should not have been granted, ...

CASE NO. 11

Hughes Co. v. Farmers' Union Produce Co. 110 Neb. 736, 194 N.W. 872, 37 A.L.R. 1314 (1923)

REDICK, D.J., delivered the opinion of the court:

Action upon certain accounts by plaintiff against defendants, seeking to charge them as partners in an unincorporated association doing business as Farmers' Union Produce Company. There was judgment against defendants individually, and they appeal. There is no dispute as to the amount due plaintiff, the only contentions of defendants being (1) that they constituted a corporation de facto, ...

Plaintiff produced certificates from the secretary of state and county clerk to the effect that no articles of incorporation had been filed by the Farmers' Union Produce Company, and evidence showing certain of defendants to be members of the association, and rested.

Defendants then introduced the record of a meeting held October 5, 1918, showing the adoption of the "constitution and by-laws" of "Farmers' Union Produce Company." This document contains no declaration of an intention to form a corporation,—the company being called an association,—the only reference to a corporation being a provision for amendment of "the articles of incorporation." . . . The original document was not produced, the evidence fails to show it was ever signed or acknowledged, and no copy was ever filed anywhere. . . . An organization similar to that of a corporation was effected, however, by the election of a board of directors and officers of the company; meetings were held and minutes kept in a crude sort of way; and, while the question is not free from doubt, it may be assumed that the parties attempted to form a corporation and believed they had done so. The business was carried on in the name of "Farmers' Union Produce Company," and all letters and statements from plaintiff were so addressed. . . . That they are not a corporation de jure is conceded, so the question is whether, under the evidence, they were one de facto. . . .

There is some apparent difference of opinion as to what facts are necessary to be shown to establish the existence of a corporation de facto, and it is not intended to hold that the filing of the articles is the only act which will authorize the requisite inference; but the authorities are practically unanimous upon the point that there must be some color of a corporate franchise before even an inference of such a corporation is permissible; and to acquire this requisite color, some effort, springing directly from its requirements, must have been made to comply with the statute. This does not mean a substantial compliance, because that is all that is requisite for a corporation de jure, as suggested in Finnegan v. Noerenberg, 52 Minn. 239, 18 L.R.A. 778, 38 Am. St. Rep. 552, 53 N.W. 1150, and it is there stated:

> "But there must be an apparent attempt to perfect an organization under the law. There being such apparent attempt to perfect an organization, the failure as to some substantial requirement will prevent the body being a corporation de jure; but, if there be user pursuant to such attempted organization, it will not prevent it being a corporation de facto, ..."

This case clearly distinguishes between persons acting with and those acting without color of organization, and holds that the mere existence of a law under which a corporation might be formed, unaccompanied by any attempt to do anything required thereby looking toward a franchise, will not satisfy the requirement of a colorable compliance, to support a claim of a de facto corporation. The reasoning of this case is convincing.

In Abbott v. Omaha Smelting & Ref. Co. supra, it was said:

> " 'Organization' . . . means simply the process of forming and arranging into suitable disposition the parts which are to act together in, and in defining the objects of, the compound body, and that this process, even when completed in all its parts, does not confer the franchise, either valid or defective, but, on the contrary, it is only the act of the individuals, and therefore something else must be done to secure the franchise."

These acts necessarily precede the filing of the articles, which is the first step to initiate a franchise. Up to the filing of the articles the power and authority of the state is not invoked, and the body has not received the breath of life necessary to its existence as a legal entity, defective or perfect. That case has never been criticized, so far as we are advised, but has been cited with approval many times in this and other states. . . .

In the case at bar no step was taken which gave defendants any color of right to a corporate franchise. The most that can be said is that they prepared to secure a franchise, but stopped short of any act which would secure their purpose. . . .

Our conclusion is that defendants are not entitled to claim that they are a corporation de facto.

Affirmed.

CASE NO. 12

Meyers v. Wells. 252 Wis. 35, 31 N.W. (2d) 512 (1948)

Nicholas S. Meyers commenced an action against Diamond Coal and Dock Company, a corporation, on February 9, 1945, to recover wages claimed to be due him. . . .

During the fall of 1938 Nicholas S. Meyers and A. C. Wells discussed entering into the wholesale and retail coal business at Marinette, Wisconsin. Meyers had twenty-seven years' experience in the coal business. . . . On March 10, 1939, after numerous conferences, they agreed to form a corporation to carry on the business. Wells personally executed a written contract employing Meyers as manager for three years from that date at $5,000 a year payable in semi-monthly installments. Wells and his two sons subscribed for seventy-five hundred shares of stock and Meyers for one thousand shares of stock in the corporation, which was organized as the Diamond Coal and Dock Company on April 3, 1939, at an organization meeting. . . .

Meyers started to work under his contract with Wells March 15, 1939, and continued as manager of the company until he was discharged in May, 1944. . . .

BARLOW, J. The first question is whether appellant adopted the contract entered into between Wells and Meyers. It must be conceded that Wells entered into this contract in order to obtain Meyers' services to manage the coal company, wherein he was to be the majority stockholder of a family corporation, where Meyers was the only outside stockholder, all stockholders being officers of the corporation. Appellant relies on the fact that the board of directors of the corporation never took any action adopting the Wells-Meyers contract and never agreed upon the compensation which Meyers was to receive. It is argued that the Wells contract in no way bound the corporation.

The corporation was not in existence at the time the contract was entered into but it was a contract made by one of the promoters in the interest of the future corporation and constituted an offer which could be accepted by the corporation when it came into existence. The failure to formally accept or adopt the contract by formal action of the board of directors does not mean its adoption cannot be implied from conduct and circumstances following its incorporation. If the corporation accepts the benefits of a contract made on its behalf by its promoters this amounts to an adoption and it must accept the contract and its burdens as well as its benefits. . . . Meyers . . . was paid by the corporation for the services rendered during the two weeks prior to the time it was organized, and at all times thereafter for a period of more than five years. The acts of the officers clearly establish its adoption as found by the trial court. . . .

On the question of whether the terms of the contract extended beyond the three year term, it is undisputed that no new written contract was entered into at the expiration of the original contract although Meyers several times requested that one be entered into. He continued to work. It is a general rule of law that if an employee continues working after his contract expires and no new contract is made it will be presumed the parties intended he should be paid the same wages he received under the original contract. . . . Meyers continued to render services as manager of appellant corporation after the original contract expired. The salary he was entitled to while the contract was in effect continued after the expiration of the contract where no new agreement was entered into. This affirms the decision of the trial court.

CASE NO. 13

King Features Syndicate v. Courrier. 43 N.W. (2d) 718 (Iowa) (1950)

MULRONEY, J. This is a suit for specific performance of a written contract whereby it is alleged plaintiff agreed to furnish leased wire news reports to defendants for broadcasting in Fort Madison. The petition set forth a copy of the contract sued upon and prayed in the alternative for judgment against defendants for damages in the sum of $1,918.80 for breach of said contract. The trial court dismissed plaintiff's petition.

The plaintiff, King Features Syndicate, is a department of the Hearst Corporation and is engaged in the business of gathering news and furnishing news reports over leased wires to newspapers and radio broadcasting stations throughout the country. In the latter part of 1946, or the early part of 1947, John F. Courrier contacted plaintiff's agent, John Moran, in Chicago, relative to obtaining news report service on behalf of a proposed corporation. Mr. Courrier told Mr. Moran that he and defendant Barron proposed to form a corporation under the name of the Mississippi Valley Broadcasting Corporation to operate a broadcasting station in Fort Madison, Iowa. On February 24, 1947, the contract in suit was executed.

The contract states in its opening paragraph that it is between the King Features Syndicate and the "Mississippi Valley Broadcasting Corporation, the owner of the Radio Station hereinafter named, hereinafter called the Broadcaster." The contract goes on to provide that the King Features Syndicate would furnish printer-telegraph machines to be installed in the broadcaster's place and the broadcaster was to pay $70 a week ($10 less if another client was obtained within a radius of 50 miles) for the daily news reports. The contract provided, "This agreement shall continue for five years from date broadcasting starts" and it was signed, on behalf of the broadcaster, "Mississippi Valley Broadcasting Corp. by John F. Courrier, Manager."

There is some dispute in the record as to whether Barron and Ashby were present when Courrier signed his name to the contract, and as to whether Ashby was associated with the other two when the contract was signed. . . . No corporation was ever organized but sometime later Courrier, Barron, and Ashby went into partnership under the name of the Hawkeye Broadcasting Company and in February of 1948, the partnership commenced operating a broadcasting station in Fort Madison. Mr. Courrier notified Moran of the partnership and he said he would have the partnership sign a new contract and Mr. Courrier said that would be all right. No new contract was ever signed. . . .

Plaintiff's theory of the liability of defendants on the contract is that Courrier, Barron, and Ashby were promoters of a proposed corporation, and, as such, liable under this contract executed by one of them for the rest.

In Telegraph v. Loetscher, 127 Iowa 383, 101 N.W. 773, 774, 4 Ann. Cas. 667, we defined a promoter as "one who brings about the incorporation and organization of a company." There too we set forth the much quoted observation from 2 Cook on Stockholders that the term promoter is a business and not a legal term

> "usually summing up in a single word a number of business operations, familiar to the commercial

world, by which a company is generally brought into existence."

It is settled by the authorities that a promoter, though he may assume to act on behalf of the projected corporation and not for himself, will be personally liable on his contract unless the other party agreed to look to some other person or fund for payment. An apt statement of the rule is contained in 18 C.J.S., Corporations, § 132, p. 532:

"Promoters of a corporation are personally liable on contracts which they have entered into personally, even though they have contracted for the benefit of the projected corporation, and although the corporation has been formed and has received the benefit of the contract; and they are not discharged from liability by the subsequent adoption of the contract by the corporation when formed. . . ."

In 18 C.J.S., Corporations, § 132, the rule is stated:

"So, if they [promoters] assume to make contracts in the name of the proposed corporation and then voluntarily abandon their purpose of forming it, they become personally liable to make good those contracts, and each becomes liable to make good such as he has directly or indirectly authorized or ratified."

Applying the law set forth in the foregoing authorities to the facts in this case we find the individual defendants were promoters. They were "prospective incorporators." All of the evidence points to a joint enterprise on the part of the individual defendants. The contract was well within the scope of the adventure. The representation that their association was soon to merge into a corporate entity was honestly made but their subsequent decision to substitute a partnership for the proposed corporation would not end their liability. As pointed out, the authorities generally are to the effect that their individual liability would not have ended if they had formed the corporation. Why then should it be said their individual liability ceased when they abandoned the plan to incorporate? We hold the individual defendants jointly and severally liable under the contract.

Review Questions

1. What characteristics make the corporation an ideal form of business organization for the conduct of large-scale enterprise?
2. Distinguish private stock corporations from nonstock corporations.
3. What are the characteristics of quasi-public corporations which distinguish them from private corporations?
4. In what respect does a public corporation differ from the so-called quasi-public corporation?
5. Explain the statement that "a corporation is a legal entity."
6. Who owns the property of a corporation?
7. Are the members of a corporation agents of the corporation, as the members of a partnership are agents of the partnership?
8. What basic consideration should determine to what extent a corporation is to be regarded as a legal entity?
9. Every corporation is possessed of the character of continuous succession. Explain this statement.
10. In what sense of the word are stockholders the owners of corporate property?

11. Are corporations regarded as persons within the meaning of the due process clause found in the Fourteenth Amendment to the Federal Constitution?
12. Construct a fact situation under which the courts would disregard the entity theory of a corporation.
13. What is the source of authority for the creation of a corporation?
14. Does the federal government have authority to create corporations?
15. How does the present-day method of incorporation under general enabling statutes differ from that which was originally employed?
16. What is the statutory procedure for the formation of a corporation in your state?
17. Why may it be important to determine the point of time at which a corporation came into existence?
18. What is a corporate charter, and of what does it consist?
19. Distinguish a corporation de jure from a corporation de facto.
20. How does the liability of the associating members of a corporation de facto differ from that of the members of a corporation de jure?
21. Is a corporation liable upon the contracts entered into by the promoter prior to the formation of the corporation?
22. Is a promoter relieved from his contractual liability by the fact that the contracts have been adopted by the corporation?
23. Should a promoter be able to recover for his services rendered in bringing the corporation into being?

Problems for Discussion

1. Prior to 1946, Belt-Modes, Inc., manufactured ladies' belts. In the early part of 1946 it began to or desired to manufacture children's and ladies' handbags. To make belts it had to sign a contract with the Beltmakers' Union, and to make pocketbooks a contract had to be signed with the Pocketbook Workers' Union.

   Rather than combine both operations, on January 22, 1946, Daniel Rubin, the principal stockholder of Belt-Modes, Inc., organized a new corporation, Danin, Inc., for the purpose of manufacturing pocketbooks, and Belt-Modes, Inc., continued to make belts.

   Danin, Inc. was a separate entity. It rented its own premises, hired its own help, owned the fixtures, machinery and equipment, had its own complete set of books and records, stationery, bank account, issued its own checks, paid its own taxes, issued financial statements, purchased insurance for itself, and participated in other normal business procedures.

   The transactions between the two corporations, (Danin, Inc., and the bankrupt) followed the usual pattern found in a jobber-contractor relationship. At the end of every month Danin, Inc., rendered a bill to Belt-Modes, Inc. This bill was entered on the Danin, Inc., books as a debit to accounts receivable and a credit to sales and was entered on the Belt-Modes, Inc. books by a debit to "purchases-contractors, labor and materials" and a credit to contractors payable.

   Danin, Inc., was only one of several contractors with whom Belt-Modes had business negotiations. The same entries were made for all contracts on Belt-Modes, Inc., books.

All of the payrolls of Danin, Inc., were paid out of Danin's bank account.

On or about the middle of 1947, Danin, Inc., moved into the same premises occupied by Belt-Modes, Inc., but continued to operate separately as it had previously done until Belt-Modes was adjudicated a bankrupt. Danin, Inc., is still in existence and is not involved in this bankruptcy proceeding.

In spite of the fact that the claimants herein were the employees of Danin, Inc., they filed wage claims against the estate of the bankrupt. The trustee objected to such claims on the grounds that the bankrupt was in no way obligated to said claimants, in that the claimants were never employed by the bankrupt and never rendered any work, labor, or services for the bankrupt.

The referee overruled these objections and allowed these claims on the ground that the said employees were actually the employees of the bankrupt. Decide. (In re *Belt-Modes,* 88 F. Supp. 141, 1950)

2. A retail grocer, A, insured his building and stock with the B Fire Insurance Co. The building and merchandise were destroyed by fire, and difficulties arose in effecting a settlement. During the course of the negotiations between A and an agent of B, the latter openly and publicly accused A of having set the fire. Does A have a cause of action for slander against B?
3. A Delaware corporation is prohibited from doing business in Iowa upon its failure to pay a fee, as required of all foreign corporations. Is this in violation of the clause of the Federal Constitution which provides, "the citizens of each state shall be entitled to all privileges and immunities of the citizens in the several states?"
4. An Arkansas statute provided that the railway commission should consider all petitions relating to train service, etc., provided the petition is signed by fifteen bona fide citizens residing in the territory affected. The commission took action upon a petition containing eighteen signatures of corporations and partnerships. The order of the commission is attacked as being void. Decide. (*St. L. and San Francisco R. Co.* v. *State,* 120 Ark. 182)
5. A state utilities commission establishes rates that prevent the Power Electric Corporation from earning any return upon its investment. Is this in violation of the Fourteenth Amendment to the United States Constitution?
6. The plaintiff since 1907 has been engaged in the manufacture and sale of furniture of all kinds in Grand Rapids under its present corporate name. It specializes in living-room and dining-room furniture and library tables. It advertises extensively in the trade journals and in metropolitan papers. For several years the defendant has been engaged in the manufacture and sale of furniture in Grand Rapids. Before May, 1921, its corporate name was the "John D. Raab Chair Company." At that time it amended its articles by changing its corporate name to "Grand Rapids Furniture Shops." Both companies market their furniture in the same way, through the furniture exhibitions held annually in Grand Rapids, by soliciting salesmen, and by filling mail orders. The trial court dismissed plaintiff's bill to enjoin the defendant's use of the name. Decide. (*Grand Rapids Fur. Co.* v. *Grand Rapids Fur. Shops,* 221 Mich. 548)
7. A, B, C, and D operating as a partnership sold their business establishment—including good will—to X. It was agreed that for the protection of the good will of the business the partnership would not compete with X. The partners

and others then organized a corporation for the purpose of engaging in the same business as that which had been purchased by X. X brings an action to enjoin the corporation from competing with him. The corporation defends by contending that it is a legal entity, existing separate and apart from its stockholders, and consequently cannot be held for contracts entered into by its members. Decide.

8. You are president of a corporation and you receive the following request from a stockholder: "I would like to have a framed copy of the corporation's charter." How would you reply?
9. The incorporators of the X corporation failed to state the corporation's principal place of business in the articles of incorporation, as they were by law required to do. Y, a creditor, seeks to hold the incorporators individually liable upon the theory that no corporation had been formed. Decide.
10. A promoter engaged the services of an attorney to draft the articles of incorporation and by-laws of a proposed corporation. After the corporation came into being, the attorney sued the corporation to recover his fee. Decide.
11. A promoter contracted to buy certain property from Black. After the corporation came into being, it formally adopted the contract. Does this relieve the promoter from liability upon the contract?

38 BUSINESS ORGANIZATIONS:

POWERS, DURATION, AND TERMINATION OF CORPORATIONS

► I. SOURCE OF AUTHORITY TO ACT

A. IN STATE OF INCORPORATION

The powers that a corporation can exercise within the borders of the incorporating state are those which have been conferred upon it by its corporate charter. Since a corporation's charter consists of (1) its articles of incorporation and (2) the laws of the state of incorporation, it may engage in those activities that are specifically enumerated in its articles and that are permissible under the laws of the state. Whereas a natural person can do all things not prohibited by law, a corporation can do only those things to which the state has given its consent, as evidenced by the charter.

The powers that a corporation can acquire under modern enabling statutes are very broad. The fact is that in most of the states a corporation can include in its articles of incorporation any or all activities not specifically prohibited by law. The modern tendency is for corporations to make their articles of incorporation as all-inclusive as possible. In addition to the specific enumeration of activities, the articles will provide that the corporation may "carry on any other lawful business whatsoever." In addition, a corporation may at any time amend its charter and so enlarge its powers.

Generally, corporations are denied the right to engage in public utility, insurance, and banking enterprises in conjunction with their other activities. Corporations engaged in these activities are organized under special statutory provisions. Nor do corporations have the right to engage in the practice of a profession, such as law, medicine, or dentistry.[1]

B. IN FOREIGN STATE

The rights of a corporation in states other than the state of incorporation are dependent upon whether the corporation's activities are interstate (commerce between the states) or intrastate (purely within the state).

1. *Right to Transact Interstate Business*

The Constitution of the United States gives the Federal Government exclusive power to regulate *interstate* commerce, leaving the control of intrastate commerce to the various states. Consequently, a corporation engaged in interstate commerce has the right to transact such business in the various states without undue inter-

[1] State v. Nat. Optical Stores Co., p. 964.

ference from the states.* The rights of a foreign corporation were in *Butler Bros. Shoe Co.* v. *U.S. Rubber Co.*, 156 Fed. 1, stated thus:

> "It is not now, and it never has been the law . . . that other states may exclude all the corporations of any state from doing any business within them, or that they may condition their transaction of such business by such terms as they may think proper to impose.
>
> "The Constitution of the United States and the acts of Congress in pursuance thereof are the supreme law of the land. Under that Constitution and those laws a corporation of one state has at least three absolute rights which it may freely exercise in every other state in the Union, without let or hindrance from its legislation, or action:
>
> "Every corporation empowered to engage in interstate commerce by the state in which it is created, may carry on interstate commerce in every state in the Union, free of every prohibition and condition imposed by the latter.
>
> "Every corporation of any state in the employ of the United States has the right to exercise the necessary corporate powers and to transact the business requisite to discharge the duties of that employment in every other state in the Union without permission granted, or conditions imposed by the latter.
>
> "Every corporation of each state has the absolute right to institute and maintain in the federal courts, and to remove to those courts for trial and decision, its suits in every other state, in the cases and on the terms prescribed by the acts of Congress.
>
> "Every law of a state which attempts to destroy these rights or to burden their exercise is violative of the Constitution of the United States and void."

2. *Right to Transact Intrastate Business*

The right of a foreign corporation to carry on intrastate business is entirely subject to the will of the various states.

> "A corporation exists by right only within the State that gave it the right to exist. . . . Consequently, it cannot as a matter of right immigrate into another State, and no other State is bound to receive it within its borders. The permit which authorizes a foreign corporation to come into this State rests not on any right belonging to the corporation, but alone on comity, and the permission may be withheld for a good or a bad reason, or for no reason at all, and it may be granted upon such conditions as the State may see fit to impose. . . ." *State* v. *Blake*, 241 Mo. 100

It is the general practice for states to permit foreign corporations to do business within their borders upon the same basis as their own corporations. A corporation wishing to operate in a state other than that of its incorporation must make application in accordance with the requirements of the state statutes. Upon receiving approval, the corporation is then qualified to engage in (1) those activities specified in its charter which are not prohibited by the laws of the foreign incorpo-

* Foreign corporations engaged in interstate commerce are, however, subject to the police power of the states. The states may exercise such control and regulation as is necessary for the public health, public morals, and public safety.

rating state, and (2) those activities which are permissible under the laws of the state granting it the right to do business within its borders.

a. Penalties for Noncompliance. A corporation which undertakes to do business in a foreign state without having properly applied and obtained permission subjects itself to such penalties as are by statute provided. The penalties take the following forms:

(1) Fines upon the corporation. Approximately thirty-six states make provision for such in widely varying amounts. The Iowa statute provides for a fine of $100 for every day of violation and Virginia provides for a fine of $10 to $1,000 for each offense. Local statutes should be consulted.

(2) Fines upon the officers, agents, or representatives of the corporation. Approximately twenty-six states so provide. In some instances the statute provides for fines and/or imprisonment.

(3) Personal liability of officers or agents for the obligations of the corporation. Such is provided for in approximately one sixth of the states.

(4) The unenforceability of the corporation's contracts. In the majority of states it is provided that the corporation may not use the courts of the state to enforce its contracts.[2]

b. Activities Constituting Doing Business. A foreign corporation to be subject to the penalty provisions of a state statute must be established to have been doing or carrying on intrastate business within the state. The problem of determining what activities constitute doing business is one which is constantly coming before the courts.[3, 4] It is a matter not easy of determination. The general rule as to what is doing business was stated by the court in *Inter-Amusement Co.* v. *Alber,* 128 Tenn. 417, 161 S.W. 488, thus:

> "A corporation is doing business within a particular State when it transacts therein some substantial part of its ordinary business continuous in character as distinguished from merely casual or occasional transactions."

And in *Penn Collieries Co.* v. *McKeever,* 183 N.Y. 98, 75 N.E. 935, the court said:

> "To be 'doing business in this State' implies corporate continuity of conduct in that respect, such as might be evidenced by the investment of capital here, with the maintenance of an office for the transaction of its business, and those incidental circumstances, which attest the corporate intent to avail itself of the privilege to carry on a business. In short it should appear . . . that the corporation . . . intended to establish a continuous business in the City of New York and not one of a temporary character." *

The following illustrate the application of the above rule:

(1) In *General Fire Extinguisher Co.* v. *Northwestern Auto Supply Co.,* 65 Mont. 371, the plaintiff, a foreign corporation, not having obtained permission to

---

* See, however, Smythe Co. v. Fort Worth Glass, 105 Tex. 8, 142 S.W. 1157.

2 Woods v. Interstate Realty Co., p. 965.

3 Lichtenberg v. Bullis School Inc., p. 966.

4 Hastings v. Piper Aircraft Corp., p. 968.

do business within the state of Montana, sold and installed for the defendant two sprinkler systems. The question for determination was whether this constituted doing business in the state. The court in resolving the question said:

"We entertain the view that isolated transactions, whereby a foreign corporation sells goods or other manufactured products on sample or specifications, the same being fabricated in another state and shipped into this state by such corporation for use or installation, does not constitute the doing of business in this state, within contemplation of the statute. Were the law given a contrary construction, it is easy to see the far-reaching and absurd consequences which would result. Transactions of this character were never in legislative contemplation. It is our opinion that the two isolated transactions of the plaintiff in this case, under the facts recited, do not constitute the 'doing of business' in this state within the intent of the statute."

(2) The facts in *Fleishmann Construction Co.* v. *Blauner's*, 190 N.Y. App. Div. 95, were that the defendant, a Pennsylvania corporation, employed a buyer in New York to "get a line" on merchandise. The manager and fifteen buyers then made weekly trips to New York to make purchases. The court concluded that

"the continued and organized buying of goods in New York City by defendant is as much a part of its business operations as the sale of these goods to the public. If the defendant was engaged in selling its goods in New York City by the same agents and in the same manner, it is evident that under the authorities, it would be doing business in New York . . . City. It must follow that a regular and long-continued practice of buying instead of selling is equally doing business."

(3) In *Mayer* v. *Wright*, et al. 234 Iowa 1158, 15 N.W. (2d) 268 (1944), the question was presented whether the Dr. Pepper Company, a foreign corporation, was, upon the basis of the following facts, doing business in the state of Iowa.

The Dr. Pepper Company, a Colorado corporation, licensed the Dr. Pepper Bottling Company of Des Moines, Iowa, to prepare and bottle beverages from syrups furnished by the Dr. Pepper Company. It was also agreed between the parties that the Dr. Pepper Company would have the right of supervision over the manufacture of the product and would furnish advice as to the manufacture and sale of the bottled goods. Other than that, it was the private business of the Dr. Pepper Bottling Company.

In holding that the Dr. Pepper Company was not doing business in Iowa, the court said:

"The general rule deducible from all our decisions is that the business must be of such nature and character as to warrant the inference that the corporation has subjected itself to the local jurisdiction, and is by its duly authorized officers or agents present within the state. . . .

"As previously stated the facts in each case must disclose circumstances from which an inference must be drawn that the foreign corporation is doing business within the state. . . . We do not see how this inference can be drawn from the facts disclosed in the record of the present case. Dr. Pepper Company has no interest in Dr. Pepper Bottling Company of Des Moines, Iowa. The bottling company is a separate entity. Dr. Pepper Company has no selling agent in the State of Iowa and has no display room. It maintained no office within the state and has no control over the bottling company. It did act in an advisory capacity in connection with the sale and promotion of the manufactured product made from the syrup furnished by it but this activity when carried on within the state was only temporary and at infrequent intervals. Such activities do not constitute doing business within the state. It is therefore our conclusion that Dr. Pepper Company was not doing business within the State of Iowa so as to warrant a holding that jurisdiction might be obtained of it by service of an original notice upon a claimed agent within this state."

3. *Interstate and Intrastate Distinguished*

We have in the preceding sections established (1) that a foreign corporation is not subject to regulation when it is engaged in *interstate* business and (2) that a foreign corporation is subject to regulation when it is engaged in *intrastate* business. So, granted that a corporation is doing business, there is the problem of determining whether such business is *interstate* or *intrastate* in character.[5, 6]

This is a problem of magnitude and difficulty; one which is constantly before the courts. The following illustrations will indicate the nature of the problem as it relates to some of the important commercial practices.

(1) The transportation of persons or things from one estate to another is of the very essence of interstate commerce. The major problem that has confronted the courts has been to determine what acts in addition to transportation were to be regarded as interstate rather than intrastate. In conjunction with the shipment of goods there are such closely allied acts as solicitation of orders, delivery of goods, warehousing prior to delivery, work upon the goods sold (such as the installation of a product), and sale by consignment.

(2) The courts have uniformly held that the acts of an agent in soliciting orders or entering into contracts of sale for a foreign principle, are interstate when shipment from another state is contemplated. The acts of the agent are a part of the whole transaction.

(3) Delivery of the goods within the state after they have been transported from another state is also a part of the whole transaction and is regarded as interstate commerce. This rule is subject to the limitation that the goods must be delivered in the original package in which they are imported. When the original package is broken for the purpose of selling or delivering in smaller units, the articles become the subject of intrastate commerce and are subject to state regulation. In *State* v. *Flannelly*, 96 Kan. 372, the court said:

"The original package of gas is broken when the first gas is taken out of the pipe lines and sold in this state. Thereafter the gas ceases to be an article of interstate commerce. . . . Interstate commerce is at an end when the bulk

[5] Gross Income Tax Div. v. J. L. Cox & Son, p. 969.

[6] State v. Western Transp. Co., p. 972.

of the imported gas is broken up for indiscriminate distribution to individual purchasers at retail sale."

(4) The act of warehousing goods when not related to the delivery of the goods to a buyer is intrastate commerce. Thus, if the X corporation maintains a warehouse in a foreign state for the purpose of carrying out the continuous process of delivery of goods that have been sold, the act is a part of the interstate transaction. If, however, goods are placed in the warehouse and then sold, the acts of warehousing and sale would be regarded as intrastate in character.

(5) Contracts of sale will frequently require the installation of the goods sold at the expense of the vendor. Whether the act of installation is part of the interstate transaction or purely local in character is dependent upon the complexity of the article and the degree of skill required to accomplish the task. Thus, in *Aeolian Co.* v. *Fischer,* 35 F. (2d) 34, the court said, "The agreement of the organ manufacturer to install is not only relevant and appropriate to the interstate sale, but is essential if an organ, as distinguished from its parts, may be sold at all."

Such acts as the construction of buildings, erection of signs and billboards, and installation of furniture would be classified as intrastate. In *Mandel Bros., Inc.* v. *Henry A. O'Neil, Inc.,* 69 F. (2d) 452, the plaintiff, a Delaware corporation, had sold to the defendant furnishings and equipment as its contract of sale required. The plaintiff in bringing an action to recover on certain unpaid promissory notes was met with the defense that the notes were void since they arose out of an intrastate transaction for which the plaintiff had not been licensed. The court in affirming the judgment for the defendant said,

> "In all cases bearing upon the subject the distinction is carefully drawn between situations requiring local work as essential to a complete delivery in interstate commerce, because of the peculiar nature of the subject matter of the contract, and those in which the local work done is inherently and intrinsically intrastate. In our judgment, the installation of these furnishings in the hotel falls within the latter classification."

► II. EXPRESS POWERS

A corporation's express powers are enumerated in the corporate charter. Consequently, these powers may be found expressly declared in the corporation's articles or certificate of incorporation (sometimes called the *charter*) and in the enabling statute under which the corporation was formed. A particular corporation has the right to exercise the powers provided for in its articles or certificate of incorporation, and all corporations created under the same enabling statute are endowed with the powers as therein enumerated.

An example of a relatively simple *purpose and powers clause* in the certificate of a corporation engaged in the general garage business might be:

(1) To buy, sell, deal in, operate, and let for hire automobiles and motor vehicles of every kind and description;

(2) to generally buy, sell, and deal in goods, wares, merchandise, appliances,

and accessories necessary or incidental to the operation, repair, or equipment of automobiles and motor vehicles of any and all kinds and description;

(3) to build, maintain, and operate buildings such as are necessary to the accomplishing of the above purposes;

(4) to buy, sell, and convey property, both personal and real, as the same shall be necessary for the purpose of carrying on the above businesses;

(5) to do all things that may be necessary and incidental to the accomplishing of the purposes stated above.

The courts have long recognized that certain powers are the natural concomitant of corporate existence—powers that are essentially necessary to put into effect and operation the corporate method of conducting its affairs. These powers are largely the result of giving recognition to the corporation as being a legal entity. Present-day enabling statutes generally enumerate these so-called *incidental powers.* Illustrative of such is Section 8341 of the 1939 Iowa Code, which provides:

Among the powers of such corporations are the following:

(1) To have perpetual succession.

(2) To sue and be sued by its corporate name.

(3) To have a common seal, which it may alter at pleasure.

(4) To render the interests of the stockholders transferable.

(5) To exempt the private property of its members from liability for corporate debts, except as otherwise declared.

(6) To make contracts, acquire and transfer property—possessing the same powers in such respects as natural persons.

(7) To establish by-laws, and make all rules and regulations necessary for the management of its affairs.

These powers will be impliedly attributed to the corporation as being incidentally necessary to the corporate scheme, even though they are not enumerated in the statute under which a corporation is formed or in a corporation's articles or certificate of incorporation.

► III. POWERS IMPLIED FROM THOSE EXPRESSLY CONFERRED

In addition to authorizing the exercise of powers expressly provided for, a charter, by implication, gives the corporation the right to take such action as is reasonably necessary to accomplish the expressly delegated powers.

> ". . . it has long been an established principle in the law of corporations, that they may exercise all the powers within the fair intent and purpose of their creation, which are reasonably proper to give effect to powers expressly granted. In doing this, they must have a choice of means adapted to ends, and are not to be confined to any one mode of operation." *Bridgeport* v. *Housatonic Ry Co.,* 15 Conn. 475

The application of this rule in any given instance is entirely a matter of placing an interpretation upon the phrase "reasonably necessary and proper." Obviously there is no absolute and certain test. There is no doubt, however, that the modern tendency is to give the corporation greater freedom of action. This trend is expressed by the court in *Keating* v. *American Brewing Co.,* 71 N.Y.S. 95, where it said:

> "In these days, when corporations are organized for so many and various purposes, and their business extends in so many directions, it would be difficult to say that any business act is not within the power of a business corporation."

A corporation will be denied the exercise of acts that depart fundamentally from the purposes for which it was formed. Illustrative of such are the following situations taken from decided cases.

(1) The power to manufacture "firearms and other implements of war" does not carry with it the right to manufacture and sell railroad locks. *Whitney Arms Co.* v. *Barlow,* 38 N.Y. Super. 554

(2) A corporation authorized "to buy and sell dairy products" has no right to deal in oysters. *Bowman Dairy Co.* v. *Mooney,* 41 Mo. App. 665

(3) A corporation chartered to publish a newspaper has no right to engage in any form of life insurance enterprise. *Brisay* v. *Star Co.,* 35 N.Y.S. 99

(4) The right to engage in booming lumber does not carry with it the implied authority to drive lumber. *Bangor Boom Corp.* v. *Whiting,* 29 Me. 123

(5) And, in *People* v. *Pullman's Palace Car Co.,* 175 Ill. 125, it was held that a corporation expressly empowered to manufacture railway cars and to purchase and hold real estate as might be reasonably necessary for the conduct of its business could not lay out a town with its various appurtenances, designed to furnish its employees with homes and the necessities and conveniences of life.

The following are a few illustrations of what the courts have regarded as being necessary and proper to the fulfillment of certain declared powers and purposes.

(1) In *Steinway* v. *Steinway,* 40 N.Y.S. 718, it was held that a manufacturing corporation had the implied powers to do substantially the same things which were denied in *People* v. *Pullman Palace Car Co., supra.*

(2) The power to manufacture automobiles carries with it the right to smelt ore for that purpose. *Dodge* v. *Ford,* 170 N.W. 668

(3) The right to dig for minerals by implication includes the right to drill for oil. *Alberta Co.* v. *Dome Oil Co.,* 8 Alta. 340

(4) The manufacture by a corporation of an inferior product at a lower price to meet an unexpected competitive situation is not a fundamental departure from the corporate purpose. *Carter* v. *Spring Perch Co.,* 113 Conn. 636

(5) In *Central Lumber Co.* v. *Kelter,* 201 Ill. 503, the lumber company became surety upon a contractor's bond for the purpose of obtaining a contract for the sale of lumber. The court said:

> "The company was organized for 'the purchase and sale of lumber and all adjuncts for carrying on a general lumber business.' If the bond was executed . . . for the purpose of securing a sale of lumber to the contractor, the making of the bond was within its implied powers."

A. IMPLIED POWER TO USE IDLE PROPERTY

It has been held that a corporation may employ its idle property outside of the scope of activities. To illustrate:

(1) In *Brown* v. *Winnisimmet Co.,* 11 Allen (Mass.) 346, it was held that a ferry company had the implied authority to charter one of its boats for temporary use in another business when not needed in its own business. The court said:

> "It may also enter into contracts and engage in transactions which are incidental or auxiliary to its main business, or which may become necessary, expedient or profitable, in the care and management of the property which it is authorized to hold."

(2) In *Garrison Canning Co.* v. *Stanley,* 133 Iowa 57, the court said:

> "While it is true as a general proposition that a corporation authorized by its articles only to carry on a mercantile or manufacturing business has no authority to engage in the business of loaning money, it does not follow that it has not the power in the management of its funds to loan them out temporarily at interest when not needed in the prosecution of its business. The loaning of money not being expressly prohibited to the corporation it may as we think without any question make such temporary disposition of the funds which it has on hand from time to time as to secure a profit, the very object of its organization being to earn money for its stockholders in the prosecution of its business. Such a temporary and incidental loaning of money is not the engaging in the business of making loans which is outside the scope of the authority of manufacturing corporations."

B. RIGHT OF CORPORATIONS TO ACQUIRE THEIR OWN STOCK

It is the general common law rule in this country that a corporation has the power to reacquire its own stock by purchase, providing such a practice does not deprive creditors of the security upon which their claims are founded or does not defeat the rights of nonassenting stockholders.[7] In any event, a corporation cannot deplete its resources to the point where the claims of creditors can no longer be discharged; this would be a fraud upon the creditors.[8] Were such a practice to be allowed without limitation, a corporation could effect a complete dissolution, leaving the creditors only assets not spent in the purchase of the stock. Where stock is purchased, nonassenting stockholders hold the right to have the corporation make the purchase at a proper price. Payment of an excessive price would be a dilution of the remaining stockholders' equity interest in the corporation. The reason upon which this majority rule is based was declared in *Coleman* v. *Tepel,* 230 Fed. 63, to be:

> "The doctrine that the purchase of stock by a corporation is legal save under circumstances producing injury, is based upon the theory that capital is not a trust fund; that a solvent corporation may employ its capital in the pur-

[7] Gilchrist v. Highfield, p. 974.

[8] Nipp v. Puritan Mfg. & Supply Co., p. 975.

chase of its own stock, when not prohibited by law, so long as it acts in good faith."

The minority rule to the effect that a corporation does not have the implied power to purchase its own stock is founded upon the theory that the capital stock is a trust fund for the benefit of those who deal with the corporation. At least two states have, by statute, prohibited a corporation from purchasing its own stock.

Some jurisdictions qualify the majority rule by holding that the purchase can be made only out of surplus funds or profits. A considerable number of the states have so provided by statute. It is to be noted that at least one half of our jurisdictions have statutory provisions relating to a corporation's right to purchase its own stock. It should also be noted that restrictions have been imposed upon the right of corporations to deal in their own shares; these restrictions were made by the New York Stock Exchange and again more recently by the Securities and Exchange Commission.

All jurisdictions recognize the right of a corporation to acquire its stock for certain so-called *legitimate causes.* The right of a corporation to receive its own stock as a gift is universally accepted. A corporation may also take its own stock in compromise of a dispute or under circumstances where such action is necessary to prevent a loss. For example, it may be necessary for a corporation to take a shareholder's stock in discharge of an obligation to the corporation.

C. RIGHT TO ACQUIRE STOCK IN OTHER CORPORATIONS

It would be far from the truth to say that a corporation does not have the power to purchase or subscribe to stock of another corporation. By the weight of American authority, corporations are denied this right only when it cannot be reasonably implied as being necessary and appropriate to the corporate ends. It is a question of fact, depending upon the circumstances in the particular case, whether such an acquisition of stock is in keeping with the purposes of the enterprise or whether it is entirely foreign and irrelative to the furthering of the objectives for which the corporation was formed. A small minority of the states have held that such a right cannot be exercised unless it is expressly conferred. Statutes should be consulted for limitations upon the right of corporations to purchase stock in other concerns.

The reader should take cognizance of the fact that corporations usually make provision in their articles for authority to acquire stock in other corporations. The liberality of many of our present-day enabling statutes make this possible without limitation. The following is taken from the articles of incorporation of the United States Steel Corporation:

"To engage in any other manufacturing, mining, construction or transportation business of any kind or character whatsoever, and to that end to acquire, hold, own and dispose of any and all property, assets, stocks, bonds and rights of any and every kind.

"To acquire by purchase, subscription or otherwise and to hold or to dispose of stocks, bonds, or any other obligations of any corporation formed for, or then or theretofore engaged in or pursuing, any one or more of the kinds of business, purposes, objects or operations above indicated. . . ."

As a general rule, a corporation may invest surplus funds—funds not needed for current operations—in stock of another corporation. A corporation should not be denied the right to employ idle funds until such time when the funds will be needed. The right of a corporation to take stock in payment of, or as security for, a debt has been given both statutory and judicial sanction.

► IV. ULTRA VIRES ACTS

A. NATURE OF ULTRA VIRES ACTS

"The term ultra vires is the modern legal nomenclature for acts of a corporation through any of its instrumentalities which are beyond the powers conferred by law upon the legal entity." *Fifth Ave. Coach Co.* v. *New York,* 111 N.Y.S. 759

By engaging in the manufacture of bicycle tires when, by its charter it is empowered to manufacture only ice cream, a corporation would be committing an *ultra vires act*—an act beyond its powers. All contracts relating to the tire-manufacturing phase of operations would be ultra vires. Ultra vires acts are not to be confused with acts that constitute torts or crimes. A corporation, like a natural person, has the duty to observe all positive rules of law, but a failure in this respect is, properly speaking, not an ultra vires act. Whether an act is ultra vires is dependent upon a determination of what the express, implied, or incidental powers of a corporation are.

B. RIGHT TO OBJECT TO AND PENALTY FOR ULTRA VIRES ACTS

A corporation is bound by a contract with the state and with its own stockholders not to exceed its express, incidental, or implied powers. A corporate charter is a contract binding between the state of incorporation and the corporation, and it also stands as a contract between the corporation and its stockholders. Consequently, either the state or an individual stockholder may resort to action against the corporation for a violation of its charter authority.

By usurping its charter powers, a corporation subjects itself to the possibility of quo warranto proceedings by the state. The state may institute a legal action demanding that the corporate charter be forfeited. It is only the state that can take action to invoke the extreme penalty of corporate death by order of court for a misuse of corporate authority. It is also within the province of the state to take steps to enjoin a corporation from exceeding its powers.

Ultra vires acts are done in violation of the duty owed by the corporation to its stockholders. The equitable owners of a corporation have the right to demand that the capital shall not be subjected to risks not provided for in the charter. When a corporate management fails in this duty, an individual shareholder may bring an action to enjoin further violations and under certain circumstances to have the act set aside.

It has been held that creditors may object to ultra vires transactions if these imperil their security. Creditors have the right to prevent the diversion of assets that should be used to pay corporate obligations.

C. STATUS OF ULTRA VIRES CONTRACTS

There is no harmony of agreement among the courts as to the rights of the parties under a contract that transcends the contracting corporation's powers. The basic difficulty lies in the diverse hypotheses employed by the courts regarding the legal status of ultra vires acts. Some courts choose to accept such an act as an absolute nullity under which no rights nor liabilities can accrue, while others indulge in the assumption that an ultra vires act is valid and that the defense of ultra vires should be allowed—either for or against the corporation—only where it serves the ends of justice.

> "The plea of ultra vires is not to be understood as an absolute and peremptory defense in all cases of excess power without regard to other circumstances and considerations." *Denver Fire Ins. Co.* v. *McClelland,* 9 Colo. 11

This view was somewhat more succinctly stated by Lord St. Leonards in *Hawkes* v. *Eastern Counties Ry. Co.,* 42 Reprint 739, when he said:

> "In my opinion nothing can be more indecent than for a great company like this to allege, by way of defense, that a solemn contract which they have entered into is void on the ground of its not being within their powers, not from any mistake, misapprehension, or subsequent accident, but because they thought fit to enter into it, if it turned out for their benefit, and to take advantage of the illegality in case the contract should prove onerous, and they should desire to get rid of it."

This doctrine is criticized chiefly upon the grounds that to sanction ultra vires acts is in effect extending the powers of a corporation, and that such an extension is presumably without limit unless the rights of innocent third parties are involved.

The conflict of opinion is further enhanced by the fact that the courts vary the application of the above basic philosophies depending upon the extent to which the contract has been performed. The decisions seem to resolve themselves into the following pattern.

1. *Contract Fully Executed*

The general rule is that a contract that has been fully performed will stand for and against both contracting parties.

> "If such a contract has been completely executed upon both sides, the courts will ordinarily refuse any relief to either. The usurpation is at an end. Each party has received from the other what he bargained for. Neither of them has any cause to complain. The contract has ceased to be a living thing. The courts will leave it in its grave." 197 Fed. 374

2. *Executed on One Side*

The great weight of authority in the state courts is to the effect that a contract fully executed by one of the contracting parties is enforceable according to its terms and provisions. The U.S. Supreme Court, as well as the English courts and some state courts, adhere to the rule that such performance cannot serve to lend validity to the contract. This is based upon the theory that it is unlawful for a corporation to go beyond the powers conferred upon it, and ultra vires contracts are consequently void and of no legal effect.

3. *Executory Contract*

Where the contract is wholly executory, the general rule is that the defense of ultra vires prevails in full force and effect, and the contract is not enforceable.[9] However, on the basis that only the state can challenge such unauthorized acts, decisions are found to the effect that, in the absence of unusual circumstances, neither party will be allowed to defeat its enforcement.

4. *Partly Executed on One Side*

As a general rule, a contract partially performed by one of the parties is treated as an executory contract in respect to its future and further performance. This means that the defense of ultra vires can be set up as a defense in an action to enforce the unexecuted part of the contract. The courts hold that, in order to deny its liability beyond the amount of such benefits actually received, a corporation need not return that which was received by virtue of the partial performance. There is authority to the effect that where there has been partial performance, the corporation will be estopped from asserting that the contract is ultra vires. Other courts limit the estoppel to situations where the performance has been substantial rather than merely partial.

The reasons for which it is asserted that a corporation is not liable upon a contract ultra vires usually are:

(1) In the public interest, corporations should not be allowed to transcend the powers granted. To accept ultra vires acts as being valid would be to extend a corporation's granted powers.

(2) The interests of the stockholders require that the capital shall not be subjected to risks not contemplated by the charter.

(3) Everyone entering into a contract with a corporation has the obligation to take notice of the legal limits of its powers. A corporation's articles can be found of public record, which serves as constructive notice to the world.

In those instances where the courts do allow the avoidance of liability upon an ultra vires contract, they will allow recovery on the basis of an implied contract for any benefits that have been knowingly received unless such benefits have been returned. Allowing such recovery is not an affirmance of the act but rather a disaffirmance.

---

[9] Jemison v. Citizens' Sav. Bank of Jefferson, p. 976.

D. EFFECT OF ULTRA VIRES UNDER UNIFORM ACT

The Uniform Business Corporation Act, as it has been adopted in a few jurisdictions, provides for the enforceability of all ultra vires contracts. The state or any stockholder may take action to prevent the commission of an ultra vires act by the corporation, but all contracts that have been entered into are binding, regardless of the extent of performance. The Uniform Act has to date been enacted in Idaho, Louisiana, and Washington.

► V. DURATION AND TERMINATION

A. PERIOD OF DURATION [10]

One of the attributes of corporate life is said to be the right of perpetual succession. Most enabling statutes so provide. The term *perpetual succession* does not, as is at times thought, mean the right to unending life. Many statutes, for example, provide that one of the powers of a corporation consists of having perpetual succession, and likewise make provision that the duration of a corporation is not to exceed a specified term of years. The term has reference to the corporate characteristic of continuous succession, regardless of any change in membership or personnel, until such time when the corporation is legally terminated. This term characterizes a corporation as being free of that high degree of fatal vulnerability of which a partnership is possessed.

At common law the corporation was conceived as capable of endless life. The enabling statutes of most of the states contain a codification of this principle and grant corporations the right of perpetual existence. Consequently, the clause, "The duration of the corporation shall be perpetual," is found in numerous articles of incorporation. Approximately one third of the states limit the life of a corporation to specified terms, ranging from twenty to one hundred years. In those instances, however, the ease and right of obtaining a charter renewal in effect likewise assures a corporation an unending life.

B. METHODS OF TERMINATION

1. *Expiration of Charter*

It is not infrequent that incorporators, even though organizing in a state authorizing perpetual existence, will limit the life of a corporation to a certain period of years. If a corporation's duration is specified in its charter, corporate life will automatically cease upon the expiration of the stated period. Any attempted corporate action subsequent to that time is void, and such a defense can be used either for or against the organization. The life of a corporation may also be made contingent upon the happening of a specified event. The occurrence of the contingency will serve to terminate the corporate existence.

---

[10] Nardis Sportswear v. Simmons, p. 977.

2. Consent of Stockholders

A corporation may be brought to an end by the required vote of its membership. Usually the charter specifies what percentage of the stockholders' votes are required to effect a dissolution. The Iowa statute provides in Section 8363:

> "A corporation may be dissolved prior to the period fixed in the articles of incorporation, by unanimous consent, or in accordance with the provisions of its articles. . . ."

In those instances where the statute and articles are silent in regard to the vote required for a dissolution, the majority rule applies unless the charter specifies a period of time for which the corporation is to exist. In such an event, a unanimous consent of the stockholders is necessary. This requirement is based upon the theory that, if a corporation is organized to exist for a definite period of time, each and every stockholder has the right to fulfillment of this obligation on the part of the corporation.

3. Dissolution by State

For varying reasons, a corporation may cause its charter to be forfeited to the state. A charter is a contract between the corporation and the state of incorporation, a contract of which the state can demand substantial performance from the corporation. A serious disregard of the charter provisions will warrant the state's action in demanding an adjudication of forfeiture. Illegal and ultra vires acts, the use of corporate powers in such a way that the corporate purposes are not being accomplished, or the nonuse of corporate powers for a considerable period of time are reasons for which the state may petition a court of equity for a decree of corporate death.

However, the courts will not grant the remedy of forfeiture for slight cause. The conduct on the part of the offending corporation must be a serious breach of the standards set up by the charter (a breach such as has produced, or tends to produce, injury to the public) before a court of equity will take it upon itself to decree a forfeiture. The attitude of the courts is well reflected by the statement found in *People* v. *N. River Sugar Refining Co.,* 121 N.Y. 582, which reads:

> "The judgment sought against the defendant is one of corporate death. The state, which created, asks us to destroy; and the penalty invoked represents the extreme rigor of the law. Its infliction must rest upon grave cause, and be warranted by material misconduct. The life of a corporation is indeed less than that of the humblest citizen, and yet it envelops great accumulations of property, moves and carries in large volume the business and enterprise of the people, and may not be destroyed without clear and abundant reason. That would be true even if the legislature should debate the destruction of the corporate life by a repeal of the corporate charter; but it is beyond dispute where the State summons the offender before its judicial tribunals, and submits its complaint to their judgment and review. By that process it assumes

the burden of establishing the charges which it has made, and must show us warrant in the facts for the relief which it seeks."

A greater reluctance to invoke the penalty of forfeiture has been displayed by the courts in cases where the corporation is a solvent going concern rather than where it is beset with financial difficulties. Moreover, the courts are disinclined to sound the death knell for public utility corporations because of the public interest involved.

Usually the forfeiture of a corporate charter cannot be effected without a quo warranto action brought by the state in which the corporation is allowed a full opportunity for defense. If the attorney general can show cause why the corporation should be deprived of its charter, the court will so decree.

By virtue of their wording, some statutes make it unnecessary to effect a forfeiture by a legal proceeding. A statute may be constructed to show an intention that a failure to meet a condition will automatically work a dissolution without need of resort to a court. A statute was held to be self-executing and automatically worked a forfeiture upon a failure of the condition, for example, in a case in which the statute read that upon a corporation's failure to comply with a condition "the rights and privileges . . . granted to said corporation shall revert to the Commonwealth." Such expressions as "shall work a forfeiture" and "shall be dissolved" have been held not to dispense with necessary legal procedure.

4. *Legislative Repeal*

The famous *Dartmouth College* case established what is the accepted principle today that a charter is a contract and as such is entitled to the protection afforded by Article I, Section 10, of the Federal Constitution, which declares: "No state shall . . . pass any . . . Law impairing the Obligation of Contracts."

The observance of this principle prevents the incorporating state from repealing a corporate charter unless such a right has been reserved in the constitution, the enabling statute, or the corporation's articles. A legislative right of repeal, unless based upon the happening of a contingency, may be exercised for such cause as the legislature deems sufficient.

5. *Court Decree*

Courts of equity have the right to grant a decree of dissolution upon a petition by stockholders. This power will not be exercised, however, unless no other adequate relief can be made available to the aggrieved stockholders.[11, 12]

[11] Petition of Collins-Doan Co., p. 979.
[12] Stott Realty Co. v. Orloff, p. 981.

CASES

CASE NO. 1

State v. National Optical Stores Co. 189 Tenn. 433, 225 S.W. (2d) 263 (1949)

GAILOR, J. The bill in this cause, as it was finally amended, and heard by the Chancellor, is a proceeding in the nature of quo warranto, . . . against the National Optical Stores Company, a Tennessee corporation. The prayer of the bill was that because the Defendant corporation, without license or other authority, was practicing optometry in Tennessee, that the Defendant be permanently enjoined from the practice of optometry, and that its charter be forfeited and revoked, and that the officers, agents and employees of the Defendant be perpetually enjoined from the practice of optometry until or unless they had been duly licensed as such optometrists.

. . . the Chancellor, on motion of the Complainant, heard the case on oral testimony and granted the prayer of the bill as amended, by revoking the charter of the corporation and perpetually enjoining the officers, servants, agents and employees of the Defendant from practicing optometry until or unless they were duly licensed. The Defendant has appealed.

. . . It is admitted that, as charged by the State, the Defendant corporation has no license to practice "optometry as a profession," that a license is a legal prerequisite of such practice, Code, § 7026 et seq.; that optometry is a branch of the "healing arts," and that Defendant corporation has no license to practice a "healing art" as required by Chapter 9, Public Acts of 1947. . . .

According to Defendant's brief, the essential facts are not disputed, and the Chancellor, in an excellent opinion, found them as follows:

"The proof in this record shows that the defendant is in the business of making lenses and fitting and selling eye glasses. It is a Tennessee corporation, but is a part of a National Chain Store operation. Prescriptions written in local stores are filled in Chicago, and the glasses sold in Tennessee are made up in Chicago at the factory of the parent corporation, and shipped to Nashville, Knoxville, and Chattanooga for delivery to the purchaser.

"The defendant corporation employs, or has an arrangement with a medical doctor in each of its three stores, by which arrangement each doctor occupies a small space or office inside the store building of the defendant. The doctors' names generally do not appear on the front of the store, and are not listed in the telephone directory. These doctors, by arrangement with the defendant, are present during the time the store is open except for perhaps a short lunch period or possibly an afternoon off each week in some cases. The doctors devote their full time, while present at the store, to examining the eyes of customers who are directed to them by the employees of the corporation, and these doctors are guaranteed a fixed minimum weekly income by the corporation.

"The doctors charge a fixed examination fee of $2.00 per customer or patient, and after examining the patient's eyes, and writing the prescription, the patient is then ushered back into the sales room of the store where the manager, or an employee of the store, proceeds to sell the patient glasses by showing samples of frames, etc., and, after agreeing with the customer on the type of frame, glasses, etc., and the price, the order for the glasses is sent to Chicago and shipped from there back to the store for the customer.

"If in any week the doctor's examination fees from the patients so directed to him by the corporate employees, fails to amount to the agreed stipulated weekly income, a voucher is sent in and a check from the corporation for the difference is paid him.

"While, in some instances, the doctors have an ostensible agreement to pay some small amount as rent for the office space occupied, the record shows that they, in fact, do not pay rent. . . ."

As found by the Chancellor, the Defendant, though a Tennessee corporation, is a branch of a large chain of optical goods stores operating throughout the United States and Canada. The chief executive authority of this chain is one B. D. Ritholz, who signed and swore to the answer in the present case, and the business operation, including the employment of licensed physicians, as it is presented by the present record, has been reviewed by the highest Courts of many other states, and by them determined to be unlawful. These cases, with the single exception of State ex rel. Bierring v. Ritholz, 226 Iowa 70, 283 N.W. 268, 121 A.L.R. 1450, have held that the physicians under contract were servants and employees of the corporation or of Ritholz, and that the business operation was, therefore, unlawful and to be enjoined. . . .

Although, since the passage of the Acts of 1939 and 1947, a decision whether "optometry" is a business or a profession, has not been required of us, it is well established by our cases that the word "person" as it is used in our statutes and decisions which have to do with the eligibility to practice a profession, means *natural persons,* and does not include corporations. In the case of Grocers & Merchants' Bureau v. Gray, 6 Tenn. Civ. App. 87, 92, in language particularly applicable here, it was said:

"A corporation can neither practice law nor hire lawyers to carry on the business of practicing law for it *any more than it can practice medicine or dentistry* by *hiring doctors or dentists to act for it.*" (Emphasis supplied.) . . .

. . . the decree below is affirmed. . . . The case is remanded to the Chancery Court for such further proceedings as may be necessary to effectuate the decree.

CASE NO. 2

Woods v. Interstate Realty Co. 168 F. (2d) 701 (1949)

. . . . .

DOUGLAS, J., delivered the opinion of the Court:

This case was brought in the District Court for Mississippi on the grounds of diversity of citizenship. Respondent, a Tennessee corporation, sued petitioner, a resident of Mississippi, for a broker's commission alleged to be due for the sale of real estate of petitioner in Mississippi. The District Court found on motion for summary judgment that the contract was void under Mississippi law, since respondent was doing business in Mississippi without qualifying under a Mississippi statute.* It there-

* Mississippi Code 1942, § 5319, requires a foreign corporation doing business in the State to file a written power of attorney designating an agent on whom service of process may be had. It also provides, "Any foreign corporation failing to comply with the above provisions shall not be permitted to bring or maintain any action or suit in any of the courts of this state."

fore dismissed the complaint with prejudice.

The Court of Appeals reversed. It reviewed the Mississippi decisions under the Mississippi statute and concluded that the contract was not void but only unenforcible in the Mississippi courts. It held in reliance on David Lupton's Sons Co. v. Automobile Club, 225 U.S. 489, 56 L.Ed. 1177, 32 Sup. Ct. 711, Ann. Cas. 1914A 699, that the fact that respondent could not sue in the Mississippi courts did not close the doors of the federal court sitting in that State. Accordingly it reversed the judgment of the District Court. 168 F. (2d) 701.

. . . If the Lupton's Sons Case controls, it is clear that the Court of Appeals was right in allowing the action to be maintained in the federal court. In that case a New York statute provided that no foreign corporation could "maintain any action in this state" without a certificate that it had qualified to do business there. The court held that a contract on which the corporation could not sue in the courts of New York by reason of that statute nevertheless could be enforced in the federal court in a diversity suit. The Court said, 225 U.S. p. 500, 56 L.Ed. 1181, 32 Sup. Ct. 711, Ann. Cas. 1914A 699:

> "The State could not prescribe the qualifications of suitors in the courts of the United States, and could not deprive of their privileges those who were entitled under the Constitution and laws of the United States to resort to the Federal courts for the enforcement of a valid contract."

We said in Angel v. Bullington that the case of Lupton's Sons had become "obsolete" insofar as it was "based on a view of diversity jurisdiction which came to an end with Erie R. Co. v. Tompkins, 304 U.S. 64, 82 L.Ed. 1188, 58 Sup. Ct. 817, 114 A.L.R. 1487." 330 U.S. p. 192, 91 L.Ed. 838, 67 Sup. Ct. 657. . . .

Angel v. Bullington . . . followed the view of Guaranty Trust Co. v. York, 326 U.S. 99, 108, 89 L.Ed. 2079, 2085, 65 Sup. Ct. 1464, 160 A.L.R. 1231, that for purposes of diversity jurisdiction a federal court is "in effect, only another court of the State. . . ." In that case we required the federal court in a diversity case to apply the statute of limitations of the State in equity actions and thus to follow local law, . . . The York Case was premised on the theory that a right which local law creates but which it does not supply with a remedy is no right at all for purposes of enforcement in a federal court in a diversity case; that where in such cases one is barred from recovery in the state court, he should likewise be barred in the federal court. The contrary result would create discriminations against citizens of the State in favor of those authorized to invoke the diversity jurisdiction of the federal courts. It was that element of discrimination that Erie R. Co. v. Tompkins was designed to eliminate.

Reversed.

CASE NO. 3

Lichtenberg v. Bullis School, Inc. D. of C., 68 A. (2d) 586 (1949)

. . . . . .

CAYTON, CH.J. This appeal presents the much disputed and frequently litigated question of when a foreign corporation is "doing business" in the District of Columbia so as to become amenable to service of process here and to the jurisdiction of our courts. . . .

The case has been brought here for review by a plaintiff who had sued Bullis School, Inc., on a contract claim. . . .

. . . the assistant principal of the school testified that it is a non-stock corporation organized under the laws of Maryland as a non-profit educational institution,—a school for boys, and that all the educational activities of the school were carried on in Maryland and none in the District. He also testified that the school had advertised in a Washington newspaper as well as in the New York Times and in Cosmopolitan Magazine; that from 30 to 40 per cent of the students came from and lived in the District of Columbia, and that others came from a number of states, . . . that until February, 1949 the school maintained a checking account at a Washington bank; that the school purchases food, equipment and supplies from stores in Washington as well as in Maryland, some by personal visits but most by telephoned orders; that William F. Bullis, principal of the school and president of its board of trustees, and his wife, who is treasurer of the school, both live in Washington; that "sometimes" he conferred on school business with Mr. Bullis from the school office in Maryland to Mr. Bullis' home in Washington, by telephone. An affidavit sworn to by plaintiff's counsel recited among other things that the defendant has for many years been listed in the Washington telephone directory, and also in the classified directory under "Schools"; that during the early part of the school year out-of-town students are conducted on a sightseeing tour of Washington.

. . . We think it cannot be said that the Bullis School was "doing business" in the District of Columbia within the meaning of our statute. The record stands uncontradicted that all the educational activities of the school are conducted in Maryland and none in this jurisdiction. That, of course, is the basic question in the case. Nevertheless, certain other aspects of the situation seem to require discussion.

It is true that Mr. Bullis and his wife, officers of the corporation, reside in this jurisdiction. But this circumstance does not establish that the school is "doing business" here. Riverside & Dan River Cotton Mills v. Menefee, 237 U.S. 189, . . .

It is also true that at the time the suit was filed the defendant maintained an account in a bank in this city. But we rule that this fact, standing alone, does not amount to "doing business" here. Honeyman v. Colorado Fuel & Iron Co., C.C.E.D.N.Y., 133 Fed. 96; . . .

Likewise it is true that defendant school makes purchases of food, equipment and supplies from stores in the District of Columbia, but the decisions are emphatic that by making such purchases a foreign corporation does not bring itself within the jurisdiction of a neighboring state. The Supreme Court has said:

> "Visits on such business, even if occurring at regular intervals, would not warrant the inference that the corporation was present within the jurisdiction of the state." Rosenberg Bros. & Co. v. Curtis Brown Co., 260 U.S. 516, . . .

Of even less help to plaintiff is the fact that the school advertises in a local newspaper and is listed in the local telephone directory. Philadelphia & Reading Railway Co. v. McKibbin, 243 U.S. 264, 37 Sup. Ct. 280, 61 L.Ed. 710; People's Tobacco Co. v. American Tobacco Co., 246 U.S. 79, ...

We also rule that the defendant school cannot be held to be "doing business" here, merely because the president, from his home in Washington, "sometimes" discusses school business by telephone with the assistant principal at the school in Maryland. . . .

Looking at all the circumstances of the case and considering them separately or together, we are satisfied that they do not spell out a case of "doing business" as contemplated by our statute. We do not attempt to lay down a rule to cover all situations for we realize that

> "A basic concept of sufficient precision to yield certain results in all cases of this sort has not yet been formulated." Mueller Brass Co. v. Alexander Milburn Co., 80 U.S. App. D.C. 274, 152 F. (2d) 142, 145.

But we are clear in our view that under the facts of this case it would be unrealistic to hold that this defendant ever brought its corporate presence into our jurisdiction or ever became liable to suit in our courts. In addition to the cases we have cited others lend solid support to our conclusions. . . .

CASE NO. 4

Hastings v. Piper Aircraft Corporation. 84 N.Y.S. (2d) 580 (1948)

CALLAHAN, J. Plaintiff sues to recover damages for the wrongful death of her intestate in Florida on May 26, 1947, as a result of the alleged negligence of defendant.

On December 18, 1947, the summons and complaint in this action were allegedly served on defendant by leaving a copy of the same with one Stanley M. Lambert at 120 Wall Street, in the City of New York. The person thus served was an employee of Frank Sheridan Jonas, Inc. (hereinafter called "Jonas"). Defendant appearing specially moved to vacate the service and for dismissal of the action on the ground that it is a foreign corporation not doing business in the State of New York and that the court has no jurisdiction over its person. The Special Term denied the motion, and defendant appeals from the order entered on such denial.

Defendant is a foreign corporation organized under the laws of Pennsylvania. It is engaged in the manufacture and sale of airplanes with its office and principal place of business in the City of Lock Haven, Pennsylvania. Defendant is not licensed to do business and has no employees soliciting business or otherwise working for it in this state.

The name of defendant, however, was listed in the telephone directory as having an export department at 120 Wall Street, in the city of New York. The Jonas company maintained an office at this address. Defendant's name was carried on the building directory and outer door of the Jonas office as occupying the same quarters. It further appears that a business letterhead listed the same address for the export department of defendant and its cable address as "Jonasnell, N.Y." There is no proof to show that defendant arranged for the telephone or building listings or that the letterhead in question was prepared or printed by it. The Jonas corporation was an export company specializing in the foreign sale of products and articles of all descriptions made by American manufacturers. It was wholly independent of defendant, with which it had a contract as exclusive distributor of defendant's product in specified foreign territory. The Jonas company purchased airplanes from defendant by transactions completed in Pennsylvania. These were shipped and delivered to the purchaser in New York packed for export. They were resold by the Jonas Company to its own customers in the foreign territory assigned by defendant on resale terms fixed by Jonas itself. Defendant did not exercise any supervision or control over the employees of the Jonas company, nor contribute to the maintenance of the office or salaries of its employees.

It likewise appears that the defendant had a telephone listing for a showroom at 332 West 57th Street, in the City of New York. This was the place of business of Safair Corporation, which was defendant's local distributor. This company, however, not only sold and distributed airplanes made by different manufacturers, but also arranged for flying lessons and did charter transportation work as a regular part of its business. Defendant as an advertising charge made a contribution to the Safair organization, which was applied towards the rental paid by this company. But this corporation, too, was wholly independent of defendant.

Further, defendant maintained a substantial and active bank account with Manufacturers Trust Company in the City of New York. The deposits were made by transmittal of funds or checks from Pennsylvania, and withdrawals made by checks issued at the home office. Defendant likewise occasionally borrowed money from the bank after negotiations conducted by its officers or representatives at the office of the lender in this jurisdiction.

In addition, defendant retained a New York law firm as its general counsel and on various matters consulted with these attorneys at their offices in the City of New York.

. . . we think that the proof fails to show that defendant was present and doing business in the State so as to be amenable to the service of process in this action. . . .

A non-resident manufacturer such as defendant does not conduct business in the jurisdictional sense in the absence of continuous and systematic solicitation within the State merely because it delivers or sends goods into the State to local buyers on sales transactions completed elsewhere.

Plaintiff relies on Chaplin v. Selznick, 293 N.Y. 529, 58 N.E. (2d) 719, supra, and Melvin Pine & Co. v. McConnell, 273 App. Div. 218, 76 N.Y.S. (2d) 279, affirmed 298 N.Y. 27, 80 N.E. (2d) 137, as authorities for a holding that the activities of defendant were sufficient to constitute the doing of business. . . .

In the Chaplin case, supra, the court refused to vacate the service of a summons on a foreign corporation which was actually maintaining an office in the city of New York at a substantial annual rent, with three salaried employees, and which had been actively soliciting business here as a continuous and systematic course of conduct. These are significant factors that serve to distinguish the present case by their absence.

CASE NO. 5

Gross Income Tax Div. v. J. L. Cox & Son. 227 Ind. 468, 86 N.E. (2d) 693, 10 A.L.R. (2d) 642 (1949)

GILKISON, C.J. Appellees brought this action to recover from appellant the sum of $3911.76 which appellant had required appellees to pay as gross income tax and interest, on March 1, 1945. . . .

The cause was tried by the court resulting in a finding and judgment for appellees in the sum of $3911.76 plus interest. . . .

. . . appellees are a partnership, composed of Joseph L. and Leroy Cox, with their home office at Raytown, Missouri, and that the partners are residents of Missouri. That during the year 1943 there was constructed for Defense Plant Corporation two pipe lines, one a 24-inch line and the other a 20-inch line. The 20-inch line was located parallel and adjacent to the 24-inch line across Indiana. Both lines were built at the expense of the United States Government. A corporate entity, War Emergency Pipe Lines, Inc., acted for and on behalf of Defense Plant Corporation in supervising and in the construction of said lines. All the pipe and material used in the construction of these lines were manufactured outside of the state of Indiana. Engineers for the construction corporations selected convenient transfer points in Indiana to which the pipe and material concerned in this case, could be shipped by rail, which points are referred to as "railheads." From certain of these railheads, appellees were engaged to unload the pipe and material from the railroad cars, and then by trucks and tractors to haul it to, and string it along the pipe lines right of way in Indiana. . . .

Appellees held a certificate of public convenience and necessity issued to them February 4, 1942, by the Interstate Commerce Commission.

Appellant contends that since all of the receipts of gross income of appellees, upon which the gross income tax was assessed and collected, were derived from activities, businesses and sources within the state of Indiana, occurring after the complete termination of the interstate transportation, that the right and duty of the state to impose the gross income tax is definitely fixed and established by the Indiana Income Tax Law. . . .

It is appellees' contention that they were residents of the state of Missouri, and that during the time involved in this case, their activities, transactions and business, and their income received therefrom, were all from their engagements in interstate commerce in Indiana and that their income so received may not be taxed by appellant.

Interstate commerce is a term of such wide implications and ramifications that the courts have carefully avoided any attempt to give it a comprehensive definition. . . .

The Supreme Court of the United States, so far as we are informed, has seen fit to determine each case on its own facts, circumstances and general situation to ascertain whether or not the particular transaction or activity is in interstate commerce to such an extent as to forbid the states to tax it. . . .

As supporting their position that their activities under their contract with War Emergency Pipe Lines, Inc., and all their income received therefrom were engagements in interstate commerce, appellees rely upon the decision in Puget Sound Stevedoring Co. v. Tax Commission of State of Washington et al., 1937, 302 U.S. 90, 58 Sup. Ct. 72, 73, 82 L.Ed. 68. In many respects that case presents facts similar to the case before us and the law there announced by Mr. Justice Cardozo is applicable in this case. However, in that case it is stated that the work done by the Stevedores was formerly done by the ship's crew. And so it was held that "The longshoreman busied in the same task bears the same relation as the crew to the commerce that he serves." But in that case the interstate or foreign commerce nature of the work was limited thus:

> "True, the service did not begin or end at the ship's side, where the cargo is placed upon a sling attached to the ship's tackle. It took in the work of carriage to and from the 'first place of rest,' which means that it covered the space between the hold of the vessel and a convenient point of discharge upon the dock."

In that case it was stipulated that,

> ". . . 'stevedoring services are essential to water borne commerce, and always commence in the hold of the vessel and end at the first place of rest, and vice versa.' "

And the court said:

> "In such circumstances services beginning or ending in the hold or on the dock stand on the same plane for

the purposes of this case as those of the ship's sling. The movement is continuous, is covered by a single contract, and is necessary in all its stages if transportation is to be accomplished without unreasonable impediments."

The court further said:

"The business of loading and unloading being interstate or foreign commerce, the state of Washington is not at liberty to tax the privilege of doing it by exacting in return therefor a percentage of the gross receipts. Decisions to that effect are many and controlling." . . What is decisive is the nature of the act, not the person of the actor. . . ."

We cannot say that a workman engaged in unloading freight from railroad cars that have been engaged in interstate commerce, under employment of the consignee is in the same situation as one engaged in unloading freight from vessels engaged in interstate or foreign commerce under employment of the carrier. There seems to be a material difference in the historical custom and usage with respect to such activities, and that difference may well cause a different conclusion with respect to the right to tax wages received from the activity.

So far as we can learn it never has been the duty of train crews to unload the freight from loaded cars engaged in interstate transportation when they arrive at the point of destination. On the contrary that always has been and is now a duty of the consignee. Thus in overland transportation of freight in loaded cars it cannot be said that the unloading of the cars is a part of the transportation. It is otherwise with waterborne transportation as noted in the Puget Sound Stevedoring case. In this there is a controlling difference between that case and the case at bar. Following the reasoning in that case we must say that, in unloading the freight cars at the railheads in Indiana, appellees were doing only that which their employer was required to do as the consignee of the freight, after its interstate transportation had ended, and it definitely had come to rest at the several railheads in Indiana. There was no element of interstate commerce in this activity of appellees or their employer. . . . See Central Greyhound Lines v. Mealey, 1947, 334 U.S. 653, . . . Wages received by appellees from this work are a proper subject for taxation under the Indiana Gross Income Tax law.

It is contended that the transportation of the freight by appellees by autotrucks from the freight cars or the points of storage at the railheads to the lines where the pipes were laid and the stringing of the pipe along the line in an appropriate position for putting it underground was a part of the interstate transportation. To ascertain whether this contention can be sustained we must look to the stipulation of facts.

Stipulation VII contains this sentence:

"All 'materials' were shipped to said railheads under bills of lading designating Defense Plant Corporation or War Emergency Pipelines, Inc., as consignees."

Stipulation VIII contains this sentence:

"At the time said 'materials' were ordered from the factories by War Emergency Pipelines, Inc., it was specified in a bill of lading that such 'materials' should be transported by rail to War Emergency Pipelines, Inc., at the designated railheads."

It thus appears from the stipulation of facts that the bills of lading issued for all of the interstate shipments made the railheads the point of destination for such shipments.

The contract of appellees with

War Emergency Pipe Lines Inc., . . . in so far as it is for the transportation of freight from the railheads in Indiana to the pipelines site in Indiana, is not a contract in interstate commerce so far as the remuneration earned in Indiana therefrom is concerned. It is a local contract between appellees and War Emergency Pipe Lines, Inc., to do certain work in Indiana for an agreed price. The fact that neither of the parties to the contract are residents of Indiana; that appellees held a certificate of public convenience and necessity issued by the Interstate Commerce Commission, . . . do not make the transactions activities in Interstate Commerce. . . .

CASE NO. 6

State v. Western Transp. Co. 43 N.W. (2d) 739 (Iowa) (1950)

GARFIELD, C.J. An officer of the state motor vehicle department filed in the municipal court of the city of Clinton an information accusing defendant Western Transportation Co. of a misdemeanor in violating section 321.54, Code, 1946, I.C.A., by operating a motor vehicle within this state for the intrastate transportation of property for compensation without registering such vehicle and paying the required fee. Defendant's manager appeared without counsel, the facts were stipulated, the court found defendant guilty and imposed a fine of $100 and costs. Defendant has appealed.

It was stipulated that on July 13, 1949, a truck driver employed by defendant drove one of its tractors, registered in Illinois, to the DuPont plant within the industrial limits of Clinton, Iowa, and transported a semitrailer, also registered in Illinois, containing merchandise consigned to a point in Chicago, Illinois, to defendant's dock located in Clinton. The tractor was then disengaged and another tractor belonging to defendant transported the semitrailer to the consignee in Chicago.

It seems also to be agreed, although the stipulation does not so state, defendant is a nonresident owner of foreign vehicles operated within this state for compensation and neither tractor nor semitrailer was registered in Iowa nor a fee paid therefor.

Code section 321.54, I.C.A., provides:

> "Nonresident carriers. Nonresident owners of foreign vehicles operated within this state for the intrastate transportation of persons or property for compensation . . . shall register each such vehicle and pay the same fees therefor as is required with reference to like vehicles owned by residents of this state." . . .

Defendant contends the stipulated facts do now show it engaged in "intrastate transportation" of property in violation of 321.54 but that the transportation was interstate. . . .

. . . The state does not contend the portion of the movement between defendant's dock in Clinton and Chicago was intrastate. Nor does it argue that any part of the trip would be intrastate if it were not for the stop at the dock in Clinton and the change of tractors there. . . .

Whether transportation is interstate or intrastate is determined by its essential character from a consideration of all pertinent circumstances. Probably the most important test—some authorities say it is controlling—is the intention of the parties in respect thereto and the manner of carrying out such intention. Here intent by the owner to make an interstate shipment or preparatory gathering of goods at a depot for that purpose are not sufficient to constitute interstate transportation. It must appear that goods have entered upon transportation to another state or have been delivered to a carrier for that purpose. . . . 11 Am. Jur., Commerce, § 70.

It is settled by numerous decisions that a shipment is not divested of its interstate character by a temporary break in the transportation at an intermediate point to serve some necessity or convenience of the carrier. Change in the method of transportation, as from rail to boat, or in identity of the carriers, or rebilling from intermediate points do not destroy its interstate character. Such circumstances are mere incidents or "accidents" of the transportation that do not change its essential character. . . . 15 C.J.S., Commerce, § 25; 11 Am. Jur., Commerce, § 71.

Courts have frequently gone further in sustaining the interstate character of transportation than defendant asks of us here. We will notice a few of these decisions. In Railroad Commission of Ohio v. Worthington, supra, 225 U.S. 101, 108, 32 Sup. Ct. 653, 656, 56 L.Ed. 1004, 1008, coal was carried by rail from Ohio mines to lake ports in that state, there placed upon vessels and carried to upper lake ports outside the state. The carriage by rail was held to be interstate and not subject to rates fixed by the state railroad commission. The opinion says:

> "By every fair test the transportation of this coal from the mine to the upper lake ports is an interstate carriage, intended by the parties to be such. . . ."

Texas & N.O.R. Co. v. Sabine Tram Co., supra, 227 U.S. 111, 126, 33 Sup. Ct. 229, 234, 57 L.Ed. 442, 448, considers shipments of lumber from a mill in interior Texas over two railroads on local bills of lading to a point on the Gulf in the same state, destined for export to a foreign port, although the particular destination of any definite part of the lumber had not been fixed. The court holds the shipments by rail were interstate. The opinion states:

> "The determining circumstance is that the shipment of the lumber to Sabine was but a step in its transportation to its real and ultimate destination in foreign countries. In other words, the essential character of the commerce, not its mere accidents, should determine."

In Western Oil Refining Co. v. Lipscomb, supra, 244 U.S. 346, 350, 37 Sup. Ct. 623, 625, 61 L.Ed. 1181, 1184, plaintiff had an oil refinery in Illinois and a barrel factory in Indiana. To fill orders for its products in Tennessee it shipped two cars to Columbia, Tennessee, where the orders from that place were filled and then the cars were rebilled to Mt. Pleasant, Tennessee, where the orders from there were filled. The entire movement from Illinois and Indiana to Mt. Pleasant, Tennessee, was held to be interstate. We quote from the opinion:

> "Certainly the transportation of the merchandise destined to Mount Pleasant was not completed when it reached Columbia; nor was the continuity of its movement broken by its temporary stop at that place. As to that merchandise the journey to Columbia and the journey from there to Mount Pleasant were not independent, each of the other, but in fact and in legal contemplation were connected parts of a continuing interstate movement to the latter place."

In Hughes Bros. Timber Co. v. State of Minnesota, supra, 272 U.S. 469, 474, 475, 47 Sup. Ct. 170, 172, 71 L.Ed. 359, 361, 362, logs were floated down the Swamp river into the Pigeon river and delivered on board ships at the mouth of the Pigeon river. The court holds the entire movement was interstate in character. The opinion states:

"The drive in the two rivers . . . was not gathering the logs for subsequent interstate shipment, it was the interstate movement itself. . . . The delays in the continuity of movement were only incidental to the journey. . . ."

In United States v. Erie R. Co., supra, 280 U.S. 98, 50 Sup. Ct. 51, 74 L.Ed. 187, wood pulp was imported through Hoboken, N.J., and shipped from there by rail to another point in New Jersey, under a new, local bill of lading. It was held the rail movement in New Jersey was not intrastate but an integral part of foreign commerce.

In United States v. Capital Transit Co., 325 U.S. 357, 363, 65 Sup. Ct. 1176, 1179, 89 L.Ed. 1663, 1669, government employees in Washington, D.C., worked in Virginia and traveled to and from work by bus or street car between their homes and the terminal in Washington and by another bus between that terminal and Virginia. The court holds the entire trip was interstate.

United States v. Yellow Cab Co., 332 U.S. 218, 67 Sup. Ct. 1560, 1566, 91 L.Ed. 2010, 2019, holds the transfer of interstate passengers between railroad stations in Chicago by Parmelee limousines is an interstate movement. . . .

The meager stipulation of facts upon which this cause was determined is silent as to the intention of the parties. Presumably the Dupont company intended the merchandise to be transported by defendant without delay from its plant in or near Clinton to the consignee in Chicago. The goods were delivered to the carrier for that purpose and started toward their destination. So far as shown (and the state had the burden to prove defendant's guilt), there was no appreciable delay at defendant's dock in Clinton or elsewhere—the goods proceeded on their way as soon as one tractor could be disengaged and another coupled to the semitrailer. There was no storage awaiting shipment at some future time. It does not appear there was any attempt to divert the shipment to some destination in Iowa nor even any reservation by the shipper, consignee or carrier of a right so to do. . . .

Reversed. . . .

CASE NO. 7

Gilchrist v. Highfield. 140 Wis. 476, 123 N.W. 102 (1909)

This action was brought by plaintiffs, as executors of Ella J. Potter, a stockholder in the Webster Manufacturing Company, to declare invalid a purchase of 364 shares of its stock by the corporation and the payment therefor of $25,480 of corporate money, and to compel the three directors voting for such purchase, namely, Highfield, Gard, and Alvord, to refund to the company such sum so paid. Webster Manufacturing Company was organized for the general purpose of manufacturing chairs. It had $225,000 of nominal stock, divided into 2,250 shares, all of which, except 119 shares, were outstanding. Highfield and Brigham, in equal partnership, owned 1,126 shares. For several years they had been the two active managing officers for the company, Highfield as business manager and Brigham as superintendent of manufacture. Their personal relations had become strained, so that they could not work harmoniously together, and Brigham had insisted that one or the other must get out, and either his stock must be bought, so that he could retire from the company, or Highfield must sell out and withdraw. In pursuance of this view he gave an option to sell his 564 shares of stock, at $70 per share, to Highfield or the corporation in July, 1907. . . . Highfield availed himself of the option to buy 200 shares, which, it appears, was up to the extent of his financial ability. A directors' meeting was then held, at which the three defendant directors and Brigham voted that the corporation purchase the remaining 364 shares upon the option. . . . At the next ensuing stockholders' meeting the act of the directors in making such purchase was fully ratified; such ratification, however, requiring the support of Highfield's votes to supply the majority. The court held that the purchase of the stock was in accordance with good business judgment, in the interest of the corporation, and for no ulterior or improper purpose, and rendered judgment dismissing the action, from which plaintiffs appeal. . . .

DODGE, J. (after stating the facts as above) The purchase of the 364 shares of stock by the corporation from Brigham is claimed to be wholly void upon the ground asserted that a corporation has no power to buy its own capital stock. This contention seems to need little discussion. While the English authorities are to that effect, and while similar holdings have been made in some of the states, the great weight of authority is in favor of such power, when exercised with no illegitimate or fraudulent purpose, and when no rights of creditors suffer thereby. In the face of this conflict of decision, this court long ago, upon support from the Supreme Court of the United States, adopted the view that, generally speaking, corporations have such power, and has persisted therein so long that we have no doubt property rights of great magnitude have grown up in reliance thereon. . . .

Another contention is that, conceding such power in the corporation, the defendants, acting on the board of directors and also voting their stock in ratification of the directors' act, were actuated by a purpose to deprive the plaintiffs of their just rights in the corporation, especially by reducing the amount of the voting stock, so that defendants would hold a majority thereof —a purpose which was condemned in Luther v. Luther, 118 Wis. 112, 94 N.W. 69, 99 Am. St. Rep. 977. But the trial court has found against the existence of any such motive, or any ulterior or illegitimate intent or purpose, other than the promotion of the best interests of the corporation, according to the honest judgment of the defendants. This finding, we think, is fully supported by a preponderance of the evidence, and must preclude any interference by a court with acts in pursuance of the business policy, adopted in good faith by the holders of a majority of the capital stock. . . .

CASE NO. 8

Nipp v. Puritan Manufacturing & Supply Co. 128 Neb. 459, 259 N.W. 53 (1935)

CARTER, J. This is an action in the nature of a creditor's bill brought by Elinor Nipp, as special administratrix of the estate of Gilbert E. Nipp, deceased, against the Puritan Manufacturing Company, a corporation, Walter J. Charnley, A. J. Schmitz and L. V. Stout, impleaded with the Puritan Manufacturing & Supply Company, a corporation, appellees herein. From an adverse decree in the district court, the plaintiff below brings the case to this court for review.

It appears from the evidence that on and for a number of years prior to January 15, 1927, Gilbert E. Nipp had been president and general manager of the Puritan Manufacturing & Supply Company. At the beginning of the year 1927, the debts of the company amounted to $14,997.98. It also appears that at this time the company, under

Nipp's management, had suffered losses on its contracts in a sum aggregating $15,781.13. On January 15, 1927, Nipp sold his stock in the company to the company for the sum of $8,876.66, payable $876.66 in cash or its equivalent, and the balance in thirty monthly instalments represented by the company's promissory notes. Nipp left the company immediately and was succeeded as president by Walter J. Charnley, one of the appellees herein, who, together with the other appellees Stout and Schmitz, was a stockholder in the company until it ceased to do business. . . .

That the company had the right to purchase its own stock is not seriously disputed. The weight of authority seems to be that, if it does not appear to be in bad faith and injurious to the rights of its creditors or stockholders, a corporation, when not prevented by its articles or by statute, may buy and sell its own stock, and hold, issue, or retire the same. . . . That the sale of the stock to the corporation in the case at bar was injurious to the rights of creditors is amply shown by the evidence. . . . In the case of In re Fechheimer Fishel Co. (C.C.A.) 212 Fed. 357, 363, it was held:

> "If at the time the stockholder receives payment for his stock the payment prejudices the creditors, payment cannot be enforced. If a stockholder sells his stock to a corporation which issued it, he sells at his peril and assumes the risk of the consummation of the transaction without encroachment upon the funds which belong to the corporation in trust for the payment of its creditors. . . ."

It is clear, therefore, in the case at bar, that Gilbert E. Nipp and his personal representative were at all times mentioned herein subsequent in their rights to those of general creditors. . . .

Affirmed.

CASE NO. 9

Jemison v. Citizens' Savings Bank of Jefferson, Texas. 122 N.Y. 135, 25 N.E. 264 (1890)

Plaintiff, commission merchants and members of the Cotton Exchange, brought this action to recover commissions and money claimed expended for defendant on the purchase and sale of cotton futures. Defendant, a savings bank and trust corporation, set up the defense of ultra vires.

HAIGHT, J. Corporations are artificial creations, existing by virtue of some statute, and organized for the purposes defined in their charters. A person dealing with a corporation is chargeable with notice of its powers and the purposes for which it is formed, and, when dealing with its agents or officers, is bound to know the extent of their power or authority.

Savings banks are designed to encourage economy and frugality among persons of small means, and are organized with restrictions and provisions intended to secure depositors against loss. Speculative contracts entered into for the sale or purchase of stock by a savings bank at the stock board or elsewhere, subject to the hazard and contingency of gain or loss, are ultra vires, and a perversion of the powers conferred by its charter. Contracts of corporations are ultra vires when they involve adventures or undertakings outside and not within the scope or power given by their charters. The acts under which they are organized were framed in view of the rights of the public and the interests of the stockholders. As artificial creations, they possess only the powers with which they were endowed. . . .

It is contended that the defense of ultra vires is not available in this case, for the reason that the contract had been executed on the part of the plaintiffs, and that the defendant is estopped from setting up the defense. In the case of Whitney Arms Co. v. Barrow, 63 N.Y. 62, the plaintiff was a corporation organized for the purpose of manufacturing every variety of firearms and other implements of war, and all kinds of machinery adapted to the construction thereof. It entered into a contract with the American Seal Lock Company to manufacture and deliver ten thousand locks. The locks having been delivered, it was held that the contract was fully executed, and that the plea of ultra vires would not prevail as a defense to an action brought to recover the contract price. We do not question the rule thus invoked. It has been repeatedly declared in other cases, as, for instance, in Parrish v. Wheeler, 22 N.Y. 494, in which it was held that a railroad company, having purchased and received a steamboat, could be compelled to pay for it, although the power to purchase such boat was not included in its charter. But this doctrine has no application to executory contracts which are sought to be made the foundation of an action, or to contracts that are prohibited as against public policy, or immoral.

In the case at bar, the transaction, as we have seen, was not only immoral and in violation of the rights of the stockholders and depositors, but the defendant had received nothing by virtue of it. The cotton had been purchased by the plaintiffs in their own name, they taking title thereto, and holding it upon the defendant's account. . . . There has been no delivery of any cotton or property of any kind, or transfer of any title to such property, to the defendant. If the steamboat had never been delivered to the railroad company so as to transfer the title thereto, or if the ten thousand locks had never been delivered to the American Seal Lock Company, very different questions would have been presented in the cases to which we have called attention. We consequently are of the opinion that, under the circumstances of this case, the defense of ultra vires is available to the defendant.

Judgment for defendant affirmed.

CASE NO. 10

Nardis Sportswear v. Simmons. 213 S.W. (2d) 864 (Tex.) (1948)

Appellant Nardis Sportswear, a dissolved corporation, by its former directors as trustees, acting under authority of Art. 1388, Vernon's Annotated Civil Statutes, instituted this suit on October 15, 1946 against appellee John J. Simmons for specific performance of an option contract to purchase certain real estate. . . . The trial court . . . entered judgment that appellant recover nothing by the suit. . . .

LOONEY, J. . . . Nardis Sportswear, Inc., the appellant, was a Texas corporation chartered for the purpose of transacting the manufacturing business of making ladies' skirts, robes, and sportswear, and to purchase and sell goods, wares and merchandise used for such business. The corporation leased from Mr. John J. Simmons, appellee, the real estate involved, as a place to conduct its business, agreeing to pay a monthly rental of $625 for five years, beginning July 1, 1943, and ending June 30, 1948. Appellant was also given an option to purchase the real estate outright for a cash consideration of $75,000. This option could have been exercised at any time during the life of the lease contract. The corporation was dissolved on April 30, 1945, on the consent in writing of all its stockholders, as authorized by 3 Vernon's Ann. Civ. St. subdv. 4 of Art.

1387; and its President, Bernard L. Gold, its Treasurer, Irving Gold, and its Secretary, Viola Ray, officers and stockholders, became trustees of the creditors and stockholders of the corporation and were given by law power to settle the affairs, collect outstanding debts, and divide money and other property among stockholders after paying the debts of the corporation and reasonable expenses of the administration, as provided in 3 Vernon's Ann. Civ. St. Art. 1388. For the limited purpose of enabling the trustees to settle up the affairs of the corporation, its existence was continued for three years after the dissolution, as provided in 3 Vernon's Ann. Civ. St. Art. 1389.

Prior to its dissolution the corporation had not exercised the option to purchase the real property. However, on December 17, 1945, the trustees sought to exercise the option, and, to that end, Bernard L. Gold, President, in the name of the corporation, so advised Mr. Simmons by letter. Without reciting immaterial matters that supervened after the attempted exercise of the option, suffice it to say the offer to purchase, or the exercise of the option, was rejected by Mr. Simmons and this suit was instituted in the name of the corporation by the trustees for specific performance of the alleged contract. The case was tried to a jury and at conclusion of the evidence each party moved for an instructed verdict. The motion of plaintiff was denied and that of defendant sustained, and on the directed verdict in favor of the defendant, the court rendered judgment in his favor, that the plaintiffs take nothing from which this appeal was prosecuted.

The only question that I care to discuss, in my opinion the pivotal question on which the decision of this case turns, is: Were these trustees, acting in the name of and for the dissolved corporation, authorized, in the proper settlement and administration of its affairs, to exercise the option to purchase the real estate involved? Or to compel specific performance of the executory contract?

There are several valid reasons, in my opinion, why these questions should be answered in the negative. The powers left to a corporation after dissolution, and the scope of the authority of the trustees in winding up its affairs, were well stated by Judge Brewster in McBride v. Clayton, 140 Tex. 71, 166 S.W. (2d) 125, 128, as follows; he said:

"Although the statutes give McBride, Inc., a continued existence for as long as three years after the surrender of its charter, it clearly could not be so continued to purchase and sell goods, wares and merchandise and to transact a general retail mercantile business. Its charter ceased on December 15, 1937, to have any force as such, and McBride, Inc., could derive no power from it, could not engage in retail merchandising under it. Whatever powers remained came by virtue of the statute and only for the specific and limited purposes named therein. Its qualified existence was in the nature of an administration of its estate, with all its corporate rights fixed and determined as of the date of its dissolution. Crease v. Babcock, 23 Pic. (Mass.) 334, 34 Am. Dec. 61. It was continued only to collect what was due it, to pay what it owed and to distribute what was left of its assets to those entitled to them. Jaffee v. Commissioner of Internal Revenue, 2 Cir., 45 F. (2d) 679; 13 Am. Jur., § 1366, p. 1206; 19 C.J.S., Corporations, § 1743(4), at page 1509. In other words, the powers of its officers had become restricted to those of liquidating agents. 11 Tex. Jur., § 470, p. 136."

Opinion adopted by the Supreme Court.

The power of these trustees is clearly defined in 3 Vernon's Art. 1388, and does not include the power to purchase real estate. After stating that the trustees

"shall be trustees of the creditors and stockholders of such corporation, with power to settle the affairs, collect the outstanding debts, and divide the moneys and other property among the stockholders after paying the debts due and owing by such corporation at the time of its dissolution, as far as such money and property will enable them after paying all just and reasonable expenses," . . .

Thus I think the conclusion inescapable that the dissolved corporation was wholly without power to purchase real estate, or anything else, as it was out of business, and its trustees were not authorized in the winding-up procedure to exercise powers greater than those remaining with the dissolved corporation.

CASE NO. 11

Petition of Collins-Doan Co. 3 N.J. 382 70 A. (2d) 159 (1949)

HEHER, J. The question here is whether the respondent corporation, Collins-Doan Company, is subject to dissolution under R.S. 14:13–15, N.J.S.A. The issue was resolved in the affirmative by Judge Grimshaw in the Chancery Division of the Superior Court and in the negative by the Appellate Division of that court. . . .

. . . The articles of incorporation declared that the primary object of the company was "to acquire and take over as a going concern" the commercial printing business then carried on in Jersey City by the appellant Israel Doan and the respondent Samuel B. Collins as co-partners under the firm name and style of Collins and Doan. The company was thereby authorized to issue 250 shares of capital stock of the par value of $100 each, consisting of 100 shares of preferred stock and 150 shares of common stock. There was provision for a cumulative dividend of 6 per cent per annum on the preferred stock, payable semi-annually out of the surplus or net earnings before the payment of any dividend on the common stock. The preferred stockholders were given the usual priority on the liquidation or dissolution of the company; and there was a stipulation for the redemption of this class of stock "by vote of a majority of the whole board of directors," at any time after three years from issue, "at a price not less than par value." It was provided also that the holders of the preferred stock "shall have equal representation on the board of directors with the holders of the common stock." 105 shares of the common stock were issued to Collins; 100 shares of the preferred stock were issued to Doan; and five shares of the common stock were issued to Moe, a lawyer, for legal services rendered in "the organization of the company." Thus, the corporation commenced business with a capital fund of $21,000, represented by the property and assets of the partnership transferred and conveyed to the corporation in consideration of the issue of the stock.

. . . The directorate now comprise Doan and Morten, elected by the preferred stockholders to afford that class the "representation" provided by the articles of incorporation and the by-laws, and Collins and Moe, chosen to "represent" the interests of the holders of the common stock.

But differences between these independent interests have resulted in a deadlock in the board of directors and in the stock ownership and a consequent failure of corporate function in the manner provided by the statute governing such entities. The plan devised to afford the holders of each class of stock an equal voice in the management of the corporate affairs has made for corporate inaction. While there have been annual elections of directors, the board has been chosen in conformity with the cited provisions of the articles of incorporation and the by-laws for equal representation in the Company's directorate of the holders of preferred and common stock, each class as a unit; and thus the disagreements, beginning in 1937, as to policy and management could not be resolved by corporate action. These controversies are now insoluble so much so that Moe joins in the petition for dissolution of the corporation. Moe testified that he considered himself "morally obligated to vote in the same manner as Mr. Collins"; and he is convinced the differences are irreconcilable.

. . . Thus, dissension has rendered the directorate impotent; and the like equal division of interest and voting power among the stockholders put it beyond their power to cure this paralysis of function by the election of a directorate of an uneven number.

The act of incorporation is a compact between the corporation and the sovereignty whence its powers came, and as well between the corporation and its stockholders and between the stockholders inter se. . . . The duration of the franchise grant is ordinarily indeterminate; but where, as here, corporate function can no longer be had due to irreconcilable differences between two independent classes or groups of stockholders of equal voting power, the corporation is subject to dissolution in the interest of the public and the shareholders who may suffer injury. Dissolution does not constitute an impairment of the obligation of contracts made with creditors and others, for resort may be had to the property of the corporation in the mode provided by statute, or, if there be no adequate statutory remedy, by the processes of equity. A corporation does not have an absolute right to existence in perpetuity. The obligation of the contract between the sovereign power and the corporate entity is not so far-reaching; it is fundamental in every such contract that the corporation is subject to dissolution at the instance of the state of its creation, as for condition broken, by a forfeiture of its franchises for wilful misuser and nonuser or for like cause, adversely affecting the essence of the contract, whereby its continued existence would run afoul of the interests and public policy of the State. This is of the very nature of such bodies politic; and the contracts between the corporate entity and its stockholders and creditors are all conditioned accordingly. . . .

. . . A corporate charter granted under a general enabling act embodies all the provisions of the constitution and the statute under which it is issued and all other applicable general laws; and if there be conflict in this regard the charter yields to the constitution and the statute. . . . It is within the competency of the legislature to reserve the right of alteration and repeal of a corporate charter by general statute; and such reservation, as to charters thereafter issued,

> "will have precisely the same effect as if inserted in the charter. Under a general statute of this description, charters of incorporated companies thereafter granted, are repealable, although there is no clause in the charter reserving such right." State, Morris & Essex R. Co., Pros. v. Commissioner of Railroad Taxation, 37 N.J.L. 228, 237 . . .

Here, the corporation has an even number of directors who are equally divided respecting the management of its affairs; the voting shares of the corporation are equally divided into two independent ownerships or interests with the same division of view as to policy and management as the deadlocked directorate; the shareholders for the same reason cannot terminate the stalemate by the election of a directorate of an uneven number, and the holders of shares consisting of one-half or more of the voting power have joined in this petition for dissolution; and thus the statutory prerequisites for the exercise of the dissolutional power are met.

There is no alternative course. For ten years or more the Company has not functioned as ordained by the laws; and irreconcilable differences between the equally divided shareholders and directors render a resumption of function impossible. . . .

The judgment of the Appellate Division of the Superior Court is reversed and the judgment of dissolution rendered in the Superior Court is affirmed. . . .

CASE NO. 12

Stott Realty Co. v. Orloff. 262 Mich. 375, 247 N.W. 698 (1933)

FEAD, J. This is appeal from decree dissolving the Stott Realty Company, a corporation.

In 1916 David Stott died, leaving a large estate, including controlling interests in several corporations. Among them was the Stott Realty Company, his stock in which he left to . . . his four daughters, Bertha, Eleanor, Ethel, and Julia, and his three sons, David, Ernest, and Arthur. . . .

At David Stott's death the assets were worth $2,000,000. In 1929 their value was $8,000,000 or over. The properties were substantially the same, but with some remodeling of buildings. The enhancement in worth was due largely to increase in real estate values in Detroit. Management conserving the estate was also a factor. Dividends of 16 per cent. annually have been paid regularly until 1929, when, after payment of 8 per cent., further dividends were suspended because of business conditions. . . .

In 1928, the corporation began the erection of the thirty-five story David Stott building. It cost $2,400,000. It was mortgaged for $1,300,000. About $725,-000 of the cost was borrowed from the Detroit Savings Bank, $150,000 secured by mortgage on the Arcadia property, and the balance unsecured. In 1929 the Detroit Savings Bank called the loans, commenced suit, and garnished the tenants of the corporation.

On November 1st a meeting of the stockholders of the Stott Realty Company was called, and various proposals of financing the bank claims discussed. Because of the condition of the real estate market, a majority favored a mortgage upon the real property, which had been authorized by the board of directors in August. Julia, Ernest, and Arthur voted against a mortgage, thereby defeating it because the statute requires approval of two-thirds of the stock. They presented no feasible plan of financing. November 29th, in the absence of Julia and Ernest, who were directors but from whom the plan was concealed, the board of directors authorized commencement of this suit. The bill was for appointment of a temporary receiver, with hope of authority to execute a mortgage. Julia, Ernest, and Arthur filed cross-bills praying dissolution of the corporation.

The record contains 2,430 pages, . . .

The record depicts a course of family controversy and dissension, beginning before the death of the father and continuing to the present, characterized by ill will, accusations, recriminations, extensive and expensive litigation, and physical violence. So far as it affects the Stott Realty Company, much of the dissension has been between David E. Stott and Arthur, and has arisen out of David's desire to keep the corporation intact and rule it and Arthur's desire to divide it into individual ownership. In their differences, David usually has been supported by Bertha, Eleanor, and Ethel. Julia is often on the side of Arthur, and Ernest is rather independent. . . .

Dissolution is not a remedy to be lightly decreed. The court has ample power in other ways to give relief for substantially all corporate ills. . . . It may require an accounting for misappropriation of funds, secret profits, and the like. It may restrain or compel the corporation and its officers to lawful conduct and ordinarily protect the stockholders in all their rights without dissolution. Dissolution is a last resort remedy, to be applied when no other will give relief.

The ultimate test of dissolution is that, with any other remedy, the corporation cannot be made to function for the purpose of its creation. The test of failure of corporate purpose is whether ruin will inevitably follow continuance of the management. 43 A.L.R. 305, note.

Undoubtedly, the case presents some conduct by the majority stockholders for which a court of equity would provide a remedy, notably the failure to hold stockholders' meetings in 1930 and 1931, prevented by the majority absenting themselves. Perhaps the court, on showing that the plan to institute this suit was concealed from some of the directors, would have dismissed the bill. It may be that some of David's conduct would warrant proceedings against him personally. But the record discloses no act of the majority which, needing correction, could not be remedied by the ordinary processes of the court. And there are outstanding facts, most of which are undisputed, which preclude the remedy of dissolution.

Dissolution is opposed by six stockholders owning over five-sevenths of the stock. It is asked by two stockholders. The contrast between them, in respect of their regard for the corporate good, does not incline a court of equity in favor of the minority. The minority complain of loans of $5,000 by the corporation to each of two of the majority, while each minority member owes the corporation over $100,000. The majority advanced $40,000 to save the corporate property from execution and mortgage sale. The minority refused to contribute and would have permitted loss of most of the corporation property. To save the corporation for the benefit of the minority as well as themselves, four majority members obligated themselves personally for $750,000 on the corporation mortgage debt. The minority assumed nothing.

The majority oppose dissolution for the valid reasons that they consider the diversification of properties through corporate control more profitable and more likely to conserve the assets than individual ownership, and also because some of them feel unable or unwilling to manage separate properties. The minority are concerned with obtaining personal control and individual ownership. . . .

The record of the corporation as to profits demonstrates competent management. Whether other persons could have produced more earnings over a period of years is not only not the test of competent management, but must necessarily be largely or wholly speculative. . . .

The corporate purpose has not failed. The Stott Realty Company is a going concern. When the cross-bills were filed, and afterwards, it was profitable. So far as the record shows, it is able to pay its current liabilities, at least as readily as most corporations. It has failed to perform only the one function of executing mortgages, and such failure has been temporary and due to the refusal of the minority to assent. No one can surely prophesy what the present economic depression will bring to any concern. The corporation may lose all its property by foreclosure and execution. But "hard times" is not a cause for dissolution. . . .

In our opinion, the case presents no right to the remedy of dissolution.

Review Questions

1. What powers may a corporation exercise within the state of incorporation?
2. What powers may a corporation exercise in a foreign state?
3. May a state prohibit a foreign corporation engaged in interstate commerce from doing business within its borders?
4. What is the concept of a corporation's incidental powers?
5. What powers are bestowed upon a corporation by implication?
6. What are the limitations upon the right of a corporation to acquire its own stock?
7. What is the reasoning underlying the minority rule that a corporation may not acquire its own stock?
8. Does a corporation have the right to purchase stock in other corporations?
9. What is an ultra vires act?
10. Upon what basis does the right of the incorporating state and the stockholder to object to ultra vires acts rest?
11. What is the status of ultra vires contracts under the Uniform Business Corporation Act?
12. Does the phrase "the corporation has the right of perpetual succession" mean the same as "the life of the corporation shall be perpetual"?
13. By what methods may corporate life come to an end?
14. To what penalty does a corporation subject itself by a violation of its charter powers?
15. What principle in relation to corporate charters was established by the *Dartmouth College* case, and how has this interfered with the right of legislative bodies to repeal corporate charters?

Problems for Discussion

1. This action was brought by the plaintiff corporation to recover of the defendant life insurance company the amount of a policy issued by it for the benefit of the plaintiff upon the life of B. F. Board, its president and general manager. Defendant takes the position that the contract of insurance was an ultra vires act. Decide. (*Mut. L. Ins. Co.* v. *Board, Armstrong & Co.*, 115 Va. 836)
2. The State of Texas took action to restrain the defendant corporation from selling gas and electrical appliances, from maintaining salesrooms and salesmen to such purpose for which in excess of $150,000 of the corporation's assets were

used. The defendant corporation was authorized to manufacture, supply, and sell electricity and gas for light, heat, and power. Decide. (*State* v. *San Antonio Public Service Co.*, 69 S.W. (2d) 38)

3. A manufacturing corporation A guaranteed the payment of B's rent upon consideration that B would continue to sell the products of A. Is this within the implied powers of A?
4. A newspaper corporation chartered a yacht for the purpose of collecting news. One of the stockholders objected that this was beyond the corporation's powers. Decide.
5. Corporation A was engaged in the making of motion pictures. Corporation B contracted with Corporation A to furnish costumes for a play to be filmed by Corporation A. Corporation C contracted to furnish A with lumber and materials to be used in the staging of the production. Shortly after C started to supply the materials, A defaulted in its payments. Corporation B then guaranteed the payments of A to C, whereupon the remainder of the materials was supplied. B's objective was to make it possible for A to proceed with the production so that the costumes contracted for could be furnished. In an action by C against B, based upon the guaranty, the issue was whether the act of guaranteeing A's obligation was within the implied powers of Corporation B. Decide. (*Woods Lbr. Co.* v. *Moore,* 183 Calif. 497)
6. A corporation organized to carry passengers for hire sold advertising space on the exterior of its vehicles. Is this within the corporate powers?
7. The A Corporation was given the power to manufacture, supply, and sell gas and electricity to the public. It undertook to sell electric and gas appliances to the public, although it had no express authority to do so. The state commenced a proceeding to perpetually enjoin A from engaging in such activities, alleging that such acts are ultra vires. Result?
8. Would a cotton-gin corporation have the implied power to buy and sell cottonseed to farmers who patronize the corporation?
9. Would a railroad corporation have the implied power to acquire and operate hotels in towns which it serves?
10. The X Corporation, having been unprofitable for the past six years, voted to purchase one half of each stockholder's shares at $20 a share. This would require $200,000. The corporation has liquid assets of $250,000, other assets of $210,000 (including a good-will item of $50,000) and liabilities to creditors of $300,000. Can the creditors block this action?
11. The defendant corporation was by its charter authorized as follows:

    "For the upbuilding of the cities of Little Rock and Argenta, Pulaski county, and the state of Arkansas, encouraging and assisting in public improvements of all kinds therein, including streets, highways, sewers, public buildings, and any and all things which are for the public good; locating schools and colleges, locating, developing and assisting in location and development therein manufactures and other industries, conducting a merchant association, board of trade, real estate exchange; for organizing and conducting any other bureau or bureaus, exchanges, which the board of governors may decide will be beneficial or necessary in the building up of said cities and state, for the best interest thereof and of the organization; shall have full power to do any and all things deemed necessary in carrying on any and all of the above objects; to foster and promote the commercial, industrial, physical, and moral development of the cities of Little Rock, Argenta, and vicinity."

This is an action to restrain the defendant from using funds to "subsidize and establish a boat line for the navigation of the Arkansas river. Decide. (*Gregg* v. *Little Rock Chamber of Commerce,* 120 Ark. 426)

12. Service was had upon J. H. Wood, Jr., the sales manager of the Atlanta branch of the Ford Motor Company. At time of service Mr. Wood was in Birmingham calling upon local Ford dealers relative to sales promotion. The Ford Motor Company had no agents in Alabama at that time. It was operating exclusively through dealers under "dealer contracts." At time of service representatives of the Atlanta branch of the Ford Motor Company called upon local dealers to assist them in "pushing the sale of cars," and to demonstrate to employees of the dealers as to how to improve service and to contact prospective customers. The validity of the service was dependent upon whether Ford Motor Co. was doing business in Alabama. Decide. (*Ford Motor Co.* v. *Hall Auto Co.,* 226 Ala. 385)
13. The X Corporation was organized for the purpose of dealing in livestock. The venture proved to be profitable and the corporation invested its surplus funds in stock of the Y Bank to an extent that it acquired a controlling interest. One of the stockholders objects. Decide.
14. The charter of the X Corporation provides for a twenty-five year life. No statutory or other provision is made in regard to the vote required for dissolution. Can the corporation be dissolved by a 99 per cent vote?
15. The X Corporation has been dormant and inactive for a period of five years. Is this cause for dissolution of the corporation by the state?

39 BUSINESS ORGANIZATIONS:

STOCKHOLDERS' POSITION

► I. METHODS OF BECOMING STOCKHOLDERS

Individuals acquire membership in a corporation by ownership or the right to ownership of shares of the corporation's capital stock. The methods by which a share interest in a corporation can be acquired are:

(1) by subscription to stock prior or subsequent to the formation of the corporation;

(2) by purchase from the corporation or an underwriter subsequent to its formation of either original stock or treasury stock; and

(3) by acquisition of an existing stockholder's share interest in the corporation. (This method may be carried out through any of the means by which title to personal property can be acquired.)

A. SHARES DISTINGUISHED FROM CERTIFICATES OF STOCK

Shares of stock such as are owned by corporate stockholders are intangible and invisible things. A stockholder's share interest in a corporation is merely his right to participate in the business enterprise in that proportion which his share interest in the corporation bears to the total shares of stock outstanding. For example, if a stockholder owns 100 shares out of a total of 400 outstanding shares, he would be entitled to participate in profits, management, and distribution of assets upon dissolution to the extent of 25 per cent.

This intangible right to participation is usually evidenced by a *stock certificate.*[1] In many jurisdictions the certificate is regarded as a quasi-negotiable document of title and by statutes and court decisions has been given many of the attributes of negotiable instruments. A share interest as evidenced by the certificate can thus be easily transferred from one owner to another by indorsement and delivery of the certificate. The transferee, however, does not become a shareholder in relation to the corporation until his name is registered upon the stock transfer books of the corporation.

The right to membership in a corporation is not absolutely dependent upon a stock certificate. A party to a subscription contract has the position of a stockholder even though a certificate has never been issued—his name upon the books of the corporation may constitute sufficient evidence of membership.

The court in *Cecil Nat. Bank* v. *Watsontown Bank,* 105 U.S. 217, said:

"This legal relation (corporate membership) and proprietary interest, on which it is based, are quite independent of the certificate of ownership, which

[1] Continental Ins. Co. v. Minn., etc. Co., p. 1000.

is mere evidence of title. The complete fact of title may very well exist without it. All that is necessary, when the transfer is required by law to be made upon the books of the corporation, is that the fact should be appropriately recorded in some suitable register or stock list, or otherwise formally entered upon its books. For this purpose the account in a stock ledger, showing the name of the stockholders, the number and amount of the shares belonging to each, and the source of their title, whether by original subscription and payment or by derivation from others, is quite suitable, and fully meets the requirements of the law."

B. SUBSCRIPTION CONTRACTS

1. *Subscription and Purchase Distinguished*

Upon entering into a *subscription contract* with a corporation, one acquires membership in the corporation. A subscriber to corporate stock occupies the status of a stockholder from the moment the contract is entered into. *A contract to purchase stock* of a corporation differs from a subscription contract in that the purchaser acquires no rights as a stockholder until the contract is consummated, that is, until the stock certificate has been formally issued to him.[2]

A *subscriber* can force specific performance of his contract, and he is liable for the subscription price even though no stock certificate has been issued to him. On the other hand, a *purchaser* is not liable for the price agreed upon until the stock certificate is issued to him. Nor can he specifically enforce his contract; his remedy for a breach by the corporation is limited to money damages.

Whether an agreement is one to purchase or to subscribe is a matter of determining what the intent of the contracting parties was. The use of the words *subscription* or *purchase,* while being evidential, is not conclusive.

2. *Subscriptions Prior to Incorporation*

The predominating view is that a subscription to stock of a proposed corporation is a mere offer by the subscriber to become a stockholder if and when the corporation comes into existence. Consequently, prior to its acceptance, the offer can be revoked at the pleasure of the subscriber. The formation of the corporation is usually regarded as an acceptance of the subscription offer without need of any further act on the part of the corporation. In those instances where the charter prescribes any conditions or special methods of becoming a member, there must be a substantial compliance before the subscriber becomes a stockholder.

3. *Subscription Contracts Between Subscribers*

When individuals enter into a mutual undertaking with each other to subscribe to stock in a proposed corporation, the various subscription offers will be regarded as irrevocable. The mutual promises of the parties constitute the consideration to support the offers to subscribe, thus making them binding.[3] For this

---

[2] Schwartz v. Mfgs.' Cas. Ins. Co., p. 1001.

[3] Coleman Hotel Co. v. Crawford, p. 1002.

reason, subscriptions become continuing irrevocable offers to the contemplated corporation, and these offers are translated into contracts upon the creation of the corporation.

4. *Subscriptions after Incorporation*

A subscription contract with an existing corporation differs in no respect from a subscription contract entered into with a corporation upon its creation. At the time of the acceptance of a subscription offer, the subscriber in either instance occupies the status of a stockholder. The offer to subscribe may originate either with the subscriber or with the corporation. For example, the corporation may open its subscription books and advertise for offers, or it may make an offer to specified individuals or to the public in general.

▶ II. TRANSFER OF STOCK

A stockholder's interest in a corporation is personal property, intangible in form, and carries with it the right of disposition in the absence of any contractual restrictions. Probably no other form of property, other than money, changes ownership more often than does that represented by stock certificates. Share interests in corporations change hands daily within the portals of the various organized exchanges, in over-the-counter transactions, and in personal dealings.

A. METHOD OF TRANSFER

It is generally provided by the articles of incorporation or by statute that a transfer of shares in a corporate enterprise is to be accomplished by indorsement and delivery of the certificate.[4] The registered owner of stock will upon sale usually indorse the certificate (or a separate assignment form which is then attached to the certificate) in blank—without designating the transferee. There is, however, no reason why the owner may not at the time of the indorsement include the name of the transferee if known. Following is a copy of a separate assignment form which is the same as the form found on the back of a stock certificate.

The complete transfer of title from one owner to another involves two steps. The *first step* is the indorsement and delivery of the certificate by the transferor to the transferee. As between these parties, the transferee will become by this act the owner of the property that the certificate represents. This will not entitle him to the status of a stockholder in relation to the corporation.

It is essential for a corporation to have a record of all shareholders for the purpose of knowing to whom it shall accord the rights of membership. It is by the corporation's records, for example, that the right to vote and the right to dividends are determined. Consequently, the *second step* to complete the transaction is the registration of the transfer with the corporation or with its designated transfer agent. Specifically this is accomplished by a surrender of the certificate that repre-

[4] Cliff's Corp. v. U.S., p. 1003.

sents the property to be transferred. A new certificate will then be issued to the transferee. This transaction in effect constitutes a *novation*—the substitution of the new stockholder in the position of the former.

STOCK

ASSIGNMENT SEPARATE FROM CERTIFICATE

For Value Received, ...

hereby sell, assign and transfer unto ....

.................................(......) Shares of the ....

Capital Stock of the ....

standing in .... name on the Books of said ....

.................................represented by Certificate No. .... herewith

and do hereby irrevocably constitute and appoint ....

.... attorney to transfer the said stock on the books of the within named Company with full power of substitution in the premises.

Dated ....

....

IN PRESENCE OF

....

It will be noted that the above transfer form makes provision for the appointment of an agent (attorney in fact) by the indorser who is authorized to transfer the stock upon the books of the corporation. This is in compliance with the usual by-law provision to the effect that

> "The stock of this corporation shall be transferred on the books of this corporation by the person named in the certificate (owner) or by his attorney, lawfully constituted in writing, and upon surrender of this certificate."

This part of the transfer form is at the time of its execution left blank. The name of the person who makes the transfer upon the corporation's books is put in at that time.

B. RIGHT OF TRANSFER

The right of disposition is one of the fundamental characteristics of our institution of private property. It is the policy of our law that as few restrictions as possible be placed upon the free transferability of property. Based upon this philosophy is the general rule that, in the absence of statutory authority, a corporation has no power, either on the basis of its by-laws or other corporate regulations, to prevent or restrict its stockholders from transferring their share interests. As a matter of public policy, shareholders should be able to change their investments or use their property interests in a corporation to their own best advantage without unreasonable restrictions.

> "The transfer of stock has been uniformly regarded as a legitimate subject of corporate legislation, to enable the company to know who are stock-

holders, to whom dividends are to be paid, who are entitled to vote, and, where the company has a lien on the stock for debts due to it from the stockholders, to enable it to prevent a transfer in derogation of its own rights. But such legislation will not be enforced beyond what is necessary to serve those purposes, where its enforcement would operate as an infringement on the property rights of others, or as an unreasonable restraint upon the disposition of property in the stock of the corporation." *Miller* v. *Farmers' Milling etc. Co.*, 78 Neb. 441.

As a matter of practice, few corporate managements place unreasonable limitations upon the right to transfer shares of stock from one owner to another. Ownership in most of our present-day corporations is open to the public. However, there are instances in which provision is made with a view to controlling and selecting membership.[5]

1. *Particular Restrictions Considered*

Generally the courts will not enforce provisions to the effect that transfers can be brought about only with the consent of specified corporation officials or with the consent of all stockholders. Provisions of this nature are looked upon as being contrary to public policy. Such a right vested in the management would give it the effective power to perpetuate its tenure of office.

It is generally held that provisions are valid when they reserve the right to the corporation or stockholders to purchase any stock offered for sale.[6] The reasoning underlying this majority view is well expressed in the following statements:

"It is sometimes necessary and often desirable that a corporation protect itself against the acquisition of shares of its stock by rivals in business or other disturbers who might purchase shares merely for the purpose of acquiring information which might thereafter be used against the interests of the company." In re *Laun*, 146 Wis. 252.

"The personal element is as important in the make-up and management of a corporation as it is in almost every other undertaking. Restrictions, therefore, reasonably protecting incorporators or stockholders in their interests by permitting them first to purchase stock offered for sale, should be held lawful as promotive of good management and sound business enterprise." *Casper* v. *Kalt-Zimmers Mfg. Co.*, 159 Wis. 517.

A corporation's charter or by-laws may give it a lien on its stockholders' shares for obligations due from the stockholders to the corporation. A provision of such a nature represents a restriction upon the right to transfer; this restriction is binding upon the stockholders. Transferees are not, however, bound by such a limitation unless they have actual or constructive notice of its existence. Third persons would be charged with notice where such a provision is contained in either the articles of incorporation or in a statutory enactment. Unless third parties are in some manner charged with notice of the contents of a corporation's by-laws, they

---

[5] Searles v. Bar Harbor Banking & T. Co., p. 1004.

[6] Guaranty Laundry Co. v. Pulliam, p. 1005.

can take a transfer free from the lien as therein provided. The Uniform Stock Transfer Act provides that no lien can exist in favor of a corporation unless the lien is stated upon the certificate.

2. *Restrictions by Contract*

"A distinction must be observed . . . between those conditions when created by contract . . . and when attempted to be imposed by a by-law upon an unwilling minority. . . ." In re *Laun,* 146 Wis. 252.

A contract between the various stockholders or between the stockholders and the corporation which absolutely restricts the sale or transfer of stock is illegal. If stockholders agree among themselves not to transfer their stock, such an agreement is unreasonably in restraint of trade and therefore unenforceable.

On the other hand, a contract is legal which merely imposes reasonable conditions upon the right of transfer—conditions that are designed for the benefit of the corporation or the individual stockholders. To illustrate:

In *Williams* v. *Montgomery,* 148 N.Y. 519, a contract was held to be binding which provided for the exclusion of shares of stock from the market during a period when treasury stock of the corporation was to be sold. The court said that such a restriction was reasonable, being calculated to promote the interests of both the corporation and the stockholders.

C. NEGOTIABLE CHARACTER OF CERTIFICATES

Stock certificates are not negotiable instruments under the Uniform Negotiable Instruments Law. Many of our courts have taken the view that a transfer of stock by indorsement and delivery of the certificate places the purchaser in no better position than that occupied by the transferor, that the quality of the transferor's right to the property represented by the certificate cannot be improved by the transfer. Thus, if a properly indorsed certificate is stolen from its rightful owner and then transferred to a bona fide purchaser, the latter can get no better title than his transferor had. The holder stands in the same position as the holder of a non-negotiable instrument.

Many of the states, notably those that have adopted the Uniform Stock Transfer Act, have endowed stock certificates with negotiable characteristics by statute. In some instances, the courts have taken it upon themselves to recognize commercial practices in the use of stock certificates and have accorded them a negotiable character.

"The nature and extent of the dealings in such certificates, in which they are passed from hand to hand like negotiable paper and in so many ways enter into the basis of credit, have influenced courts to accord to them the character of negotiability in order to meet a commercial need." *Basset* v. *Perkins,* 119 N.Y.S. 354.

The legal consequences of this view are stated in the Uniform Stock Transfer Act thus:

"Section 5. The delivery of a certificate to transfer title in accordance with the provisions of section 1, is effectual, except as provided in section 7, though made by one having no right of possession and having no authority from the owner of the certificate or from the person purporting to transfer the title.

"Section 6. The indorsement of a certificate by the person appearing by the certificate to be the owner of the shares represented thereby is effectual, except as provided in section 7, though the indorser or transferor,

(a) was induced by fraud, duress or mistake, to make the indorsement or delivery, or

(b) has revoked the delivery of the certificate, or the authority given by the indorsement or delivery of the certificate, or

(c) has died or become legally incapacitated after the indorsement, whether before or after the delivery of the certificate, or

(d) has received no consideration.

"Section 7. If the indorsement or delivery of a certificate,

(a) was procured by fraud or duress, or

(b) was made under such mistake as to make the indorsement or delivery inequitable; or

If the delivery of a certificate was made

(c) without authority from the owner, or

(d) after the owner's death or legal incapacity, the possession of the certificate may be reclaimed and the transfer thereof rescinded, unless:

(1) The certificate has been transferred to a purchaser for value in good faith without notice of any facts making the transfer wrongful, or

(2) The injured person has elected to waive the injury, or has been guilty of laches in endeavoring to enforce his rights."

Any court of appropriate jurisdiction may enforce specifically such right to reclaim the possession of the certificate or to rescind the transfer thereof, and, pending litigation, may enjoin the further transfer of the certificate or impound it.

D. LOST OR STOLEN CERTIFICATES

A stockholder has the right to compel a corporation to issue him a stock certificate if his original has been lost or stolen. On the other hand, since such a situation presents the possibility that the properly indorsed certificate may at some later date appear in the hands of a third person, the corporation has the right to demand an indemnity bond for its protection.

► III. RIGHTS OF STOCKHOLDERS

That stockholders are in fact the owners of the corporation is recognized by the many rights afforded them at common law and by statute for the protection of their interests. In practice, many of these rights are waived by the stockholders in the articles of incorporation or the by-laws of the corporation. Usually stockholders find that their legal rights avail them of naught unless concerted and collective action is taken.

A. RIGHT TO INFORMATION—INSPECTION OF BOOKS

Since stockholders are so thoroughly estranged from the affairs of the business enterprise that is being carried on in their behalf, it is necessary that they have the right to be informed concerning them. Every stockholder has the right to knowledge and information relating to the conduct of the corporate business. It is the duty of the officers to keep the stockholders properly informed.

The primary source of information is the books and records of the corporation. Under common law, a stockholder has the right of their inspection and examination with the qualification that it be at a proper time and place and for a proper purpose. The examination must be based upon a legitimate purpose—a purpose that will subserve the interests of the stockholder or the corporation. For example, a stockholder cannot demand an examination merely in order to obtain information for his personal benefit to the injury of the other stockholders or the corporation, to satisfy his idle curiosity, or to vex or harass the management.[7, 8]

In instances this common law right of inspection has been considerably changed by constitutional or statutory provisions. In some jurisdictions the common law rule has been substantially codified and is so recognized by the courts. In other states, owing to the wording of the provisions or to the attitude of the courts, we find the qualifications removed from the common law right, making the right of inspection absolute. Where the right is guaranteed by statute, the great weight of authority is to the effect that the motive or purpose in seeking to exercise the right of inspection is not the proper subject of judicial inquiry.

In some cases the common law right of inspection is restricted by statutes providing a prerequisite of ownership as to time and amount. In Michigan, to qualify for an inspection the stockholder must have owned not less than 2 per cent of the outstanding stock for not less than three months prior to the demand.

1. *Books Subject to Inspection*

At common law the right of inspection applies to all books and records of the corporation without limitation. It has been held that the right includes even contracts that have been entered into by the corporation. Under some statutes this right is equally inclusive, while under others the right is greatly limited. In some instances it is restricted to the records of stock ownership.

2. *Inspection of Property*

Stockholders have the right to inspect the corporation's property as a means of obtaining information. As the court said in *Hobbs* v. *Tom Reed Gold Mining Co.*, 164 Cal. 497:

[7] Ontjes v. Harrer, p. 1007.
[8] Day & Co. v. Booth, p. 1008.

"It is settled that at common law a stockholder has the right to inspect the books of the corporation. The reasoning on which this rule is founded is that a stockholder has an interest in the assets and business of the corporation and that such inspection may be necessary or proper for the protection of his interest or for his information as to the condition of the corporation and the value of his interests therein. There is not a feature of this reasoning that does not apply with equal force to the claim of a right to examine the property of the corporation, especially where it is mining property, the condition and value of which is so easily concealed or misrepresented. The books would often afford no information of the nature of the ore bodies exposed or of the manner in which the work was carried on."

B. RIGHT TO SHARE IN DIVIDENDS

The stockholders have no right to compel the corporation to distribute business profits to them. Like other corporate property, the profits belong to the corporation and can be used by the management for legitimate corporate purposes. A stockholder has no right to share pro rata in the profits or assets of the corporation unless a distribution has been properly declared by the board of directors.[9] It is only then that a stockholder acquires an individual interest in the profits or assets of the corporation. The declaration of a dividend constitutes the creation of a debt obligation from the corporation to the stockholder.

While the declaration of dividends is entirely within the discretion of the board of directors, a distribution can be forced when that discretion is abused. In withholding profits from distribution, the directors must be acting reasonably and in the best interests of the corporation. Diverting corporate earnings to noncorporate purposes would clearly constitute the basis for an equitable action to force the directors to make distribution to the stockholders. Unequivocal evidence that the surplus is more than adequate for corporate purposes might also afford the stockholders grounds for equitable relief. And, of course, where dividends are being arbitrarily and wantonly withheld in a display of petty malice toward certain stockholders or with a view to freezing them out, a court of equity will issue a mandate that a distribution be made. To illustrate:

(1) In *Seitz* v. *Union Brass & Metal Mfg. Co.*, 152 Minn. 460, the court upheld a finding of the trial court that the defendant corporation be required to declare a 10 per cent special dividend. The decision was based upon a finding of fact that the management was not acting in good faith toward the minority stockholders—that the management had carried earnings into surplus for the purpose of excluding them from participating in profits and for the purpose of depressing stock values.

(2) In *Dodge* v. *Ford Motor Co.*, 204 Mich. 459, the court ordered the defendant corporation to distribute $19,000,000 to the stockholders. The decision was based upon the conclusion that the corporation's surplus was in excess of corporate needs. This conclusion was based upon a public declaration by Mr. Ford to the

[9] Franzen v. Fred Rueping Leather Co., p. 1009.

effect that it was his ambition "to employ still more men; to spread the benefits of this industrial system to the greatest possible number. . . . To do this we are putting the greatest share of our profits back into the business." The court said:

> "The discretion of directors . . . does not extend . . . to the reduction of profits or to the nondistribution of profits among stockholders in order to devote them to other purposes."

1. *Position of Stockholder after Declaration*

The legal effect of a dividend declaration is the creation of a debtor and creditor relationship between the corporation and the stockholder.[10] In *Staats* v. *Biograph Co.,* 236 Fed. 454, the court said:

> "The declaration of the dividend sets apart from the profits of the corporation a sum which is to be paid the stockholders . . . and creates a debt due from the corporation to each shareholder."

After a dividend has been declared, it cannot be revoked or rescinded by the corporation. However, if the dividend is in stock of the corporation rather than in cash, it may be rescinded any time prior to distribution. The reason for this rule was stated in *McLaran* v. *Crescent Planing Mill Co.,* 117 Mo. App. 40, thus:

> "Inasmuch as the act of declaring the cash dividend not only creates a debt but thereupon severs the amount thereof from the mass of the corporate funds and property, and cannot be recalled for the reason the debtor cannot cancel a debt and rehabilitate or reestablish the fruit on the tree. . . . Whereas the act of declaring a stock dividend does not, of itself, operate to sever the stock to be thereafter issued from the other corporate property, inasmuch as there is no stock to be severed and as the new stock cannot be issued until certain precedent conditions and formalities are complied with, such as issuing stock, and the filing of certificates with the proper authorities. . . ."

2. *Legal Limitations to Dividend Distribution*

Aside from the financial expediency of declaring and distributing dividends, directors must take cognizance of the statutory limitations imposed by law. Depending upon the jurisdiction, directors may make themselves criminally liable as well as civilly liable to the corporation and its creditors for an illegal distribution.

Unfortunately, there is no universally accepted legal standard governing the declaration and distribution of dividends, but fortunately the majority of corporate managements gauge their actions by business expediency rather than by the limits set by law. The explanation of the diversity of rules attempting to establish bases for dividend declaration will be fully appreciated by those versed in the art of accounting, by those who recognize the historical change in the concepts of—and the difficulties in—defining such terms as profits, earnings, and earned surplus. Then there is the even greater difficulty of establishing as a fact the amount of assets owned by a corporation at any given point of time. Let it be emphasized that this is no attempt at evaluation, justification, or condemnation of the legal stand-

[10] State v. Standard Oil Co., p. 1010.

ards in vogue. It is, rather, an attempt at a realistic statement of the rules of law so as to give the reader a realization of the diversity of thought and an appreciation of the fact that the problems involved are of a nature other than mere legalistic declaration.

The various legislative enactments embody three basic rules, which, in many instances, are used in combination and to which there are important exceptions. According to these rules, the limitations to the right to distribute dividends are:

(1) Dividends shall be distributed out of profits (earned surplus) only.

(2) A distribution shall not be made if the corporation is insolvent or the distribution would produce insolvency.

(3) A distribution shall not be made so as to diminish the assets to an amount less than the amount of its capital stock.

a. Profits Rule. Certainly, the historical concept of dividends was that they were derived from profits resulting from the operation of the business enterprise—not profits realized over a short accounting period but rather the net aggregate realized from operations to date. In a few jurisdictions this is still the required source of dividend payments.

The Delaware statute represents an extreme modification in that it allows dividends to be distributed out of the profits shown by the current and/or preceding accounting period even though previous operating deficits have depleted the capital stock, providing the corporation's assets have not been depleted below the amount represented by the preferred stock.

b. Insolvency Rule. In its pure form, the insolvency rule presents no limitations as to what assets can be used to mollify stockholders so long as the corporation retains a status of solvency. In very few jurisdictions does the insolvency rule stand alone. It is, however, frequently employed in modification of the other two rules.

c. Impairment of Capital Rule. It is a prominent rule in our present-day legislation that dividends shall not be paid when such payment would diminish the assets to an amount less than the amount of the capital stock. The rule is based upon the philosophy that a corporation's assets in the amount of the capital stock constitute a trust fund for the benefit of creditors. This rule, in its broadest application, allows that dividends can legally be paid out of any surplus, regardless of how that surplus was acquired—regardless of whether it was earned or created by a revaluation of assets or a reduction in the capital stock.

This rule is frequently modified by the insolvency rule. Thus, the Uniform Corporation Act, Section 24, Paragraph IV, provides that dividends shall not be paid by a corporation,

> ". . . except from the surplus of the aggregate of its assets over the aggregate of its liabilities, including in the latter the amount of its capital stock."

Recent statutory modifications of the rule as originally contained in the Uniform Corporation Act have gone further in the direction of the earned surplus basis of dividend declaration. In Ohio, for example, the statute adds to the above,

". . . after deducting from such aggregate of its assets the amount by which such aggregate was increased by unrealized appreciation in value or revaluation of fixed assets."

This represents a step in the direction of establishing what the ethical business community accepts as the source out of which dividends should come.

3. *Stockholders' Liability for Illegal Distribution* *

In the event of insolvency of a corporation, the directors are personally liable to the creditors for the amount of dividends that have been illegally declared and distributed. Usually stockholders have the same liability to the insolvent corporation's creditors. In some few instances, statutes declare that stockholders have no liability unless the dividends were received in bad faith.

C. RIGHT TO ATTEND MEETINGS AND VOTE

A stockholder's right to vote constitutes his right of management. It is this right of franchise that, theoretically, vests the right of management in the stockholders collectively. The common law right to vote consisted of one vote for every stockholder, regardless of the number of shares owned. The modern practice is to give each share one vote, making the shares of stock rather that the stockholders the voting units.

The right to vote is, of course, dependent upon the right to notice of, and attendance at, the stockholders' meetings. However, usually the right to vote is not contingent upon attendance. A stockholder is almost invariably given the right to exercise his voice through an agent, a proxy. It is more usual than not that stockholders delegate to the management of the corporation the burden of voting their stock for them. There can be no objection to such a procedure if the proxy executed by the stockholder clearly defines the limits of authority given the management.

1. *Nature of Proxy*

A proxy by which a stockholder authorizes another to vote for him is, in every sense of the word, a power of attorney. Like any other gratuitous delegation of authority by a principal, a proxy can be revoked at any time before it is exercised. Where more than one proxy has been executed, conferring the right to vote the same stock, the proxy last in point of time prevails. It serves as a revocation of all prior proxies.

2. *Cumulative Voting*

Cumulative voting, as at times employed in the election of directors, presents a departure from the general rule that every share of stock has the right of one vote. Under the cumulative plan of voting, a stockholder has as many votes as the number of shares he owns, multiplied by the number of directors

* Section 25 of the Uniform Corporation Act provides for the stockholders' liability (1) when no guilty or negligent director is so liable or (2) when recovery from guilty directors is impossible.

to be elected. These votes can then be cast for one director or be apportioned among the various candidates as the voter sees fit. The purpose of this scheme of electing directors is to make it possible for the minority to concentrate its vote on one or two or more directors and thus obtain representation upon the board. Wherever this right obtains, it is conferred by constitutional, statutory, or charter provision.

The following simple formula can be used in determining the minimum number of shares that are necessary to elect a given number of directors under this system of voting:

$$\frac{S \times N}{D + 1} + 1 = R$$

S = total shares voting

N = number of directors desired to be elected

D = total number of directors to be elected

R = required shares to elect *N* directors

To illustrate:

A minority group in a corporation that has 500,000 shares of stock outstanding, desires to elect two directors in an election at which seven directors are to be elected. Applying these facts to the above formula we find $\frac{500{,}000 \times 2}{7 + 1} + 1 =$ 125,001 as the number of shares of stock necessary to elect two directors.

PROXY

ANNUAL MEETING OF STOCKHOLDERS

ACME SERVICE CORPORATION

The undersigned hereby constitutes and appoints ________________ and ________________, and each of them, attorneys and proxies, with full power of substitution and revocation, for and in the name, place and stead of the undersigned, to vote at the Annual Meeting of Stockholders of the Company to be held on March 25, 1947, at 2 P.M., Eastern Standard Time, at the office of the Company at Room 1204, 1401 Park Avenue, New York, N.Y., and at all adjournments of said meeting, according to the number of votes that the undersigned would be entitled to vote if personally present thereat, to vote: (1) for the election of directors to hold office for one year and until their successors are elected; (2) for the approval of independent public accountants for the year 1947; and (3) for the transaction of such other business as may properly come before the meeting, including election of Inspectors of Election.

The undersigned hereby revokes all proxies heretofore given to vote upon or act with respect to said stock and hereby ratifies and confirms all that said attorneys or proxies, or either of them, or his or their substitutes, may do by virtue hereof. If only one of said attorneys or proxies shall be present and act, then that one shall have and may exercise all the powers of both hereunder.

IN WITNESS WHEREOF the undersigned has hereunto set his hand and seal this ___ day of March, 1947.

Number of shares ....(L.S.)..

D. STOCKHOLDERS' RIGHT TO NEW STOCK

A stockholder has the right that his proportionate voting control and interest in the assets of the corporation be maintained. To accomplish this, he must be given the right to subscribe ratably to any new issues of stock. An owner of 50 per cent of the corporation's common stock would have the right to subscribe to one half of any new stock issued.

It is to be noted that this so-called pre-emptive right is commonly waived by the stockholders by a provision in the charter or by-laws of the corporation. As a matter of practice, however, the stockholders are usually given the right to subscribe. Usually these rights are valuable in that the subscription price is less than the market price of the stock.

In most jurisdictions the pre-emptive right of subscription is held to apply to unissued stock of the original issue under which the stockholder acquired membership. This is especially true if the stock has remained unissued for a considerable time so that the interests of the existing stockholders have come to be regarded as fixed. Some courts have taken the stand that such unissued stock can be used by the corporation for any legitimate and lawful purpose, as it sees fit.

It is generally held that the pre-emptive right does not apply to treasury stock. A resale of such stock leaves the individual stockholder in the same proportionate position that he occupied originally. Seemingly, the stockholders do not acquire a vested right to the increased voting control that they enjoy while stock is being held by the corporation or by trustees on its behalf. Since treasury stock cannot be voted, it follows logically that a stockholder's proportionate voting control is increased whenever treasury stock is created.

► IV. LIMITED LIABILITY

One of the primary characteristics of the corporate form of doing business is the limited liability of the stockholders. Their liability is limited to the full value of the stock they hold in the corporation. Thus, if the stock they receive from the corporation has been fully paid for, they cannot be looked to by the creditors of the corporation.

> "It has been again and again decided, that the unpaid subscriptions to the capital stock of a corporation constitute a trust fund for the benefit of the general creditors of the corporation; and that this trust cannot be defeated or the fund impaired by a simulated or pretended payment for the stock taken, nor by any device short of actual payment in good faith. Any arrangement, therefore, among the stockholders, or those in charge of the affairs of the corporation, by which the stock is but nominally paid for, whether in money or property, the corporation not in fact getting the benefit of the price in good faith, will be regarded as a sham, and not as a valid payment, as against the creditors of the corporation, however it may be regarded as between the corporation and the subscriber." *Crawford* v. *Rohrer,* 59 Md. 599.

The liability of a stockholder to creditors of the corporation may arise because of:

(1) An unpaid stock subscription;

(2) An acceptance of stock from the corporation in payment of over-valued property or services;

(3) An acceptance of stock as a bonus (unless such is treasury stock);

(4) Payment of less than par or stated value (the value fixed by the directors at the time of issue) of the stock.

The liability for stock that is not fully paid does not carry over to a transferee who acquires the stock in good faith and for value. To illustrate:

X received 100 shares of stock from the Y Corporation in payment for property transferred to the corporation. The property had been valued at $10,000 (an overvaluation of 50 per cent), which corresponded with the value of the stock. X then sold the stock to A, who accepted it for value and in the belief that it was fully paid. In the event of the corporation's insolvency, X and not A could be looked to by the creditors.

CASES

CASE NO. 1

Continental Ins. Co. v. Minneapolis, St. P. & S. Ste. M.R. Co. 290 Fed. 87, 31 A.L.R. 1320 (1923)

LEWIS, C.J., delivered the opinion of the court:

This suit was instituted by appellants, two preferred stockholders in appellee company, to enjoin the carrying out of a resolution passed by its board of directors on March 10, 1922, declaring a dividend of $2 per share on both the common and preferred stock, payable out of the accumulated surplus earnings of the years ending December 31, 1909, to 1919, inclusive, both dividends to be paid April 15, 1922. The part of the resolution to which objection was made and injunctive order sought was the dividend declared and directed to be paid on the common stock; the contention being that inasmuch as a dividend of 7 per cent on the preferred stock had not been declared theretofore in 1922, the common stock was not entitled to receive a dividend until that was done. . . .

Appellee, in justification of its action in passing the resolution, relies on article 11 of its articles of consolidation, by which four railway companies were consolidated in 1888 into and under the name of appellee company, ...

The trial court held that the article . . . was controlling, that it authorized the board to pass the resolution, and dismissed the bill of complaint. . . .

6 Fletcher, Cyc. Corp. p. 6028, says that the terms of the contract are generally set forth in the certificate, but that those terms are not the only evidence of the contract, and that they must be read in connection with the charter and by-laws in force at the time the stock was issued, to ascertain the true terms of the contract, and that all of these enter into and form a part of it. The same is found in Cook, § 269. It is a misconception to say that the certificate discloses the whole contract, and that to look to charter, resolutions, or

by-laws is an attempt to vary that contract. They are all to be consulted for the purpose of ascertaining what the contractual rights of the holders of preferred shares are. . . .

Affirmed.

CASE NO. 2

Schwartz v. Manufacturers' Casualty Ins. Co. 335 Pa. 103, 6 A. (2d) 299, 122 A.L.R. 1045 (1939)

DREW, J., delivered the opinion of the court:

Plaintiff brought this action of assumpsit on August 11, 1938, alleging that he is a stockholder in defendant company and claiming that he is entitled to recover $8,322.65 in dividends, plus interest, on shares of which he is owner. To the bill of complaint defendant filed a statutory demurrer, averring that the statement of claim was insufficient in that plaintiff had failed to show that he was the owner of any shares of stock in defendant company, . . . The court below sustained the demurrer, and, from the judgment thereupon entered for defendant, plaintiff has appealed.

The bill of complaint discloses the following facts: On August 9, 1916, the Lehigh Valley Silk Mills subscribed for 100 shares of stock of the defendant company at $20 per share, the purchase price to be paid in nine monthly installments. Subsequently the Lehigh Valley made another subscription for 150 more shares upon the same terms. After having paid seven installments on the first subscription and only two on the second, the Lehigh Valley made no further payments. From March 2, 1917, when the last payment was made until the time the present suit was brought, nothing was done by the Lehigh Valley with reference to the stock. During the 21 years following these subscriptions, numerous stock and cash dividends were declared by the defendant company on its capital stock, but none of these were ever paid to the Lehigh Valley and during all these years it made no claim to any dividends. In May, 1937, the Lehigh Valley was adjudged a bankrupt and on December 29, 1937, the Trustee in Bankruptcy assigned the two certificates of subscription to plaintiff.

. . . it is clear that the demurrer was properly sustained, since plaintiff has failed to show that he is a shareholder in defendant company.

. . . we must presume that the agreements relied on by plaintiff were not for an original subscription in a corporation to be formed, but were rather subscriptions for shares in an existing corporation. The subscriptions were thus simply contracts of purchase and sale and the failure of the subscriber to fully execute its part of the contracts prevented it from acquiring the status of a shareholder. . . .

This court has consistently recognized a distinction between original subscriptions for stock in a corporation to be formed, and subscriptions for shares in an existing corporation.

> "In the one case the engagement between the subscribers is created directly by the act of subscription. . . . By the act of incorporation, without more, the original subscribers become members of the corporation. . . . In the other case the contract is not between the subscribers . . . but between each individual subscriber and the corporation as it exists, and is simply a contract of purchase and sale." Bole v. Fulton, . . . 233 Pa., p. 611, . . .

In the instant case plaintiff makes no allegation that the defendant company released the subscriber from its obligation to complete performance. Since its default was not excused or waived it thus caused a breach of the contract, and hence did not acquire the status of a shareholder. That both the original parties to the agreements realized that they were but contracts for the purchase of shares and that upon their breach the subscriber did not become a shareholder is obvious from the facts set forth by plaintiff. No stock certificates were ever issued to the Lehigh Valley and during the 21 years since the breach of the agreements the dividends to which the Lehigh Valley would have been entitled, had it owned 250 shares of defendant's stock, would have totaled $8,322.65. Yet at no time during these many years did the Lehigh Valley ever make a claim for any dividends. These facts alone clearly indicate that both the defendant company and the Lehigh Valley realized that the latter, because of its failure to complete the contracts, never became a shareholder. The statement of claim fails to show that the subscription agreements were anything more than contracts for the purchase of shares which were never fully performed, and the facts alleged by plaintiff show that the parties so construed them. After having secured an assignment of the subscription contracts 21 years after their abandonment, plaintiff cannot now set himself up as a shareholder for the sole purpose of attempting to recover dividends for which the defendant company never became liable.

CASE NO. 3

Coleman Hotel Co. v. Crawford. 3 S.W. (2d) 1109 (Tex.) (1928)

LEDDY, J. A number of citizens of the City of Coleman were desirous of organizing a corporation, with a minimum capital stock of $50,000, for the purpose of building and operating a modern hotel in said city . . . the following subscription agreement was prepared and signed by the interested parties, viz.:

"September 7, 1925

"We hereby subscribe the amount set opposite our names for the purpose of organizing a corporation to purchase site, construct and own a modern fire proof hotel of not less than fifty rooms in Coleman. This subscription to be valid only upon condition of not less than $50,000.00 total solvent subscriptions being obtained. When $50,000.00 or more has been subscribed a meeting, at which all subscribers are invited, shall be held for the purposes of selecting site and making all proper arrangements for construction of such hotel, collecting subscriptions, etc. It is understood that 20 per cent shall be payable when called for and the balance as needed, not exceeding 10 per cent monthly until fully paid."

Among those signing such subscription was the defendant in error. . . .

At the close of the testimony offered by plaintiff in error, the trial court peremptorily instructed the jury to render a verdict in favor of defendant in error. Upon appeal the Court of Civil Appeals . . . concluded that the subscription agreement did not constitute a valid contract. . . .

The undisputed evidence shows that defendant in error gave notice of the withdrawal of his subscription before the formation of the corporation, and at a time when no expenses had been incurred on account of the enterprise. . . . The question is squarely presented whether such subscription agreement constitutes a valid contract from which a subscriber could not withdraw without the unanimous consent of the other subscribers.

It may be stated at the outset that

there is considerable conflict in the authorities on this question. The courts which refused to enforce such subscription agreements, as a rule, base their holdings either upon the proposition that such agreements are without sufficient consideration to constitute a binding and enforceable contract, or upon the supposed want of sufficiency of parties to the agreement.

We are not impressed with the soundness of either of these reasons for declining to sustain such agreements as valid and enforceable ones. We think the better view is expressed by the authorities holding that a subscription agreement by a number of persons to the capital stock of a corporation to be thereafter formed by them constitutes a contract between the subscribers themselves to become stockholders when the corporation is formed on the condition expressed in the agreement, and, as such, is binding and irrevocable. . . .

When several patries agree to contribute to a common object which they wish to accomplish, the promise of each is a good consideration for the promise of others. . . .

Likewise our courts have frequently upheld contracts between parties as based upon a valid consideration which are made for the benefit of a third party, even though no consideration moves from such third party. . . .

CASE NO. 4

Cliff's Corporation v. United States. 103 F. (2d) 77 (1939)

HAMILTON, C.J. . . . The stockholders of the Cleveland Cliffs Iron Company, an Ohio corporation, owning all of its common stock consisting of 408,296 shares by proper inter-company and integrated corporate action exchanged all of their stock for 402,867 shares, or one-half of the common stock, of the appellant, the Cliffs Corporation, another Ohio corporation.

The exchanges took place under mutual concurrent agreements that the shares of stock would be placed with depositaries, without indorsement of transfers on the respective books of either corporation to be held in voting trusts for a period of ten years under Section 8623-34 of Page's Annotated Ohio General Code. While in the trust the respective shares of stock were nontransferable on the books of the corporations. Voting trust certificates in the name of the individual stockholders were issued in lieu of the stock and were transferable on the books of the stock depositaries. . . .

During the life of the trust all voting and consenting rights were vested in its trustees except the consent of two-thirds in interest of the owners of the voting trust certificates were to be secured in writing before voting the stock for a merger or consolidation. The trustees, or two-thirds in number of shares of the holders of the voting trust certificates, were authorized to terminate the trust at any time during its life if they deemed it advisable and in the interest of the holders of the voting trust certificates.

During the life of the trust the trustees were to receive all dividends paid on the stock and distribute them to the holders of voting trust certificates.

At the time of the transactions under consideration, Subdivision 3 of Schedule A, Title 8 of the Revenue Act of 1926 (c. 27, 44 Stat. 101), 26 U.S.C.A. § 902(b), contained the following provisions:

> "On all sales, or agreements to sell, or memoranda of sales or deliveries of, or transfers of legal title to shares or certificates of stock . . . whether made upon or shown by the books of the corporation, or by any assignment

in blank, or by any delivery, or by any paper or agreement or memorandum or other evidence of transfer or sale, whether entitling the holder in any manner to the benefit of such stock, interest, or rights, or not, on each $100 of face value or fraction thereof, 2 cents, and where such shares are without par or face value, the tax shall be 2 cents on the transfer or sale or agreement to sell on each share."

The Commissioner of Internal Revenue decided pursuant to the above statutes that the delivery of the respective shares of stock in the two corporations to the depositaries under the voting trust was a taxable transfer and assessed against appellant on account thereof taxes of $16,223.26 which it paid to the Collector and in this action seeks to recover. . . .

The single issue for decision is whether there was a transfer of the shares within the meaning of the Statute. . . .

There is a substantial difference between a trustee and a proxy. The latter is an agent who represents and acts for his principal who is bound by what is done in the discharge of that agency. A trustee is not an agent, but a person in whom there is vested, for the benefit of another, some estate, interest, or power in or affecting property. A trustee contracts for and binds only himself as he has no principal.

The method of transferring title to shares of corporate stock is a subject of importance but, unless a particular mode of transfer is prescribed by statute or in the corporate charter or bylaws, the owner may dispose of his shares in such manner as would be sufficient to pass title to any chose in action or intangible property.

Stock certificates are assignable and pass by indorsement or delivery as do bills of exchange and promissory notes. A stockholder's rights or his passing of title to them are not determinable conclusively or exclusively by the provisions of his certificate of stock, but title may pass by evidences in writing other than an indorsement on the certificate or transfer on the books. Continental Insurance Company v. Minneapolis Railroad Company, 8 Cir., 290 Fed. 87, 31 A.L.R. 1320. The execution by the stockholders of the two voting trusts here involved pursuant to the Ohio Statutes, passed title and all indicia of ownership to the trustees, without indorsement on the certificates or transfer on the corporate records.

. . . It therefore follows that the taxes were properly assessed and collected by the United States. Judgment of the District Court is affirmed.

CASE NO. 5

Searles v. Bar Harbor Banking & T. Co. 128 Me. 34, 145 Atl. 391, 65 A.L.R. 1154 (1929)

WILSON, CH.J., delivered the opinion of the court:

A bill in equity brought, as the prayers set forth, to declare a by-law of the defendant company invalid and that the defendant be required to issue to the plaintiff stock free of any of the restrictions against free alienation imposed by the by-law. . . .

At the meeting held on July 11, 1927, it was voted to increase the stock as proposed in the call for the meeting and that the new shares be issued to the old stockholders in proportion to their present holdings and charged to undivided profits, it being in the nature of a stock dividend, and also to adopt a bylaw restricting the alienation of the new stock when coming into the hands of any person by will, inheritance, or by a conveyance to take effect after death. . . .

It is contended by the plaintiff . . . that such a by-law was not within the power of the defendant company to adopt; that it is contrary to public policy inasmuch as it constitutes a restraint upon the free alienation of his property, and is, therefore, void.

There is a seeming lack of harmony among the authorities on the question involved. As a general rule, the cases holding invalid by-laws restricting the alienation of stock are cases where alienation is made dependent on the consent of all the other stockholders or the board of directors or some official of the company . . . or such restriction is held invalid by reason of lack of legislative authority to pass such a by-law. . . .

The cases in which a limited restriction upon alienation of stock issued after the passage of the by-law have been upheld have been either under by-laws adopted under legislative authority and providing only for an option to the corporation or other stockholders to purchase for a limited period . . . or where even without express legislative authority to enact, the acceptance of stock issued in pursuance of such a by-law is held to constitute an enforceable contract between the corporation and a stockholder if the by-law is reasonable and its purpose the promotion of the purposes of the corporation. . . .

The by-law in this case is not objectionable on the ground that it imposes an absolute restriction on alienation without the consent of the officers or other stockholders. It does not even impose any restriction on present holders or during the lifetime of any one acquiring the stock by purchase. Only in case it is acquired by will or inheritance or a conveyance taking effect at death is the person so acquiring obliged to give such person as the directors may designate a 30-day option thereon. If not exercised in that period, all restrictions are removed. . . .

. . . the weight of the authority and we think the tendency of the more recent decisions, as the reasons for maintaining the integrity of the stockholding body have become more manifest, is to sustain such restrictions if reasonable and the stock has been accepted following the adoption of the restriction and with knowledge of its provisions, whether valid as a by-law or not, on the ground that it constitutes a valid agreement between the stockholder and the corporation, especially if it goes no farther than to give an option on the stock for a limited period. . . .

Bill dismissed, ...

CASE NO. 6

Guaranty Laundry Co. v. Pulliam. 198 Okla. 667, 181 P. (2d) 1007, 2 A.L.R. (2d) 738 (1947)

WELCH, J. In this action Evelyn Pulliam, as plaintiff, sues the Guaranty Laundry Company, an Oklahoma corporation, and Willis G. Sautbine, its President, to compel transfer to her of twenty-five shares of stock of the corporation which she had purchased from one Short.

Prior to this purchase plaintiff owned about one-eighth or one-ninth of the stock of the corporation, Carl B. Short owned one-fourth of such stock, Willis G. Sautbine owned nearly one-half of such stock and the remaining stock was owned by others. At the commencement of this action plaintiff was secretary of the corporation and serious controversy had arisen between plaintiff and the defendant Sautbine. Defendant Sautbine declined to join as president in the transfer of the Short twenty-five shares of stock to the plaintiff, and following demand and presentation of stock certificate for his signature this action was brought. . . .

Defendant Sautbine sought to justify his action by his answer in the case in which he alleged in effect that before plaintiff became a stockholder in the corporation, at a meeting attended by the then owners of all the stock, it was specifically agreed by all of the stockholders that in the event one of the stockholders should consider selling his stock he would give the remaining stockholders or stockholder the first and last chance to purchase his stock; that the plaintiff, then an employee of the corporation, had actual notice or knowledge of such agreement which was written into the minutes of the annual directors meeting at the time it was made; that therefore the plaintiff had no right to buy the Short stock for herself; that her holding of the Short stock was for the benefit of all of the stockholders other than Short, each in proportion to the balance of the stock as then owned, and that therefore the corporation should not be required to issue a certificate for the Short stock to plaintiff.

Defendant further alleged in his answer in effect that the plaintiff, being secretary-treasurer of the corporation, was thereby bound to a fiduciary relationship with the corporation and each of its other officers and stockholders, and that her attempted purchase of the Short stock for herself and without permitting the other stockholders the opportunity to acquire same or a proper portion thereof, was in violation of her obligation and duties as a fiduciary, ...

The chief question is whether the stockholders' agreement above referred to precluded plaintiff, a stockholder, from purchasing for herself from the stockholder Short.

As to the construction to be placed on the stockholders' agreement defendants contend that the Short stock could only be sold to all of the remaining stockholders in proportionate shares, while the plaintiff contends that the stockholders' agreement is satisfied by a sale of the Short stock to any one of the remaining stockholders, and that she, being one of such stockholders, was fully entitled to buy it for herself.

The trial court construed the stockholders' agreement to have the meaning contended for by plaintiff, and we must review that construction.

We have observed the authorities cited dealing with similar stockholders' agreements. It is emphasized that such agreements generally have the purpose of preventing stock transfers to outsiders without first providing an opportunity by which the stock desired to be sold may be left with another stockholder or stockholders . . . it has been said the restriction will be strictly construed, and not enlarged by implication. . . .

. . . the stockholders' agreement as to stock sale is written into the minutes . . . in the following language:

> "It is agreed by all stockholders that in the event one of the stockholders considers selling his stock he will give the remaining stockholders or stockholder, the first and last chance to purchase his stock."

While this agreement undoubtedly might have gone further so as to state that any transfer of stock should first be made available to all the other stockholders in proportion to their holdings of stock, as contended for by defendants here, it did not do so. . . .

As stated above we conclude that it may reasonably be construed as held by the trial court that the agreement was satisfied by sale to a remaining stockholder, as well as to all of the remaining stockholders. . . .

We conclude that the defendant Sautbine was not justified in his refusal as president of the corporation to so transfer such stock, and that the judgment of the trial court is correct. . . .

CASE NO. 7

Ontjes v. Harrer. 208 Iowa 1217, 227 N.W. 101 (1929)

DE GRAFF, J. The plaintiff-appellee is a minority stockholder in Jacob E. Decker & Sons, a corporation. . . . The prayer of the petition is for an alternative writ of mandamus directing and commanding the defendants (appellants) to exhibit to the plaintiff, for inspection, examination, and copy, the original stock records, stock ledgers, stock transfer books, of both preferred and common stock of the said corporation, and to submit to the plaintiff for inspection and examination the books and records of the corporation showing the financial condition of the corporation. . . . The order and decree entered by the trial court adjudged and decreed that a writ of mandamus issue, directing the defendants and each of them to exhibit during office hours to plaintiff for inspection, examination, and copy, forthwith, at the offices of the corporation, the original stock records, stock ledger, and stock transfer books of both the preferred and common stock of said corporation, and to submit at its corporate offices at convenient times and during office hours, or after office hours on Saturday afternoons, at the election of defendants, to the plaintiff for inspection and examination, the following books and records which show the financial condition of the corporation, ...

We now turn to the legal principles involved in this cause, and it may be observed in the first instance, that two demands were made by the plaintiff in his petition: (1) That the plaintiff be furnished, in conformity to his prior written request, a list of the stockholders, both common and preferred; and (2) that the plaintiff be permitted to inspect certain books and records of the corporation which would show the financial status of said corporation.

I. With the first proposition, there is little occasion on our part to comment. It is a matter of statutory regulation. Section 8384, Code 1927. By the terms of said section the secretary of any corporation, upon a written request, shall furnish to a stockholder of said corporation a printed or typewritten list giving the names of the stockholders, their post office address, and the number of shares owned by each stockholder. . . .

II. Was the plaintiff entitled to the right to inspect and examine such books and records which showed, or tended to show, the financial status of the corporation? . . .

It is said in Guthrie v. Harkness, 199 U.S. 148, 26 Sup. Ct. 4, 5, 50 L.Ed. 130, 4 Ann. Cas. 433:

"There can be no question that the decisive weight of American authority recognizes the common-law right of the shareholder, for proper purposes and under reasonable regulations as to place and time, to inspect the books of the corporation of which he is a member. . . ."

There was no burden resting upon the plaintiff to establish his motive or purpose as a stockholder in demanding the inspection and examination of the records of the defendant corporation. . . .

There is no presumption that a stockholder seeking information does so with a bad motive, or with intent to inflict injury upon the corporation. This is a matter of defense to be pleaded and proved. . . .

We are satisfied, under the record, that the decree entered by the trial court should be affirmed, and it is affirmed.

CASE NO. 8

Day & Co. v. Booth. 123 Me. 443, 123 Atl. 557, 43 A.L.R. 780 (1924)

PHILBROOK, J., delivered the opinion of the court: . . .

After careful and repeated examination of the record and briefs of counsel, and the extended findings of the justice before whom the case was heard, we find it difficult to state the case, the contentions of the parties, and the conclusions of law and fact, in more clear, correct, and appropriate language than that used by the sitting justice. We therefore adopt that finding as the opinion of the court, and quote in full therefrom:

"These proceedings are upon petitions for writs of mandamus against the respondents, to permit the petitioner to inspect the stock books of the corporation, of which the respondents are respectively clerks, to take copies and minutes therefrom of such parts as concern the interests of the petitioner, and to make lists of stockholders of the respective corporations. . . .

"I think, however, that the decision of these cases must depend upon whether the petitioner has shown itself entitled to the right which it claims. The petitioner relies upon Rev. Stat. 1916, Chap. 51, § 22, which provides that the corporate records and stock books 'shall be open at all reasonable hours to the inspection of persons interested, who may take copies and minutes therefrom of such parts as concern their interests,' etc.

"Has the petitioner shown itself 'interested' in the affairs of the several corporations, within the meaning of the statute? I think that this question must be answered in the negative. . . .

"I find that the petitioner is the owner of only 1 share of stock in each of the corporations concerned; that each of these shares was acquired for the sole purpose of laying a foundation to demand a list of stockholders in each company . . . that the business of the petitioner is dealing in unlisted and inactive securities, occasionally in listed securities; that the petitioner and its predecessor, the firm of Charles A. Day & Co., have acquired for the purpose of said business approximately two thousand lists of stockholders in various corporations, which the petitioner circularizes in the pursuit of its business; that a large proportion of these lists have been obtained by becoming a stockholder and demanding as the privilege of a stockholder, a list of the stockholders in the corporation; . . . that it is the general policy of the petitioner following the policy of its predecessor, the firm, to dispose of the share or shares of stock which it has obtained for the purposes of obtaining stock lists, after such lists have been obtained; . . . that the purpose of the petitioner in obtaining the lists of stockholders in the three corporations here concerned is to trade in the stocks of those corporations. . . .

". . . where it is shown that such stockholding is only colorable, or solely for the purpose of maintaining proceedings of this kind, I fail to see how the petitioner can be said to be a 'person interested,' entitled as of right to inspect the records and stock books of a corporation, and to take copies and minutes therefrom, of such parts as concern his interest.

"I therefore rule that upon the facts

> appearing in these cases the petitioner has failed to show that it is a person interested within the meaning of Rev. Stat. 1916, chap. 51, § 22, entitled to inspect the records and stock books of the respondent. . ."

Finding no error in the statement of the case or rulings of law . . . exceptions over-ruled.

CASE NO. 9

Franzen v. Fred Rueping Leather Co.
255 Wis. 265, 38 N.W. (2d) 517 (1949)

ROSENBERRY, CH.J. The articles of organization, as amended, provided that the holders of the 6 per cent preferred stock were entitled to receive dividends at the rate of, but not to exceed, 6 per cent per share per annum when earned, during a fiscal year ending on October 31, payable quarterly on the first days of January, April, July and October in the subsequent year. . . .

The amended articles provided further that the 6 per cent preferred stock or any part thereof was *subject to redemption on any dividend date on or after the first day of May, 1936 at $105 per share, together with accrued earned dividends due thereon.* . . .

On January 20, 1948, the corporation notified its 6 per cent preferred stockholders that the 6 per cent preferred stock would be called for redemption on April 1, 1948, at the price of $106.50 per share,

> "being $105 plus a sum equal to the accrued earned dividends due thereon to and including April 1, 1948, in the amount of $1.50 per share."

On January 27, 1948, the board of directors of the corporation passed a resolution calling all of the issued and outstanding 6 per cent preferred stock for redemption on April 1, 1948. Notice of redemption was sent to the stockholders on February 15, 1948.

The plaintiff contends and the trial court held that there must be added to the call price of $106.50 per share named by the defendant (1) the quarterly dividends which would have been payable on July 1 and October 1, 1948, by reason of the 1947 earnings, in other words, $3 per share, and (2) an additional dividend of $2.50 per share by reason of earnings in the first five months of the year ending October 31, 1948.

Stated more briefly, the defendant contends that the call price should be $106.50 per share, while the plaintiff contends that the call price should be $112.00 per share.

The first question we will consider is: Is the preferred stock under the provisions of the articles of incorporation subject to redemption only on the last day of a fiscal year, October 31st?

From 1941 to 1947 inclusive, dividends were paid on the first days of January, April, July and October, with few exceptions. A determination of what was meant by the term "dividend date" may be determined in part at least by the nature of a "dividend."

In Estate of Gerlach, 1922, 177 Wis. 251, 188 N.W. 94, 96, it was said:

> "It is fundamental that until profits of a corporation are distributed in the form of a dividend or otherwise the stockholder obtains no right or title thereto. Such profits belong exclusively to the corporation. They may be retained by the corporation and added to corpus."

In this case neither the general law governing corporations nor the articles of incorporation prescribe when a dividend upon preferred stock shall be declared. The language already quoted provides that the preferred stock shall be subject to redemption on any dividend date, clearly indicating that there is more than one dividend date.

We can reach no other conclusion than that the company itself and its stockholders recognized that the four quarterly dividends payable on the first days of January, April, July and October of each year were intended to make available in the form of payment the dividend which had been earned during the preceding fiscal year ending October 31st, on those dates. Those dates are the only dates which can properly be referred to as dividend dates. No other date referring to dividends is stated in the articles. The fiscal year ends October 31st, but dividends are not required to be declared on that date.

We arrive at a conclusion contrary to that of the trial court. . . .

The question for decision is: Were the dividends payable on July 1 and October 1, 1948, due? Dividends covering those dates had not been declared at any time before the preferred stock was called for retirement. The funds out of which the directors might have declared those dividends remained in the treasury of the defendant unallocated to the holders of the preferred stock. A preferred stockholder cannot maintain an action at law for a dividend which has not been declared even though it has been earned and is accrued.

This for the reason that until the dividend is declared the earned and accrued profits are the property of the corporation.

CASE NO. 10

State v. Standard Oil Co. 5 N.J. 281, 74 A. (2d) 565 (1950)

HEHER, J. The primary question here is the constitutional sufficiency of ch. 155 of the Session Laws of 1946, as amended by ch. 357 of the Session Laws of 1947 (N.J.S.A. 2:53-15, et seq.), providing for the escheat in certain circumstances of

> "moneys, negotiable instruments, choses in action, interest, debts or demands due to the escheated estate, stocks, bonds, deposits, machinery, farm crops, livestock, fixtures, and every other kind of tangible or intangible property and the accretion thereon,"

but excluding "real property or property" in *custodia legis* and "unclaimed bank deposits" made subject to escheat by ch. 199 of the Session Laws of 1945, N.J.S.A. 17:9-18 et seq.

The statute escheats to the State such personal property "within this State" of one who has died, or shall die, intestate, "without heirs or known kindred capable of inheriting the same and without leaving a surviving spouse" the personal property "within this State" of an "owner, beneficial owner, or person entitled" thereto who "has been or shall be and remain unknown for the period of fourteen successive years," or whose "whereabouts . . . has been or shall be and remain unknown for the period of fourteen successive years"; and personal property "wherever situate" which "has been or shall be and remain unclaimed for the period of fourteen successive years." . . .

The judgment under review escheated to the State the following personal property found to be in the possession of the defendant corporation.

Unpaid dividends declared upon shares of its capital stock. . . .

It is the insistence of the defendant corporation that there was error in construing the Escheat Act as applicable to choses in action barred by the statute of limitations "at the time the right of the State accrued:" . . .

The argument, in brief, is that the

property subject to escheat under R.S. 2:53-17, N.J.S.A., considered in relation to the definitive terms of R.S. 2:53-15, N.J.S.A., . . .

"is property to which some person is entitled and which is in the possession or custody of some other person who is to be the defendant in the escheat proceedings";

that in the case of debts,

"it is the claim or chose in action which is escheated, not the property of the debtor out of which the chose in action, if enforced, would be satisfied";

that the State

"takes the claim which the owner has . . . , subject to all defenses which the debtor is entitled to assert against the owner who has failed to claim the debt";

and that the defendant has a vested right to interpose the defense of the bar of the statute of limitations. . . .

In modern usage "escheat" signified the falling of property to the sovereign for want of an owner; and this category embraces not only property which has no other owner, but also property whose owner or whose owner's whereabouts is unknown. Under the common law of England escheats came to be classified as "another branch of the king's ordinary revenue." Blackstone's Comm. 302

It is a corollary of the foregoing principles that where all remedy upon the intangibles has been barred by the statute of limitations, there is no property to escheat under the act now before us. The State's right is purely derivative; it takes only the interest of the unknown or absentee owner. If the remedy has been extinguished by the statute of limitations, the State is under like incapacity. The State takes only the creditor's right; it cannot create or revive an obligation that had no existence or had become extinct. . . . Here, defendant invokes the bar of the statute of limitations; and where that defense is insufficient in law, there is no property subject to escheat. . . .

Our next inquiry is as to whether the unpaid dividends declared on the common capital stock of the defendant corporation constitute rights of property which have not been rendered unenforceable by the operation of the statute of limitations.

The contention is that when a declared dividend becomes payable the relation of debtor and creditor comes into being, and the "debt" is recoverable in assumpsit, . . . a remedy barred under R.S. 2:24-1, N.J.S.A., after the lapse of six years from the accrual of the cause of action. . . .

The trust fund theory is a more realistic concept of the substance of the transaction here and the relationship between the parties than that of a mere debt within the operation of the statute of limitations. There was a segregation from the Company's funds of the moneys to be devoted to the payment of the dividends. The mere declaration of a dividend by a corporation gives rise to a debt as against it in favor of the individual stockholders; but where

"the fund for its payment has been actually set apart and distinguished from the general mass of the company's funds, the fund so set apart becomes a trust fund for the payment of the dividend, which cannot be reached by the general creditors of the corporation, and when it becomes a trust fund for the payment of dividends it cannot be diverted and used for any other purpose. . . . There seems to be a fundamental distinction between a fund set apart for the payment of a dividend and a fund set apart for the payment of an ordinary indebtedness." In re Interborough 334, 344, 32 A.L.R. 932 (1923); certiorari denied, Porges v. Sheffield, 262 U.S. 752, 43 Sup. Ct. 700, 67 L.Ed. 1215 (1923). . . .

It results that the limitations of R.S. 2:24-1, N.J.S.A., are not operative to extinguish the stockholders' right to the dividends in question. . . .

Review Questions

1. By what various methods may membership in a corporation be acquired?
2. In what respect does a share of stock differ from a stock certificate?
3. May one be a stockholder in a corporation even though no stock certificate has been issued?
4. Does one become a stockholder upon entering into a contract with a corporation for the purchase of its stock?
5. What is the status of a subscriber to corporation stock prior to the formation of the corporation?
6. Distinguish a transfer of title to shares in a corporation from a transfer of ownership upon the books of the corporation.
7. May a corporation by its by-laws arbitrarily restrict the right to transfer shares of its stock?
8. Upon what is a corporation's right of lien against a stockholder's shares dependent?
9. Are stock certificates negotiable instruments under the Uniform Negotiable Instruments Law?
10. Can a corporation be required to replace lost or stolen stock certificates?
11. How extensive is a stockholder's right to the inspection of the corporate books?
12. May the stockholders in a corporation vote themselves a dividend?
13. Construct a fact situation under which the stockholders might conceivably be able to force a distribution of dividends.
14. What is the status of a dividend after it has been properly declared?
15. What is the impairment of capital rule as it presents a limitation to the right to declare dividends?
16. Are stockholders liable for an illegal distribution of dividends?
17. What is the nature of a proxy, and to what extent is it binding upon the stockholder before it is exercised?
18. What is the cumulative plan of voting stock?
19. Of what advantage is this plan of voting?
20. Is the transferee of stock that has not been fully paid liable to the creditors of the corporation?

Problems for Discussion

1. Felt subscribed for 1,000 shares of stock in a proposed corporation. Prior to the formation of the corporation, Felt notified all interested parties that he was withdrawing his subscription. After the corporation came into being, it accepted all subscriptions. What will determine whether Felt is bound? (*Bryants Pond Stream Mill Co.* v. *Felt*, 87 Me. 234)

2. A, B, and C agree among themselves to organize a corporation with a capitalization of $90,000, to be represented by 30,000 shares of stock, which were subscribed by A, B, and C equally. The corporation is formed, and 10,000 shares are tendered to C, who refuses to accept them. Can the corporation recover the subscription price?
3. Schilletter transferred to Blake a stock certificate representing ten shares in the Acme Corporation. Blake fails to have the transfer registered upon the books of the corporation. What will be the consequences of this?
4. The management of the X Corporation introduced a provision into the corporation's by-laws to the effect that members could not transfer their stock until sixty days after a notice of intent to transfer had been filed with the treasurer of the corporation. Is this binding?
5. A corporation by-law was enacted to the effect that stock in the corporation could not be transferred without the approval of the president of the corporation. Is this binding?
6. Marks subscribed for stock in the X Corporation. Upon payment of 75 per cent of the purchase price and an agreement to pay the balance in six months, a stock certificate was issued to him. Before he paid the balance, Marks transferred the stock to Nims. Does the X Corporation have a lien against the stock for the unpaid balance?
7. The owner of 100 shares of stock in the X Corporation, A, was fraudulently induced to deliver the certificate indorsed in blank to B. The certificate was transferred to C, who knew nothing of the fraud practiced by B. Can A replevy the stock certificate from C?
8. A is the owner of a business establishment that operates in competition with the X Corporation. A buys five shares of stock of the X Corporation and now demands the right to inspect the books. Decide.
9. The X Corporation, through its board of directors, adopted the following resolution: "Moved and seconded that the company declare a dividend of 6 per cent, divided into four payments, payable on February 15, April 1, July 1, and October 1, 1903." The February installment was paid and then the corporation rescinded its dividend action. Plaintiff sues to recover the April 1 installment. Assuming the corporation has profits out of which payment can be made, will plaintiff recover?

40 BUSINESS ORGANIZATIONS:

CORPORATION MANAGEMENT AND CONTROL

► I. STOCKHOLDERS' RIGHT OF MANAGEMENT

The control and direction of a corporation rests with the holders of a majority of the stock. They can effectively determine the course of the business enterprise in the long run by the election of directors and by voting for corporate action at stockholder's meetings.

> "It may be stated as an indisputable proposition that every person who becomes a member of a corporation aggregate by purchasing and holding shares agrees by necessary implication that he will be bound by all acts and proceedings, within the scope of the powers and authority conferred by the charter, which shall be adopted or sanctioned by the vote of the majority of the shareholders of the corporation duly taken. . . . This is the unavoidable result of the fundamental principle that the majority of the stockholders can regulate and control the lawful exercise of the powers conferred on the corporation by its charter." *Durfee* v. *Old Colony Ry. Co.*, 5 Allen (Mass.) 230.

To effect a fundamental change in the business and purposes of the corporation requires unanimous consent of all stockholders. This is based upon the fact that the charter is a contract between the corporation and the stockholders, which cannot be changed without the consent of the contracting parties. Usually the articles of incorporation provide that the articles may be changed without unanimous consent. Some states have enacted legislation bearing upon this matter. Section 38 of the Uniform Business Corporation Act provides that the articles of incorporation may be altered by two thirds of the voting power.

A. DELEGATION OF MANAGEMENT

Ordinarily the stockholders take no active part in the management and conduct of the business affairs of a corporation. As a matter of expediency, this right of management is delegated to a board of directors which is elected by the stockholders. However, it is possible for the stockholders to take an active part in management. As the court said in *Fitzpatrick* v. *O'Neill*, 43 Mont. 552:

> "It is not the universal rule that the corporation must act exclusively through its board of directors. Formal action is often dispensed with, even in the most important matters, where the members of the corporation, including the shareholders and directors, are present and concur, although there is no formal vote either of the shareholders or of the directors." *

---

* Meyers v. Wells, p. 942.

To illustrate:

In *Bryan* v. *Northwest Beverages,* 69 N.D. 274, the plaintiff had entered into a preincorporation contract with the other promoters whereby he was, upon the formation of the defendant corporation, to receive $16,000 in stock and to be made manager of the business at $150 a month. At the first meeting of the stockholder's they agreed to accept and adopt this preincorporation agreement. In an action for breach of this contract, the defendant corporation contended that the contract was not binding since it had never been formally adopted by corporation. The court, however, held that the action taken by stockholders at their first meeting constituted a sufficient adoption to make the contract binding upon the corporation.

Usually stockholders reserve to themselves the right to pass upon those things which fundamentally affect the corporate enterprise. This right of collective action, which can be taken only at duly called and properly constituted stockholders' meetings, relates to such matters as the making and amending of by-laws, electing directors, amending the corporate charter, sale or mortgaging of corporate assets, and consolidations or mergers. It is common that a vote of at least two thirds or three fourths of the stockholders is required to effect some of the changes in the affairs or the position of the corporation. Unusual circumstances, however, may give the right of action to the board of directors where ordinarily it would reside with the stockholders.[1] To illustrate:

In *Oskaloosa S. Bank* v. *Mahaska County State Bank,* 205 Iowa 1351, the court said:

> "It is urged, however, that this being a sale of all of the property of a corporation, it could not be considered valid because it was not ordered or directed at a meeting of the stockholders. We are not unmindful of the general rule that ordinarily the directors of a corporation have not the power to sell all of the corporate property without the consent of the stockholders or a majority thereof. The answer to this contention, however, is twofold: First, the record does show that the officers and directors of this corporation who participated in this sale owned a majority of the stock; and second, it is an exception to the general rule that where a business is in a failing condition and has become financially involved and insolvent, and the creditors are pressing their claims, the power of the directors to alienate the property is conceded where it is regarded as of imperative necessity."

► II. BY-LAWS

"The function of a by-law . . . is to prescribe the rights and duties of the members with reference to the internal government of corporation, the management of its affairs, and the rights and duties existing between the members inter se." *Cummings* v. *State,* 47 Okla. 627.

The by-laws fix the details of corporate operation, the details that are neces-

---

[1] Jeppi v. Brockman Holding Co., p. 1021.

sary to make the corporation a responsive and efficient unit in the conduct of its affairs. They are in the nature of a contract and are binding upon the stockholders and officers of the corporation. They are not binding upon third persons who have no knowledge or are not charged with knowledge of their contents. Third persons have the right to assume that the actions of the officers are proper and regular. To illustrate:

In *Colcord* v. *Granzow,* 137 Okla. 194, the creditors of an insolvent corporation brought action to recover from the directors under a statute making the directors personally liable for the creation of a corporate debt in excess of the subscribed capital stock. It was the contention of the defendants that since the by-laws of the corporation had not been complied with in the transaction of the corporation's affairs, the actions taken were binding upon neither the corporation nor the directors, that third parties dealing with the corporation were under duty to take note whether the actions of the directors were in accordance with the by-law provisions. The court, in holding the directors liable, said:

> "It would be inequitable and unjust to place upon third persons, dealing with a corporation, the duty of first ascertaining whether the directing officers had complied with its own regulations adopted for its own convenience and safety."

In some states, corporations are required by statute to post their by-laws as a means of giving notice of the by-law provisions to third persons. Section 1624 of the 1939 Iowa Code is an illustration of such; it reads:

> "A copy of the by-laws of the corporation, with names of all of its officers, must be posted in the principal places of business subject to public inspection."

To illustrate:

In *Iowa-Missouri Grain Co.* v. *Powers,* 198 Iowa 208, the court in passing upon this statute said:

> "Constructive notice of the provisions of the by-laws will be imputed to third parties only if a copy thereof is posted in the principal place of business of the corporation so as to be subject to public inspection, and, unless the statute is complied with in respect to posting, a stranger will not be bound thereby. . . ."

In this case it was held that placing the by-laws upon a desk in the corporation's office did not meet the requirement of posting so as to charge the plaintiff with notice of a by-law provision giving the corporation a right of lien upon stock acquired by the plaintiff from a third party.

By-laws usually relate to such essential matters as:

(1) the issue and transfer of stock;

(2) the time, place, and notice for stockholders' meetings;

(3) powers and limitations of the directors in the management of corporate affairs;

(4) appointment of officers, their powers, duties and compensation;

(5) the handling of funds and declaration of dividends;

(6) the right to amend by-laws.

By-laws are subordinate and supplementary to a corporation's charter provisions. By-laws cannot enlarge the powers granted in the charter but serve merely to provide the procedure whereby the powers granted can be made effective. Obviously, a by-law that is repugnant to the charter is void.

As a matter of common law, the right to make and to amend by-laws is vested in the stockholders. In many instances, statutes and provisions in the articles of incorporation alter this rule. There is no uniformity of practice in respect to this matter. The modern tendency has been to give the board of directors a greater hand in the making and the amending of by-laws. Nevertheless, directors cannot exercise this right when it relates to their own powers. For example, they cannot legislate away a limitation that has been placed upon their right of action.

► III. DIRECTORS

The directors of a corporation are those individuals selected by the stockholders to conduct collectively the ordinary business affairs of the corporation. Thus, to the chosen few is delegated the right of management which the common law bestows upon the stockholders. Such a procedure is necessary to obtain an expeditious conduct of the corporation's affairs. The large number of widely scattered, disinterested stockholders in the modern corporation makes direct management by the stockholders an impossibility.

> "It is common knowledge that the affairs of a corporation are generally directed and controlled by a board of directors. The board of directors is an essential element of the corporation, and it is through such board that a corporation usually acts." *Reuter Hub Co.* v. *Hicks,* 181 Mich. 250.

A. POWERS

The limits to the control and management of the corporation by the board of directors are those established by the laws of the state of incorporation, the articles of incorporation, the by-laws, and rules and regulations invoked for special and temporary purposes.

In the individual instance, the actual extent of powers enjoyed by a board of directors is dependent upon the degree to which the stockholders have been divested of their common law right. It is characteristic that stockholders rely almost entirely upon the business sagacity of the directors for the success of the enterprise and reserve to themselves only the right to act in some few matters not directly related to the conduct of the commercial venture.

The board of directors, as distinguished from the administrative officers of the corporation, is the policy determining body of the corporation. It falls within their function to make decisions relative to the exercise of the powers with which the corporation has been endowed. Directors are in a limited sense agents of the corporation; they are authorized to do only those things which the charter empowers the corporation to do. The corporation is not bound by unauthorized acts of the board of directors. In *Sullivan Timber Co.* v. *Black,* 159 Ala. 570, the court said:

> "Directors, in the absence of restrictions in the charter or by-laws, or of statutory or constitutional inhibition, have all the authority of the corporation itself in the conduct of its ordinary business."

It is entirely discretionary with the directors as to the methods or means whereby the purposes of the corporation shall be accomplished. It is left to the judgment of the directors as to what business policies are to be followed and the methods of their execution.

> "Individual stockholders cannot question, in judicial proceedings, the acts of directors, if the same are within the powers of the corporation, and, in furtherance of its purposes, are not unlawful . . . and are done in good faith and in the exercise of honest judgment." *Ellerman* v. *Chicago Jct. R. Co.,* 49 N.J. Eq. 217.

B. COLLECTIVE ACTION REQUIRED

Directors are invested with authority to act for the corporation as a board and not as individuals. Their actions are not binding upon the corporation unless taken at a *properly called and duly constituted* meeting of the board as is provided for in the by-laws.[2] However, an informal meeting without benefit of minutes may be sufficient.* The by-laws usually provide for the time and place of meeting and the method by which the directors shall be notified of such. It is usual that a majority of the directors constitutes a quorum and that a majority of the quorum shall have the power to decide any matters that may come before the meeting. The functions of a director cannot be exercised through a proxy.

C. NATURE OF POSITION

Directors stand as fiduciaries to the corporation and to the stockholders as a body.[3,4] Theirs is a fiduciary relationship of a high order; they frequently are referred to as being trustees.

> "Directors are not express trustees. The language of Special Judge Ingersoll in *Shea* v. *Mabry,* I Lea (Tenn.) 319, that 'directors are trustees,' etc., is rhetorically sound, but technically inexact. It is a statement often found in opinions, but is true only to a limited extent . . . ; they are agents; they are trustees in the sense that every agent is a trustee for his principal, and bound to exercise diligence and good faith; they do not hold the legal title, and more often than otherwise are not the officer of the corporation having possession of the corporate property; they are equally interested with those they represent; they more nearly represent the managing partners in a business firm than a technical trustee." *Wallace* v. *Lincoln Savings Bank,* 89 Tenn. 630.

---

* Jeppi v. Brockman Holding Co., p. 1021.

2 Doernbecher v. Columbia City Lbr. Co., p. 1022.

3 Anderson v. Albert etc. Mfg. Co., p. 1023.

4 In re Estate of Johnson, p. 1025.

D. LIABILITIES

The position of trust and confidence occupied by directors requires of them such conduct as will best serve the interests of the corporation and the stockholders. They are not only required to act in absolute good faith toward those whose interests they represent but are also required to exercise reasonable care, diligence, and skill in the discharge of their duties, such as would be used by an ordinarily prudent and careful man in the conduct of his own affairs. A director cannot defend himself by alleging that he did not have the requisite skill to cope with a situation such as might ordinarily arise. By accepting his post, a director warrants that he has such skill as is necessary for a proper discharge of his duties. The plea of "I'm too ignorant" will avail him naught.

There is, of course, no question concerning the liability of directors for complete failure in the discharge of the duties imposed upon them. To avoid personal liability, they must operate within the limits established by the charter and bylaws. For example, losses caused by ultra vires acts, by the issuance of stock as paid in full when such is not the fact, or by the illegal declaration and distribution of dividends are the personal responsibility of the directors. Directors are also personally responsible to corporate creditors who have suffered losses by virtue of the formers' wrongdoing, when such in effect constitutes a fraud upon the creditors.[5]

Many of the states impose statutory penalties upon directors for an abuse and misuse of their powers. This applies especially to such matters as the misuse of corporate funds and the falsification of reports.

1. *Right to Deal with Corporation*

Although a director is not permitted to use his office to his own personal profit or advantage, there seems to be little reason why a director should not be able to contract with the corporation in his individual capacity. There is authority to the effect that, regardless of the circumstances, by reason of his position of trust, a director is precluded from contracting where his interests are adverse to those of the corporation. Under this extreme view, a contract entered into against this rule is absolutely void. In some jurisdictions, on the other hand, such contracts are regarded as being not void but merely voidable by the corporation within a reasonable time.[6]

By far the majority of the states accept the view that a director can deal with the corporation with the qualification that he must act in good faith—which would require a full disclosure of all information pertinent to the transaction—and that the corporation is represented by a quorum of disinterested directors. The contracting director should avoid the meeting at which his contract is given consideration. Courts of equity have declared that such contracts will be subjected to the closest scrutiny for evidence of bad faith.

Some corporations provide in their articles that the directors and officers shall have the right to contract with the corporation personally.

[5] Hirsch v. Phily, p. 1027.

[6] Minn. Loan & Trust Co. v. Peteler Car Co., p. 1029.

E. COMPENSATION

Directors and officers are not entitled to compensation for the performance of their ordinary duties unless such has been expressly contracted for.

"The principle underlying the rule respecting directors is that they are trustees for the stockholders, and that in the absence of express contract they should not be permitted to recover for services rendered in the performance of the ordinary duties pertaining to their offices upon any implied contract therefor." *Goodwin* v. *Dixie-Portland Cement Co.,* 79 W. Va. 83.

"The rule is just as applicable to presidents and treasurers or to other officers as to directors." *Kilpatrick* v. *Penrose Ferry Bridge Co.,* 49 Pa. 118.

As a general rule, a contract for compensation will be implied when a director or officer has rendered services not usual to his office. To illustrate:

In *Blom* v. *Blom Codfish Co.,* 71 Wash. 41, it was held that the president of the defendant corporation could recover compensation under an implied contract for his services as general manager.

F. TENURE OF OFFICE

A director's tenure of office is fixed by the charter or by-laws of the corporation. However, the term of office does not necessarily terminate upon the expiration of the specified term.

"Unless the charter of a corporation provides that an office shall become vacant at the expiration of the term of office for which the officer was selected or appointed, the general rule is to allow the officer to hold over until his successor is duly and legally elected and qualified. Mere failure of a corporation to elect officers does not terminate the terms of existing officers." *Quitman Oil Co.* v. *Peacock,* 14 Ga. App. 550.

Directors may not be removed from office by the stockholders without cause—as a breach of faith—or with provision for such action in the charter or by-laws. It is usual to provide for the exercise of this right because of "negligence, misconduct in office, or other reasonable cause." This gives stockholders a great deal of discretion since, in the absence of fraud, it is entirely up to them to determine what constitutes "other reasonable cause."

► IV. ADMINISTRATIVE OFFICERS

The directors are usually given the power to select officers whose function it is to conduct the business of the corporation in accordance with policies determined by the board of directors.[7] The officers of a corporation stand in the relationship of agents to the corporation. Their rights, duties, and liabilities are those of agents generally.[*, 8, 9]

* For a detailed discussion of the functions of corporate officers see Peterson and Plowman, *Business Organization and Management,* Chap. V.

[7] Uline Loan Co. v. Standard Oil Co., p. 1030.

[8] Miller v. Wick, p. 1031.

[9] Sacks v. Helene Curtis Ind., p. 1032.

CASES

CASE NO. 1

Jeppi v. Brockman Holding Co. 34 Cal. (2d) (Adv. 10), 206 P. (2d) 847, 9 A.L.R. (2d) 1297 (1949)

EDMONDS, J. Frank Jeppi and W. B. Camp, Sr., are suing for damages assertedly sustained by them because of the refusal of Brockman Holding Company, Inc. and Mary C. Spalding, its president to convey certain real property. . . .

. . . Brockman Holding Company, Inc. was organized in 1930 to manage and dispose of the estate of I. W. Brockman, deceased. The corporation's principal place of business was at Pomona, where most of the directors lived. Mrs. Spalding was a resident of Santa Cruz. It was the custom to hold only one directors' meeting each year; during the interim matters were handled informally by the directors.

At the annual meeting held on May 1, 1944, the following resolution was adopted:

"Motion was made by Bert Harvey, seconded by Spalding, that the property of Brockman Holding Company be sold in order to close up the company as soon as possible."

In May of the following year, at the conclusion of the stockholders' meeting, a majority of the directors, who controlled 29,000 shares of the 42,000 shares outstanding, held a meeting and, among other matters considered, informally discussed the sale of the land which is the subject of the present controversy.

. . . The minutes of the board meeting make no reference to the informal discussion. However, according to the testimony it was agreed that Mrs. Spalding should go to Bakersfield and negotiate a sale of the property. . . .

Three weeks after this meeting, Mrs. Spalding, Tupman and Jeppi visited the property and Jeppi made an offer of $27,500 for it. Mrs. Spalding said: "It suits me all right, and I will get in touch with my people in Pomona by phone and let you know. . . ." The next day at the office of a title company, an escrow agreement was signed by Mrs. Spalding, as the president of the corporation, and Jeppi and he deposited his check for $27,500 in escrow. By the terms of this agreement, title was to be conveyed to Jeppi and W. B. Camp, Sr.

On the same day, the title company sent a letter to the corporation requesting that it forward deeds as called for by the escrow agreement concerning the sale of the land. A week later, the following telegram was received in reply:

"Brockman Holding Company sale not approved by directors and better offer has been received. Directors meeting to consider all proposals will be held June 14th."

Jeppi was advised that the corporation had received an offer of $30,000 for the property. . . .

From the evidence in regard to the informal nature of the corporation's conduct of business, the general declaration of policy made by the directors in 1944 to sell the remaining property, the informal discussion immediately prior to Mrs. Spalding's trip to Kern County, and her execution of the escrow agreement after a delay in the negotiations for the express purpose of getting approval from her "people," it reasonably may be inferred that the board of directors had authorized her to enter into the contract and to bind the corporation. It is not material that the authorization was given at an informal meeting of the directors of which no minutes were kept.

The corporation relies upon section 343 of the Civil Code, now sec. 3901, Corporations Code, which reads:

"No corporation shall sell . . . all or substantially all of its property and assets . . . unless under authority of a resolution of its board of directors and with the approval of the principal terms of the transaction and the nature and amount of the consideration by vote or written consent of (the) shareholders. . . ."

. . . the California courts have not been called upon to determine the question of whether the statute in question applies to a wasting assets corporation, but authority from other jurisdictions places no restriction upon sales made in the ordinary course of business.

"It is the rule at common law . . . that the directors of an ordinary business corporation have no power to dispose of all of its assets without the consent of all its stockholders. This rule has been modified . . . by statute, so that the corporation may dispose of all its assets and wind up its business when authorized by a majority vote of the outstanding stock. . . . The reason for this limitation is that a corporation is organized for the purpose of doing business of some nature, and, if so, its shareholders have the right to insist that the corporation continue for the purpose for which it was organized. A sale, therefore, of all its property, or so much thereof as would prevent it from continuing in such business, would constitute a violation of the corporate contract. 7 R.C.L. 574. To this rule there are . . . exceptions. . . . If the conversion of all assets into cash . . . is in furtherance of the business for which the corporation was organized, the transaction is not ultra vires. For instance, if a corporation is organized for the purpose of buying, selling, and dealing in real estate, it would naturally have the power to sell all the real estate it owned at a particular time because that is the very object of its organization. The sale of its tangible assets under such circumstances furthers rather than hinders the carrying out of its contract with its stockholders . . ." Thayer v. Valley Bank, 35 Ariz. 238, 276 Pac. 526, 527.

The undisputed evidence in the present case is that the Brockman Holding Company was organized for the sole purpose of managing and disposing of the property of a decedent's estate. Further, at the 1944 meeting of the stockholders a motion was made that the remaining assets should be sold "in order to close up the company as soon as possible." The contract of sale, therefore, was made in the normal course of business and cannot be held subject to the restrictive provisions of former section 343 of the Civil Code. . . .

The evidence of the appellants, with inferences which reasonably may be drawn therefrom, would amply support a finding that Mrs. Spalding was authorized to enter into the escrow agreement. Having that authority, she could of course bind the respondent corporation by her execution of the escrow agreement.

The judgment is reversed. . . .

CASE NO. 2

Doernbecher v. Columbia City Lumber Co. 21 Ore. 573, 28 Pac. 899 (1892)

BEAN, J. The company being largely indebted to William Lowe . . . Lowe assigned his claim to plaintiff, who on that day duly commenced an action against the company to recover the amount due thereon, which finally resulted in a judgment in plaintiff's favor. After the commencement of this action and before final judgment, directors Dunbar, Wallace, and McDougall without any notice to the other directors, assembled by mutual consent at the office of Emmons & Emmons in the city of Portland, and pretended to pass a resolution authorizing the president and secretary of that company to assign all its property to R. W. Emmons for the benefit of its creditors, after which a deed of assignment was executed in due form. It is claimed by plaintiff that the proceedings of this meeting are illegal and void, because it was convened without notice, verbal or written, to the directors who did not attend; and in this we think he is abundantly supported both by reason and authority.

It is indispensable to a legal meeting of the directors of a corporation for the transaction of business, that all the directors have notice, actual or constructive, of the time and place of the meetings. Otherwise, it might happen that a bare majority of the quorum present being a minority of the whole, would do some act contrary and in opposition to the will of the majority. The stockholders and other persons interested in the corporation are entitled to the combined wisdom of all the directors. Where the time and place have not been fixed by some other competent authority, such meetings must be called by personal notice to each member of the board of directors.

It is no excuse to say that the three who were present all voted for the resolution, and had the other two been present the result would have been the same. The right to deliberate, and by their advice and counsel convince their associates, if possible, is the right of the minority, of which they cannot be deprived by the arbitrary will of the majority.

All persons interested in the corporation are entitled to the advice and influence as well as the votes of all the directors. And, says Mr. Morawetz,

> "while it may not be the duty of every director to be present at every meeting of the board, yet it is certainly the intention of the shareholders that every director shall have a right to be present at every meeting, in order to acquire full information concerning the affairs of the corporation and to give the other directors the benefit of his judgment and advice. If meetings could be held by a bare quorum without notifying the other directors, the majority might virtually exclude the minority from all participation in the management of the company." Morawetz Corp., Sec. 532.

Where the meeting is a general or stated one provided for in some resolution or by-law, notice of the time and place of the meeting is perhaps, in the absence of a different provision in the charter or by-laws of the company, not necessary. In such case each member is presumed to have notice of the day fixed for the meeting. But if the meeting be a special one, personal notice, if practicable, is necessary to each member unless all are present and participate in the proceedings. And such notice is essential to the power of the board to do any act which will bind the corporation. . . .

CASE NO. 3

Anderson et al. v. Albert & J. M. Anderson Mfg. Co. et al. 90 N.E. (2d) 541 (Mass.) (1950)

RONAN, J. This is an appeal by the plaintiffs from a final decree dismissing as to the defendant corporation a bill in equity brought by the plaintiffs as minority stockholders, and such other stockholders as might become parties, against the corporation, a majority of its directors, and certain other officers, to compel the defendants to sell to the plaintiffs five hundred shares of treasury stock of the corporation. . . .

The bill alleges that the defendants Alf E. Anderson, Andreas Anderson, and W. Lloyd Allen up to December 31, 1945, were minority stockholders and that they entered into an arrangement with the defendant Maxwell McConnell by which the latter sold one hundred eight shares of the stock of the defendant corporation to Alf E. Anderson, one hundred eight and two thirds shares to Andreas Anderson, and seven hundred fifty shares to the corporation which the latter has since held as treasury stock; that as a result of these purchases the defendants Alf E. Anderson, Andreas Anderson, and Allen became the holders of a majority of the stock; that this arrangement with McConnell was made for the sole purpose of ousting the other stockholders from control of the corporation and to secure control of the corporation and to secure control for themselves; and that, although the by-laws of the corporation require the directors to sell the treasury stock when in their discretion they deem it for the best interest of the corporation to do so, they have refused to sell this treasury stock and have retained the same for the primary purpose of maintaining the control of the corporation. The bill further alleges that the plaintiffs on November 27, 1947, made an offer in writing to purchase five hundred shares of this treasury stock for $100 a share, the value which the directors had placed upon the shares of stock of the corporation in the previous September, but that the defendants Alf E. Anderson, Andreas Anderson, Allen, and McConnell, constituting a majority of the directors, in order to perpetuate the control of the corporation in Alf E. Anderson, Andreas Anderson, and Allen, have refused to accept this offer. The bill prays that the defendants be compelled to accept this offer. . . .

The directors stand in a fiduciary relation to the corporation, and are bound to act honestly and in good faith solely in the interests of the corporation, and to subordinate to that paramount duty their own individual benefit and personal gain. . . . A corporation has a vital interest in seeing that its business is conducted in an orderly manner in compliance with its by-laws, and that its directors act faithfully in administering its affairs, including the issuance and purchase of its capital stock. . . .

A corporation unless forbidden by statute has the right to purchase its shares of stock and to retain them in its treasury until in the judgment of the directors a favorable opportunity is presented for their disposal. . . . No question is raised here as to the authority of the directors to purchase stock of the corporation. In the case at bar the purchase of the stock in behalf of the corporation is only a part of the transaction. The acquisition of some of the stock by two of the directors, the purchase of the remainder to be held as treasury stock, and the consequent reduction of the number of outstanding shares resulted in ousting the other stockholders, who were not parties to the purchase, from the control of the corporation and transferring control to those who participated in the arrangement by which the McConnell stock was acquired. Seventy-five thousand dollars of corporate funds were expended in the purchase of this stock. Directors cannot take advantage of their official position to manipulate the issue and purchase of shares of the stock of the corporation in order to secure for themselves the control of the corporation and then to place the ownership of the stock in such a position as will perpetuate that control. Such action constitutes a breach of their fiduciary obligations to the corporation and a wilful disregard of the rights of the other stockholders. . . .

The remaining question is the remedy available to the plaintiffs. They do not seek to set aside the transfer of the stock from McConnell to the two Andersons and to the corporation. Their efforts apparently are directed toward the disposal of the treasury shares or at least five hundred of them. It is plain that upon the allegations of the bill the defendants should not be ordered to accept the plaintiffs' offer to purchase five hundred shares. It is not the function of a stockholder's bill to secure individual relief for a stockholder. . . .

There has been no trial upon the merits, and until the facts are established it is difficult to state in advance what the final decree should contain in the event that the material allegations in the bill are sustained. . . .

. . . the suit is to stand for a hearing in the Superior Court in accordance with this opinion.

So ordered.

CASE NO. 4

In re Estate of Johnson. 339 Ill. App. 110 (1950)

TUOHY, J. Plaintiff filed his claim in the probate court of Cook county against defendant Alex Thomson, administrator of the estate of Victor S. Johnson, to recover 6142.5 shares of the common stock of Tennessee Gas & Transmission Company valued at $132,831.56. The probate court dismissed the claim upon the grounds that the contract upon which it is based is invalid and void, and contrary to public policy. The circuit court, on an appeal from the probate court, held likewise . . .

. . . The petition sets forth an agreement whereby plaintiff and decedent entered into a joint venture to promote a pipe line company for the transmission of natural gas from northern Louisiana to middle Tennessee and which contemplated the acquisition of certain natural gas interests from the Eastern Tennessee Oil and Gas Company, of which decedent was president. . . . The financing of this company provided for an initial authorized capitalization of $150,000 of preferred stock and in excess of 90,000 shares of common stock, the latter stock to be issued as a bonus for the purchase of preferred stock in the proportion of 10 shares of common to one share of preferred. The following significant paragraph with reference to this stock appears:

"4. . . . It is further agreed between us that as a result of our joint efforts, if we can save 90,000 shares of the 'A' Corporation's common stock in connection with the raising of $75,000.00 of a $150,000.00 program, that you and I are to personally share on a fifty-fifty basis said 90,000 shares or any part thereof which we may be able to save and which stock shall accrue to us in some legal manner with a nominal consideration to meet with any existing laws of the State of Tennessee."

The agreement further specifies that the plaintiff and decedent should have the right to designate and change, to suit their convenience, the directors of the corporation to be formed except that Johnson, Dall, and one A. Faison Dixon might not be replaced. . . .

. . . the courts below dismissed the petition . . . on the grounds that it is apparent in the face of the contract that it is void . . . as being in violation of public policy in providing for a plan of organization disregarding basic principles of corporation law and the fiduciary obligations of corporate promoters and directors. . . .

We are also of the opinion that the

alleged contract violates public policy in providing for a plan of organization which disregards well established principles of law governing the obligations of corporate promoters and directors.

The shares of stock sought to be recovered by plaintiff are part of the 30,000 shares issued under a resolution of the board of directors of May 4, 1940, and are shares mentioned in paragraph 4 of the contract which evidently were "saved" from the bonus stock which was to be distributed to purchasers of preferred stock on a ratio of 10 common for each share of preferred purchased. Just how the shares were to be "saved" does not appear—but presumably at the expense of the preferred stockholders. Neither does it appear by what authority Dall and Johnson could contract to divide these 30,000 shares in derogation of the rights of all the other participants in the enterprise. . . .

. . . It is to be considered that the resolution authorizing this payment was passed by a board of directors selected by prearrangement between decedent and plaintiff, one of the beneficiaries of the arrangement, in disregard of the clear right of stockholders to pass upon the legitimacy of the claim through directors of their own selection. The arrangement is extremely suspect and seems to us to come within the prohibition in the cases of De La Motte v. Northwestern Clearance Co., 126 Minn. 197, Gerdes v. Reynolds, 260 App. Div. 906, 915, 28 N.Y.S. (2d) 622, and Ballantine v. Ferretti, 28 N.Y.S. (2d) 668. In the last-mentioned case it is said (p. 680):

> ". . . contracts by which corporate officers or directors take pay for their action as such have such harmful potentialities where there are other stock or creditor interests in the corporation that they are condemned as contrary to public policy because of their nature and general tendency, without inquiry in any given case as to whether harm in fact resulted or complaint actually is made. . . ."

In the case at bar it was Dall's duty as president and a director of the Tennessee Gas & Transmission Company so to act that the stock to be issued to Johnson for his prior services and expenditures should be such stock, and only such stock, as was fairly compensatory for the considerations received by the company therefor. In this situation a contract looking to a fifty-fifty split of all such stock with Dall under the circumstances here existing is in our opinion violative of public policy. Furthermore, the agreement to issue such stock upon "a nominal consideration" is not to be approved. It is elementary law of corporations that corporate stock must be issued for something the corporation receives for it. To say in a contract that stock shall be issued for a nominal consideration "in some legal manner" is indicative of an intention to reward the promoters of this enterprise without reference to any benefit to the corporation. This is particularly so when it is considered that under paragraph 2 of the alleged agreement it was provided that the joint adventurers should have the right to name the board of directors. It is well-established principle that an agreement by which the selection of corporate directors is reposed in anybody except the majority of stockholders is in violation of public policy and unenforceable. . . . The plain inference to be drawn from a reading of the contract is that Dall and Johnson controlled the board of directors by this prearranged plan and voted to themselves the 30,000 shares of common stock in addition to salary and other outlays for Dall with money furnished by the general public from the sale of stock.

Plaintiff cites a number of cases to the effect that there is nothing inherently illegal in an agreement to elect or continue in office certain persons as directors or officers of a corporation or corporations proposed to be formed. These cases are to be distinguished from the case at bar by the fact that in the cases cited there was being dealt with a situation of a closed corporation where the stock was substantially all owned by the officers and directors and that the stockholders united in an agreement to elect particular directors and officers; however, in the instant case it appears from the pleading that it was not only not contemplated that Johnson, Dall and Dixon should own all the stock of the proposed company, but the petition itself shows conclusively that the whole enterprise was to be financed with money of the public to be gotten for the stock.

. . . the judgment . . . is affirmed.

CASE NO. 5

Hirsch v. Phily. 4 N.J. 408, 73 A. (2d) 173 (1950)

VANDERBILT, C.J. The plaintiff appealed to the Appellate Division of the Superior Court from a judgment of the Chancery Division of that court dismissing his complaint and we have certified the appeal here on our own motion.

The plaintiff, who is in the business of discounting accounts receivable, advanced to the Artex Dyeing & Finishing Co. Inc. over a period of five years various sums for which Artex gave him demand promissory notes in the amount of each advance and, as collateral security therefor, assignments of accounts receivable. At the time of the matters complained of herein the notes aggregated $23,700 and the accounts receivable $31,261.13. Each of these assignments, all of which are in the same form, sets forth the name of the debtor, his address, and the gross amount of the invoice, and contains the following language:

"For value received, we do hereby sell, transfer, and set over to S. Hirsch, their successors, assigns and legal representatives, the claim and account set forth above, and all our right, title and interest therein and to any and all of the merchandise therein described, and any and all of the merchandise returned or unaccepted thereon. . . .

"And hereby constitute and appoint, and by these presents do constitute and appoint S. Hirsch our true and lawful attorney irrevocable, for us and in name and stead, but to its own use and benefit to sell, assign, transfer or set over, demand, compromise or discharge, pledge, sue for and collect the foregoing accounts, and to receive all moneys due or to grow due thereon. . . ."

. . . As checks were received from the customers of Artex in payment of the accounts assigned to the plaintiff, the checks would be noted on a collection report by Artex and both the checks and the collection report would be held for Leslie J. Cotter, the plaintiff's agent in charge of the Artex account, who would usually call at the Artex office twice a week. Cotter would examine the checks and the collection report and receive from Artex its check drawn on its general account to the order of the plaintiff for the amount of the promissory note secured by the particular assigned accounts represented by the customers' checks. Artex then deposited the customers' checks in its own account. This procedure was consistently followed for a period of about five years, on each occasion the customers' checks being retained by Artex until they had been examined and the collection report approved by Cotter. The customers of Artex were never notified of these assignments to the plaintiff and on no occasion did the plaintiff collect or attempt to collect the accounts directly from the customers. There was nothing in the assignment of accounts, however, which precluded the plaintiff from dealing directly with the customers of Artex, but on the contrary the assignments, as is shown by the language above quoted, expressly gave the plaintiff that right.

On July 19, 1948, at which time Artex was indebted to the plaintiff in the sum of $23,700, secured by assigned accounts totalling $31,261.13, Cotter appeared as usual at the office of Artex and was shown the customers' checks aggregating $11,179.97, and was told that this was all the money that had been collected from the customers on the assigned accounts. Cotter was then given two checks of Artex, one for $5,893.02 and another for $5,286.95. The second of these two checks Cotter was requested by the defendant White, who had succeeded the defendant Scialla as secretary of Artex, to withhold from deposit for several days, but when this check was deposited it was returned because there were insufficient funds in the Artex account to meet it. This check, however, was later made good by White. On several occasions thereafter Cotter made attempts to obtain further payments, but each time he was informed that no collections had been made. Finally at a meeting in August, White told Cotter that Artex had ceased operations. When asked by Cotter what had happened to the assigned accounts, White replied, "The collections, they have been used up, dissipated, they are gone." . . .

The present action was brought by the plaintiff against the defendants Phily, Scialla and White, officers of Artex, on the grounds that they had converted to their own use or to the use of Artex funds of the plaintiff amounting to $12,520.03. . . .

. . . The individual defendants . . . assert that they are not personally liable for the plaintiff's loss, because there is no proof that they individually participated in the misappropriation of the moneys collected on the accounts receivable or that they received any of them, the only evidence in the question of what became of the missing proceeds of the assigned accounts being the statement made by White to Cotter that "the collections, they have been used up, dissipated, they are gone." This contention of the defendants overlooks entirely the inferences that may legitimately be drawn from the fact that the defendants as officers of the corporation are presumed to direct its activities and to have knowledge of its affairs. It ignores the fact that the defendants were active in handling these financial transactions with the plaintiff over a long period of time and were well informed as to the plaintiff's rights in these accounts receivable. These facts constitute at least a *prima facie* case against the defendants. . . .

It is well settled by the great weight of authority in this country that the officers of a corporation are personally liable to one whose money or property has been misappropriated or converted by them to the uses of the corporation, although they derived no personal benefit therefrom and acted merely as agents of the corporation. The underlying reason for this rule is that an officer should not be permitted to escape the consequences of his individual wrongdoing by saying that he acted on behalf of a corporation in which he was interested. 152 A.L.R. 703; 3 Fletcher on Corporations, §§ 1140–1142.

The judgment below is reversed and the cause is remanded to the Chancery Division of the Superior Court with direction to enter judgment for the plaintiff and against the defendants in the amount of $12,520.03, with interest and costs.

CASE NO. 6

Minnesota Loan & Trust Co. v. Peteler Car Co. 132 Minn. 277, 156 N.W. 255 (1916)

DIBELL, C. . . . In the summer of 1913, the Peteler Car Company was in need of additional funds. The defendants were then its directors. An arrangement of this kind was made: The defendants guaranteed the obligations of the company to the extent of $30,000, and upon the faith of this guaranty the First National Bank of Minneapolis loaned the company this amount. As security for their guaranty the company mortgaged to the defendants the Coma property. Afterwards, the company being unable to pay, the defendants paid the bank the $30,000, and they now claim the right to enforce their mortgage.

. . . The directors of a corporation may loan the corporation money or pledge their credit, and take a mortgage for security, if they act fairly and in good faith, and without wronging others. The defendants acted fairly and in good faith and did no wrong.

"Undoubtedly his relation as a director and officer, or as a stockholder, of the company, does not preclude him from entering into contracts with it, making loans to it and taking its bonds as collateral security; but courts of equity regard such personal transactions of a party in either of these positions not, perhaps, with distrust, but with a large measure of watchful care; and unless satisfied by the proof that the transaction was entered into in good faith, with a view to the benefit of the company as well as of its creditors, and not solely with a view to their own benefit, they refuse to lend their aid to its enforcement." Richardson v. Green, 133 U.S. 30, 10 Sup. Ct. 280, 33 L.Ed. 516.

But it is urged that the mortgage is voidable without a showing of fraud or bad faith or breach of fiduciary duty or resultant injury because the mortgagees were directors, and took part in the transaction which resulted in the making of it.

The mortgagees were a majority of the directors. They participated in the meeting of the directors which authorized the mortgage, and the presence of a majority of them were necessary to a quorum. Some of the cases make a mortgage so executed void; but the weight of authority is not with them. Others make it voidable. Some of these make it voidable at the election of a corporation or of a stockholder, though fraud or breach of duty or prejudice are not present. . . . Others make the mortgage valid if it is affirmatively shown that the transaction is fair, involves no breach of fiduciary duty, and results in no harm to the corporation or others nor undue advantage to the directors; and otherwise they hold it voidable. . . .

We take the rule to be that a transaction between the corporation and a majority of its directors acting in its execution, whereby they advance money or procure it to be advanced on their guaranty, and take security, if affirmatively shown upon close scrutiny to be fair and not to involve a breach of fiduciary duty and not to result in wrong, will be upheld, and that if otherwise, it may be avoided. Such a transaction as is before us is not uncommon. Corporations find it necessary to borrow money. It is usual for the directors to provide it. Often it can be provided only by their lending their credit. The rule stated and applied to loans of money or of credit by the directors is a sensible and an easily workable one.

CASE NO. 7

Uline Loan Co. v. Standard Oil Co. 45 S.D. 81, 185 N.W. 1012, 27 A.L.R. 585 (1921)

GATES, J., delivered the opinion of the court:

Action to quiet title. Counter-claim by defendant, seeking specific performance of the contract hereinafter mentioned. Findings and judgment for plaintiff. . . .

The secretary-treasurer of respondent, in the name of respondent, executed an option contract giving appellant a thirty-day option within which to buy certain business lots in Dell Rapids for a price specified. Within such period appellant exercised the option, and a contract in writing was executed, by which appellant was to deposit the purchase price in a designated bank, to be delivered to respondent upon the delivery by it to the bank of a deed to the premises running to appellant, after the abstract of title was approved by appellant. On the part of respondent the contract was executed in the name of Uline Loan Company, by E. J. Elliott, secretary. Appellant deposited the money as agreed. Respondent sent the abstract of title to appellant, together with an unsigned deed, which described the property and the parties. After title was perfected to the satisfaction of appellant, the board of directors of respondent met and adopted a resolution repudiating the transaction, and refused to permit a deed of the premises to be executed to appellant. The basis of such refusal and the contention of respondent upon this appeal are the want of authority in Elliott, the secretary-treasurer of respondent, to bind the corporation by the contract, because it is claimed that the making of the contract was not within the scope of Elliott's authority.

Of course, if Elliott is to be considered as the agent of respondent, within the meaning of the clause, "or his agent thereunto authorized in writing," found in § 856, Rev. Code 1919, then the conclusion of the trial court was right. Not only was there no authorization in writing to Elliott to make the contract, but the by-laws of respondent required contracts to be signed by the president and countersigned by the secretary. But appellant was not bound by the by-laws of respondent. In American Nat. Bank v. Wheeler-Adams Auto Co. 31 S.D. 524, 141 N.W. 396, we said:

> "It is settled that a by-law of a corporation binds only officers, directors, and stockholders of the corporation, or third persons who have knowledge of and have been brought into privity with it, so that it may operate to establish a contractual relation between the corporation and such third parties."

The respondent corporation was organized for the purpose of loaning money on real estate and other security, and it was also expressly authorized "to take, buy, hold, sell, mortgage, use, and lease real estate." Its directors were Wilhelmina Uline (president), Alma C. Uline (vice president), and E. J. Elliott (secretary-treasurer). The directors met only when dividends were to be declared. The only acts performed by the officers, other than Elliott, were the signing of releases of mortgages. Elliott was the sole officer in charge of the operations of respondent, and the only person employed in its place of business. The by-laws denominate the secretary as the executive officer of the corporation, and as a matter of fact the directors turned over the complete management and control of the corporation to him.

He was held out to the public by its directors as the general manager of the corporation. In 7 R.C.L. 623, we find the following statement:

"It is now well settled that when, in the usual course of the business of a corporation, an officer has been allowed to manage its affairs, his authority to represent the corporation may be implied from the manner in which he has been permitted by the directors to transact its business. . . ."

Elliott was clothed by the directors with the authority of a general manager. Therefore his acts, within the scope of the business of the corporation, were the acts of the corporation itself, and not the acts of an agent, within the ordinary meaning of the word "agent."

. . . The judgment and order appealed from are reversed.

CASE NO. 8

Miller v. Wick Bldg. Co. 154 Ohio 93, 93 N.E. 2d 467 (1950)

TAFT, J. It is the contention of Miller that there is substantial evidence in the record tending to prove that Paul Wick, assuming to act on behalf of the building company, entered into an oral agreement with Miller; that, under such agreement, the building company was to pay Miller a commission for securing a buyer, ready, willing and able to purchase the Wick building at a price of $800,000 net cash to the building company, and such commission was to be whatever amount such buyer agreed to pay in addition to such price; and that Miller and Rand did secure such a buyer who agreed to pay $850,000 for the building. It is conceded that the building was not sold by the building company.

The trial judge determined, as a matter of law, that Wick had authority to enter into such an agreement for the building company and so instructed the jury. . . .

The Court of Appeals' decision was based upon the conclusion that, as a matter of law, Wick had no authority to enter into such an agreement. . . .

Of course, the fact, that one undertakes to make a contract as agent for a party, does not necessarily result in such party being bound by the contract made. . . . In order to enforce any rights against such party under such a contract, it is necessary to establish that the one who assumed to act as agent for that party had power to make the contract for that party. . . .

In the instant case, it is conceded that the building company never expressly authorized Wick to enter into an agreement such as the one which Miller seeks to enforce. . . .

There is substantial evidence, including the testimony of Wick, that he was general manager of the building company and had general charge of the conduct of its business. Miller argues that, in the absence of any evidence disclosing a limitation on Wick's powers, it follows that Wick had actual implied authority to exercise, on behalf of the corporation, as full corporate powers including the power to sell real estate.

In the instant case, there is no claim that the board had ratified the making of the contract relied upon by Miller; there is no evidence that Wick had ever previously made, or that the board knew that he had endeavored to make, any contract relating to sale of any of the building company's assets; and there was no evidence that the building company ever actually carried on the business of buying and selling real estate.

As stated by Lockwood, J., in Lois

Grunow Memorial Clinic v. Davis, 49 Ariz. 277, 286, 66 P. (2d) 238, 242:

"The usual language of the text-writers is that a general manager has the power to do anything which the corporation itself might do. On examining the cases, however, we think that this statement of the powers of a general manager is too broad, and that the better authorities hold that his authority is limited to that which is usual and necessary *in the ordinary course of the business actually followed by the corporation,* and not to extraordinary powers conferred, indeed, upon the corporation by its charter and which may be exercised by its board of directors, but outside the scope and purpose of the business of the corporation as actually carried on. We think the confusion has arisen to a great extent from the difference in the powers granted corporations by their charters in past and in modern times. Most corporations organized many years ago were limited in their powers as set forth in their charter to the particular business in which they actually intended to engage and those things naturally correlative thereto. The charter powers and the actual operations of the corporation coincided and it was quite proper to say in general language that the manager could do anything which the corporation itself could do. But of more recent times, for some reason, the charters of corporations organized under general statutes usually attempt to include the right to do everything which a private individual can do, and many things which he cannot, although the incorporators have no intention of ever exercising a tithe of the powers conferred by the charter, and as a matter of fact limit their activities to one or two of those powers. Under such circumstances, language quite appropriate to the older charters becomes wholly inappropriate when applied to the later ones."

See, also, annotation, 159 A.L.R. 796, 802.

In our opinion, in the absence of evidence to the contrary, the implied authority of a general manager of a corporation does not extend beyond authority to do that which is usual and necessary in the ordinary course of the business which has actually been engaged in by the corporation.

Judgment affirmed.

CASE NO. 9

Sacks v. Helene Curtis Industries, Inc. 340 Ill. App. 76 (1950)

BURKE, J. Harry A. Sacks filed a complaint in the circuit court of Cook county against Helene Curtis Industries, Inc., an Illinois corporation, charging that on or about January 2, 1937, the defendant offered him, a salesman in its employ, the position of sales manager and educational director; that he accepted the offer, assumed the position and responsibilities of the office, proceeded to perform the work and duties thereof; that contemporaneously with the offer the defendant agreed to pay and he agreed to accept for his services, in addition to his salary, a commission of 1 per cent of the amount by which defendant's annual sales would exceed the volume of its sales for the year 1936; that defendant from time to time made payments on account of the commissions due; that under the agreement he earned commissions totaling $190,483.96; and that he received on account thereof the sum of $6,500 in cash and $18,928.80 in merchandise. He asked judgment for the balance of $165,055.16. Defendant in its answer denied that such a contract was made, denied that plaintiff was at any time sales manager and educational director, alleged that at no time was he given any executive responsibilities, denied making payments on account of any commissions due him. . . . A trial before the court and a jury resulted in a verdict against defendant for $75,000. Motions by defendant for a directed verdict, for judgment notwithstanding the verdict and for a new trial were overruled, and judgment was entered on the verdict. Defendant appeals.

Plaintiff's theory is that an oral contract was entered into between him and the defendant, acting through Louis P. Stein, its president and general manager, early in January 1937, whereby the defendant employed him as its sales manager and educational director, and agreed to pay him as additional compensation for his services in those capacities a commission of 1 per cent on the volume by which its sales were increased over those for the year 1936. . . . Defendant's theory is that . . . the president of defendant had no authority to make the alleged agreement on behalf of defendant; that the alleged agreement was kept secret and was not adopted or ratified by defendant. . . .

Defendant maintains that there is a complete absence of proof of authority of Louis P. Stein to bind it to the contract on which plaintiff bases his action, that plaintiff has the burden of proving Stein's authority to bind it to the particular contract, and that the law will not permit enforcement of a contract against a corporation which is not disclosed to the corporation. . . . Plaintiff states that in dealing with the president and general manager of defendant he was not required to inquire as to whether there were any limitations on the latter's authority by way of by-laws of the corporation or special resolutions of its board of directors; that even if the by-laws or special resolutions limited the authority of the president and general manager, such limitation would not be binding upon plaintiff unless he had notice or knowledge thereof; that the defendant having had the benefit of the contract of employment entered into by its president in its behalf, cannot now assert lack of authority of the president to negotiate the contract; that the general rule of law is that the president of a corporation, by virtue of his office, is the business head of the corporation, and in the absence of affirmative proof to the contrary, is presumed to have been authorized by the corporation to contract or to act otherwise on behalf of the corporation with reference to any matter pertaining to ordinary corporate affairs within the general powers of the corporation; that the contract between plaintiff and defendant, by its president and general manager, was not one which required defendant to pay a percentage of its profits; and that the agreement entered into between plaintiff and defendant through Mr. Louis Stein was neither secret nor unusual and extraordinary.

. . . We cannot agree with plaintiff. It is well settled that one dealing with an agent of a corporation has the burden of proving the agent's authority to bind the principal to the particular contract on which he rests his claim. . . .

It is well settled that a president of a corporation has no implied authority to make a contract on its behalf which is unusual and extraordinary . . . Fletcher Cyc. Corp. (Perm. Ed.) § 671. It is universally held that a contract to pay as compensation a percentage of the profits of a corporation is not the usual and ordinary contract which one authorized to employ on behalf of the corporation may make without specific authority of the corporation. Warszawa v. White Eagle Brewing Co., 299 Ill. App. 509, 517; Howard v. Winton Co., 199 Cal. 374, 249 Pac. 511, 512; Defenbaugh v. Jackson Paper Mfg. Co., 120 Mich. 242, 79 N.W. 197, 198. There is a complete absence of evidence in this case as to the authority of Mr. Stein with respect to the hiring of employees and fixing of their compensation, except as appears from the testimony of witnesses that he hired salesmen and other subordinate employees in the sales department of which he was the head, and that he fixed their salaries and determined their allowances for expenses. He was not the general manager of the business and affairs of defendant and there is no evidence that he ever made a contract on behalf of defendant which was other than the usual and ordinary contract of hiring on a salary basis. The fact that no other employee or officer of defendant ever had a contract which gave him as compensation a percentage of defendant's gross sales is strong proof that Stein never had and never claimed to have the authority to make such an unusual and extraordinary contract as plaintiff asserts.

. . . For the reasons stated the judgment of the circuit court of Cook county is reversed and the cause remanded with directions to enter judgment for defendant and against plaintiff. . . .

Review Questions

1. With whom does the ultimate control of a corporation reside? Through what medium is this control exercised?
2. In respect to what matters do the stockholders of a corporation usually reserve the right of action to themselves?
3. Under what circumstances may the directors dispose of the corporation's property even though such a right has been reserved to the stockholders?
4. What is the function of a corporation's by-laws? To what extent are they binding upon the corporate management? To what extent are they binding upon third persons dealing with the corporation?
5. Who has the right to make and amend by-laws?
6. What, in general, is the function of the officers of a corporation?
7. Do directors represent the corporation in their individual capacities as agents?
8. May a director vote by means of a proxy?
9. To what extent is a director personally liable for the acts of the board of directors?
10. May a director of a corporation enter into binding contracts with the corporation in his individual capacity?
11. Is a director entitled to compensation?
12. How may a director's tenure of office be terminated?

Problems for Discussion

1. The holders of a majority of a corporation's stock vote to engage in activities not provided for in the corporation's articles of incorporation. Is this action binding upon the minority stockholders?
2. The holders of a bare majority of the Economy Engineering Corporation's

stock voted to obtain a bank loan for the purpose of purchasing new equipment. Is this action binding upon the minority stockholders?

3. The Livestock Sales Corporation was chartered in the State of Iowa for the purpose of buying and selling livestock. The holders of a majority of the stock voted by a ten-vote margin to amend the charter to include the buying and selling of livestock feeds. The minority stockholders contend that this action is not binding upon them. Decide.
4. The stockholders of a corporation seek to enjoin the management of the corporation from selling its products at a loss in competition with a rival corporation. Result?
5. The board of directors of the Acme Publishing Co. voted unanimously to merge with the Republic Printing Co. Is this within their powers?
6. A contacted the five directors of the X Corporation individually and obtained their written consent and approval of a sale of certain machinery to the X Corporation. Is this action binding upon the corporation?
7. The directors of a corporation organized for the purpose of giving instruction in commercial subjects amended the by-laws to the effect that the corporation would give instruction in dancing, music, and fine arts. Upon the basis of this authority, the directors immediately proceeded to make expenditures for the purpose of carrying out these declared functions. Within a month this venture was abandoned with heavy financial loss to the corporation. The stockholders seek to hold the directors liable upon the basis that such acts were unauthorized. Decide.
8. The directors and controlling stockholders of the X Corporation borrowed corporate funds with which to discharge their personal obligations and then sold the corporation forty shares of its stock for $15,000, crediting the corporation with the money they had borrowed and accepting the corporation's notes for the unpaid balance. The stock had no market value and a book value of 80 per cent of par. A stockholder brings action to have the transaction declared void and set aside. Result?
9. The directors of the X Corporation entrusted its management almost entirely to the president and made only superficial inquiry into the corporation's affairs at directors' meetings. It was discovered that the president had consistently used corporate funds for personal speculative purposes and to the ultimate loss of the corporation. Are the directors responsible for the injury caused the corporation by the president's acts?
10. The directors of the X Corporation entered into a contract with A, acting upon the advice of the legal counsel for the corporation to the effect that the act would not be ultra vires. Subsequently a stockholder succeeded in having the contract set aside as being beyond the corporation's powers. May the stockholders recover from the directors the losses suffered by virtue of this transaction?

Suretyship and Insurance

Chapter

41. SURETYSHIP

42. CONTRACTS OF INSURANCE

41 SURETYSHIP AND INSURANCE

SURETYSHIP

► I. NATURE OF RELATIONSHIP

Broadly speaking, if one person—the *surety* or *guarantor*—stands liable for a debt, default, or miscarriage of another—the *principal debtor*—a suretyship relation exists. It is a situation in which the personal credit of the surety stands as a pledge to secure an obligation of the principal debtor. Consequently, upon a default in performance, the surety can be looked to for satisfaction; that is, he can be called upon to make good the debt, default, or miscarriage of the principal debtor.

► II. CREATION

Suretyship relations may arise in various ways. For example:

(1) A may induce his friend B to place his name upon a promissory note as a comaker or an indorser so that A may obtain a loan from the C bank. In this way, B lends his name for the purpose of securing A's obligation. In the event that the note is not paid at maturity, B can be looked to for satisfaction. If B has placed his name upon the note as a comaker, he is liable as a primary party upon the instrument; as an indorser, he is liable as a secondary party. In either case, as between A and B, the latter stands as a surety.

(2) It is common for employers to require employees to furnish bonds for faithful performance.[1] Thus, if X employs Y as his cashier, he will want some protection against the possibility that Y may fall to temptation. The usual method by which such protection is obtained is a bond, upon which some third party (usually a surety company) obligates himself to make good for any default. The bond is a suretyship contract between the party obligated to perform and the obligor upon the bond. Fidelity bonds are extensively used in the business world.

In those instances where one person assumes the personal responsibility to pay another's obligations, in effect a suretyship relation arises. To illustrate:

Let it be assumed that A, B, and C are partners. A sells his interest in the business venture to B and C, who agree to pay, as part of the purchase price, all the partnership obligations. A has not thereby relieved himself of his personal obligation to the partnership creditors. He has merely delegated to the remaining partners, B and C, his duty to pay. Among the partners, however, B and C are the ones who are bound to pay, and thus they stand as the principal debtors, with A as the surety for their obligations. If the partnership obligations are not paid by B and C, then A can still be looked to for satisfaction.

---

[1] Town of Clayton v. Wall, p. 1046.

The same is true when the purchaser of property assumes the mortgage obligation of his grantor. The purchaser thereby becomes the principle debtor, and the mortgagor—the grantor—stands as his surety in the event of default of payment.*

► III. NATURE AND EXTENT OF SURETY'S LIABILITY

The nature and extent of a surety's liability are determined by the contract of suretyship under which he became liable. Whether or not the surety's liability is primary or secondary is dependent upon the nature of his undertaking—whether he occupies the position of a strict surety or of a guarantor.

A. STRICT SURETYSHIP

A *strict surety* is equally liable with the principal debtor. His is a primary undertaking not dependent upon any default by the party to whom he lent his name as security. Thus, if A signs a promissory note as an accommodation comaker with B, he is primarily liable and can be looked to immediately upon the maturity of the instrument. The strict surety's undertaking is not collateral to the obligation of the principal debtor but is identical in nature. It usually arises on the same instrument, executed at the same time and based upon the same consideration.†

B. GUARANTY

A guarantor's liability arises from an independent contract and is collateral to the obligation of the principal debtor. A guarantor, in the true sense, undertakes to pay the debt, default, or miscarriage of another. His is a secondary liability, and, to be enforceable against him, his undertaking must be evidenced by a writing, as required by the Statute of Frauds.

The distinction between the undertaking of a guarantor and a strict surety was stated in *First Nat. Bank* v. *Drake,* 185 Iowa 879, thus:

> "A surety's promise is to pay the debt. A guarantor's undertaking is to pay the debt if the debtor cannot. A guarantor is never the maker of the note. The undertaking of a guarantor is collateral. In the case of a surety, there is a direct promise to perform the original contract; while a guarantor's promise is only to perform the promise of another in case he cannot perform."

Since a guarantor's liability is secondary, it is conditional and not absolute; that is, before his liability attaches, certain conditions must first be met. The conditions upon which a guarantor's liability is dependent vary with the type of guaranty contract.

1. *Absolute Guarantors*

An absolute guarantor is one whose liability is contingent only upon a default by the principal debtor. The party who is entitled to performance need do nothing to fix the liability of the absolute guarantor after a default of performance by

---

* See p. 785.
† See Elkhorn Production Credit Assoc. v. Johnson, p. 548.

the principal obligor has taken place. Bonds for faithful performance operate in this way. To illustrate:

If the A Surety Company furnishes B a bond by which it guarantees that C will faithfully perform his contract with B, the surety company's liability is contingent only upon a failure of performance by C. Upon default by C, B can immediately proceed against the A Surety Company.

Contracts by which one guarantees the payment of a sum of money are also of this nature. To illustrate:

Let us suppose that A writes to B as follows: "If you will let C have $1,000 upon his promissory note for sixty days at 5 per cent, I will see that you are paid at maturity if C does not pay the debt." This is an absolute promise to pay, conditioned only upon the failure of the principal debtor to pay at maturity.

2. *Conditional Guarantors*

The liability of a conditional guarantor is contingent upon some condition or conditions other than a default of the principal debtor. The creditor is required to meet certain conditions before the guarantor's liability attaches. These conditions are whatever may be contracted for by the guarantor.

The so-called *contract* or *guarantee of collectibility* is the best illustration of this type of undertaking. If one guarantees that the obligation of another is "good" or is "good and collectible," he is merely promising to pay in the event that the principal debtor cannot pay.[2] Before the liability of the guarantor attaches, the creditor must demonstrate that he has exhausted his legal remedies against the principal debtor. The guarantor is also entitled to notice of default within a reasonable length of time.

3. *Indorsers*

As has been seen, an indorser assumes the responsibility of paying, if required, the obligation evidenced by the instrument in the event of its proper presentment, dishonor, notice, and protest. An indorser therefore occupies a position of a conditional guarantor. Unless the prerequisites to his liability are fully met, he is completely discharged.*

C. LIABILITY AS TO AMOUNT AND TIME

One who undertakes to stand good for another's obligations should protect himself as to the amount for which he can be held. It is likewise desirable to establish the period of time over which the undertaking is to be valid. If A writes to B, "I will hold myself responsible for the purchase price of all goods sold to C," he has established no limit as to the amount or the period of time over which he will be liable. This would be an unlimited and continuing guaranty, good until revoked by the guarantor or otherwise terminated.

---

* See p. 537.

[2] General Phoenix Corp. v. Cabot, p. 1047.

► IV. RIGHTS OF SURETY OR GUARANTOR

The term *surety* is used here in its broadest sense and includes both the strict surety and the guarantor.

A. RIGHT OF INDEMNITY

Whenever a surety is called upon to pay or to perform the principal debtor's obligation, he is entitled to indemnity from the latter. This right of the surety to be reimbursed arises from an implied promise on the part of the principal debtor to pay. The right of reimbursement may also be based upon the equitable principle that he who is morally bound to pay should be made to pay. It is thus possible for a surety to recover from the principal debtor even though he guaranteed the debtor's obligations without the latter's consent or knowledge.

The surety can recover only the amount that he has been called upon to pay. Consequently, if the surety compromises a claim for less than the full amount, he can recover only the amount paid under the settlement. Any costs that the surety incurs in resisting collection of the claim cannot be assessed to the principal debtor. The surety can avoid such expenses by the simple expedient of performing as he has agreed to do.

B. RIGHT OF SUBROGATION

The court, in *Millowners' Mutual Life Ins. Co.* v. *Goff*, 232 N.W. 504 (Iowa), defined subrogation as being:

> "A legal fiction whereby a debt or obligation which has been paid by a third person is treated as still subsisting for the benefit of the one so paying so that by means thereof, one creditor is substituted to the rights, remedies, and securities of another."

Upon performing the principal debtor's obligation, a surety is substituted for the creditor; he acquires all rights that the creditor had against the principal debtor. If the creditor has obtained a judgment against the debtor, the surety in effect becomes the judgment creditor. The surety has the right to avail himself of the debt and all evidences of such, upon which he can take action against the principal debtor for reimbursement. And the surety becomes entitled to any securities that the principal debtor has pledged with the creditor as security for the obligation.

C. RIGHT OF CONTRIBUTION FROM COSURETIES

It is not uncommon that there will be more than one surety upon the same obligation. In such an event, the creditor can look to any or all of the sureties for satisfaction. He may proceed against one surety only and recover the whole of the obligation.

Between the sureties, however, each one stands in equal liability for the obligation of the principal debtor unless the sureties have agreed to the contrary. Consequently, if one of several sureties has been called upon to pay more than his proportionate share, he has the right of contribution from the other sureties. To illustrate:

Let us suppose that A, B, and C are cosureties upon a $300 obligation and that the whole amount is paid by A. Thereupon, he has the right to get a contribution of $100 from B and a like amount from C. Now let us suppose that A only paid $250 of the obligation. In that event he could compel a contribution of $100 from either B or C and $50 from the other. In no event can a cosurety be forced to contribute more than his proportionate share.

The right of contribution between cosureties is not dependent upon a contractual agreement. It is said to rest upon the equitable maxim "Equality is equity." The court, in *Assets Realization Co.* v. *American Bonding Co.*, 88 Ohio St. 216, stated the reason for this rule thus:

> "It equalizes burdens and recognizes and enforces the reasonable expectations of co-sureties, because it is just and right in good morals, and not because of any supposed promise between them."

Cosureties also stand in a position of equality in respect to any collateral held as security. Should one of the cosureties acquire collateral from the principal debtor, he could not use it for his personal benefit. It would inure equally to the protection of all the cosureties.

► V. DEFENSES AVAILABLE TO SURETY

A. DEFENSES OF PRINCIPAL

As a general rule, the defenses that are available to the principal debtor are also available to the surety. Of course, this does not include defenses that are entirely personal to the principal, such as infancy, bankruptcy, and the statute of limitations. The surety cannot rely upon the statute of limitations as a defense until his promise, as distinguished from the principal debtor's promise, has been outlawed by the required lapse of time. There is, however, authority to the contrary.[3]

If a contractual obligation is not binding upon the principal debtor because of a lack or failure of consideration, that obligation is not binding upon the surety either. Obviously, a surety cannot be held liable upon a contract that is void because of illegality. It seems to be the general rule that the surety cannot avail himself of the defense of fraud that was practiced upon the principal unless the principal first elects to avoid the contract upon that basis.

B. DEFENSES PERSONAL TO SURETY

The surety has available all defenses that are personal to him. Where the creditor has induced the surety by misrepresentation to assume the obligation, the latter can use such as a defense. Ordinarily, a nondisclosure of facts is not regarded as constituting fraud. However, the relationship existing between a creditor—

[3] First Nat. Bank v. Drake, p. 1048.

the obligee—and a surety is regarded as being sufficiently of a fiduciary character as to require the creditor to disclose unusual facts that bear upon the risk of the surety. For example, an employer, in accepting a bond for faithful performance, is bound to disclose all facts pertaining to the honesty and integrity of the employee being bonded. A failure to disclose previous misconduct on the part of the employee would constitute fraud.

Any claims that the surety has against the creditor can be asserted as a setoff against the amount for which the surety is liable. If the surety is called upon to pay the principal debtor's obligation, the surety may deduct any amounts that the creditor owes him.

► VI. DISCHARGE OF SURETY BY ACTS OF CREDITOR

The courts have gone far in the direction of protecting the surety against acts or conduct of the creditor or obligee that might be to the surety's prejudice or that in any way might alter the position of the parties as of the time he assented to being a surety. The creditor must realize that certain conduct on his part may serve to discharge the surety from liability.

A. CHANGE IN TERMS OF CONTRACT WITH PRINCIPAL DEBTOR

It can be stated as a general rule that the surety will be discharged by any material alteration in the contract existing between the principal debtor and the creditor.[4] Such changes as relate to the mode, time, or place of performance would be regarded as material. Even a reduction of the interest rate is held by the majority of the courts to constitute such a material alteration as will discharge the surety.

It is by far the majority rule that, even though the alteration operates to the benefit of the surety, he is nevertheless discharged. This is based upon the theory that the altered contract represents an obligation to which the surety did not consent to be bound. However, some courts have taken the view that, to effect a discharge of the surety, the alteration must be of such a nature as to present a possibility of prejudice to him. Thus, an extension of the time of payment is regarded as prejudicial to the surety in that during that time the principal debtor's financial condition might become impaired. The surety cannot be made to take a risk for a period of time longer than that to which he consented. In a few instances, the view has been taken that the surety is not discharged unless he has actually been prejudiced by the alteration. The moral to be derived from this discussion is that a contract with the principal debtor should not be altered in any material respect without the consent of the surety.

B. EXTENSION OF TIME

The extension of the time of payment or performance to the principal debtor constitutes a material alteration of the contract and, consequently, discharges the surety. However, the extension agreement must be based upon a good considera-

[4] Becker v. Faber, p. 1050.

tion if it is to be binding upon the principal debtor and the creditor. A gratuitous promise to the debtor would not discharge the surety from his obligation to perform.

Upon granting an extension of time to the principal debtor, the creditor can preserve the liability of the surety by the simple expedient of reserving all rights against the surety. The extension agreement must contain a provision to the effect that the creditor is reserving all rights against the surety the same as though no extension had been granted. Such a provision makes the extension agreement conditional between the creditor and principal debtor. It is a recognition of the right of the surety to discharge the obligation at maturity and proceed immediately to pursue his legal rights for reimbursement. The extension of time is conditioned upon the election of the surety not to discharge the obligation when it matures.

C. RELEASE OF PRINCIPAL DEBTOR

Obviously, the surety will be released from liability by payment or performance of the obligation for which he stands as security. A tender of performance by, or on behalf of, the principal debtor will have a like effect. And if the creditor unconditionally releases the principal debtor from the obligation, the surety is also discharged. However, if the creditor conditions the release by an express reservation of his rights against the surety, a discharge of the latter will not be effected.* As in the case of a reservation upon an extension of time, this is a recognition of the right of the surety to meet the obligation at maturity and to exercise his right of reimbursement against the principal debtor.

D. ACTS IN RELATION TO COLLATERAL SECURITY

> "It is a settled principle that a surety is entitled to the benefit of all securities for the debts that are held by the creditor, and it follows from this right of subrogation that the creditor cannot, without the surety's assent, surrender, release, waste or render unavailable to the surety any of such securities." *Weik v. Pugh,* 92 Ind. 382

The creditor has no duty to resort to the collateral held as a means of satisfying the obligation. The surety cannot object to the failure of the creditor to sell the collateral to satisfy the debt even though it subsequently declines in value. It is within the surety's power to prevent such by discharging the obligation at maturity and obtaining the collateral by his right of subrogation.

However, the creditor does have the duty not to deal with or treat the collateral security in such a way as to impair the surety's security position. The surety will be released from his obligation to the extent of the loss caused by the misconduct of the creditor. Thus, if the creditor holds two $500 bonds to secure a $1,000 obligation and he negligently loses one of the bonds, the surety would be discharged to the extent of $500.

A creditor should not resort to an acceptance of substitute collateral without the consent of the surety. Should, for example, a creditor release to the principal

* See p. 594.

debtor certain stocks and bonds which he had pledged to secure the obligation and accept instead a chattel mortgage as security, the surety upon the obligation would be discharged.

E. FAILURE TO DISCHARGE DISHONEST EMPLOYEE

An employer has the duty to discharge immediately a bonded employee who has proved himself untrustworthy. Should the employer, with knowledge of the employee's dishonest conduct, allow him to remain in his employ, he would thereby release the surety from any future liability. Any reform movement is entirely at the risk of the employer unless the surety's assent is obtained.

CASES

CASE NO. 1

Town of Clayton v. Wall. 217 N.C. 365, 8 S.E. (2d) 223, 127 A.L.R. 854 (1940)

SCHENCK, J., delivered the opinion of the court:

This is an appeal by the plaintiff from judgment sustaining demurrer filed by the corporate defendant.

The complaint alleges that the individual defendant, N. Clyde Wall, was duly appointed by the governing body of the Town of Clayton collector of delinquent taxes, and executed and filed his bond in the sum of one thousand dollars with the corporate defendant, the National Surety Corporation, as surety thereon; that said bond contained the following provision:

> "The condition of the foregoing obligation is such that if the said principal shall well and truly perform all the duties of his said office or position, and shall pay over and account for all funds coming into his hands by virtue of his said office or position as required by law, then this obligation shall be null and void, otherwise it shall be and remain in full force";

and further alleges that on September 7, 1939, when said bond was in effect, the plaintiff was arrested by the individual defendant, without any warrant, on the public streets of Clayton in view of divers persons, and was unlawfully, wrongfully, purposely, wilfully, wantonly and in a high-handed manner, restrained of his liberty, and forcibly made to accompany the individual defendant and the chief of police through the streets of Clayton to the city jail, . . . ; that later in the day of September 7, 1939, the individual defendant informed the plaintiff that if he would promise to pay a stated amount from his pay checks received from the W.P.A. projects he would be released and discharged; and

> "that while the plaintiff was confined in the said city jail . . . the said defendant was unlawfully . . . demanding and coercing the plaintiff into paying an alleged debt, . . . in order that he might collect a commission on taxes alleged to be due by the plaintiff; that the said defendant's conduct herein was not warranted by law, was done in a high-handed manner in violation of the duties and authorities conferred upon him and in violation of the duties of his said office and the terms of his bond, and thereupon he committed a breach of his bond."

The question presented for answer is: Does the complaint allege a breach of the condition of the bond which reads:

"... that if the said principal shall well and truly perform all the duties of his office or position."

The answer is in the negative.

It cannot be held, even by a most liberal construction, that "the duties of his office or position" as delinquent tax collector authorized or contemplated that the individual defendant would or could arrest and imprison any one in order to coerce the payment of taxes alleged to be due. Ordinarily the nonpayment of taxes is not a criminal offense, and if a tax collector arrests and imprisons a tax delinquent in an effort to enforce payment of a tax he is not acting colore officii but acting beyond his official authority and therefore in his individual capacity. . . .

In the case at bar the alleged arrest and imprisonment of the plaintiff by the individual defendant were not acts within the scope of his authority or duties as a delinquent tax collector, but were acts entirely foreign to and beyond even any apparent power or right vested in him as such tax collector, and were not contemplated by the corporate defendant, the surety, when it executed the bond.

The condition of the bond as written does not impose on the surety the obligation that the principal should do no wrong and should in all respects observe the law. The phrase "well and truly perform all the duties of his said office or position" obviously refers to the duties incumbent upon him as delinquent tax collector. The principal and his surety are liable under a contract expressed in definite terms and their liability cannot be carried beyond the fair meaning of those terms. The clause only binds the principal affirmatively to the faithful performance of the duties of his office or position and does not cover the case of an abuse or usurpation of power. There are no negative words that the principal will commit no wrong nor do any thing unauthorized by law.

The judgment of the Superior Court is affirmed.

CASE NO. 2

General Phoenix Corporation v. Cabot. 89 N.E. (2d) 241 (N.Y.) (1949)

BROMLEY, J. In March, 1947, defendant Cabot, the president, director and sole stockholder of a corporation known as Pluto Corporation, executed an instrument guaranteeing the payment of certain loans to be made to the corporation by plaintiff, General Phoenix Corporation. . . . The loans, aggregating over $150,000 and represented by three promissory notes and open account, were not paid at maturity . . . Cabot claimed the action was premature since all remedies had not been exhausted against the debtor. . . .

The interpretation of a contract of suretyship is governed by the standards which govern the interpretation of contracts in general (Restatement, Security, § 88). Whether a surety is a guarantor of payment or a guarantor of collection depends upon the intention of the parties as expressed in the surety contract. If he binds himself to pay immediately upon default of the debtor, he becomes a guarantor of payment; if he binds himself to pay only after all attempts to obtain payment from the debtor have failed, he becomes a guarantor of collection (1 Brandt, the Law of Suretyship and Guaranty, pp. 241–249). Where the intention of the parties may be gathered from the four corners of the instrument, interpretation of the contract is a question of law, and parol evidence is not admissible as an aid in interpretation; no trial is necessary to determine the legal effect of the contract. . . . A contract of suretyship does not depend upon the use of technical words but upon a clear intent that one party as surety binds himself to the second party as creditor to pay a debt contracted by a third party, either immediately upon default of the third party or after attempts to effect collection from the third party have failed.

An examination of the surety agreement involved herein compels the conclusion that defendant obligated himself thereunder as a guarantor of payment. The ambiguities which defendant claims inhere in the instrument stem mainly from the use of the word "indemnity" in certain portions of the instrument. Upon a reading of the instrument as a whole, however, the ambiguity claimed by defendant becomes nonexistent. The contract is explicit: John B. Cabot guarantees and warrants "the full and prompt payment at maturity of any part of the principal"; "in case default is made at any time in payment of any of the . . . obligations" he "agrees to pay the same to General, its successors and assigns, upon demand"; he agrees that "the undersigned will upon demand pay and perform the undersigned's obligation under this guaranty and indemnity without requiring any proceeding or action to be taken against the Borrower." As opposed to this clear language there appears in the body of the instrument a reference to the contract as an "indemnity" and the instrument is entitled "Bond of Indemnity." In view of the clear and unmistakable language indicating that defendant guarantees payment at maturity, the use of the word "indemnity" cannot obscure the intention of the surety or give a different meaning to the instrument. Moreover, a contract of indemnity runs not to the creditor but to a third person who is or will become a debtor upon the imposition of a contingent liability. . . . Cabot's liability under the surety contract attached as soon as there was default by Pluto in the payment of its obligations. An action against such a surety brought before all efforts to collect from the principal obligor have failed is not premature.

CASE NO. 3

First Nat. Bank v. Drake. 185 Iowa 879, 171 N.W. 115 (1919)

GAYNOR, J. In this action, plaintiff seeks judgment against defendant Francis Drake, on his guaranty of payment of a certain note. . . .

At the time the note was executed, and before it was delivered, Francis Drake . . . guaranteed its payment, in writing, on the back thereof, in the following words:

> "For value received we hereby guarantee the payment of the within note at maturity, waiving demand, notice of nonpayment and protest."

The action against Francis Drake is upon this guaranty. Before the commencement of this action, the note was barred by the statute of limitations as to Sutton. Before it became barred, Francis Drake moved to California, and has resided there ever since. The action, therefore, is not barred, as to him, under the statute. It is claimed, however, that, inasmuch as the action on the note was barred at the time this action was commenced, as to J. B. Sutton (the maker) . . . it is barred as to him. No action or proceeding of any kind was ever had against the principal, Sutton, or his estate. It is apparent that, if the defendant's contention is correct, and the fact that the statute has run against Sutton bars the action as to this defendant, the controversy is at an end. There is no claim that Drake was other than guarantor of the payment of the note. . . . Sutton was primarily liable upon the note. Drake's guaranty was of the payment. He assumed, therefore, a secondary liability. . . .

A surety's promise is to pay the debt. A guarantor's undertaking is to pay the debt if the debtor cannot. A guarantor is never the maker of the note. The undertaking of a guarantor is collateral. In the case of a surety, there is a direct promise to perform the original contract; while a guarantor's promise is only to perform the promise of another in case he cannot perform.

It is true, in this case, that the guaranty is absolute, but it is the guaranty of the performance of a contract made by another. It is a guaranty that the other will pay what he has contracted to pay in the original obligation. It is true that the defendant waived demand, notice, and protest, yet he stood as one pledging his credit to secure the obligation of another. His promise was, therefore, collateral to the promise of the other. The original promise of the maker was to pay. The promise of the guarantor was that the maker would pay. He made no direct promise to pay. The simple legal import of his promise was to protect the promise of another; to make good the promise of the other. His promise, therefore, though, in a sense, original and absolute, was collateral, and his liability secondary. . . . See 2 Randolph on Commercial Paper (2d ed.), Chap. 26, § 849, in which it is said:

"A guaranty is a promise to answer for the payment of some debt or the performance of some duty in case of the failure of another person who is liable in the first instance. A guarantor differs from a surety in this: that a surety is liable absolutely as principal upon default. . . ."

A surety is usually bound with his principal, in the same instrument, executed at the same time and on the same consideration. He is an original promisor and debtor from the beginning. Usually, he will not be protected either by a mere indulgence of the principal or by want of notice of default of the principal, no matter how much he may be injured thereby. . . .

. . . we think this case is controlled and ruled by what was said by this court in Auchampaugh v. Schmidt, 70 Iowa 642, in which it was held that a claim which is barred by the statute of limitations, as against the principal debtor, is, by reason thereof, barred also as against the surety. In that case, like the case at bar, the surety was a nonresident, and as to him, under the statute, the suit was not barred. The maker of the note, however, was a resident of this state, and as to him an action was barred. The surety pleaded the bar against the maker as available to himself as surety, and his contention was sustained. This case has stood unchallenged in this court over 30 years. Some cases, however, hold to a different doctrine. See Willis & Bro. v. Chowning, 90 Tex. 617 (40 S.W. 395, 59 Am. St. 842, and notes to the case as reported in 59 Am. St.). See, also, 12 Ruling Case Law, under the head of "Guaranty," §§ 52 and 55. . . .

Following the rule in the Auchampaugh case, we think the court was wrong in entering judgment against this defendant. . . . The cause is reversed, with direction to sustain defendant's plea of the statute of limitations, and to dismiss the cause as to both defendants.

CASE NO. 4

Becker v. Faber. 280 N.Y. 146, 19 N.E. (2d) 997, 121 A.L.R. 1010 (1939)

LEHMAN, J., delivered the opinion of the court:

The plaintiff has brought this action to foreclose a mortgage upon real property in Nassau county. Payment of the principal and interest of the bond, secured by the mortgage, was guaranteed in October, 1923, by John A. Kolle. Asking a deficiency judgment against the executors of the last will and testament of John A. Kolle, deceased, the plaintiff made them parties to the foreclosure action. The complaint against them has been dismissed on the ground that the mortgagor and mortgagee modified the terms of the mortgage agreement without the knowledge or consent of the guarantor, and by force of such modification the guarantor was released.

. . . In January, 1933, the mortgagee agreed that the mortgagor would be permitted to meet the installment of interest which had become due on December 1, 1932, by monthly payments of $50 each and that similar monthly payments might be made upon subsequent installments after they became due semi-annually. In 1935 the mortgagee informed the mortgagor that when past due interest was paid up to June 1, 1934, she

> "is willing to charge you and accept 4 per cent, but only on condition that you clean up the back taxes, and that interest rate to be effective for only one year, namely June, 1935."

Though the mortgagor did not comply with the stipulated condition, the mortgagee accepted, for more than two years, monthly checks for interest at the rate of 4 per cent. It is said that through the leniency thus shown to the mortgagor, the mortgagee has released the surety.

A contractual obligation may not be altered without the consent of the person who has assumed the obligation. The obligation of a surety or guarantor of due performance of a contract cannot be extended, without the surety's consent, to cover performance of a different contract. Alteration of the contractual obligation of the principal releases the surety, for the principal is no longer bound to perform the obligation guaranteed by the surety and the surety cannot be held responsible for the failure of the principal to perform any other obligation.

By "alteration" in the obligation of the principal, the principal is discharged from performance of the obligation in its original form and, in effect, a new obligation is substituted for the old. In those cases where we have held that alteration of any kind in the obligation of the principal discharges the surety, there has been a change in the nature of the obligation which might be required of the principal, performance of the old obligation might be more onerous but relief from the burden of the old was accompanied by the creation of rights and duties different from those which arose out of the original agreement. We have in such cases refused to balance the advantage of relief from the old burden against possible disadvantage imposed by the new.

Nothing said or decided by this court conflicts with the general rule that

> "A surety is none the less discharged by a change in the terms of the principal's contract for the performance of which the surety has bound himself when the change might not be disadvantageous to him. But an agreement merely to remit part of the performance due from the principal without changing its character as by lessening the amount of rent to be paid under a guaranteed lease, or by providing for a lower rate of interest on a debt than

> the contract provides for or by waiving a portion of the performance of a contract will not discharge the surety." (Williston on Contracts (Rev. ed.), § 1240.)

It follows that remission of a part of the interest even if such remission had been made by valid contract would not discharge the surety. Cambridge Sav. Bank v. Hyde, 131 Mass. 77, 41 Am. Rep. 193.

The effect of the agreement to accept, in monthly installments, interest which under the terms of the bond was payable every six months, presents a similar question though in different form. It is said that such agreement followed by acceptance of monthly check extended the time for the payment of the principal sum. The doctrine that extension of time for payment of the principal debt even for a few days discharges the surety, has been established by a long line of decisions. . . . In this case it is said that such a binding agreement arises from the receipt of checks for $50 intended as monthly payments of interest on the principal debt.

. . . The principal of the mortgage debt was long since due. The mortgagee might have demanded at any time payment both of principal and past due interest. There was no contract, express or implied, which would have given the principal debtor the right to refuse payment of principal and past due interest and there never was an instant of time when some interest was not past due. Even a binding agreement to accept payment of past due interest in monthly installments—and we do not intimate that here the mortgagee's agreement constituted more than a proffered favor without binding effect—would not have discharged the surety. . . .

. . . The surety guaranteed the performance of the obligation of the principal debtor. The creditor's agreement to forego part of his rights does not discharge the surety from responsibility for failure of performance by the principal debtor of that part of the original obligation which still remains and which remains untouched and unaffected by the creditor's remission of the remainder of the obligation. The surety is held to no obligation which he did not assume and if the surety meets that obligation he will be subrogated to the creditor's cause of action against the principal debtor, in accordance with the terms of the original contract.

. . . judgment granted for the plaintiff, ...

Review Questions

1. Distinguish between the broad concept of suretyship and the strict suretyship relation.
2. How does the undertaking of the strict surety differ from that of the guarantor?
3. Distinguish absolute guarantors from conditional guarantors.
4. Illustrate a surety relation employed as a credit device. Also illustrate a surety relation employed as a risk-bearing device.
5. Factually illustrate an unlimited and continuing guaranty.
6. What is the legal basis of the surety's right of indemnity?
7. Construct a fact situation under which the surety would be entitled to exercise his right of subrogation.
8. What is a surety's right of contribution?
9. What limitations must be placed upon the rule that such defenses as are available to the principal debtor are also available to the surety?

10. Illustrate a situation under which a surety would have a right of set-off against the person to whom he is obligated as a surety.
11. What acts or conduct on the part of the principal debtor and creditor may serve to discharge the surety from liability?
12. Is the surety discharged from liability by a material alteration of the contract between the principal debtor and creditor even though the alteration inures to his benefit?
13. By what expedient may the liability of the surety be preserved upon a release of the principal debtor?
14. Will a gratuitous promise from the creditor to the debtor to extend the time of payment discharge the surety?

Problems for Discussion

1. Rust called Yancey on the telephone and told him to let Grace have a two-horsepower motor, saying, "I believe his credit is good and anyway I will see that you are paid." Yancey is not paid and he looks to Rust for payment. Can Yancey recover from Rust?
2. X sells his business establishment to Y, who agrees to assume all existing business obligations. What is the relationship between X and Y?
3. Wills, a traveling salesman, had taken a large order for goods from Carrol. Upon the employer's refusal to send the goods on credit, Wills wrote: "If my indorsement is worth anything, send the goods to Carrol." The goods were sent and the employer, never having received payment, looks to Wills for satisfaction. Result?
4. Sims owed plaintiff a sum of money on open book account that was past due. Defendant, in consideration of an extension of time to Sims, indorsed on the account, "This bill will be paid in thirty days." The bill was not paid and plaintiff looks to defendant as an absolute guarantor. Defendant contends he is liable as a conditional guarantor. Decide.
5. An indorser upon a promissory note has waived presentment, notice, and protest. What is the nature of his liability?
6. Grant was surety on Lemke's obligation to Wall. Lemke had pledged certain bonds as security, which Wall held. The debt was not paid and Wall indulgently waited for three years. In the meantime, the bonds depreciated to a point where they were worthless. Wall now looks to Grant for payment. Grant resists upon the contention that Wall's failure to look to Lemke for payment and his failure to satisfy the obligation from the collateral securities discharged him from liability. Will Wall succeed?
7. Suppose that in the problem above Grant had limited his undertaking to that of a conditional guarantor. Would your conclusion be different?
8. Defendant executed the following agreement to plaintiff: "I will be responsible for Austin up to $500." Plaintiff extended credit to Austin to the amount of $1,634.73. Defendant contended that this was in violation of his agreement and that consequently he was relieved of all liability to plaintiff. Do you agree?
9. X contracted to erect a structure for plaintiff; upon this contract defendant was surety on his bond. X was in default of performance of the contract and plaintiff sent him the following letter: "Inasmuch as you are in default of

your performance, consider the contract between us terminated, cancelled, and at an end as of this day." Plaintiff then took over and completed the work and brought suit against defendant upon his surety bond to recover the damages suffered by X's breach of contract. Can he recover?

10. A borrowed $5,000 from the X bank, giving the bank his promissory note, which his wife signed as surety. Some days before the maturity of the note, A and the bank entered into an agreement to extend the note for one year. The note was not paid at its extended maturity and, since A was insolvent, the wife is looked to for payment. Can she be held?

42 SURETYSHIP AND INSURANCE

CONTRACTS OF INSURANCE

Under modern conditions the businessman faces the possibility of great financial loss because of the many risks to which he and his property are exposed. Few are the individuals who can afford to assume these risks. Insurance presents a method whereby the individual can shift these risks to others. In essence, insurance companies take contributions from the various policyholders for distribution to those who suffer an insured loss. It is thus possible for the individual by the payment of a relatively small fee (premium) to shift his risk of loss to the shoulders of the many like policyholders.

In recent years, the principle of insurance has been extended to almost every conceivable risk confronting the businessman. He can insure against death, injury, or illness to himself or his employees; against losses to his property that could result from natural causes or acts of man; against the infidelity of his employees; and against various types of personal liability that he might incur. It will be impossible to consider all the various types of insurance in vogue. The basic principles of the law of insurance will be presented with their application to the insurance of life and property.*

► I. INSURANCE DISTINGUISHED

In the interest of the public, insurers are subject to regulations by the state. Insurers may, for example, be required to obtain a license, deposit a specified sum of money with the superintendent of insurance, and make various reports. It thus becomes necessary to determine whether certain contracts are for insurance or for some other indemnity purpose as, for example, contracts of guaranty.† A mere risk-shifting contract is not a contract of insurance.

The elements by which an insurance contract is recognized are:

(1) The insured must have an interest that is subject to risk of loss—an insurable interest—

(2) which risk of loss the insurer assumes,

(3) for a premium paid by the insured,

(4) which premium is placed into a general fund with premiums from those who have insured like risks,

(5) out of which fund the insurer pays losses to those insured.

An insurance contract is, thus, not only a *risk-shifting* contract but also a *risk-distributing* contract.[1]

---

* See p. 257 for beneficiaries under life insurance contracts.
† See Young v. Stephenson, p. 239.
[1] In re Smiley's Estate, p. 1062.

► II. INSURABLE INTEREST

The basis of an insurance contract is that the insurer assumes a risk of the insured. If the element of risk is lacking, there can be no contract of insurance. This risk element is called *insurable interest,* and unless it exists, the contractual undertaking is a wager and unenforceable.* [2]

► III. INSURANCE CONTRACTS

A. FORM

As a matter of practice, insurance contracts are usually in written form. A contract of insurance *need* not, however, be in writing to be enforceable, except in a few states where such is required by statute. The obligation of an insurer is primary rather than secondary and does not come under the requirements of the Statute of Frauds.†

B. TIME OF ACCEPTANCE OF RISK

It is a matter of real importance for the insured to determine at what point of time his protection will begin. The basic rule is that the contract of insurance becomes effective at such time as all terms are agreed upon and accepted by the insurer and insured. This depends primarily upon (1) the intention of the parties (their agreement) and (2) the authority of the agent.

1. *Life Insurance*

A life insurance contract is entered into upon the basis of an application—an offer—by the insured. The unconditional acceptance of this application by the insurer will constitute the consummation of the contract of insurance. In *Bowman* v. *Northern Acc. Co.,* 124 Mo. App. 477, the court said that acceptance by the insurer must be indicated by "some outward manifestation of . . . assent." Issuance of the policy and delivery to the insured would in any event be an acceptance. However, some lesser act, such as notice of acceptance, could be sufficient to constitute an acceptance of the application.

As a matter of practice, insurance applications usually specify the conditions upon which the contract—assumption of risk—will become effective.[3] Usual provisions are the following:

(1) It is most common, for example, to provide that the applicant will become an insured risk from the date of his physical examination, providing the risk factors (such as health and family history) are as of that date in conformity with the standards of the insurer. If the applicant is an acceptable risk, he will be pro-

---

* See p. 224 for insurable interest.

† See p. 186.

[2] Cherokee Foundation v. Imperial Assur. Co., p. 1065.

[3] Smiley v. Prudential Ins. Co. of Am., p. 1066.

tected from such date without the need of a subsequent act of acceptance on the part of the insurer.

(2) The application or policy may specify that the contract of insurance is not effective until the policy has been delivered. This is typical when a physical examination of the applicant is not required.

(3) It may be provided that the policy is not effective until accepted by the applicant. Ordinarily, acceptance is not essential to the validity of the insurance contract. Where, however, the terms in the policy are substantially different from those contained in the application, the policy would be a counter offer and would require acceptance by the applicant before a contract could exist.

(4) It may be provided that the contract of insurance is not effective until the premium has been paid. In the absence of such a provision, the payment of the initial premium is not generally regarded as being essential to the existence of the contract.

Life insurance policies usually provide that the policy shall after the expiration of a stated period of time no longer be contestable by the insurer.[4]

2. *Fire Insurance*

Agents for fire insurance companies are very generally authorized to accept insurance applications. The acceptance of the application constitutes a preliminary or temporary contract of insurance, giving the applicant immediate protection until the policy of insurance is issued. This preliminary agreement can be of a very informal nature. Any oral or written understanding covering the essentials of (1) the property to be insured, (2) the amount of insurance, (3) the period of insurance, and (4) the premium to be paid is sufficient. To illustrate:

A orally requests B, agent of the X Insurance Company, to insure his business establishment for $20,000 for a period of three years. B assures A that he is covered and that the policy will be mailed to him. This constitutes a temporary insurance contract providing B has authority to contract for his principal. Even though the amount of the premium has not been determined, it is understood between the parties that the usual standardized rate will apply.

Of course, if it cannot be established that the agent has authority to bind the insurance company, an acceptance of the application must be made by the latter before there can be a contract.

► IV. REASONS PERMITTING AVOIDANCE OF CONTRACT

A. CONCEALMENT

Concealment consists of the failure of the applicant to disclose any fact that has a bearing upon the risk he is seeking to insure. It is the applicant's duty to disclose all facts known to him that enter into an evaluation of the risk. His in-

[4] Richardson v. Travelers Ins. Co., p. 1068.

tentional failure to do so gives the insurer basis for avoiding the contract. To illustrate:

(1) In *Orient Ins. Co.* v. *Peiser,* 91 Ill. App. 278, it was said that where the applicant failed to disclose his knowledge of a fire in the neighborhood of the property he was insuring, the contract of insurance could be avoided.

(2) In *Goldstein* v. *New York Life Ins. Co.,* 162 N.Y.S. 1088, the applicant, before delivery of the policy, failed to disclose that he had undergone a serious operation just prior to the delivery of the policy. The court held this to be fraudulent concealment defeating recovery on the policy.

B. MISREPRESENTATIONS

A representation is a statement made by the applicant to the insurer as an inducement to enter into the contract. If the representation is false and the facts misrepresented are *material* to the risk, the contract may be avoided by the insurer.[5] This is true whether the misrepresentation is intentionally or innocently made. In either event, the insurer has been misled.

Unless the fact misrepresented is material to the risk, it will have no effect upon the contract. In *Schwarzbach* v. *Ohio Valley Protective Union,* 25 W. Va. 622, the court defined a material fact as being "one which would probably have caused the policy not to be issued or caused a change of the terms, on which it was issued." To illustrate:

(1) In *National Mutual Fire Ins. Co.* v. *Duncan,* 44 Colo. 472, it was held that representing a building as being twenty by thirty feet when in fact it was sixteen by twenty-four feet was in itself not material to the risk.

(2) A statement by an applicant that he is solvent when in fact he is insolvent would be material to the risk. As the courts have said, "It affects the moral hazard."

(3) In *Metropolitan Life Ins. Co.* v. *Moravec,* 214 Ill. 186, it was held that a misrepresentation by the applicant that he had never had heart disease was material although the applicant was not suffering from heart disease at the time of the application.

By agreement, the parties may make any representation of fact material. For example, the policy may provide that it will be void if any fact has been misrepresented.

C. WARRANTIES

A warranty, as distinguished from a representation, is a statement by the insured that is made a part of the contract. As such, under the common law rule, the validity of the contract is conditioned upon the literal truth of the statement, regardless of its materiality to the risk.[6]

In most of the states, the harshness of this common law rule has been removed by statutory provision to the effect that the policy cannot be avoided for failure

[5] Sorter v. Citizens Fund Mut. Fire Ins. Co., p. 1069.

[6] Michigan Millers Mut. F. Ins. Co. v. Grange Oil Co., p. 1070.

of a warranty unless, like misrepresentations, it is material to the risk. Under the common law rule, it has been held that where the statements in the application for life insurance are made warranties, a false statement of the applicant's place of residence makes the policy voidable even though it is not material to the risk.

D. CONDITIONS SUBSEQUENT—PROMISSORY WARRANTIES

Insurance policies contain various conditions upon which the continued validity of the policies depend.[7, 8] These provisions are called *conditions subsequent* or *promissory warranties.*

1. *Life Insurance*

Conditions subsequent as found in life insurance policies usually relate to such things as residence, occupation, travel, and habits of the insured. Thus, a policy may provide that the insured may not change his occupation without the consent of the insurer. A breach of such a condition will relieve the insurer from further liability.

2. *Fire Insurance*

Conditions found in fire insurance policies are most varied. The following, as contained in the Iowa Standard Optional Coverage Policy, are typical.

"III. This policy shall be void if the insured has concealed or misrepresented any material fact or circumstance concerning this insurance or the subject thereof.

"IV. Unless otherwise provided by agreement of this company this policy shall be void:

(a) If the insured now has or shall hereafter procure any other contract of insurance, valid or invalid, on the property covered in whole or in part by this policy; or

(b) If the subject of insurance be a manufacturing establishment, and it cease to be operated for more than ten consecutive days; or

(c) If the building herein described, whether intended for occupancy by the owner or tenant, be or become vacant or unoccupied and so remain for ten consecutive days; or

(d) If the interest of the insured be other than unconditional and sole ownership; or

(e) If the subject of insurance be a building on ground not owned by the insured; or

(f) If any change other than by death of the insured, whether by legal proceedings, judgment, voluntary act of the insured or otherwise, take place in the interest, title, possession or use of the subject of insurance, if such change in the possession or use makes the risk more hazardous; or

(g) If the subject of insurance or a part thereof (as to the part so encum-

---

[7] Mitter v. Home Ins. Co., p. 1070.

[8] Wallace v. Virginia Surety Co., p. 1072.

bered) be or become encumbered by lien, mortgage or otherwise created by voluntary act of the insured or within his control; or

(h) If the property insured or any part thereof (as to the part so removed) be removed to any other building or location than that specified in the policy; or

(i) If this policy be assigned before loss.

"V. Unless otherwise provided by agreement of this company, this policy shall be void:

(a) If the subject of insurance be a manufacturing establishment, and it be operated in whole or in part at night later than 10 o'clock; or

(b) If the hazard be increased by any means within the knowledge of the insured; or

(c) If mechanics be employed in building, altering or repairing the within described premises for more than fifteen days at any one time; or

(d) If illuminating gas or vapor be generated in any building covered hereby, or on any premises adjacent thereto for use upon the insured premises; or

(e) If there be kept, used, or allowed on the within described premises benzine, benzole, dynamite, ether, fireworks, gasoline, Greek fire, gunpowder exceeding twenty-five pounds in quantity, naphtha, nitroglycerine, or other explosives, phosphorus, calcium carbide, petroleum or any of its products of greater inflammability than kerosene of lawful standard, which last named article may be used for lights and kept for sale according to law, in quantities not exceeding five barrels; or

(f) If the insured permits the property which is the subject of insurance, or any part thereof, to be used for any unlawful purpose.

"Provided that nothing contained in paragraph five herein shall operate to avoid this policy in any case, if the insured shall establish that the failure to observe and comply with such provisions and conditions did not contribute to the loss.

"VI. This company shall not be liable for loss caused directly or indirectly by invasion, insurrection, riot, civil war, or military or usurped power, or by theft, or by neglect of the insured to use all reasonable means to save and preserve the property during and after a fire, or when the property is endangered by fire in neighboring premises; or (unless fire ensues, and, in that event, for damage by fire only) by explosion of any kind or by lightning; but liability for direct damage by lightning may be assumed by specific agreement.

"VII. This company shall not be liable for loss or damage to any property covered by this policy if the insured shall fail to pay any written obligation given to the company for the premium or any assessment or installment of premium when due; provided the company shall have given the insured notice as required by law. Upon payment and acceptance by the company of the delinquent premium, assessment or installment of premium before loss occurs, or after loss, if the company shall have had notice thereof and accepts such payment, this policy shall be revived and in full force according to its terms.

"VIII. If a building or any part thereof fall, except as the result of fire, all insurance by this policy on such building, or its contents, shall immediately cease."

V. EXTENT OF RECOVERY

A. FIRE INSURANCE

The amount that the insured can recover under a contract of insurance is dependent upon the (1) extent of the loss and (2) nature of the policy, whether it is an *open policy* or a *valued policy.*

1. *Valued Policy*

Many of the states have enacted what are called *valued policy laws.* These laws provide that

> "whenever . . . the property insured shall be wholly destroyed without criminal fault on the part of the insured . . . , the amount of the insurance written in such policy shall be taken conclusively to be the true loss and measure of damages when destroyed."

This means, then, that under such a policy the insured can recover the face value if there is a total destruction of the property.

If the property insured under a valued policy is only partially destroyed, the measure of recovery is the fair cash or market value of the property at the time of its destruction, but not to exceed the face value of the policy.

2. *Open Policy*

Under an open policy, the insured can recover only the actual loss he has sustained—such loss as he is prepared to prove. The measure of the loss is the fair cash or market value at the time of the loss. In no event can the insured recover in excess of the value of the policy. To illustrate:

A insures his house for the sum of $10,000, and it is totally destroyed by fire. Being an open policy, A can recover only the actual loss, which may be less than $10,000. Under a valued policy, A could recover the $10,000 regardless of the actual loss.

3. *Partial or Total Loss*

Regardless of the type of policy, in the event of a partial loss, the insured can recover only the actual amount of the loss but not exceeding the amount fixed in the policy. Whether a loss is total or partial is entirely a question of fact. In general, the test of a total loss is not whether the property has been physically destroyed but whether it has been rendered useless for the purposes for which it was employed at the time it was insured. To illustrate:

In *Teter* v. *Franklin Fire Ins. Co.,* 74 W. Va. 344, it was held that a total loss had been suffered although the walls of the building were still standing after the fire, they being, however, so out of plumb that a prudent man would not use them in restoring the building.

► VI. COINSURANCE CLAUSES

Owners are frequently inclined to insure their property against fire for considerably less than its value. To encourage owners to carry a greater degree of coverage, insurance companies use what is called a *coinsurance clause* in the policy. The encouragement to insure the property more fully is obtained by provision in the coinsurance clause that (1) if the owner insures his property up to a designated percentage (ordinarily 80 per cent) of its value, he will be given a lower insurance rate (premium) and (2) if he fails to carry coverage up to the designated percentage, he will bear a part of the loss. He would thus become a coinsurer of his own property. To illustrate:

A insures his $40,000 business house for $20,000 under a policy that contains an 80 per cent coinsurance clause. In the event of a $16,000 loss, the insured could recover only that percentage of the loss as the amount of the insurance bears to 80 per cent of the value of the property. This would be $\frac{\$20{,}000}{\$32{,}000\ (80\%\ \text{of}\ \$40{,}000)}$ which would be five eighths of the loss of $16,000. Thus the insurance company would be liable for only $10,000 of the loss and the owner would be a coinsurer for the balance of $6,000.

► VII. CONCURRENT INSURANCE

It is a common practice for owners to insure their property with more than one insurance company. But, regardless of the total amount of the insurance carried, the insured can recover only the amount of the actual loss suffered. Consequently, there is no point in carrying an excessive amount of insurance.

It is the practice for the insurer to provide in the policy for the division of loss where the insured carries insurance with several companies. The usual provision is that the insurer will not be responsible for a greater proportion of the loss than the amount of the policy bears to the total insurance on the property. To illustrate:

A insures his business property with the X insurance Co. for $10,000, with the Y Insurance Co. for $10,000, and with the Z Insurance Co. for $5,000. He now suffers a total fire loss which is determined to be $20,000. The policy of the X Insurance Co. is two fifths of the total insurance upon the property, which would make them liable for two fifths of the loss, namely, $8,000. The Y Insurance Co. would, by the same token, be liable for $8,000, and the Z Insurance Co. for the balance of $4,000.

► VIII. SUBROGATION *

In the event that the insured suffers a loss for which a third person—wrongdoer—is responsible, the insurer might be relieved of liability. The position of the insurer is dependent upon whether the insured receives payment for the loss from the wrongdoer, the one who is legally responsible for the loss. The right of subrogation does not apply to life insurance contracts, but only to those in which the insurer undertakes to indemnify the insured for an actual loss suffered.

A. PAYMENT MADE BY WRONGDOER

When the insured receives satisfaction from the wrongdoer, the insurer is relieved from liability. The purpose of insurance (other than life insurance) is to compensate the insured for the actual loss suffered. Consequently, if he is fully indemnified for the loss, the insurer has no responsibility to him.

B. PAYMENT MADE BY INSURER

When the insurer compensates the insured for the loss, he acquires the right of the insured to recover from the wrongdoer. This right of substitution is called *subrogation.* To illustrate:

If A's property is destroyed by fire due to the negligence of B, the latter is legally responsible for the loss. Should the X Insurance Co., with whom the property is insured, pay A the loss, they will acquire A's right of recovery against B, the wrongdoer.

CASES

CASE NO. 1

In re Smiley's Estate. 216 P. (2d) 212 (Wash.) (1950)

GRADY, J. This case is before the court to review a judgment approving a determination made by the inheritance tax and escheat division that the proceeds of "single premium policies" were not insurance exemptions provided in Rem. Rev. Stat. (Sup.) § 1121 1b. The appellant is the executor of the will of Eva B. Smiley, deceased, and the respondent is the supervisor of the inheritance tax and escheat division.

On September 28, 1935, Eva B. Smiley deposited with The Equitable Life Assurance Society of the United States the sum of $18,770.00 and received what was designated a single premium life insurance policy in the sum of $20,000.00 payable upon her death to certain named beneficiaries. On that date the decedent paid to the same society the sum of $2,430.00 and received from it a non-refund life annuity by which the society promised to pay to her the sum of $73.91 quarterly during her lifetime. On October 1, 1935, she deposited with Equitable Life Insurance Company of Iowa the sum of $18,700.60 and received what was designated a single payment life insurance policy for the sum of $20,000.00 payable upon death substantially as provided in the other similar contract. On that date she

* See p. 1042.

paid to the same company the sum of $3,299.40 and received a non-refund life annuity payable in the sum of $480.39 annually during her lifetime. At that time the decedent was of the age of seventy-eight years. She was not required to take any physical examination as to her suitability as an insurance risk. At the time of her death, which occurred on November 4, 1945, the decedent was eighty-seven years of age.

A controversy arose between the executor and the inheritance tax and escheat division as to whether the amounts derived from the two policies were taxable. If they were insurance proceeds they were subject to an exemption to the extent of $40,000.00, but if the moneys represented by them were transfers or gifts made or intended to take effect in possession or enjoyment after the death of the decedent, the estate was indebted to the state in the sum of $8,824.71. For convenience we shall refer to the documents as contracts and annuities respectively.

The theory advanced by respondent is that the contract and annuity in each case must be considered together as one transaction, and when this is done and the substance and reality of the transactions are considered, it becomes apparent that regardless of what they are labeled the contracts are not life insurance policies because the essential characteristics of risk-shifting and risk-distributing historically and commonly involved in a life insurance contract are absent. . . .

In support of its contention that the contracts constitute life insurance policies appellant advances the theory that the annuities are separate and distinct from the respective contracts made on the same dates, and they were not dependent upon each other; that the statutory definition of "insurance," formerly set forth in Rem. Rev. Stat. § 7032, and the essential elements of an insurance contract mentioned in State ex rel. Fishback v. Universal Service Agency, 87 Wash. 413, 151 Pac. 768, Ann. Cas. 1916C, 1017, bring the contracts into the field of insurance in that there existed a peril or risk, to the decedent which was insured against, and thereby the situation presented is distinguishable from those appearing in the cases upon which respondent relies. The appellant argues that in those cases it was found as a fact that the respective contracts and annuities were dependent upon each other in that the insurance company would not have made one without the other, and when thus considered it was concluded that as the total consideration was prepaid and exceeded the face value of the "insurance" policy, any risk taken by the insurance company that the prepayment would earn less than the amount paid to the "insured" as an annuity was an investment risk similar to the risk assumed by a bank but was not an insurance risk. The distinction sought to be drawn is that by our statutory definition of insurance the risk element is a risk to the insured rather than to the insurer.

We are of the opinion that each contract and annuity must be construed together for the purposes of this case. The question before the court is the nature of the contracts between the decedent and the companies and whether the amounts derived from the contracts are proceeds of insurance within the meaning of the inheritance tax statutes. In our determination of this question we must be guided by the substance or effect of the transaction rather than the particular form or label adopted. This maxim has had frequent application in inheritance tax cases. . . .

We are not in accord with the contention of appellant that our statutory definition of insurance as applied to a life insurance policy is limited to a risk to the insured. The statutory definition was a part of Rem. Rev. Stat. § 7032, and was as follows:

> "Insurance is a contract whereby one party called the 'insurer,' for a consideration, undertakes to pay money or its equivalent, or to do an act valuable to another party called the 'insured,' or to his 'beneficiary,' upon the happening of the hazard or peril insured against, whereby the party insured or his beneficiary suffers loss or injury."

. . .

In effect this definition of insurance is no different than set forth in In re Knight's Estate, 31 Wash. (2d) 813, 199 P. (2d) 89. Inherent in all life insurance is a general scheme to distribute actual losses among a large group of persons bearing similar risks, and as a consideration for the insurer's promise the insured makes a ratable contribution to a general insurance fund called a premium. Life insurance involves both risk-shifting and risk-distributing. A contract may be a risk-shifting device, but to be a contract of insurance, which is a risk-distributing device, it must possess both features, and unless it does it is not a contract of insurance whatever be its name or its form. Helvering v. Le Gierse, 312 U.S. 531, 61 Sup. Ct. 646, 85 L.Ed. 996; Vance on Insurance (2d ed.) 1, §§ 1–3. The ordinary life insurance policy is a contract by which the insured pays to the insurance company a sum of money at fixed intervals of time, and in return the insurance company promises to pay a stated sum of money upon his death to the beneficiary named therein. The beneficiary is usually some person who is beneficially interested in the continuity of life of the insured, and the purpose of the insurance is to protect him against the hazard of death and compensate him for the loss sustained by the death of the insured. The hazard or risk taken by the insurance company is that the insured may die before he had paid enough premiums, which together with any income therefrom makes an amount less than the amount the insurance company has undertaken to pay. The hazard or risk taken by the insured or the beneficiaries is the death of the former. The contracts in question contain many of the usual provisions to be found in life insurance policies, but the inclusion of these provisions is not determinative. When we look to the substance of both transactions and consider realities we find in the case of one company that it received from the decedent the sum of $21,200.00. The company promised to pay to the decedent a total of $295.64 annually during her lifetime. This amounted to nothing more than interest on the total amount received at the rate of approximately 1.4 per cent. In the case of the other company it received $22,000.00 and promised to pay to the decedent $480.39 per annum during her lifetime. This would amount to interest on the total amount received at the rate of approximately 2.2 per cent. The objective to be attained was not insurance upon the life of the decedent, but a method and means whereby she might place a part of her property in safe and responsible hands to be delivered upon her death to certain named persons, and we cannot find in such an arrangement any hazard or risk to any one. We do not wish to be understood by anything we have said in this opinion that there may not be a valid life insurance policy with a lump sum premium paid in advance, but it must be insurance in fact and not a tax-evading device. . . .

The judgment is affirmed.

CASE NO. 2

Cherokee Foundries v. Imperial Assur. Co. 188 Tenn. 349, 219 S.W. (2d) 203, 9 A.L.R. (2d) 177 (1949)

TOMLINSON, J. Fry and Stewart, trading as Cherokee Foundries, Inc., sued Imperial Assurance Company for $12,000.00 on an alleged insurance contract for damages done to an iron foundry by a fire of unknown origin on the night of April 30–May 1, 1946. . . .

Cherokee Foundries entered into an oral contract of purchase of this foundry from its owners, Jones Machinery & Foundry Company, for a cash consideration of $25,000.00. . . .

The deed of conveyance from Jones Machinery & Foundry Company to Cherokee Foundries, the deed of trust and the note to be executed by the latter and opinion on title, were all prepared during the day of April 30, 1946, and placed in the keeping of American Trust and Banking Company. The parties were to meet at this bank on the morning of May 1 for the purpose of executing and delivery of these various instruments and payment of the purchase price, thereby completing the transaction.

During the afternoon of April 30, Cherokee Foundries, acting through Stewart, called at the office of L. W. Rhodes, who was the agent in Chattanooga for Imperial Assurance Company, for the purpose of procuring fire insurance of $12,000.00 upon the building and equipment of this foundry. Rhodes issued on that date an invoice wherein it was recited that fire insurance policy in the amount of $12,000.00 of Imperial Assurance Company covered "building and contents of foundry, the policy to expire 4-30-47." This invoice was placed in the mail and received by Cherokee Foundries in due course on May 1, 1946. The policy was never issued and premium therefor was never paid, though tendered and refused some days later. The policy which would have been issued did not contain a clause providing for sole and unconditional ownership of the property by the insured.

At the close of the work day at the foundry on April 30, the key to the place was turned over to Cherokee Foundries. The employees were assembled and told by Cherokee Foundries that their employment would continue except that commencing the next morning (May 1) their employer would be Cherokee Foundries.

Some time during that night the foundry building and its contents were almost completely destroyed by the aforesaid fire. The deed, note and deed of trust heretofore mentioned were never executed. Jones Machinery and Foundry Company collected fire insurance in an unknown amount on a policy or policies which it carried. About three weeks later it conveyed the real estate upon which the foundry had been located and the damaged equipment to Cherokee Foundries for a consideration of $5,500.00. . . .

The question is whether Cherokee Foundries had an insurable interest in the property damaged or destroyed by the fire. It is elementary that it cannot recover if it did not have such interest. Our search has failed to find any case of our own deciding this question on the facts which we have here.

Baird v. Fidelity-Phoenix Fire Ins. Co., 178 Tenn. 653, 663, 667, 162 S.W. (2d) 384, 390, 140 A.L.R. 1226, by quotation from Aetna Ins. Co. v. Miers, 37 Tenn. 139, 141, said:

" 'What is an insurable interest in property, is not very clearly and distinctly settled in the books. It is said that it may be proved, without the evidence of any legal or equitable title to the property insured . . . any interest in the subject matter, or property insured, is sufficient to sustain an insurance of real estate.'"

Undoubtedly, the majority rule, and possibly the unanimous rule, by which it is to be determined whether the insured had an insurable interest in the destroyed property is that stated by the decision in 1896 of the U.S. Supreme Court in Harrison v. Fortlage, 161 U.S. 57, 16 Sup. Ct. 488, 490, 40 L.Ed. 616, 619, as follows:

"It is well settled that any person has an insurable interest in property, by the existence of which he will gain an advantage, or by the destruction of which he will suffer a loss, whether he has or has not any title in, or lien upon, or possession of the property."

The point upon which Courts disagree is whether there is any insurable interest in a prospective purchaser under a contract that is unenforceable by or against such person. That is the situation we have here, because the oral contract in question comes within the provisions of our Statute of Frauds. . . .

The text of 29 American Jurisprudence, page 294, referring to a party to the contract is this:

"However, one has no insurable interest in a thing the only right to which arises under a contract which is void or unenforceable, either at law or in equity."

From the moment Cherokee Foundries applied for this insurance to the moment of the next day when the parties were to meet at the bank and complete the transaction, it was a matter entirely within the whim and caprice of Cherokee Foundries as to whether it would pay the purchase price and take the property if the seller elected (a matter, too, entirely subject to its whim) to let the Cherokee Foundries have the property for the stated purchase price, or at all. Either could repudiate the oral agreement with impunity, because of the Statute of Frauds. . . .

So, whether the insurance policy in question was a policy coupled with an interest was eventually dependent upon the whim of either the Cherokee Foundries or the seller. As a matter of fact, one or both of the parties did elect not to go on with the contract on the next morning. The deeds, etc., remained unexecuted. The proposed seller collected the insurance which it carried as the owner of the property partially destroyed by the fire. It subsequently sold what was left of it to Cherokee Foundries under a new agreement.

On principle, the sound rule seems to be that one whose only right of purchase is under an oral contract which is unenforceable against him or the seller, and who, in fact, either at his own instance or that of the seller, or both, elected finally to reject the contract, ought not to be allowed to recover on an insurance policy for a fire which occurred during the existence of that status between the parties. An opposite conclusion can lead only to confusion and doubt as to when such an insurance contract is a wager policy or one coupled with an insurable interest, and would be, it seems to us, contrary to sound public policy.

For the reasons stated, we are in agreement with the holding of the Court of Appeals that under the facts of this case Cherokee Foundries did not have an insurable interest in the foundry. . . .

CASE NO. 3

Smiley v. Prudential Ins. Co. of America. 321 Mich. 60, 32 N.W. (2d) 48 (1948)

SHARPE, J. This is an action by the beneficiary named in an application for a life insurance policy.

The material facts are as follows:

On July 14, 1943, Errol Smiley made application to the Detroit office of the Prudential Life Insurance Company of America for a ten-year term policy of life insurance in the amount of $9,000. At the time the application was signed, Errol Smiley paid the first annual premium in the amount of $118.80 and signed the following statement which was a part of the application:

"I agree that: . . .

"(4) unless the full first premium is paid at the time of making this application, the policy shall take effect only if issued by the Company and received by me or by the other applicant, if any, and the full first premium thereon is paid, all while my health, habits and occupation and any other conditions remain as described in the application, in which case the insurance shall be deemed to have taken effect as of the date on the face of the policy; (5) if at the time of signing this application the full first premium is paid, the insurance shall be deemed to have taken effect as of the date of Part 1 or 2 of this application, whichever is the later, unless otherwise specifically requested in this application, provided the application is approved and accepted by the Company at its Home Office in Newark, New Jersey, in accordance with the plan, premium and amount of insurance applied for."

On the same day, Mr. Smiley was given a physical examination by a physician employed by the insurance company and an assistant district superintendent recommended the risk for acceptance. On July 17, 1943, Errol Smiley developed severe pains in the stomach, later found to be caused by a ruptured ulcer. He was taken to a hospital, operated on and died July 23, 1943. The application did not reach the desk of the person at the home office, authorized to accept or reject it, until July 26th, three days after the death of Smiley. On the same day the home office had information that an operation had been performed on Mr. Smiley. It then rejected the application and later refused to pay the claim.

In Olson v. American Central States Life Insurance Co., 172 Minn. 511, 216 N.W. 225, 226, the application, which was signed by the applicant on September 12, 1925, read in part as follows:

"I desire policy issued as of date, and I agree that the period to cover which the first premium is paid shall end one year after said date and that each policy year shall end on successive anniversaries of said date. I also agree that the insurance hereby applied for shall not take effect until the payment of the first premium thereon, and the approval of this application by the company."

The applicant was examined by defendant's medical examiner on September 14, 1925, and paid the first premium on September 16, 1925. The application was received at the home office on September 16, 1925, and the medical examiner's report arrived on September 17, 1925. On September 18, 1925, the applicant was stricken with infantile paralysis and died therefrom on September 23, 1925. On September 25, 1925, notice of the applicant's illness reached the home office and the application was rejected two days after the applicant died.

The court said:

"It is well settled that an application for life insurance is a mere proposal and like any other offer does not become a contract until accepted. . . . But plaintiff argues that unless the insurance began on the date of the application the premium would cover a period during which defendant did not assume the risk, and the insured would be paying for insurance for a period when he was not insured. . . .

"That the assent of both parties to the same set of terms is necessary to create a contract is axiomatic. An offer never becomes a contract until accepted. Where an application provides that the insurance shall not take effect until the approval of the application by the insurer, no contract of insurance exists prior to such approval, although the application also provides that the policy shall bear the same date as the application and that the time covered by the premium shall be measured from that date." . . .

In the case at bar the application and receipt for premium paid contained a promise to return the premium paid if the policy applied for was not issued. It also contained a proviso that the policy would be issued as applied for provided said application is approved and accepted at the home office. Under the application the insurance company reserved the right to accept the application and until the same was accepted there was no binding contract between the applicant and the insurance company. It also follows that there was no interim insurance.

CASE NO. 4

Richardson v. Travelers Ins. Co. 171 F. (2d) 699, 7 A.L.R. (2d) 501 (1948)

ORR, C.J. In 1926 appellant, then and now living in the state of California, made application to appellee for a policy of life insurance in the amount of $10,000 on a so-called "Uniform Premium Plan." Through an alleged mistake of its officers and scriveners at its home office in Hartford, Connecticut, appellee issued appellant a $10,000 policy known as a "Pension Policy, age 65." The one difference between the policy alleged to have been applied for and the one issued is that under the latter the insured is entitled upon maturity to receive benefits in twice the amount afforded by the former. The premium inscribed on the issued contract, which was paid by appellant throughout the life of the policy, was somewhat over one-half the premium appellee normally requires for its "Pension Policy, age 65."

Although the policy was in the hands of the insurance company for loan purposes on several occasions after its issuance, the alleged error was not discovered because the company's loan division has no connection with its policy writing division. In March of 1946 appellee first became aware of the alleged mistake and sought appellant's consent to a substitution of the policy applied for in place of the one issued. Upon appellant's refusal to agree to the substitution, appellee brought this action for reformation of the insurance contract. . . . The trial court ordered the policy to be reformed, relying on cases supporting its finding that a suit for reformation of an insurance policy is not a contest of the policy. . . .

. . . the important question is the construction that should be placed on the incontestable clause contained in the policy issued. The clause reads:

"This contract shall be incontestable after one year from date of issue, except for non-payment of premiums."

. . . The provisions setting forth optional payments upon maturity of the policy are integral parts of the written contract, and are included in the reference, "this contract shall be incontestable. . . ." It seems logical to assume that an action to reform portions of a document involves contesting their validity.

We believe this conclusion is supported by a consideration of the purposes for which incontestable clauses have been inserted in life insurance policies. It is generally agreed that the origin of the clause may be found in the competitive idea of offering to policy holders assurance that their dependents would be the recipients of a protective fund rather than a lawsuit. . . . Too often had an insurer obtained a judicial determination upon maturity of a policy that the insured had made an inaccurate statement in his application, or was guilty of fraud which resulted in the avoidance of liability under the policy. . . . The clause remedied this situation by rendering the insurer's promise to perform in accordance with the statements and terms in the policy absolute upon the passing of a specified time, expressly subject only to the non-payment of premiums. Many states have evidenced their favor toward the incontestable clause by enacting legislation requiring it in life insurance policies. . . .

Logically the coverage of this clause should extend to those defenses of the insurer which could be conceivably raised within the contractual period of contestability. . . . These inception defenses would include misrepresentation, fraud, breach of condition or warranty, mistake and lack of insurable interest . . . but the other inception defenses, without exception, are the very objects for which the incontestable clause was originated. . . .

Reversed. . . .

CASE NO. 5

Sorter v. Citizens Fund Mut. Fire Ins. Co. 151 Neb. 686, 39 N.W. (2d) 276 (1949)

BOSLAUGH, J. This is an action at law by appellant to recover on a policy of insurance issued to him by appellee, the amount of loss claimed to have been sustained by appellant from the destruction by fire of the property described in the policy.

Appellee . . . asserted that the contract of insurance was obtained by fraud and misrepresentation; that to secure the policy of insurance appellant represented that he was the owner and in lawful possession of the real estate described in the policy; . . . that he was not the owner of the real estate and had no interest therein; . . . that the insurance contract contains a provision that it shall be void if the interest of the insured is other than unconditional and sole ownership, or if the subject of insurance is a building on ground not owned by the insured in fee simple; . . .

The provision that no representation or warranty made in the negotiation for a contract of insurance by the insured is material or can defeat or avoid a policy of insurance unless the representation or warranty deceived the insurer to its injury is pertinent to the disposition of this case. S. 44-358, R.S. 1943. . . . If untrue statements of the insured, material to the risk, are made to the company and they are believed and acted upon by it in the issuance and delivery of a contract so that the company is obligated when it would not have done so had a truthful disclosure been made in the negotiations, it is clear that the company was deceived to its injury, and the statute does not deprive it of a remedy. . .

The representations of appellant as shown by the evidence above related were concerning matters peculiarly within his knowledge and were material to the risk. The general agent of appellee . . . testified he relied and acted upon the representations of appellant, and that the company would not have issued and delivered the policy of insurance if the appellant had reported the fact that the building was not located on land belonging to him but was in a public street of the city of Lincoln.

There is nothing to dispute his statements in this record. . . .

Affirmed.

CASE NO. 6

Michigan Millers Mut. F. Ins. Co. v. Grange Oil Co. 175 F. (2d) 540, 10 A.L.R. (2d) 209 (1949)

ORR, C.J. This appeal is from a judgment awarding appellee the sum of $16,352.20, balance due on a fire insurance policy.

The policy was of the provisional stock type, designed to provide coverage for a fluctuating stock of goods in such a manner that the goods are at all times fully protected but never over-insured when the stocks are low. By its terms the insured was required to make monthly reports of the value of stock on hand and the amount of nonprovisional insurance carried on the stock. . . .

The value of the stock destroyed by fire is admitted to be $121,410.31. During the period in question appellee was actually carrying non-provisional insurance in the sum of $33,333.00. Through mistake appellee reported the amount of non-provisional insurance as $50,000. In settling for the fire loss appellant used $50,000, the amount of the reported non-provisional insurance, in arriving at its liability. Appellee contended, and the trial court found, that $33,333, the actual amount of non-provisional insurance carried by it, should have been used. . . .

Appellant argues that failure of appellee to make correct reports of non-provisional insurance constituted a breach of a promissory warranty. There is no stipulation, provision or agreement in the insurance policy to the effect that appellee's failure to furnish true reports shall constitute a condition or warranty. Such a stipulation, provision or agreement is required under the laws of Oregon (which control here), in the absence of which, the provisions in the policy under consideration in this case must be construed as a simple covenant. . . .

CASE NO. 7

Mitter et al. v. Home Insurance Co. 49 S.D. 319, 207 N.W. 49 (1926)

The plaintiff brought action for theft of an automobile insured by the defendant. The policy provided:

"(2) It is a condition of this policy that it shall be null and void: (a) If the automobile . . . shall be used for carrying passengers for compensation . . . during the term of this policy. . . .

"This policy is made and accepted subject to provisions, exclusions, conditions, and warranties set forth. . . ."

While the automobile was being used to transport a passenger for hire from the plaintiff's farm to Martin, S.D., it was stolen by the passenger.

MORIARTY, J. In dealing with warranties such as that now under consideration the courts have devoted most of their attention to the force of the word *use, using* or *used,* as found in policies of insurance. What treatment of property is sufficient to constitute using it in a manner prohibited by the terms of the policy?

Upon the question there is great divergence of authority. With reference to their position on this question the decisions may be classified under three distinct heads:

First, those which hold that a single instance of the property being treated contrary to the strict wording of the prohibition is sufficient to constitute a breach of the warranty.

Second, those which hold that

single, occasional, or incidental treatment of the property is not sufficient to constitute a breach; that using, keeping, storing, allowing, etc., mean repeated, usual or customary treatment of the property or of the prohibited substance.

Third, those holding that single, occasional, or unusual treatment of the property, or of the prohibited substance, merely suspends the liability while such treatment continues; that if no loss results from the prohibited treatment the insurance is revived by the cessation of the treatment, . . .

. . . Farmers' State Bank of Parker v. Tri-State Fire Ins. Co., 41 S.D. 398, 170 N.W. 638, . . . cites with approval authorities holding that:

> "What is intended to be prohibited is the habitual use of such articles, not their exceptional use upon some emergency."

In that case the provision was that the policy should become void if gasoline " 'be kept, used, or allowed' on the insured premises." The court held that a single instance of using a mixture of kerosene and gasoline to remove rust from the machinery in the insured building did not avoid the liability of the insurer. But it is evident that the court did not intend to pass upon the effect of the prohibition where the loss is admittedly due to the presence of the prohibited substances, for the court says:

> "Whether the presence of the above mixture of gasoline and kerosene was the cause of the fire or not is by no means clear."

This language would be entirely unnecessary had the court intended to hold that the question whether the prohibited substance caused the loss was immaterial. The use of the language indicates that the court recognized the existence of the distinction, and did not wish to be understood as passing upon it. . . .

To hold that a prohibited use must have become usual or habitual to avoid the liability is equivalent to saying that, if an insurer seeks to exempt itself from liability for a loss occasioned by a use so perilous that loss is almost certain to result from the first occasion of such use, the insurer's effort to escape liability must fail, because there is no possibility of the use being repeated frequently enough to make it habitual or usual use. In other words, the more glaring and certain the peril the more nearly impossible becomes the effort to avoid liability for the loss occasioned by it.

To do this is to destroy the right to make a binding contract. The only escape from such fallacious doctrine is either to hold with those courts which construe the words of the contract strictly and say that a single instance of the prohibited act absolutely terminates the contract beyond revival, and those which seeking to avoid inequitable forfeitures, hold that even a single instance of a prohibited use of condition suspends the liability while the prohibited use of condition continues, but the insurance is revived when such use of condition ceases. . . .

The doctrine necessarily requires release from liability where the loss occurs during the violation and is caused by such violation.

The general rule as to the suspension of liability is thus stated in Elliott on Insurance, § 205:

> "The weight of authority seems to support the view that a violation of a condition that works a forfeiture of the policy merely suspends the insurance during the violation, and if the violation is discontinued during the life of the policy, and does not exist at the time of the loss, the policy

revives and the company is liable."

As the car involved in the instant case was being used in violation of the provisions of the policy at the time of the loss, and the loss would not have occurred but for the excepted peril, the insurance was suspended at the time of the loss, and the learned trial court erred in denying the defendant's motion for the direction of a verdict in its favor. . . .

CASE NO. 8

Wallace v. Virginia Surety Co. 80 Ga. App. 50, 55 S.E. (2d) 259 (1949)

WORRILL, J. In this case the question for determination is did the plaintiff, Wallace, have a contract of insurance with the defendant, Virginia Surety Company, Inc., under which the Surety Company was obligated to defend him against suits arising from a collision which occurred 275 miles from Atlanta where the vehicle involved, being one listed as insured under the policy, was returning from a trip to Miami, Florida, where Miami is admittedly a distance of 725 miles from Atlanta? . . .

It is elementary that an insurance company is discharged from liability under its policy if the risk is materially increased. . . . In Southern Mutual Ins. Co. v. Hudson, 113 Ga. 434, at page 440, 38 S.E. 964, the court recognizes the principle that a change in use which materially increases the hazard of the insurance releases the insurance company from liability on a loss directly resulting as a consequence of such increase in risk.

We think the terms of the covenants of the insurance policy are plain and unambiguous. The plaintiff agreed in the first paragraph of the quoted "commercial radius endorsement" not to drive the automobile beyond the 500 mile radius. This agreement showing on its face a consideration therefor constituted a promissory warranty on the part of the plaintiff, which when violated by him in sending his vehicle covered by the policy on a trip to Miami, Florida, beyond that radius, entitled the defendant to declare the policy, for the purposes of that trip, or operation, in its entirety, void. Such action by the plaintiff constituted a breach of the contract which released the defendant from the obligation to perform its covenants under the contract of insurance in so far as that particular trip was concerned.

We cannot say as a matter of law that a trip of 1450 miles does not subject the vehicle involved to greater hazards and risks over the entire trip than would one of only 1000 miles, or less. We think it is clear that it was the intention of the parties that the vehicles insured be not used as long haul carriers, and that under the rules of law set forth above the liability of the insurance company under the policy was at an end when the plaintiff sent his truck beyond the 500 mile radius from Atlanta, thus increasing the hazard and risks that the truck was subject to, and that the company was not obligated to take any action to defend the plaintiff from the suits arising from a collision which occurred as a direct and proximate result of this long haul trip. . . .

Review Questions

1. How does a risk-shifting contract differ from a risk-distributing contract?
2. What is the policy underlying the requirement of an insurable interest in insurance contracts?
3. What does an insurable interest in property consist of?

4. Is it possible for one to have an insurable interest in property owned by another?
5. What does an insurable interest in a life consist of?
6. Would a creditor have an insurable interest in the life of his debtor?
7. What determines the point of time at which a life insurance contract becomes effective?
8. Is the payment of the initial premium generally necessary to the existence of a contract of life insurance?
9. How is it possible to obtain fire insurance protection before the policy of insurance is issued?
10. Illustrate a factual situation under which a contract of insurance could be avoided because of concealment of fact by the insured.
11. What determines whether misrepresentation of fact by the insured will make the contract of insurance voidable?
12. What determines whether the failure of a warranty contained in a contract of insurance will make the contract voidable?
13. What are promissory warranties or conditions subsequent?
14. How does an open policy differ from a valued policy?
15. Can there be a total loss under a fire insurance contract even though the insured property has not been completely destroyed?
16. What is the purpose of coinsurance clauses in fire insurance contracts?
17. Illustrate the operation of a coinsurance clause.
18. What is the insurer's right of subrogation?

Problems for Discussion

1. Plaintiff, a watch manufacturer, contracted with purchasers of its watches as follows: "To replace such watch with a new . . . watch of like quality and value . . . provided the first watch aforesaid is lost . . . through Burglary or Robbery as herein defined." Is this an insurance contract subjecting plaintiff to state regulation as an insurer?
2. Mills contracts to construct a house for James. Does Mills have an insurable interest in the house while it is in process of construction?
3. Would Martin have an insurable interest in the life of his mother-in-law?
4. Nelson owes Boots $3,000. Boots insures Nelson's life for a like amount. Nelson pays the debt to Boots. Nelson then dies. Can Boots recover on the policy?
5. X contemplates the purchase of certain property and in anticipation he insures the property. One week later he acquires title. The property is then destroyed by fire. Is the insurance contract valid?
6. Fall entered into an oral fire insurance contract with the agent of the Fire Insurance Co. whereby it was agreed that Fall's building was to be insured for a period of five years. Before the policy was written the building burned. The Fire Insurance Co. contends that the oral contract was one of long duration and consequently unenforceable under the Statute of Frauds. Decide.
7. Burns contracted for insurance under an application that provided that the insurance was not to become effective until the policy was delivered to Burns while he was in good health. The policy was delivered by the company to the agent who had taken the application. The agent procrastinated in determining

the health of Burns and thirty days later Burns died without ever having received delivery of the policy. Can the beneficiary named on the policy recover?

8. This was a suit based on a theft policy covering an automobile. On the trial it appeared that the automobile was described in the portion of the policy entitled "Warranties" as model of 1916, when in fact it was of model 1913. The trial judge was asked, and refused, to find for defendant on the ground that this was a breach of warranty, which was expressed by the terms of the policy as to "the description of the automobile insured" and other matters. Decide. (*Felakos* v. *Aetna Ins. Co.*, 119 Alt. 277)
9. Copp applied for fire insurance upon his warehouse, failing to disclose the fact that he had received anonymous letters threatening to burn the warehouse. The policy was issued and a fire loss was suffered as a result of an overheated stove. The insurance company upon discovering the concealed fact refused to pay the loss. Can Copp recover?
10. Dill had acquired a building by inheritance and in making application for fire insurance he represented that the building had a tile roof. Unknown to Dill, the tile roof had been replaced by a wood shingle roof. The building was destroyed by fire and the insurance company refused to pay the loss. Result?
11. A fire insurance policy provides, "This Company shall not be liable beyond the actual cash value of the property covered by this policy." Is this a valued or open policy?
12. X insures his $100,000 business house for $50,000 under a policy that contains an 80 per cent coinsurance clause. The property suffers a $40,000 loss. What is the liability of the insurance company to X?
13. Identify the following clause taken from a fire insurance policy: "This company shall not be liable under this policy for a greater proportion of any loss on the described property . . . than the amount hereby insured shall bear to the whole amount of valid and collectible insurance covering such property."

Table of Cases

TABLE OF CASES

Advance Amusement Company v. Franke, 287
Aetna Insurance Company v. Murray, 849
Allegheny College v. Nat'l Chautauqua County Bank of Jamestown, 123
Allen v. Bissinger, 48
Allison v. Hollenbeak, 465
American National Bank v. West, 172
American T. Insurance Company v. Williams, 117
Anderson v. Albert etc. Manufacturing Company, 1023
Anderson v. Stewart, 69
Anderson v. Wisconsin Cent. Ry. Company, 56
Andre v. Ellison, 214
Ashbrook v. Briner, 792
Austin v. Burge, 57
Austin, Inc. v. Kelly, 934
Aviation Industries v. East & West Insurance Company, 324
Azevedo v. Sequeria, 854

Babb v. Bolyard, 164
Bader v. Williams, 465
Barber Agency Company v. Co-operative Barrel Company, 401
Barker v. Barker, 770
Barnwell v. Hanson, 475
Baum v. McBride, 910
Baumgartner v. Glesener, 667
Beaman v. Testori, 674
Becker v. Faber, 1050
Bekkevold v. Potts, 673
Berkovitz v. Morton-Gregson Company, 360
Binghamton Pharmacy v. First National Bank, 567
Bisner v. Mantell, 678
Block v. Means, 148
Bomberger v. McKelvey, 289
Bond Rubber Corp. v. Oates Brothers, 344
Bonnette v. Ponthieux, 517
Bozeman Mortuary Association v. Fairchild, 631
Breeding v. Melson, 830
Broadway v. Jeffers, 60
Buckalew v. Niehuss, 229
Byford v. Gates Brothers Lumber Company, 66

Caldwell v. Cline, 61
California Animal Products Company v. Lappin, 665
Capitol City Lumber Company v. Cash, 336
Carbon Fuel Company v. Gregory, 813
Cartwright v. Coppersmith, 494
Cassella v. Tiberio, 146
Castelli v. Tolibia, 77
Cherokee Foundation v. Imperial Assurance Company, 1065
Claflin v. Cont. Jersey Works, 362
Clarksburg Casket Company v. Valley Undertaking Company, 732
Cleveland C. C. Company v. Green, 366
Cliett v. Lauderdale Biltmore Corporation, 677
Cliff's Corporation v. U.S., 1003
Coast National Bank v. Bloom, 100
Coens v. Marousis, 847
Cohen v. Eggers, 299
Cole-McIntyre-Norfleet Company v. Holloway, 73
Coleman Hotel Company v. Crawford, 1002
Collier v. Brown, 194
Colonell v. Goodman, 408
Columbia Grocery Company v. Marshall, 531
Columbian Banking Company v. Bowen, 569
Commercial Trust Company v. New England Macaroni Manufacturing Company, 574
Continental Insurance Company v. Minn. etc. Ry. Company, 1000
Cornelius v. Cook, 322
Corthell v. Summit Thread Company, 75
Costello v. Costello, 775
Costello v. Sykes, 174
Cottrell v. Nurnberger, 199
Crane Ice Cream v. Terminal, 260
Crawford v. Baker, 108
Cunningham v. Roto. Company, 169
Cutler-Hammer, Inc. v. Wayne, 829

Dahl v. Moss & Son, 307
Davis v. Union Planters National Bank & Trust Company, 469
Day & Company v. Booth, 1008
Day v. Power, 868
Delgado v. Delgado, 245
Delta Asbestos Company v. Sanders, 866
Dermer v. Faunce, 618
Dixon v. Koplar, 855
Dodge v. Galuska, 303
Doernbecher v. Columbia City Lumber Company, 1022

Dorsey v. Old Surety Life Insurance Company, 624
Drzewieki v. Stempowski, 492
Dunbar v. Farnum, 852
Duris v. Iozzi, 298

Eagle Indemnity Company v. Cherry, 404
Eckert-Fair Construction Company v. Capitol Steel & Iron Company, 115
Eckhard v. Comm. of Internal Revenue, 850
Edwards v. Ollen Restaurant Corporation, 817
Electric Contracting Company v. Brown, 832
Elkhorn Production Credit Association v. Johnson, 548
Ellison v. Ind. Life, 238
Enequist v. Bemis, 175
Engbretson v. Seiberling, 120
Engleman v. Kalamazoo, 767

Farmers' Fertilizer Company v. Lillie, 434
Faultersack v. Clintonville Sales Corporation, 420
Field v. Lukowiak, 464
First National Bank of Appleton v. Court, 523
First National Bank v. Drake, 1048
First National Bank v. Hattaway, 734
First National Bank of Mandan v. Larsson, 410
First National Bank of Pipestone v. Siman, 390
First National Bank of Sioux City v. John Morrell & Company, 495
Fischetto v. Quigley Company, 153
Fitzsimons v. Eagle Brewing Company, 243
Flynn v. Kenrick, 793
Franco v. Voursney, 166
Franzen v. Rueping Leather Company, 1009
Froess v. Froess, 905
Funk Brothers Company v. Kalo Company, 627

Gardner v. Reed, 228
Garrison v. Marshall, 123
General Phoenix Corporation v. Cabot, 1047
Georgeson v. Nielsen, 342
Geyler v. Daily, 435
Gibson Oil Company v. Hayes, 739
Gilbert v. Pioneer National Bank of Duluth, 529
Gilchrist v. Highfield, 974
Gilman v. Kestral Corporation, 626
Gilpin v. Savage, 573
Ginsberg v. Kugler, 703
Glasscock v. First National Bank, 526
Glendora Bank v. Davis, 466
Glenn, Collector of Internal Revenue v. Beard, 335
Glenn v. Weill, 887
Glennan v. Rochester Trust Company, 437
Glens Falls Ind. Company v. Perscall, 294
Goerke v. Nicholson, 149
Goldberg v. Mitchell, 241
Gordon v. Marburger, 866
Gottlieb v. Rinaldo, 666
Graben Motor Company v. Brown Garage Company, 732
Graham v. Atchison, T. & S.F. Ry. Company, 171
Grand Rapids Trust Company v. Haney School Fur. Company, 939
Grant v. The Aerodraulics Company, 104
Green v. Smith, 50
Greene v. Birkmeyer, 242
Greenlease-Lied Motors v. Sadler, 704
Gregory v. Lee, 150
Griffen v. Northwestern Fish Company, 663
Gross v. Housner, 777
Gross Income Tax Division v. J. L. Cox & Son, 969
Guaranty Laundry Company v. Pulliam, 1005
Guardian Depositors Corporation v. Brown, 268

Haggard v. Mutual Oil & Refining Company, 478
Hale v. Wilmarth, 902
Halligan v. Frey, 198
Halpern v. Silver, 807
Handy v. C.I.T. Corporation, 741
Hansen v. Kuhn, 737
Harris v. Railway Express Agency, 372
Hastings v. Piper Aircraft Corporation, 968
Heath v. Stoddard, 373
Henderson Baker Lbr. Company v. Headley, 791
Henning v. Kyle, 165
Heuer v. Rubin, 230
Hibbard v. Furlong, 415
Higgins v. Beauchamp, 868
Hillman v. Kropp Forge Company, 479
Hirsch v. Phily, 1027
Hogue v. National Automotive Parts Association, 116
Hood v. Cline, 106
Hoyd v. Citizens Bank of Albany Company, 790
Hughes Company v. Farmers' Union Produce Company, 940
Hunt v. Lyndonville Savings Bank & Trust Company, 122

Iglehart v. Farmers National Bank, 472
In re Estate of Johnson, 1025
In re Estate of Wilson, 636
In re Fox's Estate, 59
In re Ganaposki, 846
In re Garland's Will, 436
In re Smiley's Estate, 1062
In re Vitelli's Estate, 906
Industrial Bank of Commerce v. Shapiro, 595
Intermountain Realty Company v. Allen, 771

International Harvester Company v. Watkins, 471
International Shoe Company v. Herndon, 107
Iron Fireman Coal Stoker Company v. Brown, 676
Irving Investment Corporation v. Gordon, 232
Iselin & Company v. Saunders, 263

Jasper v. Rossman, 237
Jemison v. Citizens' Savings Bank of Jefferson, 976
Jeppi v. Brockman Holding Company, 1021
John Hancock Mutual Life Insurance Company v. Mann, 474

Kadota Fig Association v. Case-Swayne Company, 402
Katz v. Brewington, 881
Keller v. Fredericktown Savings Inst., 587
Kent Storage Company v. Grand Rapids Lumber Company, 617
King v. Duluth, 112
King Features Syndicate v. Courrier, 943
Kirkpatrick v. Williams, 345
Klapka v. Shrauger, 302
Kolt v. Cleveland Trust Company, 708
Kuhns v. Live Stock National Bank, 497

Ladd v. Reed, 675
Lamm v. Charles Stores Company, 366
Lamm v. Shingleton, 284
Lamm v. Stoen, 930
Law Reporting Company v. Elwood Grain Company, 369
Leekley v. Short, 545
Leggett v. Vinson, 110
Leigh v. Gerber, 622
Leonard v. Woodward, 549
Lerback v. Re Mine, 64
Lichtenberg v. Bullis School, Inc., 966
Lindsey v. Stalder, 669
Linsky v. U.S., 588
Loney Company v. Nelson, 628
Losquadro v. Rubel Corporation, 233
Luedtke v. Phillips, 816
Lumberman's Mutual Insurance Company v. Slide Rule Company, 363

M. & J. Finance Corporation v. Hodges, 829
McCornick & Company, Bankers v. Gem State Oil & Products Company, 476
McGirr v. Campbell, 202
McIntyre & Lyon, 160
Mair v. Southern Minn. Broadcasting Company, 412
Malone v. Santora, 698
Mansfield Lbr. Company v. First State Bank of Vian, 831
Markey v. Corey, 495
Marquette Cloak & Suit Company v. Netter & Meyer, 908
Marsh v. Am. Locker Company, Inc., 702
Marshall & Company v. Kirschbraun & Sons, 516
Martin v. Hartley, 321
Martin v. Seigel, 212
Maryatt v. Hubbard, 205
May v. Young, 235
Mayer v. Randolph, 204
Merchants' National Bank v. Detroit Trust Company, 522
Meridian Yellow Cab Company v. City Yellow Cabs, 938
Meyers v. Wells, 942
Meylink v. Minnehaha Co-op. Oil Company, 177
Michigan Millers Mutual Fire Insurance Company v. Grange Oil Company, 1070
Miller v. Bank of Holly Springs, 99
Miller Laboratories, Inc. v. Griffen, 234
Miller & Sons Bakery Company v. Selikowitz, 309
Miller v. Wick, 1031
Minnesota Linseed Company v. Collier White Lead Company, 63
Minn. Loan & Trust Company v. Peteler Car Company, 1029
Mitter v. Home Insurance Company, 1070
Moore v. Vaughn, 515
Mulkey v. Anglin, 907
Murphy v. Henry, 118
Murphy v. Munson, 207
Myers v. Ellison, 405

Nardis Sportswear v. Simmons, 977
National City Bank of Chicago v. National Bank of Republic, 544
Nebraska Seed Company v. Harsh, 54
New Port Rickey v. Fidelity Company, 520
N.Y. Society for S.V. v. MacFadden Pub., 931
Nickerson v. Harvard College, 201
Night & Day Bank v. First National Bank of Shreveport, 543
Nipp v. Puritan Manufacturing & Supply Company, 975
Nissen v. Nissen Trampoline Company, 411
Norris v. Williams, 761
Northern Drug Company v. Abbett, 596

Oates v. Taylor, 155
O'Connell v. Brady, 269
Ohio Edison Company v. Warner Coal Corporation, 935
Oleson v. Albers, 374
O'Neal v. Clark, 575

Ontjes v. Harrer, 1007
Owen v. Schwartz, 161
Ozan Lumber Company v. McNeeley, 340

Packard Fort Worth v. Van Zandt, 76
Party Cab Company v. U.S., 338
Pauls Valley Milling Company v. Gabbert, 668
Payne v. Jennings, 370
Penn Bowling Recreation Center v. Hot Shoppes, 765
Perry v. Manufacturers National Bank of Lynn, 530
Petition of Collins-Doan Company, 979
Petrovich v. Felco Chemical Corporation, 931
Phillips v. Phillips, 848
Pitck v. McGuire, 208
Plowman v. Indian Refining Company, 102
Polis v. Heizmann, 869
Potter v. Brown, 903
Pro-Phy-Lac-Tic Brush Company v. Hudson Products, 613
Pugh v. Newburn, 883

Quanah, Acme, & P. R. Company v. Wichita State Bank, 518
Quest v. Barge, 406
Quinn v. Phipps, 403

Railway Express Agency v. Schoen, 706
Raiser v. Jackson, 292
Rankin v. Ridge, 195
Raymond v. Davis, 421
Reed v. Ind. Acci. Com., 853
Reno Sales Company v. Pritchard Industries, 681
Richardson v. Travelers Insurance Company, 1068
Rock-Ola Manufacturing Company v. Leopold, 680
Rosasco Creameries v. Cohen, 227
Rosen Company v. Eksterowicz, 418
Rothchild Brothers v. Lomas, 67
Rotzin v. Miller, 414
Rubio Savings Bank v. Acme Farm Products Company, 466
Rudin v. Steinbugler, 932
Rye v. Phillips, 119

Sabine v. Paine, 528
Sacks v. Helene Curtis Ind., 1032
Safier's Inc. v. Bialer, 615
Sanderson v. Cooke, 882
Schell v. Kneedler, 774
Schnell v. Perlmon, 114
Schwab v. Getty, 385
Schwartz v. Mfgs'. Cas. Ins. Company, 1001
Scire v. American Export Lines, 389
Scott v. Duthie, 111
Scott v. People's Monthly Company, 68
Searles v. Bar Harbor Banking & T. Company, 1004
Seitz v. Brewer's Refining Company, 193
Sell v. General Electric Supply Corporation, 72
Shatz Realty Company v. King, 417
Shelley v. Kraemer, 762
Shoenthal v. Bernstein, 387
Short v. Milby, 770
Silverstein v. Macy Company, 368
Simms v. Bovee, 286
Sinclair v. Travis, 630
Smiley v. Prudential Insurance Company of America, 1066
Smith v. Vernon County, 52
Smith v. Zuckman, 265
Smyth Sales Corporation v. Norfolk Building & Loan Association, 619
Snipes Mt. Company v. Benz Brothers, 297
Somers & Sons v. LeClerc, 320
Sorter v. Citizens Fund Mutual Fire Insurance Company, 1069
Southern Pac. Company v. Bank of America, 683
Sparrowhawk v. Erwin, 151
Spencer v. Staines, 739
Speroff v. First-Central Trust Company, 101
Spires v. Hanover Insurance Company, 266
Spiritwood Grain Company v. Northern Pac. Ry. Company, 808
Spratt v. Paramount Pictures, Inc., 71
State Bank of East Moline v. Standaert, 577
State Bank of Lehr v. Lehr Auto & Machine Company, 546
State Bank of Siloam Springs v. Marshall, 586
State of Maryland v. Manor Real Estate & Trust Company, 818
State ex rel. McConnell v. People's Bank, 733
State v. National Optical Stores Company, 964
State v. Standard Oil Company, 1010
State Street Furniture Company v. Armour & Company, 259
State v. Western Transportation Company, 972
Steele v. Brooks, 737
Steinmeyer v. Schroeppel, 168
Stephens v. Neely, 870
Stevens v. Berger, 247
Stewart v. Clemens, 735
Stieber v. Vanderlip, 178
Stone v. Freeman, 244
Stott Realty Company v. Orloff, 981
Sullivan v. Bennett, 346
Sunderman v. Roberts, 53
Sunshine Cloak v. Roquette, 305
Sward v. Nash, 300

Tatum v. Montgomery Banking Company, 145
Tetreault v. Campbell, 157

Texas Company v. Christian, 815
Theobald v. Satterthwaite, 700
Thomason v. Bescher, 125
Toole v. Crafts, 579
Town of Clayton v. Wall, 1046
Traylor Eng. Company v. National Cont. Corporation, 158

Uline Loan Company v. Standard Oil Company, 1030
Undercliff Ave. Corporation v. Consolidated Edison Company, 79
Union Properties v. Cleveland Trust Company, 634
U.S. Fidelity & Guaranty Company v. First National Bank of Omaha, 525
U.S. Fidelity v. Parsons, 295
U.S. v. Huff, 293

Valaske v. Wirtz, 343
Valley Shoe Corporation v. Stout, 372
Vanlandingham v. Jenkins, 78
Verney Corporation v. Rose Fabric Converters Corporation, 623
Viles v. S. D. Warren Company, 571
Von Wedel v. McGrath, 362

Wachova Bank & Trust Company v. Crafton, 547
Walker v. Walker, 195
Wallace v. Virginia Surety Company, 1072
Waller v. Waller, 271
Walthall v. Yohn, 773
Warner Brothers & Company v. Israel, 662
Warren v. 536 Broad Street Corporation, 937
Weber v. De Cecco, 213
Welch v. Bank of Manhattan Company, 589
Welk v. Bidwell, 811
Westlake Mercantile Finance Corporation v. Merritt, 468
White Tower Management Corporation v. Taglino, 376
Whiting & Sons Company v. Barton, 936
Williams v. Green, 167
Williams v. Mutual Benefit Association, 309
Williams v. Pedersen, 887
Wilson v. Malenock, 731
Wilson v. Moline, 884
Wilson v. Waters, 768
Winkelman Company v. Barr, 306
Wold v. Patterson, 422
Wood Company v. Finkelstein, 814
Wood v. Hutchinson Coal Company, 431
Woods v. Interstate Realty Company, 965
Woodward-Holmes Company v. Nudd, 885
Workman, Inc. v. Lincoln, 193

Young v. Stephenson, 239

Index

INDEX

A

Abstracts of title, 759
Acceleration provisions, 460
Acceptance
  of bills of exchange, 558
  of goods sold—part acceptance under Statute of Frauds, 190
  of offer, 42
Accession
  defined, 610
  title by, 610
Accommodation parties
  defined, 542
  liability, 542
Acknowledgment of instruments, 192
Act of God
  carrier's liability affected by, 696
  defined, 696
  as excuse for nonperformance of contract, 278
Adverse possession
  title by, 757
Agency
  by appointment, 331
  by estoppel, 334
  independent contractor relationship distinguished, 329
  irrevocable, 430
  master and servant distinguished, 329
  by ratification, 332
  termination of
    by acts of the parties, 427
    coupled with an interest, 430
    notice of termination required, 429
    by operation of law, 429
    undisclosed, 384
    (*See also* Agents; Principals)
Agents
  authority to act
    apparent, 353
    by conduct of principal, 355
    by custom, 354
    emergency powers, 354
    express, 351
    implied, 353
    power of attorney, 352
    secret limitations, 355
  capacity to be, 331
  duties to principal
Agents (*cont.*)
    to account, 397
    to be loyal, 394
    to inform the principal, 396
    to obey instructions, 397
    not to be negligent, 398
    not to have or represent an adverse interest, 395
    not to profit or obtain personal advantage, 394
  liability to third persons
    improperly executed contract, 381
    upon personal undertaking, 381
    tort liability, 356, 384
    when authority has been exceeded, 382
    when principal is nonexistent or incompetent, 383
    when principal is undisclosed, 384
  notice to agent, notice to principal, 396
  right to be reimbursed, 399
  right to compensation, 399
  right of indemnity, 400
  right of lien, 400
Alteration of instruments, 318, 509, 514
Anticipatory breach of contract, 283
Anti-Trust Act, 222
Arbitration and award, 318
Articles of copartnership, 840
Articles of incorporation, 952
Artisans' liens, 716
Assignment
  contractual rights generally
    delegation of duties distinguished, 255
    limitations to assignment of rights, 251
    notice of assignment, 254
    position of assignee, 252

B

Bailments
  care of property, 694
  classification, 694
  consignment distinguished, 693
  nature and elements, 691
  sale distinguished, 692
Bearer instruments
  defined, 463
  transfer by delivery, 491
Bilateral contracts, 34

Bill of Sale, 647
Bills of exchange, 445
Bills of lading, 649, 659
Blank indorsements, 464, 489
By-laws, 1015

C

Capacity to contract, 130
Carriers
  as bailees, 695
  common, defined, 695
  exceptions to liability, 696
  limitations of liability, 697
Case law, 9
Certified checks, 584
Chattel mortgages
  on after-acquired property, 722
  on crops, 722
  defined, 720
  description of property, 720
  foreclosure, 724
  on merchandise for resale (stock in trade), 723
  mortgagee's interest, 721
  recording, 721
  rights and duties of mortgagor, 723
Checks, 583
C.O.D., 648
Common carriers, 695
Common law, 8
Communication of acceptance, 44
Communication of offer, 37
Community property, 756
Composition with creditors, 96
Compromise settlements, 93
Conditional sales
  defined, 725
  goods to be resold, 726
  interest of seller, 725
  notes, 444
  position of buyer, 726
  recording, 725
  retaking of property by seller, 727
  rights of seller upon default, 727
Conditions in contracts, 278
Confession of judgment, 456
Consideration, 88, 506
Consignments, 693
Contracts
  acceptance of offer
    by accepting paper containing terms, 48
    by act, unilateral offer, 42
    communication of acceptance, mode of, 44
    conditional acceptance—counter offer, 42
    by promise—bilateral offer, 44
    silence as, 45
    time when effective, 44
Contracts (*cont.*)
  bilateral, 34
  capacity to contract
    corporations, 134
    infants, 130
    insane persons, 134
    intoxicated persons, 134
  certainty, 46
  classified, 33
  conditions in, 278
  consideration
    adequacy, 90
    in composition with creditors, 96
    in compromise and settlement, 93
    defined and explained, 88
    in discharge of unliquidated or disputed claims, 94
    past consideration, 89
    in payment of a lesser sum, 95
    pre-existing obligations as, 92
    promise to pay debt barred by bankruptcy, 97
    promise to pay debt barred by Statute of Limitations, 97
    return of, in infant's contracts, 131
    seals, contracts under, 98
    in subscription offer cases, 98
  damages, money
    duty to prevent or reduce, 275
    liquidated, 274
    measure of, 274
  defined, 31, 36
  discharge, methods of
    accord and satisfaction, 317
    arbitration and award, 318
    bankruptcy, 316
    material alteration, 318, 509, 514
    mutual rescission, 317
    novation, 317
    Statute of Limitations, 316
  elements of, 32
  executed and executory, 34
  express, 33
  form required, 185
    (*See also* Statute of Frauds)
  fraud, effect on, 138
  illegal agreements
    defined, 219
    effect of illegality, 226
    insurance contracts, 224
    Sherman Anti-Trust Law, 222
    Sunday contracts, 226
    usurious agreements, 226
    wagering contracts, 224
    when contrary to public policy, 220
    when in interference with governmental functions, 223

Contracts (*cont.*)
when in restraint of trade, 221
implied, 35
impossibility of performance, 276
infants'
for necessities, 133
right to disaffirm, 131
insane persons', 134
money damages, 274
offer
advertisements and price quotations, 39
bids as, 39
defined, 36
duration of, 40
implied, 40
methods of termination
by death or insanity, 41
by lapse of time, 41
by provision in the offer, 40
by rejection—counteroffer, 42
revocation by offeror, 40
revocation of public offers, 41
revocation of unilateral offers, 42
need of certainty, 46
need of communication, 37
need of intent to contract, 38
preliminary negotiations, 39
time of acceptance, 44
parties, capacity of, 130
performance
dependent upon conditions, 278
excuses for nonperformance, 276
to satisfaction of another, 281
substantial, 279
tender of, 319
time for, 280
waiver of, 278
personal, not assignable, 251
quasi-, 33, 36
remedies
for breach, 18, 274
for failure of a condition, 278
third-party beneficiary, 256
unilateral, 34
void and voidable, 34, 130, 219
Co-owners
community property, 756
joint tenancy, 613, 755
tenancy in common, 613, 755
tenancy by entirety, 756
Copyright, 606
Corporations
as an association, 921
by-laws, 1015
capital stock as trust fund for creditors, 996
charters
method of obtaining, 924
Corporations (*cont.*)
nature of, 926
revocation by state, 962
as source of powers, 948
as citizen or resident, 920
classified, 916
cumulative voting, 997
de facto and de jure distinguished, 927
defined, 917
directors
compensation, 1020
liabilities, 1019
meetings, 1018
powers, 1017
right to deal with corporation, 1019
tenure of office, 1020
dividends
liability for illegal distribution, 997, 1019
limitations to distribution, 995
duration, 961
express powers, 952
foreign, 948
formation procedure, 925
implied powers, 954
as a legal entity, 917
name, 926
nonprofit, 916
nonstock, 916
organization
beginning of corporate life, 925
effect of defective incorporation, 927
procedure, 925
powers
to acquire own stock, 956
to acquire stock in other corporations, 957
charter, the source, 948
express, 952
implied, 954
promoter
defined, 927
duties as fiduciary, 929
liability of corporation for acts of, 928
liability of promoter, 928
right to recover for services, 929
public, 917
quasi-public, 916
shares of stock
limitations upon right to transfer, 990
method of transfer, 988
nature of, 986
negotiable character, 991
right to transfer, 989
subscription to, 987
stockholders
defined, 986
delegation of management by, 1014
liability of, 999

Corporations (*cont.*)
right to
attend meetings, 997
force distribution of dividends, 994
inspect books, 993
make and amend by-laws, 1017
management, 997
subscribe ratably to new stock, 999
transfer shares, 989
subscriptions to stock, 987
termination
by consent of stockholders, 962
by court decree, 963
by expiration of charter, 961
by state of incorporation, 962
trust fund, capital stock as, 996
ultra vires acts
defined, 958
liability for ultra vires acts, 959
right to object to, 958
status of ultra vires contracts, 959
Counterclaim, 22
Counteroffer, 42
Courts
appeal, 23
equity, 16
federal, 24
law, 16
review, 23
state, 26
trial, 19
Crimes, 16
Cumulative voting, 997
Curtesy, 754

D

Damages
for anticipatory breach, 283
distinguished from specific performance and rescission, 18
duty to prevent or reduce, 275
liquidated, 274
measure of, 274
De facto corporations, 927
Deeds
delivery of, 760
execution of, 760
quitclaim, 757
recording, 759
warranty, 756
Demurrer, 21
Destruction of subject matter as excuse for non-performance, 277
Detriment theory of consideration, 89
Discharge of contracts, 316, 591
Dower, 754
Due process of law, 20
Duress, 144

E

Easements, 752
Entirety, tenancy by, 756
Equitable remedies, 16, 19
Equitable titles, 19
Equity of redemption, 783
Escrow delivery, 761
Estoppel, 334, 844
Exempt property, 823

F

Fee simple, 751
Forbearance as consideration, 94
Fraud
by act, 136
actionable, elements of, 135
concealment as, 136
concept of, 135
effect of, 138
innocent misrepresentation distinguished, 139
nondisclosure of fact as, 136
opinions distinguished, 137
warranties in sale of goods distinguished, 650
Frauds, Statute of, 186
Fungible goods, 645
Futures contracts, 225

G

Gambling contracts, 224
Good will, 222
Growing crops, nature of property in, 604
Guaranty contracts, 1040

I

Illegality
as a personal defense, 512
as a real defense, 509
(*See also* Contracts)
Impossibility of performance, 276
Incompetent parties, 130
Independent contractors, 329
Indorsements, 489
(*See also* Negotiable instruments)
Infants
as agent, 331
defined, 130
liability for necessities, 133
right to disaffirm contracts generally, 131
time for disaffirmance, 131
Injunctions, 18

Insane persons, contracts of, 134
Insurance
  avoidance of contract, 1056
  coinsurance, 1061
  concurrent insurance, 1061
  contract of, 1055
  distinguished from guaranty, 1054
  fire insurance, 1056
  insurable interest, 224
  insurer's right of subrogation, 1062
  life insurance, 1055
Intoxicated persons, contracts of, 134
Involuntary transfers of title, 610
Irrevocable agencies, 430

J

Joint owners, 613
Joint tenancy, 613
Judgment notes, 444, 456

L

Landlord and tenant
  eviction, 803
  improvements, 806
  landlord's lien, 807
  lease, 798
  nature of the relationship, 797
  rent, 806
  repairs, 805
  tenancies classified, 798
  tenant's right to remove crops, 801
  termination of tenancies, 799
  use of the premises, 802
Law
  as agency of control, 3
  common, 8
  constitutional, 13
  equity distinguished, 16
  nature of, 3
  ordinances, 11
  statute, 11
  unwritten, 8
Legal Procedure, 19
Liens
  agents', 400
  artisans', 716
  common law, 715
  enforcement of, 715
  judgment, 823
  landlords', 807
  mechanics', 824
  possession, necessity of, 715
  special, 715
  statutory, 716
  tax, 828
Life estates, 754
Limitation of liability
  by bailees generally, 697
  by carriers, 697
Limited partnership, 844
Liquidated damages, 274
Lost property, title to, when found, 613

M

Marshaling of assets, 902
Materialmen, right of lien, 824
Mechanics' liens
  extent of, 828
  nature of, 824
  owner's liability, 827
  persons entitled to, 825
  property subject to, 826
  time of commencement, 826
  waiver of, 828
Merchantable title, 760
Minors, 130
  (*See also* Infants)
Misrepresentations, 135, 139
Mistake, effect upon contract
  when bilateral, 142
  when unilateral, 140
Mitigation of damages, 275
Mortgages
  chattel, 720
  real estate, 782

N

Necessities, infants' liability for, 133
Negotiable documents of title
  bills of lading, 649, 659
  warehouse receipts, 659
Negotiable instruments
  acceleration clauses, 640
  acceptance
    effect of, 538, 558
  accommodation parties, 542
  alteration of, 509, 514
  antedating, 459
  assignment of, 447
  authority to complete, 459
  bearer paper
    defined, 462
    transfer by delivery, 491
  blank indorsements, 464, 489
  certification of checks, 584
  checks
    drawer's liability, 585
    stop-payment orders, 583
  classified, 443, 487
  conditional promise or order, 452

Negotiable instruments (*cont.*)
  confession of judgment, 456
  consideration, failure of, 512
  date, 459
  defenses
    personal
      discharge before maturity, 515
      fraud, 513
      illegality, 513
      lack of delivery, 513
      lack or failure of consideration, 512
      material alteration, 514
    real
      forgery, 509
      fraud as to nature of instrument, 511
      illegality, 511
      incapacity, 512
      material alteration, 509
      want of execution and delivery, 511
  delivery
    of completed instrument, 513
    conditional delivery, 514
    of incompleted instrument, 511
    as a negotiation of bearer paper, 491
  demand paper
    defined, 459
    time for presentment for payment
      bills of exchange, 555
      checks, 555
      notes, 555
    when overdue, 504
  discharge
    of drawer of check, 583
    of instruments
      by act sufficient to discharge simple contract, 593
      by cancellation, 592
      by material alteration, 593
      by payment, 591
      by renunciation, 593
    of secondary parties
      by failure of proper presentment or notice, 537, 553
      under rules of suretyship, 594
      Section 120 of N.I.L., 594
  drawees
    implied admissions by acceptance, 540
    liability based upon acceptance, 538
    liability upon raised instrument, 539
    surrender of instrument to drawee not a negotiation, 491
  drawers
    liability of, 540
  fictitious payee, 463
  forgery, 509
  holders in due course
    defenses available against, 508

Negotiable instruments (*cont.*)
    payee as holder in due course, 507
    requisites to qualify as
      complete and regular instrument, 502
      holder for value, 506
      purchaser before maturity, 503
      purchaser in good faith, 504
  holders through holders in due course, 501
  hours for presentment, 556
  indorsements
    blank, 464, 489
    conditional, 490
    qualified, 490
    restrictive, 489
    special, 489
  indorsers
    accommodation, 542
    discharge as secondary parties, 553
    liability of
      qualified, 541
      unqualified, 541
    judgment notes, 444, 456
  makers
    liability as primary parties, 537
  negotiability
    factors not affecting
      acts in addition to payment of money, 455
      reference to security contract, 454
      reference to source of payment, 452
    requirements for
      certainty of time of payment, acceleration provisions, 458, 460
      date, 458
      payable to order or bearer, 462
      unconditional promise or order, 451
      writing and signature, 450
  negotiation
    assignment distinguished, 447
    by delivery, 491
    by indorsement and delivery, 488
    surrender to drawee distinguished, 491
    transfer of unindorsed order paper, 487
  notice of dishonor
    form, 565
    manner of giving, 561
    parties entitled to give, 562
    time for giving, 560
    when not required or delay excused, 563
    where must be sent, 561
    to whom must be given, 562
  order paper, 462
  postdating, 459
  presentment
    for acceptance
      time for, 559
      when excused, 559
      when required, 558

Negotiable instruments (*cont.*)
for payment
day of making, 554
hour of making, 556
manner of making, 557
place of presentment, 554
when excused, 557
to whom made, 558
primary parties, 553
protest
defined, 564
purpose of, 565
time for protesting or noting, 566
when required, 567
secondary parties, 554
Novation, 256, 553

O

Offers, 37
(*See also* Contracts)
Opinions, 137
Options, 47
Ordinances, 11

P

Parol evidence rule, 185
Partners
acts requiring unanimous consent, 862
as agents, 859
authority to act
by agreement, 862
after dissolution, 898
by estoppel, 862
by implication, 859
in nontrading partnership, 861
by ratification, 862
in trading partnership, 860
fiduciary character of relationship, 874
liability
on contracts, 863
after dissolution, 899
extent of, 863
of incoming partners, 865
for losses, 880
nature of, 863
for torts, 864
notice to one, notice to all, 863
notice by retiring partner, 899
rights
to an accounting, 877
to compensation, 878
of contribution, 878
Partners (*cont.*)
to information, 876
of managements, 875
in partnership property, 879
to profits, 880
of reimbursement, 878
to return of capital, 880
to surplus, 880
Partnerships
agency character, 859
articles of association, 840
authority of partner, 859
creation of, formal requirements, 840
defective incorporations as, 844
dissolution
by act of partners, 893
by agreement, 892
continuation after dissolution, 898
by court decree
business unprofitable, 897
dissension among partners, 897
incapacity of partner, 896
misconduct of partner, 896
notice of, 899
by operation of law
bankruptcy, 895
death, 894
illegality, 895
right to liquidate, 898
termination distinguished, 892
distribution of assets, order of, 901
elements of, 837
as an entity, 841
by estoppel, 844
limited, distinguished, 845
management of, 839, 875
marshaling of assets, 902
name, 841
nontrading, 859
notice of dissolution, 899
profits and losses, 880
property
nature of, 842
partners' interest in, 879
right of partner's creditors to levy on, 880
title to, 843
tests of
interest in capital employed, 838
interest in profits and losses, 839
power of administration, 839
trading, 859
Patents, 608
Performance, 274
(*See also* Contracts)
Personal defenses, 512
Personal property
acquisition of title, 605

Personal property (*cont.*)
change to realty or vice versa, 602
classification of, 605
copyright, 606
crops as, 604
defined, 601
joint ownership to, 613
lost property, 613
patents, 608
real property distinguished, 602
Pleading, 21
Pledges
elements of, 717
nature of, 717
pledgee
duty as bailee, 718
right to income or increase, 719
right of reimbursement, 719
rights upon default, 719
pledgor
right to surplus, 720
as security for future debts, 718
Power of attorney, 352
Presentment, 553
(*See also* Negotiable instruments)
Principal and surety, 1040
(*See also* Suretyship)
Principals
acts which can be accomplished by, 330
duties to agent
to compensate, 399
to indemnify, 400
to reimburse, 399
liability of
for acts of agent, 351
for tort, 356
when undisclosed, 357
notice to agent, notice to principal, 396
undisclosed principal, when not liable
contracts under seal, 357
negotiable instruments, 358
personal agreements, 358
settlement between principal and agent, 358
(*See also* Agency)
Promissory estoppel, 123
Promissory notes, 443
Property in general, 601
Protest, 564
(*See also* Negotiable instruments)
Proxy, 997

Q

Qualified indorsements, 489
Quasi-contracts, 35
Quitclaim deeds, 757

R

Real defenses, 509
Real estate mortgages
absolute deed as, 784
assignment of mortgage or debt, 785
assumption by purchaser of mortgaged property, 785
deeds of trust, 785
deficiency, judgment for, 786
execution of, form required, 783
foreclosure, 788
form and contents, 783
mortgagee's interest, 782
payment and release, 787
power of sale, mortgages with, 789
recording, 783
redemption, right of, 790
transfer of mortgaged property, 785
Real property
abstracts of title, 759
adverse possession, title by, 757
community property, 756
crops as, 188, 604
curtesy, 754
deeds
execution and delivery, 760
quitclaim, 757
recording, 759
warranty, 756
defined, 602, 751
dower, 754
easements, 752
estates in
easements, 752
fee simple, 751
life estates, 754
remainders, 752
reversions, 752
joint ownership
community property, 756
joint tenancy, 755
tenancy in common, 755
tenancy in entirety, 756
modes of acquisition, 756
mortgages, 782
personal property distinguished, 602
recording instruments affecting, 759
Remainders, 752
Remedies, 16
Rescission, 18
Restraint of trade, 221
Reversions, 752
Revocation of offer, 40

S

Sale or return, 647
Sale on trial and approval, 647
Sales
  bill of, 647
  C.O.D. shipments, 648
  consignment for sale, 693
  contract of sale, 642
  contract to sell, 642
  on return, 647
  rights and remedies of buyer
    for breach of contract, 657
    for breach of warranty, 658
    right of inspection, 658
  rights and remedies of seller
    for breach of contract, 654
    right of lien, 655
    right of resale, 657
    right of rescission, 657
    stoppage in transit, 656
  risk of loss, 643
  Statute of Frauds, 190
  time of passing of title
    ascertained goods, 644
    under C.O.D., 648
    fungible goods, 645
    intention rule, 643
    under order bill of lading, 649
    on trial, 647
    unascertained goods, 646
  warranties
    defined, 650
    express, 650
    implied, 652
      of fitness, 653
      of merchantability, 652
      in sale of food products, 653
      in sale by sample or description, 652
      of title, 652
Seals, 98
Silence as acceptance of offer, 45
Specific performance, 18
Statute of Frauds
  contracts as affected by
    in consideration of marriage, 186
    of guaranty, 186
    of long duration, 189
    pertaining to personal property, 190
    pertaining to real estate, 188
Statute of Frauds (*cont.*)
  parol evidence rule, 185
  purpose of, 185
  signature required, 191
  writing, nature of required, 191
Statute of Limitations, 97, 316
Stockholders, 986
Stoppage in transit, 656
Subrogation, 1042, 1062
Subscriptions to stock, 987
Summons, 20
Sunday contracts, 226
Suretyship relations
  cosureties, 1042
  creation of, 1039
  defenses available to surety, 1043
  discharge of surety by acts of creditor, 1044
  guarantor and strict surety distinguished, 1040
  liability of surety
    as to amount and time, 1041
    nature of, 1040
  nature of, 1039
  rights of surety or guarantor
    contribution from cosureties, 1042
    indemnity, 1042
    subrogation, 1042

T

Tenancy in common, 613, 755
Tenancy by entirety, 756
Tender of performance, 319
Third-party beneficiary contracts, 256
Trial procedure, 19, 24
Trust deeds, 785
Trust receipts, 729

U

Ultra vires, 958
Undisclosed principal, 384
Undue influence, 144
Unilateral contracts, 34
Usury, 226

W

Wagering contracts, 224
Warehouse receipts, 659
Warranties, 650
Warranty deeds, 756